contemporary educational psychology

contemporary educational psychology

FIFTH EDITION

Thomas L. Good
University of Arizona

Jere Brophy
Michigan State University

 **Longman** *Publishers USA*

Contemporary Educational Psychology, Fifth Edition

Copyright © 1995, 1990, 1986, 1980 by Longman Publishers USA.
All rights reserved.
No part of this publication may be reproduced,
stored in a retrieval system, or transmitted
in any form or by any means, electronic, mechanical,
photocopying, recording, or otherwise,
without prior permission of the publisher.

Longman, 10 Bank Street, White Plains, N.Y. 10606

Associated companies:
Longman Group Ltd., London
Longman Cheshire Pty., Melbourne
Longman Paul Pty., Auckland
Copp Clark Longman Ltd., Toronto

Senior acquisitions editor: Laura McKenna
Development editor: Virginia L. Blanford
Production editor: Ann P. Kearns
Text design: Circa 86
Cover design: A Good Thing
Cover image: Unlimited Images
Text art: Circa 86
Photos: Stuart Spates, A Clear Image

Library of Congress Cataloging-in-Publication Data

Good, Thomas L., date.
  Contemporary educational psychology / by
Thomas L. Good, Jere E.
Brophy. – 5th ed.
      p.   cm.
Rev. ed. of: Educational psychology. © 1990.
  Includes bibliographical references and index.
  ISBN 0-8013-0775-9
  1. Educational psychology.   I. Brophy, Jere E.   II. Good, Thomas   93-50862
L., date. Educational psychology.   III Title.   CIP
LB1051.G5927   1995
370.15—dc20

    4 5 6 7 8 9 10 – VH – 99

brief contents

contents

6   the behavioral approach to learning   147

7   cognitive and constructivist views of learning   178

11 teaching for understanding and the social construction of knowledge 292

12 skills for learning: systematic studying, problem solving, and critical thinking 321

21 socioeconomic status, cultural, and gender differences 545

preface

Contemporary Educational Psychology, Fifth Edition, provides comprehensive and balanced coverage of the theories and basic concepts of educational psychology, shows how they can be applied in a variety of learning situations, and offers concrete advice for planning, implementing, and improving instruction. Our goal is to help teachers to understand the realities of teaching, to comprehend and organize relevant psychological theory, and to become competent at tasks instructors perform. The current edition includes these classic features, praised by past users.

focus on integration of theory and practice

We continue to stress the integration of concepts and theories of educational psychology with the task of teaching. Although prospective instructors need to master psychological concepts and principles, we take the position that the key to successful teaching is the integration of theoretical concepts and instructional strategies that are responsive to the learning needs of particular groups of students.

emphasis on informed decision making

Successful teaching requires a fundamental understanding of how students learn and develop as well as the ability to apply this knowledge in coordinating student learning in particular instructional contexts. Thus *Contemporary Educational Psychology*, Fifth Edition, is organized around applications designed to enable readers to become decision makers who can stimulate student learning.

research-based presentation of content and applications

In keeping with previous editions, *Contemporary Educational Psychology*, Fifth Edition, is research oriented, but eclectic in its approach to theory, research, and practice. We believe that no single approach can solve all of the problems teachers confront, but that an integration of ideas drawn from a variety of viewpoints can provide the basis for planning instruction. We encourage this approach in the text.

realistic approach to students and teaching

Our stress is on teaching and our aim is to prepare our readers for their future profession. Although our approach to both learning and teaching is optimistic and moral, we want our readers to be realistic in recognizing problems, constraints, and limitations in students, in classes, and in themselves. Through this practical approach, readers are prepared to face the challenges and rewards of teaching others.

new to this text

The current book, *Contemporary Educational Psychology,* Fifth Edition, has evolved from our textbook, *Educational Psychology: A Realistic Approach.* Although the present textbook retains the decision-making focus and the integration of educational psychology content with realistic and appropriate applications, the text represents a *major* revision. Indeed, the content revisions and additions throughout the book have been so substantial that we have changed the title to reflect this.

updated, streamlined coverage

Our reviewers have consistently indicated that this text is the most current and comprehensive one available on the market. Their feedback has been invaluable in planning this edition, which features new research, shifts in course emphases, and instructional applications in several key areas, including the following.

development Along with coverage of traditionally emphasized topics and theorists such as Piaget, Erickson, and Kohlberg, the present book has considerably expanded coverage of current topics such as language development and the connections between thought and language; Vygotsky and the zone of proximal development; the research of Marcia and others on Erikson's stages; the work of Gilligan and others in critiquing Kohlberg and developing theories about moral reasoning in families; the work of Bronfenbrenner and others on development in context; and recent research on children's friendships and other topics in social development.

learning and cognition The learning section, already strong in the treatment of instructional objectives, Gestalt psychology, behaviorism, and cognitive views as represented by Ausubel and Bruner, now includes coverage of cognitive science views of learning as well as situated learning, constructivism, and the social constructivist influence of Vygotsky. The new edition now also includes recent work on constructivist approaches to teaching school subjects for understanding, appreciation, and use of knowledge. Stress is, of course, placed on application. Included in the learning sections are rich concepts and guidelines for engaging students in reflective discussion and dialogue about subject matter, for focusing in depth around powerful ideas, and for engaging students in authentic application of what they are learning.

classroom realities The text continues to address the challenging problems teachers face in the classroom as they build appropriate conditions that support students' learning, but has been thoroughly revised and updated to include new research. For example, the classroom management section now provides increased coverage of approaches to classroom management that support students' self-regulation of their learning and collaboration with peers in the social contruction of knowledge.

We also include a photo essay showing examples of a variety of classroom realities.

multicultural classrooms Throughout the revision we emphasize the need for teachers to cope with student diversity and to teach within a multicultural context. The section on socio-economic status and other home background factors that influence student's school experience now includes much more discussion of culture and ethnicity.

individual differences In the individual differences section, the material on gender is updated to include the most current research and thinking on meeting the needs of both male and female students. Implications for elementary and secondary teaching have been provided throughout the text, and we've also devoted a photo essay to this important topic.

tests and measurements The educational measurement section continues to provide extensive coverage of concepts related to constructing appropriate classroom assessments, and issues involved in grading students' performance. The revision includes sections on current topics such as portfolio assessement, performance assessment, and other alternatives to traditional testing, as well as a photo essay on these topics.

modular organization

The amount of material covered in an educational psychology course varies from campus to campus. The number of credit hours for the course can also vary, as can the topics covered (e.g., sometimes material on special education, classroom management, mainstreaming, or development is taught in separate courses). So that it will be easier to use in these different situations, we have taken a modular approach to the book's organization. That is, except for the chapters on instructional applications (which assume prior mastery of the chapters on learning), sections can be taken up in any order and do not require mastery of the material in other sections. Thus, instructors may omit certain entire sections or chapters within sections, and cover material in a different order from the one we have used.

improved pedagogy

We have added a number of new elements and design features to make the book's content more clear, integrative, and reader-friendly. These include:

- *key terms*, which now appear in context in boldface and are immediately followed by a definition in italics;

- *learning objectives* at the beginning of each chapter to help readers focus more on principles and applications than on the specifics of content covered in the chapters;

- *key points*, now in color for easy reference and review;

- *Research at Work* boxes to illustrate the relevance of research to important classroom issues;

- *Implications for Teachers*, which provide organized suggestions about how teachers might consider applying relevant psychological information;

- *Questions for Reflection*, which emphasize engaging students in authentic applications and personal confrontation of key schooling issues, often in collaboration with their peers.

- *vignettes* and select *Cases to Consider* at the end of every chapter, which present situations that call for decision making or problem solving using principles developed in the chapter;

Summaries, tables, and *charts* in the text and study guide to help students focus on main ideas;

Critical Topic Photo Essays, all in full color, which have been added to help students integrate information across chapters and to reinforce our judgment that instructional methodologies, individual differences, classroom realities, and assessment are important themes in the study of educational psychology.

Combined, these features should help students to appreciate the relevance of the text material they read and to assess their ability to integrate and apply it in a variety of learning situations.

complete learning and teaching package

A fully integrated ancillary package, greatly expanded over previous editions, now accompanies *Contemporary Educational Psychology.* All ideas and suggestions included in the package are based upon or extend text discussions.

Instructor's Toolbox Written by Sharon McNeeley of Northern Illinois University, the Instructor's Toolbox is designed to help professors focus their students on learning actively and making real-world applications of theory. Using a two-part format, the Instructor's Toolbox encourages classroom interaction between instructor and students in and out of the classroom. Part I, the Comprehensive Activities Guide, provides ideas for implementing five to six class projects designed to help students learn chapter material and synthesize material across chapters. Some of these activities allow instructors to use multimedia programs commonly found in school settings as tools; many others involve cooperative learning, so that readers experience personally the effectiveness of this important instructional methodology. Part II provides teaching suggestions and tips; innovative assignments and projects; and a media resource section with brief descriptions and sources of the best videos, films, and hypermedia currently on the market, cross-referenced to chapters in the text.

study guide Written by Elizabeth Popiel of the University of Idaho, the study guide synthesizes, distills, and thoroughly reviews text material chapter-by-chapter; helps students focus on key terms, concepts, and theories; and utilizes a variety of learning strategies to encourage deep learning and real-world application of psychological theories. Study aids include concept maps; visuals that integrate theoretical knowledge; step-by-step guidelines that encourage implementation of theories; checklists; activities that tie theory to practice; "Thoughts to Ponder" guidelines for end-of-chapter *Cases to Consider,* and practice tests.

printed and computerized test banks Constructed by Thomas Fetsco of Northern Arizona University, test bank questions are designed to test both understanding of theory and appropriate application of concepts. All questions are referenced to text pages and are labeled by level of difficulty. Question formats include multiple choice, essay/short answer, and active learning exercises, and require students to think critically. Some questions are based on realistic scenarios or cases, and involve "if and why" answers. Questions that require students to synthesize information across chapters are also included. Available in printed form or on disk for IBM and Macintosh computers, this supplement is free to instructors upon adoption of the text.

Longman Educational Psychology Transparency Program The Transparency Program includes 20 color acetates and 60 blackline masters that highlight key concepts of *Contemporary Educational Psychology,* as well as core information about the field. It features many easy-to-read lists and summary tables, and is free to instructors upon adoption of the text.

Case Studies of Beginning Teachers Written by Theodore Kowalski, Roy Weaver, and Kenneth Henson, this reasonably-priced supplement offers a collection of 35 case studies of first-year teaching experiences that are a mixture of true dilemmas and best solution scenarios. Bridging theory and practice, the cases bring to life actual problems and challenges that educational psychology students will most likely face in their own teaching. Readers are encouraged to apply the general principles of education psychology, become active learners, and develop their decision-making skills.

Contemporary Educational Psychology provides a comprehensive and modern treatment of educational psychology that emphasizes the rich value of theory, concepts, and research for practice in a decision-making framework. We are optimistic that you will be pleased with the improvements made in this revision, and encourage you to continue to write us with suggestions for future editions.

acknowledgments

We want to thank Jo Ann Santoro and June Benson, who generously helped us prepare the manuscript. Special thanks are also given to Gail Hinkel, who read a draft of the manuscript and offered insightful editorial advice, and Mary Heller, who contributed the writing portfolio materials for the photo essay on assessment. Mary McCaslin provided substantial critiques of several chapters. We especially thank the many reviewers who provided extensive and helpful suggestions about style and content:

Keith Allred—Brigham Young University

Padma Anand—Slippery Rock University

Charles Bacon—Indiana University/Purdue University at Fort Wayne

Andrea Clements—West Georgia College

Theodore Coladarci—University of Maine

Lynn Diaz-Rico—California State University, San Bernadino

Beth Doll—University of Colorado at Denver

Beverly Dretzke—University of Wisconsin, Eau Claire

Keith Eicher—University of Richmond

Thomas Fetsco—Northern Arizona University

Diane Friedman—Radford University

Sherryl Browne Graves—Hunter College

Andrew Hanson—California State University, Chico

Craig Jones—Arkansas State University

Catherine King—Elon College

Hellmut Lang—University of Regina, Saskatchewan

Golam Mannan—Indiana University/Purdue University at Indianapolis

Tess Mehring—Emporia State University

Gary Negin—California State University, San Bernadino

Peggy Perkins—University of Nevada, Las Vegas

Maryanne Reid—Texas Technical University

Robert Reilly—University of Arkansas

Dawn Schrader—Cornell University

Nancy Smuckler—University of Wisconsin, Milwaukee

Lani Van Dusen—Utah State University

Paul Wagner—University of Houston, Clear Lake

Robert Weiseman—Auburn University at Montgomery

Victor Willson—Texas A&M University

Ann Wilson—Buena Vista College

part I.

introduction

Jane Lawton, *a junior at State University majoring in secondary education and a diligent student, worried after her mother called to inform her that Jane's father was ill and to ask her to come home. Jane wondered how and when to approach Dr. Shelton, the professor of her learning theories course, to say she needed to miss the first examination. She wondered what she would do if she were a teacher in that situation. Is it fair to extend extra time to some students but not to all? When do teachers make exceptions?*

Ruth Mentor, *a fifth-grade teacher at Casis Elementary School, noticed that Robbie Baker was extremely inattentive and doing poorly on his assignments since he was moved to the back of the room for excessive talking. Did Robbie need the extra structure and contact with the teacher that he had gotten when he was in the front of the room? Perhaps Robbie couldn't see the board or hear well now. Ruth started to think about what she would do next to determine which of these possibilities was most likely. She was concerned and wanted to get Robbie back on track.*

Mr. Chu *circulated around the biology lab as his students worked on an experiment. Passing one table, he heard Joe say to Penny, "Why aren't you wearing a sexy outfit? I like coming to class when you're good to look at!"*

Tim Coleman *was a seventh-grade teacher at Ames Junior High. He was teaching one of his favorite topics—converting base 10 to other number systems. However, most of the students seemed to be bored with the material and assignments. "Why do we have to study this stuff? We'll never use it!" and they would moan. Tim lamented the fact that he had not been able to convey to them the importance of the work he was presenting.*

Carolyn Lanier *listened as Alicia and Manuel, two of her star pupils, complained about the exam she had just handed back. "That test was so unfair," said Alicia irritably. "We only spent 20 percent of class time on the material on that exam! That's not a test; that's a guessing game!" Ms. Lanier wondered if she should start using portfolio and performance evaluation, as a fellow teacher had begun to do.*

teaching is complex. It demands the ability to analyze rapidly changing social and instructional interactions carefully and to respond quickly to a variety of competing concerns. *Successful* teaching requires that teachers have thorough understanding of human development, learning and instructional theory, motivation, and classroom management theory, as well as knowledge of how to assess student learning.

Some contend that teachers make more decisions, under worse conditions, than any other managers in society. The preceding vignettes present examples of some problems classroom teachers face. Instructors like Harry Shelton must determine how much to consider social and personal factors when making decisions about course requirements.

Teachers must often make inferences about whether student difficulties are caused by developmental factors, motivational factors, or instructional factors, as the example involving Ruth Mentor and her inattentive student indicates. Mr. Chu's experience illustrates that classroom instruction always takes place in a social context and that at times teachers have to deal with issues like harassment. Teachers also must consider friendships, peer pressure, and social aggression when planning

instructional environments. The example involving Tim Coleman's bored students, and Carolyn Lanier's tests that drew criticism, illustrates two other challenges teachers face if they are to be successful: motivating students to learn assigned material actively, and developing evaluation systems that accurately and objectively measure student ability. The first step teachers must take to deal with an issue or solve a problem effectively is understanding the cause of the student's difficulty. Teachers who have good subject-matter backgrounds and who know how students learn and develop will have more tools with which to assess student problems than less well-prepared teachers.

We believe teachers can have a major, positive influence on the way students learn and develop if they have a genuine interest in students, can express that interest, know their subject matter, and possess detailed information about instructional processes and the ways students learn and develop. In Part I we explore the knowledge and conceptual skills emphasized in this textbook. We look at ideas that have a rich history as well as current authoritative views of motivation. Note that educational psychology provides an important framework for looking at learners and the learning process.

chapter **1.**

classrooms, teachers, instruction, and educational psychology

objectives

When you have mastered the material in this chapter, you will be able to

1. Discuss the component skills of teaching and explain how the study of educational psychology can help one become a successful instructor
2. Describe the relationship between theories and hypotheses and between teaching and decision making
3. Describe Good and Brophy's general model of teacher decision making, using a practical example
4. Explain how the common features of classrooms noted by Doyle (1986) shape the task of teaching

5. Describe and explain Shavelson's model of teachers' preinstructional decisions
6. Distinguish successful from less successful teachers on the basis of their expectations and attitudes toward students
7. Describe how the classroom environment, its routines, and the role expectations for teachers and students constrain teacher decision making
8. Understand how group pressure affects individual student performance
9. Use a decision-making framework to analyze the case studies that appear at the end of the chapter

teachers make decisions

Jan Reisch was irritated because class discussion wasn't going well, and she thought that few of the students had read the material. She was also upset and distracted by the minor but constant misbehavior of a few students. Finally, she responded: "Ralph Jordan, give Terri her pencil back and get in your seat now! You've been fooling around for two weeks! I've had it! For the next two afternoons, I want you to report to detention period." After class, Ralph came to her desk and said, "I'm sorry about being out of my seat playing with Terri. I know I've been a pain recently. I've had problems at home and . . . well, I don't want to talk about it." He hesitated a moment and then said, "Look, I'm really sorry and I'll shape up, but I just started to work at a grocery store and I need to be there after school. I really need the job. Can we work something else out?"

Should Jan stick with her statement so as not to undermine her credibility with students? Should she compromise? (She could give Ralph a couple of days to rearrange his schedule with his employer.) If she cancels the punishment or provides a substitute, should she say anything to the class?

Alan Mirabella looked at his fifth graders' test results on the math unit. Half of the class had less than 60 percent correct—a miserable performance. He asked himself, "Should I reteach this unit? It's an important one, but it's getting late in the year and I've only covered half the text. At this rate they won't be ready to do sixth-grade work. Maybe I should go on but assign some type of homework review."

Should Alan reteach the unit? Are students having difficulty because the work is too hard for them or because of lack of effort—or because of inadequate teaching? If he assigns homework but students still do relatively poorly, what then? Is the "sixth-grade curriculum" a relevant restriction on a fifth-grade teacher?

John Dalton paused and tried to think of a way to rephrase a question to help Helen answer. He believed that she really knew the material. However, Helen and two other students, Rick and Hector, were so shy that it was difficult to determine whether they didn't respond because they didn't know the answer or because they lacked confidence.

Should John ask Helen, Rick, and Hector easier questions than he asks other students? Or will this just increase their embarrassment? If they don't answer his first question, should he ask additional questions until they give a response? Or would such persistence only increase their insecurity in public response situations?

As these vignettes indicate, teaching requires countless decisions, some of which need to be made on the spot. Teachers need to decide what to teach, how to present the material, and how to determine whether students understand and can apply it. Successful teachers use principles of educational psychology to make such decisions.

educational psychology and instructional decision making

what is educational psychology?

Anyone who attempts to help others learn (not only classroom teachers but parents teaching children, supervisors teaching trainees, etc.) can benefit from knowledge of educational psychology and decision-making models. For example, a nutrition educator needs to determine the amount of information to present in one training session and the sequence in which to present it, as well as what material students can master through self-study and how to design self-study units that will motivate learners to complete them successfully. Nutrition educators, like all educators, need to define their goals, determine criteria for meeting those goals, and then assess conditions that will enhance the learners' motivation to master the material.

In this chapter the examples of decision making focus on classroom teaching; keep in mind, however, that the decision-making model is applicable to all instructional settings and teaching roles. Educational psychology provides a framework for looking at the student, the learning process, and the learning situation. The study of educational psychology includes the following areas:

1. Educational objectives and instructional design
2. Student development, personality, and aptitude
3. The learning process; theories of learning and motivation
4. The psychology of teaching methods (selecting, organizing, motivating, explaining, scaffolding students' learning efforts)
5. Social dynamics (e.g., knowledge of how to organize students for collaborative group work, social cognition)
6. Classroom management (preventing and responding to behavior problems, obtaining student cooperation, allowing students to assume appropriate responsibility for managing their own learning)
7. Evaluation of results

Good teaching requires mastery of three areas: knowledge and conceptual skills (the content of educational psychology), teaching skills, and decision-making skills. Our goal in this book is to provide a format for integrating these three areas. Good teaching involves the integration of knowledge of teaching with knowledge of content and of students and, more broadly, the enactment of curriculum.

why emphasize decision making?

Effective instructors know that the method of instruction used affects learning, so they apply principles drawn from the study of learning, motivation, development, and teaching to tailor their approach to the situation. We stress a decision-making approach to teaching because there is no simple formula for classroom success. Research yields valuable concepts and ways of looking at classrooms, not answers.

Consider Adams and Biddle's (1970) finding that students who sit in the *action zone* (the middle front-row seats and the seats extending directly up the middle aisle) receive more opportunities to participate in class than do other students. The action zone concept is important for analyzing classroom participation patterns. If Adams and Biddle's study were interpreted too literally, however, we might conclude that the action zone is always centered on the front row and the middle aisle. More recently, Alhajri (1981) studied thirty-two classrooms and found only one with an action zone that matched the pattern Adams and Biddle described. Alhajri found many classrooms in which a different kind of action zone was present. If observers had been monitoring these classes for only one type of action zone, they might not have perceived the action zones that were present but took a different form.

The research literature is replete with valuable concepts and findings that have rich potential for classroom application. However, teachers have to apply research by combining their knowledge of the classroom with other types of evidence. For example, Rowe (1969) found that some teachers waited less time after asking a question for lower-achieving students than for more capable students. Brophy and Good (1970) observed that many teachers called on low achievers less frequently than high achievers. One might conclude that teachers should call on low achievers more frequently and wait longer for them to respond. However, teachers need to integrate such research knowledge with other general knowledge (e.g., students' developmental level), as well as knowledge of particular students (e.g., Is the student excessively shy? How knowledgeable is the student about

the topic under discussion?). Subsequent research (see Good & Brophy, 1994) has illustrated that teachers must integrate several types of knowledge when making decisions about how long to wait.

using research to support decision making

structural elaboration versus personal elaboration It is important to distinguish between two possible uses of research findings. Fenstermacher (1983) noted that sometimes research is used to generate answers or specific guidelines for how to teach, and he referred to this use as *structural elaboration*. A school district, for example, might urge teachers to teach in a specific way because of findings obtained in another school district. This approach often leads to the misapplication of research findings. What makes good sense in a rural district may not work as well in a suburban district. Similarly, what works well in seventh-grade math may be less effective or even counterproductive in second-grade math or seventh-grade history. Thus, research findings should not be used for structural elaboration but instead for *personal elaboration* (consider the relevancy of research findings in one's own context), to stimulate informed and thoughtful action.

In this book we stress that theoretical principles and research findings provide a basis for planning and implementing instruction. Teachers, however, must act as independent decision makers when applying these general concepts and principles, keeping their particular students and goals in mind. The text provides information and introduces concepts that teachers can use to develop solutions to problems such as those that Jan Reisch, Alan Mirabella, and John Dalton faced. We see this text and the field of educational psychology generally as the systematization of information and concepts that help teachers to become more aware of classroom behavior, to interpret its significance (e.g., to understand the motivation that is associated with it), and to bring about desired changes in students.

subject-matter knowledge versus action-system knowledge Unfortunately, some teachers never become active decision makers or effective instructors. Some fail because they do not have adequate knowledge of the content they teach. Others know the subject matter but fail because they do not understand students or classrooms. Leinhardt and Smith (1984) distinguished between action-system knowledge and subject-matter knowledge. **Subject-matter knowledge** includes the *specific information necessary to understand and present content.* **Action-system knowledge** refers to *skills for planning the lesson, making decisions about lesson pace, explaining material clearly, and responding to individual differences in how students learn.*

teaching: a combination of processes

This book presents knowledge that will help you to understand how students learn and develop, how classrooms can be managed, and how to present information, general concepts, and learning assignments effectively. This information will complement the subject-matter knowledge you gain in other courses by providing you with a knowledge of educational psychology—action-system knowledge that will help you to become a successful teacher.

Doyle (1992a) argues that pedagogical processes are deeply embedded in issues of curriculum. For example, in most acts of teaching

there are both general processes (providing explanations, asking questions) and domain-specific content knowledge (e.g., of good examples to use for teaching particular content). Doyle suggests that teaching is best viewed as "curriculum enactment" or the synthesis of curriculum content, pedagogical processes, and classroom management. We, too, believe that teaching involves the orchestration of various types of knowledge and skills. The focus of this book is on action-system knowledge, but this knowledge needs to be combined with subject-matter knowledge and subject-matter pedagogy if teaching is to be successful.

The study of educational psychology will help you turn content knowledge (gained in other courses) into what Shulman (1986) referred to as pedagogical content knowledge, or knowledge for teaching. Principles of educational psychology are useful for transforming subject-matter knowledge (e.g., concepts like gravity and density) into information that students can comprehend.

reflective teaching

An important goal of this book is to encourage instruction that is deliberate and based on reflection. Many decisions that teachers make are not reflective or considered. They teach the way they were taught or discipline students the way their cooperating teacher supervisor did.

Carlsen (1991a) studied the effects of four biology teachers' subject-matter knowledge on discourse and activity focus in their classrooms. Teachers were observed as they presented an equal number of lessons on topics about which they had either high or low knowledge. They were more likely to use lectures and relatively open-ended laboratory activities when teaching high-knowledge topics but to use seatwork assignments and nonlaboratory projects for topics about which they had low knowledge. It appears unlikely that these teachers considered

Teachers as decision makers: how to present the material, how to pace the material, what responses to look for, how much time to spend.

how their knowledge of subject matter might influence their choice of instructional format and thus, their students' opportunities to learn. Thus, many teaching decisions are made at an implicit level.

Even with both action-system knowledge and subject-matter knowledge, some teachers may not apply the knowledge they possess. Such teachers may have inappropriately low expectations for students' ability to learn or for their own ability to teach. Or they may not be active decision makers. Lacking an integrated set of theories and belief systems to provide a personal framework for informed decision making, they do not have effective strategies for organizing information gleaned from numerous, rapidly occurring classroom events.

common beliefs and assumptions

Many beliefs that are common among teachers turn out to be myths when subjected to systematic study. For example, the view that frequent teacher praise of student performance facilitates achievement has been shown to be false. Selective praise is useful, but excessive praise may interfere with learning. The timing and quality of praise are generally more important than its frequency (Brophy, 1981). Moreover, teachers have to consider how students interpret "praise." Students may react differently to the same teacher or action (McCaslin, 1990). Such complexities, even about seemingly obvious matters, illustrate why teachers must continually think and make decisions. Research does not yield simple answers like "praise is always good."

importance of educational psychology

Some educators have estimated that roughly one-half of effective teaching acts require only common sense but the other half are counterintuitive (Coker, Medley, & Soar, 1980). Hence, to make a correct decision requires knowledge in order not to do what seems obvious. Furthermore, it is clear that teaching requires continuous decision making (Billups & Rauth, 1987). Indeed, Berliner (1984) noting the complexity of teaching, has contended that even after careful planning a typical teacher will still have to make at least ten nontrivial decisions an hour. Thus, if teachers are to make good decisions, a thorough grounding in educational psychology is required.

Gage (1963, pp. 94–95) described the view that all persons are theorists this way: "They differ not in whether they use theory, but in the degree to which they are aware of the theory they use. The choice facing the man in the street and the research worker alike is not whether to theorize but whether to articulate his theory, to make it explicit, to get it out in the open where he can examine it. Implicit theories . . . are used by all of us in our everyday affairs."

Educational psychologists develop explicit assumptions about the conditions that facilitate learning and then collect data to verify or refute these assumptions. Some readers probably raised a puzzled eyebrow upon reading the previous sentence. They prefer the facts—"Just tell me what works; that's all I want to know." Unfortunately, if we were to restrict ourselves to a discussion of what *always* works, we would end the book here. No teaching strategy will work for all students, goals, or settings. However, some teaching behaviors and learning experiences have high probabilities of bringing about desired responses. For example, correcting a minor disturbance nonverbally (with perhaps a shake of the head) is usually, but not always, more efficient and less disruptive than a verbal strategy. Similarly, preventing

behavioral problems is generally more effective than correcting students after misbehavior has occurred (Good & Brophy, 1994). Holding students accountable for explaining and understanding material (not just memorizing discrete facts) is more likely to encourage students to integrate material (Blumenfeld, 1992a).

The study of educational psychology provides a way of *formulating hypotheses* about effective classroom strategies. **Hypotheses** are seen by researchers as *a description about the relationship between variables*. A less formal way of thinking about hypotheses is to view them as simply intelligent guesses based on all available information. The more information we have, the more confident we can be about our strategy decisions. The less information we have, the greater the risk that our strategy will fail. One may hypothesize, for example, that an attractive stranger is "dateable" because there is no ring on the "key" finger. However, many married people do not wear wedding rings because the ring is lost, is too small, or irritates the skin.

In this chapter we introduce a model of classroom decision making illustrating that teachers who make good decisions (and who are willing to correct poor ones) are most likely to foster student motivation and learning. After presenting a decision-making model, we discuss a few problems that almost all teachers must solve if they are to make good decisions. Finally, we discuss some of the special problems that many beginning teachers face.

teaching decisions and goals

Decisions about teaching strategies operate in the same way. Often we make decisions using only minimal knowledge ("Will my students integrate ideas better if I require them to prepare for a formal exam or if I assign a take-home exam on this new topic that I am teach-

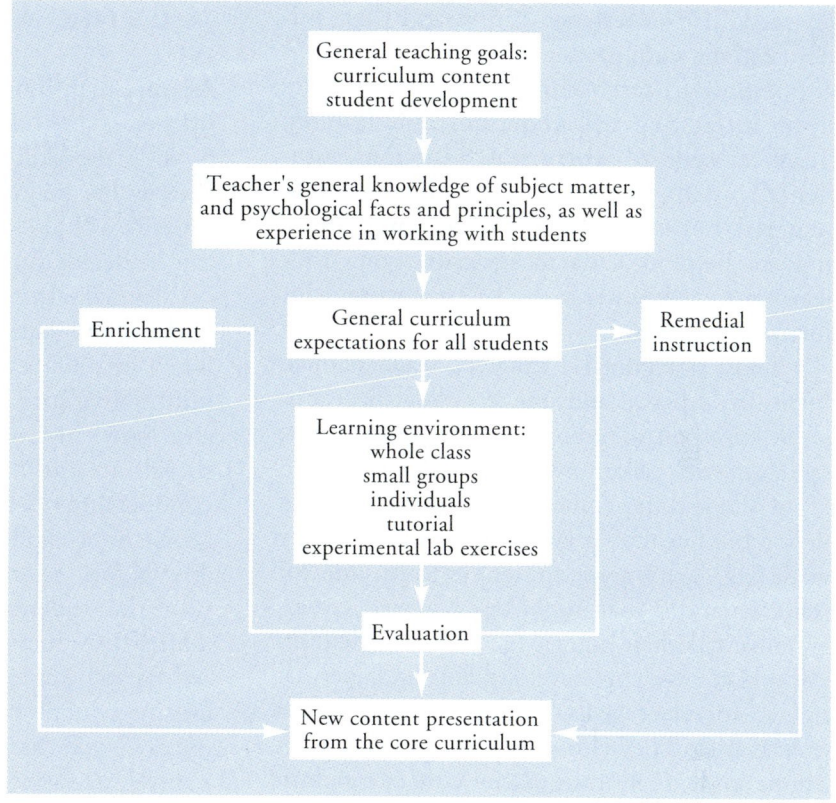

Figure 1.1 Good and Brophy's general decision model

Note: Once a teacher makes a decision to structure the learning environment (e.g., chooses to use a whole-class or small-group format), it is possible to produce more explicit models of decision making.

SOURCE: T. Good and J. Brophy, "Teaching the Lesson," in R. Slavin (Ed.), *School and Classroom Organization* (Hillsdale, NJ: Lawrence Erlbaum, 1988). Reprinted by permission.

ing for the first time?"). Other decisions can be based on considerable knowledge—research or past experience with students—but there is still a risk that the strategy will not work. If we are explicit about our teaching goals and about what we will accept as evidence that students are making satisfactory progress, we can identify untenable hypotheses and change teaching plans. Some decisions can be made through better use of our own time and resources (e.g., talk to students who are having difficulty and attempt to see the problem from their perspective), but others can be made only after obtaining information from other teachers or parents (Rosenholtz, 1989; Strike, 1993).

a model for decision making
instructional goals

The model represented in Figure 1.1 suggests that intelligent decision making begins with a clear statement of instructional goals. Teachers need clear goals, ordered according to their relative importance, if they are to make optimal use of classroom time and resources. However, it is impossible for teachers, especially beginning teachers, to be explicit about all decisions. For example, a new third-grade teacher who observed in a first-grade classroom during an early field-experience course and then student taught sixth graders must make decisions about how to teach third-grade mathematics in an interesting and understandable fashion. Teachers have to worry not only about students' initial acquisition and integration of material but they also have to worry about how to help students to structure what they learn around key ideas and to remember it for future application.

Thus, as Figure 1.1 suggests, teachers must form hypotheses and make many decisions about how best to arrange learning tasks so that students will make good progress. First, given all of the specific content (e.g., understanding how a bill becomes a law) and general learning goals (e.g., helping the student to learn skills for self-evaluation) that might be addressed, teachers must use their knowledge about curriculum goals and student development and performance to select goals that are reasonable for their classes. They also must determine to what extent students need to master core curriculum content (and at what level—80 percent, 95 percent) and develop procedures for dealing with students who fail to meet their goals initially (i.e., remedial programs) as well those who master core material quickly (enrichment). Further, teachers need to make decisions about how students learn (alone, with computer instruction, in a small group, etc.).

Even teachers who have taught at the same grade level for several years must be decision makers. Although they will develop good knowledge about age-appropriate pacing of assignments and so on, many factors will change. For example, the students many teachers instruct today are vastly different from those they taught ten years ago (Natriello, McDill, & Pallas, 1990). In addition, there have been significant changes in technology and in the goals that teachers must accomplish. For example, many teachers today must learn how to design and how to assess student portfolios (Mitchell, 1992).

using the model

Assume that Ted Wilson, a high-school speech teacher, wants his students to develop the ability to make skillful extemporaneous speeches. This is his major goal. But when should Ted teach this skill—early or late in the year? How can he decide (make a hypothesis)?

To make this decision, Ted must first specify the other goals he has in mind (e.g., the ability to introduce a speaker; to deliver a formal, informative speech; to deliver a formal, persuasive speech; to make an extemporaneous speech; to lead a committee discussion; and to conduct interviews). Next, he must define his goals more explicitly. What does he mean by "the ability to introduce a speaker"? Does he want the student to be able to deliver with ease a brief introduction that someone else has written, or to be able to write and deliver appropriate introductions for different types of audiences (such as audiences who are hostile, neutral, or supportive toward the speaker)?

Teachers must also consider students' goals and interests. Part of any effective instructional program is helping students to set goals and to make decisions. Hence, teachers also have to help students develop skills for self-regulating their own learning (McCaslin, 1990).

After defining what he wants to accomplish, Ted will be in a better position to estimate the time it will take to fulfill each goal. If he determines that the ability to deliver a formal, informative speech is his most important goal, he probably should introduce informative speeches early in the year. This will enable each student to present several such speeches and to improve in response to Ted's feedback. In contrast, if interview technique is relatively unimportant, he may want to schedule it toward the end of the year, where it can be eliminated if some units take more time than anticipated.

After becoming more explicit about their goals, teachers may want to evaluate their students' entering achievement through pretesting.

For Ted, this might mean having everyone make a one-minute, ungraded presentation to the class. Even from brief performances, Ted can gain valuable information about the general ability of the class and predict how fast he can proceed in the course. Furthermore, he can identify students who are likely to make excellent presentations and use this information profitably when he arranges the order of speakers for the first assignment.

decision making: a continuing process

planning and evaluating instructional goals

The system we describe here is active and dynamic. Teachers make plans and set goals based on their professional judgment, the policies of the schools in which they teach, and their students' characteristics. Once objectives are set, effective teachers select instructional strategies and establish appropriate learning environments, then monitor student progress and alter instruction as necessary. It is important to monitor student progress closely, because students may interpret teacher explanations and class assignments in different ways (Wittrock, 1986), and some will develop misunderstandings that need to be corrected. Good teachers are open to the possibility that lessons or units that have worked in the past may be less successful now with certain students or classes.

Teachers' decision making is more complex when enacting certain types of classroom instructional plans. For example, small-group instructional models are becoming more popular and place new types of cognitive demands on teachers. It is difficult to monitor student performance when teaching the whole class but even more complex when trying to make inferences about the thinking and performance of students who are working in groups of three or four. Given that teachers cannot monitor directly much of what occurs while students work in pairs or small groups, they will need to find ways to gather data about student work in these settings (McCaslin & Good, in press, a; Mulryan, 1992).

Even without such preliminary evaluative information, teachers can start making instructional decisions based on their understanding of general learning principles, instructional methods, and knowledge acquired from past experience with students. However, they must evaluate the wisdom of their initial decisions regularly by using feedback (student comments, observation of student behavior) from day-to-day teaching activities and from formal evaluation (classroom tests, themes). Goals or strategies may change in a class as new information is gathered. Teachers may see that some students have already mastered certain objectives, so they can replace these objectives with new ones or encourage students to set their own plans. Conversely, teachers may realize that they cannot reach some of their instructional objectives. Thus, evaluation is an important and continuous aspect of teaching.

logical sequencing of objectives

Teachers' plans are influenced not only by the relative importance of various instruction objectives but also by their *logical sequencing*. Some objectives involve skills that must be mastered as prerequisites (e.g., students need to learn subtraction before tackling division).

In Ted's speech class, the simplest task is the introduction of a speaker. This task contains key elements common to all other tasks (assumption of leadership role, public utterances, and so on), but it is more structured, briefer, and requires few memory or timing skills. The limited scope of this task, its minimal anxiety-arousal properties, and the high probability that students can complete it successfully combine to make it a good first presentation.

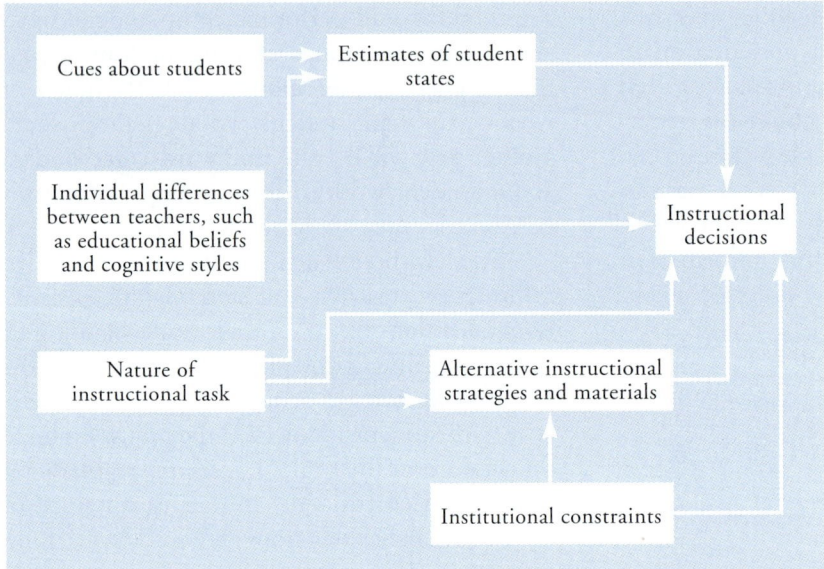

Figure 1.2 some factors contributing to teachers' preinstructional decisions

SOURCE: Adapted from "A Model of Decision Making" by R. Shavelson. Paper presented at the annual meeting of the American Educational Research Association, Toronto, March 1978. Reprinted by permission.

task analysis **Task analysis**, the attempt to find logical starting and connecting points in sequencing instruction, is an important activity. It is *the specification of the various subordinate skills, information, and knowledge that students must possess if they are to achieve a new educational objective.* In this particular example, with relatively mature high-school students, Ted could probably start with any of the goals. There is no critical starting point, as there often is with more sequentially organized subject matter. Still, some arrangements would be more efficient than others.

In addition to goal and task analysis, *information about students*—their general aptitudes, their interests, and other learner characteristics such as achievement motivation or anxiety—is essential for making effective instructional decisions. Concepts of intelligence (Gardner, 1983) and motivation (Ames, 1992) are useful in making instructional decisions. If most of Ted's students are highly capable, he may decide to start the course with challenging assignments and move along at a rapid pace. If his students are less capable, he may

initially decide to cover fewer skills and move at a slower pace so that students can review key skills frequently. He may also spend some time in gamelike activities to maintain student interest. His larger goal, though, will be to build student interest to the point where he can increase the pace and level of difficulty of assigned work. If the class has a wide range of abilities, he may choose other strategies (Hiebert, 1991).

Motivation can be conceptualized in various ways, and it is important to adjust the motivational focus to the students and the task. Teachers who see student ability as fixed (compared to teachers who see it as flexible) are less likely to assign novel and challenging tasks to students perceived as low in ability. They also are less likely to teach these students metacognitive strategies for controlling their own learning (Pressley & El-Dinary, 1993; Weinstein & Mayer, 1986).

It is possible to develop more specific models depicting different types of teacher decisions. Figure 1.2, based on Shavelson's (1978, 1983) work, illustrates how teachers make pre-

Figure 1.3 the relationship between teachers' expectations and students' performance

SOURCE: Adapted from "An Analysis of Teacher Expectation Effects" by T. Good, in D. Berliner and B. Rosenshine (Eds.), *Talks to Teacher*, 1978. New York, McGraw-Hill. Reprinted by permission.

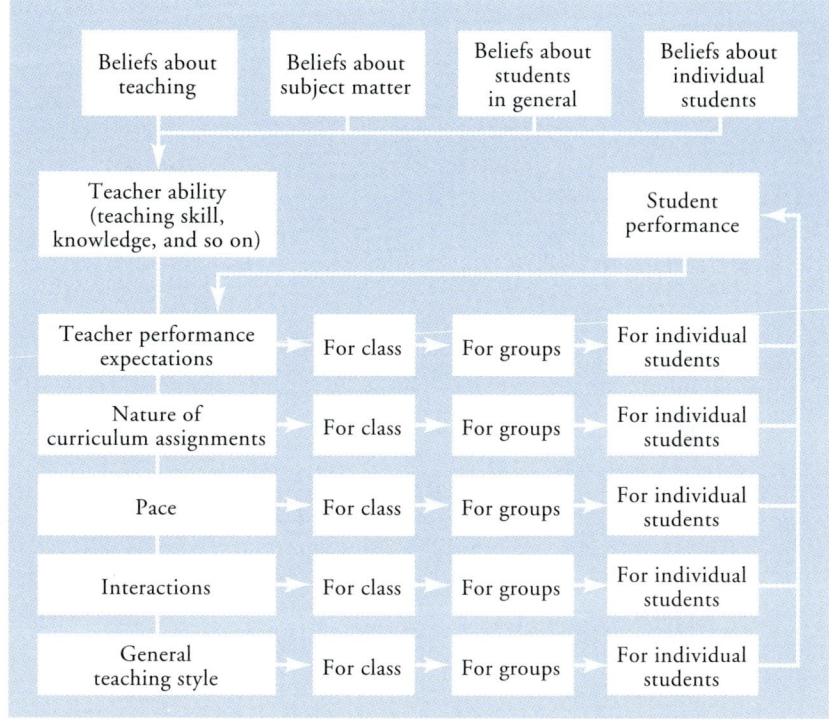

instructional decisions and shows some of the factors involved in planning instruction.

Teachers possess much information about students from observations of previous class performance, standardized test scores, and reports from other teachers. Teachers make judgments about what students can do, what they are interested in, and so forth. Such information can improve instructional planning *if teachers use it appropriately*. Sometimes teachers—especially when dealing with special-education students—focus too much on students' reputations or backgrounds rather than on what these students can do (Brantlinger & Guskin, 1987). As Figure 1.3 illustrates, how teachers form and communicate expectations for the class and for individual students is complex. Of course, as Figure 1.4 illustrates, how students internalize expectations is equally complex.

setting teaching goals

Teachers also have personal beliefs about the purposes and nature of instruction that vary widely and affect instructional decisions in many ways (Carlsen, 1991a; Clark & Peterson, 1986; Pajares, 1992). Teachers interested in affective goals (how students *feel* about content, themselves, and others) are more likely to consider different instructional strategies than do teachers who are more interested in cognitive goals (subject-matter knowledge). Teachers who emphasize affective goals may group students frequently and allow them to work cooperatively. In contrast, teachers who want to maximize cognitive growth may individualize the curriculum and encourage students to learn at a rapid pace.

Shavelson's model (see Figure 1.2) suggests

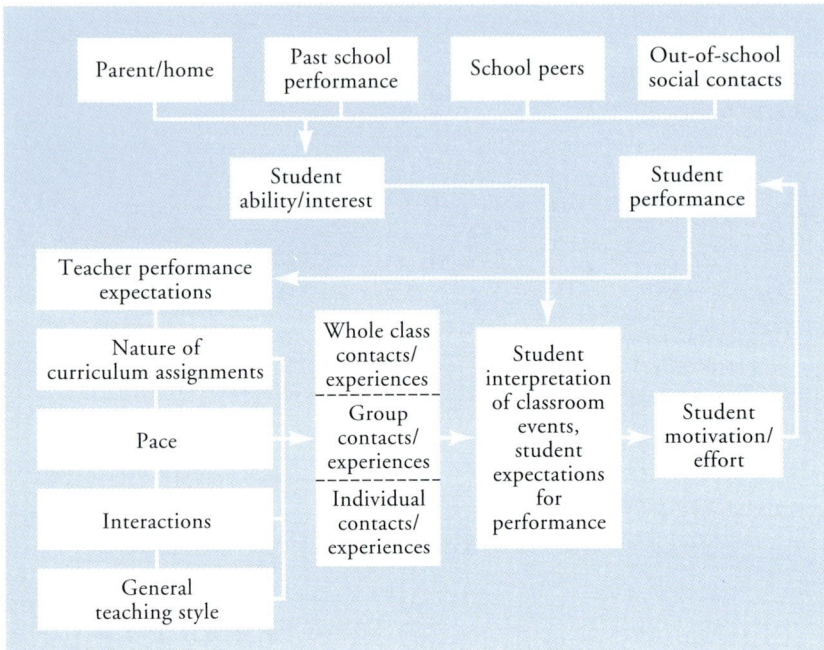

Figure 1.4 individual students' performance expectations

SOURCE: Adapted from "An Analysis of Teacher Expectation Effects" by T. Good, in D. Berliner and B. Rosenshine (Eds.), *Talks to Teacher*, 1978. New York, McGraw-Hill. Reprinted by permission.

that the nature of instructional tasks is another source of influence on instructional decisions. At present there is a great deal of research interest in the possibility that different types of teaching may be needed in different subjects (Stodolsky, 1988). Particular texts or curricula will lead a teacher toward certain instructional strategies, activities, assignments, or cues to student progress and away from others. Again, teachers who are aware of how they make decisions and who monitor progress toward their goals will be more effective than teachers who operate with vague theories.

making hypotheses

Analyses indicate that teachers have to make complex decisions rapidly and under adverse conditions. Consider a few of the decisions Ted must make. When his students make their presentations, should the focus be on the entire skill (speaker introduction), or is it better for students to do only a part of the task (e.g., deliver an effective opening sentence that avoids triteness)? When students complete their speeches, should they get public or private feedback? Should feedback be from peers as well as from the teacher? Should the teacher systematize the feedback by providing a form, or should it be spontaneous? When students make good presentations early in the year, should they receive praise, just matter-of-fact feedback, or criticism designed to encourage them to try harder?

Similarly, Ted must be concerned with the listeners and their learning needs. When should students read about a topic before hearing a speech about it? When might prior knowledge be a disadvantage? Should students be taught to be "active listeners"? Should they be taught to take notes (see Pressley & El-Dinary, 1993; Weinstein

& Mayer, 1986)? Should they focus only on skills for critiquing speeches, or will they also be expected to learn content from the presentations?

day-to-day decision making

The decisions discussed so far are ones that teachers can make before instruction and student performance. Many decisions, however, have to be made on a day-to-day basis. Suppose that five students are talking quietly but persistently in the middle of the room as George shakily delivers his first extemporaneous speech. Should Ted stop the disturbance, reassure George, and then allow him to continue? Or should Ted wait until the speech is over? What if several students do not participate in the feedback discussions that follow each presentation? Should Ted ask these students to outline speeches as they listen to them? Should he call on reluctant students directly rather than allow participation in the discussion to be voluntary? Now assume that students are performing a new speech skill and that the first two students do poorly. Ted suspects that the students have misunderstood the assignment. Should he continue with the next three presentations planned that day? What other options does he have? Another day, Ted decides to allow students, for variety, to analyze presentations in small groups. However, the groups engage in little substantive exchange. Should he continue with the small groups, perhaps after giving more guidance about what he expects? What information does he need to make the decision?

The psychological concepts presented in this text are useful tools for assessing classroom behavior and making on-the-spot decisions. If teachers can see and analyze problems as they occur, they can make appropriate modifications immediately or the next day rather than delaying until they can collect formal evaluative information (perhaps a week or two later).

Teaching experience and insight into the teaching-learning process provide a base for making intelligent decisions about the design of instruction, but it is equally important that teachers examine day-to-day instructional processes to be sure that learners are making progress. Research on teacher planning has shown that most teachers do not monitor their day-to-day activities in terms of general instructional goals (Clark & Yinger, 1979).

schools are complex places: impediments to effective decision making

Teachers who have teaching skill, knowledge of the learning process, and a can-do attitude can have significant effects on learners. Teachers do not always make decisions independently, however. Many decisions are influenced by the behavior of previous teachers or by parents, students' peers, and school policies (see, e.g., Schwille et al., 1983), and by their own unacknowledged or explicit assumptions. Frequently, too, teachers' ability to make decisions is limited by a lack of time or other factors of the learning environment.

unacknowledged assumptions and unexamined beliefs

Some instructional decisions are not made in a conscious, deliberate way, often because teachers simply do not see a problem. One teacher may view a pupil as pleasant, capable, and hardworking, whereas another teacher might realize that this student is anxious and excessively dependent on teachers, performing capably because he or she is a compulsive worker but socially withdrawn, seldom engaging in conversations with peers. If teachers are unaware of such problems, the decisions they make about handling the students will be less than optimal. Careful monitoring of one's teaching behavior and periodic reexamination of assumptions about individual students or instructional strategies help to reduce errors and to minimize their effects.

Teachers frequently make decisions on the basis of enthusiastic allegiance to an idea that has never been carefully examined. Some teachers believe in structure and teacher control whereas other teachers believe in student control and discovery approaches. However, there is growing awareness that the quality of classroom organizational structure—the way it is implemented—is much more important than the form (Ames, 1992; Blumenfeld, 1992a; Mason & Good, 1993). Hence, teachers will need to be adept at knowing when and how to use several methods.

how effective teachers respond

examination of assumptions Effective teachers must be aware of the implicit assumptions they hold regarding learners' progress and must periodically reexamine these assumptions. To accept a strategy as the truth regardless of its effect on learning is blind faith, not careful thinking and creative adaptation. Indeed, a procedure that has worked for five consecutive classes may prove to be ineffective for the sixth class.

appropriate expectations To function as decision makers, teachers must believe that they can make a difference, that they can be effective in the classroom. Teaching skills and knowledge are important, but if a teacher is not motivated to use them consistently, little will be accomplished.

Brophy and Evertson (1976) provided an interesting description of how relatively effec-tive and ineffective teachers see themselves. They reported that the most pervasive differences between teachers who enabled students to make good learning gains and less effective teachers were in the teachers' basic role definitions. Successful teachers saw teaching as an interesting and worthwhile challenge that they approached by assuming personal responsibility for the learning of their students. These teachers saw problems but believed that the problems could be overcome and were therefore motivated to search for solutions. Less successful teachers discussed problems as if they were too serious to be solved, and their behavior often guaranteed that the problems would remain unsolved. They did not believe that they could make a difference, and therefore they did not. Positive expectations alone are not sufficient to ensure teaching success, but without them no teacher will be effective in the classroom.

Brophy and Evertson also observed that teachers who reported a sense of inner control and personal responsibility clearly reflected this in their classroom behavior. More successful teachers were prepared to work with slow students, helping them to overcome failure by reteaching and providing extra practice. More recent research has produced similar findings (Brophy & McCaslin, 1992).

limitations in the learning environment

limited time

school environment The school environment is also an important determinant of what teachers are able to accomplish. Some schools produce higher achievement than other schools with comparable student populations and resources (Good & Brophy, 1986). Some principals are more supportive and active leaders than others, and it is easier to teach in some schools than in others (Rosenholtz, 1989). If most teachers in a school support its curriculum and standards of excellence, for example, it is easier for beginning teachers to maintain standards of excellence than it would be in a school where most teachers simply kept students busy.

schools are busy places Classroom settings impose constraints on what can and cannot be accomplished. Whether teachers instruct the whole class, divide the class into three or four groups, or allow students to work individually, they have limited time for one-to-one contact with students. Teachers must therefore decide which students to interact with and under what circumstances.

Teachers are best viewed as managers making executive decisions in a fast-paced environment (Berliner, 1983). As managers, teachers have a doable but difficult job.

limited resources

Jackson (1968) contends that classrooms guarantee there are crowds as well as frequent and pervasive evaluations. Large groups of students are under one teacher's direction and share limited resources, so the life of an individual student is filled with interruption, delay, denial, distraction, and boredom. No matter how teachers behave or what characteristics they possess, they have to deal with these inherent characteristics of classrooms that will affect their decisions.

Jackson (1968) reported that teachers commonly engage in as many as a thousand interpersonal exchanges each day. When teachers talk with individual students they must do so with only partial attention, because they must also monitor the class and respond to students' questions and behavior. Teachers interpret students' behavior partly on the basis of what they have just witnessed and partly on the basis of their

previous interactions with these students and the general expectations they hold for them.

Thus, teachers may interpret an ambiguous expression such as a puzzled look as evidence of thinking when it appears on the face of a high achiever but as evidence of confusion on the face of a low achiever. The decision is rapid and has immediate consequences—the teacher pauses and waits for the "thinking" student to answer but asks another student to help the "confused" peer. Teachers may misinterpret an expression or give up too soon on a student because they must make almost instantaneous decisions. It is impossible to interpret correctly everything that occurs in a short time, so they must learn to observe selectively and to monitor key aspects of their interaction with students.

how effective teachers respond Teachers not only have to explain concepts and demonstrate skills, but they also have to monitor students for apparent understanding and provide feedback to students' responses. Furthermore, they must do this within a classroom context where they must maintain pupil attention, respond to interruptions, and move through activities at an appropriate pace. Consequently, teachers' interactive decision making usually cannot involve much deliberation about alternate courses of action. Instead, like other skilled individuals required to make expert decisions in complex situations, teachers develop routines and rely on heuristics (implicit rules people use without conscious awareness) to reduce the complexity of the classroom (e.g., Shavelson & Stern, 1981).

Teachers are well advised to obtain supplementary information from students in order to more accurately understand students' attitudes and needs as well as as their understanding of subject-matter concepts (McCaslin and Good, in press, b). For example, teachers might request from students on occasion brief reaction papers—how the class is going, what I'm excited about, what I'm confused by, what I want to learn more about. Teachers might also find time to have personal and private conversations with a few students each week.

the student's role

Similarly, if teachers have taught long enough in a particular school, students will bring expectations about them to the class. "She'll read mystery stories to the students who don't go to music." "Chemistry lab exercises don't mean anything." "Don't sweat it; he only grades on tests, and they're straight from the book." Such preconceptions no doubt make it either easier or more difficult to start the year. Students may overreact or respond inappropriately to the ambiguous expressions or statements of teachers who have poor reputations.

Thus, students who have spent thousands of hours sitting in classrooms will have expectations about what should take place in the room. Many also know how well they perform various classroom activities and whether they enjoy doing them. By middle childhood (ages nine through twelve), most students have developed relatively stable views of themselves and often reject information that describes them as better or worse than they believe themselves to be. Such expectations about school life and personal performance can be changed only by systematic effort.

Students' rigid expectations (e.g., that they don't like and/or can't do math well) may lead them to avoid applying themselves to new mathematical assignments (e.g., problem-solving tasks) at which they might succeed if they worked hard. Both teacher and student can become lulled into accepting as normal that the student is uninterested in math; hence, the teacher stops trying new ways to make math understandable. Expectations and routines can become so entrenched or rigid that teachers (and students) begin to do things without thinking about them or realizing that they are in effect making decisions by choosing certain options over others without assessing the wisdom of those decisions.

contemporary student problems

Although schools are relatively stable and predictable settings, students often live in environments that are unpredictable. And at times, students are exposed to dangerous situations in schools. Hence, teachers must make school decisions within the context of understanding that school events may have unintended consequences on the playground or after school.

However, problems vary widely from school to school. O'Neill (1994) noted that the results from a 1991 survey conducted by the National Center for Education Statistics found that in terms of opinions about school safety, tardiness, absenteeism, and fighting were top complaints and drug use fell near the bottom of the list. He concluded:

> The lists are not facts but a fundamental expression of attitudes and emotions. They overlook the successes of American public education, its great expansion since 1940, and its high quality despite taxpayer resistance. The lists' broad sweep ignores that some public schools are devastated by violence and substance use, and others hardly touched at all. (p. 49)

Covington (1992) argues, "In some ghetto schools, the rate of student deaths caused by peer violence and drug overdoses approaches the rate of American combat fatalities in the Vietnam War. Things have become so desperate in some urban areas that black teenage males have literally become an endangered group. And speaking of violence, consider suicide. Estimates of unsuccessful suicide attempts among our youth run as high as 600,000 per year nationwide with 6,000 actual deaths reported in 1986" (p. 7).

Thus, teachers in the 1990s are dealing with students who are coping with significant problems. Students face monumental problems that youth in other generations have not had to face.

Covington notes that 13 million students—or about one-half of all school-age youngsters—are at serious risk for failing academically.

the pressure to "look good" Group life affects the performance of individual students. Groups exert pressure on an individual to play a role (attentive participant, class clown, class rebel), and group pressure makes it difficult for teachers to have sustained, open dialogues with individual students. The presence of others, whether strangers or friends, is sufficient to alter behavior.

Holt (1964) and Covington (1992) both describe a number of self-defeating strategies that students engage in to prevent them from looking bad in the classroom. In particular, Holt suggests that many dependent students read the teacher like a traffic light. They begin their answers slowly and softly. If the teacher smiles, nods, or in any way indicates approval, the answers become more animated (louder, quicker) and more relaxed. If the teacher nonverbally signals dissatisfaction, the student shifts into a "thinking act"—a furrowed brow and a remark such as "let me think about that" followed by "no, what I meant to say—."

student strategies Students learn to use countless games and strategies, and no doubt you can recall many of them from your own experience. We suspect that most of you who took a language course in high school or college occasionally did not do all of the required translation. At such times you may have tried to be called on to read one of the first five or so paragraphs that you did translate by tactics such as waving your hand energetically, feigning sleep, or staring out the window, depending on the teacher. Your desire to look good to peers and the teacher and possibly your wish for good grades motivated such behavior (along with your wish not to look bad by saying, "I don't know; I didn't do the translation").

Such strategies for camouflaging lack of knowledge often work, largely because the interactions occur in a group setting. Pressure to "perform for the group" leads many students to adopt strategies that are ultimately self-defeating or at least ineffective. The strategies work temporarily because the teacher either feels the pressure to move on or is embarrassed by the student's failure to respond. In the long run, however, students profit little from such activities because they are not learning the material.

impression management Social pressure such as being compared with peers may encourage students to spend considerable time in impression management—trying to look good by projecting the image of listening to the teacher or perhaps developing self-defeating behavior patterns such as learned helplessness. There is growing evidence that students' beliefs about why they do well or poorly on a task are important because they influence how much time students will spend on similar tasks in the future (see Stipek, 1993, for a discussion of related work).

In an interesting ethnographic study, Spencer-Hall (1976) found that some students are better impression managers than others. She contended that students' different rates of misbehavior are not as important in cuing teachers' evaluations of students as are their styles of misbehavior. Many students are able to maintain favorable evaluations from teachers and peers alike by being careful to misbehave in ways that escape teacher attention.

Hence, the actions of some students may "encourage" teachers to monitor their behavior closely and over time make it more likely that these students' misbehavior will be detected and that teachers will blame them in ambiguous situations. More generally, students' responses to pressure to look good (not to ask for information when needed) sometimes cause them to mislead teachers, thus making teachers' interpretations of student behavior more difficult.

research at work
common classroom features

We have been discussing many aspects of classrooms that are complex and confusing, and this makes decision making difficult. Doyle (1986a) has captured many of these aspects of teaching in his list of common features seen in any classroom. He argues that the following features are common across classrooms.

1. Multidimensionality: Many different tasks and events occur in the classroom. Records and schedules must be kept, and work must be monitored, collected, and evaluated. A single event can have multiple consequences. Waiting a few seconds for one student to answer a question may support that student's motivation but reduce the interest of another student who would like to respond, and it slows the pace of the lesson for the rest of the class.
2. Simultaneity: Many things happen at the same time in classrooms. During a discussion a teacher not only listens and helps improve students' answers but also monitors students who do not respond for signs of comprehension and then tries to keep the lesson moving at a good pace.
3. Immediacy: The pace of classroom events is rapid. Sieber (1979) found that teachers evaluated pupil conduct an average of 15.89 times per hour, or 87 times a day, or an estimated 16,000 times a year.
4. Unpredictable and public classroom climate: Things often happen in ways that are unanticipated. Furthermore, much of what happens to a student is seen by many other students. Clearly, students can infer how the teacher feels about certain students by the way the teacher interacts with them in class.
5. History: Classes meet for several weeks or months, so common norms and understandings develop. Emmer, Evertson, and Anderson (1980) showed how events that happen early in the year sometimes influence how classrooms function the rest of the year. To a student teacher or observer, some classes appear easy to manage; events that took place earlier in the school year, however, may explain why things run smoothly the time of observation.

aids to effective decision making

Not all is complexity and confusion, however, since Doyle's fifth factor, history, makes for predictability. Various enduring aspects of schools allow stable predictions and thus make it possible to develop routines and shared assumptions that allow teachers to act as decision makers.

predictability

Although many classrooms now have nontraditional physical arrangements such as group-discussion corners, independent-study cubicles, learning stations, and microcomputer and word-processing corners, even such open or individualized classrooms remain stable for a variety of reasons. The same students use the committee table together, individual study comes at the same time each day, class routines remain the same, and so on.

To the extent that students have shared experiences in the past, expectations for the forthcoming year become narrower and more predictable. Mary and Arlene, for instance, represented the homeroom on student council last year, and it is likely that one or both of them will be nominated again this year. Bob is expected to complain about homework, and Terri will probably push the teacher for information about what will be covered on tests. Bill and Alice will have their hands up 90 percent of the time, but Tina and Jim will rarely raise their hands and will seldom respond if the teacher calls on them.

how effective teachers respond

Successful teachers held realistic attitudes toward students. They liked them and enjoyed interpersonal interaction with them but mostly within teaching-learning contexts. Less successful teachers tended to fall into one or two groups, both of which represented extreme responses to students. One group romanticized students as warm and wonderful. These teachers concentrated on their personal relationships with students, often to the point of failing to manage the classroom effectively or to meet students' instructional needs. Such teachers'

expectations were unrealistic, and their behavior, despite its warmth, was inappropriate because it met their own needs rather than the needs of their students. The second group of unsuccessful teachers was disillusioned and bitter, looking upon their students as enemies.

Successful teachers see themselves as instructors and problem solvers rather than as parent substitutes or disciplinarians. Their goal is to design educational environments that work—to help students learn and not to accept classroom problems and student limitations as unchangeable. This requires facing problems and working toward their resolution. Other researchers also have found that teachers' efficacy perceptions (can I teach? can I make a difference?) as well as their attitudes toward students' learning capacities can affect classroom learning (Ashton & Webb, 1986; Gibson & Dembo, 1984; Rosenholtz, 1989).

Effective teachers also create reasonable structure and predictability by articulating expectations, establishing routines and procedures, and in general by managing the classroom in ways that encourage students to engage in the kinds of learning behavior that are consistent with the teacher's instructional philosophy. Further, teachers help to make classrooms more predictable learning environments, by helping students to become more explicit about their own learning goals and methods.

implications for teachers

the beginning teacher

student teaching Student teachers' classroom behavior is influenced by their cooperating teachers (Good & Brophy, 1994). Even though student teachers may not approve of the styles their cooperating teachers use, they may prac-

tice the cooperating teachers' styles in hopes of getting a good grade. This may become second nature to them and resurface later when they have their own classrooms. Many cooperating teachers encourage student teachers to develop their own styles, so the pressure to conform is not a problem. Other cooperating teachers, however, believe that their role is to help student teachers teach as they do. Furthermore, during the first year of teaching, a new teacher may encounter peer teachers with strong preferences.

Unfortunately, many student teachers are not encouraged to think analytically and to discuss why they make certain decisions (Stout, 1989). Verloop (1989) also notes that cooperating teachers seldom provide student teachers with any theoretical perspectives. Action-system knowledge is seldom part of discussions between cooperating and student teachers. Griffin and associates (1983) found that during such discussions little attention was paid to developing a knowledge base that would help student teachers later when they had their own classrooms. Interactions focused on immediate, specific issues and a "let's see if this works" approach without explanation of rationales or references to learning theory, child development, or instructional models. Interaction was dominated by the cooperating teacher, who selected the topics and controlled how they were discussed. Conversations usually focused on a particular classroom at a specific time; they rarely concerned alternative ways to understand and respond to classroom events. Some cooperating teachers enjoy discussing why they make decisions and how they evaluate them. Others function differently. As a student teacher, however, you can be analytical even if your cooperating teacher is not. Think about each instructional day. Consider, for example, the motivational structures that the teacher used, such as how lessons were introduced or ended and the types of feedback that were given, and speculate about their effects on various students. On another day, think about the management system in the classroom. What types of alerting and accountability systems were used? Was the structure too rigid or too loose for specific

students? By using the vocabulary and concepts in this text, you can become a more educated observer of classroom events—the first step in becoming an active classroom decision maker.

Peer teacher exchanges also exhibit some of the same characteristics as cooperating teacher-student teacher exchanges. Rosenholtz (1989) noted that teachers often avoid discussing instructional problems and hence deny themselves potentially useful information. If teachers are to be active decision makers they must seek useful information from peers.

the first year Beginning teachers have an especially difficult task because in addition to facing the enduring demands of teaching, they worry about things such as whether students will like them and follow their directions or whether they will enjoy teaching. New teachers must also prepare lessons and develop tests while trying to apply action-system knowledge.

Because of increased awareness that the first years of teaching can be difficult even for talented college graduates, many states now have induction programs to assist beginning teachers. These programs vary from state to state; however, most offer beginning teachers more assistance than newcomers have traditionally received (e.g., a mentor teacher, observation and feedback). Although the objective of induction programs is to ease adjustment to teaching, they also bring special pressures (e.g., the need to demonstrate selected action-knowledge teaching skills in the classroom) and may even mandate that a teacher teach in a certain way. (For more information on induction, see Brookhart and Freeman, 1992; Carter and Richardson-Koehler, 1989; Howey and Zimpher, 1989).

Secondary teachers must get to know as many as 180 students quickly, and elementary teachers have to prepare daily lessons in several subjects. Teachers must also implement different teaching formats and plan activities. Yinger

(1977) reported on one teacher who used fifty-three activities during a twelve-week period, including tasks such as book reports, creative writing, cooking, newspaper assignments, spelling bees, field trips, and reading groups. Thus, if teachers do not have a theoretical perspective or have inappropriate perspectives when they enter the classroom, it will be difficult to be reflective decision makers because teachers must respond to so many immediate issues. As we shall see in this text, successful teaching is considerably more than dispensing information (see also Jackson, 1986), and there is increasing evidence that many beginning teachers do not adequately understand the structural aspects of teaching (cognitive objectives, classroom management, etc.).

Brookhart and Freeman (1992) reviewed the literature dealing with the knowledge, beliefs, motivation, and so on that preservice teachers bring to teacher education programs. The findings these authors report are complex (and often conflicting); however, two themes emerge from research. First, beginning teacher education students consider the interpersonal and nurturing aspects of a teacher's role as much more important than the academic aspects, and they view teaching as dispensing information. Hence, some teachers are entering classrooms with inappropriate conceptions.

Whatever help may or may not be available to you in the form of induction programs and assistance from principals or peers when you begin working as an inservice teacher, you can prepare now to make decisions about teaching by articulating and organizing your own theory of teaching that will allow you to be a proactive teacher.

s u m m a r y

Teachers can have a major, positive influence on the way students learn and develop. Some teachers are vital forces; others have only minor effects. Teachers who significantly affect students' lives communicate a genuine interest in students, know subject matter, and possess detailed information about instructional processes and the way students learn and develop.

In this chapter we have presented a decision-making instructional model, because we believe there are no simple answers to successful teaching. We stress that theoretical principles and research findings provide a basis for planning and implementing instruction. Teachers, however, have to act as independent decision makers and apply these general concepts and principles in relation to their students and educational objectives. The model illustrates that teachers who make good decisions and are willing to correct poor ones foster student motivation and learning.

Effective teachers see their roles as positive and worthwhile, whereas ineffective teachers see teaching as a dull job. Effective teachers exhibit inner control, personal responsibility, realistic attitudes, and a problem-solving orientation. They are successful in developing positive relations with both students and peers.

Factors that restrict a teacher's decision-making ability are lack of awareness of students' problems, allegiance to unworkable ideas, limited resources, and a lack of feedback about the effects of instruction. Also, both student and teacher expectations, coupled with the self-defeating strategies that some students adopt, can interfere with learning.

We believe it is difficult for new teachers to be active decision makers unless they want to be and are willing to work to develop the necessary skills. It is easy for them to be overwhelmed by the rapid pace of classrooms and simply to react to classroom events. To be proactive, it will be important for you to consider how to apply the ideas of educational psychology as you read them, as you observe classes, and when you student teach.

The best way to become a proactive teacher is to develop an explicit theory of teaching. You must also master subject-matter content, understand and apply the concepts presented in this text, and develop an explicit approach to teaching (e.g., know when you will group pupils for instruction and when you will teach the entire class, know the bases for your decisions and how to collect evidence to determine their appropriateness).

Although we have stressed that teaching is complex, we are confident that you will learn to handle such complexities. As you master course material and persist in becoming a proactive teacher, you will be able to influence classroom interactions in a positive fashion.

Educational psychology provides a framework for looking at the learner, the learning process, and the learning situation. It includes an understanding of educational objectives, student development and personality, the learning process, the psychology of teaching methods, classroom management, and evaluation procedures. Students who apply educational psychology in their preservice and inservice teaching will understand their own students better and design more appropriate instruction. Our goal in this book is to provide basic knowledge of psychological concepts that can be combined with subject-matter knowledge and teaching experience to allow you to become an effective teacher.

questions for reflection

1. How did you decide to become a teacher (or nurse or whatever your vocational aspiration may be)? What explicit assumptions did you hold? In retrospect, what implicit assumptions and hypotheses did you make?

2. What are your own theories of teaching? On what are they based? Be explicit. Think about a particular lesson for a certain group of students. What five things would you need to do to be successful? Why?

3. How do instructional goals influence planning?

4. What does it mean to say that some classroom decisions "aren't made"? What is the difference between explicit and implicit decisions? What sorts of things happen in classrooms without teacher intent or awareness?

5. Considering the complexities of teaching,

shouldn't we provide you with a few clear, prescriptive guidelines rather than urge you to master a broad range of concepts and skills to draw on later when you are teaching and making decisions under pressure?

6. Think about the teachers you have had. Which were the most effective? Why? Were they equally effective for all students?

7. What sort of "front" have you presented to your teachers in the past?

8. How does classroom teaching differ from teaching patients about the effects of a pending operation and how they can help their own recovery by performing certain exercises?

9. As a beginning teacher, how might pressures to "look good" interfere with your ability to learn from experienced peers?

cases to consider

Disturbing first encounter Tim is apprehensive because he knows that Mr. Wilson, his cooperating teacher, had given his previous semester's student teacher a "D" and was an abrasive man. Tim anxiously knocks on the door and shivers as Mr. Wilson says loudly, "Come in!" As Tim hesitantly enters, Mr. Wilson says, "Oh! You must be my new aide from the university! I thought you'd have been here 15 minutes ago!" What would you do if you were Tim?

Rick strikes out Rick felt like a fool. "Why didn't I read the assignment more carefully?" he asked himself. Last night, to get ready to teach his first class, he spent considerable time preparing a ten-minute introduction and even more time working on discussion questions. But the lesson hadn't gone as planned. His ninth graders didn't seem to want to talk. And so, foolishly, he later thought, he asked for questions. He fielded the first three or four questions poorly. Finally, one student said with irritation, "I still can't understand the point of the experiment." Rick simply couldn't think; his mind went blank. After a full minute of awkward silence he threw the question back to the class. Weakly, he asked, "Can anybody help (pause) I'm sorry, I forgot your name." What should Rick do now? What should he do the next day?

Jim begins Jim Miller, a recent college graduate, will teach chemistry for the first time at a large high school that serves a full range of student abilities. However, only college-bound students take chemistry. What are some of the decisions that Jim must make immediately? List ten to fifteen.

A challenge for Nancy Nancy Litton has never taught reading before. She is both excited and frightened by the prospect of teaching first graders because she did her student teaching in a third-grade classroom. She has never observed first-grade reading instruction, nor has she seen a teacher start the school year. It is a week before the year begins. If you were Nancy what information would you try to obtain and what are the major decisions that must be made?

part II.

development

I pledge allegiance to the flag of the United States of America, and to the republic for which it stands, one nation, under God, indivisible, with liberty and justice for all.

The pledge of allegiance is familiar to you if you attended K-12 schools in the United States. In fact, you may have skimmed over it once you realized what it was. If so, look at it again as you think about these questions: Do you understand what all the words and phrases mean? Do you understand the connotations about loyalty to the nation that are implied in these brief statements? Do you now notice anything in the pledge that you never noticed before, even though you probably have recited it many times? If so, does this change your understanding of its meaning?

For example, you may be aware that the pledge is not a statement to the flag as such, but a loyalty oath to the nation. If you think about it, you can see that a loyalty oath to the United States does not require mention of its flag. Furthermore, the meaning of the pledge would remain the same even if the design of the flag should change, as it did when new states entered the Union.

From the point of view of developmental psychologists, you are in the stage of formal operations, so you are capable of understanding the abstract aspects of knowledge. In contrast, fourth graders would have difficulty with some of the vocabulary of the pledge, would interpret it as a pledge to the flag more so than the nation, and would not be able to follow much of this discussion. Their understandings of the pledge are limited to their familiar, concrete experiences, although within these limits their interpretations are quite logical.

For first graders, saying the pledge is a rela-

tively meaningless experience. It is associated with standing and holding the right hand over the heart while reciting the words in the presence of the flag. First graders have a general idea that the pledge relates to the flag (not the country), but not much understanding of what its words mean. In fact, if you listen to them carefully when they say the pledge, you will find that many of them distort its wording.

This example illustrates some of the insights that developmental psychologists offer. By identifying the changes that occur as children get older and the limitations that apply when they have not yet acquired insights associated with higher stages of development, psychologists help us to understand children of different ages by enabling us to see things from their perspectives. This ability is essential if we are to interact with children meaningfully and interpret their diffi-

culties when they do not understand something that an adult would understand with ease. It also enables us to appreciate how children's ideas are logical, given their point of view, but naive because they do not take into account other things that make a difference.

In the three chapters in this section we will elaborate on children's stages of development in relation to their ability to learn and to be taught. Chapter 2 presents basic principles focusing on the theory of Jean Piaget; Chapter 3 summarizes more recent theory and research on children's cognitive development as it affects their learning; and Chapter 4 deals with social and moral development. These chapters are intended to help you understand the nature and schooling needs of K-12 students, especially those at grade levels at which you intend to teach.

chapter 2.

cognitive development: Piagetian foundations

objectives

When you have mastered the material in this chapter you will be able to

1. Explain the implications of *development* (in contrast to mere *growth*) in physical and cognitive capacities during childhood and ado-lescence, especially with reference to students' readiness to learn
2. Explain how Piaget's view of learning differs from the behaviorist view and identify its implications for curriculum and instruction
3. Explain how thought and behavior develop through four major periods via assimilation and accommodation of schemes guided by equilibration processes
4. Define operational thought, identify the key characteristics of concrete versus formal operational thinking, and explain the implications of these developments for students' learning capabilities
5. Contrast Piaget's views on teaching readiness and on the extent to which cognitive development can be speeded up with the views of learning and cognition theorists, and articulate your own position on these issues
6. Explain the implications of Piaget's work for deciding what should be taught, and how it should be taught, at the grade level at which you intend to teach
7. Explain the progression from absolutist to relativist to pragmatic thinking that tends to occur among college students, and its implications concerning your personal develop-ment as a student and a professional

the concept of development

To provide effective support for learning, it is helpful to know where students have been and where they are likely to be going, not just where they are now. This requires a *developmental perspective*, a concern with changes that occur over time. Psychologists discuss three aspects of such changes:

- **sequence,** *the order in which changes occur*;
- **rate**, *the speed with which changes occur*; and
- **form**, *the shape or appearance of the developing entity at any point in time.*

True developmental sequences are fixed and universal. A always precedes B, which always precedes C, and so on. One cannot get from A to C without first going through stage B. Many of these sequences involve physical growth and development under the control of genetics and maturation. However, universal sequences have been proposed for aspects of psychological development as well (Kohlberg & Ryncarz, 1990).

It is useful to distinguish growth from development when discussing physical changes. **Growth** refers to *increases in height, weight, or physical size.* **Development**, a term that can refer to the mind and the emotions as well as the body, is *an orderly progression to increasingly higher levels of both differentiation and integration of the components of a system.*

Development can occur when no growth is taking place. For example, children of similar age and size differ in ability to ride a tricycle or use a pencil. One reason is that differences in rates of maturation of the nervous system produce differences in the ability to control and coordinate different parts of the body. Children lacking the physical maturation needed to succeed at such tasks are unlikely to master them until this maturation takes place, even if they have lots of instruction and time to practice. Persistent developmental immaturities plague certain students throughout childhood and even into adolescence. For example, children with hand-eye coordination problems may have difficulty learning to write, hyperactive students may have difficulty concentrating their attention or inhibiting physical movement, and students with poor coordination may embarrass themselves in the gym or on the playground.

Most physical development involving differentiation of new body parts occurs in the early weeks following conception. At birth, almost all parts are differentiated, except for the myelin sheaths that cover nerve cells in the brain. These sheaths, which apparently help speed up neural transmission and thus make the brain more efficient, continue to develop for at least a few years. By the time children start school, though, they are essentially fully differentiated. Consequently, their further physical development consists of simple growth and progress toward higher levels of organization and coordination of existing body parts. At adolescence, development in the form of maturation of the sexual organs occurs, along with a noteworthy spurt in overall physical growth.

intellectual development

A century ago, intellectual development was treated primarily as a growth process: Children's minds were considered to be the same as those of adults, only smaller, and they were thought to expand gradually as knowledge and experience accumulated. The Swiss psychologist Jean Piaget rejected this notion that intellectual development was a smooth, gradual process in which each new concept was just another brick added to a pile. He and others like him were called stage theorists. **Stage theorists** are *theorists who postulate that development progresses through a series of qualitatively different phases.* Each new phase represents a new level of organization of knowledge and adds a different kind of knowledge, not just more of the same kind as before.

The stage concept of development includes the concepts of maturation and readiness. In physical development, for example, infants cannot learn to walk until the maturation of biological structures takes place. Gesell and Thompson (1929) demonstrated this by studying the development of physical skills such as climbing stairs in identical twins. In each study, one twin was given special training and practice in a skill but the other was not. Did the treatment speed up development? In most cases, it did not. The special help did not have much effect until almost the time that the ability usually developed naturally, and the twin who had not been given special help soon caught up.

These studies seemed to imply that one should not try to teach a skill until children develop *readiness*—the capability of learning a skill with relative ease. The concept of readiness sometimes is taken to include cognition and interest: If children lack the prerequisite knowledge to learn a skill, or are not interested in learning it, do not try to teach it until both knowledge and interest have developed.

Piaget's theory encompasses the notion of readiness and especially emphasizes cognitive readiness. Cognitive readiness is established not only by biological maturation but also by prior learning accumulated through personal exploration and social experiences. Piaget viewed the mind as a structure that develops through successively higher levels of organization and integration. The sequence of stages is invariant; children always progress through the same stages in the same sequence. However, development is transformative, so that the quality of later intellectual behavior depends on the quality of the experiences that preceded it.

At any particular stage children will be oriented toward information that is moderately novel—new enough to be interesting but familiar enough to be comprehensible (Ginsburg & Opper, 1988). They will lack interest (at least for now) in further exploration of overly familiar topics, and they will lack both interest in and readiness for topics that are beyond their present ability to comprehend.

Not everyone agrees with Piaget on these points. Most learning and cognition theorists, for example, reject or downplay the notion of

research at work
cognitive readiness

What are your beliefs about cognitive readiness and its implications for schooling?

- At what age should children begin formal academic schooling? Why?
- Should children who seem cognitively "ready" be allowed to start school early or to skip grades?
- Should children who appear "unready" be required to start school later or to repeat grades?
- To what degree should the curriculum be organized to follow students' developing interests? Should we mostly teach students

what they want to learn when they want to learn it, or should we expect them to adapt by learning whatever our society decides they should learn at their grade level?

- Children become more differentiated with age. By adolescence it is clear that some should easily succeed at college but others will have to work hard just to graduate from high school. Should schools adapt to these differences by tracking the students into separate groups that do not see much of one another, or should they keep them together through heterogeneous grouping in at least some subjects?

qualitative stages in general intellectual development. Instead, they view learning as the gradual accumulation of expertise in particular domains of knowledge. If readiness does not exist, it can be created by moving learners through successive approximations from where they are now to where one wants them to go. Even Jerome Bruner (1966), an American psychologist who otherwise is similar to Piaget in his general ideas about development, believes that any subject can be taught to any child to at least some degree, if the content is selected carefully and represented in a form suited to the child's level of cognitive development.

Piaget's theory

Jean Piaget (1983) produced a staggering number of books and articles on cognitive development. He is usually ranked with Freud and

Skinner as one of the most influential psychologists of all time. By the 1970s, his ideas about developmental changes in the nature and structuring of children's knowledge had become the framework within which most discussions of cognitive development took place (including debates about curriculum and instruction in the schools). Since then, attention has turned away from general stages in cognitive restructuring toward the study of children's learning within particular knowledge domains (Flavell, 1992). Even so, Piaget's ideas remain influential and useful for conceptualizing the larger developmental trends within which more specific kinds of learning occur (Beilin & Pufall, 1992).

knowledge as constructed

Piaget was one of the first psychologists to recognize in his theorizing that we are born as active and exploratory information processors who construct our knowledge rather than taking it in ready-made in response to experience or instruction. He viewed us as constantly striving to adapt to our environments, constructing knowledge that enables us to perceive meaning and exert control through adaptive mechanisms. Key insights that derive from his theory and research are captured in the following quotations.

> One major impetus to cognitive development is the child himself. Much of cognitive development is *self-motivated.* Children are knowledge seekers, they develop their own theories about the world around them, and continually subject their theories to tests, even in the absence of external feedback. They perform thought and action experiments on their own, continually, and without external pressure. Children as well as adults "play" with their developing knowledge. . . . They engage in knowledge-extending and knowledge-refining activities spontaneously, arguing with themselves via an internal dialogue. They question the veracity or range of applicability of their theories, they perform *thought experiments,* question their own basic assumptions, provide counterexamples to their own rules, and reason on the basis of whatever knowledge they have, even though it may be incomplete, or their logic may be faulty. . . . This metaphor of the child as *little scientist* is compelling and central to many theories of development. (Brown, 1983, pp. 31–32)

Children are clearly not blank slates that passively and unselectively copy whatever the environment presents to them. Rather, the cognitive structures and processing strategies available to them at that point in their development lead them to select from the input what is meaningful to them and to represent and transform what is selected in accordance with their cognitive structures. As Piaget correctly taught us, children's cognitive structures dictate both what they accommodate to (notice) in the environment and how what is accommodated to is assimilated (interpreted). The active nature of their intellectual commerce with the environment makes them to a large degree the manufacturers of their own development. (Flavell, 1992, p. 998)

physical action as the basis for cognitive development

Piaget viewed learning as rooted in physical actions. We observe and conceptualize our own behavior, so that, at least initially, *what we learn is what we do.* Through activity we learn what stimuli we can use to do certain things, and what the outcomes will be if we do those things. Piaget viewed the acquisition of concepts and skills as internally motivated and actively directed, not merely "elicited" by external cues.

Consider children learning to ride bicycles. To **behaviorists**—*theorists who focus on external, measurable behaviors rather than on thoughts or other internal mediators of action*—both the bicycle itself and the input it provides when one tries to ride it are cues that elicit responses. Successful responses lead to reinforcement (sustained riding), and thus are retained and perfected. Unsuccessful responses are not reinforced (the child has difficulty maintaining balance and forward motion), and are extinguished. As practice continues, the child learns to recognize meaningful stimulus events (cues), respond accordingly, and achieve increasing efficiency. The ability to ride a bike, then, is elicited in raw form and then shaped into smooth efficiency through cues and reinforcement.

Piaget would say that the child's present interests focus attention on aspects of the stimulus situation that are relevant to learning to ride the bike (i.e., rather than just looking at it or turning it upside down and spinning the wheels). Having selected these stimuli, the child manipulates them by pumping the pedals, moving the handlebars, and so on, and uses the feedback from these actions to make corrections to increase efficiency. The child actively controls this learning. The bike is a prop for the child to use in perfecting skills, not a stimulus that somehow elicits responses. Consequences are important because they provide feedback relevant for adapting how the child thinks about riding the bicycle rather than because they function as rewards or punishments. In short, whereas behaviorists would see the child as learning how to respond to a bike, Piaget would say that the child is learning what to do with a bike. This same difference in theorizing would apply to more advanced activities such as learning to play tennis or use a computer.

Most of Piaget's theory and research focused on the cognitive operations involved in thinking and problem solving. He believed that these cognitive operations developed originally as mental reconstructions of the behavioral operations that infants and children constructed in the process of exploring the environment and solving the problems encountered there. He often spoke of thought as internalized action (Wood, 1988).

schemes

Scheme is *Piaget's term for cognitive, verbal, and behavioral frameworks that are developed to organize learning and to guide behavior.* With development, knowledge about the environment and how to respond to it is encoded and stored in the form of schemes, and these schemes are continually refined. It is useful to distinguish different kinds of schemes. *Sensorimotor (or perceptual and behavioral) schemes* are prelogical, intuitive forms of knowledge acquired by observing and manipulating the environment. They provide the basis for developing skills such as walking, turning doorknobs, or opening bottles. *Cognitive schemes* are concepts, images, and thinking abilities such as understanding the differences between plants and animals, being able to envision a triangle, or reasoning from causes to effects. *Verbal schemes* are word meanings and communication skills such as associating names with their referents or mastering grammar and syntax.

Cognitive development occurs not just through the construction of new schemes but also through the differentiation and integration of existing schemes. Differentiation occurs whenever we encounter a new (to us) subtype of a familiar scheme. For example, we may possess a "lamp" scheme that includes a shade, a light, and an on-off switch as key elements. If we were to encounter a lamp that could be turned on and off by touching it instead of by operating a switch, our existing "lamp" scheme would need to be differentiated to accommodate this newly discovered subtype.

As knowledge in a particular domain develops, existing schemes become coordinated into more complex ones that integrate previously separate constructions. For example, early knowledge about the alphabet and about letter-sound relationships gets connected with other developing knowledge about reading as the child achieves successively more powerful schemes for decoding and comprehending text. Similarly, foreign-language students become able to read the new language with more immediate comprehension, yet less conscious effort, as they begin to coordinate their developing word and phrase recognition skills with their developing knowledge of the language's verb forms and sentence construction patterns.

adaptation

Adaptation is *the continuous process of interacting with the environment and learning to predict and control it.* Adaptation experiences lead to the development of new schemes, initially through trial-and-error exploration, but increasingly through systematic experimentation as schemes begin to accumulate. Each new discovery is a revelation to the child who makes it, even if it is common knowledge to adults (tires have "nothing" but air in them; hamburgers come from cattle). Knowledge literally is *constructed* as the child gains experience, resolves apparent contradictions (all daddies are men, but all men are not daddies), and coordinates isolated schemes into clusters and ultimately into a stable, internally consistent cognitive structure.

Piaget identified two fundamental adaptational mechanisms involved in every action: accommodation and assimilation. **Accommodation** is *change in response to our recognition that existing schemes are not adequate for accomplishing our current purposes.* It includes both development of entirely new schemes and significant restructuring of existing schemes that are discovered to be incorrect, overgeneralized, or otherwise invalid. Accommodation is necessary when we encounter adaptational demands that we cannot meet with existing schemes, such as when we encounter a new word or concept, an event that seems inexplicable, or an appliance that stops working for no apparent reason and requires us to initiate troubleshooting efforts.

Assimilation is *the process of responding to a stimulus situation using established schemes.* We can do this when there is nothing new or puzzling in the situation or when any new elements can be categorized easily (e.g., a breed of dog that we have never seen before, but which we recognize as a dog). We carry out everyday activities through assimilation, with some minor accommodations—we walk automatically, but make accommodations for obstacles, corners, or slippery surfaces.

All behavior includes both assimilation and accommodation. Theoretically, situations that were entirely foreign to previous experience would produce panic or paralysis, since we would have no adaptation mechanisms (existing schemes) to call on. However, virtually any situation is *partially assimilable* to existing schemes, so that we can make some systematic response to it (consider people on the *Candid Camera* show confronted with talking mailboxes and other "impossible" situations). Conversely, even the most overlearned responses require at least some accommodation, because no two situations are ever exactly the same. Consider your signature, which is probably the most automatic of all your writing schemes. Each signing situation differs from others in small ways (space available; presence or absence of a line; placement on the page; distance from the shoulder) that demand minor accommodations, so no two signatures are ever exactly the same.

Piaget saw scheme development as universal in sequence, somewhat variable in rate, and considerably variable in form. Differences in rate and form are attributed to four factors: (1) maturation; (2) individual experience; (3) social interaction (formal and informal socialization and education); and (4) equilibration (internal self-direction and regulation).

equilibration

Equilibration is the motivating force behind all learning. The **equilibration principle** is *Piaget's basic motivational assumption holding that people strive to maintain a balance between assimilation and accommodation as they impose order and meaningfulness on their experiences.* According to Piaget, humans are intrinsically active and exploratory in trying to impose order, stability, and meaning on experience. To the extent that we are unable to assimilate and therefore must accommodate new experiences, we acquire new and successively higher levels of knowledge. Our equilibration needs motivate us to continue to process both the new knowledge and any related old knowledge, so as to resolve any inconsistencies. The resulting new synthesis is a more comprehensive, sophisticated, and coherent network of knowledge than the one it replaced.

Increasingly with development, one's schemes are coordinated (assimilated to one another) to form one's unique cognitive structure. This existing cognitive structure interacts with the specific possibilities and demands presented by the current situation to determine one's actions. Certain aspects of the situation will be foreign to existing schemes and thus not assimilable. Other aspects will be familiar and easily assimilable. Finally, some aspects will be partially assimilable and will motivate adaptational or exploratory actions that involve accommodation.

The resulting accommodation will require development of new schemes or modification of existing ones, and will continue until the originally motivating sense of disequilibrium has dissipated and been replaced either by boredom or by a shift of attention to some other aspect of the situation that now produces sufficient disequilibrium (curiosity or a desire to investigate or solve some problem) to motivate adaptational activity. If nothing in the situation has this potential, one will be motivated to leave and find a situation that does.

This pattern is easy to observe in infants and toddlers. Placed next to a variety of toys, a child will inspect them and then select one for play. Different toddlers will select different toys, according to the match between the toys and their current cognitive structures. A child will select a toy that induces disequilibrium and play with it for some time, perhaps repeating the same operations but becoming more skillful. This may continue long past the point where adults would have shifted to something else, because the activity is still new and interesting to the child. Eventually, though, the

The preoperational period is characterized by thought as internalized action; children can work puzzles and shape sorters because they can visualize and remember from previously developed schemes.

child will either start a new activity with the same toy or shift to another toy.

As another example, consider your own self-guided exploration. If you develop interest in a new kind of music, dancing, or other recreational activity, it probably will be familiar enough for you to relate to, but different enough to make it interesting and enjoyable. For a time you may indulge your new interest during every spare moment, pursuing its possibilities and developing your knowledge or skills. Eventually, though, the novelty wears off and other interests emerge. Piaget would say that you (i.e., the relevant schemes within your cognitive structure) had reached a state of equilibrium with regard to the new interest and were now ready to explore something else that induced a greater sense of disequilibrium.

The equilibration principle predicts that, as we develop, our attention will focus on progressively more complex aspects of our environments. Rather than repeatedly returning to the same starting place, we construct new and more sophisticated schemes that enable us to operate with more complex cognitive structures. Therefore, much more and better integrated knowledge is needed to maintain a twenty-year-old at equilibrium than is required to maintain a five-year-old at equilibrium. The equilibration principle also implies that we are always interested in extending our current knowledge base, so that we will prefer learning new things or new responses to familiar things over continuing to apply familiar schemes (Moessinger, 1978; Block, 1982). This is seen in the developments that occur in students' reading interests, for example, and in the kinds of questions they ask.

Piaget's four developmental periods

We have discussed Piaget's four primary concepts for describing how we adapt to our environments: We approach situations with cognitive structures composed of interrelated *schemes*, *assimilating* certain aspects into existing schemes but also *accommodating* by restructuring those schemes or constructing new ones if necessary, motivated by the *equilibration* principle. The sequence of scheme acquisition is universal, but the rates at which schemes develop and the forms they take depend on individual differences in maturation, environmental experiences, acquisition of knowledge through social interaction, and unique equilibration factors. Scheme development proceeds through four qualitatively distinct periods (stages) (see Table 2.1).

the sensorimotor period (birth-2)

During the first two years of life, development is concentrated in sensorimotor schemes as the infant explores the world of objects. A great variety of behavioral skills is developed and coordinated, but development of verbal and cognitive schemes is minimal and poorly coordinated. Attention is focused on salient stimuli in the immediate "here and now" environment. As the infant develops, however, initially reflexive physical actions become refined into controlled sensorimotor schemes; an "out of sight, out of mind" attention span is replaced by knowledge of the permanence of objects and evidence of memory and searching for them if they are removed; initial understandings develop for cause-and-effect relationships that explain observable events; and the child begins to imitate the actions of others.

Starting when they approach two years of age, children begin to internalize their sensorimotor schemes (behavioral skills) in the form of cognitive schemes (imagery, thought). For example, instead of relying on laborious trial and error when working a picture puzzle or trying to construct something from blocks, they begin to guide their actions with imagery based on memories of previous experiences in the same situation. They also produce "deferred" imitations of models who are no longer performing the imitated actions in the here and now, indicating the presence of mental representations and memories of actions observed in the past.

the preoperational period (2-7)

As the development of imagery and the ability to retain images in memory progress, learning

table 2.1 Piaget's stages of cognitive development

STAGES	APPROXIMATE AGE	CHARACTERISTICS AND ACCOMPLISHMENTS
Sensorimotor	0–2 years	Gradual move from reflexive behavior to goal-directed activity and from sensorimotor responsiveness to immediate stimuli to mental representation and deferred imitation Formation of concept of "object permanence"—i.e., objects continue to exist when they are no longer in view
Preoperational	2–7 years	Development of language and the ability to think and solve problems through the use of symbols Thinking is egocentric, making it difficult to see another person's point of view
Concrete operations	7–12 years	Improved ability to think logically due to the attainments of reversible thinking, conservation, classfication, seriation, negation, identity, and compensation Able to solve concrete (hands-on) problems logically, adopt another's perspective, consider intentions in moral reasoning
Formal operations (if attained)	12 years and beyond	Hypothetical and purely symbolic (complex verbal) thinking becomes possible Thinking becomes more scientific as the person develops the ability to generate and test all of the logical combinations pertinent to a problem Concerns about identity and social issues emerge

becomes more cumulative and less dependent on immediate perception and concrete experience. This makes possible more systematic problem solving in which children relate current situational factors to previously developed schemes retained in memory by visualizing activities without carrying them out. For example, preoperational children begin to think ahead during sequential tasks like block building or letter copying, whereas previously they had to act everything out behaviorally and thus make many errors. They also begin to think logically by using cognitive schemes that represent their prior experiences with sequential or cause-effect relationships to predict the effects of potential actions.

Despite its strengths, preoperational logic is egocentric and unstable. It is egocentric because children of this age have not yet learned to "decenter" from themselves and consider things

In Piaget's notion of conservation concepts, children aged 6–7 recognize that the amount of substance does not change if you cut it into parts, roll it up into a ball, or stretch it out in length.

from other people's perspectives. They act as if everyone else thinks exactly as they do, knows exactly what they mean, and so on. Often they do not notice or are not bothered by indications that these assumptions are incorrect (Vygotsky, 1962; Flavell et al., 1968; Miller, Brownell, & Zukier, 1977). Their readiness to work or play cooperatively with peers is limited, as is their understanding of social rules, notions of justice, and the role of intentions in distinguishing lies from mistakes or aggression from accidents (Wadsworth, 1989).

Schemes are *unstable* during the preoperational period because children have not yet learned to distinguish invariant aspects of the environment from aspects that are variable and specific to particular situations. They are easily confused by *conservation problems* that require them to conserve invariant aspects of objects in their minds while variable aspects are manipulated. For example, many children will say that a ball of clay contains more (or less) clay after it has been rolled into a "hot dog" shape, even though no clay has been added or taken away. Here, manipulation of a variable property of a piece of clay (in this case, its shape)

has led the children to believe that a change has occurred in one of its invariant properties (its mass or substance).

the concrete operations period (7-12)

Starting about age seven, children *become operational.* Their cognitive schemes, especially their logical thinking and problem-solving skills, become organized into *concrete operations*—mental representations of potential actions.

One set of concrete operations involves *classification skills* for grouping and regrouping sets of objects (McCabe et al., 1982). For example, a collection of toy chairs, tables, cars, and trucks can be divided into these four groups but also into two larger groups of furniture and vehicles. Preoperational children have difficulty distinguishing between these two levels of classification, especially if asked questions such as, Are there more trucks or more vehicles? that require them to consider both levels simultaneously (Piaget & Inhelder, 1964).

Concrete operations are reversible, so children whose classification skills have become operational can handle such questions. These children can reverse combinations of subclasses into larger classes (redivide the vehicles into separate groups of cars and trucks), and can reverse divisions of larger classes into subclasses (reassemble the vehicles into a single group). Furthermore, they can perform these operations mentally, without having to move the objects around.

Another concrete operation is **seriation**— *the ability to place objects in a series that progresses from least to most in length, weight, or some other common property.* Younger children proceed laboriously on seriation tasks because they have to make paired comparisons. Concrete operational children can "see the big picture" and place ten or twelve objects in order without having to compare each of them with each of the others. Also, they are less easily confused by misleading cues. If preoperational children are asked to order objects from lightest to heaviest, they may confuse size with weight and misplace objects that are large but light or small but heavy.

As children develop through the concrete operational years, they gradually attain **conservation concepts**—*capacities for distinguishing the invariant aspects of classes of objects or events from the variant aspects, which may change if examples are replaced or transformed* (see Table 2.2). These concepts provide bases for parallel concrete operations used for reasoning about conservation problems.

Another concrete operation is **negation**— *the recognition that an action can be negated or reversed to restore the original situation.* In a liquid volume conservation task, for example, preoperational children recognize that identical pitchers contain the same amounts of water when equally filled, but they become confused if the contents of one pitcher are poured into several glasses ("Is there more water in the remaining pitcher, or in all these glasses?"). Children who have mastered the concrete operation of negation immediately recognize

that the amounts must be the same, because if you pour the contents of the glasses back into the pitcher, you will have its original contents.

Other concrete operations can be illustrated with the same example. One is **identity**— *recognition that physical substances retain their volume or quantity even if moved around, divided into parts, or otherwise transformed in appearance, so long as nothing is added or taken away.* Children using the operation of identity will say that the amounts are the same because it's the same quantity of water—it was moved but none was added or taken away.

Another concrete operation that helps children comprehend this problem is **compensation or reciprocity**—*recognition that a change in one dimension is balanced by a compensating or reciprocal change in another dimension.* Operational children will note that the pitcher holds more water than a single glass, but there are several glasses.

Concrete operations not only allow children to solve specific problems, but also help students develop learning-to-learn skills and logical reasoning abilities that aid them in making sense of their general experience. Once children become operational in their thinking, they become more systematic in moving toward higher levels of equilibrium. Their schemes, especially cognitive schemes concerning which aspects of the world are invariant and which are subject to situational changes, become more stable, dependable, and integrated into a comprehensive cognitive structure. The schemes within this structure become coordinated and mutually supportive, so that they can be used for logical reasoning and problem solving.

Even after they become capable of logical reasoning, however, children still depend on direct, concrete experiences (or at least the ability to imagine such experiences vividly) to "ground" their thinking. They cannot yet reason about abstract content that does not lend itself to concrete examples, although they can

table 2.2 children's attainment of conservation concepts

AGE	CONCEPT	INSIGHT ATTAINED
6–7	Substance	The amount of substance (e.g., a lump of clay) does not changes if you divide it into subparts or change its shape.
6–7	Length	The length of a substance (e.g., a piece of string) does not change if you cut it into parts or bend it into a curved shape.
6–7	Continuous quantity	The amount of a liquid does not change if you pour it from one container into another or from one into several.
7	Number	The number of objects does not change if they are placed close together or spread far apart.
7	Area	The total area covered by a piece of paper will not change if the paper is cut into pieces or the pieces are rearranged into new shapes.
9–12	Weight	A piece of clay weighs the same regardless of the shape that one forms it into.
11–12	Volume	A piece of clay reformed into various shapes will always occupy the same volume when immersed in a liquid.

memorize abstract statements or definitions that they do not really understand.

The concrete operational years also feature emergence from childish egocentricity. Children become more able to cooperate with others and to recognize that game rules and other social conventions are not laws written in stone but negotiated agreements that can be changed. They learn to take others' intentions into account when judging the morality of actions, so as to distinguish unintentional misstatements of fact from deliberate lies or accidental inflictions of harm from premeditated aggression. Their thinking about fairness (justice) becomes more focused around notions of reciprocity and treating others as one wants to be treated oneself, in place of an earlier focus on punishment of rule breakers (Wadsworth, 1989).

the formal operations period (12-adulthood)

The period of formal operation begins at about age twelve and gradually consolidates through the adolescent and young-adult years. Its hallmark is the ability to think in symbolic terms and comprehend abstract content meaningfully without requiring physical objects or even imagery based on past experience with such objects. Formal operations are the logical and mathematical concepts and rules of inference used in advanced reasoning, including reasoning about abstract ideas or about theoretical possibilities that have never occurred in reality.

In describing formal operations, Piaget made reference to the binary operations used in propositional logic and the "INRC group" (see below) used in algebra. *Binary operations* are logical operations that apply to attempts to draw inferences from paired propositions. People who possess well-functioning formal operations can determine the nature and logical implications of the relationship between the two propositions (e.g., that if the first is true, the second cannot be true; that if the first is true, the second must be true because it is an implication of the first, etc.). They also can use these operations to design and draw conclusions from experiments intended to develop scientific answers to testable questions.

The *INRC group* includes more formal algebraic versions of the reversibility schemes previously attained as concrete operations. People with well-integrated INRC operations can follow all of the transformations that might be included in a conservation task because they understand the structural possibilities of *identity* (I), *negation* (N), *reciprocity* (R), and *correlativity* (C). In a conservation-of-substance task, for example, formal reasoners would realize that a lump of clay remains the same material (identity) regardless of changes in its shape, that increases in length are compensated for by decreases in width (reciprocity), that thinness is related to length and fatness to height (correlativity), and that the whole process can be reversed to undo any of the changes made (negation) (Bybee & Sund, 1982). Furthermore, in contrast to concrete operational children who can deal with only one or two of these relationships at a time and only in con-

nection with observation or vivid memory of demonstrations involving actual objects, formal operational people have a more abstract and better integrated understanding that enables them to think about these relationships rapidly and without dependence on concrete props.

Development of well-functioning formal operations apparently occurs only among individuals whose cognitive structures have been well developed and integrated at the level of concrete operational thought. Evidence of formal operations is lacking in societies without formal educational systems (Dasen & Heron, 1981; Tulviste, 1991), at least when measured with the usual Piagetian methods that involve assessing understanding of the actions of a pendulum (What factors affect its frequency of oscillation?) or the bending of rods (Does the degree to which a rod will bend when a weight is placed on it depend on its composition, length, thickness, cross-sectional form, or some combination of these factors?). Critics of these experiments point out that they assume knowledge of Western classical sciences and suggest that evidence of formal operational thinking might appear if individuals in undeveloped societies were questioned about things that were familiar to them (Modgil & Modgil, 1982; Laboratory of Comparative Human Cognition, 1983). This is possible, but has yet to be demonstrated convincingly.

Within-society comparisons of individuals who have and have not experienced formal schooling suggest that schooled groups not only attain literacy but also learn to deal with abstractions, to organize objects into logically based categories that differ from the organizations encountered in natural experience, and to manipulate concepts logically without having to carry out physical actions or refer to prior experience (Laboratory of Comparative Human Cognition, 1986; Rogoff, 1990; Tulviste, 1991). This suggests that some critical mass of formal schooling may be necessary to ensure the development of well-functioning formal operations.

Even within industrialized societies, only certain individuals, perhaps a minority, develop well-functioning formal operations in which schemes are coordinated to the point where they can be expressed in purely symbolic form as abstract logical or mathematical principles that can be used without reference to concrete objects or imagery. This level of cognitive development is necessary to understand advanced concepts in philosophy, mathematics, and science, as well as many of the concepts taught in college courses in any subject. Among college students, formal operations are more developed with reference to one's major subject than to other content (DeLisi & Staudt, 1980). Also, students with more developed formal operations tend to take more math and science courses and do better in them than students with equal American College Test (ACT) scores but less developed formal operations (Commons, Miller, & Kuhn, 1982).

The period of formal operations also features developments in adolescents' moral and social understandings. Rules become understood as necessary for cooperation, lying becomes viewed as wrong because it breaks trust, justice becomes understood in relation to intentions, and ideas about punishment for social transgressions increasingly become based on notions of equity (Wadsworth, 1989). However, while adolescents learn to appreciate logic and apply criteria of what is logical to their judgments of social and societal actions, they often do so with insufficient understanding that the world is not always ordered logically and that people do not always act logically. This may result in a period of adolescent idealism and interest in reforming society, often with oversimplified or otherwise unrealistic solutions. Adolescents' idealism begins to give way to a more stable equilibrium as they continue to develop and begin to take on adult roles, especially when they complete their schooling and enter the workforce.

post-Piagetian stage theories

Theorists interested in stages have continued to critique and build on Piaget's work. Some have argued the need to distinguish preadolescents who are just developing the ability to think abstractly about concrete experiences from older adolescents who are capable of sustained logical reasoning about abstract or hypothetical issues. They refer to preadolescents just entering the formal operations period as *transitional.* The usefulness of this distinction is illustrated in Table 2.3, which shows the typical ages at which certain mathematical concepts develop. Note that certain basic concepts are fully developed in 9- to 11-year-old transitional students, but others will continue to develop through the period of formal operations, and some have not yet begun to develop to any significant extent.

Much post-Piagetian theory and research has been motivated by dissatisfaction with Piaget's description of the period of formal operations as the end point of cognitive development. Criticism has focused on two major limitations in Piaget's formulation (Alexander, Druker, & Langer, 1990). First, the notion of formal operations, with its emphasis on deductive, syllogistic reasoning, depicts adult cognition too narrowly. Important developments occur in contextual thinking, moral reasoning, and other important areas of cognition besides logical and scientific thinking. Second, the notion of the formal operations period as an end point implies that cognitive development stops when formal operations are attained in late adolescence or young adulthood, but recent work suggests that cognitive development continues well into adulthood (Kitchener et al., 1993).

Some post-Piagetian theorizing also has incorporated the notion that there are limitations as well as strengths to formal operations (Gilligan, Murphy, & Tappan, 1990; Richards

table 2.3 average ages when selected mathematical concepts develop

Concept	Late Preoperational Period	Concrete Operations Period		Period of Formal Operations
	(4–7) ages	*(7–9)* ages	*(9–11)* ages	*(12–15)* ages
Topological space	x			
Classification	xx			
Seriation	xx			
Number conservation	xx			
Length conservation	xx			
Area conservation	xx			
Closure	xx			
Addition of classes	xx	x		
Multiplication of numbers	xx	x		
Euclidian space	xx	x		
Multiple classification	xx	xx		
Identity	xx	xx		
Commutativity	xx	xx		
Associativity	xx	xx	x	
Distributivity	xx	xx	xx	
Space	xx	xx	xx	
Time	xx	xx	xx	xx
Movement, velocity	xx	xx	xx	xx
Volume	xx	xx	xx	xx
Measurement	xx	xx	xx	xx
Functions	xx	xx	xx	xx
Proportion	xx	xx	xx	xx
Deduction/ induction				xx
Formal logic				xx
Probability				xx
Proofs				xx

NOTE: The initial steps in the construction of many of these concepts can be traced to the sensorimotor period.
SOURCE: Adapted from *Piaget for the Classroom Teacher* by Barry Wadsworth. Copyright 1978, Longman. Reprinted by permission.

& Commons, 1990). Theorists who take this approach suggest that formal operations are powerful methods of accomplishing strictly logical and scientific reasoning, but that such reasoning requires some limiting assumptions that restrict its usefulness. It yields answers to questions that can be formulated within logical and scientific rules, but it does not take into account the ethical, social, or political contexts in which real-world problems are embedded. When these considerations are taken into account, we sometimes find that the logical solution (banning automobiles as a solution to the problem of deaths from traffic accidents; castration as preventive treatment for rapists) is not the wisest, fairest, or most responsible solution. Consequently, several theorists have suggested that optimal cognitive development does not stop at the attainment of formal operations but continues to include attainment of more relativistic and contextually sensitive approaches to formulating problems and assessing potential solutions. These approaches include the use of formal operations but keep the logical and scientific aspects of the problem in perspective as parts of a larger set of issues.

The concept of formal operations has been elaborated to take into account cognitive developments that occur beyond the adolescent years, especially among students who attend college (Alexander & Langer, 1990; Commons, Richards, & Armon, 1984; Pintrich, 1990). Arlin (1986) argued that a fifth stage of cognitive development occurs in adulthood. She described this as a problem-finding stage that builds on the problem-solving abilities that come with Piaget's formal operations. People who attain this fifth stage not only can solve problems but also can infer implications and think creatively and divergently about the objects of their thought.

Perry (1981) studied development in college students' reasoning, especially their reactions to the intellectual and moral relativism that they usually encounter as part of a college education. He suggested that students typically move through nine stages as they progress through college. The early stages feature moral and intellectual absolutism, the belief that there is a correct solution for every problem, and reliance on authorities for guidance. For example, education majors functioning at these initial stages might expect their instructors to tell them the one correct way to teach content or handle discipline problems. Students at the middle stages move toward the opposite extreme by emphasizing relativism and context specificity in their reasoning. They begin to view authorities as people whose views are well informed but nevertheless open to question. Education majors operating at these stages might question the relevance of research to practice or decide that one has to find out for oneself what works in the classroom. Students operating at the later stages in Perry's model develop and become committed to a set of personal values that helps them to cope with the relativity inherent in many intellectual and moral issues. This allows them to move away from absolutism and idealism toward more pragmatic reasoning and problem solving. Beginning teachers functioning at these later stages would be committed to their own preferred pedagogical practices but also would be open to new ideas and aware that other approaches have value.

Other research suggests that adolescent and adult cognitive development, especially among individuals exposed to higher education, tends to progress from absolutist thinking (statements are either right or wrong, and what is right is so obvious as to require little justification) through a period of extreme relativism (there are no general rules, knowledge is subjective and uncertain) toward a more pragmatic view that recognizes that knowledge is constructed through personal interpretations but also that some claims are supported by better evidence or arguments (Basseches, 1984; Kitchener, 1986; Pintrich, 1990).

The students studied by Perry were mostly males. Subsequent research indicating gender differences in moral reasoning (see Chapter 4) raised questions about whether Perry's model also applied to cognitive development in females. Research by Belenky et al. (1986) suggests that young women may follow the same general lines of development but rely on quite different processes. As males discover the diversity in points of view and the potential for relativistic thinking, they tend to engage in bull sessions with peers and intellectual arguments with parents and teachers. In doing so, they not only adopt particular points of view but articulate them assertively and criticize alternatives suggested by others. In contrast, gender role socialization pressures inhibit many females from engaging so assertively in intellectual exchanges:

> Bull session[s], with students assailing their opponents' logic and attacking their evidence [seem] to occur rarely among women, and teachers complain that women students are reluctant to engage in critical debate with peers in class, even when explicitly encouraged to do so. Women find it hard to see debating as a "game"; they tend to take it personally. Teachers and fathers and boyfriends assure them that arguments are not between *persons* but between *positions,* but the women continue to fear that someone may get hurt. (Belenky et al., 1986, p. 105)

Consequently, adolescent and young adult females tend to cultivate listening skills and engage in polite conversations (as opposed to more assertive debates) on value-based issues. Their intellectual advances are more likely to occur in response to private introspection, especially at times when they sense that they have been out of touch with parts of themselves. In both men and women, many of the significant cognitive advances that occur in adolescence and young adulthood are connected with the identity crisis described by Erikson (see Chapter 4).

Along with Piagetian notions such as the equilibration principle and the construction of knowledge, post-Piagetian ideas about further developments within the stage of formal operations underscore the importance of continuing to restructure and sharpen our thinking throughout life, both as persons and as professionals.

implications for teachers
the implications of Piaget's work for teachers

Piaget made few specific statements about the implications of his work for teachers, so that any curriculum or teaching method labeled "Piagetian" is an interpretation based on his work and not a direct statement from Piaget himself. For what he did say, see Piaget (1970) and Hooper and DeFrain (1980).

Piaget's work has inspired varied approaches to schooling that are claimed to be "Piagetian" or "based on Piaget" (Kuhn, 1979; Hooper & DeFrain, 1980). Some early interpreters, stressing Piaget's emphasis on self-regulated learning governed by the equilibration principle, seemed almost hostile to the notion of instructing children (rather than allowing them to learn on their own). This extremism has faded, but among Piagetians who stress self-regulated learning as a key concept, there is still an emphasis on *exploration, inquiry, and discovery learning.* In this view, teachers should minimize direct instruction in a set curriculum taught in a prescribed sequence, and instead should provide opportunities for students to discover (construct) schemes through active manipulation of concrete materials. The teacher would be oriented more toward instructing individuals than groups, and more toward responding to students' initiatives or evidence of readiness for learning experiences than toward teacher-initiated instruction (Ginsburg & Opper, 1988; Wadsworth, 1989). Perhaps these ideas can be applied in preschool classes with low student- teacher ratios, but they do not appear feasible for elementary and secondary classes. Also, there are limits as to how seriously teachers can take concepts such as readiness or developmental stages. Duckworth (1979), a writer generally sympathetic to Piagetian notions, noted that overemphasis on self-regulated learning in applying Piaget creates a dilemma for teachers, who may be led to feel that "either we're too early and they can't learn or we're too late and they know it already."

conservation training Some would-be appliers of Piaget took the opposite approach and built Piagetian tasks into the curriculum by teaching students to conserve, to solve class inclusion problems, and so on. This was contrary to the spirit of Piaget's work, although it was based on the notion that if conservation and the other key concepts and operations that he discovered were truly basic to intellectual functioning, direct instruction in them might enhance or at least accelerate cognitive development.

These efforts led to a controversy between Piaget and psychologists interested in training nonconservers to conserve (Kuhn, 1974). The conservation trainers used brief treatments designed to bring about conceptual advances that Piaget believed would require years of

broad-based natural experience. Their data seemed to show that children could learn such concepts much earlier than Piaget had claimed. However, Piaget was not impressed with these findings. He viewed attempts to stimulate general cognitive development by teaching particular Piagetian tasks as akin to attempts to increase intelligence by teaching particular items on IQ tests.

Piaget drew on a distinction between figurative and operative knowledge in describing much of the learning produced in training experiments as superficial and "merely verbal**." Operative knowledge**—*knowledge constructed in the process of operating on the environment* — comes from actions. These actions can be either overt (physical) or internal (mental). For Piaget, operative knowledge is the most basic kind of knowledge—knowledge about what we can do and how to do it. **Figurative knowledge** is *knowledge acquired by perceiving and remembering representations of experience that we internalize directly in their original form without operating on or changing.* Much figurative knowledge involves mental images of our sensory perceptions of physical objects, although it also includes imitations of others that are limited to copying their input without operating on it, such as by memorizing a definition. Figurative knowledge is meaningful to children only to the extent that they can link it to relevant operative knowledge (see Figure 2.1).

Piaget and his colleagues (Inhelder, Sinclair, & Bovet, 1974) also believed that the criteria for concept acquisition used in the conservation training studies were not strict enough, and they doubted that the new learning would generalize to natural situations. The Piagetians wanted proof that trained children could not merely answer initial questions correctly but also withstand challenges designed to confuse those who did not have a firm grasp of the new concept. They believed that true conservers not only know what is true, but know that it is

Dr. Judith Lanier of Michigan State University composed the following exercise on "Traxoline" to illustrate what happens when we present (and require application of) knowledge only at the figurative level.

TRAXOLINE

It is very important that you learn about Traxoline. Traxoline is a new form of zionter. It is montilled in Cersitanna. The Ceristannians gristerlate large amounts of fevon and then bracter it to quasel Traxoline. Traxoline may well be one of our most lukized snezlaus in the future because of our zionter lescelidge.

Please answer the following questions in complete sentences and in your best handwriting.

1. What is Traxoline?
2. Where is Traxoline montilled?
3. How is Traxoline quaselled?
4. Why is it important to know about Traxoline?

If this example seems too farfetched, consider the next one, putting yourself in the place of a 10-year-old from Luckenbach, Texas.

Pittsburgh, "Heart of the Nation," is known for its steel production. It is located in southwestern Pennsylvania, where the Allegheny and Monongahela rivers join to form the Ohio. Iron ore, especially hematite, magnetite, and taconite, is first concentrated and then purified, using limestone as a flux to combine with impurities and float the resulting slag to the top of the melted iron in the blast furnace. Then pig iron from the blast furnace is combined with scrap iron and various additives, annealed or tempered through heat treatment, and formed into steel ingots ready for shipment to finishing mills.

Questions

1. What is Pittsburgh's nickname and what is the reason for it?
2. In steel production, what is the function of a flux?
3. What types of iron ore are commonly used in Pittsburgh's steel industry?
4. What happens to the ingots of annealed or tempered steel?

This second example *should* look familiar because it is representative of the kinds of exercises included all too frequently in the social studies curricula used in elementary schools. Note that students can answer each question correctly without learning anything at all, at least not anything beyond isolated and relatively meaningless figurative knowledge.

Figure 2.1 figurative knowledge without operative knowledge

necessarily true—that it could not be otherwise. In support of their position, the Piagetians showed that many children could not withstand vigorous probing of their newly "acquired" concepts. When confronted with counter-arguments ("But how could it be the same, when there's just one pitcher over there but all these glasses over here? All these containers surely must hold more water than just that one"), they became confused, backed down, or reverted to lower-level concepts. Typically, these were the children who had shown the least readiness to achieve the concept before training began.

Work by Miller (1986) also supports Piagetian claims that true conservers view conservation as *necessarily* true. Even so, work by other investigators indicates that apparently genuine, generalizable gains can be induced by confronting conservers and nonconservers with each other's beliefs and requiring them to come to agreement (Botvin & Murray, 1975; Russell, 1982), or by asking children to pretend that their beliefs are opposite to the real ones (Murray, Ames, & Botvin, 1977).

Others have succeeded with more traditional approaches involving instruction in rules, provision of feedback, or exposure to models (Brainerd, 1977).

Attempts to teach preadolescents to use formal operations have produced the same pattern of mixed and controversial findings as the "conservation training" studies (Nagy & Griffiths, 1982). Taken together, the data suggest that cognitive development is more open to meaningful stimulation through instruction than Piaget thought, but that Piaget was correct in stating that there are limits on what can be accomplished with a given child and on whether it will be worth the effort involved (Murray, 1978; White & Tisher, 1986).

matching input to student readiness

Piaget's work implies that teachers will have to keep the level and variety of input matched to students' schemes so as to maximize disequilibrium (and thus motivation to learn). This idea is sound as a general principle but difficult to apply to particular situations. For one thing, Piaget underestimated both the extent of knowledge that children at particular ages possess and the degree to which this knowledge can be extended with relative ease (Flavell, 1985). For example, his findings concerning conservation of number seemed to imply that preoperational children do not have useful quantitative knowledge. However, later research on children's understanding of number showed that two- and three-year-olds possess notions of quantity and the ability to compare quantities even before they can count. Older preoperational children can count and also possess a variety of useful number concepts even before they can qualify as conservers on conservation of number tasks (Bideud, Meljac, & Fischer, 1992; Gelman & Gallistel, 1986). Furthermore, counting and related number concepts and operations may be more basic to development of knowledge

about numbers than ability to succeed on Piagetian tasks (Fuson, 1988).

Another problem is that Piagetian stage notions are very general, and students' thinking can be inconsistent even when they are clearly within a particular overall stage. A child may show mastery of a concept in one task or situation but not another, such as being able to conserve length but not weight, or may function at a higher stage in certain respects but at a lower stage in other respects. To assess children's readiness for learning a particular concept or operation, teachers will need to look for clues such as inconsistency in their problem solving or strategy use, mismatches between what they say and what they communicate nonverbally, or evidence that confidence in naive beliefs is giving way to doubt and uncertainty (Graham & Perry, 1993). Such indicators suggest that knowledge is in transition and the child is open to replacement of immature beliefs with more mature ones.

In addition to these ambiguities about when children are ready for instruction in particular concepts, there are ambiguities about what is meant by matching input to students' readiness. Early Piagetian interpreters assumed that such matching meant presenting students with tasks that called for schemes and operations learned during their current stage of cognitive development. Later, other interpreters began to call for **plus-one matching**—*presenting students with tasks that require schemes or operations associated with the next higher stage*. Their rationale is that matching input to existing development will merely provide for additional exercise of already well-developed schemes and operations, whereas plus-one matching will stimulate the development of schemes and operations that are just now emerging.

Vygotsky and the zone of proximal development

Russian psychologist Lev Vygotsky (1962, 1978) advanced a similar notion in arguing that instruction should concentrate on the **zone of proximal development**—*Vygotsky's* *term for knowledge and skills that the student will not master spontaneously but can master with relative ease if given instruction and assistance.* Vygotsky's notion of teaching in the zone of proximal development is currently receiving much more emphasis than the Piagetian-inspired notion of advancing cognitive development through plus-one matching. This is because Vygotsky's ideas have been applied to conceptualizing teaching in a broad range of knowledge domains, not just to stimulation of advancement through Piaget's stages. Also, whereas Piaget tended to emphasize the child's solitary explorations of the environment, Vygotsky emphasized social learning within particular cultural contexts. Ideas about teaching in the zone of proximal development are discussed in Chapters 7 and 11.

teaching readiness Critics of Piagetian ideas reject what they see as overemphasis on the need for spontaneous and self-regulated learning. For example, they note that motivation to learn something may not exist at the moment but might be stimulated easily by a teacher. Also, where it is possible to stimulate readiness easily through systematic intervention, the teacher might teach readiness rather than wait for it to occur spontaneously.

To a cognitive development specialist who describes changes that occur with age, readiness emerges slowly over time. However, to a teacher trying to induce change through systematic intervention, readiness can be something to teach if it is not already present. Within limits, a learner who is not ready to master a given concept or skill can be made ready to master it through successive approximations involving intermediate objectives. But is this worth doing? Often it is, because teaching both the intervening readiness skills and the ultimate learning objective is relatively easy. However, if readiness can be attained only with lengthy and strenuous efforts by both the teacher and the learner, it may be best to teach other things in

the meantime and wait for greater readiness to develop. Another factor affecting how much effort to put into the development of a given skill is the centrality of the skill to the primary purposes of schooling. Elementary teachers might feel justified in minimizing picture drawing or dodgeball performance pressures on students who appeared to be hampered by motor coordination difficulties, yet might feel compelled to push these students to make better progress in learning to print and write.

providing concrete props for learning Piaget's work shows why concrete objects, photos, drawings, diagrams, charts, and other visual aids facilitate learning, and why learning requires active response. If what we learn is what we do, then we must actually practice the doing, acting it out in behavior or at least formulating a plan in our own words. Just watching and listening alone will result in "merely verbal" figurative learning rather than construction of a network of related schemes. Concrete props help students to bridge the gap between the known and the unknown, thus increasing the degree to which new material is relatively assimilable. In science classes, for example, laboratory experiments illustrate, and literally make meaningful, the abstract principles being taught.

Piaget's work suggests that everything is learned most easily and thoroughly if mastered in the order in which discovery learning would occur naturally. Sensorimotor schemes would precede cognitive schemes, and concrete experience would precede formal analysis and abstraction. When anything new is taught, some students may have difficulty learning if they have not yet developed the schemes to comprehend the new information, even though most of their peers have developed these schemes. Instruction is unlikely to be successful until the schemes develop, either spontaneouly or in response to instruction (Renner et al., 1976). Successful teachers present material in a variety of ways, so that it becomes meaningful to students who differ in levels of cognitive development.

traditional schooling and Piaget's stages

The traditional school curriculum is fairly well matched to natural levels of cognitive development. Typically, the middle grades that correspond to the period of concrete operations call for more conceptual learning than do the first few grades, but they avoid highly abstract subject matter and emphasize concrete objects, specific examples, or other aids to promote meaningful understanding. Beginning around junior high school the curriculum concentrates increasingly on more abstract subject matter. For example, elementary school history stresses particular events described in narrative form and usually personalized around the motives and actions of central characters. In contrast, history courses in high school, and particularly in college, feature more abstract analysis of the political, social, and economic reasons for historical events.

Briefly, Piaget's developmental work suggests the following about matching school experiences to existing cognitive development. First, toddlers in the sensorimotor period and early in the preoperational period learn primarily through play and exploration, and their learning is concentrated on sensorimotor schemes. The way to optimize cognitive development in these early years is to provide a rich, stimulating environment that encourages learning through exploration. Attempts to teach concepts that call on schemes that would not appear naturally for several years are not likely to succeed, except in

producing "merely verbal" learning. In the late preoperational and early concrete operational stages, children can benefit increasingly from more systematic and even formal instruction, although the content and modes of presentation must be matched to their existing schemes. They can learn a great deal about many things, particularly about familiar experiences or about concrete objects that they can manipulate and explore for themselves. They also can learn words and memorize things easily, although they will not understand the meanings of memorized statements that are too abstract or refer to events that are beyond the children's experience and imagination (i.e., if figurative knowledge is not integrated with operative knowledge).

We believe that these implications do not necessarily contradict the school practices, traditional in early grades, that Piagetians have criticized. Certain things are learned much more easily from instruction than by discovery. The list is debatable, but it includes the fundamentals of reading, writing, and arithmetic taught in the early grades. Piaget's work reminds us, however, that instruction in these fundamentals should focus on meaningful learning and authentic applications. Thus, students should read for information and enjoyment (not just to practice decoding), write to communicate ideas (not just practice penmanship), learn computation skills in the context of meaningful problem solving (not just do computation worksheets), and use computers to edit compositions, conduct research, and solve problems (not just as electronic workbooks).

concluding comments

Remember, *all students operate with some type of logic, although their logic may differ from that used by most adults.* Teachers must

be able to recognize the general developmental levels and particular logical reasoning used by their students if they are to diagnose learning difficulties accurately and communicate meaningfully. All teachers, but especially those in grades two and three (when children start to become operational) and in junior high school (when some students begin to acquire formal operations), must be prepared for a great range in developmental levels. Many third graders will be preoperational in their logic, with all of the egocentrism and other childish limitations that this implies. Others will be well into the concrete operational stage, capable of reasoning logically as long as they do not have to deal with purely abstract concepts. All students in junior high classes will be logical in their thinking, but only some will be able to deal with abstract material meaningfully.

Even students who do show formal operational thinking in certain tasks may not do so in other, less familiar tasks. Martorano (1977) measured formal operations in middle-class girls who had IQs between 100 and 120, using ten different tasks. Even in this above-average group, only about 20 percent of the eighth graders and 60 percent of the tenth graders were scored for formal operations on Piaget's "pendulum" and "rods" problems. Across the set of ten tasks, the percentages of students scored for formal operations ranged from 0 to 60 percent in sixth graders, 0 to 85 percent in eighth graders, 5 to 95 percent in tenth graders, and 15 to 90 percent in twelfth graders. Thus, ability to think abstractly depends not only on age and general cognitive development, but on specific knowledge and experience with particular intellectual content.

Possession of the ability to think abstractly does not mean that one always or even often uses that ability. Nor does attaining the period of formal operations imply that previous modes of thinking are lost. On the contrary, they persist and in fact constitute the bulk of the cognitive structure. Even professors routinely use formal operational thinking only in certain situations, most obviously when theorizing in their areas of specialization. When trying to comprehend politics or the stock market or the motivational fluctuations of their colleges' athletics teams, and especially when trying to fix an appliance or automobile, they may have to make do with primarily concrete operational or even sensorimotor schemes.

summary

Piaget and other stage theorists believe that children develop through qualitatively distinct stages in acquiring and organizing knowledge. This contrasts with the step-by-step quantitative process of acquiring knowledge described by learning theorists. Piaget stressed physical actions and experience with the environment as basic to early cognitive development. He defined the scheme as the basic unit of cognition, speech, and behavior. The constant process of adaptation, accomplished via the mechanisms of assimilation and accommodation and guided by the principle of equilibration, modifies existing schemes.

Piaget divided development into four basic periods: (1) sensorimotor (the first two years), (2) preoperational (two to seven years), (3) concrete operations (seven to twelve years), and (4) formal operations (twelve years and beyond). Scheme development in the sensorimotor stage is concentrated heavily on sensorimotor skills, while the preoperational stage brings development of language and logical thinking abilities. During the period of concrete operations, children add classification and seriation skills, reversibility of operations, negation, identity, and reciprocity. Finally, the ability to use symbols, abstractions, and propositions contrary to fact develops during the period of formal operations. Post-Piagetian research has shown that many important cognitive advances in addition to the emergence of formal operations occur during the adolescent and adult years.

Piaget's work identifies some of the general developmental trends within which more

research at work
Piagetian educational principles

Perhaps the most useful implications for teaching that may be drawn from Piaget's work are some relatively general principles. Hooper and DeFrain (1980), after reviewing several "Piagetian" programs, suggest the following principles:

- Attend to the processes, and not just the products, of students' thinking. Don't concentrate just on getting correct answers; make sure that the students really understand the concepts or operations being taught.
- Appreciate the value of play along with exploration and manipulation opportunities for developing cognitive schemes, especially in the early grades.
- Be aware that children learn a great deal from interacting with one another and, in particular, from debating conflicting views.
- Remember that learning that occurs through active exploration and discovery is more likely to be retained and to be meaningful than learning that occurs through more passive response to teachers' initiatives.

Kroll and Black (1993) emphasize the following principles in what they call a "developmental" elementary teacher education program:

- Encourage children's construction of knowledge via active involvement with the curriculum rather than via imitation or memorization of facts or algorithms. Children begin to construct their own ideas of number, scientific concepts, and reading and writing before entering school. A developmental curriculum builds on these understandings. For example, focus initial instruction in addition on the children's slowly developing ability to physically compose and decompose small numbered quantities, rather than on memorization of number facts reinforced through worksheet exercises. Similarly, in literacy instruction emphasize reading and writing for meaning rather than isolated practice of skills.

- Revisit important concepts in different contexts to help students consolidate old

specific kinds of learning occur. Many kinds of knowledge develop earlier than Piaget assumed, however. Teachers can often stimulate learning readiness directly rather than having to wait for it to develop more naturally. Yet, Piaget was correct in cautioning us that a broad base of knowledge and experience accumulated over many years might be necessary to prepare students for certain kinds of learning and that instructional

knowledge through practice and extend that knowledge to new situations. For example, instead of teaching literacy skills in separate units staggered across the school year, integrate these skills throughout the school year both within language arts and across the curriculum.

- Encourage self-regulation of the knowledge-construction process by providing students with instruction and support in self-evaluation, feedback that is immediate rather than postponed, and opportunities to reflect on the results of their actions and if necessary to initiate alternatives. This can be accomplished through reading and writing conferences in literacy instruction and through opportunities to manipulate materials and discuss the results in mathematics and science instruction.

- Promote social construction of knowledge by reducing reliance on whole-class instruction followed by seat work and increasing reliance on small-group, inter-active activities. Use both teacher-student and peer conferences in literacy instruction and collaborative problem-solving groups in mathematics and science instruction.

- Promote both the differentiation of knowledge (construction of new knowledge by making finer distinctions within existing knowledge) and the integration of knowledge (linking of elements of knowledge once they are differentiated). In literacy, for example, see that children learn about the unique aspects of reading and of writing, but also integrate reading and writing activities so that they write to read and read to write.

- Rather than focusing primarily on either the learner (child-centered) or the curriculum (skills-centered), balance and integrate the two. Observe the students carefully and be ready to introduce new concepts while reaffirming old ones as skills develop.

methods that focus on figurative knowledge without developing related operative knowledge are unlikely to produce meaningful understanding. The most important implications for teachers derived from Piaget's work involve general principles for helping students to construct and integrate networks of well coordinated schemes, not more specific techniques such as teaching them conservation concepts.

questions for reflection

1. Can one teach readiness? What are the issues associated with this question?

2. If Piagetians are correct in their belief that children go through a series of qualitatively distinct stages in cognitive development, what implications does this have for the types of learning activities and content that students can be assigned?

3. What is a scheme? Differentiate, in your own words, the following types of schemes: sensorimotor, cognitive, and verbal.

4. Explain the equilibration principle and its role in motivating and regulating cognitive development.

5. At the grade level at which you intend to teach, what sorts of learning would represent mere *growth* of knowledge and what sorts would represent significant *development?*

6. What important teaching principles can be derived from Piaget's work?

7. Define the terms "plus-one matching" and "zone of proximal development." What are the implications of these concepts for curriculum planning?

8. Notice that we have accepted differences in learner capacity (both Piagetian stage differences and general IQ differences among students at the same Piagetian stage) as real. Do you? What does this imply with respect to nature-nurture issues such as tracking, special education, and IQ testing?

9. Piagetian theory and research suggest that natural learning proceeds according to the equilibration principle rather than following logical and hierarchically arranged sequences. What (if anything) does this imply about the structuring of curricula?

10. What aspects of poetry and science can be taught meaningfully to first graders? Fourth graders? Tenth graders? Which of these aspects should be taught?

11. Why is it that the sequence of development is fixed but the rate and form of development are variable?

12. How might adolescents be taught in ways that preserve the desirable aspects of their idealism while still moving them toward more pragmatic modes of thinking?

cases to consider

Ms. Herbert and a heat wave Ms. Herbert worked with her slowest second-grade reading group. She and the children perspired because it was a hot day and the inner-city school did not have air conditioning. Everyone had to strain to focus attention on the reading task, as opposed to their personal discomfort. During the lesson two students raised questions that were touched off by the story but not directly related to it. Jim asked, "Does anybody's father in this room work on a farm like the guy in the story?" Tim asked, "What do they eat?" Ms. Herbert made minimal responses to these questions in order to keep the children "on task." What principles of human development did she ignore? Specifically, how could she improve the situation?

successful practice Marilyn Kuchar is an enthusiastic seventh-grade general math teacher. She believes that most students can learn and that she can teach them. She goes through the curriculum slowly so that students repeatedly experience success on assignments. Characteristically, all students work all or almost all problems correctly, and they seem to enjoy the opportunity to continue to practice things that they can do well. To what extent do you agree with Marilyn's teaching techniques? What suggestions might you make about improving her approach? How do the concepts of plus-one matching and zone of proximal development apply to her teaching?

Mr. Robinson and book science Darrell Robinson is a second-grade teacher who enjoys presenting science to his students and spends considerable time at it (forty-five minutes per day instead of only fifteen minutes two or three times a week). He often describes famous scientists and tells how and why they did experiments. He also likes to talk about great discoveries, about the general processes of science, and about the things we might have in the year 2050 that presently are not available. However, he does not like to actually do experiments with the students, because the class is hard to control and things might break. What principles of human development is Darrell ignoring? What advice might you have for him?

supervisor on the spot Marge Guffy, the English coordinator for the school district, has just observed an eighth-grade lesson taught by Rachel Cohen. After the lesson, Marge says, "Rachel, that was generally a very good English lesson, but you taught as though the students were second graders!" Rachel thoughtfully replies, "Well, I'm not sure I agree with you. What would I need to do differently?" Based on your knowledge of developmental theory, what are the differences between teaching second graders and eighth graders that should make for differences in teaching and learning activities in the classroom?

cognitive development and education

objectives

When you have mastered the material in this chapter you will be able to

1. Explain the shift in emphasis from general stages in cognitive development to gradual accumulation of expertise in specific knowledge domains, along with its implications for teachers

2. Explain the implications for teachers of the idea that narrative and other forms of thinking do not follow the developmental sequence that Piaget identified for logico-mathematical thinking

3. Specify what and how teachers might teach to encourage meaningful learning in grades one through three versus grades four through six versus the secondary grades

4. Explain what occurs when a child "becomes operational"

5. Distinguish the thinking characteristics of concrete versus formal operational students and the types of instruction appropriate to their abilities and needs

6. Explain Chomsky's ideas about how the structural aspects of language develop via an innate language acquisition device

7. Explain how one's functional use of language develops

8. Contrast the views of Vygotsky and Piaget on the interaction of language and thinking

9. Explain methods of adapting teaching to the needs of students who come from different discourse communities

post-Piagetian theory and criticism

We noted in Chapter 2 that Piaget led the way in calling attention to the active, constructive nature of children's cognitive development and in outlining the broad stages within which this development takes place. Reassessment of Piagetian theory and research has occurred in recent years, however, as studies of children's learning and cognition have shifted from a focus on general stages to a focus on the development of expertise within particular knowledge domains. This reassessment continues, although several broad trends have emerged (Flavell, 1992).

First, there has been a gradual shift from what Flavell called "highly verbal, talky testing procedures" toward mixed verbal-nonverbal or even wholly nonverbal experimental methods (in which the child is asked to indicate which stimulus item is heavier, which group has more items, etc.). Research with these newer methods has led to revisions of Piaget's estimates of cognitive abilities: Infants and children now appear to be more competent but adults to be less competent (Flavell, 1985; Siegler, 1991). We now know that preoperational children are

less egocentric and more cognitively advanced in many respects than Piaget believed, but adult reasoning is less rational and the development of formal operations is less complete and widespread.

Opinion has also moved away from Piaget on the issue of whether the mind develops in a general, unified fashion or in a more specific, piecemeal way (Case, 1992; Demetriou, Shayer, & Efklides, 1993; Fischer & Silvern, 1985; Flavell, 1985). Piaget emphasized general, unified cognitive development proceeding through a fixed sequence of broad stages. The opposite view is that development is very specific and piecemeal, so that knowledge in each domain proceeds at its own rate, independent of the others. Contemporary developmentalists agree that cognitive development is not as general and stagelike as Piaget thought, although they disagree on the degree to which it is specific and piecemeal. "Neo-Piagetians" recognize that development is specific in many respects but still believe that it follows important general trends. Many contemporary developmentalists, however, either ignore or doubt the existence of general stage phenomena and focus instead on more specific developments within particular content domains and cultural contexts.

Finally, there has been increasing emphasis on the sociocultural environment in which cognitive development takes place. Although Piaget recognized the role of social transmission of knowledge and interactions with others in stimulating development, he usually did not include this social aspect in his experiments and examples. "Piaget's child" is often pictured as a solitary little scientist exploring the environment and constructing knowledge in response to his or her own individual equilibration needs. In contrast, Rogoff (1990), Vygotsky (1978), Wertsch (1985), and other social constructivists claim that cognitive development more often resembles apprenticeship, in which a novice (child) works closely with an expert (parent, teacher) who provides guidance and support in the use of skills to solve problems.

Sociocultural environments differ in the nature of the knowledge and skills that they emphasize to developing children. All sociocultural environments, however, offer strengths that teachers can capitalize upon if they are sufficiently aware and appreciative of them. For example, Moll (1992) described the *funds of knowledge* that parents of children enrolled in a bilingual education program had developed through participation in various labor markets. Different parents had acquired, and were passing on to their children, knowledge about farming and ranching (horsemanship, animal husbandry, soil and irrigation, crop planting, hunting), mining and timbering (extraction of minerals, use and maintenance of equipment), economics and household management (market values, loans, labor laws, budgets, cooking, appliance repair), and many other topics relevant to everyday living and economic advancement. Successful teaching of these children featured integrated units on topics such as housing construction. The children were encouraged to

apply their language arts skills (in both languages) to projects such as reports on architecture and construction methods and vocations. The units also included visits by parents with expertise on the topic and homework assignments that engaged the students in interactions with family members and visits to local work sites as part of their research. In this way, the cultural tools taught at school were connected with the funds of knowledge possessed by local subcultures so as to increase the power and relevance of the children's education.

We will consider the trends identified by Flavell in more detail, focusing on aspects that help connect work on cognitive development to issues of teaching and learning in school.

Piaget's questioning methods

Critics have noted that certain aspects of Piaget's methods of questioning may have confused children and led him to underestimate their knowledge. Part of the problem lay in the kinds of questions he asked. Given their limited vocabularies, it is likely that many of the children Piaget interviewed did not understand confusing questions such as "Are there more flowers or more tulips?" When other investigators tested for concept development using stimulus items and vocabulary terms more familiar to young children, they usually found that the children showed concept acquisition at younger ages (Donaldson, 1978; Egan, 1982).

Piaget's insistence on questioning children thoroughly to make sure that they were certain of their convictions also led to underestimates of their knowledge. Such persistent interrogation creates an uncomfortable social situation. Feeling confused and perhaps badgered, children are likely to respond by concentrating on pleasing the interviewer rather than on thinking carefully about the question (Wood, 1988).

Piaget's clinical interviewing methods were

used for conducting research, not instruction. Even so, the concerns raised about them also apply to teachers' questions in the classroom. They underscore the need for teachers to be sensitive to their students' language use (so as not to confuse them with questions that they do not understand) and to their needs for security and respect (so as not to anger or humiliate them with persistent questioning that they perceive as badgering).

children's limited information-processing capacities

Neo-Piagetian theorists (Case, 1992; Demetriou, Shayer, & Efklides, 1993) seek to preserve the strengths of Piaget's theory while correcting its weaknesses. One important weakness is Piaget's failure to take into account developments in children's information-processing capacities. Children often fail to respond correctly to Piagetian interview questions, not because they lack the concepts or operations that the questions are designed to assess, but because they cannot simultaneously keep track of and think about all of the elements built into the questions. When questions are broken down and sequenced in ways that allow children to address the issues one step at a time, they often show that they do possess the concept (e.g., conservation of liquid volume) or operation (e.g., identity) in question.

At any given age, capacity limitations will constrain the possible forms of cognition that students can enact. It is important to be sensitive to these limitations and provide students with whatever assistance is needed to circumvent them. For example, a teacher can spare students cognitive overload by breaking complex questions into series of simpler ones, helping them decide where to begin attacking a complex problem, or providing supports for learning such as lists of steps to follow or questions to ask oneself when working through an assignment. Ordinarily, instruction should focus on developing basic understandings rather than speedy responses to specific questions or problems. You can begin to gain familiarity with students' cognitive strengths and limitations by arranging to observe in classes at the grade level at which you intend to teach.

suitability of Piagetian theory across content areas

Educators differ in the degree to which they find Piaget's work relevant to their subjects. Mathematics and science educators usually find his work useful because Piaget focused on logico-mathematical operations applied to scientific and mathematical problems. Specialists in the social sciences and especially the humanities complain that Piagetian concepts do not capture key cognitive developments that are central to their subjects. These tend to be developments in knowledge about the human condition generally and about people's motivations and related goal-directed behaviors, rather than operations for reasoning about mathematical and physical problems.

Recently, interest has developed around *narrative knowledge structures* as an alternative to Piaget's logico-mathematical knowledge structures as bases for developing understandings in the humanities and social sciences. Bruner (1990) and Egan (1988, 1990), among others, have noted that even very young children are familiar with and adept at using narrative modes of thinking for describing and remembering things that are important to them. That is, they formulate and remember in story form. The stories are built around a central figure or hero and include attention to this person's goals, behavior undertaken to accomplish those goals, and the outcomes of this behavior for the hero and other figures in the story. The narrative format provides a natural way to remember a great many details used to fill out the story, organized within the goal-strategy-outcome sequence. As long as children can understand the hero's goal, the behavior undertaken as a strategy for accomplishing the goal, and the outcomes that resulted, they can follow and remember the story. This is true even for stories about fantasy characters or people from the past or from faraway places.

Children's abilities to understand and learn through narratives make it possible for teachers to use language arts instruction to extend their students' thinking to people, places, and ideas they have not encountered in their personal experience but that they can understand through extrapolation from their experience. Similarly, although children may not yet be ready for highly conceptual and analytic forms of instruction in history and the social sciences, they can learn a great deal about these subjects when the material is taught with emphasis on stories and examples rendered in narrative format (Downey & Levstik, 1991). Even instruction in science and mathematics is likely to be made more interesting and comprehensible if it includes stories about the personal characteristics, motives, and activities of the scientists and mathematicians who made the original discoveries (American Association for the Advancement of Science, 1989).

the shift from general stages to specific knowledge domains

Recent cognitive development and learning research has focused on children's acquisition of expertise in particular domains of knowledge. Wellman and Gelman (1992) have reviewed evidence indicating that children develop naive, prescientific "theories" in the areas of physics, psychology, and biology. Naive physics ideas include notions about the properties and behavior of inanimate objects and about causal expla-

nations for their physical relationships. Naive psychological ideas concern the perceptions, motives, and thoughts that guide people's behavior. Naive biological ideas concern the properties of living organisms and the internal workings of the body.

Studies of learning in particular domains have addressed topics ranging from relatively general ideas about science (Carey, 1985) to the use of strategies in specific areas such as chess (Chi, 1978). These studies indicate that the learning of specialized expertise is often more influential than general stage development in determining the quality and level of organization of knowledge. People's abilities to think about and play the game of chess, for example, are determined much more by the levels of expertise they have developed than by their ages. Child chess experts resemble adult chess experts, not adult novices. Experts often solve problems quickly by recognizing familiar patterns and responding to them with readily accessible strategies. In contrast, novices have to rely on more generic reasoning processes to try to work out a solution.

Children undergo conceptual change and reconstruct their knowledge as they acquire expertise in particular domains. Sometimes the conceptual change requires only weak restructuring, which is limited to the accumulation of new facts and the formation of new relations between existing concepts (akin to Piaget's assimilation). However, some conceptual change requires radical restructuring that includes changes in core concepts, in how these concepts are structured, and in how the phenomena to be explained are perceived (akin to Piaget's accommodation). Restructuring is often slowed or distorted by the stubborn persistence of naive beliefs or misconceptions that the child has acquired previously and is not yet ready to give up (Carey, 1985; Chinn & Brewer, 1993; Keating & Crane, 1990; Linn & Songer, 1991; Vosniadou & Brewer, 1987).

It is important for teachers to become

familiar with common misconceptions that may interfere with their students' learning in particular knowledge domains, so as to be better prepared to assist the students with the often-difficult process of conceptual change. Again, you can begin to do this by observing in classrooms and talking to teachers and students at the grade level you intend to teach.

implications for teachers

Piaget in the classroom

the preoperational years Children show the capacity for operational thinking at five or six, but they usually do not become functionally operational (use operational thinking most of the time) until they are at least a year or two older. Thus, in effect, the preoperational period extends until second or third grade for most children. Preoperational students are ready to learn about familiar experiences and observable phenomena, especially through exploration and manipulation of concrete objects. They are also able to learn basic literacy and mathematics skills and those aspects of content area knowledge that can be linked to their experience base.

teaching basic tool skills Basic literacy and mathematics skills should be taught in ways that connect with knowledge about language, print, counting, and numbers that children develop through their preschool experiences. These tool skills should be taught in an integrated way that stresses explanation for meaningful understanding and opportunities for authentic application (Adams, 1990; Anderson et al., 1985; Hooper & DeFrain, 1980).

Preschool and primary grade children will require demonstration and explanation of skills, guided practice with feedback, and frequent opportunities to develop mastery through application. Good demonstrations and visual aids provide concrete models for children to watch or imitate, so that they do not have to struggle to follow purely verbal instruction. Complex tasks should be broken into subtasks that children can

master in sequences that gradually connect until the ultimate task is learned. When children work on their own, they might need cues, reminders, or other *learning scaffolds* that will help them overcome their limited attention spans and difficulty in following purely verbal directions. Models of completed tasks might be placed in learning centers, and worksheets might include features such as spacing and lines to keep things separate; arrows, boxes, and lines to indicate where responses should be placed or where to go next; and division of assignments into modular units that can be presented, corrected, and discussed separately.

eliciting and monitoring responses Basic knowledge and skills will need to be learned thoroughly enough to enable students to use them in appropriate application situations. Teachers will need to monitor progress by frequently asking their students questions and providing them with opportunities to apply what they are learning.

Teachers cannot reliably evaluate understanding through questions that can be answered yes or no or that merely ask which of two or three alternatives is correct. It is too easy for children to guess the answers to such questions. To find out whether they really understand, the teacher needs to ask questions that require them to demonstrate mastery (Nagy & Griffiths, 1982). For skills, this means having them perform the skill, observing to see if they use the proper process and achieve the desired outcomes, and providing helpful feedback if they do not. For verbal learning, fact questions ("who," "what," "when," "where," or "how many") and explanation questions ("how" or "why") will require the children to produce answers from memory or to figure them out.

In the early grades, teachers should elicit responses frequently from each individual student. Young children have only limited ability to learn from watching and listening to others without making overt responses themselves; therefore, it is important to elicit responses and provide feedback to each individual (Brophy & Good, 1986).

grounding the content in operative knowledge Teaching in subject areas other than basic skills should either emphasize familiar content or make the strange familiar by using concrete props or other media. Actual objects are best, but substitutes such as films or photos also are useful. Because young children have major gaps in their vocabularies and difficulties in following purely verbal presentations, they may need such props to enable them to understand what the teacher is talking about (Renner et al., 1976).

It is unwise to emphasize complex or abstract content when teaching preoperational children, especially if this content is organized around the conceptual structures used in the academic disciplines rather than around children's emerging knowledge structures. Certain curricula, such as the "new math" of the 1960s and 1970s, encountered difficulties in the early grades for this reason (American Institute for Research, 1976). These curricula were organized quite logically from an adult perspective, but were ill-suited to children's learning needs. Children tend to learn specifics first and to build up abstract generalizations only gradually

as they accumulate experience; they have trouble following the logical pattern (flowing from general rules to specific examples) that adults find helpful.

It is important to focus instruction on familiar and observable events, or at least events that are easily assimilated into the students' existing schemes. Attempts to discuss topics totally outside their experience will fail. So will attempts to present content at too-sophisticated levels. Fair (1977) suggested the following generalizations about difficulty level of curriculum content: (1) difficulty increases with the number of items that must be addressed simultaneously (it is harder to compare or interpret three things than two things); (2) abstract content is more difficult than more concrete content; (3) fine distinctions are more difficult than gross ones; (4) learning from print alone is more difficult than learning from multiple media; (5) it is easier to develop skills in thinking about matters that students see as closely related to their own lives than about other matters; and (6) providing structure, cues, and props makes thinking easier. Children in the primary grades need opportunities to manipulate concrete objects. They also need experience in comparing and contrasting, ordering before and after, identifying cause and effect, distinguishing true from false, and distinguishing main ideas and important points from less important supportive material.

readiness for content area learning Influenced by early Piagetian work, some scholars have argued that instruction in science and social studies should not begin until the secondary grades, when students are better able to handle the abstractions emphasized in these subjects. However, more recent research indicates that children are capable of learning many aspects of these knowledge domains with understanding (Downey & Levstik, 1991). Also, McKenzie (1986) has argued that many aspects of these knowledge domains are basic "learning-to-learn" skills, just as tool skills are. For example, children must learn stories, information, and ideas of precisely the sort that are included in history and social studies in order to comprehend the sketchy arguments that they hear or read each day or to solve problems through logical reasoning. The key is to convey this information in concrete terms that they can understand. Relatively meaningless statements about the difficulties of the "separatists," for example, become meaningful to young children when incorporated into a story about the "Pilgrims." Similarly, a problem such as "How can you determine the volume of an irregularly shaped object like a statue?" would stump most students who are able to think about volume only in geometric terms. However, a teacher might stimulate ideas about solutions

by recounting the story of Archimedes, who came to the realization that volume is related to displacement as he watched the water levels change when he entered or exited his bathtub.

Elkind (1981) pointed out that even Piaget spoke of "anticipations"—intuitive ideas and interests that will become fully elaborated only at a later stage. For example, children have an intuitive sense of the past and a spontaneous interest in people that can provide a basis for instruction in history and social studies. However, such instruction will need to get to the operative level rooted in students' concrete experiences, such as by having them investigate their own family histories, explore the geography of the neighborhood, or examine photos and artifacts from another culture. If the instruction stays at a purely figurative level (Native Americans lived in tepees, Mexicans wear sombreros, etc.), it will not have much meaning or potential for inclusion in networks of social studies knowledge structured around powerful ideas.

The preoperational years are characterized by learning that involves manipulation of concrete objects.

research at work
guidelines for developmentally appropriate practice

Organizations concerned with the education of young children (through age eight) have synthesized material from a broad range of sources in developmental and educational psychology to identify guidelines for what they call "developmentally appropriate practice" (Bredekamp, 1987; National Association for the Education of Young Children, 1991).

- The curriculum attends to social, emotional, and physical goals as well as to cognitive. It prepare children to function as fully contributing members of a democratic society.
- Knowledge and skill aquisition are accomplished in ways that encourage children to associate positive feelings with what they are learning and to be disposed to apply it in their lives outside of school. Much of the learning is accomplished through authentic applications.
- A wide variety of learning experiences, materials and equipment, and instructional strategies is used to accommodate individual differences in children's learning needs and interests.
- Curriculum and instruction support individual, cultural, and linguistic diversity and encourage positive relationships with children's families.
- Curriculum builds on what children already know and are able to do (activating prior knowledge) to consolidate their learning and foster aquisition of new concepts and skills.
- There is focus on particular topics but also integration across traditional subjects, using themes or learning experiences that provide opportunities for rich conceptual development. At the same time, the content has intellectual integrity according to the standards of relevant academic disciplines.
- The curriculum encourages children to learn actively and make meaningful choices.
- Instruction values children's constructive errors and does not prematurely limit

---

Egan (1988) argued that history, science, literature, and other subjects that include abstract elements can be made both very interesting and easily comprehensible to children if they are taught using narratives built around the intentions and actions of central figures. Even in the primary grades children can benefit from instruction in history if the material is presented primarily in the form of vivid narratives organized around concepts such as courage, cowardice, oppression, resentment, victory, and defeat that children experience in their own lives. Levstik (1986) also noted that children's literary interests include the distant and fantastic ones of adventures, fairy tales, and so on, and that they can understand content that is placed into a narrative framework and deals with motives or thoughts they have experienced or can identify with. Thus, there is no need to avoid content drawn from the academic disciplines in the early grades, so long as this con-

exploration and experimentation for the sake of encouraging "right" answers.

- Content and process are linked rather than taught in isolation, so as to encourage development of thinking, reasoning, decision making, and problem-solving abilities.
- Teaching reflects children's naturally recurring learning cycle that begins with awareness and progresses through exploration, inquiry, and use of constructed knowledge in authentic applications.
- Teachers foster awareness by providing opportunities to encounter new objects, events, and people; posing problems or questions; responding to children's interests or shared experiences; and modeling interest and enthusiasm in their own behavior.
- Teachers promote exploration by providing opportunities and support for children to observe, discover, collect information, or otherwise engage in active exploration; helping children to construct meaning by describing their activities and asking open-ended questions such as "What else could you do?"; and responding to errors in ways that communicate respect for children's thinking.
- Teachers support inquiry by helping children to focus their thinking and refine their understandings, asking questions such as "What else works like this?" or What happens if . . .?"; providing requested information; and helping children to make connections.
- Teachers help children to use their knowledge by creating vehicles for authentic application and helping children to see how learning developed previously can be applied in the current situation.

Guidelines are selected and paraphrased from a position statement published by the National Association for the Education of Young Children, "Guidelines for Appropriate Curriculum Content and Assessment in Programs Serving Children Ages 3 through 8," *Young Children*, *46* (3), 1991, pp. 21–38.

---

tent is grounded in children's operative knowledge and thus made meaningful to them.

Nor should teachers in the early grades ignore learning-to-learn skills, independent work skills, integrative concepts, or conceptual understanding (how to read for understanding, how to evaluate information and integrate it with input from elsewhere, and how to budget study time and plan work on complex tasks). These concepts and skills develop slowly as children become operational and more responsive to the student role.

It does little good to try to teach children at conceptual levels far beyond their present grasp, but teachers can develop readiness through modeling—making integrative or abstract statements about material being taught mostly at lower levels of analysis. Not all children will understand these statements, but some will, and the effect on the others will be to build readiness for more conceptual instruction later.

implications for teachers

Piaget in the classroom

becoming operational Piaget stressed four aspects of becoming operational: (1) developing the ability to discriminate between invariant and variant aspects of the environment; (2) coordinating separate schemes (e.g., counting objects in a group, comparing quantities) into larger ones, and ultimately into concrete operations organized within a unified cognitive structure; (3) achieving the ability to reason forward from causes to effects and backward from effects to causes (reversibility); and (4) decentration—beginning to move outward from the child's own purview so as to take into account the purviews of others.

Equilibration needs cause children who are in the process of becoming operational to become more active in seeking information by asking questions and (when able) by reading. Much of this information seeking involves attempts to fill gaps and resolve discrepancies so as to make the existing cognitive structure more comprehensive and internally consistent. For the first time, children become notably aware of such gaps and inconsistencies. They want to clear up confusion between concepts such as husband and father or state and nation, and they want more information about matters such as what parents do at work or what differentiates humans, animals, plants, and inanimate objects.

Researchers have noted distinct changes in children's responses to certain experimental situations as they become operational. We have already mentioned the changes in responses to conservation problems and other tasks used by Piaget. Another example occurs in responses to *transposition problems*. In a typical experiment, children first are taught to discriminate between a smaller and a larger circle by rewarding them for choosing the larger circle. Then a new set is introduced, in which the smaller circle is identical to the one that was larger before (see Figure 3.1).

Children in the sensorimotor and preoperational stages respond to this new pair by picking the circle that is now the smaller one (but is identical to the one that was rewarded in the previous trials). However, concrete operational

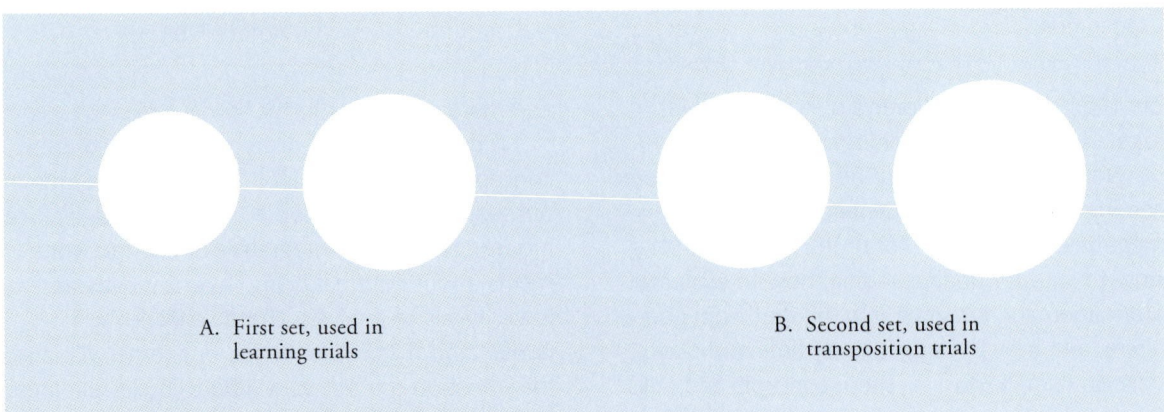

A. First set, used in learning trials

B. Second set, used in transposition trials

Figure 3.1 typical stimuli used in transposition experiments

children, as well as older children and adults, typically respond by picking the larger circle, even though they have not seen it before (Stevenson, 1970).

These and other results indicate that preoperational children tend to respond to the specific, concrete features of stimuli, and to retain what they learn in isolation without much assimilation to other schemes. Individuals at higher levels of cognitive development are less "stimulus bound" by concrete observables and more likely to approach problems with concrete or formal operational logic. In contrast to younger children who respond to the circle task as if the problem is to find the one exactly like the other one, operational children generate hypotheses such as, The relevant principle here is to find the larger one. This leads to a different definition of the task, and consequently a different mode of responding.

In the process of becoming operational, children usually begin to ask many and varied questions. It is helpful if teachers allow children time to express what they want to know, take their questions seriously, and if necessary, patiently encourage them to rephrase ambiguous questions. This will socialize them to express their needs verbally and give them practice in doing so.

concrete operations As children solidify their concrete operations and their ability to engage in inductive and deductive reasoning, teachers can place more emphasis on abstract and integrative concepts and require more verbalizing, self-monitoring, and independent work on complex projects. Children in the middle grades can work out elaborate mathematics problems or science experiments if they can carry out the operations physically, or at least sketch them or visualize them in their minds. They can also respond meaningfully to questions about the reasons for historical events or events occurring in stories if they can understand the events by putting themselves in the place of the historical or fictional characters.

When learning about Columbus's first voyage to America, children can relate to the crew's fears, to the concept of mutiny, and, with the help of a globe, to the reasons why Columbus thought he had reached "the Indies." Similarly, they can relate to lessons on modern space exploration or adventures such as the explorations of the North and South Poles. They will get more out of such lessons, however, if teachers show them objects and pictures, stimulate their imaginations by having them put themselves in the places of people they are talking about, and relate the material to familiar and observable events.

Events involving masses of people are understood more easily if personalized around the actions of specific people working from motivational systems that children can comprehend. For example, complex political and economic rivalries may be best presented as contests between individuals or countries, because children can relate to the motivations involved in trying to win a contest. The same events would be incomprehensible to them if presented using abstract terms such as "hegemony," "import-export ratio," or "expansionist doctrine."

formal operations Beginning around seventh or eighth grade, some students will enter the formal operations stage and become more able to handle abstract material. However, several cautions should be noted. First, many students (a majority in some schools) will never develop formal operations to the point that they can use these operations with efficiency in thinking and problem solving. They may memorize the formulas in algebra, for example, but never really understand them or be able to use them to solve nonroutine problems. Second, even students with very efficient formal operations will learn easier if aided by imagery, diagrams, examples, or concrete representations. Even senior high school students should not have to rely on formal operations exclusively, and in any case, only a small percentage will be capable of doing so. It is more accurate to assume that college students can handle purely abstract material, particularly in courses such as advanced mathematics or philosophy, but even at this level it is unwise to make the material any more difficult than necessary if the goal is to promote the most learning by the most students.

Teachers can assess formal operational thinking by asking their students to define concepts such as independence and justice or to induce general principles from the results of scientific experiments (e.g., determine why pendulums oscillate at different rates). Certain students will be able to produce formal responses ("length is inversely related to rate of oscillation," "justice is a condition in which all parties get the treatment they deserve"), but others will only be able to respond at a concrete level ("the short ones move the most," "justice is when a crook goes to jail and an innocent person is set free").

the use of integrative concepts To the extent that students do possess formal operations, it becomes possible to present bodies of knowledge in sequences involving articulation of general principles followed by logically deduced specifics. In other words, learning can be structured around integrative concepts that promote conceptual understanding, and curricula can be organized more according to the structures of the underlying disciplines and less according to the order in which students tend to learn things on their own.

In earlier stages, conceptually integrated levels of knowledge were the last to develop, being attained only after students had mastered a great many facts and skills and gradually assimilated them into increasingly larger schemes. This process can be reversed for students who have developed truly efficient formal operations. Instead of having to start with specifics and end up with general principles, it becomes possible to instruct by presenting the general principles first, promoting learning by using organizational

concepts to structure the content.

Formal knowledge, however, is no substitute for concrete experience. Just as a physicist who can explain why a paper airplane can fly cannot necessarily construct a good paper airplane, a student who passes a pencil-and- paper chemistry test cannot necessarily conduct laboratory demonstrations or plan worthwhile chemical research. Teachers who expect their students to be able to apply what they are learning will have to provide application opportunities. Typically, confusion about abstract principles is only one problem encountered during such applications. Students will often have problems because they know the principle but do not understand how to apply it in a specific instance (such as how to apply a theorem to an algebra problem) or because they lack concrete knowledge or experience (such as how to use a protractor to measure angles).

In fact, a challenge facing teachers at any level, but especially as instruction begins to rely on formal operations, is finding ways to help students "put it all together." It is much more difficult to teach students to integrate knowledge and skills and apply them to problem solving than it is to communicate the essence of a single concept, even a very abstract one. Thus, even at the high school level and beyond, opportunities for concrete experience and for authentic applications remain important. Knowledge must be operative, not just figurative.

Bear in mind that school curricula are tools, not ends in themselves. The larger goal is to empower students by equipping them with useful knowledge that they can access and apply whenever it would be appropriate for them to do so, in or out of school. At present, most curricula do not appear to be meeting this goal very well. To do so, they would have to adjust by addressing fewer topics but in greater depth, with emphasis on teaching for conceptual understanding (not mere memorization) of content and on applying the content in the context of critical thinking, problem solving, decision making, and other higher order applications.

thought and language

Piaget stressed thought (cognitive schemes) over language (verbal schemes), which he viewed as little more than a means for communicating thought. Others, however, place much more stress on language and its importance relative to thought (Anderson, 1990; Lakoff, 1987). This issue is important for education, which depends heavily on language to communicate concepts and skills. Clarity about the differences between thought and language can help teachers distinguish students who "have the concept" from those who have "merely verbal" learning.

Language development includes both structural and functional aspects. **Structural aspects** include *knowledge of the elements of sentences (grammar) and of how to combine these elements into sequences that conform to the language's structural requirements (syntax).* **Functional aspects** concern *the ability to use language to communicate, think, and solve problems.* Different factors influence the development of these two aspects of language.

innate language-acquisition device

Traditionally, learning theorists have explained language development using concepts such as exposure (modeling), repetition, and reinforcement. In this view, children learn to speak a particular language using particular vocabularies and idioms because they are reinforced for imitating what they hear in their homes and neighborhoods.

Noam Chomsky (1986) and other nativists reject this explanation. **Nativists** are *theorists who explain traits or capacities by referring to the genetic makeup of the species or individual rather than to learning acquired through experience.* They believe that the ability to generate language according to grammatical rules is inherent in the human brain and functions without

requiring systematic instruction or reinforcement. They argue that reinforcement cannot explain why or how children regularly generate new sentences they have never spoken or even heard before. Chomsky postulated an innate language-acquisition device that enables all humans to learn language simply by being exposed to it. Language also can be learned through systematic instruction, of course, but Chomsky's point is that typically it is not.

This is illustrated in the errors that children make as they learn language. Except for those caused by common pronunciation difficulties ("aminal," "aksed"), most of their linguistic errors are "logical." That is, the errors conform to the structural rules implicit in the language and are considered errors only because certain expressions do not follow the typical rule. For example, it is common for children to say "they goed" instead of "they went." This error indicates that, although they are using it inappropriately in this case, the children have mastered the general rule that past-tense verbs are formed by adding a "d" sound to the present-tense verb "open–opened," "lift–lifted".

Unlike errors that involve using rules that do not happen to apply in a specific instance, errors that involve violations of the basic grammatical structure of sentences are rare. Children might say "they goed to the store," or "they gone to the store," but they would not say "store to the they went," or "went they the store to." English sentence structure has an implicit "subject-then-verb-then object" rule that children know and use intuitively, even though they cannot express it verbally.

Debate continues about the degree to which language develops independently of thinking and the degree to which its development can be accomplished simply through exposure without a great deal of feedback and reinforcement (Howe, 1993). It appears that humans are born with certain language learning capabilities, but that social feedback plays a greater role than Chomsky and other nativists believe (Bohannon, MacWhinney, & Snow, 1990; Rice, 1989). Children's development of vocabulary and of functional language use is determined in part by the degree to which parents and other significant socializers engage in sustained conversations with them, ask and answer questions, and pay attention to and respond to children's comments. Innate mechanisms might be sufficient to enable children to develop a complete language structure, but the presence of such a structure is not sufficient to ensure good language functioning, especially the ability to use language to think and solve problems (Neimark & Santa, 1975; Pozner & Saltz, 1974).

learning to use language for thinking

Children have to learn how to use language for thinking and problem-solving purposes. Kendler and Kendler (1962) demonstrated *mediational deficiencies* in the responses of some children to transposition problems such as the ones shown in Figure 3.1. These were five- to seven-year-old children who possessed the verbal and cognitive schemes needed to respond to transposition problems in the developmentally sophisticated way. Nevertheless, they did not do so, even when they verbalized the problem successfully. Apparently, their language did not succeed in "carrying" (mediating) their thought processes.

Other investigators noted a similar but more frequent problem termed *production deficiency*, originally discovered in studies of memory for lists of words (Flavell, Beach, & Chinsky, 1966). A typical problem involved memorizing a list such as "apple, cow, lamp, peach, horse, table, pear, chair, pig." Preoperational children typically try to learn such lists by rote, memorizing the words in order without regrouping them. Operational children and adults tend to recognize that there are three fruits, three items of furniture, and

three animals, so they reorder the words according to these conceptual clusters and master the task much more quickly. However, some operational individuals do not use this information and instead rely on rote memorizing. In contrast to a mediational deficiency, in which the person verbalizes relevant language but the language does not mediate thought processes, a production deficiency occurs when relevant language and thought processes are available but nevertheless are not produced in the situation, and thus are not used to mediate it.

The educational implications of both mediational and production deficiency problems are the same: It is important to see that children not only master fundamental verbal and cognitive schemes but also learn to use them as tool skills or learning-to-learn skills. Production deficiency apparently occurs because the relevant schemes, while learned to some degree, are either not mastered enough individually or not coordinated enough with other schemes to allow the person to use them for solving problems. Consider, for example, the concept of area and the formulas for computing the areas of variously shaped planes. If you have mastered this geometric knowledge thoroughly, you can use it to solve everyday problems such as computing the amount of paint or fertilizer that you need to purchase. If not, you may be able to apply it only when problems are formulated for you, as they are on exercise worksheets.

the interaction between language and thought

These considerations return us to the general problem of thought and language and to the distinction between structural and functional aspects of language. Piaget represents one extreme in theorizing about the relationship between thought and language. He deemphasized language by subordinating it to thought. He saw language primarily as a vehicle for expressing thoughts, not as a precursor or cause of thought. At the other extreme are linguistic determinists who believe that language structures thought. Adherents to the *Sapir-Wharf Hypothesis*, for example, believe that a person's language determines personal perceptions and thinking about the world.

It is true that language and thought interact and that language may influence thought, although it does not seem to be true that language structures thought as a general rule (Gelman & Byrnes, 1991). Instead, it appears that cultures focus attention on certain aspects of the environment because of their importance for adaptation or cultural traditions (Moll, 1992). This focus leads both to a relatively rich conceptual understanding of these salient aspects of the environment and to a proliferation of vocabulary for discussing them. For example, most people who live in temperate climates get along with only the single noun, "snow," modified by adjectives such as "heavy" or "fluffy." However, Eskimos, skiers, and others who have interest in more specific aspects of snow have developed specialized vocabularies that facilitate communication about those aspects. A proliferation of discriminations about a topic stimulates development of a rich vocabulary about the topic.

Vygotsky's theory

The relationships between thought and language probably have been expressed best by Lev Vygotsky (1962), a Russian psychologist who was interested in many of the same topics that interested Piaget. Vygotsky showed that in the sensorimotor and early preoperational stages, thought and language develop independently. Thought is prelinguistic and language is preintellectual. Thought mostly involves nonverbal sensorimotor and cognitive schemes. Young children think, but in intuitive ways that do not involve much use of language. Meanwhile, language develops and functions primarily as a way to express personal needs, emotions, and feelings. Language is used as a method of communication during these early years, but not often as a means of thinking.

As children begin to become operational, thought and language become related. Children become increasingly able to express thoughts in language, to use language to communicate concepts, and to think and solve problems verbally. Apparently because of this, they also shift from lower to higher forms of response to transposition problems and overcome mediational and production deficiencies. In short, a confluence of developments creates qualitative changes in children's cognitive structures and in the ways that these structures function, especially in new situations that require accommodation or problem solving.

Kohlberg, Yeager, and Hjertholm (1968) produced data that support Vygotsky's findings. Their study concerned what Piaget called *egocentric speech*—overt utterances that children make in the presence of listeners that resemble ordinary social speech but do not require response from the listeners. Piaget minimized the importance of egocentric speech, seeing it as just more evidence that young children are egocentric. However, Vygotsky noted developmental changes in the rates and types of egocentric speech that occur as children develop. Among children who are clearly preoperational, egocentric speech is mostly social (verbalizations about feelings and emotions, important life events, or the child's family or possessions). Usually it has little direct bearing on what the child is doing at the moment. As children become operational, their egocentric speech shifts from such primarily social speech to what Vygotsky called inner speech. *Inner speech* is verbalized thought, the self-talk that occurs when we are thinking. Thus children playing in a sandbox, who when younger might have chattered about other matters, will begin to talk more about the sand castles they are building. Their egocentric speech

research at work

language acquisition

Children with language variations may develop through at least four of the stages in the acquisition of standard English that have been outlined by Labov (1984), if their exposure to various discourse communities is sufficiently sustained and supportive (see list of stages). When required to operate in an unfamiliar discourse community, however, they may become insecure or anxious, at least at first.

1. As preschoolers, children learn the basic grammar and lexicon of their home language in the process of communicating with family members.
2. From ages five to twelve they pick up local dialects from interacting with peers and begin learning to read at school.
3. By early adolescence, exposure to other speech styles has made teenagers aware of the social significance of their own dialect (i.e., its association with particular social class or ethnic group).
4. If they have significant exposure to discourse conventions outside of their own community (which may not occur until high school or even college for some individuals), young people learn to modify their own dialects, at least for limited periods when participating in formal settings that require the prestige standard. Others who do not have sufficient opportunities to interact extensively with people from other discourse communities never learn how to shift dialects.
5. Some people, mostly middle- and upper-class individuals raised from infancy within discourse communities that use the standard speech style, acquire the ability to use it for an extended period of time.
6. A few people, mostly college educated and possessing special interest in speech (such as bilingual college graduates) become fluent in a range of styles appropriate for a wide range of occasions.

List of stages adapted from W. Labov, "Stages in the Acquisition of Standard English." In R. Shuy (Ed.), *Social dialects and language learning*. Champaign: National Council of Teachers of English, 1984.

becomes less social, more like inner speech, and more focused on the task at hand. Increasingly, they seem to be talking to themselves. They literally think out loud about how to solve problems in building the castle. Still later, their inner speech becomes virtually unintelligible, because most of the thinking is done silently. The child may utter only a few phrases aloud, or perhaps mutter unintelligibly.

Berk (1986) reported similar patterns in her study of the private speech uttered by first graders and third graders doing math seat work. Changes over time showed increasingly task-relevant and less audible private speech. High achievers moved into and through this private speech cycle earlier than lower achieving students. High-achieving first graders used mature forms of private (but audible) speech to help them think about math problems. Later, when other students had begun to use overt private speech to guide their thinking, the private speech of the high achievers had become mostly internalized.

The results of many studies suggest that *egocentric speech is functional*, and that the changes that occur in it as the child becomes operational are part of the process of linking thought and language (Diaz & Berk, 1992; Frauenglass & Diaz, 1985; Wertsch, 1985; Zivin, 1979). Children think out loud for the same reason that they count on their fingers: It is a temporary learning aid that helps them make the transition to a new mode of functioning (e.g., thinking in words). When they no longer need to verbalize out loud, they begin to mutter and eventually to think silently. This cycle never completely ends. Most adults find it helpful to think out loud occasionally when wrestling with a complex problem.

Along with clarifying the evolving relationship between thought and language, Vygotsky (1978) contributed important ideas about the social construction of knowledge and about ways to stimulate cognitive advances by teaching children in the "zone of proximal development." These aspects of Vygotsky's work will be discussed in Chapters 7 and 11.

In summary, thought and language mostly develop separately until children begin to become operational. Verbal and cognitive schemes then become assimilated to one another and coordinated into more powerful and differentiated schemes that ultimately become learning-to-learn strategies, concrete operational logic, and other information-processing and problem-solving skills.

social aspects of language development

Language development occurs within one or more **discourse communities** (*socially or culturally self-defined groups whose members share* *norms for communicating*). Through interactions with discourse community members, children learn not only the language but "what to say to whom, and how to say it appropriately in any given situation" (Saville-Troike, 1989, p. 21). Even among speakers of the same basic language (e.g., American English), members of different discourse communities may employ somewhat different vocabularies and pronunciations, use different gestures, and develop somewhat different expectations concerning nonverbal aspects of communication such as eye contact or physical proximity.

Language variations and related *communication competencies* are usually well adapted to the needs of the discourse communities that create them, so that children socialized within a given discourse community are likely to develop into competent participants with relative ease. Their ability to adjust to the expectations of other discourse communities, however, will depend on the extent and nature of their exposure to these communities. See the accompanying Research at Work box.

Sociolinguists have pointed to these discourse community phenomena as predictors of students' adjustment to schooling (Erickson, 1987; Spindler, 1982). The less familiar students are with the discourse patterns expected at school, the more difficult their adjustment is likely to be. All students can be expected to have some adjustment problems when they begin schooling, because they will encounter discourse conventions that are rare or nonexistent even in middle-class homes. At school, students are expected to raise their hands and be called on before contributing to a discussion, and only one speaker is allowed at a time. Unlike their parents, teachers ask questions not to elicit unknown information but to see if the child can provide information that the teacher already knows. Some utterances that sound like declarative statements actually are requests for explanation ("I wonder why you thought the answer was twenty-seven"). Demands for behavioral change are often phrased indirectly ("Eyes and ears here, class" instead of "Betty, stop talking to Jean and pay attention to me!").

Children have to learn how to interpret and respond to these new types of discourse. Given sufficient time to learn the norms of the new discourse community within a supportive atmosphere, most children will do so without undue difficulty. However, their initial negative affect (confusion, anxiety) may progress to feelings of humiliation or alienation if they are made to feel devalued or excluded. This is especially likely if their existing speech patterns are associated with membership in a social or minority group that is devalued by the majority who speak "standard" or "high-prestige" language (Cummins, 1989; Ogbu, 1992).

Many children learn so-called Black English Vernacular or other variations on the standard American English that is emphasized in most schools. These dialects are structurally complete languages with their own grammatical rules, not immature forms of standard English such as those spoken by young children (Burling, 1973; Labov, 1972). Even so, dialect speakers may have difficulty with certain lessons that assume standard English. For example, children who pronounce the words "pour," "more," and "sew" as if they all rhymed with one another may have difficulty with rhyming lessons, and children who tend to drop the "t" sound in past tense verbs (saying "pass" instead of "passed") may have trouble with verb tense lessons.

Teachers need to distinguish common errors that arise in normal development and later disappear from specialized errors that are associated with subcultural dialects or unique problems in language learning. Developmental errors that come and go on their own should be ignored, although teachers should model correct language in ways that do not interrupt the natural flow of conversation or do anything to make a child feel inadequate. Thus, a teacher might respond to "He goed out" with "Yes, he went out, and then what did he do?"

Experts disagree about how teachers should handle nonstandard dialects. Advice ranges from insisting on standard English to teaching in the local dialect. Research suggests that teaching in nonstandard dialects is not a good idea, although it appears that teachers should accept local dialects rather than punish students or make them feel inferior for using them. The ideal seems to be acceptance of whatever dialect the students use to communicate, with emphasis on helping them to succeed in communicating (Harber & Bryen, 1976; Nieto, 1992).

Teachers familiar with local dialects or expressions might want to use them occasionally in the classroom. This can promote solidarity with the group when the teacher can use the local language credibly. However, attempts that come off as forced or phony are likely to undermine rather than reinforce credibility.

More important than adaptation to local dialects is adaptation to local interactional or communication styles. This has been illustrated in studies of teachers' adaptations to the kinds of questions that parents commonly address to their children in a rural African-American community (Heath, 1983), group participation in storytelling in a native Hawaiian community (Au, 1980), and traditional prohibitions against public displays of knowledge and competitiveness in a tribe of Native Americans (Phillips, 1983). In each case, when adjustments in classroom discourse patterns were made to reduce emphasis on discomforting elements and incorporate patterns used in the community, children's engagement in classroom activities became more enthusiastic and successful.

implications for teachers

literacy as a developmental tool and stimulus

Teachers can stimulate the development of both language and thinking skills in their students by promoting their progress toward functional literacy. Children who have learned to read for understanding can learn on their own by reading in the content areas, but other children will have to struggle in reading and in most other subjects until they acquire sufficient reading-to-learn abilities (Stanovich & Cunningham, 1993). Also, attaining literacy prepares the way for the emergence of more formal and logical thinking (Wood, 1988). In reading for meaning, especially when reading about hypothetical, imaginary, or abstract things that they have never experienced, children learn to pay attention to and analyze the structure and meanings of text. In writing, especially when composing authentic communications designed to accomplish particular goals with a particular audience, children learn to plan, self-regulate, edit, and correct their writing so as to communicate coherently and meet the needs of the readers (insofar as they are able to understand and anticipate them). These experiences in reading and writing require more careful and precise use of language than parallel forms of communication based on listening and speaking do, and they provide occasions for developing insights and making connections that will promote progress toward formal operations.

summary

In recent years, research on cognitive development and learning has shifted from general Piagetian stages to the development of expertise within particular knowledge domains. Critics have noted that Piaget often underestimated children's knowledge, partly because the nature and persistence of his questioning often confused them. Children are able to learn many aspects of particular knowledge domains through instruction and this learning is often comparable to that of adults. The scope and efficiency of their information-processing capacities are limited, however, so it may be necessary to break down questions for them or provide other assistance that will allow them to demonstrate their knowledge.

Piaget's work focused on logico-mathematical operations applied to scientific and mathematical problems, so his work appears to be most relevant to science and mathematics educators. Social science and humanities educators find other forms of thinking more relevant to their fields, most notably narrative modes in which children learn and remember information in the form of stories.

Researchers have been studying children's developing knowledge in particular domains, including subjects taught at school. They are finding that children often develop naive ideas or misconceptions that distort their learning until they recognize the need to reconstruct their knowledge. Some such reconstructions are difficult and time consuming to accomplish.

During the preoperational years, children learn best through exploration and manipulation of concrete objects, although they also can learn letters, numbers, sounds, words, computation, and writing skills. They have difficulty with purely verbal instruction and require demonstrations, visual aids, or concrete examples. Practice with feedback is essential at this stage. Organizations concerned with the education of young children have endorsed guidelines for "developmentally appropriate practice" in preschool and primary grade classrooms.

Piaget stressed four central aspects of becoming operational: (1) discrimination of variant from invariant environmental features, (2) coordination and integration of separate schemes into a unified cognitive structure, (3) achieving the ability to reverse operations, and (4) achieving the ability to decenter. Teachers dealing with students in the stage of concrete operations should emphasize understanding and integrative concepts. Children also thrive on "personalized" material. Beginning at about the eighth grade, some students will be able to cope with abstract material using formal operations. Many never reach that point, however, and even those who do will profit from imagery, diagrams, and concrete examples.

Piaget placed great stress on thought and relatively little on language, but others have shown that the functional aspects of language require attention because of their importance in dealing with school tasks. Vygotsky noted that in early stages language and thought develop independently, but later, egocentric speech gives way to inner speech that mediates thought processes. Students need acceptance of whatever language and communication styles they use to express their thinking, emphasis on developing understandings rather than on mere peripheral and formal uses of language, and assistance in attaining functional literacy that will allow them to study efficiently and make good progress toward formal operations.

questions for reflection

1. Assume that you teach in an inner-city high school where many students speak with foreign accents. You fear that their accents will reduce their chances for employment, but you don't want to embarrass them by calling attention to their speech. What would you do, if anything? What if you were a first-grade teacher in the same district?

2. Why are simple choice questions less useful than fact or explanation questions as a way to assess student comprehension?

3. Why can teachers who work with older students monitor learning by questioning just a few of them, whereas teachers of younger children have to question all students?

4. Why does it do little good to try to teach children at conceptual levels beyond their present ones? What distinctive materials and teaching methods do pre-operational children need that older children do not?

5. What four central aspects of becoming operational in thinking did Piaget stress?

6. What does it mean to say that young children primarily accommodate to the situation, but older individuals primarily assimilate the situation into existing cognitive structures? How might this affect the teaching of second-grade versus eighth-grade students?

7. Differentiate the structural and functional aspects of language. Which aspects are most important for teachers to emphasize? Why?

8. What is egocentric speech and what is its function? How did Piaget and Vygotsky differ in their beliefs about it?

9. Why is it important, especially with younger students, to frequently elicit overt responses or performance? How can this be done effectively when teaching humanities or social studies?

10. Suppose you teach an elementary class in which some students have well-functioning concrete operations but many do not (or a secondary class in which some have well-functioning formal operations but most do not). What organizational and instructional strategies could you use to make sure that most instruction is meaningful to all of your students?

---

cases to consider

appropriate teaching? Cheryl Speier is working with a group of fifth graders assigned to read a selection from James Michener's *Centennial*. Responding to a student's answer, Cheryl says, "Yes, Jane, that is an important point. His willingness to stake himself to the ground and fight to the death is very revealing. Well, now, we've noted twelve important events on the board. How can we use these to generalize about his basic character traits? What kind of man was he?" Describe the type of teaching that Cheryl is engaging in. If she were teaching the same material to tenth graders, how might she approach the task differently?

Sam not turned on Sam Baker, a tenth grader, achieves at an average level, but his teachers suspect that he can do better, for two reasons. First, his measured IQ has regularly exceeded 120 on a variety of tests taken over the years. Second, his performance on classroom exams is uneven. He absorbs topics he is interested in, but does not take the time to read carefully in other areas. Sam is in the college-preparatory program but has no vocational plans and only a vague commitment to college. His father manages a grocery store and his mother is a first-grade teacher. An only child without close friends, Sam's only interests are hunting with his dad on occasional weekends and reading about hunting in general and guns in particular. How could Sam's existing interests be used and eventually broadened in the following subjects: history, Spanish, physics, and geometry?

hard to tell Jane Prawat is a first-grade teacher who especially enjoys teaching reading. She tries to involve students in thinking about what they read, not just looking at words and using strategies to decode meaning. She spends considerable time talking to students about the words that they will see in stories, and after reading the stories with the children she asks them questions. The following activity is typical. With great interest and enthusiasm, she asks, "Did you believe that Mr. Martin would ever let the cats go back to Tim?" All students nod their heads approvingly. One or two say "yes" audibly. With continuing interest Ms. Prawat asks, "Do you think Tim was glad to see the kittens when they got home?" Again, the students nod affirmatively. Then she asks, "Do you think the kittens were glad to see him?" The students shake their heads, yes. Based on principles of development, what suggestions do you have for improving Ms. Prawat's teaching?

going beyond the information given Celia Navarro is in her third year of teaching at Astoria Middle School. She enjoys working with the eighth graders and tries to get them to think about the social studies reading she assigns. She especially enjoys having students challenge authors' conclusions and think of alternative ways to explain key historical figures' behavior. She also likes her students to examine economic motivation as well as individual and social motivation. She constantly reminds them that most accounts of history are written from an individual framework that does not take into consideration general economic and social factors. Some students enjoy this course but others find it vague and boring. Based on your knowledge of development, how might you account for these differences in students' reactions? How could the teacher alter some aspects of the class in order to help all students to think more fully about the material they read?

social and moral development

objectives

When you have mastered the material in this chapter you will be able to

1. Explain how social learning (environmental) factors interact with inherited (biological) factors to shape social development
2. Describe Erikson's eight stages of the human life cycle and explain how teachers can help students to cope successfully with developmental crises
3. Describe how dimensions and styles of parenting relate to children's personal and social characteristics and identify implications for teachers' interactions with students at school
4. Describe developmental trends in students' peer relationships, identify factors that influence students' acceptance by peers, and explain how teachers might help isolated or rejected students to improve their peer relationships
5. Describe some important ways in which children's development is affected by the societal and subcultural contexts in which they are raised
6. Identify some important recent social trends that have shaped the social contexts in which today's children are developing
7. Compare and contrast the typical experiences of children from different subcultures and minority groups and explain implications for teaching
8. Explain how children's understanding of morality and ability to engage in moral reasoning develop as they progress through the stages identified by Kohlberg
9. Summarize feminist critiques of Erikson's and Kohlberg's stage theories and explain what is involved in emphasizing an ethic of caring along with an ethic of justice in teaching students
10. Describe the relationships among moral judgment, moral affect, and moral behavior and explain how adults can encourage children to behave prosocially
11. Explain and critically evaluate the major approaches that have been developed for teaching about values and morality in classrooms

social development

Students are individuals and teachers will need to get to know them as such in order to identify and respond to their unique needs and interests. Even so, all students in a given class will share certain characteristics due to shared social and culture experiences. Also, certain subgroups will share additional characteristics due to shared subcultural experiences. These characteristics provide starting places for teachers seeking to address their students' developmental needs.

Over time, psychologists have emphasized three sources of explanation for observed similarities and differences in children's social and moral development. These factors include (1) characteristics present at birth, (2) age-linked social experiences considered universal across or at least within societies, and (3) social learning experiences that occur within the particular context in which a child develops. Recent theory and research have focused on the latter (contextual) influences, although with continued recognition of the role of the other two sets of factors (Cohen & Siegel, 1991; Garbarino, 1992; Lerner, 1993; Szapocznik & Kurtines, 1993).

characteristics present at birth

Psychologists continue to debate the relative influences of heredity and environment on developing social traits. In everything from food preferences (Rozin, Fallon, & Mandell, 1984) to political philosophies (Boshier & Thom, 1973), children tend to take after their parents, and siblings show lesser but still noteworthy resemblances. Environmentalists attribute these findings to social influences, suggesting that family resemblances occur because of shared family social environments whereas individual differences occur because each sibling has unique peer experiences and even unique experiences within the family. However, behavior genetics researchers claim that family resemblances are attributable primarily to shared family DNA, not shared family environment (Loehlin, 1992). They note that biologically unrelated adopted siblings are nearly as different in personality as children raised in different families, but identical twins reared apart are more alike than ordinary siblings (Dunn & Plomin, 1990; Hetherington, Reiss, & Plomin, 1993).

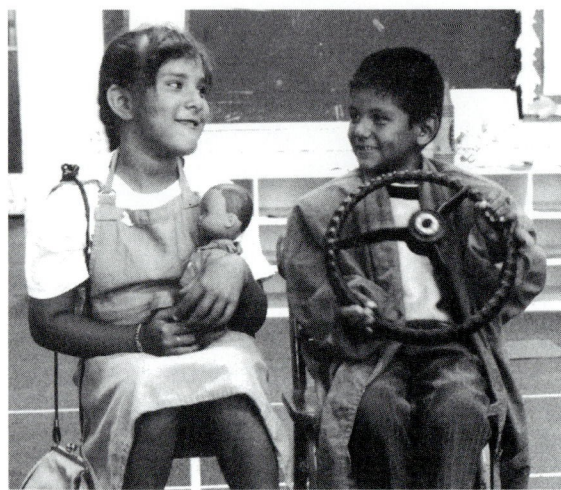 

Dress up and role play allow children to learn aspects of gender roles; the opportunity to take different roles can teach something about stereotypes, too.

Like other nature-nurture controversies, those relating to social traits are unlikely to be resolved anytime soon because findings are open to conflicting interpretations. It is clear, however, that certain stable characteristics are already in place at birth.

One of these is *gender*. Various gender differences in intellectual and social characteristics have been documented (discussed in this chapter and in Chapter 21). Some of these differences are explained in part by genetically programmed predispositions toward certain patterns of behavior. In addition or instead, however, all of them are shaped through *gender role socialization*. People treat boys and girls differently from birth, and this differential treatment communicates expectations about how males and females are expected to act. The net result is a pervasive pressure to conform to the gender roles prevalent in the society at the time, especially those emphasized in the subculture in which the child's family is situated.

Another important characteristic present at birth is *arousal level*. Some infants usually are alert and active, exploring the environment and reacting to stimulation. Others sleep much of the time, and even when awake are mostly quiet and relatively unresponsive. Similarly, newborns differ in *temperament*. Some are typically happy or at least content, but others are noticeably tense, anxious, and prone to fussing and crying. These individual differences persist and correlate with later behavior patterns (Buss & Plomin, 1984).

nature-nurture interactions Early predispositions interact with environmental influences, however. For example, one active child who has siblings or peers available may spend much time in rough-and-tumble play, but another who lacks playmates may spend a lot of time exploring the physical environment. Active children raised in an atmosphere of violence are likely to become predisposed to fighting and bullying (Huesmann et al., 1984; Rohner & Nielsen, 1978), but similar children raised in warmer, more humanistic environments tend to become assertive, but nonaggressive, peer leaders (Maccoby & Martin, 1983; Staub, 1979). Thus, although biological predispositions toward certain personal and social traits exist, environmental influences interact with these predispositions to affect behavior.

Also, we should bear in mind that individuals can shape their environments, and children may condition their parents to treat them in particular ways (Hartup & Rubin, 1986; Kuczynski & Kochanska, 1990). Many girls, for example, resist the restrictions built into the traditional female role, and succeed in defeating most pressures to conform to it. As students, they may prefer and excel at school subjects such as mathematics or science and extracurricular activities such as athletics or Junior Achievement, and as adults they may become business entrepreneurs or professional leaders.

Ahern et al. (1982) argued that most social traits are shaped by the social environment. These include cooperative, competitive, or individualistic motives and activity preferences; personal interests; status as a peer leader, follower, or isolate; optimism versus pessimism; sociability; and styles of solving problems and coping with frustrations. Such traits develop in response to the influences of *significant others,* initially parents and family members but later teachers and peers encountered at school and the real or fictional people portrayed on television and in other media. These *socializing influences* model behavior that can be imitated and project social expectations that tell developing children how they are supposed to act and what they are supposed to value, strive for, and even feel.

age-linked social experiences

Certain broad influences affect all children in a society to some degree. Along with gender roles, the most prominent of these are *age roles*—the norms for personal qualities and behavior expected of children at particular ages. As children develop social understanding, they become aware that increases in age bring not only new privileges and opportunities, but also new responsibilities and expectations.

Havighurst (1972) incorporated many age role norms in his concept of *developmental tasks*—tasks that arise at a certain period of development and if mastered lead to success on later tasks but if failed lead to unhappiness in the child, disapproval by others, and difficulty with later tasks. Some important developmental tasks are shown in Table 4.1.

Children stress both age and gender in defining themselves and their peers, and most are highly motivated to learn about and to try to fulfill the role expectations that they believe apply to themselves (Bradbard & Endsley, 1983; Kohlberg, 1966). For example, once a child understands that she is a girl (usually between ages two and three), she is likely to begin observing intensely and asking questions about what being a girl means (implications for clothing and grooming, toy and game preferences, and personal mannerisms and interests). The same thing happens to boys. One result of this preoccupation with gender differences is a preference for playmates of one's own gender. This builds to a peak sometime in midchildhood, typically around age eight in brighter and more socially mature children, but later in other children (Kohlberg & Zigler, 1967); then it recedes.

Havighurst's developmental task scheme is a relatively informal and flexible application of the notion of age-linked social experiences. It incorporates gender roles by noting that age-linked expectations will be somewhat different for boys and girls, and it implies that different developmental tasks may be emphasized in different societies or subcultures.

Erikson's stage theory

Erik Erikson (1968) used a combination of psychoanalytic ideas and ideas about age-linked social experiences to construct a more formal stage theory of personality and social develop-

table 4.1 developmental tasks

Physical/Intellectual Tasks	Social/Personal Tasks
Early Childhood	
Skill learning and general bodily control	Learning cultural rules and expectations
Fine muscle control	Learning about right and wrong
Developing and refining concepts of social and physical reality	Learning about gender roles
Learning about sex differences, developing an accurate body concept	Relating emotionally to family members and, later, to others, such as relatives and peers
Learning through exploration, manipulation, play	
Middle Childhood	
Mastering the three Rs at school	Relating to teachers and other unfamiliar adults
Learning to learn through reading and other informative activities	Achieving independence within the family
Learning basic facts of sciences and humanities	Meeting expectations of peers, reference groups
Distinguishing fact from fantasy	Coping with gender role expectations and other external pressures
Learning through hobbies and recreational activities	Developing frustration tolerance
Adolescence and Beyond	
Mastering philosophy, higher mathematics, other abstract fields	Adjusting to bodily changes, new emotions
Mastering conceptual and theoretical aspects of sciences and humanities	Achieving gradual independence from adults
Learning about and being able to apply knowledge needed for adaptation in general and one's occupation in particular	Questioning old values and reaffirming them or finding new ones
	Ultimately choosing mate, vocation, and life philosophy

ment. Erikson's theory was meant to be universal—applicable to all people in all cultures. He viewed the stages as unfolding according to the *epigenetic principle.* That is, he believed that the stages unfolded in the same sequence for everyone and that during each stage, the individual is especially vulnerable to certain influences and less sensitive to others.

Erikson identified eight stages in the life cycle, six of which occur before or during schooling (including college). Each stage involves a central developmental crisis, and one's success in coping with the crisis is seen as affecting one's more general development during and after the stage (see Table 4.2). The personality structure is resynthesized when each stage is resolved, as earlier developments are integrated with later ones.

trust versus mistrust

Erikson's first stage centers on the crisis of *trust versus mistrust.* It is a universal human experience to spend the first year or so of life totally dependent on others for food and general care. Erikson believed that fundamental dispositions toward others are formed during this dependent stage. If the infant's needs are met reasonably well, a positive social orientation and trust in others are likely to develop. If caretakers are inadequate or inconsistent in meeting basic needs, infants may develop insecurity and a fundamental mistrust of others. This lays the groundwork for a paranoid attitude of, "The world is a jungle; you have to get yours and keep others from taking it away from you." In general, people who trust others are happier, better adjusted, and better liked than those who mistrust others (Rotter, 1980).

Whether or not the first year of life has special importance, it seems clear that children whose needs are met by loving and reliable adults are likely to be secure, happy, trustful, and sociable toward others. Also, children who

suffer because apathetic or unreliable adults do not meet their basic needs consistently are likely to be insecure and mistrustful.

A common misconception regarding Erikson's stages is that one pole (e.g., trust) is totally desirable and the other (in this case, mistrust) is totally undesirable. Actually, optimal development involves attaining a favorable balance between the two poles. One can be naively or overly trusting.

autonomy versus shame and doubt

Erikson's next stage centers on the crisis of *autonomy versus shame and doubt.* The universal experience involved here is the transition from being treated as a helpless infant to being treated as a child capable of exercising self-control and therefore expected to conform to rules of conduct. At this stage, adults begin imposing rules and expectations for self-control and self-denial, and children begin self-regulating some aspects of their behavior.

If socialization is carried out with appropriate timing and methods, toddlers are likely to adjust to it smoothly, without losing their sense of personal autonomy. If parents make too many demands, make them too early, or emphasize threats and punishment in enforcing them, the children may begin to feel completely dependent on and controlled by adults. The children's failure to meet expectations may result in feelings of shame and development of doubt about their capabilities. This sets the stage for later difficulties in areas such as self-concept and impulse control.

initiative versus guilt

Erikson's next stage involves the crisis of *initiative versus guilt.* The emergent universal experience here is children's development of interest in exploring their capabilities and expanding

table 4.2 Erikson's eight stages of the human life cycle

STAGE	AGES	CENTRAL CONFLICT	PRIMARY IMPLICATIONS FOR OPTIMAL DEVELOPMENT
1	Infancy	Trust vs. mistrust	Developing general security, optimism, and trust in others (based on consistent experiences involving satisfaction of basic needs)
2	Toddlerhood	Autonomy vs. shame and doubt	Developing a sense of autonomy and confident self-reliance, taking setbacks in stride (based on consistent experiences involving encouragement and limit setting without rejection or blame)
3	Early childhood	Initiative vs. guilt	Developing initiative in exploring and manipulating the environment (based on consistent experiences of tolerance, encouragement, and reinforcement)
4	Middle childhood	Industry vs. inferiority	Enjoyment and mastery of the developmental tasks of childhood, in and out of school (based on consistent experiences of success and recognition of progress)
5	Adolescence	Identity vs. identity confusion	Achievement of stable and satisfying sense of identity and direction (based on consistent personal experiences involving success and satisfaction combined with social acceptance and recognition)
6	Young adulthood	Intimacy vs. isolation	Development of the ability to maintain intimate personal relationships (based on personal openness and confidence complemented by consistently rewarding experiences with intimate others)
7	Adulthood	Generality vs. stagnation	Satisfaction of personal and familial needs supplemented by development of interest in the welfare of others and the world in general (based on achievement of a secure and rewarding personal life and a freedom from pressures that limit one to self-preoccupation)
8	Aging	Integrity vs. despair	Recognizing and adjusting to aging and the prospect of death with a sense of satisfaction about the past and readiness about the future (based on consistent success in prior stages, which provides a real basis for satisfaction in having led a full and good life and for accepting death without morbid fears or feelings of failure)

SOURCE: Constructed from the information contained in E. Erikson, *Identity: Youth and Crisis* (New York: Norton, 1968).

their range of experiences. It is a time when children begin to explore the social world outside the family.

Children treated with acceptance and support during this stage are likely to develop the confidence and sense of well-being needed to take the initiative in trying out new things and displaying their developing capabilities. However, to the extent that these initiatives result in ridicule for failure or punishment for violating prohibitions, the children may become inhibited, initially about engaging in specific behaviors but ultimately about initiatives in general. Children may develop feelings of anxiety, inhibition, or guilt in response to a range of experiences at any age, but Erikson believed that social experiences during this stage are especially important in predisposing them to confidence versus inhibition in social situations.

industry versus inferiority

Erikson's next stage involves the crisis of *industry versus inferiority,* which is triggered by the need to cope with the expectations of the peer group and the school. In the peer group, children must learn to cooperate, share, and get along with others, as well as to master the skills involved in childhood play. In school, they must master school tasks and the role of pupil. Students who have had a good start at home attack these tasks with a sense of industry. Success breeds continued success and motivation, setting off a chain of positive self-fulfilling prophecy effects. Conversely, if children should fail in meeting these expectations (or even just feel that they failed because they did not do as well as their friends), they may develop a sense of inferiority and low self-esteem. Problems sometimes develop in this area when families move, especially if peer and school expectations in the new context are quite different from the familiar ones in the old context.

preadolescence   Thornburg (1982) and others have suggested that the transitional years between childhood and adolescence (roughly ages 11–13) also constitute a stage, at least with respect to social development. Friendships tend to become more intimate during these years, especially among girls, and early adolescents are likely to act prosocially toward their friends and to try to achieve mutually satisfying outcomes in situations where younger or older people might go their own way or compete (Berndt, 1982). Also, preadolescents who are involved in close friendships display higher levels of altruism and greater ability to assume another's perspective (McGuire & Weisz, 1982).

Thornburg (1982) noted that ages 11–14 bring shifts from same gender to both genders to the opposite gender in peer relationships, and from socializing primarily in natural environments in the home or neighborhood to socializing in contrived environments (shopping centers, movie theaters). At school, these years include a shift from identification with teachers to identification with peers, often accompanied by a degree of resentment of or even resistance to teachers' exercise of authority.

identity versus identity confusion

Erikson wrote about the crisis of *identity versus identity confusion* that arises when adolescents begin to question beliefs and value systems that they had internalized previously without much thought. As adolescents attain formal operations and greater understanding of people and ideas, they begin to see that some of the beliefs and values to which they have been exposed conflict with one another, and also that preaching and practice do not always coincide in the words and actions of parents, teachers, or other socialization agents (Wadsworth, 1989). This leads to an **identity crisis**—*a period of intense exploration and searching for acceptable commitments.*

table 4.3 Marcia's identity statuses

	HAS EXPERIENCED A CRISIS	HAS MADE SELF-CHOSEN COMMITMENTS
Diffused identity	No	No
Foreclosure status	No	Yes
Moratorium status	Yes	No
Achieved identity	Yes	Yes

Upon finding that values often are honored more in theory than in practice, many young persons become notably idealistic for a time. They not only seek values they can accept, but go out of their way to practice them conscientiously. Included in this assessment of values are questions of personal identity (Who am I? What kind of person should I be? What kind of occupational, social, and gender roles should I play?).

Adolescents who solve these dilemmas with reasonable ease tend to adjust smoothly to changes in role and status and to move into adult occupational, spousal, and parental roles without much difficulty. However, many become confused about who they are and where they are going, so it may be years before they "find themselves." They may have a continual undercurrent of dissatisfaction with their lives, a feeling of confusion that can cause difficulties in motivation, an inability to concentrate on studies, or personal adjustment problems in and out of school.

Marcia's identity statuses James Marcia (Marcia, 1980; Schiedel & Marcia, 1985) studied adolescents to determine the degree to which they had experienced crises and made commitments in five areas: occupation, religion, political philosophy, gender role attitudes, and beliefs about personal sexuality. Based on their responses to interview questions, he classified young people into four *identity status categories* (see Table 4.3): (1) *identity diffusion* (may be aware of unresolved issues but does not experience these as pressing, so has not yet experienced a crisis, has not yet made commitments, and is not especially concerned about lack of direction); (2) *foreclosure* (has made a commitment to parental positions but without ever experiencing a crisis involving serious questioning of these positions); (3) *moratorium* (currently in crisis, has not yet made firm commitments), and (4) *identity achievement* (has experienced a crisis, passed through a period of exploration, and made self-chosen commitments).

As they move through adolescence and young adulthood, most young people progress from identity diffusion through the foreclosure and moratorium statuses toward achieved identities, although advances may occur at an uneven pace and regressions are noted in some individuals (Adams & Gullotta, 1989). Progress appears to be stimulated by the development of formal operations, enrollment in school classes that require formal thinking, and opportunities to analyze and engage in dialogue on social issues. Identity statuses are associated with a variety of other personal characteristics and home background factors, at least for young people who appear to be settled within a given status rather than moving steadily through the series (Adams & Gullotta, 1989).

Diffused-identity adolescents often report feelings of inferiority, alienation, and ambivalence. They are usually not yet aware of a focused identity crisis, but they are likely to engage in behaviors that suggest an attempt to defend against anxiety stemming from an undefined identity. Some seek intense sensory experiences (fast driving, wild parties, serious drug usage), others get caught up in current fads, and still others move from one peer group to another in an effort to establish a sense of belonging through peer association. Their immaturity in identity formation tends to be part of a larger pattern of immaturity in cognitive and emotional development. They are highly susceptible to peer pressure but unlikely to have intimate relationships with friends or lovers. They tend to come from rejecting or detached families. Often the father is absent through separation or divorce, or if present, has a distant or rejecting relationship with the adolescent.

Foreclosed adolescents tend to be quiet, orderly, and industrious individuals who have a strong need for social approval, maintain dependent relationships with significant others, and endorse authoritarian values emphasizing obedience, strong leadership, and respect for authority. Their parents tend to be strongly child-centered but also to be intrusive and possessive with their children. That is, the parents combine love and concern for the children with strong pressures to conform to family values and beliefs.

Moratorium youths are currently experiencing an identity crisis, so they frequently experience feelings of anxiety or confusion. Nevertheless, they tend to be comfortable in introspecting about themselves and exploring value issues with others, and to be generally socially adept and effective. They tend to come from warm and supportive homes in which the parents accept individual differences and encourage movements toward independence.

Identity-achieved youths tend to live orderly, active, and self-directed lives that reflect a harmony between needs for individual autonomy and for social relatedness. Compared to peers, identity-achieved adolescents tend to be more confident, secure, socially adept, emotionally mature, and likely to have established intimate relationships with friends and lovers. They tend to come from highly interactive families in which parents minimize control and emphasize encouragement. Compared to diffused peers, identity-achieved adolescents are less self-conscious and more comfortable in revealing themselves to others (Adams, Abraham, & Markstrom, 1987). They also tend to engage in more extended dialogue with their parents, and in the process, to articulate and defend their own points of view more assertively (Bosma & Gerrits, 1985).

Archer (1982) studied sixth, eighth, tenth, and twelfth graders and found more advanced identity status profiles at each successive level. Still, the diffusion and foreclosure statuses were most evident at all grades. Even by twelfth grade, only a minority of students had reached the identity achievement status, and usually only in vocational choice or religious beliefs. Moratorium status was seen most frequently with vocational choice, foreclosure status with gender-role preferences, and identity diffusion status with political philosophies. The most extensive advances in identity formation usually occur during the college years rather than the high school years (Waterman, 1982).

Stage theorists and researchers clearly have contributed to our knowledge about identity formation (Adams, Gullotta, & Montemayor, 1992). They are not without their critics, however. In particular, Marcia and his colleagues have been challenged for methodological reasons, for their linear theoretical assumptions, and for insufficient sensitivity to evolving social contexts (Dimarino-Linnen, 1990; Greer, 1993).

According to Erikson, in late adolescence or young adulthood, individuals who have weathered previous developmental stages successfully enter into intimate relationships in which they share everything about themselves with a partner, particularly one of the opposite sex.

Harter's research on self-concept development

As adolescents progress toward more coherent personal identities, their self-concepts and related social behaviors become more differentiated. For example, Harter and Monsour (1992) interviewed seventh, ninth, and eleventh graders and found developmental differences in the students' abilities to project a differentiated sense of self by describing differences in their patterns of interaction with parents, with friends outside of school, and in the classroom. That is, older students were more able than younger students to report being smart at school but fun-loving with friends, being happy with friends but depressed with family, or being caring with family but inconsiderate with friends. This proliferation of role-related selves emerges in adolescence both because cognitive-developmental advances have occurred that allow adolescents to develop a more differentiated sense of self (Fischer & Lamborn, 1989; Harter, 1986) and because adolescents experience socialization pressures to develop different selves in different social contexts (Grotevant & Cooper, 1986; Rosenberg, 1986).

During adolescence, numerous potentially contradictory selves clamor for expression (Harter, 1990). Some of these are ideal selves that conflict with adolescents' understandings of their real selves (Harter, 1986; Higgins, 1987). These conflicts can be distressing as well as motivating. Harter and Monsour (1992) reported that the adolescents they interviewed often expressed confusion over the realization that they act differently in different contexts, as well as concern about discovering "the real me."

intimacy versus isolation

Erikson's next stage, *intimacy versus isolation,* focuses on the crisis faced in late adolescence or young adulthood when intimate relationships, particularly one with a single lover, become viable and desirable. Individuals who have weathered previous stages successfully will enter this one trusting others, feeling a sense of autonomy, being willing to take initiatives, having healthy self-esteem and confidence, and being reasonably sure about who they are and what they want. These strengths will prepare them to enter truly intimate relationships, sharing everything about themselves with their partners. In contrast, individuals who show mistrust of others, low self-esteem, or fear of taking initiatives will be less prepared to establish intimate relationships, even if good opportunities should appear. They may want such relationships but lack the confidence and skills needed to establish them, and thus may feel frustrated and lonely.

Marcia's intimacy statuses Marcia and his colleagues (Orlofsky, Marcia, & Lesser, 1973) have assigned individuals to *intimacy statuses* based on three criteria: (1) presence of close relationships with male and female friends, (2) presence of an enduring, committed sexual relationship, and (3) depth of peer relationships. The five intimacy statuses are: *isolate* (lives in an interpersonal void with only casual acquaintances); *stereotyped* (is pleasant but shallow and conventional in personal relationships); *pseudointimate* (is involved in a relatively permanent sexual relationship but one that is defined more by conventional roles than by sharing of self or feelings); *preintimate* (has close, open relationships with others but is ambivalent about commitment to an enduring sexual relationship); and *intimate* (committed to a long-term sexual relationship).

People whose interview responses place them in higher intimacy categories know their friends better, can predict their partners' responses to personality inventories better (Orlofsky, 1976), and are more self-disclosing with other people and able to articulate their emotional experiences (Orlofsky & Ginsburg, 1981). As predicted by Erikson's stage notions, people typically attain high status on identity measures before they attain high status on intimacy measures (Fitch & Adams, 1983; Kacerguis & Adams, 1980; Schiedel & Marcia, 1985). These findings are clearer for males than for females, however; many women resolve intimacy issues before resolving identity issues. Historically, gender role socialization has tended to orient females toward interpersonal relationships, and thus toward dealing with both identity and intimacy issues, throughout the adolescent and early adult years. In contrast, males have been oriented more toward intrapersonal soul-searching and thus toward preoccupation with identity issues during the adolescent years, followed by attention to intimacy issues in the young adult years.

generativity versus stagnation and integrity versus despair

Erikson's final two stages deal with development later in adulthood. The crisis of *generativity versus stagnation* arises in middle adulthood as peo-

ple develop concern about raising children and leaving something of themselves for future generations (Snarey, 1993). People who resolve this crisis through generativity learn to take satisfaction from contributing to the development of others (especially the young) or from dedication to other forms of altruism or creativity that transcend the self. Those who fail to renew themselves through such generativity begin to stagnate. The final stage, *integrity versus despair,* refers to the degree to which aging persons adjust to the impending reality of death. Those who do so positively become resigned to death and can look back on their lives with satisfaction, feeling that they have been generally successful, happy, and useful. Individuals who do not resolve this crisis develop morbid fear or unrealistic denial of death, or at least feel that their lives have been failures because they never amounted to anything.

personality and social development in females

Although presented as based on universal human experiences, Erikson's theory reflects a male bias because it emphasizes male experiences in cases where male and female experiences differ (Cobb, 1992). It features identity as the central crisis of adolescence and intimacy as the central crisis of early adulthood, but many females resolve the crisis of intimacy before they resolve identity issues. Also, their sense of themselves derives more from their relationships than from commitments to work and ideology (Gilligan, 1982).

Nancy Chodorow (1978) suggested that these gender differences are rooted in the fact that most children experience their first intimate relationship with a female—their mother. As they begin to develop, girls can continue to define themselves within the context of this first relationship, continuing their attachment to their mothers while they develop as females. In contrast, boys must separate themselves from their mothers much earlier than girls in order to develop as males. These gender differences orient children toward developmental paths that feature attachment and empathy for girls but separation and individuation for boys. In turn, these developments predispose females toward ease in developing relationships but difficulty in achieving individuation, whereas they predispose males toward the opposite pattern.

Like Erikson's, most stage theories are useful for helping us to understand development but need to be critiqued from a feminist perspective because they treat the age-linked social experiences of males as normative. Later in the chapter, we present another example of this problem in discussing Gilligan's critique of Kohlberg's moral development theory.

implications for teachers

assisting students through developmental stages

Erikson's stage theory helps alert teachers to major sources of conflict for students at varying levels of development. Students in the early grades are likely to be struggling with the crises of initiative versus guilt and industry versus inferiority. Teachers can help inhibited children by encouraging them to explore, satisfy their curiosity, ask questions, make suggestions, and take initiatives. Furthermore, they can reassure such children that mistakes and ventures that work out poorly are normal and expected, not causes for shame or guilt.

Children who are overly concerned about their competitive standing can be helped to attend more to their own cumulative gains and emerging abilities than to comparisons with classmates. Others who compete more successfully but tend to brag about it or to tease less successful peers might also profit from such socialization. All children need to learn the satisfactions of doing a job well through care and persistence. They also need to learn that individuals possess unique patterns of strengths and weaknesses and that everyone has something to offer everyone else, so that an atmosphere of friendliness and cooperation is desired.

In dealing with feelings of inferiority or shame, teachers need to be realistic rather than well meaning but condescending. Students know how they are doing relative to their classmates, so there is no point in trying to deny reality or distract them from failure concerns by switching the conversation to something else. To a child, this is like saying, "So what if you are stupid; I like you anyway." *Poor performance needs to be faced realistically, but in a supportive way.* If the problem is the student's fault (e.g., not listening or doing the work), point this out firmly but gently. If the problem is one of relative ability, stress absolute progress; that is, compare the student's current and past performance. When students insist that they cannot learn, vigorously reject this claim but in ways that provide support and realistic reasons for expecting improvement in the future. Instead of just offering empty reassurances, schedule individual goal-setting conferences geared to produce specific commitments and see that the student gets tutorial help if needed.

Students whose physical maturation comes very early or very late may need some assistance in handling any embarrassment that they may feel. This is especially likely to be a problem for very early maturing girls and very late maturing boys (Brooks-Gunn, Peterson, & Eichorn, 1985).

As students progress through adolescence, they shift from adult authority figures to the peer group as their primary focus for social learning through modeling and socialization. The notion that adolescence is necessarily a period of storm and stress involving conflict with parents, teachers, and other adult authority figures has been overstated, because the values of adolescent peer groups usually support or complement parental and community values (Petersen & Epstein, 1991). Still, some students who previously seemed to be well adjusted begin to experience difficulties during these years. In dealing with students who are resentful of authority, teachers should be prepared to respond in ways that do not provoke public power struggles.

Eccles's research on changing school environments

The transition from elementary to junior high school can be difficult for many students because it confronts them with a social environment that is mismatched to their developing needs (Eccles et al., 1993; Mergendoller, 1993). Compared to elementary classrooms, junior high classrooms confront students with greater emphasis on teacher control and discipline; fewer opportunities to engage in decision making, choice, or self-management; less personal and positive teacher-student relationships; more frequent use of practices such as whole-class teaching, ability grouping, and public evaluation of work; and more stringent standards for grading. Fortunately, these problems are not inevitable. When middle and junior high schools provide more personalized and supportive environments suited to their students' psychological needs, the students do not demonstrate the same declines in motivation or increases in rates of misconduct seen in more traditional schools (Bryk, Lee, & Smith, 1990; Dreyfoos, 1990; Eccles & Midgley, 1989).

Teachers who relish a socialization role and foster close relationships with students will have opportunities to help them cope with identity and intimacy crises. For a time, they may be the primary source of realistic information and feedback for some students, as when helping them to consider career options.

social development in context

We have noted that although characteristics present at birth and age-linked social experiences both play roles in shaping social development, current theory and research emphasize context-specific influences and experiences as the primary determinants. These include influences from the family, the peer group, and any relevant local subcultures, as well as influences from society at large mediated through schooling and through the news and entertainment media.

Social influences tend to be consistent at first because they are confined to the immediate family. However, as children encounter peers, schools and community organizations, and media influences, they become aware of new possibilities and of conflicting ideas. If they encounter reasonably consistent socialization pressures and adapt easily to them, they are likely to become well adjusted in the sense that their personal traits and behavior are satisfactory to them and to significant others in their lives (Kagan & Moss, 1962). However, they are likely to experience adjustment problems if they are confused by inconsistent pressures or are unable or unwilling to adapt to consistent pressures.

family influences

Of the various socializing influences, the parents or guardians exert the most powerful effects on most children's social development. For good or ill, they act as models, articulate attitudes and beliefs, and communicate and enforce behavioral demands. Children acquire many of their most pervasive attitudes and values, including religious and political beliefs, through parental modeling and socialization. In addition, parental child-rearing beliefs and practices exert far-reaching effects on children's social development. Good information about parental behavior and its effects on children is available (Baumrind, 1971, 1991; Clark, 1983; Dornbusch et al., 1987; Eisenberg & Mussen, 1989; Hess, 1970; Hoffman, 1991; Lamborn et al., 1991; Maccoby, 1980; Maccoby & Martin, 1983; Sigel, McGillicuddy-DeLisi, & Goodnow, 1992; Steinberg, Elmer, & Mounts, 1989). Many of the findings are organized around two major dimensions of parental behavior: love-hostility and restrictiveness-permissiveness.

The *love-hostility* dimension is most closely associated with the child's self-esteem and orientation toward others. Parents who love their children and treat them with acceptance, affection, and emotional support tend to develop in the children high self-esteem and an attitude of trust and sociability toward others. Parents who reject their children and treat them with hostility and abuse are likely to produce children with low self-esteem who dislike and mistrust others as well as themselves.

The *permissiveness-restrictiveness* dimension is more closely related to children's development of initiative, autonomy, and conformity. Parents who are highly controlling and restrictive tend to produce children who are conforming and well socialized, perhaps too much so. Parents who are extremely permissive tend to produce children who are nonconforming and independent, although not necessarily in productive ways. Extreme permissiveness often amounts to parental neglect of children, rather than systematic implementation of a deliberate child-rearing policy.

The love-hostility dimension and the restrictiveness-permissiveness dimension are not correlated with each other. Permissive parents are no more likely to be loving than restrictive parents, and restrictive parents are no more likely to be rejecting than permissive parents. Different combinations of these parental behaviors predispose children toward different social development patterns. These research findings are summarized in Figure 4.1.

It should be noted that the child characteristics listed in Figure 4.1 are most likely to develop when parents or guardians consistently behave at the extremes of the dimensions involved. Most parents are not extreme on either dimension, so they exert less extreme influences, although in the directions indicated. Also, the socializing influences affecting a child may not be so consistent. Where a parent lacks consistency, or where parents conflict in their child-rearing philosophies and practices, outcomes are less predictable. Finally, in some cases the relationships illustrated in the table occur in part because of child effects on parents in addition to parent effects on children. Certain types of children elicit certain kinds of parental behavior. With these cautions in mind, let us examine the table and its implications.

the two dimensions in combination

Parents who combine love with permissiveness tend to produce children who combine high self-esteem and sociability with independence and nonconformity. Such children are often social leaders or highly creative types.

Parents who combine love with restrictiveness tend to produce children who are conforming and well adjusted (in that they meet parental demands with little difficulty or resistance). However, such children may be noncreative, noninitiatory, and overly dependent on the parents.

Parents who combine permissiveness with hostility tend to produce hostile, aggressive, and paranoid children. Here, the "permissiveness" usually is apathy or a form of rejection rather than commitment to permissiveness as a child-

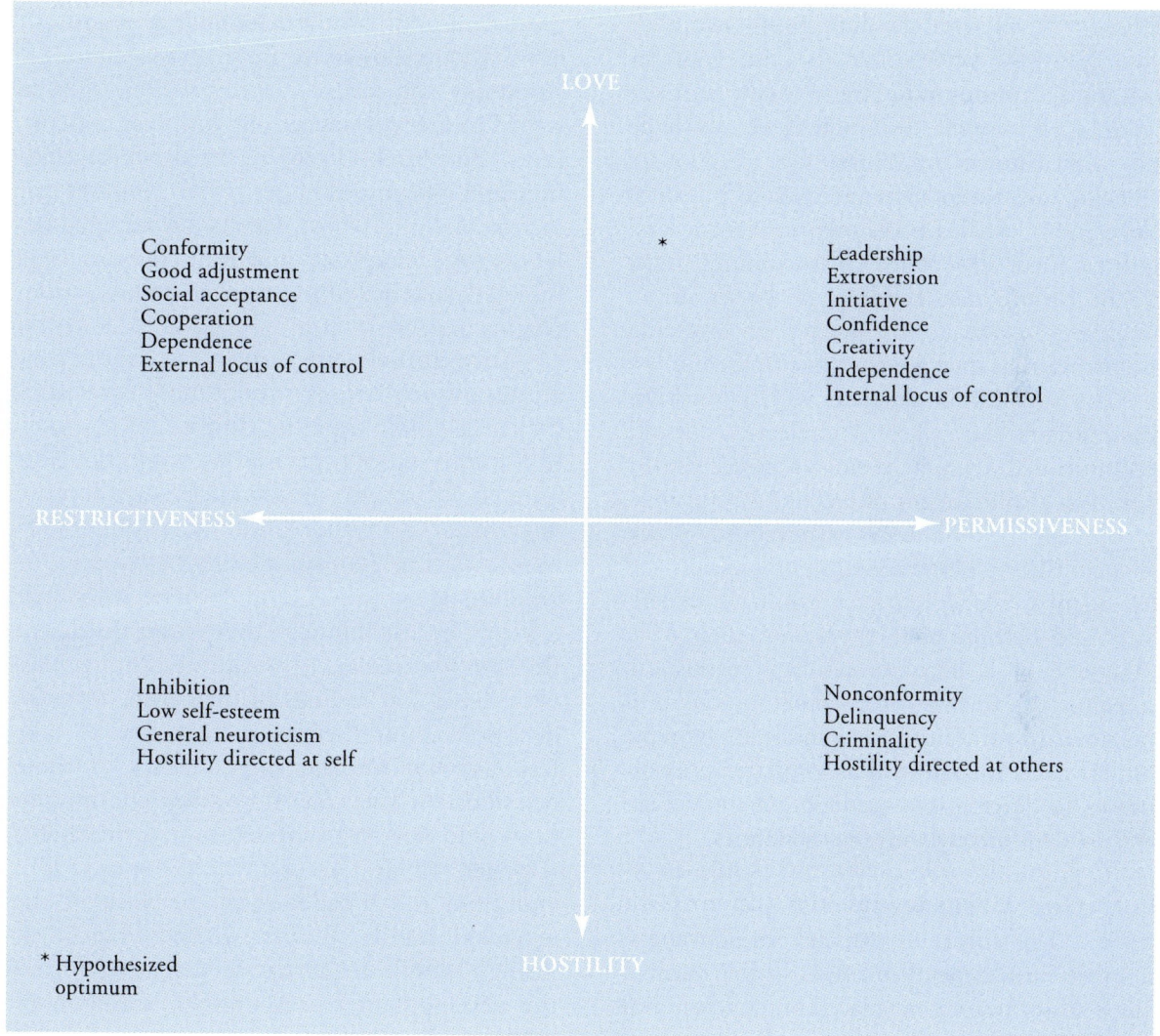

Figure 4.1 relationships between parent behaviors and child outcomes

rearing policy. In effect, such children are reject-ed and left to their own devices so long as they do not get in the parents' way. The children tend to respond by becoming hostile and reject-ing themselves. They usually have low self-esteem, although they may cover it with aggres-sive behavior.

Finally, parents who combine hostility with high restrictiveness tend to produce children who have low self-esteem, inhibitions, guilt, feelings of inadequacy, and general neurotic tendencies. Such children continually get the message "You're no good, you never were any good, and you never will be any good," and many of them come to believe it.

Determining which pattern of parental behavior is optimal requires making value judgments about desired child outcomes. Child development specialists tend to favor a combination of high love with a balance between restrictiveness and permissiveness, leaning toward permissiveness. They consider love and acceptance to be almost totally good for children, although at some point love can shade into seductiveness or undesirable affectionate behavior, and acceptance untempered by social expectations can leave children egocentric and undisciplined. Except for such extremes, most experts believe that children are better off in direct proportion to the degree of love and acceptance that they get from their parents.

The situation is different with permissiveness-restrictiveness, where a moderate course is recommended. Extreme permissiveness is usually viewed as abandonment of parental responsibility. Allowing children to do whatever they please whenever they please can result in inhibition and dependency, if children have traumatic experiences and become afraid to act on their own. Otherwise, it is likely to result in egotistical, immature personalities and contemptuous attitudes toward authority figures and rules. Extreme restrictiveness is seen as stifling children's opportunities to develop into autonomous individuals who are comfortable with their identities.

Baumrind's research on parenting styles

The effects of parental restrictiveness-permissiveness depend not just on the number and kinds of restrictions placed on children, but also on the manner in which parents exercise control. Baumrind (1971, 1991) clarified this dimension in her distinction between authoritarian and authoritative parenting. **Authoritarian parents** *make little attempt to explain the demands they make on their children.* They view obedience as an absolute virtue and expect their children to accept their demands without questioning or discussion. They boss the children around with an attitude of, You'll do it because I said so, and if you don't, you'll be punished. **Authoritative parents** may place just as many limits on their children, but they *explain the rationales for the limits.* They help their children to understand that the demands they make are for the children's own

good. Baumrind found that children of authoritative parents showed the most advanced levels of autonomy and independence for their ages, as well as greater confidence and healthier self-concepts. Buri et al. (1988) reported similar findings, and Fuligni and Eccles (1993) reported that early adolescents whose parents did not gradually reduce their power and restrictiveness were more extreme in shifting their orientations from parents to peers.

Authoritative parenting is especially important for helping children to construct their individual identities and begin to function more autonomously as they develop into and through adolescence. Adolescents need both separation from and connectedness with their families as they develop independent identities. Commensurate with their developing capabilities, they need sufficient freedom to experience themselves as individuals with needs and feelings of their own, to make decisions about their own lives, and to take responsibility for the consequences of those decisions. At the same time, they continue to need guidance and support from their parents (Conger, 1991; Grotevant & Cooper, 1985) and from the broader social network of the extended family (Levitt, Guacci-Franco, & Levitt, 1993). Authoritative parenting fosters the development of responsible, autonomous behavior. It combines appropriate exercise of control with opportunities for autonomous decision making, communication about the issues involved, and parental modeling of responsible autonomous behavior.

peer relationships

Children's experiences with their peers provide them with opportunities to learn how to interact with others, control their social behavior, develop age-relevant skills and interests, and share problems and feelings (Berndt & Ladd, 1989; Hartup, 1989). Peer relationships become espe-

research at work
authoritative socialization practices

The following socialization practices are key aspects of the authoritative pattern that promotes optimal personal and social development. They appear to be just as desirable for teachers socializing students at school as they are for parents socializing their children at home.

- Accepting the child as an individual
- Communicating this acceptance through warm, affectionate interactions
- Socializing through instruction in prosocial values and behavior, not just "discipline"
- Clarifying rules and limits, but with input from the child and with flexibility in response to developmental advances (e.g., allowing students more opportunities for autonomy and choice as they develop greater ability to handle these opportunities responsibly)
- Presenting expectations in ways that communicate respect for and concern about the child, as opposed to "laying down the law"

- Explaining the rationales underlying demands and expectations
- Justifying prohibitions by citing the effects of children's actions on themselves and others rather than by appealing to fear of punishment or essentially empty logic such as, Good children don't do that
- Practicing as well as preaching well-articulated value systems
- Continually projecting positive expectations and attitudes; treating children as if they already are, or at least are in the process of becoming, prosocial and responsible people
- Understanding and accommodating individual differences, so that children are encouraged to capitalize on their strengths and follow their interests rather than feeling pressured into becoming something else
- Advocating (and practicing) values in ways that leave children emotionally free to think about and question these values during the adolescent identity crisis

cially important in adolescence, especially in age-segregated, technologically advanced societies like ours that delay entry into the adult world of work and family responsibility (Conger, 1991). Relations with same- and opposite-sex peers begin to serve as prototypes for later adult social, work, and intimate relationships.

Developmental trends Elementary-school children tend to play primarily with same-sex peers. Friendships tend to be relatively superficial during these years, focused on pursuing shared interests and engaging in enjoyable activities. Boys' play groups tend to be larger and focused on sports and other physical activities. Girls' groups tend to be smaller and focused on social interaction. Throughout middle childhood and the preadolescent years, girls tend to have more intimate interpersonal relationships than boys (Hartup, 1989).

As they approach adolescence, children begin to develop more intimate friendships with one or a few same-sex peers. Less personal, activity-based interactions with other friends continue, but interactions with close friends begin to include more self-disclosure, emotional support, and sharing of views on intimate topics. As ties to parents become looser, adolescents become increasingly dependent on peers. More than two-thirds of them believe that a close friend understands them better than their parents do (Youniss & Smollar, 1985).

As they proceed through junior high and high school, adolescents also become involved in cliques and crowds (Coleman, 1980). *Cliques* are small groups of close friends who spend a lot of time interacting with one another, both personally and on the telephone. The exchanges of view that occur during these interactions help the adolescents to think about and prepare for upcoming activities and to evaluate them afterward. *Crowds* are larger groups, usually collections of several cliques. Crowd membership is based more on common social interests and activity preferences than on the mutual attractions that form the basis for cliques. Crowds provide the settings for larger social interactions such as parties.

During the early adolescent years, conformity to parents tends to decline and conformity to peers tends to rise. There is an increase in the perceived importance of the peer group and in felt needs to conform to the values, customs, and fads of the current youth culture, especially those aspects that are emphasized in one's crowd.

Eder (1985) documented several aspects of this in her study of the "cycle of popularity" that developed among middle school girls who were followed across grades six through eight. In grade six, there were few stable cliques among these girls and none appeared to have more status than the others. In seventh grade, however, cliques became more stable and a hierarchy began to emerge. By eighth grade, there was a clearly defined hierarchical system of stable cliques. Clique differentiation coincided with the emergence of opportunities to gain places on the student council and the school's athletic teams and cheerleading squads. Among seventh

graders, for example, the highest-status group of girls included seven of the eight cheerleaders and six student council members, including the class president. Socioeconomic backgrounds also played a part: girls in the higher status cliques tended to wear more name-brand clothes and indicate other evidence of financial advantages over girls in lower-status cliques. By eighth grade, the higher status male and female cliques had merged into a large crowd that sat together on one side of the cafeteria while the lower-status crowd sat on the other side.

Interestingly, a cycle of popularity developed, in which less popular peers' feelings toward popular girls initially became notably more positive but gradually shifted from positive to negative, eventually making many of the "popular" girls among the least-liked individuals in the school. The cycle developed as follows. First, a few girls became identified through cheerleading elections as an elite group. Immediately thereafter, these girls experienced a marked increase in popularity as other students sought to affiliate with them because friendships with popular girls are important avenues for social status among other girls. However, there are limits to the number of friendships that one person can maintain, so popular girls ended up rejecting more offers of friendship than other girls did. Also, to maintain their higher status, the girls who formed the elite group not only began associating more exclusively with one another but also began avoiding social interactions and even eye contact with less-popular girls. This led to the perception of them as stuck-up, and thus to increasing unpopularity outside of their clique. Popular girls who most actively snubbed others were the most likely to be snubbed in return, but even other girls in the popular clique who were open to initiatives from lower-status peers often began to be snubbed by those peers as a defensive "snub them before they snub you" reaction. Thus, as the popularity cycle progressed, being popular mostly meant being in

The social isolate typically suffers feelings of guilt, low self-esteem, lack of confidence, feelings of inferiority. Teachers can help by supporting unique strengths and by setting achievable goals.

the center of attention as a cheerleader or student council member, not necessarily being well liked by the full range of peers.

As development continues into middle and later adolescence, conformity to peers also begins to decline and young people become more autonomous (Steinberg & Silverberg, 1986). Even when peer conformity needs are at their peak, parental influences remain strong in several important areas. Peer influences dominate in such matters as tastes in music and entertainment, fashions in clothing and language, or patterns of interaction with peers. However, parental influences usually continue to dominate in areas such as educational plans and aspirations, moral and social values, and understandings about the adult world (Conger, 1991). This is especially the case with adolescents whose parents continually express affection for and concern about them. In contrast, adolescents whose parents are passive and neglectful tend to be more exclusively and strongly peer oriented and likely to get into trouble with school authorities and the police.

As adolescence progresses, same-sex friendships remain in place but become less intense.

At the same time, adolescents begin to develop relationships with the opposite sex. Some of these are platonic friendships that occur as male and female cliques begin to interact within larger social crowds. Others are more romantic or sexual relationships that develop as individuals begin to date and pair off in couples.

Popular and unpopular children The developmental trends in peer relationships described above are typical for children who are popular with or at least well accepted by their peers. Unfortunately, many children and adolescents are not so well accepted. Some are social isolates who are mostly ignored; others are actively disliked and socially rejected. A great deal has been learned about students who develop these contrasting peer relationships (Asher & Coie, 1990; Berndt & Ladd, 1989; Kennedy, 1990; McCallum & Bracken, 1993; Parker & Asher, 1987; Wentzel & Erdley, 1993).

Children who become popular with their peers often are physically attractive and possess special skills or talents, especially athletic ability in boys and social skills in girls. However, as children develop into adolescents, peer acceptance is most closely associated with personal characteristics that make a child liked as an individual and valued as a group member. Popular students tend to be cheerful and optimistic, open and empathic toward others, and at ease in social situations. As children, they know how to enter ongoing games, how to share, how to be an enjoyable play partner, and how to inhibit aggressive and insulting behaviors. As adolescents they make others feel accepted and involved, are able to self-disclose when appropriate, are emotionally supportive of peers, and engage in dialogue assertively but tactfully.

Unpopular students tend to lack these positive qualities and to possess certain negative qualities that impair their peer relationships. Socially isolated students who are generally neglected by their peers tend to be ill at ease and lacking in self-confidence in social situations.

Unable to assert themselves effectively, they may react to conflict with timidity, nervousness, or withdrawal. To the extent that they also say embarrassing things, they may be teased or picked on instead of merely ignored.

Students who are actively rejected tend to be angry, argumentative, and prone to start fights as children, and to be self-centered, inconsiderate, and tactless as adolescents. They usually have distrustful or even paranoid social expectations, so that they may interpret accidents as deliberate provocations and become unreasonably angry and aggressive toward peers. Consequently, peers understandably dislike and avoid them. These aggressive, rejected students are at high risk, initially for delinquency and school dropout and later for psychopathology and crime (DeBaryshe, Patterson, & Capaldi, 1993).

implications for teachers
encouraging positive peer relationships

Teachers can do several things to encourage positive peer relationships among their students (Erwin, 1993). In the process of helping class members get to know one another as individuals and begin to function as a learning community, teachers can provide all students with opportunities to present themselves in a positive light and to display their unique talents and interests. Also, teachers can incorporate cooperative learning methods that bring peers together in pairs or small groups to collaborate in working toward learning goals. Peers who collaborate in pursuit of common goals tend to get to know and value one another, so that well-structured, cooperative learning experiences can lead to positive peer relationships, including relationships that cross gender, social class, and ethnic lines. Students who are socially awkward might be paired or grouped with friendly and socially skillful students who can provide modeling as well as opportunities to develop friendships. Teachers will need to be prepared to help students learn to function productively together in pairs or small groups, however; otherwise, the experience might lead to hostility or victimization.

Teachers can help social isolates by arming them with better social understandings and skills. Although these students are usually painfully aware of their unpopularity, they are not always clear about the reasons for it. Consequently, they may benefit from sympathetically delivered feedback about the things they do that make their peers uncomfortable. Better yet, teachers can help these students develop social skills such as introducing themselves to others, initiating conversations, listening and responding appropriately to what peers have to say, and joining ongoing group activities (Asher & Coie, 1990; Bierman & Furman, 1984; L'Abate & Milan, 1985; Ladd & Mize, 1983).

Students who are rejected by their peers are more difficult to work with because they are hostile and aggressive. It is important for teachers to make it clear to these students that aggressive behavior is not acceptable and will not be tolerated (see Chapter 19). Beyond this, teachers may be able to help aggressive students by listening to them sympathetically, attempting to resocialize their beliefs and attitudes through modeling and persuasion, and teaching them more effective ways of interacting with peers and solving conflicts. Such students may benefit from being made more aware of their own behavior, how it is perceived by others, and the effects that it has on them (Patterson, Kupersmidt, & Griesler, 1990). Finally, they need counseling or instruction in more effective ways of handling frustration, controlling their tempers, solving conflicts through communication and negotiation rather than aggression, and expressing anger verbally rather than physically.

To help rejected or isolated students, teachers may have to work with the peer group as well as the students themselves (Asher & Coie, 1990). Private conferences with peers might lead to better treatment of these students, especially those who are being neglected or victimized rather than rejected because of their own antisocial behavior.

developing positive self-concepts

Teachers can help students construct positive social self-concepts. Helping students cope with developmental crises has already been discussed. Other opportunities include helping them to become aware of and develop their strong points (Hauserman, Miller, & Bond, 1976), to gain confidence and improve in areas of weakness, and

to accept limitations that cannot be changed. Some students may also need guidance in accepting their gender or their physical attributes or in developing empathy toward others ("How do you think Jenny feels when you say that to her?"), social awareness ("What do your friends think about you when you put Jenny down?"), role-taking skills ("Let's act it out. I'm Jenny, and I say, 'What are you doing?' Now, what should you say?"), or insights into self and others ("Why do you think you treat Jenny this way, when you're pleasant and friendly with everyone else?") (Eisenberg, Lennon, & Roth, 1983; Rushton & Sorrentino, 1981; Smith, 1982).

Well-established self-concepts based on long-standing status in peer groups are not easily changed, and attempts to help by thrusting individuals into unaccustomed roles may cause discomfort, even if the roles are attractive. This was shown by Klinger and McNelly (1976), who studied Boy Scout troops with established leaders and followers. The boys were asked to compete in teams of four against teams from other troops, under circumstances in which the role of captain of the team involved considerable power and responsibility. If the teams had been allowed to select their own captains, the boys with the highest existing leadership status would have been picked. However, captains were assigned so that some were the same boys who would have been selected anyway, but others were boys accustomed to follower status. Observation and interviews showed that boys who already were leaders functioned effectively as team captains and enjoyed the games, but boys accustomed to follower status who were thrust into the role of captain did not. Some even became withdrawn or anxious. These findings show that self-concepts are powerful and resistant to change through short-term or artificial interventions. Teachers can stimulate real change in students' self-concepts, but this will usually require supporting *gradual* changes, not only in self-perceptions but also in the personal characteristics and behavior on which they are based.

research at work
extrafamilial factors

Urie Bronfenbrenner (1986) has been a leading advocate calling for more attention to extrafamilial factors that impact on child development. Some of these impact directly on children (the school, the neighborhood, television and other media). Others act indirectly by influencing parents and other family members (local influences such as parents' experiences at work and interactions with relatives, friends, and social organizations, as well as broader economic or social trends that affect society as a whole). Bronfenbrenner cited the following research-based examples of extrafamilial influences on children:

- Parents' child-rearing attitudes are affected by their social class backgrounds and work experiences. Parents who work in large organizations in jobs where collaborating with others as part of a team is important tend to emphasize interpersonal skills in raising their children. In contrast, entrepreneurs tend to emphasize individual achievement and striving. Workers in jobs that require compliance with authority tend to stress obedience in raising their children, whereas more autonomous professionals tend to emphasize self-direction and independence.

- Parents' time for interaction with their children is affected by their work hours and their degree of absorption in their jobs. Parents who work late afternoon or night shifts tend to spend much less time with their children than parents who work more typical daytime hours. Parents who are absorbed in jobs that make heavy demands on their physical or mental energy also spend less time interacting with their children, and tend to be irritable and impatient when they do.

- In two-parent families, when both parents work outside the home there tends to be a positive effect on girls but a negative effect on boys. However, this general tendency is complicated by influences from other factors such as whether the work is part time or full time, whether it is perceived as necessary or voluntary, and whether it is experienced as self-enhancing or demeaning.

- Latchkey children who operate mostly independently of their working parents are at greater risk for susceptibility to antisocial peer influences and involvement in parentally disapproved behavior, although these dangers are greatly reduced when the parents keep track of their children's

Consider students who have developed stable concepts of themselves as tough or evil. Altering such self-concepts takes time, but it can be done through consistent projection of positive expectations leading to self-fulfilling prophecy effects, in which teachers reject the students' negative self-images and instead project images of them as persons who are basically well mean-

whereabouts, monitor their activities, and exert "remote control" over them.

- Child abuse and neglect rates are notably higher in families that experience economic stress and do not possess adequate social support systems for parenting. These risks are reduced when the parents are involved in strong kinship networks and attend church regularly.

- Compared to small towns and rural areas, life in urban areas offers enhanced possibilities for some families but enhanced dangers for others. Some children benefit from urban areas' richer and more differentiated cultural environments, especially older children in suburban families. However, stressful inner-city life greatly increases other children's chances for school failure, delinquency, and psychiatric disorders, especially younger children in families that feature economic stress, marital discord, or parental mental disorder or criminality.

- A deteriorating relationship between parents tends to have a negative impact on the personal, peer, and school adjustments of their children, peaking during the first year following parental separation (if this occurs). These effects can be minimized if the custodial parent receives support from friends and relatives and especially if the separated parent remains in the children's lives and cooperates with the custodial parent in providing them with physical and emotional support.

- Some resilient or "invincible" children develop into competent and well-adjusted adults despite unpromising backgrounds featuring poverty, biological risks, family instability, and inadequate parenting. Major factors that distinguish these children from similar children who fail to overcome their difficult origins include a low number of chronic, stressful life events experienced in childhood and adolescence and the presence of an informal multigenerational network of kin who provide support (Garbarino et al., 1992).

- Paid employment of high school students, which often is recommended as a way to develop responsibility in adolescents and help to prepare them for the transition into adult work roles, is actually associated with undesired outcomes such as decreased involvement in the family and school, increased use of drugs, and development of cynical work attitudes and acceptance of unethical work practices.

ing and who will do the right thing when they understand the situation fully. Students treated this way consistently can be expected to acquire and to try to live up to more positive self-concepts (Grusec et al., 1978; Lepper, 1973; Miller, Brickman, & Bolen, 1975; Rabiner & Coie, 1989). For more about self-concept development, see Damon and Hart (1988).

research at work
families and social change

Research on factors that support children's emotional well-being suggests the value of a stable and supportive home nested within a similarly stable and supportive context of neighborhood and extended family. It evokes images of Norman Rockwell paintings and *Leave It to Beaver* episodes. However, family contexts corresponding to this ideal are rapidly disappearing, if indeed they ever were very common. Social evolution during this century, and especially since World War II, has led to dramatic changes in the nature and functioning of American families (Conger, 1991; Lerner, 1993) such as the following:

- Instead of working on farms or in rural communities, the vast majority of Americans now work in urban areas. There has been a dramatic shift away from rural and small-town living, first to large cities and more recently to suburbs and smaller cities.

- In the process of relocating to live near places of employment, family members tend to spread out and live in separate nuclear family groups instead of together (or at least nearby) as a larger extended family. Today it is more the exception than the rule for aunts, uncles, and grandparents to be continually available to a child as part of a close-knit extended family.

- Fewer and fewer jobs pay enough to enable a worker to support a family comfortably in today's society. Consequently, even if a married couple should prefer that one partner act as breadwinner and the other concentrate on the home and the children, it may be difficult or impossible for them to do so. Most adults now find that they must work, whether they want to or not.

- As the nation's economy has gradually shifted emphasis from manufacturing to service activities, many high-paying industrial jobs have been lost. Most of the families involved have experienced continuing economic stress because few of the displaced workers have been able to find other jobs that pay the high salaries to which they were accustomed.

- Modern life has become increasingly impersonal, especially in urban areas. Supermarkets and shopping malls have replaced local mom-and-pop stores, consolidated schools enrolling hundreds of students have replaced smaller schools, and driving from a bedroom community to engage in organized activities or to obtain specialized services has replaced walking in the neighborhood to socialize with neighbors and patronize nearby businesses.

- Parents concerned about their children's development often feel threatened by extrafamilial influences such as violence in the streets and in the media, easy access to sex and drugs, and a youth culture that glorifies attitudes or behavior that they view as immoral.

- Even if nothing particularly unfortunate has happened to them or their children, many parents feel generally anxious and confused about social change: the nation's social mobility and racial and ethnic diversity, evolving gender roles and other social practices that clash with traditional religious teachings, and their limited knowledge of (and ability to control) their children's teachers and peers (especially once the children get to junior high school).

societal and subcultural influences

Children's interactions with family members and peers occur at particular times and places. Children growing up in the contemporary United States are exposed to the nation's traditions and values as well as its current social conditions and trends. These commonalities make for similarities in experience and outlook, but other factors make for differences. *Age cohorts* differ in the nature and import of their exposure to landmark issues and events. Issues that absorbed the youth of previous generations (civil rights, the Vietnam War) are mostly ancient history to contemporary youth who are absorbed with issues such as economic uncertainties and shifting gender and family roles. In turn, these issues may be viewed mostly as past history by today's first graders, once they begin to develop sophisticated understandings of them as high school or college students.

Within age cohorts, children's formative experiences differ according to the specifics of the contexts in which they develop. Different regions of the nation and different local settings within regions (urban, suburban, rural) emphasize somewhat different traditions and values and offer contrasting social environments. Even within local areas, children's experiences will be affected by their families' socioeconomic status and involvement in subcultures associated with particular racial or ethnic groups.

minority group families Regardless of their circumstances or backgrounds, most parents want similar things for their children (health, happiness, and a contemporary version of the American dream). Most also want similar things from schools (they usually place top priority on equipping students with the knowledge and skills they will need to prepare them for higher education and success in the workplace). Aspirations regarding children and schooling are much more similar than different across socioeconomic status levels, although higher-status parents, especially if they are more highly educated, are likely to have more knowledge about how to help their children fulfill those aspirations (Hess, 1970). A few ethnic-group differences have been reported.

Studies of Chinese-American and Japanese-American families indicate that, compared to Euro-American families, the Asian families emphasize traditional family roles and responsibilities. Socialization practices emphasize duty, maintaining control over one's emotions, and obedience to family authority figures (Huang & Yin, 1989; Nagata, 1989). In contrast, African-American family roles tend to be more flexible and less gender-specific than those in Euro-American families. About 40 percent of African-American children live in female-headed families, and most of the rest live in two-parent families where both parents work. In the latter families, parents' household responsibilities are more related to work hours and type of task than to gender-based roles, and there is less gender role differentiation in the tasks assigned to male and female children (Gibbs, 1989).

Hispanic families traditionally have been patriarchal, with fathers making the decisions and supporting the family while mothers cared for the home and children. Adolescents were socialized into these well-differentiated gender roles, and the families were embedded within strong kinship networks to provide support. These traditions have been weakening lately, however, as Hispanic women increasingly work outside the home and attain higher status and decision-making power within the family (Ramirez, 1989). It is difficult to generalize about Native American families because they represent several hundred tribal groups with varying customs and traditions. Many Native children experience culture shock when they begin school, however, especially if they live on reservations and have not had much contact with the English language or Euro-American traditions (LaFromboise & Low, 1989). These students are very much at risk for school failure unless taught by teachers who combine supportiveness and acceptance of their cultural backgrounds with positive expectations and determination to see that they succeed (Kleinfeld, 1975; Phillips, 1983).

ethnic identities Alongside their identification as Americans (and sometimes in partial opposition to it), some children and adolescents develop an identification with a racial or ethnic group. (Euro-Americans tend to have little sense of ethnicity and to identify themselves only as American, except for children of immigrants). Phinney (1990) has suggested that ethnic identity development proceeds in stages similar to the identity statuses described by Marcia (1980). Adolescents with an *unexamined* ethnic identity have internalized the values and attitudes of the dominant culture without experiencing crises or examining issues relating to their ethnicity. Adolescents involved in an ethnic identity *search* are in a moratorium stage in which they are exploring the meaning of their ethnicity. Some of them experience growing conflict between the values of the dominant culture and those of their ethnic group. Finally, adolescents with an *achieved* ethnic identity are comfortable in identifying with their ethnic heritage. They are confident rather than defensive about their ethnicity, although concerned about eliminating any stereotyping or discriminatory treatment that may be directed toward their group.

Whatever their racial or ethnic heritage, minority group children are likely to experience difficulties adjusting to school to the extent that the values, language, behavioral expectations, and other aspects of the school culture contrast with what the children have been exposed to in their families and local subcultures. These differences need not be problematic if teachers are knowledgeable about and respectful of their students' home cultures and if they work with the assets that the children bring to school with them rather than treating these as deficiencies or problems. For example,

the bilingual abilities that many Hispanic children bring to school should be viewed as a bonus and employed to promote academic achievement, not treated as a problem likely to impede progress (Garcia, 1992). Issues involved in honoring diversity and teaching in multicultural settings are addressed in Chapter 21.

Ogbu's ideas about involuntary minorities The potential for culture clash is greatest when subcultural differences are labeled as deficiencies and used as the basis for stereotyping the group's members. John Ogbu (1992) discussed this and related factors in attempting to explain why certain minority groups have more difficulty than others in adjusting to the school culture. Ogbu distinguished between *voluntary minorities* who chose to emigrate to the United States to secure political freedom or improved economic opportunities (e.g., recent immigrants from China, India, and South America) and *involuntary minorities* who became part of the United States society because of slavery, conquest, or colonization (e.g., African-Americans, Mexican-Americans, Native Americans, and Native Hawaiians). He also distinguished between *primary differences* in language or culture that existed before a group became a minority in the United States (heritage that emigrants brought with them) and *secondary differences* that arose later (especially involuntary minorities' reactions to the experience of living in subordination).

Ogbu suggested that primary differences result in a cultural frame of reference that is merely different rather than oppositional to the dominant culture. Consequently, voluntary minorities tend to accept traditional notions about strategies for getting ahead in the United States. They tend to interpret their economic hardships as temporary problems that they will overcome through education and hard work. They also tend to acquiesce in their relationships with school personnel and to view any cultural or language differences that they encounter in the school or workplace as barriers to be overcome in order to achieve their goals. In contrast, involuntary minorities who experience sustained economic and other difficulties may begin to attribute them to institutionalized discrimination, and to develop skepticism that they can get ahead by adopting mainstream beliefs and strategies. They may begin to develop secondary cultural differences that represent opposition to the dominant culture and become foci for attempts to maintain group identity and soli-

darity. This may lead to distrust of school personnel who seek to impose the dominant culture, as well as demands for modifications in schooling practices to accommodate what the group views as culturally compatible curricula, teaching and learning styles, and social interaction styles. Even if parents verbally endorse education as a means of getting ahead, these secondary cultural differences may compete with academic goals, especially where clearly oppositional cultures develop within student peer groups.

implications for teachers
teaching students from involuntary minority groups

Ogbu's ideas are controversial (Foley, 1991), in part because they imply that students from involuntary minority groups will continue to have difficulty in schools until stereotyping and discrimination directed against their groups is eliminated from society at large. Whether or not that is true, Ogbu's work suggests that, in order to help such students significantly, teachers may need to challenge and ultimately resocialize some of the students' oppositional beliefs. Openness to their cultural backgrounds and determination to build on their strengths and help them succeed may not be enough for cynical or depressed minority students who do not believe

that sustained effort will enable them to succeed despite social discrimination against their group. Focused attempts to overcome this particular form of learned helplessness may be needed for some of these students, as well as counseling in methods of handling criticism from peers who are committed to opposition to the school's agenda. In this regard, it is worth noting that teachers who are valued by minority at-risk students and their parents tend to set high standards and follow through by providing students with whatever explicit instruction and direct assistance is needed to enable them to succeed (Delpit, 1992; Siddle-Walker, 1992).

moral development

Children do not become truly moral individuals, capable of using a set of stable ethical principles to guide behavior, until they enter the concrete operational period. Sometime during the early elementary grades, they attain what theologians used to call the "age of reason," indicating an intuitive recognition of the cognitive development that occurs at this time.

Piaget (1932) was one of the first to study

the changes in moral reasoning that accompany changes in cognitive development. He found that young children tend to confuse morality with social convention and to judge the morality of an action according to its consequences, without taking intentions or situational factors into account. Consequently, they might view breaking a dish accidentally as just as wrong as breaking it on purpose. However, as children develop the cognitive abilities needed to assume the perspective of another person, they begin to take into account a person's intentions and use moral concepts such as fairness and reciprocity when making moral judgments.

the morality of justice: Kohlberg's stage theory

Lawrence Kohlberg (1969, 1984; Colby et al., 1987) elaborated on Piaget's ideas in his stage theory of the development of moral judgment. He discussed three levels of moral thinking, with two stages at each level (see Figure 4.2). As a basis for assessing moral reasoning, Kohlberg presented people with moral dilemmas and asked them to make moral judgments and explain their reasoning.

For example, one dilemma features a man named Heinz, whose wife is dying from a rare cancer. A drug that will save her is available, but Heinz can only raise half of what it costs. Its inventor refuses to sell the drug to Heinz at half the usual price, even though he would make a fivefold profit. He also refuses to take half the money now and let Heinz pay the rest later. Desperate, Heinz is considering stealing the drug. People interviewed about this dilemma are asked to say what Heinz should do and explain their reasoning. The moral reasoning strategies that they use to construct a solution (not the solution itself) are then scored according to Kohlberg's stages, and scores are averaged across dilemmas to determine the person's overall level.

Individuals at the Level I do not yet possess an organized system of moral concepts. This **preconventional** level is the *initial level of moral reasoning characterized by a focus on advancing one's own interests by maximizing rewards and minimizing punishment.* Within Level I, *Stage 1* individuals (mostly young children) are egocentric, thus concerned about their own interests. Their moral thinking emphasizes rules, sanctions, and personal consequences rather than the

concerns of others or of society as a whole. What is good or bad is seen by them as self-evident, requiring little justification beyond the identification of something as right or wrong. *Stage 2* individuals reflect a concrete, individualistic perspective. They are still primarily concerned with themselves, but they are aware of others' agendas and thus willing to enter into limited reciprocity agreements of a "you scratch my back and I'll scratch yours" nature to maximize their own interests while minimizing unwanted consequences. Most Stage 2 persons also are developing children, but some older children and adults never get beyond this stage.

Persons who reveal Level II moral thinking take a member-of-society perspective. This **conventional** level is the *intermediate level of moral reasoning in which the focus broadens from one's own interests to the good of society as a whole, with emphasis on meeting one's duties and obligations.* *Stage 3* individuals coordinate perspectives of others to develop a third-person perspective that enables them to realize that a shared set of moral norms (such as being a good or altruistic person, or having good motives) can govern relationships between people. Stage 3 individuals think in terms of doing their duty, living up to expectations, and displaying virtues for the purpose of maintaining interpersonal trust and social approval. Individuals who develop from Stage 3 to *Stage 4* change from a focus on mutual relationships between individuals to a more generalized orientation that considers the social system as a consistent set of rules and procedures that impartially apply to all members of that social system. Stage 4 persons stress the need for social order, so fulfillment of individuals' obligations to institutions and social roles is necessary to help promote the common good. Most middle school students and many high school students are predominantly conventional (Stages 3 or 4) in their moral reasoning.

Children's progression through stages in moral development is affected by the nature of their relationships with their parents. Ausubel

Level I: Preconventional Morality

Stage 1. Obedience, avoidance of punishment. Egocentric point of view, with little interest in or appreciation of the viewpoints of others. The emphasis is on literal obedience to rules and authority and avoiding doing damage to people or property. This is motivated by desires to avoid punishment and to obey for obedience's sake.

Stage 2. Individual instrumental purpose and exchange. Still primarily egocentric and concerned with own interests, but aware that others have interests that they try to pursue. Generally concentrates on meeting own needs and letting others do the same, but when needs conflict will emphasize fairness (everyone treated equally) or reciprocity (helping meet others' needs in order to get one's own needs met).

Level II: Conventional Morality

Stage 3. Mutual interpersonal expectations, relationships, and conformity. Wants to be viewed as a good person, by self and others. Not only tries to please authority figures by following rules but also tries to live up to Golden Rule expectations in interactions with relatives and friends. Seeks to maintain mutual relationships by showing concern about others and displaying virtues such as trust, loyalty, respect, and gratitude.

Stage 4. Social system and conscience maintenance. Perspective broadens from concern about the reactions of immediate others to a concern about upholding the social order and maintaining the welfare of one's society or group. Everyone has a responsibility to keep the system as a whole going by following its rules and meeting its defined obligations. Laws are to be upheld except in extreme cases where they conflict with other fixed social duties.

Level III: Postconventional and Principled Morality

Stage 5. Prior rights and social contract or utility. Sense of obligation to fulfill the social contract continues, but emphasis shifts from obeying laws to upholding the basic rights, values, and legal contracts of one's society. Recognition that laws are means to ends rather than ends in themselves, and that thinking about laws and interpersonal duties should be rooted in concern about achieving the greatest good for the greatest number of people. Recognition that the moral and the legal points of view are different and sometimes conflict, creating confusion about what is right when such conflicts occur.

Stage 6. Universal ethical principles. Moral thinking is guided by commitment to universal moral principles (justice, equality of human rights, respect for the dignity of individuals). Particular laws or social agreements are considered valid and followed to the extent that they rest on these principles, but the principles take precedence when there is conflict.

Figure 4.2 Kohlberg's six stages in the development of moral judgment

and Sullivan (1970) describe children who identify closely with their parents as satellites of the parents. They discuss the consequences of different forms of *desatellization* that occur as the children move away from parental influence. Children who desatellize gradually from accepting and facilitative homes tend not only to verbalize the value systems that they have been taught, but to use them to guide their own behavior. Ultimately, these value systems are internalized and become the basis for self-guidance. Children who experience less successful desatellization may learn to verbalize the value systems they are taught, but they are less likely to internalize these value systems and use them to guide behavior. Some are overly dominated by their parents to the point that they never seriously question what they have been taught, so they remain at conventional levels of thinking. Others never experienced enough acceptance and support from their parents to sustain their development as parental satellites, so their adolescence features rejection of parental authority and failure to articulate an integrated value system.

This process is compounded when adolescents begin to think about the meanings of their value systems and to evaluate them objectively. Those who have either limited intellectual capacities or desatellization problems do little serious thinking about their value systems. As a result, they remain fixated at the conventional or even the preconventional level, so that their moral judgments remain developmentally immature and their value systems remain mostly empty verbalizations that do not control behavior. Children who develop formal operations and spend time evaluating their value systems make important advances in moral reasoning. They switch from merely verbalizing values to consciously deliberating and adopting them (sometimes the same ones they were taught, sometimes not). To the extent that children adopt values consciously, they are likely to use the values to guide behavior.

Persons who attain Level III reasoning develop more abstract and better integrated moral concepts. This **postconventional** level is the *advanced level of moral reasoning in which people differentiate between morality and laws and emphasize fundamental values and principles in their moral reasoning*. Moving beyond the emphasis on social conventions and law and order seen at Stage 4, *Stage 5* individuals begin to view laws more flexibly by taking a reflective perspective on the reasons for establishing social systems. Stage 5 is a society-creating rather than a society-maintaining perspective. It views the social system as a contract entered into freely by its members. Basic values such as liberty or justice take precedence over laws as the bases for preserving the rights and welfare of all members of society.

Individuals who reach *Stage 6* have clear conceptions of abstract universal principles such as fairness, justice, and individual human dignity that transcend other values, even values such as the good of society. Kohlberg believed that few persons ever reach this stage. His examples tended to be persons known not only for moral teaching but for being willing to stand up and if necessary suffer for their beliefs (e.g., Socrates, Jesus, Gandhi, Martin Luther King, Jr.).

criticism of Kohlberg's theory Kohlberg's theory has been highly influential, although it has received a variety of criticism over the years. Some criticism has been relatively technical. For example, Rest (1986) and others have criticized Kohlberg's moral judgment measures and his stage sequence claims. Despite acknowledged (and since corrected) problems with his measurement methods, the weight of the evidence supports the validity of Kohlberg's stages as characterizations of developmental advances in moral judgment. That is, the findings tend to show both internal consistency and stability of moral thinking in the short term and progression through an invariant sequence of stages in the longer term (Colby et al., 1987; Kuhn, 1976; Walker, 1982; Walker & Taylor, 1991).

Findings based on the newer, stricter scoring system also show, however, that the dominant pattern of moral reasoning in most adults is conventional (Stages 3 or 4). Those who ultimately reach Stage 4 often continue to develop their moral reasoning throughout adolescence and young adulthood. A few of these (perhaps 5 percent of the total population) attain Stage 5, sometimes during the college years but more typically later.

Cross-cultural research broadly confirms the universality of Kohlberg's stage sequence through Stage 4. However, this research also indicates that Stage 5 reasoning usually appears only in urban societies. This has led to criticism of Kohlberg's characterization and scoring of Stage 5 reasoning as more suited to privileged white males in industrialized nations than to other individuals (Snarey, 1985). Shweder (1991) identified a Eurocentric bias in Kohlberg's claims for the cross-cultural universality of his stage sequence, and Cortese (1990) claimed a bias toward the thinking and experiences of socioeconomic elites.

The work of Piaget and Kohlberg on children's moral reasoning has been extended by other investigators studying reasoning about justice, social role-taking, and prosocial behavior. The first two lines of work reflected the belief that both Piaget and Kohlberg had underestimated children's moral reasoning abilities—Piaget because he asked overly complicated and confusing questions and Kohlberg because he asked about moral dilemmas that were far removed from children's everyday experiences.

justice Damon (1980) interviewed children aged 4–12 about their notions of fairness, or positive justice, in response to questions on such topics as how they would share money earned from a class project. He found that preschoolers tended to suggest egocentric solutions and to have difficulty generating logical reasons for them. Some simply reasserted their wishes rather than attempting to justify them ("I should get it because I want it"). Others attempted to justify self-serving solutions by appealing to external, observable features such as size, gender, or physical characteristics ("we

should get the most because we are girls"). Around ages 5–7, children begin to make choices based on strict equality ("everyone should get the same"). A little later (ages 6–9), ideas about merit and reciprocity emerge ("you did more work, so you should get more"). Subsequently (ages 8–10), moral relativity develops out of the understanding that different persons can have different, yet equally valid, justifications for their claims to justice. Children begin to attend to the claims of persons with special needs (such as the poor), and their choices reflect attempts to compromise among competing claims. Finally (ages 10 and up), considerations of equality and reciprocity are coordinated. Choices take into account the claims of various persons and the demands of the specific situation, and justifications reflect recognition that all persons should be given their due (which in many situations does not mean equal treatment).

role taking Damon's work indicated that children could engage in relatively sophisticated moral reasoning at younger ages than they had been credited for in the work of Piaget and Kohlberg. The work of Selman (1980) on social role-taking suggests similar conclusions. Selman's research indicates that children aged 6–8 emerge from earlier egocentricity and develop the understanding that other people have perspectives different from their own. Children aged 8–10 are better at coordinating different viewpoints because they recognize that each individual is aware of the other's perspective. These children can put themselves in another's place as a way of judging that person's intentions, purposes, and actions. Children aged 10–12 can engage in mutual role taking and also can step outside of the interaction in order to view it from a third-party perspective. Finally, children aged 12 and over engage in perspective taking from the view of the social system that all individuals share, in which social conventions and legal rules are considered.

moral principles versus social conventions

Work by several investigators who improved on Piaget's methods of interviewing children about moral issues has shown that Piaget underestimated children's capacities for making moral distinctions and engaging in moral reasoning. When interview vignettes and questions are designed to clarify the issues sufficiently to allow children to understand them, even first graders indicate that they take intentions into account in making moral judgments (i.e., they realize that breaking something or hurting someone deliberately is different from doing so accidentally). They also understand the differences between violating an important moral value and violating a mere social convention. Young children are not yet able to engage in sophisticated moral reasoning using abstract concepts and language, but they can make moral choices and justify them using experience-based notions of fairness, reciprocity, and Golden Rule behavioral expectations (Nucci, 1989).

prosocial reasoning

Kohlberg's moral dilemmas tend to emphasize situations in which laws, punishment, or formal obligations are relevant (Scott, 1987). Eisenberg (1982) extended his approach by studying children's prosocial reasoning about situations that provide opportunities to help others. She presented children with situations in which individuals were required to choose between satisfying their own wants, needs, or values or satisfying those of others by acting altruistically. She found that children's prosocial reasoning initially was hedonistic (focused on own needs), then became approval oriented (focusing on "doing good"), then became focused on empathy (putting oneself in the place of the person needing help), and finally became embedded within an internalized system of values and responsibilities. Her studies indicate that children's reasoning about prosocial issues is more advanced than their reasoning in response to Kohlberg's situations that involve constraints. Also, children's prosocial

reasoning (and behavior) tend to be more advanced when they come from supportive homes in which the parents or guardians foster empathy by explaining their expectations with reference to the effects of the children's behaviors on others' feelings.

the morality of caring: feminist views on moral development

Influential critiques of Kohlberg's views have been advanced by Carol Gilligan (1982; see also Gilligan, Ward, and Taylor, 1988) and others who approach morality from a feminist perspective. Gilligan noted that all of the subjects whose responses to moral dilemmas were used to develop the original theory were male. She further asserted that men and women speak different but equally valid moral languages: Men speak more of rights and women speak more of responsibilities. Gilligan argued that men are more likely to view moral dilemmas as conflicts of rights between individuals who rationally pursue their own self-interests, whereas women tend to stress resolutions that involve concern, continued attachment, responsibility, sacrifice, and avoiding hurting others. Men are seen as searching for general principles that can be applied to any moral dilemma (justice), and women as concentrating on particular situations, relationships, and people (caring).

To the extent that such differences appear in people's responses to moral dilemmas, they would tend to cause conventional women to be scored at Stage 3, but conventional men to be scored at Stage 4, and to make men more likely than women to be scored at Stage 5. Thus, there was reason for concern that Kohlberg's scoring scheme might have been biased against women (Pratt, Golding, & Hunter, 1984). However, Kohlberg's measurement methods and scoring schemes do not

research at work
a vision of schooling based on the ethic of caring

Nel Noddings (1984, 1992) has recommended emphasizing the ethic of caring to the extent that education would be organized around themes of care rather than the traditional disciplines. Students would be engaged in a general education that guided them in caring for self, intimate others, global others, plants, animals, the environment, the human-made world, and ideas. Moral life would be thus defined and embraced as the main goal of education. Noddings recommended that schools get started by taking the following steps:

- Adopt the primary aim of designing education to produce competent, caring, loving, and lovable people.
- Take care of affiliative needs by legitimizing time spent building relations of care and trust, keeping students and teachers together (by mutual consent) for several consecutive years, and keeping them in the same building and helping them to think of the school as theirs.
- Relax the impulse to control by giving teachers and students more responsibility

for exercising judgment, getting rid of competitive grading, reducing the emphasis on testing, increasing the emphasis on exploration and self-assessment of competence, involving students in governing their classes and schools, and accepting the challenge to care by teaching well the things that students want to learn.
- Phase out program hierarchies by abandoning uniform requirements for college entrance and providing all students with genuine opportunities to explore the questions central to human life
- Give at least part of every day to themes of care by discussing existential and spiritual matters freely, helping students to treat one another ethically and avoid behaviors that create rivals and enemies, and encouraging caring as a general approach to life.
- Teach that a commitment to caring implies accepting the responsibility to work continuously on our own competence so that the recipient of our care (whether a person, animal, object, or idea) benefits from it.

yield reliable gender differences in moral judgment scores (Mednick, 1989; Walker, 1991). Even so, Gilligan's ideas about gender differences in moral reasoning have value in broadening our notions about moral development in general and the experiences of females in particular (Larrabee, 1992).

In conclusion, Kohlberg's ideas and methods appear to be valid but focused on cognition (moral judgment), without a compara-

ble focus on moral affect and behavior (Darley & Schutz, 1990). In addition to learning about rights, rules, and the application of an impartial justice, students need to learn about sensitivity toward others and feelings of connectedness with and responsibility toward others. Students of both genders stand to benefit from socialization into an *ethic of caring,* in which interpersonal relationships and moral dilemmas are managed in ways that not only promote fairness but also minimize hurt feelings and maintain positive interpersonal relationships (Brabeck, 1987; Gilligan, Lyons, & Hammer, 1989; Oliner, 1983).

moral judgment, moral affect, and moral behavior

Most teachers will not be satisfied to concentrate only on moral judgment, because moral reasoning does not always control behavior. In fact, research generally reveals only modest correlations between levels of moral reasoning, quality and intensity of moral affect (feelings of satisfaction following good deeds or guilt following misdeeds), and moral behavior (prosocial, cooperative versus antisocial or otherwise objectionable behavior).

Early studies suggested almost no correlation at all between moral judgment and moral behavior, but more recent studies have revealed moderate relationships, at least at the extremes of the moral judgment scale. That is, students who score particularly low in moral judgment are likely to be disruptive at school (Bear & Richards, 1981; Geiger & Turiel, 1983) and delinquent outside of school (Fleetwood & Parish, 1976; Hains & Miller, 1980; Wright, 1978). In contrast, high scorers are the most likely to engage in principled moral behavior, such as helping a stranger having a bad trip on drugs (McNamee, 1978) or working actively to bring about social justice (Blasi, 1980).

implications for teachers

promoting moral development

The parents of students who show higher levels of moral reasoning tend to use inductive socialization techniques, stressing the harmful consequences of inappropriate behavior on others, whereas the parents of those who show lower levels tend to use power assertive techniques, displaying frequent threats and punishment (Eisikovits & Sagi, 1982; Hoffman, 1979; Olejnik, 1980). Thus, there is reason to believe that programs that increase moral judgment will also increase moral behavior, although comprehensive programs aimed at all facets of moral development likely will be more effective than programs restricted to just one of them.

In general, *teachers can promote moral development by both modeling and articulating prosocial values* (i.e., treating others as one wishes to be treated oneself). The socialization strategies that will be most successful in the classroom are providing guidelines and limits, offering explanations of why these are appropriate, and minimizing threats and punishment. It is also helpful to discuss idealized conduct and the reason why it is valued. Degeneration of the discussion into a listing of punishments threatened for specific violations is unlikely to change students' ideas about these forbidden activities or their tendencies to engage in them.

values and moral education in schools

Some people believe that public schools should concentrate on teaching knowledge and skills, leaving values education to the family and the church. However, most state and district curriculum guidelines call for values education, often as part of the health and guidance curriculum or the social studies curriculum. Guidelines usually call for teaching of "democratic" or "American creed" values (human dignity and the worth of the individual, the Bill of Rights, equality and respect for the rights of all people, etc.). Some also call for teaching of personal and social values (the Golden Rule, honesty, caring about others). The latter values have been receiving increasing emphasis lately, in part because they are involved in preparing students to engage in cooperative learning methods and in part because they are featured in feminist theorizing that calls for balancing an emphasis on justice with an emphasis on caring. Four major instructional approaches to values education are values inculcation, values clarification, values analysis, and Kohlberg's "Just Community" approach.

values inculcation

Values inculcation approaches attempt to impress on the minds of students a specific set of predetermined values through frequent and emphatic repetition and reinforcement of these values. It has been advocated recently under the title of **character education,** *a general term for efforts to instill moral values and related character traits and habits by teaching them directly as part of the school curriculum.* Inculcation approaches emphasize obedience, honesty, respect, cour-

tesy, and promptness, reinforced by academic standards and discipline codes, daily flag salutes, and frequent assemblies and recognition programs. Proponents argue that inculcation is a natural, necessary, and inevitable part of schooling, expected by the public and needed to ensure that students understand and internalize key values (Benninga, 1991; Lickona, 1991; Ryan & McLean, 1987; Vitz, 1990; Wynne, 1982).

Not enough research has been done to allow for an empirical evaluation of the values inculcation or character education approach. However, it has been criticized as contrary to most of the available research on moral development and behavior (Nucci, 1989; Scott, 1991) and as based on the untenable assumptions that direct instruction can effectively shape conduct and that lists of virtues can be adequate guides to behavior (Lockwood, 1991; Wainryb & Turiel, 1993). The indoctrinative methods emphasized in the approach do appear to conflict with many of the values traditionally stressed in moral education programs. Even so, several leading social educators have noted that some use of indoctrinative methods (e.g., stories and historical accounts exemplifying what are seen as basic American values and behaviors, active teacher advocacy, and reward of student expression and behavior consistent with these values) may be needed as part of a broader program of moral or values education, if instilling in youth a basic commitment to democratic values is taken seriously as a goal (Leming, 1985; Shaver & Strong, 1982; Stanley, 1981).

values clarification

The **values clarification** approach involves *engaging students in examining their attitudes,* *beliefs, and values and in the process of prizing, choosing, and acting in accordance with those values* (Raths, Harmin, & Simon, 1978). Its authors believe that we must allow students to choose values freely if we expect them to act on them consistently, so their approach concentrates on encouraging students to identify and clarify their own values rather than on trying to promote particular values as preferable to others. It follows a seven-step process of identifying and clarifying personal values:

1. choosing freely or making independent choices
2. choosing from among alternatives after considering a range of available choices
3. choosing after thoughtful consideration of the likely consequences of each alternative
4. cherishing and being happy with the choice
5. being willing to affirm the choice publicly
6. acting in a manner that is consistent with a freely chosen value
7. repeatedly acting in this manner as part of what becomes a life pattern

The approach involves students in diverse activities such as reflective thinking about the consequences of actions, searching for consistency between feelings and actions, and analyzing their lifestyles for hidden value meanings. Teachers limit themselves to attempts to clarify the different positions that one could take on an issue and the underlying values associated with these positions, without pushing the students toward any particular decision. Students are urged to clarify their values and use them consistently as a basis for decision making, but nothing is said about making sure that personal values and decisions are consistent with American creed values or other core values treated as basic.

Research data on the values clarification approach have been consistently negative, indicating its failure to affect measures of students' values or attitudes. The approach has also been criticized for an inadequate definitional and theoretical base, an implicit ethical relativism, and a seemingly haphazard conception and application of curricular interventions (Lockwood, 1978; Scott, 1991; Leming, 1985).

values analysis

The **values analysis** approach *uses inquiry, decision making, and thinking skills to investigate and analyze value conflicts* (Banks, 1985; Fraenkel, 1980; Metcalf, 1971; Shaver & Strong, 1982). As opposed to either inculcating values or merely clarifying them, it calls for analyzing values issues and making judgments in accordance with values criteria and evidence. There is assessment of the adequacy of value decisions and of the process used to make those decisions.

The values analysis approach attempts to develop in students the ability to make rationally and logically defensible moral judgments by teaching them processes of reasoning about moral or value questions: carefully identify the issue or describe the problem, identify relevant facts and potential solutions, project the probable consequences of adopting alternative solutions, arrive at a value decision, and then test and justify the decision. Justification is accomplished by showing that the value decision meets four tests: role exchange (the student would be willing to exchange positions with the least advantaged person in the agreement); universal consequences (acceptable consequences would ensue if everyone followed the same course of action); new cases (acceptable consequences would follow if the decision were applied to similar new situations); and subsumption (the justifying principle is shown to be an application of a higher principle that has already been justified).

The values analysis approach has not yet been subjected to sufficient research to allow empirical assessment of its effectiveness. However, it is widely advocated for use in social studies classes because it has good content validity for social studies and focuses on analysis of policy issues, legal cases, and other authentic applications of critical thinking to social and civic values.

Kohlberg's "Just Community" approach

Early applications of Kohlberg's ideas to educational programs involved attempts to increase children's moral judgment levels by involving them in discussions of moral dilemmas. These programs often succeeded in raising children's moral judgment levels, especially when moral dilemma discussions were supplemented by exercises in empathy training, peer counseling, role playing, listening, and communication (Damon & Killen, 1982). Research on the programs suggested that moral discussions were most successful when focused on issues of justice and human welfare, integrated within the curriculum rather than treated as a separate program or unit, and structured to promote respectful debate among the students themselves rather than depending too heavily on the teacher to confront students with levels of moral thinking that contrasted with their own (Nucci, 1987).

Despite its modest successes, the moral reasoning approach to moral education was criti-cized for using moral dilemmas that were too far removed from most students' experiences and for focusing too exclusively on the cognitive aspects of values without enough consideration of their affective and behavioral aspects (Fraenkel, 1976; Leming, 1985; Scott, 1991). Kohlberg responded by developing a broader "Just Community" approach that included not only moral dilemma discussions but also opportunities for students in groups to participate in establishing and maintaining democratic systems of governing classrooms (Power, Higgins, & Kohlberg, 1989). The approach emphasized providing opportunities for students to construct moral understandings as members of "just" communities that featured a caring and fair moral environment, interpersonal responsibility, and communal solidarity. The original just communities were school-within-a-school alternative programs in high schools in which about 100 students and their teachers operated as a participatory democracy. Each student and teacher had one vote in setting and enforcing community rules. Key features included advisor groups, community meetings, and a discipline committee.

Each student was assigned to a small group that met weekly with a faculty adviser to get to know one another and discuss school issues that would be raised in later community meetings. In the weekly community meetings, there was discussion and eventual democratic adoption of school rules and behavioral expectations. The emphasis in these meetings was on sustained discussion of the moral aspects of each issue and an attempt to forge an ultimate consensus, avoiding premature imposition of majority rule when a minority felt that the majority position was unwise or unfair. The discipline committee considered what would be fair and appropriate actions to take when rules were violated.

implications for teachers
values education

After reviewing research on values education, Leming (1985) found at least potential value in all of the approaches except for values clarification. He suggested that a complete program of values education would blend elements of values inculcation, moral reasoning, and value analysis with community involvement and social action activities, cooperative learning activities, and infusion of democratic content and practices throughout the curriculum and the school environment. **Consensus seems to be developing around the idea of teaching students to make value-related decisions that are consistent with core values, especially those expressed in the nation's basic social contracts.** Students would be encouraged to consider not just facts but values when making decisions, to predict the probable consequences of their decisions, and to justify the decisions in terms of generalizable moral values, not just narrower self-interests. These elements would be included not only in direct teaching about values but in activities involving role play and simulation, decision making, and discussion of controversial issues.

the child development project

Many of these features are incorporated into the Child Development Project (CDP) that has been designed to create a caring community within each school and classroom (Battistich et al., 1991; Schaps & Solomon, 1990). The CDP classroom contains three major elements that work together to foster prosocial development: cooperative learning, developmental discipline, and a literature-based approach to reading instruction.

The cooperative learning component emphasizes peer collaboration and adult guidance. Students collaborate with peers in work-ing toward group goals on tasks that feature division of labor and mutual helping. Teachers facilitate the process by acting as values advocates, pointing out the importance of helpfulness, fairness, concern and respect for others, and responsibility for accepting one's fair share and doing one's best. Developmental discipline is an approach to classroom management that encourages students to take an active role in classroom governance by participating in the development of classroom rules and meeting to work collaboratively with the teacher to develop solutions to discipline problems. Caring, respectfulness, and shared values, rather than imposition of authority or power, are emphasized in these interactions. The literature-based reading program is designed to develop children's understanding of how prosocial values play out in daily life by providing them with opportunities to read and discuss selections that illustrate how values such as fairness or kindness make the world a better place. Many selections reveal the inner lives of people from other cultures, ages, or circumstances as they deal with universal issues and concerns. These readings encourage children to empathize with people who are both like them and not like them, as well as to see the commonalities that underlie diversity.

Evaluation of CDP indicated that it produced a broad range of positive effects by improving students' social competence, interpersonal understanding and behavior, and endorsement of democratic values. It also increased students' reading comprehension and reduced their reporting of loneliness or social anxiety at school. For more details about moral education approaches, see Berkowitz and Oser (1985), Chazan (1985), Kurtines and Gerwirtz (1991), Nucci (1989), or the various issues of the *Journal of Moral Education.*

summary

Children's social and moral development reflects interactions among characteristics present at birth, age-linked universal social experiences, and the influences of the particular social context in which the child develops. Characteristics present at birth create social predispositions, but these interact with environmental influences, particularly socializing influences from significant others. Most children strive to fulfill gender roles and accomplish developmental tasks suited to their ages. In addition, they attempt to cope with the age-linked crises that define the stages described by Erikson. Successful accommodation to these stages leads to optimal progression toward mature functioning, whereas failure leads to fixation or distortion. The latter can be seen among children who develop inhibitions or self-concept problems and adolescents who remain at immature identity or intimacy statuses while their peers progress toward more mature statuses. Erikson's theory needs adaptation to fit the developmental experiences of women, especially the recognition that women are likely to resolve intimacy issues prior to or in conjunction with their resolution of identity issues.

Contextual influences on development include family influences, peer group influences, and broader societal or subcultural influences. Family influences are summarized in the parenting dimensions of love-hostility and permissiveness-restrictiveness considered in conjunction with Baumrind's distinction between authoritarian and authoritative parenting styles. Both social and moral development are fostered by parenting and teaching that combines acceptance and support, a balance between permissiveness and restrictiveness that places limits on the child but also provides age-appropriate opportunities for independent decision making and responsibility, and a style of socializing that articulates prosocial values and explains their underlying rationales.

Children's peer relationships become increasingly intimate and important to them as they develop into and through adolescence, although the preadolescent emphasis on peer conformity later gives way to an emphasis on intimacy and autonomy. Socially accepted students tend to be at ease and skillful in dealing with peers, but socially isolated students tend to lack these characteristics and socially rejected students additionally tend to drive peers away with inconsiderate or hostile behavior. Teachers can help students improve their peer relationships by finding ways for them to display their positive qualities, involving them in productive collaborative pair or small-group activities, and working to increase their social understanding and develop their social skills.

Students are also affected by societal and subcultural influences, some of which conflict with values emphasized at school (e.g., violence on the streets and in the media). Recent social changes have disrupted traditional gender roles and family living patterns, and students often come from diverse socioeconomic and cultural backgrounds. Nevertheless, all students appear to need a school context that is friendly and supportive of their individuality and heritage, holds positive expectations for their intellectual and personal development, and follows through by providing them with whatever resources and instruction are required to enable them to succeed.

Building on early work by Piaget, Kohlberg identified six stages in the development of moral judgment and reasoning. His work has since been criticized and elaborated in several respects, most notably by Gilligan and other feminists who have noted that it emphasizes the morality of justice that reflects the masculine experience. They have called for an equal emphasis on the morality of caring that better reflects the feminine experience. Teachers can help their students progress to higher stages of moral reasoning by discussing moral issues with them and having them discuss such issues with one another, placing emphasis not just on what ought to be done but on the moral concepts and principles that provide the rationales for such conclusions. A more complete program of values or moral education would include elements of values inculcation, values analysis, and cooperative involvement in school service and government activities.

questions for reflection

1. If children are born with certain biological predispositions (e.g., high arousal levels), do environmental influences make much difference in determining how they will develop? Why or why not?

2. Discuss Erikson's stages of industry versus inferiority and identity versus identity confusion. How can teachers help students adjust to these stages?

3. The authors present eleven adult attributes that are associated with optimal development in children. Reexamine these and identify the three or four most important. Why do you feel this way? Compare your list with the list of another student and discuss the differences between them.

4. How can teachers deal with students' feelings of inferiority, shame, guilt, or low self-esteem?

5. School success is basic to the industry versus inferiority stage and to self-concept generally. What can you do to help students who overreact to school failures by becoming depressed or withdrawn? What about students who are consistently successful but are becoming egotistical about it?

6. If you were dealing with a student who was not obeying classroom rules, would the student's level of moral judgment make any difference in how you reacted? Explain.

7. Should teachers respond differently to the same misbehavior if the culprits differ significantly in level of moral development? What effect might this have on other students in the room?

8. Gender roles often get in the way of successful instruction. What might you do when certain boys are unresponsive to literature or poetry lessons, or when certain girls are unresponsive to math or science lessons?

9. What age cohort do you identify with? What formative experiences shaped the development of your age cohort, and how might this affect your interactions with students who represent subsequent cohorts?

10. Developmental theories imply that a permanently foreclosed identity is a form of stunted growth—that foreclosed adolescents will benefit from experiencing crises and ultimately attaining an achieved identity status. However, foreclosed adolescents' parents may be delighted with their offsprings' endorsement of their values. Should teachers seek to "open up" these foreclosed adolescents, even though this may precipitate crises in the adolescents and hostile reactions in the parents?

11. How might a teacher respond to parents who ask to be kept closely informed about their child's behavior at school and pledge to cooperate by seeing that the child gets "a good whipping" if misbehavior is reported?

12. Although younger children often socialize freely, adolescents usually gravitate toward peers who are similar to themselves in racial/ethnic background and socioeconomic status. To what extent, and in what ways, should schools attempt to counter these tendencies toward voluntary social segregation?

13. Teachers' attempts to improve the peer relationships of isolated or rejected students can backfire if they are too direct or intrusive. What types of interventions are likely to be helpful in these situations, and what types are not likely to be helpful?

14. Suppose that teachers discover that certain students are drifting into delinquent behavior patterns, in part because their parents don't monitor their activities. Which interventions might be helpful in these situations? Which might be unhelpful?

15. What can teachers do to prevent development of the kinds of secondary cultural differences and oppositional peer cultures described by Ogbu? How might they respond in schools where these problems have already developed?

16. How can teachers infuse concerns about caring and about justice into the cultures they create in their classrooms?

cases to consider

Active Alice Alice Plice is a very active sixth grader—to put it nicely. She is always first in line because of her speed and willingness to shove, she has something to say about everything, and hers is the only voice that distinguishes itself from the playground hubbub. Despite her "gusto" for living, she drives people away from her and is quite lonely. Her teacher plans to try to improve her peer relationships. One way is to frequently involve Alice in cooperative group work with the same four peers. What other strategies might be used?

Dependent Dan Dan behaves anxiously in Mrs. Wang's seventh grade English class. He watches her intently and constantly nods his head in agreement as she talks. He double-checks every assignment with her, asking if he is proceeding correctly. Dan is an attractive boy with an IQ of 130. Mrs. Wang knows of no reason for his anxiety, dependency, or desperate need for her approval. In what ways could Mrs. Wang approach the problem? What types of tasks should she assign him, and how should she interact with him?

Quick Hands Jan Jan, a third grader from an affluent home, has started to "borrow" classroom supplies like scissors and jars of paste. Mrs. Dolezal notices one of her rulers sticking out of Jan's open bag. Looking more closely, she sees other classroom supplies in the bag. During recess, she asks Jan to stay in to discuss the problem. What should she say or ask Jan? Write three or four responses that Jan might make, reflecting different stages of development. How should Mrs. Dolezal respond to Jan if she determines that Jan is at a preoperational stage of development versus a concrete operational stage of development?

Sticky Hands Luke Luke, a tenth grader from an affluent home, has started to "borrow" various supplies, including school property as well as items belonging to other students. During recess he pilfers supplies from the chemistry room or the industrial education room if they are left unattended. One day Mr. Schmidt, who teaches industrial education, catches Luke putting several cans of enamel into his gym bag. This is the first time he has proof of that Luke has been taking materials. What should he say to Luke? How should Luke be treated in comparison to Jan, the third grader?

Invidious social comparisons: life in the fast lane Jim Slink is a sophomore at Eastside High School. Jim has always been a talented student who progressed rapidly in every school subject, but this year, he is doing poorly in an honors physics class composed mostly of seniors. Partly because of his concern about his poor progress in physics, his grades in other subjects are beginning to suffer as well. One day he stays after school to discuss his problems with his physics teacher. Jim discloses, "I've never been in a class like this before. Everybody else picks up the material much more quickly than I can. The other day three-fourths of them had finished the experiment before I even figured out what to do." If you were the teacher, what could you do to help Jim view himself realistically but positively?

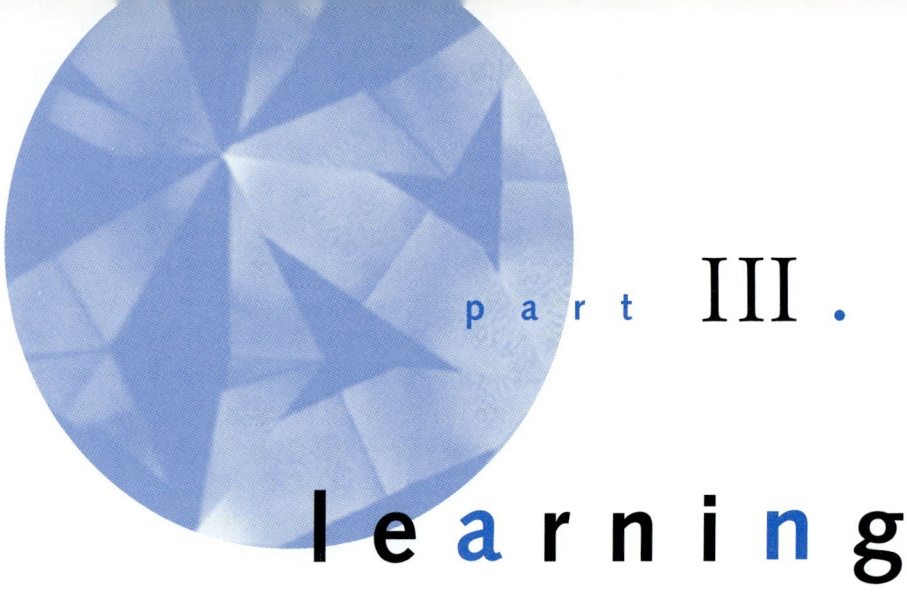

part III.

learning

Mr. Roat, *an algebra teacher, introduces each new equation clearly and demonstrates its application by working out problems on the board, and assigns more problems as homework. Students learn to solve equations with speed and accuracy; yet, their performance breaks down with word problems. Many students are completely confused or only guess. Very few think about the problem, formulate it in algebraic terms, and then solve it correctly. Why might this be?*

Ms. Brinks, *a science teacher, was pleased when her students did well on a unit test on force, gravity, and vectors. Yet they performed poorly on the final exam later. She had asked, "If you released a 2,000 pound safe and a melon at the same time from the top of the school, which would hit the ground first?" She had expected that nearly every-*

one would remember the basic principles that the two objects would hit the ground simultaneously. Few did. What had happened to that clear understanding "displayed" on the unit test?

Mrs. Abbott and Mrs. Costello *both teach American history. They use the same texts to cover the same material with similar students. Mrs. Abbott gives weekly quizzes, a midterm, and a final on the second half of the course, whereas Mrs. Costello grades according to a comprehensive final exam and a research paper on an important historical figure. Given these differences in grading, what differences would you expect in (1) amount and distribution of student study time, (2) students' attitudes toward history and interest in further study of it, and (3) how much students will remember about American history in several years?*

These vignettes illustrate just a few of the many principles of human learning discussed in the next four chapters. Mr. Roat's problem illustrates the need for curriculum alignment: logical relationships between the objectives of instruction, the content taught, the teaching methods and assignments, and the methods used to assess mastery. Mr. Roat never modeled the process of applying knowledge about equations to the solution of practical problems or gave his students sufficient practice in applications.

Mrs. Abbott and Mrs. Costello illustrate the principle that differences in assignments and assessment procedures produce differences in study patterns and in what students learn. Mrs. Abbott's students are likely to retain most of the main ideas taught in the course, because they will both study small subsets of the material for quizzes and review larger subsets for the exams. In contrast, Mrs. Costello's students probably will do little studying early on, cram for the final, and then forget most of the material. However, unlike Mrs. Abbott's class, they will learn a great deal about the topic of their term papers, gain practice in research skills, and learn to integrate information from various sources.

Teachers must be prepared to instruct their students personally rather than depending just on texts to do so, with an understanding of student learning processes. Many of the most exciting recent developments in educational psychology have advanced our knowledge about learning, and this section provides the foundation for the following section on instructional applications. Chapter 5 defines learning, identifies different types of learning and the forms of instruction associated with them, and illustrates how to establish objectives and plan instruction. The next three chapters review the theory and research behind three major paradigms of human learning—the behavioristic tradition; Bandura's social cognition theory; and contemporary applications.

Chapter 7 discusses views of learning as the construction of knowledge. Constructivists view teaching not as behavioral shaping but as assisting learners to construct new understandings. They emphasize the cognitive aspects of learning, especially the learner's own active attempts to make sense of new information and interpret it within previously developed schemes. Chapter 8 focuses on the cognitive or information processing aspects of learning and memory. It describes the findings of research on how information is remembered, coded, stored, and later retrieved, as well as the limits of human attention. Information-processing theorists stress the need to teach learners to process information in active ways by making rote learning more meaningful and making meaningful learning more systematic.

introduction to the psychology of learning

objectives

When you have mastered the material in this chapter you will be able to

1. Define learning as a covert event and distinguish it from observable changes in performance
2. Distinguish different qualitative characteristics of learning (propositional/procedural, intentional/incidental, rote/meaningful, and reception/discovery) and describe how these are used in planning instruction
3. Classify different learning objectives according to Bloom's taxonomy
4. Classify different types of learning according to the Gagné and Briggs typology
5. State the different learning conditions required to accomplish different types of learning objectives
6. Formulate learning objectives that operationalize curricular goals accurately and function as effective guides to the planning of instruction, activities, and evaluation
7. Assess sets of learning objectives for completeness and balance among the types and levels of learning addressed

definition of learning

This is the first of four chapters on the psychology of learning. In this chapter we will define learning, identify different types of learning, and show how this information is used to establish learning objectives.

Learning has been defined as *"the process of acquiring relatively permanent change in understanding, attitude, knowledge, information, ability, and skill through experience"* (Wittrock, 1977, p. ix). Learning is an internal, cognitive event. It creates the potential for changes in obeservable behavior, but the action potential acquired through learning is not the same as its application in observable performance. Furthermore, relationships between prior learning and subsequent performance are imperfect. The absence of a particular behavior does not mean that the person does not know anything about it, and the disappearance of a behavior observed in the past does not mean that the ability to perform it has been lost.

Learning is not the same as *thinking,* although these two processes are mutually supportive. **Thinking** refers to *the use of cognitive skills such as posing and answering questions, searching memory, processing information, or evaluating potential solutions to problems.* Thinking can produce learning, either when cognitive skills are used to process new input or when reflection on prior experiences yields new insights. Both kinds of learning are important, which is why we define learning as change induced through experience (including inner reflection) rather than defining it more restrictively as change induced through encounters with the external environment. Much of our learning, especially as we get older, occurs through either reflecting on past experiences or manipulating abstract concepts rather than through accommodations to new concrete experiences.

In summary, learning is a relatively permanent change in capacity for performance, acquired through experience. The experience may involve overt interaction with the external environment, but it may also involve (and sometimes will be confined to) covert cognitive processes.

qualitative distinctions

No single theory or brief list of principles fits all learning situations equally well. You will need to recognize the different kinds of learning that are called for by different instructional objectives, so that you can plan appropriate strategies for accomplishing them. We will present several qualitative distinctions and typologies that have proven useful for conceptualizing learning and instruction.

"knowledge that" versus "knowledge how"

Propositional, declarative, or theoretical knowledge is "knowledge that"—*knowledge stored in the form of verbal propositions indicating that something is the case.* It is intellectual knowledge of facts, concepts, and generalizations. **Procedural** or practical knowledge is "knowledge how"—*knowledge about how to perform tasks and solve problems.* Ideally, one possesses both forms of knowledge and can integrate them in appropriate application contexts. Propositional knowledge without corresponding procedural knowledge is inert—merely verbal knowledge that is not accessible when it would be useful for application. Procedural knowledge without corresponding propositional knowledge is inflexible—a behavioral routine mastered rotely without consideration of guiding principles, so that the routine cannot be adjusted easily to changing conditions.

One frequent criticism of schooling is that too much of what is taught is confined to inert propositional knowledge that never becomes very useful because students do not get enough opportunities to link it to procedural knowledge developed through applications. For example, if instruction in French focuses on translating text, students may acquire some

ability to read French but remain unable to communicate with French speakers because they never learned to speak French. Concern about such problems has led to the inclusion of laboratory experiences in science and foreign language classes and to greater emphasis on problem solving in mathematics classes.

intentional versus incidental learning

Intentional learning *is consciously goal directed: the person intends to learn certain things and sets out to do so.* **Incidental learning** *occurs without deliberate intention, often when the person is relatively passive, responding to the environment but not actively pursuing specific goals.* For example, you probably have watched hundreds of television dramas dealing with law enforcement, primarily to be entertained rather than to develop knowledge. Yet, in the process you have learned specialized terms used in police stations and courtrooms, and you probably could read prisoners their rights or swear in witnesses using what you remember from seeing these activities modeled by actors.

When we are actively seeking to learn, our attention focuses on the material to be learned intentionally. This is why it is important for teachers to establish clear goals to guide their instructional planning and to communicate these goals to students. Some incidental learning occurs too, however, even in highly goal-focused classrooms. For example, even while concentrating on intentional learning of course content, students incidentally learn a great deal about the mannerisms and personal attributes of their teachers.

rote versus meaningful learning

The rote/meaningful dimension of learning refers to the learners' approach to learning tasks.

To the extent that they merely try to memorize content without relating it to their existing knowledge, they are engaging in **rote learning**—*memorizing content without elaborating on it, relating it to existing knowledge, or making other attempts to understand its meanings and implications.* To the extent that they try to relate the new information to what they already know and thereby make sense of it, they are engaging in **meaningful learning**—*constructing coherent understandings of content rather than merely memorizing it.* Meaningful learning is retained longer than rote learning (material memorized for a test through cramming is soon forgotten). It also is much more efficient because a few general principles can accommodate a great many specific applications. Consequently, it is important for teachers to focus their instruction on meaningful content (networks of connected ideas rather than parades of disconnected facts) and teach their students strategies for engaging in meaningful learning (e.g., summarizing in their own words, testing themselves to see if they have accomplished the learning goals).

reception versus discovery learning

The reception/discovery dimension refers to the means by which the knowledge is made available to learners. **Reception learning** is *learning in which knowledge is presented in its final form, typically through expository instruction that states the information and then elaborates and provides examples.* **Discovery learning** is *learning in which students are exposed to experiences and guidance designed to lead them to discover the target concept or principle.* Discovery learning involves instruction in the sense that a planned series of questions or experiences is used to guide the learners toward the key insight. However, the instructor does not present this idea in its final form, except perhaps to summarize and elaborate on it after the learners have discovered it for themselves. Like the rote versus meaningful distinction, the reception versus discovery distinction refers to a continuous dimension. Combination forms involving varying degrees of reception and discovery learning occur in between the extremes of pure reception learning and pure discovery learning. Certain educational philosophies value discovery learning and disparage reception learning, but each type has a place in a well-rounded program.

David Ausubel has shown that discovery learning is not necessarily superior to reception learning (Ausubel & Robinson, 1969). Discovery learning is active learning that is likely to produce long-lasting, meaningful knowledge when successful. However, it is time consuming and can become confusing or frustrating if not handled carefully. Teaching through discovery learning requires moving students through well-planned series of structured experiences, not just exposing them to content in some haphazard way and hoping that they will discover the target learning.

Reception learning from expository lectures or demonstrations is often stereotyped as producing only parrot-like repetition or rote memorization of isolated facts. If designed to produce meaningful reception learning, however, expository teaching can be an efficient method of instruction. It is especially useful for conveying well-organized bodies of knowledge, so it is the primary method of instruction used with students who have mastered basic tool skills (partly through teacher lectures but mostly through texts). Expository instruction and reception learning can be ineffective, of course, if addressed to inappropriate content (isolated facts without general organizing principles) or if overused so that students acquire "knowledge that" but not "knowledge how."

table 5.1 outline of Bloom's taxonomy of educational objectives in the cognitive domain

CATEGORY	GENERAL DESCRIPTION OF CATEGORY	ILLUSTRATIVE ITEMS
I. Knowledge (a) of *Specifics* (terminology, facts) (b) of *Ways and Means of Dealing with Specifics* (conventions, classifications, criteria, methodology) (c) of *Universals and Abstractions* (principles, generalizations, theories)	*Recall* of specifics and universals, methods and processes, pattern, structure of setting. Knowledge objectives emphasize most the psychological processes of *remembering*.	About what proportion of the population of Canada is living in cities? 1. 10% 2. 20% 3. 40% 4. 50% 5. 60% _____ (Knowledge of specific fact) The volume of a given mass of gas varies directly as the _____ and inversely as the _____. 1. pressure and temperature 2. temperature and pressure 3. atomic weight and pressure 4. temperature and atomic weight (knowledge of principles and generalizations)
II. Comprehension (a) Translation (b) Interpretation (c) Extrapolation	Lowest level of understanding of what is communicated. Can use idea being communicated without necessarily being able to relate it to other ideas or see all its implications.	Four less than three times a certain number equals eight. In algebra this may be expressed as: 1. $4 - 3X = 8$ 3. $3X - 4 = 8$ 2. $4X - 3 = 8$ 4. $4 + 3X = 8$ (Translation)
III. Application	The use of abstractions in particular and concrete situations.	Two basic laws governing an electrical circuit are: Voltage = (Current) X (Resistance) Power = (Voltage) X (Current) If an electric iron develops greater resistance (rust, etc.) its power will: 1. increase 2. remain the same 3. decrease
IV. Analysis (a) of *Elements* (b) of *Relationships* (c) of *Organizational Principles*	Breakdown of a communication into its constituent parts, such that relative hierarchy of ideas is made clearer and/or the relations between the ideas expressed are made clear.	The given figure represents a hoop of 28 in. diameter. If the hoop is rolling without slipping in the indicated direction, how many inches has point A moved horizontally when the hoop has finished half a turn? ($\pi = 22/7$) (Analysis of Relationships)*

table 5.1 (*continued*)

CATEGORY	GENERAL DESCRIPTION OF CATEGORY	ILLUSTRATIVE ITEMS
V. Synthesis (a) Production of a unique communication (b) Production of a plan (c) Derivation of a set of abstract relations	Putting together of parts to form a whole: analyzing and combining pieces in such a way as to constitute a pattern or structure not clearly there before.	$\frac{1}{1X2} + \frac{1}{2X3} + \frac{1}{3X4} + \frac{1}{4X5} \cdots \frac{1}{98X99} + \frac{1}{99X100}$ Without adding all items, find the sum of:
VI. Evaluation (a) Judgments in terms of internal criteria (b) Judgments in terms of external evidence	Making judgments about the value of material and methods for given purposes. Judging extent to which material and methods satisfy given criteria.	The ability to indicate logical fallacies in arguments (Internal Evidence) Ability to compare a work with highest known standards in its field (External Criteria)

*Illustrative items from S. Avital and S. Shettleworth, *Mathematics Learning: Some Ideas for the Teacher* (Bulletin No. 3) (Toronto: Ontario Institute for Studies in Education. 1968).
SOURCE: Adapted from B.S. Bloom (ed.), *Taxonomy of Educational Objectives: Cognitive Domain, Book 1*, by Benjamin Bloom et al. Copyright © by Longman Publishers. Reprinted by permission of Longman Publishers USA.

learning typologies

Learning theorists have developed typologies that distinguish types of learning according to differences in what is being learned. Like the qualitative distinctions described previously, these typologies are helpful as organizers for instructional planning. Two of the best known are the taxonomy of cognitive objectives published by Bloom et al. (1956) and the learning typology published by Gagné and Briggs (1979; see also Gagné, Briggs, & Wager,1988).

Bloom's taxonomy

Recognizing the potential value of a classification scheme that would identify different learning objectives using standardized terms, a group of experts surveyed taxonomies in the early 1950s and sought to develop a common scheme. The most influential result of their work was a taxonomy of educational objectives in the cognitive domain (Bloom et al., 1956), which is often called "Bloom's taxonomy" for short. Other taxonomies were published later for objectives in the affective (Krathwohl, Bloom, & Masia, 1964) and psychomotor (Harrow, 1972) domains.

The six major categories in Bloom's taxonomy are shown in Table 5.1 (there are numerous subcategories). Educators find this taxonomy useful because it includes most of the goals stressed by schools and describes them in commonly used language. However, mathematics and science teachers may prefer the term "problem solving" to the term "analysis," which is used more in the humanities.

Like most taxonomies, this one can be criticized on several grounds. First, the boundary between comprehension and application is fuzzy; some knowledge interpretation and extrapolation tasks that the taxonomy classifies as comprehension tasks could just as easily be classified as application tasks (Ausubel & Robinson, 1969). Second, the sequencing of categories from low to high in cognitive level has been questioned on the basis of both logical considerations (Furst, 1981) and empirical data (Kunen, Cohen, & Solman, 1981; Seddon, 1978). Many believe that synthesis, rather than evaluation, should be placed at the highest level, because it requires more complete and integrated knowledge. Third, the notion of cognitive level is sometimes confused with the notion of difficulty level, but these concepts are independent. A "low-level" knowledge item (name Henry VIII's fourth wife) is extremely difficult if you don't know the answer, and yet you may be able to respond to a "high-level" task (evaluate the theory that all wars ultimately result from economic causes) with some success even if you have little organized knowledge about the topic.

Another concern is that Bloom's taxonomy (and any other taxonomy that features levels arranged into a hierarchy) misleadingly implies a clear separation of lower-level from higher-level content and suggests that one must proceed linearly from lower to higher levels when teaching content. Researchers have found that working on presumably lower-level comprehension or application tasks actually involves abstracting, making inferences, and engaging in other forms of higher-level thinking. Similarly, higher-level thinking and problem solving require the use of lower-level knowledge and skills. Therefore, rather than have students practice low-level skills in isolation and only gradually begin to combine them and apply them to higher-level tasks,

teachers should embed skills practice within a context of meaningful application right from the beginning. That is, students should learn to read, not just discriminate letters (Anderson et al., 1985), should learn to use mathematics to solve problems, not just to compute (Fennema, Carpenter, & Peterson, 1989), and so on.

Despite these imperfections, Bloom's taxonomy is a useful tool for planning or assessing instruction, a tool that probably should be used more often than it is. Implicitly, at least, we as a society want the school curriculum taught so that effective learning occurs at all levels in the taxonomy. Yet, critical analyses typically reveal that very high percentages of textbook content, practice exercises, classroom activities, and test items focus on the knowledge and comprehension levels, with little attention to higher levels (Freeman et al., 1983; Goodlad, 1984). The lesson here is obvious: to the extent that we expect students to master learning objectives that go beyond the knowledge and comprehension levels, we will need to provide instruction and application opportunities geared to these higher cognitive levels, and to assess learning accordingly.

the Gagné and Briggs typology

Gagné and Briggs (1979) identified five types of learning:

1. Attitudes: Internal states that influence personal action choices.
2. Motor skills: Organized muscle movements used to accomplish purposeful actions.
3. Information: Facts and organized knowledge about the world stored in memory.
4. Intellectual skills: Skills that permit learners to carry out symbol-based procedures (discriminations, concrete concepts, defined concepts, rules, and higher-order rules).

table 5.2 **Gagné & Briggs's Typology, using standard verbs to describe human capabilities, with examples of phrases incorporating action verbs**

CAPABILITY	CAPABILITY VERB	EXAMPLE (ACTION VERB IN ITALICS)
Intellectual skill Discrimination	DISCRIMINATES	Discriminates by *matching* French sounds of "u" and "ou"
Concrete concepts	IDENTIFIES	*Identifies* by *naming* the root, leaf, and stem of representative plants
Defined concept	CLASSIFIES	Classifies, by using a *definition,* the concept "family"
Rule	DEMONSTRATES	Demonstrates by *solving* verbally stated examples, the addition of positive and negative numbers
Higher-order rule (problem solving)	GENERATES	Generates by *synthesizing* applicable rules a paragraph describing a person's actions in a situation of fear
Cognitive strategy	ORIGINATES	Originates a solution to the reduction of air pollution by *applying model* of gaseous diffusion
Information	STATES	States orally the major issues in the presidential campaign of 1932
Motor skill	EXECUTES	Executes *backing* a car into a driveway
Attitude	CHOOSES	Chooses *playing golf* as a leisure activity

SOURCE: *Principles of Instructional Design,* second edition, by Robert Gagné and Leslie Briggs. Copyright © 1979; Holt, Rinehart & Winston. Reprinted by permission.

5. Cognitive strategies: Strategies that learners bring to bear on their own cognitive processing in order to control their learning or develop solutions to problems.

Table 5.2 shows examples of these five capabilities, as well as action verbs that apply when they are translated into performance.

Like the Bloom taxonomy, the Gagné and Briggs typology defines several categories of learning and is useful in planning or assessing instruction. Although there is some overlap, the two systems are largely complementary. The Gagné and Briggs system distinguishes among several types of learning that are included within the comprehension and application levels of the Bloom system, but the highest levels of the Bloom system are not addressed by Gagné and Briggs. Consequently, analyses of instruction that draw on both systems are likely to be more complete than analyses that use only one.

conditions of learning

Gagné and Briggs (1979) also offered guidelines about the different types of instruction that each type of learning requires. They spoke of internal and external *conditions of learning* that must be established to enable learning to occur. Internal conditions refer to events occurring within the learner, especially recall and activation of previous learning that the new learning must build on. External conditions refer to events in the environment, particularly instruction that activates and supports learning processes. Conditions of learning differ for each type of learning.

attitude learning

Attitudes are acquired primarily through exposure to respected *models* who exhibit the attitudes, rather than through more typical instruction. However, attitudes can be *stimulated through persuasive communication* (if the learner accepts the message) and can be *conditioned through experience* (people who enjoy early success at playing musical instruments or solving mathematical problems may believe that they have talent for these activities and come to enjoy them, but others who encounter early frustration may conclude that they lack talent and come to dislike them).

Clearly, we cannot teach an attitude the way we would teach the concept of a triangle. We can try to stimulate attitudes indirectly through modeling, persuasion, or manipulation of incentives, but we cannot produce them directly through instruction because they include elements of emotional involvement and personal commitment that can come only from the learners themselves. Because of these important qualitative differences between attitude learning and other forms of learning, most of what we have to say about socializing students' attitudes will appear in sections on classroom management and student motivation rather than in sections on learning and instruction.

motor learning

Motor skills are a primary focus of some classes (art, music, physical education, machine shop), and they play a role in certain academic activities (handwriting, illustrating, handling laboratory equipment). Learners develop some motor skills intuitively through experience and sustain them in the form of what Piaget (1983) called sensorimotor schemes. However, motor learning is more efficient if learners are provided with *modeling* that they can imitate, *verbal instructions* and *visual imagery* that they can use to guide their performance, and opportunities for *practice with corrective feedback.*

Practice is critical to the development and maintenance of motor skills (Newell, 1991). Although it is true that a skill (such as roller skating) that is practiced until it is thoroughly mastered will be retained indefinitely and can be recovered to some degree with relative ease when it has not been used in years, it is also true that continuous practice is needed to maintain motor skills at high levels of proficiency. That is why professional musicians, dancers, and athletes practice continually, with attention to fundamentals as well as to higher-level accomplishments.

To be useful to learners, practice must provide *feedback.* If you were to practice drawing six-inch lines with a pencil, you would get better at it and soon reach your maximum performance level if each attempt yielded feedback indicating that the line was too short, just right, or too long. Without such feedback, however, you could continue to draw lines all day without showing consistent improvement.

To the extent that learners can monitor their motor performances and assess outcomes accurately, they can generate their own feedback through knowledge of results. Some motor skill feedback is internal (Adams, 1977). Learners can learn to recognize and benefit from physical sensations, body images, and other forms of psychomotor feedback. Tennis players, for example, can learn to recognize when they are executing a stroke successfully so as to meet the ball with the "sweet spot" of the racquet. In addition to this internal feedback, motor skill performance produces external feedback in the form of results that learners can observe for themselves (the flight of the ball as it leaves the racquet). External feedback can also be supplied through opportunities to observe videotapes of performance, to get feedback from an instructor, or to compare products with ideal examples (e.g., to compare a page of printing or a product produced in the wood shop with a model).

Verbal instruction can assist motor performance, as the popularity and usefulness of how-to books attest. However, verbal instruction does not always communicate the desired motor image. Instructed to "bend your knees and shift weight as you swing," we might bend our knees too far or shift weight too soon. Thus, opportunities to observe models perform motor skills properly are valuable, especially if the models verbalize their thinking as they perform the skill so that learners can monitor the self-talk that guides behavior in addition to observing the behavior itself.

In teaching motor skills, it is important to prevent bad habits from developing. Unless they are taught basic principles and good form, learners may develop skills that are functional to an extent but inefficient or potentially counterproductive. For example, one of the authors learned to skate "the hard way" as a child and did not find out until adulthood (upon receiving instruction) that he could achieve better balance and speed, yet expend less effort, by using good skating form. Many injuries sustained from running or participating in vigorous activities occur because the person unnecessarily stresses some part of the body. Instruction in good form with attention to eliminating bad habits could minimize this problem.

information learning

The learning of verbally encoded information seems straightforward: if a message is clearly formulated, learners can understand it by relat-

ing it to the network of concepts, vocabulary, and verbally articulated experience they have accumulated. However, things are more complicated. First, the message may not be noted. Second, even if registered, the message may not be understood as it was intended by the communicator. Third, its meaning may become transformed over time.

People pick up information every day with relative ease, especially in information-rich environments such as schools. However, teachers need to direct students' attention to the most important information included in the curriculum and help them to assimilate and retain it.

This process begins by cueing student attention to the information, preferably by stimulating their interest or curiosity. It is also important to see that the students can understand the information by relating it to their existing knowledge. If the message contains undefined terms or refers to unfamiliar concepts or events, the students may not be able to understand and retain it as meaningful knowledge (although they may memorize it long enough to regurgitate it on a test). Finally, even if everything is clear and meaningful, there are limits on how much information learners can retain. More information will be remembered when it is presented in an organized fashion (in a sensible sequence, with each segment containing main ideas followed by elaboration or supportive material) and in ways that stimulate students to process it actively and encode it in their own words.

intellectual skill learning

Gagné and Briggs divided intellectual skills into five categories (ordered from simple to complex): discriminations, concrete concepts, defined concepts, rules, and higher-order rules.

Discriminations are capabilities for detecting and responding to differences in physical stimuli. Discrimination learning is especially important in early reading and writing, when students must learn to respond differently to different letters that have similar components (b, d, p, q) and to the capital and lowercase versions of the same letter (P, p). Discrimination learning also assumes importance occasionally at higher grade levels (hearing subtle sound discriminations in foreign languages that are not made in English, noting small but important differences in similar algebraic equations or chemical formulas).

Discriminations are typically taught using the principles of contiguity, feedback, and *repetition*. That is, the stimuli to be compared are presented either simultaneously (two objects, side by side), or when that is not possible, in rapid succession (one sound followed closely by another). This close contiguity between two stimuli facilitates comparison of them. Following presentation of the stimuli, learners are asked to state whether they are the same or different, and their responses are given immediate feedback. Such practice is repeated until the discrimination is mastered.

Concrete concepts are capabilities for recognizing that stimuli belong to a class that shares one or more common attributes (red color, round shape, etc.). Once learners understand the concept of red, for example, they can correctly identify objects as red even though they may differ in size, shape, or function. Gagné and Briggs suggested teaching concrete concepts by presenting a variety of stimuli that all share the defining attributes, and pointing out these attributes to learners. In teaching the concept of "apple," for example, one would present apples or pictures of apples that differed in size, shape, and color, noting that all of these were apples. Then, learners would be asked to discriminate apples from nonapples, beginning with easy discriminations (items that have nothing in common with

apples) and moving gradually toward the most difficult nonexamples (cherries, pears).

Defined concepts are capabilities for demonstrating the meanings of classes of objects, events, or relations. Unlike concrete concepts, which are based on physical attributes that one can point to directly, defined concepts are based on formal definitions (examples: prime number, iambic pentameter, potential energy, adverb). Learners who understand the concept not only can state the definition but can use the term in appropriate contexts with the appropriate meaning (e.g., they can identify iambic pentameter when they see it and can explain why a poem is or is not written in this meter).

Gagné and Briggs suggested teaching defined concepts by stating their definitions and then (as with concrete concepts) presenting examples and nonexamples. These examples and nonexamples usually must be described verbally rather than shown, however, so the meaningfulness of the instruction will depend on learners' familiarity with the vocabulary and concepts used. The terms used to identify defined concepts are often used in everyday language to refer to concrete objects or events. This may make it easier to learn the defined concept (hearing various three-sided objects called "triangles" facilitates understanding of the geometrical definition of a triangle as a three-sided plane figure). However, everyday use of defined concepts also can be confusing; in geometry, a point is a specified location in an abstractly defined space, not a dot made with a pencil or the sharpened end of some object that "comes to a point." Where a term is commonly used with colloquial meanings that differ from what is implied by the defined concept, it will be important to make students aware of this fact. They will need to learn to use defined concepts with precision and to avoid connotations that apply to their colloquial use but not to their formal use.

Rules express classes of relationships among classes of objects or events. Much human activ-

Classroom Realities

Some schools are well equipped in all areas: curriculum materials, laboratory facilities, libraries, as well as athletic and technological facilities. Unfortunately, many schools do not have these advantages.

The population served by some schools is impoverished. Children of poverty often are served by schools that also have limited resources. Differences between rich suburban schools and schools in inner city ghettos are so wide as to make meaningless statements about the quality of education in America.

The presence of security guards and metal detectors is often depersonalizing to students and teachers alike. Unfortunately, in some school situations, these are necessary to be sure that students, faculty, and staff are safe.

Although schools are generally very secure, occasionally violent behavior does occur on the playground. School staffs need to be alert to prevent these problems and to intervene appropriately when they do occur.

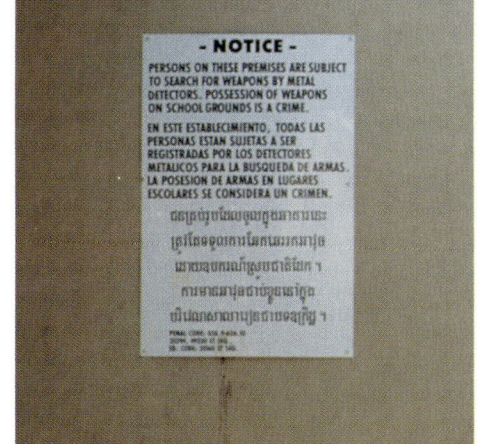

Conflict and violence have always been an issue for young people; however, the easy availability of weapons radically escalates risks that are involved in social conflict.

Some students have to cope with the threat of violence as they go to and return from schools.

Part of the need for gangs is to be seen and heard, and to form a sense of identity. This negative identity often leads to destruction of property and to the defacing of property with graffiti.

Gangs are part of the social culture. Gang membership often involves rituals that bond the individual to the group. Sometimes these are as simple as a tattoo; however, sometimes membership price is excessive, even to the point of requiring members to commit robbery or other crimes.

ity is rule-governed behavior in which general principles are applied to specific situations. We follow the rules of English grammar, for example, when speaking or writing.

We can receive formal instruction in rules and learn to apply them in specific situations. This is the rationale for instructing students in principles of science, mathematics, literary composition, historical analysis, and other academic disciplines. The ability to use defined concepts is one example of rule learning (in this case, the ability to follow a classifying rule). Other rules deal with such relationships as equal to, similar to, greater or less than, or sequential position. As with defined concepts, the ability to state a rule accurately does not necessarily mean that it is understood. Evidence of rule mastery must include demonstrated ability to apply the rule correctly in appropriate contexts.

Rules are usually taught through verbal instruction. Ordinarily this would include a statement of the rule followed by guided practice. Gagné and Briggs (1979) used as an example the rule for pronouncing words that end in a single consonant followed by a final "e." "The teacher may say, 'Notice that the letter *a* has a long sound when followed by a consonant, in a word that ends in *e*. This is true in words that you know like *made, pale, fate*. When the word does not end in *e,* the letter *a* has a short sound, as in *mad, pal, fat*. Now tell me how to pronounce these words which you may not have seen before: *dade, pate, kale'* " (pp. 68-69). The information given prior to asking students to pronounce these words helps them to remember concepts related to the rule (consonant, short and long sounds) and to arrange these related concepts in appropriate order (consonants followed by a final "e" versus consonants not followed by the final "e").

Higher-order rules are invented by learners in order to solve problems that are new to them. Once they invent a rule, they can store it in

memory and use it later to solve other problems. Higher-order rules are constructed by combining two or more simpler rules that the learner has available to bring to bear on the problem. Gagné and Briggs (1979) illustrated this process with the following example:

> Suppose that a small car has been parked near a low brick fence, and is discovered to have a flat tire on one of its front wheels. No jack is available, but there is a ten-foot two-by-four, and a piece of sturdy rope. Can the front of the car be raised? In this situation, a possible solution might be found by using the two-by-four as a lever, the wall as a fulcrum, and the rope to secure the end of the lever when the car is in a raised position. (p. 69)

Such a solution would involve accessing and combining rules that the learner knows but has never applied to such a problem before: application of force, use of a fulcrum, and using leverage to lift weights that cannot be lifted by hand.

In contrast to the previously described intellectual skills that can be taught directly through expository instruction, the discovery of higher-order rules must be stimulated indirectly by presenting learners with problem-solving situations. The problems are ones that learners cannot solve directly using rules they already know, but that they can solve by combining some of these rules into a higher order rule. The instructor may want to guide discovery by posing questions that will help learners to formulate the problem clearly or to realize that certain familiar rules are applicable to it. The instructor does not, however, put it all together for the learners by articulating the higher-order rule directly or teaching it in expository fashion. Thus, higher-order rule learning is discovery learning or problem solving.

cognitive strategy learning

Cognitive strategies are *internal control processes that learners can use to monitor and regulate their learning and problem solving.* These strategies (when present) are most evident when learners are confronted with novel problems that they must first formulate and then try to solve. To the extent that they employ cognitive strategies, learners will guide their problem solving with verbally articulated self-talk that includes generating relevant questions about the problem, formulating answers, and organizing the information into a systematic plan for working out and evaluating tentative solutions. This activity may also include internal dialogues or "metacognitive monitoring" in which learners describe, comment on, review, and criticize their problem-solving efforts to assess the appropriateness of their strategies and formulate plans for what to do next (Zimmerman & Schunk, 1989). This subjective monitoring and evaluation is directed toward learners' own thinking and problem-solving efforts, which is what makes cognitive strategies different from the intellectual skills described above that are directed toward manipulation of input from the environment.

As an example of the use of self-talk to guide problem solving, consider the inner speech reported by Nora, a sixth grader who was asked to think out loud while working on a mathematics problem:

> (Rereads problem segment; quickly looks back to earlier problems.) Oh, OK . . . 1 over 8 and 5 over . . . they have to be changed to the same denominator so the common denominator is 2 and . . . oh, wait, this is just like the first one! 1/8 and 5/6, so the common denominator is 2. And then . . . what did I do the first time? . . . Oh, my god, I did it wrong the first time. Oh. 2 times 4 is 8, oh, yeah,

> (continues working through computation algorithm) . . . so it would be . . . and then take the 2 into 15, because it's an improper fraction . . . so . . . the fraction would be 11 take away 2, plus 7, is 9 and 1/2 . . . that would be . . . oh no . . . 0, 0 . . . you have to borrow . . . make this . . . you have to make that a common denominator . . . that's the same as . . . 1/2 (sigh of relief upon solving the problem after 4 minutes and 45 seconds of work on it, which included revising her initially incorrect formulation of the problem and in the process, recognizing that she had done a previous problem incorrectly). (McCaslin Rohrkemper, 1989)

Gagné and Briggs stated that cognitive strategies cannot be taught directly or even stimulated in direct ways through guided discovery methods. Beyond arming learners with prerequisite information and skills, teachers can only create favorable conditions for allowing learners to develop cognitive strategies by frequently providing them with opportunities to think creatively or solve novel problems. Other writers, however, believe that cognitive strategy development can be stimulated more directly through modeling, especially when the model thinks out loud to allow learners to see how he or she generates and uses cognitive strategies in a particular situation (Palincsar & Brown, 1984; Weinstein & Mayer, 1986).

learning hierarchies and task analysis

Sometimes hierarchical relationships exist between learning types. Where this is true, learning types can be ordered from simple to complex in such a way that each new type combines or in some way builds on simpler types. The intellectual skill section of the Gagné and Briggs (1979) typology shown in Table 5.2 is one such hierarchy.

Note that *Gagné and Briggs postulate hierarchical relationships only among the subtypes of intellectual skills.* Their five major categories (attitudes, motor skills, information, intellectual skills, and cognitive strategies) are considered qualitatively different from one another, representing separate domains. However, the five subcategories in the domain of intellectual skills are seen as forming a hierarchy with higher-order rules at the top, followed next by rules and defined concepts (these are considered equivalent in the hierarchy), then by concrete concepts, and finally by discriminations. This is because in order to discover a higher-order rule, learners must know its prerequisite rules and defined concepts. Also, rules specify relationships between concepts, so knowledge of these concepts is prerequisite to rule learning. Similarly, defined concepts often have concrete concepts as referents. Finally, before a concept can be learned, one must be able to make discriminations between critical attributes.

Dunn (1984) characterized this hierarchy as incomplete (some intellectual skills are probably left out) but as correct as far as it goes (the hypothesized hierarchical relationships are apparently correct). He went on to show that although these hierarchies are used mostly for developing instruction in science and mathematics, they are also applicable to other school subjects such as social studies or driver education, and even to skills such as "knowing when to hold 'em, and knowing when to fold 'em" in poker.

Information about learning hierarchies can be used for **task analysis,** which is *Gagné's term for identifying a task's component parts and deciding what needs to be taught and in what order.* Curriculum designers routinely rely on task analysis in their work, and teachers find it useful for designing their own lessons and for preparing to teach lessons using published materials. Lessons often fail because they assume that students have certain prerequisite knowledge or skills that they do not actually possess. Preparation that includes task analysis designed to identify these potential problems and formulate ways to deal with them by providing on-the-spot instruction can transform potential lesson failures into mere rough spots. Such preparation also leaves the teacher in good position to plan remedial instruction for students who need it.

Figure 5.1 shows a learning hierarchy produced by analyzing the prerequisite subtasks involved in oral reading (decoding) of printed text. It is useful for diagnosing the errors that students make in oral reading. For example, one student might mispronounce certain syllables, while another might pronounce individual syllables correctly but fail to blend them properly. The first student needs instruction in one set of subskills while the second student needs instruction in a different set.

There is no single correct way to conduct task analyses and identify learning hierarchies, because the number of component parts that could be identified is theoretically infinite. However, it is usually easy to identify major parts that correspond to learning objectives taught previously, and thus to plan systematic ways to help students progress from where they are now toward ultimate objectives.

Task analysis will be treated in more detail in Chapter 9. For now, bear in mind that wise teachers prepare for instruction not only by thinking about their own teaching goals but also by putting themselves in their students' places by analyzing the assumptions and demands built into the tasks they assign. Instructions may be confusing or ambiguous, examples may be misleading or ill-suited to the backgrounds of the students in the class, or tasks may call for a concept or skill that the students do not possess.

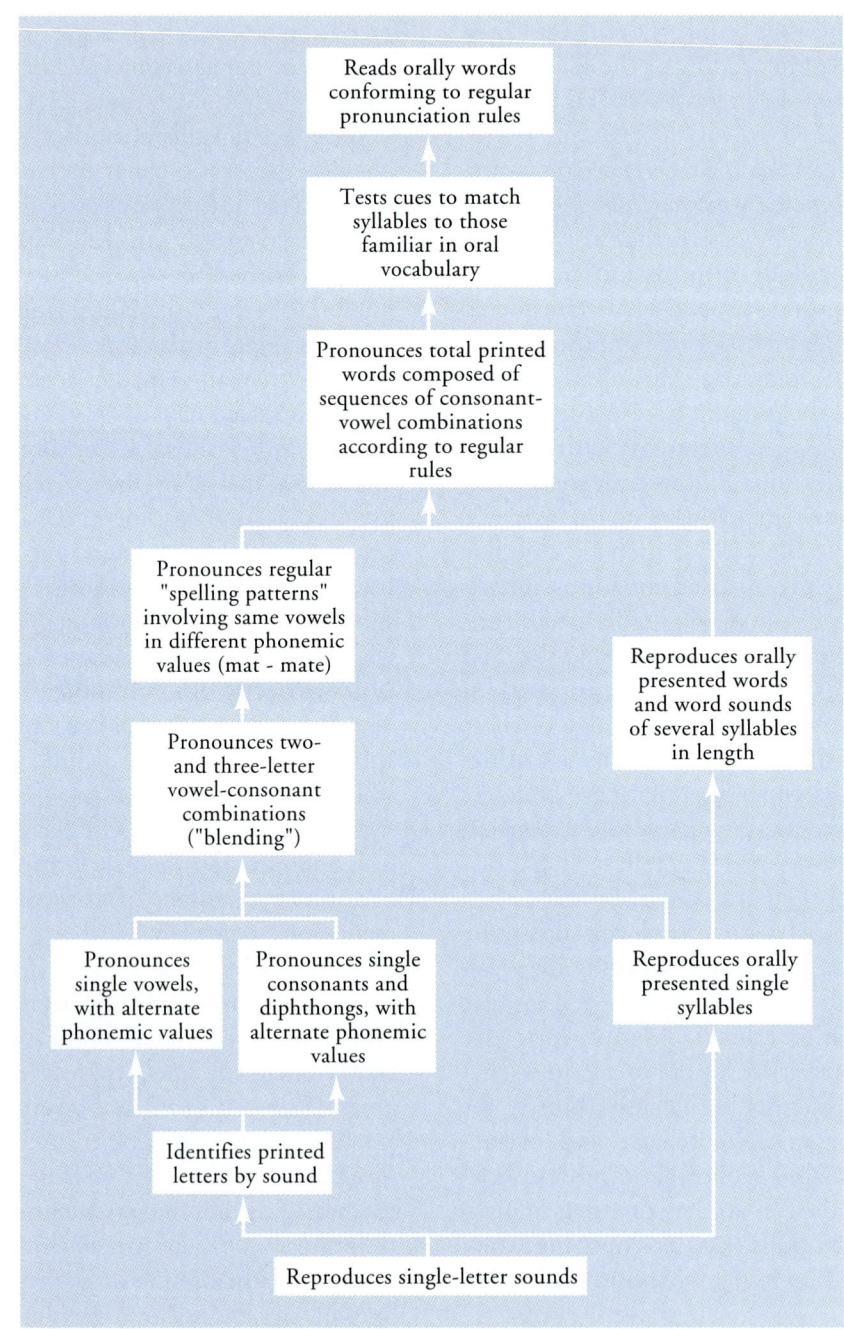

Figure 5.1 a learning hierarchy for basic reading skill ("decoding")
SOURCE: Adapted from the *The Conditions of Learning*, second edition, by Robert M. Gagné. Copyright © 1970 by Holt, Rinehart and Winston, Inc. Reprinted by permission of CBS College Publishing.

Teachers who make themselves aware of these problems can prevent needless confusion and frustration by improving on assignments or by providing more clarity, better examples, or needed preparatory instruction when presenting the assignments to the students.

instructional objectives

Teachers and students need to be aware of the purposes of activities and how they fit within the overall curriculum. One way to do this is to formulate and use *instructional objectives* in planning instructional sequences. Clear objectives provide guidance to teachers about what to teach and how to teach it, about what students should have learned and how to evaluate it, and about what kinds of feedback to give to students. They also provide guidance to students about what to study and how to study it (Hamilton, 1985; Muth et al., 1988). These benefits are most likely to occur when attention is focused on the students, rather than on the content to be taught, in formulating instructional objectives. Instructional objectives are best formulated by stating what students should be able to do following completion of the instruction.

This approach to instructional objectives was popularized by Mager (1962, 1993). He stressed that instructional objectives should be stated with reference to specific behaviors that can be observed and measured. Thus, he argued that objectives statements such as "the student will understand two-digit subtraction" should be avoided in favor of statements such as "the student will be able to solve fifty two-digit subtraction problems in eight minutes, with no more than one error." Mager's version of instructional objectives called for specification of three key elements: (1) the target behavior (solve two-digit subtraction problems correctly); (2) the conditions under which this behavior will be demonstrated (a fifty-item test); and

(3) the criteria for acceptable performance (completion of the fifty problems within eight minutes with no more than one error).

Even though Mager used the term "instructional objectives," his emphasis on stating objectives in precise behavioral terms led to the popularizing of the term "behavioral objectives." **Instructional objectives** are *statements about the goals of instruction, phrased in terms of intended student outcomes rather than in terms of content coverage or learning activities.* **Behavioral objectives** are *instructional objectives stated in behavioral terms that specify the target behavioral capacity to be induced, the conditions under which it is to be demonstrated, and the criteria for acceptable performance.* Behavioral objectives were associated with an approach to curriculum planning and control that involved expressing the entire curriculum as behavioral objectives, sequencing these objectives in some sensible way, and developing materials and methods for both instruction and evaluation of each objective.

The most extreme versions of the behavioral objectives approach were unwieldy and overly rigid, confronting teachers with hundreds of objectives to be taught in a given order using particular materials and following prescribed practices. In less extreme versions, teachers continued to use the instructional materials they were using, but were pressured to justify all of their instructional activities by stating behavioral objectives for the activities, even when the objectives were more cognitive or affective (enjoyment, appreciation) than behavioral. Sometimes, teachers were required to drop activities that could not be so "justified." Consequently, the term "behavioral objectives" carries negative connotations for many educators. For this reason, and also because we do not believe that all instructional objectives can or should be stated strictly according to Mager's criteria, we will not use the term "behavioral objectives." Instead, we will speak of "instructional objectives" or simply "objectives."

Gronlund (1991) distinguished between general objectives and more specific statements of intended learning outcomes. He recommended that general objectives be stated using verb forms that communicate what students should be able to do on completion of instruction, but are general enough to encompass a domain of student performance that would include many more specific activities. He suggested that teachers identify eight to twelve general objectives for an entire course, and perhaps two to four for a briefer unit. General objectives for a science course, for example, might include: (1) knows the meaning of terms; (2) knows specific facts; (3) knows laboratory procedures; (4) understands concepts and principles; (5) applies concepts and principles to new situations; (6) demonstrates abilities needed to conduct an experiment; (7) interprets data in scientific reports; and (8) displays a scientific attitude.

More specific objectives would be developed for particular activities. The general objective "knows laboratory procedures," for example, might be broken into subobjectives such as selecting appropriate equipment for a given experiment, assembling it correctly, manipulating it appropriately, measuring accurately with measuring devices, following safety rules, and cleaning and returning the equipment properly. Similarly, a general language arts objective such as "writes effective compositions" might be broken into subobjectives such as expressing ideas clearly, relating ideas to the main thesis, developing the thesis in an organized way, writing well-structured paragraphs, using correct grammar, and minimizing spelling errors.

Gronlund's ideas about objectives are especially helpful in planning content coverage and instructional activities. Gagné and Briggs (1979) outlined an approach to objectives that is especially helpful in planning assessment tasks. They suggested that a complete operational definition of an objective includes five components: (1) the *action* that the learner is to perform; (2) the *object* of this performance; (3) the *situation* in which the action is to be performed; (4) *tools*

and other constraints indicating how the aciton is to be performed or what limits might be placed on it; and (5) the *capability to be learned* that provides the rationale for the assessment item and will be assumed to have been achieved if the learner performs acceptably.

As an example, Gagné and Briggs noted that the ability to type a letter might be listed as an objective of a typing course or as a criterion for employment as a typist. To design an assessment task based on this objective, one would need to specify it more fully by indicating whether the typist is to compose the letter or merely reporduce it, to use a personal computer or a typewriter, and so on. If it were determined that the task was to compose a letter concerned with orders and shipping, without help from anyone concerning the letter's contents, the total performance might be described as follows:

Given a received letter inquiring about the shipping of an order	(Situation)
The student or applicant generates	(The learned capability, implying a problem-solving process)
A letter in reply	(Object)
By typing,	(Action)
Using a personal computer, making an original and a copy of a one-page letter.	(Tools and other constraints)

We believe that attention to objectives should be an important part of instructional planning. As long as it is not carried to extremes, the process of formulating instructional objectives and using them to guide the development and evaluation of instruction is likely to have the beneficial effects just mentioned.

implications for teachers

making decisions about using instructional objectives—an example

Mrs. Wolfe is a junior high physical education teacher who plans to teach a six-week unit on basketball. How can she use this time most effectively? Which knowledge and skill objectives should she concentrate on as the core curriculum and which should she cover only briefly or not at all? There are no simple right answers to these questions. A range of objectives and associated activities might be appropriate, depending on the students' current knowledge and skill levels and on how basketball instruction fits into the school's larger physical education program (as seen by Mrs. Wolfe and the other physical education teachers).

Given these considerations and her knowledge about what can be accomplished in a six-week unit, Mrs. Wolfe will have to formulate instructional objectives that address one or more of the three major domains of learning: (1) *affective objectives* (stimulate appreciation for the game by emphasizing teamwork, sharing, coordinated body movement, and general aspects of play); (2) *cognitive objectives* (develop knowledge of rules, infractions, and concepts underlying strategies for offensive and defensive play); and (3) *psychomotor objectives* (teach the students to dribble, pass, shoot, and rebound). Mrs. Wolfe's objectives will determine what activities will be included in her unit, how much time will be allocated to each, and what she will stress in evaluating the effectiveness of her instruction.

To the extent that Mrs. Wolfe decides to emphasize cognitive objectives, she will need to provide the students with topic outlines and textual material, to deliver lectures and present slides or films, to conduct recitation and discussion lessons, and to administer written tests. In contrast, to the extent that she wishes to emphasize psychomotor objectives, she will need

Mrs. Wolfe effectively demonstrates basketball skills while verbally describing the procedure

to explain and demonstrate skills, observe and provide feedback to students as they practice these skills in the gym, provide opportunities for students to blend and apply these skills during drills and controlled scrimmages, and (possibly) evaluate skill development using performance checklists or other methods of rating the quality of physical performance.

Mrs. Wolfe probably will want to integrate her approach to cognitive and psychomotor objectives. In teaching the jump shot, for example, she would provide information about when and how to use the shot, verbal description of procedures to follow in executing it, and modeling accompanied by verbalization of the self-talk, visual-motor imagery, or kinesthetic feedback that can be used to guide the shot during its execution. However, if she wants her students to become skilled jump shooters, she will have to give them opportunities to practice jump shooting in skill drills and game situations. Furthermore, if she wants to assess whether her objective has been met, she will need to assess actual jump shooting under specified conditions, and not merely assess whether students can label a picture of a jump shot correctly or answer essay questions about jump-shooting technique.

In the process of expressing her general goal (teaching basketball) in terms of specific instructional objectives, Mrs. Wolfe will develop *clarity about her own values and priorities* (what she thinks that these students should learn about basketball). These may differ from the priorities of another teacher assigned to the same course, even one who is ostensibly teaching the same things. For example, two teachers may agree to concentrate on psychomotor skills, but one may stress general body skills (running, jumping, pivoting) while the other stresses ball skills (passing, dribbling, shooting). Thus, attention

to instructional objectives helps teachers to become aware of similarities and differences in "the same" course as it is taught in different sections. Such information is important for *curriculum control* (making sure that objectives considered essential are covered adequately in each section), and discussion of differences helps to broaden teachers' perspectives on how instruction can be approached.

Once a list of instructional objectives is drawn up, the teacher can assess it for feasibility and consider its implications for the nature and sequencing of instructional activities to be included in the unit. Often it will be necessary to compromise by reducing the number of objectives to be addressed or by addressing certain objectives in less depth than the teacher would prefer. Mrs. Wolfe, for example, may decide that her students need to know about basic rule infractions so that they can avoid them in playing the game, but that they will not need to know the referees' signals associated with various infractions. Similarly, she may decide that she has time to cover both jump shots and hook shots, but only if she sticks to the basic forms and only teaches the students to shoot directly at the basket. Another teacher might decide to ignore hook shots and concentrate on jump shots, but to teach several variations on basic jump shooting form and to teach the students to use the backboard in addition to shooting directly at the basket. Each teacher's choices can be supported with a sensible rationale, but each involves trade-offs (some things are learned at the expense of others). However, because both teachers are clear about their respective objectives, both are likely to achieve them. The same could not be said of teachers who teach haphazardly or who try to cram so much into the unit that nothing is covered in sufficient depth.

guidelines for using instructional objectives

Learning situations are likely to be most effective when most of the learning is intentional—when you as the teacher know what you want to accomplish and how you intend to accomplish it, and your students know what is expected of them. This is especially true when *planning includes attention to the steps that students must go through* (i.e., not merely attention to what the teacher will do) in the process of moving toward the ultimate objectives. It is useful to formulate instructional objectives and use them to plan both instruction and evaluation. In doing so, keep in mind three general principles.

1. *State a few major objectives rather than a great many trivial ones for a given unit.* Concentrate on the objectives that represent new advances over previous learning or terminal objectives that culminate curricular strands. Where appropriate, perform task analyses, identify learning hierarchies, and provide instruction and practice on whatever subskills need work before smooth performance of the ultimate target skill will become possible. However, keep in mind that you are building toward the ultimate target skill, which will need to be taught, practiced, and evaluated in its final form. Don't lose the forest for the trees.

2. *Don't be unnecessarily behavioral or precise* in formulating objectives. For psychomotor objectives and for many of the cognitive objectives taught in the early grades, it is possible and usually desirable to express objectives in specific behavioral terms as advocated by Mager (1962). However, for affective objectives and for higher-level cognitive objectives that do not translate directly into behavioral skills, it is better to formulate instructional objectives in less behavioral terms. Even so, try to formulate objectives in terms of changes in the students that will occur as a result of instruction (rather than in terms of content coverage or other teacher behavior). Objectives should be stated specifically enough so that both you and the students can easily determine whether or not they have been reached.

3. *Don't be overly rigid in using objectives to guide instruction.* Research on teacher planning (Clark & Peterson, 1986) suggests that most teachers do not pay nearly enough attention to goals and objectives when planning instruction (they read the teacher's manual to learn how a lesson is to be conducted, but give little thought to the purpose of the lesson or how it might be adapted if it doesn't succeed). However, among teachers who do pay attention to objectives, some respond to them in an overly rigid manner. They develop lesson plans that are admirably specific and detailed, but then they implement these plans so rigidly that they are unable or unwilling to adapt them when events dictate. Wise teachers formulate and use objectives to guide instruction, but they are flexible enough to deviate from their plans when unanticipated problems occur or when they have a chance to take advantage of a "teachable moment" by following up on a relevant student question or comment.

summary

Learning is the process of acquiring relatively permanent change in understanding, attitude, knowledge, or skill through experience. It is a change in capacity for performance that must be distinguished from performance itself and from thinking. There are different kinds of learning. Common qualitative distinctions include "knowledge that" versus "knowledge how," intentional versus incidental learning, rote versus meaningful learning, and reception versus discovery learning.

The Bloom taxonomy distinguishes between knowledge, comprehension, application, analysis, synthesis, and evaluation objectives. Gagné and Briggs distinguish between five major types of learning: attitudes, motor skills, information, intellectual skills, and cognitive strategies, and further divide intellectual skills into discriminations, concrete concepts, defined concepts, rules, and higher order rules.

Gagné and Briggs also present guidelines concerning the different conditions of learning required for each learning type. Attitudes are learned primarily through exposure to models, persuasive communication, or conditioning. Motor learning is stimulated through modeling, verbal instructions combined with visual imagery, and practice with feedback. Information learning is stimulated by presenting the input in organized fashion and helping students to relate it to their existing knowledge, process it actively, and encode in their own words.

Discriminations are taught using the principles of contiguity, feedback, and repetition. Concrete concepts are taught by presenting a variety of stimuli that all share the defining attributes of the concept, pointing out these attributes to the learners, and then having them discriminate examples from nonexamples. Defined concepts are taught by stating their definitions and then presenting examples and nonexamples. Rules are taught through rule statements followed by guided practice in applying the rule to specific examples. Higher-order rules cannot be taught directly, but their discovery can be stimulated by presenting learners with problem-solving situations that require them to invent the rules. Gagné and Briggs believe that cognitive strategies can be neither taught nor stimulated directly, although they believe that teachers can encourage students to develop such strategies by giving them frequent opportunities to think creatively and solve novel problems. Other writers believe that cognitive strategy development can be stimulated more directly through modeling of the self-talk that occurs when cognitive strategies are applied to particular situations.

Gagné and Briggs hold that the five categories of intellectual skills form a hierarchy with higher-order rules at the top, followed by rules and defined concepts, then by concrete concepts, and finally by discriminations. They suggest using information about such learning hierarchies for conducting task analyses to identify the component parts of tasks and decide what needs to be taught and in what order.

Instructional planning begins with formulation of clear instructional objectives. Objectives are best formulated by stating what students should be able to do following completion of the instruction. This provides guidance about what to teach, how to teach it, and how to evaluate the effects of instruction. It also provides guidance to students about where to focus their learning efforts. The authors believe that teachers should formulate instructional objectives to guide their planning and teaching, although they suggest that teachers state only a few major objectives rather than a great many trivial ones, that they do not attempt to be unnecessarily behavioral or precise in stating those objectives, and that they not be overly rigid in confining their instructional activities to those that are related directly to the objectives. Planning should allow for enough flexibility to take advantage of unanticipated "teachable moments."

questions for reflection

1. In your own terms, differentiate between learning, performance, and thinking. Why are these distinctions important? How might they influence the decisions you make as a teacher?

2. Distinguish between propositional and procedural knowledge. Which is more difficult to achieve? Why? Which is more important? Why? Think about the courses that you took as a college freshman. Did these courses emphasize propositional or procedural knowledge? How do you account for this?

3. What are the important differences between the Bloom taxonomy and the Gagné and Briggs typology? Think about the teaching situation that you want to be in. Which of the two systems would be more useful to you? Why?

4. Examine a test that you have taken at some point during your college career. Try to determine, for each question, the level it represents in the Bloom taxonomy and the Gagné and Briggs typology. How difficult is it to classify the questions? How useful are these classifications for summarizing the cognitive demands of the test?

5. Classify the questions that appeared at the ends of Chapters 2, 3, and 4 in this text, using the Bloom and the Gagné and Briggs systems.

Does your analysis suggest any needed improvements?

6. Some teachers emphasize a great deal of drill. In some mathematics classes, for example, students may spend 60 to 70 percent of the period practicing number facts. However, this material often has to be retaught the following year. How can you account for this? What is the role of practice in retaining information? What are the conditions for successful practice?

7. How would you apply the material presented on motor learning in this chapter if you were teaching someone the basics of ice skating? How would you apply it if you were teaching freestyle skating?

8. What is the appropriate role of objectives in effective instruction? Reread the objectives that we presented at the beginning of this chapter. How effective were they for guiding your study of the chapter? If you were writing objectives for the chapter, what changes you would make in those that were presented?

9. Apply Gronlund's approach to write objectives for a course that you expect to teach. State eight to twelve general objectives for the course as a whole, then state more specific objectives for a particular unit.

cases to consider

What's the big idea? Miss Ditto and Miss Freehand both devoted considerable attention to the topic of main idea in language arts instruction. Each introduced it in a lesson that described the process of organizing lengthy texts into sections and paragraphs and suggested that each paragraph should have a single main idea. The two teachers differed considerably, however, in the nature of the follow-up activities they assigned. Miss Ditto emphasized seat-work assignments calling for students to identify the main idea sentence in a paragraph. She began by passing out pages full of short, disconnected paragraphs and having students underline the main idea sentence. Later, she assigned them increasingly longer sections of connected text to read, and had them copy the main idea sentence or state the main idea of a paragraph in their own words if they believed that no single sentence captured it adequately. For variety, she occasionally distributed several pages of uninterrupted connected text and assigned the students to mark the places where new paragraphs should begin. In contrast, Miss Freehand followed up on the main idea lesson mostly in her writing assignments. She assigned several compositions each week, and in addition to giving guidelines for the type of composition, the desired length, and so on, she reminded the students that the compositions should be divided into paragraphs such that each paragraph is built around a main idea. Sometimes she had the students underline the main idea in each of their paragraphs.

Given these differences in approach, how would you characterize what Miss Ditto's and Miss Freehand's students are learning about main idea, using concepts presented in this chapter? In particular, how would their learning compare in terms of propositional versus procedural knowledge, and how would it be classified according to the Bloom taxonomy and the Gagné and Briggs typology? What does this suggest about the relative effectiveness of these two approaches?

everything you always wanted to know about apple pie Merry Cook is a home economics teacher who offers a "carbo cooking" course as a high school elective. The course centers on baking treats and desserts, but Merry wants to make sure that it includes appropriate cognitive content (chemical composition and nutritional value of foods, changes induced by various cooking methods, trade-offs involved in serving at various temperatures, etc.). In one activity, the students will work in small groups preparing apple pies. What might she teach about this topic if she were to set out to include at least one worthwhile objective at each of the six levels of the Bloom taxonomy and each of the nine types of learning described in the Gagné and Briggs typology (counting each of the five types of intellectual skill as separate types)? If she were to ask your help in drawing up such a list of objectives, what would you suggest? Keep in mind that each objective should be worthwhile in its own right and should fit together with the other objectives to form a coherent sequence of instruction.

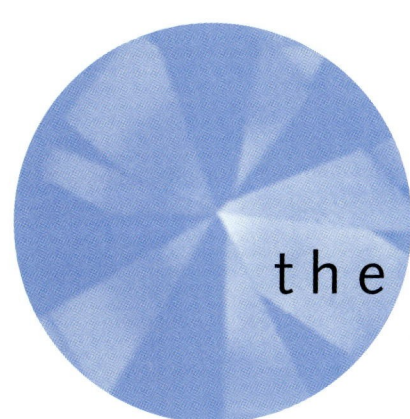

chapter **6.**

the behavioral approach to learning

objectives

When you have mastered the material in this chapter you will be able to

1. Describe the behavioral approach to learning and describe its differences from other approaches
2. Define key classical-conditioning concepts (unconditioned stimulus, unconditioned response, conditioned stimulus, conditioned response, contiguity, and repetition) and identify classroom applications of the classical conditioning paradigm
3. Describe Thorndike's work on instrumental conditioning and explain how it differs from classical conditioning
4. Explain the law of exercise and the law of effect
5. Explain the key findings of the functionalists concerning overlearning and massed versus distributed (spaced) practice
6. Define the key concepts associated with Skinner's operant conditioning (positive reinforcement, negative reinforcement, extinction, punishment, behavioral shaping, reinforcement schedules), and explain how operant conditioning differs from classical conditioning and instrumental conditioning

7. State the similarities and the differences between Skinnerian approaches to operant conditioning of animals in the laboratory and Skinnerian approaches to instructing students in the classroom
8. Define the key concepts associated with the work of Bandura and other social learning theorists (modeling, imitation, vicarious learning)
9. Describe the similarities and differences between modeling as used in traditional behavioral approaches to instruction and the combination of modeling with verbalized self-instruction as used in cognitive behavior modification approaches
10. Define the key concepts used in programmed instruction (modules, frames, linear versus branched programming, self-pacing, learner control), and explain the basic principles of instruction used in Keller's PSI system and in mastery learning
11. Describe the potential advantages that computerized instruction offers over traditional instruction, and then describe its current limitations
12. Identify the key weaknesses in proposed instructional innovations that attempt to work around, rather than through, teachers

In this chapter, we describe the contributions of learning theorists known as behaviorists. Behaviorists study learning by concentrating on overt behaviors that can be observed and measured. They view behaviors as determined by events external to the learner—by stimuli that elicit or cue responses and by reinforcement that maintains these stimulus-response relationships. Radical behaviorists believe that behavior is the subject matter of psychology and that all psychological explanations should be made at the level of behavior without reference to hypothetical mediators within the organism. Most other behaviorists recognize in their theorizing that learning is mediated by perceptions, thoughts, and other covert processes. However, even these cognitively oriented behaviorists prefer to minimize their reliance on hypothetical constructs that must be inferred rather than observed directly. This is a major difference between behaviorists and other learning theorists (discussed in the next two chapters) who stress cognitive structures and information processing.

Behaviorists have developed many theoretical principles and instructional techniques designed to induce learning. These instructional applications of behaviorism are discussed in this chapter. Behaviorists also have produced principles and techniques designed to *control behavior* (i.e., to increase or decrease the frequencies of already learned behaviors). These classroom management applications are discussed in Chapter 18.

the roots of modern behaviorism

Since at least the time of Aristotle, educators have known that much learning involves recognizing associations between repeated observations (e.g., the sight of lightning is regularly followed by the sound of thunder). The key to such recognition is **contiguity**—*the associated stimulus items regularly occur together, either simultaneously or in rapid succession.* If they are salient (e.g., a brilliant flash of lightning followed by a loud clap of thunder), or if we happen to be paying attention to them, we may learn the association from just one exposure. Usually, however, associations develop gradually through a combination of contiguity and repetition; through repeated encounters with the associated items, we become *conditioned* to expect them to occur together.

Pavlov and classical conditioning

Early in the twentieth century, Russian psychologist Ivan Pavlov (1927) conducted experiments on learning through conditioning. He had been studying the salivation response by presenting dogs with food under controlled conditions. The salivation response is a reflex action in which an unconditioned stimulus (the taste of food in the mouth) elicits an unconditioned response (increased salivation that promotes digestion). An **unconditioned stimulus** is *an event that naturally elicits and unconditioned response because this connection is built into the organism's nervous system.* The **unconditioned response** is *a biologically programmed response to an unconditioned stimulus, and is elicited automatically; no process of conditioning or learning is involved.*

Pavlov noticed, however, that his dogs sometimes salivated in anticipation of feeding. The arrival of the laboratory assistant who fed the dogs could elicit salivation, well before any food was presented. This led to a series of experiments in which Pavlov showed that a previously **neutral stimulus** (*one that produced no particular response* from the dog) could become a conditioned stimulus for the salivation response if it were routinely presented immediately prior to the unconditioned stimulus (food). This **conditioned stimulus** is *a stimulus that does not initially elicit a response but through its pairing with an unconditioned stimulus acquires the capability*

of eliciting a conditioned response. A **conditioned response** *originates as an unconditioned response to an unconditioned stimulus but is learned by the organism as a similar response elicited by a conditioned stimulus.* For example, if Pavlov routinely sounded a bell right before presenting food, the dog soon began to salivate at the sound of that bell. The bell had become a **conditioned stimulus** capable of producing salivation as a **conditioned response.**

The type of conditioning studied by Pavlov is known as classical conditioning. Narrowly defined, **classical conditioning** refers only to situations in which *reflex actions become responsive to conditioned stimuli in addition to the unconditioned stimuli that normally elicit them.* However, the term is sometimes used more broadly to refer to any *stimulus substitution learning* or *signal learning* in which contiguity and repetition are used to induce learners to generalize an existing stimulus-response connection to some new stimulus. This kind of conditioning can be used in teaching vocabulary, for example, by showing pictures paired with the printed names of the things pictured, or by showing Spanish words paired with their English equivalents.

Anxiety and other undesirable emotional reactions can become attached to classroom stimulus situations through classical conditioning processes. Whenever students experience failure or embarrassment, but especially if this occurs publicly in front of their peers, they may become flooded with anxiety or even experience panic reactions during which they find themselves unable to breathe, think, or speak normally. Should such experiences occur repeatedly during certain classroom situations (e.g., working math problems on the board, making an oral presentation, or taking a particular type of test), the student may begin to dread these situations and seek to avoid them. The best approach to such conditioned anxiety problems is to minimize their occurrence by treating students with sensitivity and creating a supportive climate for learning in the classroom. Where such problems are encountered, the students will need encouragement and assistance in overcoming them. It may be necessary to move in small steps and proceed by successive approximations to the ultimate goal. **Successive approximations** are *small steps in a progression from an originally crude version of the target response to be shaped to the ultimate, precise version.* Students who fear making public oral presentations, for example, might be allowed to make their presentations privately just to the teacher at first, then encouraged to make the presentations to small groups as they gain confidence, and finally, when they are ready, to make them to the entire class.

Thorndike and instrumental conditioning

Early behaviorists supplemented classical conditioning research by studying adaptive behavior, not just instinctive reflexes. E. L. Thorndike (1913) placed animals in problem-solving situations in his studies of **instrumental conditioning,** which involved *using conditioning and reinforcement principles to teach problem-solving methods or other behaviors that were instrumental to goal accomplishment.* For example, a hungry cat might be put in a cage where it could see food but not reach it. The cat could escape from the cage by working a latch, but it would have to discover this for itself. Typically, the first few escapes would be accidental—the cat would happen to release the latch while clawing at the cage. However, the principle of contiguity would be in effect: the cage would open immediately after the "correct" response was made. After several repetitions, clawing would evolve into "scientific" search behavior. The cat would have learned that there was a "trick" to getting out of the cage, so it would concentrate on discovering the trick and then become more effi-

cient at performing it.

These studies extended Pavlov's work on classical conditioning by showing that environmental manipulations could produce entirely new conditioned responses. Cats that learned to escape their cages were not acting reflexively by making unconditioned responses. Instead, they were discovering and refining new responses adapted to novel stimulus situations.

Thorndike postulated "laws" of learning, most notably the laws of exercise and effect. According to the **law of exercise**, *repetition of a conditioned response would strengthen the stimulus-response bond.* According to the **law of effect**, *responses followed by reward would be strengthened and responses followed by punishment would be weakened.* These principles were largely correct but had to be modified in view of later findings. The law of exercise had to be modified to take into account the need for variation in responding and for feedback about the effects of responses. Repeated practice does not necessarily improve performance. However, when practice includes systematic testing of alternative forms of response by using knowledge of results as feedback, performance tends to improve to peak efficiency. The law of effect had to be modified to allow for certain exceptions. Sometimes consequences that are usually considered rewarding do not motivate performance, and consequences that are usually considered punishing do not suppress it.

Thorndike was influential for his attacks on "faculty psychology" and the "mental discipline" approach to education. This approach held that courses in science, mathematics, languages, and classical literature provided "mental discipline" that made people more perceptive and incisive in their thinking, whereas courses in practical subjects such as business, agriculture, or home economics did not have these effects on general mental faculties. Thorndike (1924) disproved this theory by showing that there was no evidence that there were special mental faculties that could be "disciplined" or that classical sub-

Immediate feedback helps make practice of skills useful. If feedback is delayed it may not do much good.

jects were any more valuable than practical subjects for stimulating intellectual development. After Thorndike's attack, the school curriculum began to include more practical subjects.

Thorndike's conclusions hold up as well today as when he stated them: there still is no evidence that particular subject matter has general mind-broadening effects. However, certain disciplines (psychology, law, medicine) do have more modest transfer effects on students' logical or statistical reasoning abilities (Lehman, Lempert, & Nisbett, 1988), and training in study skills and information processing strategies will improve students' abilities to learn efficiently.

functionalists and practice effects

While Thorndike was developing general laws, other behaviorists were developing information about factors that influence learning in particular situations. They were known as *functionalists* because their experiments were designed to

show that performance in particular situations is a function of some determining factor, so that specified changes in the determining factor produce predictable changes in performance.

Functionalists discovered much useful information about how learning varies as a function of practice. For example, they found that skills practiced to the point of **overlearning** (*the performance peak, or the point at which practice no longer produces improvement*) tend to be retained indefinitely and to be recovered with relative ease, whereas skills that are mastered only partially tend to deteriorate. If you did a lot of skating or cycling as a child, you could perform these skills competently now with little or no practice, even though you may not have done so in years. However, if you were exposed to these skills only briefly and never really mastered them, you would have to start over virtually from scratch.

Functionalists also discovered that progress in learning depended not merely on the number of practice trials, but on how this practice was distributed. *Massed practice* is concentrated into one or just a few lengthy sessions spaced

	Classical Conditioning (Pavlov)	Operant Conditioning (Skinner)
Order of stimulus and response	S-R conditioning	R-S conditioning
Nature of the process	Stimulus substitution	Response modification
Psychological principle involved	Contiguity (no reinforcement)	Reinforcement
	Adhesive principle	Feedback principle
The basic paradigm	S_1 $\searrow$ S_2 $\dashrightarrow$ R	R $\leftarrow$ S

Figure 6.1 two basic forms of stimulus-response conditioning

SOURCE: "Basic Forms of Stimulus-Response Conditioning" from *Learning Theories for Teachers*, fourth edition, by Morris L. Bigge. Copyright © 1982 by Harper & Row Publishers, Inc. Reprinted by permission of HarperCollins Publishers, Inc.

close together. In contrast, *distributed practice* involves a larger number of shorter sessions, spaced further apart. Massed practice is efficient for simple skills that can be mastered to overlearning with relative ease. Distributed practice is more efficient for most learning, however, including most of what is taught in school. This is why curricula are divided into brief lessons and assignments that address limited content. It is also why frequent reviews and quizzes are important, and why a progressive series of tests spaced throughout the term usually produces more learning than a single final exam at the end. The benefit of distributed practice (or the *spacing effect* as it is sometimes called) has been reaffirmed more recently by cognitive psychologists interested in the mechanisms that may explain it (Dempster & Farris, 1990; Glover & Corkill, 1987; Smith & Rothkopf, 1984).

Practice is one of the most important yet least appreciated aspects of learning in classrooms. Little or no practice may be needed for simple behaviors like pronouncing words, but practice becomes more important as learning becomes more complex. To be useful, practice must involve opportunities not only to exercise skills but to receive feedback, preferably *immediate feedback*. At times when teachers are not able to provide feedback to their students personally,

they should arrange for them to get it by consulting answer keys, comparing their work with ideal models, or providing feedback to one another.

If feedback is delayed several days and limited to a grade and a few remarks, it may be too little and too late to do much good. In fact, if students are operating from misconceptions or using erroneous response patterns, continued practice without correction will only strengthen these tendencies (e.g., second graders who always subtract the smaller number in each column from the larger one instead of always subtracting the bottom number from the top one and "borrowing" if necessary; secondary students who don't pay attention to parentheses when trying to combine algebraic expressions). Successful practice involves polishing skills that are already established at rudimentary levels to make them smoother, more efficient, and more automatic, not trying to establish such skills through trial and error.

Skinner and operant conditioning

As behaviorism evolved, it began to be applied not merely as a method of studying learning, but as a set of principles for producing learning and controlling behavior. The work of B. F. Skinner on operant conditioning was the most influential of these developments (Nye, 1992).

Skinner used the term operant conditioning because he studied operant behaviors. **Operant conditioning** *applies reinforcement principles to condition or shape operant behaviors.* **Operant behaviors** *are voluntary responses, not elicited automatically by any known stimulus, that are used to operate on the environment.* This distinguished his work from research on classical conditioning of **respondent behaviors** (*involuntary reflex actions*). Skinner's operant conditioning was more like instrumental conditioning, except that Skinner was not content merely to record animals' behavior when they were placed in particular environments and allowed to discover tricks for responding to them. Instead, Skinner assumed a more active role by manipulating the environment to shape the animal's behavior in desired directions (see Figure 6.1).

contingent reinforcement

The primary mechanism for accomplishing behavioral shaping is **contingent reinforcement** which involves *reinforcing the performance of a target behavior by delivering reinforcements only when the behavior has been performed to some criterion.* One can increase the frequency of an operant behavior by rewarding the animal for performing it. Delivery of reinforcement is contingent on such performance, so the animal has to perform the behavior to get the reward.

Skinner's work on contingent reinforcement reformulated and applied Thorndike's law of effect, but with two important differences. First, Skinner used contingent reinforcement in an active way to shape behavior and speed the learning process; he did not wait for animals to learn through exploration and discovery. Second, Skinner defined reinforcers in terms of their situational effects on behavior (thus avoiding the problem that even consequences usually thought

of as rewarding are not experienced as rewarding by everyone). Skinner defined a *reinforcer* as any consequence that increased the frequency of some operant behavior when it was made contingent on performance of that behavior. This definition is circular, but it has proven extremely useful.

conditioning mechanisms

Operant conditioning is accomplished through four basic mechanisms:

- *Positive reinforcement* or reward: Responses that are rewarded are likely to be repeated (credit toward grades as reinforcement for participation in lessons).
- *Negative reinforcement:* Responses that allow avoidance of or escape from undesired situations are likely to be repeated (exemption from a major test as reinforcement for good performance on quizzes).
- *Extinction* or nonreinforcement: Responses that are not reinforced are unlikely to be repeated (ignoring students who call out answers without first raising their hands and being recognized should extinguish this tendency to call out).
- *Punishment:* Responses that bring painful or undesirable consequences will be suppressed (penalizing students who call out answers by withdrawing privileges should cause the students to suppress their calling out). The behavioral potential will remain, however, so the response may reappear if reinforcement contingencies change.

behavioral shaping

Skinner showed that operant conditioning could be used to teach animals to do things they would never learn through natural experience (such as teaching pigeons to dance or play Ping-

Pong). He accomplished this through **behavioral shaping** *using reinforcement principles to shape successively more refined versions of a behavior, continuing until the target criterion was met* **Successive approximations** of the ultimate target behavior were reinforced until the animal produced the target behavior itself.

Teaching a pigeon to "dance," for example, might begin with reinforcement (delivery of a food pellet) following any lifting of the left leg. Once the pigeon learned to lift the left leg to earn a food pellet, the reinforcement contingency would be changed so that, for example, the pigeon first had to lift the left leg and then replace it on the floor again before being reinforced. When this sequence was learned, reinforcement contingencies would change again so that the pigeon would first have to go through the sequence with the left leg and then repeat it with the right leg. At that point, the pigeon would have developed a hopping sequence resembling dancing, which could be extended into a "routine" through additional shaping.

A great range of behaviors could be shaped in this manner with a process called **chaining**— *using reinforcement procedures to produce a sequence of behaviors by first shaping the initial step, then adding the second step, and so on.* If a target behavior was in the animal's present or potential repertoire, it could be produced by initially reinforcing a partial or primitive version and then systematically reinforcing successive approximations of the final form. To produce a sequence of behaviors, one could teach the first step, then the second, and so on.

discrimination training

Contingent reinforcement can be used not only to shape behavior but also to bring the behavior under stimulus control by applying the principles of contiguity and repetition. **Stimulus control** is *the goal of operant conditioning, achieved when a given stimulus reliably cues a given response.* Just as

Pavlov had shown that a conditioned stimulus could become a signal for the appearance of an unconditioned stimulus, Skinner showed that a conditioned stimulus could become a signal for the availability of contingent reinforcement. For example, if he reinforced a pigeon's dancing behavior only when a particular light was on, the pigeon would learn to dance when the light was on but not when the light was off. The light had become a *discriminative stimulus* (or *cue)* for the dancing behavior, which was now under stimulus control (it would occur only when the light was on).

Contingent reinforcement could also be used to develop *stimulus discrimination*: the pigeon could learn to dance only in the presence of a particular light. Here, only the "right" light would function as a discriminative stimulus to cue the dancing behavior. Other light sources would remain neutral stimuli without special significance, or perhaps become discriminative stimuli cueing the pigeon to produce some behavior other than dancing.

Contingent reinforcement could also be used to produce *response discrimination*. A pigeon could learn to dance when cued by one light source but to press a lever when cued by a different light source. Eventually, the pigeon would learn that a particular situation (in this case, a specially designed experimental cage that came to be called a "Skinner box") offered a range of stimuli. Some had no special significance, but others functioned as cues indicating the chance to earn rewards by producing particular responses.

Much of what is taught in school involves discrimination training. Students must learn not only to distinguish between relevant stimuli, but also to respond appropriately to each: a plus sign cues addition operations, but a "times" sign cues multiplication operations. In some school cafeterias, an adaptation of a traffic light remains green when the level of conversational noise is acceptable, turns yellow if it starts to get too loud, and turns red if a period of silence and verbal reminders about behavioral expectations is needed.

In the classroom, cuing can be accomplished through directions ("Watch what happens when I add acid to the test tube"), as well as remarks such as, "I wonder what will happen when I push this button. Oh, look!" Cueing can also be accomplished through pointing, holding objects up for viewing, telling students where to look, or asking questions that cause them to process information and find the appropriate stimulus. Attention should be directed through cueing whenever students may be confused about where to look or what to listen to.

partial reinforcement schedules

Operant responses are established most rapidly when the target behavior is reinforced immediately each time it is produced, not just some of the time. It has also been shown that the way responses are maintained is important. This is done with **schedules of reinforcement**—*specifications concerning relationships between performances of the target behavior and deliveries of reinforcement, phrased in terms of the intervals of time that must elapse or the repetitions of the target behavior that must occur before the next delivery of reinforcement.* Prior to Skinner's work on schedules of reinforcement (Ferster & Skinner, 1957), it was assumed that a **continuous reinforcement schedule** (*reinforcing the target response every time it occurs following presentation of the controlling cue stimulus*) also would maximize the strength and persistence of the response. However, Skinner showed that once responses were established, they could be maintained better through partial reinforcement schedules than through continuous reinforcement schedules.

Partial reinforcement schedules are *schedules that call for delivering reinforcement following only some, rather than all, of the performances of the target behavior.* Partial reinforcement schedules include interval schedules and ratio schedules, and each of these can be either fixed or variable. Interval schedules are based on the time interval that has elapsed since the last reinforcement. In **fixed interval schedules**, *the target response is reinforced after a fixed amount of time (such as sixty seconds) has elapsed.* In **variable interval schedules**, *opportunities to earn reinforcement are also scheduled according to the time elapsed since the previous reinforcement, but the time intervals vary (randomly or according to some predetermined scheme) within set limits.*

Ratio schedules are based on the number of target responses that have occurred—rather than the time that has elapsed—since the previous reinforcement. In **fixed ratio schedules**, a *fixed number of target response repetitions must occur before reinforcement is delivered* (e.g., on a 1:25 schedule, a reward is delivered after every twenty-fifth response repetition). In **variable ratio schedules**, *the number of response repetitions required varies within set limits.* For example, under a variable 1:25 ratio schedule, opportunity for reinforcement may recur following anywhere from one through fifty repetitions of the target response.

Different schedules of partial reinforcement have different effects on response rate. Under fixed schedules, where reinforcement delivery is predictable, learners adjust their behavior accordingly. When they know that a fixed time interval must elapse before the next reinforcement opportunity, they will simply wait (or do something else) while the time elapses, and then begin producing the target response around the time that the next reinforcement is due. Under fixed ratio schedules they learn that a fixed amount of work is required to earn reinforcement, so they tend to repeat the target behavior rapidly at times when they particularly desire the reinforcement, but with less frequency when they are satiated. Variable interval and (especially) variable ratio schedules produce steadier rates of response, because learners know that their efforts will pay off eventually even though they cannot predict when. For example, you may have noticed that you tend to keep up by maintaining a steady study schedule in courses where unannounced quizzes are expected (variable schedule), but to concentrate your studying in days prior to exams in courses that follow a fixed exam schedule.

The power of partial reinforcement schedules to maintain responses is quite remarkable, at least in laboratory studies of animals. A response that would extinguish quickly following termination of a continuous reinforcement schedule can be sustained through thousands of unreinforced repetitions using a variable ratio schedule. Schedules of reinforcement have less extreme and less predictable effects on humans, especially older children and adults in nonlaboratory settings (Sulzer-Azaroff & Mayer, 1991). Still, there are some human examples. For example, if you often purchase snacks from a particular vending machine, you are on a continuous reinforcement schedule because each time you put in money and make a selection, you get reinforced with the desired snack. Yet, this behavior would extinguish quickly (probably in just one trial) if the machine retained your money but did not deliver the snack, and it would not reappear until the machine had been repaired. Contrast this with responses to slot machines. Most people will continue to put money into slot machines even though pulling the lever yields no payoff most of the time, because they know that the machine will pay off eventually. Response persistence is sustained through a variable ratio schedule of reinforcement. State lotteries and most other gambling devices operate on the same principle.

fading

Skinner discovered that responses maintained through continuous reinforcement could be switched to partial reinforcement schedules through **fading**—*gradually decreasing the schedule of reinforcement by increasing the number of repititions or the time interval that must occur before reinforcement is delivered*. Like shaping, fading is accomplished through successive approximations. To introduce an interval schedule, one would initially delay just a second or two before delivering reinforcement, and then gradually extend this interval as the learner became accustomed to waiting. To introduce a ratio schedule, one would occasionally skip a response or two before reinforcing, and then gradually reduce the reinforcement rate as the learner became more accustomed to repeating the response several times before being reinforced. Once begun in this manner, fading would continue until the desired schedule of reinforcement was established (typically, the lowest rate of reinforcement that would still maintain the response at the desired rate).

rule governance

We have noted that humans respond less predictably to schedules of reinforcement than animals do. A major reason for this is that much human behavior is governed by rules. Rules are instructions or other verbal formulas that govern behavior by specifying contingencies. Human learners typically acquire rules through verbal communication, but they sometimes generate their own rules from their own experiences. For example, in a typical experiment, humans might be asked to depress a telegraph key in order to earn points worth money, and they might be placed on a schedule calling for reinforcing the first response made following a fixed interval of time (e.g., thirty seconds) since the last reinforcement. In this situation, animals would show low rates of responding early in the thirty-second interval and high rates toward the end. However, humans tend to show either relatively high and steady rates or else very low overall rates but with a few responses occurring near the end of the interval. When asked to explain their behavior, those who show high rates of responding usually report thinking that they were on a rate-based schedule, whereas those showing low rates of responding usually report thinking (correctly) that they were on an interval schedule. If human subjects in this situation are told that the schedule will be rate based, they tend to show high response rates, but if told that the schedule will be interval based, they tend to show low rates and often count off the seconds between reinforcements (Hayes, 1993).

Radical behaviorists who share Skinner's philosophy and approach to theory building have been developing knowledge about rule-governed behavior and using it as a basis for behaviorist approaches to education. This allows them to take advantage of human capacities for verbal communication. Also, educational applications based on rule governance are more feasible than applications based on contingent reinforcement principles because a single teacher attempting to instruct twenty or thirty students cannot consistently provide contingent reinforcement to these students. Information about rule-governed behavior and its educational applications can be found in Hayes (1989) and Hayes and Hayes (1992). Information about a particularly well-developed application called precision teaching can be found in Lindsley (1992).

Skinner's approach to education

Skinner advocated behaviorism not only as an approach to psychology (Skinner, 1974) but also as a way to perfect the human condition. He wrote *Walden Two* (Skinner, 1948), a novel about a Utopian community in which reinforcement principles were used to maintain cooperation in the service of the common good. In this vision, credits accumulated through work were exchanged for reinforcement (basic necessities, opportunities for recreation or pleasure). People willing to do the least desirable jobs could accumulate credits more quickly.

Skinner believed that we are controlled by our reinforcement histories, so that our notions of self-determination are mere illusions (Skinner, 1971). His ideas about using operant conditioning to perfect the human condition are essentially humanistic in that they are designed to minimize suffering, meet basic needs, and maximize quality of life for all. However, many find his approach too cold and impersonal, and some fear that its manipulative aspects would lead to the sort of totalitarian "Big Brotherism" depicted by George Orwell in *1984*. The information in Table 6.1 summarizes some fundamentals of Skinner's approach to behaviorism.

Skinner's principles for teaching students are the same ones used in the laboratory for teaching animals:

1. Elicit desirable responses in the presence of discriminative stimuli (cues) and reinforce these responses immediately.
2. Continue cueing and reinforcing until the responses become well established.
3. Shape the ultimate target behavior through successive approximations.
4. Fade reinforcement once the established stimulus-response connection can be maintained without it.

There are two major differences, however, between conditioning animals and instructing students. First, students can understand language, so teachers can cue responses directly by calling for them, without having to shape them gradually. Thus, classroom instruction is more efficient than animal conditioning, and it emphasizes cueing of responses in advance at least as much as reinforcing them afterward (Martens & Kelly, 1993). Second, responses are reinforced primarily through feedback; there is no need to rely on food or other material rewards.

table 6.1 some fundamentals of Skinner's behaviorism

- The primary purpose of science is the prediction and control of behavior.
- The subject matter of psychological science is behavior and behavior only.
- Scientific knowledge about behavior is developed through functional analyses that relate environmental independent variables to behavioral dependent variables.
- Behavior is determined and lawful.
- The causes of behavior are located in the environment.
- Selection by consequences is the primary causal mode by which the environment determines outcomes in living systems.
- The two major classes of functional relations are respondent behaviors and operant behaviors.
- Operant behaviors can be brought under the control of antecedent stimuli.
- Behavioral principles apply to even the most complex human activities, including language, thinking, consciousness, and science.

SOURCE: Constructed from information contained in D. Delprato and B. Midgley (1992). "Some Fundamentals of B.F. Skinner's Behaviorism," *American Psychologist, 47* (1507–1520).

In summary, the Skinnerian approach to instruction involves building stimulus-response associations by cuing learners as to the nature of the response desired and then providing immediate feedback about the correctness of the response elicited, so that correct responses are reinforced and incorrect responses are extinguished. Where necessary, programs are sequenced to move learners through successive approximations toward the ultimate target responses. If applied properly, these principles should produce learning that is not only efficient according to cold criteria such as number of trials required to reach criterion, but also desirable according to humanistic criteria. Learning should be more enjoyable to the learners because they get to respond actively, their responses yield immediate feedback, they can move along at their own pace, and the emphasis is on producing success experiences through reward.

Skinner (1968) also applied operant conditioning principles in developing technologies for classroom management and instruction. Teaching machines, programmed instruction, and computerized instruction are among the technologies developed at least in part on the basis of his ideas. These educational technologies are discussed later in the chapter. For more information about classroom applications of Skinner's principles, see Engelmann & Carnine, 1982; Greenwood et al., 1992; Johnson & Layng, 1992; Lindsley, 1991; or recent issues of the *Journal of Behavioral Education*.

social learning theory

Radical behaviorists continue to believe that behaviorism can get along without explanations based on cognitive information processing or subjective experience. However, most behaviorists have integrated at least some of these covert processes into their theorizing. This is especially true of behaviorists who study human learning that occurs in social situations. Much of this learning is not easily explained without reference to covert mental activities.

forms of social learning that require cognitive mediation

imitation of models Humans learn to speak, to use tools, and to behave appropriately in various social situations mostly by imitating others. Sometimes we learn complex sequences of behavior from just a single observation of a model, without any deliberate cuing or behavioral shaping. We also learn about the situational specificity of various social behaviors, usually without systematic discrimination training. Seemingly effortlessly, we learn to act one way in a library, another at a party, and yet another at a formal meeting. These examples of learning from models appear to require theorizing about types of learning that are different from operant conditioning—covert learning that occurs before learners even begin to make overt behavioral responses, let alone to have those responses reinforced.

delayed imitation Sometimes, behavioral capacities acquired through observation of models are not acted out until much later. For example, when teaching a particular topic, teachers may use the same approach that was used to teach them when they were students at the same grade level.

vicarious learning We can learn not only by imitating what other people do, but also by observing how they are affected by events in their lives. By putting ourselves in their place (i.e., by identifying with them), we experience their thoughts and emotions vicariously. For example, much of what we know about interpersonal relationships and the emotions that accompany them has been learned from books, movies, or television programs about real or fictional people.

To accommodate observational learning phenomena such as imitation of models and vicarious learning, social learning theorists have broadened behaviorism to include cognition and emotion in addition to behavior. Learning is defined as cognitively mediated capacity for performance rather than identified with performance itself. It can be acquired merely through observation of models, and it includes information about stimulus-response-reinforcement linkages, not just behav-

ioral possibilities. We learn not only about potential responses but also about the situations in which those responses may be relevant, the stimuli that may cue them, and the consequences that they are likely to bring about. Such learning is mediated through cognitive processes such as attention, encoding of input, and retention in long-term memory.

Bandura and social cognitive theory

Albert Bandura (1977, 1986) is a leading social learning theorist whose ideas are important for thinking about learning, motivation, and classroom management. Bandura believes that human behavior must be described in terms of reciprocal interaction between cognitive, behavioral, and environmental determinants, not just shaping through reinforcement. Reinforcement remains important, but human mediation capacities make it unnecessary to wait for responses to occur before being able to use it. Instead, one can use modeling or verbal explanation to inform learners about the consequences of producing desired behavior, and thus motivate them to begin to produce the behavior. Here, reinforcement has effects even before it occurs, because learners anticipate its delivery.

Learners' cognitive mediations of their environments also determine their attention to competing stimuli, which is why different people will respond differently to "the same" situation. For example, if you and two friends were to visit a classroom together and then discuss the teacher's effectiveness, you might disagree because of differences in what each of you paid attention to. One might have concentrated on classroom management, another on rapport with students, and the third on the clarity of explanations.

Such phenomena have led social learning theorists to distinguish between the **nominal stimulus** (*the situation's observable and measur-*

able characteristics) and the **functional stimulus** (*the situation as observed and interpreted by the learner*). To understand learning in complex environments, and especially to understand why different individuals learn different things from "the same" experience, one must identify the functional stimulus that cues each learner's response.

When teaching, one needs to see that students attend to the right things (i.e., to see that each student's functional stimulus is the one that the student should focus on). Modeling and verbal explanation can be used to enhance the salience and distinctiveness of cues, and thus to focus students' attention.

Bandura has done a great deal of research on learning induced through modeling. Initially, this form of learning was called "imitation" because learners first were exposed to filmed models who acted out a series of discrete behaviors in exaggerated fashion, and then were observed to see how much they imitated these models when placed in the same situation. For example, children would watch a model take out frustration against an inflated rubber Bobo doll, and then would be observed to see if they responded to the same frustration in the same way. These early studies showed that learners seldom duplicated the model's behavior precisely. They did develop general notions about how to respond in the situation, but then they acted on these notions in their own ways. In the Bobo doll example, the children observing the model did not imitate the specific sequence of behaviors they had observed (first punch the doll with the right hand, then kick the doll with the right foot, etc.). Instead, they learned a general principle (take out frustration by attacking the Bobo doll) that could be implemented in a variety of ways (various combinations of the aggressive responses that had been modeled, along with other forms of aggression that were not shown in the film).

Because the term "imitation" is somewhat misleading, Bandura uses the term **modeling** to refer to *learning that occurs as a result of observing models*. Much human learning occurs through modeling, including much of what we learn about coping with everyday situations. For example, most adults typically behave much as their parents did when they respond to frustration (calm and analytical versus hysterical versus resigned), discipline their own children (forgiving versus punitive), or perform household repairs (skillful versus inept).

Modeling is responsible for much classroom learning as well. Three general types of such modeling can be identified. First, teachers continuously model ways to think about the academic curriculum and about social, political, and value issues. To the extent that this modeling is done systematically, it can be a significant factor in socializing students' attitudes, beliefs, and behavior. The other two types of classroom modeling are more specifically instructional. One involves *modeling of cognitive skills*, especially skills such as creative thinking or problem solving that cannot be taught directly in step-by-step fashion, but can be stimulated indirectly through modeling. The third type of modeling does involve step-by-step demonstration of procedures, which is often the most efficient way to teach motor skills and low-level cognitive skills.

As Bandura has developed his theorizing, he has placed more emphasis on cognition and less on reinforcement. In his social cognitive theory, even learning through directly experienced response consequences is no longer explained using concepts of conditioning through reinforcement. Instead, such learning is viewed as simply a special case of observational learning. That is, humans learn all the time through cognitive mediation of what they observe about relationships between behavior and its consequences; this applies to observations about our own behavior as well as the behavior of others. Bandura (1986) believes that we mediate our learning using five basic cognitive capabilities:

- *Symbolization:* Based on our social experiences, we construct cognitive models of social reality to guide our thinking and decision making about social behavior.

- *Vicarious learning:* By observing others, we learn about potential actions and their probable consequences in various social situations. Gradually, we integrate this learning into a social knowledge structure that includes skills, values, attitudes, and expectations.

- *Forethought:* We can draw upon our accumulated social learning in order to generate ideas about potential actions, assess these actions for appropriateness to the situation, and predict their probable consequences.

- *Self-regulation:* In response to modeling and socialization from significant others, we develop standards concerning acceptable and unacceptable behavior. Some of these are standards concerning what is ethically moral or socially appropriate. Others are personal aspiration standards that we use in setting goals and evaluating the worth of our accomplishments.

- *Self-reflection:* We can monitor our thoughts and actions, look back at them, and draw inferences about the future. One important class of inferences developed in this manner are self-efficacy beliefs—judgments about whether or not we are capable of doing what it takes to accomplish a particular goal. These beliefs influence the kinds of goals we set for ourselves and the levels of effort we are willing to invest in various activities, including classroom learning activities and assignments.

behavior modification

Behavior modification is a *general term for the use of techniques based on behavioristic principles to shape and control behavior.* Just as behavioristic theorizing ranges from the radical behaviorism of Skinner to the social cognitive approach of Bandura, so do the approaches taken to behavior modification. The most "conservative" approach is called **applied behavior analysis**, which is *based on Skinner's ideas and concentrates on using reinforcement principles to bring behavior under stimulus control.* More "liberal" approaches that combine reinforcement techniques with techniques drawn from pedagogy, instructional psychology, and psychotherapy are called cognitive behavior modification.

cognitive behavior modification

As described by Meichenbaum (1977), **cognitive behavior modification** techniques are *designed to develop in learners the capacity for controlling their own behavior through goal setting, planning, self-instruction, self-monitoring, and self-reinforcement.* These techniques feature modeling combined with *verbalized self-instruction,* in which models not only perform tasks but think out loud as they do so, enabling learners to see how to use self-talk to guide them in searching for relevant cues, developing ideas about how to respond, monitoring the effectiveness of responses, and so on.

Meichenbaum and Goodman (1971) used these techniques to train a group of boys to respond analytically, rather than impulsively, to matching-to-sample tasks. The tasks involved inspecting a sample stimulus and then identifying its duplicate among a set of alternative choices (the alternatives were all similar to the sample, but only one was identical to it). The boys had been doing poorly on such tasks because they impulsively selected the first choice that looked right, rather than taking time to study all of the choices carefully. In this experiment, the models used exaggerated gestures and motions to make it clear that they were comparing each alternative to the sample stimulus before reaching a final decision. As they did so, they verbalized such thoughts as "Let's see, I'm going to have to compare each of these to make sure I don't get the wrong one by mistake. How about this one? Is this ear the same? How about the other ear? No, this one has a round ear, and that one has a long ear. . . ." This approach was effective in improving the boys' performance on such tasks, even though other approaches (such as urging the boys to slow down and take their time) were not effective. Classroom management applications of the approach are discussed in Chapter 18.

Over the years, many of the instructional techniques originally associated with cognitive behavior modification have been combined with instructional techniques developed by educators working from very different theoretical backgrounds. They are often included, for example, in interventions currently known as "strategy training" (see Chapter 12). Reviewers disagree in their assessments of the value of self-instructional training and other applications of cognitive behavior modification. Proponents point to significant improvements in behavior or academic performance, but critics claim that any such improvements tend to be limited, of unknown durability, and unlikely to transfer to tasks or situations different from those used during the training (Abikoff et al., 1988; Diaz & Berk, 1992a; Hobbs et al., 1980; Kendall & Braswell, 1985).

We believe that the combination of modeling with verbalized self-instructions is a powerful instructional technique, especially when teaching complex processes that are guided by covert self-talk that remains hidden from learners unless the teacher shares it with them (Fox & Kendall, 1983; Meichenbaum & Asarnow, 1979; Sarason & Sarason, 1981). Students will not learn much from watching a teacher identify

Figure 6.2 a set of frames designed to teach a third- or fourth-grade pupil to spell the word "manufacture"

---

1. **Manufacture** means to make or build. *Chair factories manufacture chairs.* Copy the word here:

❑ ❑ ❑ ❑ ❑ ❑ ❑ ❑ ❑ ❑ ❑

2. Part of the word is like part of the word **factory**. Both parts come from an old word meaning *make* or *build*.

manu ❑ ❑ ❑ ❑ ure

3. Part of the word is like part of the word **manual**. Both parts come from an old word for *hand*. Many things used to be made by hand.

❑ ❑ ❑ ❑ facture

4. The same letter goes in both spaces:

m ❑ nuf ❑ cture

5. The same letter goes in both spaces:

man ❑ fact ❑ re

6. **Chair factories** ❑ ❑ ❑ ❑ ❑ ❑ ❑ ❑ ❑ ❑ chairs

---

the main ideas in a series of paragraphs, solve mathematics problems on the board, or perform experiments in the laboratory if these "demonstrations" do not include verbalization of the thinking that guides the observable actions. When teachers do share this thinking, however, students not only can understand what the teachers are doing and why, but can learn the general approach used in solving the problem and apply it later when working on their own. This makes modeling combined with verbalized self-instruction more effective than traditional lecture/demonstration methods. Such modeling in first-person language provides students with an integrated, within-context demonstration of how to approach and solve the problem. This is easier for them to retain and use than general information presented in third-person language or even instructions presented in second-person language ("First you do this, then you do this . . .") that must be first internalized and then translated into first-person language that can be used to guide behavior.

Figure 6.3 part of a program in high school physics

Sentence to be completed	Word to be supplied
1. The important parts of a flashlight are the battery and the bulb. When we "turn on" a flashlight, we close a switch that connects the battery with the _____	bulb
2. When we turn on a flashlight, an electric current flows through the fine wire in the _____ and causes it to grow hot.	bulb
3. When the hot wire glows brightly, we say that it gives off or sends out heat and _____	light
4. The fine wire in the bulb is called a filament. The bulb "lights up" when the filament is heated by the passage of a(n) _____ current	electric
5. When a weak battery produces little current the fine wire or _____ does not get very hot.	filament
6. A filament which is less hot sends out or gives off _____ light	less
7. "Emit" means "send out." The amount of light sent out or "emitted" by a filament depends on how _____ the filament is	hot
8. The higher the temperature of the filament the _____ the light emitted by it.	brighter, stronger

The machine presents one item at a time. The student completes the item and then uncovers the corresponding word or phrase shown at the right.

Teachers also should encourage students to verbalize their thinking about a task or problem. This is the only way that teachers can be sure their students have achieved desired understandings and are able to integrate and apply them effectively. Also, in attempting to verbalize their thinking overtly, students will construct new learning more actively and assess it more reflectively than they might have otherwise. For more information about classroom applications of cognitive behavioral approaches, see Hughes and Hall (1989) and Manning (1991).

educational technologies

In addition to generating principles that teachers can use during lectures, discussions, and other traditional forms of instruction, educational psychologists have developed technologies designed to enhance teacher-delivered instruction or replace it with instruction from some other source. Most of the early innovations in educational technology were based on behavioristic principles.

teaching machines

Pressey (1932) invented *teaching machines*, which were self-teaching devices that presented learners with questions, required them to respond, and then allowed them to get feedback by turning a knob or opening a slot to reveal the answer. Nothing much came of Pressey's ideas, however, until Skinner (1954, 1958) and others began to tout teaching machines as practical alternatives to traditional schooling. By then it had become clear that the "machine" aspects of such instruction (knobs, viewing windows, etc.) were not essential, and that the key elements were design principles such as sequencing the instruction, providing corrective feedback, and programming for consistent success. Consequently, educational technologies began to focus on programmed instruction (Skinner, 1986).

programmed instruction

Programmed instruction *moves learners in small steps from entry level of performance to the target objective*. Typically, programs are designed to be self-contained and ready for independent use by learners who have the appropriate entry characteristics (i.e., the program will be neither too easy nor too difficult for them). Programs are divided into segments called *modules*. Modules are divided into frames that build knowledge step-by-step. Examples are shown in Figures 6.2 and 6.3.

Programs reflect careful task analysis. Frames are sequenced so as to minimize errors and maximize reinforcement. Prerequisite knowledge is taught or cued prior to its application to higher-level tasks. Each frame presents any review considered necessary, then introduces the next step in the chain of learning. The new step may be a new concept, a check on mastery of previously introduced concepts (requiring the learner to make a discrimination or inference), or a change in focus from learning to application. The frame ends with the requirement that the learner make some active response such as answering a question by filling in a blank.

Correct responses lead to reinforcement in the form of positive feedback. Extended praise statements may be frequent early in the program, but these soon evolve into simple feedback statements with just occasional praise (i.e., reinforcement is faded). There is also *fading of cues* (also called *vanishing of prompts*): early frames provide all of the information needed to answer questions correctly, but later frames require learners to draw inferences from information presented earlier. For example, a module may begin with questions about a fully labeled map, then ask about a version of the map that has some parts missing, and then ask questions without showing any map at all.

Program sequencing may be linear or branched. *Linear programming* moves learners through a fixed sequence of objectives. It is used when there is reason to believe that the same program will enable all learners to achieve the objective with few if any errors and no need for individualized remediation. If errors should occur, learners are recycled through earlier segments in the program. *Branched programs* are designed to meet individual needs. Learners skip certain modules when their performance

on pretest frames indicates that they already know this material. Also, when learners fail to master certain modules even after being recycled through them, they are branched into special modules that provide remedial instruction before being returned to the main program.

Programmed instruction is said to be *self-paced* or under *learner control*. Students progress quickly through material that they already know or can master easily, but they spend more time on material that they find difficult. Errors are private, and feedback is immediate and constructive. In branched programs, persistent errors lead to different or more thorough remedial instruction, not just repetition of the instruction that has not worked so far. Programmed instruction requires learners to attend actively to the information presented and respond thoughtfully to the questions asked, but it also reinforces these learning efforts by allowing learners to respond overtly, receive immediate feedback, achieve consistent success, and progress at their own pace.

Most programmed instruction is designed for use by learners working privately. However, some variations allow for teacher-student interaction. Also, some programs emphasize particular learning modalities (visual, auditory) or are designed for students who lack independent work skills or functional reading ability. Reading is minimized by using tape recorded information and instructions, but active responding is retained by using worksheets. After presenting information and a question, the recorded instructions will tell students to respond, give them time to do so, and then provide feedback. Recently, additional and more flexible forms of programmed instruction adapted to the special needs of individual learners have been developed using computer technology.

research on programmed instruction

Research on programmed instruction has shown the need to qualify some of its basic principles. For example, carefully sequenced programs often produce no better learning than the same programs presented in randomly mixed or even reversed order. Usually this occurs when the learners are sophisticated (college students) and the programs are brief and easy, so that poor sequencing does not make enough of a difference to impair learning. When learners are less sophisticated or the material is sufficiently lengthy and difficult, carefully sequenced instruction produces better learning.

Initially puzzling results also were obtained when programs that required learners to respond actively and repeat frames on which they made mistakes were compared with programs that only required them to read the material without making overt responses. These studies often showed no differences and sometimes showed differences favoring the group that merely read the material. As with optimal sequencing, it appears that the value of active responses and remedial subprograms depends on the length and difficulty of the material for the learners (Tobias & Ingber, 1976; Abramson & Kagen, 1975). Sophisticated students working on a brief program they can learn easily may get as much information from reading alone as from responding overtly (in fact, having to respond to each frame may be more time consuming and irritating than helpful).

Some constructivist theorists have used these findings to question the very assumptions underlying programmed instruction. They interpret the findings involving scrambled sequences as evidence that incongruity stimulates discovery learning, and interpret findings favoring reading over active responding as evidence of the futility of trying to make learners conform to logic imposed by someone else rather than letting them encode and organize material in their own ways.

Effectiveness comparisons between programmed instruction and conventional instruction are about evenly split, and the differences tend to be small in any case (Bangert, Kulik, & Kulik, 1983; Jamison, Suppes, & Wells, 1974).

Interest in conventional forms of programmed instruction has waned in recent years, but computerized versions appear to be quite popular.

Keller and PSI

Working from principles of operant conditioning, Fred Keller (1968) developed a method of individualizing instruction that he called the *Personalized System of Instruction* (PSI) and that since has become known as the *Keller Plan*. The Keller Plan was developed originally for use in a college psychology course, and is presently used in a variety of college courses. Its main features are self-pacing (within limits, students can go as fast or as slow as they choose), mastery orientation (students move on to a new unit only after mastering the preceding unit to criterion), and student control of the examination schedule (students take tests when they decide that they are ready, and may repeat tests until they reach criterion). Following an initial orientation to the course, there are few if any class meetings. Instead, students work individually or with one another to learn from textbooks or programmed materials, and consult with the teacher or with assistants called *proctors* to get help (Keller & Sherman, 1982).

PSI is popular with college students, or at least with those who enroll in PSI courses (Robin, 1976). These students enjoy the self-pacing, individualized tutoring, and contract options that guarantee particular grades for particular levels of performance. PSI students typically achieve as well as or better than students in conventional sections, partly because they tend to put in more time and effort.

PSI works best for students who have the self-discipline and inclination to learn independently (Johnson & Ruskin, 1977). Procrastination and high withdrawal rates are commonly reported in PSI courses, although stiff mastery requirements may minimize this problem for some students. Robin (1976) reported that students with low-grade point averages began studying earlier and studied more often in PSI courses with 100 percent mastery criteria than in PSI courses using 50 percent criteria. Many students were not willing to make this effort, though, and withdrew from the PSI sections. Thus, PSI courses demand more self-discipline than many students are willing or able to exert.

PSI has much in common with mastery learning (see the discussion under "Bloom and Mastery Learning"). In fact, it is often described as a form of mastery learning and studies of PSI courses are often included in reviews of mastery learning research. However, PSI depends on individualized use of programmed instructional materials (supplemented by tutoring from proctors), whereas mastery learning, at least in its more common forms, is an adaptation of conventional classroom teaching using conventional instructional materials.

Bloom and mastery learning

Benjamin Bloom (1968) developed mastery learning as a form of individualized instruction, but the concept has since been expanded to include group-based methods. Bloom's ideas were a reaction against the notion that individual differences in general aptitudes and abilities necessarily make for individual differences in levels of curriculum mastery. Bloom was influenced by John Carroll (1963), who had argued that if students receive optimal instruction, any differences in their mastery levels will not be produced by inherent differences in their learning potential, but by differences in the time they need to learn (some students may take longer, but they will master the material if given enough time). Carroll expressed the argument in the following equation:

$$\text{degree of learning} = \frac{\text{time actually spent}}{\text{time needed}}$$

Bloom (1968, 1976, 1980) elaborated on Carroll's model to develop the concept of mastery learning. Bloom's model included student entry characteristics (both cognitive and affective), the learning task itself, the quality of the instruction provided, and a variety of learning outcomes (level and type of achievement, rate of learning, affective outcomes). Bloom suggested that the outcome of a student's encounter with a learning task will be determined not only by the time available for learning but also by the appropriateness of the task for the learner (its cognitive level and affective appeal) and by the quality of the instruction provided. Learning will proceed most smoothly when students are taught effectively on tasks they are motivated to engage in and able to master with relative ease. In suggesting guidelines for quality of instruction, Bloom stressed four aspects: (1) *cues* or directions about what to do, (2) *active learner participation* in the task, (3) *reinforcement* derived from experiencing success on the task, and (4) *feedback/correction* from the instructor.

Bloom argued that an effective combination of these elements should enable 80 percent of students to reach mastery levels that only the top 20 percent reach in traditional classrooms. He also argued that the extra time and instruction provided to slow learners when they are working on tasks that come early in a hierarchical sequence not only will allow these students to master these tasks but also will reduce the time they need to learn tasks that appear later in the sequence. Taken together, these assumptions imply that mastery learning should increase the percentage of students who master a given objective from about 20 percent to 80 percent, reduce the variance (individual differences) in mastery of any particular objective and the curriculum as a whole, and over time, reduce the variance in time needed to learn (because as slower students master more and more prerequisites, they will become able to master higher-level tasks with relative ease).

Initial applications of these ideas were at the high school and college levels and called for students to learn primarily on their own from instructional materials. Later, Block and Anderson (1975) adapted the approach for use by elementary and secondary teachers in tandem with, rather than instead of, traditional instruction. Most mastery learning programs in the schools feature group rather than individualized instruction (Block, Efthim, & Burns, 1988; Guskey, 1985; Levine, 1985). Anderson (1985) suggested that the following six features will be found in any true mastery learning program: (1) a sequence of learning units, (2) clearly specified learning objectives, (3) preset mastery performance standards, (4) short, highly valid assessment procedures, (5) provision of feedback about learning progress to students, and (6) provision of additional time and help to students who fail to achieve mastery on their first try.

cycle of mastery learning The heart of mastery learning is the cycle of teaching, testing, reteaching, and retesting. Students are informed of the objectives of a unit and then receive instruction designed to enable them to master those objectives. After completing the instruction and related practice activities, they take tests designed to assess their mastery levels. Those who achieve preset performance standards (usually 80 percent, but sometimes 90 percent or more) are certified as having mastered the unit. These students will move on to the next unit, or more typically, will work on enrichment activities or activities of their own choosing until the rest of the class is ready to move on. Meanwhile, the students who did not meet mastery criteria will receive corrective instruction and additional practice, then retake the test.

Theoretically, these cycles of assessment and reteaching would continue until all students reached mastery, but in practice, the class usually moves on to the next unit after the second test. Thus, typical group-based mastery learning programs are a compromise between traditional teaching that allows little if any extra time to slow learners and ideal mastery programs that would allow all learners as much time as they needed. Even so, half or more of the total time devoted to a unit in a typical group-based mastery program is spent on corrective instruction with students who failed to reach mastery criteria on the first test (Slavin & Karweit, 1984).

problems with mastery learning The mastery learning philosophy is very appealing in many respects. However, critics have suggested that individual differences in learning ability are too stable and powerful to be compensated for by relatively minor adjustments in time for learning. They also question the goal of reducing individual differences in achievement levels, arguing that this can be accomplished only by holding back high achievers in addition to providing extra time and instruction to low achievers. Research on mastery learning has not resolved these issues clearly.

Comparisons of mastery learning with traditional instruction usually show both better attitudes and higher achievement in mastery classes, and in particular, show that a much higher percentage of mastery students master the content believed to be basic (Guskey & Pigott, 1988; Kulik, Kulik, & Bangert-Drowns, 1990). However, these highly favorable findings are misleading. First, a great deal of additional learning time is required to achieve the gains in mastery. Arrangements must be made to provide corrective instruction before or after school, or more typically, to do so during class time and thus hold back the faster learners while the teacher works with the slower ones. If these extra time needs are taken into account, there may be little or no advantage to the mastery learning.

Second, research does not support the key assumption that taking time to ensure mastery of early objectives will reduce the time that students need to learn later ones (Arlin, 1984). A few studies have shown modest time savings (Guskey & Pigott, 1988), but on the whole, it appears that mastery learning does not really solve the dilemma of having to choose between fixing learning time and accepting individual differences in mastery levels or fixing mastery levels and accepting individual differences in time to learn. Instead, mastery learning merely substitutes the second choice for the first.

A third problem is that the findings that are most favorable to mastery learning tend to come from the least impressive studies (Slavin, 1987). More favorable results have been reported from brief studies (lasting less than four weeks) involving instruction in content not normally taught at school than in studies of instruction in basic school subjects assessed over significant time periods. Also, results have been more impressive on criterion-referenced tests than on standardized tests. Slavin argued that the criterion-referenced tests used in the mastery programs are by definition biased in favor of these programs and thus ought to be viewed with suspicion, especially because their results are much more favorable to mastery learning programs than are the results of standardized tests. Defenders of mastery programs raise issues of curriculum alignment, however, noting that the criterion-referenced tests assess mastery of the specific objectives addressed in the program, whereas this may not be true of items on standardized tests (Guskey & Pigott, 1988).

Finally, even though mastery learning was developed with low achievers in mind, it appears to be especially difficult to implement in inner-city schools populated largely by low achievers. Slavin (1987) has suggested that this is because the corrective sequence of mastery learning is designed to correct relatively minor errors or misunderstandings, whereas students in inner-city schools may have a great many serious and idiosyncratic problems that need

individualized attention. Another possibility is that, due to differences in cultural backgrounds and experiences, many of the teachers working in inner-city schools have only limited knowledge of the examples and metaphors that would be best suited to their students, so that they may take longer to make adaptive corrections or may fail to make them successfully. Whatever the reason, Slavin and Karweit (1984) found no advantage to mastery learning over traditional instruction in ninth-grade general mathematics classes in inner-city Philadelphia schools studied over the course of an entire semester. Similarly, the Chicago schools initiated a large-scale mastery learning program with a great deal of enthusiasm in the early 1980s (Jones et al., 1985), but dropped it just a few years later after teacher complaints about the curriculum materials and about difficulties in implementing the program.

In conclusion, it appears that some attempt to implement the mastery learning philosophy would be desirable because of the achievement and motivation benefits it is likely to bring to low achievers. However, we believe that teachers should seek to maximize each student's individual progress, not merely to reduce variance in achievement levels. It appears that mastery learning will not succeed in reducing the time that slow learners need to learn (relative to the time that faster learners need), so that one can reduce individual differences in achievement progress only by deliberately holding back the faster learners. This is not to say that faster learners should be continually pushed to higher curriculum levels instead of being allowed to engage in enrichment activities or other alternatives to acceleration through the curriculum. It is to say, however, that activities planned for faster learners should be selected for sound pedagogical reasons and not as mere time fillers designed to slow their progress in order to give slower learners more time to catch up. A sensible compromise here would be to identify those learning objectives that seem most

The computer as a technological teaching tool has grown rapidly in recent years, with applications for everything from language learning, information retrieval, tutorial programs for drill and practice, and coaching.

essential and see that all students master these, while tolerating more variable performance on objectives considered less essential.

outcome-based education

Towers (1992b) noted that current movements toward outcome-based education depend heavily on the mastery learning literature for their rationales and notions about curriculum, instruction, and assessment. He quoted the following definition of outcome-based education that has been adopted by the Minnesota Department of Education (1991): Education that is outcome-based is a learner-centered, results-oriented system founded on the belief that all individuals can learn. In this system:

1. What is to be learned is clearly identified.
2. Learners' progress is based on demonstrated achievement.
3. Multiple instructional and assessment strategies are available to meet the needs of each learner.
4. Time and assistance are provided for each learner to reach maximum potential.

Based on earlier debates over mastery learning, Towers (1992b) adopted a mixed but primarily negative position on outcome-based education. Along with some of the concerns expressed here, Towers expressed concern that the record keeping and individualization requirements of outcome-based education would be too complicated for teachers to implement successfully, that the most capable students would not be taught effectively, and that instruction would focus on low-level and easily measured knowledge and skills at the expense of important higher-level cognitive objectives as well as objectives in the personal, social, and moral domains. We agree with Towers that outcome-based education carries the potential for such problems. The degree to which they emerge in particular cases will depend on the degree to which mastery learning principles are applied sensibly, as well as on the numbers and kinds of outcomes identified as the lynchpins of the program (see guidelines for using instructional objectives in Chapter 5).

computerized instruction

The ultimate in educational technology is computerized instruction, which uses the computer's information storage and retrieval capacity to enhance the possibilities for offering students varied and individualized instruction.

The earliest forms of computerized instruction were called **computer assisted instruction** (CAI), which was *instruction that included opportunities for learners to make responses and get feedback by interacting with a computer program.* Much early CAI involved nothing more than computerized workbooks, and even today this remains true of most computer-based drill and practice programs. From the standpoint of instructional theory, these CAI programs offer no advantages over traditional programmed instruction, and the need for learners to type in answers and conform to other computer use requirements can make CAI less efficient than traditional programmed instruction in many cases. However, the novelty and other motivational features (flashy graphics, gamelike elements) associated with computerized drill and practice make it worthwhile for certain learners. Also, because computers are perceived as impersonal and thus more "fair," students may learn to take more responsibility for their own performance under CAI than under teacher-led instruction (Griswold, 1984).

Computer managed instruction (CMI) is *instruction accomplished through computer programs that not only allow learners to make responses and get feedback but also respond to the learners' individual needs by ensuring that they meet mastery criteria and receive remedial instruction if necessary before moving on to the next stage.* CMI becomes possible when the computer can be programmed to direct learners through sequences of modules when they are progressing smoothly, to recycle or branch them through remedial modules when they are having difficulties, and to provide the teacher with records of responses and test results to use in diagnosing the probable source of the problem when special help is needed (Golden, Gersten, & Woodward, 1990). When it works well, CMI can eliminate much of the record keeping that is a major burden on teachers attempting to implement individualized learning systems. However, teachers still will need to monitor students' progress rather than depending completely on computerized management systems, because these systems sometimes evaluate performance or diagnose remediation needs incorrectly and follow up by presenting the students with inappropriate information or feedback (Hativa & Lesgold, 1991).

recent developments in computer-based education Installation and use of personal computers in schools has mushroomed in recent years. There also has been a proliferation of educational software and an enhancement of the computer's by-now familiar capabilities (information storage and retrieval, text editing, etc.) through linkage with other developing technologies such as videodiscs, CD-ROM, and hypermedia. As a result, computer-based education now can incorporate animation, time-lapse photography, and other audiovisual techniques for communicating information and demonstrating processes in ways that are not possible through conventional print materials. Also, some programs allow students to respond more actively and in more varied ways than they can respond to conventional instructional materials. Along with electronic workbooks for drill and practice, there are tutorial programs that provide not only feedback but tutorial instruction and friendly encouragement similar to what the student might receive from a tutor (Lepper & Chabay, 1985). Some programs provide opportunities for higher-level problem solving, work with complex databases, or simulation activities of a kind seldom seen in conventional seat work or programmed instruction.

As computer-based tutorial programs have grown in sophistication, their potential benefits have multiplied (Lepper & Gurtner, 1989). Many programs now pose quite complex problems for students, provide further instruction or assistance at their request, and then present them with immediate and graphic feedback. Some use Socratic tutoring methods to call students' attention to inconsistencies in their understanding of the topic. Some programs even incorporate complex "intelligence tutoring systems" that are based on detailed models of expected lines of progress from novice to expert status in the domain of knowledge involved. These programs can provide students with precise analyses and corrective instruction concerning their misconceptions (Psotka, Massey, & Mutter, 1988).

Language arts instruction is being enhanced through programs such as *Write to Read, Bank Street Writer,* and programs designed to teach students to plan, write, and edit stories or poetry (Cochran-Smith, Paris, & Kahn, 1991; Grejda & Hannafin, 1992). Mathematics education is being supplemented with applications of LOGO (Papert, 1980), *Turtle Geometry* (Abelson & diSessa, 1981) and other imaginative forms of computerized instruction (Davis, 1984). Interesting tutorial programs and simulation activities have been developed for science as well (Arons, 1984; Stewart et al., 1992). Social studies instruction can be enhanced with programs such as *Oregon Trail*, a simulation of a family's journey to the west in a covered wagon in 1847, or *Community Search*, a game in which student teams act as leaders of a primitive agricultural

society trying to decide where and how to relocate their community to a better natural environment. Recently, there has been a proliferation of simulation programs and videodisc data bases for use in social studies (Ehman et al., 1992; Laughlin, Hartoonian, & Sanders, 1989; Martorella, 1989; Savage & Armstrong, 1992; C. White, 1992). The databases are used for developing reports on nations, regions, or cultures, and the simulation programs offer opportunities to engage in critical thinking and decision making about social and civic issues.

Rapid expansion of computer-based learning in schools has been fueled by the proliferation of purchase and use of microcomputers not only in schools but in homes and throughout our society (Venezky & Osin, 1991). The percentage of U.S. schools with microcomputers reached 98 percent in 1990–91, and the ratio of students per computer in the schools was reduced from 125:1 in 1983–84 to 20:1 in 1990–91 (Quality Education Data, Inc., 1991). Microcomputers are being applied in a variety of ways in classrooms, both as sources of direct instruction or management of student learning of particular content and as more general tools or resources that students can use for a variety of purposes.

implications for teachers

computers and instruction

Venezky and Osin (1991) identified six ways in which computers can provide direct instruction or management of student learning of particular content:

• *Drill and practice:* Students use the computer to work on assigned practice tasks, and the teacher is provided with a record of their success rates.

• *Testing and practice:* Students take pretests

to determine their initial placement in a learning program, work through the program until mastery is attained, then exit or switch to other topics or levels. The teacher is provided with records of the learners' progress and weaknesses.

• *Tutorial:* The computer performs all of the instructional functions required in an explanatory mode (introduction, explication, practice, assessment, and remediation).

- *Coaching:* Students work on open-ended tasks that allow them more freedom to determine how to proceed and to interact with the computer in moving toward strategies for solving problems. The computer provides feedback to specific responses as well as advice or other cuing when students seem lost or mired in unproductive strategies.

- *Simulation:* Students work on authentic problems under realistic conditions that change in response to their strategic moves, so that they receive feedback as they go and have the opportunity to play out a simulation to its likely conclusion.

- *Game:* A simulation that includes individual or team competition or other elements designed to enhance the activity's motivational value.

Microcomputers can serve as multipurpose tools and resources. Their *text editing* capabilities can help students develop writing and communi-cation skills. Word-processing programs reduce the drudgery of writing and make it easier for students to edit and revise their work. Programs that check spelling or grammar may help students to improve those skills and programs that aid in outlining a paper may help students learn to organize their thoughts before beginning to write. The *graphics* capabilities of microcomputers have considerable potential for application in courses in design, art, and architecture. Through the *simulation* capacity of computers, students can conduct inquiry and experimentation that would be too time consuming, costly, or dangerous for them to undertake in reality. Microcomputers can provide access to dictionaries, encyclopedias, map collections, statistical abstracts, and other *databases* that students can use when preparing a research report or engaging in other forms of inquiry learning (Scardamalia et al., 1992). Videodisc technology has dramatically enhanced the potential for use of computers as sources of *visual input* to students, and material on videodiscs can be accessed much more quickly and easily than material on film or videotape.

research on computer-based learning

Research on the relative effectiveness of computer-based learning has yielded mixed findings concerning both its absolute effectiveness and its cost-effectiveness, although the general pattern of findings has become more positive recently as costs have dropped and educational software has increased in variety and advanced in sophistication (Fletcher, Hawley, & Piele, 1990). Evaluations of some of the more highly touted programs have been disappointing. The *Write to Read* program does not appear to offer any particular advantages to alternative programs as a method of fostering early achievement in reading and language arts (Freyd & Lytle, 1990; Slavin, 1991). Applications of LOGO programming in elementary schools have produced gains on skills developed directly in the programs but not the advances in general thinking and problem solving abilities that were anticipated by its creators (Lehrer, Guckenberg, & Lee, 1988; Miller, Kelly, & Kelly, 1988; Pea, Kurland, & Hawkins, 1985; Salomon & Perkins, 1987).

On the whole, however, research findings have been positive or at least promising. Reviews of more than 200 studies that have been done on computer-assisted instruction indicate that it has moderately strong effects on measures of relevant academic achievement (Lepper & Gurtner, 1989). Within this general trend, effects are stronger with programs that involve tutorials rather than simple drill and practice, with younger rather than older students, and with lower-ability or remedial students rather than other students. There has been less research on the effects of some of the newer programs designed to stimulate inductive learning through complex and interactive problem solving. However, several promising applications have been reported (Clements, 1986; Lehrer & Randle, 1987; Miller & Emihovich, 1986), and there appears to be a trend toward more positive results developing over time (Lepper & Gurtner, 1989). Finally, students usually express enthusiasm about working with computers (Becker, 1988).

Several qualifications on these positive findings should be noted, however. First, there was no control for the amount of instructional time in about half of the studies, so that much of the reported achievement advantage to computer-assisted instruction may be due to greater opportunity to learn the material rather than to use of the computer. Also, computerized instruction was just being introduced when many of these studies were conducted, so that achievement and especially attitude findings might have been inflated by the effects of novelty, additional adult attention, and other situational effects. Finally, several reviewers have cautioned that there is great variability in the findings and that more positive results are to be expected when the quality of any instruction provided through the software is good, the content is aligned with the rest of the curriculum, the activities and responses required of students are well suited to the grade level and the computer environment, and the students receive sufficient advance instruction and subsequent coaching to enable them to participate in the computer-based learning experience successfully (Bangert-Drowns, 1993; Cochran-Smith, 1991; Lepper & Gurtner, 1989). We would add that existing computerized instructional programs mostly reflect a traditional monocultural focus, so that we hope to see the development of more programs suited to students from diverse cultural backgrounds.

Limited access to computers can create feasibility problems. Even in classrooms containing eight computers, students spend as much as three-fourths of their time waiting for a turn at the computer (Center for Social Organization of Schools, 1984). However, this problem can be alleviated by having students work together in small groups on a single computer (Clements & Nastasi, 1988; Fish & Feldman, 1987). In fact, if used with software designed for group rather than individual use, computers can provide learning environments conducive to good group thinking and problem solving (Chernick, 1990).

the future of educational technology

From teaching machines through programmed instruction and educational television to computerized instruction, new educational technologies have been introduced with great enthusiasm and predictions that they will revolutionize education. So far none has, although most technological innovations have proven useful to some degree. Instead of replacing teachers, they have been assimilated into the traditional teacher-led group instruction model.

We expect that the same will be true of computerized instruction and all other innovations that depend on the independent learning efforts of the students, for two reasons. First, under these independent learning systems, students must be willing and able to maintain concentration, understand and follow directions, and correct and learn from their mistakes while working on their own for sustained periods of time. Most students in the early grades and many older students lack the reading comprehension and other independent learning skills required, and many students who do have the necessary skills lack the motivation to work on their own in this way for very long. Second, even students who have both the skills and the motivation to learn independently tend to run into trouble if left on their own too long, even when they seem to be progressing nicely. For example, Erlwanger (1975) interviewed bright students who consistently met mastery criteria on unit tests from their individualized mathematics curricula. Many students had misunderstood the material and developed mathematics misconceptions. They had invented rules of thumb that were useful for solving particular assigned problems but would not work (and would leave them confused) later when they encountered different applications of the concepts they were supposed to be learning.

Like other technological innovations, computers can improve schooling, by enhancing the effectiveness of teachers, rather than replacing them. Computers have already proven valuable for several purposes, and new ones are likely to be established as the state of the art advances. You will clearly need to be familiar with the use of microcomputers, both as tools for assisting with some of the general tasks of teaching (planning, record keeping, reporting progress to parents) and as vehicles for providing useful learning experiences to students like those whom you intend to teach.

Some of the topics addressed in this chapter underscore the need for teachers to resist getting overly caught up in current educational fads as they set goals, plan instruction, and make other professional decisions. It is fashionable these days to attack behavioristic concepts and methods as outdated, mechanistic, unnecessarily manipulative, or even immoral. Yet, they can be applied effectively and humanely in many classroom situations. It is also fashionable to tout computerized instruction and other technological advances as the wave of the future, without sufficient attention to important theoretical qualifications and feasibility limitations. Exposure to theoretical rationales

and position debates on these and other issues of the day provide useful input to teachers' critical thinking and decision making. Ultimately, however, it is the right and responsibility of individual teachers, working within their district guidelines, to determine what learning goals are most worth pursuing with their students and what curricular content and instructional methods are most likely to succeed in helping their students to achieve those goals.

summary

Behaviorists concentrate on overt, measurable behaviors and seek to discover general laws that can be used to predict and control such behaviors. They locate causality in external events that cue behavior and reinforce stimulus-response relationships.

Early behaviorists studied the conditioning that occurs as associations become established through contiguity and repetition. Pavlov developed the classical conditioning paradigm in which repeated presentation of the conditioned stimulus prior to the unconditioned stimulus develops associations between them so that learners begin to produce a conditioned response to the conditioned stimulus.

Thorndike developed the instrumental conditioning paradigm and formulated the laws of exercise and effect. Functionalists studied factors that affected the rate or extent of learning, especially the effects of massed versus distributed practice and of continuing practice to overlearning.

Skinner developed the operant conditioning paradigm for shaping behavior through contingent reinforcement. The paradigm can be used to bring behavior under stimulus control by reinforcing responses only when they occur in the presence of the cue stimulus, to develop stimulus and response discrimination, and to maintain established stimulus-response connections by fading the original continuous reinforcement schedule to some partial schedule. Animal learners adjust to fixed schedules because they allow prediction of reinforcement delivery, so variable schedules, especially variable ratio schedules, produce steadier and more persistent rates of response. Human learners' responses are less predictable because they are subject to rule governance as well as to contingent reinforcement.

Operant conditioning principles have been incorporated into behavior modification programs, teaching machines, programmed instruction, mastery learning, and computerized instruction. Over time, however, the emphasis has shifted from reinforcement to programming for continuous progress through small successive approximations.

Bandura and other social learning theorists include the covert mental activities of the learner in their theorizing, and they study learning that occurs through imitation of models or vicariously experiencing what is happening to models being observed. In the classroom, modeling is an important mechanism for demonstrating skills and for influencing students' attitudes, beliefs, and behavior.

Meichenbaum and others have developed cognitive behavior modification techniques to develop in learners the capacity for controlling their own behavior through goal setting, planning, self-instruction, self-monitoring, and self-reinforcement. Modeling combined with verbalized self-instruction is a powerful method of teaching thinking and problem solving.

Behaviorists have been prominent in developing technology for use in classrooms. Early work on teaching machines evolved into the science and technology of programmed instruction. Programs are designed to move learners in small steps with high rates of success from their initial entry level of skill to the target objective. Linear programs move all learners through a fixed sequence believed to be effective for everyone, and branched programs include options for skipping certain modules or providing remedial instruction as learner needs dictate.

The Keller Plan (also known as the Personalized System of Instruction, or PSI) features self-pacing, a mastery orientation, and student control of the examination schedule, typically coupled with a contract system for determining grades. Students learn from textbooks or programmed materials, get assistance from proctors when they need help, and take examinations when they are ready. The Keller Plan is popular with students who enjoy learning individually and effective with those who have the self-discipline to maintain the necessary study schedule.

The mastery learning approach focuses on the needs of low achievers by providing them with additional time and corrective instruction designed to enable them to master material that high achievers master more quickly and with less help. Research on mastery learning indicates that the approach does significantly increase the percentage of students in a class who eventually meet mastery criteria, but that it does not succeed in enabling low achievers to catch up with high achievers when the high achievers are not held back. Part of the mastery learning philosophy and some of its methods appear useful for teachers who wish to adapt typical instructional methods to better meet the needs of low achievers.

Computerized instruction offers several significant potential advantages over traditional methods, although it is likely to be most effective when planned to complement other teacher-guided instruction rather than as a replacement for the teacher. No approach that requires students to learn through extensive independent interaction with curriculum materials or computers in the absence of frequent input, guidance, and supervision from teachers is likely to be successful.

questions for reflection

1. Without rereading the text, differentiate between the following terms: conditioning, extinction, generalization, and discrimination. Most students have difficulty defining these terms after reading the text just one time. Why is this? What are the implications for how key terms need to be taught?

2. Without rereading the text, define Thorndike's law of exercise and law of effect. We suspect that you found it easier to remember and differentiate these terms than the terms mentioned in Question 1. Why is this? What makes one set of terms more difficult to learn than the other?

3. Why is massed practice usually less efficient than distributed practice? Cite examples where massed practice would be more efficient.

4. What is partial reinforcement? What are its unique and powerful advantages in a classroom setting?

5. How might teacher self-talk that is modeled verbally help students to become more reflective and analytical in the classroom?

6. Might you use mastery learning principles in your own teaching? Why or why not?

7. Visit a school and determine how microcomputers are being used. Do some students have more frequent or different computer experiences than others?

8. What are the advantages and disadvantages of microcomputers in the modern classroom? How will you use the technology in your own classroom?

9. Supporters of programmed instruction and related individualized learning systems tout them as solutions to the boredom and frustration problems of lockstep curricula. Critics attack them as ineffective, asocial/mechanistic/dehumanizing, and based on false assumptions about learning. Where do you stand? Why?

10. Would you rather be called a teacher or an instructional manager? Why?

cases to consider

lump in the throat Cindy Clutch, an otherwise successful student, is having a terrible time in her high school speech class. Each of her first two speeches, although short and centered on familiar content, was a disaster. She started out nervous and became increasingly so as she went on: turning red, losing her train of thought, stammering uncharacteristically, and in general, showing every sign of acute anxiety. Her speech teacher arranges a private conference to discuss the problem, and after some hemming and hawing, Cindy explains that she has dreaded making speeches ever since a traumatic experience occurred in the eighth grade. As an attractive early maturer, Cindy was the object of a great deal of attention, both desired and undesired, from the boys. She handled this well enough during informal contacts, but once while making a presentation to the class, she suddenly became acutely aware that she was wearing a tight sweater and several boys were staring at her breasts. She blushed, lost her train of thought, and had difficulty finishing the presentation. She

A speech class can evoke anxieties that interfere with success. Sometimes such anxieties are conditioned by early negative experiences.

has been anxious in public speaking situations ever since. How does the theory and research on conditioning apply to Cindy's problem? What steps might Cindy take to overcome it? How might her speech teacher help?

conditioning Shank Karen hurled the Frisbee and shouted, "Go get it, Shank!" Shank, a young German shepherd, arched his eyebrows and turned over on his back. Karen grumbled to herself, tramped to get the Frisbee, and returned to find Shank asleep. She shook Shank gently, but said with irritation, "Look at the Frisbee." Shank pawed it, then turned over. Karen reached into her jeans and pulled out a handful of dog pellets. As Shank devoured them, Karen said, "Shank, look at the Frisbee." Then she hurled the Frisbee, yelling, "Go get it, Shank!" Shank ignored her. What is Karen's training problem? Taking into account the principles of operant conditioning, how would you

advise her to change her approach? What would you do if you were a teacher experiencing problems training a messy and forgetful student to put things away and keep his desk in order?

practice makes boredom Jim Butkus, a second-grade teacher, walks to Terry Stone's desk. Terry nervously stashes a comic book as Jim asks with concern, "Terry, why aren't you practicing your spelling words?" Terry's face reddens as he shuffles through the book trying to find today's assignment. "It's okay," Mr. Butkus continues reassuringly. "Tell me why you aren't studying." Terry remains silent for a moment and then blurts out, "I'm tired of spending fifteen minutes every day studying spelling words. Practice, practice, practice—it's boring!" Assuming that Terry and his classmates need this spelling practice, how might Mr. Butkus provide more interesting (or at least varied) ways for the students to get it? List several examples.

cognitive and constructivist views of learning

objectives

When you have mastered the material in this chapter you will be able to

1. Identify the implications of the cognitive revolution in educational psychology for theories of learning and teaching
2. Contrast transmission models of learning and teaching with constructivist models
3. Define the key concepts of gestalt psychology (gestalt, patterned perception, framing and contrast, good form, learning through insight) and explain their implications for classroom instruction
4. Explain Ausubel's model of meaningful reception learning and his ideas about structuring and sequencing instruction so as to ease learning and enhance transfer
5. Define advance organizers and state their instructional functions
6. Explain Bruner's disciplined inquiry model of discovery learning, his concept of the spiral curriculum, and his ideas about how teachers can stimulate students' cognitive development
7. Identify the strengths and weaknesses of discovery learning and the circumstances under which it can and cannot be used effectively
8. Compare and contrast Ausubel's meaningful reception model and Bruner's disciplined inquiry model with each other and with other cognitive models that are more explicitly constructivist
9. Explain the meanings and instructional implications of the constructivists' notions of a network concept of knowledge, knowledge as socially constructed, situated learning and authentic tasks, and scaffolding and transfer of responsibility for managing learning from the teacher to the learner

the cognitive revolution

Behaviorism was the dominant force in American psychology until the 1960s, when the field underwent what is now commonly called "the cognitive revolution." Depictions of learning as conditioning of associations and responses through reinforcement gave way to cognitive views that depicted learning as involving the acquisition or reorganization of the cognitive structures through which we process and store information. Cognitive theorists began concentrating on human learning, especially the meaningful learning of information and intellectual skills that occurs in schools and is mediated through language. These theorists maintained that intake of information from the environment is active and purposeful rather than passive and controlled by cue stimuli, that learning involves cognitive processing of information rather than mere stimulus-response association, and that items of knowledge acquired through learning are "sorted," "filed," and "cross-indexed" rather than stored in isolation from one another. Gradually, learners develop understanding of the relationships among elements of their knowledge, and they build cognitive structures for retaining this knowledge in an organized way.

As the cognitive revolution continued, this cognitive view gradually supplanted the behavioral view as the dominant approach to learning among educational psychologists. Currently, the most active areas of debate are not between behaviorists and cognitivists but between different subgroups of cognitivists who all share the views summarized in the previous paragraph. Many of the ongoing debates among cognitive theorists relate to where they stand on a dimension that extends from a purely transmission view of learning to a radical constructivist view of learning.

Transmission models of learning *imply that teachers act as senders who transmit a fixed body of content to learners, who act as receivers.* In this view, successful teaching involves efficient transmission of the target content. Few if any cognitive theorists have explicitly articulated such a transmission view of learning. However, many of them have developed models of teaching that say a lot about goals, content, and instructional methods, but not much about students. Critics tend to label any model for moving the class as a whole toward preestablished instructional objectives as a transmission model, but especially models that call for a great deal of teacher lecturing and for stepwise progression through preestablished sequences of activities.

These critics of transmission views tend to be cognitive theorists who favor constructivist models of learning (Davis, Maher, & Noddings, 1990; Resnick & Klopfer, 1989; Steffe, Cobb, & von Glasersfeld, 1988). **Constructivist models** are *models of learning that emphasize students' development of new knowledge through active construction processes that link new knowledge to prior knowledge.* Instead of passively receiving or merely copying input from teachers or textbooks, they actively mediate the input by trying to make sense of it and relating it to what they already know about the topic. This construction process is important because unless students build representations of the new learning, "making it their own" by paraphrasing it into their own words and considering its meanings and implications, the learning will be retained only as relatively meaningless and inert rote memories. Such **inert knowledge** *is recallable when cued by questions or test items very similar to those used in practice exercises, but students will not be able to access and apply it when it might be useful in everyday living.* To develop **generative knowledge** that *is usable for interpreting new situations, solving problems, thinking and reasoning, and learning generally,* students need to elaborate and question what they are told, examine new content in relation to more familiar content, and build new knowledge structures (Resnick & Klopfer, 1989).

Constructivists differ among themselves in their ideas about the nature of knowledge. *Empiricist-oriented constructivists* believe that knowledge is anchored in the external environment and exists independently of the learner's cognitive activities, so they tend to speak about helping learners to construct accurate concepts (Case, 1982; Ginsburg & Opper, 1988; Rumelhart & Norman, 1981). In contrast, *radical constructivists* believe that knowledge resides only in the constructions of learners. Consequently, teachers cannot teach precise representations of "truth," but can only negotiate shared meanings with students and provide them with opportunities to construct useful understandings by overcoming obstacles or contradictions that arise as they engage in purposeful activity (Cobb, 1986; Cobb, Yackel, & Wood, 1992; von Glasersfeld, 1984). Whatever their underlying philosophical views, however, all constructivists emphasize that teachers need to go beyond information transmission models (teachers or texts tell, students memorize) and move toward knowledge construction models of teaching and learning. These involve structuring reflective discussions of the meanings and implications of content and providing opportunities for students to use the content as they engage in inquiry, problem solving, or decision making (Brooks, 1990).

In this chapter, we will consider several historically significant and currently influential cognitive and constructivist views of learning, along with their instructional implications. Then, in the next chapter, we will look more closely at some of the information processing and learning mechanisms involved in the knowledge construction process.

roots in gestalt psychology

Although the term "constructivist" is relatively new, many cognitive and constructivist ideas about learning can be traced to John Dewey and Jean Piaget and some go back at least as far as Socrates. Many are embodied in historically significant educational movements such as open education, inquiry learning, and discovery learning, as well as in contemporary movements such as whole-language teaching and portfolio assessment. An important precursor to all of these developments, however, was gestalt psychology.

In the first third of the twentieth century, when behaviorism dominated American psychology, a variety of approaches thrived in Europe (Freud in Vienna, Piaget in Geneva, mental measurement work in France and England). Gestalt psychology was developed in Germany by Max Wertheimer and his associates Kurt Koffka and Wolfgang Köhler, all of whom later emigrated to the United States to escape the Nazis. **Gestalt** psychologists emphasized that perception tends to be organized into *meaningful patterns that include relationships between elements in addition to the elements themselves* (*gestalt* means "pattern" or "configuration" in German). Using visual illusions and other demonstrations, the gestalt psychologists showed that perception involves instant recognition of meaningful patterns, not inferences built slowly by taking in isolated bits of information and gradually imposing meaning on them. Also, perception is subjective—different people, or even the same person at different times, may see the same input differently (see Figure 7.1).

We tend to impose *good form* on stimulus input: to perceive and remember objects and events as conforming to familiar or expected patterns. Even when the input is not simple, regular, or complete enough to justify such perception, we tend to see and remember it as if it were. Elements that conflict with our good-form interpretations tend to be ignored during the initial perception and forgotten when it is remembered later.

Interpretation depends not only on the input itself but on how this input is framed or presented. Figures can be perceived differently depending on how they contrast with other figures or with the background. A gray dot looks lighter against a dark background but darker

Figure 7.1 Do you see a younger woman or a sad-eyed older woman in this drawing?

against a light background. Such *contrast effects* also occur with more complex perceptions. For example, teachers grading compositions will tend to grade an average essay higher if it follows several poor ones than if it follows several good ones.

Although gestalt psychology dealt more with perception than learning, Wertheimer drew on it to formulate guidelines for instruction. He noted, for example, that just as highlighting, contrasting, and other framing techniques can be used to make visual stimuli stand out as figure against the background, parallel techniques can be used to make key ideas stand out when presenting information. Learners can be made aware of the structure of the content to be learned and the relationships among its elements, so that they can retain it as an organized body of knowledge. In the classroom, listener-friendly lectures and reader-friendly texts can be constructed so as to help learners to recognize which ideas are the most important ones and how these ideas connect with one another.

Köhler (1959) demonstrated that conditions could be arranged to foster **learning by discovery**—*learning through one's own self-guided* *exploration, rather than through explanation or modeling from a teacher.* In a typical experiment, chimpanzees were placed in a situation where food was in sight but could not be reached. After giving up trying to reach it by stretching or jumping, the chimps sometimes appeared to engage in thinking that culminated in an "aha" experience—a sudden *insight* that was followed by rapid solution of the problem. For example, the chimp might realize that food placed outside the cage could be moved close enough to be grasped by pushing it with a stick that was already within reach. In a more complex variation, a short stick could be used to gather in a longer stick which then could be used to gather in the food. This problem was more likely to be solved if the items were lined up in order outside the cage (first the short stick, then the longer stick, and then the food). Such experiments proved that instrumental learning could occur without Thorndike's trial and error or Skinner's shaping of successive approximations (see Chapter 6). Instead, the chimps "figured out" the solution and then demonstrated it in a single trial. If placed in the same situation again, they solved the problem immediately without the need to hesitate for thought, indicating that the learning was retained. Such experiments and related theorizing by gestalt psychologists provided a rationale for some of the early arguments favoring guided discovery over linear programming as the preferred model for classroom teaching.

Over time, the study of learning began to focus on human learning, including the highly cognitive forms of learning emphasized in classrooms. This emphasis characterized the emerging field of educational psychology and the work of two of its leaders, David Ausubel and Jerome Bruner. Both of these theorists built on the gestalt psychologists' emphasis on making learners aware of the structure of the content to be learned and conscious of the relationships among its elements. Bruner also built on the notion of discovery learning.

Ausubel and meaningful reception learning

David Ausubel described **meaningful reception learning:** *learning from expository instruction that communicates the content to be learned in its final form.* Ausubel's model would be characterized today as primarily a transmission view, although he emphasized that the teacher's task is to present the material in ways that encourage learners to make sense of it by relating it to what they already know. Compared to rote memorizing, such meaningful reception learning will be retained longer, be better integrated with other knowledge, and be more readily available for application.

Ausubel is widely quoted for his statement that "the most important factor influencing the meaningful learning of any new idea is the state of the individual's existing cognitive structure at the time of learning" (Ausubel & Robinson, 1969, p. 143). He emphasized the teaching of organized bodies of knowledge structured around key concepts and suggested ways that teachers might structure the content for their students (Ausubel, 1963; Ausubel & Robinson, 1969; Ausubel, Novak, & Hanesian, 1978).

Ausubel started with the assumption that knowledge is organized into *hierarchical structures* in which *subordinate concepts* are subsumed under higher-level *superordinate concepts.* Even if we gradually forget details, we tend to remember key ideas associated with a particular cognitive structure, and to retain the structure itself. The structure provides scaffolding that supports retention of the information as an organized body of knowledge. It also functions as a frame within which to interpret related new knowledge or efficiently relearn forgotten knowledge. For example, even if you do not remember the details of Bloom's taxonomy, you are likely to remember that there are many types and levels of learning that need to be considered in planning instruction.

signaling techniques

Mayer (1984) elaborated on Ausubel's ideas by developing signaling techniques for calling learners' attention to the structural features of presentations. **Signaling techniques** *emphasize a passage's conceptual structure or organization.* Four major types of signals are (1) *specifications of the structure of relations* (cues such as "first," "second," "third," or "the problem is . . . and the solution is"), (2) *premature presentations* of key information that will follow ("the main ideas to be discussed are . . . "), (3) *summary statements* (similar to premature presentations except that they occur at the ends of passages), and (4) *point words* that indicate the author's perspective or emphasize important information ("more importantly," "unfortunately").

Such signaling helps make the structure of a passage clearer and provides a conceptual framework for learners to use in identifying important information and organizing it coherently (Lorch, Lorch, & Inman, 1993). Passages that include such signaling elements are learned better than the same passages without such signaling (Loman & Mayer, 1983; Mayer, Dyck, & Cook, 1984).

advance organizers

Ausubel stressed organizing content in logical ways and helping learners to recognize this organization by presenting outlines, noting transitions between parts, and including summaries at the end. In addition, he advocated presenting **advance organizers:** *superordinate concepts within which learners can subsume the new material and relate it to what they already know.* For example, Ausubel (1960) had college students read a 500-word advance organizer before reading a 2,500-word text on the metallurgical properties of carbon steel. The organizer reminded them that alloys exist in addition to pure metals and that different properties affect their usefulness for various purposes. Then, the longer passage described the properties of a particular alloy—carbon steel. Although the organizer presented ideas relevant for understanding the longer passage, it did not include material given in the passage itself. Students who read the advance organizer retained more of the passage than students who read a 500-word passage on the historical development of methods used for processing iron and steel. Although both passages were relevant to the general topic of steel, only the advance organizer presented superordinate concepts within which students could subsume the longer material.

Advance organizers are not conventional previews or summaries that state the main points of the main text in briefer form. Instead, they characterize the general nature of the text (such as by describing its purpose and the line of argument taken to accomplish it) and provide superordinate concepts within which it can be subsumed. This does not mean that advance organizers should be highly abstract or difficult to understand, however. To be useful, they must be stated in terms already familiar to the learners (Anderson, 1984).

Advance organizers are especially useful when the material is not well organized and learners lack the knowledge needed to be able to organize it well for themselves (Ausubel, 1978; Corkill, 1992; Tudor, 1986). It helps if learners are not merely presented with the organizer but required to study or paraphrase it (Corkill, Glover, & Bruning, 1988; Corkill et al., 1988; Kloster & Winne, 1989; Snapp & Glover, 1990).

Types of organizers besides those described by Ausubel can be effective. These include organizers presented in oral rather than written form (Alexander, Frankiewicz, & Williams, 1979), organizers that present key terms or

research at work
organizing learning

Besides advance organizers, Ausubel studied postlesson summaries and review questions as devices to help students integrate what they learn. His work provided much support for the advice, "Tell them what you are going to tell them, then tell them, then tell them what you told them." For teachers, this would mean the following: (1) start lessons with advance organizers or at least with previews that include general principles, outlines, or questions that establish a learning set; (2) briefly describe learning objectives and alert students to key concepts; (3) present new material in small steps organized and sequenced logically; (4) elicit student responses regularly to stimulate active learning and ensure that each step is mastered before moving to the next; (5) finish with a review of the main points, stressing general integrative concepts; (6) follow up the lesson with questions or assignments that require students to encode material in their own words and apply or extend it to new contexts.

principles rather than characterizing the material to be learned with reference to previous knowledge (Mayer, 1984), and organizers that present models or illustrations rather than expository explanations (Abel & Kulhavy, 1986; Clarke, 1990; Mayer, 1989b; Tajika et al., 1988). In general, concrete models, analogies or examples, sets of higher-order rules, or discussions of main themes in familiar terms are more effective organizers than specific factual prequestions, outlines, summaries, or directions to pay attention to specific key facts or terms (Mayer, 1979b).

linking the new to the familiar

Various investigators who share Ausubel's concern with structuring content to encourage meaningful reception learning have studied other factors besides advance organizers and signaling of the organizational structure. These include analogies, metaphors, examples, and concrete models that help learners to link new concepts to familiar ones or to develop concrete referents for abstract concepts.

Analogies help link the new to the familiar. Mayer (1984) explained the principles of radar by drawing analogies between the reflection of radio waves and the reflection of sound waves that underlies familiar echo phenomena. Royer and Cable (1975) taught the crystalline structure of molecules by drawing analogies to a *model* constructed from tinker toys. *Diagrams* or *flow charts* showing simplified models of biological systems or the working of machines can make it easier to learn such information than it is when the presentation is restricted to verbal information. In general, analogies that help learners link the new to the familiar can be expected to facilitate learning (Halpern, Hansen, & Riefer, 1990; Mayer, 1975, 1979a; Hayes & Tierney, 1982; Vosniadou & Schommer, 1988), although care must be taken to ensure that any potentially misleading aspects of the analogy do not lead to misconceptions for the learners (Zook & DiVesta, 1991).

teaching for transfer

Ausubel stressed that learning should be available for transfer to new contexts. Besides being able to remember and apply it within the context in which it was originally learned, students should be able to generalize the learning to relevant application contexts and to access and build on it when extending their learning into new areas. Transfer of existing knowledge to new situations simplifies the task of learning in such new situations.

Transfer may be vertical or lateral. **Vertical transfer**—*application of knowledge acquired in the process of learning lower-level skills to facilitate learning of higher-level skills*—is desired when teaching hierarchically organized skills. To promote vertical transfer, Ausubel recommended following a sequential organization if this applies to the material, making sure that learners have whatever knowledge they need at each step, consolidating learning and ensuring mastery before going on to higher steps, and stressing general and integrative principles. Within each step, the teacher would follow a pattern of *progressive differentiation* in which more general or inclusive ideas are presented first and then broken into their component parts. In addition, the teacher would follow the principle of *integrative reconciliation* by noting the connections between ideas and the similarities and differences between overlapping concepts. Where new material appears to conflict with what has already been taught, it is important to reconcile the apparent conflicts so that the new material can be integrated within the cognitive structures already developed.

Lateral transfer is *application of knowledge acquired in learning material in one domain to facilitate learning in another domain.* Although Ausubel recognized limits on how much lateral transfer can be expected, he suggested that teachers can promote lateral transfer by concentrating on underlying principles and generalizations and by giving students opportunities to apply material in realistic situations. He also suggested emphasizing aspects of subject matter that have the most potential for lateral transfer, such as Latin language roots of modern English words or general logic and problem-solving applications of mathematics.

Research has confirmed many of these ideas. Bromage and Mayer (1981) found that organizing a technical passage around general principles produced better transfer to problem solving than organizing it by topic. Similarly, Mayer (1975) found that organizing a mathematics lesson to move from familiar prerequisite concepts toward formal definitions and algorithms produced better transfer to problem solving than organizing it to move from the formal to the familiar. In general, the text-structuring factors stressed by Ausubel appear to be especially important for ensuring that learners grasp the main ideas in a presentation and are able to transfer and apply them later (Mayer, 1979a). They fit well with currently emphasized ideas about teaching school subjects for understanding and use of knowledge (see Chapter 11).

Bruner and disciplined inquiry

Like Ausubel, Jerome Bruner (1966, 1971, 1990) is a leading educational psychologist who has stressed the importance of making learners aware of the structure of the content to be learned and the relationships among its elements so that it can be retained as an organized body of knowledge. In contrast to Ausubel's emphasis on expository teaching, however, Bruner has emphasized enabling students to learn through guided discovery, especially through disciplined inquiry.

Bruner has much in common with Piaget, including an emphasis on the importance of active exploration and problem solving as a natural and preferable way to learn. He also is pessimistic about the value of attempting to teach students how to manipulate abstract procedures (e.g., learning how to solve equations) without first establishing the deep connections between these procedures and what they represent—the activities involved in solving practical, concrete problems (Wood, 1988). However, whereas Piaget emphasized children's learning through exploration of the physical environment, Bruner emphasizes their learning at school. In particular, he emphasizes the learning of the academic disciplines, not only because these are storehouses of enduringly important knowledge but also because they introduce children to powerful ways of thinking that constitute important learning-to-learn skills (observing carefully, making comparisons, analyzing similarities and differences, etc.).

In addition to a judicious selection of the facts, concepts, generalizations, and knowledge-generating procedures that a discipline offers, Bruner wants students to learn its structure—the pattern of relationships among these elements that connect them as parts of a larger, organized body of knowledge. He also wants them to understand the intentions and purposes that led to the creation of the discipline and that motivate its practitioners. Consequently, he wants students to develop their knowledge by engaging in **disciplined inquiry**—*using the tools that mathematicians use to address problems like those that mathematicians address, using the tools that historians use to address problems like those that historians address, and so on.*

Two of Bruner's ideas that have attracted widespread attention are: each discipline's structure includes key principles that, once understood, guide insight into the field as a whole; and these principles can be imparted, in some form, to children at any stage of development (Farnham-Diggory, 1992). Bruner (1960, p.33) takes seriously the notion that "any subject can be taught effectively in some intellectually honest form to any child at any stage of development." This is not a claim that anyone can learn

anything; note the qualifier "in some intellectually honest form." However, at least some aspects of any subject can be presented so as to be both true to the spirit of the discipline from which the information is drawn (i.e., accurate, organized around important concepts, and complete in some sense, even though a subject-matter specialist might see it as just part of a much larger picture), and meaningful (i.e., learners can relate it to their existing knowledge).

According to Bruner, the key to successful teaching of disciplinary knowledge is translating it into terms that students can understand. He believes that children at different stages of development have characteristic ways of viewing and explaining the world, so that successful teaching of school subjects to children of a given age requires representing the structure of the subject in terms of the children's way of viewing things.

In elaborating on this idea, Bruner spoke of three ways in which people might "know" something: through doing it, through a picture or image of it, or through symbolic means mediated through language. Predominant in early childhood but continuing throughout life is *enactive mode* knowledge: knowledge about how to perform processes or operations. Images, words, and symbols are not involved to any significant degree. With development, thinking becomes less stimulus bound and dependent on active manipulation of concrete objects. Children become capable of understanding knowledge presented in the *iconic mode* via pictures, images, or memories of previously experienced objects or events. They can begin to think about the properties of objects rather than only about what can be done with them. Later, students become able to represent knowledge in the *symbolic mode,* and thus to understand and manipulate purely abstract concepts. They must be able to do this in order to profit from extended verbal instruction in the more formal aspects of subject-matter knowledge. More recently, Bruner (1990) has advocated emphasis on narrative rather than analytic representations of knowledge as a way to connect better with children's ways of thinking.

In Bruner's view, good instruction begins by connecting with students' current representations of knowledge about the topic. As it progresses, it develops better connections across different modes of representing existing knowledge and extends this knowledge to new aspects of the topic. In the process, it offers students a variety of educational experiences. These include active hands-on experiences in addition to verbal explanations, and examples presented in the enactive and iconic modes in addition to explanations in the symbolic mode. Teachers help students to integrate their knowledge by presenting them with organizing principles, cause-effect explanations, and other aids to seeing how things relate to one another.

the spiral curriculum

As an alternative to the notion of moving students in lockstep fashion through linear hierarchies of learning objectives, Bruner recommended the *spiral curriculum,* in which students are brought back to the same general topics periodically but encouraged to address these topics at different levels of knowledge representation and analysis. Each time the "spiral" comes around to the topic, students will have broadened and deepened their knowledge about it and therefore will be both able and motivated to explore it at a deeper level. For example, the ability to recognize and label different animals might be an appropriate initial objective. Then, students might learn classifications for animals and the similarities and differences among animal types. Later they could learn about the natural habitats and behavior of various animals, and still later, they could study animal anatomy or physiology.

Although Bruner acknowledges the value of organizing the content to be taught, he notes that often there is no single best way to structure it and argues that there are limits to what can be accomplished by imposing structure externally. He believes that learners will retain more if allowed to organize material according to their own interests. Unlike behaviorists, who emphasize linear sequencing of learning programs as a way to foster rapid progress with minimal errors, Bruner has little interest in minimizing errors. He believes that pursuing dead ends and making errors are natural parts of learning, at least if students are taught with methods that emphasize developing deep understandings rather than speed in covering material. Also, he sees errors as useful for maintaining interest and stimulating hypotheses, if students are not made to feel ashamed of making mistakes. Other educators have reached similar conclusions about the potential of errors for stimulating learning (Rohrkemper & Corno, 1988).

discovery learning

Bruner believes that the most meaningful learning is developed through discoveries that occur during exploration motivated by curiosity. He would like to see schools provide more opportunities for students to expand their knowledge by developing and testing hypotheses rather than merely reading or listening to the teacher. Consequently, he advocates instructional methods that encourage students to learn through guided discovery. Guided discovery methods involve providing students with opportunities to manipulate objects actively and transform them through direct action, as well as activities that encourage them to search, explore, analyze, or otherwise process input rather than merely respond to it. In theory, such opportunities not only will increase students' knowledge about the topic at hand but stimulate their curiosity and help them to develop

Simulations have small but positive effects on students' learning. They can be particularly useful in social studies to help students learn about other civilizations, other times.

generalized learning-to-learn strategies useful for discovering knowledge in other situations.

For example, students studying geography might be given maps indicating the physical features of an area (temperature, rainfall, elevations, and locations of natural resources and waterways) and invited to speculate about the locations of the capital city and the major seaport, the economic emphases likely to develop in particular regions, or the placement and functions of the major highways or railroads. Later, the students are given more detailed maps indicating the development that actually

occurred. This feedback generally confirms the usefulness of the principles of geography being learned, but also introduces complexity by showing that exceptions can occur due to unique local factors (capitals are not always the largest or most centrally located cities).

simulation activities

Bruner's *Toward a Theory of Instruction* (1966) was influential in encouraging educators to use simulation activities as vehicles for promoting discovery learning (Boocock & Schild, 1968; Groff & Render, 1983). Some of these are role-play activities based on actual events, such as when social studies students are divided into groups representing various special interests in a state legislature and invited to propose and seek support for budget recommendations, or science students are assigned to groups to work on problems such as figuring out how to use X-rays to kill cancerous growths without killing the patient. Some are games in which teams compete to accomplish some goal more quickly or successfully than their rivals.

Students generally respond enthusiastically to simulation activities, although they do not always generalize the principles they use in the activity to other circumstances. The most helpful simulations appear to be those that include information-processing opportunities—chances for students to develop concepts or strategies that can be used in solving a range of problems (Coleman et al., 1973). Evaluations of simulation games have yielded mixed results, but overall they indicate small but positive effects on students' learning and motivation (VanSickle, 1986).

Cohen and Bradley (1978) assessed the impact in eight fifth- and sixth-grade classes of a simulation game that included both information-processing opportunities and experiential learning. Control classes were taught the regular unit on map skills from the textbook, using normal procedures over four consecutive sixty-minute periods. Experimental classes played the game "Phantom Submarine" during these periods. The game assumes that a submarine has been sunk off the coast of Florida and lies 200 feet below the surface, but not on the floor of the ocean. The ship carries 200 tons of mercury and is believed to contain a self-triggering device that will cause it to explode if it is entered or brought to the surface. The ship is floating, however, so it may strike an object and self-destruct even if left alone. John L.

Greedy, a treasure hunter, wants to salvage the submarine because the mercury is worth $2 million. However, if the mercury should be set loose, great damage will be done to fish and plant life. The game builds toward a simulated meeting of the World Pollution Control Committee where students play assigned roles to discuss the problem and try to agree on a solution.

The class is divided into several five-person groups that begin by compiling knowledge about currents, the route of the Gulf Stream, mountain ranges on the ocean floor, and so on. Individuals gather this information and share it with the group, and then fill in verbal and graphic material on their map cards, so that eventually all students in each group have the same information. Then the group decides what to do with the submarine. Finally, the students role play the conference and try to reach a conclusion.

In this study, teachers learned to play the game and then used it as a vehicle for teaching map skills. Both groups were tested immediately following the unit and again two weeks later. There were no immediate differences, but after two weeks, the map skills of the control students had declined whereas those of the experimental students had improved. Cohen and Bradley suggested that the experience with using information from maps to solve the problem of the submarine may have caused the experimental students to develop a theory about map symbols and usage that enabled them to recognize previous errors more easily and thus to improve their performance over time.

Despite these positive findings, Cohen and Bradley suggested that simulation should not be the only method used in social studies courses, but should be combined with more traditional methods. For more information about simulation methods, see issues of the journal *Simulation and Games*.

when to use discovery learning

Discovery learning approaches were developed from the premise that learning that occurs through self-motivated, active exploration of areas of personal interest is especially likely to be retained in long-term memory and integrated with previous learning. Despite widespread acceptance of this premise, however, there has not been widespread acceptance of discovery learning as the primary approach to instruction in classrooms. Ausubel (1963), Skinner (1968), and others have noted important limitations on the discovery approach: (1) true discoveries are rare, and most of them are made by the brightest and most motivated students, (2) discovery learning is uncertain and inefficient compared to more direct instruction, (3) it places the teacher in the unnatural role of withholding information from students who are experiencing frustration or "discovering" mistaken notions that will have to be "unlearned" later, and (4) it needs careful planning and structuring—providing the students with clear goals and with needed information and skills, guiding their exploration with cues or questions, and finishing with a review to make sure that what they learn is complete and accurate.

Another problem is that many discovery activities appear to be more trouble than they are worth. For example, inquiry-oriented science curricula often include an experiment calling for comparison of plants grown in sunlight with plants grown in the dark. This experiment often does not work because the plants raised in the light fail to thrive for some reason or because the other plants are not sufficiently protected from light or are not left in the dark long enough. Furthermore, even if it does work and the expected differences in plant growth appear, the results are anticlimactic because they are so predictable and because they must be related back to concepts

taught several weeks earlier (Anderson & Smith, 1987).

Even direct comparisons with expository instruction do not always favor discovery learning. First, expository instruction is more efficient, especially if the material is well organized and geared to the students' levels of development. Second, skilled teachers usually can create student motivation to learn about academic topics, even where none existed before. Third, because discovery learning approaches assume a great deal about student motivation, background knowledge, and learning-to-learn skills, they are difficult to implement. Thus, total reliance on discovery learning approaches is rarely if ever feasible.

On the other hand, although data on the matter are spotty and provide only mixed support (Ausubel & Robinson, 1969; Breaux, 1975; Hermann, 1969; Strike, 1975), discovery learning does appear to be useful, and perhaps optimal, when students have the necessary motivation and skills. Discovery learning is essential for objectives involving problem solving or creativity. To the extent that students work on their own, it is important to select activities that they find interesting or to stimulate their interest in the process of introducing the activities to them. To the extent that students are expected to work collaboratively, it is important to see that they are prepared to collaborate productively.

constructivist views of learning

As the cognitive revolution continues to unfold, educational psychologists increasingly are depicting learning not just as the cognitive mediation of knowledge acquisition but as a constructive process in which learners proceed in their own ways to build unique representations of the content. These learner constructions may or may not include complete and accurate reconstruction of what the teacher or textbook author intended to convey. Sometimes the learning is incomplete or distorted.

Even when the basic message is reconstructed as intended, it gets connected to each learner's unique set of prior understandings. As a result, each learner constructs a unique set of meanings and implications of "the same" set of ideas, and "files" it in memory accordingly. For example, after reading a fictional or nonfictional narrative about mountain climbers who overcame potential disasters to reach the summit, one reader might remember and think about the text primarily as a story about achievement motivation, another as a story about the value of teamwork, another as a story about how shared adventure seals the bonds of friendship, and yet another as an illustration of the challenges and specialized techniques involved in mountain climbing. The students were exposed to the same narrative as constructed by its author and their reconstructions of it all include the same basic story line, but they emphasize different meanings and potential implications.

In view of such phenomena, constructivists believe that models of learning should place much more emphasis on the learner's own construction and organization of knowledge. While they prefer cognitive to behavioral models, they reject Ausubel's emphasis on careful sequencing of content according to adult logic and his primarily transmission-oriented model of teaching. They are more accepting of Bruner's ideas (especially discovery learning and the spiral curriculum), although they see some aspects of his disciplined inquiry model as overly focused on adult rather than child logic (especially his ideas about the structures of the disciplines). They prefer models that retain a role for the teacher in guiding students' learning efforts but that place more emphasis on stimulating students to develop their current knowledge in their own ways than on moving them through predetermined

sequences of objectives. There is no single dominant constructivist model, partly because constructivists interested in different grade levels and subject matter have emphasized different kinds of learning that call for different kinds of teaching. Certain key ideas are found in most constructivist models: (1) the network concept of knowledge structuring, (2) knowledge as socially constructed, (3) situated learning and authentic tasks, and (4) scaffolding and transfer of responsibility for managing learning from teacher to learner.

the network concept of knowledge structuring

Misuse of hierarchical schemes such as the Bloom taxonomy of cognitive objectives (see Chapter 5) to guide curriculum development has implanted the notion that instructional strands are hierarchies of knowledge that learners must proceed through in sequence. Thus, the teacher introduces a topic by beginning at the knowledge level and staying there until a complete base of information has been developed, then moves to the comprehension level by helping students begin to translate the information into different terms and probe its connections, then moves to the application level, and so on. Movement to higher levels (analysis, synthesis, and evaluation) occurs only after mastery of lower levels has been accomplished.

Standing in opposition to this point of view is a great deal of constructivist theorizing and some supportive research (Brophy, 1989; Marzano et al., 1988) suggesting that there is no need to impose such a rigid, linear hierarchy on teaching and learning. The argument is that, instead of viewing knowledge as composed of linear hierarchies, we should view it as composed of networks structured around key ideas. These *knowledge networks* include facts, concepts, and generalizations, along with related values, dispositions, procedural knowledge (implementation skills), and conditional knowledge (of when and why to access and apply other parts of the network).

An important instructional implication of this network conception of knowledge organization is that one can enter and begin to learn about a knowledge network almost anywhere, not just at the low end of a linear hierarchy. Learning can be couched within an application context and students can be engaged in higher-order thinking about a topic right from the beginning of instruction. For example, a teacher might begin teaching about a mathematical operation by posing a problem that requires the operation for efficient solution. Or, a teacher might begin a lesson on climate and weather by asking students to speculate about why there often is wet weather on one side of a mountain range but dry weather on the other side.

knowledge as socially constructed

Some constructivist accounts of learning, especially those that have been influenced heavily by Piaget, depict learning as primarily a solitary activity. The focus is on the individual child who develops knowledge through exploration, discovery, and reflection on everyday life experiences. However, most constructivist accounts are variants of *social constructivism*. In addition to emphasizing that learning is a process of active construction of meaning, social constructivists emphasize that the process works best in social settings in which two or more individuals engage in sustained discourse about a topic. Participation in such discussions helps participants to advance their learning in several ways. Exposure to new input from others makes them aware of things that they did not know and leads to expansion of their cognitive structures. Exposure to ideas that contra-

dict their own beliefs may cause them to examine those beliefs and perhaps restructure them. The need to communicate their ideas to others forces them to articulate those ideas more clearly, which sharpens their conceptions and often leads to recognition of new connections. As a result, cognitive structures become better developed (both better differentiated and better organized).

Vygotsky and zone theory

Social constructivist ideas have been influenced heavily by the writings of the Russian developmental psychologist, Lev Vygotsky (1962, 1978). Vygotsky believed that children's thought (cognition) and language (speech) begin as separate functions but become intimately connected during the preschool years as children learn to use language as a mechanism for thinking. Gradually, more and more of their learning is mediated through language, especially learning of cultural knowledge that is difficult if not impossible to develop through direct experience with the physical environment. Children initially acquire much of their cultural knowledge through overt speech (conversations with others, especially parents and teachers). Then they elaborate on this knowledge and connect it to other knowledge through inner speech (thinking mediated through language—self-talk).

Literacy, numeracy, and knowledge in the subjects taught at school are prominent examples of the kinds of cultural knowledge that Vygotsky viewed as socially constructed. He suggested that this learning proceeds most efficiently when children are consistently exposed to *teaching in the zone of proximal development*. The zone of proximal development refers to the range of knowledge and skills that students are not yet ready to learn on their own but could learn with help from teachers. The children already know things that are "below" the zone, or can learn them easily on their own without help. They cannot yet learn things that are "above" the zone, even with help.

Zone theory, *a set of teaching principles based on Vygotsky's notion of teaching in the zone of proximal development,* resembles in some ways the ideas connected with the notion of readiness for learning. However, readiness is passive in its implications, suggesting that teachers can do little but wait until children become ready to learn something (presumably due to maturation of needed cognitive structures) before trying to teach it to them. Zone theory assumes that children's readiness for learning something depends much more on their accumulated prior knowledge about the topic than on maturation of cognitive structures, and that advances in knowledge will be stimulated primarily through the social construction that occurs during sustained discourse, most rapidly through teaching in the zone of proximal development (Moll, 1990; Newman, Griffin, & Cole, 1989; Rogoff & Wertsch, 1984; Tharp & Gallimore, 1988; Wertsch, 1985, 1991; Wertsch & Tulviste, 1992).

Social constructivists emphasize teaching that features sustained dialogue or discussion in which participants pursue a topic in depth, exchanging views and negotiating meanings and implications as they explore its ramifications. Along with teacher-structured, whole-class discussions, this includes cooperative learning that is constructed as students work in pairs or small groups. Key features of social constructivist approaches to teaching and learning are summarized in Table 7.1.

situated learning and authentic tasks

Many social constructivists, especially those interested in teaching procedural and conditional knowledge (knowing how and when to use skills and other procedures, as opposed to know-ing facts, concepts, and other propositional knowledge) believe that instruction in schools should be modeled as much as possible on the instruction that occurs in natural settings. Schooling brings people together and thus makes possible the social construction of knowledge, but it is an artificial environment in many respects and tends to teach generic knowledge and skills that have been abstracted and removed from the application settings that gave birth to them. Too often, generic knowledge and skills are forgotten or remain inert—not easily accessible when needed outside of school.

Scholars who have studied learning in home and job settings believe that it is a mistake to separate knowing from doing, or what is learned from how it is learned and used (Brown, Collins, & Duguid, 1989; Lave & Wenger, 1991; Rogoff, 1990). They believe that *cognition is situated;* that is, that knowledge is adapted to the settings, purposes, and tasks to which it is applied (and for which it was constructed in the first place). Consequently, they argue, if we want students to learn and retain knowledge in a form that makes it usable for application, we need to make it possible for them to develop the knowledge in the natural setting, using methods and tasks suited to that setting. In this view, the ideal model for schooling is the on-the-job training that occurs as experienced mentors work with novices or apprentices.

Whatever the merits of this notion, there are obvious limits to the degree to which it is feasible to consider shifting significant portions of the school's curriculum from in-school to out-of-school settings. However, the notion of situated cognition has implications for the design of in-school instruction as well. In particular, it implies that we ought to be more conscious of potential applications when we select and plan our teaching of curriculum content, and we should emphasize those applications in presenting the content to the students.

table 7.1 contrasts between the transmission view and the social construction view of teaching and learning

TRANSMISSION VIEW	SOCIAL CONSTRUCTION VIEW
Knowledge as fixed body of information transmitted from teacher or text to students	Knowledge as developing interpretations co-constructed through discussion
Texts, teacher as authoritative sources of expert knowledge to which students defer	Authority for constructed knowledge resides in the arguments and evidence cited in its support by students as well as by texts or teacher; everyone has expertise to contribute
Teacher is responsible for managing students' learning by providing information and leading students through activities and assignments	Teacher and students share responsibility for initiating and guiding learning efforts
Teacher explains, checks for understanding, and judges correctness of students responses	Teacher acts as discussion leader who poses questions, seeks clarifications, promotes dialogue, helps group recognize areas of consensus and of continuing disagreement
Students memorize or replicate what has been explained or modeled	Students strive to make sense of new input by relating it to their prior knowledge and by collaborating in dialogue with others to co-construct shared understandings
Discourse emphasizes drill and recitation in response to convergent questions; focus is on eliciting correct answers	Discourse emphasizes reflective discussion of networks of connected knowledge; questions are more divergent but designed to develop understanding of the powerful ideas that anchor these networks; focus is on eliciting students' thinking
Activities emphasize replication of models or applications that require following step-by-step algorithms	Activities emphasize applications to authentic issues and problems that require higher-order thinking
Students work mostly alone, practicing what has been transmitted to them in order to prepare themselves to compete for rewards by reproducing it on demand	Students collaborate by acting as a learning community that constructs shared understandings through sustained dialogue

Students' errors can be opportunities for developing insights and clearing up misunderstandings, if handled properly by the teacher.

Also, as much as possible, we should allow students to learn through engagement in authentic tasks. *Authentic tasks* require using what is being learned for accomplishing the very sorts of life applications that justify the inclusion of this learning in the curriculum in the first place. If it is not possible to engage students in the actual life applications that the curriculum is supposed to prepare them for, then one can at least engage them in realistic simulations of these applications (Cognition and Technology Group at Vanderbilt, 1993). (See Research at Work: Authentic Activities for examples of authentic activities.)

The notion of situated cognition implies that students will need to learn such things as inquiry, critical thinking, and problem solving by engaging in them under realistic conditions. Teachers will have to work within the constraints imposed by students' current readiness and by access to settings and equipment, but they still can engage their students in inquiry into worthwhile and meaningful questions, critical thinking about significant policy issues, and discussion of potential methods of solving real problems.

scaffolding and transfer of responsibility for managing learning from teacher to learner

Ideas about situated learning and about teaching in the zone of proximal development tend to cluster around the notions of scaffolding and gradual transfer of responsibility for managing learning from the teacher to the student. Instructional **scaffolding** is a *general term for the task assistance or simplification strategies that teachers might use to bridge the gap between what students are capable of doing on their own and what they are capable of doing with help.* Scaffolds are forms of support provided by the teacher (or another student) to help students progress from their current abilities to the intended goal (Rosenshine & Meister, 1992). Like the scaffolds used by house painters, the support provided through scaffolding is temporary, adjustable, and removed when it is no longer needed. Examples of scaffolding include cognitive modeling (in which the teacher demonstrates task performance while verbalizing aloud the thinking that guides it), prompts or cues that help students move on to the next

research at work
authentic activities

Listed below are some examples of activities that specialists in five school subject areas would consider to be authentic learning activities.

grades K–3

Math: Apply basic four functions to problems in saving/budgeting money, sharing/dividing treats

Science: Observe and take notes on plant growth and decomposition, events occurring in the class aquarium

Social studies: Re-create the school day in a nineteenth-century one-room schoolhouse; implement Mini-Society or other economics simulations calling for students to produce, buy, and sell goods and services

Reading: Listen to and discuss story read by teacher; read good children's literature

Writing: Correspond with pen pals; write thank-you notes to classroom visitors

grades 4–6

Math: Develop specifications for a garden or construction project

Science: Monitor air pollution on each of the four sides of the school building; collect and analyze life forms and residues found in a nearby pond

Social studies: Plan an extended vacation trip, with maps and itinerary; debate whether or not the American Revolution was justified

Reading: Read genre fiction, discuss and write reactions; learn and apply content-area reading and study skills

Writing: Poems and short essays for self-expression; journals for recording observations and insights

grades 7–12

Math: Apply probabilities to making predictions about the relative effectiveness of alternative strategies for addressing a problem or issue; use algebra for solving compound-interest problems to inform decisions about loans and investments

Science: Apply scientific principles to household engineering problems (spot removal, appliance troubleshooting); develop projects for science fairs and displays

Social studies: Debate current policy issues; simulate legislative budget debates (e.g., acting as state legislators representing districts with different agendas)

Reading: Read and discuss novels on youth themes: compare and contrast different authors who work in the same genre or different works by the same author

Writing: Compose short stories, term papers, and other research reports

step when they are temporarily stuck, and questions that help them to diagnose the reasons for errors and develop repair strategies.

Wood, Bruner, and Ross (1976) suggested that appropriately scaffolded instruction includes the following six components:

1. developing student interest in accomplishing the intended goal of the task
2. demonstrating an idealized version of the act to be performed
3. simplifying the task by reducing the number of steps required to solve a problem, so that the student can manage certain components and recognize when these are being accomplished successfully
4. controlling frustration and risk in problem solving
5. providing feedback that identifies the critical features of discrepancies between what the student has produced and what is required for an ideal solution
6. motivating and directing the student's activity sufficiently to maintain continuous pursuit of the goal

Closely associated with the notion of scaffolding is the notion of *gradual transfer of responsibility for managing learning.* Early in the process, the teacher assumes most of the responsibility for structuring and managing learning activities and provides students with a great deal of information, explanation, modeling, or other input. As students develop expertise, however, they can begin to assume responsibility for regulating their own learning by asking questions and by working on increasingly complex applications with increasing degrees of autonomy. The teacher still provides coaching or other scaffolding needed to assist with challenges that students are not yet ready to handle on their own, but this assistance is reduced little by little in response to gradual increases in student readiness to engage in independent and self-regulated learning (Day & Cordón, 1993).

implications for teachers
transferring responsibility from teacher to learner

Tharp and Gallimore (1988) described a model of *assisted performance* that involves teaching in the zone of proximal development, scaffolding learning through responsive assistance, and transferring responsibility to the child as expertise develops. Teacher assistance is contingent on and responsive to the learner's level of performance. The teacher patiently allows learners to handle as much as they can on their own and to learn through their mistakes, except where mistakes might be costly or dangerous and thus must be minimized through more direct and controlling forms of instruction.

Tharp and Gallimore identified six means of providing responsive assistance: (1) modeling (especially cognitive modeling that includes overt verbalization of strategies), (2) contingency management (especially praise of good performance), (3) providing feedback about the correctness of responses, (4) instructing (telling the student specifically what to do, to be used sparingly), (5) questioning (to stimulate the student to think and communicate about the task, especially if this will produce mental operations that might not be produced otherwise), and (6) cognitive structuring (stating principles or generalizations that pull things together and make for better-organized representation of the learning). Cognitive structuring may focus on the content being learned or on the learners' cognitive activities. When focused on the content, cognitive structuring provides explanations (e.g., that the expansion of gases as they are heated during chemistry experiments occurs because molecular activity increases with temperature or that the next story in the reader is about the challenges faced by a group of mountain climbers). When cognitive structuring focuses on the learners' cognitive activity, it provides explanation or reminders of the strategies that students are expected to use as they work on academic tasks. (For example, the teacher might say, "So, whenever you come to a new word that you are not sure about, you first look for clues, then put the clues together with what you already know about the word to decide on a meaning, and then check to see if that meaning fits with the rest of the sentence.")

Similarly, Collins, Brown, and Newmann (1989; see also Collins, Brown, & Holum, 1991) have drawn on ideas about situated cognition and about learning through apprenticeship in the workplace to develop the *cognitive apprenticeship* model of schooling. The model includes four important aspects of traditional apprentice-

ship: modeling, scaffolding, fading, and coaching. The master models task performance for the apprentice, provides coaching and other forms of scaffolding as the apprentice practices portions of the task, and then fades these forms of assistance as the apprentice becomes proficient enough to accomplish tasks independently. Cognitive apprenticeship in the classroom includes these same elements, along with additional ones that are needed because of the more abstract content taught there. The modeling includes thinking out loud to make the teacher's cognition visible to students, and the teacher asks questions designed to make student cognition visible to the teacher as well (e.g., "how did you arrive at your prediction about the end of the story?" or "think out loud for me as you work the problem on the board"). Also, by emphasizing authentic tasks and contexts for learning that make sense to students, teachers attempt to build in some of the task meaningfulness and motivation that are ordinarily built into learning that is situated in the workplace. Finally, because the teacher must teach for transfer, cognitive apprenticeship exposes students to a range of tasks and encourages them to note their common elements and consider the implications for application to life outside school.

summary

As part of the continuing cognitive revolution in educational psychology, research on learning became increasingly focused on human learning of meaningful content and its theoretical base shifted from behavioral to cognitive models. Early cognitive models focused on ways to communicate and help learners understand hierarchies of knowledge as structured by the academic disciplines that generated them. More recently developed constructivist models avoid notions of imposing adult-structured knowledge on children and instead speak of helping children to construct new

understandings by building on their existing knowledge as it is currently represented and structured.

The roots of all of these cognitive models lie in gestalt psychology. Gestalt psychologists noted that perception is organized into meaningful patterns rather than built up gradually by connecting isolated bits of information. Drawing on knowledge they developed about our tendency to impose good form on our perceptions, framing and contrast effects, and learning through discovery that leads to insights, gestalt psychologists stressed the importance of making learners aware of the structure of the content to be learned and the relationships among its elements, and they showed that learners can be exposed to conditions that will guide them toward discovery of important knowledge.

David Ausubel and others have developed methods for promoting efficient meaningful reception learning through well-structured presentations. Such presentations begin with advance organizers or at least previews that include general principles, outlines, or questions that establish the desired learning set in the students; describe learning objectives and alert students to key concepts; present material in small steps sequenced in ways that are easy to follow; elicit student responses regularly in order to stimulate active learning and ensure that each step is mastered before moving to the next; finish with a review of the main points, stressing general integrative concepts; and follow up with questions or assignments that require students to encode the material in their own words and apply it to new contexts. Analogies, metaphors, examples, or concrete models are used to help learners link the new to the familiar, and the instructional plan includes provision for vertical and lateral transfer when this is part of the overall objective.

Jerome Bruner focused on teaching students discipline-based knowledge, emphasizing not just the propositional knowledge generated by the disciplines but the methods used for generating this knowledge. He recommended that students learn through disciplined inquiry, a form of guided discovery learning in which students use the tools that practitioners of a discipline ordinarily use in the process of addressing the kinds of questions that those practitioners typically address. Bruner stated that any subject matter could be taught to any learners in some intellectually honest way if it was translated into terms that the learners could understand. He advocated the spiral curriculum, in which students would be exposed to the same general topic at several different times, but in more abstract and sophisticated ways each time. He suggested that teachers instruct by stimulating students' curiosity and guiding them to explore and discover on their own.

Discovery learning approaches tend to be enjoyed by students and useful for promoting certain higher-order objectives, and thus should be used to some degree in most classrooms. However, they are time consuming and involve other practical limitations, so few teachers will be able to use them as their primary approach to instruction.

Constructivist models of learning shift emphasis from transmission of knowledge as structured by adults to helping children construct new understandings by building on their existing knowledge as it is currently represented and structured. Constructivists favor network models over hierarchical models of knowledge organization. Network models imply that one can begin learning about a knowledge network by entering it almost anywhere rather than only at the lowest level of a knowledge hierarchy. They also imply that teachers can engage students in applications and other higher-order thinking right from the beginning of instruction, without having to wait until they have established a sizeable knowledge base at the comprehension level.

Social constructivists believe that the knowledge construction process works best in social settings, so they favor methods that feature sustained discussion in which participants pursue a topic in depth, exchanging views and negotiating meanings and implications as they explore its ramifications. Social constructivists interested in teaching procedural and conditional knowledge tend to emphasize situated learning and authentic tasks. They believe that as much school learning as possible should be incorporated within the process of engaging in the very sorts of life applications that justify inclusion of the learning in the curriculum in the first place. Constructivists also emphasize teaching in the zone of proximal development using methods that feature scaffolding students' learning efforts through needed task assistance or simplification strategies, but gradually fading these forms of assistance and transferring responsibility for managing learning to the learners themselves as their expertise develops. The assisted performance model of Tharpe and Gallimore and the cognitive apprenticeship model of Collins, Brown, and Newman are examples of approaches that feature situated learning, scaffolding, and transfer of responsibility.

questions for reflection

1. Describe in your own words the differences between behavioral and cognitive approaches to learning. In contrast to the first two chapters in this unit, what new emphasis is placed on learning in the present chapter?

2. Define the term gestalt psychology. What is a gestalt? How is the gestalt psychology viewpoint useful to teachers?

3. Reexamine the general beliefs of Skinner, Bruner, and the social constructivists. Given their beliefs, what would typical homework assignments look like from each point of view? In particular, what might the length and type of these assignments be?

4. Assume that you are going to teach the following: Pledge of Allegiance, Bill of Rights, and free-form ice skating. How might you address each of these learning outcomes if you were teaching from a Skinnerian point of view? From the viewpoint of Bruner? From a situated learning perspective?

5. Define disciplined inquiry in your own terms. If you were going to teach about the presidential election in American politics and Boyle's law in physics, would it be equally important to use inquiry procedures? Why or why not?

6. Think about teaching young children to play either soccer or Monopoly, and then write an advance organizer that would convey the structure of what you would teach.

7. Can students really be taught, or must they learn on their own? Just how much should teachers realistically expect to accomplish?

8. Many behaviorists are offended by the tendency of discovery-learning theorists to view themselves as humane rather than mechanistic, so they counter by claiming that it is cruel to force students to discover things on their own when you could save them trouble by telling or showing them. Do you agree? Why or why not?

9. Are there times when it is better for teachers to prevent errors and other times when it is better to allow students to make them? What are some specific examples?

10. Considering the grade level and subject matter that you intend to teach, what would be authentic activities in which to engage your students?

11. How might you determine your students' zones of proximal development with respect to a particular curriculum unit or topic? What does this imply about forms of preinstructional assessment of student knowledge and thinking that you might incorporate into your teaching?

12. Can constructivist methods be used in situations where students are so unfamiliar with the content to be learned that they possess no readily available schemes within which to assimilate it and very little useful prior knowledge to bring to bear?

13. How would ideal scaffolding of students' learning efforts differ from forms of teacher assistance that are less desirable?

cases to consider

an act of discovery Mr. Washington feels that his American government students passively accept and take notes about whatever he says but do not carefully evaluate this input or integrate it with their prior knowledge. He wants to get them to think more actively and make discoveries on their own. One of the points to be made in his next unit is that most people elected to national offices are lawyers. How might he arrange for students to discover this fact and the reasons for it on their own?

just a game? In his government class, Mr. Johnson uses a simulation game in which students are assigned to act as state legislators working out the compromises needed to pass the annual budget. There are five groups, each representing a geographical area with unique political interests (the big city, the tourist-oriented counties along the lake, etc.) Each group is assigned goals that would involve capturing more than its share of the budget for purposes favored in its region. The budget cannot accommodate all these goals, so it will be necessary to make compromises and to form coalitions to get as much as possible for one's own group.

The game takes place over the course of a week. By Wednesday, Mr. Johnson is pleased in most respects. The students find the game absorbing and challenging, to the point that they are getting together at lunchtime to plot strategy, and calling up members of other teams after school in an attempt to cut deals. Mr. Johnson is bothered, though, about the personal competitiveness that has crept into the game. The more assertive students have emerged as group leaders and are working hard to outsmart one another. Despite his efforts to keep students aware that they are role playing state legislators representing constituencies, most interaction takes place at the level of whether Mary Bernardi and her group will outfox Ramon Torres and his group, rather than whether the farming interests will be able to pursue their agenda at the expense of the big-city interests. The game clearly has great motivational value, but Mr. Johnson wonders if it has enough pedagogical value to justify the time spent on it.

What would you tell Mr. Johnson if he explained this to you as a fellow teacher? Should he use the game again next year? Should he do anything right now to try to influence what occurs during the rest of the week?

chapter 8.

processing, remembering, and restructuring what we learn

objectives

When you have mastered the material in this chapter you will be able to

1. Describe key features of the information processing approach to learning
2. Identify similarities and differences between associationist theories and constructivist theories
3. Differentiate semantic memory from episodic memory
4. Define the key concepts in the three-stage information processing model—sensory register, short-term or working memory, rehearsal, chunking, long-term memory, levels of processing—and explain how the model depicts information processing, storage, and retrieval
5. Define the schema concept and explain how schema activation facilitates comprehension
6. Describe the factors known to affect rote learning and explain the nature of their effects: degree of meaningfulness, serial position (primacy and recency effects), stimulus distinctiveness, practice, transfer (positive versus negative, specific versus general), interference (proactive versus reactive), organization of input, levels of processing, and use of mnemonics

7. Describe and give examples of commonly used mnemonics—place method, link method, peg method, keyword method, elaboration method, pictorial mnemonics, rhymes, acronyms, and visual imagery
8. Explain the effects of factors known to affect meaningful verbal learning—abstraction of the gist of the passage, levels of organization of the passage, activation of schemas and prior knowledge, drawing of inferences, filtering of input through preexisting misconceptions, insufficient processing of input thought to have been learned previously, responding to structuring and organizational factors built into the text, and generating mathemagenic activities
9. Define adjunct questions and state the relative advantages and disadvantages of prequestions and postquestions
10. Describe the major research findings of the information processing theorists on the behavior of novices and experts and on cognitive simulation and artificial intelligence

information processing in learning and memory

In Chapters 5–7, we identified different types and levels of learning, described the behaviorist view that depicts learning as conditioning of cued responses through reinforcement, and described cognitive and constructivist views that depict learning as construction of connections between new information and existing networks of prior knowledge. In this chapter we continue our presentation of cognitive and constructivist theory and research, but we shift attention from the macro level of models of learning to the micro level of investigations of the processes involved in learning and memory.

Information processing theorists have shown that learning involves actively processing, storing, and retrieving information, and teaching involves helping learners to develop their information processing skills and apply them systematically when mastering a curriculum. Information processing theorists tend to be constructivists, emphasizing the cognitive structures built by learners themselves rather than the ways that subject matter has been structured in the underlying academic disciplines. Humans develop increasingly differentiated and integrated cognitive structures to represent and organize their knowledge. Ongoing experience is filtered through these structures: we recognize familiar aspects of input and interpret unfamiliar aspects with reference to the meanings we attach to the familiar aspects.

Relationships between particular items of input and our larger cognitive structures are surprisingly active and continuous. Because perception of new experience is filtered through existing cognitive structures, and because new input is often open to multiple interpretations, the process of making sense of experience can be seen as an interaction between the learner and the input rather than as a one-way effect of the input on the learner. Thus, in reading this textbook you do not merely take in fully specified information that has only one meaning. Instead, you interact with the material by filling in bits of meaning that are implied but not spelled out explicitly, interpreting the probable meanings of unfamiliar terms, relating the content to your knowledge, and making decisions about what content is especially important to remember for a test or for future application. You and your classmates are all using the same book, yet each of you will attend to a unique subset of the content as being of focal importance. Even where several of you focus on the same content, each will have a unique interpretation of that content and will associate it with a unique set of prior personal and cultural experiences.

Furthermore, your memory of the content itself or your ideas about its meanings may change over time if you undergo significant development in key cognitive structures such as your general self-concept, your ideas about what schools should accomplish with students, or your notions about what makes a good teacher. For example, if you have not yet taught, you may think that classroom management is the most important topic in this book, and you may find some of what is said about it to be surprising, such as the notion that skills for keeping students engaged in well-paced lessons and well-chosen assignments are more important than skills for handling defiance. As you gain experience and progress through the developmental stages that new teachers typically go through, however, your ideas will change. If you should review this text a few years from now, much of the material on classroom management will seem "obvious" and old hat, and much of the material on learning and instruction will seem more relevant and important.

associationist and constructivist views of memory

Most research on human memory has been guided by one of two influential types of theory. The first to become well established were **associationist theories**, *theories of learning and memory that assume the retention of new learning*

depends on the nature and strength of associations between the new learning and previous learning stored in memory. Much of the research supporting associationist theories has involved rote learning of relatively meaningless and disconnected input.

More recent research has led to the development of **constructivist theories**, *theories in which learners are seen not just as accessing associations but also as constructing meaning by processing new input through existing cognitive structures and then transferring it to long-term memory, where it may undergo further processing and possible reconstruction.* Constructivists assume that retention of new learning depends on the degree to which learners can activate existing cognitive structures or construct new ones to subsume the new learning and provide access to it later. They also assume that material stored in memory can be elaborated or distorted, not just retained as is or else forgotten. Most research supporting constructivist theories has involved meaningful learning of connected discourse, typically written prose. The classical work of Ebbinghaus and of Bartlett illustrate the associationist and the constructivist approaches.

Ebbinghaus and the associationist approach

Hermann Ebbinghaus (1885) pioneered what became the associationist approach. He published one of the first treatises on learning and memory that was based on empirical data (records of his own attempts to memorize various types of input under various conditions). He wanted to study "pure" memory uncontaminated by previous learning, so he avoided connected discourse and instead used nonsense syllables (such as *dev*, or *lup* in English) that are relatively free of associations to prior knowledge. He found that learning improved when material was rehearsed overtly rather than merely read silently, and when practice was distributed over several shorter trials rather than massed into a few lengthy ones. He also discovered *serial position effects*: material at the beginning and end is memorized more quickly than material in the middle. You may have noticed these effects yourself in memorizing poems or lecture notes.

Ebbinghaus was among the first to note the relationship between time and learning. He showed that increases in practice time led to increases in performance, although less so as practice time increased and he neared his peak performance level. Graphs illustrating these relationships were among the first **learning curves**, which in general are *graphs illustrating the increase and eventual leveling off of performance scores when plotted across blocks of practice trials.* (see Figure 8.1). Ebbinghaus also illustrated *forgetting curves*: following rote memorization of disconnected content, forgetting is rapid in the early minutes and hours following learning but much slower thereafter (see Figure 8.2).

Ebbinghaus adopted the *decay theory* of forgetting, which assumed that memory traces simply fade with time. However, later work caused the decay theory to be replaced by *interference theory*, which holds that forgetting is caused by new learning that interferes with the ability to remember prior learning. For example, people who memorized a word list before going to bed at night could remember more after sleeping for eight hours than could people who first learned the original list, then learned several similar lists, and then were tested on the original list only an hour later (McGeoch & McDonald, 1931).

Interference theory still holds up well for rote learning of disconnected material. Here, subsequent learning of similar material interferes with memory for the original material. However, when one is learning meaningful, connected discourse, subsequent learning of similar material is likely to facilitate memory for both sets of material. That is, transfer effects rather than interference effects occur, at least if the previous learning is sufficiently clear, stable, and discriminable from the new learning (Ausubel & Robinson, 1969). The semantic network theory and the schema theory described in the following sections apply better to such meaningful learning than the interference theory does.

Bartlett and the constructivist approach

Research by Sir Frederic Bartlett (1932) provided early examples of what became the constructivist approach. Bartlett rejected Ebbinghaus's attempts to study pure memory in favor of studying memory as it occurs in ordinary living, so he rejected nonsense syllables in favor of more natural stimuli such as human faces, pictures, and connected discourse. In his best-known experiments, learners read brief stories and then produced written versions from memory, first

Figure 8.1 learning curves

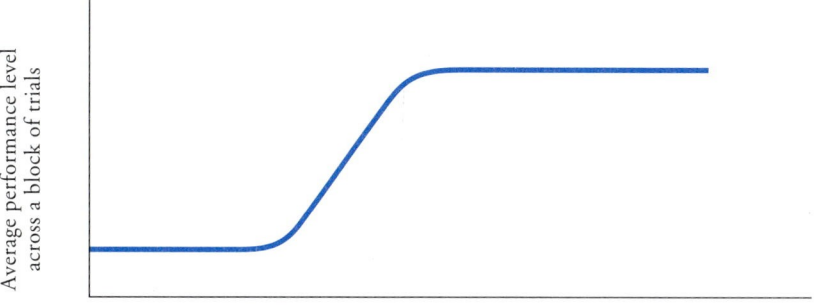

Average performance level across a block of trials

Blocks of trials repeated over time

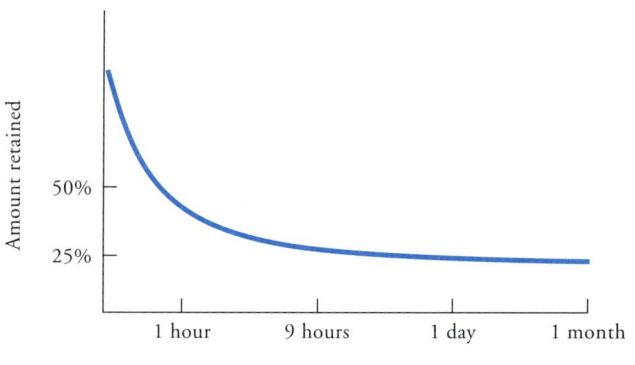

Amount retained

50%

25%

1 hour   9 hours   1 day   1 month

Time since learning (not to scale)

Figure 8.2 curve of forgetting, after Ebbinghaus

SOURCE: From *The Brain Book* by Peter Russell. Copyright © 1979 by Peter Russell. Used by permission of Dutton Signet, a division of Penguin Books USA, Inc.

after a delay of fifteen minutes and then later at intervals of several weeks or months.

Bartlett's subjects read relatively long (200- to 500-word) stories and had relatively short practice times (they read each story twice). Consequently, decay theorists such as Ebbinghaus and associationists such as Thorndike would have predicted a great deal of forgetting due to the decay of associative memory traces that were weak to begin with. They would not have predicted significant distortion, however, because no other stories that might have produced interference effects were read in between the original reading and the subsequent reproduction of the story from memory.

Bartlett's results did not confirm these associationist predictions. First, compared to the retention expected for relatively meaningless material of equal length, memory for these stories was quite good. Second, however, the story reconstructions often involved distortions and not just omissions. For example, in one study, British learners read about the cultural practices of certain Native North Americans. In recounting the story, they tended to "normalize" it by substituting thematically similar but culturally familiar content. Thus, a seal hunt became a fishing trip, and a canoe became a boat.

On the basis of such evidence, Bartlett argued that we engage in an "effort after meaning" when we read stories, seeking to understand them by connecting them to existing cognitive structures he called *schemas*. We construct a meaning that is plausible and consistent, although it might not be the same meaning intended by the author. There may be some distortion in the original learning, especially if the story contains unfamiliar elements that can be understood only partially (by filtering them through familiar schemas). Furthermore, the stories as originally constructed can undergo *reconstruction* later if changes occur in the schemas to which the stories have been connected. Subsequent research has supported and elaborated most of Bartlett's ideas (Spiro, 1977), although there is much more evidence that activation of relevant schemas affects how material is interpreted and encoded in the first place than there is that later changes in schemas produce significant reconstruction of the originally encoded material (diSibio, 1982).

information processing models

The contrasts between Ebbinghaus and Bartlett illustrate some of the diversity that exists in theory and research on human information processing and memory. Most research has focused on

Rehearsing material aloud, as one does in practicing a part in a play, is an aid to memorizing

the intentional learning of material communicated through oral or written language, as in formal education. Tulving (1985, 1993) suggested that **semantic memory,** which is *stored knowledge coded in the form of verbal propositions (language-based information),* is accomplished through systems of encoding, storage, and retrieval that differ from **episodic memory,** which involves *stored impressions of personal experiences (episodes) in one's life.* He argued that episodic memory was rich in concrete detail and stored in the form of sequences of events that occurred at particular places and times, whereas semantic memory was more abstract and stored in terms of logically

related concepts and principles. This distinction is useful, although evidence for the larger theory behind it is mixed (Horton & Mills, 1984). Most of this chapter concerns semantic memory, which regulates the storage and retrieval of most school learning. Ideas about involving episodic memory in stimulating students' learning have been advanced (Martin, 1993), but these have yet to be investigated systematically.

This chapter also concentrates on intentional rather than incidental learning. A great deal of incidental learning occurs in and out of school, but the factors that determine it are not well understood. Some aspects of experience, such as the timing, frequency, and spatial location of commonly experienced events, appear to be encoded automatically, without intention or apparent effort (Hasher & Zacks, 1984). Consequently, most people can tell about how many movies they have seen in the last year, where they sat when they last visited a favorite restaurant, or whether there are more lawyers or more tailors in the United States. Other things, such as the fact that attending to the structure of a text is useful for learning it, are learned incidentally by some people but not others. However, people in the latter group can be taught this information and can use it intentionally thereafter.

what is encoded?

Many people think of memory as a continuous, sequenced record of experience, akin to a videotape that begins with the earliest memory and proceeds linearly through the present. Certain segments have become faded or forgotten, and some may be temporarily unavailable but potentially recoverable through hypnosis, psychotherapy, or encounters with cues such as old photos that stimulate long-dormant memories. This view fits many of the known facts about memory. For example, some people have eidetic imagery (popularly known as photographic memory) that allows them to visualize and retrieve previous experience in extreme detail. Even people with ordinary memories can remember many details about important events in their lives or about what they were doing when they heard the news about John Kennedy, the Challenger disaster, or Magic Johnson (Brown & Kulick, 1977).

Despite its apparent validity, this commonsense view of memory is not correct (Wickelgren, 1981). First, it applies only to episodic memory, not semantic memory. Even if episodes in our personal lives were routinely encoded and stored as the equivalent of a run-

ning videotape, it would remain true that semantic memory for concepts and principles does not work this way. When we remember a principle, we remember it as a verbally phrased abstraction, not as an image of ourselves reliving the events that occurred when we originally learned the principle. Second, the model is not accurate even for episodic memory. Only certain experiences are encoded as "videotape segments" in the first place, and our memories for even these segments can be distorted (not just weakened) by the effects of later experiences (Loftus & Loftus, 1980).

Semantic memory is encoded and stored in the form of verbal abstractions (concept definitions and statements of rules and principles), although with associated imagery or linkages to particular prior experiences. You know that 2 + 2 = 4, for example, and although you can apply this information in concrete situations and can visualize examples of it, it is stored and retrieved primarily as a verbal abstraction—a semantically encoded number fact. Information processing theorists are concerned with how such input is encoded into semantic memory, and what happens to it after it gets there.

the three-stage information processing model

Most learning theorists accept a general three-stage model of human information processing that was developed using concepts borrowed from computer science (see Table 8.1). Versions of the model have been offered by Atkinson and Shiffrin (1971), Kintsch (1977), Klatzky (1980), and Loftus and Loftus (1976). The model proposes that input first enters a sensory register, then is processed in short-term memory, and then is transferred to long-term memory for storage and potential retrieval. The three

table 8.1 differences among the three stages of memory

FEATURE	SENSORY REGISTER	SHORT-TERM	LONG-TERM
Inputting of information	Preattentive	Requires attention but very fast	Rehearsal, relatively slow
Maintenance of information	Not possible	Very brief (c. 15–20 sec.) unless continually rehearsed	Virtually unlimited
Capacity	Large	Small (7 ± 2 chunks)	Virtually unlimited
Loss of information	Decay	Displacement, possible decay	Possibly no loss but loss of accessibility
Retrieval	Readout	Immediate	Varies depending on retrieval cues, organization, etc.

SOURCE: F. Craik and R. Lockhart (1972) from "Levels of Processing: A Framework for Memory Research." *Journal of Verbal Learning and Verbal Behavior, 11*, 671–684. Reprinted by permission of Academic Press.

stages are seen as integrated subparts of a larger system for transforming raw sensory information into forms that are more appropriate for integration with prior knowledge. All of this occurs under the executive control of the person, whose allocation of attention determines which aspects of the input available at any moment will be processed through the limited capacity of the system.

sensory register The sensory register receives input from the sensory receivers, primarily the eyes and ears. The neurological processing of this input is very brief, ranging from less than a second for visual sensations to about four seconds for auditory sensations. Then it disappears through decay or is replaced by new input. Consequently, input that enters the sensory register must be transferred to short-term memory if it is to receive focal attention and further processing. Even though it is short lived,

however, the input that enters the sensory register is monitored at some level so that we can respond to it more actively if necessary. For example, drivers attending primarily to conversations with passengers nevertheless monitor and respond to traffic conditions. Most of this visual input never enters their short-term memories, however, so that it decays quickly and is lost permanently.

short-term memory and rehearsal Sensory input that the person recognizes as important or interesting is transferred in the form of meaningful perceptions from the sensory register to **short-term memory**, *the part of the memory system that enables us to store a limited amount of information for fifteen to twenty seconds while we decide whether to process it further or shift attention to something else.* With active **rehearsal**—*the continual repetition of a piece of information (such as a telephone number)*—the information can be retained in short-term memory indefinitely. However, short-term memory has a very limited capacity. Most people can remember about seven items (numbers, words, phrases) on a list without making errors or omissions if the items are unrelated to one another. Thus, even a single phone number may be difficult to remember for even twenty seconds unless it is repeated continually or written down.

Short-term memory capacity can be increased, however, by "chunking" the input into subsets. **Chunking** is *grouping individual bits of data into larger units (chunks), thus increasing the amount of information that can be retained in short-term memory.* For example, the sequence *149210661984* is difficult to memorize as a string of twelve separate digits, but easy to remember if divided into three chunks corresponding to three famous years (*1492, 1066, 1984*). Similarly, the words *truck, cow, red, train, horse, green, plane, pig,* and *yellow* are remembered much more easily if reorganized into chunks of three vehicles, three animals, and three colors than if memorized in serial order.

George Miller (1956) showed that the chunk, and not the individual item, is the real unit determining short-term memory capacity. He estimated that this capacity averages about seven chunks of information (plus or minus two, allowing for individual differences). This implies that any particular chunk can be retained indefinitely in short-term memory through active rehearsal, but interference effects will cause memory failures once the limited capacity (7 ± 2 chunks) of short-term memory is exceeded. Subsequent estimates have been less optimistic, suggesting that the average capacity (which is attained by age six or so) is only four or five chunks, not seven (Farnham-Diggory, 1992; Kail, 1990; Schneider & Pressley, 1989).

Short-term memory is called "working memory" by theorists interested in goal-directed thinking and problem solving (Baddeley, 1986, 1990; Case, 1992). **Working memory** is *that portion of short-term memory that is available for mental operations when thinking or problem solving.* When engaged in such mental work, our ability to attend to a combination of input from the external environment and information retrieved from long-term memory is constrained by the capacity limit of working memory. Therefore, we cannot cope with complex cognitive tasks unless we can simplify them by reducing the load on working memory. Chunking is one way. Another is to break the task into subparts and take on one at a time. Another is to practice certain skills until they become automatic (i.e., they can be used with little conscious effort, thus keeping working memory free for concentration on other aspects of the larger task). Most of us have learned to walk, eat, and drive automatically, so that we can think or carry on conversations while engaged in these activities.

Basic academic skills have become automatic for successful students. For example, skilled readers have most of their working memory capacity available for making sense out of what they are reading, because basic skills such as decoding unfamiliar words and instantly recognizing familiar words have become automatic for them (Adams, 1990; Frederiksen, 1984). Most of the working memory capacity of less skilled readers is needed just to decode and understand individual words, so that little is left for putting it all together. As a result, their comprehension is poor unless they review the passage several times.

Case (1978) has stressed the importance of minimizing the load placed on students' working memory, especially when teaching young children or teaching complex new material. He suggests limiting the number of things that students must attend to at the same time, using familiar terms (that can be processed automatically) where possible, and making cues salient (so that students will not have to search for them).

long-term memory and storage Information needed for future reference is stored in long-term memory. **Long-term memory** is *the* *part of the memory system that we use for potentially permanent storage of material transferred from short-term memory.* If necessary, we can commit material to long-term memory through brute force by actively rehearsing it to the point of overlearning. This approach is inefficient and requires effortful concentration, but it may be needed for memorizing such things as phone numbers or lock combinations.

The more efficient way to intentionally store material in long-term memory is to process the information at deeper levels (Craik & Lockhart, 1972). Such deeper *levels of processing* may involve identifying or generating linkages between the new material and other material that is already retained in organized fashion, developing images to supplement the semantic form of the material, thinking about its applications, or answering questions about it.

Most theories about how material is stored in long-term memory and what happens to it after it gets there fit within one of two families: semantic network theories and schema theories. **Semantic network theories**, the modern counterparts of early associationist theories, are *theories of memory organization that assume concepts are stored in long-term memory within hierarchically organized networks of meaningful association.* (Anderson & Bower, 1973; Collins & Loftus, 1975; Kintsch, 1974; Rumelhart, Lindsey, & Norman, 1972). Some concepts have superordinate-subordinate relationships ("animal-dog-collie"). Concepts that are part of the same network share some degree of linkage, varying from direct and immediate associations ("black-white") to more distant relationships ("black-power," "black-blacksmith").

Within a network, the common attributes of the superordinate concept are stored with that concept, whereas only the particular attributes of each member of the class are stored with the member concept. Thus, the attribute "wings" is stored with the superordinate concept "birds," but only the attribute "red breast" is stored with the subordinate concept "robins."

Semantic network theories predict that the time needed to retrieve information about relationships between two concepts will depend on the distance between them in the network. Thus, it should take less time to decide whether robins are birds than to decide whether robins are animals. Similarly, it should be easier to answer the question "Does a robin have a red breast?" than "Does a robin fly?" because memory searches that begin with "robin" move quickly to "red breast." One must move up the hierarchy before encountering "able to fly," because this concept is attached to "birds" rather than "robins" (see Figure 8.3).

Most predictions based on semantic network theories have been borne out, and these theories provide useful models for the storage of information in semantic memory. Furthermore, because they can be built into computer programs, they have been useful in cognitive simulation research in which models of human information processing are constructed and then studied to see how they respond to new input.

However, semantic network theories portray long-term memory as a relatively static storage system that supports routine, predictable access and retrieval. Consequently, they have been supplemented in recent years by schema theories, which help explain the constructive encoding of input and the reconstruction of stored memories. **Schema theories** are *theories of memory organization that suggest our attempts to make sense of situations are guided by collections of related prior knowledge (schemas) that constitute models describing what to expect in the situation, the relationships among its elements, and so on.* Since Bartlett's groundbreaking work, many investigators have shown that new input is not first understood in some abstract way and only then related to existing knowledge; instead, it is interpreted from the beginning within contexts supplied by that existing knowledge. Collections of related prior knowledge that provide context for meaningful interpretation of new input are usually called

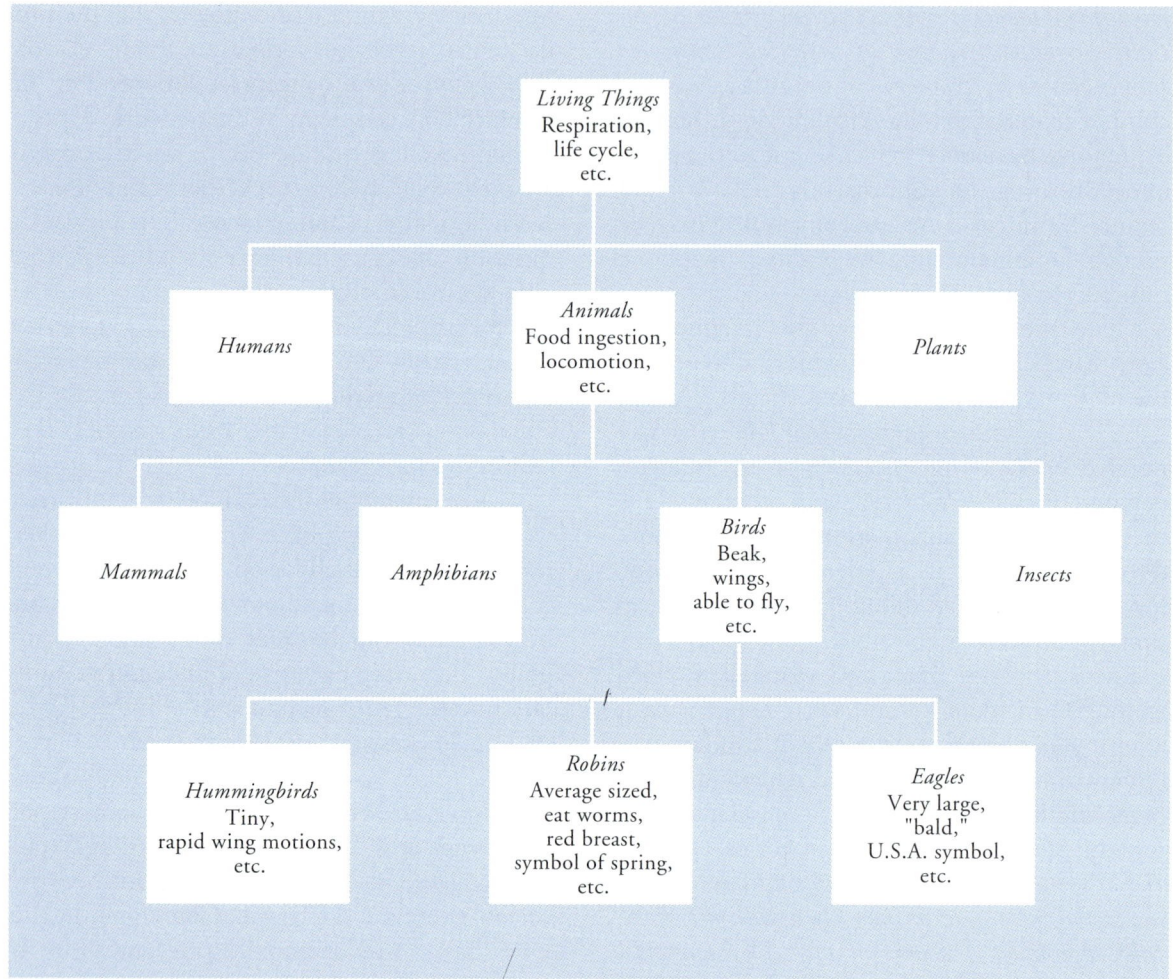

Figure 8.3 elements in a hypothetical semantic network that includes "birds" and associated groups

schemas (Rumelhart & Norman, 1978; Anderson, 1984; diSibio, 1982), *scripts* (Schank & Abelson, 1977), or *frames* (Minsky, 1975; Winograd, 1975).

Even seemingly familiar material may not have much meaning unless we can interpret it within relevant schemas. Consider the following sentence: "The notes were sour because the seam split" (Bransford & McCarrell, 1974). This sentence contains familiar words arranged according to English syntax rules, and you can even recognize it as a causal explanation for an observed event. Yet, it probably will have little meaning for you until you are given the clue "bagpipe," and can interpret it within your "bagpipe playing" schema. For a more extended example, consider the following paragraph from Dooling and Lachman (1971, p. 217):

With hocked gems financing him, our hero bravely defied all scornful laughter that tried to prevent his scheme. "Your eyes deceive," he had said, "an egg not a table correctly typifies this unexplored planet." Now three sturdy sisters sought proof, forging along sometimes through calm vastness, yet more often over turbulent peaks and valleys. Days became weeks as many doubters spread fearful rumors about the edge. At last from nowhere welcome-winged creatures appeared signifying momentous success. (p. 217)

In Dooling and Lachman's experiment, most subjects who read this paragraph without an accompanying title found it relatively meaningless and could not remember much of it later. However, subjects who read it under the title "Christopher Columbus Discovering America" found it entirely meaningful and were able to remember much more of it.

Lest you think that schema activation always leads to a single interpretation, consider the following paragraph:

Tony slowly got up from the mat, planning his escape. He hesitated a moment and thought. Things were not going well. What bothered him most was being held, especially since the charge against him had been weak. He considered his present situation. The lock that held him was strong but he thought he could break it. He knew, however, that his timing would have to be perfect. Tony was aware that it was because of his early roughness that he had been penalized so severely—much too severely from his point of view. The situation was becoming frustrating; the pressure had been grinding on him for too long. He was being ridden unmercifully. Tony was getting angry now. He felt he was ready to make his move. He knew that his success or failure would depend on what he did in the next few seconds. (Anderson, 1984, pp. 244-45)

If you are like most people, you thought that this paragraph was about a convict planning to escape from prison, and you interpreted it by relating it to schemas concerning the thinking of convicts, prison life, and prison escapes. However, if you are familiar with the sport of wrestling, you may have interpreted the paragraph as being about a wrestler trying to escape the hold of an opponent. These two interpretations are equally valid, and either yields meaningful understanding and good memory for the passage.

These specially constructed demonstrations illustrate the role of schemas in facilitating and determining the nature of text comprehension. Such schema effects occur routinely, whether we are aware of them or not. How input is encoded and stored in memory will depend on what relevant schemas are activated when interpreting it in the first place, and reconstruction of the input may occur later if changes occur in these schemas. These and other factors affecting long-term memory for connected discourse will be discussed later, following discussion of factors affecting rote learning.

factors affecting rote learning

Although most school learning involves meaningful learning of connected discourse, some of it involves primarily rote learning of disconnected material. There are school-learning parallels for each of the three major types of learning studied in verbal learning experiments (Mayer, 1982). In *serial learning*, students are given lists of items to be memorized in order, such as the alphabet or the roster of U.S. presidents. In *paired associate learning*, students must learn stimulus-response pairs so that they can supply the response item when given the stimulus item, such as with states and their capitals or foreign language synonyms for English words. Finally, in *free recall list learning*, students are given lists of items that may be recalled in any order, such as naming the countries of Europe or listing the thirteen original colonies. Rote learning of such verbal material is subject to meaningfulness effects, serial position effects, practice effects, transfer effects, interference effects, organization effects, levels-of-processing effects, and mnemonic effects (Mayer, 1982).

meaningfulness effects

Highly meaningful words are easier to learn and remember than less meaningful words (Cofer, 1971). Retention will be improved to the extent that learners are able to make relatively meaningless material more meaningful by associating it with more familiar material (see the section on mnemonic effects later in this chapter) or by substituting familiar, concrete words for unfamiliar, abstract words (Wittrock, Marks, & Doctorow, 1975).

serial position effects

Serial position effects result from the particular placement of an item within a list. Memory is better for items at the beginnings (*primacy effects*) or ends (*recency effects*) of lists than for items in the middle. An exception to these serial position effects is the *distinctiveness effect*—an item that is distinctively different from the others, such as a male name among a list of female names, will be remembered regardless of its serial position.

Serial position effects may occur because the items at the beginnings and ends of lists serve as "cognitive landmarks" that provide anchors to which the other items may be attached in memory (Mayer, 1982). Other explanations are also possible, however. For example, if the memory test follows immediately after the practice time, recency effects may occur simply because learners are able to hold the last few items of the list in short-term memory long enough to be able to reproduce them first on the test. Also, primacy effects may occur because the first few items enter an empty short-term memory register, so that more time is available and less interference is encountered in transferring them to long-term memory, compared to what happens with later items (Craik, 1979). The tendency for students to remember the beginnings of lessons better than the parts that come afterward underscores the value of advance organizers and early presentation of key ideas and structuring concepts. (see Figure 8.4).

practice effects

Active **practice (rehearsal)** is *performing a task repeatedly in an attempt to make the performance smoother, more effortless, and freer of error.* It improves retention. **Distributed (spaced) practice,** which involves *practicing for brief periods with rests or alternative activities done in between practice sessions,* is usually more effective than **massed practice,** which involves *concentrating practice into a single extended session, presumably continuing until one reaches peak performance levels.* The advantage to distributed practice is especially noticeable for long lists, fast presentation rates, or unfamiliar stimulus material (Underwood, 1961; Underwood, Kapelak, & Malmi, 1976). Apparently, massed practice allows the learner to associate a word with only one context, but distributed practice allows association with many different contexts (Glenberg, 1976).

Practice in memorizing poems, spelling words, arithmetic tables, or foreign language vocabulary is most efficient when dis-

Figure 8.4 serial position effects: memory for the beginning and end of a list or lecture is much better than for the middle segments.

SOURCE: From *The Brain Book* by Peter Russell. Copyright © 1979 by Peter Russell. Used by permission of Dutton Signet, a division of Penguin Books USA, Inc.

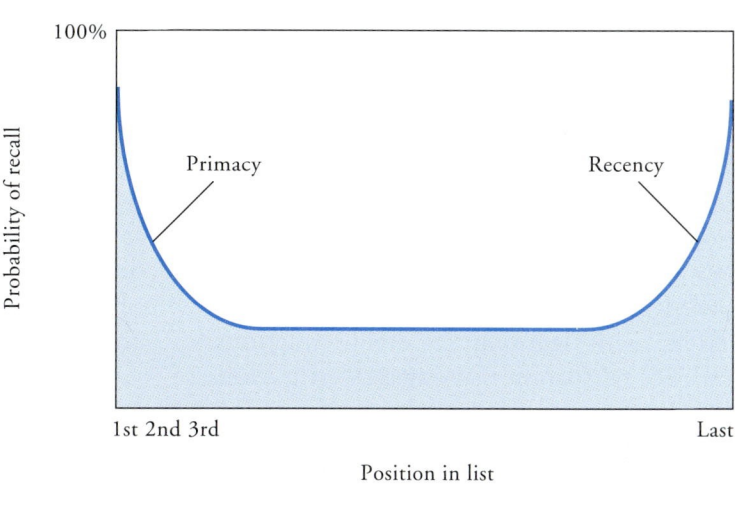

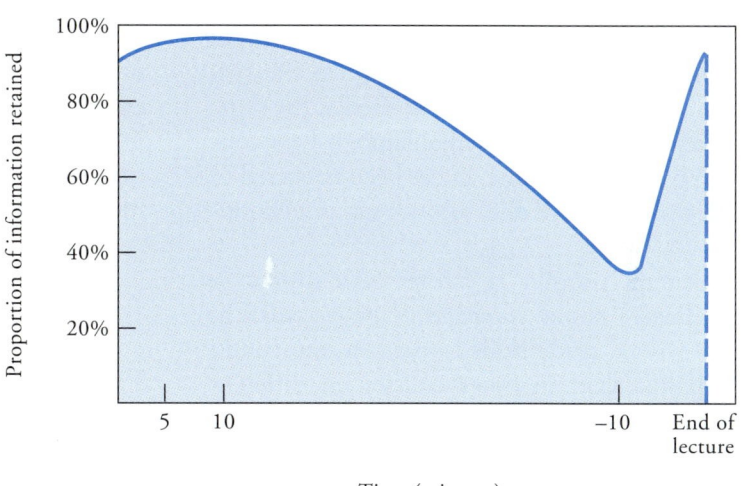

tributed over many short sessions. If the material is intended to be learned permanently or applied later, there should be practice to the point of overlearning and sufficient review thereafter to ensure that students can retrieve the learning quickly when they need it.

Also, when memorizing verbal material such as poetry or dramatic lines, overt practice is likely to be more effective than silent reading. Rehearsing the material aloud is helpful, as is accompanying it with appropriate gestures.

transfer effects

Transfer effects are effects of prior learning on the learning of new material. **Positive transfer** *occurs when previous learning makes the new learning easier*; **negative transfer** *occurs when it makes the new learning more difficult.* The more that two tasks have in common, the more likely that transfer effects will occur.

Specific transfer *occurs when tasks share components.* When the tasks involve similar stimuli and call for making similar responses, positive transfer may be expected. Thus, having learned two-column addition makes it easier to learn three-column addition, and having learned Ping-Pong makes it easier to learn tennis. When tasks involve similar stimuli but call for different responses, however, negative transfer may occur. Thus, knowledge about adding suffixes to regular words may interfere with learning of irregular words (a child says "runned" instead of "ran"), knowledge about dividing whole numbers may interfere with learning to divide fractions, knowledge of Spanish may interfere with learning of Portuguese, and knowledge of pinochle may interfere with learning to play bridge.

Unfortunately, the majority of specific transfer effects that occur in rote learning are likely to be negative (the opposite is true with meaningful learning). The danger is greatest when the two sets of similar items are being learned at the same time and neither set is well anchored. Less confusion is likely when one set has been mastered to overlearning before the second set is encountered.

General transfer is *transfer that cannot be attributed to shared components among tasks*, as when general study skills learned in one course are applied later in other courses on different topics (Cormier & Hagman, 1987; Perkins & Salomon, 1987). Such general transfer is discussed in later sections on meaningful learning. Unfortunately, rote learning offers little potential for positive general transfer, which is why schools should not place much emphasis on it.

interference effects

Interference effects occur when memory for particular material is hurt by previous or subsequent learning (Underwood, 1983). Whereas transfer effects occur when learning the new material in the first place, interference effects occur later when trying to remember it. Interference effects are always negative. *Proactive interference* occurs when previously learned material impedes ability to remember more recently learned material. For example, Americans accustomed to the traditional system of weights and measures tend to have difficulty remembering the metric system. *Retroactive interference* occurs when something learned recently interferes with ability to remember something learned previously. Students who first study Latin and then one of the Romance languages derived from Latin are likely to forget more Latin than students who first study Latin and then some unrelated language.

Interference effects are the major causes for forgetting of material learned by rote. Teachers can minimize such forgetting by varying the contexts within which practice takes place, seeing that practice continues to overlearning, and, most importantly, encouraging students to process the material in ways that make it meaningful rather than rote learning.

organization effects

Organization effects occur when learners categorize the input. Free recall of lists is better when learners organize the items into categories rather than memorizing them in serial order. Teachers can take advantage of these effects by organizing lists in logical ways and calling students' attention to this organization (Bower et al., 1969; Rabinowitz, 1988). In teaching irregularly spelled English words or irregular foreign-language verb forms, for example, teachers can group together subsets of irregularities that follow the same rule or share some other common characteristic.

levels-of-processing effects

Craik and Lockhart (1972) argued that words may be processed at several levels ranging from low-level sensory analysis of their physical characteristics to high-level semantic analysis of their meaning. They reviewed literature indicating *levels-of-processing effects*: the more deeply a word list is processed, the better it will be remembered. In particular, semantic encoding of the content leads to better memory than nonsemantic encoding. Thus, learners instructed to note whether or not each word belonged in a certain category remembered more words than learners instructed to circle every vowel (Jenkins, 1974).

The levels-of-processing notion has held up well as a general principle, although it applies better to some contexts than others and investigators do not always agree in classifying types of processing as high or low level (Craik, 1979; Horton & Mills, 1984). Consequently, some investigators prefer terms such as *distinctiveness* of encoding, *elaboration* of encoding, or *effort expended* during encoding. The common element in these ideas is that memory will be better when learners actively process the information and develop meaningful associations to it (*elaborative encoding*) than when they merely try to memorize it rotely (*maintenance rehearsal*).

Stein and Bransford (1979) showed the value of elaborative encoding. Subjects were presented with lists of sentences such as, "The bald man read the newspaper," or, "The funny man liked the ring," and then were asked memory questions such as, "Which man read the newspaper?" Memory was improved when learners were supplied with, or encouraged to generate, elaborations that made the sentences more meaningful by placing the described behaviors within cause-effect contexts ("The bald man read the newspaper to look for a hat sale," "The funny man liked the ring that squirted water"). Other elaborations that did not provide such cause-effect information were not successful in improving memory ("The bald man read the newspaper while eating breakfast," "The funny man liked the ring that he received as a present").

Bransford (1979) also spoke of *transfer-appropriate processing*—what constitutes effective processing will depend on what information the learners need and what they will be expected to do with it. Similarly, Tversky (1973) showed that learners can adjust their information processing and study strategies according to the kind of test they expect. Teachers can help their students remember what they learn by encouraging them to think about the contexts in which they will need the information and what they will do with it when they apply it.

mnemonic effects

Learners can increase the effectiveness of their rote learning by using *mnemonics*—strategies for elaborating on relatively meaningless input by associating it with more meaningful images or semantic contexts. Four well-known mnemonics methods are the place method, the link method, the peg method, and the keyword method.

The *place method* involves associating each item on a list with a particular place within a familiar location. For example, you might think of walking through your house and encountering items on the list as you move from one room to the next. The familiar sequence involved in "walking" through the house would help you to remember the items on the list in the proper sequence, and the visual imagery involved in "seeing" the items in the rooms would help you remember each one individually. The place method has received considerable support in research on human memory (Bower, 1970), and it is usually stressed in popular memory improvement books (Lorayne & Lucas, 1974).

The *link method* involves forming an image for each item and then linking them into an interactive chain. For example, if you need to pick up butter, celery, flour, ground beef, and ice cream at the food store, you might remember these items by imagining preparing a meal in which you first used the flour to make bread, stirring the mixture with celery as you did so, using the ground beef to make meat loaf, and then enjoying a meal of bread and butter and the meat loaf, with ice cream for dessert. Like the place method, the link method aids memory for specific items by tying the items to images and linking the images into a continuous "story." If necessary, the sequence of the items can be built into the story as well.

It often is easier to make a written list than to use mnemonic devices. However, such devices are useful for memorizing lists when writing is not possible or permissible, or when preparing for a speech that must be given without notes.

The *peg method* (also called the *hook method*) involves using a familiar series of items as "pegs" on which newly learned items can be "hung" as they are learned. In the most common example, the pegs are easy to visualize and their names rhyme with the number names (one is a bun, two is a shoe, three is a tree, etc.). The items to be learned are linked to the items on this peg list through imagery (Glover et al.,1987). Thus, the first item might be pictured between the halves of a bun, the second linked to the image of a shoe, and so on. Whereas the link method involves linking the items to be learned to one another, the peg method involves linking them to peg items that are easily visualized and already sequenced.

The *keyword method* began as a technique for teaching foreign language vocabulary (Atkinson, 1975). It is also useful for aiding memory for definitions of unfamiliar English words (McDaniel & Pressley, 1989) and technical terms (Jones & Hall, 1982), as well as for linking cities to their products (Pressley & Dennis-Rounds, 1980), states to their capitals (Levin et al., 1980), and proper names to events, accomplishments, or biographical information (Jones & Hall, 1982; McCormick & Levin, 1984; Shriberg et al., 1982).

The method involves identifying a keyword that links the items to be associated. For example, the Spanish word "carta" means "letter" in English. A good keyword for "carta" would be "cart," a familiar English word that is easily visualized. The keyword can then be used to link the items through either an image (of a shopping cart transporting a letter) or a sentence ("The cart carries the letter"). As another example, the state of Maryland (keyword = marry) can be linked with its capital of Annapolis (keyword = apple) using an image of two apples getting married (Levin, 1981).

The method works best when the keyword refers to something easily visualized and sounds like part of the word to be learned. Thus "car" is a good keyword for "carlin" and the image of an old woman driving a car can help one to remember that "carlin" means "old woman."

The keyword method substantially improves vocabulary learning, both in foreign language and in one's own language, across the range of grade levels (Pressley, Levin, & Miller, 1982). Furthermore, students using the keyword method learn more than students who use semantically based methods such as writing word definitions, using words in sentences, or inferring their meanings from context (Pressley et al., 1982; McDaniel & Pressley, 1984). The keyword method is especially helpful for lower-ability students who have not developed efficient methods for learning on their own (McDaniel & Pressley, 1984).

other methods There are many other mnemonic devices besides the place, link, peg, and keyword methods (Bellezza, 1981; Lorayne & Lucas, 1974). Bower and Clark (1969) reported success with the *elaboration method,* in which learners weaved together the words on a list into a running story.

Ehri, Deffner, and Wilce (1984) used *pictorial mnemonics* to help children remember the sounds associated with letters of the alphabet. In teaching the letter "f," for example, they showed an illustration in which the letter was drawn as the stem of a flower. This visual image helped the children to remember the shape of the letter "f" and the drawing depicted something whose name begins with the "f" sound (flower).

Rhymes are often useful mnemonic devices ("*I* before *e* except after *c*," "thirty days hath September, . . . "). So are *abbreviations* (YMCA, FBI), especially when they are pronounceable *acronyms* (NATO, UNICEF). You can create your own acronyms for special purposes. For example, if you are to give a speech that has five major ideas, you could employ a word (e.g., "TIGER") whose letters each stand for a key point (*T* represents the role of transportation, and so on).

Imagery and *spatial visualization* also are useful mnemonic devices. You can improve verbal learning by picturing words in your mind, solve "making change" problems easier by visualizing the coins involved, and make spatial computations by visualizing the rooms portrayed in them. In general, anything that helps you to process input more deeply, relate it to more familiar material, or supplement the verbal presentation with vivid imagery will help you to learn and remember it more easily.

factors affecting meaningful verbal learning

We have seen that the secret to learning disconnected material is to find ways to make it meaningful and thus not have to depend on purely rote-learning strategies. Meaningfulness is not a problem in learning connected discourse, however, unless the material is so unfamiliar or difficult as to make meaningful comprehension impossible. Instead, the problem is coping with the sheer volume of the material by learning it in an organized fashion and retaining it so that it can be retrieved when needed.

Mayer (1982) identified the following effects shown in research on learning connected discourse: abstraction effects, levels effects, schema effects, prior knowledge effects, interference effects, text organization effects, and mathemagenic effects. We will discuss these findings along with those on student misconception effects and know-it-all effects.

abstraction effects

Abstraction effects reflect the tendency of learners to remember the gist of a passage rather than its specific wording (Sachs, 1967; Bransford & Franks, 1971). If they assume that the goal is understanding rather than verbatim memory, and if the material can be analyzed into main ideas and supportive detail, learners will tend to concentrate on the main ideas and to retain these in semantic forms that are more abstract and generalized than the verbatim sentences in the passage.

levels effects

Levels effects occur when learners believe that some parts of the passage are more important than others. If the passage is well organized or if the learners are able to provide such organization themselves, they will tend to learn parts that occupy higher levels in the organization better than parts that occupy lower levels. Generalizations and key ideas associated with the main theme will be learned especially well (Bromage & Mayer, 1986; Meyer, 1977). Concerning Chapter 6 of this text, for example, you probably remember that behaviorists have studied methods of controlling behavior by manipulating cues and reinforcers and have shown that different schedules of reinforcement have different effects on response rates, but you probably do not remember all of the details about the names and specific effects of each type of reinforcement schedule discussed.

schema effects

We have already given several examples ("The notes were sour because the seam split," the paragraph on Christopher Columbus, and the ambiguous prisoner/wrestler story) illustrating how text comprehension is affected by existing schemas. Along with Bartlett's research indicating that memory for previously learned material can become reconstructed if the schemas to which it is attached should undergo change themselves, these are all examples of *schema effects*. Elaborating on such schema effects, Gagné and Dick (1983) suggested that: (1) newly learned information is incorporated into existing schemas; (2) recall of previously learned information is influenced by these schemas, so that remembering is a constructive act; (3) schemas not only aid retention of new material by providing frameworks for storage, but also alter the new information by making it "fit" expectations built into the schemas; (4) schemas allow learners to make inferences that fill in the gaps in stories or expository prose; (5) schemas are organized not only in terms of figurative knowledge but also in terms operative knowledge; and (6) ideally, learners will become able not only to process new information efficiently, but also to evaluate and modify their own schemas.

Similarly, Anderson (1984) identified the following six functions of schemas: (1) providing ideational scaffolding for assimilation of text information; (2) facilitating concentration on the important aspects of the text; (3) enabling us to infer details that are implied but not spelled out; (4) allowing orderly memory searches (identifying prior knowledge that will be needed to understand the text; (5) facilitating editing and summarizing (abstracting the gist for storage in long-term memory); and (6) permitting inferential reconstruction (filling in later gaps in memory by replacing lost or never-encoded details with inferences about what those details probably were).

Used in a general way, the term *schema effects* would refer not only to these effects but also to abstraction effects, levels effects, prior knowledge effects, inference effects, and student misconception effects. Mayer (1982), however, used the term *schema effects* to refer more specifically to situations in which learners recognize that the text describes an instance of a larger class of events for which they have a well-developed schema, and then use that schema both to process the information (using expectations about the probable order and degree of importance of its components) and to aid comprehension (by filling in gaps where information is implied rather than stated explicitly). Consider the following paragraph:

> When Mary arrived, the woman at the door greeted her and checked her name. A few minutes later, she was escorted to her chair and shown the day's menu. The attendant was helpful but brusque, almost to the point of being rude. Later, she paid the woman at the door and left.

Chances are that this paragraph was meaningful to you because you recognized that it took place in a restaurant, that Mary had made reservations, that she was seated by the hostess at a table (not merely in a chair), that the "attendant" was a waiter, and that the "woman at the door" was a cashier. Schank and Abelson (1977) claimed that you could infer all of this information (none of which was explicit in the text) because you possess a schema called a "restaurant script" that includes such slots as "being seated," "ordering," and "paying the check."

Similarly, Rumelhart (1975) and

Thorndyke (1977) suggested that people use specialized schemas known as *story grammars* when reading stories. A story grammar is a set of rules that specify the relationships among events or states in a story. Its four main slots are the setting, the theme, the plot, and the resolution. The setting involves a particular time and place and a cast of characters. The theme surrounds an event that the characters are involved in or a goal that they are working toward. The plot involves a series of episodes, each with a goal, behavior directed toward that goal, and the outcome of this behavior. The resolution occurs when the story reaches the climax toward which it has been building and offers some moral or conclusion relating to its theme. Younger children have poorly developed story grammars and thus tend to focus on actions rather than motives and to process stories as if they were relatively disconnected descriptions of events (Voss & Bisanz, 1982). Gradually, however, they bring to bear increasingly sophisticated schemas that help them to know what to look for as they read and how to organize their memory for the story. Setting, theme, plot, and resolution are remembered, perhaps along with some key phrases or quotations. Unimportant details and verbatim phrasing are not.

Reading comprehension theorists recommend that teachers prepare students for story reading by telling them what the story is about and asking them questions to activate schemas that they will find useful in comprehending it. These include schemas relating to the content of the story in addition to story grammars concerning the forms and functions of fictional genres.

prior knowledge effects

Even when material does not lend itself to interpretation within a well-developed schema with ready-made slots, **prior knowledge effects,** in which *learners can use existing knowledge to establish a context or construct a schema into which the new information can be assimilated,* will still occur (Bransford, 1979; Schneider, Korkel, & Weinert, 1989; Yates & Chandler, 1991). The convict/wrestler paragraph presented earlier is an example. Few people have specific "thinking about breaking a hold" schemas, but people knowledgeable about wrestling can use this prior knowledge to interpret the paragraph as being about a wrestler trying to escape a hold. Whatever the content of the text or the background of the person, we all interpret texts with reference to our personal interests and experiences, cultural backgrounds, and other aspects of our prior knowledge.

Learners can control the perspective they take in interpreting information if cued to do so (Anderson, Pichert, & Shirey, 1983). For example, Pichert and Anderson (1977) had learners read a passage describing two boys playing in a house. Some were directed to read from the perspective of a home buyer, and others from the perspective of a burglar. These assigned perspectives affected the pattern of details that were remembered later. "Home buyers" were more likely to remember that the roof leaked, but "burglars" were more likely to remember the color TV.

Providing cues about what prior knowledge is relevant to understanding a passage is one way for teachers to make vague passages more meaningful to students. For expository passages, such cuing might involve suggesting analogies or visual imagery that would link the strange to the familiar. For poetry or fiction, it might involve providing explanations or asking questions designed to alert students to metaphors and other literary devices.

inference effects

Inference effects occur when learners use schemas or other prior knowledge to make inferences about intended meanings that go beyond what is explicitly stated in the text. Three kinds of inferences are case-grammar presuppositions, conceptual dependency inferences, and logical deductions.

Fillmore (1968) used the term *case grammar* to refer to the assumptions and implications that are built into the use of language. For example, declarative sentences typically take a subject-verb-object form, and the verb implies that the subject took some action on the object. In the context of baseball, the verb "hit" implies a subject (the batter), an object (the ball), and in this case, an instrument for accomplishing the action (the bat). These logical relationships and the imagery associated with them are brought to bear in interpreting statements that are not completely explicit. Thus, people familiar with baseball will infer that the ball was pitched and that the batter hit a fair ball and reached base safely when they hear, "It's a hit," or, "He drives a single to left" (Kintsch, 1974; Meyer, 1977).

Conceptual dependency inferences occur when learners recognize cause-effect relationships or other dependencies among ideas in a passage. For example, Kintsch (1977) had students read a story containing the sentences, "A burning cigarette was carelessly discarded. The fire destroyed many acres of virgin forest." Students who read this version of the story were just as likely to report that the cigarette started the fire as were students who read a version that spelled this out explicitly.

Logical deductions occur when readers are given premises that compel certain conclusions. For example, if told that A is taller than B and B is taller than C, they will be able to answer the question "Is A taller than C?" correctly.

Inference effects simplify communication enormously. Instead of having to specify everything that we say in complete detail, we can convey the gist and rely on the listener or reader to infer the rest. In teaching, however, it is wise to be sure that learners get the complete picture when it is important for them to do so.

Teachers ordinarily should spell out cause-and-effect relationships, logical deductions, and the implications of examples or experiments. They should also be alert to the failures of textbooks to be explicit. In recent years, publishers have sought to simplify texts by substituting shorter words and sentences for longer ones. Ironically, this often reduces clarity because vague terms are substituted for precise terms and because important logical connectives ("because," "therefore," etc.) are omitted when longer sentences are divided into shorter ones (Anderson & Armbruster, 1984).

student misconception effects

So far, our discussion of schema, prior knowledge, and inference effects has emphasized the positive by showing how schemas allow us to embed input within meaningful contexts and fill in gaps whenever the message is not complete. However, there is a negative side to this process. Schema activation also makes possible the *student misconception effects* that occur when input is filtered through schemas that are oversimplified, distorted, or otherwise incorrect. This happens routinely with young children whose thinking is still in the process of becoming operational. It also happens frequently with older students and adults, especially when they are learning abstract scientific concepts that contrast with naive ideas about the world that they have built through concrete experiences.

For example, Anderson and Smith (1987) studied the teaching of a fifth-grade science unit on light. One point made repeatedly was that sunlight reflects off other objects to our eyes, and that it is this reflected sunlight that we process when we see. This scientific conception of vision differs from the naive conception that most people develop, namely, that the sun brightens the objects themselves. A test item shows the sun, a tree, and a boy, and asks the students to show

how sunlight enables the boy to see the tree. The correct answer is to draw rays coming from the sun to the tree and then reflecting off the tree to the boy's eyes. On pretests, only about 5 percent of the students answered this item correctly. Of the remaining students who responded at all, the majority drew rays from the sun to the tree but did not show these rays being reflected into the boy's eyes.

So far, this was unremarkable. However, the students then spent several weeks on the unit, which covered light reflection and vision several times in different contexts. Yet, on the post test only 24 percent of the students showed light rays reflecting off the tree to the boy's eyes, and the majority still thought that we see objects because the sun "brightens them up." Replications of this work have yielded similar results, even in classrooms taught by teachers considered to be generally effective who were using widely adopted curriculum materials.

How could this happen? One reason was that the curriculum materials were not as explicit as they needed to be. Also, however, many students never became aware of the conflict between their current beliefs and what the text was saying. They read the words, but they did not appreciate their full implications. Consequently, they sailed right through the unit with the same misconceptions that they brought into it.

These findings are not unusual. Many common misconceptions have been discovered in mathematics (Davis, 1984) and science (Champagne, Klopfer, & Anderson, 1980; diSessa, 1982), and others are being discovered in other subjects (Brophy, VanSledright, & Bredin, 1992; Nicholson, 1984). For example, Davis and McKnight (1980) found that few third or fourth graders solved the following subtraction problem correctly the first time they saw it: 7,002 - 25. Furthermore, because of a common misconception about the process of borrowing, one particular incorrect answer was common: 5,087. Nor are such misconceptions confined

to young children. Matz (1980) included the following in a list of thirty-three algebra errors commonly made by high school and college students:

Evaluating $4X$ when X equals 6 as 46 or $46X$

Evaluating XY when X equals -3 and Y equals -5 as -8

Computing $2X$ divided by $2X$ to be 0.

Claiming that one can't multiply by X because "you don't know what X is"

Such misconceptions can be difficult to remove, and they often reappear after learners seemingly have mastered the correct concepts. Anderson and Smith (1987) made adjustments in the way that the fifth-grade light unit was taught and managed to raise scores on the sun/tree/boy item from 24 percent to 79 percent correct. However, this took both special teacher training (alerting the teachers to probable student misconceptions and ways to confront them) and special curriculum materials (a revised text that was more explicit about the difference between the scientific concept and the naive concept, supplemented by illustrations).

Student misconception effects remind us that teaching involves *conceptual change* rather than infusion of knowledge into a vacuum. Students usually have at least some background knowledge to bring to bear in processing new input, and often they have considerable knowledge organized into powerful schemas. Consequently, they may process the new input primarily by assimilating it (or a distorted version of it) into old schemas, rather than by accommodating the old schemas to take into account the new input. This may be desirable when existing schemas are accurate, but if they are not, it will lead to student misconception effects. Therefore, in addition to merely explaining material, teachers need to

Students who edit their own work, organizing their thoughts and ideas, are better able to encode and remember the content.

confront common misconceptions by making students aware of them and helping them to see how and why they are incorrect (Alvermann & Hynd, 1989; Maria & MacGinitie, 1987).

know-it-all effects

Know-it-all effects occur when possession of a high level of prior knowledge causes learners to process a lecture or text at a relatively low level because they believe that they already know the information that it contains (Yates & Chandler, 1991). It is understandable that listeners might begin to tune out a lecture or readers might begin to skim through a text when they discover that it focuses on highly familiar material, but in the process, they may fail to pay sufficient attention to important aspects of the material that they do not already know. When such know-it-all effects can be anticipated, teachers might take action

designed to minimize them by calling students' attention to the fact that, although the general topic is a familiar one, they will be exploring new aspects or applications of it. For example, an instructor teaching college freshmen about differential equations might note that the course begins with review of some basic algebraic principles, despite the fact that all of the students entered with algebraic prerequisites, because more than 80 percent of previous students in the course have been vague or confused about these principles, and their grades have suffered because of it. Thus, the review is an attempt to improve the students' understanding of some important ideas that they will need to apply to new content that will be introduced as the course develops.

text organization effects

Text organization effects refer to the effects that the organization built into a passage has on what learners encode and remember. We described in the previous chapter the value of structuring elements such as advance organizers, previews, logical sequencing, outline formats, highlighting of main ideas, and summaries. These structuring elements make it possible for learners to retain more by facilitating chunking, subsumption of material into existing schemas, and encoding of it as an organized body of knowledge rather than a list of unrelated items.

In addition, text organization elements cue learners to important aspects of the material. Kintsch and Yarbrough (1982), for example, had learners read essays written in either good or poor rhetorical form. Later tests showed that the two groups were equally good at supplying specific facts, but that the group that had read the well-organized essays were better at answering open-ended questions about main points. Thus, a well-organized text or lecture sequences material in a sensible way and helps learners to encode it as a series of major ideas supported by elaborative details. This organization also helps them to retrieve more of the information later when they need it.

mathemagenic effects

Rothkopf (1970) coined the term *mathemagenic activities* to refer to the things that learners do to assist their own learning (get ready to concentrate, approach the material with the intention of studying and remembering it, etc.). *Mathemagenic effects* are effects of engaging in active information processing methods such as answering adjunct questions or taking notes.

adjunct questions *Adjunct questions* are questions included with text passages: *prequestions* at the beginning, *inserted questions* embedded within the passage itself, or *postquestions* at the end. Students who study passages that include such adjunct questions retain more than students who read the same material without them (Andre, 1987; Rickards, 1979; Reynolds & Anderson, 1982; Walczyk & Hall, 1989). More specifically, adjunct questions tend to increase intentional learning of material directly related to the questions; they do not improve and may even reduce incidental learning.

Much research on adjunct questions has focused on where such questions should be inserted. Most investigators have concluded that postquestions are more valuable than prequestions. *Prequestions* are effective in alerting learners to important issues (Pressley et al., 1992), but they interfere with the learning of material not addressed in the questions (McConkie, 1977; Sagaria & DiVesta, 1978; Klauer, 1984). Prequestions tend to be most effective when they deal with the most general or important ideas, and they are most helpful to low-ability learners (Wilhite, 1983).

Postquestions are less likely to reduce incidental learning by constricting attention to the material addressed in the questions. In addition, they allow learners to assess their understanding of the material and aid retention by encouraging them to encode the material in their own words (Sagaria & DiVesta, 1978). Postquestions that direct attention to points that are often misunderstood or missed altogether because of student misconception effects are especially valuable (McConkie, 1977). In general, postquestions facilitate learning by causing learners to review the material systematically (King, 1992; Sagerman & Mayer, 1987; Wixson, 1984).

other mathemagenic activities Besides responding to adjunct questions, learners can engage in *self-initiated mathemagenic activities* that will enhance learning. One of these is *note taking*. Note taking is an effective way to enhance learning from reading text (and also from listening to lectures, if the lectures are presented at a slow enough rate to allow both monitoring of the input and writing of notes) (Faw & Waller, 1976; Weinstein & Mayer, 1986). Note taking is especially effective when students use outline formats and concentrate on main ideas (Mayer, 1984; Carrier & Titus, 1981).

Another useful mathemagenic activity when reading text is *underlining*, apparently because it helps students to remember key terms and ideas (Rickards & August, 1975). A parallel technique for aiding memory of orally presented material is *shadowing*. After presenting a key word or phrase, the teacher pauses to let the students repeat it aloud (Mayer & Cook, 1981). Shadowing should be particularly useful in early reading instruction and foreign language instruction. The learnng and study skills discussed in detail in Chapter 12 could also be considered mathemagenic activities, although the term is not used in that chapter.

research on novice versus expert information processing

Many exciting advances in contemporary educational psychology are being contributed by investigators studying the information processing aspects of human learning and memory. Many of these involve modeling the thinking of novices and experts in particular knowledge domains and then developing methods for efficiently guiding novices toward expert functioning.

By asking people to think aloud as they solve problems, information processing theorists have been studying how people use their knowledge for thinking about specialized areas such as physics, radiology, or chess (Bédard & Chi, 1992; Chi, Glaser, & Rees, 1981; Larkin, 1981; Newell & Simon, 1972). Often this research involves comparing skilled and experienced experts with novices in the same field, both to describe how experts do it and to identify the problems that novices experience. Such knowledge can become the basis for instruction designed to move novices toward expert status by teaching them to think as experts do (Bereiter & Scardamalia, 1986; Bruer, 1993; Glaser & Bassok, 1989).

DeGroot (1965) compared expert and novice chess players and found that if twenty to twenty-five pieces were arranged randomly on a chess board, experts were no better than novices at reconstructing the arrangement from memory. Both groups placed about seven pieces correctly. However, when the arrangements were recreations of actual chess games, the experts reconstructed the positions of most or even all of the pieces, whereas the novices did little better than before.

How can expert chess players reconstruct twenty-five pieces after seeing them in place for only five or ten seconds? Apparently, they do it by relying on chunking strategies and by activating familiar chess strategy schemas (Simon, 1979). Instead of trying to keep track of twenty-five individual pieces, the experts chunk by conceptualizing the progress of the game in terms of the placement of several *groups* of pieces (perhaps five or six groups with three to five pieces each). Given what they know about chess strategy, they recognize relationships among the pieces within groups and relationships of groups to one another. Besides enabling them to reconstruct games from memory, this kind of chunking and schema activation enables chess experts to play, and usually defeat, a large number of novices at the same time by circulating continuously and taking only a few seconds to decide on a move (Chase & Chi, 1980).

Experts can bring to bear much more **domain-specific knowledge**, *knowledge about a particular domain of learning or expertise,* and their knowledge is much better organized to allow smooth movement between levels ranging from concrete particulars to abstract generalities. In addition, experts are more efficient in using their knowledge. They do not have to work through all logical possibilities when classifying problems or identifying likely solution strategies. Instead, they create a workable *problem space* (cut the problem down to size) by identifying one or a small number of schemas that probably apply to the problem. There may be some initial checking to make sure that the right schema has been chosen (this is why experts analyze the problem first before trying to solve it), but once the problem is properly categorized, they solve it rapidly.

novice and expert teachers

Expert-novice comparisons have been used in studying how experienced teachers know when to use specific strategies with specific students, and how novice teachers can develop this knowledge (Borko & Livingston, 1989; Carter et al., 1987; Fogarty, Wang, & Creek, 1983; Leinhardt, 1988; Peterson & Comeaux, 1987; Swanson, O'Connor, & Cooney, 1990). Like experts in other fields, expert teachers use chunking and schema activation to keep track of more things, to recognize (diagnose) student needs more quickly and accurately, and to bring to bear more strategies with better understanding of why the strategies are appropriate to the situation.

Leinhardt and Greeno (1986) showed this in their comparison of an expert teacher and a novice teacher opening elementary mathematics lessons with homework review. During these homework review activities the expert used established routines for taking attendance, signaled the beginnings and endings of lesson segments, and regulated when students would respond chorally and when they would need to raise their hands and be called on. This teacher efficiently recorded information about attendance and about who did and did not do the homework, elicited mostly correct answers throughout the activity, managed to get all of the homework corrected, and noted who would need individualized help later. Most of her behavior each day was systematically adapted to the time constraints, the goals of the lesson, and its place within the larger mathematics curriculum.

In contrast, the novice teacher was less clear about the purposes of the activity and she lacked established routines for accomplishing them efficiently. Consequently, she had problems with taking attendance, was not clear about who had done the homework, asked ambiguous questions that caused her to misjudge the difficulty of the homework for the students, had trouble controlling the pace, and failed to identify the students who would need individualized follow-up. As more is learned about how expert teachers cut through the complexities of the classroom in order to instruct efficiently, it should become possible to move novices toward such expert levels of functioning more quickly and systematically.

students as intelligent novices

Interesting research is also being done on the development of expertise in novice academic learners (Bereiter & Scardamalia, 1986). Children's mathematics learning provides several examples. Groen and Parkman (1972) have shown that preschool children typically use a "counting all" method for solving simple addition problems. For 3 + 4, for example, these children will recite, "1, 2, 3, 4, 5, 6, 7." By first grade, however, most children use a "choice plus counting on" procedure in which they first choose the larger of the two numbers to be added and then "count on" the additional numbers. Thus, for 3 + 4, they would begin with 4 and then recite "5, 6, 7." Most children discover this more sophisticated strategy on their own, without having to be taught explicitly.

They also discover various shortcuts. Fuson (1982) has shown that first graders are fast at adding "doubles" (2 + 2, 3 + 3, etc.) because they have memorized the answers and do not need to count at all. They also use their "doubles" knowledge for solving other problems (i.e., they can recognize 5 + 7 as the equivalent of 6 + 6, and thus solve it without needing the "counting on" procedure). Expert algebra students estimate answers as a way to check their work as they go along. In combining the expression $a/b + c/d$, for example, they may substitute numbers for the letters (1/2 + 3/4) and work out the numerical version as a way to make sure that they have combined properly (in this case, by first dividing and then adding), something that is not so obvious when just the letters are used (Davis, 1984).

These data suggest several implications for teachers to consider as they make planning decisions. First, there appear to be no shortcuts to expert knowledge. Detailed domain-specific knowledge is needed, not just a few general principles. Second, learners not only need to acquire knowledge and master strategies; they also need to know when the knowledge is relevant and how to use the strategies in various situations. They should be treated as intelligent novices capable of learning the processes involved in formulating problems and working through solutions, not as rote memorizers concerned only with using the right formula or getting the right answer. Third, linkages between the abstract and the concrete need to be made explicit. Students should understand why they are working through a geometric proof or conducting a scientific experiment, so that they appreciate the larger meanings of the exercise and come away from it with more than just the notion that they got it right. Finally, students need opportunities to apply and synthesize their knowledge. Just listening to lectures and watching demonstrations is not enough.

cognitive simulation and artificial intelligence

Many cognitive scientists develop and test models of human information processing using computers. One approach is known as *artificial intelligence*—applying what is known about knowledge, logic, and communication to develop computer programs that can process information and solve problems (Simon, 1981). Computers have been programmed to translate text from one language to another, to interpret pictures, and to "learn" or solve problems by operating on input and making decisions. The programs involve such strategies as *means-end analysis* (comparing the present state to the desired end state to identify the difference and develop ideas about how it might be reduced), *hypothesize and test* (using available information to develop and test hypotheses), and *best-first search* (evaluating hypotheses to identify the one most likely to be correct, and then beginning with this "best" one).

Artificial intelligence work has produced impressive practical demonstrations, such as chess programs that defeat all but the most expert chess players. Yet, these programs are successful only because of the huge memory capacities and rapid information processing capabilities of computers. They approach strategic thinking in thorough and logical but inefficient ways, more like novices than experts. Also, they are not good at certain things that human experts do routinely, such as distinguishing relevant from irrelevant information, responding to situational particulars, and in general, using "common sense." For example, Waldrop (1984) noted Minsky's "dead duck" example: Using rules of logic, computers would be programmed to conclude that Charlie can fly given information that ducks can fly and Charlie is a duck. If Charlie is dead, however, he cannot fly. Humans easily accommodate this information, but artificial intelligence programs can do so only with enormous increases in programming complexity and memory capacity.

Cognitive scientists also work on the *simulation of human cognition*. Here, programs are developed on the basis of actual thinking of humans engaged in problem solving, rather than on the basis of purely logical considerations. Many of these are "expert systems" programs that model the behavior of experts in various fields, although programs have also been developed to model the learning of young children (Klahr & Wallace, 1976), including the *buggy algorithms* (systematic but erroneous methods) developed by novice learners for solving mathematics problems (Brown & Burton, 1978). Such work has been the basis for the development of the computer-based "intelligent tutoring systems" described in Chapter 6.

Cognition simulation proceeds according to a bootstrapping procedure in which scientists first identify the essential elements of the behavior to be modeled, then develop a model that includes these elements and build it into a computer program, then test and improve the model's ability to "predict" the originally observed behavior in similar situations, and then use the model to process new input. One program of research, for example, began with analysis of the behavior of reading specialists trying to diagnose and prescribe treatments for students encountering reading difficulties. What sorts of information did the experts request? Which of this information did they actually use in developing a diagnosis? Which specific diagnoses were used, and what were their critical indicators? What treatments were prescribed for remediating the diagnosed reading skill deficiencies? No two reading experts handled a given case in exactly the same way, but commonalities observed across experts and cases enabled the researchers to construct a simulated "consensus expert" that diagnosed and prescribed for reading difficulties more reliably than individual experts did. Furthermore, computer-assisted instruction involving application of this program to actual cases of reading difficulty has been used to train teachers to diagnose such cases (Vinsonhaler et al., 1983). Heller and Reif (1984) followed similar procedures in developing a model of expert problem solving in physics that has proven useful for teaching students to represent mechanics problems accurately, and thus to solve them more efficiently.

Until recently, most simulations of human thinking and problem solving have used *production-function* (or *rule-based*) *models* that assume that mental processes work like programs running on a computer. In these models, thinking and problem solving are treated as rule-governed processes, so learning is treated as development of knowledge about the nature and application of the rules that govern any particular domain.

Recently, these rule-based models have been challenged by *connectionist models* that are influenced not so much by the functioning of computers as by what is known about the functioning of the brain itself (Bereiter, 1991; McClelland & Rumelhart, 1988; Schneider &

Graham, 1992; Smolensky, 1988). Connectionist models have been more successful than rule-based models for handling problems that involve recognizing patterns and similarities, making intelligent guesses and capitalizing on partial information when known rules do not fit the situation, and monitoring the big picture as they gradually move from vagueness and uncertainty toward clarity and decisiveness in dealing with messy and complex problems.

Rule-based models assume that knowledge of networks of interconnected elements is located primarily in the elements themselves, whereas connectionist models assume that knowledge resides in the connections. Through repeated exposure to a knowledge domain, learners develop appreciation of it as a network that encompasses various recognizable patterns, and this knowledge of network patterns is brought to bear when thinking about the domain or attempting to solve problems to which it applies. Connectionist approaches have been used successfully for modeling learning in such domains as regular and irregular past tenses of English verbs (Rumelhart & McClelland, 1986), foreign languages (Ney & Pearson, 1990), and early arithmetic performance (Schneider & Graham, 1992).

Connectionist models appeal to cognitive scientists who believe that rule-based cognition is too neat and orderly to be realistic as a model for brain functioning. They note that people often think and attempt to solve problems using informal reasoning, analogies, rules of thumb, and so on, rather than systematic logic. Connectionist models reflect these informal aspects of mental functioning better than rule-based models do.

Some cognitive scientists believe that both kinds of models are needed because human knowledge depends on two distinct cognitive systems—one an explicit system that produces declarative knowledge through conscious, controlled reflection and the other an implicit system that produces procedural knowledge through unconscious but automatically functioning reflexive processes (Holyoak & Spellman, 1993). Both kinds of models have been successful as bases for simulating human intelligence, and some of this work has led to practical applications in classrooms. Along with some of the computerized tutorial programs described in Chapter 6, this includes some of the recently developed methods for teaching particular school subjects described in Chapter 11.

summary

Information processing theorists study information processing, storage, and retrieval in human learning. Associationist theorists assume that new learning depends on the nature and strength of associations between new input and previous learning stored in memory. Constructivist theorists construe learning as a cognitive representation constructed actively by a learner attempting to make sense out of experiences. This cognitive representation is subject to change over time as it interacts with previously stored memories and is affected by newer experiences. The rote-memory experiments of Ebbinghaus and the story-reconstruction studies of Bartlett are examples of the associationist and constructivist approaches, respectively.

Experiences are encoded and stored in memory in different ways. Episodes in our personal lives are stored in episodic memory, which features images of ourselves reliving those events. However, intentional learning of material communicated through language is encoded in semantic memory, which features concept definitions, statements, principles, and other verbal abstractions.

Most information processing theorists accept the three-stage information processing model, in which input first enters the sensory register, then short-term or working memory, and then long-term memory. The sensory register has a capacity of 7 + 2 items of information,

perhaps less, so that rehearsal and chunking strategies must be used when this limited capacity is strained by the need to consider many items of input at once. Chunking can greatly increase the capacity of working memory to accommodate individual items. Information about concepts and relationships appears to be stored in long-term memory in the form of semantic networks organized hierarchically.

Learning is an active process of sense making in which the learner activates prior knowledge to generate frameworks within which to interpret new input. The learner "goes beyond the information given" by filling in gaps and assuming meanings that are implied but not stated directly.

Learners must rely on rote processes when input is not very meaningful or organized. Besides the level of meaningfulness of the input, rote learning is affected by serial position effects (primacy and recency effects), item distinctiveness, amount and distribution of practice, and the effects of transfer, interference, organization, levels of processing, and mnemonics. The place, link, peg, and keyword methods, along with other mnemonics such as the elaboration method and the use of pictures, images, rhymes, and acronyms, assist learning of relatively meaningless material by associating it with meaningful and organized material.

The meaningful verbal learning of connected discourse shows abstraction effects, level effects, schema effects, prior knowledge effects, inference effects, student misconception effects, know-it-all effects, text organization effects, and mathemagenic effects. Adjunct questions (prequestions, inserted questions, and postquestions) help to elicit mathemagenic effects.

Recent research on information processing features comparisons between novices and experts, as well as cognitive simulation and artificial intelligence. These lines of research advance our understanding of sophisticated human cognition in various domains, and suggest potential methods for moving novices efficiently toward expert status.

questions for reflection

1. Without reexamining the text or looking at notes, outline what you remember from what was presented about human development in Chapters 2-4. Why have you remembered some things and forgotten others? How do the models presented in this chapter for how memory works account for your learning?

2. Describe the conditions under which students are most likely to retain information for future use. How can teachers help students to retain information meaningfully?

3. Can teachers present too much as well as too little information? List conditions under which detailed information may be inappropriate. If you took a behavioral view instead of a cognitive view of learning, would you answer this question differently? Why or why not?

4. In your own words, explain the "7 + 2" rule and its implications for designing instruction.

5. Reexamine the guidelines that Case (1978) has presented for minimizing the load placed on students' working memory. If you were teaching seventh graders the differences between red and white blood cells and their role in body functioning, how would you proceed?

6. How might encouraging students to ask questions about material facilitate or inhibit their learning?

7. Differentiate between transfer effects and interference effects. How do these differ from organization and levels-of-processing effects?

8. Explain how distinctiveness of encoding, elaboration of encoding, and effort expended during encoding influence how much information is retained in long-term memory.

9. To what extent should teachers cue students to the sorts of questions that they will ask on tests? What are the advantages and disadvantages of sharing this information?

10. Should we as authors raise questions with you before or after you read a chapter? If so, what kind? What are the relative advantages of different types of prequestions and postquestions?

11. What are useful mathemagenic activities for students to engage in? How can teachers encourage them to do so?

12. Using the concepts discussed in this chapter, explain why you could not do as well on a high school history test today as you did when you took it. In particular, what was the long-term effect of studying for the test?

13. As a teacher, how can you help students to learn material so that they will retain it in long-term memory?

cases to consider

can't put it all together Mrs. Romberg is unhappy with her algebra students' performance on word problems. They solve equations quickly, and most can complete a page of forty problems with no errors. Yet, with word problems, it's as if they had never heard of algebra. Some can't even begin, others guess answers without showing any work, and still others represent the problem incorrectly and end up solving the wrong equation. Even the students who get the right answer seem unsure of themselves when questioned.

Even more puzzling and frustrating, the students usually can respond correctly when she guides them through these problems by asking a series of questions. Thus, it's not that they lack knowledge; it's that they are unable to put it all together when asked to apply this knowledge to problems that are not already formulated algebraically. Using concepts such as information storage and retrieval, limited capacity of working memory, or novice versus expert problem solving, develop an explanation for the production deficiency problems that Mrs. Romberg's students are experiencing. What can she do to help them overcome these problems?

two different worlds Mrs. Karo and Mrs. Tapper both use the same second-grade science text. They are teaching a unit on trees and leaves, and today's lesson focuses on maple trees and the process of collecting sap to use in making maple syrup. Mrs. Tapper teaches in a small town in Michigan. Most of her students are familiar with maple trees because they are surrounded by them. Furthermore, many have had firsthand experience with the sap-collecting process, either through their own relatives or through attending demonstrations and tasting experiences offered to the public by commercial sap collectors.

Mrs. Karo teaches in inner-city Phoenix. Few of her students have ever been outside of the city, let alone traveled the country, so most of them have never even seen a maple tree. In fact, most of the local vegetation has needles rather than leaves, and none of it looks much like maple trees.

Given what was said about how learners activate prior knowledge when responding to input, what will be the similarities and differences in the responses of Mrs. Tapper's students and Mrs. Karo's students to the science lesson? How meaningful will the information be, and how are they likely to process and store it? How might the two teachers adapt this lesson to their students? How can Mrs. Tapper work around her students' belief that they "already know that," and get them to learn something? How can Mrs. Karo make the material meaningful and interesting to her students? Which teacher should do more demonstrating and explaining, and which should allocate more time to discussion?

part IV.

instructional applications

Some of Mrs. Fitz's *students learn division of decimals easily, some divide correctly but misplace the decimal points, and a few don't even divide correctly. The latter students need remedial instruction in the number facts and math skills taught in lower grades. How can Mrs. Fitz determine what to include in this instruction, and how to choose materials and activities?*

Mr. Becker and Mr. Rowe *both emphasize teacher-led group instruction featuring class presentations, recitation activities, and independent seat work, and are quite successful. However, Mr. Becker's presentations last only a few minutes before engaging students in several short, fast-paced activities. In contrast, Mr. Rowe lectures for twenty to thirty minutes, then leads only two or three slower-paced activities. How can two teachers modify an approach to instruction so*

much and still achieve similar success?

Susan Melnick *is very dissatisfied with the textbooks she must use to teach. They cover too many things, in too much detail, making her students feel overwhelmed. Everything seems driven by the textbook: initial reading and recitation to introduce new content, seat work to reinforce it, and tests for accountability and grading. Unfortunately, students forget most of this learning or it remains inert—recoverable if cued sufficiently but not really usable in appropriate application situations. What can Ms. Melnick do to teach more productively?*

Charlie Curvesetter and Frank Frustrated *are in the same history class. They are similar in ability and time spent studying history, but Charlie consistently outperforms Frank on tests and assignments. How can this be?*

In Part IV (Chapters 9-12), we discuss some of the instructional applications of the theories, concepts, and research discussed in Part III on learning. Chapter 9 presents concepts and procedures for conceptualizing curricula, establishing sequences of objectives, and designing instruction. More generally, it explains how to design instruction that moves students efficiently from the simple/familiar to the complex/unfamiliar, drawing examples from research on the teaching of concepts. Using these ideas, Mrs. Fitz might do a task analysis of the hierarchy of skills required for successful division of decimals and then work backward from the target objective to her students' present skill levels to establish a starting point for remedial instruction.

Chapter 10 presents principles for adapting basic instructional methods to the students and the teaching situations. It encourages teacher-led, group-based instruction (known as *active teaching*) as a basic approach, with modifications to suit the grade level, the subject matter, and the students. Given the descriptions of their classes, Mr. Becker probably teaches in the primary grades and spends most of his time working on basic skills, while Mr. Rowe teaches at the secondary level in a subject matter (such as history) that emphasizes knowledge more than skills.

Chapter 11 addresses the principles involved in teaching school subjects for understanding and social construction of knowledge. It illustrates how research findings on the role of prior knowledge in new learning, knowledge restructuring and conceptual change, and how the social construction of situated knowledge are being used to teach students to understand, appreciate, and apply their learning. This research indicates that the principles summarized in this chapter underlie how Susan Melnick could change her teaching to make it more powerful.

Chapter 12 provides information about developing students' skills for systematic studying, problem solving, and critical thinking. It explains how differences between Charlie Curvesetter's and Frank Frustrated's note-taking and study skills may account for the differences in their performances. Charlie outlines a presentation and paraphrases its gist in his notes, but Frank writes haphazardly rather than creating an organized synopsis of it. Also, when studying, Charlie underlines sparingly and chunks information according to how the author has structured, organized, and sequenced the text, whereas Frank underlines much of the material and tries to memorize it. Chapter 12 explains how students like Frank can learn to study more effectively.

designing instruction

objectives

1. Define instructional design and explain the steps in the Gagné and Briggs systems approach
2. Define a curriculum scope and sequence statement and describe the preparation and decision making involved in developing one
3. Describe how curriculum-sequencing decisions are made with the assistance of information processing analysis, task classification, and learning task analysis
4. List the instructional events that Gagné and Briggs believe must be planned for each instructional objective
5. Describe the practical considerations involved in developing or selecting materials and media
6. Apply Gropper's ideas for designing an easy-to-difficult sequencing into tasks by manipulating the treatment tools used in teaching the tasks
7. Contrast Skinner's behavioral approach, Gagné's task analysis approach, and Case and Bereiter's cognitive development approach to instructional design
8. Define concepts and concept learning tasks
9. Apply Owen, Blount, and Moscow's model for teaching concepts
10. Distinguish the role of positive examples from the role of negative examples in teaching concepts, and explain how to use rational sets of examples to teach concepts efficiently
11. Define Engelmann and Carnine's key concepts (faultless communication, juxtaposition of examples, stipulation, interpolation, extrapolation), and explain their procedures for teaching object concepts, comparative concepts, and transformation sequences

instructional design: an overview

In previous chapters, we discussed learning hierarchies and task analysis, programmed instruction with its emphasis on careful sequencing of frames, and ideas about structuring and sequencing information around key concepts. We also described findings indicating that certain texts are more "considerate" than others because they are organized around structuring devices that provide coherence and flow. All of these ideas suggest that instruction will be most effective when the content is divided into units and ultimately individual lessons that are structured and sequenced to maximize clarity and ease of learning and to minimize potential for confusion.

Instructional design is *the art (and applied science) of creating clear and effective instruction.* It requires attention to the materials and activities as well as the methods of instruction, and includes testing and revision cycles in addition to creation of original versions (Gagné, Briggs, & Wager, 1988; Posner & Rudnitsky, 1986). Our coverage of instructional design begins with the systems approach

that originally defined the field. Next, we consider more recently developed approaches that are more compatible with currently employed constructivist models of teaching (see Bonner, 1988; Kember, 1991; Merrill, Li, & Jones, 1990; Reigeluth, 1989; Tennyson & Rasch, 1988). Finally, we illustrate some of the complexities involved in designing instruction, using concept teaching as our context for drawing examples.

the Gagné and Briggs systems approach

Gagné and Briggs (1979) stated that instructional design is most effectively conducted using a **systems approach**, *an approach that begins with analysis of needs and goals, proceeds through development and application of detailed plans for selecting and testing instructional materials and procedures designed to accomplish*

Figure 9.1 stages in designing instructional systems

System level	1. Analysis of needs, goals, and priorities
	2. Analysis of resources, constraints, and alternate delivery systems
	3. Determination of scope and sequence of curriculum and courses: delivery system design
Course level	4. Determining course structure and sequence
	5. Analysis of course objectives
Lesson level	6. Definition of performance objectives
	7. Preparing lesson plans or modules
	8. Developing or selecting materials and media
	9. Assessing student performance (performance measures)
Final system level	10. Teacher preparation
	11. Formative evaluation
	12. Field testing, revision
	13. Summative evaluation
	14. Installation and diffusion

SOURCE: *Principles of Instructional Design*, second edition, by Robert Gagné and Leslie Briggs. Copyright © 1979; Holt, Rinehart & Winston. Reprinted by permission.

these goals, and continues through as many revision cycles as may be needed to produce acceptable results. (see Figure 9.1). The systems approach begins with whatever goals have been adopted (by the designers themselves or by others empowered to do so), and then draws on teaching models, learning theories, and other relevant sources to construct a suitable instructional system. The components included in the system should be mutually reinforcing, but they need not be identical in format nor derived from a single theory, so long as they are suited to the students and the objectives. For example, instructional designers might use lecturing and modeling to develop knowledge and comprehension, but use questioning and discussion followed by exercises to promote application.

The systems approach implies that publishers of instructional materials should routinely go through all fourteen of the stages shown in Figure 9.1, continuing to recycle through them until an instructional system has proven its effectiveness. This is seldom done, however. Consequently, the materials that teachers work with are typically less than ideal and sometimes seriously flawed. Therefore, even though most teachers will not be expected to design instructional systems that extend across several grade levels, they will need to know basic principles of instructional design in order to identify and correct flaws in the materials they are given. Furthermore, most teachers will be expected to adapt materials to their classes and to develop remedial programs for students who need them. These activities require the ability to execute the first nine of the stages in Figure 9.1.

Gagné and Briggs identified system-level stages, course-level stages, and lesson-level stages. *System-level stages* concern the development of the system as a whole, including all courses or other subdivisions within it. In developing an elementary mathematics curriculum, for example, system-level work would include deciding what to teach, sequencing these objectives, and then assigning a portion of the sequence to each grade. There would be reviews at the beginning of each year and when introducing new topics that build on content taught earlier, but in general, overlearned material would be phased out and new material phased in. Some system-level stages (1–3) concern initial planning prior to development of lessons and materials, and others (10–14) concern the testing, revision, and dissemination that would follow such development. *Course-level stages* (4–5) concern the development of separate courses within the larger system, and *lesson-level stages* (6–9) concern the development of individual lessons within these courses.

initial system-level stages

stage 1: analysis of needs, goals, and priorities Planning begins with establishing consensus on needs, setting priorities among them, and stating their instructional implications. Instructional designers need to make decisions about what content to teach, to what levels of depth and mastery, to what students, and in what sequence. Once consensus is reached on these decisions, the designers develop a *curriculum scope and sequence statement* listing the instructional objectives in the order in which they will be addressed.

stage 2: analysis of resources, constraints, and alternative delivery systems Given the scope and sequence statement, the designers next consider how each objective can be accomplished. What methods are known or believed to be effective? What materials will be needed? What activities might support the students' learning?

These questions are addressed within any known constraints. Some equipment is too expensive, bulky, noisy, or dangerous to use. Some activities are not suited to the physical setting of the classroom, and some are not feasible for use by a single teacher who must work with twenty to forty students. Consequently, compromises may have to be made, and certain objectives may have to be dropped or reduced in priority. Ultimately, the work of Stage 2 culminates in feasible plans for teaching the anticipated students within the anticipated constraints.

stage 3: determination of scope and sequence of curriculum and courses: delivery system design At this stage, the designers elaborate the scope and sequence statement by assigning sequences of objectives to courses, stating objectives in terms of learner performance, and clarifying the details of the delivery system to be developed. Objectives are stated in terms of learner performance (rather than content coverage) so that learning measures can be developed and used later for evaluating the system. Clarifying the details of the delivery system involves identifying the materials, equipment, and media to be purchased or developed, the learning activities to be included, and the manuals and procedures needed for training teachers. Upon completion of Stage 3, the focus shifts to course- and lesson-level work.

course-level stages

stage 4: determining course structure and sequence Gagné and Briggs distinguished between *target objectives* (major objectives to be reached by the end of the course) and *enabling objectives* (steps toward attainment of the target objectives). At Stage 4, the target objectives of each course are clustered into units of instruction that will require perhaps one to three weeks to complete. **Sequencing**—*arranging for students to encounter clusters of instructional materials and learning activities in a developmental or logical order that facilitates systemic learning*—is then considered, first for units and then for objectives within units.

Sequencing may or may not be crucial. To teach a hierarchically ordered series of mathematics skills, most designers would begin with the simplest skills and proceed in orderly fashion up the hierarchy. In a course on western Europe, however, units on Germany, France, and Great Britain might be presented in any order.

Sometimes different sequences offer trade-offs that must be considered with reference to the instructional objectives. For example, courses in history or in developmental psychology can be organized either *chronologically* (taking up the developmental or historical periods in order and embedding coverage of each major topic within the presentations on each of the periods) or *topically* (treating each topic separately and embedding discussion of change over time within these topical units). The chronological approach highlights the big picture and shows how it changed over time, but it results in fragmented discussion of particular topics. The topical approach offers more coherent treatments of each topic but fragments the big picture.

If the objectives do not need to be addressed in a particular sequence, designers may want to *modularize* their units (make them self-contained and usable in any order) so as to provide instructors with flexibility. This strategy was followed in designing the present text. Part IV of this text, on instructional applications, assumes mastery of Part III on learning, but otherwise, the units have been prepared as modules that do not depend on mastery of prior units. The book has been prepared this way because some instructors will not have enough time to cover everything; some will want to omit certain material because their students take an entire course on that topic in addition to a course in educational psychology; and instructors differ in what topics they want to emphasize and in how they want to sequence those topics.

stage 5: analysis of course objectives

At this stage, the instructional designer performs detailed analyses of the target objectives in each course. Gagné and Briggs recommended three kinds of analysis: (1) *information processing analysis* to reveal the sequence of mental operations required to perform the objectives, (2) *task classification* to categorize learning outcomes and identify the conditions of learning that will have to be established, and (3) *learning task analysis* to identify the enabling objectives that will need to be taught as steps toward the ultimate target objectives. The point of these analyses is to anticipate the prior knowledge that learners will need and the types of information processing, thinking, or problem solving that they will need to engage in if they are to accomplish the target objectives. Subsequently, the instruction will be designed to supply needed prior knowledge and guide learners through the anticipated learning processes, so as to make their learning as smooth and efficient as possible.

information processing analysis This identifies the sequence of steps involved in a

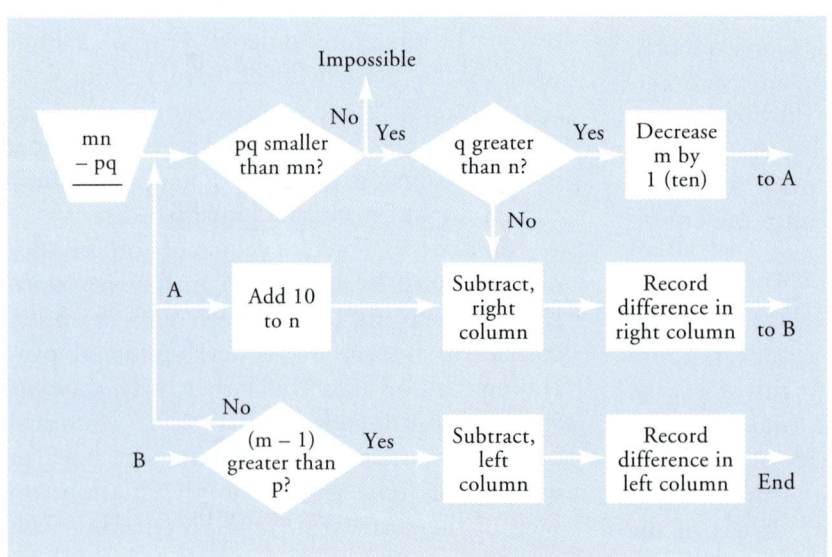

Figure 9.2 an information processing analysis of the subtraction of two-place numbers
SOURCE: *Principles of Instructional Design*, second edition by Robert Gagné and Leslie Briggs. Copyright © 1979; Holt, Rinehart & Winston. Reprinted by permission.

target performance. Gagné and Briggs advocated using *flow charts* to depict these steps. Figure 9.2 shows a flow chart of the information processing involved in subtracting two-place numbers. The figure uses trapezoids to represent inputs, rectangles to represent actions, and diamonds to represent decisions.

Information processing analyses provide clear descriptions of target objectives and thus help sharpen planning for both instruction and assessment. Also, they often reveal steps in the process that might not have been recognized otherwise. For example, Figure 9.2 clarifies that learners must be able to distinguish the larger from the smaller of the two numbers before subtracting. If they do not already possess this capability, it will have to be taught as an enabling objective.

task classification This involves classifying course objectives into task categories that imply different conditions of learning. Gagné and Briggs classify tasks as involving intellectual skills, cognitive strategies, information, attitudes, or motor skills. Intellectual skills are further classified as discriminations, concrete concepts, defined concepts, rules, or higher order rules. Different conditions of learning are associated with each of these categories (see Chapter 5), so that awareness of task type is helpful in planning instruction.

learning task analysis This involves identifying the prerequisites for learning each objective. In the case of intellectual skills, learning task analysis produces a formal **learning hierarchy**: *an ordering of related learning activities from simpler tasks such as discriminations through more complex ones such as concrete concepts, rules, and higher-order rules, with mastery of simpler tasks being prerequisite to learning of more complex tasks.* A *learning hierarchy* for subtraction of whole numbers is shown in Figure 9.3. Such hierarchies, in combination with more detailed information processing analyses such as those shown in

Figure 9.2, help identify which skills need to be taught and in what order.

Learning objectives other than intellectual skills (verbal information, cognitive strategies, motor skills, attitudes) are not embedded within hierarchies, but they may include certain ideas or skills that are logically prerequisite to other ones. For example, in teaching a mnemonic device (i.e., a cognitive strategy) to help learners remember a list of rules, it makes sense to teach the rules first so that the learners understand the meaning and usefulness of the mnemonic device when they learn it.

lesson-level stages

stage 6: definition of performance objectives At this stage, specific objectives are written for each lesson. These objectives will be used to guide development of the instruction (including the materials and activities) and of the evaluation devices used to assess its effectiveness.

stage 7: preparing lesson plans (or modules) The nature of these plans will depend on the nature of the instruction anticipated. If individualized, self-paced learning modules are to be developed, the plan will be addressed to the learner and will include a statement of objectives, a list of materials to be read, a guide to activities to be performed, a self-check test, and instruction about presenting the completed work and arranging to be tested (Gagné and Briggs, 1979). If teacher-led, group-based instruction is to be developed, the lesson plan is addressed to the teacher. In this text, we will concentrate on planning for teacher-led group instruction.

Each lesson objective will require a plan that: (1) lists the instructional events to occur; (2) identifies the materials, media, or agents needed to implement them; (3) specifies plans for all learning activities, including plans for

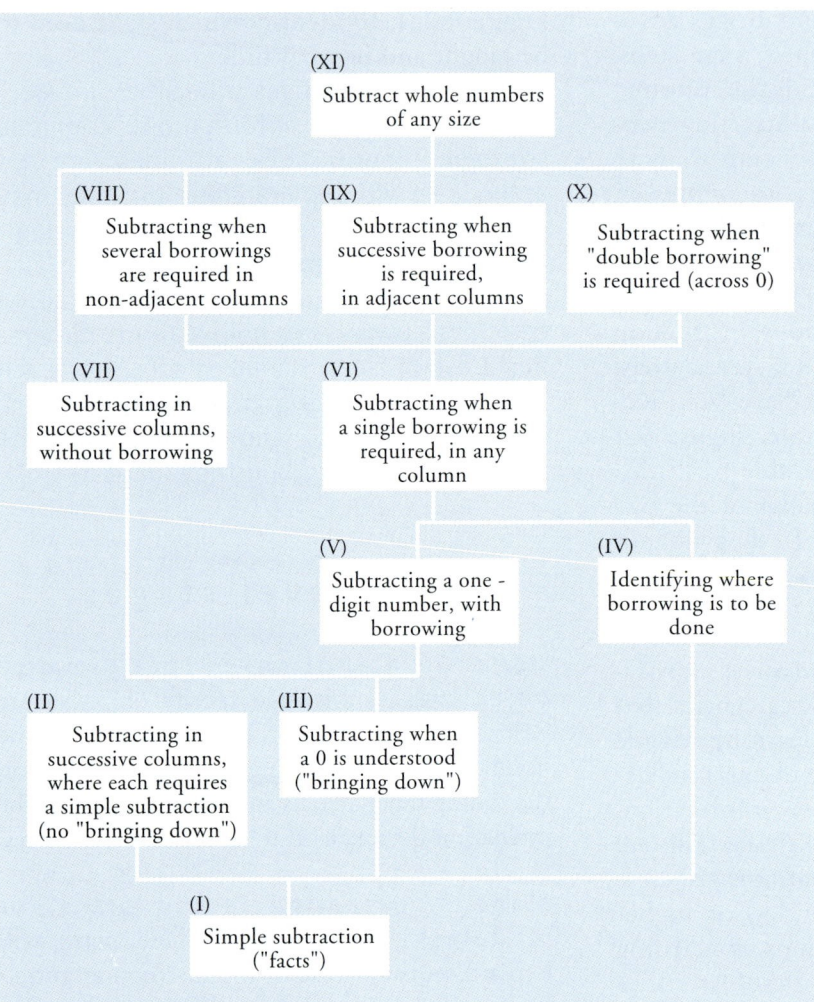

Figure 9.3 a learning hierarchy for subtracting whole numbers
SOURCE: From "Analysis of Objectives" by Robert Gagné in L. Briggs (Ed.) *Instructional Design*, Copyright © 1977. Englewood Cliffs, NJ, Educational Technology Publications. Reprinted with permission.

how media and materials are to be used; and (4) previews the selected media and materials to plan the teacher's roles during the lesson.

Instructional events are *the words and actions of the teacher*. Nine instructional events that Gagné and Briggs would include in a complete plan are shown in Table 9.1, along with the information-processing activities that they are supposed to engender in learners. Table 9.2 (p. 244) shows that instructional events take different forms depending on whether one is teaching intellectual skills, cognitive strategies, information, attitudes, or motor skills.

Here and in the next stage, the designer's creativity and knowledge of subject matter, pedagogy, and the learners come into play, so instructional design becomes an art as well as a science. Usually, there will be many ways to approach teaching a particular objective. The designer will have to decide what information to present (and at what level of difficulty and redundancy), what examples or demonstrations to use, what media or materials are important enough to justify the trouble and expense involved in including them, and what practice and application activities will be most helpful.

table 9.1 events of instruction and their relations to processes of learning

INSTRUCTIONAL EVENT	RELATION TO THE LEARNING PROCESS
1. Gaining attention	*Reception* of patterns of neural impulses
2. Informing the learner of the objective	Activating a process of *executive control*
3. Stimulating recall of prerequisite learnings	*Retrieval* to working memory
4. Presenting the stimulus material	Emphasizing features for *selective perception*
5. Providing "learning guidance"	*Semantic encoding*
6. Eliciting the performance	Activating a *response organization*
7. Providing feedback about performance correctness	Establishing *reinforcement*
8. Assessing the performance	Activating *retrieval,* making *reinforcement* possible
9. Enhancing retention and transfer	Providing cues and strategies for *retrieval*

SOURCE: *Principles of Instructional Design*, second edition, by Robert Gagné and Leslie Briggs. Copyright © 1979; Holt, Rinehart & Winston. Reprinted by permission.

Gaining attention, for example, can be accomplished by simply saying, "Look here." However, the lesson will probably be more successful if the teacher begins by arousing the students' curiosity or interest. This might be done by posing an interesting question that the lesson will answer, by showing a prop, or by telling students why they will need the knowledge or where they will use it. Depending on the objective and the students, some methods of gaining attention will be more effective than others. This is also true of other instructional events such as stimulating recall of prerequisite capabilities (can these merely be mentioned or elicited through questioning, or will a review be necessary?), presenting the stimulus material (which examples would be helpful, and which might be misleading?), or providing learning guidance (when and how should the teacher give explanations, attempt to elicit insights through questioning, or assign activities designed to stimulate discovery learning?).

stage 8: developing or selecting materials and media It may be possible to adapt needed media or other instructional materials from existing sources, although it will be important to preview them to make sure that they are appropriate. Where materials cannot be obtained elsewhere, the designer will need to develop them. Besides effectiveness in helping students to accomplish objectives, materials and media need to be assessed with an eye toward such practical factors as: the size of the group with whom the medium can be used; how easily it can be interrupted for discussion or response to questions; its probable affective impact; the need for special training in its use; the time and trouble required to set it up; and the costs involved in purchasing, storing, and maintaining it (Briggs, 1970). Many materials and media proposed for use in schools have proven to be overly time consuming, difficult to use, or otherwise impractical (Clark, 1983). This is why print materials continue to be used

table 9.2 instructional events and the conditions of learning they imply for five types of learned capabilities

INSTRUCTIONAL EVENT	TYPE OF CAPABILITY				
	Intellectual skill	*Cognitive strategy*	*Information*	*Attitude*	*Motor skill*
1. Gaining attention	Introduce stimulus change: variations in sensory mode				
2. Informing learner of objective	Provide description and example of the performance to be expected	Clarify the general nature of the solution expected	Indicate the kind of verbal question to be answered	Provide example of the kind of action choice aimed for	Provide a demonstration of the performance to be expected
3. Stimulating recall of prerequisites	Stimulate recall of subordinate concepts and rules	Stimulate recall of task strategies and associated intellectual skills	Stimulate recall of context of organized information	Stimulate recall of relevant information skills and human model identification	Stimulate recall of executive subroutine and part skills
4. Presenting the stimulus material	Present examples of concept or rule	Present novel problems	Present information in propositional form	Present human model demonstrating choice of personal action	Provide external stimuli for performance including tools or implements
5. Providing learning guidance	Provide verbal cues to proper combining sequence	Provide prompts and hints to novel solution	Provide verbal links to a larger meaningful context	Provide for observation of model's choice of action, and of reinforcement received by model	Provide practice with feedback of performance achievement
6. Eliciting the performance	Ask learner to apply rule or concept to new examples	Ask for problem solution	Ask for information in paraphrase, or in learner's own words	Ask learner ot indicate choices of action in real or simulated situations	Ask for execution of the performance
7. Providing feedback	Confirm correctness of rule or concept application	Confirm originality of problem solution	Confirm correctness of statement of information	Provide direct or vicarious reinforcement of action choice	Provide feedback on degree of accuracy and timing of performance
8. Assessing performance	Learner demonstrates application of concept or rule	Learner originates a novel solution	Learner restates information in paraphrased form	Learner makes desired choice of personal action in real or simulated situation	Learner executes performance of total skill
9. Enhancing retention and transfer	Provide spaced reviews including a variety of examples	Provide occasions for a variety of novel problem solutions	Provide verbal links to additional complexes of information	Provide additional varied situations for selected choice of action	Learner continues skill practice

SOURCE: *Principles of Instructional Design,* second edition, by Robert Gagné and Leslie Briggs. Copyright © 1979; Holt, Rinehart & Winston. Reprinted by permission.

heavily despite developments in audiovisual technology and computers.

stage 9: assessing student performance (performance measures) This stage involves preparation of performance measures for determining whether students achieve objectives. In the systems approach, instructional planning is not complete without preparation for assessment, and instructional development is not complete until success in achieving its objectives has been demonstrated.

final system-level stages

Stages 10-14 in the Gagné and Briggs scheme apply only to the designers of comprehensive learning systems, and will not be considered in detail here. They involve: designing methods for training teachers to use the new system, conducting **formative evaluation** by *pilot testing courses or individual lessons in a few classes to identify revision needs;* **field testing** by *implementing the system as a whole in a few sites, evaluating it, and making further revisions;* conducting **summative evaluation** in which *the revised system is implemented in enough sites to allow statistical analysis of its effectiveness, based on measures of the primary learning outcomes that the system is designed to produce;* and developing methods for diffusing information about the (presumably proven) system and installing it in new sites.

other approaches to instructional design

The systems approach is the best known approach to instructional design, but there are many others (for reviews and information, see Andrews & Goodson, 1980; Braden & Sachs, 1983; Dick & Carey, 1990; Gagné & Dick, 1983; Reigeluth, 1983, 1987; and issues of the *Journal of Instructional Development*). Many of these other approaches are similar to that of Gagné and Briggs, differing only in terminology and degree of elaboration of particular points. Some, however, are worth noting because they envision a different kind of instruction from the didactic approach stressed by Gagné and Briggs or because they introduce important additional considerations.

Gropper's treatment tools

Gropper (1983, 1987) outlined a behavioral approach that uses Skinnerian terminology and focuses on skills instruction. For routine instruction that is expected to proceed smoothly, he recommended telling learners what and how to perform, providing examples of good performance, and providing opportunities for practice. However, for less routine instruction that requires behavioral shaping or other specialized treatments, he identified *treatment tools* for adjusting the design of practice tasks by varying the degree of cuing provided, the size of the unit of behavior to be practiced, the mode of stimulus and response required, the types of examples, the content of tasks, or the frequency with which tasks are practiced. He also provided guidelines for use of these treatment tools at different stages in the instructional sequence.

Cuing is frequent and specific early in a unit, but is faded gradually as mastery develops. In learning penmanship, students might first trace over model script, then copy (but not trace over) the script, and then write on their own without visual cues available. In learning French, students might first imitate French spoken on tape, then read it from printed text, and then speak it in conversation.

The *size* of the unit of behavior to be practiced would also vary across the sequence of instruction. Practice might begin with isolated subskills (punctuating sentences), proceed to combinations of intermediate steps (writing sentences or paragraphs), and then move to final practice (writing essays). In addition to varying the sheer *size* of a task, the designer can vary its *complexity* (driving in empty parking lots versus driving on the streets in traffic), or the *standards* for acceptable performance (gradual decrease in the number of errors acceptable in typing).

Variations in *response mode* can also be used to gradually increase level of demand. Initial practice might require only recognition of the correct answer (by selecting it from several alternatives), whereas intermediate practice might call for editing (correcting the answer if it is incorrect), and final practice might call for production (supplying the answer in the absence of cues). Similarly, the *stimulus mode* can be varied by beginning with concrete examples and moving toward more technical or abstract definitions, or beginning with procedures before introducing general principles.

The *types of examples* can be varied to promote generalization and transfer. Examples would be sequenced from easy to difficult according to the degree to which they were familiar to the students, similar to previously encountered examples, and salient in their defining characteristics. Thus, students would practice forming plurals for regular nouns before taking on irregular nouns, and would design experiments involving only one variable before moving to designs involving multiple interacting variables.

The *content* of practice tasks can also be varied. Early in a sequence, one might exaggerate the critical features of examples to call attention to them and prepare students for subtler variations to be presented later. For certain objectives it may be helpful to have students practice errors (usually one wants to minimize this, but sometimes it is helpful to call students' attention to common errors and help them discriminate correct from incorrect performance). Or, one might alter the typical sequence of behaviors (to disassemble something or work backward from a goal before attempting to assemble or work forward). Finally, the *frequency of practice* can be varied. Typically, a great deal of distributed practice (however much it takes to produce mastery) is programmed following introduction of a new skill, with fading to a maintenance level thereafter.

Gropper's ideas show how an easy-to-difficult sequencing can be designed into instruction not only by ordering the objectives according to difficulty, but also by manipulating the treatment tools used to teach each objective. The Gagné and Briggs system, the Gropper system, and most other approaches to instructional design developed to date are most easily applied in conjunction with transmission models of teaching that feature didactic instruction. In the following sections, we consider two recently developed approaches that are more easily applied in conjunction with constructivist models of teaching.

Case and Bereiter's cognitive development approach

Case and Bereiter (1984) credited Gagné for moving instructional design from behaviorism to cognitive behaviorism, but argued the need to develop further toward "cognitive development." Following Skinner (1954), they argued that the behavioral approach includes the following steps:

0. Identify potential reinforcers that are available and effective
1. Identify and objectively describe the desired behavior

Instructional Methodologies

Increasingly, professional groups like the National Council of Teachers of Mathematics are encouraging educators to involve students more directly in mathematics by allowing them to collect data, make inferences, and make comparisons (as, in this case, comparing shapes).

Current instruction in science recognizes the value of students *doing* science, not just learning about it.

Teachers can help develop students' conceptual knowledge by presenting them with real-world problems to solve. Here a student tests the structural strength of a paper frame he built as a lead-in to a unit on bridge-building.

Pair work can allow students to receive useful feedback in a warm, immediate, and supportive environment.

There is increasing awareness that experiences in theater, shop, and art help students to integrate curriculum areas while providing an important outlet for self-expression.

Cooperative learning allows students to appreciate that there are alternative ways of understanding subject matter and to develop skills for using other individuals as resources.

Brief presentations are often an essential part of student-driven learning.

The use of mixed-age grouping can help teachers to accommodate individual differences. For example, some fifth graders are well prepared to work with sixth graders on some topics. Mixed-age grouping provides teachers with flexibility.

Teachers can facilitate students' abilities to learn on their own by helping them to conceptualize key ideas that they will be examining and to understand the procedural details of assignments before they begin to work on them.

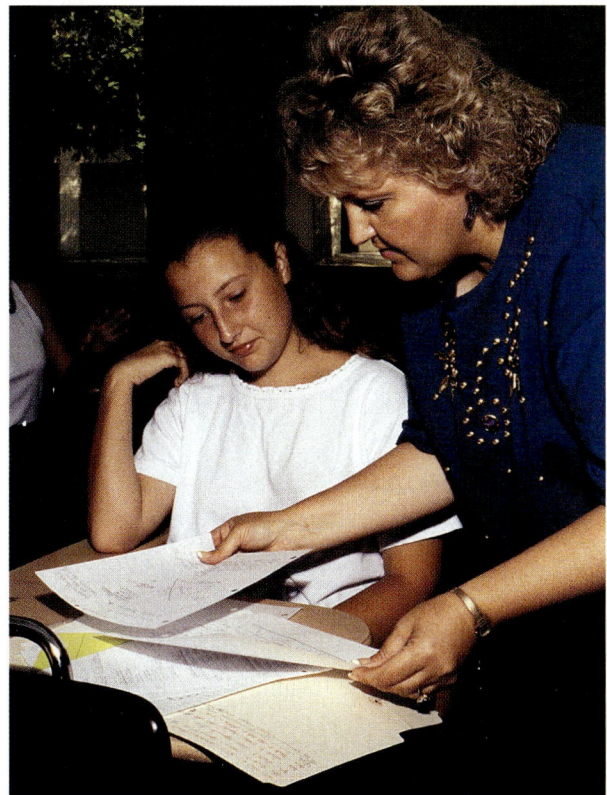

An important way to provide for diverse student learners is individual instruction. Although students can learn much in whole-class settings and in their work in small groups or pairs, it is important that they have some opportunity to pursue their own individual interests.

Well-coordinated team teaching can empower teachers to trade off responsibilities and use time and resources in creative ways that provide students with more individual attention and support.

Project presentations allow students not only to become active learners, but also to develop a sense of authenticity because they are able to see something through to completion.

Students vary in many ways, including size, cognitive development, and level of motivation; often they vary in terms of primary language and cultural background. Teachers can affirm student diversity in all areas of student life.

Technology can provide important resources to facilitate students' learning. For example, using technology, students can access massive databases, become directly involved in simulation experiments, and observe processes through video media.

2. Describe the initial or "entering" behavior of the learner
3. Define a series of behaviors leading from the entering behavior to the desired behavior, such that each successive behavior represents a small modification of the previous one
4. Move students through the sequence using demonstrations and instructions coupled with reinforcement
5. Ensure, through reinforced practice, that each behavior is learned thoroughly before advancing to the next step

Case and Bereiter credited Gagné with correcting three important weaknesses in Skinner's approach. First, Skinner emphasized reinforcement and the issue of *how* to change behavior, but Gagné showed that the more typical problem is identifying *what* needs to be taught. Gagné shifted attention from reinforcement to the nature of the behaviors themselves. Second, behavioral theory dealt exclusively with observable behaviors and thus was difficult to apply to school learning. Gagné recognized different types of learning and emphasized the intellectual skills taught in school. Third, Gagné's learning hierarchies and task analyses provided guidance about how to identify successive approximations of the terminal behavior that are small enough for learners to negotiate successfully.

Case and Bereiter suggested that the following steps characterize Gagné's approach:

1. Identify the intellectual skill to be taught and develop a measure to assess its presence
2. Using hierarchical task analysis, identify successively lower level skills until reaching a level that all students are expected to possess on entry
3. Develop assessment devices for each skill and use them to determine entering competence
4. Present instruction that progresses from existing skills to successively higher levels

5. Before beginning to teach any new skill, make sure that the student has mastered all the lower-level skills that it depends on

Case and Bereiter argued that the Gagné approach works well for many but not all instructional situations, and that its failures are typically due to one of two common problems. First, with highly difficult tasks, it sometimes yields instruction that is too difficult because it forces students to consider too many components in progressing through a hierarchy that exceeds the limits of their working memories. Second, the hierarchies yielded by purely logical analyses of tasks do not always correspond to the order in which task components are mastered developmentally, and this natural order may be more appropriate for instruction. Furthermore, students will have preconceptions about the task that should be taken into account. Accurate preconceptions will provide a good starting place for instruction. If some preconceptions happen to be incorrect, it will be necessary to show their inadequacies to students to enable them to fully appreciate the instruction and make needed accommodations in their thinking. Combining these considerations, Case and Bereiter (1984) suggested that a "cognitive development" approach includes the following steps:

1. Identify the task to be taught and develop a measure for assessing mastery of it
2. Develop a procedure for assessing the strategies that students employ in responding to the task
3. Use this procedure to assess the strategies that students use at a variety of ages, including ages where success is not achieved by current methods
4. Devise an instructional sequence for "recapitulating development" (i.e., for moving through the same sequence of steps that students would eventually move through

on their own), keeping the working memory load at each step within reasonable limits

5. Once performance at one level becomes relatively automatic, move on to the next

The ideas of Case and Bereiter are highly compatible with the ideas for teaching school subjects for understanding that are presented in Chapter 11. The major reason is that their approach emphasizes starting with students' current thinking and following its naturally occurring course of development in sequencing the instruction, rather than imposing a scheme based on adult logic.

Collins and Stevens: designing inquiry teaching

Collins and Stevens (1983) developed an approach to instructional design that uses inquiry strategies to stimulate discovery learning. Based on observations of expert teachers, they described ten instructional strategies: (1) selecting positive and negative examples; (2) varying cases systematically; (3) selecting counterexamples; (4) generating hypothetical cases; (5) forming hypotheses; (6) testing hypotheses; (7) considering alternative predictions; (8) entrapping students; (9) tracing consequences to a contradiction; and (10) questioning authority. Collins (1987) stated that this approach is intended to develop higher thought processes (cognitive strategies) more than content-specific knowledge. It is designed to work by requiring learners to formulate hypotheses (discover generalities) based on observation of varied cases (examples), and thus to force deep processing of the new knowledge.

The first three strategies are similar to those used in didactic approaches, except that they call for selecting and sequencing examples so as to create dissonance or curiosity to set the stage for inquiry, rather than using examples to illustrate didactic explanations. The strategy of generating hypothetical cases is used to challenge students' reasoning or force them to take into account factors that they are presently ignoring.

In this inquiry approach, students are challenged to form and evaluate hypotheses rather than given rules or principles, and are prodded to consider alternative predictions whenever they jump to conclusions without adequate consideration of alternatives. The strategy of entrapping students is used to expose erroneous preconceptions by showing how the students' own thinking leads to incorrect predictions or conclusions. Tracing consequences to a contradiction is a similar strategy. Finally, the strategy of questioning authority involves training students to think for themselves rather than rely on the teacher or the book for correct answers.

In addition to discussing these instructional strategies, Collins and Stevens (1983) presented rules for structuring and sequencing dialogue with students designed to achieve particular objectives. Their work illustrates that thoughtful instructional design is just as important for discovery and inquiry-oriented approaches as it is for other approaches to teaching.

power and limits of systematic instructional design

Instructional design principles can be quite helpful in planning effective instruction. They underscore the need to clarify objectives and to keep these in mind when designing and evaluating instruction, and they remind us that certain sequences, methods, examples, or activities may be more helpful than others for accomplishing those objectives. On the other hand, most instructional design approaches have yet to be tested or supported with much scientific research (Mayer, 1985).

Opinions vary on the value of the systems approach, which is rooted in behavioral psychology (Gagné & Glaser, 1987). As the cognitive revolution has progressed, critics have called for modifying the systems approach to make it more compatible with constructivist ideas about learning (Bonner, 1988; Kember, 1991; Merrill, Li, & Jones, 1990; Reigeluth, 1989; Tennyson & Rasch, 1988). Winn (1990), for example, argued that task analysis and other key components of the systems approach: (1) place too much emphasis on reducing tasks, content, and cognitive processes to their atomic components; (2) assume that what works with the students who were included in the development process will work with all students; and (3) assume that we can work out instructional procedures having orderly and predictable effects when in fact we know that humans often engage in forms of reasoning that do not follow the logical models built into design systems. Winn called for new approaches that would: (1) emphasize not just analysis (breaking tasks into their component parts and sequencing them) but also synthesis (helping students to put back together what they are learning in meaningful ways); (2) use not just instructional materials but also human teachers, especially for monitoring students' progress and adapting to the various paths that their thinking might take once instruction is underway; and (3) allow for accommodation to emerging contingencies rather than trying to do everything by the numbers.

Goldman (1991) questioned whether it is wise to plan instruction so as to minimize the cognitive load on learners and make things as easy as possible for them. Research indicates that a larger investment of initial effort in a task can sometimes have benefits in the longer term by making subsequent tasks easier. This suggests that limited-capacity theories calling for doing a lot of the work of learning for students

are less desirable as bases for instructional design than constructivist theorists calling for students to construct their own task representations and response strategies. Many behaviorally oriented instructional designers are unconvinced by such arguments, however. They argue that their models take transfer into account (Gropper, 1987), and they point to impressive results on transfer measures of learning (Sweller & Chandler, 1991). Such differences of opinion are likely to continue as part of the ongoing debate between behaviorists and constructivists.

Instructional design models provide valuable overall guidance, but they are still of limited value for suggesting ideas about how particular objectives can be taught most effectively. Task analysis and related procedures are helpful, but designers still have to rely primarily on their own knowledge of content and pedagogy, and especially on their knowledge of what the target students know about the topic and how this knowledge can be expanded. To illustrate some of the complexities involved, we will review research on the learning and teaching of concepts.

concept learning

Educational psychologists have accumulated a great deal of information about concept learning to inform the design of methods for teaching concepts. Concepts are units of thought that organize experience and provide a basis for generalizing and engaging in higher-order thinking (Keil, 1989). Following Tennyson and Park (1980), we define a **concept** as *a set of objects, symbols, or events that share common characteristics (defining attributes) and thus can be referenced by a particular name or symbol.* **Concept learning** involves *acquiring the ability to recognize valid examples of a concept (which possess its defining attributes) and to discriminate these valid examples from nonexamples.*

Early work on concept learning presented learners with a series of stimuli and asked them to state whether or not each one was an example of the concept. For example, Bruner, Goodnow, and Austin (1956) used eighty-one cards that presented stimulus combinations varying along four dimensions: shape (squares, circles, or crosses); color (red, green, or black); number of objects shown (one, two, or three); and number of borders around these objects (one, two, or three). In a typical experiment, learners were shown a chart illustrating all of the cards and asked to select one that they thought might illustrate the concept to be learned (such as that any card showing at least one red object was an instance of the concept, and all other cards were not). The learner was given feedback and then asked to select another example. This continued until the learner verbalized the concept correctly.

Such experiments revealed several factors that influence concept learning. One is *cue salience*: certain cues are noticed more easily than others. For example, Trabasso and Bower (1968) used flower designs that varied in color of flower, number and shape of leaves, and angles of branches. They found that students learned concepts based on color more quickly than concepts based on angles of branches.

Several **task variables**—*aspects of tasks that affect the degree to which the task is complex or difficult to learn*—influence learning (Bourne, Ekstrand, & Dominowski, 1971; Mayer, 1982). One is *the nature of the rule* defining the concept. Rules involving only one attribute (choose the red object) are easier than rules involving more than one (such as color and shape). Furthermore, among rules involving more than one attribute, conjunctive rules (choose red squares) are easier to learn than disjunctive rules (choose any card that contains either a red object or a square or both). Also, when rules involve more than one attribute, increasing *the number of relevant dimensions* leads to quicker solution, but increasing *the number of irrelevant dimensions* makes learning

more difficult. Finally subjects usually learn faster from *positive instances* than from negative instances.

Such findings were interesting but not very useful for developing guidelines for instruction. For one thing, the "instruction" was restricted to presentation of examples, so that learners had to learn by discovery. Concept learning is more efficient when accomplished through instruction that includes direct statements of rules and definitions in addition to presentation of examples (Clark, 1971; Francis, 1975; Klausmeier, Ghatala, & Frayer, 1974; Woodson, 1974).

A second limitation of the early work on concept learning was that many of the concepts studied were artificial, and stimuli were limited to examples that clearly were or were not instances of these concepts. For example, squares, circles, and crosses are obviously different from one another, as are red, green, and black colors. Under more normal learning conditions, however, stimuli often differ less starkly and concepts can be difficult to discriminate clearly.

For example, Rosch (1978) showed that natural categories learned through experience (bird, furniture, student) are *fuzzy*—their boundaries are not firm. Unlike conjunctive concepts defined by specific critical attributes that are all present in each example, natural categories merely share a family resemblance based on a core of common features (Rosch & Mervis, 1975). Any example of the category contains some of these features, but usually not all. For example, "singing," "flying," and "smallness" are all attributes that help define birds. *Prototype examples* (e.g., robins) possess all of these attributes, but many birds do not have all of them, and some, like the ostrich, have none. People can rate the degree to which examples show goodness of fit to natural categories ("pillow" is a poor example of "furniture," "lamp" is better, and "chair" is prototypical). They also can answer questions about typical examples ("Is a chair furniture?") more quickly than questions about atypical examples ("Is a pillow furniture?").

research at work
teaching concepts

Owen, Blount, & Moscow (1978) suggested the following model for teaching concepts:

1. Present a definition that includes the concept's label and defining attributes.
2. Present positive examples, emphasizing the defining attributes.
3. Present negative examples that help distinguish defining attributes from irrelevant attributes.
4. Present both positive and negative examples and ask the learner to identify the positive examples and to tell why the negative examples are not examples of the concept.
5. Provide feedback, giving specific reasons for errors.

Children first learn to classify and label objects using *basic level categories* (chair, table) rather than *superordinate level categories* (furniture) or *subordinate level categories* (easy chair, kitchen table), and adults are better able to use the basic level categories for thinking (Rosch et al., 1976; Rosch & Lloyd, 1978). Such data suggest that concept teaching might proceed most efficiently by starting with basic level categories rather than with seemingly simpler or more specific concepts. The basic level is the most abstract level at which instances of a concept still have roughly the same shapes or parts. Thus "chair" is basic because all chairs share certain structural features, whereas "furniture" is not basic because it subsumes subtypes that look entirely different.

Ideas based on Rosch's work have developed into *prototype theory*, which predicts that learning is easier and retrieval from memory is quicker for prototypical examples of concepts (and their related attributes) than for other concepts (Nosofsky, 1988; Ranzijn, 1991). Prototype theory provides useful guidance for the teaching of object concepts, although it is not easily applied to abstract concepts (e.g., justice). Also, exclusive focus on prototype examples may induce learners to believe that certain non-

defining attributes are defining attributes (e.g., "lives in trees" for birds) (Eysenck, 1984). Another complication is that prototypical examples of concepts vary with culture and individual experience. Robins and eagles are prototypical examples of birds for Americans, but swans and peacocks are prototypical for Chinese. Finally, novice-expert comparisons have shown that experts in a domain often organize their knowledge quite differently than novices do. Where this is the case, applications of prototype theory would need to focus on teaching about the basic level categories used by experts rather than those used by novices (Klausmeier, 1990).

Novice-expert comparisons are part of an emerging body of research on concept development which emphasizes that concepts typically are not learned in isolation but instead are assimilated into networks of organized knowledge structured around theories about the world (Keil, 1989; Medin, 1989). Thus, the relation between a concept and an example is analogous to the relation between theory and data. We recognize examples as related to one another not just because they share surface attributes, but because we possess theoretical knowledge that explains why certain shared attributes are significant and others are not (we view zebras as similar to horses but not to barber poles, even though barber poles have stripes and horses do not). The instructional implications of this recent research are not yet clear, although it appears to underscore the value of teaching networks of connected knowledge structured around key ideas rather than parades of concepts addressed in isolation from one another.

teaching concepts

Instructional designers typically call for sequencing material from the simple to the complex. Research on concept learning suggests first stating the concept's definition and its defining attributes, next presenting positive examples, and then presenting negative examples. These are useful general principles, but there are exceptions. Case and Bereiter (1984) noted the value of starting with learners' current concepts, and Rosch's work suggests beginning with basic level concepts and then working both upwards and downwards from there, rather than starting with subordinate level concepts and then working upwards. Other investigators also have suggested qualifications and elaborations of general instructional design principles.

Clark (1971) suggested that instruction should begin with positive-introductory examples, next move to positive-confirmatory examples, and then move to negative examples. *Positive-introductory examples* illustrate the defining attributes with minimal confusion or distraction by irrelevant attributes. Defining attributes for the concept of "square," for example, would include: four sides, all sides are of equal length, and all corners are right angles. Irrelevant attributes would include: how a square is oriented in space and its size. Squares

shown as positive-introductory examples would all be the same size and constructed from horizontal and vertical lines.

Positive-confirmatory examples also contain all of the defining attributes, but in addition display irrelevant attributes (e.g., squares of varying sizes and spatial rotations). These examples show learners that squares can come in any size or spatial rotation, as long as they are constructed of four equal sides joined at right angles.

Finally, *negative examples* lack one or more of the defining attributes. These range from stimuli that are not even on the same dimensions as the concept (a picture of an elephant) through those that share certain similarities but none of the defining attributes (geometric figures with more than four sides) to those that share defining attributes but are still negative examples (rectangles that are not squares). Ordinarily, negative examples are confined to those sharing the same conceptual class with positive examples (in this case, geometric figures). Within this restriction, however, an increasing variety of both positive and negative examples is displayed as instruction progresses. This makes learners aware of both the degree to which the concept generalizes (illustrated by the range of positive examples) and the limits beyond which it cannot be stretched (illustrated by negative examples, especially the near misses).

Merrill and Tennyson: rational sets of examples

Merrill and Tennyson (1977; see also Tennyson & Cocciarella, 1986) suggested similar guidelines. Their model includes definition of the concept expressed in terms of its defining attributes, expository presentation using rational sets of examples, and practice in which students differentiate examples from nonexamples and justify their choice with reference to the defining attributes.

Rational sets of examples are assembled to call attention to defining attributes and minimize errors due to overgeneralization, undergeneralization, or misconception. They include examples that are diverse in form, ordered from easy to difficult, and selected to illustrate particular points. For example, undergeneralization errors (identifying examples as nonexamples) can be minimized by making sure that the set of examples includes the full range of variation in the defining attributes (squares come in many sizes and spatial rotations). Overgeneralization errors (identifying nonexamples as examples) can be minimized by making sure that the nonexample set includes near misses (rectangles that are almost square).

To focus learners on the defining attributes, it is often helpful to use *matched pairs* of examples and nonexamples that differ on a defining attribute but not on irrelevant attributes (e.g., a square and a rectangle of the same height, shown side by side). Irrelevant attributes must be varied from one set of examples to the next, however, to avoid inducing misconceptions. If all examples shown are constructed of horizontal and vertical lines, learners might develop the misconception that this spatial orientation is essential to the definition of a square. Petty and Jansson (1987) found that rationally sequenced sets of examples (including matched pairs) were more effective than randomly ordered presentations of the same examples for teaching the concept of parallelogram to sixth graders. For more information about rational sets of examples, see Klausmeier (1990).

Engelmann and Carnine: faultless communication

Engelmann and Carnine (1982) provided suggestions about the selection and juxtaposition of examples when teaching different kinds of concepts. They argued that instruction should be designed to accomplish *faultless communication*—to communicate exactly what is intended, and nothing else. A faultless communication admits of only one interpretation. If tryout produces unexpected responses, the instruction is faulted and needs revision (different selection or sequencing of examples or better accompanying explanation).

Communications are judged faultless if they: (1) present a set of examples that are "the same" with respect to only one distinguishing quality (the one that is the basis for generalization); (2) provide two signals—one to identify every example that possesses the quality ("square") and a second to identify every example that does not ("not square"); (3) demonstrate a range of variation among positive examples that will encourage learners to induce a rule for classifying new examples on the basis of "sameness" (the defining attributes); (4) show the limits of permissible variation by presenting negative examples; and (5) provide a test of generalization (to new examples). Sameness is demonstrated through positive examples, selected and juxtaposed to show the range of examples to which the concept applies.

There are two basic *juxtaposition rules*. To show sameness, juxtapose examples that are greatly different and treat each example in the same way, To show difference, juxtapose examples that are only minimally different and treat them differently. In teaching "truck," for example, one would include pictures of a variety of trucks (panel trucks, tankers, moving vans) to make sure that the examples do not inadvertently *stipulate* that the term "truck" applies only to a particular type of truck. To clarify the limits of the concept, negative examples would concentrate on objects that are just minimally different from trucks (cars, trains, pushcarts), rather than objects that are drastically different (apples, roses).

Including the full range of variation among the positive examples allows the learner to *interpolate*—to recognize that the concept applies to all examples that fall in between these extremes. Concentrating the negative examples on objects that are just minimally different allows the learner to *extrapolate*—to recognize that the target concept does not apply to objects that are even more different than the negative examples shown.

Different concepts call for different sequencing of examples. Object concepts (nouns) are usually taught best by beginning with positive examples, but noncomparative single-dimension concepts (between, over, curved, running, pointed) are usually taught most efficiently by beginning with negative examples.

object concepts (nouns) As an example of teaching object concepts (nouns), Engelmann and Carnine (1982) recommended the following sequence in teaching the noun "vehicle" (using pictures to illustrate the examples):

example	teacher wording
1. Rowboat	This is a vehicle.
2. Train	This is a vehicle.
3. Car	This is a vehicle.
4. Truck	This is a vehicle.
5. Swing set	This is not a vehicle.
6. Power lawn mower	This is not a vehicle.
7. Tractor	Is this a vehicle?
8. Rowboat with motor	Is this a vehicle?
9. Electric drill	Is this a vehicle?
10. Treadmill	Is this a vehicle?
11. Car	Is this a vehicle?

The first four examples establish that a vehicle is something that one gets into for transportation purposes. The diversity of positive examples includes water as well as land transportation and muscle-powered as well as motor-powered transportation. The two negative examples are selected to rule out likely

misinterpretations. The swing set rules out the notion that sitting and moving is sufficient for something to be called a vehicle, and the lawn mower rules out the idea that moving and being motor powered makes something a vehicle. Presumably, learners will extrapolate from these minimally different negative examples to conclude that other things that are even more different (such as the electric drill and the treadmill in the test segment) are not vehicles, either. Note that the test segment contains positive examples not encountered previously (tractor, rowboat with motor) that fall within the range illustrated in the first four positive examples. By interpolating the information given in those first examples, learners should realize that the test segment examples are also vehicles.

If the presentation had been confined to positive examples, learners might have overgeneralized the concept of vehicles to include anything that moves or accommodates a person in a sitting position. The negative examples illustrate that these features by themselves are not sufficient to define a vehicle. They are especially well chosen because they each have two features that might be confused in identifying vehicles (the power motor has both a motor and movement; the swing has both movement and the capacity to accommodate a person in a sitting position). The same information could have been conveyed using other examples, but less efficiently (more examples would have been needed).

comparative concepts In contrast to the positive-examples-first sequence in teaching nouns, Engelmann and Carnine suggested that instruction in comparative single-dimension concepts begin with negative examples. The sequence below would be used for teaching the concept "getting heavier." The student's hand would be placed palm up on a table or flat surface, and the teacher would exert downward pressure.

example	teacher wording
Starting point:	
Pressure 3	Feel this.
1. Pressure 2	It didn't get heavier.
2. Pressure 2	It didn't get heavier.
3. Pressure 3	It got heavier.
4. Pressure 7	It got heavier.
5. Pressure 9	Did it get heavier?
6. Pressure 9	Did it get heavier?
7. Pressure 5	Did it get heavier?
8. Pressure 6	Did it get heavier?
9. Pressure 3	Did it get heavier?
10 Pressure 4	Did it get heavier?
11. Pressure 2	Did it get heavier?
12. Pressure 5	Did it get heavier?
13. Pressure 1	Did it get heavier?

Since "getting heavier" is a comparative concept, the sequence begins with a starting point that establishes the dimension ("feel this"). Then come two negative examples that are minimally different from the concept to be taught. One involves a slight decrease in pressure, and the other involves no change at all. The learner is now set up to attend to the "pressure on the palm" dimension and to anticipate a change that does involve "getting heavier." Then come two positive examples, a small change and a larger one. The examples illustrate that any increase in pressure, and not an identical increase each time or a progressively greater increase each time, is "getting heavier." This sequence should have established the concept: Examples 5 through 13 are test items to ensure that it did. The sequence as a whole and certain examples in particular are designed to focus the learner on change (getting heavier), rather than on a particular state (lightness or heaviness). At Example 6, for example, the teacher exerts heavy pressure, yet this is not "getting heavier" because it represents no change from Example 5.

transformation sequences

The previous examples involving juxtaposition of positive and negative instances are used when teaching simple concepts. *Transformation sequences* are more complicated because they require learners to produce different responses to different examples. There are no negative examples. Much of what is learned in school involves transformation sequences.

Consider teaching students to recognize the subject of a sentence. Engelmann and Carnine suggested beginning with typical examples that differ in only minor ways ("a runner went to the park"; "five runners went to the park"; "that runner sat in the park"). Then, introduce examples that illustrate the range of the concept while minimizing potential confusion due to variation on other factors ("Henry's dog ran in the park"; "those pigeons flew over the park"; "he wanted to go to the park"). Finally, introduce examples that include variation in both the target concept and other elements ("a dog and five men sat on the hill"; "the yellow pencil and the white pencil are on the desk"; "phone books are very useful").

Although recognizing the advantages of presenting examples in an easy-to-hard sequence, Engelmann and Carnine argued the need for examples chosen to prevent undesirable stipulations by learners. For example, if given only sentences in which the subject is a noun modified by an adjective (fast runners, a runner, five runners, etc.) students might infer that all sentence subjects took this form, and might be confused by other forms (pronouns, unmodified nouns, compound subjects, etc.).

Engelmann and Carnine (1982) also presented strategies (including example selection and juxtaposition) for teaching more complex concepts, cognitive operations, and behavioral skills. Their book is especially useful for those interested in designing instruction for the elementary grades, because their examples concentrate on basic skills instruction. However, their principles are general ones that should apply to the teaching of any concept at any level (e.g., catalyst, republic, self-fulfilling prophecy).

application of instructional design principles

Instruction is likely to be most effective when designed systematically, although so far there has been more theory development than research on this topic. Also, there are exceptions to even seemingly obvious principles (sometimes it is more efficient to start with the most typical or familiar concepts in a hierarchy rather than with the simplest ones; to avoid undesirable stipulations, one must introduce a broad range of positive examples early in a sequence, rather than proceeding from easy to hard examples or from regular to atypical examples).

Recent research has identified additional elaborations of and qualifications on principles for teaching concepts. One study found better concept learning when students were given both definitions and examples of concepts rather than definitions alone, although it made no difference whether they got the definition or the examples first (Crisman & Mackey, 1990). Another study found better learning when pairs of examples were presented simultaneously rather than successively (Ranzijn, 1991). A third study found that strategies based on showing examples and nonexamples were more effective when students did not have much background knowledge, but strategies based on stating definitions and analogies were more effective with more knowledgeable students (Stiff, 1989).

The principles described in this chapter will be helpful, but ultimately there is no substitute for systematic tryouts followed by revision based on evaluation data. In assessing curricula being considered for potential adoption, teachers should consider the degree to which the developers have conducted such evaluation and revision before publishing. Are claims based on substantial field testing with impressive results, or merely on unsupported assertions and testimonials? Is the content sequenced in appropriate ways? Are the clarity of exposition and the selection and juxtaposition of examples effective in creating faultless communication? If they can, teachers should replace instructional materials that fail to meet these and other criteria implied in this chapter. If they must use such materials, they will need to compensate for their weaknesses by providing students with supplementary instruction, study guides, or other assistance.

summary

Instructional design is the art (and applied science) of creating efficient methods for attaining educational objectives. Gagné and Briggs recommended a systems approach containing system-level stages, course-level stages, and lesson-level stages. The initial system-level stages involve analyzing needs, goals, and priorities and then considering resources, constraints, and potential delivery systems to develop a curriculum scope and sequence statement that specifies objectives, sequences them in a sensible order, and identifies the delivery system to be used for instruction.

Course-level stages involve dividing and sequencing the content into courses organized around target objectives and their respective enabling objectives. To accomplish this, one performs information processing analyses (perhaps using flow charts to depict the results visually), task classifications (with attention to the conditions of learning associated with each task), and learning task analyses (including identification of relevant learning hierarchies for instruction in intellectual skills).

Lesson-level stages involve identifying the objectives for each lesson and planning the instructional events (including media, materials, and evaluation) to be used. It is here that instructional designers bring to bear their creativity and knowledge of subject matter and students to decide what information to present and what examples or demonstrations, media and materials, and practice and application activities to use. Final system-level stages involve evaluating, field testing, and diffusing information about the developed learning system.

Gropper presented ideas on how to structure practice activities in an easy-to-difficult sequence by manipulating the treatment tools of degree of cuing provided, size of unit of behavior practiced, mode of stimulus and response required, variety, content, and frequency of practice. Case and Bereiter argued the need to take into account limitations on learners' working memories and to teach steps in the order in which they tend to be learned naturally rather than the subordinate-to-superordinate order suggested by logical analysis. Collins and Stevens presented ideas for designing inquiry learning. They emphasized selecting and sequencing examples so as to create dissonance or curiosity, to stimulate students to make predictions and consider alternative possibilities, and eventually to arrive at the target objective through guided discovery.

The systems approach to instructional design is useful but limited by the fact that the best ways to teach something are rarely obvious and must be established through experimentation. Some of these complexities are illustrated in research on concept learning. Early work viewed concept learning as a matter of logical deduction from clear-cut positive and negative instances. However,

Rosch showed that the natural categories involved in most concept learning are fuzzy sets based on family resemblances. Frequently, such learning begins with basic-level categories (chair) before it proceeds to either superordinate-level categories (furniture) or subordinate-level categories (easy chair). Recent research on concept development has emphasized that we learn concepts in connection with theories about the world that explain why certain of their attributes are significant and others are not.

Most advice on concept teaching stresses beginning with clear definitions that state defining attributes, next displaying positive examples, and then moving to negative examples and discrimination exercises. Merrill and Tennyson, for example, discussed presenting rational sets of examples selected to call attention to the defining attributes and minimize errors due to overgeneralization, undergeneralization, or misconception. They recommended sequencing examples from easy to difficult and making sure that the positive examples include the full range of variation in the defining attributes and that the negative examples include near misses.

Engelmann and Carnine argued the importance of designing instruction to achieve faultless communication and noted that this is not always achieved by beginning with positive examples or by proceeding in an easy-to-difficult sequence. Unlike object concepts, comparative concepts are usually taught more efficiently by beginning with negative examples. Also, instructional designers need to select and juxtapose examples in ways that will not only communicate the range of variation and limits of application of the concept, but also prevent inappropriate stipulations—beliefs that the concept applies only to a particular subset of its actual range.

questions for reflection

1. Compare scope and sequence statements for curricula designed to teach the same subject at the same grade level. Each curriculum will include objectives not included in the other, and the objectives shared in common will not always be taught in the same order. Are these differences merely matters of taste, or is one curriculum better than the other in its selection or sequencing of objectives?

2. Study instructional materials developed for the grade level and subject matter you intend to teach. Would you use them as is, or would you omit certain objectives and associated activities or supplement by bringing in or developing additional ones? If possible, compare notes with experienced teachers who have used these materials.

3. Would you prefer to select objectives and develop materials and activities yourself or have this done for you by policy makers and commercial publishers? If the former, how will you respond to administrative and parental pressures to emphasize certain objectives, and how will you evaluate and improve the materials and activities you develop? If the latter, what will you do if you find that the adopted curriculum package is not well suited to your students, or if some students need remedial work that the package does not provide?

4. Select an objective commonly taught in the grade level and subject matter you intend to teach. Perform an information-processing analysis to identify the sequence of steps leading to the target performance and construct a flow chart to depict this visually. What does this tell you about where instruction should begin, what steps should be included, and in what order?

5. The list of instructional events shown in Table 9.1 was composed with didactic instruction in mind. How might this list be changed for lessons designed to achieve higher-level cognitive objectives? For lessons that relied on inquiry procedures or discovery learning?

6. Given that special materials or media may add important dimensions to teaching but also may not be practical, what special materials and media do you foresee using in your own teaching? What advantages do these bring that make them worth the trouble?

7. For a given objective that you are likely to teach, describe how an easy-to-difficult sequence can be designed into a series of practice tasks by manipulating the treatment tools described by Gropper.

8. Gagné advocates using learning hierarchies and other tools for sequencing tasks on a logical basis, whereas Case and Bereiter advocate sequencing tasks according to the order in which their components are typically developed through ordinary experience. What students and tasks do Gagné's ideas fit best, and what students and tasks do Case and Bereiter's ideas fit best? Why?

9. Select two concepts from subject matter you are likely to teach and design instruction for each that includes a clear definition that specifies the defining attributes of the concept and a rational set of examples that illustrates both the range and limits of its application. Make sure that you do not inadvertently confine your positive examples to a subset that would cause learners to stipulate inappropriately. Also, be sure that your positive exam-

ples are not all confounded with an irrelevant attribute that learners could mistake for a defining attribute.

10. Engelmann and Carnine found that object concepts are generally taught most easily by learning with positive examples, but comparative concepts are generally taught most easily by beginning with negative examples. Why should this be? Can you formulate a more general rule about when to begin with positive examples and when to begin with negative examples? Compare your notes with your friends.

---

cases to consider

tinkering Jim Anderson is not pleased with the new science curriculum adopted by his district. The general objectives make sense—he likes what is taught and the order in which lessons are sequenced. However, many of the lessons just don't work very well. Sometimes the materials are inadequate or overly cumbersome, and some of the suggested activities and exercises seem pointless. Therefore, Jim decides to stick with the objectives but to find or develop better ways to accomplish them in the case of about half of the lessons. What potential advantages and disadvantages must be considered when teachers make wholesale changes like this? What steps could Jim take to ensure that the new materials and activities succeed in meeting the objectives and really are improvements over the old ones?

better sequencing and examples? Ed Sikes is generally pleased with his course in educational psychology, but he is aware of certain repeated failures. It always seems that many students confuse Piaget's terms assimilation and accommodation, confuse negative reinforcement with punishment, confuse cognitive level with difficulty level, and have trouble describing the differences in mental functioning between a bright six-year-old and a dull fourteen-year-old. What may be causing these problems, and what might Dr. Sikes do to eliminate them? In particular, what changes might he make in the sequencing of his instruction and in the number and kinds of examples he uses to illustrate concepts?

principles for selecting and adapting basic instructional methods

objectives

When you have mastered the material in this chapter you will be able to

1. Explain and give examples of the concept of functionally equivalent paths to the same achievement outcomes
2. Describe how effective active teaching may differ between low-SES and high-SES settings
3. Explain Good and Power's guidelines for adapting instruction to the needs of successful, social, dependent, alienated, and phantom students
4. Define process-outcome research and describe the teacher characteristics that such research showed to be associated with achievement gain
5. Describe the uses and limits of teacher-led, group-based instruction
6. Identify the strengths and weaknesses of the lecture method and the situations in which the method is appropriate
7. Describe the steps to be taken and the decisions to be made in planning effective lectures
8. Identify factors that enhance and detract from the clarity and organization of presentations
9. Describe the purposes and uses of different types of activity that involve questioning and responding to students (drills, reviews, recitations, discussions)
10. List criteria for judging the quality of teachers' questions
11. Explain how pacing and wait time should vary with the objectives of recitation activities
12. State guidelines for reacting to students' responses
13. Describe the differences between the teacher's role in recitation activities and the teacher's role in discussions
14. Describe alternatives to questioning that teachers can use for producing lengthy and insightful student responses during discussions
15. State criteria for judging the effectiveness of assignments
16. State guidelines for structuring and scaffolding students' work on assignments

instructional planning decisions

Teachers have to process a great deal of information to make intelligent decisions about how to instruct their students. Unlike curriculum designers, teachers cannot take time to devise and perfect instruction intended for individual learners. Instead, they must find ways to both manage and instruct classes of twenty to forty students, while working almost continuously in public and responding to the multidimensionality, simultaneity, immediacy, and unpredictability of classrooms as described in Chapter 1. Consequently, teachers are seldom able to sustain instruction that is ideal according to some theoretical model. Instead, they must accept compromises that enable them to accomplish the most progress possible with the most students possible under the prevailing circumstances. We now consider principles for presenting information, conducting recitations and discussions, and structuring activities and assignments.

Different learning objectives (mastering well-defined knowledge or skills versus applying them to complex problem solving or using them creatively) require different instructional methods. Furthermore, other kinds of objectives (promoting the personal development of individuals or the social development of the class as a group) require still other methods. Research can inform teachers about the relationships between teacher behaviors and student outcomes, but teachers must decide for themselves what outcomes they wish to promote and in what order of priority.

In this chapter, we review findings from research on relationships between teaching approaches and student achievement, and we consider principles involved in using three basic instructional methods: presenting information, conducting recitations and discussions, and structuring activities and assignments. In Chapter 11, we will consider methods of assisting students' efforts to construct meaning from these experiences. We begin by considering some of the complexities involved in instructional planning and decision making. Even when using basic methods, teachers need to adapt the methods to their students, their instructional goals, and a host of situational factors.

There may be different but functionally equivalent paths to the same achievement outcomes. For example, it may make no significant difference whether the three main points of a presentation are summarized at the beginning or the end, so long as they are summarized, or whether a mathematics computation review is done with flash cards during a lesson or through a seat-work assignment afterward.

Rosenshine (1983) argued that certain teaching functions must be accomplished one way or another, but a variety of methods may be available for accomplishing them. One such function is checking for student understanding after presenting new information. This might be accomplished by having students answer oral questions on the material, write answers to written questions while the teacher circulates, write answers and then check them with a partner, or discuss the information in small groups and prepare a summary for presentation to the class.

Good and Power (1976) also discussed common teaching tasks that can be accomplished through different approaches. Five such tasks and some alternative methods of accomplishing them are shown in Table 10.1. These examples imply that different teachers can achieve comparable outcomes using different approaches. Ralph Kinderstone and Judith Blondell are two such teachers.

two successful classrooms

Ralph has taught fourth grade at Grandview School for the past three years. He graduated from the state university and completed the first year of law school, but while working part-time for a law firm, he realized he would not enjoy the day-to-day roles that lawyers perform. So, he went back to school and became a teacher, which he has found to be demanding but satisfying work.

Judith has taught fourth grade for three years at Golden West School. She had always wanted to be a teacher, so she majored in education and then moved directly into the profession. Although it is more demanding than she expected, she likes her job and plans to continue teaching indefinitely.

Ralph and Judith have at least three things in common: (1) they teach fourth grade; (2) they enjoy teaching; and (3) they are successful. The fifth-grade teachers at their schools are happy to get their students because they have good study habits and have mastered basic knowledge and skills. Their students do better on standardized achievement tests than students of similar aptitude and background, and both students and parents speak favorably of them. There are both similarities and differences in the ways that they achieve this success. Consider how they teach mathematics.

Ralph Kinderstone's class

Ralph basically teaches the class as a whole group (although a few faster students work on an enriched curriculum). His presentations and demonstrations are well done. After he gives a demonstration, he may request that students repeat it, but he seldom calls on more than two. He expects students to listen, and they do. He also listens carefully to them and demonstrates genuine respect for their responses.

After his presentations (development work on a concept or a review of skills), he asks several questions. He does not let students call out answers without permission, and he insists that they listen carefully to one another's responses. When students answer incorrectly (as they do about 30 percent of the time), he tends to ask another student or else explain why the answer was wrong, but this is done briefly. The activity is rapidly paced.

Before releasing students to do seat work,

table 10.1 multiple ways to accomplish common teaching tasks

TEACHING TASK	BEHAVIORAL RESOLUTION
1. Task differentiation	A. material assigned or made available in the classroom B. grouping students C. teacher questions that vary in cognitive demand
2. Maintaining task involvement	A. highly interesting tasks B. tasks that lead to student mastery C. insulation from interruption of fellow students
3. Review	A. distribution of printed teacher summary B. students prepare their own written summary C. teacher or student oral summary D. supervised board work
4. Accountability	A. oral questions B. call for show of hands during group work followed by random check of hand raisers C. group discussions followed by student written responses to discussion questions
5. Making time for teacher to work with individual students	A. peer tutoring B. learning centers C. independent work

SOURCE: T. Good and C. Power, "Designing Successful Classroom Environments for Different Types of Students," *Journal of Curriculum Studies*, 8 (1976), 45–60.

he has them work a couple of problems and he inspects the work of several of them to ensure that they understand the task that they will do independently or in small groups. If students do poorly, he repeats the demonstration and explains more fully.

Typically, about half of a forty-five-minute period is spent reviewing homework and introducing new concepts, procedures, and assignments. Then students work individually or in small teams (whichever they choose) on assigned problems. Students usually do not finish the work before the period ends, but if they apply themselves in class, they seldom have more than fifteen to twenty minutes of homework. Those who do finish may choose from a series of interesting mathematics tasks that vary widely in difficulty.

After assigning seat work, Ralph scans the room for a minute or so, then goes to those few students who seem confused or have difficulty in settling down. Once he engages these students in the task, he retires to his desk and, depending on the circumstances, either visits with individual students (reviewing their work, helping them to set goals) or works demandingly (but genuinely) with the students who are ahead of the class. However, he is available at all times for students who need help (early in the year he consistently encouraged students to seek him out when they had difficulty). When students come to him, they receive immediate, brief, and task-relevant feedback.

Things move quickly in this classroom. The students regularly learn new material and proceed through the text rapidly. Ralph drills them for a couple of minutes each day on important skills, and occasionally conducts a general review. He gives brief (fifteen-minute) tests once or twice a week. Test scores are graphed and students see their own graphs privately each month. Students whose work reaches a specified high plateau and students who show sufficient improvement over the year will receive a gift of a math game that everybody enjoys playing. Once every two weeks or so, a math period is devoted to games in which matched teams compete against one another. The tournaments are always unannounced but students suspect that they are contingent on good performance on tests and homework.

When minor misbehavior occurs, Ralph ignores it or corrects it with a nod of his head. If it is impossible to use such techniques, or if they go unheeded, he is quick to remind students of the rules and the effect of their conduct on classmates. He is more likely to warn students than to punish them, but if he does announce a punishment he invariably carries it through.

Judith Blondell's class

Judith's mathematics program is quite different from Ralph's. She teaches math twice a day (twenty to twenty-five minutes in the morning and twenty to twenty-five minutes in the afternoon) rather than in one forty-five-minute block. Also, her pace is slower: students work on the same types of problems for several consecutive days. However, math periods often end with a few minutes of drill time accomplished within the context of games. Judith supervises this activity closely and has her students keep written records of errors they make in these games.

Judith is very active in the classroom. Much of her time is spent explaining concepts or demonstrating skills and watching students perform them in front of the class. She works hard to get participation and accepts (listens, gives feedback, praises effort, and so on) virtually any relevant response that a student makes, whether or not the student has permission to speak. Her students respond with wrong answers less frequently (15 to 20 percent of the time) than Ralph's students do. When this occurs, she typically waits for the student to correct the response, provides a clue, or repeats the question. Judith's students spend only 15 to 20 percent of their time working independently (up from only 10 percent early in the year). In contrast, Ralph's students spend 50 percent of their time working independently.

Early in the year, Judith rarely used nonverbal techniques to control students. Now she uses eye contact and will ignore minor misbehavior. She still reacts quickly, consistently, and firmly to more serious misbehavior, but she is not loud or punitive.

teaching effectively in different contexts

Some of the differences between Ralph and Judith simply reflect differences in personal preference, but several occur because these teachers work with very different students. Ralph's school is located in the nicest part of a university town. The parents of his students tend to be professors, lawyers, physicians, business executives, and others of high socioeconomic status (SES). For fourth graders, his students have very well developed skills for reading, following directions, and working independently. In contrast, Judith's school is located in an inner-city neighborhood and serves students from low-SES families in which most parents are either unemployed or working in low-paying, unskilled occupations. Few of her students have well-developed independent-study skills.

Both teachers are effective classroom managers who maximize the time that their students spend engaged in appropriate academic activities, and both are active teachers who carry the

The range of individual differences found in most classrooms means that some students will be clear about the concept and ready to move on while others are still struggling with it.

content to their students rather than depend solely on curriculum materials to do so. However, they differ in several ways that illustrate findings (reviewed in Brophy & Good, 1986) concerning teacher behaviors associated with achievement gain in low SES versus high SES classrooms.

Teachers in high SES elementary schools have to be concerned with overcompetitiveness among their students, whereas teachers in low-SES schools have to be more concerned about fear of failure and general anxiety. Consequently, Ralph works to make sure that his students do not overcompete for public response opportunities (he does not allow them to call out answers, and he encourages them to listen to one another). He does use competitive games, but he does not announce these in advance and he rotates the teams regularly to minimize possible negative consequences of such competition.

In contrast, Judith encourages her students to participate actively in academic activities, because many of them tend to be reticent (at least in public response settings). She asks easier questions (her students answer about 83 percent of her questions correctly, whereas Ralph's students answer only about 70 percent correctly). Furthermore, if her students do not respond

or respond incorrectly, she will usually stay with them and try to elicit an improved response by giving them more time, rephrasing the question, or giving clues. Ralph does not need to do this as often, because his students usually are eager to respond and will speak up if they know the answer or have a likely guess.

Most of Ralph's students achieve well above grade level. They can read assignments, have mastered basic math concepts, and are motivated to perform, so they can spend sustained time in independent work or small-group activities, although they can come to him for help or feedback when they need it. In contrast, Judith's students need more extensive explanations of the content and more structuring and supervision of their work on assignments. Consequently, it makes more sense for her to divide mathematics instruction into two shorter segments and to circulate during seat work time rather than wait for students to come to her for help.

Rather than reacting with personal praise or criticism, both teachers give feedback that focuses on the content of the students' answers or the correctness of their work. Judith's students are more in need of encouragement, however, so she provides them with more praise.

Both teachers are effective because each

has molded an instructional system that meets the needs of the students. In other words, they are successful *because* they teach differently. If they were to exchange classrooms, they would not be nearly as successful unless they changed their teaching methods.

adapting instruction to students' individual characteristics

Ralph Kinderstone and Judith Blondell both work from teacher-led group instruction as a base, but they adapt this method to the student populations served by their respective schools. In addition to making such general adaptations to their students' general characteristics, teachers can introduce a degree of differential treatment to accommodate individual differences in aptitude, personality, work mode preferences, or work habits.

Good and Power (1976) surveyed the literature on the five student types described in Research at Work: Five Student Types and Their Needs and developed suggestions about how teachers might accommodate their contrasting preferences (see Table 10.2). Although based partly on research, these suggestions should be considered tentative hypotheses rather than proven guidelines, for two reasons. First, accommodating students' preferences may not be the same as meeting their needs. Allowing students to choose their own learning methods or teaching them in ways that they prefer may produce *less* achievement gain than teaching them in some other way (Clark, 1982; Schofield, 1981; Solomon & Kendall, 1979). Second, accommodating students' personal qualities will tend to reinforce those qualities, and sometimes these are qualities that ought to be changed. It would be easy, for example, to respond reciprocally to phantom

students and passive and withdrawn alienated students by never calling on them unless they raise their hands. This might even maximize the comfort of both the teacher and the students involved. However, it would not be in the students' best interests.

Even though these complexities must be kept in mind, Table 10.2 offers ideas about how teachers can introduce a degree of individualization into their instruction while basically teaching the class as a group. Some suggestions can be incorporated with relative ease (those that merely involve interacting more often or more affectively with certain students). Others are more difficult and time consuming to implement (preparing different activities or assignments for different subgroups). Even where it is not possible to introduce such variation into daily activities and assignments, these guidelines are useful for judging the degree of variety built into a week or a unit. There should be enough balance to deliver something for everyone, rather than restriction to activities and assignments that match the needs of one or two subgroups but not the others. Along with these accommodations to students' individual characteristics and preferences, there should be attempts to adapt instruction to the racial, ethnic, or other cultural backgrounds that are represented in the classroom.

relationships between teacher behavior and student achievement

Most teachers use teacher-led, whole-class instruction as their basic method, adapting it to the general needs of their students as a group and working within it to further adapt to the needs of individuals. Many aspects of this tradi-

table 10.2 suggestions for meeting the needs of five different types of students

	SUCCESS	SOCIAL	DEPENDENT	ALIENATED	PHANTOM
I. Type of input needed from teacher					
A. substantive explanation of content	very high	very high	high	high	high
B. procedural directions	low	low	high	moderate-high	low-moderate
C. socializing, emotional support, humor	very low	low-moderate	moderate	moderate (establish private rapport)	low
II. Type of task needed					
A. reading skills required	high	high	low	low	moderate
B. task difficulty level	very high	high	low-moderate	low-moderate	moderate
C. abstractness level	high	moderate	low initially	low initially	moderate
D. cognitive level	high	moderate	low-moderate	low-moderate	moderate
E. degree of structure (specify about what to do and how to do it)	low	moderate	high	high	moderate
F. opportunity to make active, overt responses	not important	high	high	high	moderate
G. opportunity to make choices	moderate (stress on enrichment	moderate (stress on choices to work with others)	low	moderate (stress on relevance)	low
H. interest value of task to student	not important	moderate	low	high	low
III. Type of response demanded					
I. length of task	long	short	moderate	moderate	long
A. written	high	low	high	moderate	high
B. oral	low	high	low	low	low
C. physical	low	moderate	moderate	high	low
IV. Individual vs. group settings					
A. individual	high	low	high	high	high
B. group	low	moderate	low	low-moderate	low
V. Emphasis on competition	high	moderate	low-initially	low	moderate
VI. Type of feedback from teacher					
A. personal praise	low	low	moderate	moderate (private)	low
B. personal criticism	low	low	low	very low	low
C. praise of good work	low	moderate	moderate	moderate (private)	low-moderate
D. criticism of poor work	moderate	moderate	low	low (but communicate demand)	low-moderate

SOURCE: Condensed and adapted from T. Good and C. Power, "Designing Successful Classroom Environments for Different Types of Students." *Journal of Curriculum Studies* 8 (1976), 45–60

research at work
five student types and their needs

Good and Power (1976) discussed the instructional needs of five student types found in most classrooms:

1. *Successful students* are task oriented and academically successful. They participate in lessons, turn in assignments on time (usually complete and correct), and create few if any discipline problems. Teachers often direct difficult questions to them, because they get most of them right. Successful students like school and tend to be liked by both teachers and peers.

2. *Social students* are more person oriented than task oriented. They may be able to achieve but value socializing with friends more than working on assignments. Teachers tend to call on them fairly often, both to keep them involved in lessons and because they are able to answer most questions. Social students tend to be popular with peers, but may not be well liked by teachers (because their socializing creates management problems).

3. *Dependent students* look to teachers for support and encouragement, and often ask for additional directions or help. They are frequent hand raisers but usually achieve at a low level, especially in secondary schools. Teachers generally express concern about their academic progress and do what they can to assist them. Peers often reject them because they tend to be socially immature.

4. *Alienated students* are reluctant learners and potential dropouts. In the extreme, they reject the school and everything that it stands for. Some are openly hostile and create disruptions through aggression and defiance. Others remain passive and withdraw to the fringes of the classroom where they may be ignored by teachers and most peers. Teacher attitudes toward alienated students typically range between indifference and rejection.

5. *Phantom students* seem to fade into the background because they are rarely noticed or heard from. They tend to be average in everything but involvement in public settings. Some are shy or nervous, while others are quiet, independent workers of average ability. They work steadily on assignments, but are rarely involved actively in group activities because they never volunteer, and rarely involved in managerial interchanges because they never create disruption. Typically, neither teachers nor peers know these students very well.

---

tionally emphasized approach were supported by the findings of *process-outcome research* done during the 1970s and 1980s. These studies were designed to assess relationships between **processes** *(what the teacher and students do in the classroom)* and **outcomes** *changes in students' knowledge, skills, values, or dispositions).*

uses and limits of group-based instruction

Process-outcome research has reaffirmed that *teachers make a difference.* Some teachers elicit more achievement than others, and their success is based on the classroom management and

research at work
teachers who elicit strong achievement test scores

The following are the most widely replicated findings concerning the characteristics of teachers who elicit strong achievement test score gains (Brophy & Good, 1986; Cruickshank, 1990; Reynolds, 1992; Waxman & Walberg, 1991).

- *Teacher expectation/role definition/sense of efficacy.* These teachers accept responsibility for making sure that their students learn. They believe that the students are capable of learning and that they (the teachers) are capable of teaching them successfully. If students do not learn something the first time, they teach it again, and if the regular curriculum materials do not do the job, they find or make other ones.
- *Student opportunity to learn.* These teachers allocate most of their available time to instruction rather than to nonacademic activities or pastimes. Their students spend many more hours each year on academic tasks than do students of teachers who are less focused on instructional goals. Furthermore, these academic tasks allow students not just to memorize but to understand key ideas, appreciate their connections, and explore their applications.
- *Classroom management and organization.* These teachers organize their classrooms as effective learning environments and use group management approaches that maximize the time that students spend engaged in lessons and activities.
- *Curriculum pacing.* These teachers move through the curriculum rapidly but in small steps that minimize student frustration and allow continuous progress.
- *Active teaching.* These teachers actively instruct—demonstrating skills, explaining concepts and assignments, conducting participatory activities, and reviewing when necessary. They teach their students rather than expecting them to learn mostly from interacting with curriculum materials on their own.
- *Teaching to mastery.* Following active instruction on new content, these teachers provide opportunities for students to practice and apply it. They monitor each student's progress and provide feedback and remedial instruction as needed, making sure that the students achieve mastery.
- *A supportive learning environment.* Despite their strong academic focus, these teachers maintain pleasant, friendly classrooms and are perceived as enthusiastic, supportive instructors.

instructional behaviors listed above. These findings help to move the field beyond unsupported claims toward scientific statements based on credible data. Also, the findings are gratifying to most teachers because they validate many of the principles of practice that they have developed intuitively or through their own experimentation.

For example, Madeline Hunter (1984) has developed "templates" for describing, interpreting, and evaluating the quality of teaching. One such template suggests that effective lessons

Active teachers explain concepts, review when necessary, encourage participation, and do not expect students to learn on their own. Such teachers support and maintain a pleasant and friendly classroom; their enthusiasm is infectious.

contain the following elements: (1) anticipatory set (something said or done to generally prepare the students to learn and to focus them on key stimuli); (2) objective and purpose (tell students the purpose of the lesson); (3) input (new information); (4) modeling (demonstrations of skills or procedures); (5) checking for understanding (through questions or requests for performance); (6) guided practice (under direct teacher supervision); and (7) independent practice (once students know what to do and how to do it). Hunter's notions fit well with process-outcome findings about teacher effects.

Compared to the feasible alternatives, teacher-led, group-based instruction appears to be effective for classroom teaching of any body of knowledge or set of skills that has been sufficiently well analyzed and organized so that it can be presented (explained, modeled) systematically and then practiced or applied during activities that call for student performance that can be evaluated for quality and (where incorrect or imperfect) given corrective feedback. This includes much of what teachers try to accomplish, but it also excludes a lot (e.g., activities that are accomplished more effectively using inquiry or

project learning methods; creative writing; using diverse skills to conduct research or create a product of considerable complexity; art, literature, or music appreciation).

We prefer the term "active instruction" to the term "teacher-led, group-based instruction." This is because, even though we expect most lessons to be structured and led by the teacher and most instruction to be delivered to groups rather than individuals, we also expect teachers to depart from these general tendencies as circumstances dictate. We now consider principles for presenting information, conducting recitations and discussions, and structuring activities and assignments.

presenting information to students

Presenting information to the whole class is an efficient way to expose students to content. It allows the teacher to control the material taught, is easily combined with other methods, and is adjustable to fit the available time, the physical setting, and other situational constraints. Presentation of information is part of the active teaching pattern that is associated with strong student achievement gains. These teacher presentations are typically short ones interspersed with questions or activities, however, not extended lectures. In this section, we offer guidelines about when and how to present information and we review research findings on clarity and enthusiasm in teachers' presentations.

when and how to present information

Despite its continuing popularity, educators have always been ambivalent about information presentation, especially when it is stereotyped as "the lecture method" (Henson, 1988; McLeish, 1976). The approach has been criticized as follows:

- Lectures deny students the opportunity to practice social skills.
- Lectures imply the usually incorrect assumption that all students need the same information.
- Lectures often exceed students' attention spans, so that they begin to "tune out."
- Lectures only convey information; they do not develop skills or dispositions.
- Students can read facts on their own, so why not use class time for other activities?

These points are well taken. Most of us have known teachers whose lectures were ineffective because they were dull, vague, or simply too frequent and too long. However, most of these criticisms reflect overuse or inappropriate use of the lecture method, not problems inherent in the method itself. The lecture method also has much to recommend it, assuming that lectures are well organized, up to date, and pre-

sented appropriately. Ausubel (1963) pointed out that effective lectures provide students with information that would take hours for them to collect on their own. He and others would ask, "Why force students to search for information when a lecture will allow them to get it quickly and then move on to application or problem solving?" Obviously, this point has merit. The important question is not "should we lecture?" but "when should we lecture?"

Various authors (Gage & Berliner, 1984; Henson, 1988) have suggested that *the lecture method is appropriate in the following situations.*

- When the objective is to present information
- When the information is not available in a readily accessible source
- When the material must be organized in a particular way
- When it is necessary to arouse interest in the subject
- When it is necessary to introduce a topic before students read about it on their own or to provide instructions about a task
- When the information is original or must be integrated from different sources
- When the information needs to be summarized or synthesized (following discussion or inquiry)
- When curriculum materials need updating or elaborating
- When the teacher wants to present alternate points of view or to clarify issues in preparation for discussion
- When the teacher wants to provide supplementary explanations of material that students may have difficulty learning on their own

These points also are well taken. Good lectures and presentations at these times do seem preferable to available alternatives. Also, many of the criticisms of the lecture approach can be met without abandoning the approach itself.

For example, consider the criticism that lecturing does not allow students to learn actively or assist them to develop social skills. Teachers could adjust to this while retaining the advantage of lectures by giving short lectures (perhaps fifteen minutes) to structure problems and provide students with necessary information, but then breaking the class into small problem-solving groups. Also, there is no need to view lectures merely as convenient devices for presenting information. When presented in interesting, enthusiastic ways, lectures can stimulate interest and raise questions that students will want to address in follow-up activities.

Lecturing is an *appropriate* method if used for the purposes outlined. How *effective* it is will depend on the care and skill with which the lecture is prepared and delivered (Chilcoat, 1989; Duffy et al., 1986). Effective information presenters:

1. begin with advance organizers or previews that include general principles, outlines, or questions that establish a learning set.
2. briefly describe the objectives and alert students to new or key concepts.
3. present new information with reference to what students already know about the topic, proceeding in small steps sequenced in ways that are easy to follow.
4. elicit student responses regularly to stimulate active learning and ensure that each step is mastered before moving to the next.
5. finish with a review of main points, stressing general integrative concepts.
6. follow up with questions or assignments that require students to encode the material in their own words and apply or extend it to new contexts.

Three key features of good lectures are the *clarity* of the information, the *enthusiasm* with which it is presented, and the teacher's use of good *communication skills*.

clarity

Clarity is essential if students are to understand concepts and assignments. McCaleb and White (1980) identified five aspects of clarity that observers can attend to in classrooms:

1. *Understanding.* This is a prerequisite to clarity and involves matching the new information to the learners' present knowledge. Does the teacher:
   a. determine students' existing familiarity with the information presented?
   b. use terms that are unambiguous and within the students' experience?

2. *Structuring.* This involves organizing the material to promote a clear presentation: stating the purpose, reviewing main ideas, and providing transitions between sections. Does the teacher:
   a. establish the purpose of the lesson?
   b. preview the organization of the lesson?
   c. include internal summaries of the lesson?

3. *Sequencing.* This involves arranging the information in an order conducive to learning. Does the teacher order the lesson in a logical way, appropriate to the content and the learners?

4. *Explaining.* When explaining principles and relating them to facts through examples, illustrations, or analogies, does the teacher:
   a. define major concepts?
   b. give examples to illustrate these concepts?
   c. use examples that are accurate and concrete?

5. *Presenting.* This refers to volume, pacing, articulation, and other speech mechanics. Does the teacher:
   a. articulate words clearly and project speech loudly enough?
   b. pace the sections of the presentation at rates conducive to understanding?

c. support the verbal content with appropriate nonverbal communication and visual aids?

A clear explanation of the nature of the content helps students to focus on the main ideas and order their thoughts effectively. Therefore, before lecturing, teachers should see that students know what they can expect to learn from the lecture and why it is important for them to know this information. After lectures, they should summarize the main points in a few simple sentences or ask questions to elicit a summary from students.

For extended presentations, periodic internal summaries of subparts may be needed in addition to a major summary at the end. Rosenshine (1968) discussed the value of these kinds of internal summaries and in particular the "rule-example-rule" approach, in which a summary statement is given both before and after a series of examples. He also stressed the importance of "explaining links" that make causal linkages explicit—words and phrases such as "because," "in order to," "If . . . then," "therefore," and "consequently." Consider the following sentences:

1. Chicago became the major city in the Midwest and the hub of the nation's railroad system.
2. Because of its central location, Chicago became the hub of the nation's railroad system.

The first example presents relevant facts but does not link them explicitly, as the second example does. If asked, "Why did Chicago become the hub of the railroad system?" most students taught with the second example would respond, "Because of its central location," but many students taught with the first example would respond, "Because it is a big city," or in some other way that indicated failure to appreciate the linkage between a city's geographical location and the role it plays in a nation's transportation system.

In addition to these organization factors, presentations or questions can lack clarity because of vague or confusing language. Smith and Land (1981) reviewed studies indicating that the effectiveness of presentations is reduced by the presence of vagueness terms, mazes, or discontinuity. They identified nine categories of *vagueness terms*:

1. Ambiguous designation (somehow, somewhere, conditions, other)
2. Negated intensifiers (not many, not very)
3. Approximation (about, almost, kind of, pretty much, sort of)
4. "Bluffing" and recovery (actually, and so forth, anyway, as you know, basically, in other words)
5. Error admission (excuse me, I'm sorry, I guess, I'm not sure)
6. Indeterminate quantification (a bunch, a couple, a few, a lot, a little, some, several)
7. Multiplicity (aspects, kinds of, sorts of, types of)
8. Possibility (chances are, could be, maybe, perhaps)
9. Probability (frequently, generally, often, probably, sometimes, usually)

Smith and Land (1981) gave the following as a brief example indicating how vagueness terms can distract from the intended message. The vagueness terms are italicized.

This mathematics lesson *might* enable you to understand *a little more* about *some things we usually call* number patterns. *Maybe* before we get to *probably* the main idea of the lesson, you should review *a few* prerequisite concepts. *Actually*, the first concept you need to review is positive integers. *As you know*, a positive integer is any whole number greater than zero. (p. 38)

Mazes refer to false starts or halting speech, redundantly spoken words, or tangles of words. The mazes are italicized in the following example.

This mathematics lesson will *enab* . . . will get you to understand *number, uh*, number patterns. Before we get to the *main idea of the*, main idea of the lesson, you need to review *four conc* . . . four prerequisite concepts. A positive *number* . . . integer is any whole *integer, uh*, number greater than zero. (p. 38)

A third element that can detract from clarity is *discontinuity*, in which the teacher interrupts the flow of the lecture by interjecting irrelevant content, mentioning relevant content at inappropriate times, or repeatedly saying "uh."

Other research has specified indicators of clarity in more positive terms. Smith and Sanders (1981) showed that presentations were easier to follow when they were structured to create linear redundancy in the appearance of key concepts. In well-structured presentations, key concepts tend to be repeated from one sentence to the next, although new ones are gradually phased in and old ones phased out. Well-structured presentations are recognized as organized sequences of related statements, but poorly structured presentations seem random or jumbled.

enthusiasm

When teachers are enthusiastic about a subject, students are likely to develop enthusiasm of their own, and ultimately to achieve at higher levels (Rosenshine, 1970; Rosenshine & Furst, 1973). Enthusiasm includes at least two major aspects. The first is conveying sincere interest in the subject. This involves modeling, and even shy teachers should be able to demonstrate it. The second aspect is dynamic vigor. Enthusiastic teachers are alive in the room; they show surprise, suspense, joy, and other feelings in their voices and they make material more interesting to students by relating it to their experiences and showing that they themselves are interested in it. There is no need for histrionics, especially by teachers who are not comfortable "performing" for their students, but it should be clear to students that the teacher finds the content meaningful and interesting and expects the students to do so too.

communication skills

The success of a lecture will also depend on the lecturer's communication skills. *Pacing* is one crucial component. An overly slow pace will induce boredom and an overly rapid pace will leave many students confused. Pacing is often too slow, and experiments involving increasing the tempo of presentations have sometimes increased student achievement (Rippey, 1975; Carnine, 1976). On the other hand, experiments involving presentations of complex science content have shown increased achievement after teachers slowed their pacing by waiting three to five seconds following each statement (Tobin, 1980; Tobin & Capie, 1982). Thus, relatively familiar and easy content may be taught best with brisk pacing, but unfamiliar or difficult content requires slower pacing, possibly considerably slower than normal in some situations.

Gestures and movements can enhance the effectiveness of a lecture. Gestures, facial expressions, pointing, and appropriate movements can increase comprehension if they supplement the oral communication and are not overly theatrical or otherwise distracting. Gestures and movements are especially likely to enhance the comprehension of secondary students (Wyckoff, 1973).

Concluding the lecture: Rather than simply coming to a stop, lectures should end with planned conclusions designed to accomplish particular objectives. Usually the conclusion will involve review of main points, with emphasis on the structuring elements that tie them together. Following this review, the teacher invites questions, initiates discussion, or begins a follow-up activity.

effective demonstrations

When learning processes and skills, students need not only verbal explanations, but also physical demonstrations. It is important for teachers to learn to demonstrate effectively, because poor demonstrations can be more confusing than helpful. You may have discovered this for yourself if you have sought out a friend or relative for driving lessons or instructions about how to cook a complicated dish. Professional instructors teach these skills to beginners with ease and efficiency, but most other people do not, even if they are able to drive or cook very well.

What's the trick? Expert instructors tailor their demonstrations to learners' needs. They break processes down into step-by-step operations and demystify what they are doing by verbalizing the thinking that guides their movements. Also, they emphasize the general principles involved rather than just the particular applications that apply to the example at hand. As a result, learners acquire stategies that they can adapt to varying situations, not just fixed routines learned by rote. The same principles apply to teachers' demonstrations of new academic skills and instructions for assignments. A good demonstration proceeds as follows:

1. Focus attention. Be sure that all students are attentive before beginning, and focus their attention by holding up an object or pointing to where you want them to look.

2. Give a general orientation or overview. Explain what you are going to do, so that students can get mentally set to observe the key steps.

3. If new objects or concepts are introduced, label them. If necessary, have the students repeat the labels. Students cannot follow an explanation if they do not know what some of the words mean.

4. Go through the process step by step. Begin each new step with an explanation of what you are going to do, and then describe your actions as you do them.

5. If necessary, perform each action slowly with exaggerated motions.

6. Have a student repeat the demonstration. If the task is short, have the student do the whole thing and give feedback at the end. If it is longer, break it into parts at first.

7. In correcting mistakes, do *not* dwell on the mistake and the reasons for it, but instead redemonstrate the correct steps and have the student try again.

Thinking out loud at each step is crucial, especially when the task is primarily cognitive. While you demonstrate physical procedures such as pouring into a test tube, writing a number on the board, or making an incision, describe how you are filling the test tube exactly to the twenty-milliliter line, getting the sum by carrying two units of ten and adding them to the tens column, or starting your incision at the breastbone and stopping short of the hipbones. Unless you verbalize these thinking processes, some students may learn no more from watching your demonstration than they would from watching a magician perform a baffling trick.

questioning and responding to students

Teacher-led reviews, recitations, and discussions are important parts of the active teaching pattern that is associated with strong achievement gains. Teachers need to know how to plan good sequences of questions that will help their students to develop understanding of content and provide them with opportunities to apply it.

Teacher-student discourse occurs in a variety of formats. At one extreme is the *drill* or fast-paced *review* designed to test or reinforce students' knowledge of specifics. Here, the emphasis is on obtaining "right answers" and moving at a brisk pace. At the other extreme is *discussion* designed to stimulate students to respond diversely and at high cognitive levels to what they have been learning. Here, the pace is slower and the emphasis is on developing understanding and pursuing implications. In between reviews and discussions are *recitation* activities that vary in pace and cognitive level of question. They include the questioning and response segments that occur between teacher presentation segments, as well as most activities that teachers refer to as "going over the material" or "elaborating on the text."

Educational critics (e.g., Goodlad, 1984) often speak warmly of discussion but criticize drill and most forms of recitation as boring, unnecessarily teacher dominant, restricted to low-level objectives, and tending to make students passive and oriented toward producing right answers rather than thinking. Clearly, such inappropriate use of the recitation method should be avoided. However, recitation has certain legitimate uses and is in some respects well suited to classroom teaching (Farrar, 1986). It allows the teacher to work with the whole class at one time, is an efficient way to enable students to practice and receive immediate feedback on their learning of new content, is a convenient way for teachers to check on student understanding before moving on, and is much easier to manage than individualized instruction. Thus, as with lecturing, the operative question about recitation is not whether to use it but when and how to use it effectively.

The more effective forms of recitation are blended with information presentation in lecture/recitation lessons that develop students' understanding of a topic's most important ideas. Questions are not asked just to monitor comprehension but also to stimulate students to think about the content, connect it to their prior knowledge, and begin to explore its applications.

Except when intended as review or preparation for tests, recitation activities should not be rapidly paced drills or attempts to elicit right answers to miscellaneous collections of factual questions. Instead, they should be means for engaging students with the content they are learning. Questions should stimulate students to process that content actively and make it their own by rephrasing it into their own words and considering its meanings and implications. Furthermore, the questions should focus on the most important elements of the content and guide students' thinking toward key understandings. The idea is to build an integrated network of knowledge anchored around powerful ideas, not to stimulate rote memorizing of miscellaneous information.

Questions are devices for teaching, not just for testing. Advice about questioning techniques is based not only on process-outcome research but on logical analyses of different types of questions and their appropriateness to different instructional goals (Carlsen, 1991b; Dillon, 1988, 1990; Wilen, 1990).

difficulty levels of questions

The difficulty level of a question is determined by whether or not the students can answer it.

research at work
guidelines to good questioning

Groisser (1964) suggested that *good questions* are: clear, purposeful, brief, natural, and thought provoking. *Clear* questions precisely describe the specific points to which students are to respond. *Purposeful* questions are planned and sequenced with particular objectives in mind. *Brief* questions tend to be preferable to longer ones because they usually are more clear and to the point.

Questions ordinarily should be phrased in *natural* language adapted to the level of the class. If students do not understand the question, they cannot respond as desired. Finally, good questions are *thought provoking*. They arouse curiosity and interest and help students to clarify their ideas.

Most questions should be addressed to the entire class rather than to individuals. That is, the teacher first asks the question, next gives the class time to think, and then calls on someone to respond. This way, everyone is responsible for the answer. If the teacher were to name a student to respond before asking the question, only that student would be held responsible and the other students would be less likely to try to answer it in their own minds.

Questions ordinarily should be distributed widely among the students rather than addressed primarily to the same few students who provide most of the answers. This keeps most students attentive and accountable, and provides everyone with opportunities to respond and get feedback. Also, teachers who restrict their questions primarily to a small group of active (and usually high-achieving) students are likely to communicate undesirable expectations (Good & Brophy, 1974) and generally to be less aware and less effective.

Questions should be asked in a normal conversational tone rather than in a formal tone that connotes testing. *Typically, they should be asked one at a time and should not be repeated*, to condition students to the notion that each question calls for an answer. Multiple or continually revised questions are signs of poor preparation, and repeating questions merely distracts students.

Whatever the cognitive level of the response that a question demands, it is easy if most students can answer it correctly and difficult if most students cannot. The highest achievement gains are seen in classes where most questions are answered correctly, and most of the rest yield partially correct or incorrect answers rather than no responses at all. Brophy and Evertson (1976) found that the optimal percentage of correct answers averaged about 75 percent but varied according to the socioeconomic status of the students. Achievement gain was maximized when about 70 percent of questions were answered correctly in high SES classes but when about 80 percent were answered correctly in low-SES classes. Thus, students learn efficiently when they can answer most recitation questions correctly, although high-SES students profit from a somewhat greater level of challenge than the level that is optimal for low-SES students.

The 75 percent norm is just a rule of thumb. Success rates might be notably lower when teachers begin to question students about

Good questions from the teacher provoke student thought and discussion.

new material, but might approach 100 percent for review of familiar material.

cognitive levels of questions

Many investigators have used hierarchies based on the Bloom taxonomy (Bloom et al., 1956) to classify questions according to the cognitive levels of the responses that they demand from students. *Knowledge* questions are considered low in cognitive demand, *comprehension* and *application* questions intermediate, and *analysis*, *synthesis*, and *evaluation* questions high. Others have used simpler classifications such as fact versus thought questions or convergent versus divergent questions.

So far, research findings have been mixed and relatively uninformative about when and why different kinds of questions should be used. At least, they underscore the complexities involved and caution against attempts to substitute simple formulas for careful planning of question sequences. For example, higher-order questions do tend to elicit higher-order responses from students (Klinzing, Klinzing-Eurich, & Tisher, 1985) and higher frequencies

of higher-order questions often correlate positively with achievement gains (Redfield & Rousseau, 1981; Samson et al., 1987). However, students often respond at a lower cognitive level than the question called for, and high frequencies of lower-order questions often correlate positively with student achievement gains as well, even gains on higher-order objectives (Brophy & Good, 1986; Winne, 1979). Thus, it is not true that thought questions are always better than fact questions, that divergent questions are always better than convergent questions, or that higher-order or complex questions are always better than lower-order or simpler questions.

Varying combinations of questions will be needed, depending on the instructional goals. Guidelines need to focus on *sequences* of questions designed to help students develop connected understandings, not just on the cognitive levels of individual questions considered in isolation. Sequences that begin with a higher-level question and then proceed through several lower-level follow-up questions are appropriate for purposes such as asking students to suggest possible applications of an idea and then probing for details about how these applications might work. However, sequences featuring a series of lower-level questions followed by a higher-level question would be appropriate for purposes such as calling students' attention to relevant facts and then stimulating them to integrate these facts and draw a conclusion.

wait time

Students need sufficient time to think about teachers' questions. Yet, Rowe (1974a, 1974b) reported observing teachers who waited less than one second before calling on someone to respond, then waited only about another second for the student to give the answer (before supplying it themselves, calling on someone else, or giving clues). These findings did not seem to make sense because they suggested that the teachers minimized the value of their questions by failing to give students time to think.

Rowe followed up by training teachers to extend their wait times from less than one second to three to five seconds. Surprisingly, most of the teachers found this difficult to do, and some never did succeed. However, in the classrooms of teachers who did extend their wait times, the following desirable changes occurred:

- Increase in the average length of student responses
- Increase in unsolicited but appropriate student responses
- Decrease in failures to respond
- Increase in speculative responses
- Increase in student-to-student comparisons of data
- Increase in statements that involved drawing inferences from evidence
- Increase in student-initiated questions
- A greater variety of contributions by students

Subsequent research has verified that increasing wait time leads to longer and higher-quality student responses and participation by a greater number of students (Rowe, 1986; Swift, Gooding, & Swift, 1988; Tobin, 1983a, 1983b; Tobin & Capie, 1982). It also has verified that many teachers experience difficulty in extending their wait times. DeTure (1979) found that even after training, no teacher attained an average wait time longer than 1.8 seconds. Why should this be? The answer lies in the pressures on teachers to maintain lesson pacing and student attention. Some teachers are reluctant to extend their wait times because they fear that they may lose student attention, or even control of the class, if they do. This illustrates one of the continuing dilemmas that require teacher decision making and adjustment to immediate situations. Longer wait times are generally preferable to shorter ones because they allow more thinking by more students, but the teacher may have to use shorter wait times when the class is restive or when time is running out and it is necessary to finish the lesson quickly.

The appropriateness of pacing and wait time factors depends on the objectives of the activity. Most studies that have produced positive outcomes by extending wait times have focused on instruction in abstract or difficult material taught in the higher grades. In contrast, Anshutz (1975) reported no science achievement differences between short and long wait times for students in Grades 3 and 4, and Riley (1980) reported interaction effects on science achievement in Grades 1 through 5. A decrease in achievement occurred when wait time was extended for low-level questions, whereas an increase was noted when wait time was extended for higher level questions.

These studies show that pacing and wait time should be suited to the questions being asked and ultimately to the goals these questions are designed to accomplish. A fast pace and short wait times are appropriate for drill or review. However, if questions are intended to stimulate students to think about material and formulate original responses rather than

research at work
alternatives to questioning

Dillon (1988, 1990) illustrated that declarative statements by teachers can be just as effective as questions for producing lengthy and insightful responses during discussions. He also noted that questions may impede discussions at times, especially questions perceived as attempts to test students rather than to solicit their ideas. To avoid this problem, Dillon (1979) listed six *alternatives to questioning* that teachers can use to sustain discussions.

1. *Declarative statements.* In discussing the effects of war on the domestic economy, the teacher might respond to a student's statement by thinking, "When the war broke out, unemployment dropped." The teacher could introduce this idea into the discussion by stating it directly rather than putting it into the form of a question such as "What happens to the unemployment rate in wartime?" or "What causes a drop in unemployment?" The statement provides information that the students have to accommodate and respond to; compared to a question, however, it invites longer and more varied responses.

2. *Declarative restatements.* Teachers can show that they have attended to and understood what students have said by occasionally summarizing. Such summarizing may be useful to the class as a whole, and reflecting students' statements to them may stimulate additional and deeper responding.

3. *Indirect questions.* When a direct question might sound challenging or rejecting, the teacher can make a statement such as "I wonder what makes you think that" or "I was just thinking about whether that would make any difference." Such indirect questions might stimulate further thinking without generating anxiety.

4. *Imperatives.* Similarly, statements such as "Tell us more about that" or "Perhaps you could give some examples" are less threatening than direct requests for the same information.

5. *Student questions.* Rather than asking all of the questions themselves, teachers can encourage students to ask questions in response to statements made by their classmates.

6. *Deliberate silence.* Sometimes the best response to a statement is to remain silent for several seconds to allow students to absorb the content and formulate follow-up questions or comments.

merely to retrieve information from memory, it is important to allow time for these effects to occur. This is especially true for complex or involved questions. Students may need several seconds to process such questions before they can even begin to formulate responses to them.

reacting to students' responses

Students' responses to teacher questions should receive feedback, both to motivate the students and to produce learning. This probably seems obvious, but teachers sometimes fail to give feedback, especially to low achievers (Brophy & Good, 1974).

Unless it is understood that no response indicates correctness, teachers should give some sort of acknowledgment every time a student answers a question. Feedback need not be long or elaborate, although sometimes it has to be. Often a head nod or a short comment like "right" is sufficient. There is no need to praise students' answers frequently, but it is important to treat their contributions with interest and respect. When circumstances allow, teachers can both encourage the respondent and move the activity in desired directions by incorporating the respondent's ideas into their subsequent instruction, asking follow-up questions, or inviting the respondent to elaborate on the original answer.

When a student fails to respond or responds incorrectly, it is often helpful to sustain the interaction with the original respondent rather than to *terminate* it by giving the answer or calling on someone else. *Techniques for sustaining the interaction* include simply waiting patiently for a response, helping the student to answer the original question by rephrasing it or giving clues, or simplifying the response demand by substituting a series of questions that begins with easier ones but builds back toward the original question. It is not always possible to sustain interactions in this manner because the question may not lend itself to simplification, or the student may remain unable to respond. Where it is feasible to do so, however, we recommend sustaining the interaction in ways that allow it to conclude with a successful student response. This will tend to reinforce students' sense of efficacy as learners and willingness to take risks in public response situations.

responding to students' questions and comments

Besides reacting to students' responses to questions, teachers must react to their comments and questions. Teachers who elicit high achievement gains are receptive to relevant questions and comments. **Relevant questions**—student-initiated questions that are relevant to the topic under discussion—indicate a need for clarification or a desire to know more about the subject. **Relevant comments**—student-initiated comments that are relevant to the topic under discussion—suggest that students are actively thinking about the material and relating it to their experiences. Thus, such questions and comments present "teachable moments" that teachers would be foolish not to take advantage of.

Yet, some teachers cut off such questions and comments with irritation or respond in a manner that makes the students sorry that they asked the question or made the comment in the first place. Embarrassment or humiliation due to a teacher's response to one's question or comment is a frequent experience among students, and many students stop asking questions because of it (Dillon, 1981a). Thus, although responses to questions or comments occasionally may have to be kept very brief or delayed until after class because time is short or because a more complete response would move the lesson too far off topic, teachers should make clear to their students that they welcome relevant questions and comments, and when possible, should respond to them fully or incorporate them into the ongoing lesson.

conducting discussions

Although drill and recitation occur frequently in classrooms, true group discussion is rare. Even activities that teachers call "discussion" tend to be recitations in which teachers ask questions and students respond by reciting what they

Good discussions can include student-student interchanges as well as teacher-student interchanges.

already know or are presently learning. Few such activities are actual discussions in which the teacher and students share opinions in order to clarify issues, relate new knowledge to their prior experience, or attempt to answer a questions or solve a problem (Alvermann, O'Brien, & Dillon, 1990); Tharp & Gallimore, 1988).

To conduct discussions, teachers must adopt a different role from the one they play in recitation activities, where they act as the primary source of information and the authority figure who determines whether answers are correct. Teachers lead discussions by establishing a focus, setting boundaries, and facilitating interaction, but in other respects, they assume a less dominant and less judgmental role. Even if a discussion begins in a question-and-answer format, it should evolve into an exchange of views in which students respond to one another as well as to the teacher and respond to statements as well as to questions.

If ideas are being collected, the teacher should record them (listing them on the board or on an overhead projector) but not evaluate them. Once the discussion is established, the teacher may wish to participate in it periodical-

ly to point out connections between ideas, identify similarities or contrasts, request clarification or elaboration, invite students to respond to one another, summarize progress achieved so far, or suggest and test for possible consensus as it develops. However, the teacher should not push the group toward some previously determined conclusion (this would make the activity a guided discovery lesson rather than a discussion).

The pace of discussions is notably slower than that of recitations, with longer periods of silence between speech. These periods provide participants with opportunities to consider what has been said and to formulate responses to it.

In general, if teachers expect an activity to involve genuine discussion and not merely recitation, they have to make this clear to students and alter their own behavior accordingly.

structuring activities and assignments

There are three main ways that teachers help their students to learn. First, they explain,

research at work

guidelines for seat work and workbook tasks

Osborn (1984) suggested the following guidelines for seat work and workbook tasks.

- A sufficient portion should be related to current instruction in the rest of the unit.
- Another portion should provide systematic and cumulative review.
- Tasks should reflect the most important (and seat-work-appropriate) aspects of what is being taught.
- Extra tasks should be available for students who need extra practice.

- Instructions should be clear and easy to follow; brevity is a virtue.
- Response modes should be as close as possible to actual reading and writing (as opposed to circling, underlining, drawing arrows from one word to another, etc.).
- The artwork should be consistent with the prose of the task.
- Cute, nonfunctional, space- and time-consuming tasks should be avoided.
- Tasks should be accompanied by brief explanations of purpose.

demonstrate, model, or in other ways present information. Second, they lead the students in review, recitation, discussion, or other forms of discourse surrounding the content. Third, they involve students in activities or assignments that provide them with opportunities to practice or apply what they are learning. Only limited research is available on activities and assignments (Brophy, 1992a), even though most students spend half or more of their time in school working independently (Fisher et al., 1980). Similarly, although it is known that homework can provide a useful supplement to classroom instruction and may increase student achievement, at least in the secondary grades (Cooper, 1989; Epstein, 1988; Miller & Kelley, 1991; Rickards, 1982; Strother, 1984), little is known about how much or what kinds of homework to assign.

Process-outcome research suggests that independent seat work is probably overused and is not an adequate substitute either for active teacher instruction or for recitation and discussion opportunities. This is especially the case when the seat work emphasizes low-level

tasks that do not provide opportunities to think about or apply what is being learned.

Research on managing classrooms and motivating students suggests that activities and assignments should be varied and interesting enough to motivate student engagement, new or challenging enough to constitute meaningful learning experiences rather than pointless busywork, and yet easy enough to allow students to achieve high rates of success if they invest reasonable effort. The effectiveness of assignments is enhanced when teachers *explain the work and go over practice examples with students before releasing them to work independently, then circulate to monitor progress and provide help when needed.*

criteria to consider in selecting or developing activities

Assignments that provide students with opportunities to extend or deepen their knowledge and to apply what they are learning are important components of a well-rounded instructional program. However, assignments can also be pointless busy work or defective in ways that make them unlikely to accomplish their intended purposes. This is just as true of the workbooks and other assignments provided with textbook series as it is of seat work that teachers design themselves.

For teachers interested in selecting or developing their own activities and assignments, Brophy and Alleman (1991) suggested the following guidelines. First, begin with a focus on the unit's *major goals* and consider the kinds of activities that would promote progress toward those goals. Given the instructional goals, different activities might be: (1) essential, (2) useful but not essential, (3) relevant but less useful than other activities that serve the same functions more effectively, (4) relevant but tangential because they do not promote progress toward major goals, or (5) irrelevant or inappropriate to the goals. For example, an American history course designed to develop appreciation of American political traditions might feature a unit on the American Revolution that emphasized the historical events and political philosophies that shaped the thinking of the writers of the Declaration of Independence and the Constitution. Essential activities for such a unit would call for research, debate, or critical thinking about the issues that developed between England and the colonies and about the ideals, principles, and compromises that went into the construction of the Constitution. Less essential but still useful activities might include studying more about the thinking of key framers of the Constitution or about forms of oppression that different colonial groups had experienced. Activities that are similar in form but less useful in content might include studying the lives of Paul Revere or other revolutionary figures who are not known primarily for their contributions to American political traditions, or studying the details of each of the eco-

nomic restrictions that England imposed on the colonies. Irrelevant to the goals would be activities that focused on the details of particular Revolutionary War battles.

Activities that are not relevant to certain programs or courses might be highly relevant to others. For example, courses in military history would focus on the military aspects of the American Revolution, so that activities based on particular battles might be very useful. Thus, the potential pedagogical value of activities ultimately must be assessed within the context of the major goals that a curriculum is designed to accomplish.

A second set of guidelines concerns the *feasibility* and *cost-effectiveness* of a proposed activity. Is the activity feasible given its assumptions about students' prior knowledge and the time, space, and equipment that it will require? Do the benefits that the activity is expected to bring to the students justify its costs in time and trouble?

All activities considered for inclusion in an instructional program should meet these *primary criteria* of goal appropriateness, feasibility, and cost-effectiveness. In selecting from among activities that meet these primary criteria, teachers might consider several *secondary criteria*:

- Students are likely to find the activity interesting or enjoyable.
- The activity provides opportunities for interaction and reflective discourse, not just solitary seat work.
- If the activity involves writing, students will compose prose, not just fill in blanks.
- If the activity involves discourse, students will engage in critical or creative thinking, as well as articulate and defend problem-solving or decision-making approaches, not just regurgitate facts and definitions.
- The activity focuses on application of important ideas, not incidental details or interesting but trivial information.

Small group assignments or activities work best when the teacher provides coaching and feedback to help complete the assignment successfully.

structuring and scaffolding students' learning

Activities need to be effectively presented, monitored, and followed up if they are to have their full impact. This means preparing the students for the activity in advance, providing guidance and feedback during the activity, and structuring postactivity reflection (Brophy & Alleman, 1991).

In introducing activities, teachers need to stress their purposes in ways that will help students to engage in them with clear ideas about the goals they are trying to accomplish. This may need to be supplemented by statements or questions that call students' attention to relevant background knowledge, modeling of strategies for responding to the task, or scaffolding that will simplify the task for the students.

Teachers can scaffold by providing any needed information or help concerning how to go about completing task requirements. If reading is part of the task, for example, teachers might summarize the main ideas, remind students about strategies for developing and monitoring their comprehension as they read (paraphrasing, summarizing, taking notes, question-ing themselves to check understanding), or provide them with advance organizers that will help them to approach the material in the intended ways. If necessary, teachers might provide additional scaffolding in the form of partial outlines or skeletal notes (Kiewra, 1987), study guides that call attention to key ideas, or task organizers that help students to keep track of the steps involved and the strategies they are using to complete these steps.

Once students begin working on activities and assignments, teachers should monitor their progress and if necessary, help them past rough spots by providing relatively general and indirect hints or cues. If their assistance is too direct or extensive, teachers will end up doing tasks for students instead of providing them with scaffolding to enable them to do the tasks themselves.

Most tasks will not have their full effects unless they are followed by reflection or debriefing. Here, the teacher reviews the task with the students, provides general feedback about performance, and reinforces the main ideas as they relate to the overall goals. These debriefing and reflection activities should also include opportunities for students to ask follow-up questions, share task-related observations or experiences, compare opinions, or in other ways deepen their appreciation of what they have learned and how it relates to their lives outside of school.

activities and assignments that allow for cooperative learning

Although the term "activities" usually connotes something done by the whole class or a subgroup, the terms "seat work" and "assignments" traditionally connote independent work done by students working individually, typically in silence. However, it is seldom necessary for students to work in these individualized formats, and recent research suggests that there is often much to be gained by arranging for students to collaborate in pairs or small groups as they work on activities and assignments (Cohen, 1986; Good, McCaslin, & Reys, 1992; Johnson et al, 1984; McCaslin & Good, in press b; Sharan, 1990; Slavin, 1990).

Cooperative learning *allows students to interact regularly with many of their peers, to discuss interesting questions about course material, and to learn from one another.* Students in small groups have more chances to talk than they do in larger groups, and shy students are more likely to feel comfortable expressing ideas in these more intimate settings. If accountability aspects are arranged properly (students know that any one of them may be called on to answer any one of the group's questions or that they will be tested individually on what they are learning), student interaction in pairs and groups can mobilize students' attention, focus their thinking on relevant questions, and promote learning by stimulating higher-order thinking and constructive controversy. Cooperative learning can also promote affective and social benefits such as increased student interest in and valuing of subject-matter and increases in positive attitudes and social interactions among students

who differ in gender, race, ethnicity, school achievement, or other characteristics.

To prepare your students for cooperative learning, you may need to show students how to share, listen, integrate the ideas of others, and handle disagreements constructively. You also will need to assign tasks and activities that are well suited to cooperative learning. For example, if mathematics students are actually to cooperate rather than just compare answers, they will need assignments that are different from the routine computation worksheets that they are accustomed to working on alone (Good et al., 1989–90). Cooperative pairs or groups will need to work on problems with a range of formulation and solution strategies that can be discussed and debated. Alternatively, they could work on more complicated tasks to be done in stages, requiring cooperative planning and perhaps differentiation of roles for different students in the group. These activities should engage students in exploring or applying content currently being taught, so that the cooperative learning is an integral part of subject-matter teaching rather than an isolated add-on. The degree of autonomous collaboration expected from students will depend on their familiarity with both the academic content and the cooperative learning format.

summary

Few if any specific instructional behaviors are appropriate in all teaching contexts, and there may be different but functionally equivalent paths to the same achievement outcomes. Thus, it makes more sense to think in terms of instructional functions that need to be accomplished than in terms of specific behaviors to be labeled as appropriate or inappropriate. Even within the general method of active teaching that appears to be an appropriate base for most teachers, the specifics of application will vary with grade level, subject matter, and other context variables. Ralph Kinderstone and Judith Blondell provide examples of such variation.

Guidelines are given for how instruction can be expected to vary with student SES, as well as for how teachers can adapt instruction to students' individual characteristics. In particular, Good and Power (1976) present suggestions for adapting whole-class instruction to the needs of successful students, social students, dependent students, alienated students, and phantom students.

Process-outcome research links classroom processes to student outcomes. Such research has shown that achievement gains are associated with teacher expectations/role definition/sense of efficacy, student opportunity to learn, classroom management and organization, curriculum pacing, active teaching, teaching to mastery, and a supportive learning environment. Most teachers will use active teaching as their basic method of instruction. Compared to the feasible alternatives, it is effective for teaching knowledge or skills that have been sufficiently analyzed and organized so that they can be presented (explained, modeled) systematically and then practiced or applied by students, who can then be evaluated for performance quality and (where the performance is incorrect or imperfect) be given corrective feedback. Other instructional objectives will require different methods.

All teachers are likely to rely regularly on three basic sets of instructional skills—those involved in making presentations (lecturing, demonstrating, explaining), questioning and responding to students (conducting drills, recitations, and discussions), and designing and implementing activities and assignments. The lecture method can be used appropriately when the objective is to present information, especially information that is not found in readily accessible sources. Preparation for lectures begins with consideration of the objectives and of the constraints and practical considerations that may apply. This is followed by develop-

ment of an outline listing key points and then a comprehensive plan that includes attention to questions that might be asked during or after the lecture, demonstrations and visual aids to be used, handouts to be distributed, and follow-up activities or assignments.

The lecture should be clear and easy to follow. This will be accomplished if the teacher avoids vague terms, mazes, and discontinuity problems that detract from clarity. The teacher can also clarify by structuring and sequencing the material appropriately, beginning with advance organizers, using rule-example-rule patterns, and including explaining links that make explicit the causal or logical connections between elements. Comprehension will also be enhanced if the lecture is delivered with appropriate pacing, gestures, and communication of enthusiasm about the content.

Activities involving questioning and responding to students provide opportunities for the teacher to assess understanding of what has been presented and for the students to process and respond more actively to the material than merely by listening to a presentation. Questioning activities range from fast-paced drills and reviews to slow-paced discussions designed to stimulate students to respond diversely and at high cognitive levels. Teachers have been criticized for conducting too much drill and recitation and not enough discussion, and this may be true in many classrooms. However, in such cases the problem is a lack of balance between different instructional objectives and their associated activities, not something inherently inappropriate with drill or recitation.

Research on the cognitive level of teachers' questions has produced confusing and contradictory results. Assuming the appropriateness of the instructional objective in the first place, the real issue is the degree to which a planned sequence of questions makes sense as a way to accomplish that objective. Good questions are clear, purposeful, brief, adapted to the level of the class, thought provoking, addressed initially to the entire class rather than to an individual, distributed widely, asked one at a time, and asked in a conversational tone of voice. After asking a question, the teacher should wait long enough for students to process it and formulate responses. Longer wait times usually produce more active participation by a larger percentage of the students, coupled with an increase in the quality and length of responses.

Where feasible, it is better for teachers to sustain the interaction with the original respondent and attempt to elicit an improved response rather than terminate the interaction by giving the answer or calling on someone else. If the student needs help, the teacher can simplify or rephrase the question or give clues.

To conduct effective discussions, teachers must adopt a discussion-leader role that differs from the role that they play in drill and recitation activities. Although they structure the discussion and keep it on track, they act more as a collector and clarifier of opinions than as a judge of their correctness. A good discussion will proceed at a slower pace than a typical recitation activity, and although it may begin with questions and answers, it should evolve into an exchange of views in which students respond to one another as well as the teacher and respond to statements as well as questions.

Dillon suggests six alternatives to questioning that teachers can use to elicit thoughtful student responses.

Independent seat work and homework assignments are desirable elements of a balanced instructional approach, although some teachers overuse seat work. Ideally, assignments will be interesting enough to engage student interest, new or challenging enough to constitute worthwhile learning experiences or practice/application opportunities, and yet easy enough to allow success with reasonable effort. Their effectiveness is likely to depend on the degree to which teachers go over the assignments with the students before releasing them to work independently, monitor performance for completion and accuracy, supply timely and specific feedback, and follow up with appropriate remedial instruction where necessary. The primary determinant of the value of an activity or assignment is the degree to which it promotes progress toward important instructional goals.

It is often desirable for students to collaborate in pairs or groups as they work on assignments. When appropriately structured, collaborative learning activities provide opportunities for the social construction of learning, and they often bring social and affective benefits as well.

questions for reflection

1. Were you under the impression that effective teaching is simply a matter of mastering a few "crucial" behaviors? What is wrong with that statement? What would be a more accurate description of effective teaching?

2. Do the suggestions made for teaching different student types make sense to you? If so, can you see ways to do all of these things simultaneously? List some of the ways. (Remember, most if not all of these student types will exist in any classroom.)

3. Most process-outcome research has used standardized tests for measuring achievement gain. In what ways might this make the results of

such research limited or misleading? Compare notes with your friends.

4. As a teacher, you will have considerable autonomy in allocating classroom time to particular objectives. What would you see as your responsibilities and options in the following three situations? (1) The adopted curriculum contains a unit on a topic that you do not consider very important, and there is no particular pressure on you to teach it (2) You do not consider the unit important, but it is part of the official curriculum mandated by your school district (3) You recognize that the unit is important but do not feel competent to teach it effectively or do not enjoy teaching it. Would you omit the unit or reduce the time allocated to it under these circumstances? Why or why not?

5. How can you both move students through the curriculum at a brisk pace and also program for consistent success and minimal frustration? Write down some specific strategies for responding to this challenge. In particular, what should you do when 80 percent of the students have clearly mastered the objectives of a lesson but 20 percent have not?

6. If Ralph Kinderstone and Judith Blondell were to trade places, which of their present teaching strategies could they retain and which would they have to change?

7. What does it mean to say that SES is a "proxy" standing for a complex of correlated cognitive and affective differences between subgroups of students? What are the advantages and disadvantages of using such proxy variables? How can we use them in ways that help teachers to meet different student needs effectively, but do not create undesirable biases and stereotyped expectations in teachers?

8. What does it mean to say that accommodating students' preferences is not the same as meeting their needs? How should teachers define "meeting their students' needs," and how can they evaluate their degree of success in doing so?

9. In your judgment, what makes for differences in interest value, clarity, and all-around usefulness of the presentations made by instructors in your various classes? Can you identify criteria beyond those included in this chapter?

10. What types of presentation are used most typically in the grade level and subject matter you expect to teach? Given that your students will have textbooks, films, and other sources of input, what do you foresee as the role of your presentations? How will these presentations complement or supplement these other sources?

11. Using the guidelines presented in this chapter, develop a comprehensive plan for a presentation at the grade level and in the subject matter you intend to teach. Include attention to props, media, and follow-up questions and activities, in addition to the selection and organization of content. If possible, get your plan critiqued, revise it, and then try out the presentation in a classroom setting and revise it once more if necessary.

12. What types of drill/review, recitation, and discussion activities do you expect to use in your own teaching? Are these expectations realistic given the grade level and subject matter?

13. If you expect your questions to generate cognitive activity in your students rather than merely to provide an opportunity to test their knowledge, what does this imply about pacing, wait time, and distribution of response opportunities?

14. Might you be one of those teachers whose wait times are too short? If so, why? What steps could you take to inhibit your impulsiveness and increase your tolerance for the periods of silence associated with longer wait times?

15. Some students understand what they are learning, turn in assignments correctly, and earn high grades. Yet, they seldom volunteer, preferring to watch and listen rather than to contribute to classroom activities. Should you accommodate them by mostly leaving them alone, or should you frequently call on them as nonvolunteers? Why?

16. How should you handle students who feel pressured and embarrassed in public response situations when they cannot supply the correct answer immediately? Should these students be considered exceptions to the rule that teachers should sustain the interaction and try to elicit an improved response in these situations?

17. Are you prepared to adopt the change in role that is required to stimulate genuine discussion? How should you respond when a student offers a sincere but naive opinion that produces snickering by classmates?

18. What kinds of individual and collaborative assignments do you expect to use, and for what purposes? What accountability procedures and mechanisms for providing assessment and feedback will you use?

19. Will you assign homework? If so, for what purposes? How will you assess whether these purposes are being met?

20. Inspect one or more instructor's manuals for a textbook that is used in a grade and subject you expect to teach. Analyze the questions and activities suggested for use during a key unit, using criteria suggested in this chapter. Adapt or replace the ones that are not worth including, and add new ones as needed, to create a powerful curriculum unit likely to accomplish significant instructional goals.

cases to consider

Read each of the following descriptions of how a teacher conducts his or her class, and using the material presented in this chapter, critique the teacher's approach.

a mixed class Laura Stemard teaches fourth-grade mathematics. Her students are distributed fairly equally among the top, middle, and lower ranges of social class background. Two students are being mainstreamed.

Laura works with the entire class for twenty to thirty minutes a day (only the two mainstreamed students work on individual assignments). In general, she spends fifteen minutes reviewing homework and discussing the assignment. Most of her questions are easy (90 percent are answered correctly), and if students miss a question she simply goes on. The last fifteen minutes are spent completing assigned seat work. She circles the room, providing detailed feedback to students who are not finished. When students finish they are expected to find something to do (although nothing explicit is provided) and not to bother others.

an elite group "Pack" Wilson runs his algebra class as smoothly as he ran the high school football team fifteen years earlier. All his students are college bound, but, as he puts it, he likes to "let the good horses run." The top five to eight students in each section are taught as a separate group that moves through the curriculum about 25 percent faster than the other students.

Classroom discussion involves application of concepts and infrequent review. He tests twice a week, and students have one hour of homework daily. He spends roughly half of each period with each of the two groups. While he works with one group, the other works individually on clear but difficult assignments. Pack almost never talks to individual students about their work, and he actively discourages average students from approaching him unless they are totally stuck.

an inner-city speech class Toni Frick teaches a high school speech course in an inner-city school. Although the course is an elective, most students take it. Each day in the class is a bit different, although there is a general sense of purposefulness. On the average, three days a week are spent in oral speech (teacher demonstrating technique, student practice, and so on). Toni has two goals for the students: to be able to write and deliver an interesting and informative speech, and to be able to talk extemporaneously.

During most oral presentations she divides the class into outliners (who chart the flow of the speech), critics (who note the weakest parts of the speech), and helpers (who note the best parts). In addition to writing down comments relevant to their roles, students fill out general evaluations (how interesting, how clear, and so on) and may be called on to present and defend their critiques. After presenting a speech, students listen to the public evaluations carefully, because each speech is typically repeated once and major criticisms must be accommodated.

The remaining two days of each week are reserved for an analysis of written speeches (Who would have written this speech? What content is avoided? Does it engage the emotions effectively? How would an African-American audience react? Why?) and to practicing speech writing. In such activities the teacher attempts to match the complexity of the task to the students' level of mastery, although most of this work is done individually.

teaching for understanding and the social construction of knowledge

objectives

When you have mastered the material in this chapter, you will be able to

1. Define teaching for understanding and explain its implications for the planning of instruction and the assessment of learning
2. Explain the role of prior knowledge (including schema activation) in students' construction of new knowledge
3. Identify common elements that appear in various approaches to teaching for understanding and social construction of knowledge
4. Explain and give examples of approaches that emphasize understanding and social construction of knowledge in teaching language arts, mathematics, science, and social studies

5. Define and explain the instructional implications of the terms explicit instruction, responsive elaboration, reciprocal teaching, mathematical power, conceptual change, and thoughtfulness
6. Explain and give examples of ways in which different approaches to teaching are suited to different instructional goals
7. Assess the strengths and weaknesses of instructional materials and manuals, then identify any changes or additions in content sources, teacher questions, or learning activities that would be needed in order to make the materials effective for teaching students to understand, appreciate, and apply a network of knowledge structured around powerful ideas

teaching for understanding, appreciation, and application of knowledge

In Chapter 10 we reviewed process-outcome research of the 1970s and early 1980s that documented the connections between active teaching (presenting information, structuring discourse, monitoring work on assignments) and student gains on achievement tests. In the late 1980s and early 1990s, research on teaching moved on to new phases. One reason for this was increasing recognition of certain limitations in process-outcome research. First, this research focused on important but very basic aspects of teaching. Its findings differentiated the least effective teachers from other teachers, but they did not address the subtler points that distinguish the most outstanding teachers. Second, most of this research relied on standardized tests as the measures of learning. Consequently, its assessment components focused on mastery of relatively isolated knowledge items and skill components without assessing the degree to which students had developed understanding of networks of connected content or could use this content in realistic application situations.

These concerns led to new forms of research on subject-matter teaching. The new studies focused on **teaching for understanding,** which *implies that students learn not only the individual elements in a network of related content but also the connections among them, so that they can explain the content in their own words and can access and use it in appropriate application situations in and out of school* (Bereiter & Scardamalia, 1987; Brophy, 1989; Glaser, 1984; Prawat, 1989; Resnick, 1987). Students who learn content with understanding not only learn the content itself but appreciate the reasons for learning it and retain it in a form that makes it usable when needed. Recent research on subject-matter teaching has involved exemplary teachers who know their subjects thoroughly and emphasize developing understanding when planning their instruction. The research focuses intensively on particular curriculum units or lessons, taking into account the teacher's instructional goals and assessing students' learning accordingly. The researchers determine what the teacher is trying to accomplish, record detailed information about classroom processes, and then assess learning using evaluation measures keyed to the instructional goals. Often the evaluation methods include detailed interviews or collection of portfolios of student work in addition to or instead of more conventional short-answer tests.

While deepening our understanding of the role of the teacher in stimulating student learning, recent research has also emphasized the role of the student. This reflects the influence of developmental and cognitive psychologists who hold constructivist views of learning and teaching (Appleton, 1993; Carey & Smith, 1993; Davis, Maher, & Noddings, 1990; Resnick & Klopfer, 1989; Steffe, Cobb, & von Glasersfeld, 1988; von Glasersfeld, 1991).

As we noted in Chapter 7, constructivists reject linear hierarchical models of knowledge structuring and instead emphasize networks of knowledge structured around powerful ideas. These network models imply that one can begin teaching almost anywhere in a network, couch learning within an applications context, and engage students in higher-order thinking about a topic right from the beginning of instruction.

Shifting from a linear to a network conception of knowledge structuring fits well with ideas about teaching subjects for understanding, appreciation, and application. Because comprehension (i.e., understanding) is near the bottom of the Bloom taxonomy, teaching for understanding is sometimes viewed as a low-level cognitive objective. However, scholars have pointed out that, in order to achieve a reasonably complete understanding of a network of knowledge, students will have to engage in application, analysis, synthesis, and evaluation activities, not just in activities designed to build knowledge and comprehension. Consequently, the notion of separating cognitive levels of learning and addressing them in sequential order breaks down when one is planning the integrated instruction that is needed to teach for meaningful understanding.

Content should be selected and organized as means to move students toward important educational goals. That is, the content should be *worth* understanding, appreciating, and applying in the first place. If so, it will be structured as a series of networks of connected knowledge, not as a disconnected parade of facts and isolated skills. Furthermore, it will be taught with emphasis on the powerful ideas that anchor the networks and provide a basis for potential applications.

Many more things are worth teaching than we have time to teach in school, so breadth of topic coverage must be balanced against depth of development of each topic. This is an enduring challenge that can only be managed in sensible ways, not a problem that can be solved once and for all. However, recent research suggests that we have drifted in the direction of addressing far too many topics and including too many trite or pointless details. Curriculum analyses in all of the subject areas suggest the need for teacher decision making about how to reduce breadth of coverage, structure the content around powerful ideas, and develop these ideas in depth (Dempster, 1993).

the role of prior knowledge

Learners construct knowledge most smoothly when they can address new content by relating it to their prior knowledge. New content is not first understood in some abstract way and only later related to existing knowledge; instead, it is interpreted from the beginning within contexts supplied by that existing knowledge. Networks of prior knowledge that provide contexts for meaningful interpretation of new content are usually called *schemas* (Anderson, 1984; diSibio, 1982). If new content can be related to existing schemas, activation of these schemas can help learners to develop expectations about the nature of the content, identify and pay special attention to its most important elements, and fill in gaps where information is implied rather than stated explicitly.

Activation of relevant prior knowledge can make learning of new content easier and more efficient, at least if the activated schemas are suited to the instructional goals (Adams, 1990; Anderson, 1984; Gagné & Dick, 1983). Teachers can prepare students for story reading by telling them what the story is about and asking them questions to activate schemas that they will find useful in comprehending it. Teachers also can help students to activate relevant prior knowledge by drawing analogies or suggesting examples that link the new content to familiar ideas or experiences, by taking an inventory of what students know (or think they know) about the topic before beginning instruction, or by asking questions that require students to make predictions about the content or to suggest solutions to problems based on it.

knowledge restructuring and conceptual change

Learning is a constructive process that involves "seeking after meaning," so students routinely draw on prior knowledge to make sense of what they are learning. Whether schemas are activated through the students' own initiative or in response to comments or questions from the teacher, activation of relevant schemas will facilitate learning if the schemas are accurate and support accomplishment of the instructional goals. When schemas are not accurate or not well suited to the goals, however, their activation will interfere with learning (Alvermann, Smith, & Readence, 1985). If the new content is filtered through schemas that are oversimplified, distorted, or otherwise invalid, students may develop misconceptions instead of the target conceptions that the teacher is trying to

teach. For example, many students believe that the sun orbits the earth, because they have "seen" it do so. Sometimes this prior knowledge is so well entrenched that it causes certain students to miss what the teacher or textbook is saying about cycles of day and night. Such students may learn that particular parts of the earth experience daylight at times when they are exposed to the sun, yet still believe that cycles of day and night are caused by the orbiting of the sun around the earth instead of vice versa.

Besides adding new elements to an existing cognitive structure, active construction of knowledge may involve changing the structure through processes of restructuring and conceptual change. Sometimes the needed restructuring is relatively minor and easily accomplished, but sometimes students need to undergo more radical restructuring that involves simultaneous change in large networks of connected knowledge (Carey, 1985; Chinn & Brewer, 1993; Vosniadou & Brewer, 1987). Radical restructuring can be time consuming and difficult to accomplish.

Mere exposure to correct conceptions will not necessarily stimulate the needed restructuring because learners may activate long-standing and firmly held misconceptions that cause them to ignore, distort, or miss the implications of aspects of the new learning that contradict their current beliefs. It may be necessary to help students first to see the contradictions between what they currently believe and what the teacher is trying to teach, and then to appreciate that the target concepts are more valid, more powerful, more useful, or in some other way preferable to their existing concepts (Bransford & Vye, 1989; Gardner, 1991; Posner et al., 1982).

social construction of situated knowledge

Constructivists' ideas about learning (presented in Chapter 7) are reflected in their preferred methods for teaching. Viewing knowledge as socially constructed, constructivists reject transmission models and instead emphasize whole-class teaching that features sustained dialogue or discussion (not just recitation) in which participants pursue a topic in depth and negotiate shared understandings. They also emphasize cooperative learning by pairs and small groups of students who work mostly independently of the teacher. Based on notions of situated learning, constructivists emphasize engaging students in authentic activities that allow them to use their learning for accomplishing the kinds of life applications that justify the inclusion of this learning in the curriculum in the first place. Constructivists also emphasize teaching in the zone of proximal development. The teacher assists the students' knowledge construction by scaffolding their learning efforts, but gradually reduces this assistance and transfers responsibility for managing learning to the students themselves as their expertise develops.

conclusions: teaching for understanding, appreciation, and application of knowledge

Recent research on teaching school subjects for understanding, appreciation, and application has begun to move beyond the basics implied in the term "active teaching" in order to identify the subtleties involved in the best teaching. Along with ideas drawn from educators' writings about curriculum and instruction, these studies have been informed by the writings of psychologists and cognitive scientists on thought and language, cognitive development, situated cognition, and the social construction of knowledge. Different authors emphasize different theoretical rationales and instructional methods, but for the most part, their ideas are

compatible with one another and with notions about active teaching developed from earlier research. Compatibilities are especially evident when instructional goals are taken into account and it is recognized that different goals call for somewhat different approaches to curriculum and instruction.

The notion of teaching for understanding implies helping students construct connected networks of knowledge by relating new content to existing knowledge in ways that allow them to appreciate the connections and to access the knowledge for use in appropriate application situations. Students develop new knowledge through a process of active construction in which they build and integrate a network of associations linking the new content to preexisting knowledge and beliefs anchored in concrete experience. Thus teaching involves inducing conceptual change, not infusing knowledge into a vacuum. To the extent that students' preexisting beliefs about a topic are accurate, they facilitate learning and provide a natural starting place for teaching. To the extent that students harbor misconceptions, however, these misconceptions will need to be corrected so that they do not persist and distort the new learning.

When the new learning is complex, the construction of meaning required to develop clear understanding of it takes time and is facilitated by the interactive discourse that occurs during lessons and activities. Clear explanations and modeling from the teacher are important, but so are opportunities to answer questions about the content, discuss or debate its meanings and implications, and apply it in problem solving or decision making. These activities allow students to process the content actively and make it their own by paraphrasing it into their own words, exploring its relationships to other knowledge and to past experience, appreciating the insights it provides, and identifying its implications for personal decision making or action. The teacher provides whatever structuring and scaffolding the students need in order

research at work
model for subject-matter teaching

Research on teaching school subjects for understanding and social construction of knowledge is still in its infancy, but it already has produced successful experimental programs in most subjects. Even more encouraging, analyses have identified a set of principles and practices common to most or all of them (Anderson, 1989; Brophy, 1989, 1992b; Prawat, 1989). These common elements, outlined below, might be considered components in a model of powerful subject-matter teaching:

- The curriculum is designed to equip students with knowledge, skills, values, and dispositions that they will find useful both inside and outside of school.
- Instructional goals emphasize developing student expertise within an application context and with emphasis on conceptual understanding of knowledge and self-regulated application of skills.
- The curriculum balances breadth with depth by addressing limited content but developing this content sufficiently to foster conceptual understanding.
- The content is organized around a limited set of powerful ideas (basic understandings and principles).

- The teacher's role is not just to present information but also to scaffold and respond to students' learning efforts.
- The students' role is not just to absorb or copy input but also to actively make sense and construct meaning.
- Students' prior knowledge about the topic is elicited and used as a starting place for instruction, which builds on accurate prior knowledge and stimulates conceptual change if necessary.
- Activities and assignments feature tasks that call for critical thinking or problem solving, not just memory or reproduction.
- Higher-order thinking skills are not taught as a separate skills curriculum. Instead, they are developed in the process of teaching subject-matter knowledge within application contexts that call for students to relate what they are learning to their lives outside of school by thinking critically or creatively about it or by using it to solve problems or make decisions.
- The teacher creates a social environment in the classroom that could be described as a learning community featuring discourse or dialogue designed to promote understanding.

to accomplish the goals of learning activities successfully, but this assistance is faded as student expertise develops. Ultimately, students engage in independent and self-regulated learning.

Teaching for understanding requires "complete" lessons that are carried through to include higher-order applications of content,

which means that the breadth of content addressed must be limited in order to allow for more in-depth teaching of the content that is included. Unfortunately, both state and district curriculum guidelines (which often feature long lists of knowledge items and subskills to be "covered") and typical curriculum packages supplied by educational publishers (which respond to these state and district guidelines by emphasizing breadth over depth of coverage) discourage in-depth teaching of limited content. Teachers who teach for understanding and higher-order applications of subject-matter content must limit what they try to teach by focusing on what they see as most important and omitting or skimming over the rest. They must also structure what they do teach around important ideas and elaborate it considerably beyond what is in the text.

Besides presenting information and modeling application of skills, such teachers structure a great deal of content-based discourse. They use questions to stimulate students to process and reflect on the content, recognize relationships among and implications of its key ideas, think critically about it, and use it in problem solving, decision making, or other higher-order applications. Such discourse is not mere factual review or recitation featuring rapid-fire questioning and short answers, but instead is sustained and thoughtful examination of a few related topics, in which students are invited to develop explanations, make predictions, debate alternative approaches to problems, or otherwise consider the implications or applications of the content. Some of the questions admit to a range of possible correct answers, and some invite discussion or debate (e.g., concerning the relative merits of alternative suggestions for solving problems). In addition to asking questions and providing feedback, the teacher encourages students to explain or elaborate on their answers or to comment on classmates' answers. The teacher also capitalizes on "teachable moment" opportunities offered by students' comments or questions (by elaborating on the original instruction, correcting misconceptions, calling attention to implications that have not been appreciated yet, and so on).

Skills are taught holistically within the context of applying the knowledge content, rather than being practiced in isolation. Thus, most practice of reading skills is embedded within lessons involving reading and interpreting extended text; most practice of writing skills is embedded within activities calling for authentic writing; and most practice of mathematics skills is embedded within problem-solving applications. Also, skills are taught as strategies adapted to particular purposes and situations, with emphasis on modeling the cognitive and metacognitive components involved and explaining the necessary conditional knowledge (of when and why the skills would be used). Thus, students receive instruction in when and how to apply skills, not just opportunities to use them.

Activities, assignments, and evaluation methods incorporate a much greater range of tasks than the familiar workbooks and curriculum-embedded tests that focus on recognition and recall of facts, definitions, and fragmented skills. Curriculum strands or units are planned to accomplish gradual transfer of responsibility for managing learning activities from the teacher to the students in response to growing student expertise on the topic. Plans for lessons and activities are guided by the overall curriculum goals (phrased in terms of student capabilities to be developed), and evaluation efforts concentrate on assessing the progress that has been made toward accomplishing these goals.

subject-specific examples

In discussing what is involved in teaching school subjects for understanding, appreciation, and application, we have so far concentrated on generic aspects that cut across school subjects. In the following sections, we provide examples showing how these principles have been embodied in programs developed to foster such teaching in particular subjects.

reading instruction

The report *Becoming a Nation of Readers* (Anderson et al., 1985) integrates research-based principles for teaching reading for understanding and application. It calls for teaching reading as a process of extracting meaning from texts that are read for information or enjoyment (not just to get reading practice). Thus, the emphasis is on making sense of text rather than on practicing fragmented skills. Important skills such as decoding, blending, and noting main ideas are taught and practiced, but primarily within the context of application (reading for meaning). There is considerable explicit instruction and modeling of skills currently being phased in, but such skills instruction is phased out as students develop expertise. Phonics and blending, for example, receive a great deal of emphasis in the first grade but are phased out by the end of the second grade.

Activities and assignments feature more reading of extended text and less time spent with skills worksheets. Students often work cooperatively in pairs or small groups, reading to one another or discussing the meanings or implications of the text. Instead of being restricted to the rather artificial stories found in basal reading series, students often read genuine literature written to provide information or pleasure to the reader (children's literature, poetry, biography, nonfictional material about the physical or social world).

Most current innovations in reading instruction feature attempts to incorporate these principles. The principles apply at least as much to instruction of disadvantaged students or to remedial instruction of students having difficulty learning to read as they do to instruction of other students (Knapp & Shields, 1991). They are featured prominently in the Kamehameha Early Education Project (KEEP) that was developed to meet the needs of native Hawaiian children who previously had difficulty learning to read (Au et al., 1985; Tharp & Gallimore, 1988), as well as in the Reading Recovery program that is being used successfully with first graders who have failed to learn to read when taught by traditional methods (Anderson & Armbruster, 1990; Pinnell, DeFord, & Lyons, 1988). The principles are also embedded in several theoretically derived and empirically validated experimental programs.

Paris, Cross, and Lipson (1984) developed *Informed Strategies for Learning* (ISL), a program designed to increase awareness and use of effective reading strategies. The program contains fourteen weekly modules that show students what is involved in using each strategy, when to use it, and what benefits can be expected from using it. Students first observe models using the strategies and then practice the strategies themselves with guidance and feedback from the teacher. The strategies are explained and illustrated using metaphors familiar to the students. For example, a lesson on preassessment to discover clues to the topic, length, and difficulty of a passage uses the metaphor, "Be a reading detective." Similarly, comprehension-monitoring strategies are taught using analogies to traffic signs such as, "Stop—say the meaning in your own words," or, "Dead end—go back and reread the parts you don't understand." ISL has been used successfully in third- and fifth-grade classes (Cross & Paris, 1988).

Hansen and Pearson (1983) improved fourth graders' reading comprehension using a program that featured strategy training and practice in answering questions. Strategy training was conducted through story introductions in which students were asked to relate their prior knowledge about situations like those depicted in the upcoming story, then predict what the protagonist would do. They wrote down their prior knowledge answers on one sheet of paper and their predictions on another, then combined the two to demonstrate that reading involves combining what one knows with what is in a text. Following these preparations, students read the story and compared their predictions with what actually occurred.

The other part of the treatment involved changing the nature of the questions asked following story reading. Typically, students are asked about 80 percent factual questions and only 20 percent inferential questions. For this study, the students were asked only inferential questions concerning such issues as the characters' motives or the larger moral or meaning that the story was meant to communicate. Evaluation data showed that this combination of strategy training and inferential questions improved the experimental students' reading comprehension over that of control students taught in traditional ways. The treatment was especially effective with poor readers.

explicit instruction with responsive elaboration

Duffy, Roehler, and their colleagues (Duffy, 1993; Duffy & Roehler, 1987, 1989; Duffy, Roehler, & Herrmann, 1988; Duffy et al., 1987) have shown that poor readers in the intermediate grades learn to read with better comprehension and increased awareness of their strategies when they are provided with *explicit instruction* in comprehension strategies. The strategies are the same ones taught typically, such as identifying the main idea in a paragraph or using the dictionary, but they are taught much more explicitly and thoroughly than usual. Teachers learn to explain the nature of each strategy in detail, tell when and why it is used, model by verbalizing the mental processes that occur when using it, point out sequential aspects and salient features of these processes, and then provide students with opportunities to use the strategy and see its effectiveness for themselves.

During the practice and application phases, teachers provide **responsive elaboration**— *elaborating on their original instruction in response to learning difficulties or misconceptions evident in students' questions, comments, or performances.* For example, failure to use a strate-

gy when it was applicable suggests the need to clarify when and why the strategy is useful, whereas unsuccessful use of the strategy suggests the need for additional modeling. Instruction continues until students can both use the strategy effectively to make sense of what they read and explain when and why the strategy should be used.

reciprocal teaching

Palincsar and Brown (1984) developed a reciprocal teaching method for teaching four comprehension-fostering and comprehension-monitoring strategies to poor readers: summarizing, questioning, clarifying, and predicting. **Reciprocal teaching** *is an approach to instruction that features interactive dialogue between teacher and students. The teacher does most of the initial modeling and explaining but gradually turns over these responsibilities to the students, who eventually take turns acting as the teacher and leading small-group discussions of texts.*

To begin, the teacher notes the title and asks for predictions about the content of the passage. Then the group reads the first segment silently and the student "teacher" asks a question about it, summarizes it, and then offers a prediction or asks for clarification if appropriate. If necessary, the adult teacher provides guidance by prompting ("What questions do you think a teacher might ask here?"), instructing ("Remember, a summary is a shortened version; it doesn't include detail"), or modifying the activity ("If you are having a hard time thinking of a question, why don't you summarize first?"). The adult teacher also provides feedback about the quality and specificity of questions, the logic involved in making predictions, and so on.

The reciprocal teaching method has produced sizable gains on tests of reading comprehension in several studies (Palincsar & Brown, 1989). It combines key elements of teaching for understanding and self-regulated learning (modeling of strategic application of skills, scaf-

research at work
reciprocal teaching dialogue

The following dialogue (from Palincsar & Brown, 1989, pp. 42-43) illustrates reciprocal teaching as implemented in a first-grade classroom.

Teacher (reading from text): The pipefish change their color and movements to blend with their surroundings. For example, pipefish that live among green plants change their color to a shade of green to match the plants.

Claire (the child leading the discussion): One question that I had about this paragraph is: "What is special about the way that the pipefish looks?"

Keith (clarifying): Do you mean the way that it is green?

Andy (elaborating): It's not just that it's green; it's that it's the same color as the plants around it, all around it.

Claire (resuming): Yes. That's it. My summary is this part tells how the pipefish looks and that it looks like what is around it. My prediction is that this is about its enemies and how it protects itself and who the enemies are.

Monty: They also talked about how the pipefish moves . . .

Keith: It sways back and forth.

Andy: Along with the other plants.

Teacher: What do we call it when something looks like and acts like something else? The way that the walkingstick was yesterday? We clarified this word when we talked about the walkingstick.

Angel: Mimic.

Teacher: That's right. We said, we would say, that the pipefish mimics the—

Several students: Plants.

Teacher: OK! Let's see if Claire's predictions come true.

Over time, as students become more familiar with reciprocal teaching activities, the dialogue becomes less routinized and the strategies are used in more flexible ways. The teacher turns over more responsibility for leading and sustaining the dialogue to the students, gradually engaging less in modeling and instruction but more in coaching students' participation in the discussion.

---

folded instruction that gradually releases increasing responsibility to the students themselves) with provision of opportunity for students to learn cooperatively in small groups.

strategy training for high school and college students Strategy training in reading is not just for elementary students. It can be helpful to secondary students too if it is focused on strategies needed for accomplishing tasks encountered at their grade levels. Dimino and colleagues (1990) illustrated this in a study comparing two methods of improving low-achieving ninth graders' comprehension of short stories. Compared to a group taught using traditional basal instruction, students taught to analyze stories using strategies based on story grammar did significantly better on several outcome measures. These students learned to analyze stories by identifying the primary problem or conflict, the main character, the character's attempts to solve the problem or conflict, the resolution of these efforts, twists in the plot, the character's reactions to the depicted events, and the overall theme suggested. Andre and Anderson (1978–79) trained high school students to generate questions about the main points of a text as they studied it. These students learned more than a group who simply read and reread the text and also a group who were directed to ask themselves questions but were not trained in strategies for doing so.

Cook and Mayer (1988) showed that training in strategies for content area reading and text study can significantly improve learning even in college students. The students they studied initially had difficulty in sorting passages from chemistry texts into categories on the basis of their organizational structures (e.g., generalizations supported by examples or elaboration, enumeration of lists, linear sequences, classification systems, comparison and contrast passages). After training in strategies for recognizing these text structures and using this information to aid study, trained students showed considerably improved recall of highly conceptual information and ability to use what they had learned when responding to application questions.

helping students to become good strategy users Michael Pressley and his colleagues have analyzed and synthesized a great many studies of training students in strategies for improving reading comprehension. Pressley and colleagues (1989) concluded that research support is particularly strong for the following strategies: summarizing the gist of a paragraph or set of paragraphs, emphasizing the main ideas; constructing images to represent visually what the text is describing verbally; using mnemonic devices to help remember the meanings of new words; generating story grammar analyses or constructing story maps for narrative passages; generating questions to ask oneself about the meanings and implications of the text; attempting to answer any questions that have been included in the text as aids to checking for understanding; and activating relevant

prior knowledge by making predictions about the text and by comparing depicted events with one's own experiences.

Pressley and his colleagues developed what they called transactional methods to teach students to become "good strategy users" through classroom discourse and provision of support and guidance as students engage in content-area reading and study (Pressley et al., 1992). They also illustrated ways in which good strategy instruction incorporates many of the methods advocated by social constructivists, even though these approaches are often viewed as quite different or even contradictory (Pressley, Harris, & Marks, 1992). They argued that good strategy instruction differs from social constructivist recommendations in its emphasis on explicit statement, modeling, and explanation of strategies, but that otherwise it emphasizes classroom discourse, scaffolded and responsive assistance to students, and related constructivist notions.

Many students appear to develop efficient reading and study strategies on their own— and thus do not need much explicit instruction or practice—but many do not. Low-achieving students in particular stand to benefit considerably from instruction and guidance in self-regulated reading and study strategies. For more information, see Barr, Kamil, Mosenthal, and Pearson (1991), Baumann, Seifert-Kessell, and Jones (1992), Dole and others (1990), and Paris, Wasik, and Turner (1991).

writing instruction

When writing is taught for understanding and application, the instructional goals focus on teaching students to use writing for organizing and communicating their thinking to particular audiences for particular purposes, and skills are taught as strategies for accomplishing these goals. There is explicit instruction concerning when, why, and how to use the skills, and this is

The basic skills of printing and cursive writing are embedded in composition activities.

elaborated later during responsive feedback to students' composition efforts. Key basic skills such as printing and cursive writing are taught explicitly and practiced to mastery, but a great deal of this practice is embedded within writing activities that call for composition and communication of meaningful content. Composition activities emphasize "authentic" writing intended to be read for meaning and response, not mere copying or exercises focused on displaying skills for the teacher (Applebee, 1986; Bereiter & Scardamalia, 1987; Calkins, 1986; Florio-Ruane & Lensmire, 1989; Graves, 1983; Rosaen, 1989).

Thus, composition is taught, not as an impersonal exercise in writing a draft to conform to the formal requirements of a genre, but as communication and personal craftsmanship calling for developing and revising an outline, developing and revising successive drafts for meaning, and then polishing into final form. The emphasis is on the cognitive and metacognitive aspects of developing compositions, not just on writing mechanics and editing.

In helping students plan and work through successive drafts, teachers concentrate first on purpose, audience, and content and organization of the ideas to be communicated, and only later on the fine points of grammar and spelling. Writing is done for a variety of purposes and audiences, so that students learn to consider not just what they want to say but how their message will need to be phrased if it is to have the intended effects. Also, writing is used as a method of learning school subjects, via assignments calling for students to analyze, synthesize, evaluate, or in other ways use higher order thinking to respond to what they have been learning in science, social studies, literature, or other subjects.

cognitive strategies in writing One experimental program that embodies many of these principles is the *Cognitive Strategies in Writing* (CSIW) program developed by Englert and Raphael (1989). It incorporates initial explicit explanation and modeling, follow-up responsive elaboration concerning writing goals and strategies, and scaffolded assistance to students' composition efforts. Students are provided with sets of questions to guide their planning, outline forms, and suggestions for recording and organizing ideas on "think sheets."

For example, a think sheet to assist students in planning their compositions asks them to respond to the following questions: (1) Who am I writing for? (2) Why am I writing this? (3) What do I already know about my topic? and (4) How do I group my ideas? To further assist planning, the think sheet contains numbered lines under the "What do I already know about my topic?" question (so that students can enter separate ideas on separate lines), as well as boxes with lines underneath them under the "How do I group my ideas?" question (so that students can enter group labels in the boxes and then list examples on the lines under the boxes). Similarly, a think sheet for organizing information for comparison and contrast writing contains boxes for identifying the dimensions on which comparisons will be made and then separately listing the ways in which the things to be compared are alike and different. Assessment of the CSIW program indicated that it significantly improved students' knowledge of writing, including that of learning-disabled students (Englert, Raphael, & Anderson, 1992). Graham and Harris (1989) also found that scaffolded writing exercises improved the writing capabilities of learning-disabled students.

mathematics instruction

The National Council of Teachers of Mathematics (1989) has released guidelines for mathematics instruction that emphasize developing students' *mathematical power* to explore, conjecture, reason logically, and use a variety of mathematical models to solve nonroutine problems. The notion of developing mathematical power is based on the recognition that mathe-matics is more than a collection of concepts and skills to be mastered; it includes methods of investigating and reasoning, means of communication, and notions of context.

An ideal program teaches mathematical concepts as well as mathematical operations. Both the concepts and the operations are embedded in networks of knowledge structured around key ideas and taught within application contexts right from the beginning. Compared to what is typically done, students spend less time working individually on computation skills sheets and more time participating in teacher-led discourse concerning the meanings and implications of mathematical concepts and their applications to problem solving.

Teachers explain and model the mathematical reasoning used to address classes of problems, then stimulate students to engage in such reasoning themselves. In addition to well-structured exercises that merely require them to recognize problem types and then apply familiar formulas, students are exposed to the kinds of ill-structured problems that occur in real life and require us to discover and invent ways of framing and solving them. Often such applications can be approached in many different ways, thus providing opportunities for students to examine potential solution strategies. Teacher-led discourse surrounding such applications involves sustained, thoughtful examination of a small number of related questions rather than fast-paced recitation of number facts. It features a great deal of higher order mathematical reasoning in generating and debating ideas about how the problems might be approached.

cognitively guided instruction One experimental approach that embodies many of these principles is *Cognitively Guided Instruction* (CGI), a program developed by Fennema, Carpenter, and Peterson (1989) for increasing primary grade teachers' effective-

For students who are oriented toward problem solving, reasoning processes, and relationships rather than rote mastery of facts, the calculator and a chance for group dialogue serve important functions.

ness in introducing young children to mathematics. CGI places more emphasis on word problems than on computational practice. The problems emphasize applications to students' current lives, and teachers elicit and foster discussion of students' own invented strategies for solving such problems. Teachers learn that addition and subtraction problems fall into eight basic types and that children possess intuitive knowledge about and strategies for solving each problem type that can be used as a starting point for instruction (Fennema et al., 1993). Problems are taken up in the order in which children naturally develop interest in them, and the students are encouraged to discover knowledge and invent strategies in addition to learning from teacher explanation and modeling. Evaluation data revealed that stu-

dents in CGI classrooms showed significant advantages in problem solving and mathematical confidence compared to students in control classrooms, with no loss in computation skills (Carpenter et al., 1989).

developing both concepts and skills

Two other approaches to introducing mathematics in the primary grades feature similar philosophies and have achieved results similar to those described for CGI. Hiebert and Wearne (1992) provided first graders with "conceptually based" instruction on place value and addition and subtraction, using methods reflecting the guidelines published by the National Council of Teachers of Mathematics (1989). Compared to students who were taught the same content using more traditional methods, the experimental students showed more understanding of key concepts and ability to apply the strategies they had learned. Hiebert and Wearne (1993) later obtained similar results with second graders.

Cobb and his colleagues (Cobb et al., 1991; Wood, Cobb, & Yackel, 1990) drew on the same principles and on social constructivist ideas to develop a method of teaching mathematics to second graders that emphasized teacher-led discussion of alternative suggestions about solving problems. Compared to students taught more conventionally, the experimental students developed higher levels of conceptual understanding in mathematics and a preference for collaborating with others to achieve understanding rather than competing with them for rewards. Follow-up assessment indicated that these group differences continued to hold up a year later (Cobb et al., 1992).

As with the CGI program, students taught using the Hiebert and Wearne program and the Cobb group's program not only outperformed comparison students on measures of conceptual understanding and higher-order applications, but also equaled or exceeded their performance on arithmetic computations. This was true even though the experimental programs placed much more emphasis on problem solving than on computation practice. Soled (1990) achieved similar results with seventh-grade science students and ninth-grade mathematics students. Thus, within limits at least, the gains in understanding, appreciation, and strategic application of skills that can be achieved through instruction that emphasizes authentic applications over isolated skills practice apparently can be accomplished without a corresponding reduction in skills development.

collaborative construction of mathematical understandings
Lampert (1989) has emphasized teaching for understanding and developing mathematical power in the intermediate grades. She teaches not just skills but a language to use in describing mathematical phenomena, connects mathematical operations and relationships to more familiar and concrete operations and relationships, and guides students' construction of meaning concerning mathematical symbols and operations so that it centers on key ideas drawn from the discipline. Lampert instructs actively, but with stress on processes, relationships, multiple methods, and chances for students to evaluate and discuss proposed solutions to problems. Group inquiry featuring dialogue or argument is emphasized over teacher presentations, and discussion focuses on the relative merits of alternative suggestions for approaching problems rather than on finding a "right answer."

Lampert (1989) identified five keys to her approach: (1) involving learners with phenomena that feel problematic to them, so that finding solutions *matters* to them; (2) using multiple representations of concepts to ensure that students understand their meanings; (3) emphasizing dialogue (including argument, not just discourse) as the vehicle for constructing meaning; (4) diagnosing students' levels of understanding and needs for corrective explanation as the dialogue progresses, and providing the needed instruction; and (5) teaching the students to become willing and able to collaborate in solving problems and constructing new knowledge.

These approaches to mathematics teaching that have been developed recently in the United States have much in common with methods emphasized in Japan and China (Stigler & Stevenson, 1991). Mathematics classes in these countries are oriented toward problem solving rather than rote mastery of facts and procedures. Teachers use many different types of representational materials and often rely on students as sources of information. They lead the class in discussions of problems, acting as knowledgeable guides who seek to stimulate students to produce, explain, and evaluate potential solutions rather than as prime dispensers of information and arbiters of what is correct (Fernandez, Yoshida, & Stigler, 1992; Lappan & Ferrini-Mundy, 1993; Wheatley, 1992).

science instruction

Blumenfeld (1992) drew on case studies of fifth- and sixth-grade science teaching to identify practices that promote reflective student learning in science. She listed the following as characteristics of the more successful teachers:

- *Opportunities*: (1) Topic coverage focuses on a few key ideas developed in depth; (2) learning activities relate to these main ideas, focus on application rather than mere verification, and involve engagement in meaningful problems relating to children's experience or to real events; (3) the products produced through these activities also relate to the main ideas and require processing at high cognitive levels.
- *Instruction*: (1) Clear presentations highlight main points and critical information, take into account students' prior knowledge, and use examples, analogies, and metaphors; (2) these presentations build connections by linking with prior knowledge, making relationships among new ideas evident, focusing on similarities and differences among ideas, and showing their application; (3) they include scaffolding in the form of modeling of learning and of metacognitive and problem-solving strategies.
- *Press (use of questions and feedback)*: (1) Questions focus attention on main ideas; (2) teacher checks understanding by asking comprehension questions, asking for summarization, asking for application, focusing on content rather than procedures, adding higher-level questions to worksheets, and asking for alternative representations of content; (3) teacher draws out student reasoning by probing, asking for justification or clarification, and elaborating on student responses; (4) teacher uses errors to diagnose and clear up misunderstandings; (5) teacher encourages making of connections by asking about relationships of key ideas to prior knowledge, asking about relationships among new ideas, asking about how an activity's procedures relate to its content, and asking about how the results of the activity illustrate main ideas; (6) teacher ensures widespread responding by calling on many students, using debate, and using voting or asking who agrees or disagrees with a statement.
- *Support*: (1) Teacher helps students to accomplish tasks by breaking down problems, simplifying procedures, modeling procedures, or providing models and examples; (2) teacher promotes independence, self-regulation, and cooperation by encouraging students to work together, providing time for planning, asking about students' individual contributions to group work, and asking students whether they agree or disagree with their group's conclusions.
- *Evaluation*: (1) Teacher holds students accountable for understanding by adding questions to worksheets that focus on the meanings of key ideas; (2) evaluation focuses on learning rather than performance, features recognition of individual contributions and improvement, and deemphasizes grades and correct answers.

conceptual change teaching Anderson and Roth (1989) have developed an approach to teaching science. Their approach emphasizes depth over breadth and focuses on the teaching of powerful ideas in ways that encourage students not only to learn them with understanding but to recognize their value for describing, explaining, making predictions about, or gaining control over real-world systems or events. Through real-life examples and involvement of students in discussion of applications, their approach aims to make science content more meaningful to students by connecting it with their experience-based knowledge and beliefs. The focus is on producing conceptual change, building on accurate current knowledge and correcting misconceptions. **Conceptual change** is *construction of new understandings that involves abandoning or revising some of one's existing conceptions, not just adding new ones.*

Students often find science harder to learn than other subjects. In part, this is because science courses typically require them to learn a great many new concepts very quickly (the average science course introduces more new vocabulary than the average foreign language course!). An additional problem, however, is that students typically enter these courses with misconceptions about the content they will be studying. For example, most middle-school science textbooks contain units on plants that emphasize their roles as food producers via the photosynthesis process. Students typically enter these courses knowing little about photosynthesis, but a great deal about food, especially food for people. They know that food is something you consume or eat, and is taken in from the outside environment, as well as that there are many different kinds of food.

These beliefs may produce distorted understandings if they lead students to assume that, like people, plants must take in food from the environment in many different forms. In fact, plants make their own food. Neither soil nor water nor fertilizers (despite their sometimes being called "plant food") are taken in as food or consumed for energy. Nor do plants take in any other form of food. Their only source of food is that which they manufacture themselves through the photosynthesis process. They transform light energy from the sun into chemical potential energy stored in food and available for

use both by plants and by animals. The matter that they take in during this process (carbon dioxide, water, and soil minerals) is not food because it is not a source of energy. Students must go through a process of conceptual change if they are to attain understanding of photosynthesis and the food production function of plants. They must abandon their assumptions about the metabolic similarities between plants and humans and restructure their thinking about the nature of food (focusing on the scientific definition of food as potential energy for metabolism).

Unless misconceptions are corrected, they are likely to persist and distort new learning. Unfortunately, neither curriculum writers nor teachers typically are very aware of common misconceptions that students are likely to harbor about scientific content, so that the instruction they provide usually fails to confront these misconceptions directly. Often, it is presented in such general or imprecise terms that students can interpret the new input as consistent with their existing misconceptions (Anderson & Smith, 1987).

For example, Smith and Anderson (1984) found that less than a quarter of students had dropped misconceptions about plants as producers of food and acquired the correct scientific conceptions following a unit of instruction on photosynthesis. Analyses of the instruction documented ways in which students' misconceptions affected their interpretations of what they were learning.

One crucial experiment involved growing plants in the light and in the dark. To set the stage for an explanation of photosynthesis, students were to observe that the plants in the dark would begin to grow at first but then wilt. The scientific explanation for this is that the plants in the dark die because they cannot engage in photosynthesis without light, and photosynthesis is their only source of food once food stored in their seeds is used up. However, the students' misconceptions caused them to interpret the experiment differently. Because they assumed that plants take in water, minerals, and other "food" from the soil, they saw no connection between the experimental findings and the question of where plants get their food. They got the point that plants need light in order to stay green and healthy (for reasons that they were not very clear about), but they missed the point that the plants were dying of starvation because they could no longer produce food through the photosynthesis process (which requires sunlight).

None of the teachers was very successful in getting students to abandon their misconceptions in favor of scientific conceptions. *Activity-driven teachers* focused on the activities to be carried out (textbook assignments, demonstrations, experiments, etc.). They seemed to think that students would learn automatically if they engaged in these activities. However, the teachers often unknowingly modified or deleted crucial aspects of the program in ways that made it difficult if not impossible for the students to discover the intended concepts.

Didactic teachers presented information directly to students and regarded the text as a repository of knowledge to be taught. They did not seem to be aware of student misconceptions and thus did not see a need to be certain that the students had interpreted the information as intended. Also, because they did not question students in ways that would allow them to express their own thinking, these teachers denied themselves the opportunity to become aware of students' misconceptions.

Discovery-oriented teachers tried to avoid telling answers to their students and instead encouraged them to develop their own ideas about the results of the plant-growing experiment. These teachers did not realize that the program they were using, although described as a discovery program, calls for direct instruction concerning certain concepts, including photosynthesis. Also, rather than question students in ways that would challenge their misconceptions

and lead them to consider specific theoretical issues, these teachers merely invited students to interpret their own observations in their own ways. Unfortunately, most students used their *misconceptions* as the basis for interpreting the experiments.

All three types of teachers failed to develop understanding because they failed to surface and correct students' misconceptions. Posner and colleagues (1982) have suggested that four conditions must be satisfied if students are to be induced to change their understandings of key concepts: (1) dissatisfaction with existing concepts must be induced, (2) the new concepts must be intelligible, (3) the new concepts must be initially plausible, and (4) the new concepts must appear fruitful.

Anderson and Roth (1989) have developed a conceptual change teaching approach designed to accomplish these goals. Two general features of the approach are a curricular commitment to teaching limited content for understanding rather than to covering a wide range of content superficially, and recognition that teaching for conceptual change requires an array of strategies used flexibly in response to students' needs. These strategies all share an important characteristic, however: they engage students in conceptual change sense making by involving them in actively struggling with ideas rather than just witnessing the teacher's performance.

The process begins by adjusting the curriculum. In contrast to typical textbook treatments, Anderson and Roth's treatments omit much of the technical vocabulary and detail—all that can be omitted without sacrificing much explanatory power. Their materials on photosynthesis, for example, do not present the scientific formula for photosynthesis or discuss the role of chlorophyll, because these are not seen as crucial elements for developing understanding of the process. Instead, the materials are developed around the central problem of "food" for plants: What is food for plants and how is it similar to and different from food for people and animals? The unit begins by asking students to define food—and food for plants—and to respond to a problem. This provides the teacher with information about students' conceptions and makes the students more aware of these conceptions.

Next, students are given explanations about different ways of defining food, including the scientific definition of food as energy-containing matter. Then the students are asked to address questions that give them a chance to use this new definition of food to explain everyday phenomena. (Is water food? Juice? Vitamin pills? Can you live on vitamin pills alone? Why or why not?)

Throughout the unit, students use this definition of food to analyze experimental observations of plants, think about similarities and differences between plants and animals, distinguish materials taken into plants from materials made by the plants during photosynthesis, and distinguish between energy-containing and non-energy-containing materials that people consume. These activities encourage students to make connections between their own ideas and scientific concepts, as well as to use their newly structured conceptions to make predictions and to develop more satisfying explanations of familiar everyday phenomena.

Anderson and Roth speak of creating **learning communities,** *classrooms in which teacher and students work together to develop and use scientific knowledge.* Learning communities differ from classrooms in which the teacher supervises students who work individually and often compete with one another. When operating most successfully, these learning communities feature three kinds of activities.

First, the teacher establishes problems that engage students in scientific thinking. Instruction begins with questions that elicit students' reasoning about the topics they will be studying. This activates prior knowledge and

helps make the students aware of its limitations, provides diagnostic information to the teacher, and engages the teacher and students in dialogue about commonly understood issues. In the photosynthesis unit, for example, students are asked at the outset to: (1) write their ideas about how plants get food, (2) write their ideas about what kind of food plants use, and (3) draw pictures on a diagram of a plant to show how they think food moves inside the plant. At the end of the unit, the students reread what they had written and describe how their ideas have changed.

A second feature is modeling and coaching through scaffolded tasks and dialogue. The teacher models by showing how scientific knowledge can be used to solve problems, then provides problem-solving opportunities. The students' initial attempts are scaffolded through simplification or clarification of tasks and through classroom dialogues in which teacher and students listen carefully and respond to one another, sometimes critically but in ways that reflect respectful attention to the speaker's ideas. In the photosynthesis unit, students are asked at several points to answer questions that require them to make predictions and explanations about plants. Scaffolding is provided via reminders of key ideas that need to be kept in mind or provision of chart outlines to help students make key comparisons (e.g., between food for plants and food for people).

The third feature is student work that leads to independent use of scientific knowledge and integration with scientific ideas developed in other contexts. As students develop expertise, they are encouraged to work more independently to describe, explain, make predictions about, or exert control over scientific phenomena in everyday life.

The work of Anderson and Roth (1989) is representative of recent trends in science education that place greater emphasis on eliciting students' prior knowledge (including misconceptions) when introducing topics, then developing the topics through social constructivist teaching. A great deal has been learned about the kinds of misconceptions that students develop in various areas of science (Glynn, Yeany, & Britton, 1991; Novak, 1987) and about addressing these through conceptual-change teaching (Roth, 1990) and project-based learning (Blumenfeld et al., 1991). For information about programs and techniques that have been used at various elementary and secondary grade levels, see Driver (1987), Duschl (1990), Hand and Treagust (1991), Minstrell (1989), Neale, Smith, and Johnson (1990), Palincsar, Anderson, and David, (1993), and White (1992).

social studies instruction

Newmann (1990, 1992) has conducted research on social studies teaching that is built around his conception of higher order thinking. He defines **higher-order thinking** as *challenging students to interpret, analyze, or manipulate information in response to a question or problem that cannot be resolved through routine application of previously learned knowledge*. In order to meet such higher-order thinking challenges successfully, students need a combination of in-depth knowledge of content, skills in processing information, and attitudes or dispositions of reflectiveness.

Instruction is organized to offer depth on a few related topics rather than breadth in covering a great many topics, and activities encourage students to go beyond gathering information in order to participate in disciplined inquiry by scrutinizing arguments for logical consistency, distinguishing between relevant and irrelevant information and between factual claims and value judgments, using metaphor and analogy to represent problems and solutions, developing and defending positions by referring to relevant information, and making

reasoned decisions. These activities both develop and reflect a set of student dispositions that together constitute **thoughtfulness:** *a persistent desire that claims be supported by reasons (and that the reasons themselves be scrutinized), a tendency to be reflective by taking time to think problems through rather than acting impulsively or automatically accepting the views of others, a curiosity to explore new questions, and a flexibility to entertain alternative and original solutions to problems.*

teaching for thoughtfulness Newmann (1990, 1992) identified six key indicators of thoughtfulness observed in high school social studies classes:

1. Classroom interaction focuses on sustained examination of a few topics rather than superficial coverage of many.
2. Interactions are characterized by substantive coherence and continuity.
3. Students are given sufficient time to think before being required to answer questions.
4. The teacher presses students to clarify or justify their assertions, rather than accepting and reinforcing them indiscriminately.
5. The teacher models the characteristics of a thoughtful person (showing interest in students' ideas and their suggestions for solving problems, modeling problem-solving processes rather than just giving answers, acknowledging the difficulties involved in gaining a clear understanding of problematic topics).
6. Students generate original and unconventional ideas in the course of the interaction.

Thoughtfulness scores based on these scales distinguished classrooms that featured sustained and thoughtful teacher-student discourse from classrooms that featured lecture, recitation, and seat work, and those in which teachers emphasized discussion but did not foster much thoughtfulness because they skipped from topic to topic too quickly or accepted students' contributions uncritically. Other noteworthy findings were:

- Teachers with high thoughtfulness scores made writing assignments that required students to draw inferences, give reasons, integrate information from a number of sources, develop an idea or theme, or generate original responses.
- Thoughtfulness scores were unrelated to entry levels of achievement, indicating that teachers can structure thoughtful discourse with students at all ability levels.
- High-scoring teachers were more likely to mention critical thinking and problem solving as important goals.
- In talking about the satisfactions of teaching, high-scoring teachers mentioned evidence of good student thinking about the content, whereas low-scoring teachers talked about student interest or positive response to lessons (but without emphasizing good thinking).
- In talking about their goals for students, high-scoring teachers were more likely to mention long-range and far-reaching dispositional goals in addition to more immediate knowledge and skill goals.
- High-scoring teachers were more confident that they could influence the performance of below-average students.
- All teachers mentioned that students are likely to resist higher-order thinking tasks, but the high-scoring teachers nevertheless emphasized these tasks.
- All teachers felt pressure to cover more content, but high-scoring teachers experienced this primarily as external pressure and resisted it by emphasizing depth of topic development, whereas low-scoring teachers experienced it primarily as internal pressure and emphasized breadth of coverage.
- Students identified high-scoring teachers'

classes as more difficult and challenging, but also as more engaging and interesting.

Newmann's findings on teaching for thoughtfulness provide cause for optimism because they suggest that thoughtful, in-depth treatment that fosters higher-order thinking about social studies topics is feasible in most classrooms (not just those dominated by high achievers) and that teachers with the knowledge and determination to do so can overcome students' resistance to higher-order thinking activities and even bring the students to the point where they see such activities as more engaging and interesting than lower-order recitation and seat-work. Only limited research relevant to Newmann's work has been done at the elementary level, but Thornton and Wenger (1990) reported observing lessons that exhibited many of the characteristics of thoughtfulness described by Newmann, and Stodolsky (1988) reported that the quality of students' task engagement was higher during more cognitively complex activities than during lower-level activities.

Fraenkel (1992) drew on case studies of instruction in high school social studies classes, looking for factors associated with differences in effectiveness. Like Newmann (1990, 1992), Fraenkel found that the major factor determining the success of a class was the teacher, not student achievement levels, the subject matter, or other aspects. Impressive teachers were found in nonelite as well as in elite schools, and many of the teachers in the elite schools were not impressive.

The less effective teachers tended to present ideas ready-made rather than to ask students to develop ideas for themselves. They tended to talk *to* students rather than *with* them. They often did not seem to have a clear sense of where they were heading. They tended to engage students in busywork and to stress memorization and regurgitation of facts rather than understanding of ideas. These teachers often did not seem to like what they were doing, to like their students, or to be having much fun. Unsurprisingly, their students rarely were active learners and often were discipline problems.

In contrast, the more effective teachers often engaged students in discussions. When they did lecture, they combined lectures with use of the overhead or showing pictures, maps, or other visuals. Their questions tended to elicit genuine discussion and they often asked students to respond to one another's comments. Students often worked in pairs or small groups while the teacher circulated and interacted with them. They were often required to function as active learners by role playing or giving presentations in class. The teachers made a point of engaging students in activities to help them understand and require them to use the ideas they were learning.

In the process, these teachers appeared to like what they were doing, like their students, and like their subjects. They had high expectations for their students, emphasized depth over breadth of coverage, were able to explain things clearly using examples that related to the students' lives, had good wait times and were good listeners when students talked, demonstrated patience when students did not initially understand, varied their instructional approaches and types of activities, and displayed considerable command of their subject and ability to relate it to a variety of daily-life examples.

They were highly attuned to their students. They encouraged them to take public risks by contributing their opinions to discussions and publicly discussing their mistakes or confusions. Yet they were quick to notice indicators of confusion or anxiety and to react by providing additional explanations, alternative assignments, or other scaffolding. They emphasized bringing to light students' thought processes for public examination and discussion.

strategies for teaching for understanding, appreciation, and application of knowledge

For some time we have known that teachers who emphasize conceptual development in their instructional techniques are much more likely to promote student understanding than teachers who emphasize procedures and seat work (e.g., Good, Grouws, & Ebmeier, 1983). However, what is becoming clear is that designing academic tasks that encourage problem solving and pressing students for responses during dialogue that reflect their understanding are also important components of the process (Blumenfeld, 1992b; Brophy, 1992b).

Teaching well is difficult, especially if one aims high by teaching for understanding, appreciation, and application. It requires a good working knowledge of (1) the subject (including its purposes and goals, its most powerful ideas, and the ways in which these ideas are connected and applied), (2) students (their likely prior knowledge about the subject, including misconceptions, and what important knowledge and skills are within their current zones of proximal development), and (3) pedagogy (how to represent these aspects of the subject to the students and assist them in constructing new understandings). Development of this kind of expertise takes time, although researchers are beginning to learn more about it (Brophy, 1991a).

adapt plans to the teaching situation

The best teaching is adapted to the situation, including the instructional purposes and goals, the students, and the subject matter. For example, the techniques associated with the terms *active teaching, strategy instruction*, and *situated learning* are most relevant when the situation calls for presenting new information, modeling skills, or coaching students as they attempt to implement skills or procedures. In contrast, the techniques associated with terms such as *social constructivism* or *teaching for thoughtfulness* are most relevant when one wishes to develop understanding and appreciation of networks of knowledge through shared construction and negotiation of meanings and implications. A principle such as transferring responsibility for managing learning from the teacher to the students applies to all teaching situations, but figuring out exactly how to apply it (how much modeling, explanation, coaching, and other scaffolding to provide and how quickly to fade this support) takes experience with the content and the students. Even then, some trial and error may be required. What worked well with last year's class might not work well with this year's class.

Research findings sometimes reflect these complexities. Swing, Stoiber, and Peterson (1988) compared the effects of two contrasting interventions on fourth-grade students' mathematics achievement. In the "thinking skills" intervention, teachers learned how to teach the cognitive strategies of defining and describing, thinking of reasons, comparing, and summarizing. In the "learning time" intervention, teachers learned how to increase students' engagement and academic learning time. The researchers expected that the thinking skills intervention would produce better results than the learning time intervention, but the effects differed according to student achievement level. Higher-achieving classes did better with the thinking skills intervention but lower-achieving classes did better with the learning time intervention. Within the classes that received the thinking skills intervention, however, lower achievers benefited more than the higher achievers. Thus, the same treatment can have different effects on different types of students.

An approach that is well adapted to one situation might not work well in another. We noted earlier that reciprocal teaching has shown impressive results as a method of improving students' reading comprehension. However, two attempts to teach mathematical problem solving using reciprocal teaching strategies produced unsatisfactory results (Brown & Campione, 1990; Resnick, 1989). The reasons are not yet clear, but it is obvious that the reciprocal teaching method is well adapted to teaching reading comprehension but not to teaching mathematical problem solving.

Similarly, the Kamehameha Early Education Project (KEEP) that had been developed for teaching native Hawaiian children had to be adjusted when it was implemented with Navajo children. Native Hawaiian children are accustomed to learning collaboratively through lively discussions and cooperative work on tasks, so the KEEP program built on these strengths by incorporating a great deal of discussion of reading selections during group lessons and cooperative learning in independent activity centers. However, Navajo children tend to talk less in groups and to be more independent in their patterns of task engagement, so the KEEP program elements that had been specifically incorporated for and worked well with native Hawaiian children did not work well with Navajo children (Tharp & Gallimore, 1988).

Rather than viewing these complexities in research findings simply as frustrations or even as failures, researchers and teachers need to appreciate them as indications of the complexities involved in adapting instruction to students and situations. Researchers are making progress in learning about these complexities and their potential implications for instruction, and they will continue to build on this knowledge base. Still, research-based information can only inform teachers about the trade-offs involved in decision alternatives; it cannot make those decisions for them.

Working within their district's guidelines, teachers must decide what goals to pursue with their students and what combinations of content representations, instructional methods, and learning activities will be most helpful in assisting their students to accomplish the goals.

To cope with these complexities and keep their curriculum and instruction well matched to each successive class of students, you need to be reflective about your practice and prepared to engage in diagnosis and experimentation when goals are not being met. Teacher colleagues can help one another here by meeting regularly to share insights, identify and generate possible solutions to common problems, and coordinate efforts to expand students' opportunities to assume responsibility for self-regulated learning.

Opportunities for this kind of collaborative learning among teachers have been increasing recently because social constructivism, situated learning, and related cognitive science notions have begun to be applied in teacher education. This work emphasizes that teachers bring beliefs, knowledge, and experience into their teacher education activities, although their knowledge is usually anchored in classroom events and based on stories or narratives in contrast to the abstract and propositional nature of research-based knowledge about teaching. Like your students, you may construct new knowledge through interaction with peers, applying ideas in practice, and reflecting on these experiences later in ways that lead to reconstruction of knowledge. This implies that teacher educators should emphasize the same principles for teaching for understanding and use of knowledge that are emphasized for use in K–12 classrooms. Thus, teacher education efforts would begin with your current beliefs and would include opportunities for you and your colleagues to analyze, discuss, evaluate and change your own practices, assume greater responsibility for your learning, and foster the development of your own articulated theories of education. Attempts to get inservice teachers to understand and adopt innovations would include attention to difficulties or challenges that might arise in implementing the innovations and to the contextual factors that constrain the teachers' options in particular teaching situations (Calderhead & Gates, 1993; Carter, 1990; Kagan, 1992; Krajcik et al., in press; Prawat, 1992; Richardson, 1990; Schon, 1987).

Eventually, research might point to one or more highly specific methods for accomplishing each of a great many highly specific objectives. So far, research has focused on the more general goals of teaching school subjects for understanding, appreciation, and application, and it indicates the value of the principles and techniques we have reviewed in Chapter 10 and in this chapter.

keep the goals in sight

To make good decisions about what to teach and how to teach it, you need to establish worthwhile goals and keep these goals in sight as you develop and implement your plans. This can be difficult, because as curriculum guidelines get translated into separate strands and then become segmented by grade level and by units within grades and lessons within units, the goals that are supposed to guide the entire process sometimes fade into the background, along with many of the originally recognized connections and intended life applications (Brophy & Alleman, 1993). For example, consider the following goals drawn from social studies:

- *Districtwide goal*: Prepare young people to become humane, rational, participating citizens in an increasingly interdependent world.

- *Program-area goal for social studies, K–12*: Enable students to appreciate that people living in different cultures are likely to share common values but also to hold different values that are rooted in experience and are legitimate in terms of their own cultures.
- *Grade-level goal for social studies, Grade 1*: To understand and appreciate that the roles and values of family members may differ according to the structure of the family, its circumstances, and its cultural setting.
- *Unit-level goal for social studies, Grade 1*: To understand that families differ in size and composition.

The last (unit-level) goal is phrased in purely descriptive, knowledge-level language, and it is trite for a unit goal even at the first-grade level. It makes no reference to the concepts concerning cultures and roles that are referred to in the higher-level goals, nor to the related values and dispositions (multicultural appreciation and citizen participation). Unless the teacher has a coherent view of the purposes and nature of social education, or unless the manual does an unusually good job of keeping the teacher aware of how particular lessons fit within the big picture, the result is likely to be a version of social studies that is long on isolated practice of facts and skills but short on integration and application of social learning.

Unfortunately, typical manuals do little or nothing to help teachers put these lower level goals into perspective as pieces of a larger plan to move students toward major goals. Often, in fact, the curriculum materials were not even developed to accomplish major goals systematically but instead only to cover long lists of disconnected knowledge topics and isolated skills. In this case, students might learn a few obvious generalities about families (they differ in size and composition, they grow and change, and their members work and play together), but not much about variations in family roles across time and culture, the reasons for these variations, or the lifestyle trade-offs that they offer. This will not do much to advance students' knowledge of the human condition, help them put the familiar into broader perspective, or even stimulate their thinking about family as a concept.

To avoid such problems, you need to think through your goals, identifying the capabilities and dispositions that you want to develop in your students throughout the year as a whole and in each of their curriculum units. Then you can examine curriculum materials in the light of these goals. Taking the viewpoint of the students, you can first read the student text (not the teacher's manual, which contains more guidance and information) to see what information is included and emphasized and what information is not, noting places where additional structuring or input will be necessary to focus students' learning on important ideas. Then you can study the manual, assessing its suggested questions, activities, and evaluation devices to determine the degree to which they will be useful as tools for helping students accomplish their primary goals. To help your students focus on important aspects of the content, you may need to augment the text with additional input (or replace it with something else if necessary), skip pointless questions and activities, and substitute other questions and activities that support progress toward major goals.

Through such planning, you can overcome some of the limitations in materials featuring goals that are trite, content that is a parade of facts, and activities that are parades of skills exercises. Ideally, you can begin to teach for understanding, appreciation, and application to life outside school by developing a limited number of important ideas in depth, organizing the content into networks structured around these important ideas, teaching the ideas with an emphasis on their connections, and asking questions and making comments that produce reflective discourse that focuses on these key ideas. You can also engage students in activities that provide opportunities for authentic applications of what they are learning, and evaluate the learning using measures that feature authentic tasks and assess accomplishment of major goals (Shepardson, 1993).

summary

Students who learn content with understanding not only learn the content itself but appreciate the reasons for learning it and retain it in a form that makes it usable when needed. Informed by constructivist notions of learning, recent research on teaching has focused on how exemplary teachers teach school subjects for understanding, appreciation, and authentic application of what is being learned. Key principles that have emerged from this research include the following:

1. The curriculum is designed to equip students with knowledge, skills, values, and dispositions that they will find useful both inside and outside school.
2. Instructional goals emphasize developing student expertise within an application context and with emphasis on conceptual understanding of knowledge and self-regulated application of skills.
3. The curriculum balances breadth with depth by addressing limited content but developing this content sufficiently to foster conceptual understanding.
4. The content is organized around a limited set of powerful ideas (basic understandings and principles).
5. The teacher's role is not just to present information but also to scaffold and respond to students' learning efforts.

6. The students' role is not just to absorb or copy input but also to actively make sense and construct meaning.
7. Students' prior knowledge about the topic is elicited and used as a starting place for instruction, which builds on accurate prior knowledge and stimulates conceptual change if necessary.
8. Activities and assignments feature tasks that call for problem solving or critical thinking, not just memory or reproduction.
9. Higher-order thinking skills are not taught as a separate skills curriculum. Instead, they are developed in the process of teaching subject-matter knowledge within application contexts that call for students to relate what they are learning to their lives outside of school by thinking critically or creatively about it or by using it to solve problems or make decisions.
10. The teacher creates a social environment in the classroom that could be described as a learning community featuring discourse or dialogue that is designed to promote understanding.

Examples drawn from recent research illustrate how these principles have been applied in teaching reading, writing, mathematics, science, and social studies. Reading instruction focused on genuine literature rather than artificially constructed basal reader stories, and activities focused on constructing interpretations of connected text rather than practicing skills in isolation. Several programs focused on making students more aware of their reading strategies and able to use them more systematically. Writing instruction focused on teaching students to use writing for organizing and communicating their thinking to particular audiences and for particular purposes. Writing skills were taught as strategies for accomplishing these goals rather than as ends in themselves. Mathematics instruction featured reflective problem solving and sustained discussion designed to develop understanding of the mathematical relationships involved, rather than rote mastery of mathematical facts and procedures. Science instruction involved engaging students in reflectively discussing or experimenting with scientific applications. Anderson and Roth's work illustrated the conceptual change approach that involves not only building on students' accurate entering knowledge but also calling attention to students' misconceptions and helping them to restructure their knowledge accordingly. Social studies instruction focused on sustained and reflective discussion that produced higher-order thinking about important themes and issues, rather than a parade-of-facts approach that emphasized breadth of coverage over depth of development of understanding of powerful ideas.

The best teaching is adapted to the situation, including the instructional purposes and goals, the students, and the subject matter. In order to make good decisions about what to teach and how to teach it, teachers need to establish worthwhile goals and keep these goals in sight as they develop and implement their plans.

questions for reflection

1. Much of the research reviewed in this chapter was conducted by scholars who believe that standardized achievement tests are incomplete or even inappropriate as measures of student learning. To find out what you think about this, obtain samples of standardized achievement tests to study and discuss with peers. What do you see as their strengths and weaknesses as measures of learning outcomes? What does this imply about the strengths and weaknesses of the research reviewed in Chapter 10?

2. Some educators think that there are important differences between active teaching as described in Chapter 10 and helping students to construct usable knowledge as described in this chapter. Others believe that the former is subsumed within the latter and that the differences are more in underlying philosophy than in what is done in the classroom. Discuss this with peers and see if you come to agreement on implications for classroom teaching.

3. Examine K–12 textbooks that you use now or may use later. Do they present networks of connected knowledge structured around powerful ideas, or just parades of disconnected facts? What does this suggest about your use of such texts with students?

4. Learning with understanding is usually described as a process of relating new content to one's existing prior knowledge. But what if students are so unfamiliar with certain content that they possess no readily available schemas within which to assimilate it and very little useful prior knowledge to bring to bear? Is it possible to develop their understanding of such content? If so, can it be done through social constructivist methods or will it be necessary to begin by providing information through texts, teacher explanations, or other input sources? Using a realistic example from your current or future teaching, plan how you would introduce and develop a topic for which students had little or no prior knowledge.

5. How might you determine your students' zones of proximal development with respect to a particular curriculum unit or topic? What does this imply about forms of preinstructional assessment of student knowledge and thinking that you might incorporate into your teaching?

6. For each subject that you teach or plan to teach, establish a file of authentic activities and assignments that will allow your students to use what they are learning in the process of conducting inquiry, solving problems, or making decisions. Be prepared to use these activities and assignments in place of those supplied with or suggested in the manuals that accompany your curriculum materials, whenever the latter activities or assignments are not worth using.

7. How does ideal scaffolding of students' learning efforts differ from forms of teacher assistance that are less desirable?

8. Define *conceptual change teaching* in your own words. Why is more time for instruction not always effective?

9. What is the difference between teaching "main idea" as a concept and teaching about how identifying and focusing on main ideas can be a useful strategy for guiding one's efforts to learn with understanding? What does this imply about your teaching about main idea (regardless of whether or not you teach reading to your students)?

10. What is meant by the phrase "writing to learn"? What does this imply about the kinds of writing assignments you should use?

11. We suggested that there might be limits on the degree to which one could emphasize authentic applications over skills practice without experiencing reductions in skills development. What might these limits be? In the subjects that you teach, are there certain things that simply must be memorized or practiced repeatedly? If so, why?

12. The discovery-oriented teachers studied by Smith and Anderson (1984) used methods similar in many ways to those advocated by social constructivists. However, they did not get positive results. What were some crucial differences between these teachers and teachers who use social constructivist methods to teach for understanding?

13. Can you relate the goals and objectives of each of your lessons and activities to larger purposes and goals? Can you see how each lesson or activity contributes to the long-run development of knowledge, skills, values, and dispositions that school subjects are ostensibly designed to develop? Test yourself by selecting a few lessons and activities at random and seeing if you can explain to others' satisfaction why they are needed in the curriculum. If you have trouble doing this, you may need to think through larger purposes and goals and keep them in mind as you develop your teaching plans.

cases to consider

oh, shut up! Mr. Moderator likes to include a lot of discussion in his social studies classes. He particularly likes to pose some problem, invite student opinions on how it might be solved, and then assess these suggestions in discussions in which students respond to one another as well as to him. This approach has worked successfully in the past. Even though some students participated more than others, there was wide participation and students found the discussions stimulating and educational.

This year, though, the discussions have increasingly been dominated by two students who enjoy hearing themselves talk and arguing with each other. This makes for useful interchange at times, but often the two of them seem to be arguing just for the sake of arguing, and both Mr. Moderator and the rest of the class are getting tired of listening to them day after day. What can Mr. Moderator do about this? List possible options and order them in terms of their probable effectiveness in solving the problem.

curricular dilemmas and teaching anxieties Eager to apply principles for teaching school subjects for understanding and use of knowledge, the fifth-grade teachers at Sycamore school undertake a major collaborative revision of their practice. Roland Alfonso takes major responsibility for math, Marcia Griffiths for science, and Judy Mowatt for social studies. The teachers streamline and reorganize each curriculum by identifying main ideas to develop in depth, organizing supporting content into networks structured around these main ideas, and eliminating other content. They also look for opportunities to integrate skills being developed in the language arts curriculum into their revised mathematics, science, and social studies curricula. After several rounds of consultation and revision, they have plans that they believe will be feasible given the prevailing constraints and yet much more powerful in producing student understanding and use of knowledge than their previous curricula were. Their excitement is tinged by anxieties, however. They have dropped many concepts and skills, and have deemphasized others. What will happen to them if students' parents or teachers at the junior high school start to complain? Will Principal Marley follow through on his commitment to protect them from attacks and help them convince skeptics that these changes are actually improvements?

The teachers' anxieties increase once they begin to implement the new curricula during the early weeks of the new school year. Students seem confused by many of the changes—restless to move on to new topics, hesitant about breaking away from familiar recitation patterns in order to take the risks involved in engaging in genuine discussion, and conflicted about the shift in emphasis from solitary seat work to collaborative inquiry and problem solving. Some have asked, "Why don't you just tell us what we need to know?" or requested a return to textbook-based worksheets. Many of the more capable and autonomous students seem to be flourishing under the new approach, but many of the low achievers seem to be more anxious and teacher-dependent than ever.

Think about this case and discuss it with your peers, addressing the following issues: (1) Do these teachers' experiences represent expectable and manageable problems, or have they attempted an overly wrenching adjustment that will probably fail? (2) Is there anything that the principal or teachers might have done to ease the adjustment? (3) How might the teachers assess their content inclusion/exclusion decisions to provide a basis for making further adjustments in the following years? (4) Assuming that their new approach is sound, what might the teachers do to help their students adjust to it more successfully? (5) What if the students gradually catch on and the new approach appears to be working very well as the school year progresses, but the emphasis on depth reduces breadth of coverage even more than anticipated (e.g., the social studies plans called for covering U.S. history through World War II, but no teacher gets further than the Civil War)?

chapter 12.

skills for learning: systematic studying, problem solving, and critical thinking

objectives

When you have mastered the material in this chapter you will be able to

1. Explain why teachers should stimulate students to develop metacognitive awareness of their learning in addition to the learning itself

2. Define the five types of learning strategies identified by Weinstein and Mayer— rehearsal, elaboration, organizational, comprehension monitoring, and affective

3. Explain and use the SQ3R method for effective studying

4. Explain and use deep-level processing and elaboration strategies for successful studying

5. Explain and use principles for effective note taking

6. Describe commonly encountered text patterns that can be used as bases for organizing notes

7. State methods of helping students become strategic learners by studying effectively

8. Define key concepts associated with the information processing approach to human problem solving (well- versus ill-structured problems, algorithms, heuristics, task environment, problem space)

9. Describe the techniques typically used by expert problem solvers for representing and solving problems, and explain the implications of this information for teaching students to solve problems effectively

10. Explain Ohlsson's enaction theory of human thinking and its implications for teaching thinking skills to students

11. Describe the approaches taken in programs designed to teach general thinking skills (*Philosophy for Children,* the *CoRT Program,* and the *Instrumental Enrichment Program*)

generic thinking and learning skills

In previous chapters we noted that there are no easy shortcuts to expert functioning because the transfer value of particular learning is limited and a great deal of domain-specific knowledge must be accumulated before a novice can become an expert. Nevertheless, certain relatively generic skills facilitate learning in a broad range of situations: thinking critically and creatively, solving problems, making decisions, and listening, reading, and studying with conscious awareness of one's goals and control of one's strategies. Many students develop these generic skills in the process of learning and applying domain-specific knowledge, but many do not.

Some educational psychologists believe that school curricula should include instruction in generic thinking and learning skills, at least for students who do not develop them spontaneously. They offer three main arguments in support of their position. First, it is clear that not all students develop well-functioning, higher-order thinking skills in the process of studying traditionally taught subjects. Proponents of generic skills instruction argue that these stu-

dents need more direct instruction in and systematic practice of these skills if they are to develop them at all. Second, Beyer (1987) noted that questions, writing assignments, and other activities traditionally used for teaching subject matter provide occasions for practicing thinking skills but do not usually include direct instruction in these skills. He argued that the only way to ensure that such skills are learned systematically is to include them in the curriculum by allocating time for their instruction and assessing its effects. Third, Adams (1989) noted that there is a double-edged sword quality to the fact that domain-specific knowledge tends to be embedded within schemas that apply to particular situations. She argued that the same learning and memory factors that make "situated cognition" easy to access in familiar application situations also make it more difficult to access in other potential application situations that are not recognized as such. In other words, while it is true that thinking skills can be learned as abstract formulas that learners are unable to apply in particular situations, it is also true that the skills can be learned in ways that are too situation bound to allow for transfer.

Thus, although there is disagreement about how to do so most effectively, there is agreement that higher order thinking skills need to be developed in ways that will enable learners to access and use them in a broad range of application situations. Along with this emphasis on teaching for *transfer,* there is an emphasis in teaching students to use these thinking skills with **metacognitive awareness**—*conscious selection of appropriate strategies, monitoring of their effectiveness, and correcting errors or shifting to new strategies if necessary.* Children trained to monitor their problem solving are more successful than children who receive training in the same strategies but not in the process of maintaining metacognitive awareness of their use of those strategies (Delclos & Harrington, 1991; Sawyer, Graham, & Harris, 1992). One study even found that children's metacognitive knowledge about problem solving was more important than their general aptitudes in determining their problem-solving performance (Swanson, 1990).

the value of metacognitive awareness and deep processing

Learning with metacognitive awareness is fostered when the skills are taught as strategies to be accessed and used to accomplish clearly understood goals. When such instruction focuses on the skills, it teaches not just mastery of the processes or steps involved in performing a skill but also knowledge of when and why the skill is used. In particular application situations, the teacher's structuring and scaffolding of the activity helps students to remain aware of their goals and strategy decisions. To the extent needed, such structuring and scaffolding might include pre-activity instructions that emphasize the purposes and goals of the activity, questions or cues offered during the activity that help students keep aware of the processes they are using in responding to it, and post-activity debriefing sessions that focus on analyzing and appreciating what has been accomplished (Brophy & Alleman, 1991; Jones & Idol, 1990; Jones et al., 1987; Rosenshine & Guenther, 1992).

Metacognitive awareness and control of thinking and learning strategies develop slowly over time and with considerable individual differences. For example, most college students recognize that different reading and study situations make different demands on the reader. When asked by Lorch, Lorch, and Klusewitz (1993) to compare school reading with personal choice reading, college students rated school reading as involving less enjoyment, emotion, and interest; slower reading; more thinking, memorization, and self-testing of understanding; less anticipation of what is ahead in the text; more use of headings, summaries, and other learning supports built into the text; greater concentration but also greater distractibility; reading of more of the text; less visualization; more attempts to interrelate text information; more critical analysis of the content; more rereading and attention to both major points and details; more attempts to relate the material to background knowledge; and more attempts to apply the reading to specific tasks or problems. The length of this list suggests that college students have developed considerable knowledge about the differences in strategies that are appropriate for personal choice reading versus school reading.

However, the results of an exercise reported by Derry (1988-1989) suggest that relatively few college students can apply such knowledge efficiently when under pressure to do so. Derry began her course in educational and cognitive psychology with the following simulation exercise:

You are a high school student who has

arrived at school twenty minutes early. You discover that your first-period teacher is planning to give a test covering Chapter 5. Unfortunately, you have prepared the wrong chapter, and there is no one around to help you out. Skipping class is not the solution, since this results in an automatic "F," and you would never dream of cheating. So you open your book and use the next fifteen minutes as wisely as you can. (Derry, 1988–89, p. 4)

Derry next distributed the text of "Chapter 5" and gave the students fifteen minutes to study, then administered a quiz on the material. Following the quiz, she asked them to write in detail exactly what they did when they studied. She found that few students performed well on this test. Those who did reported using study strategies such as reading the chapter summary first, skimming for main ideas, and paying attention to headings. In contrast, most students reported only vague and inefficient study strategies, such as starting at the beginning of the chapter and reading as much as they could until time ran out. Also, whereas the successful learners assessed the learning situation calmly and developed a workable plan for dealing with it, the less successful learners often were occupied with worries (about lack of time, about whether the quiz would count toward their grade, etc.) instead of strategic planning.

VanRossum and Schenk (1984) reported similar findings. They had students take a pretest, then read a 400-line historical passage while having the opportunity to study it and make notes, and then take a posttest and answer questions about how they studied. About half of the students were **surface-level processors**—*they tried to memorize the material so as to be able to reproduce it.* The other half were **deeper-level processors** *who tried to understand the material, develop insights, and think about how it would be used.* For example, one student first skimmed

the text to get an overview of the content, then read more slowly with attention to the connections within and between paragraphs, and then tried to summarize the main lines of information and argument without looking at the text.

When questioned about their conception of the learning process, thirty-three of the fifty-five surface-level studiers described learning as memorizing content, trying to increase knowledge, or trying to acquire facts to be retained or used in practice. Only two described learning as the construction of meaning or as an interpretive process aimed at developing understanding. In contrast, twenty-three of the thirty-four deeper-level studiers emphasized the latter definitions of learning. The surface-level studiers were less likely to report enjoying reading the text and were more nervous in testing situations. (Benjamin et al., 1981, also found that highly anxious students tend to rely excessively on repetition and rote memorization rather than use more effective study strategies.)

Evaluation data revealed no difference in responses to factual knowledge questions, but a superior performance by the deeper-level studiers on "insight" questions. The free-response answers of the surface-level studiers were merely lists of facts with few connections between them, but those of the deeper-level processors usually were more coherent, containing main ideas linked to supportive material presented in logical lines of argument toward conclusions.

learning strategies and skills

We noted in Chapter 11 that efficient reading with comprehension is strategic: it involves allocation of attention and use of strategies to understand the meaning of what is being read and to remember it for future reference. Specifically, **strategic reading** involves *attending* *to the purposes of the reading, activating relevant schemas and background knowledge, concentrating on major points, evaluating the content for internal consistency and compatibility with prior knowledge, monitoring ongoing comprehension through periodic review and self-questioning, and testing inferences by making interpretations, predictions, and conclusions* (Paris, Wasik, & Turner, 1991). Students who do not develop such strategies for efficient reading and studying will need instruction in them. Consequently, in addition to becoming a strategic reader and studier yourself, it will be important for you to teach your students to do so, using methods appropriate to their ages and developmental levels (Pearson & Dole, 1987).

A great many learning and study strategies have been identified by various investigators. Weinstein and Mayer (1986) identified five general types:

Rehearsal strategies involve *actively repeating (saying, writing) material or focusing on key parts of it.* Examples include repeating key terms aloud, copying the material, taking verbatim notes, and underlining important parts.

Elaboration strategies involve *making connections between the new and the familiar.* Examples include paraphrasing, summarizing, creating analogies, taking notes that go beyond verbatim repetition to extend or comment on the material, answering questions (either adjunct questions already included with the text or self-generated questions), and describing how the new information relates to existing knowledge.

Organizational strategies *involve imposing structure on the material by dividing it into parts and identifying superordinate-subordinate relationships.* Examples include outlining the text, creating a hierarchy or network of concepts, and creating diagrams showing their relationships.

Comprehension monitoring strategies involve *remaining aware of what one is trying to accomplish, keeping track of the strategies one uses and the success achieved with them, and adjusting behavior accordingly.* Examples include using prequestions or statements of objectives to guide study, establishing subgoals and assessing progress in meeting them, self-questioning to check understanding, and modifying strategies if necessary.

Affective strategies include establishing and maintaining motivation, focusing attention, maintaining concentration, managing performance anxiety, and managing time effectively.

We will discuss some of these generic learning strategies and related cognitive skills as they apply to studying, problem solving, and thinking. Much has been learned about effective study strategies and about how to teach these strategies to students who have not developed them spontaneously. Most of this work has roots in the SQ3R method (Robinson, 1970).

SQ3R method

SQ3R is *an acronym that stands for the five steps in the SQ3R method: survey, question, read, recite, and review.*

1. Skim or *survey* the passage: Read the title and any introductory material to learn what the passage is about, note its length and organization to identify the author's general approach, and preview any pictures, charts, or illustrations.

2. *Question* yourself by identifying information that you want or are likely to get from reading the passage. The headings are useful in identifying such questions. On encountering the previous heading, for example, you might have asked yourself, "What are the steps in the SQ3R method?"

3. *Read* the material, paying attention to introductory paragraphs and main ideas, rereading difficult passages and looking up

unfamiliar words if necessary, and trying to understand and respond to the author's arguments.

4. *Recite* or *recall* the material. Close the book and try to answer in your own words the questions you raised earlier and to state the author's purpose and main ideas.

5. *Review.* Concentrate on passages that you find difficult or have not yet fixed in your mind, and on remembering the main ideas and the linkages between them.

The SQ3R method appears to be worth adopting as a systematic "deep-level processing" approach to studying (Darch, Carnine, & Kameenui, 1986). Also useful is the related PQ4R method for systematically studying texts: *p*review, *q*uestion, *r*ead, *r*eflect, *r*ecite, and *r*eview. The added reflection step involves relating the new material to your prior knowledge and noting its key features. For more information about SQ3R, PQ4R, and related methods, see Devine (1987) or Hayes (1992).

elaboration strategies

Weinstein (1982) trained ninth graders in *elaboration strategies* to use during study: generating verbal or imaginal elaborators to make material more meaningful, creating analogies to express new material in more familiar terms, drawing implications, and creating relationships through elaborative paraphrasing (relating the material to what is already known while also restating it in one's own words). Students trained to apply these strategies to school tasks produced better test performance than students who practiced the same tasks but did not receive the training in elaboration strategies.

Subsequent work by Weinstein has involved training college students to use these strategies in their studies. Derry (1988-89), King (1992a,b), Kourilsky and Wittrock (1992), and others have also developed meth-

ods for training students to learn more effectively from lectures or texts by using summarizing, self-questioning, schema building, and other elaboration strategies. Chi et al. (1989) showed that when studying examples of worked mechanics problems, successful students elaborated on the examples by relating them to the principles presented in the texts and by explaining each step to themselves in their own words. Less successful students failed to elaborate on the examples by generating self-explanations. Ward and Sweller (1990) showed that learning efforts in these situations can be scaffolded by providing students with carefully selected worked examples that direct their attention to key features and reduce cognitive load on working memory. Even when such support is provided, however, students who elaborate on the examples by generating self-explanations are likely to learn more than those who do not.

notetaking

To retain material for future use, it usually is necessary not only to study it in an active, systematic way, but also to take notes or in some other way preserve key ideas in a form that makes them easy to refer to later (Kiewra & Benton, 1988). Devine (1987) discussed underlining, marginal notes, summarizing, and outlining as common forms of notetaking.

Underlining and related forms of highlighting important material are among the study techniques used most by college students (Policastro, 1975). Underlining appears to be less effective than other notetaking techniques, however, because it is comparatively passive and it psychologically defers the active learning process to some future time. Also, many students use it ineffectively because they underline too much or underline before they have absorbed enough of the material to know which parts are most important. Thus, underlining

Notetaking can be done cooperatively as well as alone. Small group discussions also provide opportunity for peers to share and receive feedback on their ideas.

may be most useful if done only after reading through the material the first time.

Devine (1987) suggested supplementing underlining with marginal comments or coding systems. *Marginal comments* include questions, rephrasings of difficult sentences, and definitions of unfamiliar words. *Coding systems* include color coding (using markers) to indicate main ideas and separate them from supporting evidence, circles around new terms, arrows indicating relationships between ideas, boxes to contain related ideas, marginal numbers to indicate sequential patterns, stars to indicate important ideas, or question marks to indicate disagreement with the author. Marginal comments or coding systems involve the reader more actively in the author's presentations than mere underlining does.

These methods can only be used, however, by students who own the books and are willing to write in them. Other students will have to rely on outlining, summarizing, and other forms of notetaking. Students who learn to take notes systematically will be more successful than those who take notes haphazardly (Carrier & Titus, 1981; Kiewra et al., 1991; Ladas, 1980).

Notetaking in the form of written *summaries* is likely to facilitate learning (Doctorow,

Wittrock, & Marks, 1978; Taylor, 1982; Brown, Campione, & Day, 1981). Good summaries condense the material and focus on the important ideas.

Brown and Day (1980, cited in Armbruster & Brown, 1984) identified six rules essential to effective summarizing: (1) delete trivial material; (2) delete redundant material; (3) substitute a superordinate term for a list of subordinate items when possible; (4) substitute a superordinate event for a list of subordinate actions when possible; (5) select a topic sentence if the author has provided one; and (6) write your own topic sentence if necessary.

Simply telling students these rules was sufficient to improve performance for some. Others needed training in strategies: delete redundant information with red pencil, delete trivial information with a blue pencil, write in superordinates for any lists, underline topic sentences if provided, write topic sentences where needed. Students who practiced these strategies and also checked their performance using a checklist gained the most.

In addition to summarizing, guidelines have been developed for other forms of *notetaking*. Carrier and Titus (1981) suggested the following principles for taking notes during lectures: (1) distinguish between superordinate and subordinate information; (2) abbreviate words; (3) paraphrase in your own words; and (4) use an outline format. Notes that both condense the material and represent a conceptual gathering of main ideas or an integration of new with old information are more effective than verbatim notes or simple paraphrased lists of information (Kiewra, 1987). Notes that elaborate or process information at a deeper level are more effective than simple recording (Shimmerlick & Nolan, 1976), although verbatim copying and rote studying may be more effective for students who are so anxious as to be unable to use elaborative or deeper level processing strategies efficiently (Biggs, 1978).

using text patterns to organize notes

In taking notes from well-organized text, the author's own structuring (headings, subheads, etc.) can often be used effectively to organize notes in *outline* form. It also helps to be aware of *text structures* (organizing schemas) used in expository writing. Devine (1987), for example, identified six such structures: (1) *generalization supported by examples*; (2) *sequence* (e.g., history or narrative fiction material organized in time sequence); (3) *enumeration* (of lists of items); (4) *cause and effect*; (5) *comparison and contrast*; and (6) *question and answer* (the author poses a question and then offers answers to it).

Similarly, Meyer (1981) identified the following structures in a passage about supertankers: (1) *covariance* (lack of power and steering in supertankers leads to oil spills); (2) *comparison* (ground stations for supertankers are like control towers for aircraft); (3) *collection* (three ways to improve supertanker safety are training of officers, building safer ships, and installing ground control systems); (4) *description* (oil spills kill wildlife, as indicated by the deaths of 200,000 seabirds); and (5) *response* (a solution to the spill problem is to improve supertanker safety).

Using these text structures when taking notes and studying can improve comprehension (Armbruster, Anderson, & Ostertag, 1987; Mayer, 1984; Weinstein & Mayer, 1986). For example, Cook (1982) trained college students to recognize five structures in science texts: (1) *generalization* (explains, clarifies, or extends a main idea); (2) *enumeration* (lists); (3) *sequence* (describes a connected series of events or steps in a process); (4) *classification* (groups material into categories or classes); and (5) *compare/contrast* (examines relationship between two or more things). Students taught to recognize these text structures and outline their notes accordingly outperformed control students who were not given this training. Similarly, Benton et al. (1993) found that notes organized in a matrix form were more valuable than notes organized in an outline form when students were preparing to write compare-and-contrast essays.

comprehensive training programs

Several investigators have developed comprehensive programs for training students (especially college students) in learning strategies and study skills (O'Neil, 1978; O'Neil & Spielberger, 1979; Dansereau, 1983; Weinstein & Underwood, 1983; McCombs, 1984; Novak & Gowin, 1984). For example, Dansereau and his colleagues (Dansereau, 1983; Dansereau et al., 1979) developed a program that features two primary strategies elaborated by several substrategies and backed by several support strategies. The primary strategy designed to help learners comprehend and retain material is known as first-degree MURDER: Set the mood to study; read for understanding (mark important and difficult ideas); recall the material without referring to the text; correct the recall by amplifying and storing the material in order to digest it; expand knowledge through self-inquiry (asking and answering questions); and *review* mistakes (by learning from tests).

These first-degree MURDER strategies are elaborated through substrategies. Students are taught to paraphrase material in their own words and generate imagery to help them retain it, to identify key ideas, and to note the linkages between these ideas using a notetaking strategy known as *networking*. Networking involves using codes and symbols to underscore the following six types of linkages: (1) *part link* (e.g., the process of wound healing has three parts: the lag phase, the fibroplasia phase, and the construction phase); (2) *type link* (two types of wound are open and closed); (3) *leads to link* (the growth of a scab leads to a scar); (4) *analogy link* (a scab is like a protective bandage); (5) *characteristic link* (an open wound involves a break in the skin); and (6) *evidence link* (an X-ray test can reveal that a bone is broken).

Once basic comprehension has been accomplished using first-degree MURDER, learners prepare to recall and use the information when it will be needed (when taking a test or on the job) by invoking the second primary strategy known as second-degree MURDER: set the *m*ood, *u*nderstand the requirements of the task; *r*ecall the main ideas relevant to task requirements (using means-ends analysis and planning); *d*etail the main ideas with specific information; *e*xpand the information into an outline; and *r*eview the adequacy of the final response.

Training in these primary strategies is backed by training in support strategies such as goal setting and scheduling, managing concentration, combating anxiety, monitoring comprehension, and responding to confusion or mistakes. Students trained in these learning strategies tend to outperform other students, especially on essay questions. The strategies are especially effective with low achievers and highly anxious students. McCombs (1984) also emphasizes both cognitive and motivational aspects of learning in her program.

helping students become strategic learners

Besides teaching learning strategies and study skills, you can stimulate their use by building them into activities. In preparing students for a seat-work assignment, you can instruct them to skim the material to get an overview and note questions that they want to answer before reading the material word for word. You can also provide advance organizers or study guides that call attention to key ideas and structural elements, list key terms and provide definitions or instruct the students to look them up, and encourage students to pay attention to the author's apparent purpose and degree of success in achieving it (Devine, 1987; Thomas & Rohwer, 1993).

Providing students with partial outlines or skeletal notes to fill in while listening to a presentation or reading an assignment is particularly helpful (Kiewra, 1987). It is also helpful to see that students know how to use a textbook: help them to appreciate the information contained in the title page and preface, the index, the table of contents, the glossary, and the various structuring elements (headings, highlighting, marginal notes) and illustrations (graphs, charts, picture captions). In general, help them to appreciate that learning involves actively making sense of material and organizing it for retention and future use, and that this can be accomplished using strategies that are usually more effective than the rote learning strategies that many of them rely on.

problem-solving strategies

Students need to learn to solve problems effectively—not just in mathematics, but in any subject. A **problem** *exists where a person perceives* *a need to achieve some goal but does not immediately know how to achieve it.*

Problems differ in degree of structure (Fredericksen, 1984; Simon, 1979). *Well-structured problems* present both a clearly defined goal and all of the information needed to solve the problem using appropriate *algorithms* (fixed rules or procedures that guarantee correct answers if followed precisely, such as the rules for whole-number addition). In contrast, *ill-structured problems* are more difficult to define, let alone solve. The person is aware that a problem exists but may not be clear about what information will be needed to solve it, where this information can be obtained, or how to apply it. There may not even be a single correct answer.

Ill-structured problems must be attacked using **heuristics**—*general rules of thumb and procedural guidelines for processing information and solving problems,* such as identifying what information is given and what is needed. Heuristics do not guarantee solutions the way algorithms do, but they are applicable to a broader range of problems and allow people to discover solutions for themselves. Thus, well-structured homework problems in mathematics or science are solved using algorithms based on algebraic operations or Ohm's law, but ill-structured problems such as predicting changes in market conditions or discovering cures for diseases require heuristics.

Educational psychologists have long debated the possibilities for teaching people to solve problems effectively. Pessimists are impressed by limitations on transfer effects and the need for broad experience and development of a deep fund of domain-specific knowledge in the process of moving from novice to expert status. They believe that problem solving cannot be taught directly (although students will benefit from frequent opportunities to develop their problem solving skills through practice). Optimists believe that problem solving skills can be developed directly by teaching students

effective problem solving heuristics. So far, data appear to support the optimists by showing the teachability of specific skills for use in specific situations, but to support the pessimists by showing only limited transfer effects.

early views of problem solving

Wallas (1921) described four stages in the discovery process, reminiscent of Köhler's earlier descriptions of the discovery behavior of chimpanzees: (1) *preparation* (learning about the problem and about information that might be useful in solving it); (2) *incubation* (reflection, analysis, generation of hypotheses, and other thinking about the problem (some of which may be unconscious or may occur during sleep); (3) *illumination* (the "Aha!" experience when one suddenly becomes aware of a likely solution); and (4) *verification* (testing the proposed solution).

These discovery stages were merely descriptive, but they formed the basis for later prescriptive writings. For example, Polya (1957) offered the following guidelines for problem solving in a famous book entitled *How to Solve It:*

1. *Understand the problem.* Identify what information is given or known, and what is required.
2. *Devise a plan.* Look for connections between the given information and the unknown. Does the information fit a general principle or algorithm? Is the problem analogous to a more familiar problem that might provide guidelines for solving it?
3. *Carry out the plan.* Once a plan has been formulated, carry it out, checking to make sure that each step is included and done correctly.
4. *Look back.* Make sure that the obtained result solves the problem and squares with

all of the information given. If so, review the result itself and your method of obtaining it for information that may be useful in solving future problems.

John Dewey (1910) was among the first to suggest steps for effective problem solving:

1. *Presentation of the problem*: Become aware of the problem, or be made aware of it.
2. *Definition of the problem*: Define the problem by identifying the present state and the desired goal state, and consider the implications for solution. Sometimes a problem can be defined in different ways, with different solution implications.
3. *Development of hypotheses*: Given the problem definition, generate hypotheses for solving it.
4. *Testing of hypotheses*: Identify the advantages and disadvantages associated with each proposed solution.
5. *Selection of the best hypothesis*: Identify the solution that offers the most advantages and fewest disadvantages.

These early approaches contain good advice and are still influential today. Many modern programs for teaching people to solve problems in everyday living follow the steps first proposed by Dewey. So do many authors' suggestions to students. Clifford (1981), for example, suggested teaching students the following rules for problem solving: (1) Clearly define the problem and state the goal, (2) Formulate possible solutions, (3) Order the proposed solutions in terms of their potential, (4) Try each one in turn until the solution is found, (5) Critically evaluate the results of each solution tried, (6) Decide how the process and the product might be used to work out other problems. Similarly, Bransford and Stein (1985) described the IDEAL method of problem solving: *i*dentify the problem, *d*efine it, *e*xplore possible strategies for solving it, *a*ct on those strategies, and *l*ook at the effects of your efforts.

contemporary cognitive views of problem solving

Contemporary views of problem solving reflect recent research on human information processing, especially research comparing novice with expert problem solvers (Mayer, 1983; Tuma & Reif, 1980). For example, Chi, Feltovich, and Glaser (1981) asked expert physicists and novice physics students to sort a variety of mechanics problems into categories and explain their reasoning. Novices placed problems into the same category because they mentioned the same objects (such as pulleys or inclined planes) or the same physics concepts (such as friction). Experts, however, grouped problems because they involved the same general principle (such as conservation of energy), even though such principles usually were not mentioned explicitly. Similar findings were reported in mathematics by Schoenfeld and Herrmann (1982) and Silver (1979).

These differences in perception and organization of knowledge are paralleled by differences in thinking and problem solving. Novices tend to focus on specific features of problems and try to link them to specific information stored in memory, whereas experts tend to get the "big picture" by identifying problems as particular instances of the application of general principles and then solving them by activating associated schemas (Chi & Glaser, 1985; Gagné, 1985). Confronted with a mathematics or physics problem, for example, novice students will try to relate it to a memorized theorem, equation, or formula. This approach often leads to errors, and even when it leads to the correct answer, the novices may not really understand what they have done or why. In contrast, experts first read and think about the problem as a whole to identify its general nature and the principles that apply to it and only then begin to make calculations. They can bring to bear much more domain-specific knowledge, and this knowledge

In algebra, where Mager (1981) identified over 100 basic problem types, pattern recognition is a particularly useful problem-solving strategy.

is much better organized to allow smooth movement between levels ranging from concrete particulars to abstract generalities.

Recent research indicates that expert problem solvers do not proceed in the manner implied by Dewey's stages (in particular, they do not generate a large number of hypotheses and then test each one). Instead, they conceptualize the problem by identifying key features and relating them to background knowledge, and then identify only one or just a few promising hypotheses for testing. Physicians diagnosing medical problems, for example, do not begin by listing every conceivable source of the symptoms. Instead, they ask questions designed to quickly narrow the search to a few probable diagnoses, and then pursue these (Elstein, Shulman, & Sprafka, 1978). When used by experts with sufficient experience and domain-specific knowledge, this approach is much quicker than the classical approach, because it minimizes the time spent (and usually wasted) checking out low-probability hypotheses.

Newell and Simon (1972) described expert problem solvers as relying on heuristics to cut down complex problems to workable size. They differentiated between the task environment and the problem space. The **task environment** is *the large structure of facts, concepts, and their interrelationships within which the problem is embedded.* The **problem space** is *the problem solver's mental representation of that task environment.* The problem space must simplify the task environment enough to allow the person to address the problem within the limits of working memory, and yet be an accurate enough representation to foster effective problem-solving efforts.

The key to the success of this method is accurate representation of the problem in the first place. If key features of the problem are recognized accurately and related to appropriate background knowledge or problem solving schemas, the result is likely to be a quick and successful solution. However, if the problem is represented inappropriately, the resulting solution efforts will fail, and the person will have to begin all over again. In well-structured problems, accurate representation may be followed by activation of algorithms that lead directly to solution. In ill-structured problems, the person may have to rely on heuristics such as reasoning by analogy from more familiar problems, working on subparts before dealing with the whole, working backwards from proposed solutions, or testing the most promising hypotheses first (Newell & Simon, 1972; Polya, 1957; Simon, 1980).

Cyert (1980) suggested the following heuristics (drawn from the work of Rubenstein, 1975): (1) Keep the big picture in mind without getting lost in details, (2) Avoid committing yourself too early to a single hypothesis, (3) Create models to simplify the problem using words, images, symbols, or equations, (4) Try to change the representation of the problem if the present one is not working, (5) Use the information to generate questions to ask yourself, (6) Be willing to question the credibility of your premises, (7) Try working backwards from possible solutions, (8) Keep track of partial solutions that you may eventually be able to combine, (9) Use analogies and metaphors, (10) Talk about the problem.

Books and courses on problem solving (Bransford & Stein, 1985; Hayes, 1989; Neimark, 1987; Newell & Simon, 1972; Polya, 1957; Rubenstein, 1975; Whimbey & Lochhead, 1991) provide instruction in such heuristics and opportunities to practice them on "brain teasers" as well as on academic problems. These sources can increase your effectiveness as a problem solver by teaching you to use heuristic strategies systematically and with metcognitive awareness, although they cannot short-circuit your need for experience and domain-specific knowledge.

One approach that may accelerate development from novice to expert status within particular domains is training in *pattern recognition* as it applies to problem solving. In algebra, for example, Mayer (1981) has identified more than 100 basic problem types. Each category of problem (such as "motion problem") is represented by different subtypes (such as "overtake," "closure," "round-trip," and "speed change"). Similarly, Greeno and his colleagues (Greeno,

1980; Riley, Greeno, & Heller, 1982) have identified three types of algebra word problems: *cause/change problems* (Joe has three marbles, Tom gives him five more. How many marbles does Joe have now?); *combination problems* (Joe has three marbles. Tom has five marbles. How many do they have altogether?); and *comparison problems* (Joe has three marbles. Tom has five more marbles than Joe. How many marbles does Tom have?). Teaching students to recognize such *problem types* increases their ability to represent problems correctly and to link them to appropriate schemas and algorithms (Fennema, Carpenter, & Peterson, 1989; Mayer, 1985).

Other work in mathematics is designed to reduce novicelike reliance on formulas applied without genuine understanding and to increase expertlike concentration on representing the problem accurately before proceeding. One method is to give students *numberless problems* requiring them to conceptualize the problems and state the strategies that would be used to solve them, but without performing any actual calculations (Good & Grouws, 1979). For example, students might be asked, "You know the dimensions of a room that you want to paint, the cost of paint per gallon, and the square feet a gallon of paint will cover. How would you determine the approximate cost of the paint needed for the job?"

Bloom and Broder (1950) reported success with *strategy training* in mathematics problem solving for college students who were scoring poorly on examinations. The students were asked to think aloud and pay attention to their own problem-solving processes as they worked through problems, and then to compare these with the processes revealed in transcripts taken from students who solved the problems more effectively, stating in their own words the differences between the model's strategy and their own. This training increased the students' problem-solving confidence and performance. Schoenfeld (1979) reported similar success from training students in strategies for responding to algebra problems (draw a diagram, try to establish subgoals, consider similar problems with fewer variables, etc.).

strategies for teaching problem solving

To the extent that you expect your students to be able to apply what they are learning, you will need to provide them not only with frequent opportunities to solve problems, but also with instruction in problem-solving processes. This instruction should include heuristics such as reading the problem carefully and paraphrasing it into one's own words, identifying the information that is given and the information that must be determined, separating relevant from irrelevant information, representing the problem clearly, and sketching a general plan of attack before trying to plug in formulas or perform calculations. Students should also be taught to develop a workable problem space by dividing the problem into subproblems, reasoning by analogy from more familiar problems, working backward from possible solutions, or substituting specific examples for abstract symbols. Such instruction should include first-person modeling with thinking aloud in addition to typical lecturing, and should proceed to coaching, guided practice, student reflection on and assessment of strategies, and other activities designed to increase students' metacognitive awareness of the processes involved in solving problems successfully.

teaching thinking skills

Instruction in reading comprehension, study skills, or problem-solving strategies will tend to develop students' thinking skills (or at least to stimulate a more thoughtful approach to learning). The most direct approach, however, is to teach students key elements of the thinking process itself. The classical approach to training the mind to think called for curricular emphasis on subjects such as Latin, philosophy, mathematics, and science. Thorndike (1924) showed long ago that this approach does not yield generalized improvements in mental functioning, but it continues to be emphasized even today. A more focused variation of this same general approach is to emphasize instruction in *thinking skills* and *tools for developing knowledge.*

One approach to the teaching of thinking skills is course work in **logic**—*the use of formal rules of inference to develop conclusions from established premises.* Courses in logic teach students to deduce implications and evaluate whether conclusions follow from the premises. For example, given the premises that animals require food and that dogs are animals, it is logical to deduce that dogs require food, but not to deduce that all animals are dogs.

A related form of instruction is training in **critical-thinking skills,** *skills evaluating the credibility of information and deciding what to think or do by reasoning from the best available evidence. Critical-thinking skills* include assessing the validity of authors' premises and the soundness of their logic in developing conclusions; identifying their purposes in writing the material (distinguishing attempts to be objective from attempts to sway the reader toward particular conclusions); distinguishing relevant from irrelevant information; recognizing bias, slanted language, and rhetorical devices that appeal to emotion rather than to evidence; and distinguishing fact from opinion (Beyer, 1987; Ennis, 1987; Halpern, 1989).

Instruction in *tools for developing knowledge* usually emphasizes training in scientific methods. The emphasis here is on scientific rules of inference, and especially on the logic involved in stating questions as formal hypotheses that can be tested experimentally.

Ohlsson (1983) criticized these approaches as being limited to what he called the **deduction theory** that *views thinking as systematic application of logical rules of inference.* Ohlsson argued that human thinking is better represented by the **enaction theory** that *views thinking as mental simulation of real-world actions.* Instead of using purely verbal methods to draw verbally phrased conclusions from verbally phrased premises, Ohlsson argued, we work with multi-sensory models of what we think about, and with mental representations of concrete actions that could be performed. For example, liquids could be poured, subdivided, or boiled, and algebraic expressions could be rearranged, simplified, or converted into other expressions. Ohlsson suggested that our conceptions of the world are more similar to pictures, sculptures, holograms, toy trains, chemical formulas, musical scores, diagrams, or paintings than they are to verbal texts, and that thinking proceeds by application of operators to these mental models under the guidance of heuristics.

This implies that traditional approaches to teaching thinking skills will not generalize well because they do not include sufficient attention to the procedural knowledge and heuristics involved in deciding when and why to use a particular procedure. Even if we understand what a theorem says and why it is true, this knowledge is not sufficient to enable us to know when and how to use the theorem. To teach students to think, Ohlsson argued, teachers should emphasize the processes involved in acquiring and applying disciplinary knowledge. Each field would be thought of as being about the kinds of *change* that apply to its subject matter, rather than as a static collection of information. For example, instead of just teaching geographical facts about mountains, continents, forests, and climates, social studies teachers might emphasize mountain formation and erosion, continental drift, deforestation, and changes in average world temperature, and

might frequently ask students to predict future situations from current trends or to speculate about what would happen to the ecosystem as a whole if an important change were introduced into one part of it.

programs for teaching thinking skills

Instead of designing ways to build more emphasis on thinking into instruction in traditional subjects, some authors have developed programs designed to develop students' generic thinking skills. Some of these programs teach cognitive skills such as Piagetian conservation or the skills stressed by IQ tests (Detterman & Sternberg, 1982). Others teach students to think critically and creatively. Three of the more comprehensive "thinking" curricula are Philosophy for Children, the CoRT program, and the Instrumental Enrichment program.

philosophy for children Lipman and his colleagues (Lipman, 1985; Lipman, Sharp, & Oscanyan, 1980) have developed the *Philosophy for Children* program to introduce preschool and elementary school children to principles of logic and formal inquiry. Using fictional passages and questions about philosophical issues as the bases for initiating group discussion, teachers induce their students to function as a "community of inquiry" concerning concepts such as fairness, friendship, and truth. The children learn to use language to reason—to assume, suppose, compare, infer, contrast or judge, induce or deduce, classify, describe, explain, define, and inquire. In the process, they learn to recognize and assess chains of logic, deal with syllogisms, recognize fallacies, and develop logical reasoning and critical thinking skills. The Philosophy for Children program has achieved impressive evaluation results, relative to those reported for other generic thinking skills programs (Adams,

1989; Presseisen, 1988). Information about this program can be found in issues of the journal *Thinking: Journal of Philosophy for Children.*

the CoRT program DeBono (1985) has developed the CoRT program (CoRT is an acronym that stands for Cognitive Research Trust, an organization located in Cambridge, England). The CoRT program consists of sixty lessons on thinking intended for 9- to 11-year-olds, although it has been used with younger and older students. It focuses on thinking skills that will help students to function better in their lives outside of school. Consequently, its content avoids both specific school subjects and relatively impractical puzzles and games, and concentrates on life events such as deciding on a career, how to spend a vacation, moving to a new house, or changing jobs. Instruction focuses on the processes of thinking and decision making.

For example, the first lesson teaches a scanning tool known as PMI. The teacher invites the students to consider the merits of some idea (e.g., basic foods should be supplied free to everyone) by thinking about its implications and categorizing them into three sets labeled "*p*lus" (desirable implications), "*m*inus" (undesirable implications), and "*i*nteresting (neither good nor bad but interesting and worth noting). PMI helps students to clarify their thinking about the issue, and to state the reasons underlying the decisions they make.

The PMI exercise is the first of the sixty CoRT lessons. As the program progresses, additional tools for thinking and decision making are added, and students are encouraged to use them for thinking about real life decisions. The CoRT program has been criticized on the grounds that its curriculum is limited to variations of brainstorming and its effectiveness claims are based on unsupported assertions and testimonials rather than convincing systematic research (Halpern, 1993).

the instrumental enrichment program Feuerstein and his colleagues (Feuerstein et al.,

1980; Feuerstein et al., 1985) have developed the *Instrumental Enrichment* program for students aged nine or older. The program was originally developed as a special education tool for use with disadvantaged students or students suffering from cognitive deficiencies or learning disabilities. Its goal was to change the cognitive structures of these students and transform them into autonomous independent thinkers capable of initiating and elaborating ideas. As the program developed, it began to be used with normal students as well.

The program encourages cognitive activities such as perceptual organization of information, problem representation, planning, goal analysis, and restructuring of problems when existing plans are not working. It uses a series of progressively more demanding paper-and-pencil exercises that encourage learners to discover relationships, rules, principles, operations, and strategies. The tasks were designed on the basis of analyses of the processes involved in mental activities. Many resemble tasks used in psychometric tests and laboratory learning experiments. There are some puzzles and brainteasers as well, but in general the program is seen as a bridge between approaches based on thinking within curriculum content domains and approaches that try to develop thinking through content-free exercises.

The exercises range from simple recognition tasks to complex activities involving classification, seeing analogies, and seriation, and they make use of a variety of modalities including numerical, spatial, pictorial, and verbal. Each operation is considered to have input, elaboration, and output phases, and assessment focuses on identifying the phase that is responsible for failure when failure occurs.

The Instrumental Enrichment program requires extensive teacher training and two to three years of work (five hours per week) by students. Evaluations have shown some promising effects on low-IQ students, but data are limited and mostly inconclusive. The program failed to produce significant benefits in an evaluation study conducted in England (Blagg, 1991), but a reviewer concluded that this study was too flawed to allow confident conclusions and that the Instrumental Enrichment program has yet to be evaluated properly (Haywood, 1992).

strategies for teaching thinking skills

Thinking-skills programs are one response to the criticism that schooling concentrates too much on specific information and not enough on higher-level processes and applications. You may wish to investigate them and incorporate them into your teaching. Bear in mind, however, that despite the enthusiasm with which these programs have been received by some educators, their efficacy remains to be demonstrated. Enthusiastic testimonials abound, but few systematic data exist, and these suggest only limited effects (Adams, 1989; Chance, 1986; Idol, Jones, & Mayer, 1991; Nickerson, Perkins, & Smith, 1985; Presseisen, 1988; Sternberg & Bhana, 1986). Also, even when programs are successful in developing general thinking skills, they do not eliminate the need for broad experience and domain-specific knowledge for functioning as an expert in any particular area of application (Glaser, 1984; Klein & Hoffman, 1993; Resnick, 1987; Sternberg, 1987).

summary

This chapter concerns relatively generic learning skills—systematic studying, problem solving, and critical thinking. Weinstein and Mayer (1986) identified five general types of learning strategies: rehearsal strategies, elaboration strategies, organizational strategies, comprehension-monitoring strategies, and affective strategies.

Researchers studying learning strategies and study skills have found that some students are surface-level processors who rely primarily on rote learning, whereas more successful students are deeper-level processors who try to understand what they are learning, develop insights, and think about how to use it. Methods have been developed for teaching students to use deeper-level strategies. Many of these are variations of SQ3R (survey, question, read, recite, review). Others are built around elaboration strategies through which learners generate analogies, imagery, or other linkages relating the new to the familiar.

Teaching students to take better notes is another common strategy. Notes that use an outline format, retain key structuring elements, and summarize or paraphrase main ideas in the learner's own words tend to be more effective than merely underlining or taking less complete and organized notes. Calling students' attention to the structuring patterns used to organize presentations will help them to take organized notes.

Comprehensive training programs such as Dansereau's MURDER provide students with systematic training in learning strategies and study skills. The chapter suggests ways that teachers can help their students to study effectively by providing them with information and guidance.

Classical models viewed human problem solving as proceeding systematically from goals through the formation and testing of hypotheses to the development of conclusions. More recently, human information processing research has shown that many problems are ill-structured and thus not well suited to the classical approach, and that these are attacked with heuristics rather than systematic logic and algorithms. Experts cut a complex task environment down to a workable problem space by bringing to bear relevant schemas and prior knowledge to develop an accurate problem representation. When this occurs, solution typically follows quickly. In the absence of such expert knowledge, individuals must rely on heuristics such as working backward from proposed solutions, reasoning by analogy, or dividing the problem into subparts. Programs designed to develop problem-solving skills include instruction in such heuristics and in recognition of commonly encountered patterns of problems.

Traditional approaches to development of thinking skills feature units in logic and critical thinking. Ohlsson criticized these approaches as being limited to the deduction theory of human thinking, He argued for approaches representing the enaction theory—emphasis on procedural knowledge and heuristics in addition to figurative knowledge, and subject matter teaching that emphasizes producing and studying change rather than learning static collections of information. Others have developed comprehensive "thinking" curricula such as the Philosophy for Children program, the CoRT program, and the Instrumental Enrichment Program.

questions for reflection

1. Are you a strategic learner? Do you routinely use the five types of learning strategies described by Weinstein and Mayer (1986)? If not, what should you be doing that you are not doing now? Draw up a plan for change and use it to guide your studying in the future.

2. Think about the subject matter and grade level that you intend to teach. What strategies will you use to help students to learn strategically and with metacognitive awareness of what they are doing and why they are doing it?

3. Many teachers of social studies, mathematics, or science take the attitude that they will teach their subject matter and leave reading to the language arts teachers. However, many students in their classes have difficulty because their skills for learning from texts are not well developed. What, if anything, should such teachers do about this? Discuss this issue with classmates.

4. We discussed the value of noting the structures used to organize texts when studying or taking notes, and we gave examples of text structures commonly used in history and science texts. What structures are commonly used in the texts written for the grade level and subject matter that you intend to teach?

5. What kinds of notes do you take (underlining, outlining, summarizing)? Do you see ways to improve your note-taking abilities?

6. Given the grade level and subject matter that you intend to teach, do you expect your students to take notes when you make presentations to the class? If so, what instructions should you give them?

7. Do you believe that thinking and problem solving can be taught? Why or why not? Do you plan to teach thinking and problem solving yourself? If so, how?

8. Teaching has been described as an unusually complex task environment that requires the teacher to rely on heuristics to create a workable problem space for decision making. What

does this mean, and how does it apply to the statement that teaching is partly an art and partly an applied science?

9. If you were to apply Ohlsson's suggestion that instruction should concentrate on the kinds of change that apply to a particular subject matter, how would you teach your subject matter differently from the way it was taught to you?

---

cases to consider

preparing for a test Sue complains to her roommate Suzi, "I've got to do well on this test or I'm in trouble in the course. I really blew the first test." Suzi replies, "I wonder why that course gives you so much trouble. You get As in your other courses, even though you typically do nothing but go to class and then stay up all night before the exam to put it all together." Sue states with resignation, "All I know is that next week I had better do well or it's curtains." Then she adds with excitement, "You know, there is one thing about that course. We have to cover twice as much material as we do in any other course, and the instructor is really interested in the facts." How would you suggest that Sue prepare for the exam?

nobody ever explained it to me like that! Gregg is a bright teenager taking demanding advanced placement courses. He handles most assignments with ease, but has occasional difficulty with math problems. At these times, he comes to his father, an engineer, for help. In the past, the problem always involved mathematics that his father was familiar with, so he was able to help Gregg after studying the problem for a few minutes. Today, though, Gregg asks for help with a problem of a type that his father has never seen before. After realizing that he can't figure it out simply by studying it briefly, Gregg's father draws on his own problem-solving heuristics and begins to fire questions at Gregg. What does this term mean, and where is it explained in the book? Are there parts of the problem that Gregg recognizes and knows how to handle, and if so, which are the "extra" parts that are causing the difficulty? Has Gregg tried backtracking to the place in the book where this type of problem is introduced so as to review simpler versions?

Gregg is initially surprised and displeased. He expected an explanation of the problem, not suggestions about how he might solve it himself. Gregg's father is surprised and displeased too, because Gregg's responses to his questions don't go much beyond "I don't know" or "I never thought of that." Further questioning makes it clear that Gregg has been going through the book problem by problem without getting the big picture. He has never thought about the sequencing of the material, paid attention to the table of contents or the chapter outlines, or used the index. Nor has he fully appreciated the fact that curriculum strands are organized hierarchically and that exercises occur in an easy-to-difficult sequence, so that reviewing is wise when one is stuck on a problem.

As the reality of this sinks in, Gregg's father realizes that Gregg needs more than help with a particular problem—he needs to learn how to use a textbook and heuristics for problem solving in mathematics. If you were Gregg's father, how would you handle this situation in such a way as to widen Gregg's overly narrow concentration on getting an answer to this particular problem and help him to see that he could be using much more powerful and effective methods of studying?

part V.
motivation

Sandra *noticed her heart beating rapidly while she listened to a classmate make an extemporaneous speech. "Four more speakers, and then it's my turn," she moaned to herself. "Why do I get so nervous when I have to speak? I hate this class and this pressure!"*

Sam *flung the box against the wall. "Helen!" he screamed. "This space cruiser kit is driving me crazy! The directions say a child can assemble it in fifteen minutes, but I've been working on it for over an hour. Don't buy any more toys that need to be assembled on Christmas Eve!"*

Jane *confidently walked into the professor's office and sat down. "Jane," the professor said, "I've been pleased with your writing in this course. Your themes are interesting and you support your beliefs quite well." Jane smiled and said, "I'm glad to hear this. I've really worked on my writing until I was satisfied with my work. I'm glad your evaluation matched my own."*

Mr. Robbins *told his tenth-grade chemistry class, "This is a critical experiment. The procedures will be used often in the next three weeks. If there are any questions, ask them now." Although no student was certain of the process demonstrated and many were confused, none sought additional clarification.*

"Look, Sally, I know that Rick is going to raise hell with you, but we can make it worth your while to take the overseas job. After all, it's just two or three years. When you come back, you can expect a big promotion." Sally listed several personal objections, but after forty-five minutes of conversation, her supervisor said, "Sally, there's one thing I haven't told you: your salary would jump from $25,000 to $36,000." Within a few minutes, Sally agreed to the assignment.

these vignettes illustrate important themes in motivation. The first shows how anxiety can interfere with performance. Minor stress associated with wanting to do well is probably helpful, but too much stress undermines performance. The second vignette is central to classroom motivation. Many students learn to blame themselves when things go wrong, even though they may not be at fault. Frustration and failure in school can lead to self-castigation and eventually erode performance.

The third vignette depicts a student who is responding capably and with intrinsic motivation. She has defined the task and evaluated her performance. She is interested in feedback from others but is not overly dependent on their evaluation. Classroom teachers can help students develop such initiative and confidence.

The fourth vignette depicts a common situation in too many classrooms where students have learned that it is better to look good than to get information when they need it. The fifth vignette shows that external rewards can influence people to do things that they might not do otherwise.

In the three chapters that follow, we discuss theories of motivation and illustrate how they apply to classroom practice. Enhancing student motivation is not an easy task because students bring different levels of interest, energy, and ability to the classroom and thus vary widely in their responses to learning opportunities.

Chapter 13 presents and reviews some major distinctions and important motivational concepts and themes. It also presents an organizing framework for understanding classroom motivation: the expectancy x value model. Chapter 14 places special emphasis on the role of the teacher in increasing students' expectancies for success. Chapter 15 provides an extensive discussion of how teachers can help students to value learning. Emphasis is placed on helping students understand, integrate, and apply ideas—not memorize material.

All chapters in the motivation section stress the need for teachers to be decision makers and to tailor motivational strategies to individual students and to particular classroom social conditions.

chapter 13.

basic concepts of motivation

objectives

When you have mastered the material in this chapter, you will be able to

1. Define motivation from both the behavioristic and cognitive perspectives and be able to apply these situations to classroom settings
2. Understand how needs and drives develop and how their satisfaction affects students' motivation to learn
3. Understand how contrasting levels of achievement motivation develop and manifest themselves, and their applications for teaching
4. Be able to apply Maslow's need hierarchy to understanding student motivation in classroom settings
5. Understand the concept of attribution theory and apply it to classroom settings
6. Explain the concept of intrinsic motivation and its relationship to student effort and performance
7. Understand Corno and Rohrkemper's concept of self-regulated learning and be able to use this framework in designing classroom activities

In the past, the field of motivation and emotion was dominated by two theories—the classical Freudian and the classical behaviorist. The Freudian image of man was that of a creature driven by inherited, unconscious sexual and destructive instincts constantly seeking release in a frustrating social environment. The behaviorist view was that of a creature quietly metabolizing in the shade, occasionally goaded into action by the hot sun and the lure of a cold glass of beer. Man is not simply warding off noxious stimuli and seeking the peace of death or Nirvana. He actively interacts with the environment. He is curious, playful, and creative. He conceives great ideas, seeks meaning, and envisions new social goals (Murray, 1964, p. 119)

motivation: an evolving concept

Motivation is a *hypothetical construct used to explain the initiation, direction, intensity, and persistence of goal-directed behavior.* As Covington (1992) notes, motivation, like many concepts (e.g., gravity), is easier to describe in terms of physical characteristics than it is to define. As represented by the quote from Murray, early motivational theories depicted humans as driven by needs or manipulated by external reinforcers, but over the years theory and research on human motivation have increasingly emphasized cognitive factors. Modern conceptions of motivation recognize that motivation involves both cognition and emotion (Ames, 1992; Ames & Ames, 1984; Covington, 1992). They also recognize that similar behavior (e.g., effort) may be associated with notably different internal patterns of motivation (McCaslin, 1990). There is a growing interest in including goals and values as well as attributions in the study of motivation by examining how students think about themselves in relation to particular classroom tasks and to the process of learning. Further, modern theories of motivation have focused more on issues of persistence and volition (Corno, 1992, 1993). Finally, it is important to note that modern theories of motivation are sensitive to various individual differences and societal influences (e.g., gender, culture) and that motivation is specific to particular social or cultural contexts (Casanova, 1987).

Early work on motivation was not very useful to teachers because it involved animals. When work did focus on human motivation it tended to have limited value because it emphasized assessing individual motivational patterns and using them to predict individual differences (e.g., measures of achievement motivation as predictors of achievement-related behaviors). As we will see in this and the following chapters, there has been considerable progress in the last twenty or thirty years on general issues of motivation and especially on research on motivation in education.

Earlier work on motivation in education progressed from an emphasis on the individual to a focus on the class. More recent work has moved from studying the class to examining the school as the context for intervention and for creating a learning environment and a learning community (Ames & Stover, 1993; Blumenfeld, 1993; Buck & Green, 1993; Covington, Teel, & Parecki, 1993; Weinstein & Butterworth, 1993).

In this chapter we will discuss various motivational theories beginning with behavioral theories (seeing humans as driven primarily by needs) and turning progressively to theories that provide more recognition of cognitive factors.

Most theory and research on human motivation have been developed by psychologists working within one of three major theoretical frameworks: behaviorism, cognitive psychology, and humanism. Behaviorists believe that behavior is determined by reinforcement contingencies, so they seek to explain motivation by identifying cues that elicit behavior and reinforcement that sustains it. Cognitive psychologists believe that thought processes control behavior, so they focus on how people process information and interpret personal meanings in particular situations. Humanists also believe that people act on their environments and make choices about what to do, but they are more concerned with the general course of personal development, the actualization of potential, and the removal of obstacles to personal growth.

In this chapter we stress the cognitive approach. The humanistic perspective is presented briefly in Chapter 19. Most aspects of the behavioral approach have already been outlined in Chapter 6, but we summarize its motivational implications here.

behavioristic theory and motivation

Infants are born with primary biological drives such as hunger that motivate behavior. Certain behavior patterns become established through basic conditioning processes because they are associated with the satisfaction of primary drives. Through this association these behavior patterns eventually acquire motivating powers of their own and begin to function as secondary drives (such as dependence, social affiliation, or aggression), so that behavior that satisfies these secondary drives is reinforced and thus repeated (Mace, Belfiore, & Shea, 1989; Skinner, 1979). A history of consistent reinforcement produces strong response tendencies. Children who get attention and social rewards for clowning, for example, are likely to become "class clowns," even though better alternatives may be available to them. Different reinforcement histories lead to different interests and ultimately to different abilities. A person who is consistently rewarded for playing the piano and develops a strong interest in doing so will, in time, outperform others with similar talent that is not comparably reinforced.

Distinctions between behavioristic and cognitive approaches to motivation gradually have become blurred as behaviorists have expanded the list of potential secondary drives (e.g., curiosity, competence) and reinforcers (e.g., symbolic behavior in the form of internal statements such as "I was right! It works!"). In general, however, behaviorists place more emphasis on *external* rewards and the systematic arrangement of reinforcement contingencies, whereas cognitive theories focus on *internal* rewards and related cognitive processes (Stipek, 1993).

Bandura: a contemporary behaviorist

Albert Bandura's (1977, 1989) social learning theory is behavioristic in that it emphasizes the consequences of specific behavior, yet cognitive because it also considers how students interpret past events and set goals for themselves. According to Bandura, there are two major sources of motivation. One source involves *predicting outcomes* of behavior: "If I study hard, will I pass?" "Can I make the team?" "Will my speech be well received?" Based on consequences of past actions, the person tries to predict the consequences of contemplated actions. A second source of motivation is actively *setting goals* that become personal standards for evaluating performance. While working toward a goal, we imagine the positive things that will occur if we succeed and the negative things that will occur if we fail (Bandura, 1989; Schunk, 1989). We tend to continue our efforts until we meet the standards we have set. Upon reaching a goal, we are satisfied for a time but then begin to identify new goals or to set new (higher) standards for ourselves.

Bandura believes that **efficacy expectations**, *beliefs about one's ability to reach a goal,* determine how much effort one expends and how long one persists in the face of obstacles. The nature of the goal itself also influences behavior. Goals that are specific, moderately difficult, and seen as reachable in the not-too-distant future are most likely to stimulate persistent effort and to lead to increased efficacy expectations if reached successfully. Specific goals provide unambiguous standards for judging performance, and goals of moderate difficulty provide realistic challenges so that success in reaching them reinforces confidence in one's own abilities and thus increases efficacy perceptions.

need theories

Many of the earliest approaches to explaining human motivation were based on the concept of need. Need theories emphasize conditioning mechanisms similar to those stressed in behavioral theories, but they also include cognitive elements. Henry Murray and Abraham Maslow are two prominent need theorists.

Murray: social needs theory

Henry Murray (1938) defined need as a hypothetical construct that stands for a force that influences one's perception and behavior in the attempt to change an unsatisfying situation. A **need** is a *tension that leads one to pursue a goal, which if achieved will release the felt tension.*

A list of twenty social needs that Murray identified follows.*

1. Abasement—to surrender . . .
2. Achievement—to overcome obstacles . . .
3. Affiliation—to form friendships and associations . . .
4. Aggression—to assault or injure . . .
5. Autonomy—to resist influence on coercion . . .
6. Counteraction—proudly to refuse admission of defeat . . .
7. Deference—to admire and willingly follow . . .

---

* SOURCE: Adapted from *Explorations in Personality,* Henry A. Murray, Ed. Copyright ©1938 by Oxford University Press, renewed 1966 by Henry A. Murray.

research at work
applying Bandura's theory

Research indicates that getting students to set goals and make a commitment to try to reach those goals increases their performance (Bandura & Schunk, 1981; Tollefson et al., 1984). Goal setting is especially effective when the goals are (1) *proximal* rather than distal (they refer to performance on a task to be attempted here and now rather than to attainment of some ultimate goal in the distant future), (2) *specific* (complete a page of math problems with no more than one error) rather than global (do a good job), and (3) *challenging* (difficult but reachable) rather than too easy or too hard. Students may need help in formulating challenging but reachable goals that represent what they can expect to achieve if they consistently put forth reasonable effort. In the case of a long series of activities that ultimately leads to some distal goal, students need help in establishing specific goals for each of these activities and in understanding the connection between achieving intermediate goals and finally achieving the ultimate goal (Bandura & Schunk, 1981; Zimmerman & Schunk, 1989).

If goals are to be specific and obtainable for all students, different students need different goals. What is moderately difficult for one student may be very difficult for another. Besides assistance in learning to set goals, students may need help in learning to evaluate performance and to reinforce themselves for success. Teachers can provide such help through modeling, cuing, and reinforcing. ("That's a good list of goals to accomplish during study hall. Last week you were still trying to do too much. You should be able to complete all of these things today. Good planning.")

8. Defendance—to defend oneself against blame or belittlement . . .
9. Dominance—to influence or control others
10. Exhibition—to attract attention to one's person . . .
11. Harmavoidance—to avoid pain, physical injury . . .
12. Infavoidance—to avoid failure, shame, humiliation . . .
13. Nurturance—to nourish, aid or protect . . .
14. Order—to arrange, organize . . .
15. Play—to relax, amuse oneself . . .
16. Rejection—to snub, ignore or exlude . . .
17. Sentience—to seek and enjoy sensuous impressions . . .
18. Sex—to form and further an erotic relationship . . .
19. Succorance—to seek aid, protection or sympathy . . .
20. Understanding—to analyze experience . . .

These needs are learned through cultural experience and typically triggered by an effective **press** (*external determinant of behavior*). Together, need and press combine to form a **theme**, or *pattern, of behavior*. Murray suggested that needs become established by the frequent occurrence of a specific press. Children, for example, may develop the need to achieve if their parents begin to challenge them at an early age, expect them to meet these challenges, and reinforce their

Needs vary, so that no one classroom activity can satisfy the needs of all students simultaneously. However, teachers familiar with their students' needs can use this knowledge to motivate learning efforts. A student may be unmotivated to learn matrix arithmetic for several weeks, for example, but then develop a need for this skill in physics class and thus learn the necessary operations in a single week. Teachers can encourage this learning by involving students in meaningful or authentic tasks. The more they do so, the more likely the curriculum is to relate to students' basic needs.

Teachers need to think about ways to help students fulfill achievement needs, affiliation needs, and power needs. Some students may need more cognitively stimulating assignments, others may need more opportunities to work cooperatively with peers, and still others may need more opportunities to compete or to exercise autonomy. This implies that effective instruction requires varied organizational structures, lesson approaches, and incentives.

achievements. Children reared in different cultures or in contrasting social class settings within the same culture are exposed to different presses and thus come to school with different felt needs. For example, students from different cultures react differently toward emphasis on competition versus cooperation (Casanova, 1987; Garcia, 1991; Kagan & Knight, 1981).

Murray's view suggests that most behavior is motivated by the desire to avoid or release unpleasant tensions. Early experiences are seen as especially important because once a need is established, it tends to perpetuate itself. A child who is taught to compete, for example, may demonstrate competitiveness even in situations that do not call for it. Furthermore, behavior that reduces needs within a given context is likely to become habitual, so that it is easier to teach people new behavior in a new context than in a familiar one.

Murray's theory implies that teachers can have some effect on students' motivation, but that change gets more difficult as students get older. Unless the school effort is systematic and sustained, it is likely to have little permanent effect (as we shall see, other viewpoints are more hopeful). Few psychologists today believe that all human behavior is motivated by a need to avoid unpleasant tensions. Still, Murray was correct in noting that our needs often compel us to act in certain ways. We all know people who must achieve, compete, or dominate.

Maslow: hierarchy of needs

Abraham Maslow (1962) conceptualized a hierarchy of needs arranged in the following order of priority (see Figure 13.1):

1. Physiological needs (sleep, thirst)
2. Safety needs (freedom from danger, anxiety, or psychological threat)
3. Love needs (acceptance from parents, teachers, peers)
4. Esteem needs (mastery experiences, confidence in one's ability)

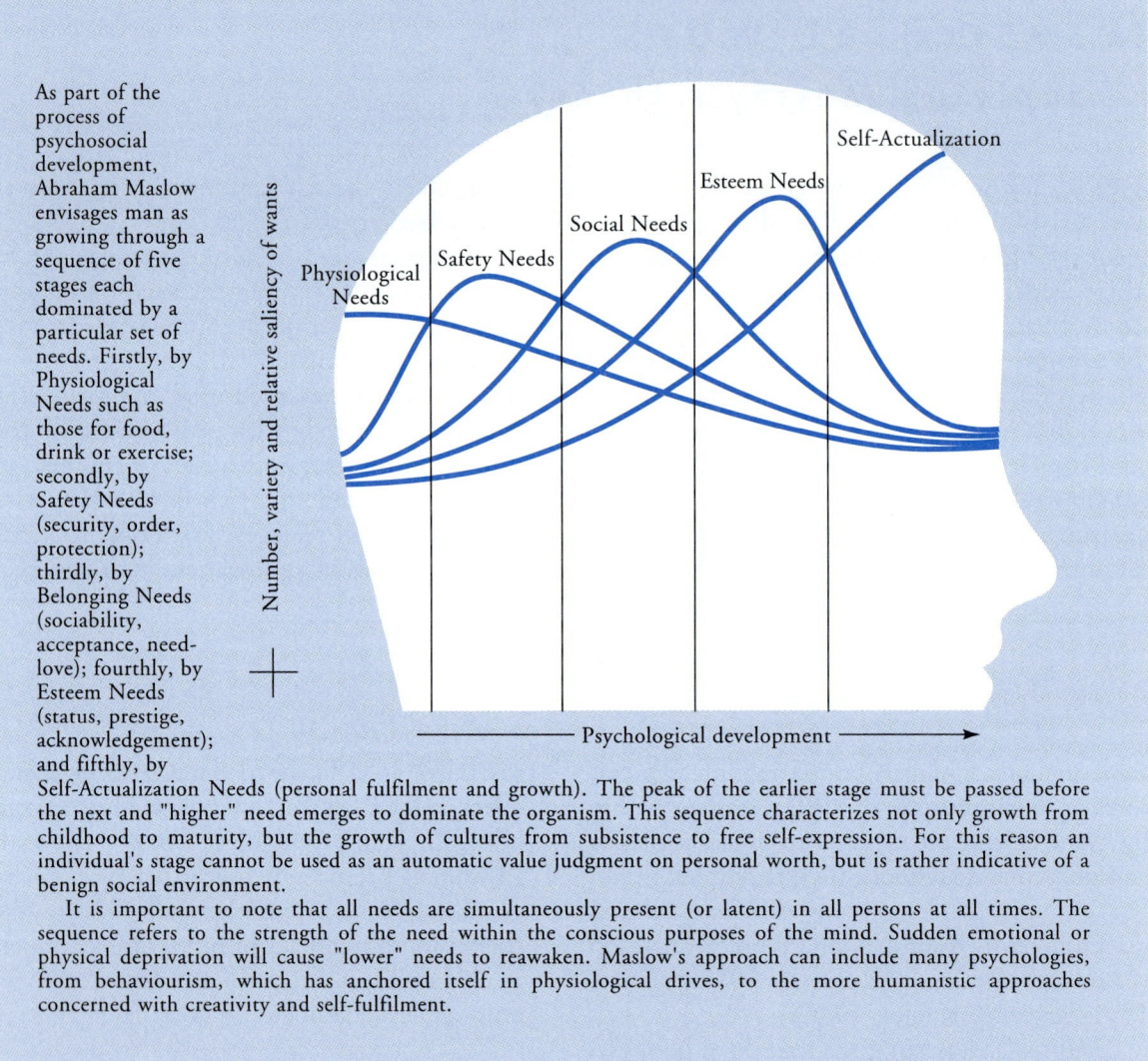

As part of the process of psychosocial development, Abraham Maslow envisages man as growing through a sequence of five stages each dominated by a particular set of needs. Firstly, by Physiological Needs such as those for food, drink or exercise; secondly, by Safety Needs (security, order, protection); thirdly, by Belonging Needs (sociability, acceptance, need-love); fourthly, by Esteem Needs (status, prestige, acknowledgement); and fifthly, by Self-Actualization Needs (personal fulfilment and growth). The peak of the earlier stage must be passed before the next and "higher" need emerges to dominate the organism. This sequence characterizes not only growth from childhood to maturity, but the growth of cultures from subsistence to free self-expression. For this reason an individual's stage cannot be used as an automatic value judgment on personal worth, but is rather indicative of a benign social environment.

It is important to note that all needs are simultaneously present (or latent) in all persons at all times. The sequence refers to the strength of the need within the conscious purposes of the mind. Sudden emotional or physical deprivation will cause "lower" needs to reawaken. Maslow's approach can include many psychologies, from behaviourism, which has anchored itself in physiological drives, to the more humanistic approaches concerned with creativity and self-fulfilment.

Figure 13.1 Abraham Maslow's hierarchy of needs

SOURCE: C. Hampden-Turner, *Maps of the Mind* (London: Mitchell Beazley Ltd., 1982). Reprinted by permission of the publisher.

5. Needs for self-actualization (creative self-expression, attempt to satisfy one's curiosity)

Maslow theorized that unless lower needs are satisfied, higher needs may not even be appreciated, let alone motivate behavior. The well-rested, psychologically secure student may seek to master academic skills and even generate questions to pursue independently, but the exhausted student has little energy for such activity.

Physiological needs are basic to survival, but once they are met, higher needs can take over. If both physiological and safety needs are satisfied, people can appreciate warm, interpersonal relationships, and love needs begin to motivate their behavior. Subsequently, they seek a stable and usually high evaluation of themselves and perhaps begin to pursue self-actualization needs.

research at work
applying Maslow's theory

Several implications of Maslow's theory are obvious. A student who comes to class hungry or tired is unlikely to become engrossed in academic activities. Similarly, students who have suffered humiliating failure will not become autonomous learners until they are convinced that the teacher will support their efforts and that they can make errors without being blamed or punished. Anxious students are likely to seek precise instruction and resist attempts to get them to take risks or make independent decisions.

Sometimes teachers try to address higher needs too soon. Students may need to feel secure in the classroom, achieve limited but real mastery, and learn to work with other students before they address higher needs. Most young children are not ready for completely autonomous functioning; to force them to shoulder such responsibility prematurely is to ask for poor progress (this was one of the reasons why the open education model never caught on). Further, students will vary greatly in terms of their preference for structure, and family and cultural experiences will influence student needs.

Building a base for future growth takes time. How can adults help students look at their actions, think about them, and plan for (rather than fear) evaluation? Maslow (1954) stated that the most stable and healthy self-esteem is based on deserved respect rather than unwarranted adulation. To allow for growth, students need to experience mastery.

There may be temporary exceptions to the order in which needs are fulfilled. People occasionally deprive themselves of a prepotent need like sleep, for example, in order to prepare for an exam, in the hope of mastering the material (an esteem need). Also, individuals are likely to pursue several goals at the same time (Covington, 1992). However, Maslow believed that people generally respond first to the more basic of two needs.

Atkinson: achievement motivation theory

Another type of cognitive theory that has been used to explain behavior is achievement motivation theory. Why do persons of similar aptitude often achieve in dramatically different ways? Some psychologists argue that this occurs because some individuals have a more powerful need to achieve than others. Achievement becomes a dominant part of their lives, and they organize their time and talents to pursue achievement goals rather than affiliative or other goals.

Richard Atkinson (1964) formulated a comprehensive theory of achievement motivation and behavior. He postulated that the tendency to approach an achievement goal, (T_s) is a product of three factors: (1) the need for achievement or the motive for success (M_s); (2) the probability of success (P_s); and (3) the incentive value of success (I_s). However, fear of failure can also be aroused in an achievement-related situation. Thus there is also a tendency to avoid failure (M_{af}), which is the product of three factors: (1) the motive to avoid failure (T_{af}); (2) the probability of failure (P_{af}); and (3) the incentive value of failure (I_{af}). M_s is conceptualized as the capacity to experience pride in achievement, and M_{af} is the capacity to experience embarrassment or shame in the face of failure.

Jane Walker, for example, has been practicing law for three years as a junior partner in an established firm. She has some regular clients but not enough to guarantee that she could maintain her present standard of living if she went into private practice. She wants to be her own boss and to decide which cases to accept, but financial security is important, too. In Atkinson's framework, Jane's decision to stay with the firm or go off on her own involves the following basic question: How much does she want to be her own boss and how probable is her success, versus how much does she fear failing to make it on her own and what is the probability of such failure?

Although the typical collegial demands that fall on a new teacher are different from those experienced by a young journalist or business person, the culture of a school or a business clearly influences how achievement motivation is expressed in the workplace. Rosenholtz (1989), for example, has illustrated that in some schools questioning one's colleagues (e.g., "How do you respond to aggressive student behavior?") is seen as a weakness, whereas in other schools consultation among teachers is seen as a sign of strength. Fortunately, more schools are emphasizing a climate where teachers can cooperate rather than compete. Hence, in many school environments (but certainly not all) teachers are encouraged to express achievement needs in collegial ways rather than to work in isolation.

According to Atkinson's theory, the strength of a person's motivation to strive for a particular goal is determined by the relative strengths of the motivation to approach the task and try to succeed at it (M_s) and the motivation to avoid failure (M_{af}). Thus a person is high in *resultant achievement motivation* when M_s exceeds M_{af}.

As Weiner (1972) pointed out, for subjects low in resultant achievement motivation, all achievement tasks are somewhat aversive and elicit fear. However, tasks that are very easy or very difficult are comparatively less aversive for these people than are tasks of intermediate difficulty.

Atkinson and Litwin (1960) showed that people high in resultant achievement motivation are much more likely to choose tasks of intermediate difficulty than are subjects low in resultant achievement motivation. The subjects in this experiment played a ring-toss game. They were free to stand wherever they wished within a range of one to fifteen feet from the target peg. Presumably, the subjective probability of success was high at one foot and low at fifteen feet. As subjects stood farther from the peg, the incentive value of success was assumed to increase and the incentive value of failure was assumed to decrease, so that a successful toss from fifteen feet would be perceived as a demonstration of competence, but failure from this distance would be "no big deal." Conversely, a successful toss from two feet would be only a minor accomplishment, and a miss from two feet would be disappointing and perhaps embarrassing. As predicted, subjects with high resultant achievement motivation (a high tendency to approach success and a low tendency to avoid failure) tossed their rings much more frequently from the moderate-risk distance (nine to eleven feet). Subjects low in achievement motivation generally made close tosses of between one and six feet or distant tosses of between twelve and fifteen feet, avoiding the intermediate distances.

An interesting test of Atkinson's theory of achievement motivation involves task choice following success or failure. In the theory, M_s (I want to achieve) and M_{af} (I don't want to fail) are viewed as relatively stable personality factors, and the incentive values of a goal depend on the person's perception of the probability of success (P_s). Weiner (1972) summarized general trends in the literature on the effects of success and failure on motivation to continue with a given activity:

1. Motivation is enhanced following failure among individuals high in resultant achievement motivation (they want to do better).
2. Motivation is inhibited following failure among individuals low in resultant achievement motivation (they are "turned off").
3. Motivation is decreased following success among individuals high in resultant achievement motivation (they have proven their skills and have no need to continue to do so).
4. Motivation is enhanced following success among individuals low in resultant achievement motivation (they are relieved to find that they are successful and want to continue with this safe, rewarding activity).

the development of achievement motivation

Deborah Stipek (1984a, 1993) analyzed the antecedent conditions of achievement motivation. She emphasized developmental issues, with particular attention to changes in *cognitions related to achievement,* such as performance expectations, self-perceptions of ability, or perceptions of causes of achievement outcomes. She also stressed the development of several related *emotions*—how children value achievement outcomes, their attitudes toward school, and their emotional responses to achievement outcomes.

Stipek's observations indicate that younger students focus on tasks rather than outcomes. They are egocentric, concerned about their own work rather than the progress of peers. However, as they mature and become more responsive to social comparisons and competi-

tion, they start to become defensive and may seek to avoid difficult tasks or even begin to demonstrate behaviors such as learned helplessness.

Developmental changes in children's cognitions appear to account for these changes in students' achievement behavior. Performance expectancy, for example, is generally high until second or third grade but then decreases through sixth grade (Stipek, 1984b). Self-perceptions of competence also generally decrease during the elementary grades. Initially overly optimistic ability perceptions drop and begin to correlate increasingly with objective performance measures (Eshel & Klien, 1981). A further, and often substantial, drop in self-perceptions occurs after students enter junior high school (Eccles, 1987). Attitudes toward school also drop as grade level increases (Eccles, 1987), with an especially steep decrease in junior high (Haladyna & Thomas, 1979).

Social comparison theory suggests that humans look to one another for information with regard to their performance when they are in ambiguous situations. In general, primary-grade children judge self-worth on the basis of self-improvement and express satisfaction at how much they are learning, no matter how others are doing. In time, self-appraisal gives way to comparing one's progress with that of others as the basis for judging ability (Frey & Ruble, 1985). Covington (1992) notes that this transition from self-comparison to social comparison roughly parallels the change in students' thinking from incremental concepts of intelligence to entity concepts. The practical consequences of this are that although upper-elementary students may believe they can become smarter by trying harder, they also are beginning to become aware of the fact that they may never be as smart as some others.

According to Covington (1992), the self-perceived ability of all students tends to decline over the junior high school years. The decline is especially steep for students who were low achievers when they began junior high (Stipek, 1984a). At this time students also become more anxious about school and consider all school subjects to be less valuable. Thus, in early adolescence, when academic ability becomes a critical factor in school success (and low ability is the cause of failure), many students begin to doubt their capability (Covington, 1992).

In seeking explanations for these changes in achievement motivation, Stipek focused on teachers' *performance evaluations,* which also change with grade level, and on students' responses to teacher feedback. Young children focus on **social feedback** (*praise or criticism*) rather than *objective feedback* (I got all problems correct), *symbolic feedback* (I got an A), or *normative feedback* (I did better than everyone else) about their performance. Older students tend to consider both objective and social feedback in developing expectations for future performance.

Stipek believes that young children focus on social feedback because they perceive their teacher's role as being similar to that of their parents and because they view adults as moral authorities and are eager to please them. She also observed that kindergarten and first-grade teachers frequently praise and rarely criticize the results of students' efforts. Brophy (1981) pointed out that teachers in early elementary grades sometimes praise students even after they make mistakes and that students view this praise as a positive reflection of their ability. Older students, however, interpret praise following failure as an indication of teacher sympathy toward students of low ability.

Symbolic feedback includes such things as grades, smiling faces, and stars. Kindergarten and first-grade students often associate these symbols with social approval. Grades begin to affect self-concept of ability and students begin to value grades for their own sake at about third grade (Eshel & Klien, 1981). Older students also come to value grades because grades allow them to compare their performance with that of their peers.

Objective feedback conveys information only about the correctness of a student's response. It becomes a more important influence on students' achievement-related cognitions over time, due to changes in students' cognitive processing. Younger students generally expect to succeed and retain high self-perceptions of ability even after failures, suggesting that they do not accurately process and integrate information about repeated failure. Even if they were able to do so, they tend not to view ability as a stable attribute and instead equate ability with effort until age ten or eleven (Dweck, 1986).

Most students do not compare their performance to that of others until about second grade, so that their self-evaluations are largely unaffected by *normative feedback* about the performance of others (Boggiano & Ruble, 1979). Stipek and Tannatt (1984) found that second and third graders were more likely to explain competency ratings of self and others in terms of relative performance and task difficulty than were younger students. Stipek believes that these developmental differences are due largely to changes in classroom organization. Classrooms become more formal in the upper grades, with more whole-class instruction, public recitation, formal testing, use of letter grades, and other factors that encourage normative comparisons of one's performance with that of peers (Eccles et al., 1993).

Once students begin to define academic success in relation to the performance of others, many begin to view themselves as failures. By sixth grade, most view ability as stable and many see increased effort as being of little use. This may account for the negative feelings that many junior high students have toward school and for the sharp decrease in students' self-perceptions of ability that occurs at this age. A major challenge facing junior high and high school teachers is sustaining their students'

research at work
applying achievement motivation theory

Teachers can maximize their students' achievement motivation by keeping criticism constructive and minimizing reasons for students to fear failure, by helping the students to set challenging but realistic goals and to take pleasure in reaching those goals, and by offering incentives for good effort and performance.

Three additional findings from achievement motivation research are worth noting. First, there is evidence that more realism in vocational aspiration is exhibited by students who are high in resultant achievement motivation than by students who are low in it. Individuals low in achievement motivation may need assistance from teachers and counselors in developing more accurate self-knowledge and making more realistic vocational choices.

Second, the difficulty of assignments affects student motivation and effort. Too often task difficulty is fixed for the entire class at a level that only stimulates average students maximally. If students are told that they will get an A if they do 90 percent of a set of math problems correctly, for example, this may be comparable to tossing a ring from two feet for

some students but more like tossing from twenty feet for others.

Third, Stipek's (1984a, 1993) review makes it clear that teachers must recognize and respond to developmental differences in students. If teachers are to function as professional decision makers, they must recognize that students' conceptions of achievement motivation and related factors (e.g., students' interpretations of success and failures) are influenced not only by classroom climate and assignments but also by students' developmental levels.

Attempts to increase achievement motivation involve teaching students the relationship between risk-taking behavior and accomplishment and helping them to understand the advantages of setting moderately difficult goals ("I want to give a better class presentation than I did last time—to hold everyone's attention and even teach the teacher something new"). Related objectives include helping students to identify problems that prevent them from completing tasks successfully and helping them to translate long-range assignments into smaller, more manageable units.

---

interest in achieving for the sake of mastering content or skills and not just for symbolic rewards such as grades.

attribution theory

Attribution theory grew out of research on achievement motivation. As researchers began to focus more on the cognitive dynamics

involved, they recognized that individuals' assessment of their levels of success achieved and attributions of success or failure to causes were key determinants of their achievement-related emotions and behavior.

Attribution theory is *a systematic analysis of the possible ways that individuals perceive the causes of their success or failure in achievement situations,* such as ability, effort, task difficulty, luck, or failure to use the right strategy for solving the problem. This is not an exhaustive list,

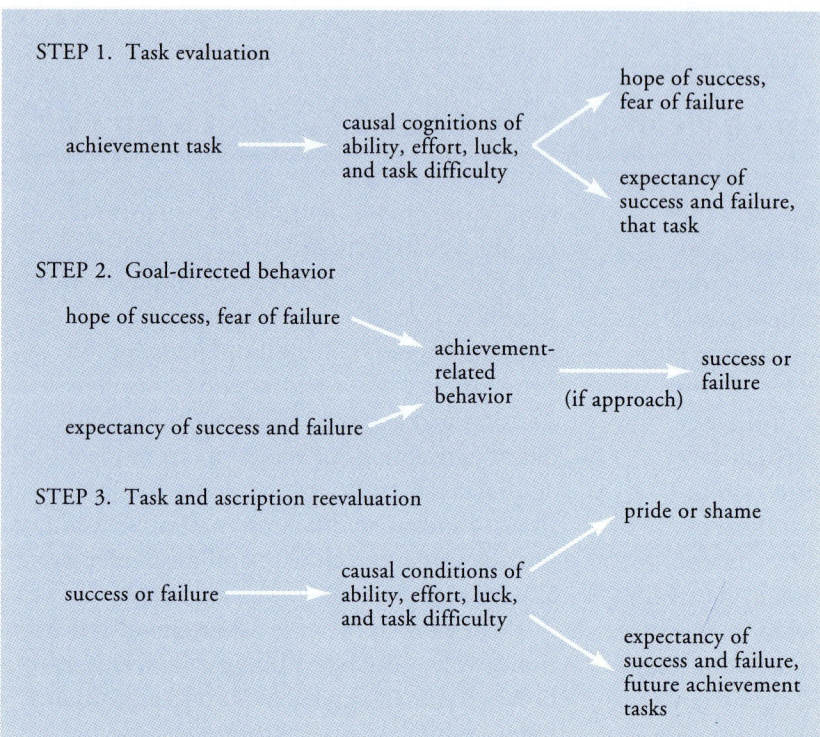

STEP 1. Task evaluation

achievement task → causal cognitions of ability, effort, luck, and task difficulty → hope of success, fear of failure

→ expectancy of success and failure, that task

STEP 2. Goal-directed behavior

hope of success, fear of failure

expectancy of success and failure

→ achievement-related behavior → (if approach) → success or failure

STEP 3. Task and ascription reevaluation

success or failure → causal conditions of ability, effort, luck, and task difficulty → pride or shame

→ expectancy of success and failure, future achievement tasks

Figure 13.2 cognitive and behavioral sequence in an attributional model of achievement behavior
SOURCE: From *Theories of Motivation* by B. Weiner. Copyright © 1972 by Rand McNally College Publishing, a Markham book.

but it does include the reasons typically offered to explain success and failure (Fiske & Taylor, 1991; Weiner, 1992).

The cognitive and behavioral aspects of task engagement as described within attribution theory are shown in Figure 13.2. In Step 1 the student assesses the task and makes causal attributions (How difficult does the task appear? Will my performance on it depend on ability, effort, or luck?). Then in Step 2 the student estimates his or her probable level of success at the task and develops an affective anticipation: hope of success or fear of failure.

Causal factors in several ways. First, they vary in *stability*. Perception of one's own general ability tends to be stable over time, as do perceptions of the difficulty of tasks. However, there is more variation in the amount of effort put out and in the role of luck as a determinant

of performance. Causal factors also vary in *controllability*. We cannot control luck, but we can control effort. Finally, causal factors vary in *internal versus external locus*. Ability and effort are internal to a person, whereas the task and its difficulty are external factors. A person brings to a task a given level of ability and may or may not put forth effort, but the nature of the task and luck (or the lack of it) are beyond the person's immediate control. Hence, in addition to looking at these three possible determinants of performance, it is possible to classify them on the basis of stability and locus of control, as shown in Table 13.1. The consequences of these attributions for achievement and social situation are further specified in Table 13.2.

The term **locus of control** *refers to how individuals tend to explain their successes and failures.* Those who perceive an external locus of control

table 13.1 determinants of achievement behavior

	STABILITY	
LOCUS OF CONTROL	*Stable*	*Unstable*
Internal	Ability	Effort
External	Task difficulty	Luck

table 13.2 perceived causes of achievement failure and social rejection on the basis of a locus × stability × controllability classification scheme

	MOTIVATIONAL DOMAIN	
DIMENSION CLASSIFICATION	*Achievement*	*Social*
Internal-stable-uncontrollable	low aptitude	physically unattractive
Internal-stable-controllable	never studies	always is unkempt
Internal-unstable-uncontrollable	sick the day of the exam	coughing when making the request
Internal-unstable-controllable	did not study for this particular test	did not call sufficiently in advance
External-stable-uncontrollable	school has hard requirements	religious restrictions
External-stable-controllable	instructor is biased	rejector always prefers to study at night
External-unstable-uncontrollable	bad luck	rejector must stay with sick mother that evening
External-unstable-controllable	friends failed to help	that night the rejector wants to watch television

SOURCE: *Human Motivation: Metaphors, Theories, and Research,* by B. Weiner. Newbury Park, CA: Sage, 1992.

Intrinsically motivated behaviors are those in which one engages in order to feel competent and self-determining. More and more frequently such behaviors have less and less to do with gender stereotypes.

see their performance as caused by external factors ("I succeeded because I was lucky"; "I failed because the teacher doesn't like me"). Individuals with an internal locus of control feel that they are responsible for their success and failure ("I was successful because I'm bright"; "I succeeded because I worked hard"; "I failed because I didn't try").

Rotter (1966) has shown that changes in expectations for future success or failure are more frequent and pronounced in skill (internal locus of control) than in chance (external locus of control) situations. Individuals with an internal locus of control prefer conditions where skill determines the outcome, whereas those with an external locus of control prefer chance conditions (Lefcourt, 1966). Because school achievement depends on development of knowledge and skill, students with an internal locus of control tend to get higher grades and achievement test scores (Crandall, Katkovsky, & Crandall, 1965), even when matched on IQ with external students (Messer, 1972), apparently because "internal" students spend more

time in intellectual activity (Crandall, Katkovsky, & Preston, 1962).

It is important to stress that locus of control is a learned perception that can be altered, although change, especially in naturalistic settings, may not occur rapidly. Success or failure on one task usually does not produce major changes in perception of ability. In general, though, performance on a task affects one's beliefs about one's ability to perform that task and others like it. To the extent that performance is attributed to internal and stable characteristics (e.g., ability), similar performance is expected in the future. To the extent that performance is attributed to external or unstable characteristics (e.g., level of effort or choice of strategy), one might expect a different outcome in the future.

Covington (1992) noted that grades can have powerful effects on the performance of individual students. It is difficult to generalize about the effects of a general grading policy on different types of students, however, because grades motivate students in quite different ways. For example, success-oriented individuals are driven to do better following failure if and when they attribute it to factors under their control. In contrast, failure-oriented persons are apt to believe that there is little they can do to improve their performance, and hence their failure does not lead to increased effort. An unexpected high grade may be mediated by failure-oriented students with disbelief because they do not think they are capable of achieving such a mark; hence, the mark must be due to luck. According to Covington, good grades are most likely to motivate students who do not need motivating and bad grades are most likely to depress the motivation of students who need encouragement the most.

Weiner: an attribution theory of student motivation

Weiner (1986, 1992), an influential theorist in the attribution tradition, summarizes the salient characteristics of students high in achievement motivation as follows: (1) they prefer situations in which performance outcomes can be ascribed to their own actions, (2) they have learned to attribute outcome to effort, and (3) they notice and react to cues indicating the importance of effort expenditure.

Weiner's general framework of motivational influences is shown in Figure 13.3. He believes a theory of student motivation that accurately reflects the complexity of classroom life must include three general principles (Weiner, 1992). First, it should incorporate the full range of *cognitive processes,* including information search and retrieval, attention, memory, categorization, judgment, and decision making. The theory must emphasize the conscious thoughts that accompany mental events and behavior, particularly students' concern with self. Second, the theory should include the full range of *emotions.* Previous theories have tended only to involve the broad pleasure-pain principle and not to distinguish among emotions within these two categories. Third, the theory must use the same concepts to explain both *rational actions* (such as when students use strategies to deal with anxiety) and *nonrational actions* (such as when students attribute failure to bad luck when poor effort was the real cause).

Weiner asserted that the basic principle of attribution theory is that persons attempt to understand *why* events occur and to search for *causes.* He presented the following classification of causes.

Figure 13.3 partial representation of an attribution theory of motivation
SOURCE: From "A Theory of Motivation for Some Classroom Experiences" by B. Weiner. *Journal of Educational Psychology*, 71, p. 18. Copyright © 1979 by the American Psychological Association. Reprinted with permission.

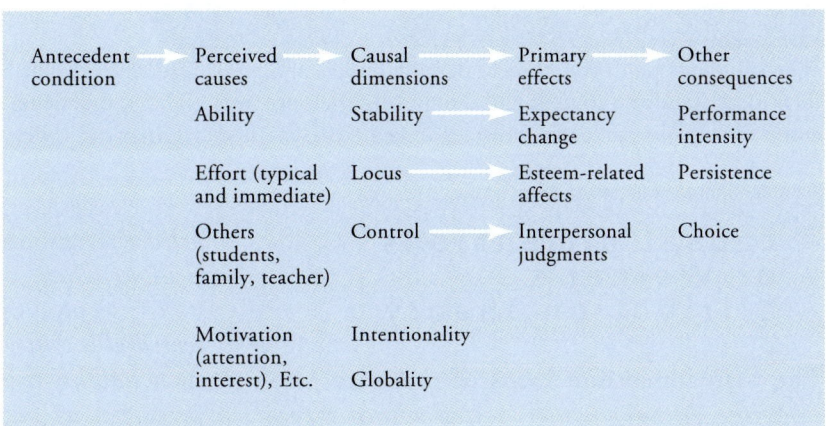

Antecedent condition	Perceived causes	Causal dimensions	Primary effects	Other consequences
	Ability	Stability	Expectancy change	Performance intensity
	Effort (typical and immediate)	Locus	Esteem-related affects	Persistence
	Others (students, family, teacher)	Control	Interpersonal judgments	Choice
	Motivation (attention, interest), Etc.	Intentionality		
		Globality		

When students put forth effort to develop understanding of academic content by deepening and manipulating their ideas about the content and monitoring their progress, they are practicing self-regulation learning. Small group discussions and cooperative learning are two methods teachers can utilize to support this kind of learning.

causal dimensions of Weiner's attribution theory

The first dimension, **locus of causality**, *distinguishes between causes located within a person, such as intelligence, effort, or physical* attractiveness, and external causes like task difficulty or luck.

A second dimension, **constancy**, *includes temporal stability and globality.* Causes differ in their *stability* over time. Ability, for example, is perceived as relatively lasting, as opposed to effort, which can vary considerably within a

research at work
applying attribution theory

Attribution theory underscores the need for tasks that are of appropriate difficulty and for helping students to perceive the relationship between effort investment and performance outcome. Many students explain their success or failure on the basis of habitual ways that they have learned to view their behavior, without noting the actual causal factors. They may say, "I failed because I am dumb," rather than "I failed because I got frustrated and gave up too easily." From an attribution theory perspective, the teacher's role is to help such students develop the capacity to use feedback appropriately. We elaborate on this in Chapter 15.

Attribution retraining programs have been developed to improve discouraged students' achievement-related behavior by reducing their tendency to attribute failures to low ability. Students are trained to attribute failure instead to internal, controllable causes such as insufficient effort or use of the wrong strategy.

---

short time. Thus outcomes perceived as caused by ability predict performance in the future more accurately than outcomes ascribed to effort. **Globality** *refers to the cross-situational generality of causes,* which may be specific (failing a math test due to low math aptitude) or general (failing because of low intelligence).

A third dimension, *responsibility,* consists of *controllability* and *intentionality* and is strongly related to evaluation consequences of behavior. **Controllability** *refers to how much control the actor has over his or her behavior.* A person is assumed to have more control over effort than over ability, for example. Similarly, **intentionality** *refers to failure due to lack of effort that is perceived as more intentional than failure due to improper choice of strategy.*

attributions and affect

There are affective consequences to success or failure. Studies show that success at achievement-related activities results in happiness, regardless of the cause of success. Other, more specific attri-bution-emotion relationships are ability–sense of competence, long-term effort–relaxation, help from others–gratitude, and luck–surprise/happiness. Contrasting affective responses follow attributions for failure (e.g., low ability–humiliation; hindrance from others–anger).

Causal dimensions also are important determinants of emotions: pride or self-esteem stem from attribution of success to self, anger from attribution of failure to the actions of others, gratitude from attribution of success to help from others, guilt from attribution of failure to one's own negative traits, pity from attribution of others' troubles to factors beyond their control, and hopelessness from attribution of failure to stable, negative, internal factors.

Studies support an attribution-emotion-action sequence (Weiner, 1992). For example, people are more likely to pity and subsequently to offer help to an individual who is in need because of factors they perceive to be beyond his or her control than a person they perceive as in need due to controllable factors. Research further shows that emotions rather than causal perceptions seem to be the immediate motivators of action (Weiner, 1992).

research at work
applying intrinsic motivation theory

It is desirable but difficult for teachers to sustain intrinsic motivation to engage in academic tasks in their students. First, a task that is interesting for one student may be uninteresting to the others. Furthermore, even if two students are initially interested in the same task, one may reach saturation much earlier than the other. Still, teachers can at least create conditions favorable to development of intrinsic motivation by allowing students choices of activity and encouraging them to regulate their own learning efforts. Also, teachers who use extrinsic rewards can strive to make them informational (helping students to see themselves as fulfilling their own goals) rather than controlling (causing students to see themselves as responding to teacher demands) by stressing the effort and accomplishment that the rewards represent.

intrinsic motivation theory

Jean Piaget and many other theorists hold that activity is intrinsic to human nature—that besides meeting basic survival needs and responding to external presses, humans display curiosity, explore their environments, amuse themselves, and seek to fulfill their potential. Even when in a state of need satisfaction, humans engage in certain activities because they find them rewarding. Intrinsic motivation theorists have tried to conceptualize such intrinsic motivation and to identify what it is about the activities that causes them to be experienced as intrinsically rewarding.

According to Edward Deci (1975, 1991), **intrinsically motivated behaviors** are *types of motivation influenced directly by personal interest, satisfaction, or enjoyment*—those behaviors in which one engages to feel competent and self-determining. He hypothesized that intrinsic motivation depends on the perception that one's behavior results from internal causes rather than external pressures and that intrinsic motivation will decrease if one's feelings of competence and self-determination are reduced.

Deci contended that consequences of actions, including feedback and rewards, have two parts—a controlling element and an informational element. If the *controlling element* is salient, the actor is likely to perceive the locus of causality of his or her behavior as external. If the *informational element* dominates, the actor tends to attribute his or her behavior to internal causes—to be intrinsically motivated. This implies that rewards may control behavior but erode intrinsic motivation unless they are used in informational as opposed to controlling ways. Evidence produced by several investigators confirms the value of distinguishing between control and information elements (Lepper & Greene, 1978).

Deci (1975) identified two types of intrinsically motivated behavior. One occurs when the person is comfortable but bored and thus motivated to find stimulation. The other involves mastering challenges or reducing incongruity (disequilibrium). Deci argued that people feel competence and self-determination when they are able to master challenges that are optimal for them (novel enough to be interesting, difficult enough to be challenging).

research at work
applying self-regulation theory

Rohrkemper and Corno (1988) suggested that teachers can set the stage for development of self-regulated learning by emphasizing classroom features that foster intrinsic motivation to learn: use of a variety of activities and teaching methods and frequent provision of student choice to accommodate individual differences in preferences and interests, classroom discourse that includes both teacher-student and student-student discussion of the content, pursuance of topics in depth through related activities that build toward understanding and application of significant networks of knowledge, and provision of feedback that is timely, informative, encouraging, and oriented toward private support of learning rather than public comparison of performance. Within this context, teachers then can promote self-regulated learning more directly by (1) clarifying goals, modeling strategies, and otherwise working to ensure that students' learning is meaningful and strategic; and (2) withdrawing these learning supports when they are no longer needed and providing opportunities for students to work with increasing autonomy on tasks that challenge them to integrate and apply what they are learning.

Corno and Rohrkemper's ideas about self-regulated learning are useful extensions of intrinsic motivation theory because they suggest that, in addition to finding ways to capitalize on students' existing intrinsic motivation to engage in other activities, teachers can model and encourage the development in students of intrinsic motivation to engage in *academic* activities (and in the process, increase the degree to which students engage in self-regulated learning). Such activities may be especially important in cases of gender differences (e.g., when females have not been encouraged to pursue mathematics seriously) or in considering culture differences (where some students may not value cooperative learning).

As McCaslin Rohrkemper (1989) notes, another important implication of this perspective is the necessity of designing classroom tasks that enhance the integration of students' affective and intellectual capacity for self-directed learning. She argues that we must carefully examine the social-instructional environments that educators design because such settings are not merely "places" for education but are an integral part of the learning process.

Corno and Rohrkemper: self-regulation theory

Lyn Corno and Mary Rohrkemper (1985) extended the notion of intrinsic motivation and linked it to ideas about teaching for strategic learning in their discussion of self-regulated learning. **Self-regulated learning** is *active learning in which students assume responsibility for motivating themselves to understand material they study.* It is the highest form of cognitive engagement that students can use to learn in classrooms—a systematic effort by students to develop meaningful understanding of academic content by deepening and manipulating the associative network of ideas they possess in relation to that content and by monitoring their progress in doing so (see Corno, 1989; McCaslin, 1990; and McCaslin Rohrkemper, 1989 for more details).

expectancy × value model: an emerging perspective

One general model that most theoretical frameworks can be subsumed within is *the expectancy × value model* (Feather, 1982). This model postulates that the effort that people are willing to expend on a task is a product of the degree to which they *expect* to be able to perform the task successfully if they apply themselves (and thus the degree to which they expect to get the rewards that successful task performance will bring) and the degree to which they *value* those rewards. Effort investment is viewed as the product rather than the sum of the expectancy and value factors because it is assumed that no effort at all will be invested in a task if one factor is missing entirely, no matter how much of the other factor may be present. People are not willing to invest effort on even highly valued tasks if they believe that they cannot succeed on these tasks no matter how hard they try. Thus, the expectancy × value model implies that teachers need both to help their students appreciate the value of school activities and to make sure that students can achieve success in these activities if they apply reasonable effort and have appropriate strategies.

The expectancy × value model subsumes many of the ideas included in the theories covered here in Chapter 13 and provides a convenient way to address additional theories and ideas that can be applied in classrooms. Chapter 14 will focus on addressing students' expectations for success, and Chapter 15 will focus on addressing their need to find value in school activities.

summary

Early motivational theories depicted humans as driven by needs or manipulated by external reinforcers. But over the years theory and research on human motivation have increasingly emphasized cognitive factors. This is not to suggest that needs, incentives, habits, or reinforcers have no value in a modern conceptual theory but to recognize that behavior is always mediated and interpreted. To be interpreted, most behavior has to be considered in terms of a particular context and individual beliefs.

Behaviorists focus on past reinforcement and present contingencies, whereas cognitive psychologists believe that people decide what they want to achieve and that perception, understanding, information processing, and curiosity are important.

Behaviorists began with the assumption that the drive to fulfill biological needs motivates behavior. Through attempts to satisfy biological drives, secondary drives such as dependence or aggression are learned. If reinforced, behavior associated with them is repeated; if not, it disappears. Murray postulated that needs interact with environmental pressure to form a pattern of behavior, or theme. Once created, needs tend to perpetuate themselves, so early experiences are especially important. Thus, at least some gender and cultural differences that students manifest are due to students' early home and environmental experiences. Murray's theory can be used to identify student needs and to predict how students might respond to given circumstances. Maslow also used the concept of needs and arranged them into a hierarchy. He believed that unfilled basic needs interfere with learning.

Cognitive explanations emphasize individuals' perceptions of events and their influences on behavior. Murray and Maslow, for example, both stressed individuals' control of their own behavior. Atkinson formulated a comprehensive theory of achievement motivation and noted how various classroom conditions influence students' motivation. In contrast, Deci argued that intrinsic motivation is a goal that teachers can promote, and Weiner emphasized the role of students' attributions and their influence on motivation.

Rohrkemper and Corno extended the notion of intrinsic motivation, linked it to ideas about teaching for strategic learning, and stressed the importance of self-regulated learning. They suggested that teachers can set the stage for development of self-regulated learning by emphasizing classroom features that foster intrinsic motivation to learn. However, features that encourage intrinsic motivation may vary widely depending upon students' gender and culture. Unfortunately, for example, some female students will be allowed (if not encouraged) by parents to express low interest in mathematics. Hence, teachers will have to address such problems directly (finding new ways to present mathematics while directly challenging old stereotypes). Further, as various researchers have noted (e.g., McCaslin & Murdock, 1991), variations in interest are wide (e.g., Anglo female students from low-income families will vary widely in their interests). Thus, teachers have to discover the interests of individual students to build on them (e.g., converse with students, visit their homes, etc.).

Finally, we have noted that the expectancy × value model subsumes many of the ideas included in the theories presented in this chapter and provides a convenient way to address additional theories and ideas for application.

questions for reflection

1. Human motivation has been debated for centuries. Pessimists believe that people must be pushed by external pressures, including threats of punishment for noncompliance. Optimists believe that the same degree of motivation can be accomplished through the pull of positive incentives. Those who are still more optimistic believe that no incentives at all are necessary, because positive and prosocial motives are basic to human nature. Where do you stand on these issues? Why? What does your stance imply concerning your approach to classroom motivation?

2. Maslow implies that students will not be very motivated to learn in school unless their basic needs are met. However, teachers rarely are in a position to meet basic needs that are not being met at home. Does this mean that teachers cannot motivate such students to learn? Why or why not?

3. Individual differences in students' motivational needs are problematic because the same teacher behavior that might motivate certain students might not motivate others. What can be done about this?

4. If you have selected teaching as your vocation, you probably are favorably disposed toward education and find learning rewarding. However, you will teach some students who are apathetic toward learning, anxious when placed in testlike situations, or even completely negative toward school. What can you do to prepare yourself to deal with these students effectively?

5. Given that students require different types of assignments because of their varying abilities, how could you make differential assignments without implying that one student is less capable than another?

cases to consider

Judy's dilemma Judy enjoys mathematics and works hard at it. Her mathematics class is individualized, and within limits, she can proceed at her own pace. Sometimes she has to wait until a few other students reach her level so that the teacher can begin another unit. Even when she has to wait to begin a new topic, however, she still enjoys the class. The teacher offers options that students can select during the delay times. Some involve straightforward review, but others involve tricky problems or novel applications of concepts. Other choice units deal with people who have discovered mathematical principles or with illustrations of ways that mathematics is used in the "real world." Judy, however, hates history. Every week is the same: Monday and Tuesday the teacher lectures ("Boring!"). Wednesday, Thursday, and Friday are devoted to small-group work, but a few students always talk even though they have little to say, and Judy dislikes answering the questions assigned each day. She often thinks, "How can one person keep asking such boring questions about an interesting subject?"

Using a motivational framework, how would you explain Judy's responses to the two subjects? Is it the content, the way the teacher presents the content, or Judy's individual needs that are most important? If you were her history teacher, how could you make the course more interesting to Judy? Are there students with needs and interests different from Judy's who might be "hurt" by these changes? If so, what types?

reticent Ryan Ryan's face flushed. He desperately tried to recall what he was going to say next. His knees became weak and he was embarrassed. Finally, he said, "Ms. Townsend, I can't remember what I was going to say. I'd better stop." She said, "That's okay, Ryan, but look at your notes, and after Jean answers the next proof I want you to explain yours." Later Ryan gave an acceptable explanation. After the class Ryan approached Ms. Townsend and said, "It's getting tougher and tougher for me in geometry. Everybody's so much better than I am. I feel like an idiot." If you were Ms. Townsend what would you say and do?

bridging cultures Ursula is a first-year teacher at Southern Middle School. She grew up in a Hispanic neighborhood and lived at home while attending college. She now teaches in a heterogeneous school setting. She wonders about the appropriateness of her motivational techniques for Anglo and Asian students. If you were Ursula, how would you attempt to further your knowledge of other cultures?

establishing and maintaining students' success expectations

objectives

When you have mastered the material in this chapter, you will be able to

1. Understand goal theory, as expressed by Ames and others, and be able to apply this theory to classroom settings
2. Explain the difference in students who have a learning orientation versus performance orientation and the consequences of these for student performance in the classroom.
3. Explain Covington's self-work theory and be able to apply it to classroom settings
4. Understand the essential preconditions necessary for student motivation and be able to discuss implications of this framework for the subject and grade level at which you intend to teach
5. Understand and be able to apply the expectancy framework for planning classroom management strategies (i.e., helping to motivate students by maintaining success expectations)
6. Conceptualize the role that teacher expectations play in setting goals, both for the class per se and for individual students
7. Generate practical strategies for helping students to reassess and to change their low performance expectations

As we noted in the previous chapter, an expectancy × value model provides a coherent framework for thinking about motivation in modern classrooms. In this chapter we deal with expectations. It is critical to note that all expectation theories imply that the classroom must be a psychologically safe place for learning in which students can concentrate on learning tasks with implicit expectations of success and without fear of failure and ridicule.

In developing appropriate success expectations, teachers must give considerable attention to classroom climate, not only from the standpoint of individual students but in terms of building a learning community in which students have mutual respect for one another. As we emphasized earlier in the learning section, meaningful learning is not focused primarily on discrete facts or isolated concepts; instead students are trying to master and integrate material so they can apply it in new contexts. Accordingly, motivation should not focus on how to get students to work faster or more expediently. Instead, teachers should encourage students to explore material thoughtfully.

As we have seen in Chapter 13, there is an emerging consensus that motivation must involve students' views of classroom opportunities. In this chapter we discuss how teachers can influence students' views of and motivation for learning assignments. In particular, we focus on the importance of an emphasis on learning goals (i.e., wanting to master and understand the material) over issues of success and failure (undue concern with performance, needing to look good, etc.).

Ames: goal theory and student motivation

Carole Ames (1992) has argued that the way in which classroom learning environments are structured (e.g., grading system, work assigned) influences how students think about themselves and their academic work and subsequently how (and to what extent) students attempt to learn. Different classroom structures are likely to make different goals salient. According to Ames, students can take either of two approaches as they attempt to define and to act on classroom achievement goals. She refers to these as mastery and performance goals (others have

The difference between mastery goal orientation and performance goal orientation: Mastery goal orientation = How can I understand this; Performance goal orientation = How fast do I need to perform?

used terms such as learning and performance goals or task involvement and ego involvement). These two goal definitions represent different conceptions of success and different ways of thinking about task performance.

Central to a *mastery goal orientation* are the student's belief that effort and outcome are related, a continuing commitment to learning, and a focus on the intrinsic value of learning (Ames, 1992). Students with a mastery goal orientation try to understand their work or to improve their competence. In contrast, the foundation of a *performance goal orientation* is a focus on one's ability and self-worth. As a result, learning typically is viewed only as a way to achieve some other goal (attention, recognition, etc.).

According to Ames (1992), mastery and performance goals are shaped by different environmental and instructional demands that over time result in qualitatively different motivational patterns. Mastery and performance goals are linked to one's view of classroom learning. A mastery goal orientation is associated with a success-seeking pattern of classroom participation, whereas a performance goal orientation fosters a failure-avoiding pattern.

Students who develop a mastery goal orientation are likely to spend more time learning tasks (Butler, 1987) and to persist longer on difficult tasks (Elliott & Dweck, 1988). Ames's analysis of extant research showed that students who are focused on a task are more likely to consider questions like "How can I understand this?" or "How can I master this task?" that lead to a motivational pattern promoting continuous and high-quality involvement in learning. Her review of the literature suggested that a performance goal orientation leads to a pattern of motivation characterized by the use of superficial or short-term learning strategies (memorizing) and a focus on doing better than others. Students with a failure-avoiding behavior pattern are motivated to avoid looking bad and are more likely to attend to surface characteristics of tasks ("How fast do I need to perform?") rather than to attempt to understand and integrate material.

Clearly, there are educational advantages in students developing a mastery approach (particularly for long-term learning goals). A fundamental question is how a classroom learning environment can be structured to make it more likely that students will develop a mastery goal

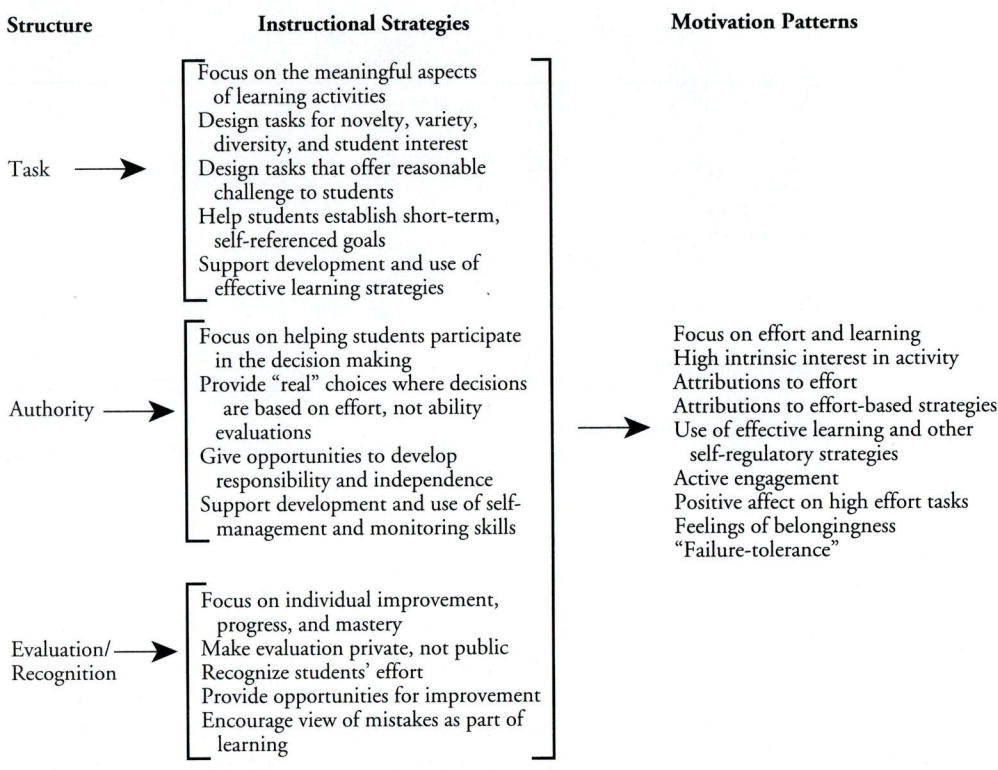

Structure	Instructional Strategies	Motivation Patterns

Task →
Focus on the meaningful aspects of learning activities
Design tasks for novelty, variety, diversity, and student interest
Design tasks that offer reasonable challenge to students
Help students establish short-term, self-referenced goals
Support development and use of effective learning strategies

Authority →
Focus on helping students participate in the decision making
Provide "real" choices where decisions are based on effort, not ability evaluations
Give opportunities to develop responsibility and independence
Support development and use of self-management and monitoring skills

→
Focus on effort and learning
High intrinsic interest in activity
Attributions to effort
Attributions to effort-based strategies
Use of effective learning and other self-regulatory strategies
Active engagement
Positive affect on high effort tasks
Feelings of belongingness
"Failure-tolerance"

Evaluation/Recognition →
Focus on individual improvement, progress, and mastery
Make evaluation private, not public
Recognize students' effort
Provide opportunities for improvement
Encourage view of mistakes as part of learning

Figure 14.1 classroom structure and instructional strategies supporting a mastery goal
SOURCE: From "Classroom Goals, Structures, and Motivation" by C. Ames. *Journal of Educational Psychology,* 84, 261–71. Copyright © 1992 by the American Psychological Association. Reprinted by permission.

orientation. As can be seen in Figure 14.1, Ames noted that three aspects of classroom structure are important in influencing students' willingness to become engaged actively in learning: the tasks, the classroom authority figure, and how evaluation and recognition are handled.

Dweck: learning goals versus performance goals

Carol Dweck (1986) contends that learning goals and performance goals (as students have accepted and internalized them) have notably different consequences for how students behave in classrooms and how they interpret performance (e.g., "How well have I done?"). Dweck found that students who develop learning goals (or mastery goals) seek appropriately challenging tasks that provide opportunities for them to develop new competencies, knowledge, and dispositions. A mastery orientation leads students of varying ability (high, middle, or low) to see classroom work as a challenge and as an opportunity to develop new skills, and to attribute initial failure to an inadequate current strategy that needs to be altered. In theory, such students are then likely to analyze their strategy, make appropriate adjustments, and to continue work on the task. In contrast, students who have developed performance goals are more likely to choose very easy tasks that allow them to look good because they are more concerned about this than about developing understanding. In the face of failure, these students tend either to develop self-defeating strategies to avoid being seen as low in ability ("I only studied for fifteen minutes") or to simply give up because they do not think that they will perform adequately (Stipek, 1993).

Students who have a mastery orientation are more likely to see their teacher as a resource—a source of helpful information. In contrast, students with a performance orientation tend to see the teacher as a judge—not of their individual progress, but of their performance relative to others'. They do not see progress on a developmental continuum but rather believe that if they do not perform adequately "now," they are incapable. Consequently, they often are immobilized by failure.

Nicholls: task-involvement theory

John Nicholls (1984) contrasted two psychological states associated with mastering a task. **Task involvement** is *the desire to master a task primarily in order to develop one's ability.* **Ego involvement** is *the desire to demonstrate successful performance to oneself or others, preferably by achieving success without having to expend too much effort.*

Generally, the tendency to become ego involved in task performance increases in the presence of cues that heighten concerns about evaluation of one's ability. Thus when a teacher announces a test of important skills, students are likely to view their performance as reflecting their abilities, and ego involvement should be high. Nicholls cited several studies that support these predictions. Testlike or competitive conditions and public performance settings heighten ego involvement (Ames, Ames, & Felker, 1977). Furthermore, these same conditions reduce intrinsic interest in the task (Deci et al., 1981; Ryan, 1982).

Nicholls (1984) predicted that *task-involved persons*, regardless of their self-perceptions of ability, will view tasks that appear to require moderate to high effort as offering them the best chance to perform well and demonstrate their ability. Consequently, they will prefer such tasks over tasks on which either success or failure seems certain. They also will show higher effort on such moderately challenging tasks. In contrast, the task preferences and performance patterns of ego-involved persons will depend on how well they expect to perform in comparison with others. *Ego-involved persons who believe that their ability is low* (those who have given up the attempt to demonstrate high ability) will avoid moderately difficult tasks offering realistic challenges and will not perform well when required to work on such tasks. Because they believe that their best efforts will not be good enough, they will tend to choose easy tasks that guarantee success. If they still desire to demonstrate high ability to others, however, they will choose extremely difficult tasks on which failure does not necessarily indicate lack of ability.

Ego-involved persons who believe that they have high ability are not threatened by ego-involving situations. They expect reasonable effort to result in success and thus expect to perform well on moderately difficult tasks. These persons also expect to do relatively well on difficult tasks, but they may relax their efforts on tasks that they perceive as easy and thus perform less well than they could. For these high-ability, ego-involved persons, easy tasks are not motivating because they do not offer the opportunity for them to demonstrate their abilities.

research at work

applying goal and task-involvement theory

Newmann and colleagues have studied the types of high school classroom environments that lead students to become engaged in meaningful academic work with the intention of mastering the material. Newmann's research is consistent with the motivational perspective discussed by Ames. He reports the following factors to be associated with student engagement: need for competence, school membership, clarity of purpose, fairness, personal support, success, caring, authentic work, and a sense of ownership (see Figure 14.2).

Newmann (1992) argues that if students are to engage in academic work they must feel a need to develop competence. When their attempts to act competently (both academically and socially) are successful, students are likely to invest more in academic work. How, then, can schools influence students so that their natural interest in expanding personal competence can be channeled into academic mastery? Newmann notes that two factors are critical: school membership and authentic work (see Figure 14.2).

School membership suggests that if students are to explore mastery goals they must perceive the school as legitimate (they want to commit to school values) and perceive that the school environment recognizes, honors, and respects them. If students experience the

conditions necessary for appropriate bonding (e.g., fairness, personal support, etc.) then it becomes relevant to explore how academic work itself can be designed to enhance student engagement.

Marshall (1987, 1988) has conducted research on strategies teachers can use to help students develop motivation to learn or develop a mastery approach. In one study, she explored how teachers in three fifth-grade classrooms explained and maintained lessons and how they discussed and actually handled responsibility for learning (Marshall, 1987). She found that twice as many lessons were introduced with motivational statements in the mastery-oriented classroom as in work-oriented and work-avoidance classrooms. Also, the mastery-oriented teacher was much more likely to use motivational statements that referred to challenge or interest rather than to external factors such as rewards. She used management and maintenance statements to maintain and encourage student interest rather than simply to redirect and reorient off-task behavior. Finally, she encouraged student responsibility for learning and developed the expectation that students should engage in self-evaluation.

Butler (1987) applied task-involvement theory in an experiment on the effects of different teacher responses to the task perfor-

Covington: self-worth theory

Martin Covington (1984, 1992) referred to a person's tendency to present a positive self-image as the **self-worth motive**, *the attempt to place a positive value on one's own academic performance.* Research on the self-worth motive in achievement situations indicates that individuals tend to attribute their successes to themselves and their failures to external conditions.

In the classroom, the self-worth motive

mance of fifth and sixth graders. One group was given comments that related specifically to each student's performance and included both a reinforcing and a goal-setting component ("You thought of quite a few ideas; maybe it is possible to think of more different ideas"). A second group was given numerical grades without comments, a third group was given global praise ("very good"), and a fourth group received no evaluation or feedback. Data collected after three repetitions of this treatment indicated that students who received individualized comments showed the most interest in the task, the highest levels of effort, higher-quality performance, and more task involvement (interest, enjoyment, desire to improve). In contrast, students who had received either numerical grades or global praise without specific comments on their performance were more likely to make attributions to ego-involved causes (desire to do better than others, concern about proving one's ability). Such findings underscore the importance of teaching students to evaluate their performance in terms of personal effort and improvement over previous performance, including the use of individualized qualitative feedback that focuses them on task involvement. If left to follow their own inclinations, most students, and low achievers in particular,

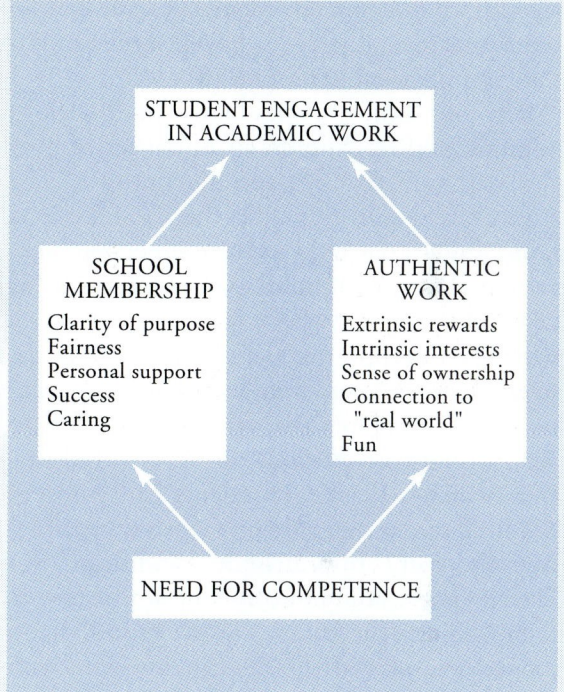

Figure 14.2 factors that influence student engagement in academic work
SOURCE: Reprinted by permission of the publisher from Newman, Fred W., *Student Engagement and Achievment in American Secondary Schools.* (New York: Teachers College Press, © 1992 by Teachers College, Columbia University. All rights reserved.) (Fig. 1.1 as it appears in the TC Press edition.)

concentrated on social comparison feedback and ego involvement rather than task involvement (Ruble & Flett, 1988).

is reflected primarily in *self-perceptions of competence*. Students want to appear competent, so they want others to attribute their success to ability rather than effort. However, the competition that typifies most classrooms makes it possible for only a few students to achieve noteworthy success. Furthermore, this competition overemphasizes the role of ability in determining achievement (Ames & Ames, 1981), causing students who fail to feel inadequate. Thus many students are likely to develop strategies designed to avoid failure and to save face.

negative effects of competition

There is ample research to suggest that when competitive goals are used, individuals typically attempt hard classroom assignments only as long as they complete them successfully. No one wants to engage in a behavior if the result is self-recrimination (Ames, 1978).

In one study, Ames and Ames (1981) administered to children an initial set of puzzles without stating a specific purpose. The study was designed so that half the subjects failed this initial task and the other half succeeded. Thus, this initial experience provided all of the subjects with a powerful lens with which to interpret the meaning of their subsequent performance. Students who were later placed in a competitive condition tended to ignore their past record. A prior record of success (which 50 percent students had enjoyed) did little to reassure students when they subsequently lost. Interestingly, winning over another person did not offset a prior history of failure. Similarly, Butler (1988) found that a preoccupation with grades can interfere with the kinds of higher-order thinking that students of superior intellect often use. Thus, competition often narrows the criteria that students use to define classroom success.

Nelson and Kagan (1972) rewarded young students with attractive toys when they cooperated in work on a problem-solving task. They found that children were motivated to cooperate when everyone received a reward; when fewer rewards were provided than players, however, the students became angry. Indeed, some even gave up their own chances of winning by sabotaging the game in order to guarantee that others would not get prizes. Similarly, Covington (1992) argued that inadequate rewards create competition that in turn discourages cooperation.

Interestingly, noncompetitive learning is not superior in all situations. Indeed, when tasks are simple and highly repetitive, competition and individual performance may lead to better learning. However, simple and highly repetitive tasks are not important components of good teaching and learning. Consequently, cooperation may be better than competition for most learning situations. If students compete while solving complex problems they are less willing to share information and may even try to undermine others' performance. In contrast, when a common goal is pursued, it is in the interest of everyone to correct mistakes and erroneous reasoning.

Despite research showing the dangers of reward, there is evidence that most teachers and parents believe that offering or denying rewards is a strategy that produces good results (Boggiano et al., 1987). However, in actuality, rewards are useful in increasing students' willingness to engage in tasks only on relatively simple and tedious tasks.

strategies to avoid failure

The most direct way to avoid failure is *not to participate*. Some students may avoid volunteering to answer questions or even "hide" from the teacher in an attempt to avoid being called on. When they are forced to participate, yet expect to fail, students may attempt to *blame failure on factors other than ability*, such as by setting unrealistically high goals, delaying work until the last minute, or expending little effort on a task. A third strategy to avoid failure involves *setting low goals* or (when possible) selecting simple tasks that are well below one's abilities. Ironically, all of these failure-avoidance strategies ultimately lead to failure, and students who use them are *failure prone*. According to Covington, the problem is not low ability but basing one's self-concept on achievement and setting unrealistically high standards for oneself.

the role of effort and excuses

Student manipulation of effort expenditure is important in avoiding the threat of failure, because failure despite high effort implies low ability and results in shame. Covington and Beery (1976) found that self-estimates of effort expenditure were low following failure. Furthermore, describing a task as very difficult improves the performance of persons who frequently worry about failure. This reduces the threat to self-esteem, because failure can be attributed to external causes rather than to one's skill deficiencies. Thus, expending little effort in failure situations may preserve one's self-perceptions of ability. However, Covington, Spratt, and Omelich (1980) found that this failure-avoidance strategy also causes students to label themselves negatively (e.g., as unmotivated or lazy).

Covington and Omelich (1979) demonstrated that, at least under hypothetical conditions, increases in college students' perceived effort enhanced their pride in success and offset the negative effects of perceptions of low ability. Because successful performance increases self-perceptions of ability, there is little need for the self-protective reports of reduced effort that people often give in failure situations. Most students are willing to accept public acknowledgement of effort that leads to success, though some try to minimize the role of effort even when they are successful. As long as students are not convinced that they lack ability, they may respond well to praise and to achieving successes even if they tend to mask their efforts by using defensive tactics.

reward and punishment from teachers

Although the primary determinant of teacher rewards is high achievement, teachers also reward effort (Blumenfeld et al., 1983). Students who teachers see as having tried hard are rewarded more for success and punished less for failure. This presents struggling students with a dilemma: high effort suggests low ability if they fail, but obvious lack of effort leads to punishment from the teacher. Covington and Omelich (1979) thus characterized effort as a *double-edged sword* and studied the role of excuses as strategies for managing effort perceptions.

Covington and Omelich asked college students to state how teachers and they as students would respond to test failure that followed high effort, low effort with an excuse, or low effort without an excuse. Results showed that the students believed that teachers would punish those who failed without making an effort more than those who tried. Students and teachers had conflicting responses to effort. Teachers were least likely to punish in the failure under high-effort condition, for example, but students in this condition would feel the most incompetent and experience the most personal dissatisfaction and shame. Low effort would reduce these negative feelings but result in more punishment by the teacher, unless the student had a plausible excuse for the low effort. In the case of success, there was little conflict between teacher and student values.

attributional factors

Successful students tend to attribute their successes to skill and effort and their failures to lack of effort or because of an ineffective strategy. Students who accept failure, however, attribute their successes to external factors such as luck and their failures to lack of ability (Ames, 1978, 1992). In its extremes, failure acceptance results in *learned helplessness*, a condition in which people do not even try to reach a goal because they believe that their efforts cannot succeed ·(Abramson, Seligman, & Teasdale, 1978).

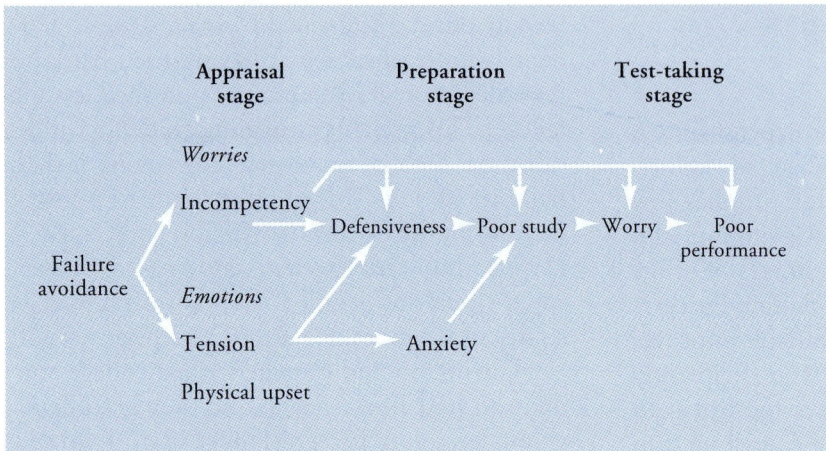

Figure 14.3 achievement dynamics: interaction of motives, thoughts, and emotions over time
SOURCE: M. Covington (1992). *Making the Grade*. Cambridge: Cambridge University Press. Reprinted by permission.

Covington (1992) depicts the pattern of negative consequences that follow when students are motivated to avoid failure (see Figure 14.3). Failure-avoiding students often doubt their ability (e.g., Salamé, 1984), feel poorly prepared (Covington & Omelich, 1988), and are consumed with anxiety (Carver & Scheirer, 1988). Students who are motivated to avoid failure are apprehensive and are often motivated to take steps to protect themselves. Students who are "primed" at the appraisal stage tend to worry as the instructor outlines details of the course or a particular assignment. Much of these students' time is spent in worry that they will be found out as being incompetent rather than in focusing on the intent and rationale of course assignments.

Covington argues that the cycle of failure continues at the preparation stage. As students begin to prepare for the exam, whenever they encounter some difficult material, their thoughts turn to self-doubts (e.g., "I'm not smart enough to be in the college-bound track." "I don't have the ability to be an engineer"). Such self-doubts trigger defensive thoughts including blame projection ("If I had a competent teacher . . ."), wishful thinking ("Maybe I'll do better on the next test"), and perhaps rationalization ("This course is not important to my

course of study"). The critical impediment for students is that they do not adaptively apply their talent to test preparation, and most of their time is spent worrying about the test performance. Hence, students enter the testing situation less prepared than they could be.

At the test-taking stage, students are engulfed by new waves of anxiety and worry. Such thoughts interfere with concentration and integration of material (e.g., "Why did those students start writing so quickly?" "I can't believe that one student is already finished with the exam—she must really be smart"). What students have learned is poorly represented because of intrusive emotions during testing. Once students fall behind and develop a skill or knowledge deficiency and a failure-avoidance orientation, they are likely to continue to fail because, instead of processing information and using time adaptively, they focus on defensive posturing.

essential preconditions for student motivation

We begin with the identification of basic assumptions and preconditions that underlie the effective use of any motivational strategies

research at work
applying self-worth theory

Research points to the need for teachers to reduce competition and make it possible for all students to succeed, so that some do not have to concentrate on avoiding failure. Techniques such as self-competition and cooperative learning are helpful in this regard.

Teachers should demonstrate to students that effort and outcome are strongly related. Students should be taught to divide a complex task into more manageable parts—for example, a process that may allow success without requiring students to set lower goals. It also helps if teachers emphasize reasons for failure that students can control: incorrect task analysis, overly high expectations, and low effort.

Teachers can promote positive effort-outcome linkages by emphasizing the quality of effort and improvement over prior accomplishments when they evaluate student performance. If tasks are appropriate in difficulty, students can achieve success by applying rea-sonable effort and experiencing pride in their accomplishments.

Covington concluded that teachers must design curricula to promote both *self-validation* and *self-accuracy* in their students. Without devaluing the role of ability in achievement, teachers must ensure that students do not equate personal worth with ability or performance. Also, students must come to view ability not as a stable trait but as a repertoire of skills that increases continuously throughout their lives.

Perhaps the most critical contribution of self-worth theory is the recognition that competition restricts performance and that students, parents, and teachers should become more sensitive to the fact that rewards and competition often undermine performance. There is increasing recognition that educators must promote mastery goals (authentic learning and integration of information) rather than performance goals (being better than someone else) (Ames, 1992; Covington, 1992).

---

in the classroom. *No motivational strategy can work effectively if these assumptions and preconditions are not in effect.*

supportive environment Anxious or alienated students are unlikely to develop motivation to learn academic content. Nor is such motivation likely to develop in a chaotic classroom. Thus, we assume the teacher (1) is a patient, encouraging person who makes students feel comfortable during academic activities and supports their learning efforts, and (2) uses class-room organization and management skills to establish the classroom as an effective learning environment. The classroom atmosphere is businesslike but relaxed and supportive. Students feel comfortable taking intellectual risks because they know the teacher will not embarrass or criticize them if they make a mistake.

appropriate level of challenge/ difficulty Activities must be of an appropriate difficulty level for students. If a task is so familiar or easy that it constitutes nothing more than busywork, and especially if it is so unfamiliar or difficult that the students cannot succeed on it even if they apply reasonable effort, no strategies to induce student motivation to learn are likely to succeed. Tasks are of appropriate difficulty when students are clear enough about what to do and how to do it so that they can achieve high levels of success if they apply reasonable effort and possess appropriate learning strategies (Pressley & El-Dinary, 1993).

meaningful learning objectives

Teachers cannot expect students to be motivated to learn if they assign pointless or meaningless activities. Therefore, we assume that teachers have selected activities with worthwhile academic objectives in mind; that is, activities *teach some knowledge or skill that is worth learning*, either in its own right or as a step toward some larger objective. The following activities will not meet this criterion: continued practice on skills already mastered thoroughly; memorizing lists for no good reason; looking up and copying definitions of terms that are never used meaningfully in readings or assignments; reading material that is too vague, technical, or abstract to allow student understanding; and working on tasks assigned merely to fill time.

moderation/optimal use

Strategies used too often may lose their effectiveness, and a strategy can become counterproductive if it is used too long or carried to extremes. Also, different activities call for different motivational strategies. When content is relatively unfamiliar and its value or meaningfulness is not obvious to students, significant motivational effort involving several of the strategies described here may be needed. In contrast, little or no special motivational effort may be needed when a task involves something that students are already eager to learn.

motivating by maintaining success expectations

Much of the best-known research on motivation has focused on the role of success expectations in determining performance (Brophy, 1987). Here we first focus on general strategies for helping students to maintain success expectations. Then we discuss expectancy issues associated with low achievers. In Chapter 15 we will deal with the value dimensions of the expectancy x value model. Research on *achievement motivation* (Ames, 1992; Dweck & Elliott, 1983) has established that effort and persistence are greater in individuals who set goals of moderate difficulty, who seriously commit themselves to pursuing these goals, and who concentrate on trying to achieve success rather than on trying to avoid failure. Research on *efficacy perceptions* (Bandura, 1989; Schunk, 1985) has shown that effort and persistence are greater in individuals who perceive that they are capable of performing a task successfully. Research on *causal attributions* for performance suggests that effort and persistence are greater in individuals who attribute their performance to internal and controllable causes rather than to external and uncontrollable causes (Weiner, 1984, 1992). In particular, better performance is associated with a tendency to attribute success to a combination of sufficient ability and reasonable effort and a tendency to attribute failure either to insufficient effort (if this was the case), confusion about what to do, or reliance on an inappropriate strategy for trying to do it (Whitley & Frieze, 1985).

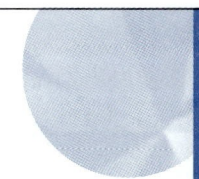

implications for teachers

helping students maintain expectations for success

Several strategies have been suggested for helping students maintain expectations for success and the desirable goal-setting behaviors, efficacy perceptions, and causal attributions that are associated with such success expectations. All of these strategies assume that students are given tasks of appropriate difficulty and receive timely and informative feedback about the correctness of their responses and about the progress they are making toward objectives. These strategies involve helping students to make and recognize genuine progress rather than misleading them or offering them only empty reassurances.

allow for progress Success that students can achieve on a particular task depends not only on the difficulty of the task but also on how well the teacher prepares them for the task through advance instruction and assists their learning efforts through guidance and feedback. Making sure that students know what to do and how to do it is an important factor in determining whether they will succeed.

It can be difficult for low achievers to be successful, especially in heterogeneous classrooms. You can help by providing extra instruction and assistance and by monitoring low achievers' progress more frequently. Give them briefer or easier assignments if they cannot succeed even with extra help and support, but continue to demand that they put forth reasonable effort and progress as fast as their abilities allow. If necessary, divide the class into subgroups that receive differentiated instruction and assignments, and grade according to mastery learning procedures

that do not penalize slower students for the extra time they take to achieve mastery (Levine, 1985) or according to criteria specified in individualized performance contracts.

When grades must be assigned according to fixed common standards, you may need to help low achievers learn to take satisfaction in receiving Bs or even Cs when such grades represent successful performance based on reasonable effort. For some lower achievers, achieving the grade of C is an occasion for taking pride in a job well done. When this is the case, teachers should express to these students (and to their parents as well) their recognition of the accomplishment and their appreciation of the effort that it represents.

Regardless of the range of achievement levels in a class, every student who consistently puts forth reasonable effort should be able to earn at least a grade of C. When this is not the case, the teacher should reflect on her or his teaching style and clarity or on the type of assignment or learning context as a possible issue.

teach goal setting, performance appraisal, and self-reinforcement Help your students to identify and use appropriate standards to judge their progress. This begins with *goal setting*, which is especially effective when the goals are *proximal*, *specific*, and *challenging*.

Goal setting is not enough by itself; there must also be *goal commitment*. Students must take goals seriously and commit themselves to trying to reach them. It may be necessary to negotiate appropriate goals with some students, or at least to provide them with guidance and to stimulate them to think about their performance potential. When an ultimate or cumulative level of performance that would earn a grade of A is not a realistic goal, help students to identify and commit themselves to realistic goals that, if reached, would yield grades of B or C (rather than to verbalize unrealistically high goals that they are not committed to). One way to do this is to provide a list of potential goals (graduated in terms of the effort required to meet them and the grades earned if success is achieved) and then ask students to commit themselves to particular goals and associated levels of effort.

Finally, students may need help in assessing progress toward established goals by using *appropriate standards for judging success.* In particular, they may need to learn to compare their work with absolute standards (progress toward achieving an objectively specified level of success) or with their own previous performance (improvement over time) rather than to judge only by comparing their work with that of peers. You can help by providing accurate but encouraging feedback. That is, your feedback about specific responses must be accurate (errors must be labeled as such if they are to be recognized and corrected), but your more general evaluative comments should provide encouragement by noting levels of success achieved in meeting established goals or by judging accomplishments with reference to what is reasonable to expect (rather than with reference to absolute perfection or to the performance of peers).

Some students need *specific, detailed feedback* concerning both the strengths and the weaknesses of their performance (Elawar & Corno, 1985). These students may have only vague appreciation of when and why they have done well or poorly, so they may need not only general evaluative feedback but also concepts and terms they can use to describe their performance and evaluate it with precision. This is especially true for compositions, research projects, laboratory experiments, and other complex activities that are evaluated using general qualitative criteria rather than by scoring answers to specific questions as correct or incorrect. Rather than just assigning letter grades, provide your students with detailed feedback about their performance on such activities.

Students who have been working toward specific proximal goals and who have the necessary concepts and language with which to evaluate their performance accurately can recognize and value the success that they achieve. Many students do this habitually, but others need encouragement to check their work and take credit for their successes. If necessary, you can focus students' attention on their progress more directly by comparing their current accomplishments with earlier performance or by having students keep scrapbooks, graphs, or other records to document their progress.

how to maintain students' success expectations
Bear in mind that the expectancy aspects of student motivation depend less on the degree of objective success students achieve than on how they view their performance: what they see as possible for them to achieve with reasonable effort, whether they define this level of achievement as successful or not, and whether they attribute their performance to controllable factors (effort, learning effective strategies) or to uncontrollable factors (fixed general ability, luck). Therefore, whatever their ability, the motivation of all students, even the most discouraged, can be reshaped by their teachers. Empty reassurances or a few words of encouragement will not do the job, but a combination of appropriately challenging demands with systematic socialization designed to make the student see that success can be achieved with reasonable effort should be effective.

In this regard, it is worth noting that teachers (not just students) need to learn to view academic frustrations and failures realistically and respond to them adaptively. As Rohrkemper and

Corno (1988) pointed out, a manageable degree of student failure is not only inevitable but desirable—when students are challenged at optimal levels of difficulty, they will make mistakes. The important thing is that learning conditions be arranged so that students get and use feedback from mistakes and respond to them with renewed motivation rather than discouragement. Learners cannot avoid mistakes, but they can learn to respond adaptively to them.

teacher expectations

Many low-achieving students present special motivational problems because these students must work very hard just to keep up. It is especially easy for their motivation and volition to erode if they develop the anxieties, low expectations, performance orientation, and excessive concern with competition. In addition to students' expectations for their own performance, teachers' expectations for students' performance can also become part of the problem.

Teacher expectations are *inferences that teachers make about present and future academic achievement and general classroom behavior of students.* General expectations include teachers' beliefs about the changeability versus the rigidity of students' abilities, the students' potential to benefit from instruction, and the appropriate difficulty of assigned material. Expectations for individual students may be based on student record information (test data, past grades, comments by previous teachers), knowledge about the family, or initial contact with the student in the classroom. Research has shown that contact with students leads to the formation of stable (and largely accurate) differential expectations within a few days after the school year begins (Brophy & Good, 1974). The formation of expectations is normal and is inherently neither good nor bad. The critical issues are the *accuracy* of the expectations and the *flexibility* with which they are held. Inaccurate expectations will do damage if teachers not only do not correct them but begin to base instructional decisions on them.

Expectations tend to be self-sustaining. They affect both *perception*, by causing teachers to be alert for what they expect and less likely to notice what they do not expect, and *interpretation*, by causing teachers to interpret (and perhaps distort) what they see so that it is consistent with their expectations. Some expectations persist even though they do not coincide with the facts.

self-fulfilling prophecy effects of teacher expectations

Teachers' expectations can function as self-fulfilling prophecies if they influence teachers to behave in ways that confirm the teachers' original expectations. A **self-fulfilling prophecy** is a *prediction that, if accepted, works to make itself come true. For instance, once a teacher forms a certain performance assessment of a student, the teacher's judgment may help to produce the expected behavior in the student.* When a teacher's initial perceptions of students' ability or motivation are inaccurate, the teacher may treat the students as if they were different from how they really are. In time, such teacher behavior may move students in the direction of the originally erroneous perceptions, thus confirming the teacher's expectations, at least in part.

Jan Getty, *an average first grader, is the daughter of a well-known artist. Her teacher knows that the artist is bright and creative, and she attributes these same qualities to Jan even though Jan*

research at work
communication of low expectations

The following are some of the most common ways in which low teacher expectations can be expressed through teacher behavior (Good & Brophy, 1994). In presenting this list and elsewhere in the chapter we use the term "low" to refer to students who have performed relatively poorly in comparison to other students on a particular segment of classroom assignments. We use this language to describe the dynamics of expectations, not to label students nor to suggest that ability is fixed.

1. Waiting less time for lows to answer questions (compared to how long the teacher typically waits for other students to answer).
2. Giving lows the answer by calling on someone else (instead of trying to elicit the answer by giving clues or rephrasing the question).
3. Rewarding inappropriate behavior of lows. In some studies teachers have been found to inappropriately praise marginal or inaccurate student responses. Praising incor-

rect responses when peers know the answer may only emphasize the academic weakness of low achievers.

4. Criticizing lows more frequently for failure. In contrast, in some studies teachers have been found to criticize lows proportionately more frequently than highs when lows provide wrong answers. This is likely to reduce the risk-taking behavior and general initiative of lows. (The contrast between variables 3 and 4 probably reflects different teacher personalities. Teachers who praise inappropriate answers from lows may be overly sympathetic toward these students, whereas overly critical teachers may be irritated at them for delaying the class or providing evidence that instruction has not been completely successful.)
5. Praising lows less frequently for success. Some research has shown that when lows provide correct answers they are less likely to be praised than highs, even though they provide fewer correct responses.
6. Not giving feedback to public responses of

rarely exhibits behavior that others would call creative. Jan's day-to-day behavior is actually routine and marked by a dependency on others for direction. Yet the teacher consistently encourages Jan "to do her own thing." She accepts Jan's work but demands that Jan express her own thoughts. By the end of the year, Jan is among the most original thinkers in the room. She can project five or six plausible but creative alternative endings for the stories in the reader.

The process described in this example is not

magical. Nor do teacher expectations influence student behavior directly. If student behavior is influenced, it is because the expectations are expressed through teacher behavior or classroom arrangements (the types of assignments the student receives, the level of group he or she is placed in, and so on).

True instances of self-fulfilling prophecies include these three factors: (1) an originally unjustified expectation, (2) behaviors that consistently communicate that expectation, and (3) evidence that the original expectation

lows. Teachers in some studies were found simply to move on to the next question following lows' answers (especially correct answers), instead of first taking a moment to confirm those answers. This is particularly undesirable in that these students, more than others, may be unsure of the adequacy of their responses.

7. Paying less attention to lows or interacting with them less frequently.

8. Calling on lows less often (this is especially likely in the higher grades).

9. Different interaction patterns with highs and lows. In elementary classrooms, highs dominate public-response opportunities, although highs and lows receive about the same number of private teacher contacts. In secondary classrooms, highs become even more dominant in public settings, but lows receive more private conferences. Here, frequent private conferences with teachers may be a sign of inadequacy and a source of embarrassment, especially if the teacher does not initiate many such conferences with highs.

10. Demanding less from lows. This is an extension of the more focused "giving-up" behavior discussed in variable 2 and refers to activities such as giving lows easier tests (and letting them know it) or simply not asking them to do academic work.

11. Other forms of differential treatment include (a) seating lows farther from the teacher; (b) interacting with lows more privately than publicly and monitoring and structuring their activities more closely; (c) differential grading of tests and assignments in which highs but not lows are given the benefit of the doubt in borderline cases; (d) less friendly interactions with lows, including less smiling and less informative feedback to their questions; (e) less eye contact and other nonverbal communication of attention and responsiveness; (f) less use of effective but time-consuming methods with lows when time is limited; (g) less acceptance and use of lows' ideas.

has been confirmed. Self-fulfilling prophecies may occur with or without teachers' awareness that their behavior is being influenced systematically by their expectations.

sustaining effects of teacher expectations

Self-fulfilling prophecies are the most dramatic teacher-expectation effects because they involve *changes* in student behavior. Cooper and Good (1983) used the term **sustaining expectations** to refer to *situations in which teachers fail to see student potential and hence do not respond in ways that encourage the students to fulfill their potential*. If a teacher, for example, automatically places all students who were in a low group last year into a low group this year (without assessing their current abilities), the teacher will fail to capitalize on new potential that may have developed in some of these students.

In general, self-fulfilling expectations bring

Changes in teacher expectations can also motivate students beyond traditional gender roles.

about change in student performance, whereas sustaining expectations prevent change. Sustaining expectation effects are subtle but occur frequently, whereas self-fulfilling prophecy effects are more dramatic but occur less frequently. In this chapter we organize information around the concept of self-fulfilling prophecies, but both types of expectation effects are important.

teacher-expectation effects: a model

Below is a model that we developed (Brophy & Good, 1974) to describe how teachers' expectations can become self-fulfilling prophecies:

1. The teacher expects specific behavior and achievement from particular students.
2. Because of these expectations, the teacher behaves differently toward different students.

3. This treatment by the teacher tells each student what behavior and achievement the teacher expects, and it affects the student's self-concept, achievement motivation, and level of aspiration.
4. If this teacher treatment is consistent over time, and if the student does not actively resist or change it in some way, it will shape the student's achievement and behavior. High-expectation students will be led to achieve at high levels, but the achievement of low-expectation students will decline.
5. With time, the student's achievement and behavior will conform more and more closely to that expected by the teacher.

Teacher expectations are not automatically self-fulfilling. Students may prevent such expectations from becoming fulfilled by resisting them in ways that force teachers to change them.

appropriate expectations and treatment of low achievers

We begin by noting two expectations that are sometimes recommended but that we see as *inappropriate*: equal expectations for all or high expectations for all. First, we do *not* suggest that all students should receive equal (in the sense of identical) classroom treatment. Some students learn more quickly than others. Some are reticent but able to learn by actively listening and covertly responding to what they hear. Thus, *sameness* is inappropriate as an expectation and self-defeating as a strategy. Second, exceedingly high expectations are not realistic for all students. In hopes of motivating student performance, a teacher might announce: "This story is interesting and easy to read, so all of you should finish it in ten minutes." If some students need twenty minutes to read the story, they are left with two choices: They can pretend to finish it and hope they are not "found out," or they can continue to read while the teacher or their peers make remarks about their slowness. These students will feed bad either way, and if such events are repeated regularly, they will tend either to accept their inferior status or to blame the teacher. Overly high performance expectations that are consistently impossible for students to reach will eventually erode their efforts. What teachers should expect is that students will do their best.

Teachers are human and will make errors in assessing students' needs. The way to reduce errors is to obtain information about classroom behavior. Teachers need to become more aware of their classroom behavior in general and their interactions with low achievers in particular. As a starting point, teachers could review their behavior with an eye toward the following questions:

Do I praise or encourage lows when they initiate questions or comments?

Do I stay with lows in failure situations?

Do I stay with lows in success situations?

Do I avoid calling on lows in public situations?

How often do lows experience success in public situations?

Are lows needlessly criticized for wrong answers or failure to respond?

Are lows placed in a "low group" and treated as group members rather than as individuals?

How often do lows get to select a study topic?

How frequently do lows have a chance to evaluate their own work and to make important decisions?

skill development through meaningful practice

Teachers sometimes overrespond to low achievers' skill deficiencies. At first glance, this seems to be reasonable. If students are weak in word-attack skills, they need to develop such skills if they are to become independent readers. However, if they work constantly on skills without reading for meaning, their motivation to learn may be eroded. Thus, teachers who constantly interrupt poor readers when they are reading may compound their problems by reducing the time they spend practicing reading. If students are to derive personal satisfaction from any task, they must have the opportunity for meaningful and successful practice. Students who have low reading ability need the chance to practice *the act of reading* (Allington, 1991; Hiebert, 1991). It is amazing to see how little time low achievers have for reading in some classrooms. Too often they are drowned in a sea of drill work and constant reminders of inadequate performance. Teachers need to balance their demands for drill with opportunity for students to read for meaning and pleasure (in content-area books and works of fiction, not just basal readers).

Student motivation can be eroded in other ways. How would you feel if everything that you did was done better and faster by someone else? This is the situation that poor readers often face. They hear the teacher discuss a story with other students long before they have a chance to read it. If this experience is repeated daily, it is apt to lower their interest in the reading material because they have already heard others discuss the story. Furthermore, it is hard for teachers to bring the same degree of enthusiasm to each new discussion of the same story. Teacher motivation may thus influence students' response. Teachers may inadvertently focus more on the mechanics of reading than on comprehension by the time they read the story with low achievers. One way to break out of this joint trap for teachers and poor readers would be to assign different stories periodically to the low reading group. New stories would provide a chance for these students to reach their own conclusions and insights. Yet another and perhaps more fundamental strategy would be to teach high- and low-achieving students together. It may be appropriate at times to group students briefly by ability (e.g., work on vocabulary or reading fluency), but at other times it is more reasonable to teach students of diverse ability together (when discussing plot, alternative endings, etc.).

Another way that teachers can address the motivational problems of low achievers is to challenge high achievers appropriately. If teachers are exposing high achievers to material of appropriate difficulty, then these students, too, will make mistakes from time to time. Teachers will have to review word-attack and interpretive skills with highs as well. The fact that all students have to exert effort will not be lost on the low achievers.

The low-ability student frequently gets to do an activity only *after* more capable students have performed the task. In elementary schools, teachers often allow students free work *after* assigned tasks are completed. In high school chemistry classrooms, more complex experiments are performed only after simpler experiments have been completed successfully. Opportunities for independent study are often available only after certain work has been completed.

There are times when a fixed sequence has to be followed (for example, all students need to master safety procedures in the lab). If teachers analyze the situation carefully, however, if is often possible to assign tasks so that students who move through the curriculum more slowly do not always repeat the same experience as the others. These students could be asked to perform relatively simple but different experiments. Indeed, when slower students are doing such work, more advanced students might be referred to them to learn about the outcomes of experiments that they themselves did not perform. In our opinion, unless there is a clear compelling reason to group students by ability, teachers should instruct students in mixed-ability groups (Bennett & Dunne, 1992).

treating low achievers as individuals

Although teachers too often group and treat all low achievers as though they were similar, it is vital that teachers learn about the unique needs and interests of students who may view school as irrelevant or aversive. Unfortunately, when teachers visit informally with students, it is rarely with lows. Most of these students want teacher contact but do not know how to obtain it, and they may think that teachers like them less than other students and do not want to be bothered with them.

Many low achievers initially played the academic game as best they could, but teacher or peer feedback proved so disheartening that they learned that an academic question avoided is an academic battle won. Teacher criticism of any serious response attempt is inappropriate in any situation but especially for passive, low-achieving students. Students who respond with passivity have been rewarded for such behavior and have learned that making no response is better than taking a chance. Teachers need to convince such students that their responses will not be evaluated harshly and that responding is the best way to get teacher attention and help.

Other students respond to threatening situations with different strategies. For example, some students may respond to teachers with open hostility. Such behavior may bring teacher criticism for rudeness and poor attitude, but it avoids negative teacher evaluation of the student's ability and sometimes even elicits indirect compliments ("If you read and improve your attitude, you'd be one of the best students in the class!").

Student behaviors that have been institutionalized through practice and reward are difficult to change. The first step is to recognize the coping strategy that the student uses and then systematically reward competing responses (e.g., answering versus not answering). But to be able to do this, it is necessary for teachers to know individual students.

Students who are victimized by low expectations and inappropriate classroom treatment may be entirely correct when they attribute their task success to external factors. If teachers do not make it possible for such students to achieve success with reasonable effort and do not reward such effort, students are unlikely to perceive a dependable relationship between personal effort and task success.

implications for teachers

changing students' low expectations

Some students with long histories of failure tend to give up at the first sign of difficulty and need more intensive and individualized motivational encouragement than the rest of the class. These students are likely to benefit from the strategies used in mastery learning approaches: Give them tasks they should be able to handle, provide them not only with the usual group instruction but also with individualized tutoring as needed, and allow them to contract for particular levels of performance and to continue to study, practice, and take tests until that level of performance is achieved. This approach builds confidence and increases discouraged students' willingness to take the risks involved in committing themselves to challenging goals (Grabe, 1985).

You can also help by working to improve these students' beliefs, attitudes, and expectations about learning. One way is to *portray effort as investment rather than risk*. Help discouraged students to appreciate that learning may take time and involve confusion or mistakes but that persistence and careful work should eventually yield knowledge or skill mastery. Furthermore, such mastery not only represents success on the particular task involved but also empowers students by arming them with knowledge or skills that will enable them to handle higher-level tasks better in the future. If they give up on tasks that they could master if they persisted, they cheat themselves out of such growth.

It also helps to *portray skill development as incremental and domain specific*. Make sure that your students realize that their intellectual abilities are open to improvement rather than fixed and limited, that they possess many such abilities rather than just a few, and that their success depends not only on general ability but also on possession and use of a range of knowledge and strategies built up gradually through many experiences in each domain. Difficulty in learning mathematics does not necessarily imply difficulty in learning other subjects, and even within mathematics, difficulty in learning to graph coordinates does not necessarily mean difficulty in learning to solve differential equations or understand geometric relationships.

In this connection, it is helpful if you *focus on mastery* when monitoring the performance of discouraged students and giving them feedback. Stress the quality of students' task engagement and the degree to which they make continuous progress rather than compare them with peers. Treat errors as learning opportunities rather than as failures: errors should lead to remedial or additional instruction followed by additional practice opportunities. Make-up exams, credit for effort, or extra-credit assignments should be used to provide struggling students with opportunities to overcome initial failures through persistent effort.

Discouraged students may also benefit from *attribution retraining* (Craske, 1985; Dweck & Elliott, 1983). Attribution retraining involves modeling, socialization, and practice exercises designed to help students learn (1) to concentrate on doing the task at hand rather than to become distracted by fear of failure, (2) to cope with frustrations by retracing their steps to find their mistakes or by analyzing problems to find other ways to approach them (rather than to give up), and (3) to attribute their failures to insufficient effort, lack of information, or reliance on ineffective strategies rather than to lack of ability. Rather than merely telling students about these things using third-person (direction-giving) language, you are likely to communicate these cognitive strategies for coping

with academic tasks most successfully if you model them for students using first-person (thinking out loud) language—demonstrating how to do the task yourself while verbalizing the thinking ("self-talk") that guides your actions. Discouraged students are especially likely to benefit from modeling that includes verbalization of the self-talk involved in maintaining composure and focusing on developing solutions to the problem when confronted with frustration or failure (as opposed to modeling of smooth, successful performance that unfolds without confusion or difficulty). In other words, your modeling should not only convince discouraged students that *you* can do the task (they already know that, anyway) but also should convince these students that *they* can do the task (because they already possess, or can reasonably expect to learn, the necessary knowledge and skills). Such modeling demystifies the task for students and arms them with coping strategies they can use instead of giving up when they become confused or frustrated.

Finally, some students may suffer from severe *test anxiety*. These students may perform well enough in informal, pressure-free situations but become highly anxious and perform considerably below their potential on tests or during any test-like situation in which they are aware of being monitored and evaluated (Covington, 1992). You can minimize such problems by avoiding time pressures unless they are truly central to the skill being taught, stressing the feedback functions rather than the evaluation or grading function of tests when discussing tests with students; portraying tests as opportunities to assess progress in developing knowledge or skills rather than as measures of ability; when appropriate, telling students that some problems are beyond their present achievement so they should not be concerned about missing them; giving pretests to accustom students to "failure" and to provide base rates for comparison later when posttests are administered; and teaching stress-management skills and effective test-taking skills and attitudes (Hill & Wigfield, 1984; Plass & Hill, 1986).

linking outcomes to effort

A key teacher task in increasing student motivation is to help students perceive the relationship between successes and personal effort. As a starting point, teachers might ask students to discuss tasks on which they have done poorly and to explain why they thought their performances were poor. Teachers also need to assess students' ability to determine the amount of time and effort necessary to complete tasks successfully. Teachers might ask students to estimate the time required to complete a task, for example, collect followup information, and provide this information to students during conferences. Teachers could also help students to distinguish between tasks they can and cannot do. Similarly, teachers could check the accuracy of students' perceptions by asking them to indicate the extent to which they had correctly answered various examination questions. Students need to see what happens when they apply themselves to academic tasks. Thus, the next step is to create a series of tasks that are clearly tied to effort so that greater effort produces greater success.

After demonstrating that performance outcome is related to effort expenditure, teachers should inform students through individual conferences that the teacher regularly assigns tasks that they can do and that anytime they cannot find information or do not know how to proceed, they should ask for help. It is also useful to stress that tasks are assigned to facilitate learning and thus designed to benefit the student, not just to fill time. The teacher also should create the expectation that assigned tasks, although appropriately difficult and challenging, can be completed if the students want to do so. Once students see that their personal efforts are related to task success, it is more difficult for them to explain away failure.

emphasizing instructional help, not sympathy

Sympathy alone is misplaced and self-defeating. Teachers who give easier tests to low achievers, who always ask them elementary questions, or who give up on them in public-response situations do not help, and often worsen, their plight.

Kleinfeld (1975) showed this in a penetrating ethnographic analysis of teacher behavior with Native American and Eskimo students who were experiencing culture shock on moving from their native, rural schools to urban, integrated schools. She found that the most effective teachers were those who took a personal interest in students, engaged in informal conversations with them, adapted instruction to their different backgrounds and achievement levels, were highly supportive of their attempts to learn, and avoided use of criticism. In addition, these highly effective teachers elicited high intellectual performance from the village Native American and Eskimo students by creating warm personal relationships and demanding a level of academic work "that the student does not suspect he can attain." Village students interpreted the teachers' demandingness not as bossiness or hostility but rather as another expression of personal concern, so meeting the teachers' academic standards became their reciprocal obligation in an intensely personal relationship.

creating an appropriate classroom climate

Teachers can help low achievers gain more self-respect and respect from classmates if they allow them to achieve notable *public success* from time to time. This involves careful planning, because trivial or unsuccessful exposure of low achievers

Cultural differences can affect students' reactions to instruction. To teach heterogeneous classes, teachers need to value diversity and encourage students to learn from one another and to appreciate different languages and traditions.

may deepen the problem. However, public success is important and worth planning for, because most of the successes of lows are private, although many of their failures occur in public.

Often teachers can use unique talents that students already possess or can capitalize on their lifestyles. Kleinfeld (1975), for example, reported that some teachers were able to increase the prestige of village students and reduce hostility toward them by making their skills, such as "surviving in the wilderness," public knowledge. At other times, teachers need to work with students to help them learn skills (such as teaching a fifth-grade student how to run a projector or allowing the student to make a movie) that they can demonstrate publicly. Repeated public successes, especially those involving skills deemed important by the peer group, will do much to raise the esteem with which lows are regarded by their classmates.

maintaining motivation

Lyn Corno (1993) maintains that some students have sufficient motivation (their goals are appropriate) but that students' motivation is eroded by insufficient self-regulation capacity. She suggests that many students need to devel-op volitional skills (the ability to require commitment to the goal). For example, students are often distracted by a noisy or unpleasant student who sits alongside.

One strategy that Corno identifies is "meta-motivational" control, which directs emotional and intellectual energy toward academic goals. Such motivational control helps the student to concentrate even when confronted with personal or environmental distractions. The lists below present two types of volitional control strategies that students can be taught. Students who have a history of poor performance (e.g., not finishing seat work, not doing homework) may behave in this manner not because they lack motivation but because they lack volitional control.

Motivation control*

Set contingencies for performance that can be carried out mentally (e.g., self-reward; self-imposed penance; self-applied Premack).

Escalate goals by prioritizing and imagining their value.

*SOURCE: Corno, L. (1993). The Best-Laid Plans: Modern Conceptions of Volition and Educational Research. *Educational Researcher, 22*, 14-22.

Visualize doing the work successfully.

Uncover ways to make the work more fun or challenging.

Immerse yourself in plans for achieving goals.

Self-instruct.

Analyze failures to direct a second try.

Emotion control

Count to 10 in your head.

Control breathing so it is slow, steady, and deep.

Generate useful diversions (e.g., sing to yourself).

Visualize doing the work successfully and feeling good about that (change the way you respond emotionally to the task).

Recall your strengths and your available resources.

Consider any negative feelings about the experience and ways to make it more reassuring.

NOTE: Examples of strategies were derived from Kuhl (1985) and in discussions with teachers and students.

awareness of cultural differences

It is beyond the scope of this chapter to discuss in detail issues of multiculturalism. There are many excellent chapters and book-length manuscripts that focus exclusively on this topic (Agger, 1992; Appleton, 1983; Casanova, 1987). We do want to assert that teachers, especially if they have not had coursework in this area, need to explore the ethnic and cultural differences of their students. It is important to understand values and behaviors that make

people similar as well as to appreciate differences that makes them distinctive. Casanova (1987) notes that all students will react differently to instruction because of unique experiences each student brings to the classroom. Although many of these experiences do not interfere with learning, Casanova notes that some do, and that it is the teacher's responsibility to recognize such problems.

According to Casanova, it is difficult to write about cultural differences because the research base is underdeveloped and superficial discussions tend to solidify features of cultural groups in ways that lead to stereotyping. She argues that differences between cultural groups mask considerable individual differences within groups:

> In our discussion, culture and ethnicity will be considered as part of everyone's personal being rather than special characteristics of people who differ from the dominant culture. At no time will the word *culture* be used to suggest artistic or intellectual achievement, nor will it be used to refer to surface differences, such as style of dress or music. Culture includes all the ways in which people think, feel, and act as they try to solve their particular problems. Because these things are not static, we view culture as dynamic. Part of our humanity is the ability to learn and grow. Some changes, like learning that one buys fruit at the store, come easy; some, like acquiring different rules of politeness, are more difficult; and some behaviors, like looking away from or looking directly at a person to whom one is speaking, are almost impossible to change because they are unconscious. (Casanova, 1987, p. 373)

To reiterate, a comprehensive discussion of issues like cultural influences on thought, culture, and communication, social linguistic differences, nonverbal communication, and school culture versus home culture are beyond the scope of this chapter. To teach heterogeneous classes, teachers need to value diversity and to encourage students to learn from one another and to appreciate different languages and traditions. For the most part, differences among students are to be respected and understood, not altered. In addition to professional reading, teachers can best prepare themselves for dealing with cultural differences by talking with community leaders, visiting homes and discussing with parents, and most importantly, private conversations with students about schoolwork and individual aspirations.

summary

Ames stated a goal theory framework and illustrated how classroom conditions may influence the type of goals students develop. Her work stresses the importance of allowing students to develop mastery orientations, and she provides theoretical arguments and research evidence to suggest how teachers can structure classrooms to encourage mastery orientations. Related work by Dweck, Marshall, and Nicholls was also presented to further articulate both the theory and application of a goal theory framework.

Student and teacher goals are important expectations that influence classroom motivation and performance. As we argued previously, an expectancy x value model provides a useful framework for thinking about classroom motivation. Learning should not focus on discrete facts or isolated concepts but rather should encourage students to understand and integrate material so they can apply it in new contexts. Thus, motivation should not focus on quantity or speed of learning. Instead, the motivational task for the teacher is to encourage students to explore material thoughtfully (i.e., quality of learning).

In this chapter we have discussed how teachers can influence in positive ways students' views of and motivation for classroom learning assignments. In particular, we have focused on the importance of developing students' expectations for appropriate classroom orientations (mastery goals, not performance goals), and we have discussed general strategies for helping students and specific strategies for dealing with the expectations of low achievers. We have also noted that one aspect of helping students to maintain success expectations is by furthering their capacity for volitional control. Finally, we have noted that building successful motivational systems in classroom settings requires recognition both of cultural differences and individual differences in students.

questions for reflection

1. What difference does it make if students believe that their grades depend more on luck than on hard work? How might such a perception influence the way that they prepare for exams?

2. What are the major differences between achievement motivation theory and attribution theory? To what extent might one's gender or culture influence one's achievement motivation or the type of attributions that one makes following failure?

3. Define task involvement and ego involvement in your own words. If you were introducing a

new curriculum unit, what could you do to make it more likely that students would respond to it with task involvement?

4. Think about the course you are now taking from the perspective of task involvement and ego involvement. What percentage of the assignments create task involvement in you? Why is this the case?

5. Given that too much structure for one student may be too little structure for another, how can teachers apply theories of personal causation (e.g., mastery) in the classroom?

6. What do you see as implications of research on strategies to avoid failure? How can a teacher reduce the likelihood that students will feel the need to employ such strategies?

7. How might you begin and end lessons to improve their motivational value?

▶ cases to consider

middle of the road Clara Green is a tenth-grade speech teacher at a high school serving an upper-middle-class population in a small but affluent community that includes a state university. Clara's class is distinguished by infrequent disturbances but minimum student involvement. Students pay attention but do not seem interested in activities. Class periods usually involve three or four students presenting speeches, with each speech followed by a couple of minutes of critique. Types of speeches vary from month to month (e.g., a prepared sales speech, an expository speech).

The course is well organized, and Clara distributes examples of model speeches, reading lists, and evaluation sheets adapted to the different types of speeches students give. The evaluation sheets emphasize speech format rather than content (e.g., Are all parts of the expository speech there? Is too much time spent on any one part? Is the delivery acceptable?). Few students in Clara's class dread giving their speeches or feel embarrassed about the feedback they get from the other students, because she emphasizes that students should be positive and gracious in their responses. Accordingly, students often gush when they give feedback to classmates. In general, they view the course as easy and mildly interesting.

What types of students are most likely to benefit from this class? Why? How might Clara make the class more meaningful to other types of students?

overgeneralizing Hal Lanier has never worked with Hispanic students. He grew up in Wisconsin and attended school at Michigan State University. He and his wife have decided to move to Texas because she has been accepted to medical school and he wants to experience a new culture. He will now teach tenth grade English at a high school in San Antonio where he will teach classes in which 80 percent of students are Hispanic. Hal wants to do a good job and he has been reading books about Mexican culture so he can understand his students. He believes, for example, that Hispanic students like cooperative learning so he plans to use a lot of cooperative learning activities and will ask students to write on topics of personal interest (bullfighting, Native American art). What mistakes might Hal be making in his approach to planning?

playing it safe Although Frank spends an hour and a half each night studying for Spanish class, he tells his friends that he never studies. Furthermore, he tries to get the teacher's attention early in the lesson because he wants to answer any questions. When he takes part in the conversational part of the lesson (which he does only when called on), he is careful to use words that are easy to pronounce. How would you characterize Frank's problem? What, if anything, should his teacher do about it?

hostile Bill Mr. Baker hesitated to call on Bill Maddi, a large boy with a sullen look on his face who sat in the rear of the sixth-grade classroom.

Bill had acted in a distant, hostile way all day, even though nothing had transpired between the teacher and Bill on this, the opening day of school. Finally, Mr. Baker decided that he had to interact with Bill, and he said, with some uncertainty, "Bill, would you read the directions for the next set of exercises?" Bill retorted loudly and quickly, "No, I'm not interested in this stupid stuff." After quieting the class, Mr. Baker called on another student to respond, and the period continued.

During the rest of the week several similar incidents occurred. Each time Bill was asked to read he refused to do so, sometimes gracefully or humorously, but generally with belligerence or hostility. When Bill was asked to make an oral response, however, he usually did so. Finally, Mr. Baker put two and two together and concluded that Bill could not read well and was embarrassed to do so in front of the class. How could Mr. Baker verify his hypotheses during an interview with Bill? What should he say and do? If he is correct that Bill cannot read well, what should he do about it? Specifically, what instructional tasks should Bill be assigned? What should a typical school day be like for Bill?

motivation: helping students to value learning

objectives

When you have mastered the material in this chapter, you will be able to

1. Understand the four motivational tasks that teachers must perform and be able to apply how these tasks can be influenced by classroom conditions
2. Explain the value that accommodating student interest and allowing choice in learning activities has for classroom motivation
3. Apply Keller's motivational model (interest, relevance, expectancy, and satisfaction) on classroom tasks at the grade level and subject that you intend to teach
4. Understand and apply Brophy's model for encouraging students to value learning

In Chapter 13 we discussed expectancy issues associated with the expectancy × value model. Here we discuss value issues, emphasizing strategies for making student learning as stimulating, authentic, and worthwhile as possible.

Even when students are confident that they can succeed if they invest in a task, they need reasons for doing so. Unfortunately, there has not been as much research on the value aspects of motivation as on the expectancy aspects (Berndt & Miller, 1990). However, theories, models, and research do exist, and we draw on them in this chapter to suggest ways of helping students to appreciate the value of what they are learning.

Brophy (1991a) argues that intrinsic motivation is primarily an affective response to an activity (the student enjoys it or finds it interesting). Although teachers' opportunities to capitalize on intrinsic motivation by allowing students to engage in classroom activities that they enjoy are sometimes limited, inventive teachers can find various ways in which to capitalize upon classroom opportunities. Where intrinsic motivational strategies are used to increase students' enjoyment of and involvement in assignments, they do not necessarily increase students'

motivation to learn the content or skills being taught, although this might be a by-product.

Brophy (1991a) argues that to develop student motivation to learn, and for students to internalize it as an enduring disposition (rather than just associate it with a particular activity), teachers must help students come to value school learning for its self-actualization and life-application potential. To help their students develop a sense of ownership of learning, which is a personal strategy for integrating material, teachers must achieve two motivational goals. First, they must create a favorable classroom learning environment by modeling motivation to learn, minimizing students' performance anxiety, and communicating desirable expectations and attributions (e.g., that students will apply what they learn to their lives outside school). Second, teachers need to stimulate motivation to learn in connection with particular content or activities by projecting enthusiasm, inducing task interest, inducing curiosity, making abstract content personal, inducing dissonance, formulating learning goals, providing informative feedback, and helping students to learn with metacognitive awareness of goals and metacognitive control of strategies.

In this chapter we also present Newmann's ideas about how to make schoolwork more authentic and more like adult work. We also discuss Keller's principles for enhancing the motivational aspects of classroom learning. From his framework, the critical dimensions are interest, relevance, expectancy, and satisfaction. Work on motivation in education has progressed from an almost exclusive focus on the individual student to a focus that includes both individual students and the class as a unit (i.e., a learning community). More recent work has studied motivation not only at the class level but also at the school level (Ames & Stover, 1993; Blumenfeld, 1993; Weinstein & Butterworth, 1993). Accordingly, in the final section of the chapter we integrate discussion of personal investment theory with other arguments about the influence of school structure and climate on motivation.

motivational tasks for the teacher

Motivational theories cannot be interpreted literally and applied in oversimplified ways. Intrinsic-motivation theories, for example, are meant to predict behavior in free-choice situations, but students are required to attend school and learn a curriculum prescribed for them by someone else. Similarly, most students will take more risks in a casual ring-toss game where nothing much is at stake than in ego-involving classroom situations where their reputations for intellectual competence may be on the line. Helping students become adaptive risk takers in the classroom is a difficult task (Rohrkemper & Corno, 1988).

The motivational challenge facing teachers involves going beyond eliciting student cooper-

ation in meeting requirements. If students are motivated solely by grades or other extrinsic rewards or punishments, they concentrate merely on meeting minimal requirements (Covington, 1992). They do what is necessary to prepare for tests but then forget most of what they have learned. Teachers must use motivational strategies to elicit a higher quality of student engagement in classroom activities—ideally, the self-regulated learning described by Corno and Rohrkemper (1985) and McCaslin (1990). Four important subtasks are involved in the larger motivational task facing teachers: (1) structuring assignments, (2) maintaining task involvement, (3) maintaining motivation over the school year, and (4) building or enhancing students' capacity for self-evaluation. We will further discuss issues related to maintaining task involvement (see management Part VI). In the previous chapter we discussed the need for students to become better at self-evaluation and volitional control.

structuring assignments

Although students spend a great deal of their time in classrooms working on academic tasks, such tasks had not received much research attention until recently, and the findings produced so far are not encouraging (Doyle, 1992a; Good & Brophy, 1994). A virtually universal finding of surveys on educational practices, for example, is that students appear to be spending too much time on isolated skill practice in the form of workbooks or worksheets emphasizing dull repetition of primarily low-level activities. Students with low achievement motivation due to strong fear of failure may value such activities to the extent that they are both predictable and easy, but no students are likely to be genuinely enthusiastic about them. Most assignments could be much more interesting, varied in both format and cognitive level, and enjoyable than they are.

Even though assignments tend to require only low-level responses, they vary in difficulty and often are poorly matched to students' current needs, especially when teachers give everyone the same assignment. Even when teachers attempt to vary assignment difficulty, they tend to underestimate the capabilities of their highest achievers and overestimate those of their lowest achievers (Bennett & Desforges, 1988).

Academic tasks—*formal classroom assignments*—consist of four parts according to Doyle (1986a): (1) a product to be produced by the student (answers to questions, an essay); (2) operations to produce the product (remembering facts from previous instruction, looking up facts in a text, generating and organizing ideas); (3) resources (lecture notes, the text); and (4) the weight of the task in the accountability system (how much it counts toward the final grade). Doyle believes that students tend to be highly concerned about their grades and thus motivated to ask questions and negotiate with teachers to minimize task ambiguity (about exactly what must be done) and the risk of failure that a task entails. This can lead to both a proliferation of guidelines about the form that responses should take (the composition should include at least 300 words, at least four paragraphs, a clear topic sentence for each paragraph, at least three reference sources, and so on), often with an accompanying reduction in the cognitive level of the task (what was supposed to be an opportunity for creative synthesis becomes a routinized exercise in fact telling). Sometimes both teacher and students lose sight of the original academic purpose of the task and it becomes just one more thing to get done.

Blumenfeld, Mergendoller, and Swarthout (1987) described other ways in which the form of a task can defeat the academic purposes that it is intended to accomplish.

They note that task form and content are independent, so that tasks can have simple forms while being cognitively complex (workbook pages featuring difficult problems) or can be cognitively simple but complex in form (scientific experiments that demand that many materials be used by several students but require the students only to record a simple observation and not to make inferences or draw conclusions). Their research indicates that students often become confused when new or ambiguous tasks are introduced or when tasks are procedurally complex even though they may be cognitively simple. Unless teachers provide sufficient guidance in these situations, students may become overly focused on the procedural aspects of tasks so that they do not get the proper academic benefit from them (e.g., they may spend so much time gathering and preparing materials for a science experiment that they do not spend sufficient time actually carrying it out or thinking about the results). Blumenfeld and Meece (1988) found that students' cognitive engagement in tasks was low when tasks were procedurally complex, so it was important for teachers to counteract this by structuring and guiding the students' work, monitoring their task engagement, and making it clear that they expected the students to master the academic content that the task was designed to teach (not merely to have students participate in the procedural activities). Thus, student motivation and learning are affected both by the nature of assignments and by the ways teachers structure assignments.

Students need tasks that are challenging but only moderately difficult given their ability levels. The context in which students work and their interest in a task can affect its difficulty level. Tasks need to be somewhat easier, for example, when students are to work independently than when they have access to immediate feedback.

Also, assignments should capture stu-

One way to maintain interest is to schedule an activity that is unexpected and pleasurable.

dents' attention. Teachers should either choose topics that relate to students' interests or create interest in the topic. Task interest can be ensured by allowing students to choose topics whenever possible. In this regard, teachers might have students provide a brief written explanation of the reasons for their choices. Such feedback might help the teacher and student, in time, to use and understand personal preferences and interests. Teachers need to search for topics that from an educational psychology perspective are relevant to students' age, stage, or life.

Another aspect of structuring assignments well is to be sure that their goals and means to reaching those goals are clear. Otherwise, students may work hard but perform poorly on tests because they are uncertain of the expectation. Increasingly, educators have recognized the importance of classroom learning tasks in influencing the extent to which students value academic learning.

maintaining motivation throughout the year

All of us grow tired of doing the same thing day after day. One way to maintain interest is to schedule something occasionally that is both unexpected and pleasurable. Such special events can be related to academic goals. Students might prepare a classroom newspaper, for example, or construct a new learning center. At times, they might be assigned responsibilities that are fun and suited to their individual abilities and interests (e.g., writing a creative essay, interviewing peers, reporting sports results).

There are good reasons for making special events relevant to previous academic assignments. Once students complete a unit they often do not encounter the material again, so the use of previous learning in novel ways can encourage student motivation on daily assignments by helping students to see that the material they study will benefit them in the future. Knowing that the material will be used later encourages retention and integration.

If progress is to be made, much classroom work must involve hard work and persistence (Corno, 1993). Teachers need to expect this and to teach students how to mobilize their time and energy for extended periods. However, teachers also need to incorporate variety and occasional pauses into the classroom routine to reinvigorate student motivation throughout the entire school year. Although the value of an instructional technique depends on its curriculum content and learning goals, variety in learning modes and assignments is useful for motivational purposes.

implications for teachers

teachers' strategies for influencing motivation

Teachers can manipulate four major conditions in the classroom: the *tasks* students are assigned, *students' perceptions of these tasks*, their *rapport* with students, and the *reward structures* involved.

Teachers can manipulate task design features (content, difficulty, abstractness, length) as well as the settings in which tasks occur (whole class, small groups, individual) and the time allowed for completion. They also can alter the frequency of feedback, the type of feedback (conference, written), and the percentage of time students work on assigned or self-selected tasks. Many combinations are possible. For example, teachers can use student-selected assignments that are not related to student interests and teacher-assigned tasks that are, or vice versa. The point is that teachers who match learning tasks to students' cognitive abilities and interests have taken a major step in establishing the conditions necessary for learning.

Teachers can also shift students' perceptions of tasks. Here the task remains constant, but the teacher shapes the students' attitudes toward it through modeling of attitudes and clear communication of expectations.

Teachers also motivate through their rapport with students. It helps if teachers develop personal relationships with students, especially those who are suspicious of adults, so teachers can motivate through encouragement and positive feedback. In the long run, teachers' informal evaluations probably affect student behavior as much as formal grades.

A fourth major way of viewing the teacher's motivational role is through the success strategies established in the classroom. Can all students be successful, or does the way in which assignments are structured and evaluated guarantee that some students succeed at the expense of others? Teachers who set high standards and individual goals are mainly helping those students who are ready to compete and are maximizing student mastery of academic material. Teachers who place students in groups, grade group performance, and reward effort are mainly helping students who are less able to compete and are maximizing prosocial and general affective growth.

In practice, it is difficult to separate these sources of influence. The teacher who manipulates task design by allowing students to work together, for example, may affect the reward structure as well. However, it is helpful for teachers to consider all types of influence, because this may help them to plan a variety of motivational strategies (not just, for example, curriculum changes or talks with students).

authentic learning

Newmann and his colleagues have explored the relationship between student engagement and the type of motivational climate a teacher can establish to help students develop a mastery orientation (see Ames, 1992). Newmann (1992) defined student engagement in academic work as "the student's psychological investment in an effort directed toward learning, understanding, or mastering the knowledge, skills, or crafts that academic work is intended to promote" (p. 12). Newmann reported the following factors to be associated with student engagement: need for competence, school membership, clarity of purpose, fairness, personal support, success, caring, authentic work, and a sense of ownership.

Newmann (1992) explored the relationship between classroom instruction and student thoughtfulness, and in particular the extent to which thoughtfulness (as opposed to memorization of fragmented bits of information) could be influenced by teachers. He argues that if students are to engage in academic work they must feel a need to develop competence. When their attempts to act competently (both academically and socially) are successful, students are likely to invest more in academic work. How, then, can schools influence students so that their natural interest in expanding personal competence be channeled into academic mastery? Newmann notes that two factors are critical: school membership and authentic work.

School membership suggests that if students are to explore mastery goals, they must perceive the school as legitimate (they want to commit to school values) and perceive that the school environment recognizes, honors, and respects them. If students experience the conditions necessary for appropriate bonding (e.g., fairness, personal support) then it becomes relevant to explore how academic work itself can be designed to enhance student engagement.

Authentic work involves *classroom tasks and assignments that are clearly applicable to everyday living*. Newmann uses it to mean tasks that are meaningful and significant in contrast to trivial and mechanical. He argues that work entailing intrinsic rewards, meeting intrinsic interests, offering students a sense of ownership, connected to the real world, and interesting and involving fun is more likely to be authentic and to engage students directly. Many instructional tasks can be designed to yield social approval, public displays of impressive accomplishments, and various privileges. How interesting students find the material is crucial in their investment in or withdrawl from learning. Students are more likely to invest effort when tasks permit expression of diverse forms of talent.

Newmann suggests that wholehearted engagement in schoolwork depends to some extent on the opportunity students have to consider the work their own. At a minimum, there should be flexibility in the pace and procedures of learning, and ample opportunity for students to ask questions and to study topics they consider important. Further, students should have an active role in constructing and producing knowledge in terms of their own insights and language, not just reproducing the language of others. Although the extent to which students can control learning is limited, and certain definitions and processes of verification must be assimilated by students, their sense of ownership can be enhanced if learning tasks provide some autonomy in the way they explore and apply the material.

Students often complain that schoolwork is boring or irrelevant. Thus, to some extent, students' perception of schoolwork as authentic depends on the connections they see between schoolwork and society. Newmann cites at least four qualities of adult work in the real world that are often not part of schoolwork: value beyond instruction, clear and prompt feedback, collaboration, and flexible use of time. For example, it is clear that meaningful achievements outside school cannot be produced within specified periods. Adults often work overtime

research at work
Keller's strategies for motivating students' interest

Keller (1983) presented the following five strategies for stimulating and maintaining student interest and curiosity in lessons:

1. Use novel, incongruous, conflictual, or paradoxical events. Attention is aroused when there is an abrupt change in the status quo.
2. Use anecdotes and other devices to inject a personal, emotional element into otherwise purely intellectual or procedural material.
3. Give students the opportunity to learn more about things they already know about, but also give them moderate doses of the unfamiliar.
4. Use analogies to make the strange familiar and the familiar strange.
5. Guide students into a process of question generation and inquiry.

On the surface, some of these strategies seem to conflict. For example, Strategy 1 encourages teachers to use novel situations, but Strategy 3 encourages them to give individuals the opportunity to learn about what they are already interested in. Obviously people want to learn more about things that they are already interested in; this is why they join clubs, attend dinners with friends more than strangers, and so forth. As Keller noted, however, the inclusion of unusual or exotic material from time to time can help initiate or maintain curiosity. If a student is already interested in a topic, the teacher's attempts to create such interest may be counterproductive. In general, though, Keller assumed that students are more likely to be understimulated than overstimulated.

Renninger, Hidi, and Krapp (1992) reviewed research on interest, learning, and development. They distinguish between interest as a characteristic of the person, a characteristic of the learning environment, and a psychological state. Much research on classroom instruction has focused on the situational interest of students, material, and learning achievement. For example, Kubli (1987) (as cited in Renninger et al., 1992) studied factors that contribute to "interestingness" in physics and suggested changes in the instructional setting to make it more attractive to female students. He contends that females would be more interested in physics problems that are linked to social or everyday problems. (Tobias [1990] made similar argu-

or in multiple settings to solve problems, but work in schools typically must be initiated and completed in a forty-five-minute period. Hence, whatever educators can do to make some assignments more flexible, in terms of time and so on, would be useful (McCaslin & Good, 1992). Some assignments might extend for an entire week, and some projects might require a semester or a year to complete.

According to Newmann, one of the most critical criteria for authentic work is that it has value beyond the class assignment. For example, writing a newspaper editorial is more authentic than writing only for a classroom grade. More and more educators are calling for at least some of students' schoolwork to emphasize performance and exhibition (see the discussion of portfolios in Chapter 23).

ments about learning in mathematics and science.)

relevance Keller argued that personal motivation increases when individuals perceive that an instructional task will satisfy basic motives such as needs for achievement, power, or affiliation. Keller's strategies for increasing personal motivation call for (1) enhancing achievement striving by providing opportunities to achieve standards of excellence under conditions of moderate risk; (2) making instruction responsive to the power motive by providing opportunities for choice, responsibility, and interpersonal influence; and (3) satisfying the need for affiliation by establishing trust and providing opportunities for no-risk, cooperative interaction.

These three objectives cannot be met simultaneously, however. Keller's first set of strategies responds to the need for achievement, where moderate levels of competition and individual contracting may be most appropriate. The second set of strategies is related to helping individuals fulfill power needs. It is important to give students positions of genuine authority and assign activities, such as debates or argumentative essays, that allow them to satisfy power

needs. The third set of strategies helps students to initiate and maintain close working relationships with peers during cooperative activities.

expectancy Keller offered four strategies for increasing expectancy for success: (1) increase experiences with success (on meaningful tasks—not on trivial or easy tasks), (2) be clear about requirements for success, (3) use techniques that offer personal control over success, and (4) use attributional feedback and other devices that help students relate success to personal effort and ability. We have discussed students' expectations for success in Chapter 13.

outcomes Outcomes refer to the satisfaction of goal accomplishment and its effects on motivation for performing similar tasks in the future. Keller suggested several strategies for increasing the appropriateness of outcomes and for maintaining intrinsic satisfaction with instruction. His chief recommendations were to emphasize the rewards that come naturally from successful completion of the task rather than artificial extrinsic rewards and to use verbal praise and informative feedback rather than threats, surveillance, or external performance evaluation.

Newmann notes that in the workplace, feedback on the quality of work is often more clear and immediate than in school. Newmann also notes that achievements in the workplace require collaboration with peers (asking questions, receiving feedback, sharing ideas, and so forth). In contrast, most school activities involve no specific or immediate feedback, and collaboration in many classrooms is prohibited.

Keller's principles for motivational design of instruction

Keller (1983) synthesized many theories of motivation to form a model for application that features four major dimensions: (1) **interest**, or *the extent to which the learner's curiosity is aroused and sustained over time*; (2) **relevance**, or

Rewards are effective as motivators only if students believe they have a chance to receive rewards if they put forth effort. If students lack such self-perception, rewards are not effective and may backfire by causing resentment.

or *the learner's perception that instruction is related to personal needs or goals*; (3) **expectancy**, or *the learner's perceived likelihood of achieving success through personal control*; and (4) **satisfaction**, or *the learner's intrinsic motivation and responses to extrinsic rewards*. Keller's model is a valuable technique for thinking about the design of instruction in classrooms.

strategies for encouraging students to value academic activities

In Chapter 13 we focused on the expectancy factor within the expectancy *x* value approach to motivation, including strategies suggested by

Brophy (1987) for helping students to develop and maintain the expectation that they can achieve success on school activities if they put forth reasonable effort. In subsequent sections of this chapter, we present Brophy's suggestions concerning the value factor. They describe strategies for helping students to see good reasons for engaging in activities in the first place—good enough reasons to motivate them to take the activities seriously and put forth the necessary efforts.

extrinsic-motivation strategies

Strategies for supplying extrinsic motivation do not attempt to increase the value that students place on a task itself. Instead, in **extrinsic motivation**, involving *motivation that occurs from* *reinforcers, feedback, or rewards that are not inherent in the activity itself,* links successful task performance with delivery of consequences that students value. These consequences typically include grades, but may also include material rewards (money, prizes, trinkets, consumables); activity rewards and special privileges (opportunity to play games, use special equipment, or engage in self-selected activities); symbolic rewards (honor rolls, hanging up good papers on the wall); praise and social rewards; and teacher rewards (opportunities to go places or do things with the teacher).

offer rewards as incentives Rewards motivate students to put forth effort, especially if they are offered in advance as incentives for striving to reach specified levels of performance. However, rewards are more effective for stimulating intensity of effort than thoughtfulness or quality of performance, and they guide behavior more effectively when students must follow a familiar path to a clear goal than when they must discover or invent strategies for responding to a novel task. Therefore, rewards are better used with routine tasks than with novel ones, better with tasks intended to produce mastery of specific skills than with tasks designed to encourage incidental learning or discovery, and better with tasks for which speed of performance or quantity of output is of more concern than creativity, artistry, or craftsmanship. It is more appropriate, for example, to offer rewards as incentives for meeting performance standards on skills that require a great deal of drill and practice (arithmetic computation, typing, spelling) than for work on a major research or demonstration project.

It is helpful if rewards are delivered in ways that support attempts to develop student motivation to learn, so that students are encouraged to appreciate their developing knowledge and skills rather than just to think about rewards. Guidelines for accomplishing this are given in Research at Work: Guidelines for Praise. The guidelines are phrased in terms of verbal praise, but they apply to other types of rewards as well.

Rewards are effective as motivators only for students who believe they have a chance to receive the rewards if they put forth reasonable effort. With students who lack such self-efficacy perceptions, rewards are not effective and may even backfire by causing depression or resentment. Therefore, to ensure that rewards act as incentives for everyone and not just high-ability students, all students must have equal (or at least reasonable) access to the rewards.

call attention to the instrumental value of academic activities Call students' attention to applications of the knowledge and skills taught in school to their lives outside of school (especially applications that will help them cope with the demands of living in our society). When possible, note that the knowledge or skills developed by a task will enable students to meet their own needs, provide them a means of social advancement, or prepare them for success in an occupation or in life generally. Better yet, cite examples by relating personal experiences or telling anecdotes about individuals with whom the students can identify (famous people they look up to, former students from the same school, or individuals with whom they are already familiar).

Teachers probably do not employ this strategy as often as they could, and when teachers use it, they often do so in self-defeating ways. Rather than stress the positive by citing the practical value of what is learned, many teachers emphasize the negative—personal embarrassment ("You don't want people to think that you are ignorant") or future educational or occupational disasters ("You'll never get through sixth grade"; "How are you going to get a job if you can't do basic math?"). Other teachers use variations that cast the student in a more positive light but portray society as a hostile environment ("Learn to count so that merchants don't cheat you"; "Learn to read so that

research at work

guidelines for praise

Brophy (1981) recommends the following guidelines for effective and ineffective praise.*

effective praise

1. is delivered contingently
2. specifies the particulars of the accomplishment
3. shows spontaneity, variety, and other signs of credibility, suggests attention to the student's accomplishment
4. rewards attainment of specified performance criteria (which can include effort criteria, however)
5. provides information to students about their competence and the value of their accomplishments
6. orients students toward better appreciation of their own task-related behavior and thinking about problem solving
7. uses own prior accomplishments as the context for describing present accomplishments
8. is given in recognition of noteworthy effort or success at difficult tasks (for *this* student)
9. attributes success to effort and ability, implying that similar successes can be expected in the future
10. fosters endogenous attributions (students believe that they expend effort on the task because they enjoy the task and/or want to develop task-relevant skills)
11. focuses students' attention on their own task-relevant behavior
12. fosters appreciation of and desirable attributions about task-relevant behavior after the process is completed

ineffective praise

1. is delivered randomly or unsystematically
2. is restricted to global positive reactions
3. shows a bland uniformity that suggests a conditioned response made with minimal attention
4. rewards mere participation, without consideration of performance processes or outcomes
5. provides no information at all or gives students information about their status
6. orients students toward comparing themselves with others and thinking about competing
7. uses the accomplishments of peers as the context for describing students' present accomplishments
8. is given without regard to the effort expended or the meaning of the accomplishment
9. attributes success to ability alone or to external factors such as luck or task difficulty
10. fosters exogenous attributions—students believe that they expend effort on the task for external reasons like pleasing the teacher or winning a competition or reward
11. focuses students' attention on the teacher as an external authority figure who is manipulating them
12. intrudes into the ongoing process, distracting attention from task-relevant behavior

* Jere E. Brophy, "Teacher Praise: A Functional Analysis." *Review of Educational Research*, (Spring 1981): 5–32. Copyright 1981, American Educational Research Association, Washington, DC. Reprinted by permission of the publisher.

you don't get taken when signing a contract").

Therefore, besides stressing that students will need knowledge and skills in the future at school, help them appreciate applications of what they are learning to situations outside school. Basic language arts and mathematics skills are used daily when shopping, banking, driving, reading instructions, paying bills, carrying on business correspondence, and planning home maintenance projects or family vacations. General knowledge is useful for everything from coping effectively with minor everyday challenges to making good decisions in emergency situations. Knowledge of history and related social studies topics is useful for voting on local issues as well as determining national policy (as several U.S. presidents have acknowledged). In general, the information, principles, and skills taught in school prepare people to make informed decisions that result in saving time, trouble, expense, or even lives, and education prepares people to take advantage of the opportunities society offers. These benefits of schooling are well recognized and highly prized in societies in which education is still a privilege rather than a right, but they tend to go unrecognized or be taken for granted in societies like ours in which education for the masses is not only available but required. Do what you can to rekindle this appreciation in students by helping them to see academic activities as valuable opportunities rather than as demands to be resisted.

Extrinsic motivational strategies can be effective under certain circumstances, but teachers should not rely on them too heavily. If students are preoccupied with rewards or competition, they may not pay as much attention as they should to what they are supposed to be learning and may not appreciate its value. The quality of task engagement, and ultimately, achievement, are higher when students perceive themselves to be engaged in tasks for their own reasons (intrinsic motivation) than when they per-

ceive themselves to be engaged in order to please an authority figure, obtain a reward, escape punishment, or respond to some other extrinsic pressure (Deci & Ryan, 1985). More specifically, if students perceive themselves as performing tasks solely to obtain a reward, they tend to adopt a "piecework mentality" or "minimax strategy" in which they concentrate on maximizing rewards by meeting minimum performance standards (and then moving on to something else) rather than doing a high-quality job (Condry & Chambers, 1978). As a result, they may write 300-word essays containing exactly 300 words or read only those parts of a text needed to answer questions on an assignment. You can minimize students' risk of developing such undesirable attitudes by following the guidelines in Table 15.1, but bear in mind that even effective use of extrinsic motivational strategies will not help students to value academic activities. The latter requires strategies that capitalize on existing intrinsic motivation or that stimulate students' motivation to learn.

intrinsic-motivation strategies

Intrinsic motivation is *motivation resulting from personal reinforcers and interests that are inherent in the activity itself.* This approach calls for teachers to select or design academic activities that students engage in willingly because they enjoy them or because the activities incorporate content that the students are already interested in. Teachers' opportunities to capitalize on students' existing intrinsic motivation are limited by several inherent features of schooling (attendance is compulsory, the curriculum is prescribed rather than chosen by the student, mistakes may lead to public embarrassment, and teachers must assign grades and enforce school rules in addition to assisting students' learning). Furthermore, students differ from one another in the topics they find interesting and the activities they find enjoyable. Even so, teachers can sometimes take advantage of students' existing intrinsic motivation by selecting or designing classroom activities that incorporate elements that most, if not all, students find rewarding. Several such elements are discussed in the following sections.

adapt tasks to students' interests

Whenever curriculum objectives can be accomplished using a variety of examples or activities, *incorporate content that students find interesting or activities they find enjoyable*. People, fads, or events that are currently prominent in the news or the youth culture, for example, can be worked into everyday lessons as examples or applications of the concepts being learned. We observed a history teacher who pointed out that the Ark of the Covenant mentioned in the ancient history text was the same ark featured in the movie *Raiders of the Lost Ark*. Similarly, a geography teacher sparked student interest in studying the coordinates (latitude and longitude) by noting that the sunken remains of the *Titanic* can easily be located again, even though they lie on the ocean floor hundreds of miles out to sea, because the discoverers fixed the location precisely using the coordinates.

Hidi (1990) and Renninger, Hidi, and Krapp (1992) note that studies involving text illustrate that the following characteristics generate student interest: intensity of action, character identification, novelty, life themes, and imagery. Findings suggest that "interesting" texts motivate individuals to read and comprehend. However, some researchers have argued that interesting texts do not always have positive effects on learning and that, under certain conditions, interesting but unimportant material can interfere with learning (Renninger, Hidi, and Krapp, 1992). Thus, "interesting" books and assignments should involve authoritative and substantive issues (not trivial or superficial content).

Renninger, Hidi, and Krapp (1992) describe the problem this way:

> The current tendency of teachers (and textbooks) to simply employ baseball passages or word problems as a means of engaging their students is fraught with misconceptions. It is based on the assumption that students all engage passages/problems in the same way, that they share the same interests, and that studying texts results in learning. Findings from the present studies indicate that, whereas the process of students' representation is probably similar, the specific content of these representations can vary. Students do not share the same interests; in fact, one student's interest is likely to be another student's noninterest. Finally, given differences in student interest, "interesting" text does not necessarily lead to learning—the student learns as a function of how he or she poses the challenges of that text to him or herself." (p. 391)

According to Renninger, if a teacher is to adjust instruction to meet students' interest, the teacher must observe how students interpret and view assigned projects. Teachers must also consider how their own interests (how they frame questions, how they make assignments) affect the questions and interests students develop. Still, students' interests vary widely and teachers need to find time to talk with individual students and to explore their interests (perhaps interview a few students each week, have students keep diaries, etc.—for a related discussion of this issue see McCaslin & Good, in press, b).

Another way to adapt school activities to student interest is to *offer students choices of alternative tasks or autonomy in selecting among alternative ways to meet requirements*. Most writing assignments and many research projects, for

Cooperative learning situations or small group activities provide more opportunities for students to respond and to receive feedback.

example, can be adapted to student interests by allowing students to choose topics or at least by taking their interests into account when assigning topics. For students who might make undesirable choices if left completely on their own, provide them with several choices to select from or require them to get your approval of their choice before they begin work.

Finally, you can incorporate students' interests into activities by making it clear that you *encourage student comments and questions* about a topic and by asking questions or making assignments that invite students to state opinions, make evaluations, or in some other way respond to content. Relevant student-initiated questions and comments provide "teachable moments" that wise teachers take advantage of by temporarily suspending the planned

sequence of events to pursue the issue raised by the student. That a question was asked or a comment made shows interest on the part of the student who voiced it, and the chances are that other students share this interest.

It is also helpful, from both instructional and motivational points of view, to see that your questions and assignments cover both basic factual knowledge and *include divergent questions and opportunities for students to express opinions or make other personal responses to the content*. After reviewing facts about the Christians and the lions, the gladiators, and other excesses of the Roman circuses, for example, a history teacher who we observed asked the students why they thought such practices had developed in Roman society, how otherwise cultured people could take pleasure in such cruelty, and other similar questions. This led to a productive discussion in which students made contributions and developed insights about issues such as violence in sports and in contemporary society generally, the role of peer pressure in escalating aggression once a conflict flares up, and the difference between desirable enjoyment of pleasures and indulgence in excesses. The same teacher, after describing life in Athens and Sparta, asked students which city they would rather live in and why. Again, this led to a lively discussion that included parallels among modern nations and contrasted societies that focus on building military strength (at a cost in quality of civilian life) with societies that have more balanced priorities.

plan for novelty and variety Students faced with the same routines and the same types of tasks each day soon become bored. Therefore, try to make sure that something about each task (form, content, media involved, or responses demanded) is new to students or at least different from what they have been doing recently. When introducing a novel activity, call attention to its new or different elements and state that you expect students to find the activity particularly interesting, challenging, or enjoyable.

provide more opportunities for students to respond and to receive feedback Most students prefer activities that allow them to respond actively— to interact with the teacher or with one another, to manipulate materials, or in some other way to respond more actively than by merely listening or reading. This is one function of drill, recitation, discussion, board work, and seat-work activities. Ideally, however, students will often receive *active response opportunities* that go beyond the simple question-answer formats seen in typical recitation and seat-work activities in order to include projects, experiments, role play, simulations, educational

games, or creative applications of what they have been learning. Language arts instruction, for example, should include dramatic readings and prose and poetry composition, mathematics instruction should include problem-solving exercises and realistic application opportunities, science instruction should include experiments and other applications or laboratory work, and social studies instruction should include debates, research projects, and simulation exercises. Such activities show students that school learning involves *doing* something, not just having something done to them.

Activities that call for students to apply skills or processes they are learning to academic content (whether in the same or in a different subject) often can provide students with opportunities for active response and feedback and also allow them to integrate their learning. Students learning statistics, for example, typically work on assignments calling for them to find the mean, median, and mode for numerical distributions. Instead of confining such assignments to skill practice involving making computations using provided sets of numbers, teachers could include hands-on applications based on measurements that the students would take themselves (of the physical characteristics of people or objects in the classroom) or on information gathered during social studies or science activities (statistics on states or nations, findings from probability experiments). The statistical computations might be part of a larger integrative assignment calling for students to collect and analyze data and prepare a written report of their findings about some issue concerning social studies or science.

Students particularly enjoy tasks that allow them to respond actively and to receive *immediate feedback* that can be used to guide subsequent responses. Such feedback features are among the reasons for the popularity of computer games and other pastimes featured in arcades (Malone & Lepper, 1987). Automatic feedback features are built into many educational toys and

Montessori materials used in preschools and kindergartens and into programmed learning materials and other "self-correcting" materials used in elementary and secondary classrooms. The same is true for computerized learning programs that allow students to respond actively and then receive immediate feedback.

You can also build feedback features into more typical classroom activities—when you lead the class or a small group through an activity or circulate to supervise progress during seatwork. At times when you are less available for immediate response (such as when you are teaching a small group and the rest of the students are working at their seats), you can arrange for students to receive feedback by consulting answer keys, following instructions about how to check their work, consulting with an adult volunteer or appointed student helper, or reviewing work in pairs or small groups.

Among activities that allow active response with immediate feedback, students are especially likely to enjoy activities that result in *a finished product*. Industrial psychologists have shown that workers enjoy jobs that allow them to create a product they can point to and identify with more than they enjoy jobs that do not yield tangible results of their labor. It seems likely that students will respond similarly to academic tasks; that is, they are likely to prefer tasks that have meaning or integrity in their own right over tasks that are mere subparts of some larger entity and are more likely to experience a satisfying sense of completion or accomplishment when they finish such tasks. Ideally, task completion will yield a finished product that the students can use or display (a map, diagram, or some other illustration, an essay or report, a scale model, a completed puzzle, or something other than another ditto or workbook page).

implications for teachers

incorporating "fun features" in the classroom

Most academic activities can be planned to incorporate certain features that most students find enjoyable. Three of them are fantasy or simulation features, gamelike features, and opportunities to interact with peers.

When more direct applications of what is being learned are not feasible, you can *introduce fantasy or imagination elements that will engage students' emotions or allow them to experience events vicariously*. In studying poems or stories, you can tell students or encourage them to consider the authors' motives in writing the poems or stories or about formative experiences in the authors' lives that led to these writings. In studying scientific or mathematical principles and methods, you can encourage students to consider the practical problems that needed to be

solved or the personal motives of the discoverers that led to the development of the knowledge or skills being taught. Or you can set up role play or simulation activities that allow students to identify with real or fictional characters or to deal with academic content in direct, personal ways.

Rather than simply assigning students to read history, for example, you can make history come alive by arranging for students to role play Columbus and his crew debating what to do after thirty days at sea or have them take the roles of the American, British, and Russian leaders meeting at Yalta.

Simulation exercises include, but are not confined to, full-scale drama, role play, simulation games, and other "major productions." Other, more modest simulation exercises can be incorporated into everyday instruction. They include brief simulation exercises or invitations for students to use fantasy or imagination to expand their thinking about content they are learning. In teaching a mathematical procedure, for example, you might ask students to name problems that come up in everyday living that the procedure might be useful to help solve (and then list them on the board).

Practice and application activities for almost any kind of content can be presented as games or structured to include *features typically associated with games or recreational pastimes* (Covington, 1992; Keller, 1983; Malone & Lepper, 1987). With a bit of imagination, ordinary seat-work assignments can be transformed into "test-yourself" challenges, puzzles, or brainteasers. Some of these activities involve clear goals but require students to solve problems, avoid traps, or overcome obstacles to reach the goals (e.g., suggesting possible solutions to science or engineering problems or finding a shortcut for a tedious mathematical procedure). Other such activities challenge students to "find the problem" by identifying the goal itself in addition to developing a method for reaching the goal (many "explore-and-discover" activities follow this model). Some gamelike activities involve elements of suspense or hidden information that emerge as the activity is completed (puzzles that convey some message or provide the answer to some questions once they are filled in).

Covington (1992) discusses a number of games that require students to engage in cooperative and higher-order thinking. For example, he presents games that require students to understand a puzzling event (the bird migration problem), develop a more powerful technology (the X-ray problem), or pool the wisdom of all group members (e.g., Lost on the Moon Game), as well as games that encourage students to think about modern society and their career goals (e.g.,

Production-Line Game, The Career Placement Game). As Covington notes, games can be structured to help students get more information about questions, issues, and problems in their own lives. For example, young adolescents can begin to question their role in the home and anticipate career options and what family life and work roles entail for them. The spirit of inquiry can be directed to the principles of industrial psychology, labor relations, business law, management conceptions, and so on as students explore real-life events through academic games. Through the Production-Line Game students can experience directly the dynamics of mass production and division of labor in the workplace. In this activity (developed by Jamieson, Miller, and Watts, 1988) students are organized into teams that must make a finished product (e.g., paper notebooks, toy cars, etc.) out of component parts. Students quickly see that they can increase their productivity by assigning themselves subtasks that support the larger production. In some instances this division of labor becomes sufficiently complex that the group must choose supervisors who keep records and coordinate the production process. Teachers can stimulate the work environment by encouraging students to wear appropriate industrial clothes, clock in, and plan work breaks. To maximize academic time during work breaks, students might receive printouts describing the cash flow earnings of the company, production schedules, and so on.

Various business decisions can be simulated in lifelike situations. For example, Jamieson, Miller, and Watts (1988) describe the Teddytronics Game in which students are part of a company that manufactures teddy bears. The simulation activities allow students to distinguish between fixed and variable cost, to explore issues associated with yearly quotas, and to learn the relationship between production efficiency and salaries. The variable (seasonal) nature of the teddy bear market (sales are higher in winter than in summer) introduces complex data and forces difficult student decisions about such issues how to negotiate favorable interest rates with the banker.

Note that most of these gamelike features involve presenting intellectual challenges appropriate for use by individual students or groups of students working cooperatively. The term *gamelike features* is intended to have a much broader meaning than the typical meaning of the term *games*, which most teachers associate with team competitions. There is reason to believe that the gamelike features described above are likely to be less distracting from curriculum objectives and more effective than competitive games in promoting student motivation to learn, especially when competitive games emphasize speed and memorized facts rather than integration or application of knowledge.

Most students enjoy activities that allow them to interact with their peers. You can easily build *peer interaction* into whole-class activities such as discussion, debate, role play, or simulation. In addition, you can plan follow-up activities that allow students to work in pairs or small groups to tutor one another, discuss issues, develop suggested solutions to problems, prepare for competition, participate in a simulation game, or produce some group product (a report or a display, for example).

Peer interactive activities are likely to be most effective if they are sufficiently structured around curriculum objectives to make them worthwhile learning experiences rather than mere occasions for socializing. It is also important that conditions are arranged so that every student has a substantive role to play and must participate actively in carrying out the group's mission rather than so that one or two assertive students can dominate the interaction and do all the work while others watch.

intrinsic motivational strategies conclusion Schooling should be as enjoyable as possible for both teachers and students. Therefore, whenever curriculum objectives can be met through a variety of activities, wise teachers emphasize activities students find rewarding and avoid activities that they find boring or aversive. However, two important limitations on what can be accomplished through intrinsic motivational strategies should be kept in mind.

First, your opportunities to use intrinsic motivational strategies in the classroom are limited. You must teach the whole curriculum, not just the parts that appeal to students, and you must teach factual knowledge and basic skills in addition to higher-level objectives. Opportunities to provide choice or gamelike features are limited. Thus, even if you make

optimal use of these intrinsic motivational strategies, your students will still be in school rather than in a recreational setting, and all of the constraints that are built into the teacher and student roles will be in place. Learning is often enjoyable, but it requires concentration and effort. It is not "fun" of the sort implied by a visit to an arcade or an amusement park.

Although intrinsic motivational strategies should increase students' enjoyment of classroom activities, they will not increase students' motivation to learn the content or skills being taught. Therefore, as is the case with extrinsic motivational strategies, intrinsic motivational strategies need to be supplemented with strategies for stimulating motivation to learn. Otherwise, students may enjoy classroom activities but fail to derive the intended knowledge or skills from them.

implications for teachers
strategies that stimulate student motivation to learn

Brophy (1987) recommended the following strategies for stimulating students' motivation to learn (i.e., stimulating them to take academic activities seriously and acquire the knowledge or skills these activities were designed to develop). The first three strategies are general ones that describe pervasive features of the learning environment that should be established in the classroom. They involve socializing students to understand that the classroom is primarily a place for learning and that acquiring and applying knowledge and skills are important contributors to quality of life (not just to report-card grades).

model motivation to learn Throughout all of your interactions with students, routinely model interest in learning: *let students see that you value learning as a rewarding, self-actualizing activity that produces personal satisfaction and enriches your life.* In addition to teaching what is in the textbooks, discuss your interests in current events and items of general knowledge (especially as they relate to the subjects you teach). Call attention to current books, articles, television programs, or movies on a subject. Also, discuss examples or applications of subject-matter knowledge in everyday living, in the local environment, or in current events.

"Modeling" here means more than just calling students' attention to examples or applications of concepts taught in school. In addition, it means acting as a model—discussing your thinking about such examples or applications so that students can see how educated people use information and concepts learned in school to understand and respond to everyday experiences and to news about current events occurring elsewhere. Without being preachy, you can illustrate how language arts knowledge enables you to communicate or express yourself effec-

tively in important life situations, how mathematical and scientific knowledge enables you to solve everyday household engineering or repair problems, or how social studies knowledge helps you to appreciate things you see in your travels or to understand the significance of events occurring in other parts of the world. You can also describe insights or opinions about current events or questions that you are raising or predictions you are making about how current crises will be resolved. In general, let the students see that it is both stimulating and satisfying to understand (or even just to think or wonder about) what is happening in the world.

One teacher we observed used modeling effectively in connection with an assignment involving reading about current events in the newspaper. He began by noting that he read the editorial page of this newspaper regularly, finding that he sometimes agreed and sometimes disagreed with the editorials, and emphasized that in either case, the material was always informative and thought provoking. He went on to discuss the newspaper's position and his own position concerning a forthcoming summit meeting of international leaders, noting that he was initially relatively uninformed about, uninterested in, and pessimistic about the likely outcome of this summit meeting but that he had become more interested and more optimistic as he became better informed through reading the newspaper and watching news programs on television. This led to a stimulating discussion that clarified for the students and provoked many questions about the positions of the United States and Russia on major issues to be discussed at the summit meeting, the positions of the editorial writer, and the positions of the teacher. In addition, the teacher provoked further interest and curiosity from students by noting that, although he was describing his own positions on the issues being discussed that day, he often deliberately withheld his positions on issues discussed in class to encourage the students to think for themselves and avoid inhibiting students who might disagree with him. Throughout the discussion he made references to aspects of the history and geography of the United States and Russia that helped shape their present policy positions. In addition, he communicated the pride and satisfaction he took in "feeling like an expert in world affairs" when he read articles or watched television programs on the summit meeting and realized that he had a good understanding of the issues and events involved. This modeling likely increased students' interest in and appreciation of the importance and usefulness of social studies concepts and information.

communicate desirable expectations and attributions

Throughout all of your interactions with students, project attitudes, beliefs, expectations, and attributions that imply that students share your own enthusiasm for learning. To the extent that you *treat students as if they already are eager learners*, they are more likely to become eager learners. Let students know that you expect them to be curious, to want to learn facts and understand principles clearly, to master skills, and to see what they are learning as meaningful and applicable to their everyday lives (Marshall, 1987).

Minimally, this means avoiding suggestions that students dislike working on academic activities or work on them only to get good grades. Preferably, it means treating students as active, motivated learners who care about their learning and are trying to understand (Blumenfeld & Meece, 1988). One teacher we observed communicated positive expectations by announcing at the beginning of the year that her class was intended to make students into "social scientists." She referring to this idea frequently throughout the year through comments such as, "Since you are social scientists, you will recognize that the description of this area as a tropical rain forest has implications about what kinds of crops will grow there," or "Thinking as social scientists, what conclusions might we draw from this information?"

minimize students' performance anxiety

Motivation is likely to develop most fully in classrooms in which students are goal oriented but relaxed enough to be able to concentrate on the task at hand without worrying about whether or not they can meet performance expectations. You can accomplish this by clearly distinguishing between instruction or practice activities designed to promote learning and tests designed to evaluate performance. *Most classroom activities should be structured as learning experiences rather than tests*.

When instruction or practice activities include testlike items (recitation questions, practice exercises), treat them as opportunities for students to work with and apply the material rather than as attempts to see who knows the material and who does not. If you expect students to engage in academic activities with motivation to learn (which implies a willingness to take risks and make mistakes), you need to protect them from anxiety or premature concern about performance.

Still, it is necessary, to evaluate student performance and assign grades using tests or other assessment devices. Until that point in the unit, though, the emphasis should be on teaching and learning rather than on evaluation, and students should be encouraged to respond to questions and performance demands in terms of "let's assess our progress and learn from our mistakes" rather than "let's see who knows it and who doesn't." When possible, give students opportunities to correct their mistakes or improve their responses by rephrasing the question or giving a clue (i.e., do not give the answer or move on to someone else). If it is necessary to give the answer or elicit it from another student, be sure to include any explanation that may be needed to make sure that the first student gets the point and understands why the answer is correct. Have students correct their mistakes in seat-work and homework assignments. Encourage your students to treat each question and performance demand as an opportunity to check their own understanding or apply what they are learning rather than as an opportunity to gain or lose points toward their grades. When necessary, you may also want to make statements such as, "We're here to learn, and you can't do that without making mistakes," to caution students against laughing at their peers' mistakes.

If you consistently implement these three general strategies, you will establish a learning environment in which student motivation to learn can flourish, and you will subtly encourage students to develop such motivation to learn as a general trait. Then, when assigning academic activities, you can supplement these general strategies by using one or more of the following specific strategies for motivating students to learn the content or skills that a particular activity is designed to develop.

project intensity When you instruct, and especially when you present key explanations, you can often use timing, nonverbal expressions and gestures, and cuing and other verbal techniques that tell students that the material is important and deserves close attention. An intense presentation might begin with a direct statement of the importance of the message ("I'm going to show you how to invert fractions—now pay close attention and make sure that you understand these procedures"). Then, you would present the message using verbal and nonverbal public speaking techniques that convey intensity and cue attention: a slow-paced, step-by-step presentation during which you emphasize or underline key words, use

unusual voice modulations, or use exaggerated gestures to focus attention on key terms or procedural steps, scanning the group intensely following each step to look for signs of understanding or confusion (and allow anyone with a question to ask it immediately). In addition to the words you speak, everything about *your tone and manner should communicate to students that what you say is important* and that they should give it full attention and be prepared to ask questions about anything they do not understand.

Projecting intensity through slower pacing, exaggerated cuing, and related rhetorical techniques is an especially useful strategy when demonstrating procedures or problem-solving strategies (as opposed to giving or reviewing information only). Such demonstrations have built-in step-by-step structures that lend themselves to slow pacing punctuated by exaggerated cuing, and the first- or second-person language that is used in modeling or demonstrating procedures lends itself more naturally to a high-intensity communication style than the third-person language typically used to communicate information.

You should use an intense style selectively and use special intensity for times when you want to communicate that "this is important; pay especially close attention."

project enthusiasm Unless they are already familiar with a topic or assignment, students will look to you for cues about how to respond to academic activities. Consciously or not, you model attitudes and beliefs about topics and assignments, and students pick up on these cues. If you present a topic or assignment with enthusiasm, suggesting that it is interesting or important, your students are likely to adopt this same attitude (Bettencourt et al., 1983). In suggesting that you project enthusiasm, we do not mean pep talks or unnecessary theatrics. Instead, we mean that you convey to students your reasons for being interested in a topic or for finding it meaningful. Use dramatics or forceful salesmanship if you are comfortable with these techniques, but if not, low-key but sincere statements of the value you place on a topic or activity are just as effective.

One history teacher we observed generated student enthusiasm (and also related a great many concepts) by explaining to students that during the Middle Ages, the Mediterranean was the center of the world, Mediterranean seaports were major trade centers, and places like England were outposts of civilization. All of this changed drastically with the discovery of the New World and the emergence of new centers of trade and culture. He demonstrated these issues with references to maps, reminders about the primary modes of transportation at the time, and characterizations of the attitudes of the people and their knowledge about other countries and trade possibilities.

encourage task interest or appreciation

Besides projecting intensity or your own personal enthusiasm, you can increase students' interest in or appreciation for a topic or activity by verbalizing reasons students should value it or asking students to generate reasons for valuing it (consistent with the Piagetian paradigm presented earlier). If the topic or activity has connections with something that the students already recognize as interesting or important, these connections should be noted. For example, teachers discussing Japanese history or current sociopolitical influence in the world might draw students' attention to the book or the movie *Rising Sun* and have students critique issues of representations versus stereotyping. When the knowledge or skills to be taught have applications for everyday living, these should be mentioned (especially applications that allow students to solve problems or accomplish goals that are important to them). You can also mention new or challenging aspects of activities that students can anticipate, especially interesting or exotic aspects.

encourage curiosity or suspense

You can stimulate curiosity or suspense in students by posing questions that make students feel the need to resolve some ambiguity or obtain more information about a topic. You can encourage such student interest by (1) asking students to speculate or make predictions about what they will be learning; (2) raising questions that successful completion of the activity will enable them to answer; (3) when relevant, showing them that their existing knowledge is not complete enough to enable them to accomplish some valued objective, that their knowledge is internally inconsistent or inconsistent with new information, or that their present knowledge exists in scattered form but could be organized around certain general principles or powerful ideas (Malone & Lepper, 1987). More generally, you can put students into an active information processing or problem-solving mode by posing interesting questions or problems that an activity will address (Keller, 1983).

encourage dissonance or cognitive conflict

When the topic of a text is familiar, students may think they already know everything that there is to know about it and thus may read the material with little attention or thought. You can counter this tendency by pointing out unexpected, incongruous, or paradoxical aspects of the content, by calling attention to unusual or exotic elements, by noting exceptions to general rules, or by challenging students to solve the "mystery" that underlies a paradox.

We have observed several teachers using this strategy effectively. One teacher introduced a unit on the Middle Ages by telling students they would learn about "our ancestors" who chose to remain illiterate and ignorant and who persecuted people who did not share their religion. Later he noted the Moslem advances in mathematics, medicine, and the construction of libraries and then contrasted them with the illiteracy of most Christian kings and lords during the Middle Ages. Another teacher stimulated curiosity about the Persian Empire by noting that Darius was popular with the people he conquered and by asking students to anticipate reasons why this might be so. Another teacher introduced a selection on the Trojan War by telling students they would read about "how just one horse enabled the Greeks to win a major battle against the Trojans." Another teacher introduced a movie on the fall of the Roman Empire by saying, "Some say that the factors that led to the decay of the Roman Empire are presently at work in the United States—as you watch the film, see if you notice parallels."

make abstract content more personal, concrete, or familiar Definitions, principles, and other general or abstract information may have little meaning for students unless you make them more concrete or visual. One way to accomplish this is to promote personal identification with the content by relating experiences or telling anecdotes illustrating how the content applies to the lives of particular individuals (especially individuals students are interested in and likely to identify with). We observed a history teacher read to students a brief selection about Spartacus to personalize a selection that they were to read about slavery in ancient times. When covering the Crusades, this teacher emphasized the Children's Crusade, noting that the children involved were "your age and younger" and that most of them died before this crusade eventually ended in failure. She also made poignant connections to contemporary Iran, where religion-based zeal is also causing preadolescents to volunteer to go to war. Another teacher brought the medieval guilds alive for his students by describing them in detail and soliciting students' reactions to the fact that if they had lived during the Middle Ages, to become a journeyman they would have had to leave their homes as children and spend years apprenticed to a master craftsman.

You can make abstractions concrete by showing objects or pictures or by conducting demonstrations. You can also help students to relate new or strange content to their existing knowledge by using examples or analogies that refer to familiar concepts, objects, or events. We have observed teachers make the following connections: (1) effects of the Nile River flooding on Egyptian customs compared to effects of spring flooding of Michigan rivers on local customs; (2) the Washington Monument as a modern example of an obelisk; (3) three times the size of the Pontiac Silverdome as an example of the size of the largest Roman circus colosseum; (4) identifications of students in the class (or failing that, famous personalities) descended from the ancient peoples or the geographical areas studied; (5) linking of students' family names to the guilds (Smith, Tanner, Miller, Baker); (6) similarities of climate and potential for flower raising and dairy farming as reasons why the Dutch were drawn to the Holland, Michigan, area; (7) similarities in the customs associated with the Roman Saturn Festival compared to those associated with the modern Christmas festivities.

Sometimes the problem is not so much that content is too abstract or unfamiliar for the students to understand if it is explained sufficiently, but that the text simply does not provide enough explanation. It is not enough, for example, to state that Russia stopped participating in World War I because "the revolution came and a new government was established." This brief statement does not supply enough details to enable students to understand and visualize events surrounding the Russian revolution. To make these events more understandable to the students, you would have to elaborate on the text by explaining why and (especially) how the Communists and others organized political and, eventually, military resistance to the czar's regime, killed or expelled the czar's family and key officials, and established a new government. Such elaboration on the text transforms the relatively meaningless statement that "the revolution came and a new government was established" into a meaningful statement that the students can explain in their own words because they can relate it to their prior knowledge and can visualize the events to which it refers. This enables them to process the content actively instead of simply trying to memorize it. Good teachers look on texts as outlines to be elaborated on, not as the entire curriculum.

encourage students to generate their own motivation to learn
You can encourage students to generate their own motivation to learn by asking them to think about topics or activities in relation to their own interests or preconceptions. Students can identify questions about a topic that they would like to get answered, list their particular interests in the topic, or note things they find surprising as they read. Besides generating motivation in a particular situation, such exercises help students to understand that motivation to learn must come from within themselves—that it is a property of the learner rather than the task to be learned.

state learning objectives and provide advance organizers
You can prepare your students to gain more from lectures, films, or reading assignments by clarifying what you want them to concentrate on or think about as they process the information. You may want to distribute a partially filled-in outline or study guide, or to give specific guidelines about note taking. If structuring devices are built into the content (lists, generalizations followed by elaborations, comparisons or contrasts, historical narratives or other sequential descriptions, presentations of rules followed by examples, questions followed by answers, or concept definitions followed by examples and nonexamples of the concept), you could call students' attention to these structural elements to increase the likelihood that students will use them to organize and remember what they learn (Armbruster & Anderson, 1984). In general, to the extent that you are clear about how students should approach an activity (to memorize verbatim versus to get the gist and be able to explain general principles or applications

in their own words), your students are more likely to adopt the appropriate learning set.

model task-related thinking and problem solving
The information processing and problem-solving strategies you use when thinking about curricular content and responding to academic tasks are invisible to students unless you make them overt and observable by modeling them. Thus, you need to model the process by showing students what to do and by thinking out loud as you demonstrate. Include the thinking that goes into selecting the approach to use, deciding on options to take at choice points, checking progress as you go along, and satisfying yourself that you are on the right track. Also, model recovery from false starts and from use of inappropriate strategies on occasion so that students can see how one can develop a successful strategy even when one is not sure about what to do at first (Diener & Dweck, 1978).

This kind of *cognitive modeling* shows students what it means to approach a task with motivation to learn by modeling some of the general beliefs and attitudes associated with motivation (patience, confidence, persistence in seeking solutions through information processing and rational decision making, benefiting from the information supplied by mistakes rather than giving up in frustration).

Modeling opportunities occur whenever an academic activity calls for use of some cognitive process or strategy. Among other things, this includes demonstrations of how to conduct scientific experiments, understand and develop ways to solve mathematics problems, identify the main ideas in paragraphs, develop a plan for conducting a research project or an outline for writing a composition, identify the moral of a story, induce general principles from collections of facts, deduce applications of general principles to specific situations, check your own understanding of content by trying to answer questions about it or paraphrase it in your own words, or find and correct your own errors.

---

research at work

motivation to learn within the expectancy × value model

Brophy (1987) reviewed the literature on motivation to learn within the expectancy × value model. Some of his suggestions about inducing success expectations were presented in the previous chapter. In this chapter we have examined his ideas for stimulating student motivation to learn. Brophy's motivational framework follows:

A. Essential Preconditions
  1. Supportive environment
  2. Appropriate level of challenge/difficulty
  3. Meaningful learning objectives
  4. Moderation/optimal use of strategies
B. Motivating by Maintaining Success Expectations
  5. Program for success
  6. Teach goal setting, performance appraisal, and self-reinforcement
  7. Provide remedial socialization for discouraged students

a. Portray effort as investment rather than risk
b. Portray skill development as incremental and domain specific
c. Focus on mastery
d. Provide attribution retraining
e. Minimize test anxiety
C. Motivating by Supplying Extrinsic Incentives
  8. Offer rewards as incentives for good (or improved) performance
  9. Structure appropriate competition
  10. Call attention to the instrumental value of academic activities
D. Motivating by Capitalizing on Students Existing Intrinsic Motivation
  11. Adapt tasks to students' interests
    a. Incorporate content that students find interesting or activities that they find enjoyable
    b. Offer choices of alternative tasks or opportunities to exercise autonomy

---

school-level motivational influences

Rosenholtz (1989) showed that the social structure of the workplace can vary remarkably from school to school and that the social organization in which teaching takes place significantly affects teachers' commitment, leadership, cooperation, and the quality of both teachers' and students' school lives and thus, overall school effectiveness (see also Good & Brophy, 1986a). Rosenholtz noted that in some schools teachers were able to function collaboratively (to share information about curriculum, the classroom, and students) and there was a shared norm for evaluation of and experimentation with instruction and continued improvement. In other schools, however, teachers were unable to use the social resources available. Thus, teachers (and students) participate in schools in which the normative expectations for performance can vary extensively.

The school, as an institution, also influences students' perceptions and performance. Good and Weinstein (1986) argued that school and classroom processes must be considered at the same time in an attempt to identify processes

in selecting among alternative ways to meet requirements

c. Encourage student comments and questions

d. Include divergent questions and opportunities for students to express opinions or make other responses to the content

12. Plan for novelty and variety
13. Provide opportunities to respond actively
14. Provide immediate feedback to student responses
15. Allow students to create finished products
16. Incorporate "fun features" into academic activities

a. Fantasy or imagination elements
b. Simulation exercises
c. Gamelike features
d. Peer interaction opportunities

E. Strategies for Stimulating Student Motivation to Learn

17. Model interest in learning and motivation to learn
18. Communicate desirable expectations and attributions about students' motivation to learn
19. Minimize students' performance anxiety during learning activities
20. Project intensity
21. Project enthusiasm
22. Induce task interest or appreciation
23. Induce curiosity or suspense
24. Induce dissonance or cognitive conflict
25. Make abstract content more personal, concrete, or familiar
26. Induce students to generate their own motivation to learn
27. State learning objectives and provide advance organizers
28. Model task-related thinking and problem solving

SOURCE: J. Brophy, (1987). "Synthesis of Research on Strategies for Motivating Students to Learn," *Educational Leadership, 45* (2), 40–48. Reprinted by permission of the author.

and interrelationships that facilitate or hinder goals at each level. School staffs need to deal with issues such as how schools can focus on high-quality instruction at the same time that individual teachers are helping students to develop their talents as effectively as possible. How can opportunities for practice, display, and reward of learning accomplishments be improved? How best can activities such as school newspapers, journals, and assemblies be used to supplement the efforts of individual classrooms?

During the past few years, researchers studying motivation and education have developed numerous strategies that teachers can use, as this chapter illustrates. Researchers have also begun

to consolidate these findings and develop programs that integrate motivational strategies and connect them with strategies for accomplishing related goals such as establishing productive classroom and schoolwide learning environments and helping students to assume more responsibility for managing their own learning.

One example is the TARGET program for managing classrooms in ways that promote student motivation to learn (Ames, 1990). The term TARGET stands for the program's six major dimensions: task, authority, recognition, grouping, evaluation, and time. The program encourages teachers to manage these dimensions in ways that allow students to engage in activi-

TARGET AREA	FOCUS	GOALS	STRATEGIES
Task	Intrinsic value of learning	Reduce the reliance on extrinsic incentives Design programs that challenge all students Stress goals and purposes in learning Stress the fun of learning	Encourage programs that take advantage of students' backgrounds and experience Avoid payment (monetary or other) for attendance, grades, or achievement Foster programs that stress goal setting and self-regulation/management Foster programs that make use of school learning in a variety of nonschool settings (e.g., internships, field experiences, and cocurricular activities)
Authority	Student participation in learning/school decisions	Provide opportunities to develop responsibility, independence, and leadership skills Develop skills in self-regulation	Give optimal choice in instructional settings Foster participation in cocurricular and extracurricular settings Foster opportunities to learn metacognitive strategies for self-regulation
Recognition	The nature and use of recognition and reward in the school setting	Provide opportunities for all students to be recognized Recognize progress in goal attainment Recognize efforts in a broad array of learning activities	Foster "personal best" awards Foster policy in which all students and their achievements can be recognized Recognize and publicize a wide range of school-related activities of students
Grouping	Student interaction, social skills, and values	Build an environment of acceptance and appreciation of all students Broaden range of social interaction, particularly of at-risk students	Provide opportunities for group learning, problem solving, and decision making Allow time and opportunity for peer interaction to occur

table 15.1 *(continued)*

Target Area	Focus	Goals	Strategies
Grouping		Enhance social-skill development Encourage humane values Build an environment in which all can see themselves as capable of making significant contributions	Foster the development of subgroups (teams, schools within schools, etc.) within which significant interaction can occur Encourage multiple group membership to increase range of peer interaction
Evaluation	The nature and use of evaluation and assessment procedures	Increase students' sense of competence and self-efficacy Increase students' awareness of progress in developing skills and understanding Increase students' appreciation of their unique set of talents Increase students' acceptance of failure as a natural part of learning and life	Reduce emphasis on social comparisons of achievement by minimizing public reference to normative evaluation standards (e.g., grades and test scores) Establish policies and procedures which give students opportunities to improve their performance (e.g., study skills and classes) Create opportunities for students to assess progress toward goals they have set
Time	The management of time to carry out plans and reach goals	Improve rate of work completion Improve skills in planning and organization Improve self-management ability Allow the learning task and student needs to dictate scheduling	Provide experience in personal goal setting and in monitoring progress in carrying out plans for goal achievement Foster opportunities to develop time management skills Allow students to progress at their own rate whenever possible Encourage flexibility in the scheduling of learning experiences

SOURCE: M. Maehr, & C. Midgley, (1991). "Enhancing Student Motivation: A School-Wide Approach." *Educational Psychologist, 26,* 399–427. Reprinted by permission.

ties with a focus on task mastery rather than on their public performance and how it reflects on their abilities. Hence, students are encouraged to focus on understanding the task and integrating present concepts with past knowledge.

Tasks are selected in order to provide an optimal level of challenge and to emphasize activities that students find intrinsically engaging. The teacher shares authority with students and exercises it with consideration of their needs and feelings. Recognition (e.g., public assemblies) is provided to all students who make notable progress, not just to the highest achievers. Grouping is managed in ways that promote cooperative learning and minimize interpersonal competition and social comparison. Evaluation is accomplished using multiple criteria and methods, focusing on individualized assessment of progress rather than on comparisons of individuals or groups. Finally, time is used in creative ways that ease the constraints of rigid scheduling and allow for more use of activities that are widely recognized as valuable but seldom used in classrooms because they are hard to fit into a rigid schedule.

Maehr and Midgeley (1991) extended Ames's TARGET model from the classroom level to the school level (Table 15.1, pp. 420-421), reasoning that the motivational efforts of individual teachers in a school will have much more powerful cumulative effects on students if the effects reinforce one another and if the school environment supports students' motivation to learn (see also Good & Weinstein, 1986). Maehr and Midgeley have been helping school leaders to consider how their school policies might be adjusted to create a schoolwide psychological environment that reflects the principles in the TARGET model. Key principles of their approach are summarized in Table 15.1. The table illustrates ways in which motivational principles can be integrated with classroom management principles and applied at both the school and classroom levels. It builds upon previous work conducted by Carole Ames and Joyce Epstein.

summary

Motivation, the process of arousing, directing, and maintaining behavior, is heavily influenced by group context and multiple stimuli. Teachers must adjust research findings and theoretical positions to specific individuals in given settings.

In the area of structuring assignments, teachers can foster motivation by providing stimulating and appropriate tasks, capturing student attention, allowing student choices, and setting clear learning goals. They can maintain task involvement during seat work by allowing students to work without interruption, demanding attention to the tasks, and providing knowledge of results. Maintaining motivation over the year involves scheduling a change of pace occasionally, making special events relevant, breaking up the day with special brief assignments that are enjoyable, and providing feedback about academic performance.

Teachers can manipulate four major motivation-related conditions in the classroom: tasks students are assigned, student perceptions of tasks, teacher rapport with students, and the reward structure. They can employ techniques such as using student preferences, student choices, individualization, "hands-on experience," peer tutoring and cooperative group assignments, games or simulations, and other variations of standard practices.

Students often complain that schoolwork is boring. Newmann argues that to some extent students' perception of schoolwork as authentic depends on the connections they see between schoolwork and society. We have discussed various strategies for making schoolwork more authentic and have presented Newmann's arguments for making schoolwork more like adult work (collaboration, flexible use of time).

Keller provided four categories that can be used to think about classroom motivation: (1) interest (learner's curiosity); (2) relevance (learner's perception that tasks relate to personal need); (3) expectancy (learner's perceived likelihood of success); and (4) satisfaction (learner's intrinsic motivation or reaction to external rewards).

Brophy offered a comprehensive list of motivational strategies that teachers can use to stimulate students to engage productively in academic activities, and in particular, to do so with motivation to learn the academic content and skills that the activities were designed to teach.

questions for reflection

1. Summarize in your own words Keller's motivational model. Think about your own experience as a student and describe the classrooms that most and least approximated this model. What do these experiences suggest about the value of Keller's model and about strategies for motivating students?

2. Do you include student motivation in your definition of teaching success? That is, are you satisfied as long as students learn the material, or do you believe that they also must become enthusiastic about you and the subject matter? What difference does it make? Can one goal get in the way of the other goal? How?

3. Think about your own teachers. Which ones stand out in your mind as especially good or bad? How did they attempt to motivate students in general and you in particular? What does this imply about how you define motivation?

4. Do you find it intuitively obvious or perhaps confusing that students with poor motivation may be won over by teachers who concentrate mostly on instruction and only secondarily on motivation? Can you see why teachers who try to improve students' self-concepts without making demands or providing success experiences could be perceived as patronizing by such students? Explain.

5. What is your position on intrinsic motivation versus extrinsic motivation? Both research and classroom observation reveal that intrinsic motivation is not observable in certain students and that extrinsic methods seem to work under most circumstances. What does this suggest about human nature? About motivation? About your views on teaching and learning?

6. Once you have led a horse to water, can you make it drink, or not? Why? Are there students whom no teacher can motivate? If so, what does motivate these students?

7. As an exercise in stimulating your own motivation to learn, pick a chapter in this text that you have not read yet and generate a list of questions relating to its topic. Given your current knowledge and beliefs about the topic, what more would you like to know about the topic simply because the questions interest you? What would you like to know because you think you will need the information to apply in the classroom when working with students? Compare your list with the questions prepared by two or three of your classmates.

cases to consider

test review The bell rings, students dash for their seats, and conversations are left dangling in mid-sentence. The excited buzz of informal exchange becomes a formal, passive, heavy silence. Marge Hiebert audibly sighs and starts the class. "Last Friday we had an exam, so I guess I should give back your papers and tell you what you did wrong. The geography proofs were poorly done. Let me show you the really bad, silly mistakes on the test. Pay attention because you have to learn this stuff—it's going to be on the midterm exam and I don't want to see these same mistakes." How effective is this teacher feedback going to be in motivating student behavior? Why? What would be a more effective strategy?

moving fast Jim Garcia taught a senior honors course in American history at San Carlos High School. Students in the class were roughly 60 percent Hispanic and 40 percent Anglo. Virtually all students came from affluent homes and most students plan to go to college. Jim was progressively becoming more discouraged because students seemed reluctant to discuss historical ideas and how they might be applied in current political contexts. Although no student actually said it, their attitude seemed to be "just give us the facts and concepts— we want to do well on our advanced placement tests in history." Discussing ideas and their implications was seemingly as popular as going to a dentist's office! If you were Jim, what would you attempt to do and why? What are specific strategies you might use to stimulate student interest?

a poor follow-up Helen finished the experiment and walked around the class with the beaker so that all the students could see the chemical reaction. Then she placed the beaker on a lab table and turned to the front of the room. She smiled and confidently asked, "Now, are there any questions?" She waited fifteen seconds and said, "Okay, then go to your lab table and do the follow-up experiment." At first, the tables buzzed with talk and activity; however, after a couple of minutes, Helen noticed that purposeful activity was occurring at only one of the five tables. She was puzzled because she knew the students had seen her example and that the follow-up experiment was simple. How could she find out what the problem was? What should she say?

part VI.

classroom management

As Mr. Floden *heads to his desk, Huey shoots a massive spitball that rockets through the air and hits Mr. Floden squarely in the back. The class howls.*

As soon as Judy Griffin *finishes explaining the assignment, several hands wave at her frantically. Then Tim blurts out, "Do we have to do this by Monday? Why not by Friday? This is a lot of work." The class buzzes with excitement as they haggle with the teacher over the length and format of the paper to be written.*

Bill Roundtree *curtly announces to his sales staff,*

"I want biweekly reports on your sales progress; we need to get sales up by 12 percent. This is important and I expect progress immediately. Some of you are going to get big rewards out of this; however, others may be looking for new jobs if they don't get that sales performance up."

Hector *walks confidently toward Ms. Bloom's desk. Ms. Bloom stresses that students not only pick the theme for their semester-long project but also identify a pertinent reading list. She also stresses that students need to develop a time management plan for turning in their outline, rough draft, and term paper.*

These vignettes involve different aspects of classroom and societal management that teachers and students face. The first vignette deals with public misbehavior, a significant aspect of classroom life that teachers must address. The second vignette illustrates the fact that, although rules and procedures are an important part of classroom management, successful classroom managers elicit student cooperation (Doyle, 1986a). The third example highlights the importance of alerting and accountability. Teachers need to alert students that certain performances will be examined and to hold students accountable. Teachers' incentives and motivational systems depend more on logic and student cooperation than on external rewards and incentives. Teachers can engage in too much alerting as well as too little and can overstructure or understructure their classrooms. The fourth example illustrates that the goal of management is the development of students' personal resources so that they can progressively assume more responsibility. McCaslin

and Good (1992) argue that students need to be involved in thoughtful consideration of classroom management issues.

Successful classrooms do not just happen. They are created, maintained, and restored (when necessary) by teachers who exhibit certain personal qualities, spend time planning and preparing, and use effective techniques. Classroom management is usually the major concern of beginning teachers. It is basic to success in meeting cognitive and affective objectives, and principals and supervisors stress it in rating teachers. Teachers who have serious management problems spend more time reacting than teaching. In addition, students often have little respect or liking for such teachers.

The basic principles for sound classroom management are the same for all teachers. Ideally, management is a minimal concern that primarily involves preventing problems by individualizing instruction to meet students' needs. At the opposite extreme, a teacher faced with five separate classes of unruly preadolescents may spend more time on management than on all other aspects of teaching combined.

Prospective teachers therefore need to consider how their personal qualities and preferences affect their teaching. Chapter 16 discusses some personal characteristics desirable in all teachers and the factors that teachers consider in developing their roles. In Chapter 17 we discuss creating and maintaining an effective learning environment. We turn to techniques for teaching students who require more individualized instruction. Chapter 18 reviews behavioristic approaches to coping with behavior problems, and Chapter 19 presents humanistic approaches.

Several basic ideas underlie the section on classroom management. First, successful classroom managers must have certain qualities, without which they are unlikely to succeed. Second, success lies in effective planning and prevention of problems rather than in handling problems after they occur. Third, no single approach equips a teacher to handle all management tasks successfully. As Doyle (1986a) notes, maintaining a good management system requires daily attention. However, teachers can build an effective, comprehensive, and internally consistent system by combining complementary elements from different approaches.

overview of classroom management

objectives

When you have mastered the material in this chapter, you will be able to

1. Understand the implications of group and individual student differences for classroom management
2. Develop and explain your personal philosophy of classroom management
3. Explain how key aspects of classroom management and student socialization change across four developmental stages

4. Identify the problems and rewards of choosing a socialization orientation to teaching
5. List and explain the expectations and responsibilities of teachers as authority figures
6. Describe characteristics of teachers who are successful as socialization agents and be able to discuss these data with a school principal or parent
7. Describe six characteristics of successful parents, showing the relevance of each for teaching and be able to apply such knowledge

There is growing agreement both among teachers and the public that student misbehavior interferes with classroom teaching and student learning. Moreover, concern about discipline has grown in recent years (Charles, 1992; Elam, 1989). Although undergraduate students sometimes underestimate the importance of management and organization in successful teaching, it is the case that experienced teachers see classroom management as a critical part of successful teaching (Neale & Johnson, 1993). Clearly, teachers must be able to create and maintain classroom environments that allow student learning (Latz, 1993).

An April 12, 1993, editorial in the *New York Times* contended that fear for personal safety interfered with the learning of too many New York City students. The editorial noted that the board of education already spends roughly $72 million a year on unarmed security officers and metal detectors. However, even with such precautions, there were 1,880 assaults and 388 robberies in New York City schools in 1992. Indeed, the problems were of sufficient concern that an advisory panel offered suggestions for improving safety conditions including walk-through metal detectors and student photo identification cards (to cut down on nonstudents from entering the buildings). Such problems are not restricted to New York City. For example, an April 13, 1993, editorial in the *Atlanta Constitution* noted that a third of the children in metropolitan Atlanta reported that they knew someone who had taken a gun to school. Further, 22 percent of the children (ten-to twelve-year-olds) indicated that they were afraid of being shot and possibly killed by a gun at school.

Another, national survey places these data in a broader perspective. In a 1993 survey by Metropolitan Life, 13 percent of the students indicated that they had brought a weapon to school at least once, and more than one in ten teachers and roughly one in four students indicated that they had been victims of some act of violence in or around their school.

Although crime is more pervasive in urban schools than in suburban or rural ones, it is not uncommon in the latter schools (Celis, 1993). A survey of more than 10,000 youths conducted by the Justice Department in 1989 found comparatively few differences between nonmetropolitan areas, cities, and suburbs in student reports of violence, theft, or perception of the need for them to take something to school to protect themselves from possible attack.

It appears that the problem may be getting worse. For example, 64 percent of administrators interviewed in 1,261 school districts reported that violence in their schools had gotten worse in the past four years. So did 54 percent of suburban administrators, 43 percent of small-town administrators, and 34 percent of rural administrators (Celis, 1993).

promoting effective classroom management

Our discussion of classroom management stresses *problem prevention,* but we also suggest strategies for dealing with misbehavior when it does occur. We approach the topic using a cost-benefit analysis, considering strategies with an eye toward what proponents claim they accomplish, what they actually do accomplish, and what side effects they may have.

Certain practices are deemed inappropriate because they are not essential to any worthwhile goal (requiring students to remain absolutely silent at all times unless addressed by the teacher) or because their positive effects are outweighed by negative ones (persistent authoritarian and punitive techniques). In general, the optimal classroom management approach establishes the desired learning environment while simultaneously imposing the fewest restrictions (Brophy & Putnam, 1979). Further, a successful management system continually removes restrictions and external control as students develop more capacity for self-regulation (McCaslin & Good, 1992).

To manage classrooms effectively, teachers need both clear *expectations* about students' behavior and *knowledge* about what to do when their expectations are not being met. Expectations define classroom management goals and guide decisions about creating, maintaining, and restoring desirable student behavior. Teachers who have clear expectations can organize the classroom accordingly, articulate these expectations to students, and recognize when discrepancies between expectations and actual student behavior are unacceptably large and indicate a need for action.

Taken together, teachers' expectations about appropriate student behavior can be called the student role. Elements that make up the student role include: (1) mastery of basic skills, (2) development of interest in and knowledge about topics included in the formal curriculum, (3) ability to apply such knowledge in problem solving situations, and (4) participation, usually as a member of a group, in extracurricular experiences that are considered necessary for efficient institutional functioning (assemblies, fire drills), or are designed to support the program of instruction (field trips, music programs) or to develop qualities believed important for all citizens (physical education, the pledge of allegiance).

As Jackson (1968) and Doyle (1986a, 1992a) have noted, the following are also identified with the student role: regimentation of activity, restriction of movement, and subordination of individual desires to the personal authority of the teacher and the less personal but often restrictive school and classroom rules. The rules help provide for an orderly and reasonably satisfactory group living experience within an institutional setting, but they do so at a price. Much behavior considered natural and appropriate elsewhere is forbidden at school (boisterous talk and play), and many other things can be done only at certain times and in certain ways (eating and drinking, using the toilet). Sustained attention to academic activities involves inhibition of behavior appropriate in

research at work

guidelines for respecting cultural differences in the classroom

Jones (1979) offers the following guidelines to help teachers show respect for cultural differences.

- Accept and value the fact that neither individual students nor groups of students act in the same way—nor do they need to do so.
- Help students identify with the classroom and achieve a sense of value—a sense that they belong in the class.
- Treat all students with courtesy and respect, independent of whether they are boisterous, self-confident, or withdrawn. Encourage them to treat one another with that same respect.
- Demonstrate continuous commitment to helping students be successful.
- Allow extensive interaction among students as a way to build cohesiveness and pride in the class.
- Increase the amount of cooperative classroom work and help students recognize and accept differences in their learning and work styles.
- Make it clear that you expect students to help and learn from one another.
- Recognize the value of discussing class problems and explaining reasons for work assignments, classroom rules, punishments, and so on.
- Give all students a role in classroom governance and in deciding on rules of conduct and procedures for resolving conflicts.
- Avoid power struggles with students; learn not to take personal offense when misbehavior occurs but rather to focus on resolving the problem.

Jones argues that this is essential for teachers' sanity and classroom adjustment because teachers can spend considerable time responding to student apathy, failure to do assigned work, and so on.

---

other contexts. Finally, all of this takes place in a public setting.

individual and group differences in students

Individual and group differences among students have implications for classroom management. Differences in age, gender, and ethnicity come readily to mind, along with variables such as maturity and responsibility. Many of these variables, however, can be overstressed, leading to overly polarized differential prescriptions for boys versus girls or black students versus white students.

As Charles (1992) argues, classroom management decisions must reflect cultural understanding. Teachers who recognize and appreciate cultural differences increase the likelihood that all students will want to participate in classroom activities. The very recognition that behavioral diversity is natural and expected can help teachers reduce classroom misbehavior.

Requirements for sustained attention and

Differences in age, gender, ethnicity, and individual maturity and responsibility are variables that have implications for classroom management.

physical immobility are difficult for students, especially young ones. This does not imply that physical restrictions should be abandoned; all students can adjust to some degree. To identify what is required, we would ask: (1) Is the instructional model being used appropriate for the students? (2) If so, what physical restrictions are really necessary? (3) Are there multiple ways to accomplish objectives (so that students can use the methods most preferred by them)?

Besides minimizing restrictions, teachers can ease students' adjustment to them. Activities can be scheduled so that sustained concentration is required when students seem most able to handle it. Students who need more physical activity can be given opportunities to obtain it in ways that do not conflict with instructional goals.

Characteristics that vary across groups or cultures also may have implications for classroom management. Many adolescents resent being touched in any way. Teachers also may anger students by taking away or otherwise overreacting to articles of clothing, combs, or other valued possessions.

Middle-class teachers typically expect students to maintain eye contact with them during disciplinary contacts, to indicate both attention and respect. However, students from some minority groups avert their eyes in such situations because they have been taught that maintaining eye contact connotes defiance. It is important for teachers to be aware of such cultural differences and, more generally, to be open minded and tolerant in dealing with students from different cultural backgrounds (Arias & Casanova, 1993).

Casanova (1987) notes that students will react differently to classroom events because of the unique experiences that each student brings to the classroom. Although many of these students' views and experiences do not interfere with learning, Casanova notes that some do and that it is the teacher's responsibility to recognize such problems and to become aware of the culture and home backgrounds of the students

Loud talking, noisy movements, and mildly disruptive behavior are considered normal and appropriate outside the classroom.

they teach. Fortunately, there is a growing body of evidence that can be explored by teachers of students who come from a different culture or who speak a different language than the teacher (Arias & Casanova, 1993; Garcia, 1991).

Meeting these students' needs does not necessarily mean catering to their preferences or reinforcing their expectations. Students accustomed to authoritarian treatment or brutality need acceptance and warmth from their teachers. Students who behave like pawns need to learn to function more as origins (assume responsibility for their own learning, make appropriate demands on the teachers). Minority-group students who are alienated from school learning and discriminated against by majority students require a combination of warmth and determination from the teacher in demanding achievement efforts and enforcing

conduct limits (Kleinfeld, 1975). In general, the overall goals of classroom management should be similar for all students, but different methods may be used to accomplish them. Distractable students may need study carrels or other quiet places to work; slow students may need special tutoring; poor workers may need contracts for division of tasks into smaller segments.

Despite the fact that physical violence is occurring more frequently in school settings, most of the "problems" that teachers deal with are essentially minor. Loud talking, noisy movements, and similar disruptions are considered normal and appropriate outside the classroom. However, some students present more enduring and serious problems.

Based upon various studies of epidemiological research (including Costello, 1989; Offord et al., 1989; and Velez, Johnson, & Cohen, 1989),

Doll (1994) concludes that in a hypothetical elementary school of 1,000 students (particular averages would vary widely from school to school) one would expect the following types of problems:

- 45–50 students with conduct disorders
- 25–65 with attention deficit disorder
- 180–210 with anxiety disorders
- 6–14 depressed students
- 110 students are being physically abused

In secondary schools (Gelles & Straus, 1987) the above problems would be found in similar proportion except the number of depressed students per 1,000 would rise to 55. In secondary schools roughly 130 students would report heavy drinking and about 101 of these students would report using other controlled substances regularly and heavily (Murray et al., 1987) Further, many secondary students would have eating disorders (Stein & Brinza, 1989) and suicidal ideation (Joffe, Offord, & Boyle, 1988). In deciding how to respond, teachers should consider variables such as their own relationship with the student, whether the problem seems to be declining or escalating, the student's emotional state (which varies daily), whether the student's disruptive activities seem to be intentional, and the probable consequences of contemplated actions.

As Doyle (1992b) notes, little classroom management research has been conducted in classrooms with frequent violence (or the potential for violence), heavy gang activity, or drug use. It is not clear to what extent the findings of research in "regular" classrooms can be applied to classrooms where issues of order are more serious. Further, most of the management research has been conducted in elementary, middle, and junior high settings, so its application to high schools is not documented. With these qualifications, the research on classroom management has yielded rich principles and guidelines that teachers can adapt to local conditions.

choosing the teacher's role

As students progress through the grades, they undergo personal and social development that affects the role of the teacher and the goals and techniques of classroom management.

1. *Kindergarten and the early elementary grades.* Here students are being socialized into the role of student and instructed in basic skills. Most still view adults as authority figures, are predisposed to do what they are told, and are likely to feel gratified when they please teachers and upset when they do not. They turn to teachers for direction, encouragement, solace, assistance, and personalized attention. Serious disturbances usually are not yet present. Consequently, teachers function primarily as instructors and socializers who emphasize teaching students what to do rather than getting them to comply with familiar rules. These instruction and socialization aspects of classroom management are basic to the teacher's job in the early grades; indeed, it is not possible to teach young children effectively without spending considerable time on these tasks.

2. *The middle elementary grades.* This stage starts when basic socialization to the student role is completed and continues as long as most students remain adult-oriented and relatively complaint. Students are familiar with most school routines, and the serious disturbances seen frequently in later years have not yet become common. Maintaining an appropriate learning environment remains central to teaching success, but doing so takes less teacher time, and teachers concentrate on instructing students in the formal curriculum.

3. *The upper elementary and lower high school grades.* As more and more students switch orientation from pleasing teachers to pleasing the peer group, teachers begin to be resented when they act as authority figures. Certain students become more disturbed and harder to

control than they used to be. As a result, classroom management again becomes a prominent part of the teacher role. In contrast to the first stage, however, the teacher's primary problem now is motivating students to behave as they know they are supposed to, not instructing them how to do it.

4. *The upper high school grades.* As many of the most alienated students drop out of school and as students become more mature, schooling once again assumes an academic focus, and teaching becomes mostly a matter of instructing students in the formal curriculum. Classroom management remains important but requires little time (except in the first few class meetings), and group socialization almost disappears. Individual socialization occurs mostly in informal, out-of-class contacts with students.

These developmental aspects of classroom management should be considered when deciding to teach at particular grade levels. Teachers who like to provide nurturant socialization as well as instruction and have the patience and skills needed for socializing young children into the student role are well placed in the primary grades. Elementary teachers who want to concentrate mostly on instruction are better placed in the middle grades. Grades 7 to 10 are best for teachers who enjoy (or at least are not bothered by) the provocative behavior of adolescents and who see themselves as socialization agents and models at least as much as instructors. The upper high school grades are best for teachers who want to function mostly as subject-matter specialists.

There has been much debate, but little research and no ironclad findings, about how to handle the most serious problems; racial and other group tensions; severe withdrawal and refusal to communicate; hostile, antisocial acting out; truancy; refusal to work or obey; vandalism; and severe behavioral disorders or criminality problems that neither psychotherapists nor correctional institutions have achieved

much success in dealing with. Yet teachers typically are asked to cope with such problems while also coping with the needs of twenty or more other students (five times as many in junior high and high school).

Some teachers respond to this with determination to solve whatever problems come along; others conclude that it is better to concentrate on a few tasks and perform them well than to try to do everything. We prefer the former position but find the latter position understandable. A teacher who does not enjoy student socialization and chooses to teach at grades where socialization is minimized and to concentrate on becoming highly skilled at teaching subject matter probably is making a wise decision. The same is true of teachers who choose to teach at the junior high grades and concentrate on socialization. Such teachers will have different effects on students than teachers who deal with the entire spectrum of responsibilities, but their effects will tend to be positive and probably greater in the long run than they would have been if they had tried to do everything and ended up doing nothing very well.

the teacher as a socialization agent

Teachers who want to have important socialization effects on students can do so, but they need to understand the commitment involved in this decision and the frustrations to be encountered because of rules and regulations, uncooperative school officials or parents, and students who do not respond to their best efforts. A teacher who makes a commitment to deal with students' problems in addition to instructing them in the formal curriculum also may be agreeing to invest the time and energy needed to cultivate deeper personal relationships with students than are necessary for purely instructional purposes; spend considerable time outside regular school hours dealing with students and their families, perhaps even to be on call as a counselor to students who have no one else to turn to; and try to deal with complex problems that have developed over a period of years.

difficulties of socialization

Teachers who commit themselves to socialization must simultaneously expect the best and yet be prepared for the worst. Those who expect to succeed consistently or to be rewarded with expressions of love and gratitude will be disappointed. Rewarding experiences occur, but so do frustrations. Many students do not respond to continued and appropriate attempts to reach them. Others respond and make initial progress only to regress and end up worse than they started. Among "success cases," only some respond with overt gratitude or other direct reinforcement of the teacher.

If you think that you can persist in trying to reach students despite frequent frustrations, you probably have a good chance to be a successful socialization agent. In fact, if you find the prospect exciting and challenging, you might consider planning to work in grades 5 to 10 (approximately), where student socialization needs are most frequent and intense.

teachers' advantages as socializers

Teachers do not have the luxury of being able to take a purely friendly, nonauthoritative therapist's role with students. However, they have some advantages over therapists or other specialists. First, they see students every day and under a variety of conditions, so they have more and better information (therapists usually must rely on what clients choose to tell them). Also,

as authority figure they can provide consequences (both rewards and punishments) to selected student behavior. The bottom line is that teachers who want to be socialization agents can achieve reasonable success and satisfaction if they approach the task with realistic expectations and attitudes in addition to the ability to identify problems and respond to them effectively.

the teacher as authority figure

Students expect teachers to manage their classrooms effectively. Nash (1976) found six main themes in elementary students' attitudes and expectations concerning teachers: (1) keep order (strict rather than lenient, punishes if necessary); (2) teaches you (keeps you busy); (3) explains (can be understood, gives help if you need it); (4) interesting (provides variety, not boring); (5) fair (consistent, does not play favorites or pick on anyone); and (6) friendly (kind or nice, talks gently rather than shouts, can laugh when appropriate).

Metz (1978) found similar attitudes among high school students. Students in high tracks expected knowledge of the subject and continuous intellectual challenge from their teachers. They seldom rebelled but often challenged teachers on academic grounds. Students in low tracks were more concerned about teachers' personal qualities: is not mean, does not shout, does not play favorites, accuses only when justified, explains material so you can understand it. These students often tested teachers by disobeying rules and causing disruptions. They did not question the teachers' right to exert authority, even though they sometimes resisted the authority.

In general, *students expect teachers to act as authority figures* and desire a predictable structure in each classroom. They will accept a variety of leadership styles, as long as each teacher is consistent. They have little sympathy, however, for teachers who cannot or will not control their classrooms, taking the attitude that such teachers deserve all the grief they get. Regardless of the teacher role you see as ideal, some suppression of unacceptable behavior will be necessary. Behavior that is disruptive to instruction or harmonious group living must be stopped. Violence, weapons, and destruction, among other things, cannot be allowed. These "nonnegotiables" must be presented to students (when necessary) as absolutely forbidden. Violence will be punished, weapons will be confiscated, and property destruction will require restitution. Students (or parents) who refuse to accept this should be referred to the police. We speak here of situations in which serious unacceptable behavior is widespread and out of control. Such problems should not even be mentioned when they do not exist. When they exist in mild and limited forms, they should be approached in positive ways designed not only to eliminate the undesirable behavior but also to solve underlying problems and channel the students into more appropriate activities.

A basic principle should be that individuals are responsible for their own behavior; students who cause trouble despite repeated warnings must take the consequences (Glaser, 1977). It is self-defeating to try to protect such students by insulating them from the consequences of their own behavior or to minimize the seriousness of crimes such as assault and battery or mugging on the grounds that they occurred at school between students rather than on the street between strangers. The result usually is an escalation of problems, as antisocial students see that they can get away with more and other students realize that they cannot rely on school authorities to accept responsibility for controlling the situation.

Thus, no matter where you stand on the issue of the degree to which the teacher has a

responsibility to help students to solve their personal problems, you must be prepared to suppress misbehavior by students who leave no alternative. This fact must be absorbed emotionally by those of you who would prefer to create situations in which everyone cooperates humanistically and shuns hostility and violence. Almost every school exhibits continuing and inescapable problems with which every teacher must be prepared to deal at some level.

research on teacher-role orientations

Teachers' classroom behavior is affected by the way they perceive their role, abilities, and goals as teachers (Ames, 1992; Ashton & Webb, 1986; Brophy & McCaslin, 1992). Ames (1983) contended that teachers arrive at attributions about their teaching effectiveness through a belief system organized around personal values and that their causal attributions for student performance affect whether or not they see a need to change their teaching behavior. He found that teachers who believed that teaching was important and valued their competence as teachers were more likely to consider their own behavior as a possible source of influence on students than were teachers who did not believe that teachers were responsible for student learning.

It is natural for teachers to develop attributional interpretations and related emotional responses to student behavior. However, teachers are professionals and must be prepared to control their emotions and give students what they need. Gordon (1974) defined three types of problems: (1) **teacher-owned problems** *(student behavior interferes with the teacher's needs)*; (2) **teacher-student shared problems** *(the teacher and student interfere with each other's need satisfaction)*, and (3) **student-owned problems** *(student completely responsible for the prob-*

research at work
teachers' perceptions

There is evidence that teachers' perceptions of the reasons for students' misbehavior influence the ways that teachers respond when behavior problems occur (Rohrkemper & Brophy, 1983). In this study, teachers who had been identified by their principals as either outstanding or average in ability to handle problem students were asked to read vignettes depicting various problems, based on Gordon's (1974) distinctions, and to describe what they would say and do if these problems occurred in their own classrooms.

vignette instrument*

1. *(Failure syndrome student, shared problem)* Joe could be a capable student, but his self-concept is so poor that he actually describes himself as stupid. He makes no serious effort to learn, shrugging off responsibility by saying that "that stuff" is too hard for him. Right now he is dawdling instead of getting started on an assignment that you know he can do. You know that if you approach him he will begin to complain that the assignment is too hard and that he can't do it.

2. *(Hostile-aggressive student, teacher-owned problem)* This morning, several students excitedly tell you that on the way to school they saw Tom beating up Sam and taking his lunch money. Tom is the class bully and has done things like this many times.

3. *(Hyperactive student, shared problem)* Bill is an extremely active child. He seems to burst with energy, and today he is barely "keeping the lid on." This morning. the class is working on their art projects. and Bill has been in and out of his seat frequently. Suddenly, Roger lets out a yell and you look up to see that Bill has knocked Roger's sculpture off his desk. Bill says he didn't mean to do it; he was just returning to his seat.

4. *(Student rejected by peers, student-owned problem)* Mark is not well accepted by his classmates. Today he has been trying to get some of the other boys to play a particular game with him. After much pleading the boys decide to play the game but exclude Mark. Mark argues, saying that he should get to play because it was his idea in the first place, but the boys start without him. Finally, Mark gives up and slinks off, rejected again.

5. *(Perfectionist student, student-owned problem)* Beth has average ability for school work, but she is so anxious about the quality of her work that she seldom finishes an assignment because of all her "startovers." This morning you have asked the children to make pictures to decorate the room. The time allocated to art has almost run out, and Beth is far from finished with her picture. You ask her about it and find out she has "made mistakes" on the other ones and this is her third attempt at a "good picture."

6. *(Passive-aggressive student, teacher-owned problem)* The class is about to begin a test. The room is quiet. Just as you are about to begin speaking, Audrey opens her desk. Her notebook slides off the desk, spilling loose papers on the floor. Audrey begins gathering up the papers. slowly and deliberately. All eyes are upon her. Audrey stops, grins. and then slowly resumes gathering papers.

Someone laughs. Others start talking.

7. *(Distractible student, shared problem)* George's attention wanders easily. Today it has been divided between the discussion and various distractions. You ask him a question, but he is distracted and doesn't hear you.

8. *(Shy/withdrawn student, shared problem)* Linda is bright enough. but she is shy and withdrawn. She doesn't volunteer to participate in class, and when you call on her directly, she often does not respond. When she does, she usually whispers. Today. you are checking the seat-work progress. When you question her, Linda keeps her eyes lowered and says nothing.

9. *(Underachieving student, teacher-owned problem)* Carl can do good work, but he seldom does. He will try to get out of work. When you speak to him about this, he makes a show of looking serious and pledging reform, but his behavior doesn't change. Just now, you see a typical scene: Carl is making paper airplanes when he is supposed to be working.

10. *(Defiant student, teacher-owned problem)* Roger has been fooling around instead of working on his seat work for several days now. Finally, you tell him that he has to finish or stay in during recess and work on it then. He says, "I won't stay in!" and spends the rest of the period sulking. As the class begins to line up for recess, he quickly jumps up and heads for the door. You tell him that he has to stay inside and finish his assignment, but he just says, "No, I don't!" and continues out the door to recess.

11. *(Immature student, shared problem)* Betty seems younger than the other students in your class. She has difficulty getting along with them and is quick to tattle. She has just told you that she heard some of the boys use "bad words" during recess today.

12. *(Low-achieving student, student-owned problem)* Jeff tries hard but is the lowest achiever in the class. This week you taught an important sequence of lessons. You spent a lot of extra time with Jeff and thought he understood the material. Today you are reviewing. All of the other students answer your questions with ease, but when you call on Jeff, he is obviously lost.

The researchers' results indicated that teachers' attributions of students' problems to causes, as well as their beliefs about their own potential effects on students, varied across the three levels of problem ownership. Student-owned problems yielded teacher statements of sympathy and desire to help via encouragement, support, and instruction in better coping strategies, but teacher-owned problems yielded responses that were mostly restricted to attempts to exert situational control through criticism and threats of punishment. The latter responses appear to be self-defeating and unlikely to change the problem behavior. They were associated with tendencies to attribute the problems to internal and unchangeable causes and thus to assume that the chances for long-term change were poor. Lacking confidence in their abilities to bring about long-term improvements in students who presented teacher-owned problems, many teachers did not even try.

* J. Brophy & M. Rohrkemper (1988). *The Classroom Strategy Study: Summary of General Findings.* Research Series Report No. 187, pp. 32–35. East Lansing: The Institute for Research on Teaching, Michigan State University.

lem; not caused by the teacher). Students who present student-owned problems need to learn to cope effectively—teacher sympathy is not enough. Students who present teacher-owned problems could use a little sympathy or at least concern, as well as information about how to behave differently—teacher anger and punitive responses do not help the situation in any fundamental way.

These teacher responses are typical human responses: we tend to respond with sympathy to people we see as victims but to respond with anger to people we see as intentionally causing us problems. Effective professionals, however, get beyond such immediate emotional responses in two ways: controlling their emotions and suppressing the typical response to those emotions, and trying to help the student gain insight and develop more effective coping mechanisms.

general attributes of effective socializers

Inferences about relationships between teachers' general attributes and their success in classroom management can be drawn from studies of student attitudes and from information on attributes of individuals who are effective models (Bandura, 1989) or effective parents (Baumrind, 1991). First, teachers should be liked by their students. Characteristics important here are the same ones for making anyone well liked: a cheerful disposition, friendliness, emotional maturity, sincerity, and other qualities indicating good mental health and personal adjustment. Certain additional qualities are essential when teachers function in the role of classroom authority figure. Many of them involve **ego strength**, *an underlying self-confidence that enables teachers to remain calm in a*

crisis, listen actively without becoming defensive, avoid win-lose conflicts, and maintain a problem-solving orientation rather than resort to withdrawal, blaming, hysteria, or other emotional overreactions. Teachers with serious problems in these areas will not be successful classroom managers no matter what techniques they use.

parents as socialization agents

Important qualities that probably affect teachers' socialization of students can be inferred from what is known about effective parental behavior. The following traits characterize parents who are successful in getting their children to adopt their ideals and internalize their standards for behavior (Baumrind, 1991).

acceptance Parents who accept their children for what they are tend to develop in their children a sense of security, a positive self-concept, and a prosocial attitude toward other people (Coopersmith, 1967). In contrast, children who are rejected because of characteristics their parents find unacceptable, and children who are accepted only conditionally (when they do things that please the parents), may feel threatened by others and hostile toward them, may have low self-esteem and other self-concept problems, or may be generally antisocial.

firm but flexible limits Successful parents state clear limits and enforce them firmly, but they keep limits flexible and negotiable. Rules are liberalized as children assume more independence and responsibility. Parents who have too few limits tend to end up with children lacking in self-discipline and self-control, whereas the children of parents whose limits are too numerous and rigid tend to be either over-conforming, dependent, and uncreative or rebellious and resentful (Baumrind, 1991). Successful classroom managers impose clear

research at work
characteristics of good student socializers

Teachers who are good student socializers tend to have the following characteristics (Brophy & Putnam, 1979):

- *Realistic perceptions of themselves and of students:* seeing themselves and their students for what they are, without letting their perceptions become clouded by romanticism, guilt, hostility, anxiety, or other emotional reactions that can reduce contact with reality.
- *Enjoyment of students, but within a teacher-student relationship:* enjoying interacting with students and getting to know them as individuals while maintaining an identity as an adult teacher and authority figure. Being friendly but not overfamiliar, comfortable with the group but not a group member.
- *Clarity and comfort concerning roles:* being clear and consistent about their own roles and relationship to students and about the behaviors that they value or will not tolerate.
- *Patience and determination:* convincing students who persist in testing limits that the rules will be enforced.

rules and enforce them consistently but keep them to a minimum and flexible enough to allow for individual differences and changes over time.

positive expectations Children tend to acquire their parents' expectations and attitudes and to use them both for defining what is normal and for deciding what expectations and attitudes apply to themselves. One result is the self-fulfilling prophecy effect: regardless of whether expectations were accurate originally, children are likely to fulfill them if adults consistently expect them to have certain qualities and treat them accordingly. Students treated as basically good people who want to do the right things, whose lapses are treated as due to ignorance or forgetfulness, are likely to become the prosocial people they are expected to become (Miller, Brickman, & Bolen, 1975). Students treated as if they are inherently evil or under the control of powerful antisocial impulses, whose lapses are taken as evidence of immorality

rather than as isolated mistakes, are likely to become antisocial.

Thus, it is important for teachers to project positive expectations by treating students as if they already are, or at least are trying to be, the kind of people that the teachers want them to be. Admonitions such as "John, be careful with that microscope—we wouldn't want to break it," or "Mary, I was surprised to hear you ridiculing Jean when you were talking to Mary Ann today. How about trying to understand her better than just running her down?" (said in private) illustrate these principles. The teacher treats the student as a responsible person (or at least as someone who will be responsible in this regard in the future) and provides prescriptive information rather than personal criticism. In contrast, consider responses such as "I don't know why you can't sit still. Do you think it's funny to make noises like that?" or "You are going to have to find some other way to take out your frustrations. We'll have no hitting in the classroom." These criticisms not only fail to provide positive guidance but also imply that no change in the behavior is really expected.

rationales and parents' expectations Successful parents supplement their socialization demands with explanations. They not only tell children what to do but also tell them why it is important to do it. This helps children see that rules and demands are imposed for good reasons rather than as arbitrary exercises of adult power and to be aware of the implications of behavior for themselves and others (Baumrind, 1991). This ability to see implications or to take the role of the other is necessary for the development of a prosocial moral orientation, a tendency to live by the Golden Rule (treating others the way one would like to be treated oneself). Furthermore, if people do not understand the reasons underlying a demand, they are unlikely to adopt it in guiding their own behavior. Students must see ideal behavior patterns modeled by the adults around them. They also must come to see that rules support the general welfare, and are not just arbitrary demands to be followed only because they may be enforced by authority figures.

consistency in rule enforcement

Inconsistency is confusing. It is difficult to learn rules that are unclear or keep changing, and frustrating if behaviors that were acceptable yesterday are punished today. This produces resentment and the feeling that the authority figure is arbitrary and undependable, and it encourages deliberate disobedience (usually called "testing") designed to see if a rule will be enforced.

Consistency can be carried too far, however. For example, what is an effective consequence for one student might be ineffective for another (Dreikurs, Grunwald, & Pepper, 1982). A student who is often bullied on the playground might not find the denial of recess aversive, but a student who enjoys playing sports and socializing may experience such denial as punishment. According to Weinstein and Mignano (1993), a particular consequence does not have to be tied to a particular rule because this may unnecessarily force a teacher to be consistent but not fair. For example, a student who has been corrected for interrupting others five days in a row is not the same as a student who is behaving inappropriately for the first time.

Some teachers develop a list of increasingly negative consequences for violating important classroom rules. For example, Curwin and Mendler (1988a) suggest that the consequences for failure to turn in homework might result in the following sequence of consequences: reminder; warning; student must finish homework before the school day ends; student stays after school to finish the homework; conference between teacher, student, and parent or guardian.

Curwin and Mendler suggest that the teacher should explain in advance to students that "fair" does not necessarily mean "the same" when it comes to consequences for misbehavior. Just as teachers must vary instruction according to different students' cognitive needs, they also have to select consequences in terms of students' social needs. Use of a range of consequences for misbehavior can allow the teacher to be consistent but still somewhat flexible by selecting a consequence that fits the situation (Weinstein & Mignano, 1993).

modeling

Authority figures must practice what they teach. Usually, they cannot have a double standard, one for themselves and one for others. Unless they can explain any exceptions satisfactorily, they will have to live up to their own ideals and rules if they expect others to do so. Thus, teachers must model and generally live up to ideals that they verbalize. In areas such as politeness and good manners, friendliness and helpfulness, and consideration for the rights and feelings of others, teachers who do not practice what they preach by modeling it in their own behavior will be perceived as hypocrites or worse and will not be respected or obeyed (Lickona, 1975).

encouraging self-regulated students

We have stressed that teachers must progressively encourage students to take increasing responsibility for organizing and directing their own learning (Corno, 1989; Rohrkemper McCaslin, 1989; Zimmerman & Schunk, 1989). Just as teachers want students to become independent and self-reliant learners, they should want students to assume more responsibility for managing their own conduct. Over time, students should assume progressively more responsibility for classroom rules, personal management, and social responsibility.

Ironically, educators often design the curriculum to encourage students to be active learners (problem finders and problem solvers) but allow, if not insist, that students be passive, obedient, and excessively rule governed in their conduct (McCaslin & Good, 1992). Thus, an important activity for teachers is to increase students' capacity for self-regulation in all aspects of the classroom. Teachers should encourage students to develop plans for goal setting, for coordinating short-term and long-term assignments (time management), and for developing the capacity for working with other students.

physical design of classrooms

Good management involves the prevention of problems; a carefully laid out physical environment is the first step. Classroom arrangements influence student involvement and participation, and the physical arrangement should be congruent with intended objectives (Weinstein & Mignano, 1993). Physical settings can influence student behavior either directly or indirectly through teacher behavior or different task structures (Doyle, 1986a).

Rosenfeld, Lambert, and Black (1985), for example, showed that students asked to brainstorm about ideas for writing assignments did better when seated in circles than when seated in rows or clusters. Presumably, the enhanced visibility made it easier for students to participate and to be monitored during these interactions (see Figure 16.1).

Figure 16.1 SOURCE: "Desk Arrangement Effects on Pupil Classroom Behavior" by P. Rosenfeld, N. Lambert, and A. Black, *Journal of Educational Psychology, 77* (1), 101–108. Copyright ©1985 by the American Psychological Association. Reprinted by permission.

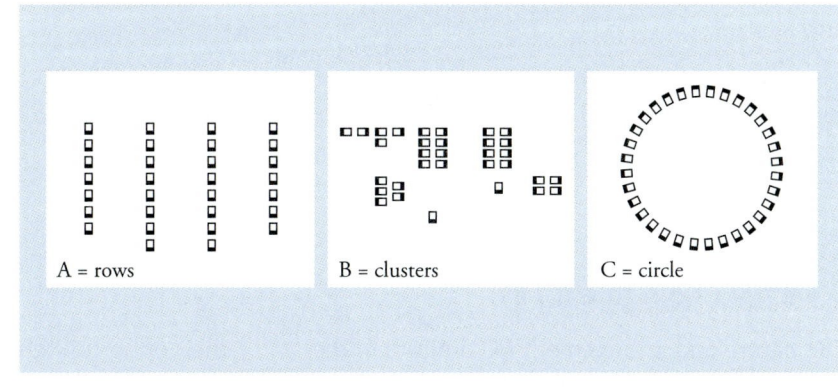

A = rows B = clusters C = circle

class size and heterogeneity

Teachers typically cannot directly affect the size of their classes, but they can divide the classes into smaller units for some instruction. By using parent volunteers and teacher aides, teachers can increase the time they spend supervising individual and group work. They also can use different organizational strategies (learning centers, peer tutoring, small groups) to reduce the size of their instructional groups.

Students and teachers may benefit from working in small groups for these reasons: (1) instruction can be geared to the specific needs of the students in the group; (2) the teacher can monitor work directly and provide corrective feedback immediately; (3) shy or slow students may feel more comfortable asking questions in small groups; (4) students may stay on task and apply themselves more consistently when they are under direct supervision; and (5) students may feel more responsible for completing tasks in small groups.

Just as small classes are easier to manage than larger classes, homogeneous classes are easier to manage than heterogeneous classes. Evertson, Sanford, and Emmer (1981) studied the ways that junior high English teachers adapted instruction to heterogenous classes compared to the ways that they taught more homogeneous classes. The heterogenous classes had eight- to ten-year spreads in grade-level

equivalent units between low and high achievers. All of the heterogeneous classes got off to a poor start because the methods and materials were poorly adapted to the students' interests and abilities, and success rates in terms of completeness and correctness of assignments were poor. This pattern continued or deteriorated further in classes in which teachers lacked the managerial skills needed to respond effectively to heterogeneity. More effective managers were, however, able to overcome these problems to an extent after about three weeks by using the following strategies; (1) special attention and help for lower-ability students; (2) limited use of within-class grouping and differentiated materials or assignments; (3) limited differential grading based on individualized effort and continuous-progress criteria; (4) limited use of peer tutoring; and (5) frequent monitoring and provision of academic feedback to all students, coupled with mechanisms to ensure student accountability for participating in lessons and completing assignments.

These adjustments were successful enough that there was no difference in achievement gain between the homogeneous and the heterogeneous classes. Still, there were limits on what could be accomplished. The pressures of meeting the greater range of instructional needs in the heterogeneous classes left the teachers with little time for personalized interaction with students, especially interaction concerning nonacademic topics.

implications for teachers
improving your classroom physical environments

The nature and arrangement of furniture in the classroom can affect the density of students, their opportunities for interaction, and the extent to which teachers can observe ongoing behavior. Weinstein (1979) reviewed research on the effects of physical features of classrooms and noted that different spatial arrangements appear to have little effect on achievement but do affect students' attitudes and conduct. In particular, it seems important to clearly separate areas serving different purposes and to design classroom traffic avenues carefully. Density appears to increase dissatisfaction and aggression and to decrease attentiveness and involvement in assigned activities.

As your classroom functions change, seating patterns should be altered. Even though many classrooms are equipped with movable desks, some teachers use one seating arrangement exclusively. Others alter the physical arrangement too frequently. You are probably better off with two or three basic room arrangements that you can use for reasons that students understand. Students should be able to move easily from one arrangement to another.

For example, the room in Figure 16.2 is arranged for students to listen to individual reports given by three students. This arrangement is acceptable for this purpose but not ideal. Most students can see the speaker (if the speaker stands), although those who have inside seats will face away from their desks and may have difficulty taking notes. If students need to pass out material or demonstrate a procedure, the clustering of students and the open space will facilitate these needs.

What makes this plan effective is the fact that the teacher plans to follow the three five-minute presentations with a half-hour of related small-group work. The arrangement is fine for small-group activity, and students can begin to work as soon as the presentations end. Furthermore, the groups are arranged so that the teacher, by selecting an appropriate position while working with one group, can also monitor the other groups easily.

space utilization Minor changes in the physical environment can lead to important changes in behavior. Weinstein (1977), for example, found that additional shelving, increased space for individual work, and more partitions encouraged the use of individual work areas in open classrooms. After these physical changes were made, management problems decreased and task-relevant behaviors increased.

Steele (1973) and Weinstein and Mignano (1993) noted that the classroom physical setting affects six factors: security and shelter; social contact; task instrumentality; pleasure; symbolic identification; and growth. Questions and issues associated with each factor can help you plan and improve upon the physical design of your classroom:

Figure 16.2 a classroom arrangement for delivery of student reports

security and shelter*
- Add elements of softness.
- Arrange space for freedom from interference.
- Create a "retreat" area.

social contact
- Consider how much interaction among students you want
- Think about whether you are making contact with *all* your students

symbolic identification
- Personalize your classroom space so that it communicates information about you and your students.

task instrumentality
- Make sure frequently used materials are accessible to students.
- Make sure it is clear where things belong.
- Plan pathways to avoid congestion and distraction.
- Arrange seats for a clear view of presentations.
- Offer students a personal space in which to keep belongings.

- Locate your desk in an appropriate place (putting it off to the side helps to ensure that you will circulate).
- Separate incompatible activities.

pleasure
- Use a variety of colors and textures to create an aesthetically pleasing environment.

growth
- Stock your room with a variety of materials, both "open" and "closed."
- Create a library corner.

Careful planning of your physical environment is an integral part of good classroom management. When you begin to design your room, think about the activities it will accommodate and invite your students to participate in the planning process. Try your arrangement, evaluate it, and redesign as needed.

*C. Weinstein & A. Mignano, Jr. (1993). *Elementary Classroom Management: Lessons from Research and Practice.* New York: McGraw-Hill.

summary

Effective classroom management requires both clear expectations about student behavior and knowledge about what to do when expectations are not met. Teachers who are friendly, mature, and sincere and who have sufficient ego strength to deal fairly and constructively with students can use a variety of techniques effectively. Such teachers consider the characteristics of various developmental stages along with past cultural experiences in dealing with students.

The role of socialization agent is difficult, but teachers have some advantages over therapists and other specialists because of their fre-

quent contact with students and students' expectations that teachers will maintain authority over classroom behavior. To be successful, teachers must be positive in their approach but determined to suppress unacceptable behavior. They must have realistic perceptions of themselves and of students, enjoy students within the confines of a professional relationship, be clear and comfortable in role portrayal, exhibit positive attitudes toward tests and challenges, and display patience and determination in dealing with persistent misbehavior.

Like parents, teachers must project acceptance and unconditional positive regard for students, set clear but flexible limits, project positive expectations for responsible behavior, provide explanations for socialization demands, be consistent in rule enforcement, and model desired behaviors that they expect students to exhibit. Progressively, students need to be involved in creating rules, generating rationales for rules, changing them when no longer needed, and so on.

Larger or more heterogeneous classes are more difficult to manage than smaller or more homogeneous ones, but teachers can adapt through grouping and other organizational strategies, limited use of peer tutoring, and differentiation of instruction, assignments, and grading standards.

Classroom environments generally can be improved by carefully considering stimuli affecting student behavior, including those originating from space utilization (e.g., furniture, displays, etc.). Physical design should support the psychological requirements for learning.

questions for reflection

1. A prospective teacher from a white, middle-class, suburban home is faced with teaching in an inner-city school. What should this person do to prepare? What should a new teacher from an inner-city background do to prepare for teaching in a silk-stocking district?

2. What is your preferred balance between instructional and managerial/counseling activities with students?

3. How can teachers be "overly" sympathetic to disturbed students?

4. What kinds of students are especially appealing to you (and thus likely to receive favoritism if you are not careful)? What kinds turn you off and will be especially hard for you to treat impartially and with positive attitudes and expectations?

5. Do you have strong preferences concerning seating arrangements or classroom groupings? What implications do these preferences have for your teaching (remember that as a teacher you will need to discover what things work best with your students and that these things may not correspond with your own preferences)?

6. How might you manipulate seat assignments for particular purposes? What if different goals conflict, such as minimizing social chatting among friends versus placing reticent students in action zones where they are more likely to participate?

cases to consider

pranksters Jim Knipp, an algebra teacher at Willow High School, sits down at his desk and immediately springs to his feet. A quick glance confirms his guess that he had sat on a melted candy bar. The class howls with laughter. What should Jim do now?

talkative Margorie Jim Heald, a first-year high school teacher, watched with interest as three girls burst into the room, glanced at him, and headed for the back of the class. As the period wore on, he became progressively more irritated because the girls talked incessantly during his presentation. Finally, in frustration he called on Margery, the loudest of the three. "Margery, I've been trying to explain the goals of our physics class. You've been talking for the past twenty minutes. Apparently, you know what our goals are here. Would you please summarize them for me?" She looked at him and half laughed as she said, "No, I think I'd better listen."

Would you have responded to Margery in the same way that Jim Heald did? If not, why not? In general, should students be allowed to choose their seats in high school classes? Why or why not? Do elementary school students need more or less choice than secondary students?

chapter **17.**

establishing and maintaining a good learning environment

objectives

When you have mastered the material in this chapter, you will be able to

1. Describe what a teacher can do to create a classroom environment that promotes learning, independence, and responsibility
2. Differentiate authoritarian, democratic, and laissez-faire leadership styles
3. Describe authoritative leadership and its effects and differentiate it from democratic leadership
4. Describe ways you can build personal trust and credibility with students and be able to apply this information to the grade level and subject you plan to teach
5. List and explain at least four characteristics of classroom rules that assist classroom management; be able to discuss how these rules influence students' long-term capacity for self-regulation
6. Understand and know how to apply the following group management skills of successful teachers: preparedness, maintaining student involvement, "withitness," overlapping, group alerting
7. Explain at least three techniques to engage and maintain students' attention during lessons or seat work.

According to Weinstein and Mignano (1993), five assumptions are helpful for understanding classroom management: (1) Most management problems can be avoided if teachers use appropriate preventive strategies. 2) The way teachers think about management (and their experience of classroom management) influences the way they behave. (3) The need for order, although important, must not become more important than the need for meaningful instruction. (4) Expectations for appropriate classroom behavior vary across classroom settings. Hence, teachers may allow students to work cooperatively in one activity or in one setting but not in another, but teachers must be careful that students understand these differential expectations. (5) Managing classrooms is a decision-making process that should be informed by relevant research; however, teachers must apply that research to their own contexts and recognize that research does not address all management problems.

As we noted in the previous chapter, research has not addressed dealing with violent behavior in the classroom (Doyle, 1992b), but most problems teachers deal with are relatively minor (Cangelosi, 1993). For example, Jones (1979) found that in the typical classroom sampled, 50 percent of allocated time was lost because of off-task behaviors. However, most misbehavior was not hostile or aggressive. Indeed, 99 percent of off-task behaviors involved talking or moving without permission. Still, on occasion teachers will have to be prepared to cope with major problems such as physical abuse. Further, as we know from Chapter 16, many students suffer from major problems (physical abuse at home, drug usage) even if those problems do not directly manifest themselves in classroom behavior.

In this chapter we first discuss the advance preparation that contributes to effective classroom management, especially the need to arrange the physical environment for efficient functioning and to develop a workable set of classroom rules. This discussion builds on material in the preceding chapter on the importance of a match between the teacher's goals and the physical arrangement of the classroom. Later we review research on group leadership styles and effective strategies for maintaining attention to lessons and engagement in seat work.

implications for teachers

preparing the physical environment

Effective management begins with preparation of the classroom itself. What can be done to make it an attractive and efficient learning environment? Regardless of how good or bad the available space and equipment may be, some arrangements are better than others. Several of these may be needed if a teacher deals with classes that vary in size or if students engage in diverse activities.

seating arrangements High priority should be given to arranging the room so that you can monitor all areas at all times. You should plan to sit or stand so that they are facing the class and should keep this in mind when identifying areas to be used for special purposes. In time children will assume more responsibility for creating and maintaining order (e.g., as they begin to work independently of the teacher in small cooperative groups).

Seats should be located to facilitate attention and minimize disruption. Usually this means keeping desks or tables in reasonably neat arrangements, with students seated facing the teacher. When students are assigned to work in groups, however, they can sit in small circles or ovals to facilitate communication among group members. If several groups meet simultaneously, they should be spread out to minimize interference. Perhaps some can meet outside the classroom, assuming that they act responsibly without supervision.

traffic, bottlenecks, and lines Heavily traveled traffic routes should be free of obstacles and wide enough to accommodate smooth, efficient movement around the classroom. This minimizes problems that occur when students bump into furniture or one another.

Problems are likely to develop when students are standing in lines, whether lines are formed by the teacher or are the result of bottlenecks. You can do many things to minimize the time students spend standing and waiting. One is to delegate authority or use students to handle time-consuming housekeeping tasks such as passing out supplies, taking attendance, and making collections. Use of the pencil sharpener or drinking fountain can be left to individual initiative within whatever limits are necessary instead of requiring groups to go at specific times or requiring students to ask permission.

Supplies like scissors or paste should be dispensed from several places around the room so that students do not have to line up and wait their turn at a single source. Checking of worksheets can be accomplished as a group activity by asking students to indicate when they are ready for checking or when they need help or when you are circulating around the room. Necessarily repetitive activities like "show and tell" or student speeches can be staggered across several days rather than massed into a single long session.

student independence and responsibility Too much time is often spent supervising students in relation to personal needs and everyday housekeeping tasks, and interruptions for this purpose are a major source of discontinuity in academic activities. You can minimize these problems by preparing the classroom and the students to handle most routine tasks on their own. This is especially important in the early grades, when students' abilities to accomplish everyday tasks may depend on the degree to which you have anticipated their needs. Young students can handle their belongings with the help of coat hooks and cubbyholes or lockers, but they should be within easy reach (not too high) and assigned individually. Color codes, pictures, and labels can be affixed to storage areas to help students remember where items belong. Everyday equipment should be stored where it can be reached and removed easily, and small items should be stored in easily opened containers that will not break. Instructions or rule reminders can be displayed prominently in activity centers so that students will not always have to come to you for help.

backup activities and supplies

Effective classroom managers have contingency plans for whenever scheduled activities are canceled or bad weather precludes outdoor recess. Prepare for these times as you would for lessons. Any needed props should be handy, and you are ready to conduct the activity smoothly. Even more important is the development of a system of backup activities, preferably including some individual student choices, that are available to them when they finish assignments. These options should include a number of attractive individual and small-group learning activities and pastimes. Students should know what their options are and be able to exercise them without getting directions from you.

general principles of group leadership

In addition to organizing the physical environment, teachers must organize the class into a cohesive group that functions effectively under their leadership. Several general principles are involved here, as well as specific techniques.

When students constitute an intact group with well-established peer leadership, teachers need to gain the cooperation of peer leaders and avoid coming into conflict with them or causing them to lose face before the group. This is especially important when teachers work with students from a different social class or ethnic background or with students whose attitudes and values contrast with those of the teacher.

group structure

Effective groups show cohesiveness and positive attitudes. Less effective groups are divided into conflicting subgroups or into a dominant ingroup and a collection of isolates. Teachers can promote group cohesiveness by arranging cooperative experiences, minimizing competition, promoting prosocial behaviors, and helping each student to identify with the class as a whole. They should avoid playing favorites, picking on scapegoats, fostering inappropriate competition, or refusing to allow students to work cooperatively (Johnson & Johnson, 1975; Slavin, 1991b).

leadership style

Lewin, Lippitt, and White (1939) conducted a classic experiment in which adults working with groups of ten-year-old boys were trained to act consistently authoritarian, democratic, or laissez-faire leaders, defined as follows: **Authoritarian leaders** are *leaders who establish firm rules and standards, but who are unwilling to discuss the reasons or negotiate about behaviors.* **Democratic leaders** are *leaders who help establish rules with the group, are willing to discuss reasons for rules or to negotiate, and involve the group in rule setting.* **Laissez-faire leaders** are *leaders who fail to establish or to maintain group* *and group direction.* The three leadership styles were evaluated for effects on group productivity (efficiency in carrying out tasks) and affect (enjoyment of the experience).

Boys in democratic-led groups developed warm feelings for one another and the leader and enjoyed the experience. These affective benefits were achieved with only slight cost in efficiency (the productivity of democratic-led groups was not quite as good as that of authoritarian-led groups). The authoritarian-led groups were the most efficient because the leaders kept everyone working at a good pace, but group members showed tension and negative feelings toward one another and the leader. Laissez-faire leadership did not succeed by either criterion. The ostensible freedom experienced in these groups did not make up for the lack of leadership, so they spent much time working at cross-purposes, produced very little, and had negative reactions to the experience.

Later studies of group leadership have produced similar results: laissez-faire leadership is generally ineffective, authoritarian leadership is efficient but otherwise unattractive, and democratic leadership produces positive attitudes and good group relations, although at some cost in efficiency. This implies that democratic leadership is best as an overall style, although more structured leadership may be required when efficiency is important.

Baumrind's (1987) research on childrearing provides some perspective for these findings. Baumrind classified parents as authoritarian, authoritative, or laissez-faire. She used "authoritative" instead of "democratic" because "democratic" leadership is not really democratic at all (decisions are not made by majority vote). It is authoritative in that the leader has a position of responsibility, speaks as an experienced and mature adult, and retains ultimate decision-making authority. Rather than act in an authoritarian manner, however, authoritative leaders solicit input, seek consensus, and make sure that everyone understands the rationales for decisions as well as the decisions themselves. Baumrind reported that children of authoritative parents show the most advanced levels of autonomy and independence for their ages and have greater confidence and healthier self-concepts.

Authoritative teachers are *teachers who establish firm expectations and performance standards, are willing to discuss the reasons for their standards, and who generally do not negotiate about them with students.* There are two reasons for stressing Baumrind's work in discussing classroom management. First, the term "authoritative" is preferable to "democratic" because it retains the notion that the teacher has the ultimate responsibility for classroom leadership. The idea that decisions should be made by majority vote was not tested or supported by Lewin, Lippitt, and White (1939), despite their use of the term "democratic." Nor does other research support the notion of truly democratic classroom leadership, although this style is often recommended on a philosophical basis (e.g., Glasser, 1969; Gordon, 1974).

Second, Baumrind's work provides a more convincing and data-based argument to support authoritative over authoritarian and laissez-faire methods. Authoritative methods are not merely *better perceived;* they are *more effective* in building the cognitive structures and behavioral control mechanisms within children that enable them to become both independent and responsible in managing their affairs. Authoritative teacher behavior should help students to see and internalize the rationales that underlie classroom rules and to choose to operate within the rules on their own initiative. Authoritarian approaches do not encourage the development of such internal control mechanisms. Instead, they generate conflict and tension even when they succeed in controlling behavior.

implications for teachers
establishing reasonable rules and limits

As a teacher you must decide what rules and limits are reasonable given your own role definition and values, the ages and number of students involved, the length of interaction with students (keeping the same ones all day versus changing classes each period), students' general levels of conformity versus rebelliousness, and the expectations of the principal and school district. Different teachers need different sets of rules. A kindergarten or first-grade teacher, for example, usually must take charge of tasks such as passing out supplies, although some children can help in the role of monitor. Fifth- or sixth-grade teachers do not need to perform this job because students can handle it on their own if guided by a few supply-distribution rules. Such rules may not even be needed in high school.

Similarly, in the early grades teachers may have to insist that no one respond to questions or make comments without first being called on. As students mature, however, you can be more flexible, especially in group discussions. Flat prohibitions against calling out can be abandoned in favor of rules such as "feel free to contribute your ideas, but wait until the person who is speaking has finished."

minimal and flexible rules Rules should be minimal in number, should refer to general qualitative aspects of behavior rather than to specific do's and don'ts, and should be flexible and open to change as situations dictate. Minimizing rules helps students remember them and makes accepting them easier than if a long and demoralizing list were involved.

Rules such as "we will treat one another with courtesy and respect" or "we will keep the classroom clean and neat" cover a great many behaviors and eliminate the need for long lists of specifics. Such rules are broad but still definitive enough for most undesirable behaviors to be obvious. Furthermore, they are phrased in positive ways that make them easier to explain in a manner likely to motivate students to accept them.

Maintaining flexibility is important because many behaviors are appropriate under some circumstances but not others. Quiet talking, for example, might be allowed among students who have finished assignments. If this gets too loud, you can simply ask the students to quiet down—there is no need to demand total silence or to revoke the talking privilege. Flexibility avoids two problems that frequently cause conflict between teachers and students: unreasonable enforcement of a rule and loss of teacher credibility resulting from inconsistency (which students perceive as teacher confusion or hypocrisy rather than reasonable adjustment to situational differences).

Some authors have suggested that rules should be extremely specific, to avoid confusion and spell out the consequences of violations. We believe, however, that any gains in avoidance of misunderstanding that might come with a large number of overly specific rules would be canceled by the needless regimentation and communication of negative expectations. Effective classroom managers usually have five to ten general rules rather than many specific ones.

getting off to a good start

Getting the year off to a good start by establishing the right expectations and routines is crucial (Doyle, 1986a; Moskowitz & Hayman, 1976). This may mean that several days or even weeks must be devoted more to getting students organized and socialized than to teaching the curriculum, but time spent this way is well worth it in the long run (Emmer, Evertson, & Anderson, 1980; Evertson & Emmer, 1982). In the early grades, teachers need to conduct actual lessons that include instruction, practice with feedback, and review to show students how to handle daily routines (such as moving from a reading group to seat work and vice versa, using the pencil sharpener, or managing the equipment in a learning center). Older students may not need such detailed instruction, but expectations should be made explicit.

In all cases, student input should be sought and used in creating appropriate expectations and routines. The joint creation of the social setting will help students to feel more connected to them and to be more likely to live up to the social expectations (for related discussion see Hamilton, 1990). Further, the sense of belonging to a social community can help to further students' positive self-esteem when they fulfill social expectations.

Emmer, Evertson, and Anderson (1980) observed in twenty-seven third-grade classrooms during the first three weeks of the school year and at three-week intervals thereafter to discover why teachers who had comparable classes at the beginning of the year differed in their **management effectiveness** (*degree of student involvement in lessons*) during the year. Their data revealed that successful managers devoted much of the first day and the first few weeks to establishing classroom procedures and rules, beginning with those of most immediate interest to the students (storage, lunch, lavatory, recess, etc.). The first few academic activities introduced were enjoyable and likely to produce success. The teachers usually worked with the whole class and supervised students the entire time, putting off grouping and sustained independent work until routines were established. They monitored students carefully so that they could move quickly when instructional help or behavioral intervention was needed. They told students precisely what they wanted them to do and then supervised them while they did it, establishing their credibility by following through on their statements so that students learned that they meant what they said.

The successful managers also revealed evidence of advanced planning and preparation. They had arranged their rooms to make the best use of whatever resources they were given to work with, often making changes in anticipation of problems with existing arrangements. They had thought out their rules and expectations so they could describe them to students in specific terms. They handled most housekeeping and paperwork before or after school, so that most classroom time was spent instructing the class. In contrast, poor managers created problems for themselves practically from the moment students arrived, because they were unclear or inconsistent about stating what they wanted, or because they failed to follow through.

Good managers also were more careful monitors of student behavior and dealt with misbehavior more quickly than poor managers. They *alerted* students to the behaviors they expected and held students *accountable* for those behaviors. As students internalized these rules, they could monitor their own behavior more continuously (e.g., they knew when and how to get help from other students about missed assignments). Such internalization of classroom norms for conduct and procedures not only makes students more efficient learners (e.g., it

A good management system allows self-motivated students to proceed and do well; for other students it allows them to learn self-control and engage in academic tasks.

minimizes the time they spend wondering about when or how to approach the teacher for feedback), it also minimizes the number of competing demands on the teacher.

why proactive management works: toward a theory

Successful managers start the year by *establishing* rules and procedures (announce some; negotiate some) and by *communicating* their expectations. Other teachers are ambiguous about their expectations and spend so much time clarifying expectations that students often wonder (sometimes justly so) whether or not their behavior is appropriate.

New teachers sometimes are advised to "clamp down" early in the year to show that they mean business. This advice can backfire if taken the wrong way. Consistency and follow-through are important, but teachers who set themselves up as "the enemy" by alienating students through vindictive behavior are in for year-long conflict. Thus, the old "rule" suggesting "don't smile until Christmas" is bad advice.

It is important to monitor actively and deal with inappropriate behavior (especially serious misbehavior). Effective managers therefore may correct student behavior more often during the first few days of the year than other teachers do. However, because their students eventually engage in fewer off-task behaviors, it soon becomes easier for them to monitor the class (there are fewer disruptions to attend to) and to respond to misbehavior appropriately (e.g., to correct the right student). If teachers establish workable rules, expect compliance, monitor the class, and insist on appropriate behavior when necessary, students understand their seriousness of purpose and internalize rules, expectations, and procedures.

Effective managers also demand that students use their time to complete assignments

research at work

organization and management

Evertson and colleagues (1984, 1993) wrote a manual summarizing management principles and guidelines for starting the school year. The manual is organized around the following eleven guidelines.*

1. *Readying the classroom*—Be certain your classroom space and materials are ready for the beginning of the year.
2. *Planning rules and procedures*—Think about what procedures students must follow to function effectively in your classroom and in the school environment; decide what behaviors are acceptable; develop a list of procedures and rules.
3. *Consequences*—Decide ahead of time consequences for appropriate and inappropriate behavior in your classroom, and communicate them to your students; follow through consistently.
4. *Teaching rules and procedures*—Teach students rules and procedures systematically; include in your lesson plans for the beginning of school sequences for teaching rules and procedures, when and how they will be taught, and when practice and review will occur.
5. *Beginning-of-school activities*—Develop activities for the first few days of school that will involve students readily and maintain a whole-group focus.
6. *Strategies for potential problems*—Plan strategies to deal with potential problems that could upset your classroom organization and management.
7. *Monitoring*—Monitor student behavior closely.
8. *Stopping inappropriate behavior*—Handle inappropriate and disruptive behavior promptly and consistently.
9. *Organizing instruction*—Organize instruction to provide learning activities at suitable levels for all students in your class.
10. *Student accountability*—Develop procedures that keep the students responsible for their work.
11. *Instructional clarity*—Be clear when you present information and give directions to your students.

* C. Evertson, E. Emer, J. Sanford, & B. Clements (1983). "Improving Classroom Management: An Experiment in Elementary School Classrooms." *Elementary School Journal, 84,* 173–188.

These researchers have also written a manual for secondary teachers (Emmer et al., 1993) indicating that such teachers do not need to do as much instructing of students in basic classroom routines as elementary teachers do. However, secondary teachers do need to be very clear and consistent in stating expectations and developing follow-up accountability procedures concerning completion of assignments. Experiments in which teachers were trained to implement the principles stressed in these manuals illustrate the effectiveness of the principles for maximizing student attention to lessons and engagement in assignments (Evertson, 1983, 1985).

In a study that compared beginning teachers with more experienced teachers nominated as "best" teachers by their students, Moskowitz and Hayman (1976) found that experienced teachers spent more time setting expectations and establishing behavior patterns on the first day of school. Even so, the experienced teachers also were more willing to accept and use student ideas. Hence, successful managers are not necessarily stern or rigid. They do appear to be skillful in stating expectations and working with students to be sure that workable rules are established and enforced. Simply put, they *teach* norms for appropriate classroom behavior.

and hold students accountable for work. Students also know what to do when they finish assignments. Thus, effective managers construct learning environments in which expectations for student behavior are *continuous*.

Some teachers make it difficult for students to know what is expected. Following a demonstration lesson, for example, they might assign seat work but say, "If you work now, you won't have homework." Such statements make students' roles ambiguous. Presumably, students can do the work now or later. Does this mean that they can choose not to do the work now? If so, what can they do while their classmates are engaged in seat work?

In contrast, more effective managers are likely to make a transition from demonstration to seat work in the following way: "Now do problems fifteen to thirty at your desks. In ten minutes we will check progress and correct any problems we encounter. If you have difficulty with a problem, do the next one. I'll be around to help you. Get started now."

As Good and Hinkel (1982) emphasized, all aspects of good management must operate for the system to work. Even if teachers establish credibility during the first few days of school, set explicit learning goals daily, and build in continuous criteria so that students always know what is expected of them, they will soon "lose" students if the students' work is not checked on a regular basis. Doyle (1986a) argued that accountability drives the task system and that students tend to take seriously only that work for which they are held accountable.

In essence, a good management system announces clear intentions and makes it possible to monitor behavior to see whether progress is being made toward shared goals. For self-motivated students, it tells how to proceed and do well. For other students, it establishes conditions to enable them to learn self-control and engage in academic tasks. These students come to understand that rewards and privileges are associated with personal progress on assigned tasks.

As McCaslin and Good (1992) have noted, implementing a management system along the lines suggested by Kounin, Evertson, Emmer, and others is an important condition for organizing environments that support thoughtful student learning. However, students need to progressively assume more responsibility for the self-regulation of their own behavior (Corno, 1989; Rohrkemper McCaslin, 1989; Schunk, 1989).

One difficulty with classroom management is what motivates one student may not motivate another student. Thus, teachers need to adjust their management plans to individual students who differ widely in their attitudes toward school, prior achievements, home and social lives, and cultural backgrounds and ethnicity (Cangelosi, 1993). Some students can progress much more quickly than others, particularly in areas such as self-alerting.

Sainato and colleagues (1990) provided evidence that even young children can learn to self-evaluate. They identified four preschool children with disabilities who frequently behaved inappropriately and then taught the students skills for determining whether they had engaged in appropriate independent seat work behaviors. Each child was photographed when behaving appropriately, and each photo was given a label describing the behavior exhibited. Next to each picture a happy face and frowning face were placed. Each child had her or his own personal folder in which the photos were placed. At the end of each independent seat work period, each child assessed the extent to which he or she had exhibited the appropriate behaviors with a "yes" or "no" (i.e., by choosing a face). The self-evaluation activities were associated with notable improvement in student behavior.

specific group management techniques

Assuming that teachers get their classes off to a good start by following the principles discussed so far, what techniques for group management should they use in everyday teaching? Kounin (1970) approached this topic by contrasting the videotaped behavior of successful classroom managers with the behavior of teachers who had continuing and severe management problems. The initial idea was to see what differentiated the two groups of teachers in their handling of student disruptions. This approach was clear and sensible, but it failed to yield a single variable that differentiated consistently between the two groups in how they responded when faced with a classroom disruption.

Fortunately, the researchers did not give up in frustration. In observing the tapes, they developed hunches about variables that *would* differentiate. Systematic follow-up analyses that involved coding these variables paid off by revealing how the successful teachers did it. Their success lay in their ability to prevent problems from occurring in the first place rather than in their ability to deal with problems once they occurred. That is, good classroom managers are not successful so much because of how they *react* to student misbehavior but because they use techniques that *prevent* misbehavior by eliciting student cooperation and involvement in assigned work.

Later, Kounin and Gump (1974) studied 596 videotaped lessons and found that teachers of lessons that had higher student involvement provided continuous, explicit cues for appropriate behavior and insulated students from external intrusions. These more successful teachers were well organized, both for teaching during lessons and for assigning and monitoring seat work. They wasted little time in making transitions from one activity to another. Less successful managers frequently had long, awkward transitions that led to student restlessness. During lessons, the successful teachers maintained high involvement by arousing motivation and holding students accountable for remaining attentive (asking a lot of questions or otherwise getting student response, being unpredictable in questioning patterns). They knew where they were going and how they intended to get there. Less successful teachers continually confused students and interrupted pacing by stopping to get something that should have been prepared in advance, stopping to check something because they were not sure what to do next, repeating themselves for no good reason or because they were vague the first time, and vacillating or even contradicting themselves. The result was slow pacing, student confusion, and low involvement.

Similar differences were observed during seat-work periods. The more successful teachers had prepared assignments that were challenging as well as instructive, whereas assignments of the less successful teachers were boring or ill suited to students' interests and abilities. Again, the result was student boredom and restlessness, leading to disruptions and other misbehavior.

teacher "withitness"

A teacher characteristic shown by Kounin (1970) to be important in both lesson and seat work contexts is **withitness**, or *the degree to which the teacher is aware of and continually monitoring what is going on in all parts of the classroom* (and thus able to take action to stop a developing disruption before it becomes serious). Successful classroom managers had this quality. Less successful ones became so involved in what they were doing that they did not monitor other parts of the room. This made them slower to recognize and respond to disruptions and more likely to make mistakes such as **timing errors** (*waiting too long to respond, so that minor problems developed into major ones*); **target errors** (*not knowing the actual culprits, failing to notice all students who were involved, or blaming some who were not*); and **overreactions** (*shouting, becoming hysterical, or otherwise overreacting when the situation called for calm control*).

Each type of error led to increased problems. Timing errors allowed routine horseplay to develop into arguments and fights. Target errors minimized student accountability by allowing culprits to get away with something and harmed teacher-student relationships when teachers mistakenly blamed the wrong students. Finally, emotional overreactions produced student resentment and sometimes led to **ripple effects**—*the rise in levels of tension and distraction that often occurs when teachers respond in strongly negative or punitive ways to student misbehavior* (sometimes the frequency and intensity of disruptions increase as well).

Experimental studies of punishment do not predict ripple effects. In theory, seeing others being punished should reduce the likelihood of misbehavior by observers, who presumably experience the punishment vicariously (Bandura, 1977). Typically, however, experiments testing this thesis involve brief experiences with strangers. In the classroom, teacher behavior is predictable after the first few days or weeks. It is likely that explosions of anger by frustrated teachers have a cathartic effect, reducing the likelihood of similar explosions in the immediate future. When this is true, alert students are likely to take advantage of it.

Thus, ironically, teachers who respond severely to current problems may be setting themselves up for extra problems in the future. In combination with the many other negative results that may occur when teachers lose their tempers and become unnecessarily punitive, this factor again underscores the need for teachers to use positive approaches to classroom management.

overlapping activities

Another important key to successful classroom management, related both to smooth pacing and to "withitness," is what Kounin (1970) called **overlapping**—*the ability to do two or more things at once*, such as responding to students who come for help without having to break the pace of a small-group lesson. Overlapping appears to be the product of preparation, ability to anticipate needs, and ability to deal with more than one thing at a time. Overlapping helps keep students engaged in productive activities by minimizing the time they spend waiting for the teacher to respond to a demand or to tell them what to do.

smooth transitions

Another important variable noted by Kounin was **smoothness of transitions** (*minimum disruption of student activities; students' task involvement is maintained*) between and within activities. This involves training students to follow daily routines that promote efficiency in changing activities, supplemented if necessary by brief instructions concerning matters specific to that day or activity. Poor transitions occur when teachers allow themselves to be distracted repeatedly by the questions or actions of individuals, give out too many and too specific instructions, repeat themselves unnecessarily, interrupt everyone to ask if previous instructions have been carried out yet, or confuse students who are trying to carry out instructions by giving new ones that may or may not be meant for these students.

Transitions within activities are often lengthy and confusing because teachers are not prepared. This leads to false starts in which orders are given and then retracted or to interruption of movement into the new activity because something omitted from the previous one is now remembered.

group alerting

Yet another aspect of effective management noted by Kounin is **group alerting**—*teacher behavior designed to maintain or reestablish attention during lessons.* In the positive sense, group alerting involves doing things to keep the rest of the group attentive while one member is reciting. This includes looking around the group before calling on someone, keeping students in suspense about who will be called on next by selecting randomly, getting around to everyone frequently, interspersing choral responses with individual responses, asking for volunteers, throwing out challenges by declaring that the next question is difficult or tricky, calling on listeners to comment on or correct a response, and presenting novel or interesting material. Negative aspects of group alerting (things to avoid) include concentrating on the responder to the point that the rest of the group is not monitored, directing new questions only to the responder, picking the responder before a question is even stated, and calling on students in a predetermined order.

accountability

Kounin documented that teachers can hold students accountable for paying attention by requiring them to hold up props, show their answers, or otherwise indicate attention to the lesson; having them respond in unison (while monitoring carefully); asking listeners to comment on peers' responses; asking for volunteers; circulating and checking performance; and calling on individuals. Many of the techniques that Kounin listed under accountability are similar to those listed under group alerting.

other studies of group management

Subsequent research by others supports most of Kounin's recommendations. In a correlational study of second- and third-grade classes (Brophy & Evertson, 1976) and in an experimental study of first-grade reading groups (Anderson, Evertson, & Brophy, 1979), "withitness," overlapping, and smoothness of lesson pacing and transitions all were associated not only with better management but also with higher achievement. These studies, however, did not support some of the group-alerting and accountability techniques. In small-group reading lessons, the more successful teachers did not try to be unpredictable in calling on students to recite. Instead, they went around the group in order, seldom calling for volunteers and not allowing students to call out answers. Good and Grouws (1975) found that group alerting was positively related to student achievement in fourth-grade mathematics, but accountability was related curvilinearly: teachers who used a moderate amount were more successful than those who used too much or too little. In general, the major management objectives during lessons involve eliciting and maintaining attention, including at times when students are supposed to "just" watch and listen. This is done primarily by making sure that lesson content is interesting and challenging and that the teacher is prepared to conduct the lesson smoothly. This should be sufficient for most students. For others, group-alerting and accountability techniques may be required periodically.

In summary, the principles of effective management at the classroom level as identified by Kounin have been consistently supported by both naturalistic and experimental research (Emmer et al., 1993; Evertson et al., 1993). Techniques drawn from Kounin and other sources are integrated in the next sections, which present guidelines for group management in the two most typical classroom contexts: group lessons and seat-work periods.

Recent research suggests that school policies can support and extend classroom policies. For example, Gottfredson, Gottfredson, and Hybl (1993) conducted a three-year study of the effects of a program designed to improve adolescents' behavior in eight middle schools. The program focused on clarity of school rules, consistency of rule enforcement, improving classroom organization, and increasing communication with parents regarding student behavior. There was also increased reinforcement of appropriate behavior and an emphasis on school organization norms that supported communication, collaboration, and planning. Hence, just as we saw in the motivation section, researchers are becoming progressively more interested in school level issues that can enhance or erode classroom-level decision making. This same emphasis is also occurring in the management area.

Techniques drawn from Kounin and other sources are integrated in the next sections, which present guidelines for group management in the two most typical classroom contexts: group lessons and seat-work periods.

implications for teachers
strategies for effective classroom management

maintaining attention during lessons

Some inattention and minor misbehavior can be expected during most lessons. This routine misbehavior is dealt with most successfully through a combination of careful monitoring of students (Kounin's "withitness"), modeling expected behavior, reinforcing expected behavior, and extinguishing undesirable behavior.

One requirement for successful monitoring is being able to see each student and to make eye contact if necessary. A second is to form the habit of continuously scanning the group or class. Students who know that the teacher regularly keeps an eye on what is going on are less likely to misbehave than students who know they have a good chance of getting away with something.

It is not enough just to see that students give the appearance of paying attention and understanding, because most students can do this without actually following the lesson (Brophy & Evertson, 1976; McCaslin & Good, in press, b). Both to ensure accountability and to sample student comprehension as a guide to lesson pacing, it is important periodically to ask questions or require students to make some kind of response. Questions usually have the greatest managerial value when students have no way of knowing in advance when the teacher might ask them or whom the teacher might call on.

Student accountability can be maintained through such questions only if you avoid three potential hazards:

1. Care should be taken not to upset or put on the spot students who regularly show anxiety and fear of failure. It is usually better to stimulate the attention of these students in more direct ways, such as by calling for it or by giving advance warning ("John, listen carefully to Ralph, because I want to ask you about his comments").

2. Concentrate on involving everyone rather than on catching the inattentive. Some teachers often call on higher-achieving students who are expected to know the answers but seldom call on low achievers or students whom they do not like.

3. The technique of maintaining student

accountability through unpredictable questioning can be overused and become obvious to students. You can counteract this by occasionally explaining the rationale for calling on a variety of students (e.g., "I want to call on most of you today, so that I can find out if you know the key concepts, or if we have to work on them some more").

So far, we have focused on conditioning attention through relatively impersonal and indirect methods. When inattention is prolonged or disruptive, however, a direct call for attention may be required. The best way to demand student attention is to do so briefly and perfunctorily (Good & Brophy, 1994). If eye contact can be made with the student, a demand for attention can be accomplished nonverbally through looks, expressions, or gestures. If verbalization is required, it should be confined to a simple directive ("Pay attention, John") delivered quickly, concisely, and with the expectation that it will be followed. Pause just long enough to make sure that the student has heard and then go on with the lesson. This minimizes the interruption of the lesson and the likelihood that other students will become distracted.

Other effective ways of stopping minor misbehavior include humorous or other responses that tell the student to change behavior but do so in a benign and generally positive way. If a student has been teasing a fellow student, for example, making faces or noises or doing something that he or she knows is inappropriate, there is no need to pause and explain the nature of the misbehavior. You need only to indicate that it must stop, using some comment such as "That's enough, John," or "Very funny, John, but now I want you to pay attention" (in a pleasant tone).

maintaining engagement in seat work Each student should have a seat-work assignment that is appropriate in difficulty and as interesting as curriculum demands allow. Also,

you should set up mechanisms that enable students to know exactly what to do if they have difficulty with assignments and what to do when they finish them. Situations in which trouble starts because a student has given up on an assignment that is too difficult or has finished an easy assignment and has nothing to do simply should not exist. Preparation here includes not only the seat work itself but other activities for students who complete their assignments.

Jones (1987) noted that there were critical times in a lesson when misbehavior was most likely to occur. One critical period he found was when seat work was assigned. Most lessons appeared to go well until students were asked to work on their own. The teacher conducted a class discussion, talked about the importance of the work, gave examples, and then asked students to work alone on assigned tasks. Students appeared to be following the lesson, but when asked to work on their own, they began to get out of their seats, seek information, and complain about the assignment.

Techniques for maintaining student engagement in seat work, assuming that the seat work is interesting and appropriate, are similar to those for maintaining attention to lessons. The major difference is that, during lessons, students tend to be seated facing the teacher, so eye contact is established more easily and monitoring is much simpler. It is easier for students to appear to be working on seat work assignments when they are not. Nevertheless, the same general principles apply: monitor as continuously as possible; set up and explain rules; communicate positive expectations; condition through a combination of modeling, reinforcement, and extinction; and intervene only when necessary and with as little disruption as possible.

Unless you are busy elsewhere (e.g., teaching a small group), you should move around the room in unpredictable patterns during seat-work times, keeping a check on progress. When you

Students should be able to maintain a focus on learning and to master material, in this case manipulative creative material, without constant teacher monitoring.

stop to give help, position yourself so that you can see the rest of the class.

It is especially important to monitor the whole class during the early part of the school year while students are still learning the work system. Doyle (1984) found that successful managers establish an activity system early in the year and closely supervise it, ushering it along and protecting it from intrusion or disruption. For the first three weeks, for example, contacts with individual students during seat work were brief, and the teacher circulated around the room to maintain a whole-group perspective. In classes with many disruptive students, successful managers tended to push the curriculum and talk about work rather than misbehavior. Less successful managers tended to focus public attention on misbehavior by their frequent reprimands, so that eventually all work ceased. By

November, observations indicated that if a work system had been established effectively, successful teachers often spent less time orchestrating the total group and more time with individuals. By this point, the work system itself imposed order in the class, and the teacher was free to attend more to individual needs.

Problems can often be stopped simply by moving close to students who are goofing off, particularly when the students know exactly what they should be doing and realize that they are not doing it. Under these circumstances, there usually is no need for you to say anything (and good reason not to, since it will distract students who are working).

Finally, interventions with students during seat-work times should involve brief stops to give help rather than prolonged tutoring and should be confined to students who really need assistance. Teachers who are overly intrusive and verbal when making rounds during seat work often interrupt students needlessly and may even create anxiety or other undesirable reactions.

self-regulation Teachers should progressively encourage students to develop their capacity for self-regulation (McCaslin & Good, 1992). What constitutes student self-regulation varies in terms of students' age, background experiences, and teachers' instructional intentions and expectations (including how teachers define their role). It is important for students to be able to regulate both their instruction and classroom behavior to the maximum extent possible. Although younger students need much more structuring, support, and teacher guidance than do older students, the goal of classroom socialization should be to help all students to become as autonomous and as adaptive as possible (McCaslin & Good, 1992).

Students should be able to maintain both a focus on learning and the intention to understand and to master material without constant teacher monitoring or encouragement (Corno, 1993). In time, students need to learn to transform information and to make it their own rather than simply accepting someone else's words or definitions. In the areas of classroom management and personal behavior, students should be encouraged to develop numerous dispositions and skills over time. For example, they should learn how to set goals and to delay gratification, and should know how to seek resources appropriately in a classroom (when to get information and how to get it) from teachers, peers, library, and computers.

Students need to develop rudimentary self-control of learning situations by judging the amount of time it will take to complete an assignment, deciding whether it is useful to do something at home or to wait for a study period the next day, and set two guidelines that help them to organize their time ("I will do at least two of the assigned problems before class ends so that I can get help if I need it"). Students must also develop the capacity for self-assessment by knowing when they understand an assignment and the topic they are dealing with and when they are confused, and should be able to encourage self-reward as appropriate by recognizing when something is finished or relatively complete. Over time, students need to develop more sophisticated strategies for intervening in their environment. Rohrkemper and Corno (1988) argue persuasively that students should be able to change themselves, change the task, or change the environment when it is appropriate to do so. For example, students should recognize inappropriate self-affect that renders them to passivity (undue thoughts about how hard the task is, how long it will take, and what will happen if they do not complete the task). These researchers indicated that students should be able to change tasks to make them more interesting ("I'll see if I can do the first two in five minutes"; "I'll see if I can come up with a general rule that explains the relationships across these problem sets") or change the environment (move away from the noisy friend who is interfering with a task completion).

As students become more sophisticated, they should become adept at allocating their personal resources adaptively (realizing how much time to spend on biology homework assignment and how much time to spend studying for a Spanish quiz). Students must recognize that an adaptive aspect of self-regulation is changing goals as well as maintaining them. That is, sometimes students have to decide to cut their losses and recognize when they have reached the point of diminishing returns. For example, after reviewing material three times, a fourth review is unlikely to help. Instead, getting new information or a new perspective or simply moving to a different area might be more productive.

summary

Effective classroom management begins with preparation of the physical environment. Classrooms should be arranged so that the teacher can monitor all areas at all times, supplies are readily accessible, and there are no obstacles to the flow of traffic. Students should be taught to complete routine tasks with minimal supervision, and contingency plans should be prepared for times when scheduled activities cannot take place.

Students should be organized into cohesive groups with positive attitudes and constructive goals. Gaining the confidence of leaders is an important step, as is developing an authoritative leadership style.

Kounin and others have found that successful classroom managers prevent discipline problems by being well organized and prepared, maintaining student involvement, recognizing and stopping disruptions promptly, overlapping activities, and maintaining individual accountability. Such teachers establish their expectations, rules, and work routines early in the school year and combine well-chosen assignments with active monitoring and follow through on accountability systems to maintain high student involvement in learning tasks.

questions for reflection

1. We have stressed the need to get off to a good start but have said that "don't smile until Christmas" is not the way to do so. Do you agree? Why?

2. Much of good management is simply good instruction in what to do and how to do it. Considering the grade at which you intend to teach, what are the routines and procedures in which you should plan to provide students with instruction and practice?

3. Do you believe good managers have a few general rules rather than many specific ones? Why? Why not?

4. Why do teachers who frequently use Kounin's group-accountability techniques tend to have management problems, even though these techniques do return attention to the lesson?

5. Considering the grade at which you intend to teach, can you state clearly the types and difficulty of seat-work assignments that will be needed? If not, how can you find out?

6. How might principles discussed in this chapter be modified for teachers working in the following situations: (a) team teaching; (b) individualized, self-paced instruction; (c) multicultural environments?

cases to consider

encouraging student self-regulation Jan Clark teaches seventh-grade mathematics. In particular, she wants students to take more responsibility for managing the classroom. How should she convey these intentions? Specifically, what changes should she expect as the year progresses? What problems might Jan encounter and how can she deal with these?

parent interest Tina Corno is a first year teacher at Laundale Elementary School. She is excited about encouraging students' capacity for self-regulation and self-evaluation. However, at the first round of parent-teacher conferences some parents complain, suggesting that Tina needs to be firmer and to take charge of the classroom. How might Tina deal with this problem?

an inattentive group Ruth Miller is distracted by the inattentiveness of two boys in the back of the room. As she continues to present information to the whole class, she notices that a third student has joined the discussion and that another is watching the three. If you were Ruth, what would you do now? Does it make any difference if it is a second-grade or twelfth-grade class? If so, how?

start of the year Jed Shulman, a history teacher in an affluent suburban high school, is teaching for the first time. Given that his students have been in the school for several years, what should Jed say to the students about classroom management? Be specific; outline comments for the first class to role-play with friends.

chapter **18.**

principles and techniques of behavior modification

objectives

When you have mastered the material in this chapter, you will be able to

1. Define modeling and its effects on observers, list three characteristics of good models, and explain how modeling can be used to teach thinking and self-control; understand the type of self-control that you would expect from students at the grade level you expect to teach
2. Discuss the role of cues in controlling behavior
3. Distinguish with illustrative examples (a) direct versus vicarious reinforcement, and (b) positive versus negative reinforcement
4. Understand how a teacher can teach and then maintain increasingly complex academic and social behavior using reinforcement techniques
5. Discuss the drawbacks of teacher praise and other external reinforcement systems
6. Define satiation and extinction techniques to stop undesirable behavior and explain when their use is appropriate
7. State how the effects of negative reinforcement and punishment differ and how punishment can be used most effectively

Previous chapters describe the personal qualities of teachers that are basic to successful classroom management, and they review principles for establishing an effective learning environment and for managing everyday group activities. Although we stress the role of the teacher in managing student behavior, we recognize that school policies and support are also important.

The principles stressed in the two previous chapters are sufficient for handling most management concerns. Some students, however, require special, individualized treatment. This may involve behavior modification techniques, covered in this chapter, or various, more in-depth humanistic approaches to be covered in Chapter 19.

Although there are various ways of describing and classifying classroom misbehavior, Charles (1992) provides one method. His approach includes five types of misbehavior: (1) aggression (physical and verbal attacks); (2) immorality (academic dishonesty, stealing); (3) defiance of authority (students refuse to follow teacher directions); (4) classroom disruptions (e.g., calling out, tossing objects); and (5) goof-ing off (fooling around, daydreaming, etc.). We will discuss ways to respond to such misbehavior when it occurs; however, we place more emphasis upon how teachers' planning and decision making can reduce or prevent misbehavior.

Behavior modification techniques are especially useful in dealing with routine problems such as persistent inattention, daydreaming or fooling around instead of working, calling out answers or unwanted comments, trying to get attention by making faces or noises, showing off personal items, changing seats, or moving around the room without permission.

Techniques for establishing and maintaining desired behavior include modeling, cuing, and reinforcement. Methods for stopping undesirable behavior include satiation, extinction, negative reinforcement, and punishment. We first cover techniques for establishing and maintaining desired behavior.

In using behavior modification techniques, teachers should realize that behavior modification is first and foremost a theory of learning—not simply a control mechanism. Hence, when teachers use the techniques we discuss in this

Learning through modeling is most successful when teachers form personal relations with their students and become the kind of individuals that students want to be like.

chapter they must realize that besides providing external incentives for students to perform behavior that they are presently incapable or unwilling to perform, they are also assuming the ethical responsibility to help students in time to control such behaviors themselves. When using behavior modification techniques, teachers need to engage in continuous reflection and recognize that just because a student needed external support or manipulation last week, they may not need it in the future. The use of behavior modification techniques must have the goal of helping students to gain control of their behavior (and decision making about the appropriateness of the behavior) as soon as possible (Lepper & Greene, 1978; McCaslin & Good, 1992).

modeling

We acquire a great deal of learning vicariously as we observe the behavior of other people (models) and its consequences for them. **Modeling** is *a form of learning in which individuals imitate the behavior of others after observing them.* Because learning through modeling goes on whenever we observe others with whom we can identify, much learning is unplanned and unsystematic.

Teachers can accomplish much in the classroom by influencing student behavior through modeling, especially if they learn to model consciously and systematically. Bandura (1977) identified three broad classes of effects that models can have on the behavior of observers:

1. Observational learning/ modeling effects: Observers acquire new response patterns that did not previously exist in their behavioral repertoires— for example, in observing a demonstration of laboratory equipment.
2. Inhibitory/disinhibitory effects: Existing response patterns in observers are inhibited when models are punished for similar behavior or disinhibited when models are reinforced for similar behavior. Students' tendencies to call out cruel or obscene comments about one another, for example,

are affected by whether or not peers who do this are reinforced or punished by the teacher or their classmates.

3. Response-facilitation effects: The behavior of the model in a particular situation cues observers to follow suit, even though they probably would have behaved differently without such modeling. Students are likely to imitate teacher behavior in response to the principal's announcements (pay respectful attention rather than ignoring).

Modeling can be a powerful instructional tool and behavior management technique for teachers. Our definition of modeling includes nonverbal behavior, verbalizations made in carrying out the behavior, and instructions and explanations given before, during, or after the behavior. These verbalizations help define the meaning of the behavior and shape observers' responses to it.

characteristics of models who are imitated

Teachers who form personal relations with their students and become the kinds of individuals that the students look up to and want to be like are more apt to be imitated than teachers who remain at a distance or stress the contrasts between themselves and their students. Another factor is the degree to which the model's behavior is rewarded. Teachers who are respected and who accomplish their goals are more likely to be imitated than teachers who are not successful.

High-prestige models are more likely to be imitated than low-prestige models, particularly when the prestige is based on qualities that potential imitators would like to possess. This implies that teachers must retain students' respect and perhaps also a degree of professional distance, but still be friendly and attractive enough to make students want to be like them.

modeling and classroom management

Everyday modeling relevant to classroom management includes listening attentively when students recite or answer questions, handling equipment carefully and replacing it properly, and remaining conspicuously quiet during times for concentrated thinking. Further, students can benefit from modeling before they have new experiences (e.g., visit a museum) or engage in new types of learning such as project activities or working with other students in a small group (Good & Brophy, 1994).

Similarly, teacher modeling is important for developing rational control of behavior by acting on well-thought-out decisions, not impulses; developing respect for others by treating them as worthwhile, valued people; developing good group climate by not making hostile criticism or scapegoating, not playing favorites, and by exhibiting emotional control by being able to accept adversity or criticism without becoming upset or angry; and responding with rational attempts to diagnose and solve problems.

Teachers can often instruct students in various classroom routines most efficiently through modeling—showing how to use the pencil sharpener or how to operate audiovisual equipment, for example (Meichenbaum, 1977). They can also use modeling to teach thinking and problem solving, especially when combined with verbalized self-instructions and other techniques of cognitive behavior modification (Meichenbaum, 1977; National Council of Teachers of Mathematics, 1989).

building self-control

Cognitive behavior modification stresses the development of self-control rather than the imposition of external control. It emphasizes thinking and subjective experience more than overt behavior, and goal setting, planning, and self-instruction rather than reinforcement. If a teacher and a student discuss a plan of action, for example, and the student writes out the plan, student behavior, classroom conduct, and academic performance become more explicit and hence potentially more controllable by the student. Such a technique also allows teachers to individualize arrangements with students, and it places more emphasis on student self-control, self-management, and self-instruction and less on one-to-one relationships between specific behaviors and rewards. Contracts can be helpful in dealing with students who are poorly motivated, easily distracted, or resistant to schoolwork or the teacher.

Experience with some of the elements involved in contingency contracting, such as goal setting and self-monitoring of behavior, revealed that these elements could have positive effects of their own, independent of reinforcement. Inducing students to set goals for themselves, for example, can lead to performance increases, especially if those goals are specific and difficult rather than vague or too easy (Rosswork, 1977; Schunk, 1989). Apparently, setting goals not only provides students with specific objectives to pursue, but it also leads them to concentrate their efforts and monitor their performances more closely. The process does not always work, however. Sagotsky, Patterson, and Lepper (1978) found that exposure to goal-setting procedures had no significant effect on students' study behavior or academic achievement, largely because many of the students did not follow through by actually using the goal-setting procedures they had been shown.

The same study did show the effectiveness of self-monitoring procedures, however. Students taught to monitor and maintain daily records of their study behavior did show significant improvement in both the study behavior and tested achievement. This is only one of many studies illustrating the effectiveness of procedures designed to help students monitor

their classroom behavior more closely and control it more effectively (Mace, Belfiore, & Shea, 1989; McLaughlin, 1976; O'Leary & Dubey, 1979; Rosenbaum & Drabman, 1979).

These procedures designed to develop self-control in students have two potential advantages over earlier procedures that depended on external control by the teacher. First, teachers cannot continuously monitor all the students and reinforce them appropriately. When responsibility for monitoring, and perhaps reinforcing, performance is shifted from the teacher to the students, this difficulty is removed. Second, behavior modification methods that depend on the reinforcing activity of the teacher tend to generalize to other settings or persist beyond the term or school year. If students can learn to monitor and control their own behavior, they may also be able to apply these self-control skills to other classrooms or even to nonschool settings.

verbalized self-instructions

Self-control skills are typically taught using procedures that Meichenbaum (1977) called **cognitive behavior modification**—*an approach to changing behavior by modifying an individual's inner, self-directive, and self-regulating speech.* One technique combines modeling with verbalized self-instructions. Rather than just telling students what to do, the model (teacher) demonstrates the process. The demonstration includes not only the physical motions involved but verbalization of the thoughts and other self-talk (self-instruction, self-monitoring, self-reinforcement) that should accompany the physical motions.

Modeling combined with verbalized self-instructions (as well as various related role play approaches) can be helpful with a variety of student problems. Meichenbaum (1977) described five stages of this approach: (1) an adult models a task while speaking aloud (cognitive modeling); (2) the child performs the task under the model's instruction (overt, external guidance); (3) the child performs the task while verbalizing self-instructions aloud (overt self-guidance); (4) the child whispers self-instructions while doing the task (faded overt self-guidance); and (5) the child performs the task under self-guidance via private speech (covert self-instruction). Variations of this approach not only have been used to teach cognitively impulsive students to approach tasks more effectively but also have been used to help social isolates learn to initiate activities with their peers, to teach students to be more creative in problem solving, to help aggressive students learn to control their anger and respond more effectively to frustration, and to help frustrated and defeated students to cope with failure and respond to mistakes with problem-solving efforts rather than withdrawal or resignation.

Applications of this approach include the "turtle" technique of Robin, Schneider, and Dolnick (1976), in which teachers teach impulsive and aggressive students to assume the "turtle" position when upset. The students learn to place their heads on their desks, close their eyes, and clench their fists. This gives them an immediate response to use in anger-provoking situations and thus enables them to delay in appropriate behavior and to think about constructive solutions to the problem. The turtle position is not essential; the key is training children to delay impulsive responding while they gradually relax and think about constructive alternatives. It is a gimmick, however, that many younger students find enjoyable, and it may also serve as a crutch to children who might otherwise not be able to delay successfully. Similarly, the "Think Aloud" program of Camp and Bash (1981) is designed to teach children to use cognitive skills to guide their social behavior and to learn to cope with social problems. It is useful with students in the early

grades, especially those prone to paranoid interpretations of peer behavior or aggressive acting out as a response to frustration.

Approaches featuring modeling, verbalized self-instructions, and other aspects of self-monitoring and self-control training, however, appear to be very promising for use in classrooms, both as instructional techniques for all students and as remediation techniques for students with emotional or behavioral problems (Hughes, 1988).

cuing

When students have difficulty remembering to perform certain behaviors, teachers can help by cuing—providing a brief direction or reminder to cue the students' attention and behavior. To be effective, cues must occur before the action occurs (Krumboltz & Krumboltz, 1972), and they should be delivered only when needed; otherwise, they begin to resemble nagging.

Cues are especially useful for problem behavior that occurs repeatedly in specific situations, such as when students get into squabbles while sharing equipment during small-group work. If the teacher is able to analyze the situation and identify the timing and reasons for trouble, problems can be short-circuited through cuing: "Your group will be going to the learning center next period. Remember, no more than three to a learning center at one time, and everyone is to share the equipment."

Cuing through advance reminders and coaching is especially useful because providing cues during the activity itself might be embarrassing or might interrupt the flow of classroom activities. Students can be prepared through discussion of how to handle the upcoming situations and by including many examples of what to do and what to avoid. Such discussions might also include modeling with verbalized self-instructions as well as more typical explana-

When a student has difficulty remembering to perform cetain behaviors, teachers can help by providing brief reminders or directions to cue student's attention.

tions or perhaps even role-play exercises to give students an opportunity to practice the expected behaviors. Verbal cuing can be supplemented with supports, such as posting instruction sheets or rule reminders in learning centers or on equipment, using arrows to indicate direction of movement, or labeling shelves to show where equipment belongs. Students who have special problems managing their time independently or remembering what they are supposed to do can be helped by assigning peers to remind or supervise them or by preparing checklists for them to use themselves.

Cuing may be particularly useful when a problem involves discrimination—certain behavior is appropriate under some circumstances but not others. Here the student needs to learn to recognize the cues indicating whether or not the behavior is appropriate rather than how to perform the behavior itself. Explanations of the rationales for the differences are important, as are multiple examples: no shouting or shriek-

ing at any time, quiet conversational talk in designated areas is allowed among students who have completed assignments, talk during work time is confined to getting help from designated persons and within designated limits, talk is not allowed during lessons and discussions except when you have the floor, talk is not allowed during tests. Students must make similar discriminations about when and how to move around the room, approach the teacher with an individual problem, or call out comments and suggestions. Teachers working with younger students, and all teachers in the first few days or weeks of school, will have to do a lot of this kind of cuing. Cuing should be reduced, both in frequency and specificity, however, as students begin to behave appropriately on their own.

Many aspects of cognitive behavior modification combine cuing with several other features (McLaughlin, 1976). Examples include self-assessment (student evaluates own performance relative to goal), self-recording (student keeps records of own relevant behaviors), self-determination of reinforcement (student establishes own contingencies between own behaviors and type or amount of reinforcement), and self-administration of reinforcement (student reinforces self upon performing contracted behaviors).

Self-reinforcement may be helpful for students who are deficient in achievement motivation or who make inappropriate attributions about the reasons for their successes. The self-reinforcement process calls students' attention to their specific accomplishments and encourages them to verbalize statements of satisfaction and praise to themselves for having achieved goals. It may also help them to attribute their accomplishments to their own efforts rather than to external factors.

Self-monitoring and self-evaluation can often be aided with checklists, scoring keys, periodic progress reports, or other devices that help students to assess systematically what they have and have not accomplished with respect to schoolwork and behavior goals. These techniques place the responsibility for monitoring and managing student behavior on the students themselves but in ways likely to be informative and attractive to them.

Extensions of these techniques include training in academic survival skills such as attending, following directions, and volunteering to answer questions (Cobb & Hops, 1973), as well as training in prosocial personal skills such as initiating interactions, helping, and sharing (Cartledge & Milburn, 1978). A combination of modeling and instruction is used to teach the skill, and self-monitoring and reinforcement procedures can be added to insure that it will be maintained.

reinforcement

Behavioristic psychologists stress reinforcement as the primary mechanism for establishing and maintaining behavior. There are difficulties in defining reinforcers. Some people are not reinforced by things that most others find rewarding, and some things commonly seen as punishments are experienced as rewards by some individuals. This has led behaviorists to use a circular definition of a **reinforcer** as being *an event or stimulus that increases or maintains the frequency of behavior when it is made contingent on performances of that behavior.* That is, if a particular consequence increases or maintains the frequency of a behavior, it is a reinforcer; if it does not affect the behavior, it is not a reinforcer.

This basic idea has many applications in school settings, especially Premack's (1965) formulation of it. The **Premack Principle** is *a principle stating that access to preferred activities can serve as a reinforcer for the performance of low-frequency behaviors.* Students who are not completing assignments, for example, can be motivated to do so by informing them that they will not be allowed to do something they want to do until they turn in the assignments. The Premack Principle provides flexibility, allowing teachers to develop reward systems suited to each individual, and to get around the problem that no single "reward" will be motivating for everyone.

positive reinforcement or reward

Reinforcers are either positive or negative. Positive reinforcers correspond roughly to what we usually call rewards. They include material rewards (food, money, prizes, or tokens that can be exchanged for something desired), social rewards (praise, grades, honors, status symbols, attention from the teacher or peers), and activity rewards (opportunities to choose and engage in desired activities, use special equipment, or play games).

negative reinforcement

Negative reinforcement is *reinforcing behavior by the removal of a negative or adversive stimulus.* The termination of the unpleasant condition (e.g., embarrassing a student who calls out an answer in class without first being recognized) serves to reinforce the desired response (e.g., waiting until the teacher calls upon the student). Negative reinforcement should not be confused with punishment. Negative reinforcement is not punishment because reinforcement *increases* the probability of desired behavior while punishment decreases behavior (more on this later in the chapter). Students can be allowed to escape failing grades, for example, through makeup work that allows them to master material they should have mastered earlier. Although negative reinforcement technically involves reinforcing desirable behavior, it also involves withholding reinforcement from students who do not meet performance demands. Typically, these students are behaving in some undesirable way, not merely failing to produce desired behavior. Consequently, negative reinforcement is discussed in more detail in a later section of the chapter dealing with techniques for stopping undesirable behavior.

vicarious reinforcement

Reinforcement may motivate not only the student who receives it but also, through modeling effects, other students who observe it. In theory, a teacher can motivate a student to work carefully not only by praising his or her careful work but also by praising careful work performed by others, especially friends or peers with whom the student identifies. Teachers cannot assume vicarious motivating effects, however, because not all students find the same consequences reinforcing. Teacher praise of a peer will vicariously motivate students who also want such praise but not those who do not value teacher praise.

using reinforcement in the classroom

Teachers can strengthen desirable student behavior by reinforcing that behavior after it occurs. The behavior can be something minor such as raising one's hand and waiting to be recognized rather than calling out an answer during a lesson or something more substantial such as turning in completed and carefully done seat-work assignments for a week. The reinforcer can be anything that the student values and is willing to work for.

When conditioning the behavior of animals, it is important to reinforce immediately after performance of the behavior, so that the animal can make the connection between performance and reinforcement. This is not as essential for humans, because this connection can be explained verbally. Language can also be used to describe the particular characteristics of the desired behavior, thus eliminating guesswork as to what is being reinforced, and to link reinforcement to a series of behaviors performed over time, as in the example just mentioned concerning seat-work performance during an entire week.

In the early stages of trying to establish a new behavior, it may be important to reinforce often, even 100 percent of the time, and perhaps also to reinforce immediately after performance of the behavior. As the behavior becomes more established, it is possible to delay reinforcement as well as to reduce its ratio or increase the intervals between deliveries. This fading of reinforcement can continue until one reaches the minimal level needed for sustaining the behavior.

In addition to reducing the frequency of reinforcement as behavior becomes established, you may want to change the nature of the reinforcers, especially if they are expensive or require too much of your time or effort. This requires substituting social and symbolic rewards for tangible reinforcers like candy or prizes. Sometimes students will not value social or symbolic rewards, so you will have to take action to build the capacity of these rewards to function as reinforcers. Krumboltz and Krumboltz (1972) suggested accomplishing this by using the principle of substitution—if a person does not value a potential reward, begin presenting it immediately before presenting a reward that is valued. This should strengthen the association of the nonvalued reward with the valued reward, so that ultimately the nonvalued reward becomes valued in its own right. Students who do not turn in assignments regularly, for example, might be given a weekly report summarizing their successes and failures in this regard. Access to a valued reward such as the opportunity to go on a special outing could be made contingent on earning positive reports. Over time, the presentation of a positive report should in itself become reinforcing to such students.

To the extent that students do respond to social and symbolic rewards, they can also be weaned from dependence on teacher reinforcement by being taught to reinforce themselves. Students can be encouraged not only to note errors but also to grade themselves and perhaps reinforce themselves for success with stars, smiling faces, or positive comments. Students who have been making progress in meeting conduct goals can learn to reinforce themselves with the help of graphs or charts.

shaping behavior through successive approximations

For reinforcement to be effective, successful performance must be elicited often enough to be reinforced frequently. When bad habits are deeply ingrained, or when students have not yet established reliable cognitive control of their own behavior, it may take some time before the desired behavior occurs, even if the motivation to change exists. You can still use reinforcement to shape behavior, however, if you analyze the total tasks facing students and divide them into subgoals that can be organized sequentially in order of difficulty. Students can then attain success and be reinforced regularly as they approach the ultimate goals one step at a time Hyperactive students who tend to leave their seats and roam the room or bother other students when they are supposed to be doing seat work, for example, could be reinforced in the following way. First, you could concentrate on getting them to stay in their seats, perhaps beginning by reinforcing them for remaining in their seats for five minutes at a time. As success is achieved, you can increase the periods gradually until they cover the entire seat-work period. When students can remain in their seats, you can add prohibitions against making noises or bothering other students. Initially, reinforcement for not bothering others might be provided separately from that dealing with staying in the seat, although eventually the two sets of criteria could be combined. If problems include careless work in addition to leaving the seat and bothering others, you could begin to phase in expectations for careful work. Ultimately, reinforcement is based not only on staying in the seat and not bothering others but also on careful and sustained application to the seat-work assignment itself.

Simple behaviors like staying in the seat can be measured in time units for successive shaping: first five minutes, then ten minutes, and so on. Meeting each successive subgoal requires the student only to persist longer with the same kind of behavior. With more complex tasks, such as a series of subgoals that lead to successful completion of seat-work assignments, meeting successive subgoals often involves more complex behaviors or more complex combinations of behaviors formerly reinforced separately. This means periodic changes in the specifications of what behaviors qualify for reinforcement. You

Contract for week of April 3–7

I, John Richardson, agree to work carefully on my seat-work assignments and complete them to the best of my ability before leaving my seat to go to the game center. I further agree to redo work done incorrectly after it is returned to me and after I have received any additional instructions or help that I need. I understand that I am free to go to the game center during any seat-work period as soon as I have completed my work assignments as described above.

Signed *John Richardson*, Student

Agreed *Sidney Weaver*, Teacher

Figure 18.1 a sample contingency contract

must handle this carefully to ensure that students do not believe that you are not keeping promises. The key here is to help your students recognize and appreciate the progress they have made and thus to see that higher expectations are now appropriate. Many teachers find contingency contracting systems to be effective in communicating these perceptions.

contingency contracts

Contingency contracts—*work agreements specifying in writing that upon completion of certain tasks, or performing tasks at a certain level of proficiency, a specific reward is given*—combine rewarding and extinguishing methods and apply them in a formalized way. After you explain the method and outline alternatives, both you and the student jointly draw up a contract specifying in precise terms the behavior the student will be expected to show and the contingent rewards that will be earned once the contract is fulfilled. A contract can be purely oral, although it is customary to formalize it by having the student write down the specific details of the agreement (see Figure 18.1). In instructional areas, such contracts call for students to complete a certain amount of work at a certain level of proficiency to obtain a reward. Behavior management contracts describe specific criteria of improvement that must be met.

The main advantage of contingency contracts is that they ensure that students see the relationship between behavior and its consequences. Furthermore, when students are required to draw up the contracts themselves, they make personal commitments that are real and meaningful to them because they express them in their own words rather than merely agree to demands that the teacher makes.

Contracts can provide needed structure for students who are distractable. Initially, contracts can be confined to short periods and a limited number of tasks and can be displayed on or near students' desks so that students can refer to them for reminders or instruction. Contracts can also be useful for students who are poorly motivated or resistant to schoolwork or the teacher. With these students, you can include a period of negotiation before the finalizing of contracts in which students have the opportunity to make suggestions and state whether or not they think the demands are reasonable.

You can use contingency contracting to control behavior during lessons and group activities, although it probably is best suited to motivating students to work carefully on seat-work assignments. Most misbehavior occurring during lessons is relatively minor; making it the object of a contingency contract tends to call too much attention to it. Contingency contracting, however, is useful for minimizing or eliminating lesson disruptions if the disruptions are serious and if they can be clearly defined (e.g., leaving one's seat or calling out insults). A contract for seat work can state that a student must get a specific number of problems correct within a certain amount of time in order to fulfill his or her obligation.

As we noted in Chapter 16, a critical goal of any school management program must be to help students become more self-reliant. Thus, in time, teachers need to help students assume more responsibility than simply sitting still. Students need, in time, to develop important life skills like setting goals, obtaining needed information, and so on. For some students, contracts may be a necessary starting point for learning rudimentary skills (listen, stay seated), but, in time, contracts should shift more burden from the teacher to the student and focus on important life skills.

implications for teachers

goal setting

Helping students to set and meet personal goals enables them to obtain reinforcement from school activities. Rosswork (1977) found that setting goals, especially specific, difficult goals, was more effective than offering monetary incentives to produce high performance. Goal setting was also more effective than nonspecific encouragement. Extrinsic incentives may be necessary when a task is not meaningful to students, but goals and goal setting probably are more relevant to meaningful tasks (Rosswork, 1977; Schunk, 1989).

The high school students studied by Ware (1978) also stressed the importance of meeting personal goals. From a list of fifteen potential rewards, students were asked to rank rewards for desirability and effectiveness. They ranked the opportunity to reach a personal goal first, followed by school scholarships; compliments and encouragement from friends; being accepted as a person or having their opinions sought; trophies, certificates, medals, or ribbons; job-related physical rewards such as raises and vacations; special privileges or responsibilities; formal letters of recognition or appreciation; having their names printed in the newspaper or repeated on a loudspeaker; teacher or employer compliments and encouragement; money for specific accomplishments; parties, picnics, trips, or banquets; election to office; being chosen to be on special programs; and being the winner in a contest. Thus not only did students rank personal goal attainment first, but they valued rewards such as peer esteem and symbolic recognition more than teacher praise and several types of concrete rewards.

Teachers did not predict students' ranking of rewards. When asked to rank the same list, teachers placed reaching personal goals and winning school scholarships at the bottom while overrating getting names printed in the newspaper or repeated on a loudspeaker, obtaining special privileges or responsibilities, and winning a contest. Interestingly, teachers ranked praise from a teacher or employer even lower than students did, demonstrating awareness that their praise is not very reinforcing compared with other potential rewards.

social reinforcement

Theorists of virtually every persuasion stress the importance of teacher praise. Functional analyses of teacher praise in the classroom, however, typically indicate that it often is not reinforcing. Many students are not motivated by it, and praise is embarrassing for some students or makes them otherwise uncomfortable so that it actually functions as punishment. Even for teachers who have the potential to use praise as reinforcement, good intentions alone are not enough. Praise is unlikely to reinforce effectively unless it is (1) sincere (ideally, spontaneous); (2) adapted in form and intensity to the specific accomplishments in question (no gushing over trivia); (3) related to the preferences of the individual (some students cringe in response to public praise but appreciate sentiments expressed privately); and (4) specifically descriptive of what the student did that was praiseworthy (Brophy, 1981; O'Leary & O'Leary, 1977).

Much "praise" commonly given in the classroom does not satisfy these criteria (Brophy, 1981). Many teachers praise students who are behaving appropriately, for example, and simultaneously to try to ignore others who are behaving inappropriately, thus trying to take advantage of the vicarious reinforcement principle. This teacher behavior is rarely reinforcing in practice. First, the praise involved is seldom praise at all. It is not spontaneous, and the target behaviors are not really praiseworthy—typically they involve being quiet or standing in line. Even when sincerely intended by the teacher, such praise often causes embarrassment, even humiliation, to the students singled out for attention.

Another common class of misguided reinforcement attempts involves praise of inhibited students who hesitate to contribute to discussion. It is important to make the experience rewarding when these students do contribute (e.g., by smiling and showing interest in their contribution), but it is not wise to call attention to them with comments such as, "See, you can speak up when you want to!"

Failure to be specific is a common problem in the praise attempts of teachers. Anderson, Evertson, and Brophy (1979), for example, found that fewer than 10 percent of the praise statements made by twenty first-grade teachers specified what was being praised. This low rate held even though ten of the teachers were in an experimental group that had been advised to specify the praiseworthy aspects of student behavior whenever they praised.

The effects of praise and criticism interact with certain students attributes. Praise and encouragement, for example, are especially reinforcing for students who are introverted, inhibited, low in self-esteem, and accustomed to failure. Students who are self-confident and accustomed to success are not as responsive to such attempts at reinforcement.

These considerations serve as reminders that teachers need to perform functional analyses of their own behavior and their students' responses to make sure that assumed "rewards" actually function as such. Teachers need to be sure that "rewards" are developmentally appropriate. Praise or symbolic rewards such as stars and smiling faces may be effective, but if they are not, teachers need to use other reinforcers. In addition to including the commonly mentioned material rewards, reinforcers can be things such as the opportunity to be first in the lunch line, use of the library, performance of tasks that students enjoy, the chance to make choices that students consider to be important, and a great many other things not often thought of as reinforcers for good conduct or good academic work.

reinforcer satiation

Even rewards that function as reinforcers may not continue to do so indefinitely. Typically, satiation sets in if students are rewarded with the same thing again and again. Even if the reward was highly prized initially, it is likely to lose some of its attraction and power as a reinforcer as students become accustomed to it. Therefore, teachers must not only make sure that classroom rewards function as reinforcement but also change reinforcers periodically or, preferably, arrange for the students to select from a variety of reinforcements (Cangelosi, 1993).

For teachers who rely heavily on reinforcement techniques applied to the class as a whole (as opposed to using them sparingly on individual students), individualizing reinforcers and combating reinforcer satiation involve extensive record keeping and other time demands.

token reinforcement systems

One way to handle these problems is with **token reinforcement systems**, which *call for reinforcing students by providing them with tokens (given after successful performance) that can later be exchanged for some reinforcement desired by students (e.g., toys, free time).* Such systems include instruction to students about the behaviors to be reinforced, a means of making potentially reinforcing stimuli (tokens) contingent on student behavior, and rules governing the exchange of these tokens for other privileges (O'Leary & O'Leary, 1977). Students are awarded points (paid in the form of tokens, punches on a punch card, check marks, or some other symbol entered in a book) and then allowed to spend these points on reinforcers they select from the menu. Points are awarded for both behaviors and academic goals (individualized, at least to some degree), and the "prices" of reinforcement selections vary according to demand. Twenty minutes in the library or twenty minutes talking quietly with friends in the classroom, for instance, might cost thirty points, whereas participation in a special field

trip or other special even might cost 500 points.

Token reinforcement systems began in hospitals and other treatment institutions, but they have also been used successfully in schools (Safer & Allen, 1976). Most typical classroom teachers find these systems to be more trouble than they are worth, but they are popular with teachers conducting special remedial classes or working in programs that emphasize individualized learning packages.

reinforcement and intrinsic motivation

Humanists and others who see reinforcement approaches as mechanistic and manipulative oppose them. Instead of bribing students, these critics argue, teachers should develop students' intrinsic motivation through methods such as building novelty and interest into the curriculum, modeling enjoyment of learning and achievement motivation, and helping them to appreciate their own growth in knowledge and skills. Such thinking has acquired some empirical support. Deci (1975) and many others have shown that the introduction of extrinsic rewards for performance of a particular behavior reduces intrinsic motivation to perform that same behavior, so sustained performance in the future becomes dependent upon extrinsic reinforcement. As Deci noted, however, behavior modifiers call for the introduction of reinforcers only if the desired behavior does not presently exist, presumably for lack of sufficient motivation, intrinsic or otherwise. Also, behavior modifiers would "fade" reinforcement by gradually reducing its frequency and intensity and by switching from concrete or immediately consumable reinforcers to more symbolic ones. Delivery of reinforcement using the principles outlined in Chapter 16 will also reduce the danger of eroding intrinsic motivation.

Eden (1975) proposed a theory of motiva-

research at work
guidelines for effective punishment

When misbeavior persists despite repeated, positive attempts to stop it, mild forms of punishment may be necessary. Threat of punishment is usually even more effective than punishment itself, particularly when phrased in a way that reminds students that it will be their own fault if punishment results.

Punishment should be flexible and tailored to the specific situation. Fear of unknown consequences usually functions as a punishment, whereas expectation of known consequences frequently does not. Other guidelines are listed below:

• Punishment should be threatened before it is actually used. This should be done in a way that makes clear to students that the teacher hopes it will not have to be used and that the students will be fully responsible if it is used.

• When punishment is used, it should be a deliberate, systematic method for suppressing misbehavior, not an involuntary emotional response, a way to get revenge,

or a spontaneous response to provocation.

• The punishment should be as short and mild as possible but unpleasant enough to motivate students to change their behavior.

• The punishment should be combined with positive statements of expectations and rules, focusing more on what the students should be doing than on what they should not be doing. The teacher should make clear to students why the rule exists, why their misbehavior cannot be tolerated, and why they have no alternative other than punishment (recall earlier discussion of Baumrind's research on parenting).

• Ideally, punishment should be combined with negative reinforcement, so that students must do something positive to show good faith and escape punishment (e.g., stating that students will lose some privilege for a specific time probably is less effective than stating that they will lose the privilege until behavior improves sufficiently to warrant removal of the punishment).

---

tion that helps explain why extrinsic reinforcement may be appropriate despite the findings of Deci (1975) and others. He noted that the motivational effects of behavioral consequences depend on the relevance of those consequences to the motive operating at the time. In theory, reinforcers congruent with operating motivational systems will have a strong positive effect

on net motivation, but other reinforcers will have a slightly negative effect. Thus teacher praise for careful work will motivate students who want that social reinforcement but will have a slightly negative effect on the motivation of students who find the task intrinsically motivating or who are working toward some material reward, such as a prize.

implications for teachers
techniques for dealing with misbehavior in the classroom

satiation This strategy eliminates certain minor misbehaviors by systematically ignoring them—it lets them run their course by allowing, or requiring, if necessary, students to repeat the behaviors until fatigue and boredom set in. According to Krumboltz and Krumboltz (1972), satiation is effective when the behavior does not lead to powerful rewards (if it does, extinction will be necessary), the behavior is counterproductive and the student can see this, and the behavior is not harmful. Such behaviors include throwing spitballs, making faces or noises, or almost any type of classroom clowning that is silly rather than really funny. Inviting students to continue to do such things allows them to get it out of their systems and takes away the novelty and desire, at least for the present.

Satiation is probably most effective if used sparingly and with minimum fanfare. If used too often, it can become an enjoyable ritual in itself, particularly if you make it an enjoyable experience. It can also become a bone of contention between you and students who feel picked on or if you appear to humiliate them.

extinction Undesirable behavior that leads to reinforcement will not decrease through satiation unless the student becomes satiated with the reinforcement it produces. You must handle such behavior with other techniques. The major means for reducing it (not merely controlling it) is extinction through nonreinforcement. To extinguish effectively, you change the conditions of reinforcement that maintain the behavior, so that performance of the behavior no longer leads to the expected reinforcement.

The most common nonreinforcement technique in the classroom is simply ignoring and getting peers to ignore behavior that is motivated by a desire for attention. Some students find attention, even negative attention involving disapproval, to be reinforcing and will repeat any behavior that brings them the attention they desire.

Extinction is not always feasible in the classroom. Certain misbehaviors are too disruptive or dangerous to be ignored, and some students assume that anything not explicitly disapproved is acceptable. Open defiance, obscenities, hostility directed specifically at the teacher, or similarly provocative behaviors demand response. Attempts to ignore such behaviors will confuse students or leave them with the impression that the teacher is not aware of what is going on, is unable to cope with it, or doesn't care.

Even when feasible, ignoring is never effective by itself; it must be coupled with reinforcement of desired behavior (O'Leary & O'Leary, 1977). Used in combination, teacher reinforcement and extinction can be effective but only for students whose behaviors are under the control of reinforcement from the teacher in the first place. Ignoring misbehaving students will have no effect on behaviors that peers reinforce.

Tanner (1978) suggested four criteria for determining when ignoring is appropriate: when the problem is momentary, when it is not serious or dangerous, when drawing attention to it would disrupt the class, and when the student involved is usually well behaved. These criteria, along with the findings of Kounin (1970), leave little room for the systematic use of ignoring in an attempt to extinguish misbehavior that is disruptive and persistent. Kounin's work suggests that some comment or signal to the inattentive student is necessary whenever the problem seems likely to escalate.

table 18.1 **reinforcing and punishing effects of consequences of behavior**

	DESIRABLE CONSEQUENCES	UNDESIRABLE CONSEQUENCES
Application of consequences following behavior	Positive reinforcement: behavior leads to reward. Increases rate of behavior.	Punishment: behavior leads to aversive consequences. Decreases rate of behavior.
Removal of consequences following behavior	Punishment: behavior leads to loss of reward. Decreases rate of behavior.	Negative reinforcement: behavior leads to escape from aversive consequences. Increases rate of behavior.

Ignoring can also have negative consequences. Students who do not realize that they are being ignored deliberately, or who do not know why they are being ignored, may increase their efforts to get attention by becoming more and more disruptive. Brief explanations to such students probably are much more effective than waiting for them to become conditioned through repeated frustration.

negative reinforcement Like modeling, cuing, and positive reinforcement, negative reinforcement is a technique for increasing desired behavior. It is discussed here among techniques for stopping misbehavior, however, because you should only use it when students have been misbehaving persistently despite more positive attempts to get them to change.

Negative reinforcement occurs when improved behavior brings about the termination of an aversive experience. For ethical reasons, you are not advised to place students in aversive situations deliberately so that you can use negative reinforcement by releasing students when their behavior improves. The natural consequences of many forms of misbehavior are aversive, however, and you can often arrange to let students escape some of these consequences by improving their behavior.

Makeup exams and extra-credit assignments, for example, allow students to avoid low grades by improving their mastery of material. Unruly classes can be kept after school until they become more cooperative. Students who have not been controlling themselves can be required to take time out from classroom activities until they regain control.

Notice that negative reinforcement is not punishment—students do not suffer aversive consequences or lose rewards as a result of misbehavior (see Table 18.1). Instead, reinforcement is withheld pending performance of desired behavior. The aversive condition persists solely because the students have not behaved appropriately, and they can terminate it at any time by changing their behavior. Negative reinforcement is most effective when the teacher warns students in advance, to underscore that the students themselves are responsible for reinforcement is not forthcoming. Ideally, such warnings stress the call for improved behavior rather than the withholding of reinforcement—for example, "Class, I know you don't like to get out late, but you're going to stay until you settle down and pay attention to this announcement."

punishment Punishment suppresses undesirable behavior by making aversive consequences contingent on such behavior. The use of punishment should be minimized because it is a stopgap measure at best. To the extent that it is effective at all, punishment only suppresses the overt performance of undesirable behaviors. It does not change students' underlying desires to misbehave or the reasons why those desires exist, does not provide guidance to students by indicating what they should do instead, and causes problems of its own by engendering resentment.

In general, effective punishment is mild rather than severe, informative rather than merely punitive, and tailored to the specific misbehavior in ways likely to help the student see why the misbehavior is inappropriate.

Redl (1966) suggested that teachers wait for the optimal moment rather than try to punish immediately, especially when students are emotionally upset. Punishing students while they are aroused and angry may only increase their alienation, while waiting until they are calm enough to listen but still concerned about the problem might be much more effective.

ineffective forms of punishment Certain forms of punishment almost never work. Suspension from school is probably the most obvious. It does remove disruptive students from class, but many of them welcome the time off from school. Also, the students lose class time and fall behind in work, and most will be resentful rather than contrite. Thus except in extreme cases such as those discussed in Chapter 19, school suspension is a mistake.

The same is true of punishing students by forcing them to do extra assignments. By assigning schoolwork as punishment, you imply that the work is just busywork.

Physical punishment is also generally ineffective. Many teachers and school administrators realize this but favor maintaining physical punishment as an option (where it is legal), intending to rely on its value as a threat without actually using it frequently. Others, including many parents, object to physical punishment on philosophical grounds. There is a simpler objection, however: Physical punishment does not work

except in unusual situations. The best examples of its failures are antisocial delinquents and criminals, who almost always come from homes in which adults relied on physical punishment to socialize children. It keeps them under control to a degree while they are still young and afraid, but it builds anger and resentment that emerge as children get older (Feshbach, 1970).

Physical punishment is a direct attack on the student, and as such it almost invariably creates anger and resentment. Furthermore, these emotions usually will be much stronger than any feelings of fear or contrition, so the punishment does not reduce the tendency for the student to misbehave. It will not help to make the physical punishment as mild as possible, either. Slaps on the wrist and light paddling do not inspire much fear, especially in students accustomed to harsher treatment. Such students may even enjoy mild physical punishment because it gets them attention from peers.

Today, most educators see physical punishment as unethical and ineffective. Even in places where it is still legal, many ethicists contend that it is immoral.

Another technique that we do not recommend is group punishment in which contingencies are arranged so that an entire class or group is punished because of the misbehavior of an individual. Some recommend this technique for extreme cases, because the peer pressure generated can be very powerful. Like physical punishment, however, it is difficult to use effectively, and the undesirable side effects are likely to outweigh any advantages. For one thing, this technique forces students to choose between the teacher and one of their classmates. Many students will choose the classmate, uniting in sullen defiance of the teacher and refusing to blame the classmate if group punishment is applied. Even if students do go along with the teacher and pressure the classmate, the technique engenders unhealthy attitudes in the target student and perhaps in the other students as well.

effective forms of punishment Some of the most effective punishments are very mild, at least from a teacher's perspective. Merely keeping students after class for a few minutes to discuss problems, for example, can have a punishing effect, especially if it prevents them from doing something they want to do immediately. A delay of even a few minutes may cause a student to have to go to the end of the lunch line or to go home alone instead of with friends. These may be more effective punishments for most students than being sent to an isolation area, sent to the principal, or physically punished.

You do not have to present punishment explicitly as such, nor does it have to be something that we usually think of as shameful or painful. If property destruction is involved, for example, the punishment should require that the students fix or replace what they have broken. If this is not possible, punishment might involve some other kind of service such as cleaning up the school grounds or performing some similar chore that requires them to make restitution. In general, destructiveness is often handled best with overcorrection methods—the student must not only change behavior but must make restitution by fixing or replacing damaged items.

Students who are upset, angry, or out of control as a result of particular situation, and hyperactive or aggressive students who are having bad days, may respond well to time out from regular classroom activities. Teachers can ask them to move to an isolated part of the room, a desk in the hall, or perhaps the principal's office, until they can collect themselves and behave appropriately. Time out usually works best if presented not as a punishment but as an opportunity for students to solve their own problems.

Abuse of privileges usually is eliminated best with response cost—making it clear that costs will be attached to certain unacceptable behaviors and that students who do not heed fair warnings will have to pay those costs. Ideally, costs are logically related to the offenses; students who abuse

library privileges will have them suspended, students who are persistently destructive with certain equipment will not get to use the equipment for a time, or students who start fights at recess will have to stay in or play alone.

Students who refuse to work on assignments usually are best handled by in-school or after-school detention during which they are required to work on assignments. This shows them that attempts to escape assignments by refusing to work or creating diversions will only result in their having to spend extra time in school.

You can best manage provocations and attention-getting behaviors by gentle and humorous put-downs. If these behaviors persist, punishment should be designed to frustrate students' intended goals completely. Students who persist in shouting out obscenities, for example, can be required to copy them repeatedly during free time until they are satiated.

Truly effective punishment does not leave students with revengeful attitudes. Instead, it provides them with feelings of guilt, shame, frustration, or embarrassment. They realize that they have gotten into trouble because of their own failures to respond to earlier, more positive attempts to curb their misbehavior.

using techniques systematically Behavior modification techniques must be used correctly and consistently with one another. Dasho (1978), for example, reported that a teacher tried the following techniques over a short period for dealing with a disobedient boy: firmly reminding the boy about the rules, moving his desk to isolate him from the class, depriving him of recess, positive reinforcement, and finally ignoring him. More generally, Dasho reported that teachers commonly vacillated among calm appeal to rationality, threatening punishment, and ignoring. Such unsystematic combining of techniques is unlikely to succeed for any length of time. This type of inconsistent teacher responding is similar to the inconsistent teaching approach that teachers often assume when teaching students believed to be less capable (Good & Brophy, 1994). Inconsistency in teachers' approaches makes it more difficult for students to learn.

Even teachers who try to implement principles of behavior modification more systematically often have trouble at first. Harris and Kapche (1978), for example, listed twenty-six errors that such teachers commonly commit. Therefore, if you intend to use these techniques systematically, carefully study sources such as Krumboltz and Krumboltz (1972) and O'Leary and O'Leary (1977) to master concepts, and try to arrange for help in the form of observation and feedback as you work on techniques in class.

assertive discipline

Assertive discipline is an approach developed by Canter (1976, 1981). The literature from this program describes the program as an in-service training workshop that allows educators to develop a "take-charge approach." **Assertive discipline** *underlines the rights of teachers to define and enforce standards for student behavior so that teachers can offer instruction that is consistent with students' capabilities and needs.* Teachers who can achieve this are described as assertive and are contrasted both with submissive teachers who fail to enforce standards and hostile teachers who do so but in ways that violate students' best interests. Teachers using assertive discipline achieve the following criteria:

- Developing clear expectations for student behavior
- Translating these into a set of rules that specify acceptable and unacceptable behavior
- Linking these to a system of rewards and punishments
- Consistently delivering promised rewards for compliance or imposing threatened punishments for noncompliance

The most widely used punishment is a penalty system in which the names of misbehaving students are written on the board and check marks are added following their names for repeated offenses. Students whose names are written on the board are subject to detention, and those whose names are followed by one or more check marks are also subject to progressively more serious punishments.

There has been much controversy over assertive discipline. Canter (1988) claims that the approach is supported by research, and both he and his supporters (e.g., McCormack, 1989) cite testimonials and survey data to suggest that the method is popular among practitioners because they are convinced that it works. However, independent reviewers have concluded that Canter and his associates have failed to conduct systematic research on the effectiveness of the approach they have been promoting for many years, and that the limited research base available on the approach simply does not support Canter's claims for its effectiveness (Emmer & Aussiker, 1987; Render, Padilla, & Krank, 1989).

Several authors have also voiced philosophical objections to the assertive discipline model. Curwin and Mendler (1988b) characterized it as an example of an obedience model, in which power-based methods are used to compel students to conform to rules. They consider such obedience models less desirable than responsibility models, in which the goal is to develop responsibility for self-guidance in students, using methods that emphasize explanations and natural consequences of behavior rather than threats and punishment. Oddly, under assertive discipline, a relatively minor student transgression can sometimes lead to a major punishment. This happens when the minor misbehavior occurs at the end of a series of other, more serious misbehaviors. Hence, because the minor misbehavior is the third or fourth offense, it leads to major complications. Such lack of congruence between severity of a misbehavior and the punishment that follows it may be difficult for many students to understand, especially young students. McDaniel (1989, p. 82) criticizes assertive discipline as being "not much more than applied behavior modification and take-charge teacher firmness with rules and consequences."

We see some value in several aspects of the assertive discipline approach—for example, its emphasis on developing and communicating clear expectations for student behavior and on the fact that teachers have a right to establish a productive and safe environment for everyone. However, we share the concerns voiced by the research reviewers and philosophical critics just cited. We believe that the approach places too much emphasis on threat and punishment, so that it is a much less desirable alternative than the eclectic approaches we outlined in this chapter and in Chapters 16 and 17—advice that is based on replicated findings obtained by several research teams working independently in different parts of the country. Further, we believe that behavior (including misbehavior) needs to be explored and understood in the context in which it occurs. That is, the reasons that students misbehave are as important as the misbehavior itself.

summary

Minor but annoying student misbehavior requires teacher command of the principles of behavior modification to shape more constructive behavior. Techniques for establishing and maintaining desired behavior include modeling, cuing, and reinforcement; methods for stopping undesirable behavior include satiation, extinction, and punishment.

Modeling is a powerful influence on behavior if teachers use it systematically. Students tend to imitate most of the behaviors of high-prestige models, especially when they can identify with the models and see that the models' desirable behaviors are rewarded. Modeling can foster a wide range of desired behaviors, especially when coupled with verbalized self-instruction to achieve self-control.

Cues for appropriate behavior can be of help when dealing with repeated problem behavior. Advance reminders, coaching, and similar supports are especially useful when students have trouble discriminating between appropriate and inappropriate times for talking, moving about, and the like. This technique can be combined with self-assessment, self-recording, and self-reinforcement.

Reinforcement is the primary behavioristic mechanism for establishing and maintaining behavior. When used in the form of the Premack Principle with appropriate schedules of reinforcement, it is applicable to classroom situations. Contingency contracting clarifies relationships between behavior and consequences, provides structure, and motivates students. Also, social reinforcement and various token reinforcement systems can support behavior.

Teachers can reduce undesirable behaviors through satiation, extinction, negative reinforcement, and punishment. All of these techniques require careful management to avoid undesirable side effects. It is especially important when using punishment to remain alert to the possibility of undesired and unintended consequences. However, the use of behavior modification requires that, ethically, teachers need to help students develop capacity for control of their behavior and decision making as soon as possible.

There are some popular in-service programs available that provide general solutions to management problems. However, we believe that although these programs have some useful advice, teachers always have to be decision makers and adjust management strategies to the context in which they teach.

questions for reflection

1. Does using reinforcement in the classroom amount to just bribing students to learn? Explain why or why not, and discuss your answer with friends.

2. Have you ever used modeling combined with verbalized self-instruction as a teaching device? What are its advantages and what are its disadvantages compared to ordinary lecture/demonstration?

3. How a message is phrased is often at least as important as the content of the message itself. What principles apply to the following situa-

tions: praise that is reinforcing to students and not condescending or patronizing and cuing that involves helpful pointers or reminders and not nagging?

4. If you use contracts, tokens, or other formalized reinforcement systems in your class, you will probably want to do so only with a few students who seem to need such extra structuring incentives. How will you explain the situation so that you do not create either self-concept problems in the few students singled out for special treatment or jealousy in the rest of the class?

cases to consider

Mr. Knight loses his cool Jim Dell, a sixth-grade student, heads for the pencil sharpener. Mr. Knight says, almost yelling, "Jim, go back to your seat! That's the fifth time I've had to tell you to get in your seat! Stay there!" Moments later Jim wanders out of his seat, sits on Wanda's desk, and begins a conversation with her. "Jim," Mr. Knight yells, "what's wrong with you? Can't you do anything right?" Jim's face muscles tighten as he stares at the floor sullenly. How would you have responded to Jim's desk-sitting behavior? What should Mr. Knight do now? In general, how would you deal with Jim's out-of-seat behavior?

in search of self-monitoring skills Jan Barnes is a tenth-grade English teacher. She bemoans the fact that when she assigns a brief research/essay paper of four to five pages, containing twenty references, students ask endless questions. How can she develop a management system for helping students to assume more responsibility for finding their own references and making independent decisions about what to include in the paper?

chapter **19.**

humanistic approaches to educating at-risk students

objectives

When you have mastered the material in this chapter, you will be able to

1. Discuss four common background experiences of students who show severe or chronic behavior problems in school
2. Explain how Rudolf Dreikurs theoretically analyzes student misbehavior and what practical advice he gives for the handling of student problems
3. Understand and be able to apply the techniques of life-space interview that deal with misbehavior problems
4. Understand Glasser's ten-step approach to dealing with problem students and the rationale that

underlies it, and be able to critique it from your perspective
5. Explain the philosophy behind Gordon's Teacher Effectiveness Training (TET), his concept of problem ownership, and the TET techniques that facilitate teacher-student communication (e.g., active listening and "I" messages)
6. Discuss Gordon's six-step "no-lose" method for solving student-teacher conflict
7. Discuss Selman and Schultz's ideas about pair therapy
8. Explain the two key elements of the authors' integrated eclectic approach to problem solving and identify the elements in a real-life illustration of problem solving

The classroom management principles discussed in the previous three chapters will enable teachers to establish and maintain an effective learning environment, manage the class as a group, and deal with routine school adjustment problems that students present. Certain students, however, will show chronic, severe problems that make it difficult for the teacher to reach them or that require frequent reliance on negative reinforcement or punishment to exert control. In this chapter, we shall discuss some characteristics of these students and some of the techniques for dealing with them that humanistic approaches to psychology and psychotherapy suggest.

paths to distorted development

The life history of each individual whose development is deflected is unique, but several themes are common. **At-risk students** are *those more likely to experience problems in the school or community*. Many come from homes in which one or both parents or guardians are seriously disturbed. In addition, students reared in homes featuring parental strife, modeling of low frustration tolerance, verbal and physical violence, and socialization based on threats and punishment are likely to mistrust adults, particularly authority figures. They are likely to have well-developed antisocial tendencies and poor self-control.

Many citizens and some teachers appear to assume that virtually all forms of emotional impairments are caused by poor parenting. However, some problems are more related to school than home issues. These include cycles of failure, feelings of inadequacy, and attempts to compensate for failure or cover up by acting out. Typically, problems start when students are in the early grades and suffer blame and rejection (usually real, but sometimes only perceived) because of school failure. Such students often develop rigid self-concepts of hopeless inadequacy in relation to school tasks. This sets in motion a series of self-fulfilling prophecy effects, since students who expect failure and

By acting hopelessly inept and alienated, students who expect failure and rejection are likely to experience failure and rejection.

rejection are likely to experience failure and rejection. By acting inept and alienated, they condition teachers to perceive and treat them as such (Covington, 1992; Dreikurs, 1968). Teachers often give up on students who are unresponsive, impulsive, wrapped up in fantasy, or virtually certain to say or do something silly if they do respond (Brophy & Evertson, 1981).

Teachers often overlook students who are alienated from learning and who are also passive. These pupils may continue to become more withdrawn and depressed if teachers do not intervene. This means changing both students' behavior and self-perceptions by helping them to learn and to realize that they are capable of learning (Covington, 1992).

Students who do not receive enough of the right kind of attention and respect from parents, teachers, or peers may strive to obtain it through clowning or disruptive behavior. Others come to be regarded as disruptive at school because of indulgence in marijuana or other drugs, drinking, obscene language, carrying weapons, or abusing peers (extortion, etc.).

Many problems can be handled successfully without a full understanding of how they develop. In most cases it is more important to understand and deal with people as they are now rather than to delve into their histories. This point is worth stressing for at least two reasons. First, there is a tendency to cite poor home backgrounds both to explain disordered behavior and to justify failure to do anything about this behavior. It is true that the more disturbed individuals are, and the longer they have been disturbed, the more difficult it will be to change them. However, this is very different from saying that nothing can or should be done. Second, partly as a holdover from early psychoanalysis, teachers frequently believe that classroom misbehavior that is part of a general pattern of disorder must be handled through psychotherapy. At one level, this is true. Even when they want to, teachers probably should not attempt to solve a student's overall adjustment problems if they are serious. It is also true, however, that teachers must take action to change misbehavior in their classrooms if they expect to stop it.

counseling techniques

Personality theory and techniques of counseling and psychotherapy are natural sources for classroom teachers to draw on in developing methods for dealing with problem students, but early attempts were not very successful. Most techniques of psychoanalysis and other early forms of intensive individual psychotherapy were not suitable for use with children, and teachers, who were busy dealing with entire classes, did not have adequate time to use them.

As counseling and psychotherapy became more diversified, new techniques that were more humanistic and behavioral were developed. These techniques are more limited but also more specific in intent and more immediate in their effects. Classroom teachers can use many of these methods effectively.

Dreikurs: interpreting the goals of problem behavior

Although the writings of Rudolf Dreikurs (1968) are psychoanalytic (Adlerian), they are intended for teachers and applicable in the classroom. Dreikurs stressed the importance of early family dynamics, tracing problems to sources such as parental overambition or overprotectiveness and sibling relationships that make certain children feel discouraged or inadequate. Dreikurs saw children as reacting to these central themes in their lives, compensating for feelings of inferiority by developing a style of life designed to protect self-esteem and avoid danger areas. He believed that children who have not worked out a satisfactory personal adjustment and place in the peer group will seek one of the following four goals (listed in increasing order of disturbance): (1) attention, (2) power, (3) revenge, or (4) display of inferiority (to get special service or attention).

The first step for teachers is to analyze problem behavior and determine what goals students are pursuing. Attention seekers are disruptive and provocative, but will not openly defy or challenge as will power seekers, who in turn will not seek to hurt or torment, as will revenge seekers. Persistent dependency and help seeking will differ in quality and purpose, depending on whether students merely want attention or have stopped coping and have opted to display inferiority and helplessness.

Dreikurs advised teachers to observe problem students, diagnose the meaning of their behavior, and then explain this diagnosis to the students in private. The teacher should help the students understand the goals of their own behavior rather than speculating about presumed causes. If the teacher is not sure about these goals, it can be helpful to speculate about them to see whether or not this strikes a responsive note in students ("I wonder if you do that just to get attention").

Dreikurs opposed artificial punishment but stressed the value of allowing the natural consequences of maladaptive behavior to occur. He stressed the linkage between maladaptive behavior and unwanted consequences as part of the attempt to develop insight and be willing to abandon self-defeating goals and make productive commitments.

research at work
guidelines for a life-space interview

Within the model of a lifespace interview, teachers should provide the following additional help that particular students need:

- Help students accept reality and abandon defensive distortions.
- Show students that inappropriate behavior is self-defeating.
- Clarify values.
- When necessary, suggest means to help students deal with problems effectively.

- Help students think for themselves and avoid being led into trouble by others.
- Help students release anger by expressing sympathy and understanding.
- Help students deal with emotions like panic, rage, or guilt following emotional explosions.
- Maintain open communication.
- Provide friendly reminders.
- Help clarify thinking and facilitate decision making.

life-space interviews

Morse (1971) described the goal of a life-space interview as fostering adjustment and obtaining a degree of behavioral compliance by providing life-space relief (improving the life conditions of the student, especially in the classroom). Incidents of defiance or serious misbehavior often provide the impetus. In this type of interview, the teachers talks to students privately, trying to obtain their perceptions of the incident and the events that led up to it. This provides an opportunity for students to experience catharsis and ventilation and for teachers to express a desire to help.

As the interview proceeds, the teacher seeks to obtain an accurate and detailed description of what happened and an indication of the meaning of the event to the student. Students may be upset by different events—one student may be concerned about being picked on by peers, and another may be upset about being blamed by the teacher. The teacher tries to communicate acceptance of the feelings the student conveys without necessarily accepting the student's actions.

Once this behavior is accomplished, discussion can move toward deciding what must be done. This involves analysis to identify places where relief can be provided or changes made. The teacher offers to work together with the student to find ways to prevent repetition of the problem. How can the problems that led up to the incident be eliminated or reduced? What will happen if there is a repetition of the incident? The teacher avoids moralizing and empty threats, confining discussion of consequences to those that the teacher seriously intends to use in the future if there should be a repetition of the behavior.

Glasser: reality therapy

In suggesting applications of what he calls "reality therapy" to the classroom, William Glasser provided guidelines for general classroom management and for problem solving with individual students. He has a wide following among teachers, and survey data indicate that systematic implementation of his program is associat-

research at work
Glasser's ten-step method

1. Select students for concentrated attention and elicit typical teacher responses to the students' disruptive behavior.

2. Analyze the list of problem-solving techniques to see which ones do and do not work, resolving not to repeat those that fail.

3. Improve personal relations with the students. Extra encouragement is provided by asking the students to perform special errands or by taking other initiatives to show concern and imply that things are going to improve.

This method continues indefinitely. If the problem behavior reappears, a new approach is added at the fourth step:

4. Instead of repeating past mistakes, ask students to describe what they are doing. This causes students to analyze their behavior, perhaps for the first time, and to begin to see their own responsibility for it, although they may try to rationalize. In any case, once students describe their own behavior accurately, the teacher simply asks them to stop it.

5. If the problem persists, call a short conference and again ask students to describe the behavior and to state whether or not it is against the rules or recognized informal expectations. Also ask the students what they should be doing instead of what they have been doing. All this is done in a warm and supportive way but with insistence that students both express the inappropriateness of their own behavior and describe what they should be doing instead.

6. If this does not work, call more conferences and get students to focus on their misbehavior, but also announce that a plan is needed to solve the problem. The plan must be more than a simple agreement to stop misbehaving, because this has not been honored in the past.

7. If the sixth step does not work, isolate the students or use time-out procedures. During their periods of isolation, charge the students with devising plans for ensuring that they follow the rules in the future. Isolation continues until the students have devised such a plan, had it approved, and made a commitment to follow it.

8. If this doesn't work, suspend the students in school. This is announced to the students firmly but matter-of-factly. Suspended students will now have to deal with the principal or someone else other than you, but this other person will repeat earlier steps in the sequence and press the students to come up with a plan that is acceptable.

9. For students who remain out of control during in-school suspension, call their parents to take them home and then start over with them the next day.

10. Remove the students from school and refer them to another agency.

ed with reductions in referrals to the office, fighting, and suspensions (Glasser, 1977). More rigorous tests of his methods are not available (or for other approaches described here). *Schools Without Failure* (1969) illustrates Glasser's interest in creating a generally facilitative atmosphere in schools, not just facilitative teacher-student relationships. He stressed that schools and classrooms be as humanistic as possible—they should be cheerful and courteous, communal, open to student input and communication, and staffed by people who believe that students are capable of exercising responsibility.

Glasser advocated that teachers and students jointly establish rules during classroom meetings and that they hold additional meetings to adjust the rules or develop new ones that apply to novel situations. Teachers adopt the role of discussion leaders and not authority figures during these meetings, setting limits only with respect to what is possible within the law and the rules of the school. Decisions are to be made by vote rather than negotiation. This part of Glasser's approach is not as well accepted as his problem-solving steps because many teachers oppose student self-government on principle, and others find it overly cumbersome.

Glasser's ten-step method of dealing with problem students does not require use of his classroom-meetings approach to rule setting, although Glasser himself stressed the latter and, in any case, insisted that everyone must recognize rules as reasonable and beneficial if they are to be effective. Glasser described his approach to discipline as no-nonsense but also as constructive and nonpunitive. It involves making clear to students that they can and must control themselves and follow school rules if they expect to stay in school.

Glasser's ten-step approach is attractive to a great many teachers because it is applicable in the classroom and provides specific steps for dealing with problems that have not responded to normal methods. It also illustrates features common to several approaches that seem to be converging. One is insistence on minimal standards of behavior, specifically behavior in school, regardless of students' personal backgrounds. All students must follow reasonable rules of behavior. A related notion is that students are responsible for their own behavior and will be held to that responsibility. Teachers will do whatever they can to help students solve their problems, but they are the students' problems and not the teacher's. This approach may seem harsh, but it assumes that rules are reasonable and fairly administered and that teachers try to be helpful, cooperate with students in making feasible adjustments, and, in general, maintain a positive, problem-solving stance. When these assumptions do not hold, Glasser's methods, like many others, can be destructive. An authoritarian teacher, for instance, can concentrate more on building a case against problem students than on trying to help them.

Gordon: teacher effectiveness training

Thomas Gordon's (1974) Teacher Effectiveness Training (TET) programs stressed freedom, responsibility, and abandonment of power and authority in favor of negotiation of "no-lose" arrangements. He advised teachers to be open and caring toward their students but also to maintain their individuality or separateness. He urged minimizing authoritative control over students, replacing this with teacher-student interdependence and mutual meeting of needs.

Problem solving starts with identification of problem ownership. Some problems are owned strictly by teachers, some strictly by students, and others by both teachers and students. Solutions to problems are facilitated if all parties involved recognize problem ownership accurately and respond accordingly.

Student-owned problems include anxiety, inhibition, and poor self-concept. For these problems, Gordon recommended passive listening (showing that you hear and understand what students are saying), door openers (invitations for students to talk), and, especially, active listening. Active listening goes beyond simply paying attention and showing that you understand; it includes providing feedback to students that responds to the underlying meanings of their messages.

In short, Gordon recommended an updated form of Carl Rogers' nondirective counseling (Rogers, 1983) for such students, and he rejected as ineffective responses those that contain what he called "the language of unacceptance." This is any response to the students' expressed fears or anxieties that does not take them seriously. This obviously includes flat contradictions or scoffing but also takes in well-meaning attempts to cheer students by praising or distracting them.

Gordon recommended active listening as an instructional technique during class discussions as well as a management technique to use on individuals. It helps students dissipate their feelings before getting to work when something upsetting has happened, and it helps promote smooth parent-teacher conferences. Through active listening, teachers help students not by trying to assume responsibility for their problems but by helping them to find their own solutions and become more independent, confident, and self-reliant.

Teacher-owned problems occur when students behave in ways that make teachers frustrated or angry. They require a different set of techniques from those used when students own the problem. In the latter case it is important for students to communicate and for the teacher to be a listener and counselor. When the teacher owns the problem, the teacher does the communicating, sending messages to students and trying to influence them to change.

"I" and "you" messages Gordon listed a number of ineffective techniques for trying to change students. They include confrontations

that backfire, "solution" messages that students resent and that induce only dependent and artificial compliance even when they do work, put-down messages that breed resentment without bringing about constructive changes, and indirect messages that may hurt the teacher's credibility. Gordon noted that most of these ineffective messages are "you" messages, used when the situation calls for "I" messages. It is the teacher in such cases who has the problem and thus the teacher who must do the communicating. "I" **messages** are *statements in which a teacher describes the behavior, the specific effect the behavior has on the teacher, and the feelings the teacher has about the behavior.* They reveal feelings and vulnerabilities but in ways that pay off by fostering intimacy and describing the problem without imputing unfortunate motives to the students. Making the student aware of the effects of his or her behavior on the teacher is one way of attempting to change student behavior.

"I" messages have three major parts. The first part indicates the specific behavior that leads to the problem ("When I get interrupted . . ."). The second specifies the effect on the teacher (". . . I have to start over and repeat things unnecessarily . . ."). This shows students that their behavior is causing the teacher real problems, and this message alone will be sufficient to motivate most students to want to change. The third part specifies the feelings generated within the teacher because of the problem (". . . and I become frustrated"). Taken together, the three parts link specific student behavior as the cause of a specific effect on the teacher, which in turn produces undesirable feelings in the teacher.

"no-lose" method of problem solving Gordon maintained that combinations of environmental manipulation, active listening, and communication through "I" messages will solve most problems. Sometimes the needs motivating unacceptable student behav-

ior are very strong, however, or the relationship with the teacher is very poor, and conflict
will continue. Genuine conflict involves problems owned by both students and teachers. It
must be approached in ways that avoid winning or losing and that meet the needs of all
parties involved. Gordon's "no-lose" method
is a process of searching until such a solution
is found.

Prerequisites for use of the method include
active listening (students must believe that
their needs will be accepted if they are expected to risk serious negotiation), use of good "I"
messages to state teacher needs clearly and
honestly, and communication to students that
this is a new and different approach (for teachers who have not been using it regularly).
There are six steps to be followed in this
"no-lose" approach: (1) define the problem, (2) generate possible solutions, (3)
evaluate these solutions, (4) decide which
solution is best, (5) determine how to
implement the solution, and (6) assess how
well the solution is solving the problem.

Defining the problem properly includes
accuracy about problem ownership and identification of only those people who are really part
of the problem. This continues until everyone is
agreed. For this purpose, it is vital that the
problem be described in terms of conflicting
needs, not competing solutions.

When generating solutions, it is important
simply to list them and not to evaluate them
prematurely. Once evaluation starts, solutions
that are objectionable to anyone for any reason
should be eliminated. Deciding which solution
is best involves a persistent search for consensus
rather than a resort to voting. Proposed solutions can be tested by imagining the consequences. When agreement is reached, specific
implementation plans and responsibilities are
drawn up, including plans for later assessment.
The result should be a "no-lose" agreement with
which everyone explicitly states satisfaction and
readiness to honor.

Not all agreements are honored, however.
Agreements may be broken when students do
not perceive the conflict in the first place, seeing only the teacher's problem, do not believe
that their needs are heard and understood by
the teacher (this can happen even when the
solutions meets their needs), or agree to the
solution because of peer or teacher pressure.
Gordon warned teachers against using power
when students break agreements. Instead, he
suggested that they send strong "I" messages to
communicate disappointment and indicate that
now they share a new problem.

Gordon did not like the idea of power
assertion by teachers, but he admitted that it
may be necessary when there is danger
involved, when students do not understand the
logic of the teacher's position, or when there is
insufficient time for more leisurely problem
solving.

Gordon also noted that certain conflicts
involve competing value systems (dress code,
use of drugs, personal grooming, language and
manners, morality, patriotism, religion) for
which no mutually acceptable solutions are possible. "I" messages are not effective in such cases
because the teacher's logic does not make sense
to the students. Value conflicts should be
labeled as such and not as conflicts of personal
needs. Gordon still recommended self-disclosure and "I" messages to show students where
teachers stand and to open the door for possible
discussion and behavior change, but that is all.
He advised dropping the matter if the first "I"
message does not produce any positive response
from students. Teacher persistence at this point
is seen as irritating preaching or nagging.

Selman and Schultz: pair therapy

Selman and Schultz (1990) articulated a theory
of interpersonal understanding. They argued
that students of different ages have different lev-

els of ability for understanding and dealing with interpersonal interactions (e.g., conflict). Some students, such as emotionally disturbed students, exhibit developmental delays in being able to understand interpersonal issues. Clearly, students who have difficulty in conceptualizing such issues will have difficulty in reasoning about and engaging in problem solving behavior.

These researchers have used **pair therapy**—*face-to-face exchanges between students that allow them to discuss their problems*—as a format for increasing the development of interpersonal reasoning. Two students meet once or twice a week for an hour with a pair therapist who facilitates their social interaction and provides an outside perspective. Selman and Schultz's theory maintains that such dyadic exchange (and third-person facilitation) helps students learn how to make and maintain a friend. It is hoped that encouraging social understanding in relations with one peer will radiate skills and insights to other peer relationships.

Furman and McQuaid (1992) noted that pair therapy has been used primarily for socially isolated students who are emotionally disturbed. They characterized pair therapy as an interesting and innovative approach, but one that has not been evaluated systematically.

Teachers who are interested in helping students deal with problems of social isolation might use classroom adaptations of the program developed by Selman and Schultz (1990). Although students who have severe problems would need close supervision (perhaps by the school counselor) students with mild problems and students in general might benefit from the opportunity for social exchange in pairs about such matters as how to apologize or ask for help). Teachers who wish to broaden students' capacity for social adaptiveness should realize that there is a growing literature about programs designed to help students cope more adequately with affect (anger, etc.). For example, Furman and McQuaid (1992) identified programs designed to improve social skills, assertiveness, social problem solving, and controlling anger.

problem types and their treatment

Brophy and Rohrkemper (1981) and Brophy and McCaslin (1992) examined how ninety-eight elementary teachers interpreted and stated how they would cope with twelve chronic student problem types. Problem types included failure syndrome, perfectionist, underachiever, low achiever, hostile aggressive, passive aggressive, defiant, hyperactive, distractable, immature, rejected by peers, and shy-withdrawn. The teachers who were studied had been nominated by their principals as either outstanding or average in their ability to cope with problem students.

These investigators examined how teachers' managerial success, location (small or big city), and grade level affected their perceptions of a problem (whether the teacher or student owned the problem or whether they shared ownership) and how teachers dealt with different types of problem students (e.g., socialization, punishment, gathering information, soliciting student input, threat, pressure, etc.). Following Gordon (1974), Brophy and Rohrkemper (1981) classified problems as (1) teacher owned, where the students' behavior interferes with the teachers' needs or agenda; (2) student owned, where the students' needs or agenda is frustrated by people or events other than the teacher; and (3) shared problems, where the students' behavior does not directly challenge the teacher but has consequences for classroom management and control. The teachers saw students who presented teacher-owned problems as acting intentionally and thus as blameworthy for their misbehavior. Those with student-owned problems, in contrast, were seen as victims of circumstances beyond their control.

Brophy and Rohrkemper noted that teachers in this sample appeared to have limited knowledge of and skill in using the various treatment models available for these problem types and did not always believe that solving these problems was a part of their duties as classroom teachers. They were pessimistic about changing students

research at work
useful strategies to deal with problem behavior

It is useful to briefly summarize strategies that were seen as especially useful in dealing with problem behavior (detailed information can be found elsewhere, Brophy & McCaslin, 1992; Rohrkemper & Brophy, 1979).

shy-withdrawn

In general, teachers attempted to respond to these students with support, encouragement, and personal assistance. These students were seen as victims of forces beyond their control; hence, teachers were naturally sympathetic to them. Teachers who responded effectively to shyness problems took them seriously and worked to improve students' willingness to participate but did so in indirect and highly supportive ways (private talks and special activities, building students' academic self-concept). Teachers used such methods to apply pressure for change but avoided directly confronting or sharply prodding these students through demands or threats. Teachers were prepared to back off and

drop the pressure if they met resistance to work several months to make progress.

Teachers who were more highly rated by their principals (as successful managers) were able to identify differential strategies for sub-types of shy-withdrawn students. This under-scores one of our principal tenets of management—that different students need different treatments, even within categories of student behavior (e.g., shy students who lack self-confidence or less withdrawn students who are preoccupied with worries or fantasies).

hostile-aggressive students

Brophy and McCaslin (1992) found that lower-rated teachers had only vague ideas about how to respond to aggressive students. They usually referred these students to the principal rather than dealing with them directly. When they did attempt to address these students' problems, they were ineffective because they did not have well-articulated

who presented teacher-owned problems and focused on immediate control strategies rather than long-term problem-solving strategies in responding to these students. They saw students with student-owned problems as difficult to change, but they were motivated to try to do so through long-term remediation programs.

Teachers believed to be effective managers behaved in ways generally consistent with the principles advocated by Glasser and Gordon. Brophy and Rohrkemper found that teachers rated as effective by their principals and by

classroom observers were willing to assume responsibility for solving problems. They worked with problem students themselves instead of or in addition to referring them to the principal or a counselor, and they used long-term, solution-oriented approaches. In contrast, less effective teachers focused on controlling misbehavior in the immediate situation, often by using threat or punishment. Effective teachers concentrated on helping their students to understand and cope with the problems that caused their symptomatic behavior.

strategies for responding to them. Responses of higher-rated teachers were more assertive and instructive. These teachers were confident in their ability to change these students and were determined to do so. They reported taking immediate and coercive action to stop aggression. They were willing to use punishment if necessary, although usually as part of a broader approach to resocialize aggressive students. The higher-rated teachers were assertive and controlling, whereas the lower-rated teachers were punitive but ineffectual. After the aggression was curbed, more effective teachers tried to show their more effective ways for handling frustration, controlling their temper, and solving conflicts through communication and discussion.

perfectionism

Most teachers reported that the key to perfectionism problems was not students' overt behavior but rather their subjective cognitive and affective responses to potential failure. Effective teacher responses went beyond sympathetic recognition ("Don't worry about it, we all make mistakes") to teaching strategies for reducing or eliminating such problems—that is, by helping students to identify more realistic goals and to accept more balanced and differentiated performance assessment. They taught that there are always relative strengths and weaknesses no matter how good overall performance may be and that the best way to respond to mistakes is to identify corrective action rather than to become emotionally upset by the performance.

Higher-rated teachers frequently communicated approval of students' progress in order to support the success-seeking aspect of perfectionists' achievement motivation while at the same time reducing their unrealistic goal setting, helping them to avoid dichotomous thinking about evaluation, and working to reduce their excessive emotional responses to mistakes.

an integrated approach

There is so much in common among the theories of Dreikurs, Morse, Glasser, and Gordon that teachers can draw on all of them to develop an integrated, eclectic approach to problem solving. Key elements include gathering complete and accurate information and seeking genuine solutions, not just stopgap suppression measures.

gathering information

Most people realize that one should not make decisions or take action without complete and accurate information. Many people, however, are not aware that undesirable outcomes can result when authority figures behave as if they were seeking information when no information is needed or obtained. If a student, for example, should call out a provocative remark or create a disturbance, there may be no need for questioning. Unless it is so serious as to require a con-

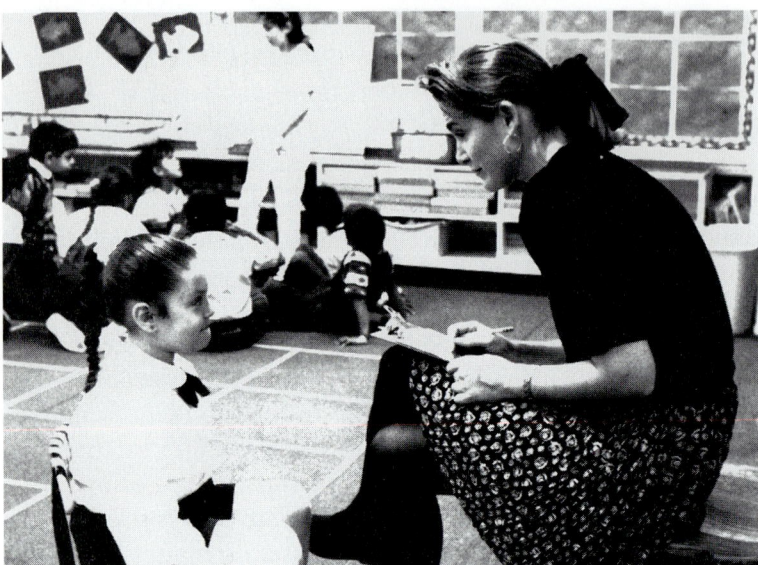

When it is necessary to gather information, the teacher should do so privately in a manner that does not cause the student to lose face.

ference, the situation should be handled with a brief or even humorous response such as, "Cool it, John." The teacher should not interrupt instruction to ask unnecessary rhetorical questions such as, "John, how many times do I have to tell you not to do that?"

When it is necessary to gather information, do so in ways that avoid causing any student to lose face. Investigations should be conducted in private, to minimize students' needs to save face, to refuse to back down no matter what, or to defy the teacher. It is also helpful to state that everything said during the discussion will be held in confidence unless some explicit agreement to the contrary is made. Insist that students keep quiet while classmates speak, reassure them that they will have a chance to give their versions later, and proceed toward the truth gradually by asking questions and pointing out discrepancies in different versions. Questions should concentrate on establishing exactly what happened and on trying to determine the motives behind the actions. The motives are important because students often misread one another's behavior—for example, by interpreting accidents as deliberate provocations or minor teasing as serious insults.

When questioning students, it is important not to be taken in by their rationalizations or attempts to project responsibility for their own behavior onto others. Students who get into regular scrapes with authority figures are usually masters of rationalization. When they cannot successfully deny or evade responsibility for their behavior, they will attempt to excuse or condone it by giving reasons such as, "He started it"; "People who leave money lying around like that *should* have it stolen"; and "He looked at me funny." For detailed and fascinating analyses of these kinds of rationalizations, see *Children Who Hate* (Redl & Wineman, 1951).

Investigations occasionally reach an impasse because one or more students are lying or withholding part of the truth. It usually is best to acknowledge this openly and to express both disappointment that the whole truth is presently not being told and the expectation that it will be told. If persistent efforts along this line still do not succeed, the teacher must decide whether the discussion itself will end the matter or some follow-up action is needed.

finding solutions

Once all needed information is collected, the next step is to work out a solution. The solution should be perceived as positive, not punitive, in intent and effect and as acceptable to everyone, not just the majority. The teacher may have to limit the range of possible solutions by stating clearly that certain things cannot be done or are outside school rules.

At this stage, attention should focus on the future and on solving the problems that led to the conflict, not the conflict itself. Attempts to rehash points already gone over in the investigation phase should be cut short, and students should be reminded that since everyone under-

stands the problem, it is time to work out a solution. Solutions do not have to be permanent or irrevocable; they can be explicitly tentative and subject to review at a designated future date.

If the students are unable to come up with realistic suggestions, teachers will have to make the suggestions themselves. They should be tentative and open to comment and evaluation. If students endorse a proposed solution, the teacher should ask them to think carefully before making final agreements, again emphasizing that students must make the decision and will be responsible for abiding by it. Students should not be allowed to come away with the idea that the teacher foisted a demand on them to which they really did not agree.

implications for teachers
problem-solving principles

Many problem-solving principles are exemplified in the following vignette:

Vera Wise is a teacher who is concerned about an increase in the frequency and seriousness of attention-getting behavior among her students over the past few weeks. The problem is worse in the last hour or so of school. Increasing numbers of students have been involved, fooling around and calling out remarks instead of working on their assignments. The primary instigators seem to be Bill, Jim, David, and Paul, four boys who sit close together and are part of a clique both in and out of school.

Vera has tried talking individually to each of these boys, as well as to other students, but the problem was worsened. The boys promise to improve their behavior, but they don't. The problem came to a head this afternoon, when one of the boys (Vera is not sure which) said something obscene and embarrassing to Mary, an attractive girl who is physically well developed and is the object of much interest and discussion among

the boys. Most of the class heard the remark and passed it along to the few who didn't hear it the first time. Vera responded by warning the class sharply that this kind of behavior had gone far enough and by telling, Bill, Jim, David, and Paul to stay after class to see her about it. Jim started to protest that he hadn't said it, but Vera cut him off with the statement that she wanted to see all four boys and would explain why later. Vera decided that this particular incident was not as important as the more general problem. Consequently, she decided to concentrate on changing the behavior of all four boys rather than on trying to find out who made the remark to Mary.

At the end of the period, as classmates prepared to leave, Jim and Paul looked surly, while Bill and David looked sheepish. The others were snickering at them and making guesses about what was going to happen. A few tried to hang around to find out, but Vera make a point of getting rid of them and closing the door before beginning the meeting. The meeting went as follows:

TEACHER: As I said in class, the remark made about Mary today was out of line, and it was just the latest of a number of things like that that have been going on recently. I think the time has come to put a stop to it, and I have kept you boys here because you four seem to be responsible for most of it.

JIM: Like I said before, I didn't do it. Besides, I can't stay because I have to go to practice and coach wants us there five minutes after the bell.

PAUL: Yeah, I didn't do it either and I have to go home and mow the lawn today.

TEACHER: Let's get a couple of things straight. First, I'm not especially interested in finding out which one of you embarrassed Mary today. I'm interested in discussing the larger problem of putting an end to this kind of thing. You four are here because you all do it more than anyone else. Furthermore, we're all going to stay here until we settle the problem for good. That includes everyone. Jim, if you like, I will call the coach and explain. Paul, if you want, I will call your home, but you are both going to stay here until we get finished. (Both Jim and Paul indicate they don't want the teacher to make calls.)

JIM: Well, David did it, not me. Besides, he does it a lot more than anyone else. When I do it, it's usually because he gets me started. (David glares but says nothing.)

The teacher begins by making it clear that she wants to talk about the general issue, not just what happened today, and that she considers all four boys to be responsible. Her behavior throughout the meeting is consistent with this opening statement.

Jim and Paul both try to get off by making excuses. The teacher offers to call and "explain," but this offer is refused. Although the offer was genuine in the sense that the teacher would have followed through if either boy had asked her to, she knew that this was unlikely because both boys probably knew that they would only compound their troubles if the teacher called the coach or a parent. With this response, the teacher both cuts off further attempts to escape the meeting and makes it clear that she intends to keep everyone there until she is satisfied. She also makes it specifically clear to Jim again that she is not interested in finding out who insulted Mary but instead is interested in the larger problem.

Now Jim tries to blame it on David. The teacher again points out that she is interested in the larger issue and she makes it

TEACHER: No good, Jim. David probably does it more, but you are responsible for your own behavior, and you can't use him for an excuse. If you didn't do it yourself a lot, you wouldn't be here now. (Jim glumly remains silent at this point.) David, if you did do it, I think you should apologize to Mary. She was very embarrassed, and whoever is responsible owes her an apology. But, as I said, I don't want to talk about what happened today; I want to talk about what's been going on over the last several weeks, and all four of you have been heavily involved in it.

PAUL: Well, we won't do it anymore. (Jim and David immediately nod and say "yes," while Bill nods solemnly.)

TEACHER: Sorry, but that's not good enough, either. I've talked to all of you, sometimes more than once. Every time you said that you wouldn't do it again, but you've kept doing it. So I'm afraid I can't take your word on it and let it go at that. We're

clear that Jim is both guilty of numerous instances of similar behavior recently and responsible for his own behavior regardless of what other students do. Her suggestion that David apologize is left simply as a suggestion with no attempt to follow up. This is appropriate, because a forced apology in front of the class would only further embarrass Mary and enrage David. The teacher has nothing to lose by suggesting this, and everyone might gain something if David follows through and does apologize to Mary sometime in the future. This statement also is consistent with the teacher's later statement that obscenity as such is not as important as respecting other people's rights and feelings. Also, by giving minimal time and attention to the information that David was responsible for today's problem, the teacher again reinforces her earlier statement that she wants to talk about the larger problem and about all four of the boys.

Under other circumstances, it probably would have been best for the teacher to take the boys at their word, perhaps ending this discussion on a more positive note, stressing happiness that they have seen the problem and are willing to respond to it in a mature fashion. However, given that these boys have pledged to change

going to have to discuss this some more and come to some kind of agreement that I can accept.

PAUL: Well, what's the big deal anyway? Words that people think are "dirty" don't hurt anybody, and besides, everyone knows what they mean.

TEACHER: In the first place, Paul, although it is true that there is nothing really wrong with these words, they are out of place in the classroom. More importantly, though, it's not just the words. It's the other things that go with them. For example, today Mary was terribly embarrassed, and no one had the right to do that to her. Also, you are distracting the whole class from their work, and let's not forget that you're supposed to be here at school to learn, not to goof off. But you're not doing your work. You know that I allow students to talk when they finish their assignments, but you four have been fooling around and making loud remarks instead of working on your assignments and then talking quietly after you finish.

JIM: Well, I can't help it. I say things without think-

in the past and have not done so, it is perfectly appropriate for the teacher to refuse to accept their pledges to change and to point out her reasons why. Furthermore, she now makes it clear that this discussion is going to continue until a real solution is reached.

Paul now takes the tack of trying to make the teacher feel guilty for being unreasonable. She counters nicely by acknowledging that his argument is valid up to a point, but then noting that it ignores certain factors in the larger context that make it impossible for schools to allow this kind of disruptive behavior. She then goes on to make the even more important point that she is more concerned about students' mutual respect for one another than about one obscenity. The boys are much more likely to feel guilt or shame about having embarrassed Mary than they are about having used obscene language. Finally, the teacher makes the additional point that the disruptive behavior of these students is interfering with their own work and that of their classmates. This is done in a way that points out implicitly that the teacher's rules are reasonable but that these four boys are abusing them.

At this point, Jim again tries to evade responsibility. In addition

ing, or else because David or somebody else gets me started. I've tried to stop, but I can't. Besides, it's not natural to try to stop from saying things that pop into your head at times like that.

TEACHER: Really! Well, suppose I invited your mother to sit in here for a few days? Do you think you might control yourself then? *(Jim's expression changes from surly self-confidence to confusion and anxiety.)*

TEACHER: You don't have to answer the question. You all know the answer; you don't use that kind of language around your mothers, and you don't have any trouble controlling yourself, either. So why don't we drop the lame excuses and start by recognizing that you can and will stop if you make the effort to do so.

PAUL: Yeah, but what are we supposed to do then? Sit there and keep our mouths shut?

TEACHER: No, I'm not asking you to do anything special. I'm only asking you to follow the rule that applies to everyone in the class: work on your assignment until you finish it. If you have time left over, then you can talk quietly, but without disrupting others.

to blaming others for "getting him started," he goes on to suggest that the teacher is asking something unreasonable and unnatural. The teacher wastes no time in dismissing this specious argument, pointing out that self-control is not a problem when the student is sufficiently motivated to show it. Her choice of an example here is particularly apt—students who use obscene language, particularly boys, almost always shrink at the thought of using it in the presence of their own mothers. The teacher closes this exchange a little roughly, characterizing what the boys have been saying as "lame excuses." However, under the circumstances, she is quite justified, because this is an accurate description of what has been happening. Also, she stresses personal responsibility for actions. Ultimately, she is not responsible for controlling these boys; they are responsible for controlling themselves.

Paul now takes a new approach, no longer attempting to rationalize the misbehavior but attacking the reasonableness of the teacher's request. She counters this by again repeating the rule, which is clearly reasonable, and also by making a point of the fact that she is only asking these boys to keep the same rule that applies to every-

PAUL: But I already said I would do that.

TEACHER: Yes, and I already said that all four of you have failed to keep your word on that. So what are we going to do? I don't want to make this into a big deal. In fact, I think it's silly to have to discuss something like this with students like yourselves, who should know better. But the problem is serious and is getting worse, and I am going to see that it stops before it gets out of hand. If I have to, I'll punish you all severely, but I don't want to do that. I asked you here to lay out the problem and to see if you had any suggestions about how it could be solved. Are there ways I could help by making some changes?

DAVID: Like what kind of changes?

TEACHER: Well, I could change your seats and separate you from one another. I could give you extra work or other things to do so that you wouldn't have time to goof off.

I could try to arrange to have some of you transferred to other classes. *(These suggestions yield negative reactions, except that Jim agrees to change seats and move away from David.)*

TEACHER: Okay, Jim, we'll

one else; she is not picking on them or asking them to do anything unusual.

Paul now goes back to repeating his pledge of reform and the teacher again points out that he has made this pledge and has broken it in the past. She then pulls together a few statements to make the situation clear to the boys: they have created the problem through their own misbehavior; she doesn't even want to discuss it but they have forced it on her; the problem is serious enough that it is going to be stopped one way or another; she is inviting them to make suggestions and expressing willingness to follow them if they are feasible and have a chance of improving the situation (even though she could simply make a decision on her own about what to do and present it to the boys with no opportunity for discussion).

In suggesting changes here, the teacher knows that they are unlikely to be acceptable to the boys. This is one way of informing them of possible negative consequences that will result if the problem is not stopped, without actually threatening such consequences. The fact that Jim agrees to change his seat is mildly surprising; it probably results from his own need to try to show that

arrange that. I hope it helps. Are there any other suggestions as to how we can solve this problem? *(Long silence.)*

PAUL: All I can think of is what I said before—I won't do it anymore, and this time I mean it. *(The others nod.)*

TEACHER: Well, I have to admit that I can't think of anything else other than punishment, and as I said, I don't want that. However, let me warn you right now that if any of you breaks his word this time, I will have to punish you. At the very least, you will have to stay after school for several days, and if there's any repeat of the kind of obscenity that went on today, I may have to contact your parents. I mention this because I want you to understand just how serious this problem is, and I want you to know that your word won't be any good in the future if you break it this time.

What about your workbooks? I know that all of you are behind, that the work you did in the past few weeks contains a lot of sloppy errors because of your fooling around. I want those workbooks brought up to date, the errors corrected, and the books turned in to me for checking shortly. How about Friday? *(Today is Wednesday.)*

JIM: *(Dejectedly.)* I'm way behind, and I have prac-

he was serious in his earlier claim that David tends to get him in trouble. In any case, it gives the teacher an opportunity to agree with a suggestion, thus showing good will on her part.

When the boys offer no more suggestions, the teacher changes from refusal to accept pledges of reform to a conditional acceptance. This is the appropriate time to make this switch, because the boys now have ceased their belligerence and rationalization, realizing that they are going to have to change their behavior and begin serious discussion of what might be appropriate in the future. As a hedge against failure to keep the pledge, the teacher threatens punishment in the future.

However, she does it in a way that does not suggest that she expects to have to use it. Also, the kinds of punishment she mentions help underscore her seriousness about this issue.

In closing the discussion, the teacher turns to the problem of incomplete and sloppy work in the workbooks. She requires the students to make this up, although she agrees to a delay when a reasonable excuse is given for it. Although this will have a punishing effect in the technical

tice again tomorrow and a game Friday night. I'm not sure I can get it in by Friday.

TEACHER: All right, what about Monday? That will give you all the rest of the week plus the weekend. *(All nod agreement.)* All right, then, we'll make it Monday.

Remember, I want you not only to catch up, but to review your work over the last three weeks or so and correct any errors you made because you weren't paying close attention to what you were doing. Work as far as the end of page 128. Okay? *(All agree.)* Is there anything else that any of you wants to add? *(After a brief silence, all shrug or shake their heads negatively.)*

TEACHER: Well, there is still the question of what to say in class tomorrow. You four are not the only ones who have been fooling around and making remarks. Tomorrow I intend to tell the class that we discussed the situation

sense, it is not the kind of behavior students typically perceive as punishment. The teacher merely is requiring them to do the same things that she requires of other students. The fact that it will cost them extra time and trouble in the next few days is their fault, not hers. This aspect of the discussion also underscores the point made earlier, that failure to do work is one of her concerns, not just hearing obscene words spoken in the classroom.

Finally, in closing the discussion, the teacher explicitly brings up the question of what is to be said to the class the next day. She makes it clear

and agreed that certain things need to stop, and I intend to remind everyone about the rules. I probably also will stress some of the other things I've pointed out to you, but I don't want to say anything more about our discussion. For your own good, I suggest that you say as little as possible about it yourselves. Perhaps just say that we had a talk and made some agreements.

Also, I would appreciate it if you urged some of your classmates to follow the rules, too, so that I don't have to hold any more sessions like this with anyone else. Anyway, I won't embarrass you or give any details about what we have said and done here, but I think some brief statement needs to be made, because everyone in the class is going to be wondering. Is this plan acceptable? *(All nod agreement.)* Is there anything else? *(All shake their heads negatively.)* O.K., get going, and let's have no more of this.

that she is going to make a statement, but also pledges not to embarrass the four boys or divulge any details of this discussion. This again underscores her intention to solve the problem rather than to punish the boys, and reiterates her earlier remarks about avoiding embarrassment of students.

Note, too, that she tries to enlist the help of the boys in this endeavor, suggesting that they minimize discussion about what went on and that they encourage their classmates to follow the rules. They may or may not do this, and she makes no attempt to check up on them. However, she has nothing to lose with this request, and it emphasizes that the boys share the problem and that they are responsible for solving it.

Note that throughout the discussion Paul and Jim have been vocal and occasionally belligerent. Under other circumstances David might have been, too, but since he was guilty of the incident that led to the discussion, he apparently has chosen to remain quiet and avoid getting into further trouble. Bill said nothing throughout the discussion, except to agree on occasion when the group agreed in unison. This may be because he is very embarrassed and remorseful,

or it may be that he regularly responds to such discussions with sullenness and unresponsiveness. If the latter is the case, it is important for the teacher to see that he agrees explicitly to what has transpired, so that he will not claim later that he never consented to it. In this case, the teacher judges that Bill has responded as have the other boys and has made the same commitment, even though he did not at any time speak out for himself.

summary

Students exhibiting behavioral problems and/or developmental lags frequently come from homes in which they have experienced cycles of failures and feelings of inadequacy, often leading them to attempt to compensate by acting out. Even if not actively aggressive, they may be alienated from learning and demand attention through clowning or disruptive behavior.

Dreikurs believed that attention, power, revenge, and displays of inadequacy (listed in increasing order of disturbance) are the four goals of student misbehavior. He advised teachers to identify the goal of misbehavior and attempt to reveal it to students in a nonthreatening, private interview. Morse recommended the life-space interview as a means for crisis intervention.

Glasser's theory, which he called "reality therapy," is based on humanistic principles involving the creating of a facilitative school atmosphere. His ten-step method is designed to be constructive and nonpunitive, with minimal but graduated responses to persistent misbehavior and self-control as the desired end result. Gordon's "Teacher Effectiveness Training" (TET) is very similar, stressing freedom and responsibility rather than authority and power. Active listening is a method he recommended for helping students find their own solutions to their behavior problems.

Because the ideas of Dreikurs, Morse, Glasser, and Gordon have much in common, teachers can draw on all of them to form an integrated, eclectic approach to problem solving, which will be illustrated in the case study that appears at the end of this chapter.

questions for reflection

1. Why do we insist that classroom problems be dealt with in the classroom when we acknowledge that they may be merely part of a much broader personality disturbance?

2. How realistic are your expectations regarding students' attitudes and behavior toward you as a teacher? Are you prepared to handle irrational hostility or defiance effectively?

3. How can teachers maintain humanistic values in harmony with their role as an authority figure? Are you prepared to punish effectively when (*when*, not *if*) you have to?

4. What should Vera Wise, the teacher in the vignette, have done if one or more of the boys blatantly failed to keep his promises? Write out your responses and analyze why certain teacher statements are desirable in dealing with blatant misbehavior.

cases to consider

Laura Simpson's problems Laura Simpson teaches English in a junior high school that draws 85 percent of its students from five nearby elementary schools. The remaining 15 percent of the population are African-American students bused from a predominantly African-American neighborhood in another part of town. As a group, the black students are of lower socioeconomic status (SES) than the white students, so they provide proportionately fewer high achievers and proportionately more low achievers. The students, as a group, have a wide range of ability, achievement, and attitudes toward the school.

Laura is a dedicated English teacher. She spends much of her time preparing both group and individualized activities, but the range of student abilities and interests with which she must cope creates many problems. Partly to accomplish desegregation and partly to avoid the elitism and other problems that usually accompany ability grouping by class, the school has a firm policy of heterogeneous grouping. Thus each of Laura's five classes contains students ranging from functional illiterates to bright high achievers capable of handling class activities such as drama or written assignments that involve composing poems or fiction. This makes it difficult to find activities with enough common ground to be interesting and worthwhile for everyone. Laura keeps searching for such activities and occasionally succeeds in finding them, but more often than not she must treat students differently.

She feels guilty about this sometimes, because it seems to contradict school policy and because it segregates the students by ability groups and, to a degree, by social class and race. The high achievers, however, seem to need and want the challenge of difficult and complex assignments, and they become understandably bored and restless when Laura tries to conduct general lessons on things they learned long ago. This almost always causes some problems of student disruption. These problems are occasionally fairly serious, such as the time that one of her brightest students caused a near-riot by publicly complaining that Laura was wasting everyone's time by trying to teach "those dummies who don't want to learn and couldn't learn even if they did."

On the other hand, when Laura attempts to involve everyone in a high-level activity such as a dramatic reading of a play, the activity is almost always ruined by the disruptive behavior of the low achievers in the class. The reading skills of some students are so limited that they can only be assigned the most simple parts. Thus their main role is to keep quiet and listen.

As if all this were not bad enough, the students are at "that age." Almost every day and in almost every class, Laura must deal more or less continually with adolescent behavior such as attention getting, defiance of authority, flirting, deliberate noise making, obscene or funny gestures and sounds, and wisecracks. In addition to these merely routine problems, occasionally there are serious ones, such as fights between students or open defiance directed at her. Laura can usually handle whatever comes up, but it takes a lot of energy, and it often leaves her wondering whether she is a teacher or a warden.

Laura sees about 150 students each day, spending about fifty-five minutes with each class. Some students present serious problems that Laura has been unable to solve. Let us look at these "problem" students.

Ben and Leon are two African-American students bused to a school where the majority of students are white and come from the adjoining neighborhood. Both are alienated from school. They are hostile and aggressive toward peers in general and whites in particular. They have been suspended in the past for racial incidents and have been sent to detention repeatedly for refusing to turn in work. Their mere presence, individually and especially together, puts everyone on edge. They are likely to overreact to even minor incidents, to complain loudly that they are being picked on, and to use any excuse for picking a fight.

George, Joan, and Marie have all made it clear that they do not like Laura, and frankly, Laura does not like them. Although George and Joan seem to do all right in other teachers' classes, and although Laura generally gets along quite well with most students, there is something about these three that bugs her, and apparently something about her that bugs them. As a result, they take every opportunity to embarrass or provoke her, and she finds herself responding with uncharacteristic defensiveness and anger.

Pete is both bright and attractive, maybe too attractive for his own good. He rarely causes serious problems, but he does not apply himself to his studies. Instead, he works at being "cool," trying to impress the other boys and charm the girls. He is often inattentive because he is busy "goofing off" with his friends or flirting with the girls. He is pleasant and outwardly cooperative when Laura tries to reach him, but he never really changes his behavior.

Art is commonly referred to as a juvenile delinquent, and in his case this is an understatement. He has frequently been suspended from school for activities such as extorting money through threats and carrying and brandishing weapons. He is part of a gang composed primarily of boys who have been thrown out or who have dropped out of school, and the word is that they spend much of their time stealing, getting drunk, using drugs, and generally engaging in petty crimes and teenage gang activities. Art is just

marking time until he can drop out or succeed in getting himself kicked out.

Laura has virtually given up serious attempts to change the fundamental problems of these students. She finds herself more and more often merely minimizing the disruptions they cause, even if it means excluding them from class, sending them to detention, or taking other measures that are likely to worsen their problems in the long run. At least, she reflects ruefully, this gets them out of her hair for a short time.

Laura Simpson is dedicated and generally successful, but her success requires constant energy and skill, and it is not total. There are some students she does not reach at all, and many others that she succeeds with only partially, often because of constraints beyond her control. If you were in Laura's position, how would you try to change this generally unsatisfactory situation?

part VII.

individual differences

Helen, Jim, Ricky, and Ruth *were assigned to conduct an experiment in chemistry class. They were good friends who had been in school together for several years. They worked well as a team. Jim prepared the equipment while Ricky sorted the chemicals and made the measurements so that they would be ready when Jim had the apparatus set up. Helen read the "cautions" in the instructions and made directive comments to Ricky or Jim from time to time. Ruth started to outline the group report and finished the purpose section just as Ricky and Jim finished their tasks.*

this unit is about individual differences. Individuals think about what happens to them and interpret events in terms of their experiences, abilities, self-concepts, and interests, so students may perceive, interpret, and evaluate the same event (a chemistry experiment) in different ways. In our example, the students automatically started to play roles they had learned in the classroom. In this instance, the roles reflect traditional gender roles. The males are setting up and conducting the experiment, and the females are observing and writing about it. The teacher did not assign them these tasks; the students simply assumed roles they had learned.

Teachers must deal with such individual differences in learning styles and personalities that students bring to the classroom. Each student is an individual and must be treated as such. This principle is clear, even simple, in the abstract, but it involves overwhelming complexities when teachers try to put it into practice. What are the important characteristics on which students differ, and what are the implications of these differences for individualized treatment?

To deal with these complexities, educators and researchers have described and labeled stu-

dents with respect to socioeconomic status, IQ, cognitive style, and creativity. Other labels describe various types of exceptional students who are deemed to require "special education." These labels and their implications for education will be considered in the present section.

There has been much opposition to such labeling in recent years, because many labels are demeaning and appear to produce undesirable self-fulfilling prophecy effects ("This child has a learning disability and can't be expected to make much progress in school."). This is a real danger, especially if the labeling of students is not accompanied by remedial instruction or other treatment designed to eliminate or compensate for their problems. When students are described with specific labels, it is helpful to ask, "So what?" If the labels are meaningful and helpful, the question should be answerable with statements such as, "Therefore, they need treatment X," or, "Therefore, they will benefit more from treatment X than from treatments Y or Z." This is clearly the case with a label like "myopic" (nearsighted): the student is fitted with corrective glasses or contact lenses. Linkages between clear-cut remedial procedures and labels such as low IQ, disadvantaged, learning disabled, or emotionally disturbed are not so clear, however. Thus the value of labels, even so-called diagnostic ones, depends not only on their accuracy but on the degree to which they provide guidance for remediating the implied problems.

In Chapter 20, we discuss students' IQ, cognitive styles, and creativity, considering how teachers can foster development in the latter areas. In Chapter 21, we discuss socioeconomic status, cultural, and gender-role differences. Finally, in Chapter 22 we consider the instruction of students whose disabilities or special needs often caused them to be labeled as abnormal and to be segregated from the educational mainstream in the past but who now are being returned to it as a result of Public Law 94–142.

chapter 20

IQ, cognitive style, and creativity

objectives

When you have mastered the material in this chapter, you will be able to

1. Discuss five common but incorrect assumptions about IQ tests, showing how the theoretical concept "intelligence" differs from the term *IQ*

2. Understand how IQ test scores can be interrelated and used properly in teaching situations

3. Differentiate Level I skills from Level II skills and identify their implications for educational practice

4. Explain how Gardner's (1983, 1988) and Sternberg's (1985) theories differ from more traditional psychometric approaches to conceptualizing and measuring intelligence

5. Explain Gregory's concepts of potential and kinetic knowledge and the value of these concepts for thinking about the role of knowledge in intelligence

6. Differentiate the concepts of fluid and crystallized intelligence

7. Define the cognitive style called conceptual

tempo, distinguishing it from simple response speed

8. Explain how differences in conceptual tempo are related to school learning and problem solving and how conceptual tempo is most effectively modified

9. Contrast the characteristics of field-dependent and field-independent persons

10. Explain how the field-dependence/field-independence cognitive style affects students' preferred learning modes and teachers' preferred instructional patterns

11. Discuss recent arguments about students' learning styles and the instructional implications of the arguments

12. Describe how creativity is measured and how it relates to IQ

13. Discuss the two general criteria of creative responses and the value of creativity measures to education

14. Describe several techniques for fostering student creativity

intelligence quotient (IQ)

The development of standardized tests of intelligence began with the work of Alfred Binet in the early 1900s in France. Binet was not trying to design a test of intelligence but to identify children likely to have difficulty in school. He analyzed the abilities that seemed necessary for school success and then worked backward to develop tests to measure these abilities. He was looking for tests that discriminated adequately between students within each grade level. Tests that were too easy or too hard were not very useful because everyone either passed or failed, so different tests were needed for each grade. Besides the ability to discriminate, Binet's primary criterion for including a test in his battery was the degree to which the test predicted later school success. Note that this is not the same as the degree to which a test measures some ability that we call "intelligence."

Binet's tests were very successful and were quickly adopted in England and America. Their outcomes were consolidated by psychologists into a single index that came to be called the **"intelligence quotient" or IQ**, which means *a score on a particular test of intelligence.*

Historically, IQ was defined as the ratio of mental age to chronological age × 100. Today, IQ is measured in notably different ways, but is still conceptualized as being on a scale (with a mean of 100 and a standard deviation of roughly 16).

By referring to Binet's tests as "intelligence tests" that yielded the IQ, the psychologists who adopted them did more that just translate them into English and use them to screen children. They abandoned Binet's detailed profiles of performance across a variety of measures, and then elaborated the notion of intelligence testing and the concept of IQ with the following ideas about IQ tests and what they could measure:

1. The tests are more than mere indicators of school success; they measure fundamental intellectual abilities.
2. Underlying these abilities is a generalized factor (usually called "g"). This factor is general intelligence.
3. General intelligence is transmitted genetically and thus it is fixed at conception.

Repeated measures may produce different scores because of situational factors or measurement errors, but theoretically, perfect measurement would yield precisely the same IQ every time for any individual.

4. Both individual and group differences are fixed and unchangeable. Differences in educational experiences or opportunities might affect the degree to which intelligence is expressed but will not affect intelligence itself.

5. Intelligence is more than simply a statistical predictor of academic achievement. It is a *cause*, usually by far the most important cause. So when students do not achieve as highly as their measured IQs lead us to expect, they are underachievers who are not working up to their abilities.

These statements combine nicely to form a consistent theory. However, not one of them is correct, at least in the extreme form in which each is stated. Humans possess a great many different intellectual abilities, even though many of them correlate highly with one another (Horn, 1986). Also, even though IQ tests can be constructed to yield a single score, they do not measure one, single ability. There is no correspondence between an IQ score and the size or functioning efficiency of the brain or any particular part of it, and there is no single ability that we can call "intelligence" (Lohman, 1993; Sternberg, 1986a, 1986b).

Researchers vary widely in how they define intelligence; and there is no standard definition that all agree upon. For example, some researchers have stressed a view of intelligence as acquiring various proficiencies (see, for example, Glaser, 1986) and other investigators have explored social aspects of intelligence (see, for example, Goodnow, 1986). Many psychologists note that intelligence is composed of various dimensions. For example, Snow (1986) suggests six aspects of intelligence: (1) Knowledge-based thinking (using organized prior knowledge in goal-directed thinking); (2) Apprehension suggests that individuals not only feel and know, but they also *know* that they have these experiences (i.e., a capacity to reflect upon experience); (3) Adaptive purposeful striving (individual can adaptively shift strategies to use strengths, etc.); (4) Fluid analytical reasoning (e.g., to recognize important features and aspects of problems and to integrate information); (5) Mental playfulness (all problems are not given, but individuals can create interesting issues and goals to pursue); (6) Idiosyncratic learning (people differ not only from others in how they approach problems, but they may differ in their own approaches over time). Clearly, the concept of intelligence carries many dimensions and scholars vary in definitions and the emphasis that they research.

diverse conceptions of intellectual abilities

As Gregory (1987) notes, there is an interesting paradox in how we think about intelligence. Someone who does well by using special knowledge (e.g., an engineer who builds a bridge) often is assumed to be intelligent. However, people who succeed without special knowledge are also viewed as intelligent. Gregory writes, "Thus, we assign intelligence both for lack and for presence of knowledge" (p. 1). From this perspective there are two interpretations of intelligence: (1) given knowledge or information, and (2) the ability to discover or build knowledge.

As we shall see in this chapter, intelligence tests attempt to measure both knowledge and especially the second type of intelligence—building knowledge and problem solving. The unique claim of intelligence tests as opposed to achievement tests is the putative claim of measuring the ability to reason. However, as Gregory notes, making such distinctions is a complex issue that is fraught with difficulties: "In this second problem-solving, 'psychologists' sense, knowledge is also important, but in a somewhat paradoxical way, as we have more knowledge so problems are more easily solved. So, as we possess more of the first sense of intelligence,—we need less of the second sense. Until, with sufficient knowledge, the problem may disappear until we need no problem-solving intelligence" (p. 6).

Diverse conceptions of intellectual abilities can be seen in the variety of tasks included on "intelligence tests." The fourth edition of the Stanford-Binet Intelligence Scale contains fifteen subtests organized into the four theoretical areas of verbal reasoning, quantitative reasoning, abstract-visual reasoning, and short-term memory. Instead of a single IQ score, the scale now yields standard age scores for each of the four areas as well as a composite for the test as a whole. This emphasis on measuring abilities across a variety of areas is closer to Binet's original intention, although the utility of the four scores yielded by the new test remains to be proved by practice and research (Sandoval & Irwin, 1988).

The Wechsler Preschool and Primary Scales of Intelligence (WPPSI) and the Wechsler Adult Intelligence Scale (WAIS) also contain a variety of tasks, although not as many as the Stanford-Binet. These tests are divided into subscales composed of verbal tasks (general information items, vocabulary words, series of digits to memorize both forward and backward, arithmetic word problems, items calling for statements of similarities between objects or concepts, and comprehension items asking how one should respond to problems such as finding a stamped, addressed, and sealed letter in the street or discovering a fire in a crowded theater) and performance tasks (finding the missing parts in incomplete drawings, putting scrambled cartoon panels into the right order, assembling jigsaw puzzles, and completing coding tasks in which each of ten digits is paired with a simple geometric symbol that must be written under the digit whenever it appears).

The Stanford-Binet and Wechsler scales are the most reliable and best validated of the intelligence tests in wide use. There also are many short-form "IQ tests" devised for group administration that focus on a few tasks or even one (typically vocabulary). These group tests are notably less reliable than the individually administered batteries (Hopkins & Bracht, 1975). In any case, even when IQ is measured reliably, it does not represent a single, clear-cut ability.

changes in IQ

IQs are not fixed at conception, either. Honzik, McFarlane, and Allen (1948) found more change than stability in a longitudinal study of middle-class children across childhood and adolescence. A majority of these children changed at least fifteen points in IQ, and a third changed twenty points or more. McCall, Appelbaum, and Hogarty (1973) reported similar findings. Changes in Stanford-Binet scores between ages two and one-half and seventeen averaged 28.5 points, and a seventh of the changes were 40 points or more. Furthermore, the changes were not random. High-SES (socioeconomic status) children tended to maintain or gain in IQ, but low-SES children tended to drop. Those who gained were described as independent and competitive in their preschool years and as independent, scholastically competitive, self-initiating, and problem solving during elementary school. Their parents were described as providing encouragement and stimulation of cognitive activities in the home and as using rational rather than fear-oriented approaches to child rearing.

intelligence test data and teaching

Intelligence testing has been controversial since its inception (Kamin, 1974). Lately, it has been under attack by those who believe that it simply labels students without doing them any good and by those who hold that intelligence tests are inherently biased in favor of white, middle-class students and against students from lower-class backgrounds and minority students (Oakland, 1977; Ogbu, 1988).

group differences

The claim that intelligence tests are biased against low-SES and minority students is debatable. Group differences in IQ are real and do not disappear when attempts are made to improve rapport with the examiner, to improve comfort in testing situations, or to use only "culture-fair" tests, although these factors may improve scores somewhat (Barrett & Depinet, 1991; Samuel, 1977). Still, talented minority students may be put under intense social pressure when they have the potential to outperform peers on intelligence tests and school assignments (Ogbu, 1988). It is important to recognize that formal testing settings, rather than the tests themselves, often place minority students in compromising situations and may not reliably measure the performance of some of these students.

Although intelligence tests do not measure any single, fixed general mental ability, they do measure important abilities such as understanding and following directions, reasoning and drawing conclusions, and solving problems. They also measure vocabulary, reading comprehension, arithmetic computation, and other skills taught in schools. Most people recognize these abilities as general cognitive skills important for everyone.

IQ tests are not perfectly objective, however. Certain vocabulary items include words that have gone out of style or are typically used only in cities or only in rural areas, and the scoring of a few items dealing with general information or comprehension occasionally is questionable. Although test makers try to identify and eliminate poor items, Gregory (1987) notes that certain types of knowledge items (that favor one gender or one culture) are difficult to determine and that separating knowledge from intelligence is fraught with difficulty. Similar problems are often found with standardized achievement tests. For example, a recent study by the American Association of University Women (AAUW, 1992) suggests that the SAT (Scholastic Aptitude Test) has a bias that favors males.

predictors of achievement

Despite controversy and criticism, IQ tests remain highly reliable predictors of school achievement. If used to measure students' potential and not as mechanisms to label or restrict them, IQ tests can enable teachers to make decisions that can improve instruction. This is especially true of students who are unfamiliar with the English language, if they are tested in their native language or with nonverbal IQ tests that eliminate the need for verbal instructions and responses.

IQ tests can identify students who are bright but score poorly on typical tests due to their verbal deficiencies. Presumably, these students will achieve better if their verbal deficiencies are eliminated through effective instruction. If testing reveals poor nonverbal skills in addition to low verbal skills, poor performance is not due solely to verbal deficiency, and remediation will require more intensive and individualized treatment.

Individual Differences

Many students will have to cope with the fact that peers mature more quickly than they do. Teachers can help students understand and accept these individual differences.

Even within gender, students of the same age often vary greatly in their rate of physical maturation.

Students with physical handicaps typically can lead exciting and vigorous lives in schools. Teachers may need to make special provisions to facilitate students' mobility, but physical handicaps are not an impediment in most classroom situations.

Social relationships may become awkward for adolescent girls, who mature more quickly on average than boys.

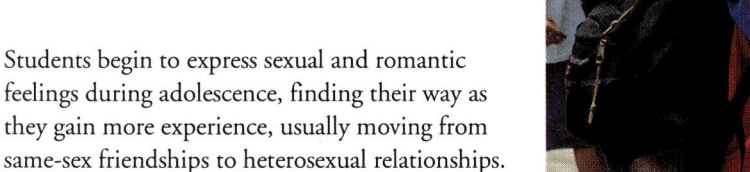

Students begin to express sexual and romantic feelings during adolescence, finding their way as they gain more experience, usually moving from same-sex friendships to heterosexual relationships.

The adolescent peer culture exerts strong pressure on students to fit in: to dress alike, listen to the same music, use the same slang, etc.

As adolescents move into their high school years, their interest in being like their peers often gives way to a stronger desire to rebel and express their individuality. This girl may have dressed and worn her hair very differently just a few years ago.

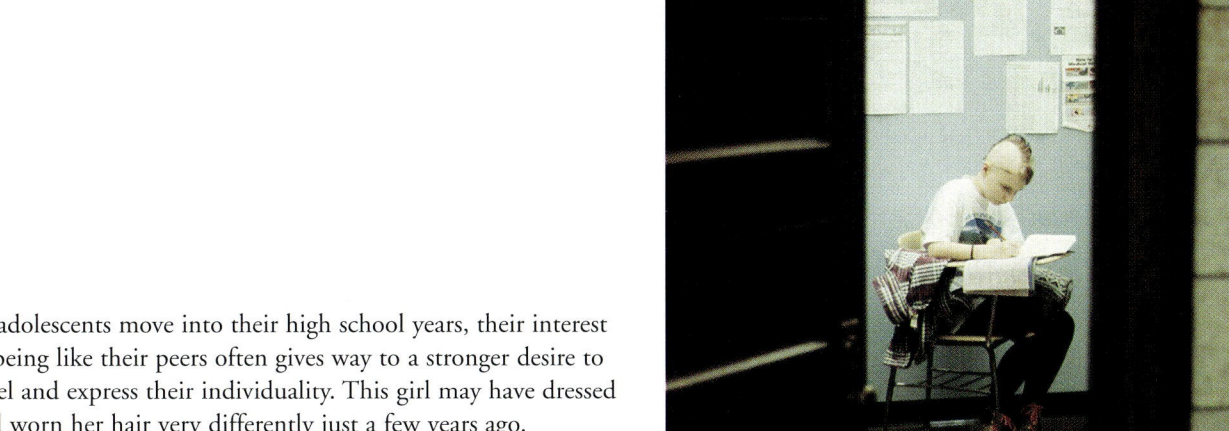

Socially popular students' experiences in schools are often quite different than those of less popular or unpopular students, who may have more difficulty navigating social and academic concerns.

Most students, like this boy in the foreground, are hurt by neglect, isolation, or rejection by peers. Unfortunately, when students cannot find rewarding peer relationships, they may withdraw and become extremely isolated and lonely. Some prefer to be loners because of their unique needs; however, most isolated students would like to be part of a group.

uses and misuses of IQ tests

There is a real danger of misuse of IQ tests by harmfully labeling students. In any case IQ tests have limited diagnostic usefulness because they rarely point to specific actions teachers should take to remediate problems. They do have some uses so that banning them altogether, which has been done in certain school districts, probably is a mistake. Still, we need to stress that the use of IQ tests has sometimes led to pupils receiving a less stimulating and less useful curriculum than they should and thereby to the erosion of human potential. Teachers need to recognize that IQ tests have limited value and should serve only as a guide about potentially appropriate curricula. Although IQ tests do predict school success, they are less useful for predicting success after graduation, and teachers should not overemphasize them.

One key is to distinguish between different kinds of IQ tests. Group-administered tests that depend heavily on reading and test-taking skills are essentially vocabulary tests that do not add anything of value to the information available from standardized achievement tests. On the other hand, individually administered omnibus IQ tests like the Stanford-Binet or the Wechsler scales provide information about a variety of abilities, and "culture-fair" tests can reveal hidden abilities among disadvantaged students or students who speak English as a second language.

types of intellectual abilities

Investigators interested in psychometric testing have searched for what Thurstone (1938) called "primary mental abilities." Some, like Cattell (1971) and Guilford (1967), developed complex models involving large numbers of specific abilities. Even these models are limited, however, because they are based on data that come only from verbal and pencil-and-paper tests and thus do not include intellectual attributes such as curiosity or social intelligence (Ford, 1986; Horn, 1986).

The distinctions between intellectual abilities that have been most useful to date are simple ones, such as the difference between associative learning and memory, and higher levels of abstract thinking and reasoning. Jensen's (1969) distinction between Level I and Level II skills, as explained in the following section, is perhaps the most useful formulation of this dimension.

level I and level II skills

Level I skills *include the association learning and rote memory that are required for tasks such as committing specific material to memory, learning to use a code that transforms the English letters into a new set of symbols, or learning to communicate in a new language. Such tasks require little reasoning or problem solving, although they do demand concentrated effort and can create cognitive strain if their demands on attention and memory are great enough.* Thus, tasks requiring only Level I skills are not necessarily easy, and some are beyond the abilities of most people (memorizing *Moby Dick*, typing 200 words a minute, or producing instantaneous translations for the United Nations). Level I abilities are primarily involved in mastering the basic skills taught in the early grades and in learning factual information.

Level II skills *include the information-processing activities involved in perceiving stimuli and the abstract thinking and reasoning needed to solve problems, especially problems not encountered previously.* They are measured in IQ test items that require one to state similarities or differences (How are an elephant and a whale alike?), supply meaningful analogies (Train is to track as automobile is to _____), or solve abstract problems (Supply the next number: 1, 4, 9, 16, _____). Level II skills are required to succeed in school tasks such as reading comprehension (understanding the connections between events in a story and drawing correct inferences about their implications, not just remembering the events themselves), solving most word problems in math, or understanding and applying abstract principles in any subject matter.

Although there are individual differences, there are no important social class or ethnic group differences in Level I skills. The development of Level I skills appears to be closely related to the quality and amount of schooling an individual receives. Schools are less successful in developing Level II skills, however, in part because Level II skills have a much stronger genetic component than Level I skills (Jensen & Figueroa, 1975; Vernon, 1981).

Also, it is harder to provide direct instruction in Level II skills. We can present students with tables containing basic number facts, help students to commit these facts to memory, and immediately judge any factual answer to be right or wrong and show why it is wrong if necessary. However, the Level II skills involved in mathematical problem solving cannot be taught so directly. We can have students practice by requiring them to solve problems, and we can even instruct them in strategies such as carefully reading the problem, systematically separating the information given from the information required, and generating and testing hypotheses. These efforts, however, may not generalize to problem situations that are very different from the ones students have practiced, even if they involve the same problem-solving principles.

Part of the reason that schooling has had only marginal effects on Level II skills may be that too little instructional time is spent on higher-order goals. Elementary school mathematics instruction, for example, focuses on computational skills, without enough emphasis on con-ceptual understanding and problem solving (Barr, 1988). Teachers appear to emphasize speed and accuracy at the expense of conceptual understanding and application. Recent evidence, however, suggests that at least under certain conditions and for certain tasks, speed and power (understanding) may be independent dimensions (Horn, 1986). Further, there is evidence that tracking in secondary schools is associated with different curriculum emphasis. Students assigned to lower-track classes often receive a curriculum aimed at Level I capacities, whereas students in higher tracks receive a curriculum that focuses on Level II capacities (Raudenbush, Rowan, and Cheong, 1993). Thus, there is reason to be hopeful that as schools place more emphasis on teaching for understanding, they may have greater effects on Level II abilities.

kinetic and potential intelligence

Earlier, in posing Gregory's (1987) paradox, we noted that the word "intelligence" has at least two meanings. Gregory's own way out of the paradox is to suggest that the acquisition of knowledge is always acquired through some type of problem solving. Thus, the acquisition of knowledge can be conceptualized as a "frozen" problem. Knowledge once acquired (how to use a computer, a formula for finding area, etc.) is stored for subsequent use. Gregory argues that a useful comparison point is the concept of *kinetic energy*, or the building up of *potential energy*, which can be used in different ways (e.g., pump water to a reservoir to produce electricity for many uses). Thus, one can conceptualize knowledge production as kinetic intelligence and power of knowledge to solve problems as potential intelligence.

Gregory puts it this way:

> On this account, potential intelligence is *available* solutions and answers—

which were *created* (perhaps in the distant past) by kinetic intelligence. If our present knowledge is adequate for a current problem or task, then little or no problem-solving—and so little or no kinetic intelligence—is required. Similar for tools; if we have the right tools a job is much easier than if we have to invent a new tool or process. In this sense tools, as well as books and computer programs, are potential intelligence though they are not in brains. Kinetic intelligence is needed whenever a solution is somewhat novel; for then it is necessary to see how the available tools or symbolically stored knowledge may be applied—which requires an inventive leap or kinetic intelligence. (Gregory, 1987, pp. 6-7)

It seems better to view intelligence as flexible and as in transition. As we gain more knowledge and experience we continue to enhance our pool of potential intelligence. Increasingly scholars have concluded that capacity for intelligent performance is not fixed but rather increases with gains in knowledge and experience.

fluid and crystallized intelligence

Somewhat similar arguments have been made about crystallized intelligence (knowledge) and fluid intelligence, a distinction originally proposed by Cattell (1943). Although different researchers have integrated crystallized and fluid intelligence in different ways, there is general agreement that fluid intelligence is the ability not only to understand what one has learned, but being able to see the relevancy of the knowledge in a given problem situation and to be able to use knowledge creatively in a new

situation (see, for example, Baltes, 1986; Snow, 1986; and Sternberg & Detterman, 1986). Over time fluid ability (problem solving, adapting information to a context) came to be viewed by some psychologists as innate potential or general intelligence. However, as Lohman (1993) has argued, the evidence is clear that intelligence can improve with schooling and that the type of education can influence particular abilities. For example, Balke-Aurell (1982) in large studies of Swedish males has found that ability changed as a function of education and occupation—a verbal curriculum was associated with gains in verbal ability, technical education was associated with gains in spatial intelligence, and so forth. Hence, whether studies develop more crystallized knowledge or ability to use such knowledge depends upon the educational systems (i.e., are students encouraged to use ideas or to memorize facts?).

Lohman argues that part of the reason that students are not fluid (able to use the information they have adaptively) is because they have not been encouraged to impose an organizational structure on their knowledge. He puts the problem this way: "The problem is *not* the learning of facts, but the learning of disconnected facts. Students cannot use what they may know about Piaget's theory in their writing or speaking or thinking unless they can bring it to mind easily. This means that they have organized it." (p. 19).

Lohman argues that if students are to become more fluid they need to be able to use crystallized knowledge to solve increasingly unfamiliar problems (i.e., practice transferring knowledge) and to be able to organize information in flexible ways. He puts it this way: "A clear understanding of the key events, controversies, or concepts in a domain, along with the ability to connect these ideas both to each other and to a larger scheme is more important than a much larger base of fact and skill knowledge that is disconnected, is not tied with other learning, and can be applied only locally" (p. 21). Thus, as argued earlier there is reason to be optimistic that schools can affect students' ability to reason if curriculum emphasis is placed upon ordering and using knowledge.

process approaches to intelligence

Psychometric theorizing was the primary approach to the study of intelligence from about 1900 to 1950. Many of those working within this approach based their measures on the theory of Charles Spearman (1927), who conceived of intelligence as a single, general ability. Thurstone (1938) distinguished among primary mental abilities such as verbal comprehension, number ability, and reasoning ability.

Sternberg (1988) argued that these psychometric approaches fail to measure mental *processes*. He used the following example to make the point.

> George is taller than Bill. Bill is taller than Sam. Who is the shortest?

According to Sternberg, people can use different strategies to solve this problem. One person might use a *verbal* approach and decode the problem into linguistic propositions. Another might use a *spatial* approach by visualizing George, Bill, and Sam. Conventional psychometric scoring would credit both individuals with getting the right answer but would miss the differences in their mental processing.

Psychometric tests sometimes confuse different mental abilities that they purport to measure. Verbal analogies, for example, are often used to assess verbal reasoning. But if a student does not know the meaning of a word used in an analogy item, the student's failure on the item will be due to a lack of word knowledge rather than to a verbal reasoning error. It appears necessary to separate the measurement of different kinds of processes (verbal versus spatial) and also to separate the measurement of mental processes from the measurement of knowledge.

cognitive-components approach

Information processing theorists have tried to separate measurements by analyzing the items and tasks that appear on tests of intelligence into their underlying cognitive components (Sternberg, 1988). By definition, this cognitive-components approach deals with a level of complexity that is at least equal to the dimensions being measured on a test. For example, with a verbal analogy such as, "Lawyer is to client as doctor is to (a) medicine, (b) nurse, (c) patient, and (d) kill," one would not simply score the item as correct or incorrect (as in the psychometric approach) but would attempt to look at how the individual used (or failed to use) available information and processes. For example, one might examine encoding to see what process the person used to figure out what each word meant. Or, one might examine inference—the process used to analyze the relation between the first two terms and the third term. Finally, one might examine how the person applied this relation to the third term to decide among the answer options (application). In this way, one can investigate the speed and accuracy with which each component of information processing is performed and assess how adequately the process is carried out. The cognitive-component approach offers a new means of examining information processing but does not fundamentally challenge or alter the content of conventional intelligence tests.

Gardner and Sternberg: systems of theorizing

Those who propose systems viewpoints believe that intelligence is much more integrated and complicated than psychometric and informa-

Musical ability is one of the seven discrete intellectual abilities that Gardner identified.

tion processing theories suggest. Rather than search for static or even dynamic processes that produce relatively stable assessments of individual abilities, they attempt to understand an integrated whole consisting of various parts. Two good examples of systems theorizing are Gardner's (1983, 1988) and Sternberg's (1985, 1988) theories of human intelligence.

Gardner's multiple intelligences

Gardner (1983, 1988) argued that intelligence is not a single entity composed of multiple abilities but, instead, that there are multiple intelligences, each important in its own right and independent of the others. Gardner defined *intelligence* as the ability to solve problems or to develop outcomes and products that are valued in one or more cultural settings. Ability to solve a verbal analogy is not suffi-

cient reason to believe that an individual can identify and solve problems in actual social settings. In studying intelligence, Gardner argued the need to move away from tests and to look instead at more naturalistic sources of information about how individuals develop skills that are important to their way of life. What aspects, for example, define intelligent practices for surgeons, hunters, choreographers, tribal chiefs, and athletic coaches?

Gardner and his colleagues have considered diverse abilities that might be defined as intelligence and have examined what is known about the development of different skills in normal children and about what happens when various types of brain damage occur. His research group has studied special populations, such as prodigies and children with learning disabilities. They have trained individuals in certain skills to

Interpersonal abilities, another of the seven intellectual abiliites named by Gardner, is characterized by the ability to notice and make distinctions among other people; exhibited by politicians, salespeople, and religious leaders.

see if the training transfers to other skills (Does training in musical ability influence mathematical or verbal performance?).

Gardner's work has resulted in a list of seven intelligences, although he makes no claim that this is a final or complete list. The list includes two types of intelligence that have been stressed in the psychometric tradition: *linguistic-verbal* and *logical-mathematical*. Gardner noted that our society emphasizes linguistic and logical-mathematical intelligences because much testing is historically based on this combination of skills. A third intelligence is *spatial intelligence*—the ability to form a mental model of a spatial setting and to operate using that model. Sailors, surgeons, and painters are examples of individuals who have developed spatial intelligence. The fourth ability is *musical intelligence*, and the fifth

is *bodily-kinesthetic intelligence*—the ability to solve problems or to fashion products using one's body (as dancers and craftspeople must do).

Gardner also identified two forms of personal intelligence that are important in a complex modern world. *Interpersonal intelligence* is the ability to understand what motivates other people and how to work with them. Successful salespeople, politicians, teachers, and religious leaders are all likely to possess high interpersonal intelligence. *Intrapersonal intelligence* is the capacity to form an accurate model of oneself and to use that model to function effectively in everyday living.

Gardner argued that these seven intelligences work together (as a system) to solve problems and to yield useful personal and societal outcomes. He suggested that all persons are different because we all have unique combinations of intelligences.

implications for teachers

Gardner's approach to schooling

Schools Gardner questioned the meaningfulness of an education in which there is a core curriculum and a set of facts that everybody should know. He suggested that there should be more adjustment of curriculum and instruction to individuals' combinations of aptitudes. His vision of the ideal school is based on two assumptions: (1) not all people have the same interests and abilities, and we learn in somewhat different ways; (2) no one can learn everything because there is simply too much to learn. Therefore, informed choice is necessary. Gardner called for an individual-centered school that is rich in assessment of individual abilities and proclivities and seeks to match individuals to both curriculum areas and methods of instruction. After a few years of schooling, an attempt would be made to match individuals with various kinds of jobs that are available in their cultures.

Gardner proposed new roles for educators that might make this vision a reality. Assessment specialists would try to understand the abilities and interests that students bring to school. Student curriculum brokers would match students' profiles, goals, and interests to particular curricula and styles of learning. Teachers would be free to do what they are supposed to do—teach subject matter in their preferred style of teaching. The job of master teacher would be demanding and involve supervising and guiding other teachers and making sure that the curriculum was appropriately balanced.

Sternberg's triarchic theory Sternberg (1985) contended that intelligence is composed of three basic parts: *conceptual, creative,* and *contextual.* The conceptual part includes the information processing components used in intelligent thought (e.g., to solve analogies or comprehend text). These conceptual processes are of three basic kinds: **executive processes** are *used to plan what one is going to do, to monitor the strategy, and to evaluate it after a task is completed;* **nonexecutive processes** are *the performance components used to do a task;* and **knowledge-acquisition components** are *learning processes used to figure out how to do a task in the first place.*

Sternberg (1988) argued that the components of intelligence do not operate in a vacuum; rather, they are affected by a person's experience with a task or practical situation. Triarchic theory suggests that good tests of intelligence should measure coping with relative novelty and automatization of information-processing components. Hence, when we confront problems, we should bring a set of well-functioning skills for processing information as well as an ability to adapt to new situations.

In the triarchic theory, information processing is measured in ways similar to strategies used in the cognitive-components approach. Sternberg has developed new and useful techniques for measuring novelty by creating tests of a person's ability to see old problems in new ways or new problems in old ways. He proposed the following example as one way to deal with an individual's ability to respond to novel situations creatively. Rather than presenting only the analogy, "Hero is to admiration as villain is to (a) treachery, (b) contempt, (c) wonder, (d) affection," one can make the analogy more a test of dealing with novelty by adding hypothetical conditions. Individuals might be asked to suppose that villains were lovable, for example: then what would the solution to this problem be?

The third aspect of the triarchic theory is contextual—the application of intelligence to everyday contexts. *Practical intelligence* is essentially what many people refer to as common sense. However, intelligence tests do not measure practical intelligence directly. Sternberg argues that one must distinguish between practical and academic intelligence because it is possible that individuals may be high in one area but not in the other.

Sternberg stresses the need for assessing practical intelligence. This might include recognizing the logical fallacy that is presented in a newspaper or television advertisement or assessing *tacit knowledge*—the informal knowledge one needs to get ahead in specific situations but that rarely is taught explicitly. To assess tacit knowledge one might ask a person to suppose that he or she is in the first year in a new job and has too many activities to get done in the time allocated. The question would require the person to prioritize activities and select which to pursue in the next three weeks.

According to Sternberg, progress has been made in measuring adaptation to everyday environments, but sometimes the best answer to a problem of adjustment is to change the environment to suit oneself. He contended that really successful people—the ones who make a difference in the world—tend to be "shapers" who know what they are good at and try to influence the environment so that they can use these skills in most of their work. They either minimize the importance of their weaknesses or find someone else to compensate for them.

Sternberg argued that both the theory of multiple intelligences and the triarchic theory of intelligence are broader than standard psychometric theories. The psychometric point of view still dominates the testing of both children and adults, although we are beginning to measure intelligence in much more diversified and interesting ways.

cognitive style

Cognitive style refers to the way people process information and use strategies to respond to tasks. Several cognitive-style dimensions have been identified (Sigel & Coop, 1974), including (1) attention to global features versus fine details of stimuli; (2) classification of stimuli into a few large categories versus many small ones; (3) tendency to classify items on the basis of observable characteristics such as similarities in function, time, or space versus common possession of some abstract attribute; (4) quick, impulsive versus slow, painstaking problem-solving behavior; (5) intuitive, inductive versus logical, deductive thinking; and (6) tendency to impose one's own structure on what is perceived versus allowing perceptions to be structured by features of the focal stimulus, influences of the context in which it is embedded, or other external sources.

Inspection of this list reveals why cognitive styles are called styles rather than abilities. They refer to *how* people process information and solve problems, not *how well*. Sometimes they do affect the quality of performance, however, because each style is helpful in performing certain tasks but not others. In this chapter we discuss two cognitive-style dimensions that have some relevancy for education: conceptual tempo (cognitive reflectivity versus cognitive impulsivity) and psychological differentiation (field independence versus field dependence).

conceptual tempo

Conceptual tempo refers to *the degree to which people are cognitively impulsive versus reflective in deciding on a response when two or more alternatives are plausible*. Differences in conceptual tempo are most obvious (and are measured) in matching-to-sample tasks, in which people are shown a drawing of an object or figure and asked to indicate which of several other drawings is identical to the sample. The other drawings are all similar to the sample in varying degrees, but only one is exactly like it.

- **Cognitively impulsive people** are *those who inspect the alternatives briefly and then quickly select one*. They have short response latencies (they respond quickly), but they may make a lot of errors because they do not take the time to compare carefully. Often they do not even inspect all of the alternatives (Kagan & Kogan, 1970), responding instead as soon as they come to one that is not obviously wrong.
- **Cognitively reflective people** are *those who deliberate before responding, carefully considering each alternative*. They take longer to respond but make fewer errors.

When conceptual tempo was first described (Kagan et al., 1964), the emphasis was on speed of response. Since then, it has become clear that other qualitative characteristics that affect accuracy must be considered. In addition to those who are either fast and inaccurate or slow and accurate, some people are both fast and accurate or both slow and inaccurate. Thus, some people respond quickly because they are efficient at a task rather than impulsive in their problem-solving behavior. Also, fast responders—even fast/inaccurate responders—are not necessarily impulsive. Speed of response in matching-to-sample tasks does not correlate consistently with personal traits other than speed of response in other problem-solving situations in which more than one plausible alternative is available (Block, Gjerde, & Block, 1986). Specifically, fast responders are not especially likely to be hyperactive, unable to delay gratification, or otherwise impulsive in the classroom or in everyday life. Thus, the term *cognitively impulsive* is misleading because it connotes general behavioral impulsivity. If anything, individuals who are both fast and inaccurate in problem solving can be described as *anxious* or *defensive* rather than impulsive (Wapner & Connor, 1986). Far from being carefree and unconcerned about making mistakes, they are anxious and vulnerable, so they respond "impulsively" in an attempt to cope with (and to escape from) stressful problem-solving situations.

Conceptual tempo is related to early reading progress (Kagan & Kogan, 1970) and to performance on other school tasks that require careful discrimination of similar yet different stimuli (*p* versus *q*, *if* versus *it*). Students predisposed to notice such fine differences in detail and to withhold interpretation until first impressions are verified are likely to read more accurately than other students.

Differences in conceptual tempo are believed to be shaped by modeling and socialization in the home, although Kagan, Pearson, and Welch (1966) showed that conceptual tempo can be socialized in school as well. They found that cognitively impulsive boys who spent a year in the classroom of a very reflective teacher became notably more reflective themselves. This does not have clear implications for teachers, however, because not all teachers are cognitively reflective and because a reflective conceptual tempo is not always superior to an "impulsive" one. Rollins and Genser (1977) found the reflective tempo to be superior for problem solving in simple tasks that offered only a few plausible response alternatives. In complex tasks involving many dimensions and possible response alternatives, however, "impulsive" responders who moved immediately to consideration of the most likely solutions generally solved faster and with fewer errors than extreme reflectives who tested each possible solution systematically and thus wasted a lot of time examining unlikely solutions.

The point is that success in problem solving is determined by the match between the strategy a person uses and the demands of a task. This can be seen in the results of attempts to modify conceptual tempo. The earliest interventions concentrated on slowing response speed but not on changing children's information processing or problem-solving strategies. Cognitively impulsive children were cautioned to take their time and "pay attention," but they were not directed to attend to anything specific. Typically, they learned to respond more slowly but made just as many errors as before.

Investigators who trained children to use more efficient problem-solving skills obtained much better results. Meichenbaum and Goodman (1971), for example, used a cognitive behavior-modification approach involving modeling and verbalized self-instructions to teach fast/inaccurate responders to talk to themselves to provide guidance during problem solving. The experimenter's modeling stressed not only the importance of responding slowly and carefully but also the actual process:

> I have to remember to go slowly to get it right. Look carefully at this one (*the standard*). Now look at these carefully (*the response alternatives*). Is this one different? Yes, it has an extra leaf. Good, I can eliminate this one. Now, let's look at this one (*another response alternative*). I think it's this one, but let me first check the others.

The modeling also included errors and how to cope with them, a feature that probably was especially valuable for fast/inaccurate responders who tend to be anxious in problem-solving situations:

> It's OK, just be careful. I should have looked more carefully. Follow the plan to check each one. Good, I am going slowly.

Even this explicit modeling was not enough by itself, however, because children exposed only to the modeling learned to respond more slowly but did not improve their accuracy. Only the children who received self-instructional

training in addition to modeling became more accurate problem solvers. These children were trained to perform the task as the experimenter did, giving themselves verbal instructions as they worked. As they began to achieve consistent success, the verbalized self-instructions were reduced to whispering and finally to silent (inner) speech. These results have clear implications for teachers dealing with fast/inaccurate responders or any students whose information processing or problem-solving strategies are inappropriate. Self-instructional training may be especially useful for anxious students who are unlikely to remain calm and rational when they must solve problems on their own. Teacher demonstrations or even extensive modeling may not be enough for these students, who may need opportunities to role-play successful problem-solving strategies by verbalizing self-talk out loud and getting feedback.

Perhaps the key educational value of cognitive style research is its demonstrations that students do use various styles as they approach learning tasks. Thus, as teachers examine students' performance they need to understand that cognitive style also influences how students perform (not just cognitive ability or past achievement).

psychological differentiation

A second cognitive-style dimension with implications for education is *psychological differentiation*, also known as *field dependence versus field independence* or as *global versus analytic perceptual style* (Witkin et al., 1977). People who are low in psychological differentiation (*field dependent*) have difficulty differentiating stimuli from the contexts in which they are embedded, so their perceptions are easily affected by manipulations of the surrounding context. People who are high in psychological differentiation (*field independent*) perceive more analytically. They can separate stimuli from context, so their perceptions are less affected when changes in contexts are introduced.

Psychological differentiation is exhibited in a remarkable variety of situations. One of the most basic is when the stimulus in question is the person's own body. Witkin and colleagues (1962) observed persons seated in specially constructed chairs in rooms that made use of optical illusions to confuse them about directionality and gravity. Field-dependent people were very confused by these situations and did not do well when asked to estimate the degree to which their bodily positions differed from the vertical upright. Some were off as much as forty-five degrees, so that they literally did not know which way was up. Field-independent people were less affected by these manipulations.

Similar results were obtained with the "rod and frame" test. Here, people in a darkened room are presented with a luminous rod that could be tilted in any direction and asked to adjust the rod until it was vertical. To make the task even more difficult, the rod was surrounded by a luminous frame that also could be tilted in any direction. Certain tilts produced optical illusions like those in the "tilted rooms" at amusement parks. Again, field-independent people were more successful than field-dependent people in adjusting the rod to the true vertical and resisting optical illusions.

Psychological differentiation also occurs in cognitive tasks such as embedded-figure tests, in which familiar stimuli are embedded in more complex configurations that mask them ("Can you find five animals in this picture?"). Field-independent people are good at such tasks, but field-dependent people have trouble with them. More generally, field-independent people are likely to impose their own organization on a perceptual field, but field-dependent people tend to adhere to the existing structure. This is true for social perceptions as well as for perceptions of the physical world. Field-dependent people's perceptions and opinions are strongly affected by those of other people, whereas field-independent people are more likely to resist social pressures and make up their minds on the basis of their own perceptions.

The adaptive values of these cognitive styles vary with culture and with the role demands of the situation. In social situations, especially ambiguous ones, field-dependent people are more attentive to and make more use of prevailing social frames of reference, look at the faces of others more frequently for cues as to what they are thinking, attend more to verbal messages with social content, and get physically closer to and interact more with others. In general, they prefer to be with people in social situations (Witkin et al., 1977). As a result, field-dependent people tend to be better liked by others; to be perceived as warm, tactful, considerate, socially outgoing, and affectionate; and to know and be known to more people than are field-independent people. The latter have a more abstract, theoretical, analytical, and impersonal orientation. This makes them more able to resist external pressures toward conformity, but it also makes them more likely to be perceived as cold, distant, or insensitive. These statements apply to people at the extremes of the dimension of psychological differentiation. Most people are not nearly so extreme, although they may tend more toward one set of attributes than the other. (We will return to this issue later.)

Note that neither cognitive style is superior in all situations. Field-independent people are better equipped to deal with situations that call for impersonal analysis, but field-dependent people are better equipped for situations that place a premium on social perceptiveness and interpersonal skills.

implications for teachers

psychological differentiation

Psychological differentiation affects students' preference for, and response to, different teaching methods (Witkin et al., 1977). Field-dependent students tend to prefer to learn in groups and to interact frequently with the teacher, whereas field-independent students may respond better to more independent and individualized learning opportunities. Field-independent students prefer and generally do better in math and science, whereas field-dependent ones generally prefer and do better in the humanities and social sciences. Field-independent people prefer occupations that place a premium on theoretical and analytic interests: mathematician, scientist, architect, engineer, dentist, production manager, carpenter, forest service worker, farmer, mechanic, artist. Field-dependent students tend to choose occupations that stress social skills: social worker, minister, counselor, probation officer, teacher, salesperson, advertising manager, administrator, politician (Witkin et al., 1977).

Within the education profession, field independence is likely among math, science, and industrial-arts teachers, but field dependence is likely among social studies, humanities, or general elementary school teachers (Frank, 1986). *Psychological differentiation affects the ways that teachers instruct.* Field-independent teachers prefer impersonal teaching situations and emphasize the more cognitive or theoretical aspects of teaching, whereas field-dependent teachers prefer frequent interaction with students and class discussion. Field-independent teachers use questions mostly as instructional tools to be used when introducing topics or inducing students to process information, whereas field-dependent teachers use questions primarily to check on student learning following instruction. Field-independent teachers tend to

emphasize their own standards and to formulate principles themselves when explaining material to students, but field-dependent teachers tend to involve students more in organizing the content and to encourage them to formulate principles themselves (Gordon & Gross, 1978; Witkin et al., 1977).

Field-independent teachers are more likely to inform students when they are incorrect, to tell them why they are incorrect, and to express displeasure with those who are performing below capacity. Field-dependent teachers are less likely to criticize. They are interested primarily in creating and maintaining positive attitudes and good group dynamics, and only secondarily in subject content, whereas field-independent teachers have the opposite priorities. Finally, students perceive field-independent teachers as emphasizing application of general principles, but see field-dependent teachers as teaching facts (Witkin et al., 1977).

The psychological differentiation dimension also is associated with learning outcomes. Field independence correlates with mathematics and spatial abilities even when IQ is controlled (Satterly, 1976). More generally, students tend to achieve more in academic subjects that they prefer, and field-independent students do better when matched in cognitive style with their teachers (Garlinger & Frank, 1986; Witkin et al., 1977).

Even so, it is not clear that students or even teachers would be better off if matched so as to reinforce their preferences, especially not if they lie at the extremes of the psychological differentiation dimension. Extreme field independents have social adjustment problems, and extreme field dependents are conforming to the point that they seem to lack minds of their own. Such individuals might be better off in the long run if they could learn to appreciate and function more frequently in their nonpreferred orientation.

Teachers need to learn to recognize and respect both orientations, to build on students' strengths, and to avoid letting stylistic differences lead to discriminatory practices or personality clashes. Field-independent teachers can help meet the needs of field-dependent students by structuring their learning experiences enough to enable them to cope effectively, providing encouragement and praise, being objective and supportive when criticizing mistakes, generally developing a positive personal relationship with them, and using cooperative learning methods.

Field-dependent instructors accustomed to indirect communication that depends on perception of subtle social cues need to be more direct with field-independent students who may not recognize critical feedback unless it is presented explicitly (nor are they likely to resent or become upset by such criticism). Also, field-independent students are not likely to respond strongly or even positively to warmth or praise from the teacher (nor should the teacher feel rejected when this occurs). Finally, it is important that field-dependent teachers respect field-independent students' needs for privacy and distance and that they avoid penalizing these students unreasonably for low social participation.

The value of teacher consideration of students' cognitive styles was shown in a study by Doebler and Eicke (1979). Fifth-grade teachers in the experimental group were given information about their students' field dependence-independence, along with suggested strategies for teaching each type. Compared to students in control classes whose teachers were not given this information, the experimental students developed better self-concepts and attitudes toward school. Teachers usually do not have access to such data, but they should be able to identify students' cognitive styles by observing and interacting with them.

Frank (1984) studied field-independent and field-dependent students' learning of content from taped lectures under four conditions: (1) no notes, (2) student's notes only; (3) outline framework plus student's notes, and (4) complete outline plus student's notes. Frank found that field-independent students performed well under the student's-notes-only condition, because they tended to take efficient notes and to organize them within an outline format. The field-dependent students, however, seemed to need the teacher-provided outline.

Frank contended that the typical classroom procedure in which the teacher lectures and students take notes may favor the performance of field-independent students. To reduce this effect, he suggested that teachers provide students with external aids (e.g., an outline on the board or a handout that organizes the presentation) that may help the field-dependent students without harming the field-independent students.

Meng and Patty (1991) have noted that many students are not field-dependent or field-independent but rather that degree of field-dependence varies. They provide evidence that students' use of organizers varied by student cognitive style (field-dependent, field-independent, and field-intermediate) and by the timing of organizer presentations (before or after instruction). Instruction was most effective for field-dependent students when illustrative advance organizers were used. In contrast, field-intermediate subjects achieved better when illustrative post organizers were used. Field-independent students' achievement was not affected by either type of organizer (perhaps because these students could generate their own structure).

research at work
students' learning styles

Recently there has been great interest in exploring students' learning-style preferences with the expectation that such analyses have educational implications. Research on learning-style preferences involves questions such as the following: Do students like to learn in a noisy environment, with music, or in silence? Do students prefer to learn alone or with others? Do students prefer to listen to information or see information? Do students prefer to learn by studying for frequent short periods or for fewer longer periods?

Some advocates argue strongly that attention to students' learning styles can have important effects on their achievement (Dunn, Beaudry, & Klavas, 1989; McCarthy, 1990; O'Neil, 1990). McCarthy (1990) argues, for example, that students vary on two major continuums: perceiving (sensing/feeling versus thinking) and processing (doing versus watching), so they can be located in one of four major learning styles.

- *Imaginative learners* perceive information concretely and process it reflectively. They listen, share, and seek to integrate school experience with self-experience.
- *Analytic learners* perceive information abstractly and process it reflectively. They appreciate both details and ideas, tend to think sequentially, and value ideas more than people.

- *Common sense learners* perceive information abstractly and process it actively. They tend to be pragmatic learners who value concrete problem solving. They like to "tinker" and experiment.
- *Dynamic learners* perceive information concretely and process it actively. They tend to integrate experience and application and are enthusiastic about new learning. They are ready to engage in trial-and-error learning and are adept at risk taking.

McCarthy argued that by using the four typologies, teachers can accommodate instruction by building on students' strengths. However, she noted that such information also can be used to help students to "stretch" and function in learning modes that they use infrequently.

We think that such ideas can stimulate teacher reflection (i.e., realizing that school tasks, if not varied, will have considerably more appeal for some students than others). However, we suspect that students vary in multiple ways so that it is not possible to rely on only a few dimensions when designing instruction. For example, a student who has a history of poor achievement in mathematics and who is a dynamic learner may have quite different needs from a dynamic learner who has a history of success in mathematics.

Recent research has called into question the bipolar value-free characteristic of field-dependence theory (i.e., that these styles are different but equally effective). For example, Davis (1991) reports two recent research studies that challenge the view that field-dependent students are better at learning social information. However, in both cases, the dependent measures focused on social information rather than use of social informa-

research at work
multiple abilities

Curry (1990) noted that research and development on learning styles have suffered from three major problems.

- Confusing and incomplete definitions (e.g., some may define a particular trait as initiative, whereas someone else labels it as aggression)
- Poor reliability and questionable validity
- Weak classroom treatments (failure to identify creative alternative ways of representing curriculum and instruction—i.e., actual changes in classrooms have been superficial in this research)

Curry also noted that many studies have shown that matching on the basis of learning style had no effect on achievement. According to Curry, even when positive findings have been reported, the results may have been due to factors other than the matching of learning style and learning assignment.

- Most learning-style theorists have not distinguished their constructs and measures from measures of intelligence. Hence, results may be due to intelligence, not to learning styles.
- The concepts of individual differences and adaptive education have had a long history in educational research and practice (see Corno & Snow, 1986). Creative and competent teachers have been individualizing instruction for many years. Thus, if needed adjustments were simple interventions, they would have been identified a long time ago.
- Instructional alignment (closer association between teacher goals, classroom instruction, and assessment of methods) may account for the greater achievement. Thus, it is possible to argue that effects occur because of more precision in teaching, not because of matching per se.

---

tion or social perceptions (see Frank & Noble, 1985; Marx & Winne, 1987). There is growing evidence that field-independent learners are generally more efficient than field-dependent learners, especially in situations that have high-information processing demands (Davis, 1991). Frank and Keene (1993) note that there is growing empirical evidence "that field-independent learners actively process information and have strong cognitive restructuring skills, whereas field-dependent learners display a more passive, spectator approach to learning in which they rely on the immediate characteristics of the learning task" (pp. 23-24).

matching instruction

Various student abilities and dispositions other than cognitive differentiation have been examined for their importance in designing instruction. Students' *conceptual level* is one of these variables. A student at a high conceptual level can see many sides of an issue, can tolerate ambiguity, and can think abstractly. Students who operate at a low conceptual level tend to focus on one set of ideas and to see concepts and issues as one-dimensional rather than multifaceted. Thus, high-conceptual-level students might perform better under relatively unstructured techniques (discovery), whereas low-conceptual level students might perform better under more didactic instruction.

Some empirical studies support such a prediction. Siegel and Siegel (1965) identified fact-oriented and concept-oriented students who were enrolled in a college biology course and given study sessions that included quizzes on factual or conceptual information. Students with high general ability showed an interaction between instruction and performance on a final exam that contained both types of questions. That is, conceptually oriented students did better on the final exam when their study sections were conceptually driven, and factually oriented students did better when their study sessions focused on factual material. Again, these interactions were obtained only for students high in general ability or prior knowledge. It seems that unless students have sufficient knowledge or ability, style preferences are secondary to knowledge considerations.

In similar research, Pask and Scott (1972, 1973) identified students as "serialist" or "wholist" on the basis of their performance on a learning task. The wholists attempted to organize all information logically and to focus on the whole situation and on higher-order relations. Thus, wholist students had many of the characteristics of high-conceptual-level students. In contrast, serialists tended to remember information in lists and to focus on relatively lower order relations (hence, a low conceptual orientation). The researchers found that students mastered more material when the method of instruction matched their cognitive style.

According to Mayer (1987), because some students score better on tests of visual ability and others score better on tests of verbal abilities, some students could be classified as visual processors and others as verbal processors. One might expect visual processors do better when given visual instruction (videotapes of experiments, diagrams, etc.). Despite the simple logic of the argument, Mayer (1987) noted that the evidence is not very compelling that verbal

processors do better when given verbal instruction and that visual processors do better when given visual instruction.

Part of the issue may be that multiple abilities are commonly called for in any task. For example, both verbal and visual abilities are required to some extent when students are watching films and when students are working in small groups discussing geometric shapes. When students are learning a concept, many factors other than the primary way in which the material is presented must be considered (Cronbach & Snow, 1977; Mayer, 1987). For example, a high visual learner who is presented with a visual task in which his or her prior knowledge of the concept involved in the task is limited is quite different from a visual learner who has considerable expertise and knowledge of the concept.

It is clear that cognitive style is one dimension on which teachers can plan for individual differences in students. Teachers, however, need to use cognitive-style information as stimulation for thinking about individuals rather than as a basis for treating students as groups (Good & Stipek, 1984; Messick, 1984).

Others have reached similar conclusions. For example, according to Mayer (1987):

> It seems premature to advocate the development of separate instructional programs for students with different learning styles. In short, the current results do not warrant the development of one comprehensive program for one type of student and a different type of comprehensive program for another type of student. Instead, teachers should be sensitive to the idea that, for a given instructional domain, not all students learn in the same way. (p. 501)

Numerous educators have attempted to measure learning styles (Dunn, 1987; Gregorc,

1982; Keefe, 1982), and several instruments are available for doing so (Dunn, Dunn, & Price, 1984; Keefe & Monk, 1986; Renzulli & Smith, 1978). Although the idea of assessing learning styles and accommodating student preferences is attractive, evidence does not support the enthusiasm that many advocates have expressed. Various educators have noted the lack of evidence on reliability and validity (Snider, 1990). Also, there is increasing recognition that accommodating to preferences may not maximize learning in the long run, and that many students can benefit from developing new (and eventually perhaps more powerful) ways of learning.

Others who have examined the research evidence have reached conclusions similar to Curry's. For example, Stahl (1989) noted that although the idea of matching style and instruction is appealing, the research base supporting the idea is not well established. Some research has shown that basing instruction on student preferences may result in lower student achievement (Strom, Hocevar, & Zimmer, 1990). Although there are some encouraging developments in research on individual differences in students' reactions to particular types of instruction (Snow & Swanson, 1992; Whitener, 1989), students react in complex ways and there is no single simple system for adjusting instruction.

creativity

Most of us value and can recognize creativity when we encounter it, but it is difficult to define and measure (Glover, Ronning, and Reynolds, 1989). Thus, part of the problem of exploring creativity is that it is a complicated, multi-faceted concept. Further, people can be creative in many, varied ways (Baer, 1993; Davis, 1989). For example, some people may be creative in their professional life but not in their personal life. Many writers argue that creativity is part of (or the same as) general

intelligence, but contrasts in the creative achievements of people with equal IQs dispute this (MacKinnon, 1962). Creativity is associated with IQ, but IQ tests do not measure it directly (Hattie & Rogers, 1986; Sternberg, 1986a, 1986b, 1988).

Guilford (1959) provided a perspective on creativity in his model of mental abilities that he believed collectively form a map or structure of intelligence. Included in the model is a list of mental operations, of which one is basic to what many investigators mean by the creativity process (see Figure 20.1). Guilford contended that information retrieval from memory storage can involve two kinds of operations—convergent production or divergent production. **Convergent production** *involves searching for specific information to solve a problem that requires a single, logically necessary, correct answer* (If Mary is taller than Sally and Sally is taller than Gwen, who is the tallest?). In contrast, **divergent production** *is required for problems that can be answered in many different and equally acceptable ways* (What can we do with a pencil besides use it for writing? How can we make ancient history meaningful to today's students?).

Guilford (1959) determined that creativity involves divergent thinking, as represented by the fluency, flexibility, and originality of thought processes. Individuals high in ideational fluency produce a great many problem-solving ideas in a short time. Those high in flexibility can shift easily from the problem-solving approach they have been using if new problems or conditions call for new approaches. Individuals high in originality can make unusual or even unique suggestions. Thus, highly creative individuals can generate ideas at a rapid pace (fluency), "break set" in order to attack problems from a new perspective (flexibility), and generate new and genuinely different ideas (originality). (For an extended discussion of recent research on divergent thinking, see Baer, 1993.)

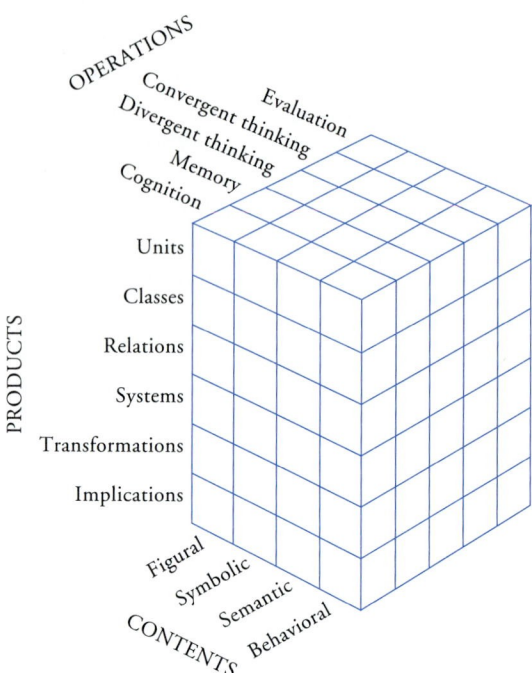

Figure 20.1 Guilford's model of the structure of the intellect. Guilford identifies five basic mental operations: cognition, memory, divergent thinking, convergent thinking, and evaluation. Each of these operations can process each of four kinds of content (behavioral, semantic, symbolic, and figural), and each of these twenty combinations of mental operations with content categories can produce any of six kinds of mental products: units, classes, relations, systems, transformations, and implications. Creativity tests call for divergent thinking, usually to produce transformation of figural or symbolic content.

SOURCE: From J. Guilford, "Three Faces of Intellect." *American Psychologist*, 1959, *14*, 469–479. Copyright © 1959 by the American Psychological Association. Reprinted by permission of the publisher and author.

measures of creativity

Torrance (1966, 1990) has developed a variety of tests for measuring divergent thinking. They include generating unusual uses for a box or a brick, completing an ambiguous partial sketch by turning it into an interesting picture, and

suggesting how a stuffed animal might be improved to make it more interesting to play with. Responses to these tasks are scored for fluency, flexibility, and originality.

These tests have low but significant correlations with IQ, averaging about 0.20 (Torrance, 1975). In general, there is a closer relationship between divergent production ability and IQ at the lower levels of the IQ range than at the higher levels; that is, individuals with low IQs generally do not score very well on divergent production tests. People who score highly on such tests usually have at least average IQs, but a high IQ does not guarantee high divergent production ability.

Wallach and Kogan (1965) discovered that the relationship between IQ and scores on so-called creativity tests varies with the test used. Moderate or even high correlations with IQ may occur if a "creativity test" has a time limit and includes convergent production tasks in addition to divergent production tasks. On the other hand, if the "creativity test" is confined to divergent production tasks, and if testing is conducted under relaxed or playful conditions, the relationships between fluency, flexibility, and originality scores and IQs drop almost to zero.

Getzels and Jackson (1962) were early leaders in exploring the relationship between divergent thinking, intelligence, and creative performance. Within a sample composed primarily of extremely bright students, they noted some striking differences between those highest in IQ but low in divergent thinking and those highest in divergent thinking but lower in IQ. The following excepts are responses to a stimulus card showing a man seated in an airplane and another showing a man alone in an office.

A low-divergent thinking student: "Mr. Smith is on his way home from a successful business trip. He is very happy and he is thinking about his wonderful family and how glad he will be to see them again. He can picture it, about an

research at work
teachers and student creativity

Mayer (1989a) argued that teachers can help students to develop their creative talents. He suggested that the following factors are useful to consider.

- The material to be presented must be potentially meaningful—it is one thing to memorize a list of the causes of the Civil War but another to try to understand how "Northerners" and "Southerners" viewed the causes of the war.
- Students must possess relevant prior knowledge if they are to engage in active thinking. It is difficult to speculate creatively about the reasons for the Civil War if one does not understand the eco-

nomic and political conditions that preceded it.

- The instructional material needs to be designed to encourage students to use active learning processes. For example, providing analogical models is one strategy for helping students to link current instruction to what they already know, whereas the provision of colorful background scenes is not (i.e., making the learning stimulus salient).
- Evaluation of learning should stress application and creative thought. Students should be asked to transfer and to use knowledge to solve problems, not to generate memorized lists.

hour from now, his plane landing at the airport and Mrs. Smith and their three children all there welcoming him home again."

A high-divergent thinking student: "This man is flying back from Reno where he has won a divorce from his wife. He couldn't stand to live with her anymore, he told the judge, because she wore so much cold cream on her face at night that her head would skid across the pillow. He's now contemplating a new skid-proof face cream."

A low-divergent thinking student: "There's ambitious Bob down at the office at 6:30 in the morning. Every morning it's the same. He's trying to show his boss how energetic he is. Now, thinks Bob, maybe

the boss will give me a raise for all my extra work. The trouble is that Bob has been doing this for the last three years, and the boss still hasn't given him a raise. He'll come in at 9:00, not even noticing that Bob has been there so long, and poor Bob won't get his raise."

A high-divergent thinking student: "This man has just broken into this office of a new cereal company. He is a private eye employed by a competitive firm to find out the formula that makes the cereal bend, sag, and sway. After a thorough search of the office he comes upon what he thinks is the current formula. It turns out that it is the wrong formula and the competitor's factory blows up. Poetic justice!" (Getzels & Jackson, 1962, pp. 39–40)

Getzels and Csikszentmihalyi (1975) have stressed that the high-divergent students could free themselves from the stimulus, but the low-divergent students were fixated by it.

> For the low-divergent students the problem was essentially one of following up on what others had given them. If the picture stimulus is of a man in an airplane, he tells a story about travel . . . For the high-divergent thinking subject, the problem was one of constructing something that he wants to give. The picture may be of a man in an airplane, but the story he wants to tell is about a divorce. (p. 99)

Such differences have led Getzels and Csikszentmihalyi to view creativity as *problem finding* more than as *problem solving*.

v a l i d a t i o n   o f   c r e a t i v i t y   t e s t s

Torrance, Tan, and Allman (1970) reported that undergraduate teacher trainees who scored higher on situational tests of creativity demonstrated more creative teaching behavior in the classroom six years later. Predictive validity studies of Torrance's creativity tests are supportive but not decisive. They predict achievement in areas such as writing better than in fields such as business (Torrance, 1975), perhaps because the tests best measure verbal fluency.

There is still little evidence that situational creativity measures can predict creative and original performance later in life. At present, it appears that such measures do *not* predict creative performance among adult professionals, although they usually correlate positively (but weakly) with indicators of creativity in nonprofessional endeavors (Mansfield, Busse, & Krepelka, 1978).

What, then, is **creativity**? Although there is no universally accepted definition, two criteria are widely accepted. *First, a product must be novel if it is to be called creative. The second criterion is value.* A creative product must reflect value by being judged correct (a technical solution works) or good (the music is satisfying). Additional criteria have been proposed, but novelty and value are the two most general standards.

i m p l i c a t i o n s   f o r   t e a c h e r s

f o s t e r i n g   c r e a t i v i t y   i n   t h e   c l a s s r o o m

How can teachers foster creativity in the classroom? Probably the first step is to *learn to value it*. Nearly everyone values the abstract concept of creativity, but student creativity in the classroom can be irritating, disruptive, or even threatening to teachers. Getzels and Jackson (1962) found that teachers preferred students low in divergent thinking to those higher in divergent thinking, even though all of the students were bright and even though the divergent thinkers produced more imaginative and original responses. This is not really surprising. Schools are inherently rule-bound and conservative institutions (necessarily, to a degree), so much student creativity contrasts or even conflicts with what is routine, expected, and "correct." If students are urged to think and act creatively, some of their responses will be both novel and valuable, but others will be silly, obscene, outrageous, or bizarre. Teachers who intend to foster creativity must accept this.

Clues about factors that may foster creativity have been gathered in retrospective reports of the childhood experiences of creative adults, who typically report being exposed to a rich variety of experiences as children and being encouraged to ask questions and test their ideas thorough active experimentation. Also, they usually were encouraged to pursue their interests thorough collections, hobbies, development of specialized knowledge, or pursuit of talents or skills (Wallach, 1970).

Torrance (1962) included such ideas in his recommendations for developing creativity in the classroom and added several others: encourage manipulation of objects and ideas, teach students to test their ideas systematically, teach students to value creative thinking, caution against premature or unwarranted dismissal of "wild" ideas, teach students that everyone has creative potential (creativity is not something possessed only by a few "geniuses"), and induce creative thinking by asking students to generate alternative solutions to problems, to speculate on what might have happened if historical events had been different, to suggest worthwhile inventions or improvements, or to solve other problems that call on their divergent production abilities.

Note that most of these suggestions can be incorporated into the regular school curriculum without special materials or the scheduling of special "creativity time." Teachers can learn to do many of these things automatically by habitually asking themselves, when planning activities and assignments, "Have I included opportunities for students to think and solve problems in connection with this topic? Have I included opportunities for them to use their divergent production abilities?" The result of this should be teacher behavior like that described above, as well as assignments involving creative writing or action projects requiring research and development of a sophisticated (for the student) product.

Special programs designed to facilitate divergent thinking or other aspects of creativity are available. The *Productive Thinking Program* (Covington et al., 1974) is a self-instructional program for fifth and sixth graders. It attempts to develop creative problem-solving abilities and attitudes through booklets that teach problem-solving skills in a cartoon format.

Many of the problems involve convergent thinking, but some involve divergent thinking as well. Evaluations suggest that the program improves student performance on tests of divergent thinking, although best results are obtained when teachers instruct students rather than distribute the materials for use in self-instruction, as the developers intended (Mansfield, Busse, & Krepelka, 1978).

Parnes (1967) developed a program that emphasizes a technique called **brainstorming**—*generating ideas in response to some question or problem (typically in a group)*. Students are encouraged to volunteer whatever ideas occur to them, regardless of whether the ideas seem reasonable or correct. Ideas are recorded for later evaluation, but no criticism is permitted until after everyone's ideas have been contributed. The Parnes program is used mostly in college and high school courses, where it has been generally successful in increasing divergent thinking scores. Subsequently Parnes developed The Creative Studies Project, which was organized around a semester-long course for freshmen that focused on awareness, creative problem solving, and creative analysis. See Parnes (1987) for a systematic account of the program and its subsequent effects on students' academic and career performance.

Myers and Torrance (1966) developed sets of workbooks designed to foster creativity in elementary school children. Their approach involves teaching students to value creative thinking and provides practice in a variety of divergent production tasks. It may be useful in improving divergent-thinking ability, especially when teachers guide students in the use of workbooks, although no clear data are yet available (Mansfield, Busse, & Krepelka, 1978).

Davis (1986) has developed a variety of methods for teaching students to think creatively. In one study, college students were asked to think of improvements for a doorknob. Three methods of encouraging creative thinking were tested, two of which proved effective. One group was given a list of seventy-three possible ways to make changes. This method was not very effective, apparently because students did not try to think creatively but instead simply worked their way through the list, following as many of the suggestions as they could. Most of the creative thinking had already been done for them.

A second group received lists containing only seven suggestions: add or subtract something, change color, change the material, rearrange the parts, change shapes, change size, change design or style. This short list effectively stimulated creative thinking in that the students produced about twice as many ideas as those with the long list or those who received no suggestions. The list was specific enough to stimulate a variety of ideas but not so complete as to inhibit creativity.

The group that produced the most ideas, however, used a matrix or checkerboard technique that involved analyzing the stimulus into its various dimensions and then combining the values of these dimensions into new arrangements. To generate new solutions to the energy crisis, for example, one axis of a two-dimensional checkerboard matrix could be the source of power (wind, solar, ocean tides, geothermal). Each of these power sources could be combined with ideas arranged along another axis indicating uses for the power (heating homes, transportation, cooking, manufacturing). Cross-referencing these two lists produces novel combinations that stimulate creative thinking. In this vein, ideas about changing doorknobs might be stimulated by combining consideration of where the knob is placed on the door with various lock arrangements (deadbolt

versus spring lock versus no lock at all; key versus no key). Students using this method produced more ideas for the doorknob problem than students in any other group, even though they did not work as long as students using the short list of seven suggestions. Thus, different approaches affected fluency (rate of idea generation), although there were no significant group differences in the originality of ideas.

New creativity training programs and materials appear regularly. Torrance (1987) provides a systematic account of many diverse programs that have attempted to enhance student creativity and the effects of such training on students' attitudes and performance. Most have at least some value in that students usually enjoy them and find them stimulating. However, it is questionable whether such programs actually produce any genuine, lasting, or generalizable improvements in creative-thinking abilities (c.f. Parnes, 1987; Torrance, 1987). Results are mixed, and even supportive results involve scores on tests of divergent production rather than more rigorous criteria such as evidence of increased creativity in schoolwork or in everyday life. Furthermore, higher divergent production scores can be due to increased persistence on criterion tests by students who know that they are expected to perform well, to the advantages provided by training on tasks that are very similar to the items on the tests, or even to improved attitudes or confidence.

The last factor may be the most important. Manske and Davis (1968) found that students gave more original responses to problems when they were merely instructed to be original and more practical responses when they were instructed to be practical. Wallach and Kogan (1965) concluded that students who were intelligent but not highly creative were merely disinclined, rather than unable, to use their imaginations. Many students' barriers to creative thinking reside solely in their own minds: social inhibition, fear of failure, lack of confidence, or even the belief that they lack creativity (Davis, 1986). Similarly, students may not respond with creativity because they are either satisfied or have no interest in a particular issue (today's mousetrap is OK!). If this is true, student creativity may be fostered most effectively not by special training programs (although they may be useful) but by teachers who model and encourage creativity every day and create a classroom atmosphere that values originality and playful consideration of ideas.

Recent work on creativity has focused on domain specific creativity (e.g., Glover, Ronning, & Reynolds (1989). The Glover team's work provides information about problem solving in domains such as writing, social science, reader response to literature, and so on. It is plausible that more powerful effects will be obtained in the future by the use of programs that integrate general approaches with subject-matter-specific approaches.

implications for teachers

maintaining and enhancing creativity

As Amabile (1987) notes, students may approach a writing task with various motivational patterns. Some patterns are primarily intrinsic (self-motivated) such as when one feels relaxed when writing, finds pleasure in expressing one's views in a clear articulate fashion, or enjoys reading one's own writing and attempts to play with words. Other reasons are more extrinsic (done because of external reasons), including enjoyment of public recognition, awareness that writing ability is helpful in obtaining a good job or entering graduate school. Her research and review of related research show that social constraints can reduce creativity in important ways. Amabile suggests that it is easier to kill creativity by external constraints than it is to increase or create it. Some of the factors that she finds counterproductive include:

- Not giving students (or employees, etc.) sufficient choice in selecting tasks—students who have more intrinsic motivation are typically more creative than students who are externally motivated

- Excessive concern with external evaluation, more so as students become older (according to research on well-known creative scholars)
- Excessive surveillance; constant or frequent questions from someone which may detract from the task to a focus on pleasing the person
- Rewards, by lowering intrinsic motivation and, subsequently, creative performance
- Competition (though the picture is complex because there is some evidence that competition is helpful in some contexts—specifically, there is evidence that group competition may enhance creative effort, at least in the short run)
- Restricted choice (imposing specific techniques for solving a problem; limited or no choice in task selection lowers intrinsic motivation; limited choice in how to proceed on a task or problem is especially detrimental)
- Unreasonable time pressures which appear to reduce intrinsic motivation.

Teachers and school districts vary in how much they emphasize developing creativity. Schools have many goals, and much important learning does not involve creativity per se. We believe that most teaching and learning should be directed at meaningful understanding and recognition of the application value of material that is understood. Although intelligent and thoughtful understanding is always the goal, an original or new response is not always required. You need to help students understand the type of performance expected of them. When you want students to use and perhaps develop their creativity without undermining intrinsic motivation, you need to (1) allow them to select tasks as much as possible; (2) minimize unneeded process accountability, rewards, and competition; (3) allow students considerable latitude in how they will develop and exhibit their ideas; and (4) provide students with sufficient time for conceptualization, reflection, and adaptation.

summary

Informal teacher assessments of students' academic aptitudes may be supplemented by standardized intelligence and achievement tests. Binet developed a test to measure abilities related to school success, but American and British psychologists later established the notion of a single IQ score based on a number of questionable assumptions. The Stanford-Binet and Wechsler scales are reliable and well-validated as predictors of school success, but they do not measure any single, easily definable ability. Also, although IQ scores predict school achievement, they are not powerful predictors of accomplishments beyond school graduation. Finally, even though there is a strong genetic component, scores vary widely with time and other variables over a considerable range.

Intelligence tests have value as predictors of academic performance and may be especially useful for identifying potential that is currently masked by disadvantaged home backgrounds or difficulties with the English language. However, intelligence tests can also be used simply to label students without helping them deal with their problems, or to help students from disadvantaged home backgrounds or those who have difficulty with the English language.

Current work in intelligence testing emphasizes the variety of human abilities and the need to consider the processes that people use in responding to problems along with the outcomes of their problem-solving efforts. Gardner identified seven forms of intelligence and advocated that schools be organized to foster the development of all seven types and to respond to individual differences in patterns. Sternberg developed a triarchic theory of intelligence and called for assessment and follow-up that would consider the conceptual, creative, and contextual aspects of intellectual functioning. Other investigators are concerned with developing measures of practical or social intelligence to complement the paper-and-pencil measures that have been emphasized to date.

Scholars are increasingly recognizing that intelligence is not fixed and that rich environments and appropriate experience foster enhanced capacity for intelligent problem-solving. Gregory (1987) distinguished between kinetic intelligence and potential intelligence. From this theoretical perspective, knowledge and intelligence are always aggregated. Cattell (1943) distinguished fluid and crystallized intelligence. Some educators have contended that much teaching in today's schools emphasizes discrete facts over the application of an integrated knowledge base (fluid intelligence).

Cognitive style and creativity involve elements of both cognition and personality. They refer to how people process information and solve problems, not how well they do so. Conceptual tempo is a cognitive-style dimension dealing with impulsivity versus reflectivity in choosing between two or more plausible alternatives. Psychological differentiation is a second dimension involving field dependence versus field independence or global versus analytical perceptual style. Both dimensions have implications for students' preferences for and responses to different learning situations, as well as for teachers' approaches to teaching.

Creativity is difficult to define or measure. It is associated with IQ, but IQ tests do not measure it directly. Elements such as divergent production, fluency, flexibility, and originality are involved. Guilford, Torrance, and Getzels and Jackson have done extensive work in the area, but valid and reliable tests of creativity—with strong predictive validity—have yet to be developed.

Teachers can foster student creativity in several ways. Valuing creativity and accepting divergent thinking are critical, as is the provision of a wide variety of experiences and opportunities for students to use creative talents. Activities such as brainstorming, searching for novel solutions to problems, and dealing with several dimensions of a problem simultaneously appear to have value as well. Further, students need opportunities to select tasks and have sufficient time for conceptualization, reflection, and adaptation when they are expected to produce creative products.

questions for reflection

1. If a parent asked you to tell them what an IQ score means, how would you respond?

2. Under what circumstances, if any, would you request IQ testing for a student? Why? How would you use the results?

3. Is it possible for a student to do well in school as measured both by teachers' grades and by standardized achievement scores, and yet show no gain in IQ?

4. What is the difference between potential and kinetic knowledge? How does knowledge per se relate to intelligence?

5. As a teacher, when should you teach to a student's strength (in a way that matches the student's cognitive style)? When should a student be required to learn in a way that forces the student to develop new skills (e.g., require a field-independent student to work in a group)?

6. Some students having problems learning to read make errors because of cognitive impulsivity; others make errors because of more serious deficiencies in perception or memory. How can teachers distinguish these types of students?

7. Why is it not enough to teach cognitively impulsive students to slow down and take their time before responding?

8. Although psychologists are unable to define and measure creativity satisfactorily, most people think they know what the word means and can recognize creativity when they see it. How do you define creativity? What are some of the things that indicate it?

9. Do you think of creativity as a genetic trait, as an ability that is learned but not teachable, or as something that is teachable?

10. What implications does this have for your teaching?

11. Would you supplement the regular curriculum with special activities designed to foster creativity? Why or why not?

12. Summarize in your own words how field-dependent students differ from field-independent students. What does this imply about your teaching?

cases to consider

mental mathematics and estimation Jane Keystone is a sixth-grade mathematics teacher who works in a large, departmentalized school where she teaches five math classes a day. She stresses that mathematics does not merely involve obtaining correct answers but is also a way to organize information quantitatively so that decisions can be made. Her instruction is similar to that of other teachers, except that every day she takes fifteen minutes for mental mathematics and work on estimation. Which students are most likely to benefit from Jane's teaching? Why? How can Jane adjust instruction so that more students can benefit?

drill Royal Grind wants to make sure that his junior high English students know their grammar, so most class time is devoted to workbook exercises (underline the right word, cross out the wrong word, correct the misspelled words) and diagraming sentences. Students work individually, and Royal spends much of this time correcting their papers. What changes could he introduce that would still allow him to stress grammar but introduce elements that would be more appealing to field-dependent students and would allow all students to make more use of their creativity?

chapter **21.**

socioeconomic status, cultural, and gender differences

objectives

When you have mastered the material in this chapter, you will be able to

1. Describe differences between high- and low-socioeconomic-status (SES) families in the cognitive environments created for children
2. Discuss how structural variables (community resources) affect students' progress
3. Describe the key features of the type of teaching that is most successful with disadvantaged students
4. Discuss assimilationist and cultural pluralist positions and their implications for educational practice. Understand the value of cultural diversity and language and how school experiences can help to integrate home and school cultures
5. Describe how ethnic minorities' academic performance of is affected by cultural expectations
6. Describe how females' and males' academic performance is affected by cultural expectations
7. Explain how teacher praise and criticism might differentially affect females and males and the implications for improving the classroom performance of both groups
8. Understand and be able to explain why cultural expectations in learning are relatively more important than biology in determining differences between students who differ in gender or culture in reading and mathematics performance

socioeconomic status (ses)

Among individual difference variables used to describe particular students or even entire school populations, the most important may be socioeconomic status (SES) and social class. The two terms are often used interchangeably, but they are defined and measured differently.

- **SES** is *an individual or group status based upon educational level, financial wealth, quality of housing, place of residence, and occupational level.* SES is a cold, impersonal statistic compiled from indices such as type of occupation, years of education, size of income, quality of housing, and desirability of neighborhood.
- **Social class,** usually defined in a more personal way, *ascribes high or low status to individuals and is a more subjective measure than SES, expressing local prestige and respectability.* Persons are high in social class to the extent that people in their community describe them as respectable, influential, or prestigious (Mueller & Parcel, 1981).

Both SES and social class are "proxy" variables that represent a complex of intercorrelated attributes that partially describe people and are useful for making educated guesses about them but do not substitute for detailed information about the individual. We use the term "SES" in this book because it is more objectively measured, although we usually intend it to refer to lifestyle variables associated more closely with the term "social class" than with variables such as income.

All of the variables mentioned above, along with race, ethnicity, and various religious, political, and social customs, tend to correlate together into clusters (Blau, 1981; Yando, Seitz, & Zigler, 1979). No single SES variable causes all of the others in any simple way, but the educational level of parents is probably the most basic because the other variables lose most of their power for predicting things such as student achievement once the educational level of the parents is statistically controlled (Hess, 1970; Stevenson et al., 1978). In any case, parental education level is especially important to teachers because it is linked to parental interest in and attitudes toward education (Laosa, 1982).

Parents who are well educated generally value education and expect their children to become well educated, too. They usually show interest in their children's progress and in meeting and collaborating with teachers, and they typically volunteer, participate in PTA and fund-raising activities, and help supervise field trips. The situation is different with low-SES parents. Many quit or were expelled before finishing high school, and most of the rest ended their schooling at high school graduation. Most of them know the value of education and want their children to go as far as possible (Hess, 1970), but few are knowledgeable about schools or accustomed to dealing with them. Many are awed or even afraid when faced with the prospect of talking to teachers. Often these parents had difficult times themselves as students, so they look upon teachers with a mixture of respect for their expertise and authority (as they see it) and discomfort or even resentment based on fear, mistrust, or hostility. For these reasons, and because they often have less leisure time and less flexible schedules, low-SES parents tend to have fewer interactions with teachers. Thus, teachers may need to assume a special role in communicating with low-SES parents and finding ways that they can participate in school-related activities. In addition to apprehension about coming to school, many low-SES parents and guardians have inflexible work schedules that make it difficult, if not impossible, to come to the school during the day.

Even so, most low-SES parents value education highly, including most of those who are uncomfortable around schools and teachers. They tend to be both grateful and cooperative if teachers establish themselves as people devoted to their children's best interests (and not as authority figures threatening to expel these children).

the disadvantaged

People at the lowest SES levels are often referred to as "the disadvantaged." In our view, there has been too much emphasis on the problems and difficulties of these people (which are clearly real and not likely to go away in the immediate future) and not enough on their potential (also real but relatively unfulfilled as yet). Too often, being labeled as disadvantaged results in being written off as lost causes rather than receiving special, effective treatment likely to enable them to succeed at school. Educators also recognize this issue—overreaction to deficiencies—in other areas as well (e.g., when students have limited English proficiency) (Casanova & Arias, 1993).

It is worth noting who the disadvantaged are and how they got to be that way. According to economic indicators, about 20 percent of the population is disadvantaged because they are on welfare or have inadequate incomes. In terms of race and urban versus rural status, the majority of disadvantaged families are white and a large proportion are rural. So much attention has been focused on urban African-Americans that many people think terms like "disadvantaged" refer primarily to this group. It is true that a greater percentage of blacks than whites is disadvantaged, but it is also true that this percentage is a minority of the total number of disadvantaged.

The term "educationally disadvantaged" is defined in various ways. **Educationally disadvantaged** students are *students who have been exposed to insufficient educational experience, either in the school, home, or community*. However, the number of disadvantaged students in U.S. schools is certain to increase in the coming years. According to one research team, "Some students will have suffered from a lack of appropriate formal educational experiences, others will have suffered from a lack of intellectual experiences in the family, and still others will have suffered from a lack of educational experiences in the community" (Natriello, McDill, and Pallas, 1990, p. 13).

Although figures vary according to their source (and the assumptions authors make), educators agree that teachers in the 1990s (and beyond) will face a more diverse population of students than any previous group of teachers. Ross and Smith (1992) indicate that in the fifteen largest school districts, minority enrollments range from 70 percent to 96 percent, and that 20 percent of American students live in families earning less than the official government poverty rate.

Casanova and Arias (1993) note that, using conservative estimates, in 1990 about 32 millon people aged five and over spoke a language other than English in their homes. According to Natriello and colleagues (1990), between 1988 and 2020 the number of Hispanic children under age eighteen will triple and the population of African-American youth under eighteen will increase by 9 percent. At the same time, the number of white students under eighteen is expected to decline by about 27 percent. Some experts (e.g., Vobeda, 1992) estimate that Asian-Americans will be the fastest growing group.

The projected change in the composition of the school-age population suggests a substantial rise in the percentage of educationally disadvantaged students (Natriello et al., 1990). Unfortunately, racial and ethnic group status are correlated with other indicators of educational disadvantage. Assuming a continuing relationship between race and poverty, as the proportion of ethnic minority children increases, more children living in poverty will attend public schools. Although new intervention programs (food programs, job training, educational programs, etc.) may reduce the relationship between socioeconomic status and educational progress, the number of educationally disadvantaged students will still grow, and the total student population will become more diverse.

For a time, it was thought that SES differences could be eliminated entirely through educational enrichment, especially during the first few years of life. A few still take this position, but most experts do not believe that SES differences can be eliminated through any quick and easy method. Thus, Head Start, Chapter 1, and other education-related programs aimed at the disadvantaged no longer are expected to eliminate SES differences in IQ, although they are considered helpful because of their health and nutrition benefits and because they facilitate school achievement and ultimately educational attainment (Lazar & Darlington, 1982).

The disadvantaged are often stereotyped as having values and attitudes contrary to "middle-class values," although this is not the case. To the extent that disadvantaged parents fail to nurture their children's intellectual development or mental health, this typically is not because they do not mean well or do not want the same kinds of things for their children that other parents want. The major difference between disadvantaged and advantaged parents is that the former lack the knowledge that would enable them to obtain things they want (Hess, 1970).

Furthermore, relevant knowledge and experience, not financial resources, determine the cognitive environment a home provides (Clark, 1983; Sigel, 1985). **Cognitive environment** is the *intellectual stimulation provided by home, including the availability of books and the quality and amount of time that parents spend with children providing intellectual stimulation (taking them to the zoo and explaining about animals, asking them to explain why they feel a particular way, etc.).* That is, children's cognitive development depends more on the modeling and intellectual stimulation they get from their parents than on the mere presence of material possessions. Parents who provide a rich cognitive environment interact with their children often (not just when they need to), frequently at length, and in ways likely to stimulate thinking (Brophy, 1977; Hess, 1970). They label objects and events, explain causal relationships, discuss future activities in advance, and accompany discipline with instructions containing informa-

Parents who provide a rich cognitive environment interact in ways that stimulate thinking, explain causal relationships, discuss future activities, and answer children's questions.

tion as well as demands. They also answer children's questions, encourage their exploratory efforts, and, in general, provide them with a rich context of meaning within which to understand and assimilate new experiences. They model intellectual activity and verbal communication in everyday activities: reading newspapers and books for both information and pleasure; using computers for educational purposes as well as for challenging games; watching educational as well as purely entertaining television programs, and discussing their content; conversing about daily events at mealtimes; participating in social and political organizations; and visiting zoos, museums, and other educational settings.

Students who are truly disadvantaged do not get much of this kind of stimulation. Their parents may not even be aware of the importance of providing a stimulating cognitive environment in the home and, even if they are, may lack knowledge of what to do and how to do it. For the most part, these students need instruction that follows the same general principles outlined in the rest of this book, not something different from what is effective with other stu-

dents. However, they do especially well with teachers who share warm, personal interactions with them but also hold high expectations for their academic progress, require them to perform up to their capacities, and move them along at the most rapid pace possible. In short, effective teachers break through social-class differences and other potential barriers to communication in order to form close relationships with disadvantaged students, but they use these relationships to maximize students' academic progress, not merely to provide friendship or sympathy (Delpit, 1992; Kleinfeld, 1975; Siddle-Walker, 1992).

structural influences

As various educators have indicated, few recent studies allow an examination of student achievement by race or ethnicity, gender, and socioeconomic status (AAUW, 1992; Kaufman & Rosenbaum, 1992). It is well known that SES is a powerful predictor of school grades and student performance on standardized tests. However, we suspect that many of these differences are due to structural reasons and not simply to the socioeconomic status of parents. That is, the resources available in the community (e.g., the types of schools and the materials in them) influence students' performance just as the home environment does. Interestingly, despite considerable research on school integration, neighborhood or residential integration has rarely been studied. Even today, racial and socioeconomic integration seldom occurs in American society (Hackerman, 1992; Kozol, 1991; West, 1993).

Kaufman and Rosenbaum (1992) explored the effects of community setting on student achievement. A ruling by the U.S. Supreme Court against the Chicago Housing Authority and the Department of Housing and Urban Development stated that these agencies had employed racially discriminatory policies in managing the low-rent public housing program in Chicago. One outcome of the Supreme Court's ruling was the Gautreaux program, which gave public housing residents certificates that allowed families to move to private apartments, either in mostly white suburbs or in other areas of Chicago. This program resulted in low-income African-American families moving to environments that differed not only in housing but also in community factors, income, and race.

Kaufman and Rosenbaum (1992) studied the development of African-American youth after their families moved from primarily African-American urban housing projects to either mostly white suburbs or other mostly African-American urban areas. As they note, there are various reasons why low-income youth may not do well in suburban schools.

- Racial bias may keep them from having full access to suburban resources.
- A low-income background may leave them less prepared educationally or less motivated to succeed.
- Their low SES may result in attitudes and

behavior that are interpreted as unacceptable by middle-income school staffs and/or employers.

However, a different and more positive expectation is that students who move to the suburbs will benefit because of higher educational and employment opportunities in the suburbs and more appropriate student role models. The data from their study indicate that African-American youth who moved to white suburbs fared more favorably than those who moved to new urban locations. In particular, African-American youth in suburban schools were more likely to be in high school, in a college preparatory high school track, employed, employed with benefits, or inside of the educational and employment systems.

As Kaufman and Rosenbaum (1992) note, relatively few Americans have resided both in the inner city and in suburbia. Thus, the families who move to the suburbs had a distinctive perspective from which to compare relevant dimensions of these two environments.

When participants were asked to speculate about how youths' lives would have been different if they had not moved, all participants were most likely to mention safety. That is, both those who moved to suburban and other city locations indicated that students were better off because they were away from dangerous elements such as drugs or gangs. However, other than safety, the two groups gave notably different types of responses. Those who moved within the city were likely to mention improved finances (from rent supplements) and improved quality of housing; however, they did not mention motivational or educational changes. In most respects, the schools that these students moved to were not much different from the schools they had been enrolled in when living in public housing.

In striking contrast, those who moved to suburbs noted that the new environment provided better educational opportunities and was more effective in stimulating their motivation. Respondents said that suburban schools had higher standards for achievement and provided better preparation for college. They also said that teachers in the two environments taught differently. Suburban teachers not only held students accountable to higher standards but also were available to provide help. These teachers were more likely to stay with students after school and to give them special attention when they needed it. Indeed, Kaufman and Rosenbaum noted that, even in high school, teachers were about twice as likely to offer academic help in suburban schools (as compared to city schools).

Thus, many of the consequences of low SES are structural in nature. They are not a direct outcome of the resources provided in the family but rather represent the total pattern of resources available to students. Students who moved from inner-city public housing to suburbs received many more opportunities (better teaching, better role models, more opportunities for better jobs, etc.) than did students who moved elsewhere in the city. These data indicate the powerful factors operating when socioeconomic and racial integration occur. We agree with the recent AAUW report (1992), which argues that "public schools must do more to provide educational opportunity for children of low socioeconomic status, who do less well in school regardless of race/ethnicity or sex. . . . Educational excellence and equity can never be achieved until we devote substantial financial resources to poor children" (p. 36). Although there may be some structural elements that educators cannot influence (e.g., job opportunities), teachers can directly affect the quality of education and teaching students receive. At least some of the correlation between low SES and poor performance in school is probably associated with poor instruction (McCaslin & Good, in press, a; Oakes, 1990).

If teachers are to be effective decision mak-

ers in adjusting curriculum and instruction to the needs of individual students, they must be knowledgeable about family and community factors that influence student understanding and motivation (Kozol, 1991; Moll, 1992; Nieto, 1992). Further, teachers need to become aware of strategies for working effectively with parents and building home-school-community bridges (Brantlinger, 1991; Comer & Haynes, 1991; Hoffman, 1991; Powell, 1991).

students who are culturally different

Students differ not only in SES but also in the families and the communities in which they reside. Some students grow up reading and participating in a culture that is valued and sanctioned in schools. Other students grow up in hostile environments, or in homes in which school-related readings and discussions do not occur. Students who come to school speaking Spanish or Korean are frequently encouraged not to use their native language and in some cases punished for doing so.

Grosjean (reported in Secada & Lightfoot, 1993) interviewed bilingual individuals who recounted the discomfort they felt when they were forced to give up their home language for the language of school. One of Grosjean's informants expressed the problem this way:

> As a child my life seemed strange and confusing. At home, which meant brothers, parents, an aunt, and an uncle . . . and grandparents, the language was Spanish, and the culture was distinctly Mexican. At school the language was a cold and distant way of being treated—like the re-molding process of an army boot camp. When my parents first told me I had to learn English in order to survive in this country, the impact of

the statement had little immediate effect. But later, as a young person, I began to associate my feelings of alienation with the need to identify with the group, a cultural group. My capacity to use Spanish had dwindled to nothing. Identification with the dominant group seemed impossible, but recreating my group sense seemed equally impossible without the help of Spanish. . . . My years without Spanish now appear tragic. How can I ever make up that loss? I barely communicated with my grandparents. They died, in fact, before I relearned Spanish." (Secada & Lightfoot, 1993, p. 51)

Although it is beyond our scope in this chapter to discuss cultural diversity, cultural pluralism, and multicultural education in detail, we do want to identify some significant issues and suggest curriculum decisions that teachers must make.

assimilationists versus cultural pluralists

As Secada and Lightfoot (1993) have noted, how to deal with ethnic and gender diversity in American education is a complex issue and one that involves a dynamic process (the curriculum and political boundaries are in constant change). According to these authors, as a heuristic for organizing discussion, arguments on bilingual education can be expressed as a dichotomy—cultural pluralists versus assimilationists. **Assimilationists** *seek to move non-English-speaking students into an all-English-speaking environment as rapidly as possible and encourage students to accept as completely as possible the norms and values of the dominant society.* These individuals believe that, to be successful, students have to learn English as rapidly as possible. They place little emphasis on helping stu-

dents retain their native language or culture. The dominant questions become, how rapidly and under what circumstances can these students become English language users?

In contrast, **cultural pluralists** *argue that bilingual education should help students understand and appreciate the various cultural heritages and languages that comprise American society.* Predictably, some advocates of cultural pluralism are more assertive than others. Some pluralists want schools to do more than help students identify and understand their own cultural heritage and those of other groups; they want schools to communicate to students that some of the academic curriculum is based on denying the contribution of this country's most diverse individuals (Secada & Lightfoot, 1993). Thus, multiculturalism should set the historical record straight and increase minority students' self-esteem and self-respect.

Secada and Lightfoot (1993) describe problems with the curriculum:

For example, history is often presented in schools as a linear progression of events whose flow is inevitable and is governed by natural laws. Such accounts hide the uncertain nature of historical events and render conflicts as aberrations that were dealt with quickly and efficiently by the victors, thereby granting legitimacy to their victories. This view of history does not help many students from culturally diverse backgrounds to understand that their own situations are the results of historical events that could have turned out differently. Moreover, this presentation of history does not help students to understand present-day conflicts.

The development and maintenance of non-English languages can also become a matter of cultural right and of opposition to forces that would take away people's cultural heritages and backgrounds. Not just among Hispanic but also among American Indians, the reclamation of languages has become a matter of cultural pride in rebuilding a heritage that was forcibly taken away from them and their ancestors. (pp. 52–53)

The argument for acculturation is that if people abandon their language and cultural background, they are given an opportunity to participate widely in the country's economic system. However, as Secada and Lightfoot note, this negotiated "trade" was often quite uneven. ("Give up your language and your values and you might have the opportunity to participate.")

According to scholars such as Ogbu (1991), anger builds up among minorities over time when those promises have not been fulfilled. Ogbu indicates that many students from diverse ethnic backgrounds conceptualize academic success as "acting white" and view it as weakening their identification with their cultural group. Some persons see school success as an immoral contract in which minority youth are asked to assimilate and join a society that discriminates against them by requiring them to give up their ethnic identity. We agree with Secada and Lightfoot (1993), who write, "One wonders what the achievements of such students would be if their energies were liberated by an environment in which they no longer needed to trade ethnicity for school learning" (p. 53).

pejorative deficit models

The term **perjorative deficit model** refers to *the tendency to describe the skills that students lack, rather that the strengths they possess.* One problem of those who support strong assimilationism is that language, cultural experiences, and values that differ from those of the dominant society are typically discussed in negative and limiting terms (Estrada, 1993). Part of the issue is that

educators do not possess an adequate language for discussing issues of race, gender, culture, and so on. According to Estrada (1993),

What I consider to be the most significant, most depressing aspect of our existing language, especially with regard to our students, is that it is overwhelmingly negative and exploitative. Few positive, affirmative discourses on race, ethnic identity, multiculturalism, and/or gender have made their way into mainstream schooling or, for that matter, into mainstream society except as tokenisms (e.g., Cinco De Mayo Day, Martin Luther King Day). (p. 29)

Delpit (1992) contends that she has met many progressive and sympathetic literacy teachers who have a strong need and interest to empower and politicize their students. She notes that some of these teachers define empowerment by refusing to teach grammar, form, or strategies for communicating in the dominant language. These teachers attempt to develop literacy primarily, if not solely, within the language the students use at home. However, Delpit strongly argues that learning to utilize the dominant language to express oneself does not mean that one necessarily must reject one's home identity and values. She contends that "teachers must acknowledge and validate students' home language without using it to limit students' potential" (p. 301). She notes that students' home language or discourse is connected in a central way to students' perception of self. Thus, a teacher teaching the discourse of general literacy must do so in a way that allows students to still feel comfortable and to utilize their home language and values while also addressing issues associated with learning school discourse.

Clearly some educators feel that neither extreme position on assimilation or cultural pluralism is required and that integrative approaches are possible. Just as one can be oppressive by forcing students to abandon local culture and language, it is possible to be equally insensitive to real needs by denying students the chance to develop skills and insights for dealing with majority societal discourse. Indeed there is a shared perception among some authors that many African-American students especially value teachers who are directive and authoritative in the classroom. Certain teacher behaviors—refusing to answer questions completely or not explaining material clearly—is seen as unhelpful by these students and they may resent such behaviors (Siddle-Walker 1992).

sensitivity to social differences

Casanova and Arias (1993) stress the important effects of the larger social context on students' identity and school achievement. They note that Korean students do not generally achieve well in Japan but are often considered outstanding students in the United States. Similarly, Finnish students tend to perform poorly in Sweden but excel in Australia. As teachers deal with students who differ from them, they need to continually question how they can support and respect students' differences while helping them become active learners who integrate new knowledge with their cultural backgrounds but also prepare to participate in a broader society.

responding to cultural differences

Although there is growing interest in multicultural awareness and in helping teachers to deal with students from different cultures, it is not always clear how to accomplish such goals. McDiarmid (1992) argues that providing information alone is probably insufficient. He examined teachers' attitudes before and after they attended a series of presentations entitled Multicultural Week, and concluded that the presentations had little effect on teachers' views of cul-

turally diverse students. The content of the program encouraged teachers to:

- respect students whose values, language, dress, and so on differed from their own
- be sure to include information during teaching and references to the role and the contributions of minorities in American society
- not stereotype students on the basis of language or membership in a particular ethnic group
- know the history, customs, language, and family values and patterns of the students they teach.

In addition to accounts of this program in the Los Angeles public schools, McDiarmid discusses similar results (lack of change in teacher attitudes) that were obtained with a program in Michigan that was sponsored by the State Department of Education. He puzzles over the dilemma inherent in generalizing about cultural groups while at the same time trying to emphasize unique individual differences in learners. If educators are not careful, they may stereotype and trivialize individuals even as they attempt to recognize cultural differences.

This is not to suggest that information about minorities is irrelevant, only that it is insufficient. Of course, knowledge about students from various ethnic groups may be useful to a teacher. For example, it may be relevant to know that on average young Hispanic students respond to *abrazo* (personal support), that students from Hispanic homes may be more collaboratively than competitively oriented (hence, may work better in small groups than individually), or that Hispanic students are more sensitive and that aggressiveness is often inhibited in females (see Udall, 1989). American Indians value group membership and cohesiveness (hence, recognition from teachers needs to be private) and are committed to the value and survival of their tribe and culture (Maker & Schieber, 1989). Asian-Americans value family honor and personal responsibility, tend to lack assertiveness and risk-taking skills, but have high levels of academic orientation and persistence (Kitano, 1989; Tanaka, 1989). It may be important for teachers to recognize that African-Americans are the only immigrants who did not come to this country voluntarily and that a culture of poverty has followed forced slavery. In some schools, teachers should know that parental influence is more conduct oriented than task oriented. Further it may be useful to know that many African-American students prefer authoritative teaching styles (Siddle-Walker, 1992).

However, knowledge of general characteristics masks a great deal of information about individual students. Although some Japanese-American students may resist group work, some will relish it, and all students need to develop skills to work productively in small groups. Although many Hispanic students will have cooperative orientations, some will resist group work more strongly than most Asian-Americans. Some Hispanic students may dislike individual work and some white rural poor students may love it; however, both groups of students need to develop skills for both solitary and group work. Although some African-American students may be perceived to overquestion authority and some Asian-American students are viewed as too compulsively obedient, both groups of students will have to develop a reasonable respect for authority and a capacity for self-direction.

If teachers are not careful, they may use information about race or culture in ways that have unproductive and limiting consequences. According to Woo (1989),

Many Asian-Americans have been stereotyped as having little creative ability, and thus have been channelled into careers in science and mathematics that emphasize technical expertise. Asian-American parents, who tend to err on the side of conservatism and practicality, can be blamed as much as the schools for restricting the goals and dreams of their children. I have known many Asian-American physicians and engineers who are frustrated actors, writers, and inventors because, as Gallagher so ably states, they were never afforded the opportunity to develop strong communication skills—the kinds of skills that might have made them feel more comfortable about exploring themselves and the world of choices that are open to people with the self-assuredness to seek such opportunities. (pp. 180–181)

recognizing strengths

As various researchers have noted (McCaslin & Good, 1992; Moll, 1992), instruction in schools serving high-income families tends to focus on problem-solving and application, whereas working-class schools, particularly those serving ethnic groups, emphasize low-level skills and practice.

Moll (1992) urges bilingual educators to move away from a pervasive examination of language issues to a sociocultural approach to instruction. This perspective suggests that students in bilingual education classes need to be active learners, using either English or Spanish (or their native language) as a tool for inquiry, thinking, and communication. Although learning English is a part of the program, it is only a part. Teachers need to engage all students in social and academic tasks that are meaningful to students and involve them in relevant educational goals. According to Moll, "This emphasis on active research and learning leads to the realization that these children (and their families)

table 21.1 a sample of household funds of knowledge

Agriculture and Mining	Economics	Household Management	Material and Scientific Knowledge	Medicine	Religion
Ranching and farming	Business	Budgets	Construction	Contemporary medicine	Catechism
Horsemanship (cowboys)	Market values	Child care	Carpentry	Drugs	Baptisms
Animal husbandry	Appraising	Cooking	Roofing	First-aid procedures	Bible studies
Soil and irrigation systems	Renting and selling	Appliance repairs	Masonry	Anatomy	Moral knowledge and ethics
Crop planting	Loans		Painting	Midwifery	
Hunting, tracking, dressing	Labor Laws		Design and architecture		
	Building codes				
	Consumer knowledge				
	Accounting		Repair	Folk medicine	
	Sales		Airplane	Herbal knowledge	
Mining			Automobile	Folk cures	
Timbering			Tractor	Folk veterinary cures	
Minerals			House maintenance		
Blasting					
Equipment operation and maintenance					

SOURCE: L. Moll (1992). Bilingual classroom studies and community analysis. *Educational Researcher, 21,* 20–24. Reprinted by permission.

contain ample resources, which we termed "funds of knowledge," that can form the basis for an education that far exceeds what working-class students usually receive" (p. 21). Moll and other researchers argue that too often school programs for students from working-class homes (both in monolingual and bilingual classrooms) are aimed at remedying students' (and their homes') putative weaknesses and limitations. An emerging and important perspective is that schools need to take advantage of all the resources available in the community.

For example, ethnic or minority neighborhood households, unlike many classrooms, do not function alone or in isolation but are connected in diverse social networks (Moll, 1992). These networks are essential for enabling households with limited funds to share expertise that lowers economic cost. Important neighborhood ties help students to develop vital social information about the community.

For an illustration of this point, examine Table 21.1, which presents a description of the *funds of knowledge* that are available in a community. Moll (1992) notes that the descriptive table was drawn from interviews with thirty families. Teachers could usefully integrate such knowledge into classrooms in various ways (having students research on community issues, understanding architectural principles used in building community houses, awareness of how the community developed socially, etc.) (Moll, 1992). However, the important principle is integrating parents intellectually into the life of the school.

Casanova and Arias (1993) also comment about the value of the sociocultural approach, noting that students may learn or fail to thrive as the sociopolitical context changes. Many educators are influenced by the rich theoretical arguments of Vygotsky, who also advocates a social approach that stresses the connection and integration of all learning environments a student experiences (community, school, and home).

bilingual education

It is beyond the scope of this chapter to provide an extensive discussion of bilingual education. Most students will receive detailed coverage of this issue in other courses (curriculum, English methods, or bilingual education). However, because it is critically important, we want to address some of the psychological and research issues associated with bilingual education here.

Any attempt to describe individual differences in students would be remiss if some attention was not paid to one of the primary ways in which American students differ—fluency in English. Recent research illustrates that students benefit from extended use of their primary language in school settings. We contend that opportunity for academic instruction in one's primary language in the early school years strengthens rather than weakens subsequent development in English.

bilingual education: multiple models

There are many different models of bilingual instruction that have been implemented across the United States. To further complicate the issue of what constitutes appropriate practice, what occurs within a "program" varies widely. Two programs that have the same name may vary more than two presumably different programs. As Dolson (1986) notes, two of the most common bilingual designs are types of transitional programs: early transitional and full bilingual (for extended discussion of various programs, see Dolson, 1986).

The difference between these two basic programs is the amount of time students spend in instruction in their primary language (L_1). In early transitional programs, students exit after they have developed fluent listening and speaking skills in English (typically, this occurs in two to three years). In contrast, students in full bilingual programs continue to receive primary instruction in their primary language (L_1), not only until they have mastered fluency in English, but also until they have mastered English literacy skills that are equivalent to native English speakers at the same grade level and same age group. (This typically occurs after four to seven years of formal instruction in a full bilingual program.)

While we again stress that what happens in a particular bilingual program varies widely, Dolson (1986) provides a general description:

> Bilingual programs commonly provide initial literacy and some subject matter instruction in the students' native language. At the same time, program participants receive English as a second language instruction and usually participate in a substantial amount of mainstream classroom activities conducted in English. In bilingual programs, the proportion of English instruction increases over time. In early transitional programs, English is usually the only language of instruction by the end of the second or third year of instruction. In full bilingual models, L_1 instruction usually continues across all grade levels included in the program. Even in the full bilingual designs, however, by about the fourth or fifth year, L_1 instruction is frequently reduced to approximately 20 percent of the school day. (pp. 9–10)

In recent times there has been increased interest in an immersion model following the use of such programs in Canada. Students in immersion programs receive instruction in the second language not only in language classes, but also in all academic subjects. Although immersion programs are logically appealing (more focus on a language should lead to more proficiency), recent data suggest that transitional and maintenance programs appear to be more viable.

Upon careful scrutiny, however, it is evident that there are notable differences between bilingual education programs in Canada and in the United States. As noted in a personal conversation by Carol Evans, a colleague at the University of Arizona with one of the authors of this book, the goal of Canadian immersion programs is bilingualism and biliteracy, in contrast to the typical goal of English immersion programs—to develop monolingual English ability.

recent research

Evaluation and research studies on bilingual programs indicate that such programs vary in effectiveness (Baker & Dekanter, 1983; Dolson, in press). Thus, a critical issue has to be the quality of the program. Even though it is difficult to make recommendations for particular programs, a recent comprehensive research study suggests that total immersion programs may be less effective than many have contended (Ramírez, 1992).

Ramírez and colleagues (1991a, 1991b) compared English immersion programs and early-exit and late-exit programs. The findings provide clear evidence that increased emphasis upon English usage did not increase students' academic ability to achieve (in English) in various subject areas. Cummins (1992), commenting upon the Ramírez et al. study and related research, writes: "If anything, the bulk of the evidence suggests an inverse relation between exposure to English instruction and English achievement for Latino students in the United States" (p. 98).

Cummins (1992) notes that the Ramírez team's study refutes the expectations of many policy makers who believe that immersion programs are less costly and as effective as bilingual programs and that students should be "immersed." One clear finding from the study was that students following the immersion strategy did not leave the program more quickly than students who participated in early-exit programs. Thus, costs for bilingual and immersion programs are apt to be comparable.

As Cummins notes, these results do not demonstrate that early-exit bilingual programs are better than English immersion programs. But they clearly illustrate that the "time-on-task" argument is a flawed concept (i.e., the contention that there is a direct relation between the amount of time spent in English instruction and academic growth in English). On the basis of the time-on-task hypothesis, the early-exit bilingual students should have performed less capably than did the English immersion students—but they did not.

However, what is more compelling is the comparison between English immersion programs and late-exit bilingual programs that make extensive use of students' primary language for a longer period. Cummins (1992) describes the results:

> The "time-on-task" notion suffers even further indignity from the late-exit bilingual program results. In contrast, to students in the immersion and early-exit programs, the late-exit students in the two sites that continued primary language instruction for at least 40 percent of the time were catching up academically to students in the general population. This is despite the fact that these students received considerably less instruction in English than students in the early-exit and immersion programs and proportionately more of their families came from the lowest income levels than was the case for students in the other two programs. (p. 97)

Cummins notes that all language programs were deficient in the sense that language use by students was relatively passive. Students, in general, were simply responding to the teacher with short statements; they were not actively involved in extended speech. Students in bilingual programs were as passive as students in typical classrooms. These findings were similar to those presented by Goodlad (1984) and colleagues a decade earlier.

For example, writing on data collected in the project directed by Goodlad, Sirotnik (1983) suggests that a hidden, informal curriculum is communicated to students in many classrooms. Given that teachers talk a lot and students mainly listen, when students do talk they often are responding only to relatively closed, factual questions, an environment that exudes little affect and enthusiasm—by students for learning or by teachers for students. Sirotnik (1983) contends that "we are implicitly teaching dependence upon authority, linear thinking, social apathy, passive involvement, and hands-off learning" (p. 29).

Although there may come a time in school where a more immersion-oriented program has academic value (after a student has made considerable progress in learning academic content in her or his primary language), the need for students to receive much academic instruction in their primary language in the elementary school years and to maintain that language in subsequent years seems clearly documented. Further, it would seem that all students would benefit if active language use was stressed more in American classrooms.

policy recommendations

Based upon his research study, Ramírez (1992) contends the following:

1. LEP (limited proficiency in English skills) students need to be provided with language support for at least six years or until they fully demonstrate language skills that are appropriate for functioning in an English-only, mainstream classroom.

2. LEP students should be provided with content instruction and primary language until such time as they are fully able to function from English-only classroom instruction.

3. LEP students cannot be denied access to the core curriculum until they develop English-language skills. Students need immediate instruction in the content areas in Spanish (or their language) so that skill differences between them and mainstream English-speaking peers are not exaggerated and extended.

4. In mixed-language settings, teachers should be certain that each student's primary language is used.

5. When parent resources are integrated to help support their children's learning, their home language should be used for instruction and planning. If schools are to integrate parent resources, they must be able to communicate effectively with parents.

6. On the basis of these data, it would appear optimal for LEP students in the primary grades to receive most of their content instruction in the primary language, and to receive a limited amount of formal instruction in English. In contrast, in upper primary grades, the amount of time and content-based ESL instruction would increase and content instruction in the students' primary language would decrease (i.e., as the student becomes more proficient in English).

school and classroom climate

Although classroom teachers may not be able to determine how much English or Spanish is offered in the classroom, teachers' attitudes about students' language programs can have a profound impact upon students' self-concepts and performance. Similarly, the way the school qua school deals with student diversity in culture and language has important implications for students' affect and school performance.

Various educators have discussed the important role of the overall school environment affirming and celebrating different types of student preferences and achievement (Good & Weinstein, 1986a). For example, Kuykendall (1992), writing on the importance of a good *school climate*, contends, "Schools can enhance the motivation of youth when they provide a climate where cultural diversity is celebrated, not just in what we teach, but also in how we teach. The entire culture of school must be expanded to accept and celebrate student differences" (p. 91).

However, teachers can do a great deal to promote student growth by accepting student diversity in their own classrooms. There is a great deal of literature to suggest the powerful influence of individual teachers' expectations on student performance (Good & Brophy, 1994; Good & Weinstein, 1986b). Kuykendall (1992) writes about how teachers can make a difference in classroom climate:

> Teachers must foster freedom of expression. When students feel uncomfortable about expressing themselves, they are more likely to disengage themselves from the learning process. Teachers can encourage freedom by accepting various means of expression, by being willing to listen, and showing empathetic understanding and an interest in the child as a person.
>
> Some Black and Hispanic students express themselves through poetry, art work, songs, "rap," dance, or other media. While it is necessary that all students learn how to express themselves in socially acceptable manners, i.e., through the use of standard English in speaking and writing, students should be encouraged to engage in various

Affirmation, solidarity, and critique are the greatest benefits of multicultural education.

means of expression which may reflect individual or cultural strengths.

Once students get the message that teachers are unwilling to listen to their concerns or responses, these youths are less likely to express themselves. Remember, good teachers must be able to listen to verbal communication and understand what is communicated through nonverbal behavior. Many underachieving students feel trapped in schools, where teachers and administrators just "don't understand" them. Even though some teachers may not know what a child might be internalizing, experiencing, or feeling, teachers can show a willingness to accept and validate the feelings of that particular child. Children, especially Black and Hispanic children, need to feel that perceived barriers to understanding can be eradicated. (pp. 91–92)

Carol Evans (personal communication) recently shared a powerful instance of a teacher communicating low expectations and prejudice concerning the use of Spanish in the classroom (for related discussion, see Chapter 14). In a transition maintenance classroom, the teacher acknowledged the absence of two students one day by expressing, "Oh, good. Manuel and Alicia are not here so we won't have to speak Spanish today." (Manuel and Alicia were the two students with the least amount of English proficiency in the class.) This teacher's utterance was a powerful and unfortunate expression of the limited value that the teacher holds toward speaking Spanish. The teacher's attitude seemingly implies that Spanish is to be tolerated (barely, until we can move on to real instruction in English). In sharing her experience, Evans stressed that this was a well-respected bilingual teacher—a truly good teacher in most respects. She noted that the teacher was responding to the social context and the subtle messages about primacy of English and the relative lack of importance of Spanish. Unfortunately, the invidious social message that is often derived (even on occasion by bilingual teachers) from the influence of various sources is that the real business of school is English. One of the difficult problems faced by most bilingual teachers are students' own resistance to the use of Spanish (because the message of "Spanish as low priority" is communicated to them as well). As we will see later, many educators are forcefully criticizing educational practice that implicitly, if not explicitly, forces students to feel shame about their culture or language.

implications for teachers

affirming cultural diversity in the classroom

Educators need to become aware that students they instruct come from diverse cultures and that individual development both within a family and within a school is heavily influenced by the community context in which the student is socialized (Szapocznik & Kurtines, 1993). Nieto (1992) argues that educators must move away from an exclusive focus on presenting the monocultural perspective in schools and represent a multicultural perspective that is consistent with the pluralistic values of our society. However, Nieto emphasizes that a multicultural perspective will mean different things to different people and that it can be analyzed from at least four different levels: tolerance; acceptance; respect; and affirmation, solidarity, and critique.

The first level is *tolerance*, which suggests the capacity to endure something while not necessarily embracing it. What is tolerated today may be rejected tomorrow; thus, tolerance is the lowest level of multicultural education in the school. It suggests that linguistic and cultural differences are tolerated as the inescapable obligation of a culturally pluralistic society.

Acceptance is the next level of dealing with diversity, and it suggests that at a minimum we acknowledge differences without denying their importance. If schools accept diversity, programs acknowledging students' language and cultures would be visible in the school (e.g., perhaps a transitional bilingual program that uses students' primary language), and acceptance might suggest that some differences are celebrated (e.g., multicultural fairs, cookbooks).

Respect is the third level of multicultural education. When diversity is respected, it provides an organizing base for much of the school program. For example, teachers might offer programs of bilingual education using students' native language not only as a bridge to English but also throughout their education. Students' values and experiences would be used as a basis for literacy development and students would be exposed to different ways of approaching the same reality.

Affirmation, solidarity, and *critique* together are the highest level of multicultural education (Nieto, 1992). According to Nieto, It [this level] means accepting the culture and language of students and their families as legitimate and embracing them as valid vehicles for learning. It also means understanding the culture is not fixed or unchanged, and thus one is able to critique its manifestations and outcomes. Because multicultural education is concerned with equity and social justice for all people, and because basic values of different groups are diametrically opposed, conflict is inevitable. Passively accepting the status quo of any culture is inconsistent with multicultural education. (p. 277)

The differences between monocultural education and various levels of multicultural education are further delineated in Table 21.2 (pp. 564–565). As we begin to think about the implications of SES, culture, family, and other factors on the social development of students, it is important to remember that there are varying perspectives on multicultural education and that in part these definitions and their implications for practice are mediated by political and legal orientations in a given school district. Educators and policy makers vary notably in what they mean when they talk about multicultural education and when they urge teachers to become more sensitive to multicultural issues. However, we believe that school districts must move beyond tolerance and accept and respect multicultural differences.

gender differences

As a result of the women's liberation movement and a host of related social and cultural changes that have occurred since World War II, gender segregation in schooling and in society in general has for the most part disappeared, along with many of the cultural beliefs and practices that accompanied it. Still, it is clear that many forms of gender discrimination still exist (e.g., women, especially minority women, often are charged more for a new car than men).

But according to Biklen and Pollard (1993): "Being male or female carries few meanings in and of itself; its most potent meanings come from the social and cultural meanings attached to it. These meanings we call gender, the social construction of gender" (p. 1). Thus, as these authors note, we are not just male or female but we are also Japanese-American, Native American, upper class, or homeless. Although we discuss gender issues here, it is useful to note that there is no generic concept of gender—to some extent gender interacts with class and ethnic identity.

Gender roles are no longer as rigid and pervasive as they used to be, although most of us still expect certain differences between males and females and still view certain behaviors as either masculine or feminine (Deaux, 1985). Some of the beliefs about gen-der-role differentiation are expressed in relatively direct ways. Beliefs that boys have more aptitude for, interest in, or future occupational need for science and mathematics than girls do, for example, appear to lead a great many parents, teachers, and school counselors to encourage boys to develop positive learner self-concepts in mathematics and science and to continue to take courses in these areas, but to discourage girls from doing so (Eccles, 1987). Other beliefs about gender-role differentiation are expressed much more subtly. Analyses of children's literature and of the stories included in basal readers and literature anthologies at school, for example, have shown that male characters are much more likely than female characters to play a major role in stories, to be depicted within career roles, and to be active and decisive rather than passive or ineffectual (Garrett-Schau & Scott, 1984; Martin, 1992).

Reviews of the voluminous literature on gender differences in intellectual and personal attributes reveal surprisingly little support for our still-powerful cultural tendencies to expect sizable gender differences and thus to treat boys and girls differently (Maccoby, 1988, 1990). In the intellectual sphere, males tend to score higher on tests of visual-spatial ability and mathematical ability, and females to score higher on tests of verbal ability. These differences have been consistent but very small, too small to justable 21.2 **levels of multicultural education**

MONOCULTURAL EDUCATION	CHARACTERISTIC OF MULTICULTURAL EDUCATION	TOLERANCE
Racism is unacknowledged. Policies and practices that support discrimination are left in place. These include low expectations and refusal to use students' natural resources (such as language and culture) in instruction. Only a sanitized and "safe" curriculum is in place.	Antiracist/ Antidiscriminatory	Policies and practices that challenge racism and discrimination are initiated. No overt signs of discrimination are acceptable (name-calling, graffiti, blatantly racist and sexist textbooks or curriculum, etc.). ESL programs are in place for students who speak other languages.
Defines education as the 3 R's and the "canon" "Cultural literacy" is understood within a monocultural framework. All important knowledge is essentially European-American. This Eurocentric view is reflected throughout the curriculum, instructional strategies, and environment for learning.	Basic	Education is defined more expansively and includes attention to some important information about other groups.
No attention is paid to student diversity.	Pervasive	A multicultural perspective is evident in some activities, such as Black History Month and Cinco de Mayo, and in some curriculum and materials. There may be an itinerant "multicultural teacher."
Ethnic and/or women's studies, if available, are only for students from that group. This is a frill that is not important for other students to know.	Important for all students	Ethnic and women's studies are only offered as isolated courses.
Education supports the status quo. Thinking and acting are separate.	Education for social justice	Education is somewhat, although tenuously, linked to community projects and activities.
Education is primarily content: who, what, where, when. The "great White men" version of history is propagated. Education is static	Process	Education is both content and process. "Why" and "how" questions are tentatively broached.
Education is domesticating. Reality is represented as static, finished, and flat.	Critical pedagogy	Students and teachers begin to question the status quo.

ACCEPTANCE	RESPECT	AFFIRMATION, SOLIDARITY, AND CRITIQUE
Policies and practices that acknowledge differences are in place. Textbooks reflect some diversity. Transitional bilingual programs are available. Curriculum is more inclusive of the histories and perspectives of a broader range of people.	Policies and practices that respect diversity are more evident, including maintenance bilingual education. Ability grouping is not permitted. Curriculum is more explicitly antiracist and honest. It is "safe" to talk about racism, sexism, and discrimination.	Policies and practices that affirm diversity and challenge racism are developed. There are high expectations for all students; students' language and culture are used in instruction and curriculum. Two-way bilingual programs are in place wherever possible. Everyone takes responsibility. for racism and other forms of discrimination.
The diversity of lifestyles and values of groups other than the dominant one are acknowledged in some content, as can be seen in some courses and school activities.	Education is defined as that knowledge that is necessary for living in a complex and pluralistic society. As such, it includes much content that is multicultural. *Additive multiculturalism* is the goal.	Basic education is multicultural education. All students learn to speak a second language and are familiar with a broad range of knowledge.
Student diversity is acknowledged, as can be seen not only in "Holidays and Heroes" but also in consideration of different learning styles, values, and languages. A "multicultural program" may be in place.	The learning environment is imbued with multicultural education. It can be seen in classroom interactions, materials, and the subculture of the school.	Multicultural education pervades the curriculum, instructional strategies, and interactions among teachers, students, and the community. It can be seen everywhere: bulletin boards. the lunchroom, assemblies.
Many students are expected to take part in curriculum that stresses diversity. A variety of languages is taught.	All students take part in courses that reflect diversity. Teachers are involved in overhauling the curriculum to be more open to such diversity.	All courses are completely multicultural in essence. The curriculum for all students is enriched. "Marginal students" no longer exist.
The role of the schools in social change is acknowledged. Some changes that reflect this attitude begin to be felt: Students take part in community service.	Students take part in community activities that reflect their social concerns.	The curriculum and instructional techniques are based on an understanding of social justice as central to education. Reflection and action are important components of learning.
Education is both content and process. "Why" and "how" questions are stressed more. Sensitivity and understandings of teachers toward their students are more evident.	Education is both content and process. Students and teachers begin to ask, "What if." Teachers empathize with students and their families.	Education is an equal mix of content and process. It is dynamic. Teachers and students are empowered. Everyone in the school is becoming a multicultural person.
Students and teachers are beginning a dialogue. Students' experiences, cultures, and languages are used as one source of their learning.	Students and teachers use critical dialogue as the primary basis for their education. They see and understand different perspectives.	Students and teachers are involved in a "subversive activity." Decision-making and social action skills are the basis of the curriculum.

SOURCE: S. Nieto, (1992). *Affirming Diversity: The Sociopolitical Context of Multicultural Education* (pp. 280–81). White Plains: Longman Publishing Group.

tify the attention often given to them. Furthermore, they have become smaller still in recent years, sometimes to the point of disappearing altogether (Feingold, 1988), presumably as a result of recent cultural awareness of sexism and related reduction in gender-differentiated socialization and education.

In the personality domain, males have been found to be more aggressive (across a broad range of situations and types of aggression), and females have been found to smile and laugh more (Maccoby, 1990). In the classroom, boys are more active and salient than girls and have more of almost every kind of interaction with the teacher that can be measured. Eccles and Blumenfeld (1985) found that teachers had 10 percent more communication with boys than girls. In part this is because boys are more prone to misbehave in the classroom than girls, so teachers criticize or punish boys more often, and they initiate interactions with them more frequently to give them procedural instructions, check their progress on assignments, or generally monitor and control their activities. Sadker and Sadker (1982) reported that teachers were more likely to discipline boys; hence, boys appear to be more salient. However, teachers are also more likely to call on boys than girls during lessons, and boys are more likely than girls to call out answers without first being recognized by the teacher and thus to garner response opportunities for themselves (Good & Brophy, 1994). Sadker and Sadker (1982) also found that boys are more likely to be asked abstract and open-ended questions than were girls. These patterns are just as likely to appear in classes taught by female teachers as in classes taught by male teachers, so they are due primarily to gender differences in the behavior of the students themselves rather than to gender differences between teachers in the ways that they interact with male versus female students.

Sadker and Sadker (1986) identified the following gender differences in styles of participation in social conversation that they believe are pervasive in our society and thus carry over into the classroom: (1) Men speak more often and frequently interrupt women. (2) Listeners appear to pay more attention to male speakers, even when female speakers use similar styles and make similar points. (3) Women participate less actively in conversation but do more gazing and passive listening. (4) Women often transform declarative statements into more tentative statements ("This is a good restaurant, isn't it?") that may limit their ability to influence others. The Sadkers also claimed that teachers not only accepted these gender differences in social assertiveness but reinforced them in subtle ways. In one of their studies, for example, boys were eight times more likely than girls to call out answers rather than raise their hands and wait for teacher recognition. Yet teachers were more likely to caution girls against calling out and more likely simply accept to boys' answers without reprimanding them for failing to raise their hands and wait for recognition.

The Sadkers also suggested that teachers tended to be bland when giving feedback to girls' responses but to be more animated and also more detailed and specific when giving feedback to boys. They also cited research suggesting that when complex tasks need to be done, teachers may simply do the tasks for girls but give boys detailed instructions and feedback that will enable them to do the tasks for themselves.

Other investigators have also reported subtle differences in teacher treatment that might reinforce assertiveness and independence in boys but dependency or inhibition in girls. Grant (1984), for example, suggests that although teachers may have more positive attitudes toward and even higher expectations for girls compared to boys, this apparent advantage can work against the girls' long-run best interests if it is associated only with teacher pressures toward conformity and responsibility but not autonomous achievement striving. Much teacher encouragement and reinforcement directed at girls focuses on dress, grooming, manners, and other social role issues, whereas most of the encouragement and reinforcement directed to boys focuses on their achievement striving and accomplishments. Rennie and Parker (1988) reported that during science work girls watched and listened 400 percent more than boys, but explored and manipulated 25 percent less. Teachers need to guard against accepting such performance patterns where girls are allowed to attend to minor rather than substantive issues.

Similarly, Dweck and associates (1978) studied the evaluative feedback given by teachers in one fifth-grade and two fourth-grade classrooms. There were no gender differences in general frequencies of praise or criticism related to academic work, but there were qualitative differences in the degree to which such evaluative feedback referred to the intellectual aspects of the work (competence or correctness) or to nonintellectual aspects (neatness, following directions, speaking clearly). For positive evaluations of work, about 94 percent of statements directed to boys concerned the work's intellectual quality, but the corresponding figure for girls was only about 81 percent. Thus, boys were almost always praised for having responded correctly or having done work competently. Girls were praised for the same reasons most of the time, but relatively they were much more apt to be praised for neatness, following directions, or speaking clearly. Thus, good performance on their part was less often attributed to their own personal competence. Teachers' negative evaluations of students' work showed a different pattern. Here only about 54 percent of the criticism directed to boys referred to poor intellectual quality of work, but the corresponding figure for girls was 89 percent. Criticism of girls' work therefore almost always indicated that they lacked competence or did not understand the work, whereas criticism of boys' work often referred to nonintellectual aspects that did not imply lack of competence. Taken together, these patterns of evaluative feedback probably would have more favorable effects on boys than girls in developing self-confidence, sense of efficacy, and a tendency to attribute academic successes to internal factors (ability and effort) but to attribute failures to external factors (inappropriate or overly rigid teacher responses to the form rather than the substance of the work).

These subtle differences suggesting teacher tendencies to reinforce assertiveness and achievement striving in boys but to reinforce conformity and responsibility in girls do not appear in every classroom, and some may appear in the classrooms of only a minority of teachers. Still, they illustrate pervasive yet subtle differences in ways teachers may treat boys versus girls. Differential treatment along these lines is likely to appear in advanced courses in science and mathematics. Becker (1981) described the academic environment for boys in such courses as academically and emotionally supportive but the environment for girls as one of benign neglect. Again, this was true whether the teachers were male or female.

subject-matter achievement patterns

Becker's (1981) study is just one of many indicating that gender differences in classroom behavior interact with gender differences in patterns of motivation and achievement in various subjects. The latter differences typically favor boys in science classes and favor girls in English classes; in mathematics, patterns of achievement test scores show no differences or even favor girls in the early grades and on tests of number computation, but favor boys in the later grades and on tests of mathematical reasoning (Feingold, 1988).

It is tempting to link these subject-matter achievement differences to gender differences in related intellectual abilities and ascribe them all to genetic influences, but arguments for environmental causes are at least as compelling as those for genetic causes. For one thing, achievement differences within each gender are very large. Furthermore, there are exceptions to the typical patterns of average differences that would not occur if relatively straightforward genetic influences were at work. Scores on elementary school reading-comprehension tests, for example, favor girls in Canada and the United States but favor boys in England, Nigeria, and Germany (Johnson, 1976; Preston, 1962). Similarly, although gender differences in mathematics achievement typically favor boys in the continental United States, they favor girls in Hawaii (Brandon, Newton, & Hammond, 1987). Along with the previously mentioned finding that gender differences in cognitive ability and in patterns of achievement test scores have been decreasing in recent years, these findings suggest that gender differences in school experiences and outcomes are caused as much by *cultural socialization* of children into contrasting gender roles as by innate predispositions. We may begin to see equal achievement from boys and girls in different academic subjects as we begin to expect it.

To the extent that we expect gender differences in motivation and achievement in different subjects, however, such differences are likely to continue. Thus, at least until recently, American teachers and students tended to view reading as a feminine activity and thus to expect girls to respond more positively to it than boys, despite the preponderance of males as central characters in children's literature (Bank, Biddle, & Good, 1980). There are similar tendencies to look on math and science as masculine activities (Eccles, 1987). These differential expectations can engender self-fulfilling prophecy effects, as several researchers have noted. Leinhardt, Seewald, and Engel (1979), for example, observed second-grade classrooms during individualized reading and mathematics instruction, when teachers circulated around the room to interact with individual students. They found that teachers had more academic contacts and spent more time discussing subject matter with girls than with boys during reading instruction but showed the opposite pattern during math instruction. The greater activity and involvement of males in math and science studies has been frequently documented. For example, Tobin and Garnett (1987) studied science classrooms and reported that when teachers required assistance in carrying out a demonstration, 79 percent of such requests were given to boys. In part, science classrooms are dominated by boys because they have more extensive out-of-school familiarity and experience with the subject matter (hence, teachers may be sustaining rather than creating gender differences).

Brophy (1985) made the following two points in discussing these findings. First, these differential patterns appear to be due mostly to gender differences in the attitudes and classroom behavior of the students themselves rather than to differences in treatment of boys versus girls by teachers. Therefore, if teachers are to counteract such gender differences effectively, it will not be enough for them merely to treat boys and girls in the same ways in the same situations. In addition, it will be necessary consciously to treat them differently, such as calling on boys more often in reading and language arts and on girls more often in mathematics and science, to counteract gender differences in rates of volunteering in these subjects. Second, the findings concerning girls' progress in math and science are somewhat more serious and disturbing than those for boys in reading and language arts. Boys' problems with elementary reading seem to be primarily motivational—many boys acquire the idea that reading is primarily for girls and that they will not enjoy it. Relatively few boys, however, construe the problem as one of ability by acquiring the belief that boys lack aptitude for reading. Many girls, however, acquire the notion that they lack aptitude for mathematics and science, especially at the secondary level. When this is true, it will be necessary to motivate them not only in the sense of developing their interest in and willingness to take courses in these subjects but also in the sense of developing in them the expectation that they can achieve success if they apply reasonable effort.

The notion that motivation (as opposed to ability) is the probable cause of differential academic performance of boys and girls is strengthened by data showing that gender differences in mathematics and reading performance narrow considerably when efforts are made to increase the attractiveness of tasks (Asher & Markell, 1974; Bleakley, Westerberg, & Hopkins, 1988; Christoplos & Borden, 1978). Initially, for young males

it seems especially important to use materials that are appropriately stimulating and action oriented. For young females it is important to use materials that define sex roles more broadly. However, males especially need to learn to value a broad range of literature—including literature that at one point in time might have been called "feminine." Both genders need to learn to "care" and to realize that care and action are appropriate responses for both females and males. (See Martin, 1992, for extended discussion.)

As we move into the twenty-first century, it is time to rethink the role of schooling in a modern society. It is time to integrate home and school concerns and to help students to take the best aspects of these two institutions forward as they prepare for careers.

implications for teachers

improving classrooms for boys and girls

Noddings (1992) indicates that schools need to do more than respond to helping students develop capacity for intellectual work and deal with the world of ideas.

> Teenage pregnancies nearly doubled between 1965 and 1985; the teen suicide rate has doubled in the same period of time; teenage drinking takes a horrible toll in drunk driving accidents and dulled sensibilities; children take guns to school, and homicide is the leading cause of death among minority teens; a disgraceful number of children live in poverty. And still many school people and public officials insist that the job of the schools is to increase academic rigor. In direct opposition, I will argue that the first job of the schools is to care for our children. (p. xiv)

As a teacher, you can be helpful to girls by encouraging them to be more active in the classroom and by making systematic efforts to observe and get to know each girl as an individual. We speak of making a systematic effort because that is what will be required. If teachers merely respond passively to boys and girls, they will spend most of their time with boys. Many girls will not come to the teacher; the teacher must go to the girls. We believe that this effort is worthwhile, however, because society cannot afford to allow overrestrictive sex-role expectations to pressure girls into hiding their abilities and talents. You can help by encouraging girls to speak their minds, calling on them to participate if they do not volunteer, assigning them to leadership roles for group projects, and taking similar actions to encourage them to be more assertive.

You can also broaden the perspectives of

young girls by helping them to realize that the full spectrum of career alternatives is open to them and by using learning experiences such as stories involving females in leadership positions, or compositions or discussions about the work of female scientists. Many books detail accomplishments of women, and they should be available in classrooms. You can also help by encouraging girls to take advanced courses in science and mathematics.

You also need to provide boys with appropriate academic encouragement and reinforcement. For example, you should expect boys as much as girls to have interest and talent in poetry, literature, and the fine arts and should treat them accordingly. Further, boys need to be taught prosocial values of caring and to be taught to become as adept as girls at community building and consensus building.

To the extent that teachers treat boys ineffectively in more general ways, the problem is likely to be not so much with all of the boys as with the subset of boys who are both low achievers and hostile or alienated learners. Low-achieving girls are often dependent and conforming students who elicit teacher sympathy and concern, but many low-achieving boys are hostile and disruptive students who engender attitudes of rejection and hostility in their teachers. Teachers sometimes come to view these boys as lazy, immature, maladjusted, and troublesome and begin to treat them in ways that produce undesirable self-fulfilling prophecy effects. Teachers, especially those who fear loss of classroom control, need to work hard to sustain a professional manner in dealing with such hostile and potentially disruptive students (most of whom will be low-achieving boys).

sexual harassment

A survey conducted in 1993 by the American Association of University Women involving 1,600 students in grades 8 through 12 reported that a majority of students had experienced some form of sexual harassment. Indeed, 10 percent of the students reported extreme sexual harassment—that they had been forced to commit a sexual act beyond kissing during school hours. Although sexual harassment is outlawed in the workplace by the Civil Rights Act of 1991, few states have addressed sexual harassment in schools. However, the problem needs to be addressed, because 25 percent of female students indicated that harassment had caused them to stay home from school or cut class, an additional 24 percent indicated that the experience had made them fearful, and another 39 percent said they had been very upset by it. Roughly 50 percent of male students and two-thirds of female students indicated that they had been harassed often or occasionally. Male and female students

reported that harassment occurred in various locations including hallways, classrooms, restrooms, and locker rooms. Others have also documented sexual harassment in school settings (e.g., Strauss, 1988). As Stein (1993) notes, "Sexual harassment occurs in the mundane, daily matters of school life; in the corridors and stairwells; in the cafeteria; in the chemistry laboratory as well as in the carpentry shop; in the gym and the parking lot; on school buses, in the driver's education car, and on the practice fields for extracurricular sports" (p. 192).

Although sexual harassment is prohibited under Title IX, many forms of sex-biased peer interactions seem to be permitted in schools. Sometimes harassment is seen as "boys being boys" rather than as a form of serious misconduct (e.g., see AAUW, 1992). Teachers must be alert to both explicit and implicit forms of sexual harassment and not allow students of any gender to assert unwarranted power over other students. Sexual harassment and other forms of intimidation cannot be tolerated in schools.

research at work
guidelines for gender and racial equity

Scott and McCollum (1993) offer the following ideas for making classroom gender-and-race appropriate:

- Actively challenge misconceptions of race, culture, and gender through class lectures and discussions.
- Model sex-equitable behavior.
- Physically organize classrooms so students are not segregated by race or gender.
- Eliminate the assignment of sex-stereotyped tasks (e.g., boys dissect the frog, girls record procedures).
- Use instructional materials that are culture fair and gender fair (e.g., allow students to see active role models from a variety of professions, history from multiple viewpoints).
- Encourage girls to use equipment that is typically reserved for boys (computers, basketballs).
- Provide opportunities for cooperative learning activities to occur across gender and racial lines.

Recently the AAUW (1992) presented evidence that female students are not participating equally in the American educational system. The report offered forty recommendations that schools should act upon in order to improve education for females (see Appendix 1 of the report for the full list of recommendations). The AAUW maintains that:

- The reinforcement of Title IX must be strengthened.
- Teachers, administrators, and counselors must bring gender equity and awareness to every aspect of schooling.
- The formal school curriculum must include the experiences of women and men from various aspects of life. Young females and males must come to see women and girls as valued in the materials they study.
- Girls must be encouraged to understand that mathematics and the sciences are important and relevant to their lives.
- Attention must be paid to gender equity in vocational educational programs.
- Testing and assessment must serve as stepping stones, not terminal points. In particular, new testing techniques must accurately reflect the abilities of females and males.
- Women must play a central role in educational reform: the experiences, strengths, and needs of girls from every race and social class must be considered if excellence and equality is to be provided for all our nation's students.
- A critical goal of educational reform must be to enable students to consider effectively the realities of their lives, particularly in areas such as health and sexuality.

cultural and gender influences on student achievement

Although we have discussed gender differences and socioeconomic differences in this chapter, student performance is associated with multiple effects of gender, race or ethnic identification, and socioeconomic status. There are comparatively few studies that allow an examination of student achievement as a function of race or eth-

research at work
explanations for differential performance in the classroom

In discussing these results, the AAUW report suggests several possible explanations for differential performance.

- Racial and ethnic minorities are likely to attend schools that have fewer resources.
- Racial and ethnic minorities are more likely to live in neighborhoods that have fewer resources (including after-school jobs).
- The quality of instruction that minority females and males receive is apt to be inferior to the instruction that other students are receiving.
- Teachers' expectations for performance may lead them to offer more and less challenging environments to students based upon student race, ethnicity, and gender.
- Minority students may have less motivation to succeed in school because they believe they will still not qualify for desirable jobs because of bias (e.g., Ogbu, 1978).

nicity, sex, and socioeconomic status. The recent AAUW report (1992), *How Schools Shortchange Girls*, gives data from the National Educational Longitudinal Survey (NELS) of eighth graders for 1988 and from the High School and Beyond (HSB) study for 1980. In these sources, data are presented for African-Americans, whites, American Indians, Asian-Americans, and Hispanics. The data compare grades, test scores, and postschool plans of students.

Although there are important gender, racial, and ethnic differences, socioeconomic status is the best predictor for both grades and test scores. In general, girls do obtain better grades than boys (in both the NELS eighth-grade and HSB samples), even when socioeconomic status is controlled for. A notable exception is high-SES African-American females, whose grades are not better than their male counterparts in the HSB data set (gender performance was comparable). Asian-American girls consistently outperform all other groups.

Student performance and career plans often vary by race. Many of the differences narrow considerably when students from the same socioeconomic group are compared. Again, such data emphasize that socioeconomic status is more powerful than any other variable in predicting educational outcomes.

The powerful effects of SES on achievement are illustrated in the NELS sample. In general, low-SES students do not score well in the advanced reading or in the advanced math category; in contrast, few high-SES students fall below the basic skills level in core subjects like reading and math. These findings hold regardless of race or gender. Contrary to popular myth, low-SES Asian-American students do not do better than other low-SES students at the eighth-grade level.

There are some notable gender differences among eighth graders. Regardless of race, females of low SES are likely to do better than boys of low SES. However, in contrast, high-SES females are likely to do only as well, and often less well, than males. High-SES males, also do better than high-SES females in high school.

Racial and ethnic minorities are likely to attend schools and live in neighborhoods that have fewer resources.

As the AAUW report (1992) notes, these results raise important and provocative questions:

- Are more resources and attention given to high-SES males relative to high-SES females than are provided to low-SES males relative to low-SES females?
- Does low SES have a differential effect on the development of boys?
- Is it possible that boys of low SES invest less in school because they see their future job prospects as more diminished than girls'?

The NELS data indicate that among low-SES students, males are more likely than females to have repeated at least one grade. This pattern holds for African-American, white, and Hispanic males. However, African-American females are more like African-American males (in terms of grade retention) than females in any other group. The AAUW report (1992) indicates that one-third of all low-SES males are held back at least one grade. Recently, much media attention has focused on the retention of African-American males; however, the NELS data indicate that 29 percent of low-SES African-American females were also held back at least one grade (in contrast to 34 percent of African-American males).

Even after adjusting for SES, racial and ethnic differences are still found in the NELS and HSB data sets. Among low-SES students, grading differences by race tend to be small; however, high-SES whites and Asian-American do better than African-Americans and Hispanics. Also, comparing students from the same SES group diminishes some but not all racial differences in test scores: African-Americans and Hispanics receive lower test scores than do Asians and whites.

gender and race: classroom interaction

There is evidence that students' access to teachers is sometimes influenced by students' gender and race. Damico and Scott (1988) reported that although the achievement of white males and African-American females was comparable, teachers were more likely to reinforce the academic behavior of white males. Teachers were also more likely to encourage and support the academic behavior of white females but to pay more attention to and provide support for the social behavior of African-American females. Some teachers were more likely to call on African-Amrican females to help peers with nonacademic tasks and to ask white females to help peers with academic tasks. In part, such differences appear to be related to differential teacher expectations. Apparently some teachers may perceive African-American females to be socially, but not cognitively, mature.

Siddle-Walker (1992) notes that African-American females are likely to be perceived as responding inappropriately to teachers and are sometimes perceived by teachers as being "overactive." But Siddle-Walker notes that, according to her observations, they are actively attempting to participate in the class but do not understand teachers' rules for taking turns. Clearly for teachers to be effective in the classroom they must respect and understand cultural differences in students.

summary

SES and social class correlate with other variables such as race, ethnicity, and various religious, political, and social customs into clusters of characteristics that teachers should take into account in their planning. Well-educated, high-SES parents, for example, are likely to be more interested in school activities than are low-SES parents, especially those who have had limited educations and disappointing associations with schools. Teachers must deal with the problems that disadvantaged students present but also consider these students' needs for relevant knowledge, experience, and cognitive stimulation.

As we noted, today's schools are populated not only by students who differ in SES but also in culture. Unfortunately, students who come to school speaking a different language are often both discouraged from using their native language and actively punished. Different languages and cultural experiences are seen not as strengths but weaknesses that need to be corrected.

We have stressed in this chapter that teachers and schools need to value diversity in culture and respect student differences. Indeed, as teachers instruct culturally different students they need to reflect on how they can support and respect students' differences while helping them become active learners who integrate new knowledge with their cultural backgrounds while preparing to participate in a broader society.

The gender roles into which societies socialize their children interact with the student roles stressed in schools to create gender differences, both in the ways children respond to various school situations and in the varied ways teachers respond to boys and girls. Our society, and consequently our schooling, promotes much less extensive and rigid gender-role differentiation than in the past, which appears appropriate given data indicating that gender differences in intellectual and personal traits are few in number and very small in size and significance. Still, there are tendencies for boys to be more active and assertive in the classroom than girls, and for boys and girls to differ in their patterns of interest and achievement in various subjects. Teachers need to guard against drifting into self-defeating patterns of interaction with low-achieving and disruptive boys, as well as against interacting with girls in ways that encourage and reinforce obedience and conformity rather than intellectual assertiveness and achievement striving.

We have seen that structural variables (e.g., after-school jobs, peer cohort group) have important influences on students. Also, we have seen that gender issues and school opportunities for students who differ in race or ethnicity are influenced by the sociopolitical context in which schooling occurs. We believe that educators should perceive differences in students as resources they can build on in helping students to respect and value diversity.

questions for reflection

1. Persons promoted to supervisory positions in business and industry sometimes refuse promotion or resign their new jobs after a few weeks. They prefer to remain ordinary workers, at lower salaries and without administrative titles. Why?

2. Many Americans resist terms such as *socioeconomic status* or *social class* because they seem inconsistent with our traditional values of individualism and equality. If you feel this way, try to keep those feelings from biasing your responses when answering the following questions: (1) What is your own SES background? (2) How has it affected your development to date by influencing the experiences you have had? (3) Have you undergone changes in beliefs, attitudes, or behavior due to a change in SES? (4) How might your SES affect your interactions with students of various backgrounds?

3. How can schools and teachers simultaneously accomplish both of the following: (1) realistically take into account differences in SES, IQ, and other variables that can affect students' interest or readiness and (2) promote equal opportunity and quality education for all?

4. Gender-role socialization is so much a part of our society that we are all affected by it to

some degree. In what ways have you been affected by it?

5. If you are male, are you reluctant to show affection or emotions, or to do things traditionally associated with a woman's role? If you are female, are you inhibited about asserting yourself, exercising leadership and authority, competing, or doing things that are traditionally associated with men?

6. How do you react to men who have characteristics traditionally labeled as feminine or to women who have characteristics traditionally labeled as masculine? What does this mean for you as a teacher?

7. What is your stance on integrating multicultural issues into the school curriculum? Which of the four levels suggested by Nieto is most appealing to you? Why? How does your view compare to that of your peers?

8. As a teacher, how would you deal with a situation in which girls assume a passive role in teamwork (they take notes) while boys assume more active roles (they dissect the frog, wire the circuit, etc.)? How could you change students' attitudes and beliefs as well as their behavior?

cases to consider

language barrier Tran Van Do is a recent Vietnamese immigrant assigned to Jo Cornell's class. He is the same age as the other students but cannot participate much or do many assignments because he knows very little English. Jo arranges to have him tested, and he is given the parts of the WISC-R that do not require language facility. His performance on these subtests would translate into an IQ of 115 if matched by equivalent performance on the verbal subtests. What, if anything, does this tell Jo about how to plan instruction for Tran?

exploration in sexism Janet Trumbower and Henry Marshall team teach at the sixth grade in an integrated school. They have decided to examine the degree of monoculturalism and sexism present in their social studies instruction, including curriculum content, student-student dialogue, teacher-teacher interaction, and teacher-student conversations. They intend to involve students in the process. How might they make this a valuable learning experience for everyone? How could they collect evidence (what would be looked at and by whom)? Are there things that they should be careful to avoid in this process?

harassment Judy Burden, a ninth-grade Spanish teacher at Rockhurst Junior High, watched as students entered her third-period advanced Spanish class. She noticed as Tim "brushed up" against Alicia. Alicia (angry and red faced) said, "Tim, don't do that again." Tim smiled broadly and said, "You know you like it." If you were Judy, what would you do and say?

educating students
with special needs

objectives

When you have mastered the material in this chapter, you will be able to

1. Explain why some students' disabilities merit special classroom plans
2. Discuss three problems associated with the education of students with disabling conditions in special settings and programs
3. Explain how Public Law (P.L.) 94–142 attempts to remedy the problems of special education through mainstreaming within the least restrictive environment
4. Explain the regular education initiative (REI) and discuss how teachers can prepare themselves and their students to deal effectively with students with disabilities
5. Explain how P.L. 99-456 and P.L. 98-199 amend and extend special services offered under P.L. 94–142
6. Understand why many educators advocate non-

categorical programs and discuss the philosophy that underlies noncategorical programming
7. Define various disabilities and tell how teachers can assist students with these disabilities
8. Explain what an individualized educational program (IEP) is, how one is written, and how it attempts to ensure due process for those with disabilities
9. Define gifted education, recognize the criteria used for placing gifted students in special programs, and explain how teachers can teach these students effectively
10. Understand that many students who are intellectually gifted may also have disabling conditions that merit special consideration
11. Identify expectations that may reduce the performance of intellectually gifted students and explain how teachers can counteract this problem through appropriate curriculum assignments

Theoretically, our national policy of free public education for all means that the public schools are available to any student who wants to enroll. For much of our history, however, African-American students either received no public education or were required to attend segregated schools. Unfortunately, even today many African-American and Hispanic students receive instruction in segregated schools (Hacker, 1992; Kozol, 1991). Moreover, students initially considered appropriate for admission to public schools may be excluded from regular school programs because they are judged to disrupt normal classroom procedures.

Courts have upheld such exclusion on the basis of mental and physical deficiencies, health problems, pregnancy, flagrant or willful misbehavior, and even unconventional clothes or personal appearance. As a result, enrollment in regular public school classrooms used to be more a privilege for those who met specific criteria than a guaranteed right. More recent court decisions have struck down most of these exclusionary criteria, however, so that attendance in regular public school programs now is more

clearly established as a universal right in practice as well as in theory (Schloss, 1992a).

Understanding the legitimate needs of students with disabling conditions has increased notably in the past twenty years, as has the willingness of educators to accommodate special students. Further, there is growing recognition that all students are special and hence deserving of personalized attention (Ainscow, 1991; Stainback & Stainback, 1992). Thus, as we shall see, educators have moved from a policy of *exclusion* to policies of *inclusion*.

the traditional emphasis on special placement

Most students affected by these changes have special educational needs because of various disabilities (impairment in vision, emotional disturbances, etc.). Until recently, many of these students were placed in special institutions such as schools for the blind or deaf. Those with less extreme disabilities usually were accepted by the public schools but often were segregated from other students for part or all of the day. They attended "special-education classes" or spent much of their time in "resource rooms" where instructors could provide them with more individual attention and specialized help.

In theory, this approach made good sense: identify students who have special needs using screening procedures followed with diagnostic test batteries where indicated, follow diagnosis with needs assessment to identify the special services and forms of instruction that individual students require, and then place them in settings with special teachers who are prepared to provide appropriate educational experiences. Unfortunately, this is not what usually happened. Students who were placed in special settings often received instruction and work that were too simple or otherwise inappropriate. Disenchantment set in, and sentiment gradually switched from special placement to retaining special students in the regular classroom for various reasons including: (1) equivocal results of research on the effectiveness of special classes, (2) recognition that many of the instruments used to identify retardation were inadequate, (3) realization that the problems of being labeled and segregated into special settings might be greater than those involved in coping with disabilities in normal settings, and (4) court litigation that took the above problems into account and stressed the rights of all students to the appropriate educational treatment over the rights of schools to choose their clients.

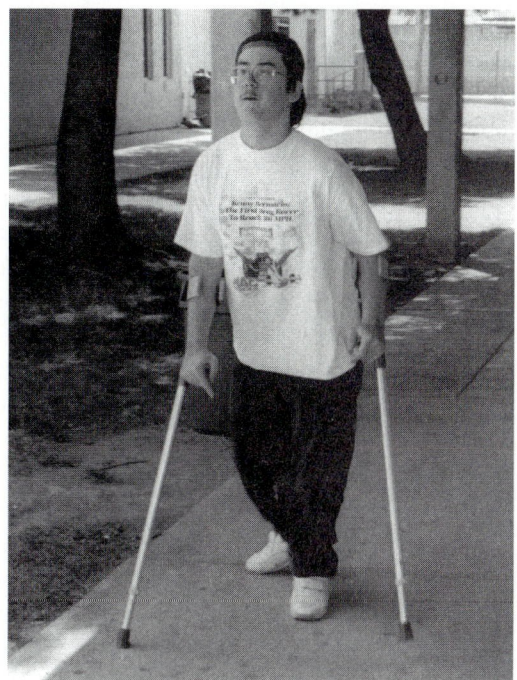
Special students have special needs.

problems with special placement

Data on the effectiveness of special settings and programs are unimpressive. Special programs for the deaf seem to work reasonably well; deaf students in special schools show higher achievement than comparable deaf students in regular schools. Beyond this, however, it is not clear that specialized programs and settings provide benefits that students with mild disabilities cannot obtain in regular classrooms (Macmillan, Keogh, & Jones, 1986; Schloss, 1992a).

The data on diagnosis are equally discouraging. First, the problem of cultural bias is serious (Brantlinger & Guskin, 1987). Brantlinger and Guskin noted that more students from lower-class homes are identified as having disabilities. But they reported that the extent of this pattern varies depending on the location and the characteristics of the sample studied and may be compounded if students are tested in English when English is not their primary language.

Diagnostic testing has been misused. Often the classroom teacher must request such testing, and many do so more out of a desire to get rid of students who present personality or behavior problems than out of concern about meeting these students' special educational needs. In some districts, special classrooms became dumping grounds for such students, whereas peers with similar abilities, test profiles, and achievement levels were kept in regular classrooms because they got along better with their teachers. This caused many low-SES and minority-group parents to resist placement of their children in special classes, even though at the same time many middle-class parents sought to expand special educational services.

In addition to problems with the instruments themselves and with the justifications for their use, there are also questions about the reliability and validity of special-education diagnoses and the presumed linkages between diagnoses and treatments. For example, specialists show poor agreement with one another and even with themselves when they encounter the same case twice (Vinsonhaler et al., 1983).

There is also reason for concern about the negative effects of labeling and segregation. Psychologists and sociologists have long recognized that being labeled as different can produce social stigma, damage the self-concept, and initiate a series of negative self-fulfilling prophecy effects (Mackie & Hamilton, 1993). The process is exaggerated if the stigma results in segregation of the "different" from the "normal" (Ianacone & Stodden, 1987).

Educators' recognition of these problems led to a change of attitudes in the early 1970s, and during the 1970s and 1980s students with mild disabilities were returned from special to regular classrooms. Court litigation gradually speeded up this process, and this legal activity culminated on a national scale with the passage of Public Law 94–142 in 1975.

the effects of Public Law 94–142

Public Law 94–142, the Education for All Handicapped Children Act, became effective in the mid 1970's. The law called for a number of sweeping changes, although its implementation was left primarily to individual states—there has been considerable variation among states. Overall, important changes in schooling have resulted from P.L. 94–142.

In short, this law commits the nation to a policy of mainstreaming and inclusion of students with disabilities by placing them in the least restrictive environment in which they will be able to function and still have their special needs met. **Mainstreaming** is *a policy by which these students will be kept in the mainstream of general public education by being placed as often as possible in regular classrooms rather than segregated into separate institutions or special classes.* Students are expected to spend as much time as possible in regular classrooms with ordinary students and function as ordinary students by participating in essentially the same ways in the same activities.

There is increasing resistance to removing students from regular classrooms unless there is a clear need for a special program. Indeed, teachers are expected to exhaust all reasonable possibilities before seeking special programs (Schloss, 1992b).

least restrictive environment principle

The **least restrictive environment** is *the educational setting most like the regular classroom (in many cases, this means placement in a regular classroom) in which an individual can succeed.* The term implies that special students are not to be classified by disability and given permanent special placement on the basis of these classifications but instead are to be moved to special settings only if necessary and only for as long as necessary. Schloss (1992a) noted that the least restrictive environment provision "encourages educators to demonstrate the ineffectiveness of regular education practices prior to referral for special education services . . . even when placement in a full-time special class setting is agreed on, the team remains vigilant for opportunities to return the student" to regular-class settings (pp. 233-34).

Individuals with Disabilities Education Act: IDEA

Bateman (1992) argued the importance of the IDEA act in the following way.

> Drastic winds of change swept across the field of learning disabilities in the mid 1970s, reforming the entire scene. With the advent of the Education for All Handicapped Children Act of 1975 (now the Individuals with Disabilities Education Act or IDEA), learning disabilities moved from the clinic to the classroom. The numbers of children identified as learning disabled grew from a few thousand to over two million. (p. 92)

However, as Bateman noted, there are still considerable gaps in the field's knowledge about learning disabilities per se and too few curriculum materials for students with disabilities.

regular education initiative: REI

Historical and continuing problems with educating students with mild disabilities in special placements have led to an increasing interest in finding solutions within the regular educational setting (Ainscow, 1991; Salend, 1990; Semmel et al., 1991; Will, 1986). The reform of existing special education services is commonly referred to as the **regular education initiative, or REI**—*the integration, inclusion, or mainstreaming of students with mild disabilities from special programs to regular classrooms.*

Although most professionals support REI, there is considerable disagreement about *which* students with particular types of disabilities should be reintegrated, *when* they should be reintegrated (that is, what skills they should possess before they enter regular classrooms), and *what* type of curriculum they should receive when they reenter the regular classroom.

Work by Semmel and associates (1991) illustrates that many regular educators have concerns that must be dealt with if transition programs are to work. For example, Semmel and associates reported that many educators did not predict positive achievement gains for special or regular students as a result of REI initiatives. Other concerns were that newly reintegrated students might slow the pace of instruction and that these students might not benefit socially from the placement in regular classrooms.

As a classroom teacher you should realize that both the law of the land and professional sentiment argue that students should be in the least restrictive environment. However, there is considerable disagreement among professionals about when students are ready for reintegration. As a teacher you will often have to make difficult decisions about when students should be removed from a classroom to a special setting or about the curriculum students should receive when they are reintegrated. Although other specialists and parents will be involved in making such decisions, a key aspect of the process is your judgment based on careful observations of and reflection on student performance (both social and academic). The goal is to place students in the least restrictive environment (Schloss, 1992a); however, for some students that environment is a special setting.

implementation of P.L. 94–142

P.L. 94–142 did not fully spell out its implementation, so this has been determined gradually by court decisions, state laws, and local practices. The law did place six major requirements on state programs as a condition of obtaining federal support:

- Students with disabling conditions must be educated, to the maximum extent appropriate, in the least restrictive environment.
- Nondiscriminatory, culture-free testing in the native language of the student is necessary before placement into special programs.
- Prior consultation with parents must take place before special placement.
- An individualized educational program (IEP) must be prepared for each disabled student.
- Public school programs must serve non-public school students if they are disabled and need services that the federal government funds.
- Staff development programs must be conducted in every school district.

Note that these guidelines concentrate on ensuring due process, provision of services, and availability of staff development programs, but they do not mandate the content of the programs. This is determined primarily by school districts. There is considerable professional advice but little research-based knowledge about how to implement mainstreaming

(policies of inclusion) optimally (Fuchs, Fuchs, & Fernstrom, 1992), so local specialists will likely determine implementation in a given school district. Available research suggests that effective reintegration or mainstreaming strategies generally involve what are considered effective teaching techniques (Scruggs & Mastropieri, 1992).

There is currently much experimentation concerning both what kinds of special students should be placed in regular classrooms and what special arrangements (if any) their regular teachers must make. Teachers can get materials and help from itinerant special-education teachers or other consultants, as well as guidelines from in-service activities and from the IEP written for each student. If there is a special-education resource room in the building, mainstreamed students may spend part of the day there being taught in a group by the resource room teacher. This teacher is also available as a consultant to regular classroom teachers.

research on mainstreaming and reintegration

Research on the effects of mainstreaming has yielded complex findings that do not lend themselves to generalizations, for at least three reasons. First, most research has been on program labels and has addressed only simple questions (e.g., Does enrollment in special programs influence student achievement?). Too little attention has been given to instruction within programs. Second, one program label often means different things in different settings. Mainstreaming and least restrictive environment may mean one thing in one seventh-grade class and something different in another (even one that is located across the hallway in the same building). Further, even when labels convey similar meanings, a par-

Some researchers feel that instruction in special and regular classrooms is often indistinguishable.

ticular philosophy may be implemented in various ways (i.e., issues of program quality).

Although the literature is complex and too few field observational studies have been completed, three generalizations can be made from research on mainstreaming. First, programs that take students with mildly disabling conditions from regular classrooms and place them in special rooms for instruction appear to have less positive effects on achievement than approaches in which students receive instruction in regular classrooms with nondisabled peers (Leinhardt, 1980; Madden & Slavin, 1983; Thompson, White, & Morgan, 1982). Even so, a second generalization is that the quality of instruction that students with mild disabilities receive in regular classrooms is still low in too many instances. Indeed, instruction for these students in special and regular classrooms is often indistinguishable (Epps & Tindal, 1987; Macmillan, Keogh, & Jones, 1986; Stainback

& Stainback, 1992). Much of what is known about how students learn is not applied to instruction of students with mildly disabling conditions. Third, many special educators believe that educators need to reduce substantially the numbers of students who are given special-education labels and assigned to be taught in pull-out programs (Ainscow, 1991; Alper & Ryndak, 1992; Fuchs, Fuchs, & Fernstrom, 1992; Peterson, 1988).

Some students with mildly disabling conditions do not make progress in regular classrooms because they are not actively taught, but others may fail because teachers do too much for them. Stipek and Sanborn (1983) observed teacher-child interactions in two preschool programs, focusing on teachers' interactions with mainstreamed children with disabilities and children perceived as "high risk" for academic problems. They found that teachers offered unrequested assistance and praise to those with disabilities and high-risk children more than to nondisabled children and suggested that this pattern resulted from the teachers' desire to compensate for the children's disabilities. By initiating the majority of their interactions with these children, however, the teachers may have conditioned the children to play a passive role. That is, the students did not need to seek information or assistance because their teachers always offered it to them. Teachers of mainstreamed students need to guard against being overly critical and demanding of these students, but they also need to realize that they can do too much for them (Cullinan, Sabornie, & Crossland, 1992). Students have to initiate and learn on their own as well as respond to teacher structuring.

To reiterate, research on mainstreaming or reintegration is incomplete because it has not focused enough on the quality and appropriateness of instruction that students with mild disabilities receive. This absence of process research is especially acute regarding the transition from special to regular settings. For example, Fuchs, Fuchs, and Fernstrom (1992) report that their examination of eight special education journals over sixteen years yielded only nine studies in which researchers had explored the process of moving students from a more restrictive to a less restrictive classroom. Although some researchers have documented the reintegration process (e.g., Fuchs, Fuchs, & Fernstrom, 1992), more studies are needed to help educators move from a policy of exclusion (separate educational programs and facilities) to inclusion.

Still, evidence leads to several broad conclusions that can guide educational practice.

1. **Pull-out instruction** (*instruction that occurs outside the regular classroom*) is overused, and too many students are assigned to special programs. Although some pull-out programs are effective, they generally result in minimal achievement gains for three reasons. First, students often receive no special instruction (geared to a particular need) and sometimes receive less instruction than they do in regular classrooms.

Second, students often receive a fragmented curriculum because there is little or no coordination between regular and pull-out programs. Furthermore, different teaching styles often result in varied and sometimes conflicting performance expectations for students in regular and pull-out programs. Third, the "special-education" label (perhaps especially when students are in regular, special education classes rather than supplemental instruction rooms) may be associated with lower student and teacher expectations for performance as well as reduced opportunity for students to interact with peers who differ in ability, learning style, or ethnicity.

2. A growing literature indicates that students who have mild disabilities learn in similar ways and generally benefit from the same type of instruction as do other students. Too often students who have mild disabilities or who are perceived as low achievers receive less reading instruction in the regular classroom or in the special program. Furthermore, the instruction they do receive is overly focused on drill and workbook exercises.

3. When possible, students with mild disabilities usually are best instructed in regular classrooms. Many students, however, have disabling conditions that benefit from some pull-out instruction, especially if it is coordinated with what occurs in the regular classroom and designed to remediate specific problems. Hence, what happens in a program—its quality—is important, not its label.

4. Considerably more research needs to focus on the process of reintegrating students with learning disabilities.

noncategorical instruction programs

Although we discuss specific types of disabilities in the sections that follow, we have some reservations about doing so because there is a tendency to overreact to a label (e.g., behavior disordered, learning disabled) as if it had some precise meaning and indicated specific instructional needs. This is not the case. Snow (1984), for example, noted that educable mentally retarded (EMR) students differ from one another in as many ways as do other students. He stressed that educators need to identify these students' particular strengths as well as their weaknesses and to prescribe treatment accordingly. According to Snow, some special-education programs simply establish lower expectations for students instead of adapting instruction to individual differences in order to achieve as many common goals as possible (i.e., goals that other students achieve).

Ysseldyke (1987) acknowledges that many students have difficulty learning in school because of cognitive deficits, perceptual problems, emotional disorders, or language problems. However, he argues that the concepts that should drive practice have lost intended meaning, so terms such as "learning disabled" or "emotionally disturbed" do not have any clear instructional implications. Some of the issues associated with labeling are summarized in Figure 22.1.

The term **noncategorical** refers to *instructional programs that include a range of students with mild disabilities and deny that classifying labels (e.g., learning disabled, mentally retarded) are important to instruction.* Few would argue for totally abandoning student classification, and even most proponents of noncategorical programs acknowledge the need for certain broad distinctions. Such proponents try to be conservative, however, in that they believe that treatments associated with pupil characteristics should have demonstrated validity before they are applied in schools.

We believe the preceding caveats are important and that teachers need to realize that definitions of disabilities are general approximations. Students who share the same label may have vastly different instructional needs. However, since categories of disabilities provide general definitions of limitations and broadly outline instructional opportunities, and because some legisla-

Figure 22.1 issues associated with labeling

Possible Benefits of Labeling

1. Categories can relate diagnosis to specific treatment.
2. Labeling may lead to a "protective" response, in which non-labeled children accept certain behaviors of their handicapped peers more fully than they would accept those same behaviors in "normal" children.
3. Labeling helps professionals to communicate with one another and to classify and assess research findings.
4. Funding of special education programs is often based on specific categories of exceptionality.
5. Labels allow special interest groups to promote specific programs and spur legislative action.
6. Labeling helps make the special needs of exceptional children more visible in the public eye.

Possible Disadvantages of Labeling

1. Labels usually focus on negative aspects of the child, causing others to think about the child only in terms of inadequacies or defects.
2. Labels may cause others to react to and hold low expectations for a child based on the label, resulting in a self-fulfilling prophecy.
3. A labeled child might develop a poor self-concept.
4. Labels might lead peers to reject or ridicule the labeled child.
5. Special education labels have a certain permanence about them. Once labeled as "retarded" or "learning disabled," it is difficult for a child ever again to achieve the status of being "just like all the other kids."
6. Labels often provide a basis by which children can be kept out of the regular classroom.
7. A disproportionate number of children from minority culture groups may be inaccurately labeled "handicapped," especially as educably mentally retarded.

SOURCE: W. Heward and M. Orlansky, *Exceptional Children*. Third Edition (Columbus, OH: Merrill Publishing Company, 1984). Reprinted by permission of the publisher.

tion still ties funding to these classifications, we will discuss these categories in this chapter.

teaching special students: general considerations

P.L. 94–142 has blurred the distinction between regular and special education, so most teachers now need training in methods of meeting the needs of special students in addition to the traditional preparation for teaching. This is especially the case since some educators even encourage teachers to assume instructional responsibility not only for students with mild disabilities but also for students with severe disabilities (Alper & Ryndak, 1992).

In preparing to work with students with disabilities, teachers need to shed any stereotypes they may have developed because of past labeling and segregation of these students. Their disabilities limit what they can do, but they are not different from other students in other respects. They develop and learn according to the same general principles, respond to the same kinds of incentives, develop the same kinds of motivational systems, and so on. For the most part, then, the principles described throughout this book apply as much to students with disabilities as to other students (Larrivee, 1985; Scruggs & Mastropieri, 1992).

In fact, most types of students who were returned from special settings to regular classrooms as part of the mainstreaming effort used to be taught in regular classrooms before special-education settings proliferated. Classroom teachers known to the authors report that these students tend *not* to be defiant or threatening. Instead, they are mostly slower and more dependent than their classmates, so their special needs are more instructional than managerial (for example, they may require more structured teaching and more use of individualized programs and perhaps contract systems). Many of them are enjoyable to teach because they want to succeed and will try hard to do so.

Teachers can prepare to reintegrate students with special needs by reading about (see, for example, Schloss, 1992b) and taking courses in special education and consulting with specialists. Recently there have been important advances in technology that assists students with disabilities to learn more effectively (Wisniewski & Sedlak, 1992). Thus, teachers could profitably consult with specialists about learning aids that may be available for particular disabilities (e.g., blindness, deafness). Teachers can also observe in classrooms where students with disabilities are mainstreamed, both to learn about techniques teachers are using and about the students themselves. It is always helpful to analyze classroom events from the perspective of students (McCaslin & Good, in press, b) but especially from the perspective of students with disabilities: What classroom tasks can they accomplish as well as other students without special provisions or help? What additional tasks might they accomplish with assistance? When they cannot accomplish tasks even with assistance, are there other approaches that might allow them to get the same benefits?

These questions illustrate a major consideration to keep in mind in dealing with special students: Instead of concentrating on their disabilities, capitalize on their strengths to help them compensate. Certain goals may have to be reduced, and some disabled students may have to be taught in unusual ways, but by and large these students should pursue the same objectives as other students. Like regular students, special students need positive but realistic expectations and instruction designed to enable them to realize those goals.

There is evidence that some teachers hold inappropriate expectations for students with disabilities. Hannah and Pilner (1983) found that although there was variation in attitudes toward particular disabling conditions, many teachers, especially secondary teachers, had negative attitudes toward these students and were somewhat reluctant to teach them. Guskin and Jones (1982) noted that attitudes toward persons with disabilities tended to be less favorable than those toward the nondisabled and that the intensity of negative attitudes varied with the type and severity of disability.

Although they acknowledge that regular classroom teachers' negative attitudes can undermine reintegration, Fuchs, Fuchs, and Fernstrom (1992) believe that negative attitudes have been overstressed and that another critical factor has gone almost unexamined. They contend that many skills and strategies taught in more restrictive environments do not transfer when students attempt to use them in less restrictive environments. Thus, many teachers see reintegrated students as unprepared. According to the Fuchs team, "we believe this perceived unpreparedness, more than some teachers' a priori biases, contributes to the negative view of children with disabilities and mainstreaming, which sometimes is reported by practitioners and documented in the literature" (p. 263). However, as we have seen, there is considerable evidence that many teachers have concerns about disabled students' ability to benefit from being in the regular classroom (Semmel et al., 1991).

implications for teachers

preparing the class for mainstreamed students

Teachers involved in mainstreaming often structure not only their own expectations and behavior but those of other students in their classes as well. What to tell a class depends on the nature of incoming mainstreamed students' disabilities and on what the students can and cannot do without assistance. If an impairment is not obvious, it may be best to say nothing at all about it to other students and to let the mainstreamed student enter the class as any other newcomer would. However, because some students have negative stereotypes about students with disabilities, teachers may want to use a student's reintegration to help classmates develop more positive attitudes toward disabling conditions. For example, Cullinan, Saborine, and Crossland (1992) suggest that teachers provide students with information about various disabilities, make them aware of the contributions made by various people with disabilities, and hold discussions about appropriate attitudes toward persons with disabilities.

In the case of obvious disabilities, students in the class should be told what to expect and how to act. You should obtain students' cooperation in welcoming new students and in helping them to participate as much as they possibly can as regular members of the class. Impairments should be described directly and matter-of-factly:

> Class, tomorrow we are going to be joined by a new member named Linda Johnson. We will need to rearrange the room a little to get ready for Linda because she uses a wheelchair. Several years ago she had an accident that left her paralyzed from about the waist down, so she can't walk. She hasn't let this stop her from keeping up with her studies and participating in most activities outside the classroom, however. You'll see for yourselves starting tomorrow. Meanwhile, though, I was thinking that she could park her wheelchair right up in front of this row here. There is a nice clear path between here and the door. She won't need a regular desk, but she will need some place to keep her things. We could move that bookcase up next to where her wheelchair will be parked . . .

You can go on to ask if there are any questions, answering any that can be answered clearly and asking students for their suggestions about how to welcome Linda to the class. You may want to clarify certain attributions that students may make about a student's behavior if they are likely to interfere with integration (e.g., discussing certain minor behaviors—like tics—that may be beyond the learner's control). A few students might be assigned as a welcoming committee to make a point of getting to know Linda and "showing her the ropes" as well as providing her with any special help she may need (peer tutoring is often valuable for meeting the needs of mainstreamed students). Since some students may be reluctant to interact with students who have disabilities, you should structure a few learning activities that allow immediate social contact (group project, peer tutoring, etc.). However, as Cullinan, Sabornie, and Crossland (1992) caution, teachers should not force interaction because this could create resentment toward the child who is being reintegrated.

In general, then, you can prepare for mainstreaming by informing yourself about, observing, and talking with students with disabilities, especially those being mainstreamed in other classrooms. Conversations with other teachers will also be useful in helping you to establish appropriate expectations and behavior in your own classroom.

preparing the disabled student for reintegration

Teachers can probably help the students being reintegrated to adjust by meeting with them in advance, being sure that they understand expected classroom behavior, and assessing students' beliefs about their academic abilities and their possible reactions to classroom assignments (see motivation chapters—especially attribution theory). Such an interview (possibly with parents or guardians as well) could help students to verbalize special interests or concerns about joining the class. Teachers' decisions about classroom grouping could be informed by such conversations: Is the new student excessively concerned about negative peer relations? Is the student reluctant to speak in front of the class? Such interviews might help teachers and classmates avoid irritating or embarrassing the student.

dealing with special disability conditions

Many students with disabilities have been taught successfully in regular classrooms all along (students who have allergies, asthma, arthritis, amputation, diabetes, epilepsy, cerebral palsy, or muscular dystrophy). We will not discuss these types of health disabilities here because of their great variety. Brantlinger and Guskin (1987) discussed educational interventions for students who are culturally, linguistically, and/or situationally unique. In particular, they analyzed instructional needs of rural children, American Indian children, children of migrant workers, and children with limited English proficiency. Suggestions for dealing with students who have major disabilities follow.

visual impairment

Two broad distinctions are often made within the larger category of visual impairment. **Blind** students have *central vision acuity of 20/200 or less in the better eye after correction.* Students whose visual fields are restricted to twenty degrees (tunnel vision) are usually classified as blind as well.

Partially sighted students have *visual limitations that interfere with their learning to the extent that they require special teaching services and aids if they are to perform up to their potential.*

identifying possible visual loss

Smith and Luckasson (1992) indicate that the following are some possible signs of visual impairment:

- Eyes water excessively
- Eyes are red
- Eyes look dull
- One or both pupils look(s) gray or white
- One or both eye(s) turn in or out, or move differently from the other
- Student frequently bumps into or trips over things
- Student has difficulty reading small print or details
- Student has trouble discriminating a letter
- Student rubs eyes often or complains of dizziness after a reading assignment
- Student uses one eye frequently (perhaps shutting or covering the other eye when reading)

strategies for helping visually impaired learners

Smith and Luckasson (1992) stress the following points for teachers when working with visually impaired learners:

1. The students' desks should be close to the teacher's desk, the blackboard, the overhead projector, and the classroom door.
2. When making demonstrations that require close examination, allow students to move as close to the presentation as they need in order to see and hear.
3. Be sure that the classroom is always free of any dangerous obstacles, including clutter and litter.
4. Be sure to open or close doors *fully*; a partially open door can be dangerous.

5. Eliminate as much unnecessary noise from the learning environment as possible.
6. Do not speak in an excessively loud voice, for this increases the volume level in a classroom—including the background noise.
7. Consider the individual's visual impairment, but do not let the impairment be an excuse for poor or unacceptable performance.
8. Always place needed materials in the same location to allow students to find them easily and thus to promote self-management.
9. Never leave the room without telling the students.

hearing impairment

Educators (e.g., Hallahan & Kauffman, 1991) stress that the age of onset of hearing impairment is important. This is because the earlier the hearing loss develops, the more difficulty a child will have in developing language (because of the close relationship between hearing loss and language delay). Professionals working with hearing-impaired children frequently distinguish between prelingual and postlingual deafness. Prelingual deafness is present at birth and postlingual deafness occurs afterward (six to eighteen months after birth).

identifying possible hearing loss

Smith and Luckasson (1992) list some of the following as possible signs or characteristics of hearing impairments:

- Has difficulty following oral instructions—even simple ones
- Watches the teacher's lips very carefully
- Turns an ear toward the speaker
- Is inattentive during lectures or class discussions
- Complains of earaches
- Has ear discharge
- Has frequent ear infections

- Turns on equipment very loudly, e.g., listening to a TV or audiotape in the room

ways in which the teacher can assist

1. Make referral to specialist for complete evaluation.
2. If the loss is slight (20 to 40 decibels), the student may benefit from a hearing aid and from extra help with new vocabulary. Favorable seating and lighting, as well as speech-reading instruction, may be needed.
3. Students with moderate (41 to 55 decibels) hearing losses can hear conversational speech at a distance of three to five feet but may miss as much as 50 percent of class discussion if they cannot see the lips of speakers or if speakers' voices are weak. Hence, teachers need to make visual cues available (speak clearly, don't turn away from the student when talking, and don't stand between the student and the window).
4. If the hearing loss is marked (56 to 70 decibels), teacher speech must be very loud to be understood. Also, the student will have difficulty participating in group discussion and is likely to have problems with vocabulary (language usage and comprehension). Listening is hard work for such students, so they may become fatigued during activities that involve prolonged listening.
5. The teacher needs to learn how hearing aids function and how to maintain them.

lectures

Hallahan and Kauffman (1991) make the following suggestions for helping teachers to improve their lectures and discussions with hearing-impaired students.

- Use an overhead projector to note important points thus allowing you to face students while you talk.
- Stay in one place in the room so that students can see your face.
- When possible make relatively short and simple verbalizations.

- Repeat main points as necessary.
- Provide appropriate nonverbal cues to enhance communication.
- Call speakers' names to reduce the time a student has to spend to locating the source of speech.
- Require students to raise their hands before they speak to reduce the noise and confusion that results from several people talking at once.

oral instruction

Garwood (1987) offers the following "speech" checklist for teachers (or other adults) to use when they are providing hearing-impaired students with oral instruction:

s	=	state the topic to be discussed
p	=	pace conversation at a moderate speed with occasional pauses to permit comprehension
e	=	enunciate clearly without exaggerated lip movements
e	=	enthusiastically communicate, using body language and natural gestures
ch	=	check comprehensions before changing topics

speech impairment

Students with speech impairments cannot comprehend the spoken language of others or cannot express themselves meaningfully with spoken words. The most frequent problems that public school teachers deal with are *articulation disorders*. There are four common articulation disorders: Omissions (*at* for *that*), substitutions (*that* for *than*), distortions (*shled* for *shed*), and additions (*puhlease* for *please*). Other problems include voice disorders (e.g., too loud, too soft, pitch too high) and stuttering.

1. Refer students to speech therapist for complete evaluation.
2. Help students to pronounce correct sounds.
3. Help students to *hear* their spoken errors.
4. Encourage students to use new words frequently once they can pronounce the words correctly.
5. Help students to rehearse oral skills (e.g., introducing someone) and allow them to practice the skills publicly.

stuttering

Stuttering is still poorly understood. No one really knows what causes it, despite a variety of explanations. Thus, advice on how to help students who stutter varies widely. However, the following suggestions are frequently made:

1. Cue these students before calling on them.
2. Focus on the content of what they say, not how they say it.
3. Do not label them as stutterers.
4. Do not allow them to use stuttering as a crutch (to avoid schoolwork). If the stuttering prohibits participation in an activity, be sure to have them do an additional written assignment (or some other substitute activity).
5. Many students stutter in one situation (e.g., when called on to answer) but not another (e.g., reading aloud). If so, continue to give them plenty of oral practice in situations that do not create problems, to build confidence that may generalize to problem situations.

mild mental retardation

Students with disabilities and with mild retardation are the largest groups of special students with which regular classroom teachers work.

Mental retardation refers to *subaverage general intellectual functioning with accompanying deficits in adaptive behavior.* To be classified as having retardation, then, a child must have both a low IQ and difficulty adapting to social situations. In general, only children with mild retardation (with an IQ of 50 to 70) are likely to be mainstreamed, not students with more severe mental limitations.

According to Smith and Luckasson (1992), the following are some of the possible precursors to or signs of mental retardation:

- A difficult delivery for the mother
- A history of alcohol and drug abuse in the family
- A home environment that provides limited stimulation and few resources
- The child is a victim of abuse or neglect
- Language development is delayed
- Physical abilities seem immature
- Social abilities seem delayed
- Student seems not to respond as quickly as age peers
- Student has difficulties in school

1. Focus on a *few* basic skills.
2. Provide concrete learning experiences as frequently as possible.
3. Present instruction in brief periods (five to ten minutes).
4. Provide frequent feedback and review.
5. Give simple, step-by-step directions.
6. Try to eliminate possible distractions.
7. Use curriculum materials that are appropriate to students' interests and reading levels.
8. Be alert to the fact that these students need more time to learn the same material.
9. After students have learned something, provide many practice/recall opportunities.
10. Do not repeatedly do for these students things that they should learn to do for themselves.

other ways of conceptualizing and responding to mental retardation

Smith and Luckasson (1992) stress that students with impaired intellectual abilities must be seen as people first—as individual students who have all of the emotions, motivations, and desires of other students. Thus, teachers need to recognize that these students have many needs that are exactly the same as their age mates. Smith and Luckasson (1992) provide the following advice and information for teachers who work with retarded students:

(1) Realize that most students with impaired intellectual ability have mild mental retardation. About 89 percent of individuals with mental retardation function at the mild level. Many of these students are not in special education at all, although most such students will spend some time in their school careers in special education programs. Only 4 percent of all students with mental retardation have severe disabilities that require extreme and creative efforts from educators and parents.

(2) Early identification and early intervention are critical. In many cases, the effects of retardation can be lessened or even prevented with early intervention.

(3) Mental retardation is caused by many factors (including both enviornmental and biological causes). However, the frequency of mental retadation could be reduced in important ways through simple prevention techniques.

(4) Teachers in public schools must by law individualize students' learning needs. In some cases they will call for specialized academic instruction in reading and mathematics. However, for other students this will mean instruction in functional skills of daily living and cooperating with others. An important goal for the school is to help students to develop more capacity for self-direction and self-responsibility so that many of them can eventually live autonomous lives as adults.

behavior disorders

Behavior disorders *involve one or more of the following characteristics to a marked extent over time: (1) inability to learn that cannot be explained by intellectual deficiencies or health problems, (2) difficulty relating to peers and teachers, (3) extreme behavioral reactions to normal events, (4) general moodiness or depression, (5) frequent physical symptoms or fear associated with school problems.*

ways in which the teacher can assist

1. Verbalize to students the problems they present to the teacher or other students (i.e., tell them gently but honestly why others react to them negatively).
2. Help students to dispel the delusion of uniqueness (no one has problems like mine).
3. Model appropriate expression of emotion.
4. Stop misbehavior or emotionality before it becomes traumatic.
5. Develop firm behavioral expectations and clear managerial guidelines.
6. Provide praise when warranted (specify the praiseworthy behavior).
7. Set up places where these students can work alone occasionally.
8. Don't expect quick results or give up because you see little progress. These students' maladaptive behaviors were established over a long time. It takes time to resocialize inappropriate behavior.

orthopedic disabilities

Orthopedic disabilities include *defects of structure or function of bones, joints, or muscles.* Such disadvantages limit movement, but in the absence of other disabling conditions, students with orthopedic problems can learn the same material that nondisadvantaged students of similar aptitude learn.

1. Allow these students to do whatever they can for themselves.
2. When necessary, allow them to leave the room a couple of minutes early to avoid crowded hallways.
3. If a student is wearing orthopedic equipment, learn how it works and how to assist when simple malfunctions occur.
4. Be alert for safety problems (e.g., bad brakes on wheelchairs, worn crutch tips that will not provide stability on a slippery floor).

learning disabilities

Learning disabilities include *a range of disorders in which students have learning problems (usually language usage) that do not involve significant emotional difficulties, mental retardation, or sensory.* Hence, the definition is somewhat ambiguous and circular. For a learning disability to be present, there must be a serious discrepancy between potential and actual performance, and no other impairment substantially associated with the deficit. For an illustration of how a learning disability might be manifested, see the case study presented in Figure 22.2.

1. Recognize that each student with a learning disability is likely to have unique problems.
2. Teach at the readiness level initially (not to the potential level).
3. Structure assignments that allow immediate success.
4. Make brief assignments.
5. Review work with students frequently.
6. Observe closely and attempt to determine how each student best learns. Direct experiences and manipulative materials typically work well.
7. Frequently assess students' understanding to identify inappropriate assignments as soon as possible ("What was the story about? Tell me what you've read in your own words").
8. Give students plenty of time to respond. Processing information and searching for items in memory are usually difficult for learning-disabled students. Typically, it is best to ask students a question and wait silently for a response. Repeating or rephrasing the question confuses such students.
9. If a student is on medication, find out the effects of the medication. If it causes excessive drowsiness or activity, see if the dosage can be adjusted.

teaching learning-disabled students in the secondary school

Many secondary teachers will teach students with learning disabilities. Elementary school learning-disability programs focus on remediation and building basic academic skills, especially in reading and mathematics. When possible, teachers also emphasize higher-order thinking skills, especially in the upper-elementary grades. This trend should continue as students with learning disabilities move into secondary programs (Gearheart & Weishahn, 1984). Although some secondary students still need basic skill instruction, many benefit from instruction that requires them to synthesize, generalize, and apply information to everyday problems.

technology and disabilities

It is encouraging that new assistive technologies for particular disabilities are being developed rapidly. These have important implications for

Figure 22.2 Jim and Mark: a study of similarities and difficulties

Jim	*Mark*
Age: 9 years	Age: 9 years
Grade: 3	Grade: 3
Years in school: 4 1/2	Years in school: 4 1/2
Reading achievement: 1.6 (grade equivalent)	Reading achievement: 1.6 (grade equivalent)
Group IQ score: 75	Group IQ score: 75

The preceding descriptions of Jim and Mark are obviously identical. However, their IQ scores, as indicated by an *individual* test of intelligence, are quite divergent.

Full-scale WISC IQ: 68	Full-scale WISC IQ: 102

The test indicates that Jim is very likely borderline EMR, and that Mark is probably learning disabled. Additional data are then gathered.

Arithmetic: 1.8 (grade equivalent)	Arithmetic: 3.2 (grade equivalent)

Generally, EMR* students have basic skills in mathematics that are at about the same level as their reading skills, although sometimes they are higher if they mainly involve rote memory. In contrast, many learning-disabled students who have severe problems in reading may do near-grade-level work in mathematics as long as reading is not required. The reverse may also be true of learning-disabled students; they may do satisfactory work in reading but have significant problems in mathematics. It is the inconsistency in performance among various academic areas and various types of activities that characterize learning-disabled students.

Additional information about the boys' abilities in classroom interaction, apparent ability to learn from peers, and ability to conceptualize follows:

In classroom, interaction regarding relationships of planets and the sun, Jim had real difficulty following the idea of relative movement. He can follow class discussion as long as concepts are simple, but has difficulty making generalizations. Jim's speaking vocabulary is better than his reading vocabulary, but is still far below the class average.	In classroom interaction regarding relationships of planets and the sun, Mark was one of the first in the class to understand. In most topics related to science, if no classroom reading is involved, Mark does very well. On a verbal level he conceptualizes and generalizes well. Mark's reading vocabulary (words he can recognize in print) is no better than Jim's; however, his spoken vocabulary is up to the class average in all respects and is above-average in science areas.

Many learning-disabled students have a performance profile (in such areas as reading achievement, arithmetic achievement, vocabulary, ability to generalize, and ability to conceptualize) that is characterized by many ups and downs. They sometimes (or in some academic areas) seem average or perhaps above average, but in some areas they may be even less able than some EMR students. It is possible for a learning-disabled student to be low in *all* areas of achievement and class interaction, but this is unusual. In contrast, the performance profiles of EMR students are usually relatively flat.

SOURCE: B. Gearheart and M. Weishahn (1984). *The Exceptional Student in the Regular Classroom* (3rd ed.). St. Louis: Times Mirror-Moseby College Publishing. Copyright 1984 Times Mirror/Moseby College Publishing. Reprinted by permission of Charles E. Merrill Publishing Co., Columbus, OH.
*EMR = educable mentally retarded

teaching students with particular disabilities. Teachers should, accordingly, seek information from specialists in technology and review the literature annually.

It is beyond the scope of this chapter to provide a comprehensive assessment of technologies for disabilities. An example, however, may help teachers understand the potential value of such technologies. Research has illustrated that individuals who have learning disabilities can make important gains in academic achievement by using computer programs. Programs are available not only for teaching traditional materials such as spelling, but also more abstract tasks such as reasoning and problem solving (e.g., Moore & Carnine, 1989; Smith & Luckasson, 1992). In one study Carnine (1989) used laser video disk equipment to teach students concepts in earth science. The interactive format supplemented classroom learning by allowing students to learn at their own pace.

Sources of technology for use with other

research at work
guidelines for teachers

Recognizing student differences in potential, Gearheart and Weishahn (1984) make the following recommendations for secondary teachers who work with learning-disabled students.

1. For students who can express themselves orally but are unable to prepare orderly, well-conceived written reports, a carefully taped response to an assignment might be permitted and evaluated. This avoids a situation in which inability to express oneself in writing masks significant content mastery.
2. If taped reports cannot be accepted, the teacher might agree to evaluate the content of reports without penalizing for poor mechanics. To prevent later claims that the student did not receive an effective education, however, students and their parents must understand and agree to such an arrangement and be told—preferably in writing—that deficiencies in writing skills are deliberately being overlooked.
3. Peer tutors may provide individualized assistance to learning-disabled students.
4. Study-skill sessions may be organized to help students explore effective ways to identify, analyze, categorize, and recall information (Pressley & El-Dinary, 1993; Sheinker & Sheinker, 1982).
5. Students can be taught to use different reading rates and study strategies for various types of materials and assignments.
6. Other skills, such as preparing for tests, taking notes, and outlining, may be emphasized (Sheinker & Sheinker, 1982). The teacher may agree to provide a student in advance with an outline of material to be learned as a framework within which to organize study.
7. The teacher may provide the student and the resource-room teacher with lists of critical new vocabulary words in advance so that the student may study them before they will be needed in class.
8. The teacher may notify the resource teacher of areas in which the student is falling behind, particularly those that will be essential in future learning.

disabilities include: communicative disorders (IBM National Support Center for Persons with Disabilities [1989]. *Resource guides for persons with speech or language impairments.* Atlanta: IBM; Fishman, I. [1987]. *Electronic communication aids: Selection and use.* Boston: Little, Brown); physical disabilities (U.S. Congress, Office of Technology Assessment. [1987]. *Technology-dependent children: Hospital versus home care. a technical memorandum.* OTA-TM-H-38 [GP0052-003-01065-8]. Washington, DC: U.S. Government Printing Office; Vanterheiten, G. [1984]. High- and low-technology approaches in the development of communication systems for severely physically handicapped persons. *Exceptional Educational Quarterly, 4,* 40–56); hearing impairment (Compton, C., & Kaplan, H. [1988]. Up close and personal: Assistive devices increase access to speech and sound. *Gallaudet Today, 18,* 18–23);

research at work
strategies for teachers of students with visual impairments

The following are suggestions for dealing with students with visual impairments (Dunn, 1973):

1. Be alert to the behavioral signs and physical symptoms of visual difficulties in *all* students. Be sure that proper referrals are made and that everything possible is done to ameliorate the problems.
2. Accept and provide for individual differences on many dimensions, of which vision is just one.
3. View visual limitation as only a difficulty, not the most important characteristic of the student. Do not let the impairments become the central focus in students' lives, allow students with visual impairments to exploit their visual limitations to get inappropriate special treatment, or exploit them by "showing them off" to classroom visitors. As much as possible, treat them as you treat other students.
4. Make visually limited students "your own" as much as other students. Do not consider them as belonging to the residential school, the resource teacher, or the itinerant teacher. Get help from these resource people but do not expect them to reteach what should have been taught in the regular classroom, and do not let the student play one teacher against another.
5. When in doubt, regular classroom teachers should do what they consider best for any student.

visual impairment (Brody, H. [1989, July]. The great equalizer: PCs empower the disabled. *PC Computing*, 82–93).

keeping disabilities in perspective

We have listed some of the characteristics of students with disabilities and suggested ways teachers can help these students succeed in regular classrooms. It is worth stressing, however, that one should not take these lists (or any material about students with disabilities) too literally or too rigidly. Neither should one apply the lists of ways that teachers can help too literally. These are just a few representative suggestions, not blueprints for solving problems. Special students probably are best served if teachers view them essentially as regular students with special needs.

active learning in special education

We stress that all students can assume more responsibility for their learning and become better at learning how to learn. This is true for all students; however, these same instructional principles also apply to special learners.

self-regulated learning

As Paris and Oka (1986) have noted, students with disabilities often appear powerless, helpless, and low in motivation. However, these characteristics, and related student self-views, can be altered through instruction. Many poor learners simply do not understand the relation between the use of learning strategies and successful performance.

Borkowski, Johnston, and Reid (1986) used "strategy training" with students in grades 2, 3, and 4 who had been labeled learning disabled and hyperactive. In comparison to control students, students who participated in the training (which involve self-management and more positive self-attributions) became more able to control impulsivity and to change their attributions for success and failure. Paris and Oka argued that students need to be taught cognitive strategies and reasonable expectations for performance, with an emphasis on control of their own learning outcomes. Students' awareness of their cognitive abilities can enable them to control their own learning, which, under certain conditions, can motive them to seek more challenging tasks and to persist in the face of difficulty.

metacognitive strategy instruction

The goals of metacognitive instruction are to teach students to plan, implement, and assess their strategic approaches to learning assigned material. Palincsar (1986) found that metacognitive strategies can enhance students' capacity for learning when teachers provide explicit instruction in efficient strategies and progressively assign more control over the application of these strategies to students, especially when students understand the purposes and consequences of using the strategies. Palincsar (1986) described a procedure called *reciprocal teaching* that she and a colleague, Ann Brown, had investigated for several years.

Most of Palincsar and Brown's research on reciprocal teaching has been conducted with junior high students enrolled in supplemental remedial-reading classes. These students usually were adequate decoders but read at least two years below grade level on standard measures of comprehension. In the initial research, adult tutors worked with students in pairs, and volunteer developmental-reading teachers supervised groups of approximately five students who read expository passages taken from basal readers written at a seventh-grade level. After reciprocal teaching was used for twenty consecutive school days, the students were retested. They were below the twentieth percentile on comprehension tests before the intervention; after the reciprocal teaching program they had moved to the fiftieth percentile and above (Brown & Palincsar, 1982; Palincsar & Brown, 1984).

Palincsar (1986) cautioned that reading material for reciprocal teaching must be selected with care. It should not present students with major decoding problems, and it should be representative of content that students will study in school. If strategy training is to transfer to school tasks, it should involve material that students will encounter in science, social studies, and other content areas.

Palincsar and Brown (1987) argued that a cognitive-instructional approach needs to be emphasized within the curriculum and that educators consider the content to be mastered as well as the thinking processes that promote mastery and learner self-control. Students identified as low ability or disabled tend to receive instruction that does not encourage them to think about the meaning of material (i.e., pay attention to words; not construct personal meaning).

Readers who would like extensive information about strategies teachers can use to expand students' self-regulation can consult a special issue on strategies instruction (November, 1993) of the *Elementary School Journal* prepared by Mike Pressley and Pam El-Dinary.

individual education programs

An **individualized educational program (IEP)** is *a unique, specialized program of educational experiences for a disabled student that includes specific objectives and particular ways that they can be achieved. Public Law 94–142 requires that an IEP be designed for each disabled student.* It should describe the student's present educational performance, short-term learning goals, and annual learning goals. It also should specify the time the student will spend in the regular classroom, which teacher is responsible for which objectives, and how the student's progress will be evaluated. Once a student has been formally referred to special-education services, a placement committee is formed to write the initial IEP and to supervise the student's progress for as long as the special services are provided. The core committee is likely to include the teachers who will instruct the student, the principal, the person who evaluates the student (a school psychologist or social worker), and, when feasible, a parent and the student.

The committee must keep the parents and the student fully informed about and included in decision making, assure confidentiality about records, recognize the student's right to be represented by a parent or guardian, conduct assessment with nondiscriminatory instruments presented in the student's native language, and demonstrate commitment to the principle of placing the student in the least restrictive environment feasible under the circumstances.

The assessment procedures should be complete and wide ranging, with information from several sources. This is a major departure from previous procedures in which a diagnostician administered a few tests, wrote a report, and made recommendations.

The placement committee is charged not merely with following recommendations but with evaluating and integrating them. Student evaluations and reports are to be judged on criteria such as the following:

- Is the report written in understandable language?
- Are the tools or processes used for evaluation identified?
- Is the setting in which the evaluation occurred described?
- Does the evaluation contain concise statements of specific results?
- Are problem areas that are identified by the evaluation procedure specified?
- Are problem areas that are identified by behavioral observations specified?
- Does the report contain concise statements of strengths and weaknesses?
- Is the information relevant to educational planning?
- Does the report describe conditions that influence ability to perform tasks?

Figure 22.3 (pp. 600–602) illustrates an IEP that follows both the spirit and the letter of the law and seems likely to organize school resources to meet the needs of the student appropriately. The program may seem deceptively simple at first, but bear in mind that the development of a successful plan involves a great deal of data gathering, resolution of differences in opinion and interpretation, compromise, and careful planning. Note the array of specific recommendations, each of which includes identification of the person responsible, specification of the time required, and provision for review and possible revision of the recommendation.

Public Laws 99–457 and 98–199

P.L. 99–457 amends P.L. 94–142 in important ways. It requires states to provide an appropriate public education to children ages three through five. This increases young children's access to educational programs and could improve the transition of infants with disabilities from home to educational settings.

Recent federal legislation has also focused on the transitional problems of youth with disabilities when they leave secondary schools and seek employment. A major aspect of P.L. 98–199, the Education of the Handicapped Amendment, specifies funds and support for secondary education and transitional services. Ianacone and Stodden (1987) noted that increased attention to transitional services stems from the fact that unnecessarily large numbers of handicapped adults are unemployed and dependent on welfare. Between 50 and 80 percent of working-age adults who report a disability, for example, are jobless, and about 8 percent of the gross national product is spent annually on disability programs. This makes it important to identify skills that enable students to be relatively independent at various transition points.

Ianacone and Stodden identify five practices that illustrate how schools have not assisted students who are mentally retarded to become independent, particularly at points of critical transition.

1. Structuring Dependence: Instruction in public schools is dominated by vertical interaction between teacher and student (teacher telling the student what to do and when to do it), especially for students perceived to be mildly or severely retarded. Ianacone and Stodden suggest that this mode of communication fosters student dependence on teachers. They argue that in secondary schools it is especially depressing to see students still lining up before leaving class and having decisions about extracurricular activity made for them rather than with them.

2. Decision Making: In many schools the opportunity for student decision making is limited, and students typically make decisions with fewer consequences and little relevance for them. Instead, decision making should be taught in order to foster student independence and self-reliance (with emphasis on helping students to understand and accept the consequences of their choices).

3. Employment Irrelevance: Ianacone and Stodden are especially disappointed that there is not more opportunity for academic content to bridge vocational- or employment-related experiences for students. For example, many secondary students in special classes were still coloring pictures or learning to name letters when they could have been focusing on vocabulary related to vocational training.

4. Self-Fulfilling Expectations: Educators often underestimate the independent functioning and employment potential of mentally retarded students. Not all individuals who are classified as moderate to severely mentally retarded are necessarily headed for sheltered employment. Because of low expectations, teachers, counselors, parents, and employers too often force these students to fit into predetermined, limited roles.

5. Focus on Disability: Consistent with the notion of self-fulfilling expectations, the processes associated with special education often lead to an emphasis on a student's disability rather than on what he or she can do. Rather than focusing on disabilities, educators need to identify ways to help students develop independence and useful competencies.

Americans with Disabilities Act

Continuing concern with the inadequacies of educational programs for helping disabled students to make successful adjustments from the

Figure 22.3 a typical Individual Education Program

INDIVIDUAL EDUCATION PROGRAM

Childs' Name   Frank West

Date Referred to Committee   March 2

School   "   Crescent Point High School

SUMMARY OF PRESENT LEVELS OF PERFORMANCE

Frank wants to stay in school. He recognizes that his reading ability is low and he wants to learn to read. Teacher observations and test scores indicate that he has a basic understanding of the concepts and operations of fundamental mathematics. He has the ability to follow through on assignments which interest him. He experiences the most difficulty when he is asked to do schoolwork which he doesn't understand or is presently incapable of doing. He is extremely unhappy in the self-contained classroom and does not associate with his classmates. He looked forward to being placed in a "regular" classroom but he has trouble controlling his anger when he can't do the required work. He does independent reading (e.g., newspapers and sports books). Teachers and school personnel often view his behavior as inappropriate for school. This has resulted in numerous suspensions.

PRIORITIZED LONG-TERM GOALS

(1) Frank will improve in his reading ability.

(2) Frank will experience success in the regular classroom.

(3) Frank will be given the opportunity to explore a range of career alternatives.

(4) Frank will develop positive relationships with peers and teachers.

(5) Frank will become more of a participant and less of a spectator in areas of interest.

Figure 22.3 *(continued)*

Short-Term Objectives	Special Education and Related Services	Person Responsible	Beginning and Ending Dates	Review Date
(1) Design a reading program building on Frank's areas of interest:				
A. Develop sight-word vocabulary builders using the newspaper and sports books.	EMR* teacher/ support from remedial-reading teacher/ supplemental materials	EMR teacher	March 7	May 1 June 1
OBJECTIVE: improve Frank's sight-word vocabulary by 25%				
B. Using math word problems designed to incorporate new vocabulary words. Frank will improve in his ability to deal with math word problems.	EMR teacher/ supplemental materials	math teacher	March 7 June 1	May 1
C. An independent reading list based on occupational opportunities will be developed. Frank will read and discuss such materials.				
D. Frank will be encouraged to report on independent reading to his teacher—later to his peers.	EMR teacher	EMR teacher	March 15 June 1	May 15
(2) Frank will remain in the regular math class.				
A. Teacher will design sequential math materials building on Frank's strengths.	math teacher/ math supervisor	math teacher	March 7 June 1	May 15
OBJECTIVE: Frank will experience academic success.				
B. Shop teacher will design math problems in that content area. Frank will be allowed to experience finishing a project from the conceptual stage through completion.		shop teacher	March 7 June 1	May 15
C. Frank will be enrolled in an intramural or P.E. program.	P.E.	P.E. instructor	March 7 June 1	May 15

(continued)

Figure 22.3 (continued)

Figure 22.3 *(continued)*

Short-Term Objectives	Special Education and Related Services	Person Responsible	Beginning and Ending Dates	Review Date
(3) Frank will spend two hours per week for three weeks with the vocational counselor discussing his readings in job opportunities.	EMR teacher	vocational counselor	March 30 June 1	April 20
(4) Frank will assume increasing amounts of responsibility for his own learning as evidenced by his willingness to complete required projects and seek help from teachers.	EMR teacher	all of Frank's teachers	March 7 June 1	May 15

PLACEMENT DECISIONS

Frank will remain in EMR class for reading and language arts. He will attend a regular math class, shop class, and be enrolled in a P.E. class.

PERCENT OF TIME IN REGULAR CLASSROOM

50 %

FOR THE COMMITTEE, RECOMMENDATIONS FOR SPECIFIC PROCEDURES/TECHNIQUES, MATERIALS, INFORMATION ABOUT LEARNING STYLE, ETC.

Frank's basic strength lies in the fact that he recognizes his weakness in reading and that he wants to stay in school. It is extremely important that he be allowed to experience success in an academic setting.

CRITERIA FOR EVALUATION OF ANNUAL GOALS

(1) Reading and math will be evaluated on the basis of teacher test and standardized test.

(2) Social behavior will be based on staff observations and Frank's observations as well as suspensions.

(3) Relations with teachers and peers (most likely dependent upon academic success) will be based on observations.

NOTES: EMR = educable mentally retarded
P.E. = physical education

Committee Members Present

_____

_____

_____

_____

Date of Meetings

_____

_____

_____

school to the workplace led to the 1990 law, Americans with Disabilities Act. Meers (1992) noted that in the 1980s the percentage of men with disabilities who were working dropped, as did incomes of workers with disabilities (compared to other workers). Somewhat larger declines occurred for women with disabilities than for disabled men. Given that 47 million Americans have disabilities (Meers, 1992), it is important to explore new ways to help students with disabilities become productive citizens. (For examples of transition programs in large school districts, see White & Bond, 1992.)

teaching gifted students

In this section we discuss the educational needs of gifted and talented students. The Jacob K. Javits Gifted and Talented Students Education Act of 1988 legally recognizes our educational responsibilities to talented youth. This legislation asserts that gifted students are a national resource and that elementary and secondary schools need to develop these students' talents responsibly.

Before we define gifted students and discuss their educational needs, we want to emphasize that all students are unique, and that many students who have a disability also may be gifted in one or more areas. Still, some students clearly are sufficiently talented that teachers must find ways to accommodate their needs in the classroom.

Fenstermacher (1982) notes that the designation of giftedness is determined by how the term is defined. If one believes that every person is in some way unique, all children are gifted. If, on the other hand, one emphasizes a single attribute (such as a high score on a standardized test of verbal ability), only those who excel on this attribute are seen as gifted. According to Fenstermacher, authors who advocate special instruction for gifted students often encourage freedom, support, challenging materials, and rich learning resources. Through unintentional implication, then, average and below-average learners should receive none or few of these instructional treatments. He argues, however, that all students deserve humor, support, encouragement, openness, enrichment, field trips, and other entitlements.

A focus on basic skills is devalued for gifted students because of the belief that they already know what is being taught or can learn it more quickly than other students. This implies, however, that other learners are well served by materials that are replete with minimum competencies and countless behavioral objectives.

Other educators assume a different stance on this issue. They argue that all individuals are unique and merit special education and that gifted education is a right not a privilege. They believe that students who are reading four grades above grade level and who are not challenged academically will soon become uninterested and discouraged learners despite their considerable intellectual skills. Many educators emphasize that what they recommend for the gifted is especially appropriate for these students—not that other students should not have some of these instructional opportunities. However, it is difficult to distinguish a student right from a privilege. Meeting the special needs of all students represents an intellectual and moral challenge to teachers. Problems of appropriate interest and challenge may be especially difficult to develop for bilingual and limited English-proficient students (Barkan & Bernal, 1991).

defining giftedness

Whitmore and Maker (1985) contend that four key cognitive abilities sometimes define **giftedness**: *(1) communication of ideas; (2) problem-solving skills; (3) creative production or thinking; and (4) retention and use of knowledge.* According to these authors, students are recog-

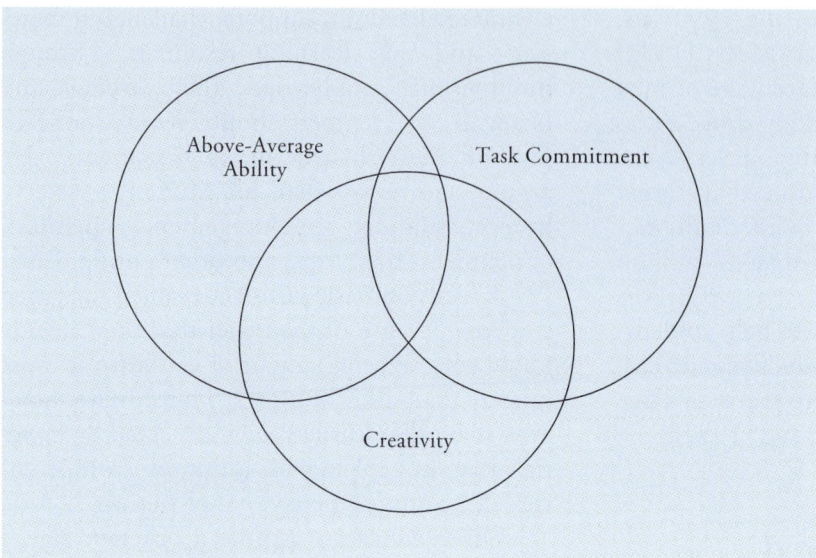

Figure 22.4 Renzulli's three-ring conception of giftedness

SOURCE: "What Makes Giftedness?" by J. Renzulli, 1979. National State Leadership Training Institute of the gifted and Talented. Reprinted by permission.

nized as gifted because of their fluent and advanced use of language and their ability to express themselves in clear and interesting ways. When solving problems, gifted students are analytical and can draw from a wide range of knowledge and relevant experience as they assess alternative solutions. They can also invent new ideas and think divergently.

IQ scores and standardized achievement test scores are only two of many ways giftedness can be measured. Students may be highly skilled at processing verbal information or may have a unique capacity for expressing themselves in artistic ways. Sternberg (1986a, 1986b) emphasizes that intelligence should not be limited to performance on academic tasks and that practical intelligence (e.g., behavior in everyday settings, getting along with others at school or at work, making progress on tasks) merits additional attention.

Gardner (1983) and Walters and Gardner (1986) suggest that it is better to view intelligence in terms of multiple intelligences because human cognitive performance is best described in terms of a set of abilities and talents. Each individual has some degree of each of seven

intelligences that these authors view as independent and of equal stature: musical, bodily-kinesthetic, logical-mathematical, linguistic, spatial, interpersonal, and intrapersonal.

One of the most widely used approaches for defining giftedness is Renzulli's three-ring conception of giftedness (see Figure 22.4). Renzulli notes that a combination of three factors leads to adult productivity and suggests that educators should focus their talent search on children who display all three characteristics. From Renzulli's viewpoint, "gifted performance" and not just gifted aptitude is required before a student is labeled as gifted. There is the problem, however, of specifying what constitutes appropriate performance for gifted students (Reis & Renzulli, 1991). For example, should instruction emphasize originality or powerful application?

According to Whitmore and Maker (1985), for too long intellectual giftedness was equated with a high IQ: usually students had to score over 130 to be placed in a gifted program. Furthermore, students were expected to have high scores in all or most school subjects on standardized achievement tests, consistently superior grades, and a recommendation from the classroom teacher. Despite a growing willingness by educators to define giftedness more broadly, older methods of identification and selection for program participation still predominate (i.e., academic achievement with emphasis on verbal and test-taking skills).

Whitmore (1982) noted that it is important for teachers not to expect outstanding performance from gifted students in all subjects but rather to recognize that there are many different ways and areas in which students can express their giftedness. Moreover, all students need many of the educational features recommended for gifted students, and programs for gifted students should differ from regular education only in degree of emphasis.

gifted students with disabilities and gifted disadvantaged students

Unfortunately, virtually all gifted persons with specific disabilities are first labeled and educated in terms of their handicapping conditions (Whitmore & Maker, 1985). Thus, many disabled students do not get the opportunity to develop their superior mental abilities in ways that would be recognized by others as giftedness. According to Whitmore and Maker, there is no accurate figure to convey the number of gifted persons with specific disabilities, but as much as 5 percent of the disabled population may be intellectually gifted. Teachers must also be able to identify gifted bilingual students. Such students who show marked talent are often bored and "put on hold" while they are drilled in spoken English (Barkan & Bernal, 1991).

Appropriate educational programming for these students would unleash a significant amount of creative productivity that could be of great value to society. In addition to well-known gifted individuals who have overcome disabilities (e.g., Helen Keller), many lesser-known gifted persons have also overcome potentially disabling conditions and had productive careers.

Many students who come from low-income or minority homes also have superior talents that go unrecognized. Torrance (1973, 1977) identified creative characteristics that frequently appear among disadvantaged children that teachers should be aware of: (1) ability to express feelings and emotions; (2) ability to improvise with commonplace materials; (3) articulateness in role playing and storytelling; (4) enjoyment of and ability in visual art; (5) enjoyment of and ability in creative movement, dance, dramatics; (6) enjoyment of and ability in music and rhythm; (7) expressive speech; (8) fluency and flexibility in nonverbal media (produces variety of ideas through drawing, dance, music, etc.); (9) enjoyment of and skills in small-group activities (tries harder in small groups or produces productive ideas in a small-group setting, skillful in group organization); (10) responsiveness to the concrete (generates ideas from concrete objects and materials); (11) responsiveness to the kinesthetic (skillful in interpreting meaning of movement); (12) expressiveness of gestures; (13) humor; (14) richness of imagery and informal language (makes people visualize when describing something in conversation); (15) originality of ideas in problem solving; (16) problem centeredness (is hard to distract); (17) emotional responsiveness; (18) quickness of warm-up (e.g., ready to engage a task quickly; may easily get tired of waiting).

As is evident, defining the "gifted student" is not an easy task. Even educators who spend much of their professional lives trying to meet the needs of gifted students vary to some extent in how they conceptualize these students.

trends in program alternatives

Historically, one of the most common ways of responding to the needs of gifted students has been the use of acceleration programs. **Acceleration activities** *allow gifted students to obtain educational experiences that are usually presented to older students (grade skipping, early admission to college, and so on).* Torrance (1986) noted that the most discussed program alternative for gifted education in recent years is *radical acceleration* (i.e., skipping several grades instead of one or two) advocated by Julian Stanley (1976, 1978). According to Torrance, there is consistent research support for programs that use moderate acceleration for mature and capable students (see Daurio, 1979; Stanley, 1976, 1978, 1980).

According to Torrance (1986), for many years arguments have been made to support individual education plans for gifted students. However, not until IEPs were mandated for learners with retardation and other disabilities did the practice become widespread. A variety of proposals have been made for implementing IEP programs, and there has been considerable experimentation with IEPs in gifted education. Most of these plans integrate several alternatives, such as regular classes with special assignments, enriched experiences, and self-directed study.

Other approaches to gifted education include curriculum compacting (Renzulli, Smith, & Reis, 1982); mentoring (Reilly, 1992; Runions, 1980); special schools (e.g., Amara & Leona, 1983); Saturday and summer school programs (Feldhusen & Sokol, 1982); special leadership training (Foster, 1981); materials in academic subjects (e.g., Rebbeck, 1983); and special instruction in forecasting and planning skills (Kolloff, 1983), research skills (Pellegrini, 1982), and computer skills (Beasley, 1984). Although it is not possible to discuss all of the trends that Torrance identified, we want to comment on mentoring, curriculum compacting, and regular-class programs.

mentoring

In the 1970s peer tutoring became an important part of education at all levels, and more than 10,000 programs involving tutoring have been reported (Runions, 1980). All students are capable of tutoring and can benefit from it, but tutoring does not necessarily result in desirable outcomes. Certain conditions make tutoring more effective (for example, when the situation is structured in terms of task, time, materials, and procedures and when students are trained in how to perform as tutors).

Mentoring is *an educative relationship between an experienced, knowledgeable performer and a relative newcomer in the same field.* It is a type of tutoring in which a student is tutored not by a peer but by an adult, and involves interaction between students and professional people in the community. A major difference between tutoring and mentoring is that much tutoring is compensatory based, because some learning difficulty is being resolved (Runions, 1980). In mentoring, both tutor and tutee are extremely talented, and participants are equal partners in the learning activity. Students who are selected for mentoring have demonstrated above-average competence in an area, are committed to learning and communicating what is learned, and are ready to assume responsibility for their own learning. Mentoring is a social contract between individuals, and learners are expected to use the mentor as a source of stimulation but not to depend on the mentor for evaluation or for identification of the learning activity (i.e., to tell them what they should learn). The mentor should support self-directed trial and error and provide appropriate feedback.

Runions noted that one potential threat to mentoring is that mentors may become surro-

research at work

strategies for instructing gifted students in regular classrooms

Treffinger offered sixty ideas for instructing gifted students in regular classrooms (although all students can benefit from many of these ideas). Ten of these ideas are as follows:

- Use pretests to enable students to "test out."
- In a part of one lesson each day, include a discussion of questions that students did not know how to answer about the topic of study. These questions can stimulate general inquiry as well as provide a basis for independent work projects or shared group activities.
- Have students develop a community resource file for the class. Students could interview potential resource people and describe the skills and insights these individuals could share with the class.
- Provide one afternoon a week during which students can explore (with parents or community volunteers) hobbies and new topics in seminars.
- Develop a series of brief experimental units in which students can explore new areas of interest without committing themselves to prolonged study.
- Have a "research-in-progress" corner where students can go to record information about new topics they are investigating.
- Encourage students to write by developing a directory of publications (community, state, national) in which students' work can be published.
- Urge students to keep journals or to use pocket notebooks to record interesting ideas and to write questions that occur to them.
- Obtain copies of textbook and curriculum materials at various grade levels to provide challenging instructional materials in a variety of subjects for advanced students.
- Promote students' use of many senses in processing information and in expressing their ideas. Provide learning opportunities that involve observation, visualization, listening, touching, and tasting.

gate teachers if they are required to evaluate and record student performance in detail. More appropriate behavior would be for these individuals to maintain their roles as scientists, academics, lawyers, newspaper people, and so on who generously provide their talents. In this sense, mentoring is not so much evaluating the student's performance as it is sharing common interests and encouraging students to think more deeply and critically about a par-

ticular area. For more information on mentoring, see the May/June, 1992, special issue of *The Gifted Child Today*.

curriculum compacting

Renzulli, Smith, and Reis (1982) pointed out that students who are academically years ahead of their peers are often frustrated because they are held accountable for classroom assignments that are repetitious and unnecessary. Teachers are often too busy to find challenging assignments for students who understand the material and need no further review.

According to Renzulli and associates, providing special services for a few hours per week is one alternative, but educators are only kidding themselves if they do not also modify the regular curriculum significantly. These authors argued that teachers need to streamline the regular curriculum to relieve gifted students of the boredom often associated with unchallenging work on basic skills, and find time for gifted students to pursue accelerated enrichment activities.

The first curriculum compacting task is for the teacher to identify an area in the curriculum in which a student shows particular strength. If a student's reading achievement scores are three years above grade level, for example, and if this student is consistently earning As in reading, the reading curriculum should be compacted. Also, most of the major curriculum packages have diagnostic instruments (especially in the basic skill areas of reading, language arts, and mathematics), and teachers who are interested in compacting the curriculum can use pretests and end-of-unit tests to assess students' mastery of major concepts to be presented. It makes little sense to expose students to a two-week instructional unit if they only need to learn a couple of vocabulary words or to review basic facts briefly.

If a curriculum does not include a series of preunit and postunit tests, teachers must review the major objectives of a unit and construct an instrument that measures most of the important content in order to identify students who do not need a particular unit or who can master the unit in one or two days.

Once students have demonstrated an understanding of the material in a unit, they need the opportunity to work on accelerated or enrichment activities. Renzulli and associates argued that the major consideration in making

these decisions is the interests of the students. It is important, for example, not to assume that students are interested in a particular area because they happen to perform exceptionally well in the area. Thus, the fact that students have earned enrichment time in mathematics class does not necessarily mean that the extra time has to be spent in mathematics. Furthermore, there is no reason that students should work on enrichment assignments alone; they can be done with other students.

regular-class programs

Treffinger (1982) noted that too many programs for the gifted are isolated from the regular classroom and that many educators settle for special programs that involve only a small part of the school week, few students, and have little if any relation to regular programs. According to Treffinger, no matter how good programs are, gifted students should spend most of their time in the regular classroom. Although a classroom teacher with limited resources cannot be everything for everyone, many valuable, stimulating activities can be provided in regular classrooms.

clarifying expectations for talented students

Coop (1982) contended that writings on the gifted tend to focus on producing "things" rather than on social processes. He advocated creating better techniques for motivating students toward positive social goals or helping them to empathize with others. The same steps that lead to the invention of products may also lead to the creation of better strategies and processes for dealing with others. Although gifted programs are paying more attention to social outcomes (e.g., leadership), we agree that these programs should focus more on social goals.

According to Coop (1982), one of the problems with recommending programs for gifted students is that there is a paucity of information linking specific programs to outcomes for students. Therefore, teachers should view the suggestions discussed here as guidelines for developing their own teaching strategies rather than rules to be followed rigidly. In this spirit, we offer some of our own observations on eight teacher expectations that cause problems for some gifted students.

implications for teachers

problematic teacher expectations for gifted students

too much too soon High-achieving students are often expected to do too much too soon (e.g., they must have clear career plans), and such expectations pressure these students too much. Their talent is seen by others as so "precious" that they are not allowed to make productive mistakes. The pressure also leads them to develop inappropriately premature, superficial commitments to goals. In addition to the expectation for academic success, many gifted students are also expected to be social leaders and to develop capacities in many different areas at the same time. Unfortunately, they are not encouraged to be flexible or allowed the leisure to delay important decisions as other students are often encouraged to do (see Figure 22.5).

fast curriculum pace Gifted students are often required to cover content more quickly than other students. They are exposed to more content but often without enough time to think about it and consolidate their knowledge. The image is of a car going down the highway, but instead of traveling at forty or fifty miles an hour, gifted students are asked to speed along at eighty miles an hour. They seldom have the opportunity to explore interesting and productive side roads, which may be more important than simply reaching a fixed destination more quickly.

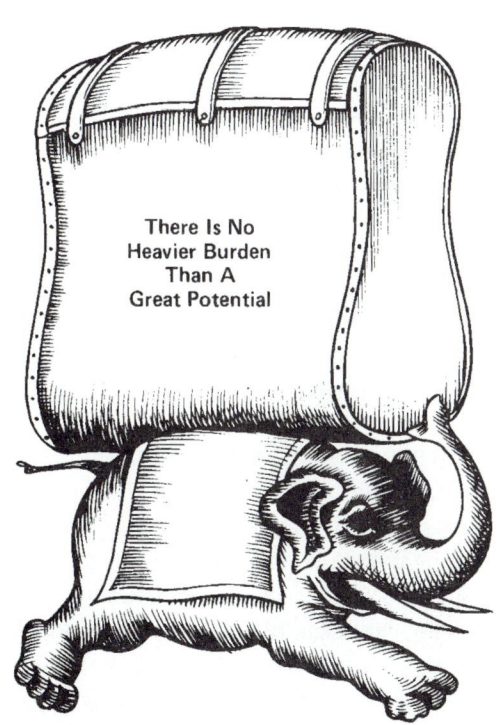

There Is No
Heavier Burden
Than A
Great Potential

Figure 22.5 No student can be at her best all the time!
SOURCE: Adapted from J. Galbraith. (1983). *The Gifted Kids Survival Guide (For Ages 11–18)*. Minneapolis, MN: Free Spirit Publishing, Inc. Reprinted by permission.

too few opportunities to reexamine and to repeat assignments It is critical that high-achieving students occasionally be asked to redo something—to do it better and more thoughtfully. After having completed an assignment, the teacher might add new dimensions for students to consider when they read the assignment or work on related activities. Gifted students often complete work and then want to know what the next task is; to them, classroom success means finishing things quickly and moving on to something else. If we want them to develop the ability to explore new topics independently, it is important to require them to revise and revisit problems or assignments.

too little assimilation It is possible for a curriculum to require too little assimilation. Students, for example, can carefully outline others' views of the pros and cons of electing senators for two-year versus four-year or six-year terms, but a student's own views of this issue are most important. Many gifted students are adept at generating lists of detailed points but have little capacity to evaluate information produced by others and develop their own beliefs. More instruction and training in this area are important.

too much analysis; too little synthesis In many curriculum areas, teachers spend a great deal of time helping gifted students to be critical of and sensitive to social issues and social problems. There is too little opportunity, however, for students to follow these analyses with syntheses that enable them to offer creative suggestions for addressing problems constructively. Although the "textbook curriculum" facilitates analysis and critical thinking skills (when taught well), most curriculum materials do too little to encourage synthesis or applications of knowledge.

too little opportunity to develop leadership skills Considering that bright students have many ideas, can reach decisions

quickly, and can successfully integrate information, they may be intolerant of students who process information less quickly or integrate it less meaningfully. Thus, gifted students often have low regard for the cognitive abilities of other students. It seems important to give bright students the opportunity to work with other bright students to discover that they can learn from others and that they can develop more insight when they use others as resources. It is also vital that talented students learn how to work constructively with others who have less talent and ability. After all, in subsequent real-world jobs, they will need to use the talents of less able coworkers. Too many gifted students cut themselves off from productive relationships with other people who, although perhaps not quite as bright, can stimulate, challenge, and extend gifted students' thinking.

too little opportunity to communicate In general, gifted students learn text material quickly and then are presented with another text assignment that provides yet another opportunity to learn new information quickly. Thus, school learning for them is a series of successes in which the key is an increase in their knowledge. These students, however, have too little opportunity to communicate what they have learned and experienced to other students or adults. A constructive use of class time would be to allow talented students to work in this area, that is, to communicate what they have learned through newspapers, critical reviews of subject matter, book reviews, or musical reviews.

infrequent self-evaluation Most talented students who go "through the curriculum" learn self-management—they learn how to set deadlines and organize their personal resources. They may be less able to engage in constructive self-evaluation, however. Too many talented students set inappropriately high expectations (Why can't I make up my mind? Why am I having difficulty with this?). They need to learn about their relative strengths and weaknesses and their emerging skills. These students need to think about their own papers, for example, and to compare them with papers that they wrote three months earlier. How have they changed their minds about earlier papers? Why?

responding to expectation problems

The following responses have the potential simultaneously to address several of the eight inappropriate expectations that have been outlined.

opportunity to learn about careers

Talented students should collect and assimilate information that enables them to consider the advantages and disadvantages of particular careers. What decisions do people have to make? What problems do they confront? Does a job call for problem finding, problem solving, or application of general knowledge to relatively straightforward issues? What are the unique challenges and satisfactions of particular careers? Discussing and comparing how different types of engineers or physicians view their careers are vital. They allow students to think about jobs and how they relate to a variety of important conditions. Considering the multiple talents that these students have, getting information that helps them to consider what they want from a work situation may have long-term benefits.

social change and implications for individual roles

It would be constructive for gifted students to see what the world looked like in 1915, 1945, 1965, and 1995 to examine how various professions and social institutions have changed with time. What was the life of a physician like in 1915 versus 1995? How and why has the role changed? How does it compare to the role of a university professor in 1915 and 1965? Why have some professions changed more than others? What constitutes the knowledge base of a profession?

How many careers might one expect an individual to engage in during the next thirty years, given the rate at which social change is occurring? What was the role of the federal government in higher education in 1920, 1940, 1990? What is it likely to be in 2000 or 2010? What are the positive and negative consequences of these changes? Assignments should help talented students to see that flexibility in career planning is desirable (i.e., changing conditions must be anticipated), that it is acceptable to consider several careers, that a degree of uncertainty is expected no matter how talented one is.

assignments that require problem identification and data collection and analysis

Many related curriculum materials can be used in classrooms, but sometimes the best assignments involve problems and issues in the local school or community or factors that are personally relevant to students. It is important that gifted students debate about the best way to collect data, what the data mean, how to analyze them, and how best to present data. Debate allows constructive criticism and exchange and helps students to realize that information alone does not solve problems.

formal communication

One frustrating issue that many talented people have to face is that others do not process information as quickly or as deeply as they do. Hence, gifted students sometimes avoid communication with others and do not attempt to improve their own ability to communicate. When problems occur, they tend to blame others. It is constructive to ask students to engage in activities such as watching newscasts to see how newscasters face the challenge of presenting information in a way in which the average citizen can comprehend it but also in a technically accurate fashion so as to stimulate more sophisticated viewers. Or students can debate how to advertise a bond issue so that it appeals to individuals in high-paying occupations but also to individuals who will be hurt economically and so that the message is ethical and fair as well as persuasive. In general, gifted students need opportunities to communicate through formal speeches, debates, television broadcasts, book reviews, evaluations of school plays, and so on to develop their capacity to share their thinking in socially constructive ways.

research skills Gifted students should have opportunities to evaluate original scholarship. They might go to the library, for example, to assess alternate sources and to see how people who were writing in 1920 viewed the coming social and economic conditions. What were the popular ways to think about the economy? What were some individual economic forecasters beginning to worry about? How did others react to their worries?

If research is done constructively in a social setting (two or three students working together), gifted students can jointly consolidate, assimilate, synthesize, and analyze information and develop constructive leadership skills. They learn how to disagree with others yet ultimately to produce a plan or document that satisfies all of them in an intellectually honest fashion by making compromises to achieve consensus that are not expedient but represent a fair view of what they believe. Courses in history and English should stress successful library research skills, courses in biology and chemistry should help students to develop research and laboratory skills, and courses in sociology and psychology should expose students to survey and observational research and allow them to collect and analyze data and to draw meaningful conclusions about the research topic.

summary

In the past, students with special needs were placed in special institutions or classes. Data on the effectiveness of special settings and programs, however, are unimpressive, so the current trend is toward retaining special students in regular classrooms. Problems in diagnosis, the reliability and validity of classifications and their treatment implications, the negative effects of labeling, and various legal changes have all contributed to this trend. Public Law 94–142 commits the nation to a policy of mainstreaming students with disabilities.

Teachers working with special students need to shed their stereotypes and recognize the many similarities of these students to their peers. Teachers should capitalize on special students' strengths, prepare other students to interact constructively with them, deal realistically and matter-of-factly with disabilities, and establish appropriate positive expectations.

Many special educators now believe that general labels are most appropriate to describe disabling conditions because it is extremely difficult reliably to identify specific disabilities and because specific labels are often associated with narrow, rigid classroom programs that focus too much on students' disabilities rather than their abilities. Labels are still widely used, however, because educators believe that they convey some useful information, if not taken too literally, and because legislation often demands that labels be used if program funds are to be obtained. In this context, we have discussed several disabling conditions and have presented broad guidelines for teachers that are associated with these specific disabilities.

Research suggests that students with mild disabilities tend to do poorly in various educational environments in which they are placed. Instruction varies widely within general program categories (e.g., resource rooms, mainstreamed regular classrooms) as well as from classroom to classroom within a category. So far, not enough attention has been placed on the quality of instruction that students with mild disabilities receive. Some data suggest, however, that many programs have not been adapted to the needs of individual students.

There is a clearly emerging philosophy that most students should be educated together in a common setting for much of the time. Currently educators favor policies of inclusion rather than exclusion. There is growing recognition that differences in students provide meaningful contexts for important learning (Stainback & Stainback, 1992).

However, the learning needs of some students are best met in a special environment. As Schloss (1992a) and others note, the appropriate least restrictive environment for many special-needs students is a special placement.

The term "gifted" can mean many different things, but school officials place a premium on one type of giftedness—verbal facility. Although this is understandable to some extent (because success on many school tasks is highly associated with verbal ability), this is only one type of giftedness, and educators must recognize and nourish other talents, particularly in disadvantaged or disabled students.

Several trends in programming for gifted students are described in the chapter. Although many useful ideas are available in the literature, few studies examine the efficacy of one model over another. Teachers need to adjust instruction to the needs of diverse learners (Stainback & Stainback, 1992), including students whose primary language is not English (Casanova & Arias, 1993). There are some distinct differences between student groups; however, many needs of students who are intellectually gifted and those who have mild disabilities are similar.

questions for reflection

1. How far can ordinary public schools go in striving to meet the ideal of free public education for all? Specifically, what categories of students, if any, should be excluded from public schools? Why? How? Who should decide, and on what basis?

2. Considering the grade and subject you expect to teach, what special provisions will you need to make for students with mild mental retardation (special teaching techniques, substitute assignments, special tests)? For students with visual or hearing impairments? For students with physical disabilities? For students who are gifted?

3. How can conflict or disagreement among participants in an IEP meeting (principal, diagnostician, special-education teacher, classroom teacher, parents) be resolved in the best inter-

ests of the student? What should be done if there is no consensus?

4. What, if anything, should a teacher say about mainstreamed students to classroom visitors (parent volunteers, observers from a college of education, PTA representatives, and so on)?

5. The needs of students with impairments is usually obvious to everyone. But what about students with emotional or behavioral disorders? Should these students sometimes be exempted from demands or given special privileges? If so, how should this be explained to classmates?

6. What are the advantages for other students of having mainstreamed students in the classroom?

7. How can the needs of intellectually gifted students be satisfied in the classroom? In what ways do special programs for the gifted differ from regular instruction?

8. If you were speaking to a PTA meeting that included parents of both students with mild disabilities and gifted students, how would you justify a gifted program?

cases to consider

special teaching techniques Jan Jones and Marilyn Martin are the two most disruptive students in Joyce Putnam's class. Both are often out of their seats, unable to concentrate on work, get into fights and arguments with classmates, and resist Joyce's authority. Jan has been diagnosed as hyperactive and takes Ritalin. Marilyn does not take medication, but she has been diagnosed as emotionally disturbed, with poor impulse control and frequent inappropriate affect. How should Joyce deal with these two girls? What special techniques or procedures should she use? Should her approach be essentially the same with both girls, or are there things she should do with one but not the other?

moving forward Sam had done terribly during the first two weeks of school. His work was poor, especially his seat work. At times Sam seemed to be doing an assignment other than the one Ms. Murphy had put on the board. Yesterday Sam got into trouble several times for talking with Molly, who is seated next to him. Today he did all of his seat work perfectly. Ms. Murphy wondered if the move (to the front of the room near her) had helped Sam. What are possible reasons for Sam's improved performance? What should Ms. Murphy do to confirm her prediction?

special interests Tim is a talented fourth-grade student who has a club foot. He loves sports and makes constant reference to college and professional teams as well as those at the local high school. However, Tim spends recess by himself and never shoots baskets or engages in any other physical activity on the playground. How could his teacher, Jeff Wilson, use Tim's interest in building classroom assignments? In what ways might Mr. Wilson help Tim become more involved in physical activities?

preparing the class Anna Molina teaches algebra at Lincoln High School. She has been informed that she will have a new student next week—a student who has previously been in a special program for students with attention disorders. How can Anna prepare herself and her class for the new student?

Assessment

The portfolio is an alternative assessment tool whereby teachers, students, and parents collaborate to provide an authentic and representative view of student performance over time. Portfolios allow us to consider assessment as an on-going process rather than an end product or grade earned in a subject area.

Michael's Portfolio is a pictorial essay containing illustrative examples of one fourth-grader's work collected during the first nine-week grading period. The portfolio model includes examples of Michael's personal goals and the initial and final drafts of his writing across several curricular areas. At the end of the assessment period, the portfolio is presented by Michael himself, during the fall parent/teacher conference.

Michael's Portfolio
First Grading Period

Table of Contents

1. Goals
2. Progress Report
3. Literature
   - Reading Projects
   - Novel Study
4. Writing
   - Special Selections
   - Publications
5. Science
   - Animal Report
   - Nutrition Folder
6. Social Studies
   - Peace Poetry
   - Civil War Unit
7. Math
   - Story Problems

The portfolio contents reflect the teacher's philosophy of integrating reading and writing into science, social studies, and mathematics assignments.

My Goals

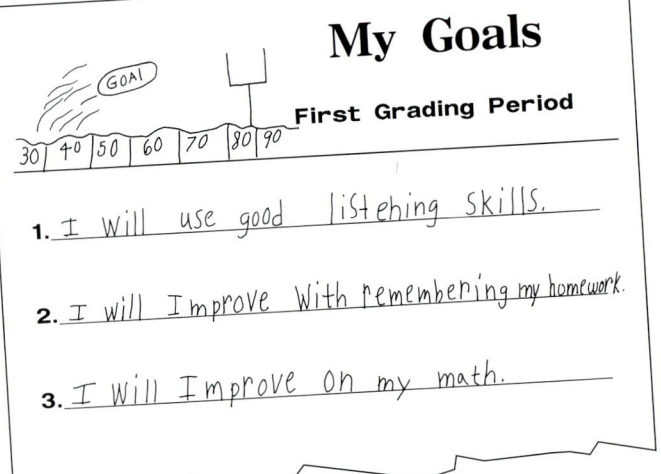

First Grading Period

1. I will use good listening skills.

2. I will improve with remembering my homework.

3. I will improve on my math.

Portfolios give students a voice in their own learning. Michael wrote his personal goals for the upcoming nine weeks, under the supervision of his teacher.

My Reading Projects

First Semester

These are the books I've read so far:
CALL It COURAGE (sperry)
Maniac Magee (Spinellie)
ON MY Honor (C Bauer)
Monster blood (CStine)

Right now I'm reading Missing May (Rylant)

This is how I choose a book to read:
I ask my friends if the book is good.

When I read I think about The characters and their problems.

Michael kept a record of what he read throughout the year. He also described his own processes for choosing books and comprehending text. Such information helped his teacher assess his reading skills, process and product.

Progress Report

Date: October 27, 1994

I'VE SHOWN IMPROVEMENT IN. . .
I've shown Improvement in math, science, social studies, and writeing.

I STILL NEED TO WORK ON. . .
I still need to work on Spelling, math, and hand writeing.

I WILL TRY TO. . .
I will try to do better in all of the above and more.

The portfolio encourages students to be self-reflective and goal-oriented. A six-week progress report gave Michael the opportunity to think positively about his school work and to develop a personal action plan for improving himself.

My Writing Projects

Special Selections

1. **My Favorite Selection:**
   I'am moveing to kansas

2. **My Best Work:**
   As the door opened

3. **My Selection for Improvement:**
   The Nightmare

Near the end of the first grading period, Michael chose several pieces of writing to include in his portfolio. These selections included works in progress as well as final drafts.

AS THE DOOR OPENed!

Michael

I sould of never opened the door that day. I was in my room playing with my toys, When I herd a noyse from the next room closet, It sounded relly wierd.

I forgot what was in my closet, More and more I herd that sound Wondering what that sound was. I asked all of my family but every body gave me the same anser, It is just your imaganation!

Finaly I had enough nerve to open the closet door but when I did, It caused chaos every thing fell on me and I could not move.

I'AM MOVEing to K.S.

Michael

I'am from eastern new york and I'am moveing to kansas, I have herd that old K.S. is known for its buffulow and sunflower-s. Whoknows maby its as good a state as new york.

Befor I buy a house I mite rent a apartment or have a conduminyum bilt for me, I know it will cost about 60,000$ but I can aford that.

The resion why I'am moveing to K.S. is because. I don't like the cars the begers and all the crimeanals. And because I love sunflowers. one thing I dont like about K.S. is that it is in tornato aley, I hate tornatos and I will never go nere one in my life!

THE Nightmare

Michael

one night I was walking down the street when, I came to a house covend with cobwebs, I yelled a loud hello! Why? because I was lost and I needed hellp so I whent in side.

I yelled another loud hello! Still no one anserd. I was all alone, It was geting late so I dicided to go to sleep. I dremed about monsters called cyclopess and aleans, They came out of the walls and down from the celeing.

I could feel the alean biteing me. I could hear the cyclops roar and when I wock up. The cyclops was still there the dream was real. grawl

Michael chose these written and illustrated stories to include in his portfolio. In his class, initial drafts were read and discussed by peers and teachers as the fourth graders worked through the composing process—revising, editing, and publishing.

Reading and writing across the curriculum enabled Michael and his peers to think like scientists, sociologists, and mathematicians. The final draft examples on this page illustrate the value of the fully integrated curriculum, as reflected in the portfolio contents.

FERRETS

By Michael

Science

Most ferrets live in North America, but you can find them in Asia and Europe. In North America they live on the central plains in prairie dog towns. Few ferrets still exist in the world.

The most interesting physical characteristic of ferrets is that they are 25 inches long and 4 inches tall. The ferrit's fur is tan with a black mask on its head. The ferret has scent glands under its tail. Also the ferret is a relative of the weasel.

The ferret takes good care of its young. A ferret spends four to five months in an underground nest with its young. Ferrets have four to eight babies at a time. It takes five weeks until the mother gives birth.

One interesting eating habit of the ferret is that it kills more than it can eat. The ferret eats squirrels, rabbits, birds, and frogs. Ferrets hide leftovers in their burrows.

Recipe For Peace

By Michael

Ingredients

- 1 cup freedom
- 1 cup fun
- 1/2 cup willing people
- 1 cup friendship
- 2 cups helpers
- 1/2 cup hard work
- 1 cup sharing
- 2 cups love
- 1 big bowl peace
- 1 cup courage
- 1/2 cup understanding

Directions

Mix all the ingredients. Add some extra ideas to the recipe. Bake it in an oven so it is nice and ripe, and then have someone eat it. It makes the nicest and happiest person ever.

For his portfolio, Michael selected a final draft science report and a poem. He composed both at the computer then revised, spell-checked, and edited them. His teacher frequently used hard copies of his and his peers' writing in published class collections of prose and poetry.

Math

Michael

Hawaii vacation

If I had $1,000 bucks I would move to Hawaii. That would cost about $200. With $800 in my pocket I would go to the Hyatt Regency maui for two nights. Wich is $200 each night.

Now I have $400 in my pocket so I'am going to buy me a gameboy wich costs about $100. So now I have $300 in my pocket. So I will buy a fur coat wich costs $100 and a shirt for my dad wich costs $50, so now I have $250. So I will buy me a plane ticket home, and give the rest to mrs. Tippin.

"What would you do if you had $1000?" Michael responded to this question by composing a story problem in which he calculated the cost of a trip to Hawaii. He shared his creation with classmates and then placed the story problem in his portfolio.

measurement and evaluation

there is a great deal of interest in improving school and teacher performance through more testing of both teachers and students. In some states teachers must pass exams before they are certified. More and more states are requiring students at selected grade levels to pass achievement tests mandated by the state. Tests can be important indicants of performance and can be very helpful in improving the quality of instruction. Most tests (e.g., multiple-choice tests) assess knowledge that is easy to measure, however, and do not measure more complex and perhaps more important cognitive abilities. As a classroom teacher, you will likely face increasing pressure in the next few years to test students, and part of your success as a teacher will depend on your ability to determine whether or not a test is related to important instructional goals. You must not allow testing to dictate the curriculum in inappropriate ways.

Measuring and evaluating student performance are important parts of a teacher's professional responsibility. Let us assume that you are a teacher who has decided to state your grading criteria at the beginning of the school year. You pass out a sheet listing a group of tests, totaling 500 credit points. Everyone who gets 450 points (90 percent) or more will get an A, those getting between 400 and 449 points will get a B, and so on down the scale. This plan seems fair and sensible, but what if at the end of the term you find that test scores are extremely high? If so, you face one of two possible results:

1. If you follow your plan, more than 50 percent of the students will get an A. You now realize, however, that your tests were much too easy. You are sure, based on questions and comments and on class discussion, that many of the students with more than 450 points did not really learn much of the material.

2. More than 50 percent of your students should get an A. In this case students' grades match your other information. The tests were of appropriate difficulty and measured mastery of key concepts and skills. Student behavior in the classroom indicated general interest in and knowledge about the subject matter, and there was no evidence of cheating or other reasons for artificially high grades.

What might you do in these situations, and what implications might there be for you and your students? What about the opposite situation, with point totals discouragingly low, when more than 50 percent of your students will get Fs?

1. You realize that your expectations were unrealistic and your test questions were too difficult or too tricky. Even your best students, who gave every evidence of interest and understanding in class discussions and activities, had difficulty with the test. You discounted student complaints that the tests were difficult. But the tests were given, and the scores are recorded. Now what?

2. In a contrasting situation, scores are very low, but this time you have no reason to question test difficulty. The questions were drawn directly from classroom presentations and assigned readings, and there were no tricky questions. You have every reason to believe that your tests were fair and valid, but your students nevertheless did poorly. Your observations suggest that lack of motivation was the reason. Students were not studying very hard, if at all, and did not learn much. Now what?

Information that will help you to avoid such dilemmas is presented in the chapter on sound test construction (Chapter 23), and in Chapter 24 we discuss principles for grading students fairly, even when the information available is less than ideal.

chapter 23.

assessing student performance

objectives

When you have mastered the material in this chapter, you will be able to

1. Understand the importance of representative sampling of content and test length
2. Discuss with your class your grading system and the role of classroom tests
3. Understand the six levels of Bloom's taxonomy of educational objectives and how the taxonomy may be used in test construction
4. Understand the advantages and disadvantages of using instructional objectives in teaching
5. Apply the six suggestions for writing good essay questions and explain how essays should be graded to minimize teacher bias and error
6. Discuss the guidelines for writing objective test questions and contrast the advantages and disadvantages of essay questions
7. Discuss and be able to use new types of assessment—portfolios and performance assessments

In this chapter, we discuss ways that teachers can assess student performance. Information is provided on traditional types of classroom testing including how to prepare different types of tests. However, it is important to recognize that adequate assessment of student performance includes more than simply testing students. The chapter discusses new techniques for classroom assessment (e.g., portfolios).

Appropriate professional practice requires that teachers make good decisions about classroom assessment both because testing requires much time and because its effects on students are so important (Crooks, 1988). Stiggins (1991) notes that teachers spend a considerable amount of time in assessment-related activities. Indeed, some teachers have been found to spend as much as 50 percent of available time on such activities as quizzes, unit tests, informal observation, and so on (Plake, 1993; Stiggins, 1991). Teachers also appear to test frequently. For example, Gullickson (1982) surveyed teachers in South Dakota and found that 89 percent of elementary school teachers and 99 percent of secondary school

teachers relied on testing for evaluation purposes. Most teachers tested at least weekly (95 percent) or biweekly.

Teachers use various assessment approaches. A joint committee composed of representatives from the American Federation of Teachers, National Council on Measurement in Education, National Educational Association (1990) has outlined important skills that teachers need to develop in the area of educational assessment. Included in their statement of professional standards are the following:

- Teachers should be skilled in choosing assessment methods for instructional decisions.
- Teachers should be skilled in developing assessment methods appropriate for instructional decisions.
- Teachers should be skilled in using assessment results when making decisions about individual students, planning teaching, developing curriculum, and school improvement.
- Teachers should be skilled in developing

valid pupil grading procedures that use pupil assessments.
- Teachers should be skilled in communicating assessment results to students, parents, other lay audiences, and other educators.

In this section of the book, we will help teachers to conceptualize problems and strategies dealing with these five standards.

test length and content coverage

Typically, tests cover only a small sample of the content and objectives taught, and decisions have to be made about what to include. This problem is most serious for final exams given at the end of the term or school year but is relevant to unit and weekly tests as well.

It is important to sample from the full range of content taught and to include enough items to allow reliable measurement. Sampling from all content taught will help ensure that the teacher recognizes areas of weakness, that students are accountable for learning all material, and that students will view the test as fair. Students may not perceive the test as fair if it emphasizes only a few areas, especially if students thought these areas were unimportant. An "unfair" fifteen-item objective test on comparative political systems, for example, might include several questions about evolutionary forces and key individuals who shaped the development of those systems, only a couple of questions about how the systems presently operate and about the practical implications of similarities and differences between countries, and no questions about probable future trends.

Let us now examine how such a test could have biased effects. Table 23.1 shows the per-

centage of time that eight students of comparable ability spent studying for the test. The student victimized the most by the test is Ruth, who spent only 20 percent of her time reviewing historical development, which turned out to be 80 percent of the exam, and 60 percent of her time studying future trends, which were not included on the exam. In contrast, Judy did well on the test. She spent 75 percent of her time preparing for the first part and the remainder of her time studying material tested on the second part. Other students made different choices and scored differently on the basis of their choices.

Table 23.2 presents the distribution of scores that students might have made on such a test. Although the distribution is not directly related to the percentage of time spent studying for key parts of the exam, it does correspond closely. In any test situation many factors operate. Bill, for example, may have scored lower than Joan because he was absent during a class discussion that dealt with material needed to answer three of the exam questions (a longer test makes such effects less likely). Joan, however, may score higher because she has better test-taking skills (for example, she notices subtle clues in two poorly written test questions that give the answers away). Alice may have scored lower than Jane or Tom because she spent too much time thinking about the first few questions and did not have a chance to respond to the last questions.

The point is that some error of measurement will occur in any test. A test that unfairly samples content will exacerbate minor problems into major ones. As can be seen in Tables 23.1 and 23.2, the test on comparative politics is not fair. It favors some students who guessed correctly about how to spend their study time.

Some of these problems may be related to the length of the test. As a rule of thumb, test reliability increases with test length, so a thirty-item test is ordinarily more reliable than a fif-

table 23.1 distribution of test items and percentage of time students spent studying three areas of comparative politics

Test	Historical Development (in Percent) 80 (12 Items)	Present Functioning (in Percent) 20 (3 Items)	Future Trends (in Percent) 0 Items
Alice	33	33	33
Jane	33	33	33
Bill	25	50	25
Ted	50	25	25
Joan	50	50	0
Judy	75	25	0
Ruth	20	20	60
Tom	33	33	33

teen-item test. This assumes that the test equally samples each of the major content areas addressed. If this is not the case, adding to the length of the test may not improve its reliability or its fairness.

If we increase our fifteen-item comparative political systems test to thirty items, for example, but ask twenty-three questions on the first part, seven questions on the second part, and none on the third part, the problems illustrated above will still exist. The test is a more reliable measure of student mastery of the first and second parts, but it still gives no information about mastery of the third part and it is still unfair to students who concentrated their study on the third part.

Even when a test does sample evenly from all content taught, test items still might favor certain students over others. Suppose that we want to test students' abilities to read and comprehend material. This requires students to read paragraphs, and these paragraphs have to be concerned with some type of content. Sally, for

example, might be knowledgeable about and interested in baseball, and Ted may not. If some material on the test deals with baseball, Sally may be able to read it more quickly and even remember more of it because she is more familiar with specialized terms, even though she may be no better than Ted in general reading ability and comprehension. However, if students must read several paragraphs dealing with various topics, these individual differences in knowledge and interest will balance out. This is the major reason why longer tests tend to be more reliable than shorter ones, other things being equal.

table 23.2 students' scores on the classroom test in comparative politics

Alice	8	Joan	12
Jane	10	Judy	14
Bill	7	Ruth	7
Ted	11	Tom	10

cognitive levels of test content

Besides sampling from the full range of topics covered, we might also wish to sample various levels of understanding of the material. The **Taxonomy of Educational Objectives** (Bloom et al., 1956) may be used to consider various cognitive demands that different kinds of test items make on students. The following taxonomy contains six levels, ordered from simplest to most complex (see Chapter 5 for more details about this taxonomy):

1. **Knowledge:** *To remember and to recall information.* (Who were the first five presidents of the United States? Recite the alphabet. What author wrote *Hamlet?*)
2. **Comprehension:** *To understand the relations between facts or concepts.* (Translate a French sentence into English. Predict the probability of rain when given key facts. Determine the relative size of a standard deviation by looking at a distribution of scores.)
3. **Application:** *To use information and procedures that are comprehended.* (Given a set of student scores, compute the mean and standard deviation. Write sentences that are grammatically correct.)
4. **Analysis:** *To break down an idea into its parts.* (Diagram sentences. Identify the setting, plot, and climax of a novel.)
5. **Synthesis:** *To rearrange parts to form a new whole.* (Write a class play. Watch a film of one's teaching and plan a better strategy.)
6. **Evaluation:** *To know the value of methods for given purposes.* (Was the play credible, well placed? Was the teaching more effective?)

To the extent that all these levels of content mastery were included as instructional goals for the curriculum sequences being tested, we might want to sample from each level. This will help yield a balanced view of each student's learning as well. (Some students are good at understanding and remembering discrete facts but have trouble synthesizing them, integrating them with general principles, and applying their knowledge in problem-solving situations; other students have the opposite pattern of strengths and weaknesses.) Table 23.3 illustrates a plan for a test that samples both the range of topics taught and a variety of levels of cognitive demand. For simplicity, the six cognitive level categories from the taxonomy are combined to form two categories. The first (terms, facts, principles) represents the first two levels of the taxonomy (knowledge and comprehension).

Table 23.3 also summarizes the teacher's plans for three units. The first unit on weather indicates that the largest percentage of instruction will focus on application of concepts to predict weather. Hence, the exam should emphasize this information, and students should know that when they prepare for the test.

The second plan indicates that understanding general facts and principles of the metric system is a key instructional goal. (Perhaps an application unit will follow this one.) Such an outline of goals helps teachers to make instructional decisions (how much time to spend in class, the type of homework to assign) and to write appropriate tests. Unfortunately, many teachers fail to provide students with this information; typically, teachers erroneously confuse general knowledge of test expectations with knowledge of specific questions.

instructional objectives

We have discussed test construction as if all content topics and all instructional objectives included in a unit were equal. However, teachers often want to stress certain topics or

table 23.3 three plans for classroom tests with specification of content and cognitive emphasis

	COGNITIVE OBJECTIVES		
CONTENT	*Terms, facts, principles*	*Applications*	*Total percentage*
Unit 1: Weather			
A. Atmosphere	20	0	20
B. Air masses and fronts	15	5	20
C. Causes of precipitation	0	15	15
D. Predicting	0	40	40
E. Control	5	0	5
Unit 2: Weights and Measures			
A. Length	10	0	10
B. Weight mass	10	0	10
C. Time	10	0	10
D. Standard measures			
1. Metric system	60	0	60
2. GCS	5	0	5
3. KMS	5	0	5
Unit 3: Comparative Politics			
A. Historical development	80	0	80
B. Present function	0	20	20
C. Future trends	0	0	0

objectives they consider to be especially important. In this case, it may make sense for the teacher not only to emphasize these key goals during instruction but to emphasize them in constructing tests and in making suggestions to students about how to allocate their preparation time.

In general, instruction is more effective to the extent that teachers have specific plans and communicate clear expectations to students about what they are to learn. These shared expectations about what course content is important and about what types of test will be used can help improve the reliability of teacher-made tests. Test construction experts contend that teachers must resolve three questions if they are to teach effectively: (1) What will I teach? (2) How will I know when students have learned it?, and (3) What materials and activities will be necessary? These three questions represent the three parts that compose an instructional objective. Three steps are involved in writing these objectives (Mager, 1962; Gronlund, 1985).

1. Name the terminal behavior—what proof would you accept that the learner has achieved your goal (Must the student swim a lap or a mile, design a blueprint, or build a garage?).
2. Specify the conditions under which the behavior will be demonstrated (Will students write essay questions or deliver a speech; will answers be picked from a list or from memory; will students evaluate a live debate or analyze written material?).
3. Announce the criteria for acceptable performance (15 out of 20 for an A; run a mile in less than 8 minutes for a B; write a theme with no grammatical errors to pass the grammar unit review).

Currently many school districts are attempting to organize schools using outcome-based educational models (e.g., Sizer 1984; Towers, 1992a, 1990b). These districts encourage specific outcomes (e.g., advanced writing ability) but allow the student options for demonstrating the performance (the student chooses the evaluation dimension). We return to this topic later.

In Chapter 5, we summarized the advantages and disadvantages of instructional objectives. Some of these arguments are presented below, as they apply to evaluation issues. Even before reading the list, however, it is useful to note that instructional objectives are neither always desirable nor always undesirable. Their value depends on how teachers use them.

advantages of instructional objectives

1. They increase teacher awareness of what students should be working on and lead to more optimal planning that includes a wider range of objectives.
2. They provide a basis for assessing continuous progress (allowing students to proceed at their own rates) because instruction focuses on specific skills.
3. Students have a better blueprint for guiding their learning activity; hence, they learn more.

disadvantages of instructional objectives

1. They unduly emphasize things that can be measured easily and therefore favor low-level objectives.
2. Once established (the teacher invests the time to write objectives and set up a measurement system), the system perpetuates itself; objectives remain the same and spontaneity is reduced.
3. A great deal of instructor time is used in writing instructional objectives; such time could be better used in other ways, such as in one-to-one conferences.

Our only major concern with instructional objectives is that at times teachers apply them too specifically or to content for which they are inappropriate.

communicating expectations to students

It may be useful for students to know what will be emphasized in testing and grading (e.g., that their themes will be graded on the basis of ideas, organization, mechanics, and sentence structure). Table 23.4 shows that such knowledge has practical consequences for students. In Ms. James's class, students know they should spend most of their time generating ideas; however, they also realize that they should polish their language and grammar. In contrast, students in Ms. Wilson's class should concentrate on developing major ideas. If she wishes to assess students'

table 23.4 four teachers' criteria for grading students' papers

TEACHER	IDEAS	ORGANIZATION	MECHANICS	SENTENCE STRUCTURE
Ms. James	70	10	10	10
Ms. Wilson	85	15	0	0
Mr. Adkins	50	10	25	15
Ms. Stanford	50	50	0	0

use of correct grammar, she will do so with separate, focused tests. Mr. Adkins's students know that they should spend about half of the time available for composition by carefully examining sentence structure, grammar, and so on. Mr. Adkins believes that the only proof of knowledge of grammar is its application in written composition. Different expectations are reflected in Ms. Stanford's objectives. She stresses organization, especially paragraphing, more than the other teachers; however, students' grammatical mistakes do not affect their scores. In the margin, she puts an "X" by any sentence that contains a grammatical error and gives students five minutes to correct their errors. Grades are lowered slightly if students cannot find their mistakes.

Teachers' performance expectations vary widely, and teachers should communicate their expectations to students before examinations. Too much information, however, may lock both teachers and students into unproductive patterns of behavior. If Mr. Adkins were to define every conceivable organizational, grammatical, and sentence-structure error and assign deduction points in advance (four points for inappropriate use of colon or semicolon, two for inappropriate use of comma, five for a sentence without subject and so forth), he might inadvertently constrict student behavior. His students could learn to write three or four short paragraphs, using very simple sentences and words. If students were left at this level, it would be an unfortunate loss.

facts versus concepts

What does a good test blueprint look like? What percentage of questions should be factual? What percentage should cover application or evaluation? There is no formula for a good plan. A plan should clarify instructional goals, assist in planning instruction, and help the teacher to prepare a test that measures intended goals. Sometimes it makes sense to have a little application and much emphasis on basic facts. At other times balance between application and facts is more appropriate, and sometimes it makes sense to stress application. The teacher should know content and cognitive goals before instruction and should match the exam to the instructional emphases. It is simply not fair to students, nor is it effective evaluation, to lead them to expect one type of test and present another.

types of test items

We have discussed the need for reliable tests and have noted that a test must cover assigned content sufficiently if it is to produce an interpretable score. Equally important is the need for questions that measure objectives appropriately. In this section, we describe two types of questions that teachers can use on classroom tests and examine some of the strengths and weaknesses of these questions.

Often teachers write essay questions that only call for factual information. To assess factual information given in response to an essay question is a waste of time. Knowledge and comprehension can be assessed more efficiently and reliably by objective tests. Teachers must decide which cognitive level they want to test before writing questions, because this decision determines the type of test they should construct. Teachers should then tell students precisely what type of response is desired.

Too often essay questions merely tell students to discuss an issue and force students to guess what the teacher really wants. Imagine yourself answering the following exam question in a teacher education class: "Discuss the factors that contribute to student learning." Does the teacher simply want a list of all factors that relate to student learning? Should you discuss the importance or role of each factor? This question does not indicate what type of answer the teacher wants.

The question is vague in other ways as well. What is meant by the term "factors"? If you apply a literal definition, hundreds of factors are involved (quality of prenatal care, and so on). A clearer question would be: "Illustrate how a teacher could hypothetically improve the performance of an anxious but capable (IQ 115) student in a speech class. Be sure that your response illustrates the use of dissonance, feedback, reward, and success in public and private discourse situations."

Essay questions, if used correctly, should require students to do more than reproduce information. Questions that ask students to predict or to write their own examples are generally better than questions that require students merely to present facts.

Asking students to solve problems is an especially good way to use essay questions.

For example, "The first paragraph that follows describes the academic problems of Ted Jenkins. The following three paragraphs describe a teacher's attempt to deal with the problems. Compare and contrast the three solutions, with special consideration to the short-term and long-term effects of the plans on Ted's general dependency, class achievement, and peer status." This question forces students to apply their learning to an authentic problem.

Some teachers, perhaps because they feel uncomfortable asking so few questions and neglecting so much content, ask too many essay questions and undermine the unique role that an essay question can play. Essay exams are useful to the extent that they provide students with an opportunity to demonstrate their ability to recall, organize, and apply facts and principles. To rush students through ten essay questions in fifty minutes, however, is self-defeating. To obtain valid information for making decisions about student learning, teachers will need to use various types of assessment (e.g., objective and short-answer tests to assess basic knowledge, essay exams or term papers to assess students' ability to write and integrate ideas).

It is also important to provide students with complete directions. Teachers may occasionally prefer, for example, that students outline their answers rather than write them out. (Teachers may not want to penalize students who write poorly, or may think that it is important to ask a few extra questions—hence, they are testing planning and organizational skills more than writing.) Such expectations should be clearly communicated to students. It is especially important to specify how many points each question is worth. Without such knowledge, students cannot effectively plan how much time to spend on various questions.

research at work
guidelines for writing essay questions

Teachers who use the following guidelines for writing essay exam questions can improve their ability to measure student performance rather than teacher bias (Kubiszyn & Borich, 1993; Thorndike & Hagen, 1977):

1. Know the mental processes you want students to use before writing test questions.
2. Write essay questions so that students have clear tasks. (Are students to recognize biased presentations? Are they to distinguish verifiable from unverifiable facts?)
3. Be sure essay questions require students to do more than reproduce information.
4. Be sure that questions are not too numerous or too lengthy.
5. Include questions that vary in difficulty.
6. Provide students with clear directions for essay tests. (Students need to know if the answer is to be outlined or written out completely, the point value of each question, and the criteria the teacher will use to evaluate their answers.)

implications for teachers
the essay test: instructions and scoring

Read the two answers that follow in response to the question: "Compare the powers and organization of the central government under the Articles of Confederation with the powers and organization of our central government today." Which grade should student A receive? Student B? Which answer is better written? Which conveys more knowledge? More comprehension?

student A Our government today has a president, a house of representatives, and a senate. Each state has two senators, but the number of representatives is different for each state. This is because of compromise at the Constitutional Convention. The Articles of Confederation had only a Congress and each state had delegates in it and had one vote. This Congress couldn't do much of anything because all the states had to say it was alright. Back then Congress couldn't make people obey the law and there wasn't no supreme court to make people obey the law. The Articles of Confederation let Congress declare war, make treaties, and borrow money and Congress can do these things today. But Congress then really didn't have any power, it had to ask the states for everything. Today Congress can tell the states what to do and tax people to raise money they don't have to ask the states to give them money. Once each state could print its own money if it wanted to but today only the U.S. Mint can make money.

student B There is a very unique difference between the Central Government under the Articles of Confederation and the National Government of today. The Confederation could not tax directly where as the National Government can. The government of today has three different bodies—Legislative, Judicial, and Executive branches. The Confederation had only one branch which had limited powers. The confederate government could not tax the states directly or an individual either. The government of today, however, has the power to tax anyone directly and if they don't respond, the government has the right to put this person in jail until they are willing to pay the taxes. The confederation government was not run nearly as efficiently as the government of today. While they could pass laws (providing most of the states voted with them) the confederate government could not enforce these laws, (something which the present day can and does do) they could only hope and urge the states to enforce the laws.

How hard is it for you to *quantify* the differences between the two responses? How much better is the response you rate higher? How do you think the grades you assigned compare to those your classmates gave? We suspect the ratings of the two responses will vary widely in your class.

Thorndike and Hagen (1969) presented these two answers (along with three others) to two groups of graduate students taking a course in tests and measurement. They asked the groups to assign a maximum of 25 points to the answers, provided them with a model answer, and stressed that the grades should be based on completeness and accuracy, not grammar or spelling. The papers received a wide variety of scores from the two groups of raters. Student A's paper received scores ranging from 5 to 25 points, and student B's paper was scored as low as 3 and as high as 25. The ratings of the papers depended on who rated them.

These findings indicate that it is important for teachers who use essay tests to develop objective criteria for scoring such tests. Is the paper assigned a 20 or 21 really inferior to the paper assigned a 24 or 25? To put it another way, you must be sure that the scores reflect

demonstrated student performance, not teacher biases. Some techniques for accomplishing this follow.

scoring essay exams Green (1975) noted that there are two generally acceptable techniques for grading an essay—the point-score method and the sorting method. The sorting method is easier to use than the point-score method, and, although not as reliable, it can be used fairly. The steps involved in **sorting** are: *(1) quickly read all the papers, sort papers into piles (A, B, C, pass, fail), and place borderline papers into the higher category with a question mark on them; (2) read the responses again, paying special attention to borderline papers; (3) assign a grade to each paper on the basis of the pile it ends up in.* Gronlund (1988) notes that this process is greatly facilitated if the teacher prepares a model answer and decides in advance how to assign points to particular aspects of responses (general organization, consistency of arguments, etc.).

The **point-score procedure** *calls for the following: (1) a grading key that includes features that should be present in student answers for full credit (partial credit for each part of the response should be determined in advance); (2) reading all responses to the same question consecutively and assigning the number of earned points to each question as it is read; (3) reading all responses to the next question; (4) when all questions have been read, totaling points and assigning a grade.*

In general, the point-score method is the best way to grade essay tests because it uses a fixed standard (an answer key) and guards against halo effects that interfere with effective grading. A **halo effect** refers to *the tendency to rate or evaluate a person or performance on the basis of a global impression rather than according to a specific trait or performance.* The sorting method also yields generally reliable scores, however, and teachers who test frequently and often use essay tests may have to rely on this technique.

Both methods of grading essay questions are applied most validly when teachers read papers anonymously. This can be done by telling students to put their names on the backs of their papers. It is easy to read something extra into an answer by a good student, and it is equally easy to demand more from a student we believe to be marginal (e.g., more proof that the student really deserves full credit). An advantage of the point-score method is that the teacher reads answers to the same question consecutively on all papers. Students who write poor responses to the first question are not as likely to be inadvertently penalized when you read answers to the second question as they would be if you read responses to the two questions one after another.

If you write the point value at the bottom of the first question (where you cannot avoid seeing it when you begin to grade the second question), however, the usefulness of this procedure is reduced somewhat. Similarly, if you repeatedly grade student B's responses after student A's, student B's score might be systematically influenced (Follman, Lowe, & Miller, 1971; Hales & Tokar, 1975). If student A is among the best in the class, the contrast between the two papers might be sufficiently glaring for B's score to suffer. Similarly, B's score might look better than it actually is if it repeatedly follows a low scorer's paper. For this reason teachers should shuffle papers after reading all responses to a particular question.

Mehrens and Lehmann (1978) recommended that teachers construct model answers to essay questions as they write the questions, not after the test is given. This procedure calls attention to faulty wording, inadequate time allotment, inappropriate difficulty level, and similar problems early enough for teachers to correct them prior to test administration.

writing objective test items

We agree with Thorndike and Hagen (1977) and Kubiszyn and Borich (1984) who contend that multiple-choice items can measure the same aspects of an educational objective as any other pen-and-paper test, except written expression and originality. Analysis, synthesis, and all other levels of cognitive processing can be tested with multiple-choice items. The multiple-choice format is the most versatile form of an objective test item. The item has two parts: the **stem**, *which represents the problem*, and three or more response choices, of which one is the correct answer and the others are **distractors**, plausible alternatives for students who do not know the answer. Consider the following illustration:

Which of the following is one of the ways that Good and Brophy suggest for helping students to value course content?

a. teaching students goal-setting strategies

b. helping students recognize effort-outcome linkages

c. incorporating gamelike features into activities

d. focusing on quick mastery of material

The answer to this question is c, and choices a, b, and d are designed to be distractors.

How can one write or recognize a good multiple-choice question? We know that a good test question must ask the student to respond to important content, but what other criteria are there?

It is not essential to present novel material in the stem of multiple-choice questions to require students to do more than just memorize facts. For example, a teacher who is interested in helping students to develop quantitative literacy abilities could give students novel data (e.g., concerning changing population demographics or sales of computers as a function of family income) in the form of a graph or table and ask students to show their ability to analyze the material by responding

research at work
guidelines for writing multiple-choice test items

Thorndike and Hagen (1977) provided a number of guidelines for writing multiple-choice items:

1. The stem must present a problem.
2. Include most of the item in the stem and keep options short.
3. Keep the stem as short as possible.
4. Use the negative infrequently in the stem but make it noticeable by underlining the "not" when it is included.
5. Use new material in stem problems and attempt to measure application.
6. Include only one correct or clearly best answer.
7. Try to make all the options plausible.
8. Do not cue the answer (by making it longer than the others or using predictable patterns—B, C, D, A, B, C, D, A, and so on).

The first four suggestions are all related to helping students know precisely the question they are answering. If a stem does not present a problem, the student has to spend valuable time trying to figure out what the problem is. Similarly, lengthy questions make it more difficult to identify the problem. Since the purpose of the test is to assess knowledge and not reading ability, a clear presentation of the problem is desirable. Using "not" in the stem is acceptable if the student is aware that it is there. When students read stems rapidly they may miss the word. If the word "not" is used it should be underlined.

Which of the following is <u>not</u> typical of successful students?

a. essentially task oriented

b. tend to be liked by peers

c. more person oriented than task oriented

d. cooperative in class

As noted, the correct answer to this question is c. The "not" is emphasized in this question, the stem presents the problem, and both the stem and the answer choices are relatively brief.

to a series of multiple-choice questions (e.g., What is the best conclusion? What are the apparent consequences?). However, the utilization of such testing could also require students to go beyond the information given by asking them to extrapolate into the future. That is, given the data presented summarizing trends over the last decade, what could be predicted ten years from now if these trends continue? An example of a data source that could easily be converted into multiple-choice items is presented in Figure 23.1. The primary advantage of the objective test, when properly constructed, is that it provides a relatively unbiased assessment of student performance. The inclusion of partially correct answers reduces the objectivity of the test because judgments have to be made about the degree of correctness, and if answer choices are not plausible, the chances that a student will guess the answer are increased. Often test questions give away answers (the right answer is often longer, the stem provides a grammatical clue, or the teacher may have a habit of

Sowing Less, Importing More

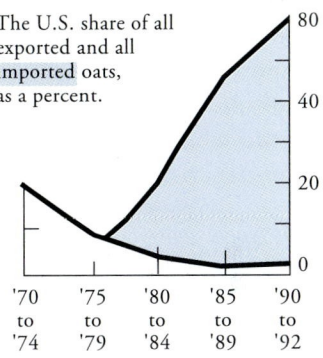

Figure 23.1 dwindling harvest of oats in the United States
SOURCE: Copyright © 1993 by The New York Times Company. Reprinted by permission.

placing the right answer in the same position). When test answers can be guessed, the test measures students' ability to take tests, not their knowledge.

criticisms of multiple-choice testing

Mitchell (1992) and other educational writers argue that for years educational evaluation has informed students that what counts is memorization and passive recognition of single correct answers. This is because in some classrooms virtually the only type of assessment is the multiple-choice test. She notes that multiple-choice tests would not be so objectionable if they were part of an evaluation package that included teachers' observations, students' collections of work, essays, and cooperative products.

Mitchell argues that assessment is as old as education itself. Throughout most of the schooling in America, educational assessment focused on recitations, oral demonstrations, and essays. She notes that this trend changed in the middle of this century and that by the

1980s, multiple-choice exams had become by far the dominant form of assessment.

Recently, educators have been calling for assessment that allows students to present and defend their ideas and to show what they can do (Frechtling, 1991; Sizer, 1984). Mitchell contends, "Learning does not mean memorizing facts or algorithms; it means the ability to use them appropriately by weighing conflicting values, arguing with reasoned propositions, selecting facts, using evidence, and thinking clearly. . . . If students should be able to analyze, synthesize, interpret, and evaluate facts and ideas, then their progress should be charted by direct performances. If students should write well, they should be tested by reading their writing" (p. 21).

Mitchell concludes that multiple-choice tests interrupt the teaching and learning process for these reasons:

1. Even at their best, multiple-choice tests ask students to select a response in a selective fashion. Students are not required to think.
2. Multiple-choice tests imply that a right or wrong answer is available. Few situations in life have a correct or incorrect answer.

3. The tests rely on memorization and recall of algorithms instead of allowing students to show their understanding of the algorithms.
4. Too often multiple-choice tests include content that is easily assessed rather than important.
5. Multiple-choice tests do not accurately record what a student knows and can do.
6. The tests trivialize teaching and learning.

We share the belief of Mitchell and other educators that multiple-choice exams are overused and that their extensive use is undesirable. However, we think that they are useful for assessing whether students possess an essential knowledge base to inform their thinking and problem solving. For example, knowledge that there was a Republican president for twelve years before Bill Clinton took office is important information if one is attempting to understand how various coalitions in the Democratic party respond to policy initiatives from the executive branch. Similarly, we suspect that knowledge that certain chemicals cannot be mixed in the lab may not only be associated with improved lab safety but may transfer more readily to real-life situations (alcohol and quaaludes cannot be mixed and are often deadly) than platitudes like "just say no." Education has a tendency to move from fad to fad: one current fad is to devalue factual knowledge and objective testing.

To reiterate, some objective testing is essential in most classrooms. When used appropriately and when used in combination with other types of assessment, multiple-choice tests can provide dependable and useful information. The issue is not whether or not to use objective tests but when and how to use them.

other forms of objective questions

We emphasize the multiple-choice question because it is the most versatile form of objective test. There are other forms of objective tests, however, and each has advantages and limitations. Three other popular objective test formats are true-false, completion, and matching.

In general, true-false questions can be constructed much more quickly than multiple-choice items. Unlike multiple-choice questions, the **true-false** format *forces students to choose between two alternatives rather than four or five.* For example, "true or false: assimilation occurs when the child integrates a new idea into a scheme he or she already has."

Brown (1976) noted that true-false questions can be used to good advantage with young children, especially when only a general estimate of student performance is necessary. A major limitation on the use of true-false questions is that much content is difficult to express in true-false form. Furthermore, students will be correct 50 percent of the time by guessing; hence, the diagnostic power of true-false questions is low.

Short-answer and completion items *require students to finish a statement from recall rather than recognition.* On a multiple-choice test students select (recognize) the best answer from a series of choices. In contrast, in a short-answer format, students provide their own answers. It is considerably more difficult to construct a multiple-choice item that presents four or five carefully written and plausible alternatives than it is to write a stem and to allow students to provide their own answers.

Consider this question: "Motivation can be defined as _____?" Obviously, it takes considerably more time to present this question in a multiple-choice format than to write the question in its present form. The ease of scoring multiple-choice questions, however, typically compensates for the time needed to construct the items and often yields more reliable scores than those obtained from a completion test. Indeed, some forms of completion tests possess some of the same scoring problems as essay tests. For questions like the one presented above, for example, many responses can be partially or wholly correct. Teachers must invariably use their judgment in scoring some responses to completion questions. However, brief short-answer questions do give teachers an idea of how students think.

Short-answer and completion items are especially useful in math and science courses, where formulas or equations can be requested, and for testing spelling and language, where specific bits of information often are required in order to do more complex problem-solving tasks. In any subject, they are good for testing knowledge of definitions and technical terms (Mehrens & Lehmann, 1978).

Matching exercises require students to link items in one column with corresponding items in another column:

Column A	Column B
___ 1. Intelligence tests	A. Freud
___ 2. Cognitive development	B. Skinner
	C. Erikson
___ 3. Trust vs. mistrust	D. Piaget
___ 4. Reinforcement	E. Kounin
___ 5. Modeling	F. Binet
___ 6. Formal operations	G. None of the above

In this example, students would receive credit for answering F, D, C, B, G, and D for items 1–6, respectively. Matching exercises are useful for testing memory of specific facts: terms, definitions, dates, events, and so on. They are easy to construct and score, as long as each item has just one clearly correct answer. To avoid cuing answers, it is helpful to have more response alternatives (column B in this example) than items (column A) or to include response alternatives that may be used more than once (D in the example).

conclusions: types of test items

No type of test or test item is best in all circumstances. Advocates sometimes claim that essay tests are better for measuring higher-level objectives and that objective tests are better for measuring factual recall or other low-level objectives. Things are not that simple, however. Essay tests can be used purely to grade low-level skills (punctuation, capitalization, spelling), with no attention to the creativity of the essay, or they can be used to measure factors such as sentence structure, paragraph structure, or story theme. Similarly, multiple-choice tests can measure learning objectives at almost any level of difficulty or sophistication; they are not restricted to low-level objectives. However, it is probably easier to write an essay test that can appropriately measure higher-order thinking than it is to write objective tests to accomplish that same purpose. Thus, in terms of both validity (does the test measure what it purports to measure?) and economy (how much time it takes to prepare), it may be more appropriate to use essays (and other types of tests we will describe later) to measure higher-order objectives.

Other differences between test items are more a matter of teacher or student preference than of necessity. Essay tests, for example, allow students to organize their answers and to integrate material. To students with above-average writing skills, however, they provide an advantage not directly relevant to the course but relevant to success on essay tests. Essay tests are confined to a relatively small portion of the material covered and are time-consuming to grade, and the grading can be highly subjective.

Multiple-choice and other objective tests present different advantages and disadvantages. Advantages include speed and objectivity of scoring, sampling a much larger number of objectives in the same amount of time, quicker feedback to students, and collecting broader-based data on how well students have mastered a wide range of course objectives. Some students, however, have test-taking skills that give them an advantage on this kind of test, independent of content. Also, the items are structured completely by the teacher, so the test provides little opportunity for students to integrate material or to discuss it in their own words.

The best policy is to use a variety of tests and assignments so as to balance differential student test-taking abilities with different kinds of tests. This will also create a balance among the kinds of learning strategies that various tests foster.

Preparing (and scoring) tests is a demanding and time-consuming process. However, this investment is important because tests and expectations of what will be tested guide how students think and try to organize course content. Teachers can often save time by using tests that publishers provide with elementary and secondary series. Teachers can also reduce test-preparation time by sharing tests with other teachers (e.g., teachers who teach at the same grade). The critical factor is that the test measure the content the teacher deems most important, as well as critical issues students have been asked to consider. If a publisher's test is of high quality and measures important content, teachers can use portions of it for classroom assessment (Airasian, 1991).

additional assessment procedures

performance tests

A **performance test** *demands that an individual, or sometimes a group, make a decision, solve a problem, or perform some prescribed behavior like delivering a speech.* Some contend that student behavior—not student knowledge as shown on pen-and-paper tests—is the critical variable in determining whether students have mastered material or developed social maturity. Indeed, many teacher-education programs use student performance as a part of assessment. Similarly, several states have now adopted beginning-teacher evaluation programs in which teachers have to demonstrate classroom competency before they are allowed to become fully certified.

Some knowledge can be assessed through pen-and-paper measures. If behaviors are critically important, however, they can be assessed with rating scales and checklists by having individuals perform. The advantage of performance measures is that they provide direct evidence that a student can perform a special skill, or can apply knowledge to solve problems. The disadvantage is that the process of observing the performance of individuals is time consuming for both students and teachers.

Brown (1976) listed the following examples of skills that one might want to measure directly: painting a watercolor, typing forty words a minute, conducting an opinion poll, conducting a counseling interview, programming a computer, making a soufflé, or assembling a carburetor.

To obtain reliable scores on performance tests, as on pen-and-paper tests, students need to know precisely what they are to demonstrate and the criteria by which their performance will be judged. Similarly, teachers should prepare checklists and rating scales that adequately describe student performance.

Teachers may use performance tests or oral presentations as part of their assessment programs. The general procedure teachers follow is the same as that for construction of classroom tests: (1) identify instructional objectives (content and cognitive skills) (2) plan instructional activities and (3) assess student learning and the instructional program. A fourth, unique dimension is to help students to identify performance criteria and to internalize them so that students can progressively assume more responsibility for self-evaluation.

Thus, in performance exams—just as in pen-and-paper exams—the appropriate starting point is to conceptualize and communicate the

An industrial arts course provides a different setting from an academic classroom for evaluating performance.

essence of the learning task. For example, it is important to articulate in advance to students the elements of an appropriate term paper. Kubiszyn and Borich (1993) suggest that writing comprises various elements and that it might be useful to determine the emphasis we want to give these elements. The elements include grammar, punctuation, vocabulary, spelling, capitalization, division of words, documentation, and references.

In contrast, other teachers might emphasize the interpretation and organization of papers rather than structure and grammar. According to Kubiszyn and Borich (1993), some teachers might focus on the quality and accuracy of ideas, logical development of ideas, organization of ideas, style and individuality, and general wording and phrasing. For an example of a rating scale that applies this framework, see Figure 23.2.

Yet other teachers might emphasize effects of the writing on the reader. To what extent is the reader motivated to take action or to con-

sider a problem definition more systematically? The teacher may want to look at the uniqueness and the defendability of the thesis the writer advances. Consistent with views we have articulated earlier in the book, we think that this level of evaluation—helping students to assert, integrate, and defend their ideas—is particularly important in today's schools.

There is growing interest in reviving exercises and assignments that allow students either individually or in groups to articulate ideas orally and to explain and explore through verbal communication (Mitchell, 1992; Sizer, 1984). Often oral evaluations tend to emphasize rather mechanical features of performance that can inhibit performance if they are focused on extensively. For example, a rating suggested by Kubiszyn and Borich (1993) emphasizes enunciation, pronunciation, loudness, word usage, pitch, rate, and gestures (see Figure 23.3). Although these dimensions may have some utility, we suspect that the act of communicating involves many more important areas and

Figure 23.2 rating scale for themes and term papers that emphasizes interpretation and organization

---

Quality and accuracy of ideas

1	2	3	4	5
Very limited investigation; little or no material related to the facts.		Some investigation and attention to the facts are apparent.		Extensive investigation; good detail and representation of the facts.

Logical development of ideas

1	2	3	4	5
Very little orderly development of ideas; presentation is confusing and hard to follow.		Some logical development of ideas, but logical order needs to be improved.		Good logical development; ideas logically connected and build upon one another.

Organization of ideas

1	2	3	4	5
No apparent organization. Lack of paragraphing and transitions.		Organization is mixed; some of the ideas not adequately separated from others with appropriate transitions.		Good organization and paragraphing; clear transitions between ideas.

Style, individuality

1	2	3	4	5
Style bland and inconsistent, or "borrowed."		Some style and individuality beginning to show.		Good style and individuality; personality of writer, shows through.

Wording and phrasing

1	2	3	4	5
Wording trite; extensive use of clichés.		Some word choices awkward.		Appropriate use of words; words and phrasing work to sharpen ideas.

SOURCE: Adapted from *Educational Testing and Measurement* by T. Kubiszyn and G. Borich. Copyright 1984, Scott Foresman. Reprinted by permission of HarperCollins College Publishing.

dimensions that need to be considered if oral presentations are to be more than a mechanical exercise (a verbal multiple-choice test!). The extent to which the speaker is genuine, appropriately enthusiastic, knowledgeable, and congruent with her or his purpose (informative, entertaining, etc.) is also important.

Thus, teachers need to combine a focus on specific and narrow technical skills or discrete knowledge with a focus that fosters application and performance. We will present an example on measuring student perfor-

mance in small groups to illustrate how this might be accomplished.

measuring small-group performance

Given the growing interest in allowing students to work cooperatively, it seems that teachers will have to develop some techniques for evaluating students' ability to work in groups. One source of evidence is the products

Figure 23.3 rating scale for speaking

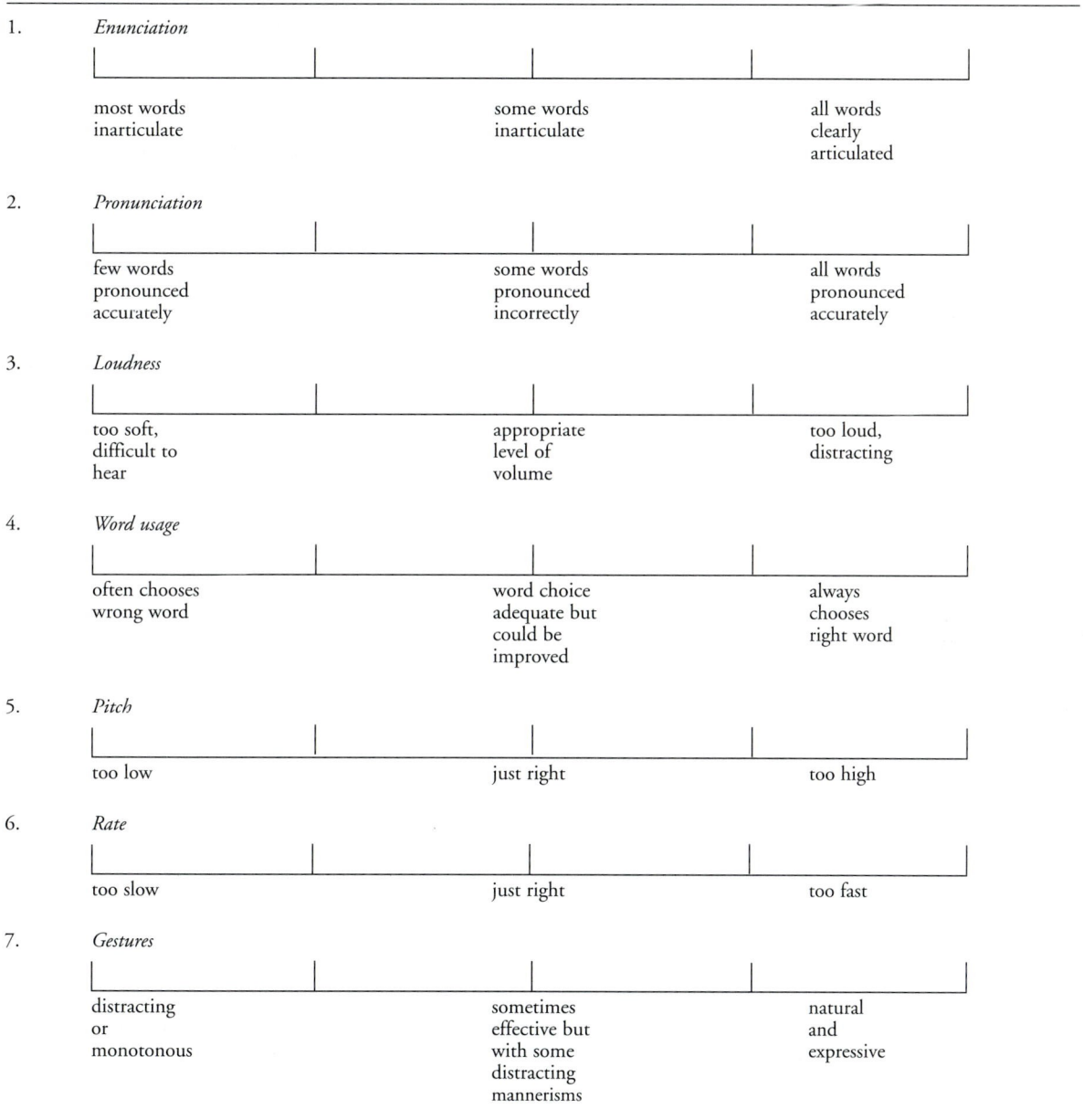

SOURCE: Adapted from *Educational Testing and Measurement* by T. Kubiszyn and G. Borich. Copyright © 1984, Scott Foresman. Reprinted by permission of HarperCollins College Publishing.

that individuals in groups create during group work. That is, teachers can examine the process (by listening to tapes) of group deliberation as well as the products (e.g., written reports) that students provide. It is also important, if students work frequently in groups, to examine their ability to perform relevant skills in a group context. Rather than simply having

Figure 23.4 small-group scale for individual members

_____ 1. Student comments show awareness of listening to peers.
_____ 2. Student comments show interest in contributing to the dicussion or solving the problem.
_____ 3. Student seems to interact with all members of the small group.
_____ 4. Student can summarize the entire group conversation when asked to do so.
_____ 5. Student can challenge peers' incorrect statements or their questionable judgment/logic in a task-relevant fashion.
_____ 6. Student can both ask for and provide information to others.

Directions: 1 implies that the student needs considerable work on the skill; 2 implies that the student is minimally competent; 3 implies a good mastery; 4 implies complete mastery of the skill

students present oral reports to classmates or having one student present a group's report, the teacher asks students to demonstrate appropriate group processes. Once a month, the teacher could have a group of students solve a problem or work collaboratively on an assignment while the rest of the class watches. The teacher could consider carefully the students' ability to work cooperatively (illustrating dimensions the teacher has been emphasizing). Because of evidence that student exchanges during cooperative learning are often not appropriate (concerning academic engagement or communicating sensitively and intelligently), it is important that students develop an appreciation and skills for collaborating productively with peers.

The measures in Figure 23.4 are designed to record an individual student's performance in a group. (The fourth item in the scale—"students can summarize the entire group conversation"—would be relevant for older students but not for primary students.) Some teachers might want to focus on the performance of the group per se rather than individual students (e.g., does group climate support risk taking?).

using rating scales

A **rating scale** does more than record the presence or absence of behavior; it _forces the rater to judge the quality of the performance._ In general, it is easier for errors to occur when using rating forms than checklists. Yet a rating is often necessary to estimate quality.

Several steps can be taken to improve the reliability of ratings. The first and most important one is to obtain several ratings on different days. All of us vary from day to day and from situation to situation. The more ratings we have the more likely we will be to describe typical, not atypical, behavior. Second, it is important to make a separate rating for each performance element. Teachers must guard against halo effects when they use rating forms. It is easy for a student's previous record of performance to influence the present rating, partly because the identity of the student cannot be masked, as it can be with written papers, and because the rating must be made immediately. Thus, the teacher may not rate students who typically give good speeches as critically as he or she rates other students.

Teachers sometimes use rating scales inappropriately because they divide tasks into too many small steps and fail to obtain a general rating of a project or presentation. Sometimes poor performance on one aspect does not negatively affect total performance (a low score for hand usage may not hurt the speech, whereas poor eye contact may make it totally ineffective). However, teachers should try to include major criteria in the rating form itself. Green (1975) offered the following criteria for evaluating a student's oral presentation:

1. Rapport with audience
2. Enthusiastic presentation
3. Effective organization
4. Clarity
5. Correct grammar
6. Good word choice
7. Adequate knowledge of subject

Special assessment measures
are needed for small-group
performance.

8. Significance of material
9. Stage presence
10. Appropriate gestures

Grading performance and progress is difficult, and errors will occur. Observation checklists and rating forms are two ways to make such assessment more systematic. Remember that ratings are judgments, not facts.

informal assessment

Formal testing is only one way that teachers can obtain information, and not always the best way. Teachers can also collect information using **informal assessment:** by *observing, questioning, or inspecting the work their students perform.*

Besides this regular, informal monitoring, teachers may wish to conduct oral tests by calling on students to answer questions or recite individually. Records of this performance can

be kept and used to guide instructional decisions or for grading, just as with student performance on written assignments. Teachers who conduct oral tests should be sure to include everyone or else to call on students at random. If they only call on students who volunteer, they will overestimate student understanding: if they only call on nonvolunteers, they will underestimate this understanding and put certain students on the spot continuously.

If everyone is to be questioned, the teacher may wish to proceed in a pattern, calling on students alphabetically or in rows. If so, the teacher probably should let the students know this, cautioning them to pay attention and think about how they would answer each question but to do so silently without calling out answers or raising their hands. This will minimize confusion and help ensure that students will get the most out of listening to exchanges between the teacher and other students.

Much useful information also can be

research at work
guidelines for effective use of portfolios

Woolfolk (1993) presents six useful guidelines for using portfolios effectively.

1. Teachers must teach students how to think about portfolios—why use them, how to create them, and so on. She suggests that teachers keep models of well-done portfolios but also convey to students that each portfolio should reflect an individual's unique thinking. Thus, we believe the model portfolios teachers use should not only be well done but also illustrate different styles of student performance. Early in the year teachers should provide constructive ideas and frequently review portfolios with students. Responsibility for identifying key aspects of the review process (What are the strengths? What are next steps?) should shift gradually from the teacher to students.

2. Students should understand that the portfolio reflects a range of their activities (library research, drawings, etc.).

3. Students should be aware that portfolios can fulfill different functions as the year progresses. For example, early in the year, rough drafts and planning documents might be prevalent and later, finished essays and self-critiques of work might predominate.

4. Portfolios should show growth (a problem is better defined, a preliminary plan is executed, a preliminary drawing is finished, etc.).

5. The portfolio should reflect personal as well as product growth. Thus, portfolios should include information that demonstrates students' self-evaluation abilities (e.g., identify strengths and weaknesses or provide advice to someone who might do a similar project in the future).

6. Students should have an active voice in determining what is included in the final course portfolio. They might be asked to consider what learning is most important for them and how to document that learning.

obtained from observing and correcting students while they work on seat-work assignments. In subjects such as elementary language arts or English composition, and in mathematics at almost any level, seat work is as good or better than formal tests for monitoring progress, although teachers may wish to test for other reasons.

portfolios

A **portfolio** is *an organized set of student work that illustrates student progress over time.* It should provide an opportunity for students' self-evaluation and self-reflection on their progress. Many types of student work may be included in a portfolio (e.g., videotapes, essays, blueprints, reports, photos, or laboratory experiments). Moreover, as Mitchell (1992) suggests, portfolios have various purposes and can take various forms. For example, a portfolio might be part of a formal standardized evaluation that all sixth or twelfth graders complete in a similar way (i.e., same amount of time, criteria) or it can be an informal requirement by a single teacher. According to Mitchell, a key objective of portfolios is to help students assess their own progress; hence, teachers should frequently ask students questions that encourage thinking (e.g., What have you learned about writing in completing this essay? Why did you select this work to include in your portfolio?).

Although performance evaluation has always been emphasized in U.S. schools, interest in portfolios and exhibitions (public demonstration of mastery and understanding) has increased dramatically since Sizer (1984) argued that course requirements and even graduation requirements should include mastery exhibitions in addition to performance on paper-and-pencil tests.

Mitchell (1992) notes that portfolios are used for various reasons including as a teaching tool (e.g., to provide student ownership, to help students and teachers set goals, or to individualize writing instruction); for the professional development of teachers (to examine writing in different disciplines, to build a sequence in writing instruction); for assessment (e.g., to serve as a grade), and for research (e.g., to evaluate how students learn a new language).

A portfolio includes only a portion of work, which students select. One virtue of portfolios is they can be designed to serve different goals at the same time (e.g., as a teaching tool and as an assessment medium). Portfolios are most likely to be used to inform students of progress and to provide feedback on the teachers' instruction, and are often ungraded.

encouraging student performance

Wiggins (1993) argues that teachers need to balance more fairly the needs of the test giver and the test taker. He argues that historically most of the burden has been on the test taker and he thinks it important to achieve a better balance between the needs of teachers and students. Indeed, he has proposed an assessment bill of rights for students that includes some of the following entitlements:

1. Students should be assigned worthwhile assessment tasks that are educative and engaging (i.e., not just memorize lists).
2. Students should be subjected to only minimal secrecy in testing and grading. They should know what constitutes adequate performance standards and what content they are responsible for.
3. There should be clear teacher criteria for grading work and students should be able to see models of excellent work that represents appropriate standards.
4. Students need ample opportunity (most especially time) to produce work that is thoughtful and complete; thus, they need time to self-assess, to redo assignments, and so on.
5. Students should be given opportunities to display and document their achievement. Tests should play to students, strengths, not only to their weaknesses (the traditional way in which many tests operate).
6. Students also need the freedom to question grades and test practices openly and without teacher constraints.

Wiggins (1993) makes the very persuasive argument that secrecy of testing often gets in the way of challenging students with authentic questions for which they have ample time to reflect, gather information, and assess themselves. Many educators would contend that assessments—especially new performance assessments (like portfolios)—should be designed to allow students to show their strengths. Along these lines, Wiggins suggests that the performance items in Figure 23.5 are illustrative of the products and performances that could be used in completing performance-based course requirements in a global studies course. He argues that such a set of criteria should be known in advance by students and, further, that such a test could be "taught" without compromising the integrity of the test, while also making it possible for students to understand explicitly the type of performance obligation for which they are accountable.

Figure 23.5 major tasks for a global studies course

1. Design a tour of the world's most holy sites.
   - Include accurate maps.
   - Prepare a guidebook, with descriptions of local norms, customs, etiquette.
   - Analyze the most cost-effective route and means of transportation.
   - Write an interesting-to-students history of the sites.
   - Compile an annotated bibliography of recommended readings for other students.
2. Write an International Bill of Rights.
   - Refer to past attempts and their strengths and weaknesses: Helsinki Accords, Communist Manifesto, U.S. Bill of Rights, and so on.
   - Convince a diverse group of peers and adults to "sign on."
3. Write a policy analysis and background report on a Latin American country for the secretary of state.
   - What should be our short-term policy goals with that country?
   - What are that country's economic and political prospects?
4. Collect and analyze media reports from *other* countries on U.S policies in the Middle East.
   - Put together a "briefing book" of photocopied press clips for the president, with commentary on the accuracy of each story.
   - Videotape/audiotape a simulated newscast summarizing world reaction to a recent U.S. policy decision.
5. Compile an oral history on a topical but historically interesting issue:
   - Interview recent American immigrants.
   - Talk to veterans of Operation Desert Storm, Vietnam, and World War II about America's role as a police officer for world-affairs.
6. Design a museum exhibit, using artifacts and facsimiles.
   - Exhibit links between a European country's geography and its economy.
   - Illustrate the local area's role in the industrial revolution.
   - Display patterns of modern emigration and their causes.
7. Write and deliver, on videotape, two speeches: the first, by the visiting head of an African country on the history of U.S.-Africa relations; the second, in response, by President Clinton's spokesperson.
8. Take part in a formal debate on a controversial issue of global significance—for example, aid to Russian republics or the U.S. role in the fall of communism.
9. Create a model United Nations (with groups of two or three representing each country) and enact a new Security Council resolution on terrorism.
10. Write a textbook chapter titled "The Primary Causes of Revolution: People, Ideas, Events, or Economic Conditions?" in which you weigh the various causes of revolution and reflect on whether the most important revolutions were "revolutionary" or "evolutionary."

SOURCE: G. Wiggins (1993). *Assessing Student Performance: Exploring the Purpose and Limits of Testing.* San Francisco: Jossey-Bass.

implications for teachers

classroom assessment and test-taking skills

Although each teacher and testing situation is unique, these general guidelines for assessment can be offered:

1. If you consider testing important, it is probably a good idea for you to test frequently over short time spans, so that you can use your test data for reteaching and individualized instruction as well as for grading.
2. Be clear about learning objectives. If you are, you are unlikely to run into problems such as lack of content validity, and you will not create tests that measure content that was taught but do not measure the objectives that you want to measure.
3. Take care that you allow students ample time to finish a test unless time is a relevant factor.
4. If you intend to test over the entire course content, be sure that your test samples equally from different parts of the course.
5. On the other hand, if you wish to stress certain content, alert students to this so that they can adjust their preparation accordingly. In fact, if you are extremely clear about the objectives, you can give students a number of potential test questions and inform

them that the test will be composed of a subset of these questions. This will ensure that the students study all of the material that you consider important.

6. Try to maintain some balance between essay tests for essay-type assignment(s) and objective tests, because certain students do notably better on one type of test than the other, independent of course content. Also, as pointed out previously, different kinds of tests promote various kinds of learning. A balance between test types is usually preferable to reliance on only one.

developing test-taking skills Even a carefully constructed test, under certain circumstances, can yield unreliable results. One of the biggest threats to obtaining accurate information about student performance is the fact that some students can take tests better than other students. Unfortunately, some students experience debilitating anxiety during testing or evaluation situations and thus underperform. As Hill and Wigfield (1984) note, several recent educational trends may increase this problem including minimal competency testing, the increased use of test scores to evaluate educational programs, and greater public pressure for high skill learning and achievement in schools (for a review of the effects of anxiety on student performance, see Hill & Wigfield, 1984).

Hill and Wigfield argue that teachers may want to help students to understand testing and to develop more adequate skills for taking both teacher-made and standardized tests. To this end they have developed an in-service training model to assist teachers in preparing students for testing situations. These authors believe that allowing students to practice with test formats, respond to difficult material, and learn good test-taking strategies will improve student effort, motivation, and performance in test situations. Evaluative data show that the in-service training program is associated with improved student test performance, particularly in language arts. The following outline of skills and motivational dispositions suggests statements teachers can make to students about taking tests.

examples of test-taking skills and motivational dispositions

1. General test skills and knowledge
   a. Be comfortable and sit where you can write easily.
   b. Pay attention when I talk.
   c. I can help you understand how to work on the test but can't tell you the answer to a problem on the test.
   d. Taking tests is something we learn to do in school.
2. Positive motivation—do your best
   a. All I ask is that you do your best. I will be really pleased if you try to do your best.
   b. If you finish a section before time is up, go back and check your answers. Don't disturb others; instead, work quietly at your desk.
   c. Before we begin, remember to listen carefully to me, be quiet, take a deep breath, and relax.
3. Positive motivation—expectancy reassurance
   a. Some tests have very hard problems. Don't worry if you can't do some problems.
   b. It's OK if you aren't sure what the right answer is. Choose the answer you think is best. It's OK to guess.
   c. If you work hard but don't finish a test, don't worry about it. The most important thing to me is that you try hard and do as well as you can. I know you'll do a good job if you try.
4. Test strategy and problem-solving skills
   a. There is only one best answer.
   b. Do what you know first. If you can't answer a problem or it's taking a lot of time, move on to the next one.

Please circle the number that best represents your response to each statement (from "strongly agree," 1, to "strongly disagree," 5).

1. This was a fair test of what we learned.   1 2 3 4 5
2. This test was easy, if you studied for it.   1 2 3 4 5
3. This kind of test really makes you think.   1 2 3 4 5
4. This kind of test is new for me.   1 2 3 4 5
5. I did a good job of preparing for this test.   1 2 3 4 5
6. You did a good job of preparing us for the test.   1 2 3 4 5
7. I was unfortunately surprised by the questions you chose.   1 2 3 4 5
8. The directions were clear.   1 2 3 4 5
9. You provided lots of different ways for us to show that we
    understand what was taught.   1 2 3 4 5
10. There was enough choice in the questions we could select
    to answer.   1 2 3 4 5
11. Some questions should have been worth more points and/or
    others worth less.   1 2 3 4 5
12. We were allowed appropriate access to resources (books, notes,
    and so on) during the test.   1 2 3 4 5
13. I expected the grade I got, once I saw the test questions and
    then later found out the right answers.   1 2 3 4 5
14. There wasn't enough time to do a good job; I know more than
    I was able to show.   1 2 3 4 5

Figure 23.6 student questionnaire on the test
SOURCE: G. Wiggins (1993). *Assessing Student Performance: Exploring the Purpose and Limits of Testing.* San Francisco: Jossey-Bass.

You can come back later if you don't have time.

c. Don't rush. If you work too fast, you can make careless errors. You have to work carefully.

d. Don't work too slowly. Do the problems at a moderate rate.

e. Pay close attention to your work.

f. Keep track of where you are working on the page by keeping one hand on this spot.

obtaining feedback from students

After teachers have students complete tests or performance assessments, it would be useful occasionally for teachers to collect information from them regarding their perceptions of the adequacy of the testing procedures and the conditions under which they completed a performance assignment (e.g., did they have sufficient time and resources to do the project?). Figure 23.6 from Wiggins (1993) illustrates a set of questions that a teacher could present to students to get more data about students' perceptions of a particular test.

In terms of the performance assessment dimensions that we have discussed in the text, the teacher could also turn the assignment into a project and allow students to construct their own test or to devise alternative procedures that the teacher could use for future assessments. The students could work in groups of three or four, or individually, for one or more periods. Teachers' interest in obtaining and using such information would help highlight the concept of two-way communication and implement the students' bill of rights discussed earlier. At a minimum, open communication between teachers and students about tests, performances, and general assessments will result in a better understanding about what the testing condition can and cannot represent.

summary

Construction of tests involves consideration of a number of issues such as content coverage, test length, item types, weighing, and related matters. Because tests only sample mastery of content taught in a course, it is important to sample from the full range of content and to include enough items to allow reliable measurement. Otherwise, a test may yield biased results and the errors of measurement are likely to be increased. Generally, test reliability increases with test length, so errors of measurement can be reduced by adding items if content coverage and other important qualities are carefully considered.

In addition to content coverage, it is important to consider the levels of understanding involved in test items. The six levels of Bloom's taxonomy provide a convenient reference for planning test items that measure different cognitive levels. Simultaneous examination of content and level permits planning of tests that will cover the instructional objectives of a course adequately. Item type is another critical factor, since essay items can be used to assess higher levels in the cognitive domain more easily than objective items. However, it is frequently more difficult to sample a wide range of content with essay than with objective items.

Teachers can use various means of assessment other than written tests. Performance tests can be used if actual performance on a test, rather than knowledge, is the essential factor.

Rating scales provide a basis for measuring the quality of performance directly. Informal assessments, perhaps based on observation supplemented by oral tests, can be used along with more formal assessments like written tests in evaluating student performance.

As in all aspects of evaluating student performance, teachers need to consider issues of reliability, validity, and grading when using portfolio assessment (Maeroff, 1991; Newman & Smolen, 1993; Tierney, Carter, & Desai, 1991; Vavrus, 1990; Wolf, LeMahieu, & Eresh, 1992). For example, developing appropriate and shared norms about what represents appropriate performance at a particular grade level is an important aspect of classroom measurement. It would seem important that teachers take the opportunity to examine portfolios of other teachers across the district (who teach at the same grade level) to develop appropriate grade level standards. Just as teachers must make decisions about what to include in portfolios—and how much choice students should have in selecting items for inclusion—so, too, must teachers make decisions about the quality of student performance and growth.

Students' test-taking skills can be improved by helping them to understand the reasons for testing and to develop appropriate skills for taking tests. Test-taking skill training can help to improve the reliability and validity of classroom tests.

questions for reflection

1. What would you do if students correctly pointed out to you that your test concentrated on only a quarter of the assigned material, thus benefitting those who studied the tested portion of the material thoroughly and penalizing those who studied all of the material?

2. Some students clearly do better on objective tests than on essay tests, and others do better on essay tests. What implication, if any, does this have for your testing and grading practices?

3. Is it better to test frequently but briefly, or is it

better to test infrequently but to test exhaustively?

4. What types of tests do you like and dislike as a student? How might these likes and dislikes affect your behavior as a teacher? Are your biases appropriate for the subject, grade, and types of students that you expect to teach?

5. Considering the grade and subject you expect to teach, how can you evaluate the progress of students who do not read or write English efficiently?

6. Prepare a model essay test on the functions of the Supreme Court for sixth-grade students and another for eleventh-grade students. How would the two tests vary? Compare the two essay tests that you prepared with those of classmates.

cases to consider

a lesson on the American Revolution Read the following material describing the American Revolution. As you read it, identify concepts and facts that you would want students to learn. Take notes as you read in order to:

1. Write four instructional objectives that will tell students what they should learn.
2. Prepare a test blueprint.
3. Write four multiple-choice items that measure objectives in your blueprint.

The American Revolution and its meaning The American Revolution grew largely out of change in Britain's colonial purposes and methods. In 1763 the American colonists seemed content with their status. If Great Britain had not attempted to tighten the loosely knit empire and to make more money out of it, the break between Britain and the colonies would probably not have come when it did or as it did.

But once the break took place, changes came fast in the Americans' attitudes toward Great Britain and toward their own society. The fears, hopes, dreams, and material pressures caused by war produced some major changes in American life. Nevertheless, America after the war years looked remarkably like colonial America. The conservative nature of the American Revolution was caused largely by two circumstances. The first is that the colonists began fighting in an effort to preserve what they had rather than to create a new order. The second is that the war did little damage to agriculture, the basis of the American economy.

Reconstructing the empire After the French and Indian War, the British decided they could no longer afford to neglect their American colonies. The government issued a series of laws and decrees aimed at establishing more effective control over the colonies.

With French power eliminated in America after 1763, colonists moved west and provoked a new Indian war, the Pontiac Conspiracy. To quiet the Indians and to gain time to organize the territory acquired from France, Parliament issued the Proclamation of 1753. This act forbade the colonists to settle west of the Appalachian Mountains. Then, in 1764, Parliament passed the Sugar Act. This act placed new duties on sugar, coffee, wine, and certain other imported products; reduced the tax on molasses; and provided ways to collect all duties more effectively.

There were only scattered protests to these first measures. But a major crisis over taxation quickly followed. In 1765 Parliament passed the Stamp Act. Colonial resistance took a number of forms. Colonial leaders refused to do any business requiring the use of stamps to show that the tax had been paid. Trade came to a halt, and courts of justice closed because virtually all legal papers needed stamps. Politicians organized bands of patriots, largely workingmen, who called themselves the Sons of Liberty. They pressured reluctant business people to support the boycott and forced Stamp Act officials to resign by their use of threats and violence.

Even more significant was a meeting in New York of delegates from nine colonies. This Stamp Act Congress was the first really effective act of political cooperation among so many colonies. It adopted a series of resolutions protesting the new tax law and other new policies, such as the trials of accused smugglers by military courts. British businesspeople hurt by the colonial boycott persuaded Parliament to repeal the Stamp Act in 1766. At the time, Parliament restated its right to pass laws for the colonies.

Parliament continued to pass new and unpopular laws that caused the division between the colonists and Great Britain to grow larger. There were occasional brawls between the colonists, and the British soldiers shot five members of an unarmed mob. Similar brawls between soldiers and colonists occurred in New York and added to the growing dislike and fear between the colonists and the British.

The lull and the storm In the spring of 1770, British-colonial relations took a marked turn for the better. The British soldiers in Boston withdrew to the fort in the harbor to prevent further incidents. A new parliamentary ministry took office. Its leader, Lord Frederick North, had all of the Townshend duties repealed except that on tea. North allowed the Quartering Act to expire and also promised that no new taxes would be imposed on the colonies. There was rejoicing in the colonies, and for more than two years there seemed to be a real reconciliation.

Then a series of episodes produced serious conflicts that finally led to independence. The first took place in June 1772, when a group of Rhode Islanders raided and burned the Gaspée, a customs vessel. The British decision to try the offenders in England, assuming they could be identified, alarmed the colonists, who saw this decision as yet another blow to the right of trial by jury. The colonists organized Committees of Correspondence to keep each other informed about local conflicts between colonial and British authority and to circulate propaganda against British rule.

In 1773 the tea crisis speeded up the final break with Great Britain. The colonists saw the British East India Company's monopoly on the sale of tea as another example of colonial exploitation for British profits. The colonists prevented the sale of tea up and down the Atlantic coast. In Boston, the center of colonial protest, a band of citizens destroyed the cargo of tea ships.

Parliament responded angrily in 1774 with the Coercive Acts, labeled the Intolerable Acts by the colonists. At the same time, Parliament passed the Quebec Act, which was not intended as a colonial punishment, but which the colonist interpreted as one.

With the Intolerable Acts, Parliament showed that it intended to enforce British authority, regardless of the cost to trade and remaining colonial goodwill. All of the colonies united firmly in support of Massachusetts. The Committees of Correspondence organized a Congress, which met in Philadelphia in September 1774 to deal with the mounting crisis. The fifty-five delegates from twelve colonies (Georgia was not represented) voted to support Massachusetts, to denounce Parliament's legislation for the colonies since 1763, and to form a Continental Association to enforce a complete boycott of trade with Britain.

By the spring of 1776, it became clear to most members of the Congress that reconciliation between the colonies and Great Britain was impossible without completely surrendering the colonial position. In all thirteen colonies, the Americans had removed the royal officials. The colonists were disillusioned with the king, who had stoutly supported Parliament. And their position was strengthened by Thomas Paine's bitter attack in Common Sense on the monarchy in general and on the king in particular. The Continental Congress responded to the events of the year by adopting the Declaration of Independence.

The war and its strategy The Americans were victorious in the War of Independence for a number of reasons. First, they fought on home ground. Second, they received considerable help from France and Spain. And third, their commander, George Washington, realized that the time was on the American side if he could avoid an early defeat. The British met with serious difficulties in using their superior strength on the distant rebellion. The war against the colonies was unpopular with many merchants, some members of Parliament, and even some generals. The British did not have the manpower needed to put down the revolt so they had to hire 30,000 mercenary soldiers from Germany. In addition, the British navy was in bad shape.

The revolution at home After the revolution against Britain, relatively few changes occurred in American institutions. State governments were established under new constitutions, beginning in 1776, but they resembled the colonial governments they replaced. Under the new constitutions, the representative assemblies held most political power. Voters in most states elected their governors, whose power was reduced. In most of the colonies, the right to vote had depended on possession of some property. During the war, nearly all property qualifications for voting and office holding were either lowered or dropped.

The new states guarded their powers jealously. They gave some authority to the new government of the United States formed under the Articles of Confederation in 1781. But they kept all authority relating to local government. The central government, which itself lacked an effective executive office, directed the army and conducted foreign relations. But it could not regulate commerce nor did it have the authority to tax citizens directly.

It had the right to request money from the states but could not enforce its requests.

Merchants and other creditors suffered from the interruption of commerce during the war. But farmers and debtors benefited from the demand for foodstuffs and the creation of a vast supply of paper money by the revolutionary government to pay its debts. Much property owned by loyalists was confiscated. In most cases, it went to property holders rather than to landless people. Stimulated by war, democratic ideas affected some relationships. Perhaps the most striking examples were the decisions of several northern states to abolish slavery. Some southern states simplified the process of freeing slaves. The numbers of freed slaves increased substantially. Most states prohibited the slave trade during the Revolution. Thus, Americans emerged from their War for Independence with a working national political system and a society and economy that were not deeply divided.

Test plan, American Revolution: Three-day unit. Assume that the test plan in the accompanying table has been given to students to guide their study of the unit on the American Revolution. How will the plan influence student behavior? Discuss the value of this blueprint. Is it good or bad? Defend your answer.

	Cognitive Objectives		
	Terms, Facts, Principles	Applications	Total Percent
A. *Causes*			
1. In England	10	0	10
2. In the colonies	10	0	10
B. *Battle strategy*			
1. General attitude—Motivation of soldiers	20	0	20
2. Specific battles	0	0	0
C. *Consequences of the war*			
1. Relationship with England	0	5	5
2. Relationship with world	0	5	5
3. Life in the colonies	0	50	50

chapter 24.

assigning grades

objectives

When you have mastered the material in this chapter, you will be able to

1. Discuss the educational and practical purposes of grading versus evaluating students and provide reasons why strict "grading on a curve" is not appropriate
2. Understand how the three basic methods of grading work and be able to discuss the system you will use
3. Describe the advantages and disadvantages of fixed-standard versus norm-referenced grading systems

4. List and explain the four considerations a teacher might use in adjusting grades and discuss how you will apply these considerations in your teaching
5. Describe individualized contracts for grades and tell when and how contracts are appropriate to use
6. Discuss the relationship between different grading methods and student motivation and perception of success
7. Make recommendations for setting up a grading system that will minimize both teacher and student anxiety about the process

You are probably familiar with the term "grading on the curve." Originally, this method assumed that student mastery of course material would be distributed normally, so grades would also follow a normal distribution: 2 percent A, 14 percent B, 68 percent C, 14 percent D, and 2 percent F. This notion did not last long, however, because it involves several faulty assumptions.

First, even if students' efforts were equal, this content mastery often would not follow a normal distribution because their aptitudes often would not follow a normal distribution. Second, students' efforts usually are not equal, and many teachers want grades to reflect effort as well as objective achievement. Third, even if both effort and achievement were distributed normally, this in itself would not necessarily mean that grades should be distributed normally. The "ideal" distribution of grades varies with their intended purpose or function: to motivate and reward effort, document progress, measure achievement relative to absolute standards or individualized expectations, or qualify students for advancement or certification, among others.

functions of grading

Most teachers intend their grades to perform several functions, typically including motivation/reward and documentation of progress. As a compromise between grading purely on the basis of effort or only according to absolute achievement, they adjust grades based on achievement to take into account effort. In addition, teachers may try to grade as highly as the facts seem to justify, believing that this will maximize the motivational value of the grades and minimize damage to students' self-concepts. The result often is a method called "grading on the curve," although it does not involve using the normal curve as just described. Instead, in **grading on the curve,** *the teacher determines in advance that the class will receive a certain percentage of each of the grades to be assigned (for example, 30 percent A, 30 percent B, 30 percent C, and 10 percent D or F). This ensures that grades will be distributed in a way that seems to make sense, assuming that differences in student performance correspond roughly* *to the percentages that the teacher has assigned.*

But does it? If the class as a whole does well on the test, adhering rigidly to this grading plan means that many students who answered more than 90 percent of the items correctly will get a grade of C despite their good performance and despite the fact that the differences between them and the students who get an A are trivial. Thus, grading on a curve is not always appropriate. Under what conditions would it be a fair and appropriate way to grade?

Another point to consider is that teacher-made tests often include questions that seem straightforward to teachers but turn out to be ambiguous to students. Sometimes more than one alternative answer is correct or at least justifiable. Should you credit the only answer you considered to be correct in the first place? Should you credit the only answer you consider to be the best answer? Should you credit all answers that are justifiable? Does it make a difference? If your answer to the last question was "no," consider the probability that students who receive no credit under one procedure but would have some under another may be outraged, especially if their final grades are affected. Sometimes, due to poor phrasing or typographical omissions, none of the response alternatives is correct. What should you do about these items when you grade the test? Should you ignore them? Give everyone credit for them?

Thinking about these hypothetical situations probably has made you realize some of the complexities involved in grading. The simplest solution, and the one that many persons favor, is to abolish grading altogether. This is a realistic solution up to a point, but not a complete one.

It is important to make a distinction between grading and evaluation. Grading may not be necessary, but evaluation is. Teachers must evaluate both their own behavior and their students' progress regularly if they are to function efficiently. Failure to do so represents only avoidance of an uncomfortable problem, not a solution to it.

Most necessary evaluation can be accomplished without formal grading, although the complexities involved in testing apply in varying degrees to other methods as well. Student progress can be assessed through a variety of evaluation methods besides tests. Students' questions and comments in class, ability to answer questions about content, performance on special assignments and projects, and written work all can help a teacher monitor their progress. When tests are used, there is no need to return them with letter grades or percentage scores. In addition, or even instead, teachers can return tests with detailed comments about the strengths and weaknesses of students' efforts, focusing on progress and on ways to improve rather than on how students did in comparison to one another.

Ultimately, though, students will have to take relatively objective tests so that their performances can be compared not only with one another but with the achievement of students in the country at large. External pressures for these test data come from citizens and state educational agencies interested in school quality. Also, colleges and universities use such information to decide about admissions and course advisement, although this could change in the future if more and more school districts elect to use outcome-based assessment or some form of evaluation other than grading.

Many employers require information about the basic literacy and mathematical skills of prospective employees. Most desirable jobs have minimal educational requirements. Furthermore, employers have become wary of grades because they have seen too many people with high school or college degrees who do not have the skills expected of such graduates. Consequently, in examining transcripts, many employers pay much more attention to scores on standardized tests than to grades. If no such scores are available, they are likely to test prospective employees themselves before offering to hire them. Thus, due to external pressures of this sort, instructors who refuse to grade or who assign very high grades to everyone regardless of performance do not do their students any favors in the long run. They are leaving to someone else the unpleasant task of making it clear to certain students that they are deficient in basic skills, have difficulty in applying basic skills to real problems, or cannot communicate their ideas effectively.

grading methods

We have just stressed the need for accurate assessment and have noted that teachers can assess student progress through formal tests and ratings as well as informal monitoring. Ultimately, this information has to be turned into a description of student progress or a grade.

Many instructional programs, especially in elementary schools, now stress continuous monitoring of student performance, which enables teachers to keep specific records of student progress. Often schools using such systems do not assign grades in the first few years. Instead, student progress is reported in terms of skills expected and skills mastered.

When teachers do assign grades, there are three basic methods they can use. The **individual-standard method** is *based on a student's progress in relation to his or her capacity.* A bright student must master more material to get an A than a slower student. Such a method demands careful testing at the beginning of the year, and students must be informed of the relative performance levels they must obtain to get specified grades. The individual-standard method is difficult to implement. If two students score 49 and 60 on a 100-item pretest, for example, how does one set fair standards for what these students must do to earn an A, B, C, or D in the

course? And how can effort be graded? Furthermore, most people, including employers and parents, want to know how much students learned or what they can do, not how their performance compares with their ability or potential. Some teachers, however, can and do grade on the basis of an individual standard or at least assign grades partly on the basis of such information.

Most teachers in American classrooms use a *fixed standard* to assign grades. (A driver's license exam is a good example of using a fixed standard—to pass the test requires a minimum standard score. In setting the exam, the state has a long history of knowing how past applicants have fared on the test.)

In the **fixed-standard method**, *levels of performance correspond with different grades on the basis of how students have performed previously.* Establishing a standard of performance is difficult for beginning teachers, who may want to obtain tests used by teachers who have taught similar students in order to begin building realistic expectations. The "fixed" standard varies from teacher to teacher. A 70 on Mr. Marx's algebra exams equals a C; in Ms. Thomas's room it's a D. Still, when a teacher uses fixed standards, students know what performance levels correspond to different grades.

Teachers who know that some parts of a course are more difficult than others may vary their standards from exam to exam. It is best to explain the current standard to students when they are ready to take the exam: "I know this material is tough, and students in the past have had more trouble on it than any other unit. Thus, on this test, any score above 80 percent will be an A." Similarly, teachers who recognize that a group of students is better or worse than the typical class they teach may alter their standards to prevent giving an excessive number of high or low marks.

Norm-referenced grading *compares a student's achievement with the performance of the class rather than a fixed standard of subject-mat-*

ter mastery. A student's grade depends on how well other students do. If a student scores 90 on an exam, but all other students score above 90, he or she has done poorly. Conversely, if a student scores 70, but all other students score below 70, he or she has done well. Teachers who use norm-referenced grading often assign grades

according to a normal distribution. However, classes differ in levels of ability and effort expenditure, so a normal curve for grading will penalize some students unfairly. Students who perform well but are part of an exceptionally capable and hard-working class, for example, would be downgraded.

implications for teachers

a class grading example

Consider the record of student performance presented in Table 24.1. Assume that there are thirty students in the class and that each student in the table represents two other students who performed identically. We can see Heather and Jeff earned the most points in the course (90 each) and shared a total class rank of 1.5%.

How can we assign grades using the three methods just discussed? To use an individual standard we would have to have information about student ability. Assume that the students as they appear in Table 24.1 are ranked in terms of course aptitude (Heather has the most; Terrill has the least). Using such criteria, we might decide that Sandra deserves an A (she had a relatively low aptitude but high performance), and that Jeff's and Heather's performances warrant a B (high aptitude, high performance). However, Heather and Jeff have scored 90, and how high a level can we demand? In part, the criteria would be determined by the differences in students' aptitudes. If Heather's IQ was 115 and Terrill's was 108, it would be inappropriate to

expect much, if any, extra performance from Heather. A difference between 140 and 85 would be a different case. The practical differences in implementing an individual standard, however, are overwhelming, and this method typically creates more misunderstanding and arbitrariness than it resolves.

A fixed standard provides a clear basis for assigning grades. It is easy to use, although it may take a great deal of time and thought to establish initial standards. The distribution of grades will vary depending on where the standards are set. Consider the three standards presented below. All would look realistic to teachers and students at the beginning of a course.

If these three standards are applied to the students in Table 24.2, however, different grades will be assigned. In general, standards A and C are higher than B, although standard A is more liberal in the D range than is standard C. Standard B establishes lower cut-off points for the assignment of As, Bs, and Cs than do standards A and C.

fixed standard A	fixed standard B	fixed standard C
A = 94% or above	A = 90% or above	A = 93% or above
B = 85–93%	B = 80–89%	B = 85–92%
C = 75–84%	C = 70–79%	C = 78–84%
D = 60–74%	D = 60–69%	D = 70–77%
F = below 60%	F = below 60%	F = below 70%

table 24.1 summary of student performance on five course assignments

	Class Presentation (30%)		Assigned Paper (10%)		Exam I (25%)		Exam II (25%)		Homework (10%)			
	Raw	Rank	Raw	Rank	Raw	Rank	Raw	Rank	Raw	Rank	Total	Rank
Heather	27/30	1.0	10	1.5	20/25	5.5	24/25	1	9/10	6.5	90	1.5
James	24/30	8.5	2	8.5	19/25	8.0	12/25	8	9/10	6.5	66	10.0
Jeff	26/30	2.5	10	1.5	24/25	1.0	20/25	4	10/10	2.5	90	1.5
Julia	25/30	5.5	6	5.5	18/25	9.0	18/25	6	10/10	2.5	77	5.0
Pat	25/30	5.5	6	5.5	20/25	5.5	21/25	2	9/10	6.5	81	4.0
Peggy	24/30	8.5	3	7.0	20/25	5.5	14/25	7	8/10	9.5	69	8.0
Sam	23/30	10.0	9	3.0	16/25	10.0	10/25	10	9/10	6.5	67	9.0
Sandra	26/30	2.5	8	4.0	22/25	2.5	20/25	4	10/10	2.5	86	3.0
Skip	25/30	5.5	2	8.5	22/25	2.5	11/25	9	10/10	2.5	70	7.0
Terrill	25/30	5.5	1	10.0	20/25	5.5	20/25	4	8/10	9.5	74	6.0

Table 24.2 is an expanded version of Table 24.1 and represents the distribution of thirty students (assuming that the performance of each student in Table 24.1 is typical of two other students in the class). An examination of Table 24.2 and the standards proposed above indicates that no students would have received As if fixed standards A and C were used in the course. Standard A would have resulted in the assignment of fifteen Ds, whereas in both standards B and C only nine Ds would have been assigned. Furthermore, standard C would have resulted in the assignment of

nine Fs, but none would have been assigned using standards A or B. It should be clear that shifting standards by even small percentages can result in different grade distributions.

One could assign grades using norm-referenced standards by inspecting the distribution of scores and allowing natural breaks to determine the assignment of letter grades. Whenever there are no explicit standards for judging student performance, as is typically the case in secondary schools, we recommend such norm-referenced comparisons.

table 24.2 **student scores and the assignment of grades using three fixed standards and a norm-referenced comparison**

STUDENT SCORE	STANDARD A	STANDARD B	STANDARD C	NORM-REFERENCED COMPARISONS
90	B	A	B	A
90	B	A	B	A
90	B	A	B	A
90	B	A	B	A
90	B	A	B	A
90	B	A	B	A
86	B	B	B	B
86	B	B	B	B
86	B	B	B	B
81	C	B	C	B
81	C	B	C	B
81	C	B	C	B
77	C	C	D	C
77	C	C	D	C
77	C	C	D	C
74	D	C	D	C
74	D	C	D	C
74	D	C	D	C
70	D	C	D	C-D+?
70	D	C	D	C-D+?
70	D	C	D	C-D+?
69	D	D	F	D
69	D	D	F	D
69	D	D	F	D
67	D	D	F	D
67	D	D	F	D
67	D	D	F	D
66	D	D	F	D
66	D	D	F	D
66	D	D	F	D

recommendations for grading

Grading should implement the philosophy of the school and the teacher as fairly as possible. Decisions about grades have to be made on the basis of one's particular situation; you may teach in a school that has fixed grading guidelines, or you may have complete freedom to set your own standards. In general, we recommend that grades not be assigned on the basis of individual standards (evaluating performance in terms of ability), except perhaps in a multiage grouping system characterized by continuous assessment. If individual standards are used in grading, they should be applied after the major decisions are made, when the teacher is choosing between two close alternatives (is the grade C- or D+?).

Fixed standards make most sense when teachers have a firm notion of what students can do, so that standards can be based on realistic expectations. In some areas such standards are readily available (the student needs to make at least fifteen out of twenty free throws over three consecutive testings to earn an A), but in other areas it may take some time to establish realistic expectations (to earn an A should a student spell correctly, on the average, 90 percent or 95 percent of the assigned vocabulary?).

Teachers who use fixed standards must be careful that a single poor performance does not prevent a student from obtaining a reasonably high mark. If they test frequently, they can do this by allowing students to drop their lowest score. However, allowing students to drop one of only two or three scores can cause as many problems as it solves (consider the situation in which Ted has a 50, 70, 90; and Jim has an 80, 70, and 70).

Teachers who are willing to take the extra time necessary to prepare and grade make-up exams can help students continue to make an effort to learn material; that is, teachers can allow students to retake one or two exams instead of dropping their lowest test score. Retesting has the obvious disadvantage of creating more work for the teacher, but it does encourage new effort by students.

By now you realize that there is no totally fair way to grade students. Each decision is really a hypothesis about how to help students perform as well as they can. Individual students are always affected differently by "class" rules. In the example just presented, we can see that Ted will be hurt if one test score is not eliminated; however, if a test score is dropped, Ted will end up with a higher grade than Jim, who has a higher average).

We recommend that beginning teachers use a combination of norm-referenced standards and common sense, unless they are teaching in a non-graded situation or a fixed-standard system (most teachers from fourth grade through high school, however, do assign grades). As teachers gain more experience and have expectations about what students can do, they can shift to fixed standards if their preference and the local situation are appropriate.

The chief advantage of the fixed system is that it puts the control of grades in students' hands. If the standards are appropriately fixed, students who work hard can earn good grades. If the standards are too low, however, students are not challenged; if the standards are too high, students will give up.

The major disadvantage to norm-referenced comparisons is that they interpret performance not in terms of some absolute standard (fifteen out of twenty free throws) but in terms of how a student performs in comparison to other students. (If the class average is 10, 15 may be excellent, but a 15 may be poor if the class average is 18.) When teachers do not have firm expectations about how students will perform, however, standards broadly imposed by the collective performance of all students will probably be fairer than fixed standards.

adjusting grades

Teachers do not have to rely totally on fixed standards or norm-referenced comparisons. Four possible considerations that a teacher might want to use in making grade adjustments are: (1) consistency of performance, (2) performance on major course objectives, (3) special-credit work, and (4) contract work. If teachers use any or all of these considerations, however, they should explain to students how they will be used and what influence they will have on grades early in the course.

After examining the distribution of scores in Table 24.2, we could use consistency of performance as a criterion in borderline cases. For example, Skip, a student with a 70 (see Table 24.1), falls short of the C cutoff. His grade is hurt by his score on the assigned paper and his performance on exam II. However, his performance on exam I is excellent. Here the criterion of consistency does not help us. If his total score was influenced by one low score, we might give him the higher grade, but his performance was inconsistent and is therefore difficult to describe with a single grade.

A second criterion that might help us is the importance of particular objectives. Skip's total course performance is heavily influenced by his performance on a minor task, the assigned paper. If the teacher found the paper difficult to grade or if the assignment was accompanied by consistent student complaints (e.g., not enough

time to write), the teacher might assign Skip a higher grade on this basis. But Skip also did poorly on the second exam, and unless the teacher has absolutely no confidence in the grade on the assigned paper, there is no basis for giving Skip a higher mark.

Although the criteria of consistency and importance of objectives may be helpful in making minor adjustments, they sometimes provide no help. For this reason teachers sometimes allow students to raise their final grades by doing special-credit work or by fulfilling contracts. Assignments that call for mastery and effort are viable ways of assessing student performance and extending teacher flexibility in grading. Credit for such assignments should be given after norm comparisons have been made. Hence, a teacher might have one or two extra assignments worth a few points during a grading period. Border-line students who earn enough extra-credit points would be assigned a higher grade.

contracting for specific grades

When individualized contracts are used, it is possible to allow students some choice concerning the degree and types of effort they will expend. This is done by promising specific grades in exchange for specific levels of accomplishment on tasks. For example, an A might require both earning 90 percent on a test and doing a project, a B might call for only earning 90 percent on the test, a C earning 80 percent on the test, and so on. Minimal requirements can be established for those who wish to receive only a passing grade, and progressively more difficult standards can be set for earning higher grades.

With this plan, students know exactly what they will need to do to get a particular grade, and they can lower their effort if they are willing to take a lower grade. In addition to providing students some choice and making a clear connection between effort and assigned grades, contracting allows the teacher to establish requirements that ensure that students master the objectives considered most important or essential to the course.

This system works well when all students are capable of achieving the highest grade, although some will require more time and effort to do so than others. Often such arrangements involve the Keller plan for personalized, self-paced instruction (Keller, 1968). In this plan, students not only can choose the effort they want to expend and the resulting grade, but they are given as much time as they need to complete their work (see Chapter 6).

Arrangements like the Keller plan are usually not feasible in the elementary and middle-school grades, partly because relatively few students have the maturity needed to exercise choices appropriately and follow through with independent work. Also, the range of individual differences is often so large that common or standard requirements for everyone in the class may not be practical. Less formalized variations of the same ideas can be developed, however, by making agreements or contracts with individual students, adjusting the requirements so that they are matched appropriately to student abilities and current levels of achievement. Teachers must explain this process to their classes, because students understandably will want to know why there are different standards for different students.

combining evaluations to form a grade

Teachers who use various types of assessment are likely not only to have more diverse infor-

mation but also more valid information about student performance. However, they must integrate that knowledge to yield a grade that fairly reflects performance across assignments. Teachers may find that some students (perhaps many) take tests better but write less capably and document portfolios less readily than other students. One logical way to solve this problem is to have multiple grades—one for each major evaluation focus in a course.

Unfortunately, in the foreseeable future most teachers can give only one grade (not four or five) per subject each quarter. Thus, teachers need to be able to combine student performance on diverse activities to create a single grade. Perhaps the most important task is to determine and communicate the weight each measure will contribute to the final grade. Teachers may use a variety of performance measures (objective tests, homework, essay exams, term papers), but students need to know how much each measure contributes to the overall grade. Does homework equal 35 percent of the grade, 10 percent, or does it count only as bonus points added after initial grades are assigned? Students need to know the value of each assignment and whether or not the teacher accepts makeup work.

In Table 24.3 the teacher has chosen to use five major assessment areas in one grading period: test A; test B; an area combining five quizzes and ten homework assignments; a theme paper; and a unit portfolio. The teacher has announced to the class that the theme and the portfolio are twice as important as each test and the homework/quiz performance. Thus, the teacher will have to double students' scores in these two areas. As can be seen in Table 24.3, the highest-scoring student is Jerry, who actually did more poorly in the highest-weighted evaluation areas, even after the scores were weighted.

To represent a student's performance fairly, one has to consider not only the magnitude of

table 24.3 three students' classroom performance

	TEST A	TEST B	QUIZ & HOMEWORK	THEME	PORTFOLIO	TOTAL
Jan	70	70	60	90	90	380
Jude	80	80	80	80	80	400
Jerry	100	100	90	75	75	440
Jan	70	70	60	90 (2)	90 (2)	560
Jude	80	80	80	80 (2)	80 (2)	560
Jerry	100	100	90	75 (2)	75 (2)	590
Jan	70	70	60	90 (2)(2)	90 (2)(2)	920
Jude	80	80	80	80 (2)(2)	80 (2)(2)	880
Jerry	100	100	90	75 (2)(2)	75 (2)(2)	890

NOTE: Raw score, weighted score, corrected for variance and weighted.

the score (e.g., is it higher than most scores?) but the variability or the range of scores (distance from highest to lowest score). For example, students' scores may be close together (all twenty-three students scored above 90 on a 100-point test) or far apart (half a class obtained 100s, one-quarter a score of 50, and one-quarter a score of zero). If teachers are not careful, tests that have more **variation** *(students are spread far apart)* will have the most influence on students' final grades—even if such tests are weighted less. However, a teacher who corrects for the spread (or variation) in scores can prevent this problem by taking both **weight** *(importance of the evaluation)* and **variability** *(the spread of scores)* into account. Testing specialists do this by converting raw test scores into standard deviation scores that reflect the raw scores' relative positions within the distribution for all students taking the test. Teachers who do not have access to conversion programs can approximate this by using the range (the distance between the highest and lowest scores on a test) as a proxy for computing the standard deviation (a tedious procedure). Thus, if a test

has 100 possible points but the highest score is 90 and the lowest score is 71, the range is 20 points.

Teachers need to think about what they are trying to do. They cannot apply any formula or correction procedure without considering the effects of the decisions they make by adjusting scores. First, in examining a set of scores, teachers may decide not to use the test at all instead of correcting variance and then computing the contribution of the test to the total score. For example, a test with low variance (all students score between 25 and 0 on a 100-point test) may convince the teacher that the test was too difficult or that students were poorly prepared for it. Accordingly, the teacher may decide that averaging in an invalid test is less appropriate than admitting that the test is inappropriate and discarding it. Similarly, a teacher might decide that a set of student scores that is uniformly high is not a valid measure of performance but rather an indication that the teacher has not developed clear criteria for grading. This often occurs when a teacher

A, B, C, D? Where to draw the line?

develops a new test or attempts to assess a new dimension of performance.

One common mistake is to allow one component (e.g., a quiz, a test) of a grade to influence the final grade too heavily. That is, after engaging in many of the steps described in the previous chapter (e.g., specifying to students intended emphasis areas and the weight of various assignments), teachers often fail to implement these criteria when they combine student work to develop a single mark. Kubiszyn and Borich (1993) argue that irrespective of how appropriate a teacher's instructional objectives, methods, and evaluation instruments are, many errors occur when teachers combine scores to create a single comprehensive grade. They note that failure to equate measures before weighing them is one of the most common errors. Given that educators are calling for more varied types of assessment, teachers in today's classrooms must be able to combine marks from different types of assessment to yield a course grade.

assessing portfolios and performance measures

One important issue is how to assess portfolio work. Figure 24.1 explains the criteria used in Vermont's statewide assessment of fourth- and eighth-grade students' mathematics portfolios. As we noted, some districts now include performance as a final examination. Although performance and portfolios offer some exciting possibilities for encouraging students to do thoughtful, integrative work, they are relatively new approaches and no data exist to confirm their effectiveness (Mitchell, 1992). Furthermore, use of these approaches could result in problems for students. For example, what happens to a student who moves from one district to another that uses notably different methods of assessment? Performance assessments that consider performance over time might be especially difficult to implement in inner-city districts that have turnover rates as high as 60 percent per year.

Figure 24.1 Vermont mathematics portfolio: explanation of criteria

A1. *Understanding of the task.* In order to solve a problem you must understand the task. Understanding can include an appreciation of relevant information, being able to interpret the problem, understanding key questions that push for clarification.

A2. *Quality of Approaches, Procedures, Strategies.* Most problems have multiple ways in which they can be solved including, among others, simple guessing and checking, systematic listing, using some form of manipulative, using Venn diagrams, using grids to record possible combinations, using formulas, or applying algorithms.

A3. *Why the Student Made the Choices Along the Way.* Good problem solvers are constantly checking their assumptions, reflecting on decisions, analyzing the effectiveness of strategies, checking for exceptions, and verifying results in other ways. These skills may be the most critical components of good problem solving.

A4. *What Decisions, Findings, Conclusions, Observations, Generalizations the Student Reached.* Mathematics is no longer simply about finding the answer to an exercise. The issue is not what did you find, but what does it mean.

B1. *Language of Mathematics.* Mathematics is a language and students gain power in their ability to communicate with one another as they grow in their facility with the language. The goal is to help students become more proficient in the use of mathematical vocabulary, notation, symbols, and structure to represent ideas and to describe relationships.

B2. *Mathematical Representations.* Beyond terminology and notation, communication power in mathematics comes from being able to communicate information through graphs, charts, tables, diagrams, models and some types of manipulatives. Visual information often communicates information more powerfully than pages of text.

B3. *Clarity of Presentation.* The presentation of ideas is at the core of this criterion and it is an essential element of portfolio based tasks. The importance of oral and written communication skills demands that they be assessed. Students must be able to organize their thoughts and present them to others in a format that is organized, coherent, and sufficiently detailed to allow another to follow the student's thinking and conclusions.

SOURCE: Ruth Mitchell, *Testing for Learning: How New Approaches to Evaluation Can Improve American Schools.* New York: 1992.

Although new theory and principles may emerge as research on portfolios and performance unfolds, at present teachers should apply guidelines for using traditional methods of grading and testing to these new approaches. However, teachers will have to address some problems as they implement performance evaluations. For example, teachers cannot grade performance exhibitions anonymously. That is, the teacher knows the student's identity and perhaps a good deal about the process of project development. One means of overcoming biases would be for teachers to grade the performance demonstrations of students in other classrooms. Research needs to be conducted in this area.

Research illustrates that teachers teach differently, depending on their knowledge of content. It thus seems probable that teachers' background knowledge (and interests) may greatly influence how they evaluate students' projects. For example, in areas where they are knowledgeable, teachers may provide more realistic and authentic feedback. Thus, teachers may need to collaborate in order to match their expertise to project topics, especially projects involving a student's year-long effort to explore and integrate knowledge in an area.

teacher evaluation standards

The reader interested in more advanced information about how teacher evaluative standards and testing practices influence students' effort could profitably consult Natriello and Dornbusch (1985). These researchers hypothesize that students will respond more favorably to evaluations and to the teachers who administer them when they see those evaluations as: (1) addressed to central rather than peripheral aspects of the task at hand, (2) influential in evaluating their progress or mastery, (3) soundly based, and (4) reliable.

Natriello and Dornbusch (1985) also offer a six-stage model for evaluation designed to improve student effort and performance. Their work provides detailed information about: (1) attention to the processes of task assignment, (2) criteria setting, (3) sampling, (4) appraisal, (5) feedback, and (6) improvement. Especially interesting is their stress on the need to teach students how to interpret and evaluate performance data reliably. Simply put, these authors contend not only that appraisals need to be technically fair (reliable, valid), but that students need to perceive them that way.

---

implications for teachers

grading: a summary

We have argued that success is necessary if students are to maintain positive self-views and involvement in assigned schoolwork. A grading system based on absolute standards, but standards that some students cannot attain, guarantees that these students will give up and expend only minimal effort in pursuing coursework. Norm-referenced comparisons will also ensure that some students reduce their time and effort in the course, for example, those who do poorly on a first exam and have no hope of improving their relative positions in the future.

We have also argued that students do not respond to gratuitous, empty praise and that when students perceive assignments as easy they will attribute good performance not to their own efforts but instead to external causes like luck or easy assignments. Hence, students' task persistence, confidence, and so on will not be maximized by easy standards.

Teachers who use grades are caught in the middle. If they assign them too leniently or too restrictively, they will not motivate students as much as they could. We encourage teachers who must use grades to set standards that allow every student to obtain at least a grade of C, or whatever grade indicates satisfactory completion of general course expectations. This does not mean that every student will achieve at best a C, but it does mean that conditions should be arranged (by offering extra work, for example) so that students who work productively can earn an acceptable mark.

We mentioned that grading is an unpleasant aspect of teaching for most teachers but that it remains necessary, despite suggestions from some persons that it be eliminated (see for example Smith, 1986). It may be helpful to point out that much teacher concern about grading is unnecessary, because low grades are not nearly as traumatic for students as most teachers think they are. First, students are realistic about their own performances, both absolutely and in comparison to classmates, so that students' expectations concerning grades are likely to conform fairly closely to the grades they receive. Second, assigned grades are often higher than those students expect, especially in this recent period of "grade inflation." Grade inflation is not necessarily good—in fact, it seems unlikely to motivate students. Also, some students are irritated when they see classmates who have accomplished much less than they have receive the same grades.

The keys to satisfactory grading are developing clearly valid methods to assess learning (measuring knowledge directly related to the course content, as opposed to general information, test-taking skills, or other student individual differences unrelated to course content) and communicating these evaluation methods and criteria precisely to students. The latter aspect is important, because many students become anxious if they do not know the basis on which grades will be assigned, and virtually all students want some assurance that grading will be reasonable and fair. One of the most common complaints against instructors that appears in studies of student evaluations of teaching is that they fail to specify the bases for grading or that they assign grades in an arbitrary manner or on the basis of insufficient information.

The "insufficient information" problem usually refers to grades that are assigned on the basis of a single final examination or an assignment that covers only a fraction of course content. In the case of grading on the basis of term papers rather than tests, the objection is that the grade may have little or nothing to do with the degree to which the student learned material taught in the course. Unless notified otherwise, students generally expect to be held responsible for material presented in class and in assignments, as measured by one or two large tests or long assignments. These preferences are understandable, and for the most part appropriate. They seem compatible with most teaching goals, including goals involving integration of all material covered in a course. The latter objective can be accomplished by testing periodically during the course for content mastery and then giving a final exam that poses more integrative questions. For more information about marking systems (e.g., grade inflation, effects on motivating students, percentage grading, pass-fail grading), see Mitzel, 1982; Natriello, 1992; and Wiggins, 1993.

grading on style and personal voice

Whether a paper should be graded for style as well as content and form (e.g., grammar and organization) is an issue that the teacher will have to decide as we noted in Chapter 23. However, we return to the issue again here because in the context of performance assessment, the issue of student voice and style is becoming more prominent. Some educators are contending that education should help students to develop an intellectual style and voice that is uniquely their own and one that they can use thoughtfully and naturally. At present, many students are encouraged (implicitly) to model and reproduce ponderous forms of intellectual writing. Although there is an appropriate time and place for a detailed research paper complete with appropriate references, it is also important that students develop the ability to transform and communicate information effectively. Wiggins (1993), in terms of encouraging students to develop style and voice, writes: "Another approach might ask students, after they have written a lengthy research paper . . . to turn the same research into a one-page paper to be delivered, in an engaging and insightful way, to an audience of lay persons, such as Rotarians" (p. 56). He further notes that some writing assessments are beginning to analyze and to score papers for personal voice—not just for grammar and organization. As a case in point, see Figure 24.2 taken from a high school writing assessment exam in Alberta, Canada.

grades as informing learning

There is evidence that high standards, an overly competitive classroom atmosphere, and a high percentage of low grades are associated with class absences and even increased dropout rates (e.g., Moos & Moos, 1978). However, it is equally clear that low grades and failure are sometimes an unavoidable aspect of school life. Clifford (1990, 1991) concluded that failure can have both positive and negative effects on subsequent performance and that efforts to protect students from failure and to guarantee easy success may be counterproductive in the long run. Clifford argues that educators must replace easy success with an appropriate challenge, teachers must recognize that students will make errors, and learning is a gradual process, not an automatic, quick process.

Section 1: Personal Response to Literature—Scoring Guide

Thought and Detail

When marking **Thought and Detail**, the marker should consider how effectively

- the assignment is addressed
- the detail supports and/or clarifies the response

5 *Excellent:* An insightful understanding of the reading selections is effectively demonstrated. The student's opinion, whether directly stated or implied, is perceptive and is appropriately supported by specific details. Support is well defined and appropriate.

4 *Proficient:* A well-considered understanding of the reading selections is appropriately demonstrated. The student's opinion, whether directly stated or implied, is thoughtful and is supported by details. Support is well defined and appropriate.

3 *Satisfactory:* A defensible understanding of the reading selection(s) is clearly demonstrated. The student's opinion, whether directly stated or implied, is conventional but is plausibly supported. Support is general but functional.

2 *Limited:* An understanding of the reading selections may be evident but is vaguely demonstrated or is not always defensible or sustained. The student's opinion may be superficial, and support is scant and/or vague, and/or redundant.

1 *Poor:* An implausible conjecture concerning the reading selections is suggested. The student's opinion, if present, is irrelevant or incomprehensible. Support is inappropriate, inadequate, or absent.

INS *Insufficient:* The marker can discern no evidence of an attempt to fulfill the assignment, or the writing is so deficient in length that it is not possible to assess thought and detail.

It is important to recognize that student responses to the Personal Response Assignment will vary from writing that treats personal views and ideas analytically and rather formally to writing that explores ideas experimentally and informally. Consequently, evaluation of the personal response on the diploma examination will be in the context of Louise Rosenblatt's suggestion:
The evaluation of the answer would be in terms of the amount of evidence that the [student] has actually read something and thought about it, not a question of whether necessarily he has thought about it in the way an adult would, or given an adult's "correct" answer. (Rosenblatt, Louise. "The Reader's Contribution in the Literary Experience." An interview with Lionel Wilson in *The English Quarterly 1* (Spring, 1981): 3–12.)

Figure 24.2 Alberta, Canada, high school leaving exam: writing assessment. SOURCE: Alberta Education (1993). *1993–94 School Year, English 33 Information Bulletin, Diploma Examinations Program.* Edmonton, Alberta. Reprinted with the permission of Alberta Education.

One chief determinant of the effects of low grades is whether students simply receive information that they have not mastered material or whether the teacher also offers feedback that allows students to understand strategies and ways in which they can improve their performance. It is not appropriate just to tell students that they are wrong (and have received a grade of D); students need to know why they are wrong (Bangert-Drowns et al., 1991). Students need realistic feedback about their performance (including appropriate criticism) and teachers should integrate criticisms with suggestions for how students can improve and build on strengths in their work.

As a case in point, Elawar and Corno (1985) reported that the appropriateness of teacher feedback was significantly improved when teachers used a framework when generating student feedback. They found it important for teachers to use four guides: (1) What is the key error? (2) What is the probable reason the student made this error? (3) How can I guide the student to avoid the error in the future? (4) What did the student do well that could be noted? Thus, in addition to summarizing the overall quality of a student's work, teachers should make certain that students understand the basis on which a grade is assigned.

communication with parents

In assigning grades, teachers and administrators need to be sensitive to the needs of parents. After all, the second reason for giving grades is to allow

research at work
common mistakes in grading

Glover and Bruning (1990) noted seven mistakes that teachers should avoid when grading. Attention to these potential problems is important if teachers are to grade fairly and effectively.

1. *Abdicating responsibility*. Don't adjust your courses so that you can use tests developed by other teachers or textbook writers, regardless of how overworked you are.
2. *Employing grades to alter attitudes*. Don't give bonus points for good behavior or subtract points for misbehavior.
3. *Becoming lazy.* No matter how much you might dislike grading, don't base students semester or course grades on a single test.
4. *Going overboard.* Don't make your courses an exercise in endurance in which students are assessed for everything short of the number of times they shift in their seat.
5. *Using "special insight".* Don't come to the conclusion that you have special insights allowing you to "see" how much students have learned without using any measurements.
6. *Increasing difficulty levels.* Don't change the difficulty level of your tests as the course progresses in an attempt to increase the standards of the course.
7. *Demanding perfection.* Students are human, too.

Grading is a complex issue without clear-cut answers. Each grading method has strong and weak points. As you develop your own grading approach you may choose one of those we summarize or work out your own. No matter what the method, however the most important factor is that grades should be a fair, objective reflection of student achievement.

---

parents and guardians to understand the progress of their child. Hence, a report card (or information that accompanies it) should communicate to parents what a grade represents. Unintended and serious consequences often follow the assignment of low grades. For example, recently one fifth-grade student was killed in a gun battle with police—a shooting caused in part by the student's despondency over poor grades. Although some might dismiss such dramatic and unfortunate consequences as rare, the incidence of child abuse following the issuance of report cards is estimated to be high.

The Baltimore Public Schools have recently developed the practice of sending an information sheet home with students when they send out report cards, so that parents know how they can obtain appropriate information and answers to their questions. By providing parents with specific phone numbers, it is more likely that parents will contact a school official or a particular social agency rather than take out frustration on their child.

microcomputers and classroom testing

Software packages are now available to help teachers with many of the technical tasks of measuring student performance. The computer is a powerful clerical aid for managing classroom instruction. Teachers can use it to identify potential instructional objectives (i.e. by noting what other eighth-grade social studies teachers emphasize), to develop test items, to analyze the effectiveness of each test item, and to analyze grade distributions.

Statistical software programs enable teachers to keep comprehensive records of student performance over several consecutive years, thus allowing them to become more adept at analyzing their behavior over time. When the teacher makes a major change in the assignments in a course, for example, what effect does this have on student performance? Computerized records make it possible for teachers to evaluate the effects of new instructional techniques on test performance and to study issues like grade inflation or declines in achievement over time (Kubiszyn & Borich, 1993).

summary

The practice of assigning grades according to a normal distribution has become less popular in recent years because it fails to take into account the fact that student aptitudes often are not normally distributed in a given classroom. Also, teachers often want grades to reflect effort as well as aptitude, since they use them for motivation and reward as well as for documentation of progress. The result is a modified system that is still called "grading on the curve" but does not follow the distribution of the normal curve.

Grading involves many complexities, but some form of evaluation of student performance is essential. It may involve alternatives to grading, such as progress reports or ratings, but the need for accurate and realistic information about progress is essential. When grades are used, teachers can choose the individual standard, which examines a student's progress in relation to capacity; the fixed standard, which uses established criteria; or the norm-referenced system, which compares each student's performance with the performance of the entire class. Each system has advantages and disadvantages, but in most classes there are no explicit standards and norm-referenced comparisons seem most practical.

Grading should implement the philosophy of the school and the teacher as fairly as possible. Since grades may affect motivation and general performance, it is important to examine the implications of all decisions carefully. Grade adjustments can be made on the basis of consistency, performance on major objectives, special-credit work, or contract work. Caution must be used, since grades assigned either too leniently or too restrictively will inhibit motivation and performance.

questions for reflection

1. The assumption that grading cannot be avoided pervades this chapter. Do you agree with this assumption? If not, what would you propose as a realistic alternative?

2. It is possible to be clear and consistent in grading by announcing your intentions to students and then following through on them. But is it possible to be fair? Does the concept of fair grading make any sense at all? If so, define it. If not, why not?

3. No matter where you draw the line between grades, some students with the highest marks in a grade range will ask if they can earn extra credit or if you would extend the range down one

more point so that they can get a higher grade. How would you respond to these students?

4. Some students, independent of their ability (high- and low-achievement students, male and female students, and so on), develop what is called "fear of success." Among other things, this may include an aversion to high grades, or at least grades that are "too high." Is this "their" problem, or is there something that you as a teacher

should try to do about it? If so, what? If you see it as "their" problem, explain your point of view.

5. How should teachers grade highly competent students who consistently do just enough to qualify for a B, even though they could do A-level work with below-average effort? Under what circumstances, if any, might it be appropriate and perhaps helpful to such students to give them less than a B?

cases to consider

evaluating test results Examine the four mathematics test scores (see the accompanying tabulation) that students have earned (each test is worth 100 points). (1) How consistent is student performance across the four tests? What problems are caused by inconsistent student performances? (2) If you were assigning grades using norm comparisons and your common sense, what would be the cut-offs for A, B, C, and D? Defend your choices for borderline students.

	Test 1 (25%)	Test 2 (25%)	Test 3 (25%)	Test 4 (25%)	Total Points
Alan	80	85	90	96	351
Candy	85	70	65	60	280
Antonio	98	92	100	90	380
Debbie	100	75	90	74	339
Ed	70	90	65	70	295
Frank	90	95	74	90	349
Gene	82	83	82	80	327
Violeta	90	91	93	94	368
Karen	70	75	70	69	284
Linda	65	60	60	60	245
Owen	70	75	70	69	284
Peter	69	78	65	70	282
Ralph	60	60	70	60	250
Reggie	65	85	60	60	270
Renee	70	70	70	70	280
Rita	90	90	90	90	360
Juanita	93	100	85	80	358
Stan	76	72	73	71	292
Stephen	100	85	90	89	364
Warren	50	60	72	80	262

bibliography

Abel, R., & Kulhavy, R. (1986). Maps, mode of text presentation, and children's prose. *American Educational Research Journal, 23,* 263–74.

Abelson, H., & diSessa, A. (1981). *Turtle geometry: The computer as a medium for exploring mathematics.* Cambridge, MA: MIT Press.

Abikoff, H., Ganeles, D., Reiter, G., Blum, C., Foley, C., & Klein, R. (1988). Cognitive training in academically deficient ADHD boys receiving stimulant medication. *Journal of Abnormal Child Psychology, 16,* 411–32.

Abramson, L., Seligman, M., & Teasdale, J. (1978). Learned helplessness in humans: Critique and reformulation. *Journal of Abnormal Psychology, 87,* 49–74.

Abramson, T., & Kagen, E. (1975). Familiarization of content and different response modes in programmed instruction. *Journal of Educational Psychology, 67,* 83–88.

Adams, G., Abraham, K., & Markstrom, C. (1987). The relations among identity development, self-consciousness, and self-focusing during middle and late adolescence. *Developmental Psychology, 23,* 292–97.

Adams, G., & Gullotta, T. (1989). *Adolescent life experiences* (2nd ed.). Pacific Grove, CA: Brooks/Cole.

Adams, G., Gullotta, T., & Montemayor, R. (Eds.). (1992). *Adolescent identity formation.* Newbury Park, CA: Sage.

Adams, J. (1977). Motor learning and retention. In M. Marx & M. Bunch (Eds.), *Fundamentals and applications of learning.* New York: Macmillan.

Adams, M. (1989). Thinking skills curricula: Their promise and progress. *Educational Psychologist, 24,* 25–77.

Adams, M. (1990). *Beginning to read: Thinking and learning about print.* Cambridge: MIT Press.

Adams, R., & Biddle, B. (1970). *Realities of teaching: Explorations with videotape.* New York: Holt, Rinehart & Winston.

Agger, B. (1992). *Cultural studies as critical theory.* London: Falmer Press.

Ahern, F., Johnson, R., Wilson, J., McClearn, G., & Vandenberg, S. (1982). Family resemblances in personality. *Behavior Genetics, 12,* 261–80.

Ainscow, M. (Ed.) (1991). *Effective schools for all.* London: David Fulton.

Airasian, P. (1991). *Classroom assessment.* NY: McGraw-Hill.

Alexander, C., Druker, S., & Langer, E. (1990). Introduction: Major issues in the exploration of adult growth. In C. Alexander & E. Langer (Eds.), *Higher stages of human development: Perspectives on adult growth* (pp. 3–32). New York: Oxford University Press.

Alexander, C., & Langer, E. (Eds.). (1990). *Higher stages of human development: Perspectives on adult growth.* New York: Oxford University Press.

Alexander, L., Frankiewicz, R., & Williams, R. (1979). Facilitation of learning and retention of oral instruction using advance and post organizers. *Journal of Educational Psychology, 71,* 701–7.

Alharjri, A. (1981). *Effect of seat position on school performances of Kuwaiti students.* Dissertation, University of Missouri-Columbia.

Allington, R. (1991). Children find learning to read difficult: School responses to diversity. In E. Hiebert (Ed.), *Literacy for a diverse society* (pp. 237–52). New York: Teachers College Press.

Alper, S., & Ryndak, D. (1992). Educating students with severe handicaps in regular classes. *Elementary School Journal, 92,* 373–88.

Alton-Lee, A., Nuthall, G., & Patrick, J. (1993). Reframing classroom research: A lesson from the private world of children. *Harvard Educational Review, 63,* 50–84.

Alvermann, D., & Hynd, C. (1989). Effects of prior knowledge activation modes and text structure on nonscience majors' comprehension of physics. *Journal of Educational Research, 83,* 97–102.

Alvermann, D., O'Brien, D., & Dillon, D. (1990). What teachers do when they say they're having discussions of content area reading assignments: A qualitative analysis. *Reading Research Quarterly, 25,* 296–322.

Alvermann, D., Smith, L., & Readence, J. (1985). Prior knowledge activation and the comprehension of compatible and incompatible text. *Reading Research Quarterly, 20,* 420–35.

Amabile, T. (1987). The motivation to be creative. In S. Isaksen (Ed.), *Frontiers of creativity research* (pp. 223–54). Buffalo, NY: Bearly Limited.

Amara, J., & Leona, M. (1983). Prep-tech: A vocational school for academically talented students. *Phi Delta Kappan, 64,* 372–73.

American Association for the Advancement of Science. (1989). *Science for all Americans: A Project 2061 report on literacy goals in science, mathematics, and technology.* Washington, DC: Author.

American Association of University Women [AAUW]. (1992). *AAUW Report: How schools shortchange girls.* Annapolis Junction, MD: AAUW Educational Foundation.

American Federation of Teachers, National Council on Measurement in Education, and National Education Association. (AFT/NCME/NEA, 1990). Standards for teacher competence in educational assessment of students. *Educational Measurement: Issues and Practice, 9,* 30–32.

American Institute for Research. (1976). *Impact of educational innovation on student performance: Project, methods, and findings for three cohorts.* Project LONGSTEP Final Report, Vol. 1. Palo Alto: Author.

Ames, C. (1978). Children's achievement attributions and self-reinforcement: Effects of self-concept and competitive reward structure. *Journal of Educational Psychology, 70,* 345–55.

Ames, C. (1990). Motivation: What teachers need to know. *Teachers College Record, 91,* 409–21.

Ames, C. (1992). Classrooms: Goals, structures, and student motivation. *Journal of Educational Psychology, 84*(3), 261–71.

Ames, C., & Ames, R. (1981). Competitive versus individualistic goal structures: The salience of past performance information for causal attributions and affect. *Journal of Educational Psychology, 73,* 411–18.

Ames, C., & Ames, R. (1984). Systems of student and teacher motivation: Toward a qualitative definition. *Journal of Educational Psychology, 76,* 535–56.

Ames, C., Ames, R., & Felker, D. (1977). Effects of competitive reward structure and valence of outcome on children's achievement attributions. *Journal of Educational Psychology, 69,* 1–8.

Ames, C., & Stover, J. (1993). *Comprehensive classroom-based intervention involving teachers in changing classroom goals.* Paper presented at the annual meeting of the American Educational Research Association, April, Atlanta, GA.

Ames, R. (1983). Teachers' attributions for their own thinking. In J. Levine & M. Wang (Eds.), *Teacher and student perceptions: Implications for learning.* Hillsdale, NJ: Erlbaum.

Anderson, C., & Roth, K. (1989). Teaching for meaningful and self-regulated learning of science. In J. Brophy (Ed.), *Advances in research on teaching,* Vol. 1, *Teaching for meaningful understanding and self-regulated learning.* Greenwich, CT: JAI.

Anderson, C., & Smith, E. (1987). Teaching science. In V. Richardson-Koehler (Ed.), *Educators' handbook* (pp. 84–111). New York: Longman.

Anderson, J. (1990). *Cognitive psychology and its implications.* New York: Freeman.

Anderson, J. (1993). Problem solving and learning. *American Psychologist, 48,* 35–44.

Anderson, J., & Bower, G. (1973). *Human associative memory.* New York: Wiley.

Anderson, I.. (1984). The environment of instruction: The function of seatwork in a commercially developed curriculum. In G. Duffy, L. Roehler, and J. Mason (Eds.), *Comprehension instruction: Perspectives and suggestions.* New York: Longman.

Anderson, L. (1989). Implementing instructional programs to promote meaningful, self-regulated learning. In J. Brophy (Ed.), *Advances in research on teaching.* Vol. 1, *Teaching for meaningful understanding and self-regulated learning.* Greenwich, CT: JAI.

Anderson, L., Evertson, C., & Brophy, J. (1979). An experimental study of effective teaching in first-grade reading groups. *Elementary School Journal, 79,* 193–223.

Anderson, L., Evertson, C., & Brophy, J. (1982). *Principles of small-group instruction in elementary reading.* Occasional Paper No. 58. East Lansing, MI: Institute for Research on Teaching, Michigan State University.

Anderson, L. W. (1985). A retrospective and prospective view of Bloom's "Learning for Mastery." In M. Wang & H. Walberg (Eds.), *Adapting instruction to individual differences.* Berkeley, CA: McCutchan.

Anderson, R. (1984). Role of the reader's schema in comprehension, learning, and memory. In R. Anderson, J. Osborn, & R. Tierney (Eds.), *Learning to read in American schools: Basal readers and content texts.* Hillsdale, NJ: Erlbaum.

Anderson, R., & Armbruster, B. (1990). Some maxims for learning and instruction. *Teachers College Record, 91,* 396–408.

Anderson, R., Hiebert, E., Scott, J., & Wilkinson, I. (1985). *Becoming a nation of readers: A report of the Commission on Reading.* Washington, DC: National Institute of Education.

Anderson, R., Pichert, J., & Shirey, L. (1983). Effects of the reader's schema at different points in time. *Journal of Educational Psychology, 75,* 271–79.

Anderson, T., & Armbruster, B. (1984). Content area textbooks. In R. Anderson, J. Osborn, & R. Tierney (Eds.), *Learning to read in American schools: Basal readers and content texts.* Hillsdale, NJ: Erlbaum.

Andre, M., & Anderson, T. (1978–79). The development and evaluation of a self-questioning study technique. *Reading Research Quarterly, 14,* 605–23.

Andre, T. (1987). Questions and learning from reading. *Questioning Exchange, 1,* 47–86.

Andrews, G., & Goodson, L. (1980). A comparative analysis of models of instructional design. *Journal of Instructional Development, 3*(4), 2–16.

Anshutz, R. (1975). An investigation of wait-time and questioning techniques as an instructional variable for science methods students microteaching elementary school children. (Doctoral dissertation, University of Kansas, 1973). *Dissertation Abstracts International, 35,* 5978A.

Applebee, A. (1986). Problems in process approaches: Toward a reconceptualization of process instruction. In A. Petrosky & D. Bartholomae (Eds.), *85th yearbook of the National Society for the Study of Education: The teaching of writing.* Chicago: University of Chicago Press.

Appleton, K. (1993). Using theory to guide practice: Teaching science from a constructive perspective. *School Science and Mathematics, 93,* 269–74.

Appleton, N. (1983). *Cultural pluralism in education: Theoretical foundation.* White Plains, NY: Longman.

Archer, S. (1982). The lower age boundaries of identity development. *Child Development, 53,* 1551–56.

Arias, M., & Casanova, U. (1993). *92nd yearbook of the National Society for the Study of Education.* Part 2, *Bilingual education: Politics, practice, and research.* Chicago: University of Chicago Press.

Arlin, M. (1984). Time, equality, and mastery learning. *Review of Educational Research, 54,* 65–86.

Arlin, P. (1986). Problem finding and young adult cognition. In R. Mines & K. Kitchener (Eds.), *Adult cognitive development: Methods and models* (pp. 22–32). New York: Praeger.

Armbruster, B., & Anderson, T. (1984). Structures of explanations in history textbooks, or so what if Governor Stanford missed the spike and hit the rail? *Journal of Curriculum Studies, 16,* 181–94.

Armbruster, B., Anderson, T., & Ostertag, J. (1987). Does text structure/summarization facilitate learning from text? *Reading Research Quarterly, 22,* 331–46.

Armbruster, B., & Brown, A. (1984). Learning from reading: The role of metacognition. In R. Anderson, J. Osborn, & R. Tierney (Eds.), *Learning to read in American schools: Basal readers and content texts.* Hillsdale, NJ: Erlbaum.

Arons, A. (1984). Computer-based instructional dialogs in science courses. *Science, 224,* 1051–56.

Asher, S., & Coie, J. (Eds.). (1990). *Peer rejection in childhood.* Cambridge: Cambridge University Press.

Asher, S., & Markell, R. (1974). Sex differences in comprehension of high-and low-interest reading material. *Journal of Educational Psychology, 66,* 680–87.

Ashton, P., & Webb, R. (1986). *Making a difference: Teachers' sense of efficacy and student achievement.* New York: Longman.

Atkinson, J (1964). *An introduction to motivation.* Princeton, NJ: Van Nostrand.

Atkinson, J. W., & Litwin, G. H. (1960). Achievement motive and test anxiety as motives to approach success and avoid failure. *Journal of Abnormal and Social Psychology, 60,* 52–63.

Atkinson, R. (1975). Mnemotechnics in second-language learning. *American Psychologist, 30,* 821–28.

Atkinson, R., & Shiffrin, R. (1971). The control of short-term memory. *Scientific American, 225,* 82–90.

Au, K. (1980). Participant structures in a reading lesson with Hawaiian children. *Anthropology and Education Quarterly, 11,* 91–115.

Au, R., Tharp, R., Crowell, D., Jordan, C., Speidel, G., & Calkins, R. (1985). The role of research in the development of a successful reading program. In J. Osborn, P. Wilson, & R. Anderson (Eds.), *Reading education: Foundations for a literate America.* Lexington, MA: Lexington Books.

Ausubel, D. (1960). The use of advance organizers in the learning and retention of meaningful verbal material. *Journal of Educational Psychology, 51,* 267–72.

Ausubel, D. (1963). *The psychology of meaningful verbal learning: An introduction to school learning.* New York: Grune & Stratton.

Ausubel, D. (1978). In defense of advance organizers: A reply to the critics. *Review of Educational Research, 48,* 251–57.

Ausubel, D., Novak, J., & Hanesian, H. (1978). *Educational psychology: A cognitive view.* New York: Holt, Rinehart & Winston.

Ausubel, D., & Robinson, F. (1969). *School learning: An introduction to educational psychology.* New York: Holt, Rinehart & Winston.

Ausubel, D., & Sullivan, E. (1970). *Theory and problems of child development* (2nd ed.). New York: Grune & Stratton.

Baddeley, A. (1986). *Working memory.* New York: Oxford University Press.

Baddeley, A. (1990). *Human memory: Theory and practice.* Boston: Allyn & Bacon.

Baer, J. (1993). *Creativity and divergent thinking: A task-specific approach.* Hillsdale, NJ: Erlbaum.

Baker, K. (1992). Ramiréz et al.: Led by bad theory. *Bilingual Research Journal, 16,* 63–90.

Baker, K., & Dekanter, A. (1983). *Bilingual education: A reappraisal of federal policy.* Lexington, MA: D.C. Heath

Baldwin, A. (1989). The purpose of education for gifted black students. In C. Maker & S. Schieber (Eds.), *Defensible programs for cultural and ethnic minorities* (Vol. 2, pp. 237–45.) Austin, TX: Pro-Ed.

Balke-Aurell, G. (1982). Changes in ability as related to educational and occupational experience (Göteborg Studies in Educational Sciences, No. 40). Göteborg, Sweden.

Baltes, P. (1986). Notes on the concept of intelligence. In R. Sternberg & D. Detterman (Eds.), *What is intelligence? Contemporary viewpoints on its nature and definition* (pp. 133–40). Norwood, NJ: Ablex Publishing Corporation.

Bandura, A. (1977). *Social learning theory.* Englewood Cliffs, NJ: Prentice-Hall.

Bandura, A. (1986). *Social foundations of thought and action: A social cognitive theory.* Englewood Cliffs, NJ: Prentice-Hall.

Bandura, A. (1989). Human agency in social

cognitive theory. *American Psychologist, 44,* 1175–84.

Bandura, A., & Schunk, D. (1981). Cultivating competence, self-efficacy, and intrinsic interest through proximal self-motivation. *Journal of Personality and Social Psychology, 41,* 586–98.

Bangert, R., Kulik, J., & Kulik, C. (1983). Individualized systems of instruction in secondary schools. *Review of Educational Research, 53,* 143–58.

Bangert-Drowns, R. (1993). The word processor as an instructional tool: A meta-analysis of word processing in writing instruction. *Review of Educational Research, 63,* 69–93.

Bangert-Drowns, R., Kulik, C., Kulik, J., & Morgan, M. (1991). The instructional effect of feedback in test-like events. *Review of Educational Research, 61,* 213–38.

Bank, B., Biddle, B., & Good, T. (1980). Sex roles, classroom instruction, and reading achievement. *Journal of Educational Psychology, 72,* 119–32.

Banks, J. (1985). *Teaching strategies for the social studies: Inquiry, valuing and decision-making* (3rd ed.). New York: Longman.

Barkan, J., & Bernal, E. (1991). Gifted education for bilingual and limited English proficient students. *Journal of Gifted Child Quarterly, 35,* 144–47.

Barr, R. (1988). Conditions influencing content taught in nine fourth-grade mathematics classrooms. *Elementary School Journal, 88*(4), 413–26.

Barr, R., Kamil, M., Mosenthal, P., & Pearson, P.D. (Eds.). (1991). *Handbook of reading research* (Vol. 2). New York: Longman.

Barrett, G., & Depinet, R. (1991). A reconsideration of testing for competence rather than for intelligence. *American Psychologist, 46,* 1012–24.

Bartlett, F. (1932). *Remembering.* Cambridge: Cambridge University Press.

Baska, L. (1989). Standardized testing for minority students: Is it fair? In C. Maker & S. Schieber (Eds.), *Defensible programs for cultural and ethnic minorities* (Vol. 2, pp. 226–36). Austin, TX: Pro-Ed.

Basseches, M. (1984). *Dialectical thinking and adult development.* Norwood, NJ: Ablex.

Bateman, B. (1992) Learning disabilities: The changing landscape. *Journal of Learning Disabilities, 25,* 29–36.

Battistich, V., Watson, M., Solomon, D., Schaps, E., & Solomon, J. (1991). The Child Development Project: A comprehensive program for the development of prosocial character. In W. Kurtines & J. Gewirtz (Eds.), *Handbook of moral behavior and development.* Vol. 3, *Application.* Hillsdale, NJ: Erlbaum.

Baumann, J., Seifert-Kessell, N., & Jones, L. (1992). Effect of think-aloud instruction on elementary students' comprehension monitoring abilities. *Journal of Reading Behavior, 24,* 143–72.

Baumrind, D. (1971). Current patterns of parental authority. *Developmental Psychology Monograph, 4* (No. 1, Part 2).

Baumrind, D. (1987). A developmental perspective on adolescent risk taking in contemporary America. In C. Irwin, Jr. (Ed.), *Adolescent social behavior and health* (pp. 93–125). San Francisco: Jossey-Bass.

Baumrind, D. (1991). The influence of parenting style on adolescent competence and substance abuse. *Journal of Early Adolescence, 11,* 56–94.

Bear, G., & Richards, H. (1981). Moral reasoning and conduct problems in the classroom. *Journal of Educational Psychology, 73,* 644–70.

Beasley, W. (1984). *Microcomputer applications in the education of the gifted.* Unpublished doctoral dissertation, University of Georgia, Athens.

Becker, H. (1982). Microcomputers: Dreams and realities. *Curriculum Review, 21,* 381–85.

Becker, H. (1988). *The impact of computer use on children's learning: What research has shown and what it has not.* Baltimore: Johns Hopkins University, Center for Research on Elementary and Middle Schools.

Becker, J. (1981). Differential teacher treatment of males and females in mathematics classes. *Journal for Research in Mathematics Education, 12,* 40–53.

Bédard, J., & Chi, M. (1992). Expertise. *Current Directions in Psychological Science, 1,* 135–39.

Beilin, H., & Pufall, P. (Eds.) (1992). *Piaget's theory: Prospects and possibilities.* Hillsdale, NJ: Erlbaum.

Belenky, M., Clinchy, B., Goldberger, N., & Tarule, J. (1986). *Women's ways of knowing.* New York: Basic Books.

Bell, R. (1971). Stimulus control of parent or caretaker behavior by offspring. *Developmental Psychology, 4,* 61–72.

Bellezza, F. (1981). Mnemonic devices: Classification, characteristics, and criteria. *Review of Educational Research, 51,* 247–75.

Benjamin, M., McKeachie, W., Lin, Y., & Holinger, D. (1981). Test anxiety: Deficits in information processing. *Journal of Educational Psychology, 73,* 816–24.

Bennett, N., & Desforges, C. (1988). Matching classroom tasks to students' attainments. *Elementary School Journal, 88,* 221–34.

Bennett, N., & Dunne, E. (1992). *Managing small groups.* Great Britain: Simon and Schuster.

Benninga, J. (Ed.). (1991). *Moral, character, and civic education in the elementary school.* New York: Teachers College Press.

Benton, S., Kiewra, K., Whitfill, J., & Dennison, R. (1993). Encoding and external-storage effects on writing processes. *Journal of Educational Psychology, 85,* 267–80.

Bereiter, C. (1991). Implications of connectionism for thinking about rules. *Educational Researcher, 20,* 10–16.

Bereiter, C., & Scardamalia, M. (1986). Educational relevance of the study of expertise. *Interchange, 17*(2), 10–19.

Bereiter, C., & Scardamalia, M. (1987). An attainable version of high literacy: Approaches to teaching higher-order skills in reading and writing. *Curriculum Inquiry, 17*(1), 9–30.

Berk, L. (1986). Relationship of elementary school children's private speech to behavioral accompaniment to task, attention, and task performance. *Developmental Psychology, 22,* 671–80.

Berkowitz, M., & Oser, F. (Eds.). (1985). *Moral education: Theory and application.* Hillsdale, NJ: Erlbaum.

Berliner, D. (1983). The executive who manages classrooms. In B. Fraser (Ed.), *Classroom management.* Bentley, Australia: Western Australian Institute of Technology.

Berliner, D. (1984). Testimony before the governor's task force on teacher education, February 16, University of Arizona.

Berndt, T. (1982). The features and effects of friendship in early adolescence. *Child Development, 53,* 1447–60.

Berndt, T., & Ladd, G. (Eds.). (1989). *Peer relationships in child development.* New York: Wiley.

Berndt, T., & Miller, K. (1990). Expectancies, values, and achievement in junior high school. *Journal of Educational Psychology, 82,* 319–26.

Bettencourt, E., Gillett, M., Gall, M., & Hull, R. (1983). Effects of teacher enthusiasm training on student on-task behavior and achievement. *American Educational Research Journal, 20,* 435–50.

Beyer, B. (1987). *Practical strategies for the teaching of thinking.* Boston: Allyn & Bacon.

Bideaud, J., Meljac, C., & Fischer, J. P. (Eds.). (1992). *Pathways to number: Children's developing numerical abilities.* Hillsdale, NJ: Erlbaum.

Bierman, K., & Furman, W. (1984). The effects of social skills training and peer involvement on the social adjustment of preadolescents. *Child Development, 55,* 151–62.

Biggs, J. (1978). Individual and group differences in study processes. *British Journal of Educational Psychology, 48,* 266–79.

Biklen, S., & Pollard, D. (Eds.). (1993). *Gender and education: 92nd yearbook of the National Society for the Study of Education.* Chicago: University of Chicago Press.

Billups, L., & Rauth, M. (1987). Teachers and research. In V. Richardson-Koehler (Ed.), *Educators' handbook: A research perspective* (pp. 624–39). White Plains, NY: Longman.

Blagg, N. (1991). *Can we teach intelligence? A comprehensive evaluation of Feuerstein's Instrumental Enrichment program.* Hillsdale, NJ: Erlbaum.

Blank, M. (1973). *Teaching learning in the preschool: A dialogue approach.* Columbus, OH: Merrill.

Blasi, A. (1980). Bridging moral cognition and moral action: A critical review of the literature. *Psychological Bulletin, 88,* 1–45.

Blau, Z. (1981). *Black children/white children: Competence, socialization, and social structure.* New York: Free Press.

Bleakley, M., Westerberg, V., & Hopkins, K. (1988). The effect of character's sex on story interest and comprehension in children. *American Educational Research Journal, 25,* 141–55.

Block, J. (1982). Assimilation, accommodation, and the dynamics of personality development. *Child Development, 53,* 281–95.

Block, J., & Anderson, L. (1975). *Mastery learning in classroom instruction.* New York: Macmillan.

Block, J., Efthim, H., & Burns, R. (1988). *Building*

effective mastery learning schools. New York: Longman.

Block, J., Gjerde, P., & Block, J. (1986). More misgivings about the Matching Familiar Figures Test as a measure of reflection-impulsivity: Absence of construct validity in preadolescence. *Developmental Psychology, 22,* 820–31.

Bloom, B. (1968). Learning for mastery. (UCLA-CSEIP) *Evaluation Comment, 1*(2), 1–12.

Bloom, B. (1976). *Human characteristics and school learning.* New York: McGraw-Hill.

Bloom, B. (1980). *All our children learning.* Hightstown, NJ: McGraw-Hill.

Bloom, B., & Broder, L. (1950). *Problem-solving processes of college students.* Chicago: University of Chicago Press.

Bloom, B., Englehart, M., Furst, E., Hill, W., & Krathwohl, D. (1956). *Taxonomy of educational objectives: The classification of educational goals.* Handbook 1, *Cognitive domain.* New York: Longmans Green.

Blumenfeld, P. (1992a). Classroom learning and motivation: Clarifying and expanding goal theory. *Journal of Educational Psychology, 84,* 272–81.

Blumenfeld, P. (1992b). The task and the teacher: Enhancing student thoughtfulness in science. In J. Brophy (Ed.), *Advances in research on teaching.* Vol. 3, *Planning and managing learning tasks and activities* (pp. 81–114). Greenwich, CT: JAI.

Blumenfeld, P. (1993, April). *Teaching for understanding.* An invited address for Division K. Presented at the annual meeting of the American Educational Research Association, Atlanta, GA.

Blumenfeld, P., Hamilton, V., Bossert, S., Wessels, K., & Meece, J. (1983). Teacher talk and student thought: Socialization into the student role. In J. Levine & M. Wang (Eds.), *Teacher and student perceptions: Implications for learning.* Hillsdale, NJ: Erlbaum.

Blumenfeld, P., & Meece, J. (1988). Task factors, teacher behavior, and students' involvement and use of learning strategies in science. *Elementary School Journal, 88,* 234–50.

Blumenfeld, P., Mergendoller, J., & Swarthout, D. (1987). Task as a heuristic for understanding student learning and motivation. *Journal of Curriculum Studies, 19,* 135–48.

Blumenfeld, P., Soloway, E., Marx, R., Krajcik, J.,

Guzdial, M., & Palincsar, A. (1991). Motivating project-based learning: Sustaining the doing, supporting the learning. *Educational Psychologist, 26,* 369–98.

Boggiano, A., Barrett, M., Weiher, A., McClelland, G., & Lusk, C. (1987). Use of the maximal-operant principle to motivate children's intrinsic interest. *Journal of Personality and Social Psychology, 3,* 866–79.

Boggiano, A., & Ruble, D. (1979). Competence and the overjustification effect: A developmental study. *Journal of Personality and Social Psychology, 37,* 1426–68.

Bohannon III, J., MacWhinney, B., & Snow, C. (1990). No negative evidence revisited: Beyond learnability or who has to prove what to whom. *Developmental Psychology, 26,* 221–26.

Bonner, J. (1988). Implications of cognitive theory for instructional design: Revisited. *Educational Communication and Technology Journal, 36,* 3–14.

Boocock, S., & Schild, E. (1968). *Simulation games in learning.* Beverly Hills, CA: Sage.

Borko, H., & Livingston, C. (1989). Cognition and improvisation: Differences in mathematics instruction by expert and novice teachers. *American Educational Research Journal, 26,* 473–98.

Borkowski, J., Johnston, M., & Reid, M. (1986). Metacognition, motivation, and the transfer of control processes. In S. Ceci (Ed.), *Handbook of cognitive, social, and neuropsychological aspects of learning disabilities.* Hillsdale, NJ: Erlbaum.

Boshier, R., & Thom, E. (1973). Do conservative parents nurture conservative children? *Social Behavior and Personality, 1,* 108–10.

Bosma, H., & Gerrits, R. (1985). Family functioning and identity status in adolescence. *Journal of Early Adolescence, 5,* 69–80.

Botvin, G., & Murray, F. (1975). The efficacy of peer modeling and social conflict in the acquisition of conservation. *Child Development, 46,* 796–99.

Bourne, L., Ekstrand, B., & Dominowski, R. (1971). *The psychology of thinking.* Englewood Cliffs, NJ: Prentice-Hall.

Bower, G., & Clark, M. (1969). Narrative stories as mediators for serial learning. *Psychonomic Science, 14,* 181–82.

Bower, G., Clark, M., Lesgold, A., & Winzenz, D.

(1969). Hierarchical retrieval schemes in recall of categorized word lists. *Journal of Verbal Learning and Verbal Behavior, 8,* 323–43.

Brabeck, M. (Ed.). (1987). Feminist perspectives on moral education and development. Special issue, *Journal of Moral Education, 16*(3), 163–66.

Bradbard, M., & Endsley, R. (1983). The effects of sex-typed labeling on preschool children's information-seeking and retention. *Sex Roles, 9,* 247–60.

Braden, R., & Sachs, S. (1983). The most re-commended books on instructional development. *Educational Technology, 23*(2), 24–28.

Brainerd, C. (1977). Feedback, rule knowledge and conservation learning. *Child Development, 48,* 404–11.

Brandenburg, N., Friedman, R., & Silver, S. (1990). The epidemiology of childhood psychiatric disorders: Prevalence findings from recent studies. *American Academy of Child and Adolescent Psychiatry, 29,* 76–83.

Brandon, P., Newton, B., & Hammond, O. (1987). Children's mathematics achievement in Hawaii: Sex differences favoring girls. *American Educational Research Journal, 24,* 437–61.

Bransford, J. (1979). *Human cognition.* Belmont, CA: Wadsworth.

Bransford, J., & Franks, J. (1971). The abstraction of linguistic ideas. *Cognitive Psychology, 2,* 331–50.

Bransford, J., & McCarrell, N. (1974). A sketch of a cognitive approach to comprehension: Some thoughts about understanding what it means to comprehend. In W. Weimer & D. Palermo (Eds.), *Cognition and the symbolic processes.* Hillsdale, NJ: Erlbaum.

Bransford, J., & Stein, B. (1985). *The IDEAL problem solver.* San Francisco: Freeman.

Bransford, J., & Vye, N. (1989). A perspective on cognitive research and its implications for instruction. In L. Resnick & L. Klopfer (Eds.), *Toward the thinking curriculum: Current cognitive research,* 1989 yearbook (pp. 173–205). Alexandria, VA: Association for Supervision and Curriculum Development.

Brantlinger, E. (1991). Home-school partnerships that benefit children with special needs. *Elementary School Journal, 91*(3), 249–60.

Brantlinger, E., & Guskin, S. (1987). Ethnocultural social-psychological effects on learning characteristics of handicapped children. In M. Wang, M. Reynolds, & W. Walberg (Eds.), *Handbook of special education: Research in practice* (Vol. 1, pp. 7–34). Oxford: Pergamon Press.

Breaux, R. (1975). Effects of induction versus deduction and discovery versus utilization on transfer of information. *Journal of Educational Psychology, 67,* 828–32.

Bredekamp, S. (Ed.). (1987). *Developmentally appropriate practice in early childhood programs serving children from birth through age 8.* Washington, DC: National Association for the Education of Young Children.

Briggs, L. (1970). *Handbook of procedures for the design of instruction.* Pittsburgh: American Institute for Research.

Bromage, B., & Mayer, R. (1981). Relationship between what is remembered and creative problem-solving performance in science learning. *Journal of Educational Psychology, 73,* 451–61.

Bromage, B., & Mayer, R. (1986). Quantitative and qualitative effects of repetition on learning from technical texts. *Journal of Educational Psychology, 78,* 271–78.

Bronfenbrenner, U. (1986). Ecology of the family as a context for human development: Research perspectives. *Developmental Psychology, 22,* 723–42.

Brookhart, S., & Freeman, D. (1992). Characteristics of entering teacher candidates. *Review of Educational Research, 62,* 37–60.

Brooks, J. (1990). Teachers and students: Constructivists forging new connections. *Educational Leadership, 47*(5), 68–71.

Brooks-Gunn, J., & Petersen, A. (Eds.). (1983). *Girls at puberty.* New York: Plenum.

Brooks-Gunn, J., Petersen, A., & Eichorn, D. (1985). The study of maturational timing effects in adolescence. *Journal of Youth and Adolescence, 14,* 149–61.

Brophy, J. (1977). *Child development and socialization.* Chicago: Science Research Associates.

Brophy, J. (1981). Teacher praise: A functional analysis. *Review of Educational Research, 51,* 5–32.

Brophy, J. (1985). Interactions of male and female students with male and female teachers. In L.

Wilkinson & C. Marrett (Eds.), *Gender influences in classroom interaction* (pp. 115–42). Orlando, FL: Academic Press.

Brophy, J. (1987). Synthesis of research on strategies for motivating students to learn. *Educational Leadership, 45*(2), 40–48.

Brophy, J. (Ed.). (1989). *Advances in research on teaching.* Vol. 1, *Teaching for meaningful understanding and self-regulated learning.* Greenwich, CT: JAI.

Brophy, J. (Ed.). (1991a). *Advances in research on teaching.* Vol. 2, Greenwich, CT: JAI.

Brophy, J. (1991b). I know I can do this, but where's my motivation? *American Journal of Community Psychology, 19,* 371–77.

Brophy, J. (Ed.). (1992a). *Advances in research on teaching.* Vol. 3, *Planning and managing learning tasks and activities.* Greenwich, CT: JAI.

Brophy, J. (1992b). Probing the subtleties of subject-matter teaching. *Educational Leadership, 49*(7), 4–8.

Brophy, J., & Alleman, J. (1991). Activities as instructional tools: A framework for analysis and evaluation. *Educational Researcher, 20*(4), 9–23.

Brophy, J., & Alleman, J. (1993). Elementary social studies should be driven by major social education goals. *Social Education, 57,* 27–32.

Brophy, J., & Evertson, C. (1976). *Learning from teaching: A developmental perspective.* Boston: Allyn & Bacon.

Brophy, J., & Evertson, C. (1981). *Student characteristics and teaching.* New York: Longman.

Brophy, J., & Good, T. (1970). Teachers' communication of differential expectations for children's classroom performance: Some behavioral data. *Journal of Educational Psychology, 61,* 365–74.

Brophy, J., & Good, T. (1974). *Teacher-student relationships: Causes and consequences.* New York: Holt, Rinehart & Winston.

Brophy, J., & Good, T. (1986). Teacher effects. In M. Wittrock (Ed.), *Third handbook of research on teaching* (pp. 328–75). New York: Macmillan.

Brophy, J., & Hannon, P. (1985). The future of microcomputers in the classroom. *Journal of Mathematical Behavior, 4,* 47–67.

Brophy, J., & McCaslin, M. (1992). Teachers' reports of how they perceive and cope with problem students. *Elementary School Journal, 93,* 3–68.

Brophy, J., & Putnam, J. (1979). Classroom management in the elementary grades. In D. Duke (Ed.), *78th yearbook of the National Society for the Study of Education.* Part 2, *Classroom management.* Chicago: University of Chicago Press.

Brophy, J., & Rohrkemper, M. (1981). The influence of problem ownership on teachers' perceptions of and strategies for coping with problem students. *Journal of Educational Psychology, 73,* 295–311.

Brophy, J., & Rohrkemper, M. (1988). *The classroom strategy study: Summary of general findings.* Research Series Report No. 187. East Lansing: The Institute for Research on Teaching. Michigan State University.

Brophy, J., VanSledright, B., & Bredin, N. (1992). Fifth graders' ideas about history expressed before and after their introduction to the subject. *Theory and Research in Social Education, 20,* 440–89.

Brown, A. (1983). *Cognitive development.* Unpublished manuscript, National Institute of Child Health and Human Development, Bethesda, MD. Quoted in J. Flavell (1992), Cognitive development: Past, present, and future, *Developmental Psychology, 28, 998–1004.*

Brown, A., & Campione, J. (1990). Interactive learning environments and the teaching of science and mathematics. In M. Gardner, J. Greeno, F. Reif, A. Schoenfeld, A. diSessa, & E. Stage (Eds.), *Toward a scientific practice of science education* (pp. 111–39). Hillsdale, NJ: Erlbaum.

Brown, A., Campione, J., & Day, J. (1981). Learning to learn: On training students to learn from texts. *Educational Researcher, 10,* 14–21.

Brown, A., & Day, J. (1980). *Strategies and knowledge for summarizing texts: The development of expertise.* Manuscript. Urbana: University of Illinois.

Brown, A., & Palincsar, A. (1982). Inducing strategic learning from texts by means of informing, self-controlled training. *Topics in Learning and Learning Disabilities, 2,* 1–17.

Brown, F. (1976). *Principles of educational and psychological testing* (2nd ed.). New York: Holt, Rinehart & Winston.

Brown, J., & Burton, R. (1978). Diagnostic models for procedural bugs in basic mathematical skills. *Cognitive Science, 2,* 155–92.

Brown, J., Collins, A., & Duguid, P. (1989). Situated cognition and the culture of learning. *Educational Researcher, 18*(1), 32–42.

Brown, R., & Kulik, J. (1977). Flashbulb memories. *Cognition, 5,* 73–99.

Bruer, J. (1993). *Schools for thought: A science of learning in the classroom.* Cambridge: MIT Press.

Bruner, J. (1960). *The process of education.* Cambridge: Harvard University Press.

Bruner, J. (1966). *Toward a theory of instruction.* Cambridge: Harvard University Press.

Bruner, J. (1971). *The relevance of education.* New York: Norton.

Bruner, J. (1990). *Acts of meaning.* Cambridge: Harvard University Press.

Bruner, J., Goodnow, J., & Austin, G. (1956). *A study of thinking.* New York: Wiley.

Bryk, A., Lee, V., & Smith, J. (1990). High school organization and its effects on teachers and students: An interpretive summary of the research. In W. Klune & J. Witte (Eds.), *Choice and control in American education* (Vol. 1, pp. 135–226). Philadelphia: Falmer.

Buck, R., & Green, T. (1993). *Collaborating with school leaders for school wide change to enhance motivation and learning.* Paper presented at the annual meeting of the American Educational Research Association, April, Atlanta, GA.

Buri, J., Louiselle, P., Misukanis, T., & Mueller, R. (1988). Effects of authoritarianism and authoritativeness on self-esteem. *Personality and Social Psychology Bulletin, 14,* 271–82.

Burling, R. (1973). *English in black and white.* New York: Holt, Rinehart & Winston.

Buss, A., & Plomin, R. (1984). *Temperament: Early developing personality traits.* Hillsdale, NJ: Erlbaum.

Butler, R. (1987). Task-involving and ego-involving properties of evaluation: Effects of different feedback conditions on motivational perceptions, interest, and performance. *Journal of Educational Psychology, 79,* 474–82.

Butler, R. (1988). Enhancing and undermining intrinsic motivation: The effects of task-involving and ego-involving evaluation on interest and performance. *British Journal of Educational Psychology, 58,* 1–14.

Bybee, R., & Sund, R. (1982). *Piaget for educators* (2nd ed.). Columbus, OH: Merrill.

Calderhead, J., & Gates, P. (Eds.). (1993.) *Conceptualizing reflection in teacher development.* London: Falmer.

Calkins, L. (1986). *The art of teaching writing.* Exeter, NH: Heinemann.

Camp, B., & Bash, M. (1981). *Think aloud: Increasing social and cognitive skills—a problem-solving program for children, primary level.* Champaign, IL: Research Press.

Campbell, M., & Lam, D. (1993). Gender in public education: From mirrors to magnifying lens. In S. Biklen & D. Pollard (Eds.), *92nd yearbook of the National Society for the Study of Education: Gender and education* (pp. 204–20). Chicago: University of Chicago Press.

Cangelosi, J. (1993). *Classroom management strategies* (2nd ed.). White Plains, NY: Longman.

Canter, L. (1976). *Assertive discipline: A take-charge approach for today's educator.* Santa Monica, CA: Canter and Associates.

Canter, L. (1981). *Assertive discipline follow-up guidebook.* Santa Monica, CA: Canter and Associates.

Canter, L. (1988). Let the educator beware: The response to Curwin and Mendler. *Educational Leadership, 46,* 71–73.

Carey, S. (1985). *Conceptual change in childhood.* Cambridge: MIT Press.

Carey, S., & Smith, C. (1993). On understanding the nature of scientific knowledge. *Educational Psychologist, 28,* 235–51.

Carlsen, W. (1991a). Subject-matter knowledge and science teaching: A pragmatic perspective. In J. Brophy (Ed.), *Advances in research on teaching* (Vol. 2, pp. 115–44). Greenwich, CT: JAI Press.

Carlsen, W. (1991b). Questioning in the classrooms: A sociolinguistic perspective. *Review of Educational Research, 61,* 157–78.

Carnine, D. (1976). Effects of two teacher presentation rates on off-task behavior, answering correctly, and participation. *Journal of Applied Behavior Analysis, 9,* 199–206.

Carnine, D. (1989). Teaching complex content to learning disabled students: The role of technology. *Exceptional Children, 55,* 524–33.

Carpenter, T., Fennema, E., Peterson, P., Chiang, C., & Loef, M. (1989). Using knowledge of children's mathematical thinking in classroom teaching: An experimental study. *American Educational Research Journal, 26,* 499–532.

Carrier, C., & Titus, A. (1981). Effects of note-taking pretraining and test mode expectations on learning from lectures. *American Educational Research Journal, 18,* 385–97.

Carroll, J. (1963). A model of school learning. *Teachers College Record, 64,* 722–33.

Carter, K. (1990). Teachers' knowledge and learning to teach. In W. Houston, M. Haberman, & J. Sikula (Eds.), *Handbook of research on teacher education* (pp. 291–310). New York: Macmillan.

Carter, K., & Richardson-Koehler, V. (1989). A curriculum for an initial year of teaching program. *Elementary School Journal, 89*(4), 405–20.

Carter, K., Sabers, D., Cushing, K., Pinnegar, S., & Berliner, D. (1987). Processing and using information about students: A study of expert, novice, and postulant teachers. *Teaching and Teacher Education, 3,* 147–57.

Cartledge, G., & Milburn, L. (1978). The case for teaching social skills in the classroom: A review. *Review of Educational Research, 48,* 133–56.

Carver, C., & Scheirer, M. (1988). A control-process perspective on anxiety. *Anxiety Research, 1,* 17–22.

Casanova, U. (1987). Ethnic and cultural differences. In V. Richardson-Koehler (Ed.), *Educators' handbook: A research perspective* (pp. 370–93). White Plains, NY: Longman.

Casanova, U., & Arias, M. (1993). Contextualizing bilingual education. In M. Arias & U. Casanova (Eds.), *92nd yearbook of the National Society for the Study of Education.* Part 2, *Bilingual education: Politics, practice, and research* (pp. 1–35). Chicago: University of Chicago Press.

Case, R. (1978). A developmentally based theory and technology of instruction. *Review of Educational Research, 48,* 439–63.

Case, R. (1982). Learning, maturation, and the development of computation strategies in elementary arithmetic. In T. Carpenter, J. Moser, & T. Romberg (Eds.), *Addition and subtraction: A cognitive perspective* (pp. 156–70). Hillsdale, NJ: Erlbaum.

Case, R. (Ed.). (1992). *The mind's staircase: Exploring the conceptual underpinnings of children's thought and knowledge.* Hillsdale, NJ: Erlbaum.

Case, R., & Bereiter, C. (1984). From behaviourism to cognitive behaviourism to cognitive development: Steps in the evolution of instructional design. *Instructional Science, 13,* 141–58.

Cattell, R. (1943). The measurement of adult intelligence. *Psychological Bulletin, 40,* 153–93.

Cattell, R. (1971). *Abilities: Their structure, growth, and action.* Boston: Houghton-Mifflin.

Celis, W., III. (1993). School crime hits suburbs and small towns. *New York Times,* April 21, pp. A1, B8.

Center for Social Organization of Schools. (1984). *School uses of micro-computers: Reports from a national survey* (November, No. 6). Baltimore: Johns Hopkins University Press.

Champagne, A., Klopfer, L., & Anderson, J. (1980). Factors influencing the learning of classical mechanics. *American Journal of Physics, 48,* 1074–79.

Champagne, A., Klopfer, L., & Gunstone, R. (1982). Cognitive research and the design of science instruction. *Educational Psychologist, 17,* 31–53.

Chance, P. (1986). *Thinking in the classroom.* New York: Teachers College Press.

Charles, C. (1992). *Building classroom discipline* (4th ed.). White Plains, NY: Longman.

Chase, W., & Chi, M. (1980). Cognitive skill: Implications for spatial skill in large-scale environments. In J. Harvey (Ed.), *Cognition, social behavior, and the environment.* Hillsdale, NJ: Erlbaum.

Chazan, B. (1985). *Contemporary approaches to moral education.* New York: Teachers College Press.

Chernick, R. (1990). Effects of interdependent, coactive, and individualized working conditions on pupils' educational computer program performance. *Journal of Educational Psychology, 82,* 691–95.

Chi, M. (1978). Knowledge structure and memory

development. In R. Siegler (Ed.), *Children's thinking: What develops?* (pp. 73–96). Hillsdale, NJ: Erlbaum.

Chi, M., Bassok, M., Lewis, M., Raimann, P., & Glaser, R. (1989). Self-explanations: How students study and use examples in learning to solve problems. *Cognitive Science, 13,* 145–82.

Chi, M., Feltovich, P., & Glaser, R. (1981). Categorization and representation of physics problems by experts and novices. *Cognitive Science, 5,* 121–52.

Chi, M., & Glaser, R. (1985). Problem-solving ability. In R. Sternberg (Ed.), *Human abilities: An information-processing approach* (pp. 227–50). New York: Freedman.

Chi, M., & Glaser, R., & Rees, E. (1981). Expertise in problem solving. In R. Sternberg (Ed.), *Advances in the psychology of human intelligence* (Vol. 1). Hillsdale, NJ: Erlbaum.

Chilcoat, G. (1989). Instructional behaviors for clearer presentations in the classroom. *Instructional Science, 18,* 289–314.

Chinn, C., & Brewer, W. (1993). The role of anomalous data in knowledge acquisition: A theoretical framework and implications for science instruction. *Review of Educational Research, 63,* 1–49.

Chodorow, N. (1978). *The reproduction of mothering.* Los Angeles: University of California Press.

Chomsky, N. (1986). *Knowledge of language: Its nature, origin and use.* New York: Praeger.

Christoplos, F., & Borden, J. (1978). Sexism in elementary school mathematics. *Elementary School Journal, 78,* 275–77.

Clark, C., & Peterson, P. (1986). Teachers' thought processes. In M. Wittrock (Ed.), *Handbook of research on teaching* (3rd ed.). New York: Macmillan.

Clark, C., & Yinger, R. (1979). Teachers' thinking. In P. Peterson & H. Walberg (Eds.), *Research on teaching.* Berkeley, CA: McCutchan.

Clark, D. (1971). Teaching concepts in the classroom: A set of teaching prescriptions derived from experimental research. *Journal of Educational Psychology, 62,* 253–78.

Clark, R. (1982). Antagonism between achievement and enjoyment in ATI studies. *Educational Psychologist, 17,* 92–101.

Clark, R. (1983). *Family life and school achievement:*

Why poor black children succeed or fail. Chicago: University of Chicago Press.

Clark, R. E. (1983). Reconsidering research on learning from media. *Review of Educational Research, 53,* 445–59.

Clarke, J. (1990). *Patterns of thinking: Integrating learning skills in content teaching.* Boston: Allyn & Bacon.

Clements, D. (1986). Effects of LOGO and CAI environments on cognition and creativity. *Journal of Educational Psychology, 78,* 309–18.

Clements, D., & Nastasi, B. (1988). Social and cognitive interactions in educational computer environments. *American Educational Research Journal, 25,* 87–106.

Clifford, M. (1981). *Practicing educational psychology.* Boston: Houghton-Mifflin.

Clifford, M. (1990). Students need challenge, not easy success. *Educational Leadership, 48,* 22–26.

Clifford, M. (1991). Risk-taking: Empirical and educational considerations. *Educational Psychologist, 26,* 263–98.

Cobb, J., & Hops, H. (1973). Effects of academic survival skill training on low achieving first graders. *Journal of Educational Research, 67,* 108–113.

Cobb, N. (1992). *Adolescence: Continuity, change, and diversity.* Mountain View, CA: Mayfield.

Cobb, P. (1986). Making mathematics: Children's learning and the constructivist tradition. *Harvard Educational Review, 56,* 301–6.

Cobb, P., Wood, T., Yackel, E., Nicholls, J., Wheatley, G., Trigatti, B., & Perlwitz, M. (1991). Assessment of a problem-centered second-grade mathematics project. *Journal for Research in Mathematics Education, 22,* 3–29.

Cobb, P., Wood, T., Yackel, E., & Perlwitz, M. (1992). A follow-up assessment of a second-grade problem-centered mathematics project. *Educational Studies in Mathematics, 23,* 483–504.

Cobb, P., Yackel, E., & Wood, T. (1992). A constructivist alternative to the representational view of mind in mathematics education. *Journal for Research in Mathematics Education, 23,* 2–33.

Cochran-Smith, M. (1991). Word processing and writing in elementary classrooms: A critical review of related literature. *Review of Educational Research, 61,* 107–55.

Cochran-Smith, M., Paris, C., & Kahn, J. (1991).

Learning to write differently: Beginning writers and word processing. Norwood, NJ: Ablex.

Cofer, C. (1971). Properties of verbal materials and verbal learning. In J. Kling & L. Riggs (Eds.), *Woodworth and Schlosberg's experimental psychology.* New York: Holt, Rinehart & Winston.

Cognition and Technology Group at Vanderbilt (1993). Toward integrated curricula: Possibilities from anchored instruction. In M. Rabinowitz (Ed.), *Cognitive science foundations of instruction* (pp. 33–55). Hillsdale, NJ: Erlbaum.

Cohen, E. (1986). *Designing group work: Strategies for the heterogeneous classroom.* New York: Teachers College Press.

Cohen, R., & Bradley, R. (1978). Simulation games, learning, and retention. *Elementary School Journal, 78,* 247–53.

Cohen, R., & Siegel, A. (Eds.). (1991). *Context and development.* Hillsdale, NJ: Erlbaum.

Coker, H., Medley, D., & Soar, R. (1980). How valid are expert opinions about effective teaching? *Phi Delta Kappan, 62,* 131–34.

Colby, A., Kohlberg, L., & collaborators. (1987). *The measurement of moral judgment.* Vol. 1, *Theoretical foundations and research validation.* Cambridge: Cambridge University Press.

Coleman, J. (1980). *The nature of adolescence.* London: Methuen.

Coleman, J., Livingston, S., Fennessey, G., Edwards, K., & Kidder, S. (1973). The Hopkins Games Program: Conclusion from seven years of research. *Educational Researcher, 2,* 3–7.

Collier, V. (1992). A synthesis of studies examining long-term language-minority student data on academic achievement.

Collins, A. (1987). A sample dialogue based on a theory of inquiry teaching. In C. Reigeluth (Ed.), *Instructional theories in action: Lessons illustrating selected theories and models* (pp. 181–99). Hillsdale, NJ: Erlbaum.

Collins, A., Brown, J., & Holum, A. (1991). Cognitive apprenticeship: Making thinking visible. *American Educator, 15,*(3), 6–11, 38–46.

Collins, A., Brown, J., & Newman, S. (1989). Cognitive apprenticeship: Teaching the craft of reading, writing, and mathematics. In L. Resnick (Ed.), *Knowing, learning, and instruction: Essays in honor of Robert Glaser.* Hillsdale, NJ: Erlbaum.

Collins, A., & Loftus, E. (1975). A spreading activation theory of semantic processing. *Psychological Review, 82,* 407–28.

Collins, A., & Stevens, A. (1983). A cognitive theory of inquiry teaching. In C. Reigeluth (Ed.), *Instructional-design theories and models: An overview of their current status.* Hillsdale, NJ: Erlbaum.

Comer, J. P., & Haynes, N. M. (1991). Parent involvement in schools: An ecological approach. *Elementary School Journal, 91*(3), 271–78.

Commons, M., Miller, P., & Kuhn, D. (1982). The relation between formal operational reasoning and academic course selection and performance among college freshmen and sophomores. *Journal of Applied Developmental Psychology, 3,* 1–10.

Commons, M., Richards, F., & Armon, C. (Eds.). (1984). *Beyond formal operations: Late adolescent and adult cognitive development.* New York: Praeger.

Condry, J., & Chambers, J. (1978). Intrinsic motivation and the process of learning. In M. Lepper & D. Green (Eds.), *The hidden costs of reward: New perspectives on the psychology of human motivation* (pp. 61–84). Hillsdale, NJ: Erlbaum.

Conger, J. (1991). *Adolescence and youth: Psychological development in a changing world* (4th ed.). New York: Harper Collins.

Cook, L. (1982). *The effects of text structure on the comprehension of scientific prose.* Doctoral dissertation. Santa Barbara: University of California.

Cook, L., & Mayer, R. (1988). Teaching readers about the structure of scientific text. *Journal of Educational Psychology, 80,* 448–56.

Coop, R. (1982). A view of education of gifted and talented students from an educational psychologist's perspective. *Elementary School Journal, 82,* 292–97.

Cooper, H. (1989). *Homework.* New York: Longman.

Cooper, H., & Good, T. (1983). *Pygmalion grows up: Studies in the expectation communication process.* New York: Longman.

Coopersmith, S. (1967). *The antecedents of self-esteem.* San Francisco: Freeman.

Corkill, A. (1992). Advance organizers: Facilitators of recall. *Educational Psychological Review, 4,* 33–67.

Corkill, A., Glover, J., & Bruning, R. (1988). Advance organizers: Concrete versus abstract. *Journal of Educational Research, 82,* 76–81.

Corkill, A., Glover, J., Bruning, R., & Krug, D. (1988). Advance organizers: Retrieval hypotheses. *Journal of Educational Psychology, 80,* 304–11.

Cormier, S., & Hagman, J. (Eds.). (1987). *Transfer of learning: Contemporary research and applications.* San Diego: Harcourt Brace Jovanovich.

Corno, L. (1989). Self-regulated learning: A volitional analysis. In B. Zimmerman & D. Schunk (Eds.), *Self-regulated learning and academic achievement* (pp. 111–42). New York: Springer-Verlag.

Corno, L. (1992). Encouraging students to take responsibility for learning and performance. *Elementary School Journal, 93,* 69–84.

Corno, L. (1993). The best-laid plans: Modern conceptions of volition and educational research. *Educational Researcher, 22,* 14–22.

Corno, L., & Rohrkemper, M. (1985). Self-regulated learning. In C. Ames & R. Ames (Eds.), *Research on motivation in education* (Vol. 2). Orlando, FL: Academic Press.

Corno, L., & Snow, R. (1986). Adapting teaching to individual differences among learners. In M. Wittrock (Ed.), *Handbook of research on teaching* (3rd ed., pp. 605–29). New York: Macmillan.

Cortese, A. (1990). *Ethnic ethics: The restructuring of moral theory.* Albany: State University of New York Press.

Costello, E. (1989). Child psychiatric disorders and their correlates: A primary care pediatric sample. *Journal of the American Academy of Child and Adolescent Psychiatry, 28,* 851–55.

Coté, J., & Levine, C. (1983). Marcia and Erikson: The relationships among ego identity status, neuroticism, dogmatism, and purpose of life. *Journal of Youth and Adolescence, 12,* 43–53.

Covington, J., & Omelich, C. (1979). Effort: The double-edged sword in school achievement. *Journal of Educational Psychology, 71,* 169–82.

Covington, M. (1984). Strategic thinking and the fear of failure. In J. Segal, S. Chipman, & R. Glaser (Eds.), *Thinking and learning skills: Relating instruction to basic research.* Hillsdale, NJ: Erlbaum.

Covington, M. (1992). *Making the grade.* Cambridge: Cambridge University Press.

Covington, M., & Beery, R. (1976). *Self-worth and school learning.* New York: Holt, Rinehart & Winston.

Covington, M., Crutchfield, R., Davies, L., & Olton, R. (1974). *The productive thinking program: A course in learning to think.* Columbus, OH: Merrill.

Covington, M., & Omelich, C. (1988). Achievement dynamics: The interaction of motives, cognitions, and emotions over time. *Anxiety Journal, 1,* 165–83.

Covington, M., Spratt, M., & Omelich, C. (1980). Is effort enough or does diligence count too? Student and teacher reactions to effort stability in failure. *Journal of Educational Psychology, 72,* 717–29.

Covington, M., Teel, K., & Parecki, A. (1993). *Addressing achievement motivation among African-American students: A collaborative attempt to apply theory to practice.* Paper presented at the annual meeting of the American Educational Research Association, April, Atlanta, GA.

Craik, F. (1979). Human memory. In M. Rosenzweig & L. Porter (Eds.), *Annual review of psychology.* Palo Alto, CA: Annual Reviews Inc.

Craik, F., & Lockhart, R. (1972). Levels of processing: A framework for memory research. *Journal of Verbal Learning and Verbal Behavior, 11,* 671–84.

Crandall, V., Katkovsky, W., & Crandall, V. (1965). Children's beliefs in their own control of reinforcement in intellectual-academic situations. *Child Development, 36,* 91–109.

Crandall, V., Katkovsky, W., & Preston, A. (1962). Motivational and ability determinants of young children's intellectual achievement behaviors. *Child Development, 33,* 643–61.

Craske, M. (1985). Improving persistence through observational learning and attribution retaining. *British Journal of Educational Psychology, 55,* 138–47.

Crawford, J. (1993). *Bilingual education: History, politics, theory and practice.* Trenton, NJ: Crane.

Crisman, F., & Mackey, J. (1990). A comparison of oral and written techniques of concept instruction. *Theory and Research in Social Education, 18,* 139–55.

Cronbach, L., & Snow, R. (1977). *Aptitudes and instructional methods.* New York: Irvington.

Crooks, T. (1988). The impact of classroom evaluation practices on students. *Review of Educational Research, 58,* 438–81.

Cross, D., & Paris, S. (1988). Developmental and instructional analyses of children's metacognition and reading comprehension. *Journal of Educational Psychology, 80,* 131–42.

Cruickshank, D. (1990). *Research that informs teachers and teacher educators.* Bloomington, IN: Phi Delta Kappa Educational Foundation.

Cullinan, D., Sabornie, E., & Crossland, C. (1992). Social mainstreaming of mildly handicapped students. *Elementary School Journal, 92,* 339–52.

Cummins, J. (1980). The cntry and exit fallacy in bilingual education. *NABE Journal, 4,* 25–59.

Cummins, J. (1989). *Empowering minority students.* Sacramento: California Association for Bilingual Education.

Cummins, J. (1992). Bilingual education and English immersion: The Ramiréz report in theoretical perspective. *Bilingual Research Journal, 16,* 91–104.

Curry, L. (1990). A critique of the research on learning styles. *Phi Delta Kappan, 48,* 50–56.

Curwin, R., & Mendler, A. (1988a). *Discipline with dignity.* Alexandria, VA: Association for Supervision & Curriculum Development.

Curwin, R., & Mendler, A. (1988b). Packaged discipline programs: Let the buyer beware. *Educational Leadership, 46,* 68–71.

Cyert, R. (1980). Problem solving and educational policy. In D. Tuma & F. Reif (Eds.), *Problem solving and education: Issues in teaching and research.* Hillsdale, NJ: Erlbaum.

Cziko, G. (1992). The evaluation of bilingual education. *Educational Researcher, 21,* 10–15.

Damico, S., & Scott, E. (1988). Behavior differences between black and white females in desegregated schools. *Equity and Excellence, 23,* 63–66.

Damon, W. (1980). Patterns of change in children's social reasoning: A two-year longitudinal study. *Child Development, 51,* 1010–17.

Damon, W. (1988). *The moral child.* New York: Free Press.

Damon, W., & Hart, D. (1988). *Self-understanding in childhood and adolescence.* Cambridge: Cambridge University Press.

Damon, W., & Killen, M. (1982). Peer interaction and the process of change in children's moral reasoning. *Merrill-Palmer Quarterly, 28,* 347–67.

Dandonoli, P. (1987). Report on foreign language enrollments in public secondary schools. In Secondary Schools, Fall, 1985. *Foreign Language Annals, 20,* 457–470.

Dansereau, D. (1983). Learning strategy research. In J. Segal, S. Chipman, & R. Glaser (Eds.), *Relating instruction to basic research.* Hillsdale, NJ: Erlbaum.

Dansereau, D., Collins, K., McDonald, B., Holley, C., Garland, J., Diekhoff, G., & Evans, S. (1979). Development and evaluation of a learning strategy training program. *Journal of Educational Psychology, 71,* 64–73.

Darch, C., Carnine, D., & Kameenui, E. (1986). The role of graphic organizers and social structure in content area instruction. *Journal of Reading Behavior, 18,* 275–95.

Darley, J., & Schultz, T. (1990). Moral rules: Their content and acquisition. In M. Rosenzweig & L. Porter (Eds.), *Annual review of psychology* (Vol. 41, pp. 525–56). Palo Alto: Annual Reviews Inc.

Dasen, P., & Heron, A. (1981). Cross-cultural tests of Piaget's theory. In H. Triandis & A. Heron (Eds.), *Handbook of cross-cultural psychology: Developmental psychology* (Vol. 4, pp. 295–342). Boston: Allyn & Bacon.

Dasho, S. (1978). *A communications approach to classroom socialization* (Report A-78-12, Effective Teacher Education Program). San Francisco: Far West Laboratory for Educational Research and Development.

Daurio, S. (1979). Educational enrichment versus acceleration: A review of the literature. In W. George, S. Cohn, & J. Stanley (Eds.), *Educating the gifted: Acceleration and enrichment.* Baltimore: Johns Hopkins University Press.

Davis, G. (1986). *Creativity is forever* (2nd ed.). Dubuque, IA: Kendall/Hunt.

Davis, G. (1989). Testing for creative potential. *Contemporary Educational Psychology, 14,* 257–74.

Davis, J. (1991). Educational implications of field dependence-independence. In S. Wapner & J. Demick (Eds.), *Field dependence-independence: Cognitive style across the life span.* Hillsdale, NJ: Erlbaum.

Davis, R. (1984). *Learning mathematics: A cognitive science approach to mathematics education.* London: Croom Helm.

Davis, R., Maher, C., & Noddings, N. (Eds.). (1990). Constructivist views on the teaching and learning of mathematics. *Journal for Research in Mathematics Education Monograph, 4.* Reston, VA: National Council of Teachers of Mathematics.

Davis, R., & McKnight, C. (1980). The influence of semantic content on algorithmic behavior. *Journal of Mathematical Behavior, 3,* 39–87.

Day, J., & Cordón, L. (1993). Static and dynamic measures of ability: An experimental comparison. *Journal of Educational Psychology, 85,* 75–82.

Deaux, K. (1985). Sex and gender. *Annual Review of Psychology, 36,* 49–82.

deBaryshe, B., Patterson, G., & Capaldi, D. (1993). A performance model of academic achievement in early adolescent boys. *Developmental Psychology, 29,* 795–804.

deBono, E. (1985). The CoRT thinking program. In J. Segal, S. Chipman, & R. Glaser (Eds.), *Thinking and learning skills, Volume 1: Relating instruction to research.* Hillsdale, NJ: Erlbaum.

Deci, E. (1975). *Intrinsic motivation.* New York: Plenum.

Deci, E., & Ryan, R. (1985). *Intrinsic motivation and self-determination in human behavior.* New York: Plenum.

Deci, E., Schwartz, A., Sheinman, L., & Ryan, R. (1981). An instrument to assess adults' orientations toward control versus autonomy with children: Reflections on intrinsic motivation and perceived competence. *Journal of Educational Psychology, 73,* 642–50.

Deci, E., Vallerand, R., Pelletier, L., & Ryan R. (1991). Motivation and education. *Educational Psychologist, 26* (3,4), 325–46.

deFelix, J., Waxman, H., Paige, S., & Huang, S. (1993). A comparison of classroom instruction in bilingual and monolingual secondary schools. *Peabody Journal of Education, 69,* 102–16.

deGroot, A. (1965). *Thought and choice in chess.* The Hague: Mouton.

Delclos, V., & Harrington, C. (1991). Effects of strategy monitoring and proactive instruction on children's problem-solving performance. *Journal of Educational Psychology, 83,* 35–42.

DeLisi, R., & Staudt, J. (1980). Individual differences in college students' performance on formal operations tasks. *Journal of Applied Developmental Psychology, 1,* 201–8.

Delpit, L. (1992). Acquisition of literate discourse: Bowing before the master? *Theory into Practice, 31,* 296–302.

Delprato, D., & Midgley, B. (1992). Some fundamentals of B. F. Skinner's behaviorism. *American Psychologist, 47,* 1507–20.

Demetriou, A., Shayer, M., & Efklides, A. (Eds.). (1993). *Neo-Piagetian theories of cognitive development: Implications and applications for education.* New York: Routledge.

Dempster, F. (1993). Exposing our students to less should help them learn more. *Phi Delta Kappan, 74,* 433–37.

Dempster, F., & Farris, R. (1990). The spacing effect: Research and practice. *Journal of Research and Development in Education, 23,* 97–101.

Derry, S. (1988–89). Putting learning strategies to work. *Educational Leadership, 46*(4), 4–10.

Detterman, D., & Sternberg, R. (1982). *How and how much can intelligence be increased?* Norwood, NJ: Ablex.

DeTure, L. (1979). Relative effects of modeling on the acquisition of wait-time by preservice elementary teachers and concomitant changes in dialogue patterns. *Journal of Research in Science Teaching, 16,* 553–62.

Devine, T. (1987). *Teaching study skills: A guide for teachers* (2nd ed.). Boston: Allyn & Bacon.

Dewey, J. (1910). *How we think.* Boston: Heath.

Diaz, R., & Berk, L. (1992a). *Misguided assumptions of self-instructional training.* Paper presented at the annual meeting of the American Educational Research Association, April, San Francisco.

Diaz, R., & Berk, L. (Eds.). (1992b). *Private speech: From social interaction to self-regulation.* Hillsdale, NJ: Erlbaum.

Dick, W., & Carey, L. (1990). *The systematic design of instruction* (3rd ed.). New York: Harper Collins.

Diener, D., & Dweck, C. (1978). An analysis of learned helplessness: Continuous changes in performance, strategy, and achievement cognitions following failure. *Journal of*

Personality and Social Psychology, 36, 451–62.

Dillon, J. (1979). Alternatives to questioning. *High School Journal, 62,* 217–22.

Dillon, J. (1981a). A norm against student questions. *Clearing House, 55,* 136–39.

Dillon, J. (1981b). Duration of response to teacher questions and statements. *Contemporary Educational Psychology, 6,* 1–11.

Dillon, J. (Ed.). (1988). *Questioning and teaching: A manual of practice.* London: Croom Helm.

Dillon, J. (Ed.). (1990). *The practice of questioning.* New York: Routledge.

Dimarino-Linnen, E. (1990). *Identity development from a dialectical perspective: Towards a richer understanding of the identity formation process.* Unpublished doctoral dissertation, Bryn Mawr College, Bryn Mawr, PA.

Dimino, J., Gersten, R., Carnine, D., & Blake, G. (1990). Story grammar: An approach for promoting at-risk secondary students' comprehension of literature. *Elementary School Journal, 91,* 19–32.

diSessa, A. (1982). Unlearning Aristotelian physics: A study of knowledge-based learning. *Cognitive Science, 6,* 37–75.

diSibio, M. (1982). Memory for connected discourse: A constructivist view. *Review of Educational Research, 52,* 149–74.

Doctorow, M., Wittrock, M., & Marks, C. (1978). Generative processes in reading comprehension. *Journal of Educational Psychology, 70,* 109–18.

Doebler, L., & Eicke, F. (1979). Effects of teacher awareness of the educational implications of field-dependent/field-independent cognitive style on selected classroom variables. *Journal of Educational Psychology, 71,* 226–32.

Dole, J., Duffy, G., Roehler, L., & Pearson, P. (1990). Moving from the old to the new: Research on reading comprehension instruction. *Review of Educational Research, 61,* 239–64.

Doll, B. (1994). *Prevalence of psychiatric disorders in children and youth.* Manuscript submitted for publication.

Dolson, D. (1986). *The application of immersion education in the United States.* Rosslyn, VA: The Clearing House for Bilingual Education.

Dolson, D. (in press). Bilingualism and scholastic

performance: The literature revisited. *NABE Journal.*

Donaldson, M. (1978). *Children's minds.* London: Croom Helm.

Dooling, D., & Lachman, R. (1971). Effects of comprehension on retention of prose. *Journal of Experimental Psychology, 88,* 216–22.

Dornbusch, S., Ritter, P., Leiderman, P., Roberts, D., & Fraleigh, M. (1987). The relation of parenting style to adolescent school performance. *Child Development, 58,* 1244–57.

Downey, M., & Levstik, L. (1991). Teaching and learning history. In J. Shaver (Ed.), *Handbook of research on social studies teaching and learning* (pp. 400–410). New York: Macmillan.

Doyle, W. (1984). How order is achieved in classrooms: An interim report. *Journal of Curriculum Studies, 16,* 259–77.

Doyle, W. (1986a). Classroom organization and management. In M. Wittrock (Ed.), *Handbook of research on teaching* (3rd ed., pp. 392–431). New York: Macmillan.

Doyle, W. (1986b). Content representation in teachers' definitions of academic work. *Journal of Curriculum Studies, 18,* 365–79.

Doyle, W. (1992a). Curriculum and pedagogy. In P. Jackson (Ed.), *Handbook of research on curriculum* (pp. 486–516). New York: Macmillan.

Doyle, W. (1992b). *Research on classroom organization and management.* Invited paper prepared for U.S. Department of Education, Office of Educational Research and Improvement, Washington, DC.

Dreikurs, R. (1968). *Psychology in the classroom* (2nd ed.). New York: Harper & Row.

Dreikurs, R., Grunwald, B., & Pepper, F. (1982). *Maintaining sanity in the classroom: Classroom management techniques* (2nd ed.). New York: Harper & Row.

Dreyfoos, J. (1990). *Adolescents at risk: Prevalence and prevention.* London: Oxford University Press.

Driver, R. (1987). Promoting conceptual change in classroom settings: The experience of the Children's Learning in Science Project. In J. Novak (Ed.), *Proceedings of the second international seminar on misconceptions and educational strategies in science and mathematics* (Vol. 2, pp. 97–107). Ithaca, NY: Cornell University.

Duckworth, E. (1979). Either we're too early and they can't learn it or we're too late and they know it already: The dilemma of "applying Piaget." *Harvard Educational Review, 49,* 297–312.

Duffy, G. (1993). Rethinking strategy instruction: Four teachers' development and their low-achievers' understandings. *Elementary School Journal, 93,* 231–47.

Duffy, G., & Roehler, L. (1987). Improving classroom reading instruction through the use of responsive elaboration. *Reading Teacher, 40,* 514–21.

Duffy, G., & Roehler, L. (1989). The tension between information-giving and mediation: Perspectives on instructional explanation and teacher change. In J. Brophy (Ed.), *Advances in research on teaching.* Vol. 1, *Teaching for meaningful understanding and self-regulated learning.* Greenwich, CT: JAI.

Duffy, G., Roehler, L., & Herrmann, B. (1988). Modeling mental processes helps poor readers become strategic readers. *Reading Teacher, 41,* 762–67.

Duffy, G., Roehler, L., Meloth, M., & Vavrus, L. (1986). Conceptualizing instructional explanation. *Teaching and Teacher Education, 2,* 197–214.

Duffy, G., Roehler, L., Sivan, E., Rackliffe, G., Book, C., Meloth, M., Vavrus, L., Wesselman, R., Putnam, J., & Bassiri, D. (1987). Effects of explaining reasoning associated with using reading strategies. *Reading Research Quarterly, 22,* 347–68.

Dunn, J., & Plomin, R. (1990). *Separate lives: Why siblings are so different.* New York: Basic Books.

Dunn, L. (1973). *Exceptional children in the schools: Special education in transition.* New York: Holt, Rinehart & Winston.

Dunn, R. (1987). Research on instructional environments: Implications for student achievement and attitudes. *Professional School Psychology, 2,* 43–52.

Dunn, R., Beaudry, J., & Klavas, A. (1989). Survey of research on learning styles. *Educational Researcher, 70,* 50–58.

Dunn, R., Dunn, K., & Price, G. (1984). *Learning-style inventory.* Lawrence, KS: Price Systems.

Dunn, T. (1984). Learning hierarchies and cognitive psychology: An important link for instructional psychology. *Educational Psychologist, 19,* 75–93.

Duschl, R. (1990). *Restructuring science education: The importance of theories and their development.* New York: Teachers College Press.

Dweck, C. (1986). Motivational processes affecting learning. *American Psychologist, 41,* 1040–48.

Dweck, C., Davidson, W., Nelson, S., & Enna, B. (1978). Sex differences in learned helplessness: II. The contingencies of evaluative feedback in the classroom and III.: An experimental analysis. *Developmental Psychology, 14,* 268–76.

Dweck, C., & Elliott, E. (1983). Achievement motivation. In P. Mussen & E. Hetherington (Eds.), *Handbook of child psychology.* Vol. 4, *Socialization, personality and social development.* New York: Wiley.

Ebbinghaus, H. (1885). *Memory* (Translated by H. Ruger & C. Bussenius). New York: Dover, 1964 (originally published in Leipzig in 1885).

Eccles, J. (1987). Gender roles and women's achievement-related decisions. *Psychology of Women Quarterly, 11,* 135–72.

Eccles, J., & Blumenfeld, P. (1985). Classroom experiences and student gender: Are there differences and do they matter? In L. Wilkinson & C. Marrett (Eds.), *Gender influences in classroom interaction.* Orlando, FL: Academic Press.

Eccles, J., & Midgley, C. (1989). Stage/environment fit: Developmentally appropriate classrooms for early adolescents. In R. Ames & C. Ames (Eds.), *Research on motivation in education* (Vol. 3, pp. 139–86). San Diego: Academic Press.

Eccles, J., Midgley, C., Wigfield, A., Buchanan, C., Reuman, D., Flanagan, C., & MacIver, D. (1993). Development during adolescence: The impact of stage-environment fit on young adolescents' experiences in schools and in families. *American Psychologist, 48,* 90–101.

Eden, D. (1975). Intrinsic and extrinsic rewards and motives: Replication and extension with kibbutz workers. *Journal of Applied Social Psychology, 5,* 348–61.

Eder, D. (1985). The cycle of popularity: Interpersonal relations among female adolescents. *Sociology of Education, 58,* 154–65.

Educational Products Information Exchange (Epie Institute). (1986). *The educational software selector* (TESS), 1986–87 edition. New York: Teachers College Press.

Egan, K. (1982). What does Piaget's theory describe? *Teachers College Record, 84,* 453–76.

Egan, K. (1988). *Primary understanding: Education in early childhood.* New York: Routledge.

Egan, K. (1990). *Romantic understanding: The development of rationality and imagination, ages 8–15.* New York: Routledge.

Ehman, L., Glenn, A., Johnson, V., & White, C. (1992). Using computer databases in student problem solving: A study of eight social studies teachers' classrooms. *Theory and Research in Social Education, 20,* 179–206.

Ehri, L., Deffner, N., & Wilce, L. (1984). Pictorial mnemonics for phonics. *Journal of Educational Psychology, 76,* 880–93.

Eisenberg, N. (Ed.) (1982). *The development of prosocial behavior.* New York: Academic Press.

Eisenberg, N., Lennon, R., & Roth, K. (1983). Prosocial development: A longitudinal study. *Developmental Psychology, 19,* 846–55.

Eisenberg, N., & Mussen, P. (1989). *The roots of prosocial behavior in children.* Cambridge: Cambridge University Press.

Eisikovits, Z., & Sagi, A. (1982). Moral development and discipline encounter in delinquent and nondeliquent adolescents. *Journal of Youth and Adolescence, 11,* 217–30.

Elam, S. (1989). The second Gallup-Phi Delta Kappa poll of teachers' attitudes toward the public schools. *Phi Delta Kappan, 70,* June, 785–98.

Elawar, M., & Corno, L. (1985). A factual experiment in teachers' written feedback on student homework: Changing teacher behavior a little rather than a lot. *Journal of Educational Psychology, 77,* 162–73.

Elkind, D. (1981). Child development and the social science curriculum of the elementary school. *Social Education, 45,* 435–37.

Elliott, E., & Dweck, C. (1988). Goals: An approach to motivation and achievement. *Journal of Personality and Social Psychology, 79,* 474–82.

Elstein, A., Shulman, L., & Sprafka, S. (1978). *Medical problem solving: An analysis of clinical reasoning.* Cambridge: Harvard University Press.

Emmer, E., & Aussiker, A. (1987). *School and classroom discipline programs: How well do they work?* Paper presented at the annual meeting of American Educational Research Association, Washington, DC.

Emmer, E., Evertson, C., & Anderson, L. (1980). Effective management at the beginning of the school year. *Elementary School Journal, 80,* 219–31.

Emmer, E., Evertson, C., Sanford, J., Clements, B., & Worsham, M. (1993). *Classroom management for secondary teachers* (3rd ed.). Englewood Cliffs, NJ: Prentice-Hall.

Engelmann, S., & Carnine, D. (1982). *Theory of instruction: Principles and applications.* New York: Irvington.

Englert, C., & Raphael, T. (1989). Developing successful writers through cognitive strategy instruction. In J. Brophy (Ed.) *Advances in research on teaching.* Vol. 1, *Teaching for meaningful understanding and self-regulated learning.* Greenwich, CT: JAI.

Englert, C., Raphael, T., & Anderson, L. (1992). Socially mediated instruction: Improving students' knowledge and talk about writing. *Elementary School Journal, 92,* 411–49.

Ennis, R. (1987). A taxonomy of critical thinking dispositions and abilities. In J. Baron & R. Sternberg (Eds.), *Teaching thinking skills* (pp. 9–26). New York: Freeman.

Enright, R., Lapsley, D., Harris, D., & Shawver, D. (1983). Moral development interventions in early adolescence. *Theory into Practice, 22,* 134–44.

Epps, S., & Tindal, G. (1987). The effectiveness of differential programming in serving students with mild handicaps: Placement options and instructional programming. In M. Wang, M. Reynolds, & H. Walberg (Eds.), *Handbook of special education: Research in practice* (Vol. 1, pp. 213–48). Oxford: Pergamon Press.

Epstein, J. (1988). *Homework practices, achievements, and behaviors of elementary school students* (Report No. 26). Baltimore: Johns Hopkins University, Center for Research on Elementary and Middle Schools.

Epstein, J. L., & Dauber, S. L. (1991). School programs and teacher practices of parent involvement in inner-city elementary and middle schools. *Elementary School Journal, 91*(3), 289–306.

Erickson, F. (1987). Transformation and school success: The politics and culture of educational achievement. *Anthropology and Education Quarterly, 18,* 335–56.

Erikson, E. (1968). *Identity: Youth and crisis.* New York: Norton.

Erlwanger, S. (1975). Case studies of children's conceptions of mathematics (Part 1). *Journal of Children's Mathematical Behavior, 1,* 157–283.

Erwin, P. (1993). *Friendships and peer relations in children.* New York: Wiley.

Eshel, Y., & Klein, Z. (1981). Development of academic self-concept of lower-class and middle-class primary school children. *Journal of Educational Psychology, 73,* 287–93.

Estrada, K., & McLaren, P. (1993). A dialogue on multiculturalism and democratic culture. *Educational Researcher, 22,* 27–33.

Evertson, C. (1985). Training teachers in classroom management: An experimental study in secondary school classrooms. *Journal of Educational Research, 79,* 51–58.

Evertson, C., & Emmer, E. (1982). Effective management at the beginning of the school year in junior high classes. *Journal of Educational Psychology, 74,* 485–98.

Evertson, C., Emmer, E., Clements, B., Sanford, J., & Worsham, M. (1984). *Classroom management for elementary teachers* (1st ed.). Englewood Cliffs, NJ: Prentice-Hall.

Evertson, C., Emmer, E., Clements, B., Sanford, J., & Worsham, M. (1993). *Classroom management for elementary teachers* (3rd ed.). Englewood Cliffs, NJ: Prentice-Hall.

Evertson, C., Emmer, E., Sanford, J., & Clements, B. (1983). Improving classroom management: An experiment in elementary school classrooms. *Elementary School Journal, 84,* 173–88.

Evertson, C., Sanford, J., & Emmer, E. (1981). Effects of class heterogeneity in junior high school. *American Educational Research Journal, 18,* 219–32.

Eysenck, M. (1984). *A handbook of cognitive psychology.* Hillsdale, NJ: Erlbaum.

Fair, J. (1977). Skills in thinking. In D. Kurfman (Ed.), *47th yearbook: Developing decision-making skills* (pp. 29–68). Arlington, VA: National Council for the Social Studies.

Faltis, C. (1993a). Critical issues in the use of sheltered content teaching in high school bilingual programs. *Peabody Journal of Education, 69,* 136–151.

Faltis, C. (1993b). Editors' introduction. *Peabody Journal of Education, 69,* 2–5.

Faltis, C., & Arias, M. (1993). Speakers of languages other than English in the secondary school: Accomplishments and struggles. *Peabody Journal of Education, 69,* 6–29.

Farnham-Diggory, S. (1992). *Cognitive processes in education* (2nd ed.). New York: Harper Collins.

Farrar, M. (1986). Teacher questions: The complexity of the cognitively simple. *Instructional Science, 15,* 89–107.

Faw, H., & Waller, T. (1976) Mathemagenic behaviors and efficiency in learning from prose. *Review of Educational Research, 46,* 691–720.

Feather, N. (Ed.). (1982). *Expectations and actions.* Hillsdale, NJ: Erlbaum.

Feingold, A. (1988). Cognitive gender differences are disappearing. *American Psychologist, 43,* 95–103.

Feldhusen, J., & Sokol, L. (1982). Extra-school programming to meet the needs of gifted youth: Super Saturday. *Gifted Child Quarterly, 21,* 450–76.

Felker, D. (1974). *Building positive self-concepts.* Minneapolis: Burgess.

Fennema, E., Carpenter, T., & Peterson, P. (1989). Learning mathematics with understanding. In J. Brophy (Ed.), *Advances in research on teaching:* Vol. 1, *Teaching for meaningful understanding and self-regulated learning.* Greenwich, CT: JAI.

Fennema, E., Franke, M., Carpenter, T., & Carey, D. (1993). Using children's mathematical knowledge in instruction. *American Educational Research Journal, 30,* 555–83.

Fenstermacher, G. (1982). To be or not to be gifted: What is the question? *Elementary School Journal, 82,* 299–303.

Fenstermacher, G. (1983). How should implications of research on teaching be used? *Elementary School Journal, 83,* 496–99.

Ferguson, G. (1956). On transfer and the abilities of man. *Canadian Journal of Psychology, 10,* 121–31.

Fernandez, C., Yoshida, M., & Stigler, J. (1992). Learning mathematics from classroom instruction: On relating lessons to pupils' interpretations. *Journal of the Learning Sciences, 2,* 333–65.

Ferster, C., & Skinner, B. (1957). *Schedules of reinforcement.* New York: Appleton.

Feshbach, S. (1970). Aggression. In P. Mussen (Ed.), *Carmichael's manual of child psychology* (3rd ed., Vol. 2). New York: Wiley.

Feuerstein, R., Rand, Y., Hoffman, M., & Miller, R. (1980). *Instrumental enrichment: An intervention program for cognitive modifiability.* Baltimore: University Park Press.

Feuerstein, R., et al. (1985). Instrumental enrichment, an intervention program for structural cognitive modifiability: Theory and practice. In J. Segal, S. Chipman, & R. Glaser (Eds.), *Thinking and learning skills.* Vol. 1, *Relating instruction to research.* Hillsdale, NJ: Erlbaum.

Fillmore, C. (1968). The case for case. In E. Bach & R. Harms (Eds.), *Universals of linguistic theory.* New York: Holt, Rinehart & Winston.

Fischer, K., & Lamborn, S. (1989). Mechanisms of variation in developmental levels: Cognitive and emotional transitions during adolescence. In A. DeRibaupierre (Ed.), *Transition mechanisms in child perspective* (pp. 37–61). Cambridge: Cambridge University Press.

Fischer, K., & Silvern, L. (1985). Stages and individual differences in cognitive development. *Annual Review of Psychology, 36,* 613–48.

Fish, M., & Feldman, S. (1987). Teacher and student verbal behavior in microcomputer classes: An observational study. *Journal of Classroom Interaction, 23,* 15–21.

Fisher, C., Berliner, D., Filby, N., Marliave, R., Cahen, L., & Dishaw, M. (1980). Teaching behaviors, academic learning time, and student achievement: An overview. In C. Denham & A. Lieberman (Eds.), *Time to learn.* Washington, DC: National Institute of Education.

Fiske, S., & Taylor, S. (1991). *Social cognition* (2nd ed.). New York: McGraw-Hill.

Fitch, S., & Adams, G. (1983). Ego identity and intimacy status: Replication and extension. *Developmental Psychology, 19,* 839–45.

Flavell, J. (1985). *Cognitive development* (2nd ed.). Englewood Cliffs, NJ: Prentice-Hall.

Flavell, J. (1992). Cognitive development: Past, present, and future. *Developmental Psychology, 28,* 998–1005.

Flavell, J., Beach, D., & Chinsky, J. (1966). Spontaneous verbal rehearsal in a memory task as a function of age. *Child Development, 37,* 283–99.

Flavell, J., Botkin, P., Fry, C., Wright, J., & Jarvis, P. (1968). *The development of role-taking and communication skills in children.* New York: Wiley.

Fleetwood, R., & Parish, T. (1976). Relationship between moral development test scores of juvenile delinquents and their inclusion in a moral dilemma discussion group. *Psychological Reports, 39,* 1075–80.

Fletcher, J., Hawley, D., & Piele, P. (1990). Costs, effects, and utility of microcomputer assisted instruction in the classroom. *American Educational Research Journal, 27,* 783–806.

Florio-Ruane, S., & Lensmire, T. (1989). The role of instruction in learning to write. In J. Brophy (Ed.), *Advances in research on teaching.* Vol. 1, *Teaching for meaningful understanding and self-regulated learning.* Greenwich, CT: JAI.

Fogarty, J., Wang, M., & Creek, R. (1983). A descriptive study of experienced and novice teachers' interactive instructional thoughts and actions. *Journal of Educational Research, 77,* 22–32.

Foley, D. (1991). Reconsidering anthropological explanations of ethnic school failure. *Anthropology and Education Quarterly, 22,* 60–86.

Follman, J., Lowe, A., & Miller, W. (1971). Graphics variables and reliability and level of essay grades. *American Educational Research Journal, 8,* 365–73.

Ford, M. (1986). A living systems conceptualization of social intelligence: Outcomes, processes, and developmental change. In R. Sternberg (Ed.), *Advances in the psychology of human intelligence* (Vol. 3, pp. 119–71). Hillsdale, NJ: Erlbaum.

Foster, W. (1981). Leadership: A conceptual framework for recognizing and educating. *Gifted Child Quarterly, 25,* 17–25.

Fox, D., & Kendall, P. (1983). Thinking through academic problems: Application of cognitive-behavior therapy to learning. In T. Kratochwill (Ed.), *Advances in school psychology* (Vol. 3). Hillsdale, NJ: Erlbaum.

Fraenkel, J. (1976). The Kohlberg bandwagon: Some reservations. *Social Education, 40,* 216–22.

Fraenkel, J. (1980). *Helping students think and value* (2nd ed.). Englewood Cliffs, NJ: Prentice-Hall.

Fraenkel, J. (1992). *A comparison of elite and non-elite social studies classrooms.* Paper presented at the annual meeting of the National Council for the Social Studies, November, Detroit.

Francis, E. (1975). Grade level and task difficulty in learning by discovery and verbal reception methods. *Journal of Educational Psychology, 67,* 146–50.

Frank, B. (1986). Cognitive styles and teacher education: Field dependence and areas of specialization among teacher education majors. *Journal of Educational Research, 80,* 19–22.

Frank, B., & Noble, J. (1985). Field independence—dependence and cognitive restructuring. *Journal of Personality and Social Psychology, 47,* 1129–35.

Frank, M. (1984). A comparison between an individual and group goal structure contingency that differed in the behavioral contingency and performance-outcome components. Unpublished doctoral dissertation, University of Minnesota, Minneapolis.

Frank, B., & Keene, D. (1993). The effect of learners' field independence, cognitive strategy instruction, and inherent word-list organization on free-recall memory and strategy use. *Journal of Experimental Education, 62,* 14–25.

Frasier, M. (1989). Identification of gifted black students: Developing new perspectives. In C. Maker & S. Schieber (Eds.), *Defensible programs for cultural and ethnic minorities* (Vol. 2, pp. 213–25). Austin, TX: Pro-Ed.

Frauenglass, M., & Diaz, R. (1985). Self-regulatory functions of children's private speech: A critical analysis of recent challenges to Vygotsky's theory. *Developmental Psychology, 21,* 356–64.

Frechtling, J. (1991). Performance assessment: Moonstruck or the real thing? *Educational Measurement: Issues and Practice,* 23–25.

Fredericksen, N. (1984). Implications of cognitive theory for instruction in problem solving. *Review of Educational Research, 54,* 363–407.

Freeman, D., Kuhs, T., Porter, A., Floden, R., Schmidt, W., & Schwille, J. (1983). Do textbooks and tests define a national curriculum in elementary school mathematics? *Elementary School Journal, 83,* 501–13.

Frey, K., & Ruble, D. (1985). What children say when the teacher is not around: Conflicting goals and social comparison and performance assessment in the classroom. *Journal of Personality and Social Psychology, 48,* 550–62.

Freyd, P., & Lytle, J. (1990). A corporate approach to the 2R's: A critique of IBM's Writing to Read program. *Educational Leadership, 47,* 83–89.

Friedman, L. (1989). Mathematics and the gender gap: A meta-analysis of recent studies on sex differences in mathematical tasks. *Review of Educational Research, 59,* 185–213.

Fuchs, D., Fuchs, L., & Fernstrom, P. (1992). Case-by-case reintegration of students with learning disabilities. *Elementary School Journal, 92,* 261–82.

Fuligni, A., & Eccles, J. (1993). Perceived parent-child relationships and early adolescents' orientation toward peers. *Developmental Psychology, 29,* 622–32.

Fuller, F. (1969). Concerns of teachers: A developmental conceptualization. *American Educational Research Journal, 6,* 207–226.

Furman, W., & McQuaid, E. (1992). Intervention programs for the management of conflict. In C. Shantz & W. Hartup (Eds.), *Conflict in child and adolescent development* (pp. 402–29). New York: Cambridge University Press.

Furst, E. (1981). Bloom's taxonomy of educational objectives for the cognitive domain: Philosophical and educational issues. *Review of Educational Research, 51,* 441–53.

Fuson, K. (1982). An analysis of the counting-on solution procedure in addition. In T. Carpenter, J. Moser, & T. Romberg (Eds.), *Addition and subtraction: A cognitive perspective.* Hillsdale, NJ: Erlbaum.

Fuson, K. (1988). *Children's counting and concepts of number.* New York: Springer-Verlag.

Gage, N. (Ed.). (1963). *Handbook of research on teaching.* Chicago: Rand McNally.

Gage, N., & Berliner, D. (1984). *Educational psychology* (3rd ed.). Boston: Houghton-Mifflin.

Gagné, E. (1985). *The cognitive psychology of school learning.* Boston: Little, Brown & Co.

Gagné, R., & Briggs, L. (1979). *Principles of instructional design* (2nd ed.). New York: Holt, Rinehart & Winston.

Gagné, R., Briggs, L., & Wager, W. (1988). *Principles of instructional design* (3rd ed.). New York: Holt, Rinehart & Winston.

Gagné, R., & Dick, W. (1983). Instructional psychology. In M. Rosenzweig & L. Porter (Eds.), *Annual review of psychology.* Palo Alto, CA: Annual Reviews.

Gagné, R., & Glaser, R. (1987). Foundations in learning research. In R. Gagné (Ed.), *Instructional technology: Foundations.* Hillsdale, NJ: Erlbaum.

Garbarino, J. (1992). *Children and families in the social environment* (2nd ed.). New York: Aldine De Gruyter.

Garbarino, J., Dubrow, N., Kostelny, K., & Pardo, C. (1992). *Children in danger: Coping with the consequences of community violence.* San Francisco: Jossey-Bass.

Garcia, E. (1992). Hispanic children: Theoretical, empirical, and related policy issues. *Educational Psychology Review, 4,* 69–93.

Garcia, R. (1991). *Teaching in a pluralistic society* (2nd ed.). New York: HarperCollins.

Gardner, H. (1983). *Frames of mind: The theory of multiple intelligences.* New York: Basic Books.

Gardner, H. (1988). Beyond the IQ: Education and human development. *National Forum, 68*(2), 4–7.

Gardner, H. (1991). *The unschooled mind: How children think and how schools should teach.* New York: Basic Books.

Garlinger, D., & Frank, B. (1986). Teacher-student cognitive style and academic achievement: A review and mini-meta-analysis. *Journal of Classroom Interaction, 21*(2), 2–8.

Garrett-Schau, C., & Scott, K. (1984). Impact of gender characteristics of instruction materials: An integration of the research literature. *Journal of Educational Psychology, 76,* 183–93.

Garton, A. (1992). *Social interaction and the development of language and cognition.* Hillsdale, NJ: Erlbaum.

Garwood, V. (1987). Audiology in the public school setting. In F. Martin (Ed.), *Hearing disorders in children* (pp. 427–467). Austin, TX: Pro-Ed.

Gearheart, B., & Weishahn, M. (1984). *The exceptional student in the regular classroom* (3rd ed.). St. Louis: Mosby.

Geiger, K., & Turiel, E. (1983). Disruptive school behavior and concepts of social convention in early adolescence. *Journal of Educational Psychology, 75,* 677–85.

Gelles, R. J., & Straus, M. A. (1987). Is violence toward children increasing? A comparison of 1975 and 1985 national survey rates. *Journal of Interpersonal Violence, 50,* 212–22.

Gelman, R., & Gallistel, C. (1986). *The child's understanding of number* (2nd ed.). Cambridge: Harvard University Press.

Gelman, S., & Byrnes, J. (Eds.) (1991). *Perspectives on language and thought: Interrelations in development.* New York: Cambridge University Press.

Gesell, A., & Thompson, H. (1929). Learning and growth in identical infant twins. *Genetic Psychology Monographs, 6,* 1–24.

Getzels, J., & Csikszentmihalyi, M. (1975). From problem solving to problem finding. In I. Taylor & J. Getzels (Eds.), *Perspectives in creativity.* Chicago: Aldine.

Getzels, J., & Jackson, P. (1962). *Creativity and intelligence: Explorations with gifted students.* New York: Wiley.

Gibbs, J. (1989). Black American adolescents. In J. Gibbs, L. Huang et al. (Eds.), *Children of color.* San Francisco: Jossey-Bass.

Gibson, S., & Dembo, M. (1984). Teacher efficacy: A construct validation. *Journal of Educational Psychology, 76,* 569–82.

Gilligan, C. (1982). *In a different voice.* Cambridge: Harvard University Press.

Gilligan, C. (1988) *Mapping the moral domain: A contribution of women's thinking to psychological theory and education.* Cambridge, MA: Harvard University Press.

Gilligan, C., Lyons, N., & Hammer, T. (Eds.). (1989). *Making connections: The relational worlds of adolescent girls at Emma Willard School.* Cambridge: Harvard University Press.

Gilligan, C., Murphy, J., & Tappan, M. (1990). Moral development beyond adolescence. In C. Alexander & E. Langer (Eds.), *Higher stages of human development: Perspectives on adult growth* (pp. 208–25). New York: Oxford University Press.

Gilligan, C., Ward, J., & Taylor, J. (Eds.). (1988). *Mapping the moral domain: A contribution of women's thinking to psychological theory and education.* Cambridge: Harvard University Press.

Gillingham, M., & Guthrie, J. (1987). Relationships between CBI and research on teaching. *Contemporary Educational Psychology, 12,* 189–99.

Ginsburg, H., & Opper, S. (1988). *Piaget's theory of intellectual development* (3rd ed.). Englewood Cliffs, NJ: Prentice-Hall.

Glaser, R. (1977). *Adaptive education: Individualized diversity and learning.* New York: Holt, Rinehart, & Winston.

Glaser, R. (1984). Education and thinking: The role of knowledge. *American Psychology, 39,* 93–104.

Glaser, R. (1986). Intelligence as acquired proficiency. In R. Sternberg & D. Detterman (Eds.), *What is intelligence? Contemporary viewpoints on its nature and definition* (pp. 77–84). Norwood, NJ: Ablex Publishing Corporation.

Glaser, R., & Bassok, M. (1989). Learning theory and the study of instruction. In M. Rosenzweig & L. Porter (Eds.), *Annual review of psychology* (Vol. 40, pp. 631–66). Palo Alto: Annual Reviews Inc.

Glasser, W. (1969). *Schools without failure.* New York: Harper & Row.

Glasser, W. (1977). Ten steps to good discipline. *Today's Education, 66*(4), November–December, 61–63.

Glenberg, A. (1976). Monotonic and nonmonotonic lag effects in paired-associated and recognition memory paradigms. *Journal of Verbal Learning and Verbal Behavior, 15,* 1–16.

Glover, J., & Bruning, R. (1990). *Educational psychology: Principles and applications* (3rd ed.). New York: HarperCollins.

Glover, J., & Corkill, A. (1987). Influence of paraphrased repetitions on the spacing effect. *Journal of Educational Psychology, 79,* 198–99.

Glover, J., Timme, V., Deyloff, D., & Rogers, M. (1987). Memory for student-performed tasks. *Journal of Educational Psychology, 79,* 445–52.

Glover, J., Ronning, R., & Reynolds, C. (Eds.). (1989). *Handbook of creativity.* New York: Plenum Press.

Glynn, S., Yeany, R., & Britton, B. (Eds.). (1991). *The psychology of learning science.* Hillsdale, NJ: Erlbaum.

Golden, N., Gersten, R., & Woodward, J. (1990). Effectiveness of guided practice during remedial reading instruction: An application of computer-managed instruction. *Elementary School Journal, 90,* 291–304.

Goldman, S. (1991). On the derivation of instructional applications from cognitive theories: Commentary on Chandler and Sweller. *Cognition and Instruction, 8,* 333–42.

Good, T., & Brophy, J. (1974). Changing teacher and student behavior: An empirical investigation. *Journal of Educational Psychology, 66,* 390–405.

Good, T., & Brophy, J. (1986). School effects. In M. C. Wittrock (Ed.), *Handbook of research on teaching* (3rd ed., pp. 570–604). New York: Macmillan.

Good, T., & Brophy, J. (1987). *Looking in classrooms* (4th ed.). New York: Harper & Row.

Good, T., & Brophy, J. (1994). *Looking in classrooms* (6th ed.). New York: Harper Collins.

Good, T., & Grouws, D. (1975). The Missouri Mathematics Project: An experimental study of fourth-grade classrooms. *Journal of Educational Psychology, 71,* 355–62.

Good, T., Grouws, D., & Ebmeier, H. (1983). *Active mathematics teaching.* New York: Longman.

Good, T., & Hinkel, G. (1982). *Schooling in America: Some descriptive and explanatory statements.* Paper prepared for the National Commission on Excellence in Education.

Good, T., McCaslin, M., & Reys, B. (1992). Investigating work groups to promote problem solving in mathematics. In J. Brophy (Ed.), *Advances in research on teaching.* Vol. 3, *Planning and managing learning tasks and activities* (pp. 115–60). Greenwich, CT: JAI Press.

Good, T., & Power, C. (1976). Designing successful classroom environments for different types of students. *Journal of Curriculum Studies, 8,* 1–16.

Good, T., Reys, B., Grouws, D., & Mulryan, C. (1989–90). Using work groups in mathematics instruction. *Educational Leadership, 47*(4), 56–62.

Good, T., & Stipek, D. (1984). Individual differences in the classroom: A psychological perspective. In G. Fenstermacher & J. Goodlad (Eds.), *1983 yearbook of the National Society for the Study of Education.* Chicago: University of Chicago Press.

Good, T., & Weinstein, R. (1986a). Schools make a difference: Evidence, criticism, and new directions. *American Psychologist, 41,* 1900–1907.

Good, T., & Weinstein, R. (1986b). Teacher expectations: A framework for exploring classrooms. In K. Zumwalt (Ed.), *Improving teaching* (pp. 63–86). Alexandria, VA: Association for Supervision and Curriculum Development.

Goodlad, J. (1984). *A place called school.* New York: McGraw-Hill.

Goodnow, J. (1986). A social view of intelligence. In R. Sternberg & D. Detterman (Eds.), *What is intelligence? Contemporary viewpoints on its nature and definition* (pp. 85–90). Norwood, NJ: Ablex Publishing Corporation.

Gordon, R., & Gross, R. (1978). An exploration of

the interconnecting perspective of teaching style and teacher education. *Curriculum Studies, 10,* 151–57.

Gordon, T. (1974). *T.E.T.: Teacher effectiveness training.* New York: McKay.

Gottfredson, D., Gottfredson, G., & Hybl, L. (1993). Managing adolescent behavior: A multi-year, multi-school study. *American Educational Research Journal, 30,* 179–215.

Gottfried, A. (Ed.). (1984). *Home environment and early cognitive development: Longitudinal research.* New York: Academic Press.

Grabe, M. (1985). Attributions in a mastery instructional system: Is an emphasis on effort harmful? *Contemporary Educational Psychology, 10,* 113–26.

Graham, S., & Harris, K. (1989). Components analysis of cognitive strategy instruction: Effects on learning disabled students' compositions and self-efficacy. *Journal of Educational Psychology, 81,* 353–61.

Graham, T., & Perry, M. (1993). Indexing transitional knowledge. *Developmental Psychology, 29,* 774–78.

Grant, L. (1984). Black females' "place" in desegregated classrooms. *Sociology of Education, 57,* 98–111.

Graves, T. (1983). *Writing: Teachers and children at work.* Exeter, NJ: Heinemann.

Green, J. (1975). *Teacher made tests* (2nd ed.). New York: Harper & Row.

Green, M. (1993). Gender, multiplicity, and voice. In S. Biklen & D. Pollard (Eds.), *Gender and education: 92nd yearbook of the National Society for the Study of Education* (pp. 241–55). Chicago: University of Chicago Press.

Greeno, J. (1980). Some examples of cognitive task analysis with instructional implications. In R. Snow, R. Federico, & W. Montague (Eds.), *Aptitude, learning, and instruction* (Vol. 2). Hillsdale, NJ: Erlbaum.

Greenwood, C. et al. (1992). Out of the laboratory and into the community: Twenty-six years of applied behavior analysis at the Juniper Gardens Children's Project. *American Psychologist, 47,* 1464–74.

Greer, A. (1993). New directions in identity research. *Contemporary Psychology, 38,* 1088–89.

Gregorc, A. (1982). *Gregorc style delineator:*

Development, technical, and administrative manual. Maynard, MA: Gabriel Systems.

Gregory, R. (1987). Intelligence based on knowledge—knowledge based on intelligence. In R. Gregory & P. Marstrand, *Creative intelligences* (pp. 2–8). London: Frances Pinter.

Grejda, G., & Hannafin, M. (1992). Effects of word processing on sixth graders' holistic writing and revisions. *Journal of Educational Research, 85,* 144–49.

Griffin, G., Barnes, S., Huges, R., O'Neal, S., Defino, M., Edwards, S., & Hukill, H. (1983). *Clinical preservice teacher education: Final report of a descriptive study* (Report No. 9025). Austin, TX: Research and Development Center for Teacher Education.

Griswold, P. (1984). Elementary students' attitudes during two years of computer-assisted instruction. *American Educational Research Journal, 21,* 329–43.

Groen, G., & Parkman, J. (1972). A chronometric analysis of simple addition. *Psychological Review, 79,* 329–43.

Groff, E., & Render, G. (1983). The effectiveness of three classroom teaching methods: Programmed instruction, simulation and guided fantasy. *Journal of the Society for Accelerative Learning and Teaching, 8,* 5–13.

Groisser, P. (1964). *How to use the fine art of questioning.* New York: Teachers' Practical Press.

Gronlund, N. (1985). *Stating objectives for classroom instruction* (3rd ed.). New York: Macmillan.

Gronlund, N. (1988). *How to construct achievement tests* (4th ed.). Englewood, NJ: Prentice Hall.

Gronlund, N. (1991). *How to write and use instructional objectives* (4th ed.). New York: Macmillan.

Gropper, G. (1983). A behavioral approach to instructional prescription. In C. Reigeluth (Ed.), *Instructional-design theories and models: An overview of their current status.* Hillsdale, NJ: Erlbaum.

Gropper, G. (1987). A lesson based on a behavioral approach to instructional design. In C. Reigeluth (Ed.), *Instructional theories in action: Lessons illustrating selected theories and models* (pp. 45–88). Hillsdale, NJ: Erlbaum.

Grotevant, H., & Cooper, C. (1985). Patterns of

interaction in family relationships and the development of identity exploration in adolescence. *Child Development, 56,* 415–28.

Grotevant, H., & Cooper, C. (Eds.). (1986). Individuation in family relationships. *Human Development, 29,* 83–100.

Grusec, J., Kuczynski, L., Rushton, J., & Simutis, Z. (1978). Modeling, direct instruction, and attributions: Effects on altruism. *Developmental Psychology, 14,* 51–57.

Guilford, J. (1959). Three faces of intellect. *American Psychologist, 14,* 469–79.

Guilford, J. (1967). *The nature of human intelligence.* New York: McGraw-Hill.

Gullickson, A. (1982). *The practice of testing in elementary and secondary schools.* Unpublished paper, University of South Dakota. (ERIC document Reproduction Service No. ED 229 391).

Guskey, T. (1985). *Implementing mastery learning.* Belmont, CA: Wadsworth.

Guskey, T., & Pigott, T. (1988). Research on group-based mastery learning programs: A meta-analysis. *Journal of Educational Research, 81,* 197–216.

Guskin, S., & Jones, R. (1982). Attitudes toward the handicapped. In H. Mitzel (Ed.), *Encyclopedia of educational research* (5th ed., pp. 189–93). New York: Free Press.

Hacker, A. (1992). *Two nations: Black and white, separate, hostile, unequal.* New York: Scribners.

Hains, A., & Miller, D. (1980). Moral and cognitive development in delinquent and nondelinquent children and adolescents. *Journal of Genetic Psychology, 137,* 21–35.

Haladyna, T., & Thomas, G. (1979). The attitudes of elementary school children toward school and subject matters. *Journal of Experimental Education, 48,* 18–23.

Hales, L., & Tokar, E. (1975). The effect of quality of preceding responses on the grades assigned to subsequent responses to an essay question. *Journal of Educational Measurement, 12,* 115–17.

Hall, R., & Sandler, R. (1984). *Out of the classroom: A chilly campus climate for women.* Washington, DC: Project on the Status and Education of Women, Association of American Colleges.

Hallahan, D., & Kauffman, J. (1991). *Exceptional children: Introduction to special education.* Englewood Cliffs, NJ: Prentice Hall.

Halpern, D. (1989). *Thought and knowledge: An introduction to critical thinking* (2nd ed.). Hillsdale, NJ: Erlbaum.

Halpern, D. (1993). Teaching thinking: An anecdotal, atheoretical, antiempirical approach. *Contemporary Psychology, 38,* 380–81.

Halpern, D., Hansen, C., & Riefer, D. (1990). Analogies as an aid to understanding and memory. *Journal of Educational Psychology, 82,* 298–305.

Hamilton, R. (1985). A framework for the evaluation of the effectiveness of adjunct questions and objectives. *Review of Educational Research, 55,* 47–85.

Hamilton, S. (1990). *Apprenticeship for adulthood: Preparing youth for the future.* New York: The Free Press.

Hand, B., & Treagust, D. (1991). Student achievement and science curriculum development using a constructive framework. *School Science and Mathematics, 91,* 172–76.

Hannah, E., & Pilner, S. (1983). Teacher attitudes toward handicapped students: A review and synthesis. *School Psychology Review, 12,* 12–25.

Hansen, J., & Pearson, P. (1983). An instructional study: Improving the inferential comprehension of fourth-grade good and poor readers. *Journal of Educational Psychology, 75,* 821–29.

Harber, J., & Bryen, D. (1976). Black English and the task of reading. *Review of Educational Research, 46,* 387–405.

Hargreaves, D., Hester, S., & Mellor, F. (1975). *Deviance in classrooms.* London: Routledge and Kegan Paul.

Harris, A., & Kapche, R. (1978). Problems of quality control in the development and the use of behavior change techniques in public school settings. *Education and the Treatment of Children, 1,* 43–51.

Harrow, A. (1972). *A taxonomy of the psychomotor domain.* New York: David McKay.

Harter, S. (1983). Developmental perspectives on the self-system. In P. Mussen (Ed.), *Handbook of child psychology* (4th ed., Vol. 4). New York: Wiley.

Harter, S. (1986). Cognitive-developmental processes in the integration of concepts about emotion and the self. *Social Cognition, 4,* 119–51.

Harter, S. (1990). Causes, correlates and the

functional role of global self-worth: A life-span perspective. In J. Kolligian & R. Sternberg (Eds.), *Perceptions of competence and incompetence across the life-span* (pp. 67–97). New Haven: Yale University Press.

Harter, S., & Monsour, A. (1992). Developmental analysis of conflict caused by opposing attributes in the adolescent self-portrait. *Developmental Psychology, 28,* 251–60.

Hartup, W. (1989). Social relationships and their significance. *American Psychologist, 44,* 120–26.

Hartup, W., & Rubin, Z. (1986). *Relationships and development.* Hillsdale, NJ: Erlbaum.

Hasher, L., & Zacks, R. (1984). Automatic processing of fundamental information: The case of frequency of occurrence. *American Psychologist, 39,* 1372–88.

Hativa, N., & Lesgold, A. (1991). The computer as a tutor—can it adapt to the individual learner? *Instructional Science, 20,* 49–78.

Hattie, J., & Rogers, H. (1986). Factor models for assessing the relation between creativity and intel-ligence. *Journal of Educational Psychology, 78,* 482–85.

Hauserman, N., Miller, J., & Bond, F. (1976). A behavioral approach to changing self-concept in elementary school children. *Psychological Record, 26,* 111–16.

Havighurst, R. (1972). *Developmental tasks and education* (3rd ed.). New York: David McKay.

Hayes, D. (1992). *A sourcebook of interactive methods for teaching with texts.* Boston: Allyn & Bacon.

Hayes, D., & Tierney, R. (1982). Developing readers' knowledge through analogy. *Reading Research Quarterly, 17,* 256–80.

Hayes, J. (1989). *The complete problem solver* (2nd ed.). Hillsdale, NJ: Erlbaum.

Hayes, S. (1993). Rule governance: Basic behavioral research and applied implications. *Current Directions in Psychological Science, 2,* 193–97.

Hayes, S. (Ed.). (1989). *Rule-governed behavior: Cognition, contingencies, and instructional control.* New York: Plenum.

Hayes, S., & Hayes, L. (Eds.). (1992). *Understanding verbal relations.* Reno: Context Press.

Haywood, H. C. (1992). Evaluation of instrumental enrichment in England. *Contemporary Psychology, 37,* 206–7.

Heath, S. (1983). *Ways with words.* New York: Cambridge University Press.

Heller, J., & Reif, F. (1984). Prescribing effective human problem-solving processes: Problem description in physics. *Cognition and Instruction, 1,* 177–216.

Henson, K. (1988). *Methods and strategies for teaching in secondary and middle schools.* New York: Longman.

Henze, R., & Lucas, T. (1993). Shaping instruction to promote the success of language minority students: An analysis of four high school classes. *Peabody Journal of Education, 69,* 54–81.

Hermann, G. (1969). Learning by discovery: A critical review of studies. *Journal of Experimental Education, 38,* 58–71.

Hess, R. (1970). Class and ethnic influences upon socialization. In P. Mussen (Ed.), *Carmichael's manual of child psychology* (3rd ed., Vol. 2). New York: Wiley.

Hess, R., Holloway, S., Dickson, W., & Price, G. (1984). Maternal variables as predictors of children's school readiness and later achievement in vocabulary and mathematics in sixth grade. *Child Development, 55,* 1902–12.

Hess, R., & McDevitt, T. (1984). Some cognitive consequences of maternal intervention techniques: A longitudinal study. *Child Development, 55,* 2017–3030.

Hess, R., & Shipman, V. (1965). Early experience and the socialization of cognitive modes in children. *Child Development, 34,* 869–86.

Hetherington, E. M., Reiss, D., & Plomin, R. (Eds.). (1993). *The separate social worlds of siblings: The impact of nonshared environment on development.* Hillsdale, NJ: Erlbaum.

Hewett, F., & Watson, P. (1979). Classroom management and the exceptional learner. In D. Duke (Ed.), *78th yearbook of the National Society for the Study of Education.* Part 2, *Classroom management.* Chicago: University of Chicago Press.

Hidi, S. (1990). Interest and its contribution as a mental resource for learning. *Review of Educational Research, 60,* 449–571.

Hiebert, E. (Ed.). (1991). *Literacy for a diverse society.* New York: Teachers College Press.

Hiebert, J., & Wearne, D. (1992). Links between teaching and learning place value with understanding in first grade. *Journal for Research in Mathematics Education, 23,* 98–122.

Hiebert, J., & Wearne, D. (1993). Instructional tasks,

classroom discourse, and students' learning in second-grade arithmetic. *American Educational Research Journal, 30,* 393–425.

Higgins, E. (1987). Self-discrepancy: A theory relating self and affect. *Psychological Review, 94,* 319–40.

Hill, K., & Wigfield, A. (1984). Test anxiety: A major educational problem and what can be done about it. *Elementary School Journal, 85,* 105–26.

Hobbs, S., Moguin, L., Tyroler, M., & Lahey, B. (1980). Cognitive behavior therapy with children: Has clinical utility been demonstrated? *Psychological Bulletin, 87,* 147–65.

Hoffman, M. (1979). Development of moral thought, feeling, and behavior. *American Psychologist, 34,* 958–66.

Hoffman, M. (1991). Empathy development, moral principles, and action. In W. Kurtines & J. Gewirtz (Eds.), *Handbook of moral behavior and development* (Vol. 1). Hillsdale, NJ: Erlbaum.

Hoffman, S. (1991). Introduction. *Elementary School Journal, 91*(3), 193–98.

Hogrebe, M., Nist, S., & Newman, I. (1985). Are there gender differences in reading achievement? An investigation using the High School and Beyond data. *Journal of Educational Psychology, 77,* 716–24.

Holt, J. (1964). *How children fail.* New York: Pitman.

Holyoak, K. & Spellman, B. (1993). Thinking. *Annual Review of Psychology, 44,* 265–315.

Honzik, M., McFarlane, J., & Allen, L. (1948). The stability of mental test performance between 2 and 18 years. *Journal of Experimental Psychology, 4,* 309–24.

Hooper, F., & DeFrain, J. (1980). On delineating distinctly Piagetian contributions to education. *Genetic Psychology Monographs, 101,* 151–81.

Hopkins, K., & Bracht, G. (1975). Ten-year stability of verbal and nonverbal IQ scores. *American Educational Research Journal, 12,* 469–77.

Horn, J. (1986). Intellectual ability concepts. In Sternberg, R. (Ed.), *Advances in the psychology of human intelligence.* Hillsdale, NJ: Erlbaum.

Horton, D., & Mills, C. (1984). Human learning and memory. In M. Rosenzweig, & L. Porter (Eds.), *Annual review of psychology.* Palo Alto, CA: Annual Reviews Inc.

Howe, C. (1993). *Language learning: A special case for developmental psychology?* Hillsdale, NJ: Erlbaum.

Howey, K., & Zimpher, N. (1989). The role of higher

education in initial year of teaching programs. *Elementary School Journal, 89*(4), 451–70.

Huang, L., & Yin, Y. (1989). Chinese-American children and adolescents. In J. Gibbs, L. Huang et al. (Eds.), *Children of color.* San Francisco: Jossey-Bass.

Huesmann, L., Eron, L., Lefkowitz, M., & Walder, L. (1984). Stability of aggression over time and generations. *Developmental Psychology, 20,* 1120–34.

Hughes, J. (1988). Cognitive behavior therapy with children in schools. Elmsford, NJ: Pergamon.

Hughes, J., & Hall, R. (Eds.). (1989). *Cognitive-behavioral psychology in the schools: A comprehensive handbook.* New York: Guilford.

Hunter, M. (1984). Knowing, teaching and supervising. In P. Hosford (Ed.), *Using what we know about reading.* Alexandria, VA: Association for Supervision and Curriculum Development.

Hyde, J. (1991). *Half the human experience: The psychology of women.* Lexington, MA: D. C. Heath.

Hyde, J., & Linn, M. (Eds.). (1986). *The psychology of gender: Advances through meta-analysis.* Baltimore: Johns Hopkins University Press.

Ianacone, R., & Stodden, R. (1987). Overview: Transition issues and directions for individuals who are mentally retarded. In R. Ianacone & R. Stodden (Eds.), *Transition issues and directions.* Reston, VA: Council for Exceptional Children.

Idol, L., Jones, B., & Mayer, R. (1991). Classroom instruction: The teaching of thinking. In L. Idol & B. Jones (Eds.), *Educational values and cognitive instruction: Implications for reform* (pp. 65–119). Hillsdale, NJ: Erlbaum.

Inhelder, B., Sinclair, H., & Bovet, M. (1974). *Learning and the development of cognition.* Cambridge: Harvard University Press.

Jackson, P. (1968). *Life in classrooms.* New York: Holt, Rinehart & Winston.

Jackson, P. (1986). *The practice of teaching.* New York: Teachers College Press.

Jamieson, I., Miller, A., & Watts, A. (1988). *Mirrors of work: Work simulations in schools.* New York: Falmer Press.

Jamison, D., Suppes, P., & Wells, S. (1974). The effectiveness of alternative instructional media: A survey. *Review of Educational Research, 44,* 1–68.

Jenkins, J. (1974). Remember that old theory of memory? Well, forget it! *American Psychologist, 29,* 785–95.

Jensen, A. (1969). How much can we boost IQ and scholastic achievement? *Harvard Educational Review, 39,* 1–123.

Jensen, A., & Figueroa, R. (1975). Forward and backward digit span interaction with race and IQ: Predictions from Jensen's theory. *Journal of Educational Psychology, 67,* 882–93.

Joffe, R. T., Offord, D. R., & Boyle, M. H. (1988). Ontario Child Health Study: Suicidal behavior in youth age 12–16 years. *American Journal of Psychiatry. 145,* 1420–23.

Johnson, D. (1976). Cross-cultural perspectives on sex differences in reading. *Reading Teacher, 29,* 747–52.

Johnson, D., & Johnson, R. (1975). *Learning together and alone.* Englewood Cliffs, NJ: Prentice-Hall.

Johnson, D., Johnson, R., Holubec, E., & Roy, P. (1984). *Circles of learning: Cooperation in the classroom.* Alexandria, VA: Association for Supervision and Curriculum Development.

Johnson, J., & Ruskin, R. (1977). *Behavioral instruction: An evaluative review.* Washington, DC: American Psychological Association.

Johnson, K., & Layng, T. (1992). Breaking the structuralist barrier: Literacy and numeracy with fluency. *American Psychologist, 47,* 1475–90.

Jones, B., Friedman, L., Tinzmann, M., & Cox, B. (1985). Guidelines for instruction-enriched mastery learning to improve comprehension. In D. Levine (Ed.), *Improving student achievement through mastery learning programs.* San Francisco: Jossey-Bass.

Jones, B., & Hall, J. (1982). School applications and the mnemonic keyword method as a study strategy by eighth graders. *Journal of Educational Psychology, 74,* 230–37.

Jones, B., & Idol, L. (Eds.). (1990). *Dimensions of thinking and cognitive instruction.* Hillsdale, NJ: Erlbaum.

Jones, B., Palincsar, A., Ogle, D., & Carr, E. (Eds.). (1987). *Strategic teaching and learning: Cognitive instruction in the content areas.* Alexandria, VA: Association for Supervision and Curriculum Development.

Jones, F. (1987). *Positive classroom discipline.* New York: McGraw-Hill.

Jones, L. (1979). The gentle art of classroom discipline. *National Elementary Principal, 58,* 26–32.

Kacerguis, M., & Adams, G. (1980). Erikson stage resolution: The relationship between identity and intimacy. *Journal of Youth and Adolescence, 9,* 117–26.

Kagan, D. (1992). Professional growth among preservice and beginning teachers. *Review of Educational Research, 62,* 129–69.

Kagan, J., & Kogan, N. (1970). Individual variation in cognitive processes. In P. Mussen (Ed.), *Carmichael's manual of child psychology* (3rd ed., Vol. 1). New York: Wiley.

Kagan, J., & Moss, H. (1962). *Birth to maturity: A study in psychological development.* New York: Wiley.

Kagan, J., Pearson, J., & Welch, L. (1966). Modifiability of an impulsive tempo. *Journal of Educational Psychology, 57,* 357–65.

Kagan, J., Rosman, B., Day, D., Albert, J., & Phillips, W. (1964). Information processing and the child: Significance of analytic and reflective attitudes. *Psychological Monographs, 78* (No. 1, whole number 578).

Kagan, S., & Knight, G. (1981). Social motives among Anglo-American and Mexican-American children. *Journal of Research in Personality, 15,* 93–106.

Kail, R. (1990). *The development of memory in children* (3rd ed.). San Francisco: Freeman.

Kamin, L. (1974). *The science and politics of IQ.* Potomac, MD: Erlbaum.

Kaufman, J., & Rosenbaum, J. (1992). *The education and employment of low-income black youth in white suburbs* (Vol. 14, pp. 229–40).

Keating, D., & Crane, L. (1990). Domain-general and domain-specific processes in proportional reasoning: A commentary on the Merrill-Palmer Quarterly. *Merrill-Palmer Quarterly, 36,* 411–24.

Keefe, J. (1982). Assessing student learning styles: An overview. In J. Keefe, *Student learning styles and brain behavior.* Reston, VA: National Association of Secondary School Principals.

Keefe, J., & Monk, J. (1986). *Learning-style profile examiner's manual.* Reston, VA: National Association of Secondary School Principals.

Keil, F. (1989). *Concepts, kinds, and cognitive development.* Cambridge: MIT Press.

Keller, F. (1968). Good-bye, teacher . . . ! *Journal of Applied Behavioral Analysis, 1,* 79–88.

Keller, F., and Sherman, J. (1982). *The PSI handbook: Essays on personalized instruction.* Lawrence, KS: TRI.

Keller, J. (1983). Motivational design of instruction. In C. Reigeluth (Ed.), *Instructional-design theories and models: An overview of their current status.* Hillsdale, NJ: Erlbaum.

Kember, D. (1991). Instructional design for meaningful learning. *Instructional Science, 20,* 289–310.

Kendall, P., & Braswell, L. (1985). *Cognitive-behavioral therapy for impulsive children.* New York: Guilford.

Kendler, H., & Kendler, T. (1962). Vertical and horizontal processes in problem solving. *Psychological Review, 69,* 1–16.

Kennedy, J. (1990). Determinants of peer social status: Contributions of physical appearance, reputation, and behavior. *Journal of Youth and Adolescence, 19,* 233–44.

Kiewra, K. (1987). Notetaking and review: The research and its implications. *Instructional Science, 16,* 233–49.

Kiewra, K., & Benton, S. (1988). The relationship between information-processing ability and notetaking. *Contemporary Educational Psychology, 13,* 33–44.

Kiewra, K., DuBois, N., Christian, D., McShane, A., Meyerhoffer, M., & Roskelley, D. (1991). Notetaking functions and techniques. *Journal of Educational Psychology, 83,* 240–45.

King, A. (1992a). Comparison of self-questioning, summarizing, and notetaking review as strategies for learning from lectures. *American Educational Research Journal, 29,* 303–23.

King, A. (1992b). Facilitating elaborative learning through guided student-generated questioning. *Educational Psychologist, 27,* 111–26.

Kintsch, W. (1974). *The representation of meaning in memory.* Hillsdale, NJ: Erlbaum.

Kintsch, W. (1977). *Memory and cognition.* New York: Wiley.

Kintsch, W., & Yarbrough, J. (1982). Role of rhetorical structure in text comprehension. *Journal of Educational Psychology, 74,* 828–34.

Kitano, M. (1989). Critique of "identification of gifted Asian-American students." In C. Maker & S. Schieber (Eds.), *Defensible programs for cultural and ethnic minorities* (Vol. 2, pp. 163–68). Austin, TX: Pro-Ed.

Kitchener, K. (1986). The reflective judgment model: Characteristics, evidence, and measurement. In R. Mines & K. Kitchener (Eds.), *Adult cognitive development: Methods and models* (pp. 76–91). New York: Praeger.

Kitchener, K., Lynch, C., Fischer, K., & Wood, P. (1993). Developmental range of reflective judgment: The effect of contextual support and practice on developmental stage. *Developmental Psychology, 29,* 893–906.

Klahr, D., & Wallace, J. (1976). *Cognitive development: An information-processing view.* Hillsdale, NJ: Erlbaum.

Klatzky, R. (1980). *Human memory* (2nd ed.). San Francisco: Freeman.

Klauer, K. (1984). Intentional and incidental learning with instructional texts: A meta-analysis for 1970–1980. *American Educational Research Journal, 21,* 232–339.

Klausmeier, H. (1990). Conceptualizing. In B. Jones & L. Idol (Eds.), *Dimensions of thinking and cognitive instruction* (pp. 93–138). Hillsdale, NJ: Erlbaum.

Klausmeier, H., Ghatala, E., & Frayer, D. (1974). *Conceptual learning and development.* New York: Academic Press.

Klein, G., & Hoffman, R. (1993). Seeing the invisible: Perceptual-cognitive aspects of expertise. In M. Rabinowtiz (Ed.), *Cognitive science foundations of instruction* (pp. 203–26). Hillsdale, NJ: Erlbaum.

Kleinfeld, J. (1975). Effective teachers of Indian and Eskimo students. *School Review, 83,* 301–44.

Klinger, E., & McNelly, F. (1976). Self states and performance of pre-adolescent boys carrying out leadership roles inconsistent with their social status. *Child Development, 47,* 126–37.

Klinzing, G., Klinzing-Eurich, G., & Tisher, R. (1985). Higher cognitive behaviours in classroom discourse: Congruencies between teachers' questions and pupils' responses. *Australian Journal of Education, 29,* 63–75.

Kloster, A., & Winne, P. (1989). The effects of different types of organizers on students' learning from text. *Journal of Educational Psychology, 81,* 9–15.

Knapp, M., & Shields, P. (Eds.). (1991). *Better schooling for the children of poverty: Alternatives to conventional wisdom.* Berkeley: McCutchan.

Kohlberg, L. (1966). A cognitive-developmental analysis of children's sex-role concepts and attitudes. In E. Maccoby (Ed.), *The development of sex differences.* Stanford, CA: Stanford University Press.

Kohlberg, L. (1969). Stage and sequence: The cognitive-developmental approach to socialization. In D. Goslin (Ed.), *Handbook of socialization theory and research.* Chicago: Rand McNally.

Kohlberg, L. (1984). *Essays on moral development.* Vol. 2, *The psychology of moral development.* San Francisco: Harper & Row.

Kohlberg, L., & Ryncarz, R. (1990). Beyond justice reasoning: Moral development and consideration of a seventh stage. In C. Alexander & E. Langer (Eds.), *Higher stages of human development: Perspectives on adult growth* (pp. 191–207). New York: Oxford University Press.

Kohlberg, L., Yeager, J., & Hjertholm, E. (1968). Private speech: Four studies and a review of theories. *Child Development, 39,* 691–736.

Kohlberg, L., & Zigler, E. (1967). The impact of cognitive maturity upon the development of sex-role attitudes in the years 4 to 8. *Genetic Psychology Monographs, 75,* 84–165.

Kohler, W. (1959). *The mentality of apes.* New York: Vintage.

Kolloff, P. (1983). The Center for Global Futures: Meeting the needs of gifted students in a laboratory school. *Roeper Review, 5*(3), 32–33.

Kounin, J. (1970). *Discipline and group management in classrooms.* New York: Holt, Rinehart & Winston.

Kounin, J., & Gump, P. (1974). Signal systems of lesson settings and the task-related behavior of preschool children. *Journal of Educational Psychology, 66,* 554–62.

Kourilsky, M., & Wittrock, M. (1992). Generative teaching: An enhancement strategy for the learning of economics in cooperative groups. *American Educational Research Journal, 29,* 861–76.

Kozol, J. (1991). *Savage inequalities: Children in America's schools.* New York: Crown Publishers.

Krajcik, J., Blumenfeld, P., Marx, R., & Soloway, E. (in press). Supporting innovation: A collaborative model for helping teachers learn project-based instruction. *Elementary School Journal.*

Krathwohl, D., Bloom, B., & Masia, B. (1964). *Taxonomy of educational objectives.* Handbook 2, *Affective domain.* New York: McKay.

Kroll, L. & Black, A. (1993). Developmental theory and teaching methods: A pilot study of a teacher education program. *Elementary School Journal, 93,* 417–41.

Krumboltz, J., & Krumboltz, H. (1972). *Changing children's behavior.* Englewood Cliffs, NJ: Prentice-Hall.

Kubiszyn, T., & Borich, G. (1984). *Educational testing and measurement.* Glenview, IL: Scott, Foresman.

Kubiszyn, T., & Borich, G. (1993). *Educational testing and measurement: classroom application and practice* (4th ed.) New York: Harper Collins.

Kubli, F. (1987). *Interesse und Verstehen in Physik und Chemie.* Cologne: Aulis-Verlag Deubner. Cited in A. Renninger, S. Hidi, & A. Krapp (Eds.), (1992), *The role of interest in learning and development* (Hillsdale, NJ: Erlbaum).

Kuczynski, L., & Kochanska, G. (1990). Development of children's noncompliance strategies from toddlerhood to age 5. *Developmental Psychology, 26,* 398–408.

Kuhn, D. (1974). Inducing development experimentally: Comments on a research paradigm. *Developmental Psychology, 10,* 590–600.

Kuhn, D. (1976). Short-term longitudinal evidence for the sequentiality of Kohlberg's early stages of moral judgment. *Developmental Psychology, 12,* 162–66.

Kuhn, D. (1979). The application of Piaget's theory of cognitive development to education. *Harvard Educational Review, 49,* 340–60.

Kulik, C., Kulik, J., & Bangert-Drowns, R. (1990). Effectiveness of mastery learning programs: A meta-analysis. *Review of Educational Research, 60,* 265–99.

Kunen, S., Cohen, R., & Solman, R. (1981). A levels-of-processing analysis of Bloom's taxonomy. *Journal of Educational Psychology, 73,* 202–11.

Kurtines, W., & Gerwitz, J. (Eds.). (1991). *Handbook of moral behavior and development* (3 vols.). Hillsdale, NJ: Erlbaum.

Kuykendall, C. (1992). *From rage to hope: Strategies for reclaiming Black and Hispanic students.* Bloomington, IN: National Education Service.

L'Abate, L., & Milan, M. (1985). *Handbook of social skills training and research.* New York: Wiley.

Laboratory of Comparative Human Cognition. (1983). Culture and cognitive development. In P. Mussen (Ed.), *Handbook of child psychology* (4th ed., Vol. 4). New York: Wiley.

Laboratory of Comparative Human Cognition. (1986). Contributions of cross-cultural research to educational practice. *American Psychologist, 41,* 1049–58.

Labov, W. (1972). *Language in the inner-city.* Philadelphia: University of Pennsylvania Press.

Labov, W. (1984). Stages in the acquisition of standard English. In R. Shuy (Ed.), *Social dialects and language learning.* Champaign, IL: National Council of Teachers of English.

Ladas, H. (1980). Summarizing research: A case study. *Review of Educational Research, 50,* 597–624.

Ladd, G., & Mize, J. (1983). A cognitive-social learning model of social skills training. *Psychological Review, 90,* 127–57.

LaFromboise, T., & Low, K. (1989). American Indian children and adolescents. In J. Gibbs, L. Huang et al. (Eds.), *Children of color.* San Francisco: Jossey-Bass.

Lakoff, G. (1987). *Women, fire, and dangerous things: What categories reveal about the mind.* Chicago: University of Chicago Press.

Lamborn, S., Mounts, N., Steinberg, L., & Dornsbusch, S. (1991). Patterns of competence and adjustment among adolescents from authoritative, authoritarian, indulgent, and neglectful families. *Child Development, 62,* 1049–65.

Lampert, M. (1989). Choosing and using mathematical tools in classroom discourse. In J. Brophy (Ed.), *Advances in research on teaching.* Vol. 1, *Teaching for meaningful understanding and self-regulated learning.* Greenwich, CT: JAI.

Lampert, M. (1990). When the problem is not the question and the solution is not the answer: Mathematical knowing and teaching. *American Educational Research Journal, 27,* 29–63.

Laosa, L. (1982). School, occupation, culture, and family: The impact of parental schooling on the parent-child relationship. *Journal of Educational Psychology, 74,* 791–827.

Lappan, G., & Ferrini-Mundy, J. (1993). Knowing and doing mathematics: A new vision for middle grades students. *Elementary School Journal, 93,* 625–41.

Larkin, J. (1981). Cognition of learning physics. *American Journal of Physics, 49,* 534–41.

Larrabee, M. (1992). *An ethic of care: Feminist and interdisciplinary perspectives.* New York: Routledge.

Larrivee, B. (1985). *Effective teaching for successful mainstreaming.* New York: Longman.

Latz, M. (1993). *The perceptions of experienced teachers concerning management and discipline.* Paper presented at the annual meeting of the American Educational Research Association, April, Atlanta, GA.

Laughlin, M., Hartoonian, H., & Sanders, N. (Eds.). (1989). *From information to decision making: New challenges for effective citizenship* (Bulletin No. 83). Washington, DC: National Council for the Social Studies.

Lave, J., & Wenger, E. (1991). *Situated learning: Legitimate peripheral participation.* Cambridge: Cambridge University Press.

Lawlor, J. (1982). *Computers in composition instruction.* Los Angeles: Southwest Regional Laboratory for Educational Research and Development.

Lazar, I., & Darlington, R. (1982). Lasting effects of early education. *Monographs of the Society for Research in Child Development, 47* (Nos. 2–3, Serial No. 195).

Lefcourt, H. (1966). Internal versus external control of reinforcement: A review. *Psychology Bulletin, 65,* 206–20.

Lehman, D., Lempert, R., & Nisbett, R. (1988). The effects of graduate training on reasoning: Formal discipline and thinking about everyday-life events. *American Psychologist, 43,* 431–42.

Lehrer, R., Guckenberg, T., & Lee, O. (1988). Comparative study of the cognitive consequences of inquiry-based Logo instruction. *Journal of Educational Psychology, 80,* 543–53.

Lehrer, R., & Randle, L. (1987). Problem solving, metacognition and composition: The effects of interactive software for first-grade children. *Journal of Educational Computing Research, 3,* 409–27.

Leinhardt, G. (1980). Transition rooms: Promoting maturation or reducing education? *Journal of Educational Psychology, 72,* 55–61.

Leinhardt, G. (1988). Situated knowledge and expertise in teaching. In J. Calderhead (Ed.), *Teachers' professional learning.* New York: Falmer.

Leinhardt, G., & Greeno, J. (1986). The cognitive skill of teaching. *Journal of Educational Psychology, 78,* 75–95.

Leinhardt, G., Seewald, A., & Engel, M. (1979). Learning what's taught: Sex differences in instruction. *Journal of Educational Psychology, 71,* 432–39.

Leinhardt, G., & Smith, D. (1984). *Expertise in mathematics instruction: Subject matter knowledge.* Paper presented at the annual meeting of the American Educational Research Association, April, New Orleans.

Leming, J. (1985). Research on social studies curriculum and instruction: Interventions and outcomes in the socio-moral domain. In W. Stanley (Ed.), *Review of research in social studies education: 1976–1983* (pp. 123–213). Washington, DC: National Council for the Social Studies.

Lepper, M. (1973). Dissonance, self-perception, and honesty in children. *Journal of Personality and Social Psychology, 25,* 65–74.

Lepper, M., & Chabay, R. (1985). Intrinsic motivation and instruction: Conflicting views on the role of motivational processes in computer-based education. *Educational Psychologist, 20*(4), 217–30.

Lepper, M., & Greene, D. (1978). *The hidden costs of reward: New perspectives on the psychology of human motivation.* Hillsdale, NJ: Erlbaum.

Lepper, M., & Gurtner, J. (1989). Children and computers: Approaching the twenty-first century. *American Psychologist, 44,* 170–78.

Lerner, R. (Ed.). (1993). *Early adolescence: Perspectives on research, policy, and intervention.* Hillsdale, NJ: Erlbaum.

Lesgold, A. (1986). Preparing children for a computer-rich world. *Educational Leadership, 43*(6), 7–11.

Levin, J. (1981). The mnemonic '80s: Keywords in the classroom. *Educational Psychologist, 16,* 65–82.

Levin, J., Schriberg, L., Miller, C., McCormick, C., & Levin, B. (1980). The keyword method in the classroom: How to remember the states and their capitols. *Elementary School Journal, 80,* 185–91.

Levine, D. (Ed.). (1985). *Improving student achievement through mastery learning programs.* San Francisco: Jossey-Bass.

Levitt, M., Guacci-Franco, N., & Levitt, J. (1993). Convoys of social support in childhood and early adolescence: Structure and function. *Developmental Psychology, 29,* 811–18.

Levstik, L. (1986). Teaching history: A definitional and developmental dilemma. In V. Atwood (Ed.), *Elementary school social studies: Research as guide to practice* (NCSS Bulletin No. 79, pp. 68–84). Washington, DC: National Council for the Social Studies.

Lewin, K., Lippitt, R., & White, R. (1939). Patterns of aggressive behavior in experimentally created social climates. *Journal of Social Psychology, 10,* 271–91.

Lewontin, R., Rose, S., & Kamin, L. (1984). *Biology, ideology, and human nature: Not in our genes.* New York: Pantheon Books.

Lickona, T. (Ed.). (1975). *Morality: A handbook of moral behavior.* New York: Holt, Rinehart & Winston.

Lickona, T. (1991). *Educating for character: How our schools can teach respect and responsibility.* New York: Bantam.

Lindsley, O. (1991). Precision teaching's unique legacy from B. F. Skinner. *Journal of Behavioral Education, 1,* 253–66.

Lindsley, O. (1992). Precision teaching. *Journal of Applied Behavior Analysis, 25,* 51–57.

Linn, M., & Hyde, J. (1989). Gender, mathematics, and science. *Educational Researcher, 18*(8), 17–27.

Linn, M., & Songer, N. (1991). Cognitive and conceptual change in adolescence. *American Journal of Education, 99,* 379–417.

Lipman, M. (1985). Thinking skills fostered by philosophy for children. In J. Segal, S. Chipman, & R. Glaser (Eds.), *Thinking and learning skills.* Vol. 1, *Relating instruction to research.* Hillsdale, NJ: Erlbaum.

Lipman, M., Sharp, A., & Oscanyan, F. (1980). *Philosophy in the classroom* (2nd ed.). Philadelphia: Temple University Press.

Lipson, J., & Fisher, K. (1983). Technology and the classroom: Promise or threat? *Theory into Practice, 22,* 253–59.

Lockwood, A. (1978). The effects of values clarification and moral development curricula on school-age subjects: A critical review of recent research. *Review of Educational Research, 48,* 325, 364.

Lockwood, A. (1991). Character education: The ten percent solution. *Social Education, 55,* 246–48.

Loehlin, J. (1992). *Genes and environment in personality development.* Thousand Oaks, CA: Sage.

Loftus, E., & Loftus, G. (1980). On the permanence of stored information in the human brain. *American Psychologist, 35,* 409–20.

Loftus, G., & Loftus E. (1976). *Human memory: The processing of information.* Hillsdale, NJ: Erlbaum.

Lohman, D. (1993). Teaching and testing to develop fluid abilities. *Educational Researcher, 22,* 12–23.

Loman, N., & Mayer, R. (1983). Signaling techniques that increase the understandability of expository prose. *Journal of Educational Psychology, 75,* 402–12.

Lorayne, H., & Lucas, J. (1974). *The memory book.* New York: Ballantine.

Lorch, R., Lorch, E., & Inman, W. (1993). Effects of signaling topic structure on text recall. *Journal of Educational Psychology, 85,* 281–90.

Lorch, R., Lorch, E., & Klusewitz, M. (1993). College students' conditional knowledge about reading. *Journal of Educational Psychology, 85,* 239–252.

Lucker, G., Rosenfield, D., Sikes, J., & Aronson, E. (1976). Performance in the interdependent classroom: A field study. *American Educational Research Journal, 13,* 115–23.

Lynch, M., Norem-Hebeisen, A., & Gergen, K. (1981). *Self-concept: Advances in theory and research.* Cambridge, MA: Ballinger.

Maccoby, E. (1980). *Social development: Psychological growth and the parent-child relationship.* New York: Harcourt, Brace & Jovanovich.

Maccoby, E. (1988). Gender as a social category. *Developmental Psychology, 26,* 755–65.

Maccoby, E. (1990). Gender and relationships: A developmental account. *American Psychologist, 45,* 513–20.

Maccoby, E. (1992). The role of parents in the socialization of children: An historical overview. *Developmental Psychology, 28,* 1006–17.

Maccoby, E., & Martin, J. (1983). Socialization in the context of the family: Parent-child interaction. In P. Mussen (Ed.), *Handbook of child psychology* (4th ed., Vol. 4). New York: Wiley.

Mace, F., Belfiore, P., & Shea, M. (1989). Operant theory and research on self-regulation. In B. Zimmerman & D. Schunk (Eds.), *Self-regulated learning and academic achievement* (pp. 27–50). New York: Springer-Verlag.

Mackie, D., & Hamilton, D. (Eds.). (1993). *Affect, cognition, and stereotyping.* San Diego, CA: Academic Press.

MacKinnon, D. (1962). The nature and nurture of creative talent. *American Psychologist, 17,* 484–95.

Macmillan, D., Keogh, B., & Jones, R. (1986). Special educational research on mildly handicapped learners. In M. Wittrock (Ed.), *Handbook of research on teaching* (3rd ed.). New York: Macmillan.

Madden, N., & Slavin, R. (1983). Mainstreaming students with mild handicaps: Academic and social outcomes. *Review of Educational Research, 53,* 519–69.

Maehr, M., & Midgeley, C. (1991). Enhancing student motivation: A school wide approach. *Educational Psychologist, 26,* 399–427.

Maeroff, G. (1991). Assessing alternative assessment. *Phi Delta Kappan, 73,* 273–81.

Mager, R. (1962). *Preparing instructional objectives.* Palo Alto, CA: Fearon.

Mager, R. (1993). *Preparing instructional objectives* (2nd ed.).Belmont, CA: Lake.

Maker, C., & Schieber, S. (Eds.) (1989). *Defensible programs for cultural and ethnic minorities* (Vol. 2). Austin, TX: Pro-Ed.

Malone, T., & Lepper M. (1987). Making learning fun: A taxonomy of intrinsic motivation for learning. In R. Snow & M. Farr (Eds.), *Aptitude, learning, and instruction.* Vol. 3, *Cognitive and affective process analysis.* Hillsdale, NJ: Erlbaum.

Manning, B. (1991). *Cognitive self-instruction for classroom processes.* Albany: State University of New York Press.

Mansfield, R., Busse, T., & Krepelka, E. (1978). The effectiveness of creativity training. *Review of Educational Research, 48,* 517–36.

Manske, M., & Davis, G. (1968). Effects of simple instructional biases upon performance in the unusual uses test. *Journal of General Psychology, 79,* 25–33.

Marcia, J. (1980). Identity in adolescence. In J. Adelson (Ed.), *Handbook of adolescent psychology.* New York: Wiley-Interscience.

Maria, K., & MacGinitie, W. (1987). Learning from texts that refute the readers' prior knowledge. *Reading Research and Instruction, 26,* 222–38.

Marshall, H. (1987). Motivational strategies of three fifth-grade teachers. *Elementary School Journal, 88,* 136–50.

Marshall, H. (1988). In pursuit of learning-oriented classrooms. *Teaching and Teacher Education, 4,* 85–98.

Marshall, S., & Smith, J. (1987). Sex differences in learning mathematics: A longitudinal study with item and error analyses. *Journal of Educational Psychology, 79,* 372–83.

Martens, B., & Kelly, S. (1993). A behavioral analysis of effective teaching. *School Psychology Quarterly, 8,* 10–26.

Martin, J. (1992). *The schoolhome.* Cambridge, MA: Harvard University Press.

Martin, J. (1993). Episodic memory: A neglected phenomenon in the psychology of education. *Educational Psychologist, 28*(2), 169–83.

Martorano, S. (1977). A developmental analysis of performance on Piaget's formal operational tasks. *Developmental Psychology, 13,* 666–72.

Martorella, P. (1989). *Interactive video and instruction.* Washington, DC: National Education Association.

Marx, R., & Winne, P. (1987). Students' perception of instruction, cognitive style, and achievement. *Perceptual and Motor Skills, 65* (1), 123–34.

Marzano, R., Brandt, R., & Hughes, C., Jones, B., Presseisen, B., Rankin, S., & Suhor, C. (1988). *Dimensions of thinking: A framework for curriculum and instruction.* Alexandria, VA: Association for Supervision and Curriculum Development.

Maslow, A. (1954). *Motivation and personality.* New York: Harper & Row.

Maslow, A. (1962). *Toward a psychology of being.* Princeton, NJ: Van Nostrand.

Mason, D., & Good, T. (1993). Effects of two-group and whole-class teaching. *American Educational Research Journal, 30,* 328–60.

Masters, J., Ford, M., Arend, R., Grotevant, H., & Clark, L. (1979). Modeling and labeling as integrated determinants of children's sex-typed imitative behavior. *Child Development, 50,* 364–71.

Matz, M. (1980). Towards a computational model of algebraic competence. *Journal of Mathematical Behavior, 3,* 93–166.

Mayer, R. (1975). Different problem-solving competencies established in learning computer programming with and without meaningful models. *Journal of Mathematical Behavior, 3,* 93–166.

Mayer, R. (1979a). Can advance organizers influence meaningful learning? *Review of Educational Research, 49,* 371–83.

Mayer, R. (1979b). Twenty years of research on advance organizers: Assimilation theory is still the best predictor of results. *Instructional Science, 8,* 133–67.

Mayer, R. (1981). Frequency norms and structural analysis of algebraic story problems into families, categories, and templates. *Instructional Science, 10,* 135–75.

Mayer, R. (1982). Learning. In H. Mitzel (Ed.), *Encyclopedia of educational research* (5th ed., Vol. 2). New York: The Free Press.

Mayer, R. (1983). *Thinking, problem solving, and cognition.* San Francisco: Freeman.

Mayer, R. (1984). Aids to text comprehension. *Educational Psychologist, 19,* 30–42.

Mayer, R. (1985). Instructional design theories: Building a linking science? *Contemporary Psychology, 30,* 156–57.

Mayer, R. (1987). *Educational psychology: A cognitive approach.* New York: HarperCollins.

Mayer, R. (1989a). Cognitive views of creativity. *Contemporary Educational Psychology, 14,* 203–11.

Mayer, R. (1989b). Models for understanding. *Review of Educational Research, 59,* 43–64.

Mayer, R., & Cook, L. (1981). Effects of shadowing on prose comprehension and problem solving. *Memory and Cognition, 9,* 101–9.

Mayer, R., Dyck, J., & Cook, L. (1984). Techniques that help readers build mental models from scientific text: Definitions pretraining and signaling. *Journal of Educational Psychology, 76,* 1089–1105.

McCabe, A., Siegel, L., Spence, I., & Wilkenson, A. (1982). Class-inclusion reasoning: Patterns of performance from three to eight years. *Child Development, 53,* 780–85.

McCaleb, J., & White, J. (1980). Critical dimensions in evaluating teacher clarity. *Journal of Classroom Interaction, 15,* 27–30.

McCall, R., Appelbaum, M., & Hogarty, P. (1973). *Developmental changes in mental performance.* Chicago: University of Chicago Press.

McCallum, R.S., & Bracken, B. (1993). Interpersonal relations between school children and their peers, parents, and teachers. *Educational Psychology Review, 5,* 155–76.

McCarthy, B. (1990). Using the four MAT system to bring learning styles to school. *Educational Leadership, 48,* 31–37.

McCaslin, M. (1990). Motivated literacy. In J. Zutell & S. McCormick (Eds.), *Thirty-ninth yearbook of the National Reading Conference (NRC): Literacy theory and research: Analysis from multiple perspectives.* Chicago: NRC.

McCaslin, M., & Good, T. (1992). Compliant cognition: The misalliance of management and instructional goals in current school reform. *Educational Researcher, 21,* 4–17.

McCaslin, M., & Good, T. (in press, a). The informal curriculum. In R. Calfee & D. Berliner, *Handbook of educational psychology.*

McCaslin, M., & Good, T. (in press, b). *Listening to students.* New York: Harper Collins.

McCaslin, M., & Murdock, T. (1991). The emergent interaction of home and school in the development of students' adaptive learning (pp. 213–59). In M. Maehr & P. Pintrich (Eds.), *Advances in motivation and achievement* (Vol. 7, pp. 213–59). Greenwich, CT: JAI Press.

McCaslin Rohrkemper, M. (1989). Self-regulated learning and academic achievement: A Vygotskian view. In B. Zimmerman & D. Schunk (Eds.), *Self-regulated learning and academic achievement* (pp. 143–68). New York: Springer-Verlag.

McClelland, J., & Rumelhart, D. (1988). *Explorations in parallel distributed processing: A handbook of models, programs, and exercises.* Cambridge: MIT Press.

McCombs, B. (1984). Processes and skills underlying continuing intrinsic motivation to learn: Toward a definition of motivational skills training and intervention. *Educational Psychologist, 19,* 199–218.

McConkie, G. (1977). Learning from text. In L. Shulman (Ed.), *Review of research in education* (Vol. 5). Itasca, IL: Peacock.

McCormack, S. (1989). Response to Render, Padilla, and Krank: But practitioners say it works. *Educational Leadership, 47,* 77–79.

McCormick, C., & Levin, J. (1984). A comparison of different prose-learning variations of the mnemonic keyword method. *American Educational Research Journal, 21,* 379–98.

McDaniel, M., & Pressley, M. (1984). Putting the keyword method in context. *Journal of Educational Psychology, 76,* 598–609.

McDaniel, M., & Pressley, M. (1989). Keyword and context instruction of new vocabulary meanings: Effects on text comprehension and memory. *Journal of Educational Psychology, 81,* 204–13.

McDaniel, T. (1989). The discipline debate: A road through the thicket. *Educational Leadership, 47,* 81–82.

McDiarmid, G. (1992). What to do about differences? A study of multicultural education for teacher trainees in the Los Angeles Unified School District. *Journal of Teacher Education, 43,* 83–93.

McGeoch, J., & McDonald, W. (1931). Meaningful relation and retroactive inhibition. *American Journal of Psychology, 43,* 579–88.

McGuire, K., & Weisz, J. (1982). Social cognition and behavior correlates of preadolescent chumship. *Child Development, 53,* 1478–84.

McKenzie, G. (1986). Learning and instruction. In V. Atwood (Ed.), *Elementary school social studies: Research as guide to practice* (NCSS Bulletin No. 79, pp. 119–36). Washington, DC: National Council for the Social Studies.

McLaughlin, T. (1976). Self-control in the classroom. *Review of Educational Research, 46,* 631–63.

McLeish, J. (1976). The lecture method. In N. Gage (Ed.), *75th yearbook of the National Society for the Study of Education.* Part 1, *The psychology of teaching methods.* Chicago: University of Chicago Press.

McNamee, S. (1978). Moral behavior, moral development and motivation. *Journal of Moral Education, 7,* 27–31.

Medin, D. (1989). Concepts and conceptual structure. *American Psychologist, 44,* 1469–81.

Mednick, M. (1989). On the politics of psychological constructs: Stop the bandwagon, I want to get off. *American Psychologist, 44,* 1118–23.

Meers, G. (1992). Getting ready for the next century: Vocational preparation of students with disabilities. *Teaching Exceptional Children, 24,* 36–39.

Mehrens, W., & Lehmann, I. (1978). *Measurement and evaluation in education and psychology* (2nd ed.). New York: Holt, Rinehart & Winston.

Meichenbaum, D. (1977). *Cognitive-behavior modification.* New York: Plenum.

Meichenbaum, D., & Asarnow, J. (1979). Cognitive-behavioral modification and metacognitive development: Implications for the classroom. In P. Kendall & S. Hollon (Eds.), *Cognitive-behavioral intervention: Theory, research, and procedures.* New York: Academic Press.

Meichenbaum, D., & Goodman, J. (1971). Training impulsive children to talk to themselves: A means of developing self-control. *Journal of Abnormal Psychology, 77,* 115–26.

Meng, K., & Patty, D. (1991). Field-dependency and contextual organizers. *Journal of Educational Research, 84,* 183–89.

Mergendoller, J. (Guest Ed.). (1993). Middle grades research and reform [Special Issue]. *Elementary School Journal, 93,* 443–658.

Merino, B., & Samaniego, F. (in press). Language acquisition theory and classroom practices in the teaching of Spanish to the native Spanish speaker. In B. Merino, H. Trudean, and F. Samaniego (Eds.), *Culture and language in the teaching of Spanish to native Spanish speakers.* London: Falmer Press.

Merino, B., Samaniego, F., Trueba, H., Castañeda, E., & Chaudry, L. (1993). Language minority native Spanish speakers at the secondary level and the role of the foreign language teacher. *Peabody Journal of Education, 69,* 152–71.

Merrill, M., Li, Z., & Jones, M. (1990). Second generation instructional design. *Educational Technology, 30*(2), 7–14.

Merrill, M., & Tennyson, R. (1977). *Concept teaching: An instructional design guide.* Englewood Cliffs, NJ: Educational Technology.

Messer, S. (1972). The relation of internal-external control to academic performance. *Child Development, 43,* 1456–62.

Messick, S. (1984). Assessment in context: Appraising student performance in relation to instructional quality. *Educational Researcher, 13,* 3–8.

Metcalf, L. (Ed.). (1971). *Values education: Rationale, strategies, and procedures.* Washington, DC: National Council for the Social Studies.

Metz, M. (1978). *Classrooms and corridors: The crisis of authority in desegregated secondary schools.* Berkeley: University of California Press.

Meyer, B. (1977). The structure of prose: Effects of learning and memory implications for educational practice. In R. Anderson, R. Spiro, & W. Montague (Eds.), *Schooling and the acquisition of knowledge.* Hillsdale, NJ: Erlbaum.

Meyer, B. (1981). Basic research on prose comprehension: A critical review. In D. Fisher & C. Peters (Eds.), *Comprehension and the competent reader.* New York: Praeger.

Miller, D., & Kelley, M. (1991). Interventions for improving homework performance: A critical review. *School Psychology Quarterly, 6,* 174–85.

Miller G. (1956). The magical number seven, plus or minus two: Some limits on our capacity for processing information. *Psychological Review, 63,* 81–87.

Miller, G., & Emihovich, C. (1986). The effects of mediated programming instruction on preschool children's self-monitoring. *Journal of Educational Computing Research, 2,* 283–97.

Miller, L., & Bizzell, R. (1983). Long-term effects of four preschool programs: Sixth, seventh, and eighth grades. *Child Development, 54,* 727–41.

Miller, R., Brickman, P., & Bolen, D. (1975). Attribution versus persuasion as a means for modifying behavior. *Journal of Personality and Social Psychology, 31,* 430–41.

Miller, R., Kelly, G., & Kelly, J. (1988). Effects of logo computer programming experience on problem solving and spatial relations ability. *Contemporary Educational Psychology, 13,* 348–57.

Miller, S. (1986). Certainty and necessity in the understanding of Piagetian concepts. *Developmental Psychology, 22,* 3–18.

Miller, S., Brownell, C., Zukier, H. (1977). Cognitive certainty in children: Effects of concept, developmental level, and method of assessment. *Developmental Psychology, 13,* 236–45.

Minicucci, C., & Olsen, L. (1992). *Programs for secondary limited English proficient students: A California study.* Washington, DC: National Clearing House for Bilingual Education.

Minnesota State Department of Education. (1991). *Introduction to education that is outcome-based.* St. Paul: State of Minnesota Printing Office.

Minsky, M. (1975). A framework for representing knowledge. In P. Winston (Ed.), *The psychology of computer vision.* New York: McGraw-Hill.

Minstrell, J. (1989). Teaching science for understanding. In L. Resnick & L. Klopfer (Eds.), *1989 yearbook of the Association for Supervision and Curriculum Development, Toward the thinking curriculum: Current cognitive research.* Alexandria, VA: Association for Supervision and Curriculum Development.

Mitchell, R. (1992). *Testing for learning.* New York: The Free Press.

Mitzel, H. (Ed.). (1982). *Encyclopedia of educational research* (5th ed.). New York: Macmillan.

Modgil, S., & Modgil, C. (Eds.). (1982). *Jean Piaget: Consensus and controversy.* New York: Praeger.

Moessinger, P. (1978). Piaget on equilibration. *Human Development, 21,* 255–67.

Moll, L. (Ed.). (1990). *Vygotsky and education: Instructional implications and applications of sociohistorical psychology.* Cambridge: Cambridge University Press.

Moll, L. (1992). Bilingual classroom studies and community analysis. *Educational Researcher, 21,* 20–24.

Moore, L., & Carnine, D. (1989). Evaluating curriculum design in the context of active teaching. *Remedial Special Education, 10,* 28–37.

Moos, R., & Moos, B. (1978). Classroom social climate and student absences and grades. *Journal of Educational Psychology, 70,* 263–69.

Morse, W. (1971). Worksheet on life space interviewing for teachers. In N. Long, W. Morse, & R. Newman (Eds.), *Conflict in the classroom: The education of children with problems* (2nd ed.). Belmont, CA: Wadsworth.

Mosher, R. (Ed.). (1980). *Moral education: A first generation of research and development.* New York: Praeger.

Moskowitz, G., & Hayman, J. (1976). Success strategies of inner-city teachers: A year-long study. *Journal of Educational Research, 69,* 283–89.

Mueller, C., & Parcel, T. (1981). Measures of socioeconomic status: Alternatives and recommendations. *Child Development, 52,* 13–30.

Mulryan, C. (1992). Student passivity during cooperative small groups in mathematics. *Journal of Educational Research, 85,* 261–73.

Murray, D. M., Perry, C. L., O'Connell, C., & Schmid, L. (1987). Seventh-grade cigarette, alcohol and marijuana use. *The International Journal of the Addictions, 22,* 357–76.

Murray, E. (1964). *Motivation and emotion.* New York: Prentice-Hall.

Murray, F. (1978). Teaching strategies and conservation training. In A. Lesgold, J. Pellegrino, S. Fokkema, & R. Glaser (Eds.), *Cognitive psychology and instruction.* New York: Plenum.

Murray, F., Ames, G., & Botvin, G. (1977). Acquisition of conservation through cognitive dissonance. *Journal of Educational Psychology, 69,* 519–27.

Murray, H. (1938). *Explorations in personality.* New York: Oxford University Press.

Muth, K. D., Glynn, S., Britton, B., & Graves, M. (1988). Thinking out loud while studying text: Rehearsing key ideas. *Journal of Educational Psychology, 80,* 315–18.

Myers, R., & Torrance, E. (1966). *Plots, puzzles, and ploys.* Boston: Ginn.

Nagata, D. (1989). Japanese-American children and adolescents. In J. Gibbs, L. Huang et al. (Eds.), *Children of color.* San Francisco: Jossey-Bass.

Nagy, P., & Griffiths, A. (1982). Limitations of recent research relating Piaget's theory to adolescent thought. *Review of Educational Research, 52,* 513–56.

Nash, R. (1976). Pupils' expectations of their teachers. In M. Stubbs & S. Delamont (Eds.), *Explorations in classroom observation.* New York: Wiley.

National Association for the Education of Young Children. (1991). Guidelines for appropriate curriculum content and assessment in programs serving children ages 3 through 8. *Young Children, 46*(3), 21–38.

National Council of Teachers of Mathematics. (1989). *Curriculum and evaluation standards for school mathematics.* Reston, VA: Author.

Natriello, G. (1992). Marking systems. In M. Alkin (Ed.), *Encyclopedia of educational research* (6th ed., Vol. 3, pp. 772–75). New York: Macmillan.

Natriello, G., & Dornbusch, S. (1985). *Teacher evaluation standard and student effort.* New York: Longman.

Natriello, G., McDill, E., & Pallas, A. (1990). *Schooling disadvantaged children: Racing against catastrophe.* New York: Teachers College Press.

Neale, D., & Johnson, V. (1993). *The development of teachers' theories of classroom management and control.* Paper presented at the annual meeting of the American Educational Research Association, April, Atlanta, GA.

Neale, D., Smith, D., & Johnson, V. (1990). Implementing conceptual change teaching in primary science. *Elementary School Journal, 91,* 109–31.

Neimark, E. (1987). *Adventures in thinking.* San Diego: Harcourt Brace Jovanovich.

Neimark, E., & Santa, J. (1975). Thinking and concept attainment. In M. Rosenzweig & L. Porter (Eds.), *Annual review of psychology* (Vol. 26). Palo Alto, CA: Annual Reviews.

Nelson, L., & Kagan, S. (1972). Competition: The star-spangled scramble. *Psychology Today,* September, pp. 53–56, 90–91.

Newell, K. (1991). Motor skill acquisition. In M. Rosenzweig & L. Porter (Eds.), *Annual review of psychology* (Vol. 42, pp. 213–37). Palo Alto, CA: Annual Reviews Inc.

Newell, K., & Simon, H. (1972). *Human problem solving.* Englewood Cliffs, NJ: Prentice-Hall.

Newman, C., & Smolen, L. (1993). Portfolio assessment in our schools: Implementation, advantages, and concerns. *Mid-Western Educational Researcher, 6,* 28–32.

Newman, D., Griffin, P., & Cole, M. (1989). *The construction zone: Working for cognitive change in school.* Cambridge: Cambridge University Press.

Newmann, F. (1990). Qualities of thoughtful social studies classes: An empirical profile. *Journal of Curriculum Studies, 22,* 253–75.

Newmann, F. (1992). *Student engagement and achievement in American secondary schools.* New York: Teachers College Press.

Ney, J., & Pearson, B. (1990). Connectionism as a model of language learning: Parallels in foreign language teaching. *Modern Language Journal, 74,* 474–82.

Nicholls, J. (1984). Achievement motivation: Concepts of ability, subjective experience, task choice, and performance. *Psychological Review, 91,* 328–46.

Nicholson, T. (1984). Experts and novices: A study of reading in the high school classroom. *Reading Research Quarterly, 19,* 436–51.

Nickerson, R., Perkins, D., & Smith, E. (1985). *The teaching of thinking.* Hillsdale, NJ: Erlbaum.

Nieto, S. (1992). *Affirming diversity: The sociopolitical context of multicultural education.* White Plains, NY: Longman.

Noddings, N. (1984). *Caring: A feminine approach to ethics and moral education.* Berkeley: University of California Press.

Noddings, N. (1990). Feminist critiques in the profession. In C. Cazden (Ed.), *Review of research in education* (Vol. 16, pp. 393–424). Washington, DC: AERA.

Noddings, N. (1992). *The challenge to care in schools.* New York: Teachers College Press.

Nosofsky, R. (1988). Similarity, frequency, and category representations. *Journal of Experimental Psychology: Learning, Memory, and Cognition, 14,* 54–65.

Novak, J. (Ed.). (1987). *Proceedings of the second international seminar on misconceptions and educational strategies in science and mathematics* (Vol. 2). Ithaca, NY: Cornell University.

Novak, J., & Gowin, D. (1984). *Learning how to learn.* New York: Cambridge University Press.

Nucci, L. (1987). Synthesis of research on moral development. *Educational Leadership, 44*(5), 86–92.

Nucci, L. (Ed.). (1989). *Moral development and character education: A dialogue.* Berkeley, CA: McCutchan.

Nye, R. (1992). *The legacy of B. F. Skinner: Concepts and perspectives, controversies and misunderstandings.* Pacific Grove, CA: Brooks/Cole.

Oakes, J. (1990). Opportunities, achievement, and choice: Women and minority students in science and mathematics. In C. Cazden (Ed.), *Review of research in education* (Vol. 16, pp. 153–222). Washington, DC: AERA.

Oakland, T. (Ed.). (1977). *Psychological and educational assessment of minority children.* New York: Brunner-Mazel.

Offord, D. R., Boyle, M. H., Fleming, J. E., Blum, H. M., & Grant, N. R. (1989). Ontario Child Health Study: Summary of selected results. *Canadian Journal of Psychiatry, 34,* 483–91.

Ogbu, J. (1978). *Minority education and caste.* New York: Academic Press.

Ogbu, J. (1988). Human intelligence testing: A cultural-ecological perspective. *National Forum, 68,* 23–29.

Ogbu, J. (1992a). Adaptation to minority status and impact on school success. *Theory into Practice, 31,* 287–95.

Ogbu, J. (1992b). Understanding cultural diversity and learning. *Educational Researcher, 21*(8), 5–14.

Ogbu, J., & Gibson, M. (Eds.). (1991). *Minority status and schooling: A comparative study of immigrant and involuntary minorities.* New York: Garland.

Ohlsson, S. (1983). The enaction theory of thinking

and its educational implications. *Scandinavian Journal of Educational Research, 27,* 73–88.

O'Leary, K, & O'Leary, S. (Eds.). (1977). *Classroom management: The successful use of behavior modification* (2nd ed.). New York: Pergamon.

O'Leary, S., & Dubey, D. (1979). Applications of self-control procedures by children: A review. *Journal of Applied Behavior Analysis, 12,* 449–65.

Olejnik, A. (1980). Adults' moral reasoning with children. *Child Development, 51,* 1285–88.

Oliner, P. (1983). Putting "community" into citizenship education: The need for prosociality. *Theory and Research in Social Education, 11*(2), 65–81.

O'Neil, H. (Ed.). (1978). *Learning strategies.* New York: Academic Press.

O'Neil, H., & Spielberger, D. (Eds.). (1979). *Cognitive and affective learning strategies.* New York: Academic Press.

O'Neil, J. (1990). Making sense of style. *Educational Leadership, 48,* 4–9.

O'Neill, B. (1994, March 6). The history of a hoax. *The New York Times Magazine,* pp. 46–49.

Orlofsky, J. (1976). Intimacy status: Relationship to interpersonal perception. *Journal of Youth and Adolescence, 5,* 73–83.

Orlofsky, J., & Ginsburg, S. (1981). Intimacy status: Relationship to affect cognition. *Adolescence, 16,* 91–100.

Orlofsky, J., Marcia, J., & Lesser, I. (1973). Ego identity states and the intimacy vs. isolation crisis of young adulthood. *Journal of Youth and Adolescence, 27,* 211–19.

Osborn, J. (1984). Workbooks that accompany basal reading programs. In G. Duffy, L. Roehler, & J. Mason (Eds.), *Comprehension instruction: Perspectives and suggestions.* New York: Longman.

Owen, S., Blount, H., & Moscow, H. (1978). *Educational psychology: An introduction.* Boston: Little, Brown & Co.

Pajares, M. (1992). Teachers' beliefs in educational research: Cleaning up a messy construct. *Review of Educational Research, 62,* 307–32.

Palincsar, A. (1986). Metacognitive strategy instruction. *Exceptional Children, 53*(2), 118–124.

Palincsar, A., Anderson, C., & David, Y. (1993). Pursuing scientific literacy in the middle grades through collaborative problem solving. *Elementary School Journal, 93,* 643–58.

Palincsar, A., & Brown, A. (1984). Reciprocal teaching of comprehension-fostering and comprehension-monitoring activities. *Cognition and Instruction, 1,* 117–75.

Palincsar, A., & Brown, A. (1987). Advances in improving the cognitive performance of handicapped students. In M. Wang, M. Reynolds, & H. Walberg (Eds.), *Handbook of special education: Research in practice* (Vol. 1, pp. 93–112). Oxford: Pergamon.

Palincsar, A., & Brown, A. (1989). Classroom dialogues to promote self-regulated comprehension. In J. Brophy (Ed.), *Advances in research on teaching.* Vol. 1, *Teaching for meaningful understanding and self-regulated learning.* Greenwich, CT: JAI.

Papert, S. (1980). *Mindstorms: Children, computers, and powerful ideas.* New York: Basic Books.

Paris, S., Cross., D., & Lipson, M. (1984). Informed Strategies for Learning: A program to improve children's reading awareness and comprehension. *Journal of Educational Psychology, 76,* 1239–52.

Paris, S., Lipson, M., & Wixson, K. (1983). Becoming a stragetic reader. *Contemporary Educational Psychology, 8,* 293–316.

Paris, S., & Oka, E. (1986). Self-regulated learning among exceptional children. *Exceptional children, 53,* 103–8.

Paris, S., Wasik, B., & Turner, J. (1991). The development of strategic readers. In R. Barr, M. Kamil, P. Mosenthal, & P. Pearson (Eds.), *Handbook of reading research* (Vol. 2, pp. 609–40). New York: Longman.

Parker, J., & Asher, S. (1987). Peer relations and later personal adjustment: Are low accepted children at risk? *Psychological Bulletin, 102,* 357–89.

Parnes, S. (1967). *Creative behavior guidebook.* New York: Scribner's.

Parnes, S. (1987). The creative studies project. In S. Isaksen (Ed.), *Frontiers of creativity research* (pp. 156–88). Buffalo, NY: Bearly Limited.

Pask, G., & Scott, B. (1972). Learning strategies and individual competence. *International Journal of Man-Machine Studies, 4,* 217–53.

Pask, G., & Scott. B. (1973). CASTE: A system for exhibiting learning strategies and regulating uncertainties. *International Journal of Man-Machine Studies, 5,* 17–52.

Patterson, C., Kupersmidt, J., & Griesler, P. (1990). Children's perceptions of self and of relationships with others a a function of sociometric status. *Child Development, 61,* 1335–49.

Patterson, G., & Stouthamer-Loeber, M. (1984). The correlation of family management practices and delinquency. *Child Development, 55,* 1299–1307.

Pavlov, I. (1927). *Conditional reflexes.* London: Oxford University Press.

Pea, R., Kurland, D., & Hawkins, J. (1985). LOGO and the development of thinking skills. In M. Chen & W. Paisley (Eds.), *Children and microcomputers* (pp. 193–212). Beverly Hills, CA: Sage.

Pearson, P., & Dole, J. A. (1987). Explicit comprehension instruction: A review of research and a new conceptualization of instruction. *Elementary School Journal, 88,* 151–65.

Pease-Albarez, L., & Hakuta, K. (1992). Enriching our views of bilingualism and bilingual education. *Educational Researcher, 21,* 4–7.

Pellegrini, A. (1982). The effects of exploration training on young children's associative fluency. *Creative Child and Adult Quarterly, 7,* 226–33.

Peréz, B. (1993). Biliteracy practices and issues in secondary schools. *Peabody Journal of Education, 69,* 117–135.

Perkins, D., & Salomon, G. (1987). Transfer and teaching thinking. In D. Perkins, J. Lockhead, & J. Bishop (Eds.), *Thinking: The second international conference* (pp. 285–303). Hillsdale, NJ: Erlbaum.

Perry, W. (1981). Cognitive and ethical growth: The making of meaning. In A. Chickering (Ed.), *The modern American college* (pp. 76–116). San Francisco: Jossey-Bass.

Petersen, A., & Epstein, J. (Eds.). (1991). Development and education across adolescence [Special Issue]. *American Journal of Education, 99,* 373–657.

Peterson, P. (1988). Selecting students and services for compensatory education: Lessons from aptitude-treatment interaction research. *Educational Psychologist, 23,* 313–52.

Peterson, P., & Comeaux, M. (1987). Teachers' schemata for classroom events: The mental scaffolding of teachers' thinking during classroom instruction. *Teaching and Teacher Education, 3,* 319–31.

Petty, O., & Jansson, L. (1987). Sequencing examples and nonexamples to facilitate concept attain-ment. *Journal for Research in Mathematics Education, 18,* 112–25.

Philips, S. (1983). *The invisible culture: Communication in classroom and community on the Warm Springs Indian Reservation.* White Plains, NY: Longman.

Phinney, J. (1990). Ethnic identity in adolescence and adulthood: A review of research. *Psychological Bulletin, 108,* 499–514.

Piaget, J. (1932). *The moral judgment of the child* (Translated by M. Worden). New York: Harcourt, Brace & World.

Piaget, J. (1970). *Science of education and the psychology of the child.* New York: Orion.

Piaget, J. (1983). Piaget's theory. In P. Mussen (Ed.), *Handbook of child psychology* (4th ed., Vol. 1). New York: Wiley.

Piaget, J., & Inhelder, B. (1964). *The early growth of logic in the child* (Translated by L. Lunzer & D. Papert). London: Routledge & Kegan Paul.

Piattelli-Palmarini, M. (Ed.). (1980). *Language and learning: The debate between Jean Piaget and Noam Chomsky.* Cambridge: Harvard University Press.

Pichert, J., & Anderson, R. (1977). Taking different perspectives on a story. *Journal of Educational Psychology, 69,* 309–15.

Pinnell, G., DeFord, D., & Lyons, C. (1988). *Reading recovery: Early intervention for at-risk first graders.* Arlington, VA: Educational Research Service.

Pintrich, P. (1990). Implications of psychological research on student learning and college teaching for teacher education. In W. Houston (Ed.), *Handbook of research on teacher education* (pp. 826–57). New York: Macmillan.

Plake, D. (1993). Teacher assessment literacy: Teachers' competencies in the educational assessment of students. *Mid-Western Educational Researcher, 6,* 21–27.

Plass, J. & Hill, K. (1986). Children's achievement strategies and performance: The role of time pressure, evaluation anxiety, and sex. *Developmental Psychology, 22,* 31–36.

Plomin, R., & Foch, T. (1981). Sex differences and individual differences. *Child Development, 52,* 383–85.

Policastro, M. (1975). Notetaking: The key to college success. *Journal of Reading, 18,* 372–75.

Polya, G. (1957). *How to solve it* (2nd ed.). Princeton, NJ: Princeton University Press.

Posner, G., & Rudnitsky, A. (1986). *Course design: A guide to curriculum development for teachers* (3rd ed.). New York: Longman.

Posner, G., Strike, K., Hewson, K., & Gertzog, W. (1982). Accommodation of a scientific conception: Toward a theory of conceptual change. *Science Education, 66,* 211–28.

Powell, D. R. (1991). How schools support families: Critical policy tensions. *Elementary School Journal, 91*(3), 307–19.

Power, F. C., Higgins, A., & Kohlberg, L. (1989). *Lawrence Kohlberg's approach to moral education.* New York: Columbia University Press.

Pozner, J., & Saltz, E. (1974). Social class, conditional communication, and egocentric speech. *Developmental Psychology, 10,* 764–71.

Pratt, M., Golding, G., & Hunter, W. (1984). Does morality have a gender? Sex, sex role, and moral judgment relationships across the adult lifespan. *Merrill-Palmer Quarterly, 30,* 321–40.

Prawat, R. (1989). Promoting access to knowledge, strategy, and disposition in students: A research synthesis. *Review of Educational Research, 59,* 1–41.

Prawat, R. (1992). Teachers' beliefs about teaching and learning: A constructivist perspective. *American Journal of Education, 100,* 354–95.

Premack, D. (1965). Reinforcement theory. In D. Levine (Ed.), *Nebraska Symposium on Motivation* (Vol. 13). Lincoln, NE: University of Nebraska Press.

Presseisen, B. (1988). Thinking success for all students: Understanding the issues. In B. Presseisen (Ed.), *At-risk students and thinking: Perspectives from research* (pp. 38–64). Washington, DC: National Education Association.

Pressey, S. (1932). A third and fourth contribution toward the coming "industrial revolution" in education. *School and Society, 36,* 668–72.

Pressley, M., & Dennis-Rounds, J. (1980). Transfer of a mnemonic keyword strategy at two age levels. *Journal of Educational Psychology, 72,* 575–82.

Pressley, M., & El-Dinary, P. (1993). Special issue on strategies instruction. *Elementary School Journal, 94*(2).

Pressley, M., El-Dinary, P., Gaskins, I., Schuder, T., Bergman, J., Almasi, J., & Brown, R. (1992).

Beyond direct explanations: Transactional instruction of reading comprehension strategies. *Elementary School Journal, 92,* 513–55.

Pressley, M., Harris, K., & Marks, M. (1992). But good strategy instructors are constructivists! *Educational Psychology Review, 4,* 3–31.

Pressley, M., Johnson, C., Symons, S., McGoldrick, J., & Kurita, J. (1989). Strategies that improve children's memory and comprehension of text. *Elementary School Journal, 90,* 3–32.

Pressley, M., Kuiper, N., Bryant, S., & Michener, S. (1982). Mnemonic versus nonmnemonic vocabulary-learning strategies: Additional comparisons. *Journal of Educational Psychology, 74,* 693–707.

Pressley, M., Levin, J., & Miller, G. (1982). The keyword method compared to alternative vocabulary-learning strategies. *Contemporary Educational Psychology, 7,* 50–60.

Pressley, M., Wood, E., Woloshyn, V., Martin, V., King, A., & Menke, D. (1992). Encouraging mindful use of prior knowledge: Attempting to construct explanatory answers facilitates learning. *Educational Psychologist, 27,* 91–109.

Preston, R. (1962). Reading achievement of German and American children. *School and Society, 90,* 350–54.

Psotka, J., Massey, L., & Mutter, S. (Eds.). (1988). *Intelligent tutoring systems: Lessons learned.* Hillsdale, NJ: Erlbaum.

Quality Education Data, Inc. (1991). *Technology in schools 1990–91 school year.* Denver: Author.

Rabiner, D., & Coie, J. (1989). Effect of expectancy inductions on rejected children's acceptance by unfamiliar peers. *Developmental Psychology, 25*(3), 450–57.

Rabinowitz, M. (1988). On teaching cognitive strategies: The influence of accessibility of conceptual knowledge. *Contemporary Educational Psychology, 13,* 229–35.

Ramírez, J. (1992). Executive summary. *Bilingual Research Journal, 16,* 1–62.

Ramírez, J., Pasta, D., Yuen, S., Ramey, D., & Billings, D. (1991a). *Final report: Longitudinal study of structured English immersion strategy, early-exit, and late-exit bilingual education programs for language-minority children. (Vol. 2).* (Prepared for U. S. Department of Education). San Mateo, CA: Aguerra International. No. 300-87-0156.

Ramírez, J., Yuen, S., Ramey, D., & Pasta, D. (1991b). *Final report: Longitudinal study of structured English immersion strategy, early-exit, and late-exit bilingual education programs for language-minority children. (Vol. 1).* (Prepared for U.S. Department of Education). San Mateo, CA: Aguirre International. No. 300-87-0156.

Ramírez, O. (1989). Mexican American children and adolescents. In J. Gibbs, L. Huang et al. (Eds.), *Children of color.* San Francisco: Jossey-Bass.

Ranzijn, F. (1991). The sequence of conceptual information in instruction and its effect on retention. *Instructional Science, 20,* 405–18.

Raths, L., Harmin, M., & Simon, S. (1978). *Values and teaching* (2nd ed.). Columbus, OH: Merrill.

Raudenbush, S., Rowan, B., and Cheong, Y. (1993). Higher order instructional goals in secondary schools: Class, teacher, and school influences. *American Educational Research Journal, 30,* 523–53.

Rebbeck, B. J. (1983). Foreign language techniques for the gifted or watch your blooming language! *Roeper Review, 5*(4), 136–39.

Redfield, D., & Rousseau, E. (1981). A meta-analysis of experimental research on teacher questioning behavior. *Review of Educational Research, 51,* 237–45.

Redl, F. (1966). *When we deal with children.* New York: Free Press.

Redl, F., & Wineman, D. (1951). *Children who hate.* New York: Free Press.

Reigeluth, C. (Ed.). (1983). *Instructional-design theories and models: An overview of their current status.* Hillsdale, NJ: Erlbaum.

Reigeluth, C. (Ed.). (1987). *Instructional theories in action: Lessons illustrating selected theories and models.* Hillsdale, NJ: Erlbaum.

Reigeluth, C. (1989). Educational technology at the crossroads. *Educational Technology Research and Development, 37,* 67–80.

Reilly, J. (1992). When does a student really need a professional mentor? *Gifted Child Quarterly, 15,* 2–8.

Reis, S., & Renzulli, J. (1991). The assessment of creative products in programs for gifted and talented students. *Gifted Child Quarterly, 35,* 128–34.

Render, G., Padilla, J., & Krank, H. (1989). What research really shows about assertive discipline. *Educational Leadership, 47,* 72–75.

Renner, J., Stafford, D., Lawson, A., McKinnon, J., Friot, E., & Kellogg, D. (1976). *Research on teaching and learning with the Piaget model.* Norman: University of Oklahoma Press.

Rennie, L., & Parker, L. (1987) Detecting and accounting for gender differences in mixed-sex and single-sex grouping in science lessons. *Educational Review, 39,* 67–68

Renninger, A., Hidi, S., & Krapp, A. (Eds.). (1992). *The role of interest in learning and development.* Hillsdale, NJ: Erlbaum.

Renzulli, J., & Smith, L. (1978). *The learning-styles inventory: A measure of student preferences for instructional techniques.* Mansfield Center, CT: Creative Learning Press.

Renzulli, J., Smith, L., & Reis, S. (1982). Curriculum compacting: An essential strategy for working with gifted students. *Elementary School Journal, 82,* 185–94.

Resnick, L. (1987). *Education and learning to think.* Washington, DC: National Academy Press.

Resnick, L. (1989). Treating mathematics as an ill-structured discipline. In R. Charles & E. Silver (Eds.), *The teaching and assessing of mathematical problem solving.* Hillsdale, NJ: Erlbaum.

Resnick, L., & Klopfer, L. (Eds.). (1989). *Toward the thinking curriculum: Current cognitive research: 1989 Yearbook of the Association for Supervision and Curriculum Development.* Alexandria, VA: Association for Supervision and Curriculum Development.

Rest, J. (1986). *Moral development: Advances in theory and research.* New York: Praeger.

Reynolds, A. (1992). What is competent beginning teaching? A review of the literature. *Review of Educational Research, 62,* 1–35.

Reynolds, R., & Anderson, R. (1982). Influence of questions on the allocation of attention during reading. *Journal of Educational Psychology, 74,* 623–32.

Rice, M. (1989). Children's language acquisition. *American Psychologist, 44,* 149–156.

Richards, F., & Commons, M. (1990). Postformal cognitive-developmental theory and research: A review of its current status. In C. Alexander & E. Langer (Eds.), *Higher stages of human development: Perspectives on adult growth* (pp. 139–61). New York: Oxford University Press.

Richardson, K. (1991). *Understanding intelligence.* Philadelphia: Open University Press.

Richardson, V. (1990). Significant and worthwhile change in teaching practice. *Educational Researcher, 19*(7), 10–18.

Rickards, J. (1979). Adjunct postquestions in text: A critical review of methods and processes. *Review of Educational Research, 49,* 181–96.

Rickards, J. (1982). Homework. In H. Mitzel (Ed.), *Encyclopedia of educational research* (5th ed.). New York: Free Press.

Rickards, J., & August, G. (1975). Generative underlining strategies in prose recall. *Journal of Educational Psychology, 67,* 860–65.

Riley, J. (1980). *The effects of teachers' wait-time and cognitive questioning level on pupil science achievement.* Paper presented at the annual meeting of the National Association for Research in Science Teaching, Boston.

Riley, M., Greeno, J., & Heller, J. (1982). The development of children's problem solving ability in arithmetic. In H. Ginsberg (Ed.), *The development of mathematical thinking.* New York: Academic Press.

Rippey, R. (1975). Speech compressors for lecture review. *Educational Technology, 15,* 58–59.

Robin, A. (1976). Behavioral instruction in the college classroom. *Review of Educational Research, 46,* 313–54.

Robin, A., Schneider, M., & Dolnick, M. (1976). The turtle technique: An extended case study of self-control in the classroom. *Psychology in the Schools, 13,* 449–53.

Robinson, F. (1970). *Effective study* (4th ed.). New York: Harper & Row.

Rogers, C. (1983). *Freedom to learn: For the 80s.* Columbus: Merrill.

Rogers, C., Smith, M., & Coleman, J. (1978). Social comparison in the classroom: The relationship between academic achievement and self-concept. *Journal of Educational Psychology, 70,* 50–57.

Rogoff, B. (1990). *Apprenticeship in thinking: Cognitive development in social context.* New York: Oxford University Press.

Rogoff, B., & Wertsch, J. (Eds.). (1984). *Children's learning in the "zone" of proximal development.* San Francisco: Jossey-Bass.

Rohner, R., & Nielsen, C. (1978). *Parental acceptance and rejection: A review and annotated bibliography of research and theory.* New Haven: HRAF Press.

Rohrkemper, M., & Brophy, J. (1979). *The influence of teacher role definition on strategies for coping with problem students.* Paper presented at the annual meeting of the American Educational Research Association, San Francisco. ERIC Document Reproduction Service No. 179 522.

Rohrkemper, M., & Brophy, J. (1983). Teachers' thinking about problem students. In J. Levine & M. Wang (Eds.), *Teacher and student perceptions: Implications for learning.* Hillsdale, NJ: Erlbaum.

Rohrkemper, M., and Corno, L. (1988). Success and failure on classroom tasks: Adaptive learning and classroom teaching. *Elementary School Journal, 88,* 297–312.

Rohrkemper McCaslin, M. (1989). Self-regulated learning and academic achievement: A Vygotskian view. In B. Zimmerman & D. Schunk (Eds.), *Self-regulated learning and academic achievement* (pp. 143–68). New York: Springer-Verlag.

Rollins, H., & Genser, L. (1977). Role of cognitive style in a cognitive task: A case favoring the impulsive approach to problem solving. *Journal of Educational Psychology, 69,* 281–87.

Rosaen, C. (1989). Writing in the content areas: Reaching its potential in the learning process. In J. Brophy (Ed.), *Advances in research on teaching.* Vol 1, *Teaching for meaningful understanding and self-regulated learning.* Greenwich, CT: JAI.

Rosch, E. (1978). Principles of categorization. In E. Rosch & B. Lloyd (Eds.), *Cognition and categorization.* Hillsdale, NJ: Erlbaum.

Rosch, E., & Lloyd, B. (Eds.) (1978). *Cognition and categorization.* Hillsdale, NJ: Erlbaum.

Rosch, E., & Mervis, C. (1975). Family resemblances: Studies in the internal structure of categories. *Cognitive Psychology, 7,* 573–605.

Rosch, E., Mervis, C., Gray, W., Johnson, D., & Boyes-Braem, P. (1976). Basic objects in natural categories. *Cognitive Psychology, 8,* 382–439.

Rosenbaum, M., & Drabman, R. (1979). Self-control training in the classroom: A review and critique. *Journal of Applied Behavior Analysis, 12,* 467–85.

Rosenberg, M. (1986). Self-concept from middle childhood through adolescence. In J. Suls & A. Greenwald (Eds.), *Psychological perspective on the self* (Vol. 3, pp. 192–205). Hillsdale, NJ: Erlbaum.

Rosenfeld, P., Lambert, N., & Black, A. (1985). Desk arrangement effects on pupil classroom behavior. *Journal of Educational Psychology, 77*(1), 101–8.

Rosenholtz, S. (1989). *Teachers' workplace: The social organization of work.* New York: Longman.

Rosenshine, B. (1970). Enthusiastic teaching: A research review. *School Review, 78,* 499–514.

Rosenshine, B. (1983). Teaching functions in instructional programs. *Elementary School Journal, 83,* 335–51.

Rosenshine, B., & Furst, N. (1973). The use of direct observation to study teaching. In R. Travers (Ed.), *Second handbook of research on teaching.* Chicago: Rand McNally.

Rosenshine, B., & Guenther, J. (1992). Using scaffolds for teaching higher level cognitive strategies. In J. Keefe & H. Walberg (Eds.), *Teaching for thinking* (pp. 35–47). Reston, VA: National Association of Secondary School Principals.

Rosenshine, B., & Meister, C. (1992). The use of scaffolds for teaching higher-level cognitive strategies. *Educational Leadership, 49*(7), 26–33.

Rosenshine, R. (1968). To explain: A review of research. *Educational Leadership, 26,* 275–80.

Ross, D., & Smith, W. (1992). Understanding preservice teachers' perspectives on diversity. *Journal of Teacher Education, 43,* 94–103.

Rosswork, F. (1977). Goal setting: The effects on an academic task with varying magnitudes of incentive. *Journal of Educational Psychology, 69,* 710–15.

Roth, K. (1990). Developing meaningful conceptual understanding in science. In B. Jones & L. Idol (Eds.), *Dimensions of thinking and cognitive instruction* (pp. 139–75). Hillsdale, NJ: Erlbaum.

Rothkopf, E. (1970). The concept of mathemagenic activities. *Review of Educational Research, 40,* 325–36.

Rotter, J. (1966). Generalized expectancies for internal versus external control of reinforcement. *Psychological Monographs, 80,* 1–28.

Rotter, J. (1980). Interpersonal trust, trustworthiness, and gullibility. *American Psychologist, 35,* 1–7.

Rowe, M. (1974a). Science, silence, and sanctions. *Science and Children, 6,* 11–13.

Rowe, M. (1974b). Wait time and rewards as instructional variables, their influence on language, logic, and fate control. Part I—Wait time. *Journal of Research in Science Teaching, 11,* 81–94.

Rowe, M. (1986). Wait time: Slowing down may be a way of speeding up! *Journal of Teacher Education, 37,* 43–50.

Royer, J., & Cable, G. (1975). Facilitated learning in connected discourse. *Journal of Educational Psychology, 67,* 116–23.

Rozin, P., Fallon, A., & Mandell, R. (1984). Family resemblence in attitudes to foods. *Developmental Psychology, 20,* 309–14.

Rubenstein, N. (1975). Patterns of problem solving. Englewood Cliffs, NJ: Prentice-Hall.

Ruble, D., & Flett, G. (1988). Conflicting goals in self-evaluative information seeking: Developmental and ability level analysis. *Child Development, 59,* 97–106.

Ruiz, R. (1989). Considerations in the education of gifted Hispanic students. In C. Maker & S. Schieber (Eds.), *Defensible programs for cultural and ethnic minorities* (Vol. 2, pp. 60–65). Austin, TX: Pro-Ed.

Rumelhart, D. (1975). Notes on a schema for stories. In D. Bobrow & A. Collins (Eds.), *Representation and understanding.* New York: Academic Press.

Rumelhart, D., Lindsey, P., & Norman, D. (1972). A process model for long-term memory. In E. Tulving & W. Donaldson (Eds.), *Organization of memory.* New York: Academic Press.

Rumelhart, D., & McClelland, J. (1986). On learning the past tenses of English verbs. In J. McClelland & D. Rumelhart (Eds.), *Parallel distributed processing: Explorations in the microstructure of cognition.* Vol. 2, *Psychological and biological models* (pp. 216–271). Cambridge: MIT Press.

Rumelhart, D., & Norman, D. (1978). Accretion, tuning, and restructuring: Three modes of learning. In J. Cotton & R. Klatzky (Eds.), *Semantic factors in cognition.* Hillsdale, NJ: Erlbaum.

Rumelhart, D., & Norman, D. (1981). Analogical processes in learning. In J. Anderson (Ed.), *Cognitive skills and their acquisition* (pp. 335–59). Hillsdale, NJ: Erlbaum.

Runions, T. (1980). The mentor academy program: Educating the gifted/talented for the 80's. *Gifted Child Quarterly, 24*(4), 152–57.

Rushton, J., & Sorrentino, R. (Eds.). (1981). *Altruism and helping behavior: Social, personality, and developmental perspectives.* Hillsdale, NJ: Erlbaum.

Russell, J. (1982). Cognitive conflict, transmission, and justification: Conservation attainment through dyadic interaction. *Journal of Genetic Psychology, 140,* 283–97.

Ryan, K., & McLean, G. (Eds.). (1987). *Character development in schools and beyond.* New York: Praeger.

Ryan, R. (1982). Control and information in the intrapersonal sphere: An extension of cognitive evaluation theory. *Journal of Personality and Social Psychology, 43,* 450–61.

St. John, N. (1971). Thirty-six teachers: Their characteristics and outcomes for black and white pupils. *American Educational Research Journal, 8,* 635–48.

Sachs, J. (1967). Recognition memory for syntactic and semantic aspects of connected discourse. *Perception and Psychophysics, 2,* 437–42.

Sadker, M., & Sadker, D. (1982). *Sex equity handbook for schools.* New York: Longman.

Sadker, M., & Sadker, D. (1989). The treatment of sex equity in teacher education. In S. Klein (Ed.), *Handbook for achieving sex equity through education* (pp. 147–49). Baltimore: Johns Hopkins University Press.

Safer, D., & Allen, R. (1976). *Hyperactive children: Diagnosis and management.* Baltimore: University Park Press.

Safford, P. (1978). *Teaching young children with special needs.* St. Louis: Mosby.

Sagaria, S., & DiVesta, F. (1978). Learner expectations induced by adjunct questions and the retrieval of intentional and incidental information. *Journal of Educational Psychology, 17,* 280–88.

Sagerman, N., & Mayer, R. (1987). Forward transfer of different reading strategies evoked by adjunct questions in science test. *Journal of Educational Psychology, 79,* 189–91.

Sagotsky, G., Patterson, C., & Lepper, M. (1978). Training children's self-control: A field experiment in self-monitoring and goal-setting in the classroom. *Journal of Experimental Child Psychology, 25,* 242–53.

Sainato, D., Strain, P., LeFevre, D., & Rapp, N. (1990). Effects of self-evaluation on the independent work skills of preschool children with disabilities. *Exceptional Children, 56,* 540–49.

Salamé, R. (1984). Test anxiety: Its determinants, manifestations and consequences. In H. van Der Ploeg, R. Schwarzer, & C. Spielberger (Eds.), *Advances in test anxiety research* (Vol. 3, pp. 83–119). Hillsdale, NJ: Erlbaum.

Salend, S. C. (1990). *Effective mainstreaming.* New York: Macmillan.

Salomon, G., & Perkins, D. (1987). Transfer of cognitive skills from programming: When and how? *Journal of Educational Computing Research, 3,* 149–69.

Samson, G., Strykowski, B., Weinstein, T., & Walberg, H. (1987). The effects of teacher questioning levels on student achievement: A quantitative synthesis. *Journal of Educational Research, 80,* 290–95.

Samuel, W. (1977). Observed IQ as a function of test atmosphere, tester expectation, and race of tester: A replication for female subjects. *Journal of Educational Psychology, 69,* 593–604.

Sandoval, J., & Irwin, M. (1988). Review of the Stanford-Binet intelligence scale: 4th ed. *Professional School Psychology, 3,* 157–61.

Sarason, I., & Sarason, B. (1981). Teaching cognitive and social skills to high school students. *Journal of Consulting and Clinical Psychology, 49,* 908–18.

Satterly, D. (1976). Cognitive styles, spatial ability, and school achievement. *Journal of Educational Psychology, 68,* 36–42.

Savage, T., & Armstrong, D. (1992). *Effective teaching in elementary social studies* (2nd ed.). New York: Macmillan.

Saville-Troike, M. (1989). *The ethnography of communication: An introduction* (2nd ed.). Oxford: Basil Blackwell, Inc.

Sawyer, R., Graham, S., & Harris, K. (1992). Direct teaching, strategy instruction, and strategy instruction with explicit self-regulation: Effects on the composition skills and self-efficacy of students with learning disabilities. *Journal of Educational Psychology, 84,* 340–52.

Scardamalia, M., Bereiter, C., Brett, C., Burtis, P., Calhoun, C., & Lea, N. (1992). Educational applications of a networked communal database. *Interactive Learning Environments, 2,* 45–71.

Schank, R., & Abelson, R. (1977). *Scripts, plans, goals, and understanding.* Hillsdale, NJ: Erlbaum.

Schaps, E., & Solomon, D. (1990). Schools and classrooms as caring communities. *Educational Leadership, 48*(3), 38–42.

Schiedel, D., & Marcia, J. (1985). Ego identity, intimacy, sex role orientation, and gender. *Developmental Psychology, 21,* 149–60.

Schiff, M., & Lewontin, R. (1986). *Education and class: The irrelevance of IQ genetic studies.* Oxford: Clarendon Press.

Schloss, P. (1992a). Mainstreaming revisited. *Elementary School Journal, 92,* 233–44.

Schloss, P. (Ed.). (1992b). Integrating learners with disabilities in regular education programs [Special Issue]. *Elementary School Journal, 84,* January.

Schneider, W., & Graham, D. (1992). Introduction to connectionist modeling in education. *Educational Psychologist, 27,* 513–30.

Schneider, W., Korkel, J., & Weinert, F. (1989). Domain-specific knowledge and memory performance: A comparison of high-and low-aptitude children. *Journal of Educational Psychology, 81,* 306–12.

Schneider, W., & Pressley, M. (1989). *Memory development between 2 and 20.* New York: Springer-Verlag.

Schoenfeld, A. (1979). Explicitly heuristic training as a variable in problem solving performance. *Journal for Research in Mathematics Education, 10,* 173–187.

Schoenfeld, A., & Herrmann, D. (1982). Problem perception and knowledge structure in expert and novice mathematical problem solvers. *Journal of Experimental Psychology, 8,* 484–94.

Schofield, H. (1981). Teacher effects on cognitive and affective pupil outcomes in elementary school mathematics. *Journal of Educational Psychology, 73,* 462–71.

Schon, D. (1987). *Educating the reflective practitioner.* San Francisco: Jossey-Bass.

Schriberg, L., Levin, J., McCormick, C., & Pressley, M. (1982). Learning about "famous" people via the keyword method. *Journal of Educational Psychology, 74,* 238–47.

Schunk, D. (1985). Self-efficacy and classroom learning. *Psychology in the schools, 22,* 208–23.

Schunk, D. (1989). Social cognitive theory and self-regulated learning. In B. Zimmerman & D. Schunk, *Self-regulated learning and academic achievement* (pp. 83–111). New York: Springer-Verlag.

Schwille, J., Porter, A., Belli, G., Floden, R., Freeman, D., Knappen, L., Kuhs, T., & Schmidt, W. (1983). Teachers as policy brokers in the content of elementary school mathematics. In L. Shulman & G. Sykes (Eds.), *Handbook of teaching and policy.* New York: Longman.

Scott, E., & McCollum, H. (1993). Making it happen: Gender equitable classrooms. In S. Biklen & D. Pollard (Eds.), *92nd yearbook of the National Society for the Study of Education.* Part 1, *Gender and Education.* (pp. 174–90). Chicago: University of Chicago Press.

Scott, K. (1987). Missing developmental perspectives in moral education. *Theory and Research in Social Education, 15,* 257–73.

Scott, K. (1991). Achieving social studies affective aims: Values, empathy, and moral development. In J. Shaver (Ed.), *Handbook of research on social studies teaching and learning* (pp. 357–69). New York: Macmillan.

Scruggs, T., & Mastropieri, M. (1992). Effective mainstreaming strategies for mildly handicapped students. *Elementary School Journal, 92,* 389–409.

Secada, W., & Lightfoot, T. (1993). Symbols and the political context of bilingual education in the United States. In M. Arias & U. Casanova (Eds.), *Bilingual Education: Politics, practice, and research,* 92nd Yearbook of the National Society for the Study of Education (Part II), (pp. 36–64). Chicago: University of Chicago Press.

Seddon, G. (1978). The properties of Bloom's taxonomy of educational objectives for the cognitive domain. *Review of Educational Research, 48,* 303–23.

Selman, R. (1980). *The growth of interpersonal understanding.* New York: Academic Press.

Selman, R., & Schultz, L. (1990). *Making a friend in youth.* Chicago: University of Chicago Press.

Semmel, M., Abernathy, T., Butera, G., & Lesar, S. (1991). Teacher perceptions of the regular education initiative. *Journal of Exceptional Children, 58,* 9–25.

Sharan, S. (Ed.). (1990) *Cooperative learning: Theory and research.* New York: Praeger.

Shavelson, R. (1978). *A model of teacher decision making.* Paper presented at the annual meeting of the American Educational Research Association, March, Toronto.

Shavelson, R. (1983). Review of research on teachers' pedagogical judgments, plans and decisions. *Elementary School Journal, 83,* 392–413.

Shavelson, R., & Stern, P. (1981). Research on teachers' pedagogical thoughts, judgments, decisions, and behavior. *Review of Educational Research, 51*(4), 455–98.

Shaver, J., & Strong, W. (1982). *Facing value decisions: Rationale-building for teachers.* New York: Teachers College Press.

Sheinker, J., & Sheinker, A. (1982). *Study strategies: A metacognitive approach: Skimming, note taking, summarizing, outlining* (four handbooks). Rock Springs, WY: White Mountain Publishing Co.

Shepardson, D. (1993). Publisher-based science activities of the 1980s and thinking skills. *School Science and Mathematics, 93,* 264–68.

Shimmerlick, S., & Nolan, J. (1976). Organization and the recall of prose. *Journal of Educational Psychology, 68,* 779–86.

Shriberg, L., Levin, J., McCormick, C., & Pressley, M. (1982). Learning about "famous" people via the keyword method. *Journal of Educational Psychology, 74,* 238–47.

Shulman, L. (1986). Paradigms and research programs in the study of teaching: A contemporary perspective. In M. Wittrock (Ed.), *Third handbook of research on teaching* (pp. 3–36). New York: Macmillan.

Shweder, R. (1991). *Thinking through cultures: Expeditions in cultural psychology.* Cambridge: Harvard University Press.

Siddle-Walker, E. (1992). Falling asleep and failure among African-American students: Rethinking assumptions about process teaching. *Theory into Practice, 31,* 321–27.

Sieber, R. (1979). Classmates as workmates: Informal peer activity in the elementary school. *Anthropology and Education Quarterly, 10,* 207–35.

Siegel, L., & Siegel, L. (1965). Educational set: A determinant of acquisition. *Journal of Educational Psychology, 56,* 1–12.

Siegler, R. (1991). *Children's thinking* (2nd ed.). Englewood Cliffs, NJ: Prentice-Hall.

Sigel, I. (Ed.). (1985). *Parental belief systems: The psychological consequences for children.* Hillsdale, NJ: Erlbaum.

Sigel, I., & Coop, R. (1974). Cognitive style and classroom practice. In R. Coop & K. White (Eds.), *Psychological concepts in the classroom.* New York: Harper & Row.

Sigel, I., McGillicuddy-DeLisi, A., & Goodnow, J. (Eds.). (1992). *Parental belief systems: The psychological consequences for children* (2nd ed.). Hillsdale, NJ: Erlbaum.

Silver, E. (1979). Student perceptions of relatedness among mathematical verbal problems. *Journal for Research in Mathematics Education, 10,* 195–210.

Simon, H. (1979). Information processing models of cognition. In M. Rosenzweig & L. Porter (Eds.), *Annual review of psychology.* Palo Alto, CA: Annual Reviews, Inc.

Simon, H. (1980). Problem solving and education. In D. Tuma & R. Reif (Eds.), *Problem solving and education: Issues in teaching and research.* Hillsdale, NJ: Erlbaum.

Simon, H. (1981). *The sciences of the artificial* (2nd ed.). Cambridge: MIT Press.

Sirotnik, K. (1983). What you see is what you get—consistency, persistency, and mediocrity in classrooms. *Harvard Educational Review, 53,* 16–31.

Sizer, T. (1984). *Horace's compromise: The dilemma of the American high school.* Boston: Houghton Mifflin.

Skinner, B. (1948). *Walden Two.* New York: Macmillan.

Skinner, B. (1954). The science of learning and the art of teaching. *Harvard Educational Review, 24,* 86–97.

Skinner, B. (1958). Teaching machines. *Science, 128,* 969–77.

Skinner, B. (1968). *The technology of teaching.* New York: Appleton-Century-Crofts.

Skinner, B. (1971). *Beyond freedom and dignity.* New York: Knopf.

Skinner, B. (1974). *About behaviorism.* New York: Knopf.

Skinner, B. (1979). *The shaping of a behaviorist.* New York: Knopf.

Skinner, B. (1986). Programmed instruction revisited. *Phi Delta Kappan, 68,* 103–10.

Slavin, R. (1987). Mastery learning reconsidered. *Review of Educational Research, 57,* 175–213.

Slavin, R. (1990). *Cooperative learning: Theory, research, and practice.* Englewood Cliffs, NJ: Prentice-Hall.

Slavin, R. (1991a). Reading effects of IBM's "Writing to Read" program: A review of evaluations. *Educational Evaluation and Policy Analysis, 13,* 1–11.

Slavin, R. (1991b). Synthesis of research on cooperative learning. *Educational Leadership, 48,* 71–82.

Slavin, R., & Karweit, N. (1984). Mastery learning and student teams: A factorial experiment in urban general mathematics classes. *American Educational Research Journal, 21,* 725–36.

Sloan, D. (Ed.). (1985). *The computer in education: A critical perspective.* New York: Teachers College Press.

Smith, C. (1982). *Promoting the social development of young children: Strategies and activities.* Palo Alto, CA: Mayfield.

Smith, D., & Luckasson, R. (1992). *Introduction to special education: Teaching in an age of challenge.* Needham Heights, MA: Allyn & Bacon.

Smith, E., & Anderson, L. (1984). *The Planning and Teaching Intermediate Science study: Final report.* East Lansing: Michigan State University, Institute for Research on Teaching.

Smith, F. (1986). *The bureaucratic invasion of our classrooms: Insult to intelligence.* New York: Arbor House.

Smith, L. (1985). Presentational behaviors and student achievement in mathematics. *Journal of Educational Research, 78,* 292–98.

Smith, L., & Land, M. (1981). Low-inference verbal behaviors related to teacher clarity. *Journal of Classroom Interaction, 17,* 37–42.

Smith, L., & Sanders, K. (1981). The effects on student achievement and student perception of varying structure in social studies content. *Journal of Educational Research, 74,* 333–36.

Smith, S., & Rothkopf, E. (1984). Contextual enrichment and distribution of practice in the classroom. *Cognition and Instruction, 1,* 341–58.

Smolensky, P. (1988). On the proper treatment of connectionism. *Behavioral and Brain Sciences, 11,* 1–74.

Snapp, J., & Glover, J. (1990). Advance organizers and study questions. *Journal of Educational Research, 83,* 266–71.

Snarey, J. (1985). Cross-cultural universality of socio-moral development: A critical review of Kohlbergian research. *Psychological Bulletin, 97,* 202–32.

Snarey, J. (1993). *How fathers care for the next generation: A four-decade study.* Cambridge: Harvard University Press.

Snider, V. (1990). What we know about learning styles from research in special education. *Educational Leadership, 48* (2), 53.

Snow, C., Barnes, W., Chandler, J., Goodman, I., & Hemphill, L. (1991). *Unfulfilled expectations: Home and school influences on literacy.* Cambridge: Harvard University Press.

Snow, R. (1984). Placing children in special education: Some comments. *Educational Researcher, 13,* 12–14.

Snow, R. (1986). On intelligence. In R. Sternberg & D. Detterman (Eds.), *What is intelligence? Contemporary viewpoints on its nature and definition* (pp. 133–40). Norwood, NJ: Ablex Publishing Corporation.

Snow, R., & Swanson, J. (1992). Instructional psychology: Aptitude, adaptation, and assessment. In M. Rosenzweig & L. Porter (Eds.), *Annual review of psychology* (Vol. 43, pp. 583–626).

Soled, S. (1990). Teaching processes to improve both higher and lower mental process achievement. *Teaching and Teacher Education, 6,* 255–65.

Solomon, D., & Kendall, A. (1979). *Children in classrooms: An investigation of person-environment interaction.* New York: Praeger.

Spearman, C. (1927). *The abilities of man.* New York: MacMillan.

Spencer, Hall, D. (1976). *A grounded theory of aligning actions in an elementary classroom.* Doctoral dissertation, University of Missouri-Columbia.

Spindler, G. (Ed.). (1982). *Doing the ethnography of schooling: Educational anthropology in action.* New York: Holt, Rinehart & Winston.

Spiro, R. (1977). Remembering information from text: Theoretical and empirical issues concerning the "State of Schema" reconstruction hypothesis. In R. Anderson, R. Spiro, & W. Montague (Eds.), *Schooling and the acquisition of knowledge.* Hillsdale, NJ: Erlbaum.

Stahl, S. (1989). Is there evidence to support matching reading styles and initial reading methods? *Phi Delta Kappan,* 317–27.

Stainback, S., & Stainback, W. (1992). *Curriculum considerations in inclusive classrooms.* Baltimore: Brookes.

Stanley, J. (1976). The case for extreme educational acceleration of intellectually brilliant youths. *Gifted Child Quarterly, 20,* 66–75.

Stanley, J. (1978). Radical acceleration: Recent educational innovation at Johns Hopkins University. *Gifted Child Quarterly, 22,* 62–67.

Stanley, J. (1980). On educating the gifted. *Educational Researcher, 9,* 8–12.

Stanley, W. (1981). Indoctrination and social

education: A critical analysis. *Social Education, 45,* 200–204.

Stanovich, K., & Cunningham, A. (1993). Where does knowledge come from? Specific associations between print exposure and information acquisition. *Journal of Educational Psychology, 85,* 211–29.

Staub, E. (1979). *Positive social behavior and morality: Socialization and development.* New York: Academic Press.

Steele, F. (1973). *Physical settings and organization development.* Reading, MA: Addison-Wesley.

Steffe, L., Cobb, P., & von Glasersfeld, E. (1988). *Construction of arithmetical meanings and strategies.* New York: Springer-Verlag.

Stein, B., & Bransford, J. (1979). Constraints on effective elaboration: Effect of precision and subject generation. *Journal of Verbal Learning and Verbal Behavior, 18,* 769–77.

Stein, D. M., & Brinza, S. R. (1989). Bulimia: Prevalence estimates in female junior high and high school students. *Journal of Clinical Child Psychology, 18,* 206–13.

Stein, N. (1993). It happens here, too: Sexual harassment and child sexual abuse in elementary and secondary schools. In S. Biklen & D. Pollard (Eds.), *92nd yearbook of the National Society for the Study of Education.* Part 1, *Gender and Education.* (pp. 191–203). Chicago: University of Chicago Press.

Steinberg, L., Elmer, J., & Mounts, N. (1989). Authoritative parenting, psychosocial maturity, and academic success among adolescents. *Child Development, 60,* 1424–36.

Steinberg, L., & Silverberg, S. (1986). The vicissitudes of autonomy in early adolescence. *Child Development, 57,* 975–85.

Steinmetz, S. (1977). *The cycle of violence: Assertive, aggressive, and abusive family interaction.* New York: Praeger.

Sternberg, R. (1985). *Beyond IQ: A triarchic theory of human intelligence.* New York: Cambridge University Press.

Sternberg, R. (Ed.). (1986a). *Advances in the psychology of human intelligence* (Vol. 3). Hillsdale, NJ: Erlbaum.

Sternberg, R. (1986b). Intelligence, wisdom, and creativity: Three is better than one. *Educational Psychologist, 21,* 175–90.

Sternberg, R. (1987). Questions and answers about the nature and teaching of thinking skills. In J. Baron & R. Sternberg (Eds.), *Teaching thinking skills: Theory and practice.* New York: Freeman.

Sternberg, R. (Ed.). (1988). *The nature of creativity.* Cambridge: Cambridge University Press.

Sternberg, R., & Bhana, K. (1986). Synthesis of research on the effectiveness of intellectual skills programs: Snake-oil remedies or miracle cures? *Educational Leadership, 44*(2), 60–67.

Sternberg, R., & Detterman, D. (Eds.) (1986). *What is intelligence? Contemporary viewpoints on its nature and definition.* Norwood, NJ: Ablex Publishing Corporation.

Stevenson, H. (1970). Learning in children. In P. Mussen (Ed.), *Carmichael's manual of child psychology* (3rd ed., Vol. 1). New York: Wiley.

Stevenson, H., Parker, T., Wilkenson, A., Bonnevaux, B., & Gonzalez, M. (1978). Schooling, environment, and cognitive development: A cross-cultural study. *Monographs of the Society for Research in Child Development, 43*(3) (Serial No. 175).

Stewart, J., Hafner, R., Johnson, S., & Finkel, E. (1992). Science as model building: Computers and high-school genetics. *Educational Psychologist, 27,* 317–36.

Stiff, L. (1989). Effects of teaching strategy, relevant knowledge, and strategy length on learning a contrived mathematical concept. *Journal for Research in Mathematics Education, 20,* 227–41.

Stiggins, R. (1991). Relevant classroom assessment training for teachers. *Educational Measurement: Issues and Practice, 10,* 7–12.

Stigler, J., & Stevenson, H. (1991). How Asian teachers polish each lesson to perfection. *American Educator, 15*(1), 12–20, 43–47.

Stipek, D. (1984a). The development of achievement motivation. In R. Ames & C. Ames (Eds.), *Research on motivation in education* (Vol. 1). Orlando, FL: Academic Press.

Stipek, D. (1984b). Young children's performance expectations: Logical analysis or wishful thinking? In J. G. Nicholls (Ed.), *The Development of achievement motivation.* Greenwich, CT: JAI Press.

Stipek, D. (1993). *Motivation to learn: Theory to practice.* Boston: Allyn & Bacon.

Stipek, D., & Sanborn, M. (1983). *Pre-school teachers' task-related interactions with handicapped and nonhandicapped boys and girls.* Paper presented at the annual meeting of the American Educational Research Association, Montreal, Canada.

Stipek, D., & Tannatt, L. (1984). Children's judgments of their own and their peers' academic competence. *Journal of Educational Psychology, 76,* 75–84.

St. John, N. (1971). Thirty-six teachers: Their characteristics and outcomes for black and white pupils. *American Educational Research Journal, 8,* 635–48.

Stodolsky, S. (1988). *The subject matters: Classroom activity in math and social studies.* Chicago: University of Chicago Press.

Stout, C. (1989). Teachers' views of the emphasis on reflective teaching skills during their student teaching. *Elementary School Journal, 89*(4), 511–27.

Strike, K. (1975). The logic of discovery. *Review of Educational Research, 45,* 461–83.

Strike, K. (1993). Professionalism, democracy, and discursive communities: Normative reflections on restructuring. *American Educational Research Journal, 30,* 255–76.

Strom, B., Hocevar, D., & Zimmer, J. (1990). Satisfaction and achievement: Antagonists in ATI research on student-oriented instruction. *Educational Research Quarterly, 14,* 15–21.

Strother, D. (1984). Homework: Too much, just right, or not enough? *Phi Delta Kappan, 65,* 423–26.

Sullivan, H. (1953). *The interpersonal theory of psychiatry.* New York: Norton.

Sulzer-Azaroff, B., & Mayer, R. (1991). *Behavior analysis for lasting change.* Forth Worth: Holt, Rinehart & Winston.

Swanson, H., O'Connor, J., & Cooney, J. (1990). An information-processing analysis of expert and novice teachers' problem solving. *American Educational Research Journal, 27,* 533–56.

Swanson, H. L. (1990). Influence of metacognitive knowledge and aptitude on problem solving. *Journal of Educational Psychology, 82,* 306–14.

Sweller, J., & Chandler, P. (1991). Evidence for cognitive load theory. *Cognition and Instruction, 8,* 351–62.

Swift, J., Gooding, C., & Swift, P. (1988). Questions and wait time. In J. Dillon (Ed.), *Questioning and discussion: A multidisciplinary study* (pp. 192–212). Norwood, NJ: Ablex.

Swing, S., Stoiber, K., & Peterson, P. (1988). Thinking skills versus learning time: Effects of alternative classroom-based interventions on students' mathematics problem solving. *Cognition and Instruction, 5,* 123–91.

Szapocznik, J., & Kurtines, W. (1993). Family psychology and cultural diversity: Opportunities for theory, research, and application. *American Psychologist, 48,* 400–407.

Tajika, H., Taniguchi, A., Yamamoto, K., and Mayer, R. (1988). Effects of pictorial advance organizers on passage retention. *Contemporary Educational Psychology, 13,* 133–39.

Tanaka, K. (1989). A response to "Are we meeting the needs of gifted Asian-Americans?" In C. Maker & S. Schieber (Eds.), *Defensible programs for cultural and ethnic minorities* (Vol. 2, pp. 174–178). Austin, TX: Pro-Ed.

Tanner, L. (1978). *Classroom discipline for effective teaching and learning.* New York: Holt, Rinehart & Winston.

Taylor, B. (1982). Text structure and children's comprehension and memory for expository material. *Journal of Educational Psychology, 70,* 323–40.

Taylor, R. (1980). *The computer in the school: Tutor, tool, tutee.* New York: Teachers College Press.

Tennyson, R., & Cocchiarella, M. (1986). An empirically based instructional design theory for concept teaching. *Review of Educational Research, 36,* 40–71.

Tennyson, R., & Park, O. (1980). The teaching of concepts: A review of instructional design research literature. *Review of Educational Research, 50,* 55–70.

Tennyson, R., & Rasch, M. (1988). Linking cognitive learning theory to instructional prescriptions. *Instructional Science, 17,* 369–85.

Tharpe, R., & Gallimore, R. (1988). *Rousing minds to life: Teaching, learning, and schooling in social context.* Cambridge: Cambridge University Press.

Thomas, J., & Rohwer, W. (1993). Proficient autonomous learning: Problems and prospects. In M. Rabinowitz (Ed.), *Cognitive science foundations of instruction* (pp. 1–32). Hillsdale, NJ: Erlbaum.

Thompson, R., White, K., & Morgan, D. (1982). Teacher-student interaction patterns in classrooms with mainstreamed mildly handicapped students. *American Educational Research Journal, 19,* 220–36.

Thornburg, H. (1982). *Development in adolescence* (2nd ed.). Monterey: Brooks/Cole.

Thorndike, E. (1913). *The psychology of learning: Educational psychology* (Vol. 2). New York: Teachers College Press.

Thorndike, E. (1924). Mental discipline in high school studies. *Journal of Educational Psychology, 15,* 1–22, 83–98.

Thorndike, R., & Hagen, E. (1969). *Measurement and evaluation in psychology and education* (3rd ed.). New York: Wiley.

Thorndike, R., & Hagen, E. (1977). *Measurement and evaluation in psychology and education* (4th ed.). New York: Wiley.

Thorndyke, P. (1977). Cognitive structures in comprehension and memory of narrative discourse. *Cognitive Psychology, 9,* 77–110.

Thornton, S., & Wenger, R. (1990). Geography curriculum and instruction in three fourth-grade classrooms. *Elementary School Journal, 90,* 515–31.

Thurstone, L. (1938). Primary mental abilities. *Psychometric Monographs, 1.*

Tierney, R., Carter, M., & Desai, L. (1991). *Portfolio assessment in the reading-writing classroom.* Norwood, MA: Christopher-Gordon.

Tobias, S. (1990). *They're not dumb, they're different. Stalking the second tier.* Tucson, AZ: Research Corporation.

Tobias, S., & Ingber, T. (1976). Achievement-treatment interactions in programmed instruction. *Journal of Educational Psychology, 68,* 43–47.

Tobin, K. (1980). The effect of an extended teacher wait-time on science achievement. *Journal of Research in Science Teaching, 17,* 469–75.

Tobin, K. (1983a). The influence of wait-time on classroom learning. *European Journal of Science Education, 5*(1), 35–48.

Tobin, K. (1983b). Management of time in classrooms. In B. Fraser (Ed.), *Classroom management.* Bentley, Australia: Western Australia Institute of Technology.

Tobin, K., & Capie, W. (1982). Relationships between classroom process variables and middle-school science achievement. *Journal of Educational Psychology, 74,* 441–54.

Tobin, K., & Garnett, P. (1987). Gender related differences in science activities. *Science Education, 71,* 91–103.

Tollefson, N., Tracy, D., Johnsen, E., Farmer, W., & Buenning, M. (1984). Goal setting and personal responsibility for LD adolescents. *Psychology in the Schools, 21,* 224–33.

Tomlinson, T. (1993). Educational reform: The ups and downs of good intentions. In T. Tomlinson (Ed.), *Motivating students to learn: Overcoming barriers to high achievement* (pp. 3–20). Berkeley, CA: McCutchan.

Torrance, E. (1962). *Guiding creative talent.* Englewood Cliffs, NJ: Prentice-Hall.

Torrance, E. (1966). *Torrance Tests of Creative Thinking: Norms-technical manual.* Princeton, NJ: Personnel Press.

Torrance, E. (1973). Non-test indicates of creative talent among disadvantaged children. *Gifted Child Quarterly, 17*(1), 3–9.

Torrance, E. (1975). Creativity research in education: Still alive. In I. Taylor & J. Getzels (Eds.), *Perspectives in creativity.* Chicago: Aldine.

Torrance, E. (1977). *Discovery and nurturance of giftedness in the culturally different.* Reston, VA: Council for Exceptional Children.

Torrance, E. (1986). Teaching creative and gifted learners. In M. Wittrock (Ed.), *Handbook of research on teaching* (3rd ed.). New York: Macmillan.

Torrance, E. (1987). Teaching for creativity. In S. Isaksen (Ed.), *Frontiers of Creativity Research* (pp. 189–215). Buffalo, NY: Bearly Limited.

Torrance, E. (1990). *The Torrance tests of creative thinking: Norms—technical manual.* Bensonville, IL: Scholastic Testing Service.

Torrance, E., Tan, C., & Allman, T. (1970). Verbal originality and teacher behavior: A predictive validity study. *Journal of Teacher Education,* 215–341.

Towers, J. (1992a). Outcome-based education: Another bandwagon? *The Educational Forum, 56* (3), 291–305.

Towers, J. (1992b). Some concerns about outcome-based education. *Journal of Research and Development in Education, 25,* 89–95.

Trabasso, T., & Bower, G. (1968). *Attention to learning.* New York: Wiley.

Treffinger, D. (1982). Gifted students, regular classrooms: Sixty ingredients for a better blend. *Elementary School Journal, 82,* 267–83.

Tudor, I. (1986). Advance organizers as adjuncts to L2 reading comprehension. *Journal of Research in Reading, 9,* 103–15.

Tulving, E. (1985). How many memory systems are there? *American Psychologist, 40,* 385–98.

Tulving, E. (1993). What is episodic memory? *Current Directions in Psychological Science, 2,* 67–70.

Tulviste, P. (1991). *The cultural-historical development of verbal thinking.* Commack, NY: Nova Science Publishers.

Tuma, D., & Reif, R. (Eds.). (1980). *Problem solving and education: Issues in teaching and research.* Hillsdale, NJ: Erlbaum.

Tversky, B. (1973). Encoding processes in recognition and recall. *Cognitive Psychology, 5,* 275–87.

Udall, A. (1989). Curriculum for gifted Hispanic students. In C. Maker & S. Schieber (Eds.), *Defensible programs for cultural and ethnic minorities* (Vol. 2, pp. 41–56). Austin, TX: Pro-Ed.

Underwood, B. (1961). Ten years of massed practice on distributed practice. *Psychological Review, 58,* 229–47.

Underwood, B. (1983). *Attributes of memory.* Glenview, IL: Scott, Foresman.

Underwood, B., Kapelak, S., & Malmi, R. (1976). The spacing effect: Additions to the theoretical and empirical puzzles. *Memory and Cognition, 4,* 391–400.

Valdés, G., Lozano, A., & García-Moya, R. (1981). *Teaching Spanish to the Hispanic bilingual: Issues, aims, and methods.* New York: Teachers College Press.

Valencia, R. (1991). The plight of chicano students: An overview of school conditions and outcomes. In R. Valencia (Ed.), *Chicano school failure and success* (pp. 3–26). London: The Falmer Press.

VanRossum, E., & Schenk, S. (1984). The relationship between learning conception, study strategy and learning outcome. *British Journal of Educational Psychology, 54,* 73–83.

VanSickle, R. (1986). A quantitative review of research on instructional simulation gaming: A twenty-year perspective. *Theory and Research in Social Education, 14,* 245–64.

Vavrus, L. (1990). Put portfolios to the test. *Instructor, 100,* 48–53.

Velez, C. N., Johnson, J., & Cohen, P. (1989). A longitudinal analysis of selected risk factors for childhood psychopathology. *Journal of the American Academy of Child and Adolescent Psychiatry, 28,* 861–64.

Venezky, R., & Osin, L. (1991). *The intelligent design of computer-assisted instruction.* New York: Longman.

Verloop, N. (1989). *Interactive cognitions of student teachers.* Arnhem, The Netherlands: National Institute for Educational Measurement.

Vernon, P. (1981). Level I and Level II: A review. *Educational Psychologist, 16,* 45–64.

Vinsonhaler, J., Weinshank, A., Wagner, C., & Polin, R. (1983). Diagnosing children with educational problems: Characteristics of reading and learning disabilities specialists, and classroom teachers. *Reading Research Quarterly, 18,* 134–64.

Vitz, P. (1990). The uses of stories in moral development: New psychological reasons for an old education method. *American Psychologist, 45,* 709–20.

Vobeda, B. (1992). Births, immigration fuel population boom. *Washington Post.*

von Glasersfeld, E. (1984). An introduction to radical constructivism. In P. Watzlawick (Ed.), *The invented reality* (pp. 17–40). New York: Norton.

von Glasersfeld, E. (1991). *Radical constructivism in mathematics education.* Boston: Kluwer.

Vosniadou, S., & Brewer, W. (1987). Theories of knowledge restructuring in development. *Review of Educational Research, 57,* 51–67.

Vosniadou, S., & Schommer, M. (1988). Explanatory analogies can help children acquire information from expository text. *Journal of Educational Psychology, 80,* 524–36.

Voss, J., & Bisanz, G. (1982). Models and methods used in the study of prose comprehension and learning. In S. Black & B. Britton (Eds.), *Expository text.* Hillsdale, NJ: Erlbaum.

Vygotsky, L. (1962). *Thought and language.* Cambridge, MA: MIT Press.

Vygotsky, L. (1978). *Mind in society: The development of higher psychological processes* (edited by M. Cole, V. John-Steiner, S. Scribner, & E. Souberman). Cambridge: Harvard University Press.

Wadsworth, B. (1989). *Piaget's theory of cognitive and affective development* (4th ed.). New York: Longman.

Wainryb, C., & Turiel, E. (1993). Conceptual and

informational features in moral decision making. *Educational Psychologist, 28,* 205–18.

Walczyk, J., & Hall, V. (1989). Effects of examples and embedded questions on the accuracy of comprehension self-assessments. *Journal of Educational Psychology, 81,* 435–37.

Waldrop, M. (1984). The necessity of knowledge. *Science, 223,* 1279–82.

Walker, L. (1982). The sequentiality of Kohlberg's states of moral development. *Child Development, 53,* 1330–36.

Walker, L. (1991). Sex differences in moral development. In W. Kurtines & J. Gewirtz (Eds.), *Handbook of moral behavior and development* (Vol. 2). Hillsdale, NJ: Erlbaum.

Walker, L., & Taylor, J. (1991). Stage transitions in moral reasoning: A longitudinal study of developmental processes. *Developmental Psychology, 27,* 330–37.

Wallach, M. (1970). Creativity. In P. Mussen (Ed.), *Carmichael's manual of child psychology* (3rd ed., Vol. 1). New York: Wiley.

Wallach, M., & Kogan, N. (1965). *Modes of thinking in young children.* New York: Holt, Rinehart and Winston.

Wallas, G. (1921). *The art of thought.* New York: Harcourt, Brace & World.

Walters, J., & Gardner, H. (1986). The theory of multiple intelligence: Some issues and answers. In R. Sternberg & R. Wagner (Eds.), *Practical intelligence: Nature and origins of competence in the everyday world* (pp. 163–82). Cambridge: Cambridge University Press.

Wapner, J., & Conner, K. (1986). The role of defensiveness in cognitive impulsivity. *Child Development, 57,* 1370–74.

Ward, M., & Sweller, J. (1990). Structuring effective work examples. *Cognition and Instruction, 7,* 1–39.

Ware, B. (1978). What rewards do students want? *Phi Delta Kappan, 59,* 355–56.

Waterman, A. (1982). Identity development from adolescence to adulthood: An extension of theory and a review of research. *Developmental Psychology, 18,* 341–58.

Waxman, H., & Walberg, H. (Eds.). (1991). *Effective teaching: Current research.* Berkeley: McCutchan.

Weiner, B. (1972). *Theories of motivation: From mechanism to cognition.* Chicago: Rand McNally.

Weiner, B. (1984). Principles of a theory of student motivation and their application with an attributional framework. In R. Ames & C. Ames (Ed.), *Research on motivation in education* (Vol. 1). Orlando, FL: Academic Press.

Weiner, B. (1986). *An attributional theory of motivation and emotion.* New York: Springer-Verlag.

Weiner, B. (1992). *Human motivation: Metaphors, theories, and research.* Newbury Park, CA: Sage.

Weinstein, C. (1977). Modifying student behavior in an open classroom through changes in the physical design. *American Educational Research Journal, 14,* 249–62.

Weinstein, C. (1979). The physical environment of the school: A review of the research. *Review of Educational Research, 49,* 577–610.

Weinstein, C. (1982). Training students to use elaboration learning strategies. *Contemporary Educational Psychology, 7,* 301–11.

Weinstein, C., & Mayer, R. (1986). The teaching of learning strategies. In M. Wittrock (Ed.), *Handbook of research on teaching,* (3rd ed., pp. 315–27). New York: Macmillan.

Weinstein, C., & Mignano, A., Jr. (1993). *Elementary classroom management: Lessons from research and practice.* New York: McGraw-Hill.

Weinstein, C., & Underwood, V. (1983). Learning strategies: The how of learning. In J. Segal, S. Chipman, & R. Glaser (Eds.), *Relating instruction to basic research.* Hillsdale, NJ: Erlbaum.

Weinstein, R., & Butterworth, B. (1993). *Enhancing motivational opportunity in elementary schooling: A case study of the principal's role.* Paper presented at the annual meeting of the American Educational Research Association, April, Atlanta, GA.

Wellman, H., & Gelman, S. (1992). Cognitive development: Foundational theories of core domains. *Annual Review of Psychology, 43,* 337–75.

Wentzel, K., & Erdley, C. (1993). Strategies for making friends: Relations to social behavior and peer acceptance in early adolescence. *Developmental Psychology, 29,* 819–26.

Wertsch, J. (1985). *Vygotsky and the social formation of mind.* Cambridge: Harvard University Press.

Wertsch, J. (1991). *Voices of the mind: A sociocultural approach to mediated action.* Cambridge: Harvard University Press.

Wertsch, J., & Tulviste, P. (1992). L. S. Vygotsky and contemporary developmental psychology. *Developmental Psychology, 28,* 548–57.

West, C. (1993). *Race matters.* Boston: Beacon Press.

Wheatley, G. (1992). The role of reflection in mathematics learning. *Educational Studies in Mathematics, 23,* 529–41.

Whimbey, A., & Lochhead, J. (1991). *Problem solving and comprehension* (5th ed.). Hillsdale, NJ: Erlbaum.

White, B. (1975). *The first three years of life.* Englewood Cliffs, NJ: Prentice-Hall.

White, C. (1992). Software review. *Social Education, 56,* 364–65.

White, R. (1992). Implications of recent research on learning for curriculum and assessment. *Journal of Curriculum Studies, 24,* 153–64.

White, R., & Tisher, R. (1986). Research on natural sciences. In M. Wittrock (Ed.), *Handbook of research on teaching* (3rd. ed.). New York: Macmillan.

White, S., & Bond, M. (1992). Examples of transition programs in large school districts. *Teaching Exceptional Children, 24,* 44–47.

Whitener, E. (1989). A meta-analytic review of the effect on learning of the interaction between prior achievement and instructional support. *Review of Educational Research, 59,* 65–86.

Whitley, B., & Frieze, I. (1985). Children's causal attributions for success and failure in achievement settings: A meta-analysis. *Journal of Educational Psychology, 77,* 608–16.

Whitmore, J. (1982). Recognizing and developing hidden giftedness. *Elementary School Journal, 82,* 274–83.

Whitmore, J., & Maker, C. (1985). *Intellectual giftedness in disabled persons.* Rockville, MD: Aspen Systems Corporation.

Wickelgren, W. (1981). Human learning and memory. In M. Rosenzweig & L. Porter (Eds.), *Annual review of psychology.* Palo Alto, CA: Annual Reviews Inc.

Wiggins, G. (1993). *Assessing student performance: Exploring the purpose and limits of testing.* San Francisco: Jossey-Bass.

Wilen, W. (Ed.). (1990). *Teaching and learning through discussion.* Springfield, IL: Charles C. Thomas.

Wilhite, S. (1983). Prepassage questions: The influence of structural importance. *Journal of Educational Psychology, 75,* 234–44.

Will, M. (1986). Educating children with learning problems: A shared responsibility. *Journal of Exceptional Children, 52,* 411–15.

Winn, W. (1990). Some implications of cognitive theory for instructional design. *Instructional Science, 19,* 53–69.

Winne, P. (1979). Experiments relating teachers' use of higher cognitive questions to student achievement. *Review of Educational Research, 49,* 13–50.

Winograd, T. (1975). Frame representations and the declarative/procedural controversy. In B. Bobrow & A. Collins (Eds.), *Representation and understanding.* New York: Academic Press.

Wisniewski, L., & Sedlak, R. (1992). Assistive devices for students with disabilities. *Elementary School Journal, 97,* 297–314.

Witkin, H., Dyk, R., Faterson, H., Goodenough, D., & Karp, S. (1962). *Psychological differentiation.* New York: Wiley.

Witkin, H., Moore, C., Goodenough, D., & Cox, P. (1977). Field-dependent and field-independent cognitive styles and their educational implications. *Review of Educational Research, 47,* 1–64.

Wittrock, M. (Ed.). (1977). *Learning and instruction.* Berkeley, CA: McCutchan.

Wittrock, M. (1986). Students' thought processes. In M. Wittrock (Ed.), *Third handbook of research on teaching* (pp. 297–314). New York: Macmillan.

Wittrock, M., Marks, C., & Doctorow, M. (1975). Reading as a generative process. *Journal of Educational Psychology, 67,* 484–89.

Wixson, K. (1984). Level of importance of postquestions and children's learning from text. *American Educational Research Journal, 21,* 419–33.

Wolf, D., Lemahieu, P., & Eresh, J. (1992). *Good measure: Assessment as a tool for educational reform.* Paper presented at the American Educational Research Association annual meeting, San Francisco, CA.

Woo, E. (1989). Personal reflections on the purpose of special education for gifted Asian-Americans. In C. Maker & S. Schieber (Eds.), *Defensible programs for cultural and ethnic minorities* (Vol. 2, pp. 179–81).

Wood, D. (1988). *How children think and learn.* Oxford: Basil Blackwell.

Wood, D., Bruner, J., & Ross, G. (1976). The role of tutoring in problem solving. *Journal* of Child Psychology and Psychiatry, 17, 89–100.

Wood, T., Cobb, P., & Yackel, E. (1990). The contextual nature of teaching: Mathematics and reading instruction in one second-grade classroom. *Elementary School Journal, 90,* 497–513.

Woodson, M. (1974). Seven aspects of teaching concepts. *Journal of Educational Psychology, 66,* 184–88.

Woolfolk, A. (1993). *Educational psychology* (5th ed.). Boston: Allyn & Bacon.

Wright, I. (1978). Moral reasoning and conduct of selected elementary school students. *Journal of Moral Education, 7,* 199–205.

Wyckoff, W. (1973). The effect of stimulus variation on learning from lecture. *Journal of Experimental Education, 41,* 85–90.

Wynne, E. (1982). *Character policy: An emerging issue.* Washington, DC: University Press of America.

Yando, R., Seitz, V., & Zigler, E. (1979). *Intellectual and personality characteristics of children: Social class and ethnic group differences.* Hillsdale, NJ: Lawrence Erlbaum Associates.

Yates, G., & Chandler, M. (1991). The cognitive psychology of knowledge: Basic research findings and educational implications. *Australian Journal of Education, 35,* 131–53.

Yinger, R. (1977). *A study of teacher planning: Description and theory development using ethnographies and information processing methods.* Dissertation, Michigan State University, East Lansing.

Youniss, J., & Smollar, J. (1985). *Adolescent relations with mothers, fathers, and friends.* Chicago: University of Chicago Press.

Ysseldyke, J. (1987). Classification of handicapped students. In M. Wang, M. Reynolds, & H. Walberg (Eds.), *Handbook of special education: Research in practice* (Vol. 1, pp. 253–71). Oxford: Pergamon Press.

Zigler, E., & Valentine, J. (Eds.). (1979). *Project Head Start: A legacy of the war on poverty.* New York: The Free Press.

Zimmerman, B., & Schunk, D. (1989). (Eds.). *Self-regulated learning and academic achievement.* New York: Springer-Verlag.

Zivin, G. (1979). *The development of self-regulation through private speech.* New York: Wiley.

Zook, K., & DiVesta, F. (1991). Instructional analogies and conceptual misrepresentations. *Journal of Educational Psychology, 83,* 246–52.

index